OKANAGAN COLLEGE LIBRARY

03483989

S0-DRG-502

HANDBOOK OF GENDER
IN ARCHAEOLOGY

GENDER AND ARCHAEOLOGY SERIES

Series Editor
Sarah Milledge Nelson
University of Denver

This series focuses on ways to understand gender in the past through archaeology. This is a topic poised for significant advances in both method and theory, which in turn can improve all archaeology. The possibilities of new methodological rigor as well as new insights into past cultures are what make gendered archaeology a vigorous and thriving subfield. The Press welcomes single authored books on themes in this topical area, particularly ones with a comparative focus. Edited collections with a strong theoretical or methodological orientation will also be considered. Audiences are practicing archaeologists and advanced students in the field.

EDITORIAL BOARD

Philip Duke, Fort Lewis College
Alice Kehoe, Marquette University
Janet Levy, University of North Carolina, Charlotte
Margaret Nelson, Arizona State University
Thomas Patterson, University of California, Riverside
K. Anne Pyburn, Indiana University
Ruth Whitehouse, University College London

BOOKS IN THE SERIES

In Pursuit of Gender: Worldwide Archaeological Approaches, Sarah Milledge Nelson and Myriam Rosen-Ayalon, Editors (2001)
Gender and the Archaeology of Death, Bettina Arnold and Nancy L. Wicker, Editors (2001)
Ancient Maya Women, Traci Ardren, Editor (2002)
Sexual Revolutions: Gender and Labor at the Dawn of Agriculture, by Jane Peterson (2002)
Ancient Queens: Archaeological Explorations, Sarah Milledge Nelson, Editor (2003)
Gender in Ancient Cyprus: Narratives of Social Change on a Mediterranean Island, by Diane Bolger (2003)
Ambiguous Images: Gender and Rock Art, by Kelley Hays-Gilpin (2003)
Gender and Chinese Archaeology, Katheryn M. Linduff and Yan Sun, Editors (2004)
Gender in Archaeology: Analyzing Power and Prestige, Second Edition, by Sarah Milledge Nelson (2004)
The Archaeology of Childhood: Children, Gender, and Material Culture, by Jane Eva Baxter (2005)
Gender and Hide Production, edited by Lisa Frink and Kathryn Weedman (2005)
Handbook of Gender in Archaeology, edited by Sarah Milledge Nelson (2006)

SUBMISSION GUIDELINES

Prospective authors of single or co-authored books and editors of anthologies should submit a letter of introduction, the manuscript or a four to ten page proposal, a book outline, and a curriculum vitae. Please send your book manuscript/proposal packet to:

Gender and Archaeology Series
AltaMira Press
1563 Solano Avenue, #364
Berkeley, California 94707
Tel: 510-526-5315 / Fax: 510-526-5340
www.altamirapress.com

HANDBOOK OF GENDER IN ARCHAEOLOGY

EDITED BY
SARAH MILLEDGE NELSON

A Division of
ROWMAN & LITTLEFIELD PUBLISHERS, INC.
Lanham • New York • Toronto • Oxford

ALTAMIRA PRESS
A Division of Rowman & Littlefield Publishers, Inc.
A wholly owned subsidiary of
The Rowman & Littlefield Publishing Group, Inc.
4501 Forbes Boulevard, Suite 200
Lanham, MD 20706
www.altamirapress.com

PO Box 317, Oxford, OX2 9RU, UK

Copyright © 2006 by AltaMira Press

All rights reserved. No part of this publication may be reproduced, stored in a retrieval system, or transmitted in any form or by any means, electronic, mechanical, photocopying, recording, or otherwise, without the prior permission of the publisher.

British Library Cataloguing in Publication Information Available

Library of Congress Cataloguing-in-Publication Data

Handbook of gender in archaeology / edited by Sarah Milledge Nelson.
   p. cm. — (Gender and archaeology)
  Includes bibliographical references and index.
  ISBN-13: 978-0-7591-0678-9 (cloth : alk. paper)
  ISBN-10: 0-7591-0678-9 (cloth : alk. paper)
  1. Feminist archaeology. 2. Women—History—To 500. 3. Sex role—History.
  I. Nelson, Sarah Milledge.
  CC72.4.H36 2006
  930.08—dc22
                                                                    2005031960

Printed in the United States of America

∞™ The paper used in this publication meets the minimum requirements of American National Standard for Information Sciences—Permanence of Paper for Printed Library Materials, ANSI/NISO Z39.48-1992.

Contents

Acknowledgments   ix

Introduction: Archaeological Perspectives on Gender
SARAH MILLEDGE NELSON   1

Part I: Theoretical and Thematic Issues

CHAPTER 1
Methods in Feminist and Gender Archaeology: A Feeling for Difference—and Likeness   ELIZABETH M. BRUMFIEL   31

CHAPTER 2
Feminist Theory and Gender Research in Historical Archaeology
SUZANNE M. SPENCER-WOOD   59

CHAPTER 3
Gender, Things, and Material Culture   MARIE LOUISE STIG SØRENSEN   105

CHAPTER 4
Gender and Archaeological Mortuary Analysis   BETTINA ARNOLD   137

CHAPTER 5
The Engendered Household   JULIA A. HENDON   171

CHAPTER 6
Gender and Landscapes   WENDY ASHMORE   199

CHAPTER 7
Gender, Heterarchy, and Hierarchy   JANET E. LEVY   219

CHAPTER 8
Gender and Ethnoarchaeology   KATHRYN WEEDMAN   247

CHAPTER 9
Feminist Gender Research in Classical Archaeology
SUZANNE M. SPENCER-WOOD   295

Part II: Identities

CHAPTER 10
The Prism of Self: Gender and Personhood   BONNIE J. CLARK AND
LAURIE A. WILKIE   333

CHAPTER 11
Sexuality in Archaeology   BARBARA L. VOSS   365

CHAPTER 12
Archaeology, Men, and Masculinities   BENJAMIN ALBERTI   401

CHAPTER 13
The Archaeology of Nonbinary Genders in Native North American
Societies   SANDRA E. HOLLIMON   435

Part III: Subsistence Strategies

CHAPTER 14
Gender and Human Evolution   DIANE BOLGER   453

CHAPTER 15
Gender Dynamics in Hunter-Gatherer Society: Archaeological Methods
and Perspectives   HETTY JO BRUMBACH AND ROBERT JARVENPA   503

CHAPTER 16
Gender and Early Farming Societies   JANE D. PETERSON   537

CHAPTER 17
Women, Gender, and Pastoralism   PAM CRABTREE   571

Part IV: World Regions

CHAPTER 18
A Critical Appraisal of Gender Research in African Archaeology
DIANE LYONS   595

CHAPTER 19
Gender in East and Southeast Asian Archaeology   ELISABETH A. BACUS   633

CHAPTER 20
Gender and Archaeology in South and Southwest Asia   CARLA M. SINOPOLI   667

CHAPTER 21
Gender and the Disciplinary Culture of Australian Archaeology
CLAIRE SMITH AND EMER O'DONNELL   691

CHAPTER 22
Gender Archaeology in Europe   RUTH WHITEHOUSE   733

CHAPTER 23
Gender and Mesoamerican Archaeology   ROSEMARY A. JOYCE   785

CHAPTER 24
Gender Archaeology in Native North America   KAREN OLSEN BRUHNS   813

CHAPTER 25
Gender in South American Archaeology   VIRGINIA EBERT AND
THOMAS C. PATTERSON   853

Index   875

About the Contributors   907

Acknowledgments

THIS VOLUME WAS the brainchild of Mitch Allen, founder and former editor of AltaMira Press, who now is founder and editor of Left Coast Press. His original plan for the book, and his encouragement until near the final stages, contributed greatly to the final product. I begin these acknowledgments by thanking him for his vision that gender in archaeology is a growing field, for his foresight to suggest this book, and for inviting me to edit it.

Although the process of soliciting chapters from perhaps the busiest archaeologists in academe was long, and sometimes arduous, it was worth the journey, as I think readers of the book will agree. The vision of what gender in archaeology can contribute to the discipline, and to our understanding of the past, is present in each chapter. I thank the chapter authors for their willingness to view the future as well as to summarize the past. And thanks, too, to all the foremothers of gender in archaeology, a few of whom had to drop out of the project before it was completed.

Finally, thanks to the staff at AltaMira Press, who ultimately made the book production go smoothly: Erik Hanson, who took over as editor, Sarah Walker, and Jehanne Schweitzer. Many thanks to them all.

Introduction
Archaeological Perspectives on Gender

SARAH MILLEDGE NELSON

THE SEARCH FOR EVIDENCE of gender in the archaeological past, including gender roles, gender ideology, gender identity, and many other facets of gender, has become an integral part of the way archaeology is practiced in many branches of archaeology and within a variety of theoretical stances. While the development of theory and methods has been most intense in the English-speaking world, awareness of the possibilities for learning about gender in specific archaeological contexts has become global, as the chapters in this volume demonstrate. Furthermore, these chapters indicate that almost any set of data from archaeological sites can be approached with gendered questions.

The demonstrated usefulness of the concept of gender for archaeology is surprising in retrospect because barely two decades have passed since the time when papers about gender were deemed unpublishable (or even laughable) by those who controlled archaeological publications. Considerable grit was needed to pursue gender in the face of such derision. But even under those circumstances, some archaeologists, dominantly but not exclusively women, were thinking about gender in archaeological contexts, especially in terms of gender stereotypes made manifest and analyzed by the women's movement since the 1960s.

A score of years is a very short time for the astonishing variety of applications that can be appreciated in this volume. The breadth of publications on gender in archaeology can be seen in the topics covered, and the extent of the gender literature can be partially judged by the bibliographies for each chapter. These chapters and their references represent an outpouring of interest in gender—theories, methods, and ways of teaching and learning; new examination of artifacts, bodies, and sites with an eye to gender; and new attention to the ways the discipline of archaeology allows or fails to allow growth in a subfield that challenges prior assumptions.

Although some of the early attempts at doing gendered archaeology can be seen to be flawed in retrospect (and some are critiqued in this volume in several chapters), we have learned by doing. Using gender as an entry for understanding our sites has proven to be a durable approach to the archaeological past, especially as further research and thought has refined both theories and methods. The growth of the topic of gender in archaeology has rivaled the magic beans of Jack and the Beanstalk. Growth of the beanstalk has been in all directions, not simply up to the ogre's palace in the sky where the gatekeepers against gender used to sit but also outward, to all parts of the world, and inward, to all varieties of archaeology. Archaeological questions about gender have increased in sophistication and complexity. New questions have been raised by feminists about the very concepts of women (Alcoff 1995), sex (Bleier 1986), and gender (Butler 1993). While sometimes unsettling, these questions have resulted in serious explorations of gender identity (e.g., Joyce 2000), bodies (Hamilakis et al. 2002), sexuality (Voss, this volume), and masculinities (Alberti, this volume) in archaeological sites. Nonbinary genders are being considered beyond male and female (Hollimon, this volume). The topic of gender has been found to touch many archaeological subjects, from households to landscapes, from public roles to personal and group identities. Such explorations continue to be abundantly fruitful.

Gender research has spawned interest in other groups of people, such as children and the aged (Moore and Scott 1997). Class and other kinds of privilege intersect with gender, not always in expected ways. Gender has become a growing and diversifying subject within archaeology; indeed, there is no sign that the stream of papers is even beginning to slow let alone "run its course." Rather, each exploration of gender brings more avenues to explore, more ways to think about the past. Each new facet of gender suggests another beyond. This volume presents evidence of how far gender in archaeology has come and offers glimpses into new possibilities for future research.

A Brief History of Gender in Archaeology

The vibrant field of gender in archaeology was born of the women's movement of the 1960s and 1970s, and credit should be given to the ancestors. But which ancestors? There were many, and the first to explore gender questions about the past were not all archaeologists, in spite of the fact that many of the problems tackled were of interest to archaeology, and some used archaeological evidence.

Historians tackled the problem of finding past women, and social anthropologists specifically studied women who had been left out of ethnographic accounts. Paleontologists asked why "man the hunter" should be a more central character than "woman the gatherer" in forging (or perhaps foraging) human evolution (see Bolger, this volume). Sociologists looked for reasons that women were devalued in our own culture, and psychologists pointed out that definitions of many "human" traits were androcentric.

Women in several fields in addition to anthropology exposed the workings of androcentrism (Bem 1993; Coward 1983; Fee 1974; Morgan 1984; Sanday 1981). These writings were particularly useful to early thinkers about gender in archaeology, some of whom were attached to fledgling programs in women's studies. Besides, some women archaeologists inhabited departments of anthropology where both cultural and physical anthropologists provided awareness of androcentrism within what had been considered standard scholarship. Long before any feminist or gendered archaeology was deemed fit for print, a literature in other disciplines and other branches of anthropology was well established.

When archaeologists became interested in women and gender, attention was first directed to making generalizations about women's statuses in different contexts. Thus, Frances Dahlberg (1981) edited *Woman the Gatherer*, dedicated to the possibility of discovering ways gender operated in the past that might be different from the present. Primatologists challenged the way female primates were used as a model for early human females (Hrdy 1986). The distortions produced by androcentrism, even in cultural anthropology where ethnocentrism was routinely scrutinized, were uncovered by women anthropologists returning to the scenes of some very famous and even foundational anthropological publications where they discovered the other half of the story—what the women were doing (e.g., Goodale 1971; Weiner 1976).

Because the Wenner-Gren Foundation is dedicated to four-field anthropology, archaeology was included in a 1987 gender conference, "Sex and Gender Hierarchies" (Miller 1993; Silverman 2002). Discussions were a revelation to Mark Cohen and me, the archaeologists invited to the conference (Cohen and Bennett 1993; Nelson 1993). But most archaeologists were reluctant to take up the challenge. Those who pioneered the archaeology of gender in archaeology had to persevere because the topic was not taken seriously by establishment archaeologists, on whom all of us depended for our jobs, our tenure, our promotions, our salaries, our publications, and our grants. Archaeology was then a strongly male-dominated field, and successful women were reluctant to risk losing any hard-won respect they had garnered. Defying the gatekeepers in archaeology while maintaining credibility was a challenge (for an extended discussion of this point, see Nelson 2004a:18–33).

Since fledgling observations about gender in the past could not be shared with the profession in general through standard publication outlets, they were circulated among those known to be interested in the topic—a product referred to as "gray literature" (for some excellent examples that eventually were published, see Nelson et al. 1994). While archaeologists interested in questions of gender wrote and circulated their ideas, they continued to do fieldwork and to publish the kinds of work that were deemed respectable while at the same time producing papers regarding gender for the critiques of our women colleagues (Hays-Gilpin 2000; for references to some of these first efforts, see Wylie 2002:289, n. 8).

Inspired by the women's movement but choosing a different path, some archaeologists were motivated to raise issues regarding gender equity. Both statistical and anecdotal data were collected that demonstrated the systematic ways that women archaeologists were disadvantaged in the discipline of archaeology. As a result of this convincing data set, many women became politically active on behalf of women and other underrepresented groups within their workplaces, whether or not they added gender questions to their own research.

Other archaeologists turned the same questions that were being asked about women in history to the service of archaeology, especially historic archaeologists. Where were the women in historical accounts? Was it true that all kinds of women all over the world throughout prehistory as well as history had done the same (boring) things? Was it true that only men "built culture"? If all we knew about the past was what men did, wouldn't it be useful—and more complete—to know about women's activities? Although this has been decried as an "add women and stir" approach, without "adding women" archaeology would never have been stirred up to the extent that gender research has accomplished. In fact, adding women was a fundamental block in building an archaeology of gender. Once archaeological questions about women were asked, more nuanced questions, such as differences between groups of women in the same culture, demanded attention. Such nuances even became inevitable once some of the women of the past had been "found."

Whatever the reasons that moved archaeologists to seek gender, they were formed within the context of an important social movement, by individuals who were willing to work toward overcoming considerable opposition, in the forms of both inertia and antagonism. For example, students were discouraged from attempting gendered theses and dissertations, and funding agencies looked with a jaundiced eye on anything as "soft" as gender.

Although it was difficult to publish papers about gender issues in archaeology published in the 1980s, a few papers did eventually pass through the gatekeepers in spite of considerable lag time. Papers from a 1979 conference in Norway were probably the earliest. The Theoretical Archaeology Group in England devoted several sessions to archaeology, the first of which occurred in 1982, although it too suffered a time lag in publications (Arnold et al. 1988), and Scandinavian papers on gender in archaeology were also translated (Boye et al. 1984). An American publication, not widely circulated, appeared in 1983 (Gero et al. 1983). That volume concerned other topics in addition to gender since it was antiestablishment in general and as such was not destined to be widely imitated. Still, it touched on themes relevant to gender in archaeology, broached the important questions, and struck a chord that reverberated with those who were already beginning to be tuned in. In the same year, Alice Kehoe published a paper that challenged the archaeological status quo (Kehoe 1983), and Thomas Patterson's students began examining questions about the gender of leadership and state origins that undermined current thinking about gender and the state (Gailey 1985; Patterson and Gailey 1987; Silverblatt 1988).

Archaeologists interested in gender were like penguins pushing and shoving each other at the edge of the ice floe, eager to go in but fearful of predators. The publication of Margaret Conkey and Janet Spector's (1984) paper in an important archaeological series was the icebreaker. It is rightly heralded as the most important step in publishing gender in archaeology. It was celebrated as the first to be widely read beyond the circle of (mostly) women archaeologists sending each other unpublishable papers. The critical difference was that they presented the general case for gender in archaeology, and they stated it both brilliantly and thoroughly. They were allowed a platform, and they were heard, and no seals attacked them. Those elements made the paper a groundbreaking event, one that gave heart to many others who had been thinking along the same lines but had not been able to breach the barricades. The publication of that paper was a tremendous breakthrough, and the sigh of relief could be heard wherever women archaeologists congregated. Although some male archaeologists paid attention too and even applauded, the majority of archaeologists continued to dig, survey, and report their sites in familiar ways.

Detailed histories of the feminist movement in archaeology have already been written (Hays-Gilpin 2000; Nelson 1997:31–48; Wylie 2002; see also Spencer-Wood on historical archaeology, this volume). It is fair to say that many archaeologists who were inspired by feminism directly or by their feminist colleagues in cultural anthropology began experimenting with some of the early strands of gender archaeology: finding the women archaeologists who had been overlooked in histories of archaeology, probing equity issues for women archaeologists, and finding the women of the past who had been lost in the generalizations of archaeology in which the pronoun "he" stood for all humanity. It is useful to remember that in those days, archaeology books had titles like *Prehistoric Men* (Braidwood 1975), *Man Makes Himself* (Childe 1951), and *Man's Role in Changing the Face of the Earth* (Thomas 1956). It is easy now to see those first steps as simplistic, but in fact they were revolutionary.

Gender in archaeology was brought about by a social movement in addition to individual efforts. The time was ripe, ferment was occurring in many sectors, and some attempts at doing gender archaeology bubbled up higher than others, caught the attention of many, and gave the concept of gender in archaeology the boost it needed. But not all gender archaeology directed attention to women (or gender) of the past. The gendered structure of the discipline of archaeology in the present needed examination too and was in fact the cause of the lack of engendering of the discipline in the past.

Strands of Gender Archaeology

At least three strands can be teased from the original fabric of gender archaeology. Roberta Gilchrist (1991) named them political feminism, gender theory, and historical revisionism, but other categories could be named slightly differently. At first, much attention was devoted to the political in the form of equity issues, especially in America (e.g., papers in Nelson et al. 1994:sec. II; Walde and Willows 1991:177–233). Gender inequality wasn't hard to find in archaeology, but demonstrating it took some work, and obtaining the statistics to show inequality by gender (instead of other reasons for women's lesser success in archaeology as in other fields) was in some cases a major issue. Secrecy shrouded the decisions of the gatekeepers. The Committee on the Status of Women in Archaeology was first established as a standing committee of the Society for American Archaeology, patterned on a similar committee founded by the American Anthropological Association. Its founding was based on countless data sets that had been collected that demonstrated that bias against women archaeologists was real and systematic. This bias extended to appointments, salaries, promotion, tenure, success at grant getting, and various perks. It also extended to treatment by colleagues and even students in ways that came to be called the "chilly climate" (Sandler 1986), referring to accumulating small slights that would seem individually petty to complain about. But, as Sandler noted, a ton of feathers still weighs a ton.

A frequent response (which was not often expressed directly in publication) was that women couldn't succeed because of their natural deficiencies, whether related to brains, hormones, body size, or the limitations of children. In answer to such female stereotypes, studies were designed to reply to insinuations that women as a group weren't as good at archaeology as men. Did women submit as many papers to journals as men, or is the greater publication record of men due to their greater productivity? Do women coauthor papers more often than men, and, if so, does that mean they are dependent on men? Do they write about "soft" subjects (such as gender)? If a married pair includes two archaeologists, which of them is more likely to be offered a job?

The questions boil down to these: Is the fact that women are at the bottom of the totem pole their own fault? and Are women less worthy than men? These questions are still being posed today, having been given new life by Laurence Summers, president of Harvard University (Wogan 2005). Periodically rearing its ugly head, this insinuation seems to sleep but not die. The fact that it does not die in the face of overwhelming evidence to the contrary, including the recent and current achievements of women made possible in part by affirmative action laws, demonstrates that the career injustices women suffer have more to do with the structure of power than with either innate ability or biological limitations.

The second strand of gender archaeology focused on women archaeologists in the past. Once sought, it was amazing how many women's archaeological lives could be recovered (e.g., Bender 1991; Claassen 1994; Diaz-Andreu and Sørensen 1998; Levine 1991; Parezo 1993; White et al. 1999). It wasn't that women hadn't dared to "do" archaeology since archaeology began, but the "Old Boys' Club," composed of the power brokers in archaeology, largely ignored, marginalized, or trivialized them and their work. Once again, power structures worked to keep women from having too much visible success. Women didn't necessarily accept the status quo, but there were few mechanisms for seeking justice. When a woman archaeologist complained about the way she was treated (lower pay, menial jobs, not given credit for her work, sexually harassed, and so on), she was considered to be, in the immortal words of Linda Cordell (1993:30), "a pain in the ass."

Finally, we come to the topic of this volume: studying gender in the past with archaeological data. This kind of project began with simply finding the women in the past, as noted previously, because women of all cultures were treated either as if they didn't exist or as if they never produced anything of consequence. The first book-length treatment of women in archaeology was *Women in Prehistory* (Ehrenberg 1989), which was followed by *Women's Work: The First 20,000 Years* (Barber 1994). These books were written in the face of much skepticism expressed about whether "women" could be found in the past because "women's work" was invisible. Gathering, which involved vegetal matter and containers of basketry or hide, didn't leave "hard" traces in the archaeological record like men's work (read "animal bones and projectile points").

The built-in assumptions here are obvious once they were pointed out by various feminist writers who demonstrated the fallacies of this argument step by step. One of the first archaeologists to ponder this question in print was Alice Kehoe (1990), who showed that evidence of various hunting strategies that may have been pursued by women had been ignored in Paleolithic archaeology. Evidence of traps and snares was overlooked in favor of stone tools and their manufacture. Since then, the question of whether bones and stones can reveal something about women as well as men has been explored in various ways. Joan Gero (1991) insisted that gendering stone tools as products created by males only was itself an unwarranted assumption—women may have made and used the "utilized flakes" that were rarely studied from archaeological collections, or they might have made their own tools, such as scrapers, since hide working was thought to be women's work. While the field has moved to more detailed and complex studies of women as toolmakers, this foundational work continues to be important. The question of women as hunters has been explored in various ways (for a comprehensive overview, see Brumbach and Jarvenpa, this volume). But in spite of increasing data and logical arguments, not all archaeologists have been listening.

The assertion that women were hard to find in the archaeological data highlighted essentially archaeological questions, including the need to struggle with the questions of how anyone knows which gender performed particular tasks (Dobres 1995) or who made the tools to perform required production tasks (Gero 1991). How do we know whether men or women made particular stone tools? Caroline Bird (1993) showed that ethnographic evidence for women as the makers of stone tools had been overlooked. Once the topic of gender is raised, it becomes clear that many "facts" are merely assumptions based on the supposed universality of gender traits. For example, some kind of division of labor by gender occurs widely, but the nature of tasks divided by gender, as well as those divided by characteristics other than gender, is something that can be studied once we no longer make automatic assumptions about what men do and what women do. Insistence on putting aside the gender assumptions of our own culture was a fundamental breakthrough in being able to perform archaeological research on gender.

Feminist methods of presenting archaeology have been explored in various ways. Presentations using the capacities of the World Wide Web are just beginning to be developed, led by Rosemary Joyce and her students (Joyce et al. 2000; Lopiparo and Joyce 2002). The ongoing excavations of Çatalhöyük by Ian Hodder also explore ways to use the Web to allow multiple perspectives on the new excavations and encourage a variety of voices (Wolle and Tringham 2000). Ruth

Tringham has also experimented with this mode, allowing the visitor to her site to select several different outcomes consistent with the archaeological data.

Feminist pedagogy is another field of exploration (Romanowicz and Wright 1996). A course pioneered by Margaret Conkey and Ruth Tringham at Berkeley encouraged students to study in groups and prepare presentations of their research for the class in a variety of modes, from film to playlets (Conkey 1997; Conkey and Tringham 1996). Other archaeologists have used alternative forms of written material in their classes, especially novels that flesh out the archaeological record and create a space for discussing how conclusions are formed and what alternative interpretations are possible.

Ways to write archaeology as a feminist have received wide discussion. It was noted that the standard ways of writing archaeology, especially the use of the passive tense, obscured both the author's role in constructing archaeological reports and the people who left the remains studied by archaeologists (Lutz 1995). Jane Kelley and Marcia Hanen (1988) advocated "many and varied voices" in archaeological writing. Writing that is accessible and reasonably transparent allows a wider audience for archaeological discoveries and interpretations that include gender. Louise Zarmati (1998:7) recommends using gender-inclusive language, avoiding jargon, and emphasizing "the female perspective as a valid point of view." Elizabeth Brumfiel (1992) notes that universalizing obscures the controllers both in the present and in the past.

Janet Spector (1991, 1994) paved the way with *What This Awl Means*, using multiple voices, the real voices of local people who had helped interpret the site, her own voices explaining how she felt about the excavations, straight archaeological reporting, and a fictional narrative woven around an artifact. Another offshoot has led to novels that are fictional but informed by real archaeology and a feminist perspective (Nelson 1999, 2004b). The fact that archaeology is a kind of storytelling anyway, no matter how scientific (and opaque) the language, has been noted (Jameson et al. 2003; Terrell 1990). Of course, all archaeological fiction is not inspired by gender archaeology, but *Death by Theory*, written for beginning students, takes note of gender as a theory (Praetzellis 2000), which is heartening.

Gender Archaeology around the World

Women archaeologists in Norway were the bravest of all. The very first public meeting about women in the past took place in Norway in 1979, although the papers were not published until 1987 (Bertelsen et al. 1987). The conference was aptly titled "Were They All Men?" This was followed by a number of seminal (ovarian?) gatherings. An invited meeting in the United States (Gero and Conkey 1991) and meetings with volunteered papers in Canada (Walde and Willows 1991) and Australia (Balme and Beck 1993; du Cros and Smith 1993) were popular and attended with excitement. The Boone conference, organized by Cheryl Claassen (Claassen 1992; Claassen and Joyce 1997), was another early gathering dedicated to gender in archaeology. This conference continues to encourage dialogue among many different groups interested in gender in the past.

Newsletters dedicated to women or gender in archaeology sprang up, and while most eventually withered away, at least one newsletter has continued for two decades: *Rundbrief, Netzwerk Archaeologische Arbeitende Frauen*, the network of women working in archaeology, was organized in Germany by Sigrun Karlisch and Sibelle Kaestner. How well the study of gender in archaeology fared in a given region depended partly on the local power structure where women strove to promote it for (examples of differences in the way gender in archaeology is treated between and within world regions, see the regional chapters in this volume).

Sometimes the spread of gender ideas was deliberate, as when Miriam Rosen-Ayalon and I organized a conference at the Rockefeller Center in Bellagio. Archaeologists who came from eight countries and worked in archaeology in all parts of the world pondered gender in their own archaeology while listening to the possibilities imagined by the other participants. It was an enriching experience for both organizers and participants (Nelson and Rosen-Ayalon 2002:x). For example, at that meeting we learned that not all languages even have a word for gender or a concept that makes sense of the sex/gender system as the term is used in English (Shoocongdej 2002).

Regional meetings and regional edited volumes are proving useful in spreading gender archaeology within their own circles. These include Africa (Kent 1997; Wadley 1997), China (Linduff and Sun 2004), the ancient Maya (Ardren 2002), North America (Bruhns and Stothert 1999), and Italy (Whitehouse 1998), with more in the planning stages.

Theories

As already noted, the first glimmerings of gender in archaeology were based on theory created by feminists but not by archaeologists. One of the key concepts of the women's movement was patriarchy. This concept could range from the assertion of the universal dominance of men and the matching oppression of women to the more benign sense that "it's a man's world," enforcing the idea that "woman's place is in the home" (Janeway 1971). Publications that addressed patriarchy in a way that was related to archaeology dealt with questions about how male dominance arose and sometimes appealed to archaeological discoveries for their data. These included topics such as women's loss of autonomy in some cultures with the shift from matrilineality to patrilineality (Schlegel 1972), foundation myths that define and uphold gender roles (Sanday 1981), the origin of women's oppression (Rohrlich 1980), and the role of women in ancient states (Rapp 1977). Instead of probing the way patriarchy came about, other authors looked for a golden age for women in the distant past (Stone 1976), suggested archaeological sites that might represent a vanished matriarchy (Barstow 1978), or discovered ancient goddesses (Davis 1971; Gimbutas 1982).

Historians looked for ancient women in literate contexts (e.g., Boulding 1976; Fraser 1989) using documentary data that required locating unusual sources, such as women's diaries and census data. Data in public documents about women's lives in general or regarding specific women were rare. Interesting facts emerged in these studies, such as the activities of midwives (Ulrich 1990) and the way women's knowledge of healing became stigmatized as occult knowledge and witchcraft beginning in the Middle Ages. We still use the expression "old wives' tales" to denigrate women's knowledge.

When paleoanthropologists challenged the "man the hunter" model, they asserted that women's gathering of plants and even animals and their products was probably at least as important as hunting in provisioning the group (Zihlman 1978, 1991, 1993; Zihlman and Tanner 1978). Even though it was based on a model of human evolution that assumed some adaptation to the sea, there was much of interest in Elaine Morgan's *The Descent of Woman* (1972). For example, the notion that speech might have arisen from interaction between mothers and babies was one that had not been raised in the anthropological literature but was at least as reasonable as other speculations.

In spite of these forays into archaeology's backyard, it took a long time for archaeologists to apply their data to the questions of women in the past. Alison Wylie calls this a "silence . . . enforced by a lack of relevant data" (Wylie 2002:186). In this context, she refers to historic archaeologists researching the history of slavery, but the expression applies as well to the early lack of archaeological interest in women and the assumptions about women that underlay that lack of relevant data.

One of the first things that had to happen to ground gender theory was a critique of the patriarchal system itself, although this term was rarely used by archaeologists. This critique took two forms. One was to note the ways that women in the past were ignored or trivialized in archeological discourse (e.g., Conkey and Spector 1984); the other ran to philosophical critiques, including the insight that data are not given but depend on theory, explicit or unconscious. The "theory ladenness" of any scientific enterprise is inescapable. Therefore, the "micro-politics of archaeology shape the directions and results of inquiry" (Wylie 2002:188). Wylie separates critiques that have laid bare the workings of such micropolitics into four categories.

The first type of critique is that of erasure. In the case of archaeology of gender, the problems that are deemed important can obscure issues of gender and render women entirely invisible. Joan Gero's (1995) discussion of "early man" studies in North America is a case in point. She shows how the paradigm of early man as defined by projectile points and hunting leaves women out entirely—both as subjects of research on Pleistocene humans in America and as researchers.

The second category noted by Wylie is distortion. She singles out the "projection onto prehistory of presentist and ethnocentric ideas about sexual divisions of labor and the status and roles of women in prehistory" (Wylie 2002:187). Many examples of this kind of critique are found in the chapters in this volume. For example, Hetty Jo Brumbach and Robert Jarvenpa (this volume) show that current attitudes toward and beliefs about hunting actually distort the roles of women in many cultures.

The third kind of critique identified by Wylie is political resonance. When an interpretation agrees with cultural ideas of the present, it is not likely to be questioned. The "politics of objectivism" is the fourth type of critique. Wylie describes this as the "conditions under which, or the mechanisms by which, . . . political interests come to shape . . . the systematic silences and replication of stereotypes" (Wylie 2002:187). The interest in power and prestige in current archaeology has been explicitly connected to a lack of interest in gender in archaeology (Nelson 1997, 2004a).

Thus, both theory and data are constructed. The constructivist view of archaeology and of science in general derives from "critiques of the kinds . . . described [previously, which] are often seen to reveal sociopolitical dynamics that are intrinsic to disciplinary practice and are constitutive of its results at all levels. They show how external (noncognitive) factors determine what data will be collected and how they will be construed as evidence, what interpretive and explanatory hypotheses will be taken seriously and accepted (sometimes evidence notwithstanding), and what range of revisions or corrections will be considered when evidence resists being appropriated in terms of entrenched presuppositions" (Wylie 2002:189). Margaret Conkey (2005) also noted the structure of power in the production of archaeological knowledge, which marginalizes both feminist and native archaeologies.

From these critiques, standpoint theory evolved, based on a philosophical argument that there is no "view from nowhere" (Wylie 2002:22). The belief that science is not biased has been shown to be false both because the structure of knowledge is socially derived (Gero 1995) and because individuals bring their own "standpoints" to their work. "What you find, archaeologically, has everything to do with what you look for, with the questions you ask and the conceptual resources you bring to bear in attempting to answer them" (Wylie 2002: xiv). A counterargument has been that feminist archaeology, in being engaged with political issues, is itself biased. But Wylie shows that situated interests do not necessarily determine the outcome of archaeological inquiry because of the evidence itself and its capacity to surprise.

The social constructionist understanding of gender has also come under criticism from those who think it makes women "victims." This is a word that is laden with emotion, which somehow implies a perpetrator, and as such this concept is not appropriate. To point out that certain laws, social customs, or stereotypes disadvantage women and/or other categories of people is not to allege that any single person or group of people has deliberately tried to victimize someone else. Analysis of the social system may show, however, that disadvantage is systematic. Disadvantaged groups would like to promote change if they can find the means to do so, but the powerful are reluctant to share their power, and counterattacks are mounted. It is those in power who try to silence opposition by trying to trivialize it and thus move guilt to the disadvantaged party (French 1985).

As a way out of the "victim" trap, the emphasis on agency has proven to be a useful tool in feminist analysis (Dobres 1995). While it is senseless to contrast "victims" with "agents," it is useful to note that social systems allow more or less leeway for even the disadvantaged to create change. Thus, studying the possibilities for decision making by those not in power can lead to more nuanced analyses.

The processual/postprocessual debate has sometimes involved gender studies in archaeology. Is feminist archaeology processual or postprocessual? While at first the theory, goals, and methods of feminist archaeology seemed to have contributed most to the postprocessual side, gender has more recently gained strongholds within the processual paradigm. Michelle Hegmon (2003) provides interesting examples of processual archaeologists who have begun to investigate gender under a category she calls "processual plus." These papers are opening to new ideas without giving up "science," which seems to have been the fear about both gender and postprocessualism (e.g., Crown 2000).

Controversies in Gender Archaeology

Gender archaeology is not without its tensions, factions, and mutual misunderstandings. Each archaeologist who studies gender has different sets of data to interpret, and this limits some possible ways to study gender but on the other hand may suggest new possibilities. Different theoretical perspectives, based only partly on differences in the data sets, also influence the results. But, as Alison Wylie (2002) has cogently argued, data constrain the kinds of interpretations that can be offered as well as the degree of certainty with which they are proposed. Not all interpretations are possible.

Thus, there is no orthodoxy in gender archaeology, no gatekeepers decide what is or what is not gender archaeology, and a certain diffuseness about the boundaries of the topic is typical. This is not a bad thing. A lack of orthodoxy has allowed the field to continue being creative and alive. Gender in archaeology was characterized not by an initial burst of brilliance followed by "cleanup" operations but rather by many fine minds providing continuing innovation.

Tensions in gender archaeology include whether it is just about women, the disjunction that may arise between feminism and gender, whether gender is cultural and sex is natural or sex is cultural too, and whether there is "good" and "bad" work in gender archaeology.

Many critiques of writing about "women" in the past centered on the essentialism of the idea of women as a group who could be characterized by specific "feminine" traits. Some of the early publications did treat women as a timeless category, while current gender archaeology emphasizes differences. Part of that shift has been due to changes in archaeology itself as well as advances in other disciplines. We can learn so much more by examining the specificity of archaeological sites within their own context. Rather than generalizing about a category called "women," we tend to ask what makes gender different in different places.

But, with roots in the feminist movement, it is clear that gender archaeology *is* about women. It is about the missing women archaeologists, equity issues for women, and the missing women in the past. It is about the relationships between women and men. But that is not all. Early publications hedged their bets, with both "gender" and "women" in their titles (e.g., Gero and Conkey 1991), and many publications that use the word "gender" concentrate on the female gender. Yet women are not all that gender archaeology studies. Relational genders, age, and class can all be relevant to gender archaeology. Janet Spector (1998:49) recommends that the focus be on women and on gender dynamics, which allows a foot in both camps.

However, in this volume, the answer to whether gender in archaeology is just about women is a resounding "no!" Gender is about relationships between or among whatever genders a particular society recognizes. Thus, all possible kinds of genders should be considered, not just male and female. Ruth Whitehouse (1998:5) asks "whether gender should be considered a universal and primary category of social organization, and if so, whether it invariably takes the dichotomous binary form found in western society." It is clear that nonbinary genders should sometimes take center stage (Hollimon, this volume).

It is necessary to remember, though, the fact that gender archaeology has roots in the women's movement and attend to some of the basic questions that arose in response to androcentric blinders. That stage is not complete. My sister gave me a T-shirt with the slogan "I'll be a post-feminist in the post-patriarchy." Ruth Whitehouse (1998:5) worries that "women will be written out of history before they are written into it." Attention still needs to be paid to women. Feminism is about making all women count and has been a global enterprise from the start (Morgan 1984).

On the other hand, while androcentrism has not been eradicated, in the course of exposing it other blinders have been identified, such as class and ethnicity. To become aware of such unconscious attitudes, feminists insist that each person needs to be aware of one's own biases and one's own standpoint. Returning again and again to the data can be a useful check against unwarranted assumptions.

The question of feminism and gender research has additional dimensions. Feminism is necessarily political, and the point of view that asserts that science has no politics has stifled (or attempted to stifle) feminism in archaeology. However, it has become abundantly clear that people do science and that people have standpoints (Wylie 1996). The archaeology establishment created barriers against women for a very long time precisely because it was gendered male. The basic goal of feminism is to make women count, but it is not to eradicate men!

Finally, the "sex/gender system" may not always be a useful way to describe archaeological past. Sex and gender are not clearly separable. Ruth Whitehouse reminds us that "biology is not something that is either understood or experienced separately from culture, it is always culturally mediated. . . . Biology and culture continually interact from birth and throughout life (Whitehouse 1998:4).

Questions in the Public Eye

Some questions arise among the general public that have largely been set aside by those who practice gender in archaeology, but they still engage the media: Was there ever a matriarchy? Did Amazons ever exist? What about goddesses? and the recurring chestnut, Is gender all in our genes (or hormones or the wiring of our brains) after all?

The answers to these questions are elusive, but for most archaeologists these are the wrong questions because they are not framed as scholarly questions. Instead of generalizing about "women," the authors of the chapters in this volume ask more detailed and more insightful questions and are more focused on the lives of various kinds of people.

On the other hand, these kinds of questions will be asked regardless of what professional archaeologists think of them. It is useful to be prepared with answers, and some archaeologists (and others) have provided them in cogent ways (e.g., Fee 1974). For example, the problem with looking for goddesses in the past is often that they are used out of context for the purpose of women's spirituality. This is not bad; it is simply irrelevant to archaeology. The more specific uses of archaeology by Marija Gimbutas have been examined and shown to use loaded words when describing discoveries, for example, designating a building as a "shrine" or a figurine as a "goddess" (Conkey and Tringham 1995). The context of Çatalhöyök, widely used as an example of a matriarchal society, is being thoughtfully considered from all sides. It is interesting to follow the website, which includes the input of many different interest groups (Wolle and Tringham 2000).

Progress

But is the progress only skin deep? For example, a book that aspires to define *Archaeology at the Millennium*, subtitled *A Sourcebook* (Feinman and Price 2001), is not a milestone for gender in archaeology. In fact, gender has barely made a dent in the consciousness of most of these authors. If the index was constructed correctly, "woman" does not appear in the book at all (or else it was not important enough to appear in the index), and even the word "gender" appears on only three pages in the entire 508-page tome. The exceptions occur in three chapters. Jerry Sabloff and Wendy Ashmore, who discuss the history of settlement pattern studies in archaeology, do notice, as number ten in a list of eleven "topics or areas of interest," that "social variability, including gender, class, and other social identities," can be studied (Sabloff and Ashmore 2001:21). Gender is only a whisper here, but it is not altogether silent. When discussing households, Sabloff and Ashmore state that the developments in gender studies in archaeology are "still emergent." In my opinion, they have emerged, with excellent papers by Julia Hendon (this volume), among others.

The only chapter in *Archaeology at the Millennium* that comes to grips with gender as a basic component of social identity is Cathy Costin's (2001) chapter on craft production systems. It is notable that many of the leading theorists of craft production are women, many of whom are well versed in feminist theory. For this reason, the literature in this area is rich with variety and subtlety and eschews cross-cultural generalizations. Costin is to be congratulated in bringing this book truly to the millennium.

Gil Stein's (2001) chapter on ancient state societies in the Old World acknowledges gender, along with class and ethnicity, as important in considering power relationships. The connection with European archaeology is interesting since the archaeological paradigm in Europe is far more welcoming to the archaeology of gender than is that of America.

Equity issues for women in archaeology have made small inroads in the Feinman and Price volume, however. Five of the sixteen authors are women, although only three of them escape a male coauthor. Thus, of the fourteen chapters, nine are by males only, two are coauthored by a man and a woman, and three are by women. Two of the three chapters that mention gender have women authors.

Overt androcentrism has thus waned from the archaeological scene, but the paradigms that produced it have not. Feminist archaeological theory is all but invisible. This is troubling. Perhaps one glimmer of hope is an assessment of archaeological theory in America by Michelle Hegmon (2003). This paper, published in the flagship journal of archaeology in America, provides interesting evidence that gender is making some inroads even into the Americanist paradigm, although most of that progress is being made by women archaeologists. In a section that Hegmon calls "Processual Plus," gender plays a prominent role. Her examples demonstrate that the archaeology of gender can be incorporated into the eco-techno-economic paradigm.

In spite of the gloom that the previously mentioned observations might induce, other paradigms are more hopeful for gender archaeology. *Contemporary Archaeology in Theory*, edited by Robert Preucel and Ian Hodder (1996), not only acknowledges research on gender but also devotes an entire section to it. Unlike the Feinman and Price volume, which contains all new chapters, Preucel and Hodder have chosen to reprint important articles, thus acknowledging further that some feminist papers have had an impact on the field of archaeology. That volume of course has a postprocessual slant, while the Feinman and Price volume previously discussed is almost entirely within the processual paradigm. It is clear where the easiest acceptance of gender in archaeology lies.

Other evidence of progress is that gender gets some notice in the latest edition of Brian Fagan's *Archaeology: A Brief Introduction* (2006), which is widely used in introductory courses. Furthermore, *Archaeological Theory Today* (Hodder 2001) has three out of twelve chapters authored by women on a topic (theory) that once was a masculine preserve.

Who Benefits?

Which brings us to the important question for feminists: Who benefits? So far, women archaeologists, whether interested in gender or not, have benefited. There are more of us, and we are freer to pursue gender interests. But I would also insist that benefit accrues to women everywhere from the study of gender in the past. Variation of women's roles in the past is important to discover and demonstrate, especially when it is presented in terms that can be understood and adopted within archaeology as a whole.

Women (and girls) in the present can thus see that women have not always been either invisible or the "drudge on the hide" (Gifford-Gonzalez 1993) but have had important roles in societies around the world. Girls can choose from a variety of role models and behave in a variety of ways. Researching gender in archaeology has shown that there is nothing women biologically couldn't do, and archaeology has the data to prove it. Leaders, warriors, athletes, and, yes, mothers, wives, and daughters were all roles that some women could fill at some time in their lives, given their class and other circumstances. So one of the answers to "who benefits?" is that women in general benefit. Nancy Wicker and Bettina Arnold (1999:3) remind us that "research into past gender constructs has significant implications for contemporary policy-making, for the shaping of public opinion, and even for our expectations of the new millennium."

But just as important, archaeology benefits. Gender in archaeology requires closer attention to many kinds of data when one refuses to accept the assumption that males were exclusively the movers and shakers. As Janet Spector (1998:49) notes, "Our research provides the 'props' and the 'scripts' for museums, the media, textbooks, teachers and parents, about human origins, capabilities, developments, variation and change." Our work should not perpetuate stereotypes but should reason from data, look for alternative lines of data, and present clear conclusions that can be used by the general public.

About This Volume

The intention of the *Handbook of Gender in Archaeology* is to highlight the insights and increased specificity that the study of gender has brought to archaeology. The chapters in this volume are divided into four parts in order to facilitate their usefulness to students, nonspecialists, and specialists in gender archaeology. They include theoretical and thematic issues, identities, archaeological traditions, and world regions. Each chapter may include history, theory, method, and examples, depending on the subject matter. Each author also looks to the future.

Part I addresses a variety of ways to approach gender in archaeology with different data subsets. Each theme, method, or issue is explored with examples. Feminist methods, historical archaeology, classical archaeology, ethnoarchaeology, material culture, and feminist methods are more general, while the chapters that focus on heterarchy, mortuary contexts, households, and landscapes are concerned with the interaction between method and theory given that particular topic.

Part II is devoted to identities as they relate to gender. These include personhood, sexuality, masculinities, and third or fourth genders. They are on the leading edge of gender studies in many ways, as they struggle with questions that have not been posed before.

Part III describes what is known about gender within particular subsistence strategies since this is often the way that sites are categorized. Archaeological categories such as Neolithic, Archaic, or Middle Stone Age are not used in archaeology worldwide, so they are less useful for a book of this type. Furthermore, generalizations have been made about gender roles in different subsistence modes, and comparing them directly is useful. When each topic is pursued, universals in gender studies turn out to be less productive than concentrating on variables and finding the revealing differences.

Slicing the data another way, part IV describes the research on gender in archaeology that has been undertaken in different regions of the world. In some regions, there has been a great deal of study and thought about gender, while in others the study of gender is nascent. Nevertheless, it is interesting to compare the regions in terms of both the theoretical stances and the data uncovered.

A certain amount of overlap is inevitable in this kind of presentation. This enriches this volume by providing more than one perspective on the same issues. While each chapter is an overview of its subject and since gender in archaeology is an ever-growing field, the chapters cannot be comprehensive. Nevertheless, besides discussing what has been accomplished already in gender research, these chapters most excitingly present new ideas and point the way to future research. The reader will be inspired to take gender research in other new directions.

References

Alcoff, Linda
    1995   Cultural Feminism versus Post-Structuralism: The Identity Crisis in Feminist Theory. In *Culture/Power/Nature*. N. B. Dirks, G. Eley, and S. B. Ortner, eds. Pp. 96–122. Princeton, NJ: Princeton University Press.

Ardren, Traci, ed.
    2002   *Ancient Maya Women*. Walnut Creek, CA: AltaMira Press.

Arnold, Karen, Roberta Gilchrist, Pam Graves, and Sarah Taylor, eds.
    1988   Women and Archaeology. *Archaeological Review from Cambridge* 7(1):2–8.

Balme, Jane, and Wendy Beck
    1993   Archaeology and Feminism—Views on the Origins of the Division of Labour. In *Women in Archaeology: A Feminist Critique*. Occasional Papers in

Archaeology, no. 23. Hilary du Cros and Laurajane Smith, eds. Pp. 61–74. Canberra: Department of Prehistory, Research School of Pacific Studies, Australian National University.

Barber, Elizabeth Wayland
 1994 *Women's Work: The First 20,000 Years.* New York: Norton.

Barstow, Ann
 1978 The Uses of Archaeology for Women's History: James Mellaart's Work on the Neolithic Goddess at Çatal Hüyük. *Feminist Studies* 4(3):7–17.

Bem, Sandra L.
 1993 *The Lenses of Gender: Transforming the Debate on Sexual Inequality.* New Haven, CT: Yale University Press.

Bender, Susan J.
 1991 Towards a History of Women in Northeastern U.S. Archaeology. In *The Archaeology of Gender*, Proceedings of the Twenty-Second Annual Chacmool Conference. Dale Walde and Noreen D. Willows, eds. Pp. 211–16. Calgary: Department of Archaeology, University of Calgary.

Bertelsen, Reidar, Arnvid Lillehammer, and Jenny-Rita Naess, eds.
 1987 *Were They All Men? An Examination of Sex Roles in Prehistoric Society.* Acts from a workshop held at Ulstein Kloster, Rogaland, November 2–4, 1979. Stavanger: Arkeologisk Museum i Stavanger.

Bird, C. F. M.
 1993 Woman the Toolmaker: Evidence for Women's Use and Manufacture of Flaked Stone Tools in Australia and New Guinea. In *Women in Archaeology: A Feminist Critique.* Occasional Papers in Archaeology, no. 23. Hilary du Cros and Laurajane Smith, eds. Pp. 22–30. Canberra: Department of Prehistory, Research School of Pacific Studies, Australian National University.

Bleier, Ruth
 1986 Sex Differences Research: Science or Belief? In *Feminist Approaches to Science.* Ruth Bleier, ed. Pp. 147–64. New York: Pergamon Press.

Boulding, Elise
 1976 *The Underside of History: A View of Women through Time.* Boulder, CO: Westview.

Boye, L., B. Draidy, K. Hvenegaard-Lassen, and V. Odegaard
 1984 Towards an Archaeology for Women. S. Holten-Dall, trans. *Archaeological Review from Cambridge* 3(1):82–85.

Braidwood, Robert
 1975 *Prehistoric Men.* Glenview, IL: Scott, Foresman.

Bruhns, Karen Olsen, and Karen E. Stothert
 1999 *Women in Ancient America.* Norman: University of Oklahoma Press.

Brumfiel, Elizabeth M.
 1992 Distinguished Lecture in Archaeology: Breaking and Entering the Ecosystem—Gender, Class, and Faction Steal the Show. *American Anthropologist* 94(3):551–67.

Butler, Judith
   1993   *Bodies That Matter: On the Discursive Limits of Sex*. London: Routledge.
Childe, V. Gordon
   1951   *Man Makes Himself*. New York: New American Library.
Claassen, Cheryl, ed.
   1992   *Exploring Gender through Archaeology*. Madison, WI: Prehistory Press.
   1994   *Women in Archaeology*. Philadelphia: University of Pennsylvania Press.
Claassen, Cheryl, and Rosemary Joyce, eds.
   1997   *Women in Prehistory: North America and Mesoamerica*. Philadelphia: University of Pennsylvania Press.
Cohen, Mark, and Sharon Bennett
   1993   Skeletal Evidence for Sex Roles and Gender Hierarchies in Prehistory. In *Sex and Gender Hierarchies*. Barbara Diane Miller, ed. Pp. 273–96. Cambridge: Cambridge University Press.
Conkey, Margaret W.
   1997   Mobilizing Ideologies: Paleolithic "Art," Gender Trouble, and Thinking about Alternatives. In *Women in Human Evolution*. L. D. Hager, ed. Pp. 172–207. London: Routledge.
   2005   Dwelling at the Margins, Action at the Intersection? Feminist and Indigenous Archaeologies, 2005. *Archaeologies* 1(1):9–59.
Conkey, Margaret W., and Janet Spector
   1984   Archaeology and the Study of Gender. *Advances in Archaeological Method and Theory* 7:1–38.
Conkey, Margaret W., and Ruth E. Tringham
   1995   Archaeology and the Goddess: Exploring the Contours of Feminist Archaeology. In *Feminisms in the Academy*. Domna C. Stanton and Abigail J. Stewart, eds. Pp. 199–247. Ann Arbor: University of Michigan Press.
   1996   Cultivating Thinking/Challenging Authority: Some Experiments in Feminist Pedagogy in Archaeology. In *Gender and Archaeology*. R. P. Wright, ed. Pp. 224–50. Philadelphia: University of Pennsylvania Press.
Cordell, Linda S.
   1993   Women Archaeologists in the Southwest. In *Hidden Scholars: Women Anthropologists and the Native American Southwest*. Nancy J. Parezo, ed. Pp. 202–345. Albuquerque: University of New Mexico Press.
Costin, Cathy Lynne
   2001   Craft Production Systems. In *Archaeology at the Millennium: A Source Book*. G. Feinman and T. D. Price, eds. Pp. 273–327. New York: Kluwer Academic/Plenum.
Coward, Rosalind
   1983   *Patriarchal Precedents*. London: Routledge and Kegan Paul.
Crown, Patricia L.
   2000   Women's Role in Changing Cuisine. In *Women and Men in the Prehispanic South-*

west: Labor, Power, and Prestige. Patricia L. Crown, ed. Pp. 221–66. Santa Fe, NM: School of American Research Press.

Dahlberg, Frances
  1981   Woman the Gatherer. New Haven, CT: Yale University Press.

Davis, Elizabeth G.
  1971   The First Sex: The Book That Proves That Woman's Contribution to Civilization Has Been Greater Than Man's. New York: Penguin.

Diaz-Andreu, Margarita, and Marie Louise Stig Sørensen, eds.
  1998   Excavating Women: A History of Women in European Archaeology. London: Routledge.

Dobres, Marcia-Anne
  1995   Gender and Prehistoric Technology: On the Social Agency of Technical Strategies. World Archaeology 27(1):25–49.

du Cros, Hilary, and Laura Jane Smith, eds.
  1993   Women in Archaeology: A Feminist Critique. Canberra: Australian National University.

Ehrenberg, Margaret
  1989   Women in Prehistory. Norman: University of Oklahoma Press.

Fagan, Brian
  2006   Archaeology: A Brief Introduction. Upper Saddle River, NJ: Pearson Prentice Hall.

Fee, Elizabeth
  1974   The Sexual Politics of Victorian Social Anthropology. In Clio's Consciousness Raised. Mary Hartman and Lois W. Banner, eds. Pp. 86–102. New York: Harper Torchbooks.

Feinman, Gary M., and T. Douglas Price, eds.
  2001   Archaeology at the Millennium: A Source Book. New York: Kluwer Academic/Plenum.

Fraser, Antonia
  1989   The Warrior Queens. New York: Alfred A. Knopf.

French, Marilyn
  1985   Beyond Power: On Men, Women, and Morals. New York: Summit Books.

Gailey, Christine Ward
  1985   The State of the State in Anthropology. Dialectical Anthropology 8:65–89.

Gero, Joan M.
  1991   Genderlithics: Women's Roles in Stone Tool Production. In Engendering Archaeology: Women and Prehistory. Joan M. Gero and Margaret W. Conkey, eds. Pp. 163–193. Oxford: Basil Blackwell.
  1995   The Social World of Prehistoric Facts: Gender and Power in Paleo-Indian Research. In Interpretive Archaeology, A Reader. J. Thomas, ed. Pp. 304–16. London: Leicester University Press.

Gero, Joan M., and Margaret W. Conkey, eds.
  1991   Engendering Archaeology: Women and Prehistory. Oxford: Basil Blackwell.

Gero, Joan M., David M. Lacy, and Michael L. Blakey
  1983   Introduction. In The Socio-Politics of Archaeology. Joan M. Gero, David M. Lacy,

and Michael L. Blakey, eds. Pp. 1–4. Research Report, no. 23. Amherst: Department of Anthropology, University of Massachusetts.

Gifford-Gonzalez, Diane
    1993   You Can Hide, but You Can't Run: Representations of Women's Work in Illustrations of Paleolithic Life. *Visual Anthropology Review* 9(1):3–21.

Gilchrist, Roberta
    1991   Women's Archaeology? Political Feminism, Gender Theory and Historical Revision. *Antiquity* 65:495–501.

Gimbutas, Marija
    1982   *The Goddesses and Gods of Old Europe: Myths and Cult Images.* Berkeley: University of California Press.

Goodale, Jane C.
    1971   *Tiwi Wives: A Study of the Women of Melville Island, North Australia.* Seattle: University of Washington Press.

Hamilakis, Yannis, Mark Pluciennik, and Sarah Tarlow
    2002   Introduction: Thinking through the Body. In *Thinking through the Body: Archaeology of Corporeality.* Yannis Hamilakis, Mark Pluciennik, and Sarah Tarlow, eds. Pp. 1–21. New York: Kluwer Academic/Plenum.

Hays-Gilpin, Kelley
    2000   Feminist Scholarship in Archaeology. *Annals, American Academy of Political and Social Sciences* 571:89–106.

Hegmon, Michelle
    2003   Setting Theoretical Egos Aside: Issues and Theory in North American Archaeology. *American Antiquity* 68(2):213–43.

Hodder, Ian, ed.
    2001   *Archaeological Theory Today.* Cambridge: Polity Press.

Hrdy, Sarah Blaffer
    1986   Empathy, Polyandry, and the Myth of the Coy Female. In *Feminist Approaches to Science.* Ruth Bleier, ed. Pp. 119–46. New York: Pergamon Press.

Jameson, John H., Jr., John E. Ehrenhard, and Christine A. Finn
    2003   *Ancient Muses, Archaeology and the Arts.* Tuscaloosa: University of Alabama Press.

Janeway, Elizabeth
    1971   *Man's World, Woman's Place: A Study in Social Mythology.* New York: Morrow Quill Paperbacks.

Joyce, Rosemary
    2000   *Gender and Power in Prehispanic Mesoamerica.* Austin: University of Texas Press.

Joyce, Rosemary, Carolyn Guyer, and Michael Joyce
    2000   *Sister Stories.* www.nyupress.nyu.edu/sisterstories. New York: New York University Press.

Kehoe, Alice B.
    1983   The Shackles of Tradition. In *The Hidden Half: Studies of Plains Indian Women.* P. Albers and B. Medicine, eds. Pp. 53–73. Washington, DC: University Press of America.

> 1990   Points and Lines. In *Powers of Observation: Alternative Views in Archeology*. Sarah M. Nelson and Alice B. Kehoe, eds. Pp. 23–38. Archeological Papers of the American Anthropological Association 2. Washington, DC: American Anthropological Association.

Kelley, Jane H., and Marsha P. Hanen
> 1988   *Archaeology and the Methodology of Science*. Albuquerque: University of New Mexico Press.

Kent, Susan, ed.
> 1997   *Gender in African Archaeology*. Walnut Creek, CA: AltaMira Press.

Levine, Mary Ann
> 1991   An Historical Overview of Research on Women in Anthropology. In *The Archaeology of Gender*. Proceedings of the Twenty-Second Annual Chacmool Conference. Dale Walde and Noreen D. Willows, eds. Pp. 177–86. Calgary: Department of Archaeology, University of Calgary.

Linduff, Katheryn, and Yan Sun
> 2004   *Gender and Chinese Archaeology*. Walnut Creek, CA: AltaMira Press.

Lopiparo, Jean, and Rosemary A. Joyce
> 2002   Crafting Cosmos, Telling Sister Stories, and Exploring Archaeological Knowledge Graphically in Hypertext Environments. In *Ancient Muses, Archaeology and the Arts*. J. H. Jameson Jr., J. E. Ehrenhard, and C. A. Finn, eds. Pp. 193–203. Tuscaloosa: University of Alabama Press.

Lutz, Catherine
> 1995   The Gender of Theory. In *Women Writing Culture*. Ruth Behar and Deborah A. Gordon, eds. Pp. 249–66. Berkeley: University of California Press.

Miller, Barbara Diane
> 1993   The Anthropology of Sex and Gender Hierarchies. In *Sex and Gender Hierarchies*. Barbara Diane Miller, ed. Pp. 3–31. Cambridge: Cambridge University Press.

Moore, Jennifer, and Eleanor Scott, eds.
> 1997   *Invisible People and Processes: Writing Gender and Children into European Archaeology*. London: Leicester University Press.

Morgan, Elaine
> 1972   *The Descent of Woman*. New York: Bantam Books.

Morgan, Robin
> 1984   *Sisterhood Is Global: The International Women's Movement Anthology*. Garden City, NY: Anchor Press/Doubleday.

Nelson, Margaret, Sarah M. Nelson, and Alison Wylie, eds.
> 1994   *Equity Issues for Women in Archeology*. Archeological Papers of the American Anthropological Association 5. Washington, DC: American Anthropological Association.

Nelson, Sarah M.
> 1993   Gender Hierarchy and the Queens of Silla. In *Sex and Gender Hierarchies*. Bar-

            bara Diane Miller, ed. Pp. 297–315. Cambridge: Cambridge University Press.
  1997   *Gender in Archaeology, Analyzing Power and Prestige*. Walnut Creek, CA: AltaMira Press.
  1999   *Spirit Bird Journey* (a novel of prehistoric Korea). Littleton, CO: RKLOG Press.
  2004a *Gender in Archaeology, Analyzing Power and Prestige, 2nd edition*. Walnut Creek, CA: AltaMira Press.
  2004b *Jade Dragon* (a novel of prehistoric China). Littleton, CO: RKLOG Press.

Nelson, Sarah M., and Myriam Rosen-Ayalon, eds.
  2002   *In Pursuit of Gender: Worldwide Archaeological Approaches*. Walnut Creek, CA: AltaMira Press.

Parezo, Nancy J.
  1993   *Hidden Scholars: Women Anthropologists and the Native American Southwest*. Albuquerque: University of New Mexico Press.

Patterson, Thomas C., and Christine W. Gailey, eds.
  1987   *Power Relations and State Formation*. Washington, DC: American Anthropological Association.

Praetzellis, Adrian
  2000   *Death by Theory*. Walnut Creek, CA: AltaMira Press.

Preucel, Robert, and Ian Hodder, eds.
  1996   *Contemporary Archaeology in Theory*. Oxford: Blackwell Publishers.

Rapp, Rayna
  1977   Gender and Class: An Archaeology of Knowledge Concerning the Origin of State. *Dialectical Anthropology* 2:309–16.

Rohrlich, Ruby
  1980   State Formation in Sumer and the Subjugation of Women. *Feminist Studies* 61:76–102.

Romanowicz, Janet V., and Rita P. Wright
  1996   Gendered Perspectives in the Classroom. In *Gender and Archaeology*. R. P. Wright, ed. Pp. 199–223. Philadelphia: University of Pennsylvania Press.

Sabloff, Jeremy A., and Wendy Ashmore
  2001   An Aspect of Archaeology's Recent Past and Its Relevance in the New Millennium. In *Archaeology at the Millennium: A Source Book*. Gary M. Feinman and T. Douglas Price, eds. Pp. 11–32. New York: Kluwer Academic/Plenum.

Sanday, Peggy Reeves
  1981   *Female Power and Male Dominance: On the Origins of Sexual Inequality*. Cambridge: Cambridge University Press.

Sandler, Bernice R.
  1986   *The Campus Climate Revisited: Chilly for Women Faculty, Administrators, and Graduate Students*. Washington, DC: Association of American Colleges.

Schlegel, Alice
  1972   *Male Dominance and Female Autonomy*. New Haven, CT: HRAF Press.

Shoocongdej, Rasmi
    2002   Gender Roles Depicted in Rock Art: A Case from Western Thailand. In *In Pursuit of Gender: Worldwide Archaeological Approaches.* S. M. Nelson and M. Rosen-Ayalon, eds. Pp. 187–206. Walnut Creek, CA: AltaMira Press.

Silverblatt, Irene
    1988   Women in States. *Annual Review of Anthropology* 17:427–60.

Silverman, Sydel
    2002   *The Beast in the Table: Conferencing with Anthropologists.* Walnut Creek, CA: AltaMira Press.

Spector, Janet D.
    1991   What This Awl Means: Towards a Feminist Archaeology. In *Engendering Archaeology: Women and Prehistory.* Joan M. Gero and Margaret W. Conkey, eds. Pp. 388–406. Oxford: Basil Blackwell.
    1994   *What This Awl Means: Feminist Archaeology at a Wahpeton Dakota Village.* St. Paul: Minnesota Historical Society Press.
    1998   Doing Feminist Archaeology: What Difference(s) Does It Make? In *Redefining Archaeology: Feminist Perspectives.* Mary Casey, Denise Donlon, Jeannette Hope, and Sharon Wellfare, eds. Pp. 49–54. Canberra: ANH Publications.

Stein, Gil J.
    2001   Understanding Ancient State Societies in the Old World. In *Archaeology at the Millennium: A Source Book.* Gary M. Feinman and T. Douglas Price, eds. Pp. 353–79. New York: Kluwer Academic/Plenum.

Stone, Merlin
    1976   *When God Was a Woman: The Story—Archaeologically Documented—of the Most Ancient of Religions, the Religion of the Goddess, and the Role This Ancient Worship Played in Judeo-Christian Attitudes toward Women.* New York: Dial Press.

Terrell, John
    1990   Storytelling and Prehistory. In *Advances in Archaeological Method and Theory.* M. Schiffer, ed. Pp. 1–29. New York: Academic Press.

Thomas, William L., Jr.
    1956   *Man's Role of Changing the Face of the Earth.* Chicago: University of Chicago Press.

Ulrich, Laurel T.
    1990   *A Midwife's Tale: the Life of Martha Ballard Based on her Diary, 1785–1812.* New York: Knopf.

Wadley, Lyn
    1997   *Our Gendered Past: Archaeological Studies of Gender in Southern Africa.* Johannesburg: Witwatersrand University Press.

Walde, Dale and Noreen D. Willows, eds.
    1991   *The Archaeology of Gender.* Proceedings of the Twenty-Second Annual Chacmool Conference. Calgary: Department of Archaeology, University of Calgary.

Weiner, Annette B.
    1976   *Women of Value, Men of Renown: New Perspectives in Trobriand Exchange.* Austin: University of Texas Press.

White, Nancy M., Lynne P. Sullivan, and Rochelle Marrinan, eds.
    1999   *Grit Tempered: Early Women Archeologists in the Southeastern United States.* Gainesville: University of Press of Florida.

Whitehouse, Ruth, ed.
    1998   *Gender and Italian Archaeology: Challenging the Stereotypes.* Accordia Specialist Studies on Italy. London: Accordia Research Institute, University of London.

Wicker, Nancy L., and Bettina Arnold, eds.
    1999   *From the Ground Up: Beyond Gender Theory in Archaeology: Proceedings of the Fifth Gender and Archaeology Conference of University of Wisconsin—Milwaukee, October 1998.* BAR International Series 812. Oxford: BAR International.

Wogan, Lisa
    2005   Summersgate. *Ms. Magazine.* Summer 2005:57–63.

Wolle, Anna C., and Ruth Tringham
    2000   Multiple Catalhoyuks on the World Wide Web. In *Towards a Reflexive Method in Archaeology: The Example at Catalhoyuk.* I. Hodder, ed. Cambridge: MacDonald Institute for Archaeology.

Wylie, Alison
    1996   Good Science, Bad Science or Science as Usual? Feminist Critiques of Science. In *Women in Human Evolution.* L.D. Hager, ed. Pp. 29–55 London: Routledge.
    2002   *Thinking from Things: Essays in the Philosophy of Archaeology.* Berkeley: University of California Press.

Zarmati, Louise
    1998   "Archaeo-Speak": The Politics of Language in Archaeology. In *Redefining Archaeology: Feminist Perspectives.* Mary Casey, Denise Donlon, Jeannette Hope, and Sharon Wellfare, eds. Pp. 3–8. Canberra: ANH Publications.

Zihlman, Adrienne L.
    1978   Women in Evolution: Part II, Subsistence and Social Organization in Early Hominids. *Signs* 4(1):4–20.
    1991   Gender: The View from Physical Anthropology. In *The Archaeology of Gender.* Proceedings of the Twenty-Second Annual Chacmool Conference. Dale Walde and Noreen D. Willows, eds. Pp. 4–10. Calgary: Department of Archaeology, University of Calgary.
    1993   Sex Differences and Gender Hierarchies among Primates: An Evolutionary Perspective. In *Sex and Gender Hierarchies.* Barbara Diane Miller, ed. Pp. 32–56. Cambridge: Cambridge University Press.

Zihlman, Adrienne, and Nancy Tanner
    1978   Gathering and the Hominid Adaptation. In *Female Hierarchies.* Lionel Tiger and Heather T. Fowler, eds. Pp. 163–194. Chicago: Beresford Book Service.

THEORETICAL AND THEMATIC ISSUES

I

Methods in Feminist and Gender Archaeology: A Feeling for Difference—and Likeness

ELIZABETH M. BRUMFIEL

METHODOLOGIES FOR FEMINIST and gender archaeology have been sharpened by two decades of fieldwork with explicitly feminist and gender objectives, the diversification of theoretical approaches within feminist and gender archaeology, and the insights gained from twenty years of critical discussion. Feminist and gender archaeologists now ask a wider variety of research questions, draw on more forms of relevant evidence, and avoid a number of earlier pitfalls in data interpretation.[1]

Four methodological developments have been particularly important in feminist and gender archaeology: (1) increased attention to the variability in gender-relevant data; (2) increased concern with the inclusion of women, men, and other genders in a single frame of analysis; (3) increased caution in the use of ethnohistoric and ethnographic analogy in the study of gender; and (4) new methods for ascertaining how gender was experienced in the past. After reviewing these developments, I examine the strengths and weaknesses of four domains of archaeological evidence relevant to the study of gender: human skeletal remains, burials, representational art, and distributions gender-associated artifacts. I also examine some approaches to gender that do not require gender attribution.

Throughout this chapter, I highlight the contributions that archaeologists can make to the feminist goal of promoting social equality. Unlike Sørensen (2004), I do not believe that the presentist objective of achieving gender equality is in conflict with the disciplinary aim of developing a theoretically informed archaeology of gender. A scholarly archaeology of gender cannot be severed from politics because, implicitly or explicitly, all scholarship in the social sciences is rooted in political stances and has political implications (Shanks and Tilley 1987). Feminist archaeology is not exceptional in this regard. But even for the emotionally charged subject of gender, the material evidence maintains a degree of independence from the political and theoretical biases of the investigator so that feminist archaeology is much more than "just politics" (Wylie 1992, 1996; see also Brumfiel 1996b).

An empirically and theoretically informed archaeology of gender makes real contributions to the feminist goal of expanding social equality. An archaeology of gender can (1) promote self-confidence and pride for women and people of other genders, (2) create a sympathetic understanding of difference within genders and sameness across genders that will facilitate broad-based political movements capable of achieving social equality, and (3) enhance our understanding of how gender hierarchy is created and maintained so as to design effective policies for promoting equality in contemporary society.

Variability

Feminists of color have focused our attention on the existence of variability ("difference") within gender categories (Combahee River Collective 1977; hooks 1984; Mohatny 1988). These feminists argue that the meaning and consequences of gender vary, depending on the intersection of gender with other social identities, such as race, class, ethnicity, and age (see also Butler 1990; di Leonardo 1991; Sacks 1988). Inspired by this insight, archaeologists have searched for the ways that the intersection of gender with other social categories, such as age and civil status, has produced variability within gender groups. For example, Martin (1998) defines a subgroup of women at the Pueblo site of La Plata, New Mexico, with multiple skeletal trauma. Rather than interpreting this as undifferentiated "violence against women" or "wife beating," Martin suggests the existence of a special subclass of women subjected to violence, perhaps female war captives or servants. Membership in this subclass, then, would be determined by the intersection of gender with a distinctive civil status (war captive or servant). Similarly, on the basis of burial treatment, Robb (1994a) suggests that the most important division in Neolithic Italian society was not between women and men but between the subgroup of adult (initiated?) males on the one hand and subadult (uninitiated?) males and all females on the other. Both gender and initiated status (for men, a function of age) were the criteria for these social groupings (see also Joyce 2001a).

Gay and lesbian scholars have demanded that we not assume a norm of exclusive heterosexuality (e.g., Rubin 1984), and this has prompted archaeologists to search among burials sexed as male or female for individuals who represent third and other genders (Hollimon 1997; Weglian 2001). For example, Hollimon

(1997) identifies two Chumash male burials that differ in important ways from other male burials in her sample. These males show much greater degeneration in the spine as compared to other males, and they were buried with digging-stick weights and basket fragments. Hollimon concludes that these two individuals were third-gender, two-spirit undertakers known from ethnographic descriptions of Chumash culture rather than conventional men.

Archaeologists also search gender-relevant data to find variation in the expression of gender from one context to another. This is linked to the recent emphasis on the social construction and maintenance of gender through performance (Butler 1990, 1993; Morris 1995). Gender can be performed differently in different contexts, imparting a mosaic quality to gender rather than overriding consistency, and these different performances might be evident in different archaeological contexts (Cohodas 2002:28; Crown 2000; Gero and Scattolin 2002; Sørensen 2000:61). Gero and Scattolin (2002) suggest that at Yutopian, Argentina, specialized tasks such as corn grinding divided household members by age, sex, and space, while collaborative activities such as copper smelting were collaborative and erased the differences between household members.

Archaeologists also explore variation in the way that gender is represented in the different media of a single society. For example, women are often represented differently in household figurines and state-sponsored art, and the gender attributes emphasized in burial practices may be different still (Brumfiel 1996a; Cohodas 2002; Joyce 2000). These different presentations of gender often highlight the elements of gender ideology that were contested by different social groups (Cohodas 2002). Thus, by recognizing variation in the representation of gender rather than expecting uniform conventions, archaeologists can define the elements of gender that were contested and study how these disagreements were negotiated.

Archaeologists also recognize variability in the various indices of gender equality. The different measures of social well-being within a given society do not always coincide. For example, Crown and Fish (1996) found that Hohokam women who were members of high-status households could be judged advantaged by some criteria (e.g., they had access to high-prestige spaces at the tops of mounds) but disadvantaged by other criteria (e.g., their personal autonomy was limited by walls enclosing high-prestige domestic space). This suggests that gender status is a mixed bag: individuals may be offered higher standing in some areas of life (e.g., prestige) at the cost of low standing in other areas of life (e.g., autonomy). Such trade-offs are very common in social life, and rather than expecting any simple answer to the question "What was the status of women in ancient society X?," archaeologists should investigate the various dimensions of social well-being and what is gained and what is lost at each step of social change.

Women, Men, and Other Genders—Together

The consideration of men, women, and other genders in a single analysis distinguishes the newer feminist and gender archaeologies from the older feminist archaeology, which emphasized the roles and status of *women*. Studies of women in ancient societies tried to correct for the fact that women and women's activities were virtually ignored in earlier archaeological reports (Conkey and Spector 1984). Studies of women in prehistory continue to be published (Ardren 2002; Bruhns and Stothert 1999; Nelson 2003), and they continue to serve two important functions. First, these studies highlight the contributions of women in ancient societies, and, second, they demonstrate the variability of gender roles in ancient societies, with the implication that gender roles and identities cannot be attributed a universal, unchanging human biology laid down during the Paleolithic. However, it is increasingly recognized that the condition of women in past societies is best understood if women are placed in a frame of analysis that includes men and other genders. This is because different genders are defined in relation to one another through their paradigmatic relationships. That is, men and women and other genders are defined not only in terms of what they are but also in terms of what they are not. The contrasting properties between genders define the meaning of each gender. Thus, recent work in feminist and gender archaeology includes both women and men (e.g., Meskell and Joyce 2003).

In addition, different genders must be analyzed together in order to identify the extent of difference between gender categories. The degree of difference between genders provides a measure of the salience of gender as a social category, that is, the extent to which gender is an important organizing principle in any given society. Second-wave feminists were certain that gender was a universally important dimension of social differentiation, but, more recently, scholars have realized that the emphasis given gender differences varies greatly from culture to culture or even in the same culture according to different contexts. We are only beginning to explore the causes of cross-cultural differences in gender salience. Archaeologists can contribute much to this discussion by being cognizant of the areas of overlap between genders, the situations in which difference is highlighted, and how these change through history.

Cross-gender comparison is also important for assessing the relative fates of women and men and other genders during periods of cultural transformation, such as the adoption of agriculture or state formation (Peterson 2002; Pyburn

2004a). For example, if in the transition to state formation both women and men suffered parallel declines in well-being, this is very different from a situation where women but not men experienced decline.

The Uses of Ethnohistory and Ethnography

Feminist and gender archaeologists have begun to exercise increased caution in projecting ethnographic and ethnohistorical data into deep prehistory and to resist more vigorously "the tyranny of the ethnographic record" (Wobst 1978). They recognize that historical records and ethnographies often are unreliable guides to the gender systems of past societies because these records are colored by the culture, class, and gender biases of their Western authors (Pyburn 2004a; Stahl 2001). And even when these records accurately describe gender systems as they existed at the time of Western contact, the gender systems might be vastly different from their precontact predecessors, given the often cataclysmic changes wrought by the contact situation (Etienne and Leacock 1980). In addition, the unexamined projection of ethnography or ethnohistory into prehistory erases the record of culture change and thus promotes essentialist views of both gender and culture (Chance 1996; Luedke 2004; Robin, in press; Stahl 2001; Trigger 1980).

Aware of these problems, archaeologists are beginning to show more finesse in the application of ethnographic analogy. Ethnographic analogy is most convincing when archaeologists identify complexes of traits in the ethnographic record along with the functional or ideological circumstances that account for these complexes (Wylie 1985). For example, Robin (2002) examines the historical forces (e.g., nucleated settlements, schooling for children, and grants of agricultural land to village-based *ejido* committees) that have made farming an archetypically male task among contemporary Yucatec Maya. In the absence of these forces during the Classic period, Maya women and men may have collaborated on farming, which is the pattern for Maya women and men in the Lacandon area today. Robin argues that the dispersed households at ancient Chan Nòohol, Belize, are consistent with a pattern of collaborative farming during the Classic period.

Weismantel (2004) uses Melanesian and Amazonian ethnography to build a model of beliefs about sex, reproduction, lineage, and power in lineage societies. She then uses this model to convincingly explain many features of the iconography and depositional context of Moche pots. Her composite model avoids reliance on any single ethnographic case; in this way, Weismantel avoids collapsing historical change. By finding specific points of correspondence between the elements of her model and the Moche data set, Weismantel invites archaeologists to unpack the attributes of Moche style, to study the changing configurations of these attributes over time, and to track changes in Moche style and lineage ideology from the past to the present.

Experience

Phenomenology is concerned with the variable quality of human experience (Wilkerson 2000:269); it asks, "Who experienced what in prehistory?" (Gero 1991). Archaeologists have approached human experience in several different ways. One approach focuses on the *locations* of women and men and other genders on a site and the implications of these locations for gender-related statuses and roles, access to knowledge, experience, and motivation (e.g., Gero 1991; Gilchrist 1999; Hendon 1997; Sweely 1998; Tringham 1991). Another approach focuses on *embodiment*, the experience of gender and sexuality through the senses (Joyce 2004). Archaeologists study embodiment to explore how bodily experience can be used to lend an aura of naturalness and immutability to gender roles and identities (Joyce 2000; Sørensen 2000) and to demonstrate historical variation in definitions of sexuality and the body, thus undermining our belief that our conceptions of gender, sexuality, and the body are natural and self-evident (Gilchrist 1999:109–45; Meskell and Joyce 2003; Schmidt and Voss 2000; Weismantel 2004).

Phenomenological studies in archaeology have found a receptive audience. In part, this is because their concern with the individual, embodiment, identity, and agency resonates well with the ideas of the person in Western capitalist society. Phenomenological approaches can make intelligible the experiences of women or men or third genders in other times and other places and thus foster a sympathetic awareness and understanding of *differences*. This understanding of difference is important to feminist politics because it facilitates the building of political coalitions across groups, coalitions that are large enough to achieve institutional change (Hames-García 2000; Nguyen 2000).

However, interest in the experience of gender is sometimes associated with a distinct lack of interest in the organization of wealth and power that structures experience. An analysis of experience severed from its political and economic contexts runs the risk of essentializing people in the past because, in the absence of an understanding of political economy, gender subjectivity is often attributed to arbitrary sets of cultural definitions, values, and norms. To fully appreciate the experiences of others, these experiences must be related to the array of available possibilities and constraints that individuals face. Recognizing the economic and political structures that engaged individuals in past societies actually enhances our sense of them as active agents rather than cultural dupes.

I now turn to four types of archaeological evidence that are relevant to the study of gender: human skeletal material, burials, representational art, and distributions of gender-associated artifacts. I also examine some approaches to gender systems that do not require the identification of gender or the association of certain artifact classes with specific genders.

Bioarchaeological Approaches to Gender

Gender is a system of culturally defined differences that are ascribed to individuals on the basis of their biological sex. Bioarchaeology, the study of human skeletal material from archaeological contexts, has established fairly reliable methods for defining the sex of individuals on the basis of skeletal measurements.[2] Therefore, the association of particular types of grave goods and burial practices with male and female skeletons is a common point of entry into past gender systems (see the discussion later in this chapter). But of equal (or greater) interest is the fact that many types of behavior leave their marks on human bone. Since gender is socially constructed, it must be created and maintained through engendering performances, and these habitual performances result in skeletal alterations. Unlike burial ritual and art, which provide *representations* of gender, human bone records actual *enactment* of gender. Human bone is the closest thing that archaeologists have to the direct observation of gendered behavior in the prehistoric past.

Patterns of work are revealed in bone density, the size of muscle attachments, and wear on skeletal joints (Larsen 1997; Peterson 2002). Particular kinds of work are also indicated by some wear patterns on teeth (associated with the production of baskets, mats, and cordage; Molleson 1994), high rates of tooth decay (associated with the frequent intake of food and during cooking; Ardren 2002), and high frequencies of auditory exostoses (associated with deep-sea diving for shellfish; Allison 1984). Comparing indicators of sex with indicators of work, archaeologists can determine the presence of a gendered division of labor or, of equal importance, the *absence* of a gendered division of labor. They can assess changes in the work patterns of women and men during important cultural transitions, such as the adoption of agriculture (Peterson 2002), and they can provide independent assessments of the accounts of the division of labor left by Western observers (Hollimon 2000).

Archaeologists can explore variation in bone and joint alteration within sexes as well as between sexes to reveal the existence of third and other genders. For example, third genders can be identified by bone and joint patterning typically found on female skeletons but occasionally occurring on male skeletons (or vice versa) or by bone and joint patterns that are atypical for both males and females

(Hollimon 1997). Within sexes, differences in bone and joint alteration may also mark the intersection of gender with other social categories, such as age and class.

Bone can also reveal habitual participation in nonsubsistence activities. For example, ritual activities such as feasting may be evident in bone chemistry (Hastorf 1991), and sweat bathing may produce auditory exostoses (Lambert 2001). Healed fractures provide evidence of participation in warfare (Goodman and Armelagos 1985; Hollimon 2001) or exposure to violence (Martin 1998; Robb 1997; Walker 1989; Wilkinson and Van Wagenen 1993).

Bone can also distinguish native-born individuals from immigrants. Patterns of residential change are important aspects of past (and present) gender systems because social power is often a function of social alliances, and alliances are often disrupted by migration. Hence, women in societies with virilocal residence may have a more difficult time in maintaining social power than women in societies with uxorilocal residence. When individuals are buried in houses that persist over several generations, the distribution of genetic anomalies by sex can be used to identify patterns of postmarital residence (Spence 1974). Bone chemistry may also identify postmarital residence patterns and other patterns of migration (Price, Grupe, et al. 1994; Price, Johnson, et al., 1994), and it can reveal the existence of alien subgroups, such as female war captives (White et al. 2002, 2004).

Burial Data

Depositional contexts for human skeletons may provide direct evidence of behavioral patterns. For example, at least nine of sixteen skeletons recovered from precolonial gold mines in Zimbabwe were female, suggesting that the miners were women (Luedke 2004; Summers 1969). But usually, skeletons occur in burials, which are conscious creations that serve as a medium for the constitution of social relations (Arnold and Wicker 2001; Joyce 2001a). Burials reflect gender ideologies, which may or may not coincide with actual practice.

Differences in the burial programs for women, men, and other genders provide one measure of the salience of gender as a social category. For example, burials in the early levels of Çatalhöyük, Turkey, reveal no appreciable gendered differences in burial location, orientation, aspect, or grave goods. Heads were often removed from both female and male bodies and deposited in the foundations of house posts, which suggests that both females and males could qualify as honored ancestors (Meskell 2005). Gender at Çatalhöyük might have been marked in such perishable media as clothing, hairstyles, and tattoos, but archaeologists can provisionally accept the proposition that Çatalhöyük was a society where genders were not highly differentiated. Lack of gender differentiation probably indicates a condition of gender equality (see also King 2004).

When two or more contemporaneous burial programs exist in a single culture, they usually demarcate genders. When the distinctive burial programs include subadults, it is possible to define the age at which gender identity was imposed by society at large (Rega 2000). But different burial programs do not always demarcate genders, for example, in Neolithic Italy (Robb 1994a). Where men and women receive different burial treatments, gender inequality is usually implied since the whole purpose of creating gender difference is to legitimate differential access to resources and status (Sørensen 2000). But several archaeologists have argued that gender differences can signal parallel gender hierarchies rather than gender inequality (Gilchrist 1999; Hendon 1999; Moore 1993). The presence or absence of parallel gender hierarchies can be established using burial data: gender inequality is marked by differences in the labor invested in constructing female and male graves and by the quantity and quality of grave goods deposited in female and male graves (Chapman 1997; Crown and Fish 1996; Haviland 1997; Meskell 1998b).[3]

Since burials reflect gender ideologies, which may or may not coincide with actual practice, the assessment of gender equality based on burial data should be compared with skeletal indicators of material well-being in terms of health, nutrition, and violence (Ardren 2002; Cohen and Bennett 1993; Danforth et al. 1997; Gerry and Chesson 2000; Lillie 1997; Neitzel 2000; Rega 1997; Robb 1997; Savage 2000; Walker 1989; Wilkinson and Van Wagenen 1993). Archaeologists should also determine whether all members of a sex group were treated equally since only certain subgroups may have been disadvantaged. If not recognized as distinctive, a disadvantaged subgroup will drag down averages for a gender as a whole and make a special case of gender inequality appear to be a general condition (Ambrose et al. 2003; Martin 1998). Pyburn (2004a) argues that, almost always prior to Western contact, differences of class are much more salient than differences of gender in burial data, suggesting that the rise of class inequality did not uniformly entail marked gender inequality as suggested by Engels (1972 [1884]) and other gender theorists (e.g., Coontz and Henderson 1986; Gailey 1987; Leacock 1983; Sacks 1982; Silverblatt 1987; Zagarell 1986).

Grave goods have often been interpreted as indicating the activities of women, men, and other genders (Costin 1996). The persistent association of a specific artifact class with women or men or other genders implies a gendered division of labor or at least the ideology of a gendered division of labor.

In inferring activities from grave goods, archaeologists have shown a persistent tendency to invoke a double standard according to whether the patterns of activity suggested by the grave goods conform to Western gender roles (Conkey and Spector 1984; Nelson 1997; Pyburn 2004a). When the grave goods suggest activity patterns that parallel Western gender roles, the inferences are accepted as unproblematic. When the inferred patterns differ from Western gender roles, archaeologists seek alternative interpretations. For example, Winters (1968) inferred that grinding pestles found with female burials at Indian Knoll reflected women's food-processing roles but that grinding pestles found with male burials reflected male craft manufacture (Conkey and Spector 1984:11). It is always a good exercise in thought to imagine what interpretations archaeologists would give to grave goods were they strongly associated with the other sex and then to test for the likelihood of this alternate hypothesis by examining skeletal indicators of activity, the associations of this artifact with other tools and waste, or the representation of gendered activities in ancient art.

Finally, grave goods have been used to examine the life cycle in different cultures, particularly the way in which gender varies as it intersects with age and other social variables. Joyce (2001a) examines the burials of a dozen women at Early Formative Tlatilco, Mexico, showing the range of variation among them as gender intersects with age and household membership. Through this analysis, the Tlatilco women emerge as multidimensioned individuals rather than "faceless blobs" (Tringham 1991; see also Meskell 1998b).

Representational Art

Burials provide one form of gender representation; others forms include the presentation of human figures in rock art, figurines, murals, painted pottery, and sculpture. Human figures may or may not be gendered; that is, they may or may not bear anatomical features or styles of clothing suggesting gender difference. The prominence of gender difference in representational art is one indication of the salience of gender, which may change over time. For example, Hays-Gilpin (2000, 2004) has studied gender salience in the rock art of the American Southwest. In the preagricultural Archaic, only ungendered spirit beings were depicted, which Hays-Gilpin interprets as shamans' spirit helpers. During the Basketmaker era, a time of scattered, economically self-sufficient households, figures in rock art are clearly marked as male or female by anatomy or dress. In later, nucleated, Pueblo settlements, gender was no longer displayed on rock art; instead, it was enacted in public performances.

The public nature of representational art makes it a useful tool in enforcing gender norms. Thus, when representational art depicts women and men and other genders engaged in different activities, these depictions may constitute ideological statements about gender roles rather than direct reflections of reality. For example, in both Late Neolithic Italy and the Great Basin, the depiction of male figures in hunting scenes became more frequent just as hunting declined in economic importance (Robb 1994b; Whitley 1994). As in the case of gender patterns suggested by grave goods, the gendered activities depicted in representational art should be tested against skeletal indicators of activity and/or the distribution of associated tools in occupation contexts.

In addition to conveying norms of appropriate gender activities, artists may make ideological statements about gender through the differences in the sizes of female and male figures (as in Egyptian royal art) or through the relative positions of female and male figures: above/below, right/left, and front/back (Joyce 1996). The depiction of only one gender in art and the absence of the others has sometimes been interpreted as indicating gender dominance. However, like the interpretations of grave goods, the meaning of gender in art has sometimes been subject to a double standard. For example, the absence of women in Olmec art has been interpreted as an effort to exclude them from political negotiations and power (Joyce 2000), but the absence of males in Paleolithic figurines has been attributed to male fascination with the female body (Nelson 1990). In many cases, men have been considered the audience for art regardless of its content. For example, Meskell and Joyce (2003) interpret the depiction of the nude female body in ancient Egyptian art as serving male pleasure, but they also interpret the depiction of the nude male body in ancient Maya art as serving male pleasure. When women are depicted with little clothing and/or engaged in sexual acts, Western equations of nudity with sexuality and sexuality with the degradation of women lead to inferences of a low status for women. But Weismantel (2004) offers a convincing alternative reading of Moche depictions of sexuality connecting sexual acts with the nurturing of children.

Representational art provides an excellent opportunity to examine the negotiation of gender. Different art forms have different authors and different consumers. Archaeologists have begun to pay attention to differences in the way that gender is expressed in different contexts: state-sponsored art, such as monumental sculptures, versus commoner art, such as ceramic figurines, and so on (Brumfiel 1996a; Joyce 2000). In doing so, archaeologists hope to capture some of the tensions generated by the existing gender system. Cohodas (2002) distinguishes five separate strands of discourse in Maya art: sculpture in public spaces, sculpture in residential spaces, painted ceramics, mold-made figurine whistles from commoner households, and Jaina figurines from elite burials. The discourse generated by these different art forms has yet to be fully analyzed.

Gendered Tools and Spaces

Linking artifact types to one gender or another opens further avenues of inquiry by archaeologists. Changes in the frequency of gender-linked tools can be used to monitor changes in workloads and organization of labor that accompany social transitions such as emerging food production, imperial expansion, and colonialism (Brumfiel 1991; Costin 1993; Crown and Fish 1996; Deagan 2004; Hastorf 1991). The technical properties of artifacts can be used to examine the gendered dimensions of technological innovation or hidden forms of resistance in gendered labor (Brumfiel 1996a; Sassaman 1992). Artifact decoration may reflect the negotiation of gender status. For example, Hodder (1986:109) suggests that contemporary Ilchamus women decorate milk calabashes in order to call attention to the importance of women in reproduction in a society where reproduction is the central pivot of male power. Aztec women may have used decorated spindle whorls to call attention to the importance of women's production in the domestic and state economies (McCafferty and McCafferty 1991:31–32; 2000:47–48).

However, linking artifacts with gender, what Costin (1996) calls "gender attribution," is a tricky business. Ethnohistoric texts may describe the gendered division of labor in non-Western societies, but these descriptions cannot be taken at face value. The authors of these texts frequently skewed their observations to conform to their own Western, male expectations of the gendered division of labor. The association of grave goods with specific sexes in burials might represent a cultural ideal, but it might not coincide with the actual distribution of labor. The same could be true of the activities and tools associated with gender in representational art. Archaeologists have sometimes used the location of production areas to assign gender to one set of tools or activities or another. Usually, archaeologists attribute tools or activities within or adjacent to houses to women and tools or activities in more distant locales to men. But this seems to inscribe a Western, nineteenth-century "separation of spheres" ideology on all of human history (Pyburn 2004a).

The problems of gender attribution are so great that it is tempting to discard the enterprise entirely. But the valuable knowledge gained from studying gender-associated artifacts is an inducement to proceed cautiously to establish gender attributions. A gender attribution can be proposed when multiple lines of evidence (skeletal alteration, ethnohistory, burial data, and representational art) point consistently in the same direction. For example, Gero (1992) observes that *tupus* (clothes-fastening pins) and spindle whorls are consistently associated with women in ethnohistoric texts, representational art, and burials in the Andes from the Early Intermediate period to the present. Therefore, she argues, the recovery of *tupus* and spindle whorls from ritual feasting locales in Queyash, Peru, testify to the participation of women in those feasts. Her conclusion is strengthened by the fact that the spatial distributions of *tupus* and spindle whorls at Queyash overlap extensively.

Gender attribution must be argued separately for each historical case. For example, the association of spindle whorls with women in the Postclassic Basin of Mexico is strongly suggested by the ethnohistorical literature, burial data, and representational art. But the presence of spindle whorls in male graves at Cholula (McCafferty and McCafferty 2002) and Lamanai (Fekete 1996) indicates that the equation of spindle whorls with women cannot be taken for granted, even for pre-Hispanic Mesoamerica.

The distribution of gendered artifacts in different sorts of spaces has been used to infer power exercised by men and women in different social contexts (Gero 1992; Hendon 1997). Using artifacts to define gendered space is most effective for artifacts that are found in use contexts rather than trash or storage. Rapidly abandoned sites, such as Cerén, El Salvador, or Aguateca, Guatemala, are more likely to preserve artifacts in use contexts than sites that were gradually abandoned (Inomata and Stiver 1998). But even at rapidly abandoned sites, many artifacts will be found in storage spaces, and these do not necessarily represent the extent of gender segregation or blending that occurred in daily activity. Meskell (1998a) avoids problems of depositional context by basing her analysis of gendered domestic space on wall decorations and fixtures within New Kingdom Egyptian houses. Wall paintings pertaining to the sexual lives of mature women define rooms dominated by women; raised divans define the rooms devoted to men's sociability.

In general, a lack of spatial segregation by gender indicates a low degree of gender salience and inequality, as Gero (1992) argues for Queyash feasting and Hendon (1997) argues for domestic activity among the Classic Maya. The segregation of space by gender generally reflects gender inequality, although the argument has been made that the division of space by gender indicates parallel gender hierarchies (Gilchrist 1999). The scale, integration, and complexity of gendered spaces might also have implications for gender hierarchy (Blanton 1994; Hegmon et al. 2000; Hopkins 1987). Hendon (1997) and Robin (2004) suggest that Classic Maya royal courts were significantly more segregated by status, occupation, and gender than were the houses of lower-ranking nobles and commoners.

Finally, Gero and Scattolin (2002) consider the implications of a hearth at Yutopian, Argentina, that contains the debris of both food preparation (which they gender female) and copper working (which, they believe, would have engaged household members of different ages and genders). Gero and Scattolin conclude that a single household might engage in some tasks that segregate household members by age and gender and other tasks that involve the collaboration among household members of different ages and genders. In such situations, segregation and collaboration could act together to intensify household cohesion, and this would be missed if archaeologists sought only one overall measure of spatial segregation.

Beyond defining the spaces occupied by different genders, spatial distributions of gendered artifacts also suggest lines of vision that can used to reconstruct social relations. For example, Sweely (1998) uses the locations and orientations of grinding stones to establish personal interactions and relations of authority among women in the rural Maya village of Cerén. Lines of vision can also aid phenomenological analysis, as in Gilchrist's (1999) reconstruction of the experiences of noblewomen in their sequestered quarters in medieval castles.

Gender in the Absence of Gender Attribution

In a few cases, archaeologists have made inferences about gender relations without resorting to gender attribution. For example, Robin (2002) argues that the dispersion of rural Maya houses among agricultural fields at Chan Nòohol, Belize; the outdoor location of most activity areas; and the pole walls of houses that would have allowed people inside or outside the structure to peer at or talk to each other all facilitated a collaborative pattern of female and male labor among household members, with continuous communication throughout the day.

Hastorf (1991) argues that the extent of dispersion of debris from women's food-processing activities in Sausa, Peru, reflects the degree of contestation between genders. She observes that when Sausa came under Inca rule, an earlier pattern of relatively high dispersion of food debris was replaced by a pattern of decreased dispersion, suggesting that Inca dominance was accompanied by increased strain between women and men in local households. The interesting thing about this argument is that it applies equally even if food processing was not considered women's work. The heterogeneity or homogeneity of debris on household floors, regardless of their gendered affiliations, could gauge the degree of strain in household relations.

Dobres (1995:41) uses a similar line of argument to propose that site-specific technical variability in Magdalenian artifacts reflects the flexibility of social norms: "Flexibility in technical strategies practiced on a site-by-site basis may be interpreted as the embodiment of a general flexibility in social conduct situated to the specific settings in which people organized societies." Strictly defined gender roles, then, would be associated with low technical variability in artifacts; more flexible gender roles would be expected in cases of high technical variability.

Given the difficulties of gender attribution, these efforts to comment on gender without first linking artifacts to genders seem exceedingly worthwhile.

Using a Wider Lens: Proposals for Future Studies

Case studies are the most common form of research in feminist and gender archaeology. In part, this reflects the long-standing practice in archaeology of taking the site (or the region) as the unit of analysis. Archaeologists have frequently viewed themselves as the ethnographers of past societies, with a goal of reconstructing in as great a detail as possible the lifestyles, experiences, and worldviews of people in a particular time and place.

Recent efforts to avoid totalizing accounts of the past have reinforced this tradition. Many feminist archaeologists have rejected sweeping evolutionary models of prehistory because they utilize essentialized cross-cultural categories (such as "women," "progress," and "states") and mechanical models of culture change (Conkey and Gero 1991; Pyburn 2004a; Silverblatt 1988, 1991). These students of gender have emphasized the specificities of archaeological time, place, and culture, and their studies have been very useful. They have (1) refuted assumptions about the timelessness and invariability of women's roles, (2) heightened our sensitivity to gender difference, and (3) discredited evolutionary models of gender that were little more than projections of the gender biases of their Western authors (Nelson and Rosen-Ayalon 2002). Too often, however, these highly nuanced case studies leave unexamined the dynamic relationship between gender and other broad variables, such as ecology, economy, politics, and culture. The severing of connections between gender and these other broad variables threatens to marginalize the study of gender by reducing it to just another subfield of archaeology, leaving unrealized the full transformative potential of gender studies for archaeology. In addition, the case study approach in archaeology has frequently meant that archaeologists have adopted ethnographers' synchronic perspective for their own. But it was ethnography's shallow time depth that led early anthropologists to construe contemporary cultural variation as evolutionary development (Fabian 1983; Yoffee 1993), with all the essentializing and mechanistic qualities of unilineal evolutionist schemes.

The ties between gender systems and other broad variables are difficult to pursue in the absence of a comparative perspective. I suggest that we begin to broaden our focus in gender studies to include several neighboring regions and/or long-term histories. Such controlled comparisons would enable feminist and gender archaeologists to study broad social processes without falling into the essentializing traps that are so objectionable.

Archaeologists have real sequences of development at their disposal, and these sequences have analytic potential that has not yet been realized. Archaeologists can begin to examine the intertwining of identity, agency, economy, politics, and gender over the long term: how shifts in one variable open new possibilities for change in the others. Working with real sequences of development in limited regions, archaeologists can provide accounts that are *comparative but also contextual* and that deal with *structural variables*, such as economics and politics, *but also subjective variables*, such as identity and agency. Let me provide an example of work that I think would be very productive.

In Mesoamerica at the time of European contact, cloth production was a female activity laden with symbolic meaning (McCafferty and McCafferty 1991; Sullivan 1982). Archaeologists could ask, How did cloth production emerge as a symbol of women's identity? Was weaving always a female activity, given its compatibility with women's child care responsibilities (Barber 1994), or did the changing economic and political circumstances of cloth production determine that spinning and weaving would emerge as women's activities? How did these changing circumstances alter the power and status of cloth producers, the ideological meanings of cloth production and of being a woman? A broad, comparative study of the 3,500-year history of cloth production and gender in Mesoamerica would provide answers to these questions but would avoid the essentializing and mechanistic qualities of more synthetic, less historical accounts (for an initial effort at such a history, see Brumfiel 2005).

The study of long-term change in the social relations of cloth production alerts us to the likelihood of changes in the meaning of cloth production for women's identity. It encourages us to search for change in gender ideologies, identities, and experiences over time, and it makes us more (not less) aware of how gender is socially constructed through the negotiation of issues that range far beyond gender. The study of long-term change is one of the unquestioned strengths of archaeology, and the study of economic and political relations over the long term will enrich our understanding of gender subjectivity.

Feminists need real histories of weaving and farming, nursing and state formation, warfare, gender identity, and gender symbolism in Mesoamerica and in other regions of the world in order to better understand both the general principles that guide the operation of gender systems and the specific possibilities and constraints that women face under varied political, economic, and cultural circumstances. *Archaeologists* need these real long-term histories so that they can better account for both the intimate details of specific finds (e.g., Hodder 2000; Joyce 2001a; Meskell 1998b) and for the broader sweep of social change.

Notes

1. This chapter does not deal with issues of feminist epistemology, which would include the construction of basic categories in archaeology such as cultures, phases, and types; androcentric bias in the processes of data recovery, interpretation, and hypothesis testing; and feminist approaches to archaeological writing and to the teaching of archaeology. For reviews of these issues, readers should consult Conkey and Gero (1991, 1997), Conkey and Tringham (1995, 1996), Gero (1996), and Romanowicz and Wright (1996). These archaeologists argue that unreflective empiricism is not likely to yield comprehensive and reliable understandings of past gender systems and that the development of critical and reflexive research categories and procedures is the most essential goal of feminist methodology. I agree with these authors that the continuing critical assessment of basic archaeological assumptions is crucial; however, I also believe that feminist critiques in archaeology have progressed to the point where it is possible to generate reliable information about past gender systems by using amended approaches to traditional archaeological data.

I disagree with feminist archaeologists who argue that the primary contribution of archaeology to gender equality is its ability to demonstrate the *irreducible ambiguity* of all knowledge about the past. This position has been most clearly articulated by Conkey and Tringham (1995:231):

> What is empowering, in our view, is the recognition and acceptance of ambiguity, which admits the role of constructedness and the possibilities for reconfiguring and renegotiating meanings, including what constitutes evidence.... The contemporary reader ... must participate in and confront the entanglement of ambiguity, history, and the production of knowledge.

Instead, I prefer a *dialogic approach* to the presentation of archaeological data and interpretation. In a dialogic approach, investigators would present their own and others' interpretations of an archaeological data set along with the train of assumptions and inferences that underlies each interpretation. Investigators would then explain their preference for one interpretation over the others. I take as my model Warren's (1998:33–51) exposition of the arguments favoring and opposing the pan-Maya identity movement in *Indigenous Movements and Their Critics*.

The advantage of a dialogic approach is that it promotes the feminist goals of demystifying authoritative "facts" about the past and inviting readers to participate in the construction of knowledge (Longino 1994). At the same time, a dialogic approach makes it possible to argue against blatantly sexist and racist interpretations of the past, thus enabling feminists to mobilize the "emancipatory function of modern science" (Keller 1982). A dialogic approach also preserves the excitement of archaeological research, which is often carried out in the hopes of resolving at least some of the ambiguities in the archaeological record. Finally, a dialogic approach would build a reliable fund of knowledge about gender systems in the past that can be used by gender activists in the present to design effective strategies for promoting systems of gender equality.

2. In humans, biological sex is marked in several ways: by DNA, hormone levels, external genitalia, and skeletal structure. In any given individual, these may or may not coincide (Sørensen 2000:45).

3. Haviland's (1997) reconstruction of gender inequality at Classic Maya Tikal is the subject of vigorous criticism by Pyburn (2004b), but criticism seems warranted only of those who would use the Tikal data to generalize for "Maya culture" as a whole. During the Classic era, gender statuses seem to have differed from one Maya polity to the next.

References

Allison, Melvin J.
    1984   Paleopathology in Peruvian and Chilean Populations. In *Paleopathology at the Origins of Agriculture*. M. N. Cohen and G. J. Armelagos, eds. Pp. 515–30. Orlando: Academic Press.

Ambrose, Stanley H., Jane Buikstra, and Harold W. Krueger
    2003   Status and Gender Differences in Diet at Mound 72, Cahokia, Revealed by Isotopic Analysis of Bone. *Journal of Anthropological Archaeology* 22:217–26.

Ardren, Traci
    2002   Death Became Her: Images of Female Power from Yaxuna Burials. In *Ancient Maya Women*. T. Ardren, ed. Pp. 68–88. Walnut Creek, CA: AltaMira Press.

Ardren, Traci, ed.
    2002   *Ancient Maya Women*. Walnut Creek, CA: AltaMira Press.

Arnold, Bettina, and Nancy L. Wicker, eds.
    2001   *Gender and the Archaeology of Death*. Walnut Creek, CA: AltaMira Press.

Barber, Elizabeth Wayland
    1994   *Women's Work: The First 20,000 Years: Women, Cloth, and Society in Early Times*. New York: Norton.

Blanton, Richard E.
    1994   *Houses and Households: A Comparative Study*. New York: Plenum.

Bruhns, Karen Olsen, and Karen E. Stothert
    1999   *Women in Ancient America*. Norman: University of Oklahoma Press.

Brumfiel, Elizabeth M.
    1991   Weaving and Cooking: Women's Production in Aztec Mexico. In *Engendering Archaeology*. J. M. Gero and M. W. Conkey, eds. Pp. 254–51. Oxford: Blackwell.
    1996a   Figurines and the Aztec State: Testing the Effectiveness of Ideological Domination. In *Gender and Archaeology*. R. P. Wright, ed. Pp. 143–66. Philadelphia: University of Pennsylvania Press.

1996b The Quality of Tribute Cloth: The Place of Evidence in Archaeological Argument. *American Antiquity* 61:453–62.
2005 Cloth, Gender, Continuity and Change: Fabricating Unity in Anthropology. Presidential Address presented at the 104th Annual Meeting of the American Anthropological Association, Washington, DC.

Butler, Judith
1990 *Gender Trouble: Feminism and the Subversion of Identity.* London: Routledge.
1993 *Bodies That Matter: On the Discursive Limits of "Sex."* London: Routledge.

Chance, John K.
1996 Mesoamerica's Ethnographic Past. *Ethnohistory* 43:379–403.

Chapman, John
1997 Changing Gender Relations in the Later Prehistory of Eastern Hungary. In *Invisible People and Processes: Writing Gender and Childhood into European Archaeology.* J. Moore and E. Scott, eds. Pp. 131–49. London: Leicester University Press.

Cohodas, Marvin
2002 Multiplicity and Discourse in Maya Gender Relations. In *Ancient Maya Gender Identity and Relations.* L. S. Gustafson and A. M. Trevelyan, eds. Pp. 11–53. Westport, CT: Bergin & Garvey.

Combahee River Collective
1977 *The Combahee River Collective Statement.* Reprinted in *Theorizing Feminism.* A. C. Herrman and A. J. Stewart, eds. Pp. 26–33. Boulder, CO: Westview.

Cohen, Mark Nathan, and Sharon Bennett
1993 Skeletal Evidence for Sex Roles and Gender Hierarchies in Prehistory. In *Sex and Gender Hierarchies.* B. D. Miller, ed. Pp. 273–96. Cambridge: Cambridge University Press.

Conkey, Margaret W., and Joan M. Gero
1991 Tensions, Pluralities and Engendering Archaeology: An Introduction to Women and Prehistory. In *Engendering Archaeology.* J. M. Gero and M. W. Conkey, eds. Pp. 3–30. Oxford: Blackwell.
1997 Programme to Practice: Gender and Feminism in Archaeology. *Annual Review of Anthropology* 26:411–37.

Conkey, Margaret W., and Janet D. Spector
1984 Archaeology and the Study of Gender. *Advances in Archaeological Method and Theory* 7:1–38.

Conkey, Margaret W., and Ruth E. Tringham
1995 Archaeology and the Goddess: Exploring the Contours of Feminist Archaeology. In *Feminisms in the Academy*, D. C. Stanton and A. J. Stewart, eds. Pp. 199–247. Ann Arbor: University of Michigan Press.
1996 Cultivating Thinking/Challenging Authority: Some Experiments in Feminist Pedagogy in Archaeology. In *Gender and Archaeology.* R. P. Wright, ed. Pp. 224–50. Philadelphia: University of Pennsylvania Press.

Coontz, Stephanie, and Petra Henderson
    1986   Property Forms, Political Power and Female Labour in the Origins of Class and State Societies. In *Women's Work, Men's Property*. S. Coontz and P. Henderson, eds. Pp. 108–55. London: Verso.
Costin, Cathy L.
    1993   Textiles, Women, and Political Economy in Late Prehispanic Peru. *Research in Economic Anthropology* 14:3–28.
    1996   Exploring the Relationship between Gender and Craft in Complex Societies: Methodological and Theoretical Issues of Gender Attribution. In *Gender and Archaeology*. R. P. Wright, ed. Pp. 111–40. Philadelphia: University of Pennsylvania Press.
Crown, Patricia L.
    2000   Gendered Tasks, Power, and Prestige. In *Women and Men in the Prehispanic Southwest*. P. L. Crown, ed. Pp. 3–41. Santa Fe, NM: School of American Research Press.
Crown, Patricia L., and Suzanne K. Fish
    1996   Gender and Status in the Hohokam Pre-Classic to Classic Transition. *American Anthropologist* 98:803–17.
Danforth, Marie, Keith P. Jacobi, and Mark Nathan Cohen
    1997   Gender and Health among the Colonial Maya of Tipu, Belize. *Ancient Mesoamerica* 8:13–22.
Deagan, Kathleen
    2004   Reconsidering Taíno Social Dynamics after Spanish Conquest: Gender and Class in Culture Contact Studies. *American Antiquity* 69:597–626.
di Leonardo, Micaela
    1991   Introduction: Gender, Culture, and Political Economy. In *Gender at the Crossroads of Knowledge*. M. di Leonardo, ed. Pp. 1–48. Berkeley: University of California Press.
Dobres, Marcia-Anne
    1995   Gender and Prehistoric Technology: On the Social Agency of Technical Strategies. *World Archaeology* 27:25–49.
Engels, Frederick
    1972   [1884] *Origin of the Family, Private Property, and the State*. E. B. Leacock, ed. New York: International Books.
Etienne, Mona, and Eleanor Leacock, eds.
    1980   *Women and Colonization: Anthropological Perspectives*. New York: Praeger.
Fabian, Johannes
    1983   *Time and the Other: How Anthropology Makes Its Object*. New York: Columbia University Press.
Fekete, Eva
    1996   Excavating Gender: Rethinking the Archaeology of Maya Mortuary Practice. Master's thesis, York University.

Gailey, Christine W.
   1987   *From Kinship to Kingship: Gender Hierarchy and State Formation in the Tongan Islands*. Austin: University of Texas Press.

Gero, Joan M.
   1991   Who Experienced What in Prehistory? A Narrative Explanation from Queyash, Peru. In *Processual and Postprocessual Archaeologies*. R. W. Preucel, ed. Pp. 126–39. Carbondale: Southern Illinois University Center for Archaeological Investigations.
   1992   Feasts and Females: Gender Ideology and Political Meals in the Andes. *Norwegian Archaeological Review* 25:15–30.
   1996   Archaeological Practice and Gendered Encounters with Field Data. In *Gender and Archaeology*. R. P. Wright, ed. Pp. 251–80. Philadelphia: University of Pennsylvania Press.

Gero, Joan M., and M. Cristina Scattolin
   2002   Beyond Complementarity and Hierarchy: New Definitions for Archaeological Gender Relations. In *In Pursuit of Gender: Worldwide Archaeological Approaches*. S. M. Nelson and M. Rosen-Ayalon, eds. Pp. 155–71. Walnut Creek, CA: AltaMira Press.

Gerry, John P., and Meredith S. Chesson
   2000   Classic Maya Diet and Gender Relationships. In *Gender and Material Culture in Archaeological Perspective*. M. Donald and L. Hurcombe, eds. Pp. 250–64. New York: St. Martin's Press.

Gilchrist, Roberta
   1999   *Gender and Archaeology: Contesting the Past*. London: Routledge.

Goodman, Alan H., and George J. Armelagos
   1985   Disease and Death at Dr. Dickson's Mounds. *Natural History* 94(9):12–18.

Hames-García, Michael R.
   2000   "Who Are Our Own People?": Challenges for a Theory of Social Identity. In *Reclaiming Identity: Realist Theory and the Predicament of Postmodernism*. P. M. L. Moya and M. R. Hames-García, eds. Pp. 102–29. Berkeley: University of California Press.

Hastorf, Christine A.
   1991   Gender, Space, and Food in Prehistory. In *Engendering Archaeology: Women and Prehistory*. J. M. Gero and M. W. Conkey, eds. Pp. 132–59. Oxford: Blackwell.

Haviland, William A.
   1997   The Rise and Fall of Sexual Inequality: Death and Gender at Tikal, Guatemala. *Ancient Mesoamerica* 8:1–12.

Hays-Gilpin, Kelley
   1999   Beyond Mother Earth and Father Sky: Sex and Gender in Ancient Southwestern Visual Arts. In *Reading the Body*. A. E. Rautman, ed. Pp. 165–86. Philadelphia: University of Pennsylvania Press.

2004   *Ambiguous Images: Gender and Rock Art.* Walnut Creek, CA: AltaMira Press.
Hegmon, Michelle, Scott G. Ortman, and Jeannette L. Mobley-Tanaka
   2000   Women, Men, and the Organization of Space. In *Women and Men in the Prehispanic Southwest.* P. L. Crown, ed. Pp. 43–90. Santa Fe, NM: School of American Research Press.
Hendon, Julia A.
   1997   Women's Work, Women's Space, and Women's Status among the Classic-Period Maya Elite of the Copan Valley, Honduras. In *Women in Prehistory: North America and Mesoamerica.* C. Claassen and R. A. Joyce, eds. Pp. 33–46. Philadelphia: University of Pennsylvania Press.
   1999   Multiple Sources of Prestige and the Social Evaluation of Women in Prehispanic Mesoamerica. In *Material Symbols.* J. E. Robb, ed. Pp. 257–76. Occasional Paper 26. Carbondale: Center for Archaeological Investigations, Southern Illinois University.
Hodder, Ian
   1986   *Reading the Past.* Cambridge: Cambridge University Press.
   2000   Agency and Individuals in Long-Term Processes. In *Agency in Archaeology.* M. A. Dobres and J. Robb, eds. Pp. 21–33. London: Routledge.
Hollimon, Sandra E.
   1997   The Third Gender in Native California: Two-Spirit Undertakers among the Chumash and Their Neighbors. In *Women in Prehistory: North America and Mesoamerica.* C. Claassen and R. A. Joyce, eds. Pp. 173–88. Philadelphia: University of Pennsylvania Press.
   2000   Sex, Health, and Gender Roles among the Arikara of the Northern Plains. In *Reading the Body: Representations and Remains in the Archaeological Record.* A. E. Rautman, ed. Pp. 25–37. Philadelphia: University of Pennsylvania Press.
   2001   Warfare and Gender in the Northern Plains: Osteological Evidence of Trauma Reconsidered. In *Gender and the Archaeology of Death.* B. Arnold and N. L. Wicker, eds. Pp. 179–93. Walnut Creek, CA: AltaMira Press.
hooks, bell
   1984   *Feminist Theory from Margin to Center.* Boston: South End Press.
Hopkins, Mary R.
   1987   An Explication of the Plans of Some Teotihuacan Apartment Compounds. In *Teotihuacan: Nuevos Datos, Nuevas Síntesis, Nuevos Problemas.* E. McClung and E. Rattray, eds. Pp. 369–88. Mexico City: Universidad Nacional Autónoma de México.
Inomata, Takeshi, and Laura R. Stiver
   1998   Floor Assemblages from Burned Structures at Aguateca, Guatemala: A Study of Classic Maya Households. *Journal of Field Archaeology* 25:431–52.
Joyce, Rosemary A.
   1996   The Construction of Gender in Classic Maya Monuments. In *Gender and Archaeology.* R. P. Wright, ed. Pp. 167–95. Philadelphia: University of Pennsylvania Press.

2000   *Gender and Power in Prehispanic Mesoamerica.* Austin: University of Texas Press.

2001a   Burying the Dead at Tlatilco: Social Memory and Social Identities. In *Social Memory, Identity and Death: Anthropological Perspectives on Mortuary Rituals.* M. S. Chesson, ed. Pp. 12–26. Archaeological Papers of the American Anthropological Association 10. Washington, DC: American Anthropological Association.

2001b   Negotiating Sex and Gender in Classic Maya Society. In *Gender in Pre-Hispanic America.* C. F. Klein, ed. Pp. 109–41. Washington, DC: Dumbarton Oaks.

2004   Embodied Subjectivity: Gender, Femininity, Masculinity, Sexuality. In *A Companion to Social Archaeology.* L. Meskell and R. W. Preucel, eds. Pp. 82–95. Oxford: Blackwell.

Keller, Evelyn Fox

    1982   Feminism and Science. *Signs* 7:589–602.

King, Stacie M.

    2004   Spinning and Weaving in Early Postclassic Coastal Oaxaca. Paper presented at the 69th Annual Meeting of the Society for American Archaeology, Montreal.

Lambert, Patricia M.

    2001   Auditory Exostoses: A Clue to Gender in Prehistoric and Historic Farming Communities of North Carolina and Virginia. In *Archaeological Studies of Gender in the Southeastern United States.* J. M. Eastman and C. B. Rodning, eds. Pp. 152–72. Gainesville: University Press of Florida.

Larsen, Clark S.

    1997   *Bioarchaeology.* Cambridge: Cambridge University Press.

Leacock, Eleanor

    1983   Interpreting the Origins of Gender Inequality. *Dialectical Anthropology* 7:163–83.

Lillie, M. C.

    1997   Women and Children in Prehistory: Resource Sharing and Social Stratification at the Mesolithic-Neolithic Transition in Ukraine. In *Invisible People and Processes.* J. Moore and E. Scott, eds. Pp. 213–28. London: Leicester University Press.

Longino, Helen

    1994   In Search of Feminist Epistemology. *The Monist* 77:472–85.

Luedke, Tracy

    2004   Gendered States: Gender and Agency in Economic Models of Great Zimbabwe. In *Ungendering Archaeology.* K. A. Pyburn, ed. Pp. 47–70. New York: Routledge.

Martin, Debra L.

    1998   Violence against Women in the La Plata River Valley (A.D. 1000–1300). In *Troubled Times: Violence and Warfare in the Past.* D. L. Martin and D. W. Frayer, eds. Pp. 45–75. Amsterdam: Gordon and Breach.

McCafferty, Geoffrey G., and Sharisse D. McCafferty
    2002   Boys and Girls Interrupted: Mortuary Evidence on the Children of Postclassic Cholula, Puebla. Paper presented at the 101st Annual Meeting of the American Anthropological Association, New Orleans.
McCafferty, Sharisse D., and Geoffrey G. McCafferty
    1991   Spinning and Weaving as Female Gender Identity in Post-Classic Mexico. In *Textile Traditions of Mesoamerica and the Andes*. M. B. Schevill, J. C. Berlo, and E. B. Dwyer, eds. Pp. 19–44. Austin: University of Texas Press.
    2000   Textile Production in Postclassic Cholula, Mexico. *Ancient Mesoamerica* 11:39–54.
Meskell, Lynn
    1998a   An Archaeology of Social Relations in an Egyptian Village. *Journal of Archaeological Method and Theory* 5:209–43.
    1998b   Intimate Archaeologies: The Case of Kha and Merit. *World Archaeology* 29:363–79.
    2005   De/Naturalizing Gender in Prehistory. In *Complexities: Beyond Nature and Nurture*. S. McKinnon and S. Silverman, eds. Pp. 157–75. Chicago: University of Chicago Press.
Meskell, Lynn M., and Rosemary A. Joyce
    2003   *Embodied Lives: Figuring Ancient Maya and Egyptian Experience*. London: Routledge.
Mohatny, Chandra
    1988   Under Western Eyes: Feminist Scholarship and Colonial Discourses. *Feminist Review* 30:61–88.
Molleson, Theya
    1994   The Eloquent Bones of Abu Hureyra. *Scientific American* 271(2):70–75.
Moore, Henrietta L.
    1993   The Differences Within and the Differences Between. In *Gendered Anthropology*. T. Del Valle, ed. Pp. 193–203. London: Routledge.
Morris, Rosalind C.
    1995   All Made Up: Performance Theory and the New Anthropology of Sex and Gender. *Annual Review of Anthropology* 24:567–92.
Neitzel, Jill E.
    2000   Gender Hierarchies: A Comparative Analysis of Mortuary Data. In *Women and Men in the Prehispanic Southwest*. P. L. Crown, ed. Pp. 137–68. Santa Fe, NM: School of American Research Press.
Nelson, Sarah M.
    1990   Diversity of the Upper Paleolithic "Venus" Figurines and Archeological Mythology. In *Powers of Observation*. S. M. Nelson and A. B. Kehoe, eds. Pp. 11–22. Archaeological Papers of the American Anthropological Association 2. Washington, DC: American Anthropological Association.
    1997   *Gender in Archaeology*. Walnut Creek, CA: AltaMira Press.
        Nelson, Sarah M., ed.

2003　*Ancient Queens: Archaeological Explorations.* Walnut Creek, CA: AltaMira Press.
Nelson, Sarah M., and Myriam Rosen-Ayalon, eds.
2002　*In Pursuit of Gender: Worldwide Archaeological Approaches.* Walnut Creek, CA: AltaMira Press.
Nguyen, Minh T.
2000　"It Matters to Get the Facts Straight": Joy Kogawa, Realism, and Objectivity of Values. In *Reclaiming Identity: Realist Theory and the Predicament of Postmodernism.* P. M. L. Moya and M. R. Hames-García, eds. Pp. 171–204. Berkeley: University of California Press.
Peterson, Jane
2002　*Sexual Revolutions: Gender and Labor at the Dawn of Agriculture.* Walnut Creek, CA: AltaMira Press.
Price, T. Douglas, G. Grupe, and P. Schrörter
1994　Reconstruction of Migration Patterns in the Bell Beaker Period by Stable Strontium Isotope Analysis. *Applied Geochemistry* 9:413–17.
Price, T. Douglas, C. M. Johnson, J. A. Ezzo, J. H. Burton, and J. A. Ericson
1994　Residential Mobility in the Prehistoric Southwest United States. *Journal of Archaeological Science* 24:315–30.
Pyburn, K. Anne
2004a　Rethinking Complex Society. In *Ungendering Civilization.* K. A. Pyburn, ed. Pp. 1–46. New York: Routledge.
2004b　Ungendering the Maya. In *Ungendering Civilization.* K. A. Pyburn, ed. Pp. 216–33. New York: Routledge.
Rega, Elizabeth
1996　Age, Gender and Biological Reality in the Early Bronze Age Cemetery at Mokrin. In *Invisible People and Processes.* J. Moore and E. Scott, eds. Pp. 229–47. London: Leicester University Press.
2000　The Gendering of Children in the EBA Cemetery at Mokrin. In *Gender and Material Culture in Archaeological Perspective.* M. Donald and L. Hurcombe, eds. Pp. 238–49. New York: St. Martin's Press.
Robb, John E.
1994a　Burial and Social Reproduction in the Peninsular Italian Neolithic. *Journal of Mediterranean Archaeology* 7:27–71.
1994b　Gender Contradictions, Moral Coalitions, and Inequality in Prehistoric Italy. *Journal of European Archaeology* 2:20–49.
1997　Violence and Gender in Early Italy. In *Troubled Times: Violence and Warfare in the Past.* D. L. Martin and D. W. Frayer, eds. Pp. 111–44. Amsterdam: Gordon and Breach.
Robin, Cynthia
2002　Gender and Maya Farming: Chan Nòohol, Belize. In *Ancient Maya Women.* T. Ardren, ed. Pp. 12–30. Walnut Creek, CA: AltaMira Press.
2004　Social Diversity and Everyday Life within Classic Maya Settlements. In *Meso-*

american Archaeology. J. A. Hendon and R. A. Joyce, eds. Pp. 148–68. Oxford: Blackwell.
 In press   Gender, Farming, and Long-Term Change: Maya Historical and Archaeological Perspectives. *Current Anthropology*.
Romanowicz, Janet V., and Rita P. Wright
 1996   Gendered Perspectives in the Classroom. In *Gender and Archaeology*. R. P. Wright, ed. Pp. 199–223. Philadelphia: University of Pennsylvania Press.
Rubin, Gayle
 1984   Thinking Sex. In *Pleasure and Danger: Exploring Female Sexuality*. C. S. Vance, ed. Pp. 267–319. London: Routledge and Kegan Paul.
Sacks, Karen B.
 1982   *Sisters and Wives: The Past and Future of Sexual Equality*. Urbana: University of Illinois Press.
 1988   *Caring by the Hour: Women, Work and Organizing at Duke Medical Center*. Urbana: University of Illinois Press.
Sassaman, Kenneth E.
 1992   Gender and Technology at the Archaic-Woodland "Transition." In *Exploring Gender through Archaeology*. C. Claassen, ed. Pp. 71–79. Madison, WI: Prehistory Press.
Savage, Stephen H.
 2000   The Status of Women in Predynastic Egypt as Revealed through Mortuary Analysis. In *Reading the Body*. A. E. Rautman, ed. Pp. 77–92. Philadelphia: University of Pennsylvania Press.
Schmidt, Robert A., and Barbara L. Voss, eds.
 2000   *Archaeologies of Sexuality*. London: Routledge.
Shanks, Michael, and Christopher Tilley
 1987   *Re-Constructing Archaeology*. Cambridge: Cambridge University Press.
Silverblatt, Irene
 1987   *Moon, Sun, and Witches: Gender Ideologies and Class in Inca and Colonial Peru*. Princeton, NJ: Princeton University Press.
 1988   Women in States. *Annual Review in Anthropology* 17:427–60.
 1991   Interpreting Women in States. In *Gender at the Crossroads of Knowledge*, M. di Leonardo, ed. Pp. 140–71. Berkeley: University of California Press.
Sørensen, Marie Louise Stig
 2000   *Gender Archaeology*. Cambridge: Polity Press.
 2004   The Archaeology of Gender. In *A Companion to Archaeology*. J. Bintliff, ed. Pp. 75–91. Oxford: Blackwell.
Spence, Michael W.
 1974   Residential Practices and the Distribution of Skeletal Traits in Teotihuacán. *Man* 9:262–73.
Stahl, Ann B.
 2001   *Making History in Banda: Anthropological Visions of Africa's Past*. Cambridge: Cambridge University Press.

Sullivan, Thelma D.
  1982   Tlazolteotl-Ixcuina: The Great Spinner and Weaver. In *The Art and Iconography of Late Post-Classic Central Mexico*. E. H. Boone, ed. Pp. 7–35. Washington, DC: Dumbarton Oaks.
Summers, Roger
  1969   *Ancient Mining in Rhodesia and Adjacent Areas*. Salisbury: Trustees of the National Museums of Rhodesia.
Sweely, Tracy L.
  1998   Personal Interactions: The Implications of Spatial Arrangements for Power Relations at Cerén, El Salvador. *World Archaeology* 29:393–406.
Trigger, Bruce G.
  1980   Archaeology and the Image of the American Indian. *American Antiquity* 45:662–76.
Tringham, Ruth E.
  1991   Households with Faces: The Challenge of Gender in Prehistoric Architectural Remains. In *Engendering Archaeology*. J. M. Gero and M. W. Conkey, eds. Pp. 93–131. Oxford: Blackwell.
Walker, P. L.
  1989   Cranial Injuries as Evidence of Violence in Prehistoric Southern California. *American Journal of Physical Anthropology* 80:313–23.
Warren, Kay B.
  1998   *Indigenous Movements and Their Critics*. Princeton, NJ: Princeton University Press.
Weglian, Emily
  2001   Grave Goods Do Not a Gender Make: A Case Study from Singen am Hohentwiel, Germany. In *Gender and the Archaeology of Death*. B. Arnold and N. L. Wicker, eds. Pp. 137–55. Walnut Creek, CA: AltaMira Press.
Weismantel, Mary
  2004   Moche Sex Pots: Reproduction and Temporality in Ancient South America. *American Anthropologist* 106:495–505.
White, Christine D., Michael W. Spence, Fred J. Longstaffe, Hilary Stuart-Williams, and Kimberley R. Law
  2002   Geographic Identities of the Sacrificial Victims from the Feathered Serpent Pyramid, Teotihuacan: Implications for the Nature of State Power. *Latin American Antiquity* 13:217–36.
White, Christine D., Rebecca Storey, Fred J. Longstaffe, and Michael W. Spence
  2004   Immigration, Assimilation, and Status in the Ancient City of Teotihuacan: Stable Isotopic Evidence from Tlajinga 22. *Latin American Antiquity* 15:176–98.
Whitley, David S.
  1994   By the Hunter, for the Gatherer: Art, Social Relations and Subsistence Change in the Prehistoric Great Basin. *World Archaeology* 25:356–72.

Wilkerson, William S.
  2000 Is There Something You Need to Tell Me? In *Reclaiming Identity*. P. M. L. Moya and M. R. Hames-García, eds. Pp. 251–78. Berkeley: University of California Press.
Wilkinson, Richard G., and Karen M. Van Wagenen
  1993 Violence against Women: Prehistoric Skeletal Evidence from Michigan. *Midcontinental Journal of Archaeology* 18:190–216.
Winters, Howard D.
  1968 Value Systems and Trade Cycles of the Late Archaic in the Midwest. In *New Perspectives in Archaeology*. S. R. Binford and L. R. Binford, eds. Pp. 175–222. Chicago: Aldine.
Wobst, Martin
  1977 The Archaeo-Ethnology of Hunter-Gatherers and the Tyranny of the Ethnographic Record in Archaeology. *American Antiquity* 43:303–9.
Wylie, Alison
  1985 The Reaction against Analogy. *Advances in Archaeological Method and Theory* 8:63–111.
  1992 The Interplay of Evidential Constraints and Political Interests: Recent Archaeological Research on Gender. *American Antiquity* 57:15–35.
  1996 The Constitution of Archaeological Evidence: Gender Politics and Science. In *The Disunity of Science*. P. Galison and P. Stump, eds. Pp. 311–43. Palo Alto, CA: Stanford University Press.
Yoffee, Norman
  1993 Too Many Chiefs? (or, Safe Texts for the '90s). In *Archaeological Theory: Who Sets the Agenda?* N. Yoffee and A. Sherratt, eds. Pp. 60–78. Cambridge: Cambridge University Press.
Zagarell, Allen
  1986 Trade, Women, Class, and Society in Ancient Western Asia. *Current Anthropology* 27:415–30.

Feminist Theory and Gender Research in Historical Archaeology

SUZANNE M. SPENCER-WOOD

IN THIS CHAPTER, I use the development of feminist theory as a framework to survey gender research in historical archaeology. My aim is to increase awareness, overt expression, and disciplinary dialogue concerning the application of feminist theoretical approaches in gender research. To this end, I analyze the feminist theoretical approaches that are implicit in much gender research in historical archaeology. In the final section of this chapter, I consider issues in feminist theory and how they may be addressed by synthesizing different feminist approaches.

This chapter selects from a wide variety of gender research in historical archaeology to outline the scope of the field. Although technically historical archaeology includes all societies with written records, this chapter is limited to Deetz's (1977:5) definition of historical archaeology as the archaeology of European colonies, particularly America and Australia. Despite the continued predominance of ungendered discourse in historical archaeology, the amount of gender research in America and Australia has grown rapidly since groundbreaking feminist publications in the late 1980s (Bickford 1987; Spencer-Wood 1987a).

All feminist research is concerned with gender, but not all gender research applies feminist concepts, theories, or methods. Feminists are unified by the theoretical standpoint that gender is a foundational social structure that always needs to be analyzed in archaeological research as much as class has been and ethnicity and race increasingly are. The feminist standpoint that gender must be analyzed leads to new questions that push archaeological research, method, and theory beyond existing epistemological assumptions about what kinds of archaeological knowledge can be created (e.g., Conkey and Gero 1991; Gero 1991; Linton 1971; Wylie 1991a, 1991b).

A core difference between feminist and nonfeminist archaeology is the definition of the concept of gender. Early gender research in historical archaeology followed the traditional practice of equating gender with biological sex. In the 1970s, feminist theory distinguished biological sex from the cultural construction of gender as a social structure (Spencer-Wood 1992). The feminist conceptualization of gender—and, more recently, sexuality—as separate from biological sex reveals the foundational role of feminist critique as the first step in the development of feminist concepts, theories, frameworks, methods, and research. If the process of feminist critique of androcentrism is not first undertaken, then gender is uncritically explained using received male-biased theoretical perspectives, frameworks, concepts, and methods (Spencer-Wood 1995).

Another major distinction is that feminist research *analyzes* gender power dynamics, while nonfeminists uncritically accept the dominant patriarchal gender ideology as universally descriptive of past gender practices. Nonfeminist gender research assumes and reifies stereotypic asymmetrical constructions of gender roles and power dynamics as innate and unchanging, naturalizing and legitimating the devaluation and subordination of women in modern patriarchal society. Feminist critique has exposed the androcentrism involved in legitimating Western gender inequalities by projecting them onto other cultures as universal (Spencer-Wood 1992).

This chapter is presented according to the historical development of feminist theories, although these theories have been simultaneously applied and sometimes combined in historical archaeology. Feminist theory developed as a process of critique of androcentric biases and reflexive critique that can be metaphorically understood in analogy with the process of peeling an onion, in this case the androcentric onion of male bias. Peeling away one layer of androcentrism reveals deeper layers of male bias that need to be critiqued and corrected. Male biases in different layers support and reinforce each other, creating a complex androcentric structure of knowledge that is internally consistent and difficult to critique from within the framework (Spencer-Wood 1991c, 1995).

Feminist critique first revealed male biases in the surface layer of ungendered paradigms, frameworks, method, and theory that have been traditionally used to construct supposedly ungendered pasts that often generalize men's experiences as universal and disappear women. This critique led to remedial feminist research making visible the importance of women's public and/or domestic roles. However, sometimes women's stereotypic domestic roles were just added to androcentric constructions of the past, using what has been called the "add women and stir" approach (Bunch 1987:140). Postmodern feminist theory critiques binary constructions of gender and has instead researched the diversity and fluidity of gender ideologies, identities, roles, relationships, and power dynamics due to the complex intersections of gender, class, race, ethnicity, and other social dimensions (Spencer-Wood 1995).

Feminist Critiques of Male Biases in Historical Archaeology

Correcting male-centered bias requires a critical paradigm starting from feminist standpoint epistemology rather than an androcentric epistemology. Feminist critiques developed as a process of asking critical questions, from the standpoint of a feminist analysis of women's experiences, about what was missing or androcentric in ungendered and stereotypic constructions of the past.

Androcentric Paradigms and Models

Feminist critiques in fields with predominantly ungendered discourse, including archaeology, have asked why and how such a fundamental social structure as gender has been excluded from the research paradigm (e.g., Conkey and Spector 1984; Englestad 1991; Spencer-Wood 1992; Wylie 1991a, 1991b). Social stratification had always been considered important to research. In historical archaeology, race relations on plantations had been analyzed since the 1970s (Singleton 1990), and ethnicity was highlighted as a topic in 1980 (e.g., Schuyler 1980).

Much of historical archaeology had followed the predominant practice in anthropology analyzing cultures as monolithic wholes with some level of social stratification. Gender systems were seldom analyzed because they were assumed to involve the same innate tasks worldwide, so there was no variation through time or between cultures that required explanation with archaeological theory or research (Wylie 1991b:34).

Historical archaeology in America developed into a field in the late 1960s and was first taught in Australia in 1974 (Lydon 1995:73). In the 1960s, the rise of Binford's new archaeology included the systems theory model of culture that either excluded gender entirely or subsumed it within the social system. Wylie (1991a, 1991b) critiqued systems theory for excluding gender as a foundational subsystem that cannot be reduced to any other subsystem. Further, feminist archaeologists critiqued how the scientific focus on large-scale patterns and processes led to ignoring the importance of small-scale internal variables, particularly gender and ethnicity (Conkey and Spector 1984; Spencer-Wood 1995, 2000; Wylie 1991a, 1991b).

Binford (1962) also theorized a hierarchical ladder of inference in which ideological and social information were more difficult to analyze from archaeological data than information about technology or subsistence. This widely accepted hegemonic model of inference effectively took gender ideology and gender power dynamics off the historical archaeological research agenda until feminists began to reclaim them (e.g., Spencer-Wood 1987a, 1989a, 1991b; Weber 1991; Yentsch 1991a, 1991b, 1991c).

Historical archaeology drew on the dominant ungendered cultural paradigm reified in both anthropology and history in which elite white men's roles, activities, and viewpoints were represented as the genderless norm. Because white men are the dominant cultural group, their accounts of historic men's ideas and behaviors were considered representative of the entire culture. The underlying assumption of this paradigm is that men have always been the significant members of society who made the important public history, while women's domestic roles and activities were not significant to history. The disappearance of women and other minorities from the past was facilitated by the low frequency of their voices in historical documents, which were written mostly by elite white men and a few elite women (Spencer-Wood 1992, 1995).

Feminist Critiques of Androcentrism in Ungendered Constructions of the Past

Historical archaeologists have often uncritically adopted historians' unitary ungendered overgeneralizations of men's viewpoints as *the* American colonial mind or universal meanings of material culture (e.g., Boorstin and Boorstin 1989; Glassie 1975). Drawing on Glassie (1975), Deetz (1988) constructed a supposedly ungendered structural analysis of the stylistic evolution of Anglo-American architecture, ceramics, and gravestones from the seventeenth century to the nineteenth century. He described these styles as evolving progressively from chaotic, irrational, natural colors in the seventeenth century to orderly, cultural, intellectual, white-colored architecture and artifacts in the nineteenth century. This supposedly ungendered evolutionary construction in fact de-genders and masks the well-known ideological dichotomy between irrational, chaotic, natural, inferior women in opposition to cultural, rational, orderly, superior men. In addition, Deetz's framework also carries racist undertones in the evolutionary progress from colored artifacts to white ones (critiqued by Spencer-Wood 1993, 1995). Deetz was no doubt unaware of the sexist and racist dichotomies underlying Glassie's construction of architectural evolution that Deetz applied to other kinds of artifacts.

Androcentric Biases in Ungendered Theoretical Frameworks, Epistemology, and Language

Deetz (1988) justified his construction of the evolution of American colonial culture in dichotomies with a structuralist argument that binary thinking is universal and natural. In the paradigm of structuralism, the principal contention that all thought and culture can be reduced to a set of binary oppositions is based on the heterosexist binary construction of gender and biological sex in mutually exclusive *either* male *or* female opposed categories, ignoring other genders such as berdache or transvestites and the biological diversity that includes hermaphrodites. Structuralism is deeply embedded in Western thought and belief, as represented in the ungendered paradigm of logic that insists on categorizing something as *either* P *or* not P (Spencer-Wood 1992, 1995). Hodder and Hutson (2003:68, 90) have critiqued how structuralism constructs cultures in ahistorical dichotomies that cannot analyze or explain processes of culture change.

Feminist epistemological critiques have unmasked purportedly objective and ungendered paradigms such as structuralism to show that they actually represent men's interests, perspectives, questions, and experiences. Similarly, at the deeper level of supposedly generic language, the use of androcentric nouns such as "mankind" or "man" and the male pronoun "he" often represent a male-biased view as universal (Spencer-Wood 1992). Scientific methodology and language predominantly used in archaeology have misrepresented archaeological research as completely objective, masking the subjectivity involved in what research theories and questions are considered important, the methods used to select and analyze data, and the resulting conclusions (Longino and Doell 1983).

The use of the scientific omniscient third-person passive voice stating what the facts or data show masks the subjective processes of interpretation and inference, making them more difficult to challenge (Spencer-Wood 1992, 1995). Thus, feminists argue for including the researcher as a person, as the I who explains how s/he made the subjective decisions in the research process (Longino 1989; Spencer-Wood 1995:130). It is particularly important for archaeologists to reveal their subjective decisions because interpretations are often underdetermined by data (Wylie 1992). Janet Spector's 1993 book *What This Awl Means* exemplifies the value of the use of the first-person active voice by archaeologists to reveal how gendered narratives about people's lives in the past can be imaginatively constructed from ethnohistorical and archaeological evidence.

The storytelling school in historical archaeology, inspired by Spector's book, shows how telling the stories of real people in the past requires addressing the complex intersections of gender identities, roles, relationships, and power dynamics with class, age, race, religion, and other social dimensions (e.g., Costello 2000; Praetzellis and Praetzellis 1998; Yamin 2004). While storytelling may require some imagination when documentary data are lacking, this school has increased the reconstruction of *documented* individual life histories that are at least as interesting as the more imaginative stories (compare Cook 1998 with Heck and Balicki 1998).

Feminist Critiques of Androcentric Methods

Methodologically, women have been disappeared from the past by the practice of using male-defined ungendered categories of analysis. For instance, a male viewpoint was evident in calling brothels "sporting culture" or "entertainment" sites, when for the prostitutes brothels were primarily workplaces and secondarily domiciles (e.g., Baker 1983, critiqued in Spencer-Wood 1991c:238; Kennedy 1989; Lawrence-Cheney 1991). Deetz (1977) used supposedly ungendered language in discussing the yeo*man*'s dairy but did not discuss the normative importance of women's roles in dairying, as did Yentsch (1991b). Henretta (1971) presented an ungendered account of the socioeconomic structure of Boston based on men's occupations without even mentioning women. Classes defined by men's occupations reify in modern discourse the historic Western legal practice of the male head of household representing his wife and children in the public sphere (Millett 1970).

The patriarchal dominance of men as a group has also been reified by the usual practice of naming domestic sites and gardens for the surname or whole name of the male head of household. While it is perfectly valid to research the male head of household's relationship to his house and garden, feminists have critiqued the exclusive androcentric focus on men. They call this the "male power-garden syndrome" of interpreting gardens as expressing the prestige of only the male head of household, ignoring his wife's prestige and the work of servants or slaves who created the garden (Spencer-Wood 1991c:237). Weber (1991) critiqued the neglect of elite women's gardens and gardening expertise in historical archaeology.

Some feminist historical archaeologists have critiqued the androcentric practice of constructing the past in the shape of essentialist binary gender stereotypes (Seifert 1991a; Spencer-Wood 1989a, 1989c, 1991a, 1991c:237, 1992, 1995). The dominant gender dichotomy has led to the tendency to dichotomize the classification of sites into *either* female-domestic *or* male-public sites. Women's roles have been ignored at "public" sites occupied predominantly by men, such as military sites (Clements 1993; Starbuck 1994), mining camps (Hardesty 1989), and lumber camps (Brashler 1991) in America and a railroad construction camp and telegraph station in Australia (Bickford 1993:198). On the other hand, men are often overlooked at domestic sites that are associated with women in the gender dichotomy. Further, sites where women are prominent have often been labeled domestic sites even if they also held public significance for women. For instance, brothels have been stereotypically labeled primarily domestic sites because they were associated with women (e.g., Seifert 1991b, 1994), ignoring or downplaying the fact that they were women's public entrepreneurial businesses.

Many historical archaeologists use South's (1977) ungendered classification system of artifacts into functional categories such as architectural, kitchen, and personal artifacts. Spencer-Wood (1991c:236, 1995:126) has critiqued the androcentrism in South's ungendered personal and kitchen categories. Yentsch (1991a:254) further unpacked South's kitchen artifact group, showing that it lumped together in a meaningless category ceramics used in very different gendered activities, ranging from food preparation and storage usually by women in the kitchen, pantry, or basement to food service tableware used by women and men in the dining room.

Although South's categories appear ungendered, implicit assumptions gendering these categories may have contributed to androcentric analyses. For instance, Seifert (1991b) followed South's classification of cosmetics as personal artifacts, although she was analyzing a brothel site where cosmetics held their most significant meanings as work-related artifacts. She failed to analyze cosmetics as work-related artifacts because she uncritically accepted and used South's categorization of cosmetics as personal artifacts (Spencer-Wood 1995).

Feminist Theories in Historical Archaeology

The historical development of feminist theory is often simplified into three "waves." However, these three waves do not capture the full range of diversity in feminist theories or their frequent use in complex combinations. Further, the wave metaphor gives the incorrect impression that each wave of theory was replaced by the subsequent wave. In actual fact, each wave of theory has continued to be developed as subsequent waves of theory were created, often through reflexive critique of previous theories (Nelson 2002). What the wave image does correctly represent is that the most recent wave of feminist theory is the most prevalent.

Another problem is that different feminists define the waves of feminist theory in a variety of ways. This chapter resolves this issue by using the framework that includes the widest range of feminist theories that have been developed throughout history. This framework is the most widely accepted and used because it is most inclusive of the variety in feminist theory. In this framework, the first wave of feminist theory started in the Enlightenment, the second wave began with Betty Friedan's *Feminine Mystique* in 1963 (although it has precedents from the mid-nineteenth century), and the third wave started in the 1980s (Donovan 2001; Lorber 2001).

First-Wave Feminist Egalitarian Liberal Theory

Liberal egalitarian feminist theory critiques the patriarchal gender ideology that devalues women and their domestic roles and conducts research demonstrating that women exercised social agency in a variety of important roles in both public and domestic spheres. Liberal feminist theory and research demonstrates that gender stereotypes were not universally practiced through three different kinds of research paradigms concerning the ways that women have been social agents as much as men (Donovan 2001).

Research on Women's Public Roles

The first egalitarian feminist paradigm critiques sexist stereotypes of a biologically determined universal dominance of men in public roles. Instead, this corrective paradigm involves asking about and seeking evidence that historic women had important public roles, even in patriarchal societies (e.g., Lorber 2001:25–28, Nelson 2003; Valian 1998; Wertheimer 1977). This paradigm measures women against the standard of public men and does not challenge the status hierarchy in which public roles are judged to be more important than domestic roles. However, neither this paradigmatic limitation nor the persistence of patriarchy can be used to dismiss the significance of women's social agency in public roles.

In America, archaeologists have researched native women who had important public positions in the European fur trade (Frink 2005; Holliman 2005; Jackson 1994). Archaeologists have researched some Euro-American women who managed plantations (Anderson 2004), founded and led utopian communes (Spencer-Wood, in press), overcame legal restrictions to own land as wives (e.g., Bell 2001; Lewis 2003), or operated merchant businesses or shops with their husbands or as widows (Elliott 1977; Goodwin 1999; Jamieson 2000:146; Little 1994; Spencer-Wood 1987b:336–37; Wheeler 2000). Research has also been undertaken on white women who were doctors (Sipe 2003; Spencer-Wood 1994b, 2003); ship captains and navigators (Smith 1989); schoolteachers and principals (Gibb and Preston 2003), hotel operators (Hardesty 1994); day care workers, dietitians, social workers, nurses, librarians, and street inspectors (Spencer-Wood

1987a, 1991b, 1994a, 1994b); prison matrons (Spencer-Wood 2001b); craftswomen (Hautaniemi and Rotman 2003); seamstresses, laundresses, and entrepreneurs (Hardesty 1994); and factory workers (e.g., Beaudry and Mrozowski 2004). Archaeologists have further researched slave women who produced pottery (McEwan 1991:33–34) and agricultural produce and cooked food that they took to markets in southern cities (Franklin 2001; Yentsch 1994:243, 246). Postbellum African American women have been researched who worked as midwives (e.g., Wilkie 2003), laundresses, domestic servants, shop owners (Davidson 2004:88–102), beauty salon owners, and entrepreneurs, such as the famous Madame C. J. Walker, founder of a major company selling African American skin whitening and hair straightening (Mullins 1999:63–64).

Excavations in the Five Points area of New York City have revealed occupation-related artifacts discarded by women as well as men of different ethnicities working in the needle trades (Griggs 2001). A very large deposit of materials and tools from a Jewish commercial tailoring business was found, including thimbles inscribed "Forget Me Not," "Love," "A Present," and "From a Friend" that were usually given to women by men (Griggs 2001:82). Griggs (2001:77–78) analyzed how gender stereotypes resulted in discrimination against women, including requiring more work for lower wages than men and exclusion of women from the better-paid needlework undertaken by men.

Groups of elite philanthropic reform women in both America and Australia founded and operated a wide variety of public institutions and landscapes. Among the earliest were female orphan asylums in the early 1800s and industrial schools for girls, which trained predominantly poor girls for domestic service. In Sydney, Australia, the first governor's wife founded the earliest female orphan asylum, and the second governor's wife designed its grounds. The governor's wife in Tasmania designed the island's first museum and gardens (for Australia, see Bickford 1998:196–97; for the United States, see Spencer-Wood 1994a). In Boston, Spencer-Wood (1987a, 1994a, 1996) located sites of public charitable cooperative homes founded by Anglo-American, African American and Jewish, Catholic, and Protestant middle-class women, such as homes for working women, aged women, intemperate women, "fallen" girls and women, and unwed mothers. De Cunzo (1995, 2001) researched the site of the Philadelphia Magdalen Asylum for fallen women.

Liberal egalitarian research on the importance of women's domestic roles derived from cultural feminist theory valorizing women's domestic roles. Androcentric devaluations of women's domestic work have been corrected with feminist analyses demonstrating the importance of women's social agency in domestic roles (Donovan 2001). Feminists seek and find evidence that women's domestic roles are in many cases either as important as men's public roles or significant to the culture in general. If women's domestic roles are measured against the importance of men's public roles, then this paradigm does not challenge the dominance of public men in the gender status hierarchy. However, in some cases the importance of women's domestic roles to the culture in general is discussed.

Feminist historians and archaeologists have found evidence that native American women and American colonial women shaped domestic lifeways and sites as social actors, even in male-dominated situations (e.g., Deagan 1983:181–85, 234; Jackson 1994; McEwan 1991; Wheeler 2001; Woodhouse-Beyer 1999; Yentsch 1991b, 1994). Some research has involved finding evidence that historic white women's domestic roles were important in maintaining lifeways at a variety of male-dominated types of sites (Brashler 1991; Clements 1993; Purser 1991; Smith 1989; Starbuck 1994).

Yentsch (1994:196–217) researched the documentary and archaeological evidence that slave women maintained African lifeways and also altered white foodways with imported African squashes, birds, and spices. Slave women were domestic social agents in manufacturing African-style colonoware cooking pots, wattle and daub cooking huts, and hearthstones (Armstrong 1990:266). The importance of slave women's cooking in separate kitchen buildings has been researched in relation to American white urban house site layout (Stewart-Abernathy 2004). In Connecticut houses, caches of amulets, charms, bones, and so on found buried at kitchen thresholds or in corners have been interpreted as part of magical rituals by slave women (Woodruff 2005). On the Oakley Plantation in Louisiana, Wilkie (1996) found that women were often in charge of the medical care of the African American community, shifting from homemade concoctions to patent medicines as the plantation labor system evolved from slavery to tenant farming and sharecroppers.

In some household research, women's life cycle in the household has been important in changing the use of household space as well as in creating archaeological deposits. Archaeologists researching consumer choice have long related family life cycle to household consumer choices of ceramics (e.g., Garrow 1987; Leedecker et al. 1987). At two house sites of white people near Boston, Massachusetts, Wheeler (2001) identified the construction of new kitchens with new female heads of household. Further, at one site two separate discard areas were identified with the old and new kitchen locations. Women's role in maintaining the hearth provided them with social agency to construct new kitchens and discard previous tableware in order to acquire their own.

Spencer-Wood (1996:418–25, 1999d:181–85) researched how white middle-class reform women developed new gender ideologies to justify designing household spaces to raise the status of women in a number of ways. The central importance of women's domestic roles was symbolized by raising the kitchen from the basement, where it had been used by servants, to the main public floor in the center of the house, permitting surveillance by mothers of children's and adults' activities in the two first-floor parlors, while working in the kitchen. As the "sovereign of her empire," mothers were to organize their children's cooperative labor. Further, potted plants were to be brought into the conservatory to morally educate children through contact with God's nature that was associated with women's sphere.

In an excavation of an Australian sheep station household in the outback, Allison (2003) found evidence under floorboards of women's uses of different rooms, verandas, and outbuildings. Similar to urban households in the American south (e.g., Stewart-Abernathy 2004), a separate kitchen building was identified. However, in the late nineteenth century, a kitchen was built in the main house when meal preparation devolved from servants to the wife of the station owner. This process of loss of ability by the middle class to afford servants was important in the Beecher sisters' design of a potentially servantless house with its central kitchen in 1869 (Beecher and Stowe 1975:22). Allison (2003) found archaeological evidence that in the summer women had tea and coffee on the veranda and also sewed there as they watched their children playing with dolls.

Gendering the Historical Archaeology of Mothering and Child Rearing

In *The Archaeology of Mothering*, Wilkie (2003:6–7) notes the neglect of mothering in historical archaeological analyses and cites three out of a number of publications that have addressed child rearing and mothering or parenting (see Clark and Wilkie, this volume). Contextual differences at three sites affected the parenting interpretations of similar children's toys, particularly white dolls. Yamin and Bridges (2002) analyzed working-class parenting practices from nineteenth-century children's toys at working-class house sites in Paterson, New Jersey, and in the poor Five Points neighborhood of New York City. Yamin concluded from slate pencils and writing slate fragments that parents were teaching children to write at home since documentary data recorded working-class objections that public schools taught their children middle-class values. Yamin usually considers the working class and reformers as monolithic opposed groups and does not address how differences in income, number and gender of children, or parenting styles within her working-class sample could account for the diversity that she found in amounts of children's toys, such as dolls and marbles. Yamin glossed over these differences in order to make universal generalizations about the working class, rejecting the possibility that some might be upwardly mobile. In contrast, Brighton (2001:27–28) interprets children's artifacts found at Five Points, such as children's mugs with names as well as doll parts and cloth remnants, as indicating an upwardly mobile parenting style that emulated middle-class respectability and gentility. In Wilkie's (2003:107–9) analysis of mothering in the African American Perryman family living in Mobile, Alabama, she concluded that remains of four white dolls and a toy tea set expressed the family's desire for upward mobility as well as the sanctity of motherhood rather than the emulation of whites.

Research on the Importance of Women's Combined Domestic and Public Roles

Some research has combined both of the egalitarian feminist approaches to show that women's domestic and public roles were both culturally significant. Further, in some cases women's roles or activities combined aspects of the traditional domestic and public spheres. This feminist approach shows that the ideology of gender dichotomy between *either* female-domestic *or* male-public roles did not accurately express the complexity of actual gender practices (Spencer-Wood 1991a, 1992, 1995, 1996, 2003).

During the American contact period in the Spanish American colonies, McEwan (1991) analyzed the importance of Native American women's roles as public traders of their domestically produced pottery and foodstuffs as well as the cultural importance of the domestic roles of Spanish women and female African slaves who may also have produced pottery. Jackson (1994:47–48) found in records of the Russian American trading company that native Alaskan women were paid both for domestic work such as making clothes and for public work stringing trade beads and as translators.

Gardens at domestic sites have been analyzed as expressing the public prestige of men at some sites and women at other sites. Feminist historical archaeologists countered the previously exclusive construction of gardens as expressing male power with evidence of elite European and American women who publicly displayed their prestige or public image through ornamental household gardens in the eighteenth and nineteenth centuries (Spencer-Wood 1991c, 1999a; Weber 1991, 1996). Others have researched how wives were involved in designing gardens for the public image of elites at house sites in America (e.g., Bescherer Metheny et al. 1996), including President Jackson's plantation (McKee 1996), and at the Australian governor's estate (Casey 2002).

Research in Australia and America has revealed the significance of women's domestic roles in household production not only for household consumption but also for public markets. In particular, the importance of women's household dairy products has been researched both for the Australian colonial system by Casey (1999) and for the American international cheese and butter markets by Yentsch (1991b:136). Women frequently conducted underpaid waged labor in their homes, such as seamstresses and laundresses. By the twentieth century, African American women also frequently set up hair-straightening and manicure businesses in their homes (Mullins 1999:63). Excavations of households conducting outwork have yielded both work-related artifacts and domestic artifacts providing information about lifeways and consumer choices. For instance, in New York City's Five Points area, a domestic deposit included jewelry, pottery, and children's toys with a few sewing-related items, in contrast to another deposit with a large number and variety of discarded sewing materials from thirteen poor Irish women in the tenement who were documented working in the needle trades from 1850 to 1880 (Griggs 2001:80).

Women could gain income and status by operating boardinghouses in their homes. Archaeologists have excavated nineteenth-century American boardinghouse sites in Harper's Ferry, West Virginia (Lucas 1994); Lowell and Lawrence, Massachusetts (Mrozowski 2000:288–89); and Portsmouth, New Hampshire (Agnew 1995:68–71) and an Australian one in Sydney (Lydon 1993a, 1993b). Lucas (1994:84) has pointed out that boarders' tableware consumer choices were made by the boardinghouse keeper and represent the meaning of meals to the keeper. In addition, keepers were conducting a business in which they had to weigh the costs of tableware and food against the quality of boarders they wished to attract as customers. The boardinghouses at Harper's Ferry (Lucas 1994:89–90) and in Sydney (Lydon 1993b:143, 1993a:38) both signaled their respectability with unmatched transfer-printed breakfast sets plus additional special tableware at Harper's Ferry. Plain white tableware predominated at all the boardinghouse sites, possibly symbolizing women's domestic morality and surveillance since most had rules against alcohol consumption. However, at Lowell numerous hidden alcohol bottles, as well as patent medicines at all the sites, testified to the ability of boarders to circumvent the rules, although the medicines were connected to children's diseases at Harper's Ferry (Larsen 1994:70). The Sydney boardinghouse served beef, the preferred meat (Lydon 1993a:37–38, 1993b). The Lowell textile company boardinghouse was also documented as serving mostly beef, but parasitological analysis of the privies revealed that horse meat was also being served. A further contrast was found between company propaganda about the cleanliness of their boardinghouses and the documented objections of the "millgirls" to the crowding in Lowell boardinghouses (Beaudry 1993:96–100).

Some gender research has found that women's domestic roles were important in linking households into a public community. For instance, excavations at two eighteenth-century Spanish colonial house sites near the Rio Grande in Texas yielded identical chocolaterias that could have been from the same set, suggesting that the households were kin (Bonine 2004:31). At President Jackson's nineteenth-century Hermitage plantation, slave women and men created community by sharing yards between their houses that hid their activities from surveillance by whites in the plantation house (Battle 2004). Wilkie (2003:119–42) has shown how African American midwifery not only was an occupation but also provided symbolic mothering for a community and taught each young mother child-rearing practices after she gave birth to her first child (Wilkie 2000; for further details, see Voss, this volume).

American reform women constructed new kinds of connections to resolve the perceived conflict between individual households and the public sphere in the nineteenth century. The predominantly middle-class reform women sought to increase women's powers by combining and conflating the domestic and public spheres in two ways. Some reformers applied men's scientific-industrial technology to raise the status of housework to a profession, arguing that women should control the domestic sphere (Spencer-Wood 1999d:181–85). Second, reform women transformed private domestic mothering and housekeeping tasks into a variety of female public professions in public cooperative housekeeping institutions, from orphan asylums and public kitchens to day nurseries, kindergartens, playgrounds, and children's gardens. In the municipal housekeeping movement, reform women argued that they were the symbolic mothers and housekeepers of the community, gaining appointments from male government officials to positions from juvenile parole officers to school committee members, elementary school teachers, playground supervisors, and factory inspectors. Reform women living cooperatively in social settlements in working-class neighborhoods further acted as community mothers by offering a wide variety of after-school programs for children of working mothers, organizing local children to clean up the streets, and provided hot-water showers, baths, child clinics, and laundries for the majority of working-class families living in cold-water tenements (Spencer-Wood 1991b:234, 1994a:179–80, 1994b:126, 2002b, 2003).

Public institutional community mothering was evident from turn-of-the-century deposits excavated at the Daughters of Charity Catholic orphanage for white children at Schuyler mansion in Albany, New York. Middle-class child-rearing practices were indicated from the variety of middle-class doll parts and miniature tea set fragments found along the south wall of the mansion, indicating that girls played there. Few other toys were found, including buff clay marbles, a jack, and a pocketknife, which may have been associated with boys' play (Feister 1991). Feister (2003) concluded that boys played farther away from the house.

Second-Wave Feminist Theoretical Approaches to Analyses of Patriarchy

The second wave of feminist theory, starting in the 1970s, is concerned with explaining and analyzing how patriarchy, as a culturally constructed ideology and societal institution, maintains gender inequalities (e.g., Ortner 1974; Rosaldo 1974; Rosaldo and Lamphere 1974). Second-wave feminist theory was developed by white Western middle-class women and essentialized their experiences in the dichotomy between domestic women and public men (Gilchrist 1999:6; Spencer-Wood 2002a:207).

Second-wave feminist theory has been critiqued for essentializing men's and women's actual behaviors as universally conforming to patriarchal gender ideology (e.g., Rosaldo 1980). Women's public roles were either categorized as domestic or dismissed as exceptions that prove the rule of women's domesticity. Such constructions of other cultures reify gender stereotypes and fail to show the diversity in actual gender practices.

Second-Wave Analyses of Dominant Gender Ideology and Women's Social Agency

Some second-wave research has not overgeneralized gender practices as universally conforming to dominant binary gender ideology but has instead analyzed the specific situations and circumstances in which historic patriarchal gender ideology was or was not materially expressed. Some of these analyses, exemplified here, have also considered the possibility of women's social agency or resistance to patriarchy.

At the nineteenth-century Magdalen Asylum for fallen women in Philadelphia, De Cunzo (1995) researched how inmates' lives were controlled using the dominant patriarchal ideology that blamed women rather than men for sexual promiscuity. The institution sought to reform women by isolating them in a walled institution with convent-type cells. Inmates were forced to perform domestic work, ostensibly to learn their appropriate role so they could be transformed into domestic servants. However, a number of inmates demonstrated social agency by escaping over the walls. Although higher walls were continually constructed, some inmates continued to escape.

Spencer-Wood's (2004) research analyzed how the social agency of mid-nineteenth-century Harvard faculty wives in establishing the Cambridge Cooperative Housekeeping Society was thwarted by their husbands, who exerted their patriarchal male dominance to prevent their wives from participating in the cooperative. However, Melusina Fay Peirce, who founded the cooperative, divorced her husband after a number of years and became renowned as the leading theorist of housekeeping cooperatives, which became one of the most numerous types of domestic reform sites.

In a case study from early twentieth-century Deerfield, Massachusetts, patriarchal male dominance was found to be expressed in the location of municipal water spigots near barns rather than houses at some sites after local women had raised the money to pay for the municipal water system. Married women seldom got a water spigot at the house because their husbands had it installed near the barn to facilitate tending hogs and other livestock. However, financially independent widows with income from participating in the Arts and Crafts movement were successful in getting water spigots at the back of the house to facilitate washing laundry (Huateniemi and Rotman 2003).

Marxist-Feminist and Postcolonial Feminist Approaches to Gender Research

In the 1970s, Marxist-feminism emerged by making an analogy between the way the bourgeois capitalist class exploited the oppressed working classes and the ways men as a class and capitalism as a whole benefited from exploiting women's unpaid domestic labor (Delphy 1984; Guettel 1974; Hartsock 1983; Kuhn and Wolpe 1978). In contrast to the essentialist/structuralist analysis of dominant gender ideology as congruent with actual practice, Marxist-feminist theory was concerned with women's actual gender practices that resisted the gender ideology legitimating public men's domination over subordinate domestic women. Thus, feminists adopted the Marxian framework of domination and resistance and applied it to gender relationships.

Marxism and Marxist-feminism have been useful in analyzing some of the structural sources of sexism and discrimination against women. However, Marxism and Marxist-feminism are essentializing in considering only the dominant gender ideology and overgeneralizing about women and men as homogeneous groups. Marxist-feminism focused on women's domestic work and tended to neglect women's public wage labor aside from proposing it as the solution to the devaluation of women's domestic labor (Engels 1884:148, cited in Donovan 2001:88). These limitations stemmed from the development of Marxist-feminism as part of the second-wave feminist focus on the experiences of white middle-class women, most of whom only worked at home in the 1960s and 1970s (Donovan 2001:79–105).

Postcolonial feminist theory relates the Western devaluation of women's unpaid domestic labor to the devaluation of and lower wages in women's paid work in Western capitalist enterprises in Third World countries. Postcolonial feminist theory critiques the imposition of Western gender categories and values to often degrade women's traditional precolonial status, roles, economic independence, and identities. It is also concerned with women's resistance to their exploitation and the breakdown of their traditional subsistence economy (Lorber 2001:55–73).

Marxist-feminist theory was first advocated for historical archaeology gender research by Elizabeth Scott in a paper presented at the 1991 Society for Historical Archaeology conference in a miniplenary titled "Shaken, Not Stirred" organized by Margaret Purser. In the introduction to her edited volume, Scott (1994) discussed the application of the Marxist paradigm of domination and resistance to gender research.

Contact-period gender research in historical archaeology frequently addresses changes in native American gender systems due to colonization, although feminist postcolonial theory has not yet been applied. Change toward more patriarchal gender roles due to indigenous interaction with western European culture was researched by Bassett (1994) for the Apache, Devens (1991) for the Cree, and Birmingham (1993) for Australian aborigines. The fur trade undermined Eskimo women's traditional status in clothing manufacture (Frink 2005), and the Russian American company required native women to produce food for them, resulting in starvation for native families (Woodhouse-Beyer 1999:141).

Some Marxist-feminist research in historical archaeology has speculated on women's resistance to European patriarchy, including Australian aboriginal women resisting Victorian missionaries' gender ideology of a clean, neat, Christian home (Birmingham 1993:122–23); native American women retaining matrilineal tribes (Clements 2005) and traditional powers (Frink 2005); African American free women retaining their land despite capitalist pressures (Muller 1994); white women keeping forbidden personal items in an Australian asylum (Piddock 2001); American white women in Shaker communes resisting the men's attempts to get women to undertake work traditionally accomplished by men (Savulis 2003:180–84); and white women resisting the appropriation of their household cheese production by men's factories in the second half of the nineteenth century (Yentsch 1991b). However, in some cases women did not retain their household cheese production by choice, according to interviews with them (McMurray 1987).

Marxist-Feminist Postmodern Analyses

Scott (1991a) applied Spector's (1983) task differentiation framework to conduct an explicitly Marxist-feminist analysis of who did what for whom in gender relationships at eighteenth-century British Fort Michilimackinac in Michigan. Scott used Spector's (1983) Marxist analytic framework to analyze the complexity of gender roles and interactions among English, French, and native Americans. Spector's framework holds implications for power dynamics that have yet to be explicitly addressed.

Delle (2000) combines a Marxist analysis of colonial slave labor on Jamaican coffee plantations with a postmodern comparison of idealistic writings and actual gender practices. Idealistic writings advocated methods by which plantation owners could control slave women's sexual behavior and reproduction. Delle compares these idealistic writings with evidence for actual gender practices such as infanticide, which Delle interprets as slave women's resistance to white men's attempts to control women's reproduction.

Third-Wave Postmodern Feminist Theoretical Approaches to Gender Research

Postmodern feminist theory critiques and corrects essentialist second-wave feminist theory that constructed actual gender practices as a heterosexist dichotomy (Spencer-Wood 1992, 1997a). Postmodern feminist theory constructs gender and sexuality as diverse, complex, fluid performances that cannot be monolithically described for any social group. The heterosexist construction of biological sex as a dichotomy is critiqued with evidence of biological diversity in physical sexual characteristics and hormones. Diversity and flexibility in gender identities, roles, performances, relationships, practices, and power dynamics are related to the complex intersections of gender, race, class, ethnicity, and other social dimensions. Sexism is related to racism and classism. Finally, postmodern feminism theorizes performances and representations of gender and sexuality as texts and discourses that can be understood through the process of deconstruction (Lorber 2001:147–63, 203).

Inclusive Feminist Theory and Continuum Models in Historical Archaeology

Spencer-Wood (1991a, 1991c, 1992, 1995, 1997a) drew on postmodern feminist theory to critique binary structuralist either/or thinking used to classify a range of variation in phenomena into two opposed categories. Instead, she argued for the use of feminist "both/and" thinking to create inclusive models of the actual range of variation and nuance of meanings in social dimensions, including but not limited to the two opposed binary categories that are constructed by structuralism as the only categories. Spencer-Wood (1995:130, 1997a) proposed replacing structural dichotomies with continuum models of social dimensions to represent their entire range of variation.

The diversity of an individual's identity can be represented as the intersection point of a number of continuum lines for different social dimensions. The situational fluidity of identity can be dynamically represented as the potential for movement along each continuum and the extent to which the intersection point between different continuums can move dynamically (Spencer-Wood 2002a:207, 1997a).

Diversity in Historic Women's Gender Ideologies of the Home

In the Cult of Female Invalidism, elite and middle-class white women used the dominant ideology of women's inherent physical weakness as a way to control their sexual relationships with their husbands. In the Cult of Republican Motherhood, middle-class white women emphasized the importance of women's child-rearing skills and morality for raising the next generation of male leaders of the new republic of the United States. The Cult of Republican Motherhood transformed child rearing from a supposedly simple innate female function into scientific child rearing, a complex learned behavior that required special tools, advice books, and higher education, leading to the growth of the academic fields researching child development and education (Beecher and Stowe 1975:13–14, 275–86; Spencer-Wood 1996:421, 1999d:172–79). Wilkie (2003:11, 177–204) has followed historians who further divide "republican mothering" ideologies into "intensive mothering" accompanying the separation of the domestic and public spheres and "scientific mothering" due to the development of male-dominated medicine and childbirth, accompanied by advertising of mass-produced mothering products.

Wilkie (2003:70–74) analyzed a different ideology of motherhood developed among African American slaves that stressed love, nurturing, protection, and strength in adversity. African American women often came from matrilineal African societies and developed strong roles and an ideology of female strength in slavery that seems incompatible with the Cult of Female Invalidism (e.g., Muller 1994). However, distrust of white male medicine also led to the use of patent medicines (Wilkie 2000) that often contained labels illustrating delicate white women. Since patent medicines illustrating African American women were not available, African American use of these patent medicines is not necessarily evidence that African American women ascribed to the Cult of Female Invalidism, as has been argued by Hautaniemi (1994).

The Cult of True Womanhood or Domesticity claimed that white middle-class and elite women were innately more pious, moral, modest, and domestic than men (Larson 1994; Wall 1994; Welter 1966) and, by assumption, African American women (Wilkie 2003:84). The Cult of True Womanhood or Domesticity was used to elaborate and increase the significance of women's domestic roles as a source of power (Spencer-Wood 1989a:114, 1991b:237, 250–55, 1991c:240). Wall (1991:78–79, 2000:111) identified the Cult of Domesticity with mid-nineteenth-century Gothic white paneled ceramics that were interpreted as symbolizing the sanctity of the home and community at meals and tea taken by the family, in opposition to capitalist competitive status display.

In the Cult of Home Religion, middle-class white domestic reformers further argued that women's housework should be equivalent in status to the male ministry because women sacrificed for their family flock just as ministers sacrificed for their religious flock. Women's role as home ministers was symbolized in the Gothic house style, ceramics, glassware, and furnishings as well as a round table with a Bible. Cut flowers and potted plants were ideally used in household conservatories to symbolize women's innately higher piety due to the closeness of their domestic sphere to God's nature, removed from men's sinful capitalistic sphere (Spencer-Wood 1994a, 1996:418–19, 1999d:181–83).

Wilkie (2003:56–59) discusses how elite white gender ideology depended on the opposite stereotypes of African American women as oversexed Jezebels and dominating matriarchs, who by definition were unnatural mothers for supposedly not exhibiting the unsexed purity and higher morality of white mothers in the sanctified home of the cult of domesticity. These negative stereotypes of African American women were compounded with the stereotype of the oversexed promiscuous working woman that was applied to all working-class women but especially African American working women, who were considered "public women," akin to prostitutes for transgressing men's sphere and walking public streets without a male protector and guarantor of her purity (Ryan 1990:67; Stansell 1986:125–27, 148). This was part of the dominant elite gender ideology that domestic reformers significantly manipulated to make it acceptable for women to have public professions (Spencer-Wood 1991b, 1994a).

Archaeologists and historians have defined the Cult of Gentility in diverse ways. A few archaeologists have identified the cult with eighteenth-century men (e.g., Crass et al. 1999), but most identify it with nineteenth-century women. Wall (1991:79; 2000:111, 122, 135–36) has identified the Cult of Gentility with competitive status display using secular gilt and floral tea sets and tableware. In contrast, Linda Young (2003) has included the Cult of Domesticity in the Cult of Gentility, and Fitts (1999:53–55) further associates the two cults with Gothic paneled ceramics.

Lawrence argued that the desire to display middle-class domestic respectability led Euro-Australian miners and their wives to line their tents or cabins with decorative cloth or wallpaper, construct whitewashed fireplaces, and display some fashionable middle-class artifacts, such as a gilt clock, transfer-printed ceramic tewares and tablewares, glass tumblers, and pressed-glass stemmed bowls. In addition, a few remains of women's jewelry were found, and Christian temperance was indicated by low numbers of alcohol bottles (Lawrence 1999:1129, 1133). The decorated tablewares may be an expression of respectability involved in the Cult of Gentility more than the sanctity of the home symbolized by undecorated white ceramics. Purser (1991) found the Cult of Gentility expressed in western American mining household decoration and the practice of women visiting each others' homes.

Public Domestic Reform Ideologies

Women's domestic reform ideologies transformed Western culture by making it acceptable in the dominant gender ideology for women to have public professions and be economically independent. In the communitarian ideology of domestic reform, women argued for the socialization of women's household tasks in public cooperative housekeeping institutions in order to eliminate the isolated repetitive labor of women in individual households (Spencer-Wood 1994a). The ideology and practice of cooperative housekeeping was adopted by urban reform women from American utopian communes, which often called themselves families (Spencer-Wood 1987a, 1999d, in press).

Domestic reformers further used a cultural feminist ideology in municipal housekeeping and City Beautiful movements to argue that women's innately superior domestic morality was needed to reform men's sinful capitalist cities, where youth were corrupted by dirty streets and the lack of contact with God's nature, which was associated with women (Spencer-Wood 2003). Based on this ideology, reform women used their feminine powers of moral suasion to gain the assistance of government officials in establishing urban green spaces and park playgrounds (Spencer-Wood 1994b, 1999c, 2003).

In other ideologies, women developed justifications for having public professions. The Cult of Single Blessedness (1740–1910s) advocated that women not marry men but instead marry their professions as religious callings, in analogy with nuns who became celibate brides of Christ (Chambers-Schiller 1984, cited in Spencer-Wood 1999c:172). The Cult of Real Womanhood, starting in the 1890s, advocated that women marry carefully, undertake exercise for health, and be trained in a profession in case they needed to work to support their family (Cogan 1989, cited in Spencer-Wood 1999d:172).

Diversity and Change in Gender Ideologies and Practices in Different Religions

Postmodern gender research analyzes the polyvocal nature of women's and men's actions in constantly renegotiating gender ideologies and actual gender practices (Spencer-Wood 1991c:239). Religious beliefs can have a major effect on negotiations over consumer choices. For instance, Kruczek-Aaron (2002) found unusual letters documenting negotiations concerning gender ideology and practice between Gerrit Smith and his wife and daughter. Gerrit was a prominent abolitionist and temperance reformer who experienced an Evangelical Protestant conversion and sought to present himself as a plain man who eschewed ostentation. His wife and daughter wished to display fashionable Victorian gentility, especially at dinner parties. Negotiations resulted in the compromise of fancy decorated ceramics but not matched sets (Nickolai 2003:154) for the dinner parties in a house that was plainly furnished. It may be that the unmatched decorated ceramics were justified for use because they were secondhand or heirlooms. In any case, during the 1850s, when Gerrit was a congressman in Washington, D.C., he materially betrayed his religious beliefs by adding an ostentatious two-story Greek Revival porch with Doric columns to his Federal-style mansion.

Different Jewish sects developed distinct gender ideologies and practices as they moved across Boston's landscape from 1840 to 1930. In poor, orthodox eastern European communities, women were segregated in screened balconies in synagogues, were provided ritual bath buildings called *mikvehs*, and practiced kosher foodways with separate pots and dishes for meat and milk. In contrast, over time middle-class western European Reformed Jews increasingly adopted Protestant mixed-gender seating and singing in synagogues and stopped building *mikvehs* and practicing kosher foodways (Spencer-Wood 1999b).

Postmodern Research Contrasting the Dominant Gender Ideology with Household Gender Practices

A major theme in postmodern feminist historical archaeology are analyses separating and comparing dominant gender ideology with the diversity and fluidity in actual gender practices due to the complex intersections of gender, class, race, ethnicity, religion, and other social dimensions. This approach contrasts with the second-wave structuralist approach of uncritically projecting the dominant gender ideology as the universal reality of actual practice.

Some historical archaeological research shows that "separate spheres" gender ideology often contrasted with actual practices that combined domestic and public spheres. In both America and Australia, colonial homes often housed women's as well as men's businesses. Gibb and King (1991) found little evidence of segregation in the deposition of traditionally gendered artifacts around seventeenth-century houses in Maryland, in contrast to the ideology of gender dichotomy in the use of household spaces (Yentsch 1991c). Further, neither American, African American, nor Australian colonial or working-class houses of one to three multi-purpose rooms had the separate dining room and gender-segregated rooms required for the cult of gentility, although Australian photos show that part of a room could be used for women's genteel ritual of tea using decorated ceramics, though usually not the tea sets used by the middle class (Baker 1980; Deetz 1977; Karskens 2003:41; Russell 1993:30). In the Sydney Rocks neighborhood, a working-class house site yielded middle-class decorated ceramics for genteel dining but inexpensive cuts of meat (Karskens 2003:45–50). Mullins (1999:174–75) found that tableware at an African American house site in Annapolis, Maryland, did not fit the genteel ideal but instead consisted of a variety of old, worn, unmatched ceramics.

Gendered household research in historical archaeology has progressed from a second-wave structuralist construction of household spaces as universally conforming to the elite gender ideology of fixed mutually exclusive male versus female spheres (e.g., Yentsch 1991c) to postmodern contrasting of this dominant separate-spheres gender ideology with the actual diversity and fluidity in the use of household spaces. Research on nineteenth-century house sites in western Michigan contrasted the elite ideology of separate domestic spaces for women and men with actual practices involving different degrees of gender mixing and segregation in household spaces due to class. Generally, more mixed-gender use of domestic spaces was found in the working-class households and more gender segregation in the use of spaces in upper-class houses (Nassaney et al. 2001:251–52; Rotman and Nassaney 1997). In contrast, fewer gender segregation tasks were found on middle-class farm landscapes employing hired hands (Rotman and Nassaney 1997; Sayers and Nassaney 1999).

Postmodern Historical Archaeological Research on Diversity, Fluidity, and Negotiations in Gender Systems

A variety of publications in historical archaeology have conducted postmodern analyses of diversity in gender roles, behaviors, practices, and identities due to complex intersections of gender, class, race, and ethnicity. In America, archaeologists have analyzed how gender roles in the colonies varied among native Americans, African Americans, and white colonists as well as how these groups related to each other (e.g., McEwan 1991; Scott 1991a).

Class differences in ability to practice the cult of gentility have been found in both Australia (Russell 1993) and America (Wall 1991, 1994, 2000). Two archaeological studies of the use of household spaces for the performance of gentility, one each in Australia and America, have found documentary evidence of negotiations between elite women and servants over the proper performance of elite dining rituals and housecleaning (e.g., Kruczek-Aaron 2002; Russell 1993).

Some historical archaeologists have analyzed the complex intersections between gender, race, and class. Wilkie (2000:56–58, 96) argues that unmatched plain white ironstone tableware, a white porcelain set, and sets of pressed-glass goblets, tumblers and bowls found at the turn-of-the-century African American Perryman house site in Mobile, Alabama, do not indicate simple middle-class emulation but rather symbolize the purity of sacred motherhood in the cult of domesticity in order to counteract negative stereotypes of African American women as oversexed immoral Jezebels who were unnatural bad mothers. A "Rebekah at the Well" pitcher and two white cherub figurines are also interpreted as domestic symbols of the importance of full-time mothering and domesticity, displaying not only middle-class domesticity but also the freedom from previous work in plantation fields that limited slave women's time for mothering their children (Wilkie 2003:106, 113–14). It is interesting to note that the earlier tableware set is blue, suggesting, along with the recovery of numerous blue bottles, materialization of African American ideology of hoodoo magic, in which using blue is believed to bring good luck (pointed out by Wilkie 2000).

Brandon (2004) analyzed the gendered racial identities and relationships symbolized in one artifact, the topsy-turvy doll that was popular in nineteenth-century America. Brandon (2004:197) states, "It is effectively two dolls in one—one end an elegant white 'missy' and the other a manifestation of the well-used stereotype of the 'wild-eyed pickaninny.'" The skirt on this doll covered the head of one manifestation when the other was in view, making it a horrific metaphor for racialization in America: the two are inextricably attached and cannot exist without the other, while simultaneously they are unarguably in two different worlds as they cannot be seen together." Stewart-Abernathy (2004) is one of the few historical archaeologists who has interpreted race relations between slave women and their white mistresses from the separation of the elite house from the kitchen, where slave women had some independence in preparing meals for both the slave and white residents of the house site.

Intersecting gender, class, and ethnic inequalities can be expressed in cultural landscapes. Archaeological investigations of the grounds of Sailor's Snug Harbor on Staten Island found that the prestige and wealth of the white Anglo male benefactor was expressed through a formal public front lawn with his tomb in front of a row of five Greek temple building facades. The institution's inmates constructed an elaborate garden landscape, including a fish pond, around the large fashionable Italianate house of the white Anglo male governor of the institution. The lower-status white doctor's house was adjacent to a corner of the front lawn of the institution. The lowest-status maintenance workers lived behind the institution in closely spaced buildings with no lawns and dumps in back, including the Irish women who were domestic servants for the institution. The landscape expressed the low status of these women in terms of both their gender and their ethnicity (Baugher and Baragli 1987).

Some research has shown how women were social agents in using gender solidarity to create connections across cultural, ethnic, and class differences. At the nineteenth-century Locust Grove plantation near Louisville, Kentucky, excavations yielded ceramics of the same patterns in different slave houses, which were interpreted as gifts between slave women to create community solidarity among women who may or may not have been kin. Community solidarity was important in resisting the oppressions of slavery (A. Young 2003:108–13). Research at an early twentieth-century mining town in Berwind, Colorado, found that women's networks linked miners' households both within and across ethnic boundaries, permitting them to organize a strike that was suppressed by the 1914 Ludlow massacre of miners' families by the Colorado National Guard (Wood 2004). A survey of women's domestic reform sites in Boston from 1865 to 1925 found that annual reports of social settlements and other organizations expressed the middle-class reformers' goal of reaching across social barriers separating women (Spencer-Wood 1994a:197; 1996).

Documentary and archaeological data have revealed the gendered social agency of children in using play landscapes. For instance, at the early twentieth-century racially integrated Cambridge Pine Street playground for young children, older girls did not passively accept their exclusion, but instead successfully negotiated to be admitted in order to "mind baby in the sand" (Spencer-Wood 1994b:133). In excavations at a turn-of-the-century orphan asylum site in New York and at a state home for older children in Rhode Island, evidence of children's social agency was expressed through gendered differences in children's use of institutional landscapes for play. Excavations revealed that girls played close to the buildings and lost toys such as dolls there, while boys played in the woods farther away from the buildings and lost toys identified with boys, such as marbles or toy soldiers (Feister 2003; Morenon 2003).

Spencer-Wood (1994a, 1996) has researched complex class and ethnic dialogues between Boston reform women and program participants who were not passive but negotiated with reformers over the content and material culture of programs. Some reform women viewed their programs as social experiments rather than social control and therefore recorded and responded to participants' reactions to programs. For instance, in the Denison House settlement annual reports, Anglo reform women recorded their response to the voices of immigrant women who complained that their production of ethnic textiles for sale ought to be put on a business basis instead of a charitable basis. In 1881 at the North Bennet Street Industrial School for Girls in Boston, boys did not passively accept their exclusion but instead successfully argued with reform women to provide the boys with a carpentry class taught by a man who worked for the women, inverting the normal gender hierarchy (Spencer-Wood 1996:433–34).

Reform women were not a monolithic group. While some worked for women's unions and had programs to create a pluralistic society by preserving ethnic cultures, others attempted social control with classes to train domestic servants, which nonpassive working-class women refused to attend (Spencer-Wood 2002b:121). In contrast to the secular college women's settlements in Boston, the New York Ladies' Home Missionary Society of the Methodist Episcopal Church sought to morally reform the poor working class living in Five Points by converting immigrant Catholics to Methodism and the cult of domesticity, requiring material expression in middle-class genteel consumer choices. The missionaries produced three publications characterizing Five Points as the most notoriously dirty and immoral slum, rife with crime, violence, and promiscuity. Working-class lifeways, including mixed-gender crowded sleeping quarters, open sexuality, drinking, smoking, and racial and ethnic miscegenation, were viewed by the middle-class missionaries as immoral. These reports justified the mission and neighboring House of Industry in boasting that they had "rescued" 60,000 children by the early 1890s, separating them from their natural (usually Catholic) parents and sending them to a Protestant family in the country (Fitts 2001).

Methods in Postmodern Feminist Historical Archaeology

Feminists have analyzed archaeological data in new ways to establish the gender identity of site occupants as well as the diversity in distinctive gendered behavior patterns at different types of sites. The gender identity of site occupants was found to be best determined from personal artifacts. Gendered differences in consumption patterns were compared at different types of sites, finding the highest alcohol consumption at brothels, a police station, and a hotel, where single men apparently ate and drank since their tent sites did not include these types of artifacts (Spude 2001). Households were found to vary in alcohol consumption, but their generally lower rates of consumption than brothels and hotels has been related to the influence of wives subscribing to the cult of domesticity and temperance (Blee 1991; Lawrence-Cheney 1991, 1993). However, a priest's privy revealed hidden alcohol bottles, although he vocally supported the local temperance law (Spude 1999).

Beaudry and Mrozowski (2004) analyzed how consumer choices of Lowell factory operatives indicated their intersections of gender, ethnic, and class identities. Costume jewelry and fancy imitation jet buttons were interpreted as expressions of female factory operatives' identities as working-class women (Ziesing 1989:141–68). Irish pipes that were found were associated with men's ethnic identities (Beaudry and Mrozowski 2004) since women who smoked were considered "loose," and working women were more likely to smoke cigarettes than pipes when they did smoke (Cook 1997). Thus, consumer choices were shown to be affected by intersections of gender, class, and ethnic identities.

Postmodern Queer Theory and Masculinity Theory

The most recent development of postmodern feminist theory is the critique and correction of heterosexist biases in feminist theory in order to analyze the diversity and fluidity in sexual orientations and performance, masculine identities, and bodily identities. Historical archaeological research has found a variety of sexual ideologies, practices, and identities at different sites, from utopian communes (Spencer-Wood, in press) to brothels (see Voss, this volume; Andretti, this volume).

The Future

Postmodern approaches appear to be developing most in part because this approach facilitates extending research into the diversity and fluidity among cultural subgroups and individuals in gender ideologies, identities, actual gender roles, practices, behaviors, and performances. Postmodern feminist theoretical approaches to gender research have progressed from considering complex intersections with class, ethnicity, and age in 1991 (e.g., Scott 1991a, 1991b; Spencer-Wood 1991b; Whelan 1991), to further analyzing their intersections with race, religion, and sexual orientation (e.g., Delle et al. 2000; Knapp 1998; Scott 1994; Spencer-Wood 1999b, 1999d, in press). Marxist-feminist theoretical approaches have been and will continue to be important in the analysis of gender power dynamics and social agency among subcultural groups (e.g., Delle 2000).

Postmodern feminist theory has synthesized the first and second waves of feminist theory by separating the analysis of patriarchal gender ideology from the analysis of actual gender practices. This paradigm can also be useful in analyzing how gender ideologies and practices are mutually constituted and constantly renegotiated between individuals, cultural subgroups, and social institutions.

There are a number of theoretical and methodological issues concerning gender research in historical archaeology that are gaining increasing attention. One fundamental concern is that the analysis of gender become as prevalent as analyses of class. In the past two Society for Historical Archaeology conferences (2004, 2005), the number of papers on gender research has declined. While no one would fail to consider class in historical archaeological research, it is still acceptable to conduct and publish ungendered research, even in analyzing households, where gender is a primary organizing principle.

At the deeper level of epistemology, it is essential that postmodern feminist theory's concern for diversity not be extended into a nihilistic relativistic epistemology in which all claims to knowledge are considered equally valid, as has been claimed in postprocessual archaeology by Hodder (1991b). The consideration of feminist and androcentric interpretations of the past as equally valid dismisses the feminist critique of androcentric archaeology and the feminist claim to more inclusive analysis and resulting knowledge (Spencer-Wood 1992). The claim that feminist and androcentric constructions of the past are equally valid reveals how relativism is a tool of the dominant group used to discredit claims to more valid knowledge by subordinate groups (Harding 1993). Both Hodder (1991a) and Englestad (1991) have noted that the dominant male elite in archaeology decides which interpretations are most valid, given that interpretations are underdetermined by data (Wylie 1992).

Feminist philosophers have written about the need to balance postmodern theories of gender diversity with the feminist epistemological standpoint argument privileging feminist knowledge as more inclusive and less partial than androcentric knowledge (Harding 1987). Harding (1993) has created the term "strong objectivity" to express the argument that recognition of the researcher's political standpoint creates more objective knowledge than the impossible attempt in traditional science to eliminate all researcher biases (Spencer-Wood 1992). The postmodern diversity of perspectives due to class, race, ethnicity, and other social variables can be reconciled with feminist standpoint theory by retaining a feminist theoretical approach starting from women's lives that critiques and corrects androcentrism.

Feminist historical archaeology needs more conscious choice and justification of the appropriateness of a feminist theoretical approach to a research project. The field would benefit greatly from more overt discussion about the value and limitations of different feminist theoretical approaches for a variety of gender research projects in historical archaeology. Postmodern feminist theory can assist archaeologists in the construction of frameworks for interpreting material culture from the standpoint of women in a variety of classes, races, and ethnic groups. Bickford (1998); Brandon (2004); Franklin (2001); Lawrence (1999); Mrozowski et al. (2000:xviii–xx); Scott (1991a, 1994); Spencer-Wood (1989a, 1989b, 1991a, 1991b, 1991c, 1992, 1994a, 1995, 1996, 1997a, 1997b, 1999a, 1999b, 1999c, 1999d, 2000, 2001b, 2002a, 2004, 2005, in press); Wilkie (2003); and Yentsch (1991c) have been among the minority in overtly discussing different feminist theoretical approaches to gender research in historical archaeology. It is hoped that this volume will lead more archaeologists researching gender to overtly discuss their theoretical approach. Discussions of feminist theory can only lead to more informed and nuanced analyses of historic gender systems by archaeologists.

Acknowledgments

I would like to thank the following colleagues for their generous assistance in providing me with information on gender research in historical archaeology of Australia: Penelope Allison, Judy Birmingham, Annie Bickford, Mary Casey, and Jane Lydon. My thanks to Sherene Baugher for sending me references from Northeast Historical Archaeology. My deepest thanks to Sarah Nelson for her thoughtful editing. Of course, any errors are my own.

References

Agnew, Aileen B.
    1995   Women and Property in Early 19th Century Portsmouth, New Hampshire. *Historical Archaeology* 29(1):62–75.

Allison, Penelope M.
    2003   The Old Kinchega Homestead: Doing Household Archaeology in Outback

New South Wales, Australia. *International Journal of Historical Archaeology* 7(3):161–94.

Anderson, Nesta
    2004   Finding the Space between Spatial Boundaries and Social Dynamics: The Archaeology of Nested Households. In *Household Chores and Household Choices: Theorizing the Domestic Sphere in Historical Archaeology.* Kerri S. Barile and Jamie C. Brandon, eds. Pp. 109–38. Tuscaloosa: University of Alabama Press.

Armstrong, Douglas V.
    1990   *The Old Village and the Great House: An Archaeological and Historical Examination of Drax Hall Plantation, St. Ann's Bay, Jamaica.* Urbana: University of Illinois Press.

Baker, Vernon G.
    1980   Archaeological Visibility of Afro-American Culture: An Example from Black Lucy's Garden, Andover, Massachusetts. In *Archaeological Perspectives on Ethnicity in America.* R. L. Schuyler, ed. Pp. 29–38. New York: Baywood Publishing.

Baker, Steven
    1983   A Quantitative Archaeological Study of the "Sporting Subculture": The Victorian Brothels of Ouray, Colorado. Paper presented at the 16th annual meeting of the Society for Historical Archaeology, Denver, January.

Bassett, Everett
    1994   "We Took Care of Each Other Like Families Were Meant To": Gender, Social Organization, and Wage Labor among the Apache at Roosevelt. In *"Those of Little Note": Gender, Race and Class in Historical Archaeology.* E. M. Scott, ed. Pp. 55–81. Tucson: University of Arizona Press.

Battle, Whitney
    2004   A Space of Our Own: Redefining the Enslaved Household at Andrew Jackson's Hermitage Plantation. In *Household Chores and Household Choices: Theorizing the Domestic Sphere in Historical Archaeology.* Kerri S. Barile and Jamie C. Brandon, eds. Pp. 33–51. Tuscaloosa: University of Alabama Press.

Baugher, Sherene, and Judith Baragli
    1987   *The Archaeological Investigation at the Matron's Cottage, Snug Harbor Cultural Center, Staten Island, New York.* New York: New York City Landmarks Preservation Commission.

Beaudry, Mary C.
    1993   Public Aesthetics versus Personal Experience: Worker Health and Well-Being in 19th-Century Lowell, Massachusetts. *Historical Archaeology* 27(2):90–106.

Beaudry, Mary C., and Stephen A. Mrozowski
    2004   Cultural Space and Worker Identity in the Company Town: Lowell, Massachusetts. In *The Archaeology of Urban Landscapes: Explorations in Slumland.* Alan Mayne and Tim Murray, eds. Pp. 118–32. Cambridge: Cambridge University Press.

Beecher, Catharine E., and Harriet Beecher Stowe
  [1869] 1975   *The American Woman's Home, or Principles of Domestic Science*. Reprint, with an introduction by Joseph Van Why. Hartford, CT: Stowe-Day Foundation.
Bell, Alison
  2001   "The Strong Prejudice of Propinquity": Inheritance Patterns and Women's Empowerment in 19th Century Virginia. Paper presented at a 2001 Society for Historical Archaeology symposium, Long Beach, CA, January 12.
Bescherer Metheny, Karen, Judson Kratzer, Anne Elizabeth Yentsch, and Conrad M. Goodwin
  1996   Method in Landscape Archaeology: Research Strategies in a Historic New Jersey Garden. In *Landscape Archaeology: Reading and Interpreting the American Historical Landscape*. R. Yamin and K. Bescherer Metheny, eds. Pp. 6–32. Knoxville: University of Tennessee Press.
Bickford, Anne
  1987   *Calthorpe's House: A Museum Guide*. Canberra: Australian Government Publishing Service.
  1993   Women's Historic Sites. In *Women in Archaeology: A Feminist Critique*. Hilary du Cros and Laurajane Smith, eds. Pp. 195–205. Canberra: Australian National University.
Binford, Lewis R.
  1962   Archaeology as Anthropology. *American Antiquity* 28(2):217–25.
  1983   *Working at Archaeology*. New York: Academic Press.
Birmingham, Judy
  1993   Engenderdynamics: Women in the Archaeological Record at Wybalenna, Flinders Island 1835–1840. In *Women in Archaeology: A Feminist Critique*. Hilary du Cros and Laurajane Smith, eds. Pp. 121–28. Canberra: Australian National University.
Bonine, Mindy
  2004   Analysis of Household and Family at a Spanish Colonial Rancho along the Rio Grande. In *Household Chores and Household Choices: Theorizing the Domestic Sphere in Historical Archaeology*. Kerri S. Barile and Jamie C. Brandon, eds. Pp. 15–33. Tuscaloosa: University of Alabama Press.
Boorstin, Daniel J., and Ruth F. Boorstin
  1989   *Hidden History: Our Secret Past*. New York: Vintage Books.
Brandon, Jamie C.
  2004   Reconstructing Domesticity and Segregating Households: The Intersections of Gender and Race in the Postbellum South. In *Household Chores and Household Choices: Theorizing the Domestic Sphere in Historical Archaeology*. Kerri S. Barile and Jamie C. Brandon, eds. Pp. 197–210. Tuscaloosa: University of Alabama Press.

Brashler, Janet G.
- 1991 When Daddy Was a Shanty Boy: The Role of Gender in the Organization of the Logging Industry in Highland West Virginia. *Historical Archaeology* 25(4):54–68.

Brighton, Stephen A.
- 2001 Prices That Suit the Times: Shopping for Ceramics at the Five Points. *Historical Archaeology* 35(3):16–31.

Bunch, Charlotte
- 1987 *Passionate Politics: Essays 1968–1986—Feminist Theory in Action.* New York: St. Martin's Press.

Casey, Mary
- 1999 Local Pottery and Dairying at the DMR Site, Brickfields, Sydney, NSW. *Australasian Historical Archaeology* 17:3–38.
- 2002 Remaking the Government Domain, 1788–1821: Landscape, Archaeology and Meaning. Ph.D. dissertation, University of Sydney.

Chambers-Schiller, Lee Virginia
- 1984 *Liberty a Better Husband. Single Women in America: The Generations of 1780–1840.* New Haven, CT: Yale University Press.

Clements, Joyce M.
- 1993 The Cultural Creation of the Feminine Gender: An Example from 19th Century Military Households at Fort Independence, Boston. *Historical Archaeology* 27(4):39–64.
- 2005 ". . . A Winding Sheet for Deborah George . . ." Searching for the Women of Ponkapoag. Ph.D. dissertation, York University.

Cogan, Frances B.
- 1989 *All-American Girl: The Ideal of Real Womanhood in Mid-Nineteenth-Century America.* Athens: University of Georgia Press.

Conkey, Margaret W., and Joan M. Gero
- 1991 Tensions, Pluralities, and Engendering Archaeology: An Introduction to Women and Prehistory. In *Engendering Archaeology: Women and Prehistory.* J. M. Gero and M. W. Conkey, eds. Pp. 3–30. Oxford: Basil Blackwell.

Conkey, Margaret W., and Janet D. Spector
- 1984 Archaeology and the Study of Gender. *Advances in Archaeological Method and Theory* 7:1–38.

Cook, Lauren J.
- 1997 "Promiscuous Smoking": Interpreting Gender and Tobacco Use in the Archaeological Record. *Northeast Historical Archaeology* 26:23–38.
- 1998 "Kathrine Nanny, Alias Naylor": A Life in Puritan Boston. *Historical Archaeology* 32(1):15–20.

Costello, Julia G.
- 2000 Red Light Voices: An Archaeological Drama of Late Nineteenth-Century

Prostitution. In *Archaeologies of Sexuality*. Peter A. Schmidt and Barbara L. Voss, eds. Pp. 160–79. London: Routledge.

Crass, David C., Bruce R. Penner, and Tammery R. Forehand
    1999   Gentility and Material Culture on the Carolina Frontier. *Historical Archaeology* 33(3):14–31.

Davidson, James M.
    2004   "Living Symbols of Their Lifelong Struggles": In Search of the Home and Household in the Heart of Freedman's Town, Dallas, Texas. In *Household Chores and Household Choices: Theorizing the Domestic Sphere in Historical Archaeology*. Kerri S. Barile and Jamie C. Brandon, eds. Pp. 75–108. Tuscaloosa: University of Alabama Press.

Deagan, Kathleen A.
    1983   *Spanish St. Augustine: The Archaeology of a Colonial Creole Community*. New York: Academic Press.

De Cunzo, Lu Ann
    1995   Reform, Respite, Ritual: An Archaeology of Institutions; the Magdalen Society of Philadelphia, 1800–1850. *Historical Archaeology* 29(3).
    2001   On Reforming the "Fallen" and Beyond: Transforming Continuity at the Magdalen Society of Philadelphia, 1845–1916. *International Journal of Historical Archaeology* 5(1):19–45.

Deetz, James F.
    1977   *In Small Things Forgotten*. Garden City, NY: Anchor Press/Doubleday.
    1988   Material Culture and Worldview in Colonial Anglo-America. In *The Recovery of Meaning: Historical Archaeology in the Eastern United States*. Mark P. Leone and Parker B. Potter Jr., eds. Pp. 219–34. Washington, DC: Smithsonian Institution Press.

Delle, James A.
    2000   Gender, Power, and Space: Negotiating Social Relations under Slavery on Coffee Plantations in Jamaica 1790–1834. In *Lines That Divide: Historical Archaeologies of Race, Class, and Gender*. J. A. Delle, S. A. Mrozowski, and R. Paynter, eds. Pp. 168–205. Knoxville: University of Tennessee Press.

Delphy, Christine
    1984   *Close to Home: A Materialist Analysis of Women's Oppression*. Diana Leonard, trans. and ed. Amherst: University of Massachusetts Press.

Devens, Carol
    1991   Gender and Colonization in Native Canadian Communities: Examining the Historical Record. In *The Archaeology of Gender*. Proceedings of the 22nd Annual Chacmool Conference. Dale Walde and Noreen D. Willows, eds. Pp. 510–14. Calgary: Department of Archaeology.

Donovan, Josephine
    2001   *Feminist Theory: The Intellectual Traditions*. 3rd ed. New York. Continuum.

Elliott, Suzanne W.
    1977   Historical Archaeology and the National Market: A Vermont Perspective, 1795–1920. Ph.D. dissertation, University of Massachusetts, Amherst.

Englestad, Erica
    1991   Feminist Theory and Post-Processual Archaeology. In *The Archaeology of Gender*. Proceedings of the 22nd Annual Chacmool Conference. Dale Walde and Noreen D. Willows, eds. Pp. 116–20. Calgary: Department of Archaeology, University of Calgary.

Feister, Lois M.
    1991   The Orphanage at Schuyler Mansion. *Northeast Historical Archaeology* 20:27–36.
    2003   Archaeology at a 19th-Century Orphanage: Why Toys? Paper presented at the 36th Annual Conference on Historical and Underwater Archaeology, Providence, RI, January 14–18.

Fitts, Robert K.
    1999   The Archaeology of Middle-Class Domesticity and Gentility in Victorian Brooklyn. *Historical Archaeology* 33(1):39–63.
    2001   The Rhetoric of Reform: The Five Points Missions and the Cult of Domesticity. *Historical Archaeology* 35(3):115–33.

Franklin, Maria
    2001   Black Feminist-Inspired Archaeology? *Journal of Social Archaeology* 1(1):108–25.

Frink, Lisa
    2005   Gender and the Hide Production Process in Colonial Western Alaska. In *Gender and Hide Production*. Lisa Frink and Kathryn Weedman, eds. Pp. 89–105. Walnut Creek, CA: AltaMira Press.

Garrow, Patrick H.
    1987   The Use of Converging Lines of Evidence for Determining Socioeconomic Status. In *Consumer Choice in Historical Archaeology*. Suzanne M. Spencer-Wood, ed. Pp. 217–33. New York: Plenum.

Gero, Joan M.
    1991   Genderlithics: Women's Roles in Stone Tool Production. In *Engendering Archaeology: Women and Prehistory*. Joan M. Gero and Margaret W. Conkey, eds. Pp. 163–94. Oxford: Basil Blackwell.

Gibb, James G., and Julia A. King
    1991   Gender, Activity Areas, and Homelots in the 19th Century Chesapeake Region. *Historical Archaeology* 25(4):109–31.

Gibb, James G., and Lee Preston
    2003   Patapsco Female Institute (1837–1890): A Light upon a Hill Relit. Paper presented at the 36th Annual Conference on Historical and Underwater Archaeology, Providence, RI, January 14–18.

Glassie, Henry
    1975   *Folk Housing in Middle Virginia*. Knoxville: University of Tennessee Press.

Goodwin, Lorinda B. R.
    1999   *An Archaeology of Manners: The Polite World of the Merchant Elite of Colonial Massachusetts*. New York: Kluwer Academic/Plenum.

Griggs, Heather J.
    2001   "By Virtue of Reason and Nature": Competition and Economic Strategy in the Needletrades at New York's Five Points, 1855–1880. *Historical Archaeology* 35(3):76–89.

Guettel, Charnie
    1974   *Marxism and Feminism*. Toronto: Women's Educational Press.

Hardesty, Donald L.
    1989   Gender Roles on the American Mining Frontier: Documentary Models and Archaeological Strategies. Paper presented at the 22nd Annual Chacmool Conference, Calgary, November.
    1994   Class, Gender Strategies, and Material Culture in the Mining West. In *"Those of Little Note": Gender, Race and Class in Historical Archaeology*. Elizabeth M. Scott, ed. Pp. 129–49. Tucson: University of Arizona Press.

Harding, Sandra
    1987   Conclusion: Epistemological Questions. In *Feminism and Methodology*. Sandra Harding, ed. Pp. 181–90. Bloomington: Indiana University Press.
    1993   Rethinking Standpoint Epistemology: "What Is Strong Objectivity"? In *Feminist Epistemologies*. Linda Alcoff and Elizabeth Potter, eds. Pp. 49–83. New York: Routledge.

Hartsock, Nancy C. M.
    1983   *Money, Sex and Power: Toward a Feminist Historical Materialism*. New York: Longman.

Hautaniemi, Susan
    1994   Race, Gender, and Health at the W. E. B. DuBois Boyhood Homesite. *Bulletin of the Massachusetts Archaeological Society* 55(1):1–7.

Hautaniemi, Susan I., and Deborah L. Rotman
    2003   To the Hogs or to the House? Municipal Water and Gender Relations at the Moors Site in Deerfield, Massachusetts. In *Shared Spaces and Divided Places: Material Dimensions of Gender Relations and the American Historical Landscape*. Deborah L. Rotman and Ellen-Rose Savulis, eds. Pp. 135–60. Knoxville: University of Tennessee Press.

Heck, Dana B., and Joseph F. Balicki
    1998   Katherine Naylor's "Home of Office": A Seventeenth-Century Privy. *Historical Archaeology* 32(3):24–38.

Henretta, J. A.
    1971   Economic Development and Social Structure in Colonial Boston. In *The Reinterpretation of American Economic History*. R. W. Fogel and S. W. Engerman, eds. Pp. 54–63. New York: Harper and Row.

Hodder, Ian, and Scott Hutson
    2003   *Reading the Past: Current Approaches to Interpretation in Archaeology.* 3rd ed. Cambridge: Cambridge University Press.

Hodder, I.
    1991a.   Gender Representation and Social Reality. In *The Archaeology of Gender.* Proceedings of the 22nd Annual Chacmool Conference. Dale Walde and Noreen D. Willows, eds. Pp. 11–17. Calgary: Department of Archaeology, University of Calgary.
    1991b.   Postprocessual Archaeology and the Current Debate. In *Processual and Postprocessual Archaeologies: Multiple Ways of Knowing the Past.* Robert W. Preucel, ed. Pp. 30–41. Occasional Paper 10. Carbondale: Center for Archaeological Investigations, Southern Illinois University.

Holliman, Sandra E.
    2005   Hideworking and Changes in Women's Status among the Arikara 1700–1862. In *Gender and Hide Production.* Lisa Frink and Kathryn Weedman, eds. Pp. 77–89. Walnut Creek, CA: AltaMira Press.

Jackson, Louise M.
    1994   Cloth, Clothing and Related Paraphernalia: A Key to Gender Visibility in the Archaeological Record of Russian America. In *"Those of Little Note": Gender, Race and Class in Historical Archaeology.* E. M. Scott, ed. Pp. 27–55. Tucson: University of Arizona Press.

Jamieson, Ross W.
    2000   Doña Luisa and Her Two Houses. In *Lines That Divide: Historical Archaeologies of Race, Class, and Gender.* J. A. Delle, S. A. Mrozowski, and R. Paynter, eds. Pp. 142–68. Knoxville: University of Tennessee Press.

Karskens, Grace
    2003   Revisiting the Worldview: The Archaeology of Convict Households in Sydney's Rocks Neighborhood. *Historical Archaeology* 37(1):34–55.

Kennedy, Margaret
    1989   Houses with Red Lights: The Nature of Female Households in the Sporting Subculture Community. In *Households and Communities.* Proceedings of the 21st Annual Chacmool Conference. Scott MacEachern, David J. W. Archer, and Richard D. Garvin, eds. Pp. 93–101. Calgary: Department of Archaeology, University of Calgary.

Knapp, Bernard
    1998   Boys Will Be Boys: Masculinist Approaches to a Gendered Archaeology. In *Reader in Gender Archaeology.* Kelley Hays-Gilpin and David S. Whitley, eds. Pp. 365–74. London: Routledge.

Kruczek-Aaron, Hadley
    2002   Choice Flowers and Well-Ordered Tables: Struggling over Gender in a Nineteenth-Century Household. *International Journal of Historical Archaeology* 6(3):173–87.

Kuhn, Annette, and Ann Marie Wolpe, eds.
  1978 *Feminism and Materialism: Women and Modes of Production*. Boston: Routledge and Kegan Paul.
Larsen, Eric L.
  1994 A Boardinghouse Madonna—Beyond the Aesthetics of a Portrait Created through Medicine Bottles. In *An Archaeology of Harpers Ferry's Commercial and Residential District*. Paul A. Shackle and Susan E. Winter, eds. *Historical Archaeology* 28(4):68–80.
Lawrence, Susan
  1999 Towards a Feminist Archaeology of Households: Gender and Household Structure on the Australian Goldfields. In *The Archaeology of Household Activities: Gender Ideologies, Domestic Spaces and Material Culture*. Penelope M. Allison, ed. Pp. 121–42. London: Routledge.
Lawrence-Cheney, Susan
  1991 Women and Alcohol: Female Influence on Recreational Patterns in the West 1880–1890. In *The Archaeology of Gender*. Proceedings of the 22nd Annual Chacmool Conference. Dale Walden and Noreen D. Willows, eds. Pp. 479–89. Calgary: Department of Archaeology, University of Calgary.
  1993 Gender on Colonial Peripheries. In *Women in Archaeology: A Feminist Critique*. Hilary du Cros and Laurajane Smith, eds. Pp. 134–37. Canberra: Australian National University.
Leedecker, Charles H., Terry H. Klein, Cheryl A. Holt, and Amy Friedlander
  1987 Nineteenth-Century Households and Consumer Behavior in Wilmington, Delaware. In *Consumer Choice in Historical Archaeology*. Suzanne M. Spencer-Wood, ed. Pp. 233–61. New York: Plenum.
Lewis, Kenneth E.
  2003 The Tin Worker's Widow: Gender and the Formation of the Archaeological Record in the South Carolina Backcountry. In *Shared Spaces and Divided Places: Material Dimensions of Gender Relations and the American Historical Landscape*. Deborah L. Rotman and Ellen-Rose Savulis, eds. Pp. 86–104. Knoxville: University of Tennessee Press.
Little, Barbara J.
  1994 "She Was . . . an Example to Her Sex": Possibilities for a Feminist Historical Archaeology. In *Historical Archaeology of the Chesapeake*. Paul A. Shackel and Barbara J. Little, eds. Pp. 189–201. Washington, DC: Smithsonian Institution Press.
Longino, Helen
  1989 Can There Be a Feminist Science? In *Feminism and Science*. Nancy Tuana, ed. Pp. 45–58. Bloomington: Indiana University Press.
Longino, Helen, and Ruth Doell
  1983 Body, Bias and Behavior: A Comparative Analysis of Reasoning in Two Areas of Biological Science. *Signs: Journal of Women in Culture and Society* 9(2):206–27.

Lorber, Judith
    2001   *Gender Inequality: Feminist Theories and Politics.* 2nd ed. Los Angeles: Roxbury.

Lucas, Michael T.
    1994   A la Russe, a la Pell-Mell, or a la Practicall: Ideology and Compromise in the Late Nineteenth-Century Dinner Table. In *An Archaeology of Harpers Ferry's Commercial and Residential District.* Paul A. Shackle and Susan E. Winter, eds. Historical Archaeology 28(4):80–94.

Lydon, Jane
    1993a.   Archaeology in The Rocks, Sydney, 1979–1993: From Old Sydney Gaol to Mrs Lewis' Boarding House. *Australasian Historical Archaeology* 11:33–42.
    1993b   Task Differentiation in Historical Archaeology: Sewing as Material Culture. In *Women in Archaeology: A Feminist Critique.* Hilary du Cros and Laurajane Smith, eds. Pp. 129–33. Canberra: Australian National University.
    1995   Gender in Australian Historical Archaeology. In *Gendered Archaeology: The Second Australian Women in Archaeology Conference.* Jane Balme and Wendy Beck, eds. Pp. 72–80. Canberra: ANH Publications, Research School of Pacific Studies, Australian National University.

McEwan, Bonnie G.
    1991   The Archaeology of Women in the Spanish New World. *Historical Archaeology* 25(4):33–41.

McKee, Larry
    1996   The Archaeology of Rachel's Garden. In *Landscape Archaeology: Reading and Interpreting the American Historical Landscape.* R. Yamin and K. Bescherer Metheny, eds. Pp. 70–91. Knoxville: University of Tennessee Press.

McMurray, Sally
    1987   Women and the Expansion of Dairying: The Cheesemaking Industry in Oneida County, New York, 1830–1860. Paper presented at the annual Berkshire History Conference, Wellesley, MA, June.

Millett, Kate
    1970   *Sexual Politics: A Surprising Examination of Society's Most Arbitrary Folly.* Garden City, NY: Doubleday.

Morenon, E. Pierre
    2003   Children at Play: Archaeological Studies of Toys, Buildings and Institutions. Paper presented at the 36th Annual Conference on Historical and Underwater Archaeology, Providence, RI.

Mrozowski, Stephen A.
    2000   The Growth of Managerial Capitalism and the Subtleties of Class Analysis in Historical Archaeology. In *Lines That Divide: Historical Archaeologies of Race, Class, and Gender.* J. A. Delle, S. A. Mrozowski, and R. Paynter, eds. Pp. 276–307. Knoxville: University of Tennessee Press.

Mrozowski, Stephen A., James A. Delle, and Robert Paynter
    2000   Introduction. In *Lines That Divide: Historical Archaeologies of Race, Class, and Gender.*

J. A. Delle, S. A. Mrozowski, and R. Paynter, eds. Pp. xi–xxxi. Knoxville: University of Tennessee Press.

Muller, Nancy Ladd
    1994   The House of the Black Burghardts: An Investigation of Gender, Race and Class at the W. E. B. DuBois Boyhood Homesite. In *"Those of Little Note": Gender, Race and Class in Historical Archaeology*. E. M. Scott, ed. Pp. 81–97. Tucson: University of Arizona Press.

Mullins, Paul R.
    1999   *Race and Affluence: An Archaeology of African America and Consumer Culture*. New York: Kluwer Academic/Plenum.

Nassaney, Michael S., D. L. Rotman, D. O. Sayers, and C. A. Nickolai
    2001   The Southwest Michigan Historic Landscape Project: Exploring Class, Gender, and Ethnicity from the Ground Up. *International Journal of Historical Archaeology* 5(3):219–61.
    2002   Gender in Archaeology: The Professional Is Political. Paper presented at the 2002 centennial meetings of the American Anthropological Association, New Orleans.
    2003   *Ancient Queens: Archaeological Explorations*. Walnut Creek, CA: AltaMira Press.

Nickolai, Carol A.
    2003   Class and Gender in Nineteenth-Century Rural Michigan: The Merriman-Sharp Hillside Farm. *Historical Archaeology* 37(4):69–83.

Ortner, Sherry B.
    1974   Is Female to Male as Nature Is to Culture? In *Woman, Culture and Society*. Michelle Z. Rosaldo and Louise Lamphere, eds. Pp. 67–88. Stanford, CA: Stanford University Press.

Piddock, Susan
    2001   "An Irregular and Inconvenient Pile of Buildings": The Destitute Asylum of Adelaide, South Australia and the English Workhouse. *International Journal of Historical Archaeology* 5(1):73–97.

Praetzellis, Adrian, and Mary Praetzellis, eds.
    1998   Archaeologists as Storytellers. *Historical Archaeology* 32(1).

Purser, Margaret
    1991   "Several Paradise Ladies Are Visiting in Town": Gender Strategies in the Early Industrial West. *Historical Archaeology* 25(4):6–16.

Rosaldo, Michele Zimbalist
    1974   Woman, Culture, and Society: A Theoretical Overview. In *Woman, Culture and Society*. Michelle Z. Rosaldo and Louise Lamphere, eds. Pp. 17–42. Stanford, CA: Stanford University Press.
    1980   The Use and Abuse of Anthropology: Reflections on Feminism and Cross-Cultural Understanding. *Signs* 5(3):389–417.

Rosaldo, Michele Z., and Louise Lamphere
    1974   Introduction. In *Woman, Culture and Society*. Michelle Z. Rosaldo and Louise Lamphere, eds. Pp. 1–16. Stanford, CA: Stanford University Press.

Rotman, Deborah L., and Michael S. Nassaney
　1997　Class, Gender and the Built Environment: Deriving Social Relations from Cultural Landscapes in Southwest Michigan. *Historical Archaeology* 331(2):42–62.

Russell, Penny
　1993　In Search of Woman's Place: An Historical Survey of Gender and Space in Nineteenth-Century Australia. *Australasian Historical Archaeology* 11:28–32.

Ryan, Mary P.
　1990　*Women in Public: Between Banners and Ballots, 1825–1880*. Baltimore: The Johns Hopkins University Press.

Savulis, Ellen-Rose
　2003　Zion's Zeal: Negotiating Identity in Shaker Communities. In *Shared Spaces and Divided Places: Material Dimensions of Gender Relations and the American Historical Landscape*. Deborah L. Rotman and Ellen-Rose Savulis, eds. Pp. 160–90. Knoxville: University of Tennessee Press.

Sayers, D. O., and Michael S. Nassaney
　1999　Antebellum Landscapes and Agrarian Political Economies: Modeling Progressive Farmsteads in Southwest Michigan. *The Michigan Archaeologist* 45(3):74–117.

Schuyler, Robert L., ed.
　1980　*Archaeological Perspectives on Ethnicity in America: Afro-American and Asian American Culture History*. Farmingdale, NY: Baywood.

Scott, Elizabeth M.
　1991a　A Feminist Approach to Historical Archaeology: Eighteenth-Century Fur Trade Society at Michilimackinac. *Historical Archaeology* 25(4):82–109.
　1991b　Gender in Complex Colonial Society: The Material Goods of Everyday Life in a Late Eighteenth Century Fur Trading Community. In *The Archaeology of Gender*. Proceedings of the 22nd Annual Chacmool Conference. Dale Walde and Noreen D. Willows, eds. Pp. 270–79. Calgary: Department of Archaeology, University of Calgary.
　1994　Through the Lens of Gender: Archaeology, Inequality and "Those of Little Note." In *"Those of Little Note": Gender, Race and Class in Historical Archaeology*. E. M. Scott, ed. Pp. 3–27. Tucson: University of Arizona Press.

Seifert, Donna J.
　1991a　Introduction. In *Gender in Historical Archaeology*. D. J. Seifert, ed. *Historical Archaeology* 25(4):1–5.
　1991b　Within Sight of the White House: The Archaeology of Working Women. *Historical Archaeology* 25(4):82–108.
　1994　Mrs. Starr's Profession. In *"Those of Little Note": Gender, Race and Class in Historical Archaeology*. E. M. Scott, ed. Pp. 149–74. Tucson: University of Arizona Press.

Singleton, Theresa L.
　1990　The Archaeology of the Plantation South: A Review of Approaches and Goals. *Historical Archaeology* 24(4):70–78.

Sipe, Amy E. S.
- 2003 Understanding Gender, Reform, and Social Change in 19th Century Central New York. Paper presented at the Society for Historical Archaeology 36th Annual Conference on Historical and Underwater Archaeology, Providence, RI, January.

Slocum, Sally
- 1975 Woman the Gatherer: Male Bias in Anthropology. In *Towards an Anthropology of Women*. Rayna R. Reiter, ed. Pp. 36–51. New York: Monthly Review Press.

Smith, Sheli O.
- 1989 Women and Seafaring. Paper presented at the 22nd Annual Chacmool Conference, Calgary, November 11.

South, Stanley
- 1977 *Method and Theory in Historical Archaeology*. New York: Academic Press.

Spector, Janet D.
- 1983 Male/Female Task Differentiation among the Hidatsa: Toward the Development of an Archaeological Approach to the Study of Gender. In *The Hidden Half: Studies of Plains Indian Women*. P. Albers and B. Medicine, eds. Pp. 77–99. Washington, DC: University Press of America.
- 1993 *What This Awl Means: Feminist Archaeology at a Wahpeton Dakota Village*. St. Paul: Minnesota Historical Society Press.

Spencer-Wood, Suzanne M. A.
- 1987a A Survey of Domestic Reform Movement Sites in Boston and Cambridge, ca. 1865–1905. *Historical Archaeology* 21(2):7–36.
- 1987b Miller's Indices and Consumer Choice Profiles: Status-Related Behaviors and White Ceramics. In *Consumer Choice in Historical Archaeology*. Suzanne Spencer-Wood, ed. Pp. 321–58. New York: Plenum.
- 1989a The Community as Household: Domestic Reform, Mid-Range Theory and the Domestication of Public Space. In *Household and Communities*. Proceedings of the 21st Annual Chacmool Conference. S. MacEachern, D. J. W. Archer, and R. D. Garvin, eds. Pp. 113–22. Calgary: Department of Archaeology, University of Calgary.
- 1989b Feminist Historical Archaeology. Symposium organized for the 22nd Annual Chacmool Conference, Calgary, November.
- 1989c Making Women Visible through Historical Archaeology. Symposium organized at the First Joint Archaeological Congress, Baltimore, January 8.
- 1991a Feminist Empiricism: A More Holistic Theoretical Approach. Paper presented at the Conference on Historical and Underwater Archaeology, Richmond, VA, January.
- 1991b Toward an Historical Archaeology of Domestic Reform. In *The Archaeology of Inequality*. R. McGuire and R. Paynter, eds. Pp. 231–86. Oxford: Basil Blackwell.
- 1991c Towards a Feminist Historical Archaeology of the Construction of Gender.

In *The Archaeology of Gender*. Proceedings of the 22nd Chacmool Conference. Dale Walde and Noreen D. Willows, eds. Pp. 234–44. Calgary: Department of Archaeology, University of Calgary.

1992   A Feminist Program for a Non-Sexist Archaeology. In *Quandaries and Quests: Visions of Archaeology's Future*. LuAnn Wandsnider, ed. Pp. 98–113. Occasional Paper 20. Carbondale: Center for Archaeological Investigations, Southern Illinois University.

1993   Review of "The Recovery of Meaning: Historical Archaeology in the Eastern United States," by Mark P. Leone and Parker B. Potter. *Bulletin of the History of Archaeology* 3(1):27–35.

1994a   Diversity in 19th Century Domestic Reform: Relationships among Classes and Ethnic Groups. In *"Those of Little Note": Gender, Race and Class in Historical Archaeology*. Elizabeth Scott, ed. Tucson: University of Arizona Press.

1994b   Turn of the Century Women's Organizations, Urban Design, and the Origin of the American Playground Movement. *Landscape Journal* 13(2, fall):125–38.

1995   Toward the Further Development of Feminist Historical Archaeology. *World Archaeological Bulletin* 7:118–36.

1996   Feminist Historical Archaeology and the Transformation of American Culture by Domestic Reform Movements, 1840–1925. In *Historical Archaeology and the Study of American Culture*. L. A. De Cunzo and B. L. Herman, eds. Pp. 397–46. Knoxville: Winterthur Museum and University of Tennessee Press.

1997a   Feminist Inclusive Theory: Crossing Boundaries in Theory and Practice. Paper invited for the Fourth Australian Women in Archaeology Conference, Cairns, Australia, July 3–5.

1997b   Pragmatism and Feminism. Paper invited for an American Anthropological Association symposium, Washington, DC, November 19–23.

1999a   Archaeology and the Gendering of American Historical Landscapes: A Brief Overview. Paper presented at the Fifth Australian Women in Archaeology Conference, Sydney, Australia, July 2–4.

1999b   The Formation of Ethnic-American Identities: Jewish Communities in Boston. In *Historical Archaeology: Back from the Edge*. Pedro Paulo A. Funari, Martin Hall, and Siân Jones, eds. Pp. 284–307. London: Routledge.

1999c   Gendering Power. In *Manifesting Power: Gender and the Interpretation of Power in Archaeology*. Tracy L. Sweely, ed. Pp. 175–83. London: Routledge.

1999d   The World Their Household: Changing Meanings of the Domestic Sphere in the Nineteenth Century. In *The Archaeology of Household Activities: Gender Ideologies, Domestic Spaces and Material Culture*. Penelope M. Allison, ed. Pp. 162–89. London: Routledge.

2000   Strange Attractors: Non-Linear Systems Theory and Feminist Theory. In *Exploring Social Theory in Archaeology*. Michael B. Schiffer, ed. Pp. 112–26. Salt Lake City: University of Utah Press.

2001a   Introduction. In *The Archaeology of Seventeenth and Eighteenth Century Almshouses*.

Sherene Baugher and S. M. Spencer-Wood, eds. *International Journal of Historical Archaeology* 5(2):115–22.

2001b What Difference Does Feminist Theory Make? In *The Archaeology of Nineteenth Century Institutions for Reform*. Suzanne M. Spencer-Wood and Sherene Baugher, eds. *International Journal of Historical Archaeology* 5(1):97–114.

2002a Feminist Theory. Entry invited for the *Encyclopedia of Historical Archaeology*. Charles E. Orser, ed. Pp. 205–9. London: Routledge.

2002b Utopian Visions and Architectural Designs of Turn-of-the-Century Social Settlements. In *Embodied Utopias: Gender, Social Change and the Modern Metropolis*. Amy Bingaman, Lise Shapiro, and Rebecca Zorach, eds. Pp. 116–32. London: Routledge.

2003 Gendering the Creation of Green Urban Landscapes in America at the Turn of the Century. In *Shared Spaces and Divided Places: Material Dimensions of Gender Relations and the American Historical Landscape*. Deborah L. Rotman and Ellen-Rose Savulis, eds. Pp. 24–62. Knoxville: University of Tennessee Press.

2004 A Historic Pay-for-Housework Community Household: The Cambridge Cooperative Housekeeping Society. In *Household Chores and Household Choices: Theorizing the Domestic Sphere in Historical Archaeology*. Kerri Barrile and Jamie Brandon, eds. Pp. 138–58. Tuscaloosa: University of Alabama Press.

2005 Feminist Boundary Crossings: Challenging Androcentric Assumptions and Stereotypes about Hideworking. Invited commentary chapter in *Gender and Hide Production*. Lisa Frink and Kathryn Weedman, eds. Pp. 197–215. Walnut Creek, CA: AltaMira Press.

In press A Feminist Theoretical Approach to the Historical Archaeology of Utopian Communities. *Historical Archaeology*.

Spencer-Wood, Suzanne M., and Sherene Baugher
  2001 Introduction. In *The Archaeology of Nineteenth Century Institutions for Reform*. Suzanne M. Spencer-Wood and Sherene Baugher, eds. *International Journal of Historical Archaeology* 5(1):3–17.

Spude, Cathy H.
  1999 Predicting Gender in Archaeological Assemblages: A Klondike Example. In *Restoring Women's History through Historic Preservation*. Gail Dubrow and J. Goodman, eds. Baltimore: The Johns Hopkins University Press.

Stansell, Christine
  1986 *City of Women: Sex and Class in New York 1789–1860*. New York: Alfred A. Knopf.

Starbuck, David R.
  1994 The Identification of Gender at Northern Military Sites of the Late Eighteenth Century. In *"Those of Little Note": Gender, Race and Class in Historical Archaeology*. E. M. Scott, ed. Pp. 115–29. Tucson: University of Arizona Press.

Stewart-Abernathy, Leslie C.
  2004 Separate Kitchens and Intimate Archaeology: Constructing Urban Slavery on

the Antebellum Cotton Frontier in Washington, Arkansas. In *Household Chores and Household Choices: Theorizing the Domestic Sphere in Historical Archaeology.* Kerri S. Barile and Jamie C. Brandon, eds. Pp. 51–75. Tuscaloosa: University of Alabama Press.

Valian, Virginia
 1998 *Why so Slow? The Advancement of Women.* Cambridge, MA: MIT Press.

Wall, Diana di Zerega
 1991 Sacred Dinners and Secular Teas: Constructing Domesticity in Mid-19th-Century New York. *Historical Archaeology* 25(4):69–81.
 1994 *The Archaeology of Gender: Separating the Spheres in Urban America.* New York: Plenum.
 2000 Family Meals and Evening Parties: Constructing Domesticity in Nineteenth-Century Middle-Class New York. In *Lines That Divide: Historical Archaeologies of Race, Class, and Gender.* J. A. Delle, S. A. Mrozowski, and R. Paynter, eds. Pp. 109–42. Knoxville: University of Tennessee Press.

Weber, Carmen A.
 1991 The Genius of the Orangery: Women and Eighteenth Century Chesapeake Gardens. In *The Archaeology of Gender.* Proceedings of the 22nd Annual Chacmool Conference. Dale Walde and Noreen D. Willows, eds. Pp. 263–69. Calgary: Department of Archaeology.
 1996 The Greenhouse Effect: Gender-Related Traditions in Eighteenth-Century Gardening. In *Landscape Archaeology: Reading and Interpreting the American Historical Landscape.* R. Yamin and K. Bescherer Metheny, eds. Pp. 32–52. Knoxville: University of Tennessee Press.

Welter, Barbara
 1966 The Cult of True Womanhood: 1820–1860. *American Quarterly* 18:151–74.

Wertheimer, Barbara M.
 1977 *We Were There: The Story of Working Women in America.* New York: Pantheon Books/Random House.

Wheeler, Kathleen L.
 2000 Using archaeology to debunk the myth of the "poor widow." Paper presented at the 99th annual meeting of the American Anthropological Association, San Francisco, November 22.
 2001 Women, Architecture and Artifact. Paper presented at a 2001 Society for Historical Archaeology conference symposium, Long Beach, CA, January 12.

Whelan, Mary K.
 1991 Gender and Historical Archaeology: Eastern Dakota Patterns in the 19th Century. *Historical Archaeology* 25(4):17–32.

Wilkie, Laurie A.
 1996 Medicinal Teas and Patent Medicines: African American Women's Consumer Choices and Ethnomedical Traditions at a Louisiana Plantation. *Southeastern Archaeology* 14(2):136–48.

2000 Not Merely Child's Play: Creating a Historical Archaeology of Children and Childhood. In *Children and Material Culture*. Joanna S. Derevenski, ed. Pp. 100–115. London: Routledge.

2003 *The Archaeology of Mothering: An African-American Midwife's Tale*. Berkeley: University of California Press.

Wood, Margaret C.
    2004 Working-Class Households as Sites of Social Change. In *Household Chores and Household Choices: Theorizing the Domestic Sphere in Historical Archaeology*. Kerri S. Barile and Jamie C. Brandon, eds. Pp. 210–35. Tuscaloosa: University of Alabama Press.

Woodhouse-Beyer, K.
    1999 Artels and Identities: Gender, Power and Russian America. In *Manifesting Power: Gender and the Interpretation of Power in Archaeology*. Tracy L. Sweely, ed. Pp. 129–55. London: Routledge.

Woodruff, Janet
    2005 African Spiritual Practices in the Diaspora: A Preliminary Look at Connecticut. Paper presented at the 38th Annual Conference on Historical and Underwater Archaeology, York.

Wylie, Alison
    1991a Feminist Critiques and Archaeological Challenges. In *The Archaeology of Gender*. Proceedings of the 22nd Annual Chacmool Conference. Dale Walde and Noreen D. Willows, eds. Pp. 17–23. Calgary: Department of Archaeology, University of Calgary.
    1991b Gender Theory and the Archaeological Record: Why Is There No Archaeology of Gender? In *Engendering Archaeology: Women and Prehistory*. J. M. Gero and M. W. Conkey, eds. Pp. 31–54. Oxford: Basil Blackwell.
    1992 The Interplay of Evidential Constraints and Political Interests: Recent Archaeological Research on Gender. *American Antiquity* 57:15–35.

Yamin, Rebecca
    2004 Alternative Narratives: Respectability at New York's Five Points. In *The Archaeology of Urban Landscapes: Explorations in Slumland*. Alan Mayne and Tim Murray, eds. Pp. 154–71. Cambridge: Cambridge University Press.

Yamin, Rebecca, and Sarah T. Bridges
    2002 Children's Strikes, Parents' Rights: Paterson and Five Points. *International Journal of Historical Archaeology* 6(2):113–27.

Yentsch, Anne E.
    1991a Access and Space, Symbolic and Material, in Historical Archaeology. In *The Archaeology of Gender*. Proceedings of the 22nd Chacmool Conference. Dale Walde and Noreen D. Willows, eds. Pp. 252–63. Calgary: Department of Archaeology, University of Calgary.
    1991b Engendering Visible and Invisible Ceramic Artifacts, Especially Dairy Vessels. *Historical Archaeology* 25(4):17–32.

1991c The Symbolic Divisions of Pottery: Sex-Related Attributes of English and Anglo-American Household Pots. In *The Archaeology of Inequality*. R. H. McGuire and R. Paynter, eds. Pp. 192–230. Cambridge: Basil Blackwell.

1994 *A Chesapeake Family and Their Slaves: A Study in Historical Archaeology*. Cambridge: Cambridge University Press.

Young, Amy

2003 Gender and Landscape: A View from the Plantation Slave Community. In *Shared Spaces and Divided Places: Material Dimensions of Gender Relations and the American Historical Landscape*. Deborah L. Rotman and Ellen-Rose Savulis, eds. Pp. 104–35. Knoxville: University of Tennessee Press.

Young, Linda

2003 *Middle-Class Culture in the Nineteenth Century: America, Australia and Britain*. New York: Palgrave Macmillan.

Zeising, Grace H.

1989 Analysis of Personal Effects from the Excavations of the Boott Mills Boardinghouse Backlots in Lowell, Massachusetts. In *Interdisciplinary Investigations of the Boott Mills, Lowell, Massachusetts. Vol. 3: The Boardinghouse System as a Way of Life*. Boston: National Park Service, North Atlantic Regional Office.

Gender, Things, and Material Culture   3

MARIE LOUISE STIG SØRENSEN

THE ASPECT OF GENDER that archaeology can investigate with the greatest expertise is the way in which gender construction and the living of gendered lives involve and are affected by material culture. Material culture is not, however, merely things. Rather, it is an extremely interesting and flexible medium that is used both to create notions of traditions, the maintenance of conventions, and normative behavior and as a means of defiance against and disrupting these same norms. Material culture is therefore not just a source for the finding of representations of gender; rather, it is in itself implicated in the construction of gender at different levels. Conceptualizing the meaning of things should therefore be thought of as a dynamic rather than a decoding process (Kirkham and Attfield 1996:11, n. 2). We should think of material culture as a place of creation as well as resistance, and both qualities come into play in the construction and experience of gender. One of the distinct achievements of gender research has therefore been its explicit attention to this intricate relationship between material culture and social and psychological ideas about and categories of gender. In the history of gender archaeology, we can accordingly identify a distinct line of argument concerned with analyzing and utilizing the connections between gender (as both a social construction and a personal experience) and the external physical means through which such constructions and experiences are formulated. We have seen the debate move quickly from a position in the 1970s to 1980s in which objects were approached as the reflections, symbols, or signs of gender without in themselves adding any dynamic to the situations studied to the current one in which different theoretical positions are used to explore material culture as a medium intimately involved in the construction of meaning. During this development, a number of key concerns have been raised, and substantially different perceptions of gender have become apparent, all of which contribute to the current self-critical and explorative stage in the development of gender archaeology. In particular, these discussions manage to show archaeological data in a new light, they outline complex and potentially contradictory understandings of gender, and they provide challenges to and links with developments in other disciplines, such as design history, material culture study, and history—in other words, they add to our means of exploring how people and communities construct gendered worlds around themselves.

The following discussion of material culture and gender begins by outlining some of the main changes in our understanding and analyses of this relationship since the first explicit discussions of gender in archaeology. Thereafter, two main thematic foci will be used to provide exemplars that outline some of the arguments of recent developments. One theme is the relationship between the learning and acquiring of gender identity and the use of objects to fabricate differences in people's appearances. The other theme is the manner in which gender ideology can be manifest in the construction of space and the development of routines or *habitus* that this encourages. Finally, some reflections on the advances currently taking place and the emergence of a new range of arguments will be given. The overall aim throughout is to illuminate the explicit yet intricate relationship between different dimensions of gender and the production, circulation, and consumption of material culture and to give some insights into with what strength and thoughtfulness archaeology has been exploring this relationship to the benefit of the study of gender, the discipline, and material culture studies more generally.

On the Changing Role of Material Culture in Gender Studies

Material Objects as Reflection of Gender

The first explicit studies of gender and material culture were motivated by a strong desire to find women's past, to locate their roles and contribution in society, and to find evidence of their importance. Epistemologically, this work was guided by an understanding of material culture that saw it as passive and its role to be the representation of social relations. The analyses were also often influenced by an expectation that association with wealth of various kinds would evidence the importance of women; studies were accordingly formulated within an analytical framework that focused on general patterns, repetition, and various quantitative measures. This led in particular to studies looking for evidence of women's rank and wealth in mortuary data. These studies were theoretically influenced by approaches to mortuary studies that equated objects found in a person's grave (in particular, their amount and rarity) with the importance of that person; they searched for "correlations." An early example of this kind of approach is found in Dommasnes's investigation of Norwegian Iron Age graves in which she aimed to answer why some women obtain rank seemingly equal to men in a society that written testimony shows was male dominated (Dommasnes 1987:69). Her initial analysis is based on a simple proposition, very similar to others used in mortuary studies at the time, as she states, "The ratio of male/female graves is here used as a measure of the general status of women within an area" (Dommasnes 1987:71). The analysis of the number of graves is, however, supplemented by further analysis of possible socioeconomic factors, such as affinity to good agricultural land and differentiation between locations in terms of their access to wider trade networks (Dommasnes 1987:72). Through these additional analyses, Dommasnes was able to answer her question by proposing that "women achieved high rank when they took over male tasks and responsibilities. In the period in question this happened because men invested their energy in other fields than farming [e.g., expedition of war and trade]" (Dommasnes 1987:76).

Another clear emphasis arose from the desire to show women's importance in past societies. This often took the form of reassigning value to what was considered to be undervalued or downgraded elements of women's material culture, such as domestic utensils or weaving equipments (e.g., Bevan 1997; Brumfiel 1991; Wright 1996; see also the discussion in Nelson 1997:85–111), or, alternatively, studies aimed to insert women as participants into what had typically been considered male spheres of activities. The former often took the form of arguing that the resources or activities represented by these objects were central to the sustenance and reproduction of society, and in this light objects associated with gathering or cooking were highlighted. The latter emphasis was often formed around theoretical propositions, such as the idea of gendered division of labor (e.g., Wright 1991), or it took the form of a challenge to existing interpretations, as in the case of the debate around women's contribution to hunting in the Palaeolithic (e.g., papers in Balme and Beck 1993; Hager 1997). Where historical sources were available, this interest in identifying women doing what was traditionally seen as men's work is even more obvious with examples ranging from discussions of women in the coal mining industry (Preece 1996) to analyses of the involvement of women in various crafts and guilds, such as women working as smiths (Weinstein 1996). Regardless of these differences, these early attempts at finding women's past share an understanding of the relationship between gender and material culture in which the latter is thought of as essentially passive.

The attempts at looking for women's past outside the sphere of mortuary practices largely had to develop their own interpretative framework for the analysis of domestic activities and the material remains of production since existing ones provided little guidance beyond economic analysis. These restraints caused a lack of subtleties in the interpretations put forward, but this phase was nonetheless significant for further developments, as it brought attention to neglected aspects of past societies and also increasingly raised questions about how we assess the social significance of objects. It became, for example, apparent that some artifacts were difficult to rank without using our own value judgment regarding the activities they represent. In particular, mundane artifacts, such as the spindle whorl, provided interesting challenges insofar as they at one level were clearly not very valuable while at another level might be seen as expressing women's relationship to and control over certain products and thus as a sign of their specific social roles and therefore also their economic significance. As part of domestic production, these objects were typically associated with women as well as with low value and rank, and there was a clear need for reconsidering how we analyze such artifacts and understand their incorporation in different contexts.

These early gender studies used material culture as an essentially passive component of gender construction, seeing objects as the outward sign or representation of gender roles rather than as partners to the production of gendered meaning. Material culture was still perceived primarily as a fossil record of chronology, as an expression of material and stylistic variation, as evidence of craft and technologies, as a means of investigating trade and exchange relationships, and as a value in and of itself. These aspects of objects are still being pursued, but we have added to them an interest in understanding the involvement that material culture has with its context of production and consumption: how is material culture partner to the maintenance as well as the transformation of social and cultural conditions, including the conditions of gender?

From Things to Contexts

There were different responses to the challenges emerging from the first flow of studies that had aimed to return to women (in the past and the present) their history and their material culture. One important reaction was to reconsider the meaning of objects and to foreground the question of to whom this meaning "belongs." Another was to make the relationship between objects and people personal and intimate, part of the life histories of both (e.g., Tringham 1991). For these budding ideas, Spector's work in the 1990s was seminal, as it provided an innovative way of framing and responding to such needs. As her device, she focused on an awl found during the excavation of a nineteenth-century Wahpeton Dakota village in Minnesota and used it to connect to and construct a narrative of events in the life of an individual woman known to have lived on the site (Spector 1991, 1993).

A somewhat different solution to the problem of how objects were valued and therefore how women's work was considered was provided by Conkey (1991). Reinterpreting the assemblage from the Palaeolithic rock-shelter site at Cuerto de la Mina, Spain, her solution was to sensitize our research questions to how objects are embedded within contexts of action and therefore that they cannot be interpreted in isolation. Rather than demonstrating the presence of women, her concern was to explore how the material culture revealed a range of different activities and contexts that were likely to have involved gender. This study is one of the earliest and clearest advocates of an approach where "engendering" is dependent not on the physical identification of women but rather on a different way of investigating the material culture. As an example, Conkey used the worked bone and antler from the site to argue that extensive bone and antler industry took place in the site, and on this basis she made inferences about supplementary activities, such as the making and use of cord, string, line, and, by extension, perhaps even weaving (Conkey 1991:76). The objects were interpreted as relating to contexts of action, and using this as an interpretative device, a dense and interconnected range of activities were demonstrated to have taken place on and close to the site. It was also clearly demonstrated how the performance of these activities would have involved social differentiation of different kinds and at different scales (Conkey 1991:77f.). On this basis, an argument about women's active engagement with several levels of productive activities could be made (Conkey 1991:78). Conkey also suggested that these technologies are simultaneously partitioned by the occupants and generate such partitioning and that such divisions give rise to both social order and tension inasmuch as the different tasks have to be scheduled and may be dependent on each other (Conkey 1991:80).

Others used the classic concern with women's seclusion in the domestic sphere as their starting point. Tools used in textile productions, especially spindle whorls and loom weights, were often singled out, and interesting arguments about ways of interpreting them were made. Gräslund (2001:96–97), for instance, making the simple point that "in earlier times, one of women's main tasks was to produce textiles needed on the farm, which was absolutely crucial work," was able to use this to show how the discipline was now ready to work from such propositions and to use them to reinterpret complex social and economic relations. Gräslund also used studies showing that for southern German Merovingian women, social differentiation based on grave goods generally corresponded with differences in what tools they had to remind us that potentially complex relations may exist between women within many domestic contexts (i.e., all women are not necessarily equal) (96–97). Furthermore, she used her review of evidence for the tasks and roles associated with Viking women to show that even when women's place was inside, within the domestic sphere, this does not necessarily mean she had no value; on the contrary, being the head of the domestic sphere could be the basis of powerful positions (99).

Another focus that developed was concerned with how material culture, as various kinds of resources, is central to and entrenched in the negotiation over and legitimization of power. It was recognized that material culture becomes absorbed into the political economy and therefore that gender can become one of the structures through which power relations seep into the very fabric of communities. This intrinsic relationship was clearly outlined in a case study by Hastorf (1991). She showed how the expansion of the Inca Empire influenced local gender relations in the intermontane Mantaro Valley in Peru. Using palaeo-ethnobotanical data from two different Sausa compounds, one from the later pre-Hispanic period just before the Inca expansion (Wanka II, A.D. 1300–1460) and the other from during the period of Inca control (Wanka III, A.D. 1460–1532), Hastorf made a comparison between the two phases in terms of the distribution of equipments and residues related to food processing and consumption. These data were further supplemented by isotope analysis of human bones. It was well known that communities such as that of Wanka III were transformed and incorporated into the Inca state through imperial conquest, but Hastorf's study demonstrated how during this transformation local gender relations were affected. In particular, she used the changing distribution of equipments and food residues to suggest that the period saw increased circumscription of certain, presumably female activities associated with food preparation (Hastorf 1991:148), while the isotope analysis showed that entry into the Inca state locally resulted in differential access to certain types of food and in particular beer, which was consumed by selected males as part of ritual, political, and social meetings (Hastorf 1991:150–52).

Brumfiel's various studies of textile and weaving activities in Aztec societies similarly provide a challenging connection between the distribution of apparently mundane weaving equipments, such as spindle whorl, and the complexity of economic strategies and dependencies that they were part of. The written record states that women were the weavers; but using the numbers and size of spindle whorls from different sites in the Valley of Mexico, Brumfiel (1991) was able to argue that weaving played different economic roles on different sites. The implication of this analysis is that women's participation in different kinds of work varied between sites, and their contribution to the market economy varied accordingly. It was through studies like these, which were finding new ways of identifying women as producers and partners in complex production strategies, that new approaches to how women's contribution to society could be reclaimed were being formulated.

One may also see Dommasnes's (1987) arguments, outlined previously, about the effect that Late Iron Age raids had on the domestic power relations of those left behind as bringing together the political economy, material culture, and gender, while Stalsberg's (2001) study of Varangian women (the Scandinavians in Old Russia during the Viking period) in Russia illustrates another dimension of the relationship between gender and the economy. In her work, the common occurrence of weighing equipment in women's graves is used to mount a strong argument for women taking part in the trading of the family (Stalsberg 1991, 2001:73) and for seeing men and women not as equals but both as "indispensable members of their economic micro-unit (i.e. their family), but with sharply separated tasks" (Stalsberg 2001:75).

The subtleties of such studies come from their concerns with gender as part of wider social and economic relations and as shaped around the opportunities and restrictions arising from particular historical conditions. They did, however, in the main continue to approach material culture in a limited fashion in which remains were seen as symbols of positions and roles, as representing certain value, and as means of empowerment but not yet as dynamically involved in the processes through which meanings and understandings of the world and of ways of acting in it are formed.

During this phase, mortuary studies continued to be an area of gender analysis, as graves often provide the least ambiguous evidence about gender roles and ideologies. Gradually, however, the focus of such studies shifted from being about establishing women's positions in past societies to a concern with identifying key aspects of gender as part of social relations more widely (e.g., papers in Arnold and Wicker 2001; Moore and Scott 1997). The examples vary, covering the whole time period of archaeology and various regions and including detailed comparison between communities or investigating specific conditions within them, such as food allocation.

The latter is exemplified by Rega's (1997) study of an Early Bronze Age cemetery in the former Yugoslavia. She used isotope analysis (to establish the proportion of meat and plant food in a diet) in combination with dental caries rates and attrition (as an indirect indication of dietary carbohydrate consumption) to investigate differences in diet. For this population, the analysis showed that males and females had similar diets, while, on the other hand, differences in food consumption were observed between groups within the cemetery interpreted as representing family or residence groups (Rega 1997:238–39). The Early Bronze Age is a period of considerable change in material culture partly because of the rapid development and elaboration of bronze metallurgy and extensive exchange systems. So far, it has been common to suggest that the social impact of these changes resulted in growing asymmetries between men and women, as it is assumed that men became the metalworkers and were the ones engaged in and controlling exchange (Shennan 1993). Rega's analysis, although based on only one cemetery, may suggest that social responses to these changes were more complex and less divided along gender lines than we have assumed. Another example of dietary variance that is interpreted as resulting from social differences comes from Early Iron Age temperate Europe. Here skeletal differences were used to argue that the people buried in some of the richest graves, in contrast to the rest of the population, "came from a privileged background on several generations of good food" (Oliver 1992:57). Central to this kind of study is the question of how differences within communities affect resource allocations and in turn may consolidate and legitimize difference.

From these attempts at engaging with ways of contextualizing how objects were used and of recognizing their diverse meanings arose an interest in theoretical approaches that not only granted objects an active role in society but also explicitly aimed to discuss the nature and quality of objects. Prominent among the influences behind this shift were arguments, such as that by Appadurai (1986), about the "social life of things" that led to increased interest in the life history or bibliography of objects. Bourdieau (1977) was another central influence. His concept of *habitus*, with its focus on the enactment of everyday life, its opening up of new ways of understanding the social impact of routine action, and its valorization of practical logic, introduced new avenues of thought. It also brought intellectual legitimacy to the study of "the small things" and to domesticity. It is furthermore of significance that such arguments reinserted the social into the relationship between things and people, readdressing the risk of treating things as if their meanings and impacts were totally separate from human actions and perceptions.

From Contexts to Materiality, Norms, and Subversion

Arising out of these arguments, the focus of gender archaeology has recently shifted further, and its early preoccupation with the presence and status of gender has in general been replaced with an interest in how gender is constructed and negotiated. Our approaches to and exploration of material culture have changed accordingly. Following on critiques that argued that gender is neither static nor stable and an emphasis on gender as made and not given, the media through which gender is constructed and experienced have come into sharper focus. This has fueled further attention to the characteristics of material culture as objects, including discussions of "what they do" (e.g., Fisher and Loren 2003; Sørensen 2000). Moving beyond the recognition that material culture arguably is central to discourses about identity and power as well as a basic medium for the performance and staging of social categorization, investigation and arguments about how these processes unfold have come into the foreground. This has included arguments by Joyce (2002), based on Butler (1990), who sees material culture as providing a means of reiteration through citation and quotations. For Butler, "Gendered identity is created through the repetition of postures, gestures, dress language and so on, performed as the repeated citation of a gendered norm" (Gilchrist 1999:82).

The proposition that material culture can be understood as a medium of performance has also been explored, and this has provided new ways of approaching and of deconstructing the significant metaphors and messages in, for example, elaborate burial contexts (e.g., Arwill-Nordbladh 1998; Sørensen 2004). In short, the call for gender studies to focus on the discursive construction of gender has in itself given rise to a need to deconstruct how such discourses are shaped. Along the way, substantial and methodological innovative studies have been conducted, and our insight into the relationship between gender and material culture has been formed through a range of case studies as well as theoretical debate.

One approach emerging from this emphasis has been concerned with the explicit materiality of gender and how this affects its perception and the practices of gendered life. It is argued that objects and action make gender "real" and give it material consequences and impact (Sørensen 2000). In other words, it is emphasized that it is through objects and their associated activities that gender is enacted and becomes an affective dimension of both personal and social life. Objects simultaneously represent and affect gender, and it is essential that our analyses encompass both qualities. Such arguments have changed the outlook of gender archaeology from a perspective that saw objects as mere things reflecting or representing norms, values, and roles to one that approaches objects as dynamic and actively involved with the construction of contexts and meaning to the current concern with the very nature of material culture as a medium of or partner to social discourse.

Another focus has been formulated around the concern with maintaining embodiment as our central focus, as "it is the experience of the body in the landscape, constituted through material culture in daily praxis and situated in the discourse of bodily representation, that frame the lived experience of the body and that informs us about constructions of identity. . . . And it is this process that we are just coming to grips with in archaeological inquiry" (Fisher and Loren

2003:227). In this emphasis, the articulation of embodiment becomes key to understanding the use of material culture in the formation of different identities (Fisher and Loren 2003:228).

In response to these developments, it has, for example, been argued that the tangible physical character as well as the affective properties of objects give them particular qualities in social discourses (Sørensen 2000). They are the material and substantive form of meaning and understandings as well as a media of repetition of association, and they are therefore one of the means through which meaning shifts from the individual to become part of social corporate spheres of meaning making. It is further argued that objects are made and used within contexts of meaning; that they are produced with intentions and shaped according to assumptions about how, when, and who may be using them; and that in their use they reinforce or alter such expectations. At the same time, objects exist beyond such intentions, and their potentials are not preset. Many different areas of study have now begun to recognize and respond to these qualities, as when Smart Martin, working in material culture studies, states that "material objects matter because they are complex, symbolic bundles of social, cultural and individual meanings fused onto something we can touch, see and own. That very quality is the reason that social value can so quickly penetrate into and evaporate out of common objects" (Taylor 2002:72). It is because of such qualities that material culture and gender are so intricately linked. Gender gains material reality and affects individual and groups as it becomes acted out and experienced through material culture (Sørensen 2000). In the process of "learning" how to act in the material world, including learning the use and meaning of material culture, people built up an understanding of the self in its relationship to other—an understanding that sits at the heart of acquiring and transforming one's gender identity through life (Sofaer 2006).

Moreover, the use of objects always involves negotiation, and material culture is always involved in social processes. It is, for example, partner to processes and actions through which differently constituted groups (such as develop around kin, age set, gender, ethnicity, or rank) participate in social dialogues about identity and associated distribution of demands and responsibilities. There are significant and interesting consequences of this connectedness between material culture, social discourse, and experience. For instance, ornaments are never just emblems of status or wealth but are also in themselves involved with the creation of such qualities. And following on from this, the same objects do not mean the same regardless of contexts: a sword does not necessarily signify the same in a grave, in a hoard, or as part of a depiction, although it brings the quality of "sword-ness" to each of these contexts. Such arguments identify social actions and intentions as the context of meaning while not necessarily the sole arbiter of meaning-content. This strongly suggests that analyses of gender should always aim to identify its context as well as its discursive qualities.

Such contextualized use of objects in the construction and performance of gender is by now demonstrated by a range of examples from different branches of archaeology and neighboring disciplines. They show how material culture is incorporated into and used as a medium for the construction of gender (including its very meaning) as well as in the negotiation and transformation of existing gender arrangements. Kirkham and Attfield (1996:10) have labeled this "people-object relations," arguing that objects lend meaning to people's lives and that people construct their identities through these relations.

Gilchrist's (1999:50) arguments about the relationship between gender and textile production may be seen as an example of this concern with the dynamic of gender. She argues that female labor can be a crucial means of the construction of femininity and a basis for the definition of gender roles as ideological constructions. She illustrates this complex relationship by showing how changes in the technology of weaving by the eleventh century A.D. affected the value, visibility, and social significance of textile production in England. As textile production was moved out of its domestic context, "female labour was not automatically accorded lower prestige, although there were attempts to confine it to a non-professional, domestic context, and to limit its financial reward" (Gilchrist 1999:50–51), while at the same time textile production as such became the affairs of guilds and in the control predominantly of men. Another point about textile production has been pursued by Arwill-Nordbladh (1998:204–6), who argues that textile production, just like many other activities, within itself contains the possibility of differentiation between its practitioners as well as contact and dependency with other spheres, as the production is constituted by many different stages that may involve different skills. The spinning (and thus the spindle whorl) is particularly interesting in this regard; it is easily learned and can be done in combination with other activities, as known from ethnographic and historical sources. This means that spinning, which so consistently is assumed to have been done by women in the past, is in fact a fluid practice that can be fitted in between other activities and can potentially be done by anyone and at anytime. The fluidity of such practices opens interesting questions about how they are made gendered. It also makes it clear how easily categorizations may become blurred and therefore that social "instruments" are needed to maintain differentiation.

Mortuary studies have also become influenced by these concerns, and their focus has recently turned in particular to the interconnection between gender and the life cycle (e.g., papers in Struwe et al. 2004). Studies have been carried out that focus on how material objects or material practices (such as head shaping [Lorentz 2005]) may be used to mark life cycle changes; they argue for the intertwining of life, objects, and practices. Theoretical arguments as well as case studies have also been used to argue that "gender is not static throughout the life course, but must be constantly negotiated in the light of increased gendered knowledge and changes in social situations. The acquisition of gender knowledge is time dependent" (Sofaer-Derevenski 1997:487). In these studies, material culture is often assigned a role as the mediator of gender relations.

This means that mortuary studies, in addition to identifying the presence and roles of different members of society, are increasingly also being seen as a way of accessing how social understandings and articulation of difference are variously constructed by societies. The question of how differences between people's bodies (including apparent perceptions held about such bodies) were explored in the construction of ideals and ideas about the social person has therefore become a major trend within this part of gender archaeology (e.g., Sofaer-Derevenski and Sørensen 2002). Crucial to these approaches is the recognition that "these dimensions [gender and age] of our identities are both individual characteristics and fluid social potentials that will be shaped and reinforced as part of specific social discourses. Gender . . . while emerging from universal characteristics of the human body are nonetheless also always cultural and relational" (Sørensen 2004).

The materialization and performance of gender are in many societies particularly clearly articulated during burial rituals. It has been suggested (Sørensen 2004) that in order to elucidate the insertion of gender into the social discourse that burials constitute, it is helpful to recognize that these events were composed of distinct stages and that each of these may have provided an opportunity for gender negotiation and performance. In particular, the preparation of the body for the funeral (i.e., how it was dressed and what happened around it) and the burial itself are two obvious contexts of action in which gender may have been emphasized and distinctions performed. For instance, during the late third millennium B.C., a burial practice developed throughout most of central and western Europe (the Bell Beaker culture and the Earliest Bronze Age) that rigidly emphasized people as belonging in one of two categories. What is interesting here, however, is how these categories become expressed during the burial rituals as the bodies are placed differently in the grave (i.e., the orientation and/or positioning of the body) depending on their biological sex. Thus, the burial would have expressed and been designed around a social understanding of what kind of body was being buried, including its similarities with and differences from other bodies, and a normative understanding of the appropriate position of such bodies. Further analysis of the objects found with the bodies confirms that these categories were also emphasized during the stage when the body was dressed for the funeral. In particular, differential use of dress accessories depending on biological sex was commonly maintained (Sørensen 2004).

This focus on gender as part of the processes through which society maintains and regulates itself and how it creates traditions and norms makes gender archaeology a partner to the larger projects and concerns about the relationship between the individual and society that are currently being put forward by the humanities. Our special role in this debate must be the analysis of how difference was conceptualized and materialized by communities living lives that were distinctly different from ours.

Appearance: The Construction of the Social Person

Dress or items of dress are significant elements of material culture and associated practices. This importance of dress is vividly illustrated by contemporary discussions of the use of Muslim head coverings and the veil in western Europe. Such discussions show how both the objects per se and the act of using them can become embroiled in symbolic and political discourses. This is not a new phenomenon, however. The veil, for example, as discussed by Yeğenoğlu (1998), has a complex history of involvement with politics, and it has often been used as a central object-partner in complex identity constructions. With reference to the political struggle between Islamism and secular/Western nationalism in Turkey during the late nineteenth and early twentieth centuries, Yeğenoğlu (1998:126) argues that "it is the veil which becomes one of the most effective and convenient instruments of this battle. The visible cultural effects one can induce by veiling or unveiling woman makes it a convenient signifier for the contending parties to fight out their differences through manipulating this highly charged symbol." The political and cultural-symbolic dimensions of dress are also well illustrated by the many instances of sumptuary laws that through time have been used to dictate how different social groups could be dressed. Schama's (1988) study of sumptuary laws in the Netherlands during the sixteenth to seventeenth century is a classic case, but similar directives and measures aimed at social control over the means of appearance are widespread (e.g., Gilchrist 1999:114; Roach and Eicher 1979:12). Hall (2000:70–71), for instance, in his study of the colonial world, discusses the emphasis on cultural display—the use of dress to make it known that one matters. He exemplifies this by showing how in the Cape the colonial administration used sumptuary laws to enforce a tight connection between status and its material signifiers, including dictates for the clothes to be worn by slaves

(Hall 2000:72–73). The Romans (Harlow 2004) formulated similar laws encoding social rules about dress. In fact, social restrictions and regulations of appearance are probably common features of complex societies and in particular early states even if they do not all take the same legalistic form.

This explicit social and political significance of dress has recently guided many different disciplines to more focused investigation of the practices and objects used to construct our outward appearances. This has led to associated questions about how the manipulation of the surface of the body affects the experience of being in the body as well as questions about how societies perceive, use, and make restrictions on the dressed body. Arising from an earlier interest in the body's signal, where clothing was seen as costumes and as a system of communication, the interest has recently become more broadly based and now embraces questions such as how dress is part of social learning (including the acquiring of gender identity) and a means of constructing dialogues between the self and society. The recent development of the distinct field of dress history and the approaches and aims it has come to entail over the past two decades outline the transformation of this general area of study very well (e.g., Taylor 2002). Prior to the 1980s, textile was investigated primarily as part of economic history; it was recognized as a significant commodity and as an important area of production and employment. Textile was therefore part of the history of the transformation of labor organization, of technological advances, and of economic transformative processes. During the 1980s to 1990s, we see a seminal shift, as the focus became dress rather than textiles and textile/dress became a subject of social history and more particular consumption studies (Taylor 2002:69f.). This shift was followed by explicit theoretical work on dimensions such as fashion, use, style, communication, and identity with gender playing a central role in the latter. Attention has also moved to the cultural processes surrounding the exploitation of dress in the construction of identities, be it gender, race, or class, and the formation of subculture or counterculture dress codes. It has been pointed out, however, that in this shift of interest from the object of dress to the practice of dressing, the actuality of objects risk becoming marginalized again (Taylor 2002:83); this is similar to the concerns recently expressed by Olsen (2003) with regard to archaeology. If, however, our analysis of dress can combine both objects and practice, then the study of clothing can indeed be seen, as suggested by Crane, as "a strategic site for studying changes in meanings of cultural goods in relation to changes in social structures, in the character of cultural organisations and in other forms of culture" (Taylor 2002:84).

Through this and parallel developments within other academic fields, the study of clothing has become an area fueled by curiosity about how differences, such as masculinity and femininity, are made and understood. Inspired by such debates and challenged by its own data, gender archaeology has turned the tradition of the archaeological study of textiles and ornaments into a study of how the construction of the external appearance of the person is part of social dialogues about identity and membership. Moreover, the effectiveness of visual representation of the categorization of people is being recognized and drawn into our analyses. The challenge remains, however, to understand more fully (and through more case studies, especially from nonliterate societies) how objects mediate between the self and social ideals and to recognize the distinction between discourse about identity and actual lived identity experiences (Fisher and Loren 2003:225–26).

Archaeological examples of intricate uses and rules governing dress and the use of accessories in prehistoric as well as historic societies have become abundant over recent years. For instance, mortuary data have been used to show how during the Middle Bronze Age in central Europe the arrangement of dress accessories (such as pins, rings for different parts of the body, and belts) in every region and regardless of local typological differences follows one of two set schema in their composition on the body. This differentiation seemed to have separated biological women into two groups: one with ornament sets mainly arranged on the chest and one with the ornaments placed around the waist (Sørensen 1997). In contrast, analyses of the Bell Beaker culture and the Early Bronze Age from central Europe show remarkable widespread consistency in the association of certain type of dress accessories, in particular, items used on the head and around the neck, with only either men or women without any obvious further visual distinctions in the appearance of members of these groups. Furthermore, detailed analyses of Early Bronze Age cemeteries have also begun to show how the acquiring of gender identity in these communities was tied in with the life cycle. For some communities, for instance, it can be argued that separate gender identities are first fully emerging among subadults, as male and female children, while treated differently in their positions in the graves, are nonetheless associated with the same range of objects, a similarity that is in contrast to what we see among adults (e.g., Neugebauer 1991). In other areas, apparently similar communities seem to emphasize difference and act on people in terms of separate gender categories from a young age (e.g., Sofaer-Derevenski 1997).

The social significance of dress codes is by now widely demonstrated not only by studies based on textual evidence but also increasingly through archaeological sources. Attitudes to dress in the Roman world have, for example, been extensively discussed. Harlow (2004) has most recently used a combination of pictorial and literary representations to study change in the dress of the elite man in order to investigate changing expressions of gender in the later Roman world. She showed how the traditional Roman dress of tunic and toga was transformed by the inclusion of new elements and concluded, "When the earlier Roman fought to obscure outside influences, later Roman man embraced them and, in so doing, accepted a transformation both in the individuals who held power and in the way they expressed that power in dress code" (Harlow 2004: 69).

Studies of one of the largest groups of artifacts from later prehistory in Europe, namely, the fibulae and brooches, have witnessed similar shifts (e.g., Effros 2004). Such dress accessories were commonly elements of the costume. They were meant to be seen, and they were often affected by regulation about how and where they were worn (Jundi and Hill 1997:125). Such details of dress often play a role in commenting on the identity of the wearer, and the political and social dimensions of these comments are demonstrated by change in dress styles and fashions during periods of rapid political change. For instance, in Britain, brooches changed during the first century A.D., the conquest period, and Jundi and Hill (1997:134) interpret the appearance of the visually distinct dragonesque brooches at this time as a way of "asserting a new, and possible non-military, non-Roman identity in the years following conquest."

To advance the archaeological study of the gendered aspects of appearance, it is, however, crucial to appreciate the specific qualities that come with dress and dressing. Two distinct set of practices are involved with dress. One is the putting together of the dress, the "getting dressed" part, where decisions are made about how elements are composed, while the other arises from being dressed. This difference gives dress and dressing some distinct temporal qualities that are different from, for example, those associated with the experience of architecture discussed later in this chapter. It is, therefore, analytically helpful to separate the composition of a dress from the act of wearing it. The composition of a dress is about decisions and the negotiation of possibilities within available resources, while the wearing of it involves primarily performance of the body and social communication rather than further manipulation of the material possibilities. Therefore, while gender is a decisive influence at both stages, different aspects of gender may come into play at each. The archaeology of gender can with great benefit aim to investigate both the distinct elements used and the choices made in the composition of dress in different contexts and the social implications of the dresses worn by different people within particular societies, but it will also benefit from recognizing these as separate practices.

The Material Culture of Space

The other main theme, one that will be used to exemplify current development, is that of the relationship between space and the performance of gender, with particular attention to space in the form of the built environment and architecture. This theme arises from increased attention to the intersection of gendered ideals and practices with material culture and how spatial constructions provide an arena for the performance and experience of gender. This in turn is based on the recognition that spatial constructions encourage routine; they are a means of repetition, and within them are embodied separations, privileges, and emphasis, qualities that bring an explicit awareness of the lived practices of gendered lives to our interpretative engagement with the past.

The intersection is the main point here, as space otherwise would become reduced to a place in which gender is enacted. This, however, can also be seen as involving, on the one hand, the material building and, on the other, both ways of doing things and their timing. Space is then "not a prior condition of something else ('place'), but rather the outcome, the product of an activity, and so it necessarily has a temporal dimension" (Morris 1992:3). This emphasis on the timing of action in space, on temporarily and embodied movement, shows clear similarities to some of the arguments put forward when phenomenology is used in archaeological studies of the landscape (e.g., Tilley 1994). It seems, however, that phenomenology tends to lessen the significance of gender, as it sees it as just one of the formative aspects of the experiencing subject, and it does not provide a clear basis for analyzing both gender and space as simultaneously social constructs and materialities. There are, therefore, other layers of meaning and representation affecting the intersection of gender and space that need to be detailed and explored beyond recognizing how they are produced in the action. Colomina (1992a) makes these points clear when, commenting on the relationship between sexuality and space, she reminds us, "It is not a question of looking at how sexuality acts itself out in space, but rather to ask: How is the question of space already inscribed in the question of sexuality? This formulation required that we abandon the traditional thought of architecture as object, a bounded entity addressed by an independent subject and experienced by a body. Instead, architecture must be thought of as a system of representation. . . . Likewise, the body has to be understood as a political structure, a product of such systems of representation rather than the means by which we encounter them." Later, she also points out that "architecture is not simply a platform that accommodates the viewing subject. It is a viewing mechanism that produces the subject. It precedes and frames its occupant" (Colomina 1992b:83).

To explore these arguments further in terms of their relevance to our analysis of the built environments of past communities, we now look at some of the main propositions used in archaeology when attempting to interpret the relationship between social relations and architecture in terms of value and meaning. One of these is the argument that power relations commonly are embedded within spatial relations and that gender, as part of power relations, therefore will be reflected as well as reproduced in spatial constructions. This has been most vividly argued in studies of households, ranging from analyses of the British prehistoric roundhouses (e.g., Parker Pearson and Richards 1994) to domestic settings (Allison 2002) to Greek houses from the Iron Age (e.g., Nevett 2001) to historical archaeology (Kinchin 1996; Wall 1994). Such studies become especially powerful when they simultaneously analyze the particular historical manifestation of this relationship and explore the mechanisms through which space affects or allows specific understandings and performances of gender and other social identities.

Different analytical approaches have also been explored (see also the discussion in Gilchrist 1999:111–13). Among these, the spatial syntax model, developed by Hillier and Hansen (1984), represents an interesting early approach, as it proposes a method for evaluating the social significance and value of the different parts of an architectural construction. It is also an early example of critical awareness of the significance of movement for understanding architectural space. Focusing on two axes of significance, one being spatial depth and the other the degrees of connectedness between different parts of a structure, the model proposes that the different rooms, passages, and courtyards that may make up a building can be analyzed in terms of their degree of hierarchy. The model also makes it possible to characterize differences between spaces in value terms and includes among these seclusion and access. In architecture, this model and related approaches have been used to characterize, for example, the social changes expressed in vernacular architecture and their grammar (Glassie 1975) and in historical studies of the institutional architecture of the modern city (Hillier and Hansen 1984). In archaeology, the method on its own has been used mainly to track changes in social organization, such as the emergence of social elites (e.g., Foster's [1989] comparison of Early and Later Iron Age brochs at Orkney). The general approach can be criticized for its mechanical and ahistorical dissection of spatial construction, but it nonetheless injected a helpful concern with the differential value and composite nature of such constructions, and the echoes of this concern are found in some of the most interesting and influential archaeological investigations of gender and architecture (e.g., Gilchrist 1994, 1997, 1999). Approaches like the spatial syntax model can be obviously strengthened if combined with historical or ethnographic evidence that help discriminate between different social scenarios. Brusasco's (2004) comparison of houses from Ur with, on the one hand, houses from the patrilineal and patrilocal society of modern Iraq and, on the other, houses from the Ashanti, who live in a matrilineal and matrilocal society, is a case in point. In this case, the richness of the ethnographic data provides the insights needed to connect the spatial pattern with the differential use of the various elements of the architecture. Lacking such data, another response would be to explore in greater depth how and why such architectural qualities are valued and responded to in social strategies. Among such analyses, Gilchrist's as well as Nevett's studies are excellent examples of how gender archaeology has explored and further developed these kinds of arguments with specific regard to the phenomenon of seclusion and the subversion of spatial constraints. Nevett's (1994, 2001) work has focused on the architectural structures of the house in ancient Greece. It is known from other sources that women were secluded within the house during this period, but Nevett's (1994) study showed the greater subtleties of what this seclusion was about. She investigated the routes of access and lines of vision that characterize the interior space of the house and its connection to the world outside, and on this basis she demonstrated that the space was not constructed to create absolute segregation between men and women within the household, as previously argued, but rather functioned to seclude women from contact with strangers. Seclusion and segregation have also been a central concern in Gilchrist's (1994, 1999, 2000) work. She has investigated the relationship between the materiality of space and gender ideologies with particular reference to medieval buildings. She has, for example, identified some of the specific ways in which the overall architectural plan of nunneries as well as details in their construction were used both to segregate the nuns from other communities and to provide access for men representing the religious hierarchy. She further showed how the enclosure of women, both through architectural mechanisms, such as interior enclosing walls, and through observances was particularly strict as the women were perceived as in need of particularly rigid seclusion because of their untamed sexuality (Gilchrist 2000:94). Her analyses show how churches, when shared by a nunnery and the parish congregation, often became divided along distinct lines by the addition of architectural elements, such as gallery-choirs, screened aisles, or a separation between choir and nave (Gilchrist 2000:95–96). Gilchrist (2000:89) also proposes that the coupling of such strict physical enclosures with an emphasis on sexual denials meant that the sexuality of medieval religious women "was turned inside out: sexuality became an interior space, a place of elevated senses and ecstatic states of consciousness." Gilchrist's (1999) work has expanded to include analysis of the later medieval castle and the seclusion of the high-ranking women within them. Throughout Gilchrist's work on the link between space and the embodiment of gender, the underlying argument has been that "such embodiment is perceived materially through the concrete, everyday world, and the physical processes of the life cycle" (Gilchrist

1999:109). This means that the gendered constructs and relations within, for example, the castle can be studied through "the contrasting locales, concerns and textures surrounding its men and women" (Gilchrist 1999:110).

Another distinct influence has been to analyze architecture and in particular houses as symbolic signifiers of the body or the world inhabited. A particular approach has been to explore binary oppositions as the basic structuring principles affecting the layout and the use of a house. Hingley (1990), for instance, used this as a means of investigating the organization of activities within the different rooms of the Romano-British aisled house, while Parker Pearson (1996, 1999) linked the significance of cosmologies and binary oppositions in his analysis of the British Iron Age roundhouse, demonstrating the consistency in the division of activities within the houses.

The study of gender and the built environment has also moved in another direction explicitly concerned with the concept of domesticity and with the social dynamic embedded within the organization of households. In such approaches, the house is understood as a social and semantic "stage" as well as an arena of routine practices. Differences in architectural plans, such as entranceways and internal divisions, are emphasized as influential for how ideas such as home, house, and households are conceptualized and materialized and how these differences would have impacted life in and around the domestic center in various ways. The architectural form affects the organization and flow of a wide range of practices performed within and in relationship to the house, including the engendering of labor divisions and collaborations of various kinds. Simply put, domestic life is always affected by and structured in response to the different physical and logistic constraints as well as the allowances provided by the space in which it takes place. Historical archaeology has provided some extremely useful case studies of these relationships and their historical contingency. Wall's (1994) analysis of the developing middle-class New York in the period from 1790 to 1840 shows how architecture and space was becoming gendered as well as class based. Her analysis shows a growing distinction of male versus female spheres, and it tracks how this was expressed and manufactured through an increasing range of minor as well as more noteworthy means of differentiations, such as etiquettes at mealtimes, architectural details, and increased physical and social distance between people. The male sphere became one of the public life of commerce, while women's was the private one of domesticity. Kitchen's (1996:12) study of the nineteenth-century interior space of the English middle-class home shows a similar scenario but adds to it the further gendered division within the house, as rooms were often designed as explicitly masculine or feminine. The emergence of literature guiding women on household taste further shows the extent to which these views were codified and the deliberate use of architecture to assign strikingly different ideological roles to men and to women. Colomina's (1992b) discussion of the expression of sexuality within houses built by Adolf Loo and by Le Corbusier shows how these central structures are transformed yet repeated even in architecture that is more recent. The tension between the interior and exterior is, for instance, also here responding to the difference between private and public spheres (Colomina 1992b:85–94), while architectural depth and seclusions are associated with female spaces (Colomina 1992b:81). Such case studies enforce views that see the body as a political construct rather than as solely a means of experience (e.g., Colomina 1992a).

When we consider these various points and reflect on the methods used and the arguments made by the archaeological case studies that have added most to current understanding of gender and space, a few proposals may be put forward. First, the various arguments that stress that the gendering of space involves temporality and movement make important points. It is, however, equally crucial that we do not stop there but make the connection between this and practice—the act of doing things. It is in the living within built structures, responding to their qualities and differences and to their existing gender templates and ideologies, that space and people connect. The archaeological investigation of gender and space therefore needs a dual focus on the material construction and the doing of things within them. Second, built structures are composed of different kinds of spaces and therefore also of points of connections and transitions. It is around these points that practices are most poignantly revealing meanings and change in meaning. An obvious example of this is the transition from the nunnery part of a medieval church to the part used by the congregation and the need to construct discontinuity of meaning within the continuity of the building. In practice, the solution is often different types of physical segregation, such as screens (as discussed by Gilchrist 2000). Archaeological investigation of spatial control of meanings should therefore pay particular attention to such pivotal points in the architecture and how they are embellished or in other ways accentuated and made to direct the meaning of the spatial encounter or how they may allow change in meaning. This means that the meeting points of different rooms or kinds of spaces, the liminal areas that may be neutral or in-between spaces, are places that may reveal some of the dialogues about identity that are performed through routine practices in the house. Thresholds, entrances, doorways, corridors, and boundaries and the remains and traces accumulated there are therefore archaeologically important parts of buildings (Gilchrist 1999:112; Sørensen 2000).

Recent Developments

Within current arguments and the enlarged scope of gender studies in archaeology, one can outline a number of central trajectories for the further exploration of the relationship between gender and material culture. One of these is the continuous investigation of the nature and qualities of material culture and its role or incorporation into social discourse (e.g., Olsen 2003). It is interesting here to note how earlier propositions that in various ways tried to comprehend material culture through its similarities to other cultural products or practices, such as the analogy drawn between material culture and text (e.g., Hodder 1986, 1989), are generally being abandoned in favor of approaches that focus on the material qualities of objects.

One approach has been to emphasize the thing-ness of material culture (e.g., Olsen 2003; Sørensen 2000) in reaction to the emerging inclination to present things entirely and only as social discourse (Olsen 2003:88). Olsen (2003:88), expanding on Schiffer's criticism of the current tendency to marginalize the thing and how this treats people–artifact interaction as secondary to processes of culture, has argued for a different way of seeing material culture as "things, all those physical entities we refer to as material culture, are beings in the world alongside other beings, such as humans, plants and animals. All these beings are kindred, sharing substances ('flesh') and memberships in a dwelt-in-world. . . . [Through time] humans have extended their social relations to non-human agents with whom they have swapped properties and formed collectives."

One response that is in line with arguments made in other disciplines is to move attention to how we can investigate the effects of objects, including the significance of their evocative and affective qualities. For some time, archaeologists have been investigating material culture as active, but to this is now added a language that animates it and places it centrally in social understanding. The material culture we are trying to explore is now seen by some as never neutral but rather as contaminated and affected by intentions (Joyce 2002; Riegel 1996:99–100). This position is producing a perspective in which the object becomes social and directly involved with notions of difference. This approach to material culture has already been explored for some time by prominent feminist museologists (e.g., Porter 1991, 1996; Sandahl 1995), and it provides new interpretative potentials for understanding, for example, the gender dimension of complex material situations like the adaptation of technological innovations (e.g., Sofaer-Derenvenski and Sørensen 2002). This kind of reflection is also providing a different background for mortuary studies insofar as it gives us a means of discriminating interpretatively between different objects in terms of what meanings they may bring to the specific burial construction. Arwill-Nordbladh's (1998) study of the rich Viking-period grave at Oseberg, Norway, is an interesting example of this approach. Her focus is not the objects per se but rather how they are incorporated into the grave, the choreography of their inclusion, and the meanings and associations they draw with them into the construction. Arwill-Nordbladh uses the concept of "contexts of actions" (based on Conkey 1991) to group the objects used in the funerary setting in terms of what spheres of actions, social relations, and interests they represent and bring with them into the grave construction. This approach shows that in the construction of this grave, objects are used to make references to four main contexts of actions: the productive activities of a farm, textile production, communication and movement, and rituals. She further proposes that these contexts of actions in the construction of the burial may be perceived as preunderstandings attached to the objects and that it is within this that the essence of their significance can be found. Arwill-Nordbladh (1998:257) states, "The act of bringing the objects from their different preunderstandings on board the ship, could be read as the creation of a material metaphor.... In this way a completely new meaning is created. This meaning is expressed by the artefacts, and can only be expressed in this particular way."

Another distinct development has emerged in reaction to the separation usually made between the body and material culture. Recognizing that the body is a malleable cultural material, various authors have been linking the construction of gender with various types of technologies of the body. Some of these studies follow arguments made by Foucault (1978) and others about the body being the product of discourse (e.g., Treherne 1995), while Sofaer in particular has taken this argument further to argue that the body can be approached not just as material manifestation but as material culture itself. In her most recent work, Sofaer (2006) has advanced from her earlier studies of gender and the life cycle to even more fundamental questions about the nature of bodies. She aims to problematize the tendency to draw a distinction between the material body and the materialized body that has evolved in the wake of embodiment theories. In response to arguments that see the enactment of cultural practices as leading to the materiality of the body, she proposes that "the material qualities of the human body are key to its materiality" (Sofaer 2006). She bases this argument on the very physicality of the body, the recognition that it is materially constituted and that embodiment is about acting within and on the material possibilities and restraints imposed by the body through its life cycle. She therefore also argues that the materiality of the body is the product of social relations in that the traditions, values, and skills of the living may be expressed as a result of the plasticity of the body, but that it is not produced in a purely discursive manner. The body exists in a very real way where actions have the potential for often predictable material consequences (Sofaer 2006). This proposition, furthermore, is not merely a rhetorical shift in position but rather a fundamental change in orientation in which the body is seen to have specific material qualities that go beyond the meanings they may have in social discourse or how they may be used as signifiers.

There are interesting resonances between the points made by Sofaer and those of Olsen (2003) about the nature of material culture referred to earlier. While their starting points seem to be at opposite ends, one discussing the body and the other the things, both argue for the necessity of dissolving the perceived dichotomy between persons and things.

A different trajectory is outlined by Joyce (2002:141), who suggests that material remains in archaeological sites can be viewed as utterances by people in the past who made and used them. She makes it clear that this is neither a return to a simple textual analogy nor a concern with recovering past communicative intentions. Based on self-critical reflection about her own earlier analyses and publications of the burials at Tlatilco (a central Mexican pre-Classic site, for which the interpretation has undergone several changes from being focused on spatial patterns as evidence of the habitual practices of social groups to a concern with the effects of life cycle changes), she traces how she came to this position (2002:138–142). In her words, viewing objects as utterances "is to say that the object created was expressive, that it is a representation of, at the very least, a social engagement with the past world in which the people of Tlatilco lived. It is to say that objects recovered archaeologically are comparable to each other because they were manufactured by people engaged in dialogically seeking responses from those around them" (Joyce 2002:142). She further suggests that "the evidence of the dialogic communication of utterances is present in the chain of their reproduction" and that our task "is at least partly to respond to the objects produced in terms of their existence as unique entries in a dialogue, responses to prior material utterances" (Joyce 2002:142).

In various ways, these most recent developments emerge from and react to long-standing concerns within any historical analysis of social relations, including archaeology's. For instance, they are responding critically and self-reflexively to archaeology's classic angst about the nature of its knowledge claims, and they show strong affinities to its traditional concern with investigating change as well as continuity. These concerns are, however, shown in a new light because of the emphasis on self-reflection and the concern with investigating the conditions of real people who lived at another time and on the psychical as well as cultural qualities of objects. The commitment to analyses that aim to investigate gender as simultaneously integrated within society and in the process of becoming also ensure depth to our studies. A core view of many of these recent arguments is therefore that the meaning of gender is never fixed but is part of ongoing dialogues about and between people and material culture.

Conclusion

Gender archaeology has changed in its theoretical position toward material culture and the ways in which it has seen this as a means of identifying women or as a way of exploring the construction and experiences of gender. Rather than growing toward a collective view and a shared understanding of what material culture is and how we can best harness it to our research questions, this development has spawned a number of positions, differences, and debates. Despite these differences, there is a common interest in what gender may be, how it is experienced and expressed, and how this was part of the conditions and possibilities affecting the lives of individuals and groups in past societies. Regardless of period and area, material culture can be used to focus analysis on how society needs and constructs meaning around and attitudes toward fundamental differences between people. This can then be followed up by exploration of how these understandings became expressed in ideologies and its prescribed practices and regulative mechanisms, and that gets us back to people.

References

Allison, Penelope M.
    2002   *The Archaeology of Household Activities*. London: Routledge.
Appadurai, Arjun
    1986   *The Social Life of Things: Commodities in Cultural Perspective*. Cambridge: Cambridge University Press.
Arnold, Bettina, and Nancy L. Wicker, eds.
    2001   *Gender and the Archaeology of Death*. Walnut Creek, CA: AltaMira Press.
Arwill-Nordbladh, Elisabeth
    1998   *Genuskonstruktioner i Nordisk Vikingatid: Förr och nu*. Gothenburg: Gothenburg University.
Balme, Jane, and Wendy Beck, eds.
    1993   *Gendered Archaeology: The Second Australian Women in Archaeology Conference*. Research Papers in Archaeology and Natural History 26. Canberra: Australian National University.
Bevan, Lynn
    1997   Skin Scrapers and Pottery Makers? "Invisible" Women in Prehistory. In *Invisible People and Processes: Writing Gender and Childhood into European Archaeology*. Jenny

Moore and Eleanor Scott, eds. Pp. 81–87. London: Leicester University Press.

Bourdieu, Pierre
 1977   Outline of a Theory of Practice. Cambridge: Cambridge University Press.

Brumfiel, Elizabeth M.
 1991   Weaving and Cooking: Women's Production in Aztec Mexico. In *Engendering Archaeology: Women and Prehistory*. Joan W. Gero and Margaret W. Conkey, eds. Pp. 224–54. Oxford: Blackwell.

Brusasco, Paolo
 2004   Theory and Practice in the Study of Mesopotamian Domestic Space. *Antiquity* 78(299, March 2004):142–57.

Butler, Judith
 1990   *Gender Trouble: Feminism and the Subversion of Identity*. London: Routledge.

Colomina, Beatriz
 1992a   Introduction. In *Sexuality and Space*. Beatriz Colomina, ed. New York: Princeton Architectural Press.
 1992b   The Split Wall: Domestic Voyeurism. In *Sexuality and Space*. Beatriz Colomina, ed. Pp. 73–128. New York: Princeton Architectural Press.

Conkey, Margaret W.
 1991   Contexts of Action, Contexts for Power: Material Culture and Gender in the Magdalenian. In *Engendering Archaeology: Women and Prehistory*. Joan W. Gero and Margaret W. Conkey, eds. Pp. 57–92. Oxford: Blackwell.

Dommasness, Liv Helga
 1987   Male/Female Roles and Ranks in Late Iron Age Norway. In *Were They All Men? An Examination of Sex Roles in Prehistoric Society*. Acts from a workshop held in Utstein Kloster, Rogaland, November 2–4, 1979. Reidar Bertelsen, Arnvid Lillehammer, and Jenny-Rita Næss, eds. Pp. 65–77. Stavanger: Arkeologisk Museum i Stavanger.

Effros, Bonnie
 2004   Dressing Conservatively: Women's Brooches as Markers of Ethnic Identity? In *Gender in the Medieval World: East and West, 300–900*. Leslie Brubaker and Julia M. H. Smith, eds. Pp. 165–84. Cambridge: Cambridge University Press.

Fisher, Genevieve, and Diana DiPaolo Loren
 2003   Introduction. Special Section: Embodying Identity in Archaeology. *Cambridge Archaeological Journal* 13(2, October 2003):225–30.

Foster, Sally M.
 1989   Analysis of Spatial Patterns in Buildings (Access Analysis) as an Insight into Social Structure: Example from the Scottish Atlantic Iron Age. *Antiquity* 63(238, March 1989):40–50.

Foucault, Michel
 1978   *The History of Sexuality*. Harmondsworth: Penguin.

Gilchrist, Roberta
  1994 *Gender and Material Culture: The Archaeology of Religious Women*. London: Routledge.
  1997 Gender and Medieval Women. In *Invisible People and Processes: Writing Gender and Childhood into European Archaeology*. Jenny Moore and Eleanor Scott, eds. Pp. 42–58. London: Leicester University Press.
  1999 *Gender and Archaeology: Contesting the Past*. London: Routledge.
  2000 Unsexing the Body: The Interior Sexuality of Medieval Religious Women. In *Archaeologies of Sexuality*. Robert A. Schmidt and Barbara L. Voss, eds. Pp. 89–103. London: Routledge.

Glassie, Henry H.
  1975 *Folk Housing in Middle Virginia: A Structural Analysis of Historic Artefacts*. Knoxville: University of Tennessee Press.

Gräslund, Anne-Sofia
  2001 The Position of Iron Age Scandinavian Women: Evidence from Graves and Rune Stones. In *Gender and the Archaeology of Death*. Bettina Arnold and Nancy L. Wicker, eds. Pp. 81–102. Walnut Creek, CA: AltaMira Press.

Hager, Lori D., ed.
  1997 *Women in Human Origins*. London: Routledge.

Hall, Martin
  2000 *Archaeology and the Modern World: Colonial Transcripts in South Africa and the Chesapeake*. London: Routledge.

Harlow, Mary
  2004 Clothes Maketh the Man: Power Dressing and Elite Masculinity in the Later Roman World. In *Gender in the Medieval World: East and West, 300–900*. Leslie Brubaker and Julia M. H. Smith, eds. Pp. 44–69. Cambridge: Cambridge University Press.

Hastorf, Christine A.
  1991 Gender, Space, and Food in Prehistory. In *Engendering Archaeology: Women and Prehistory*. Joan W. Gero and Margaret W. Conkey, eds. Pp. 132–59. Oxford: Blackwell.

Hillier, Bill, and Julienne Hansen
  1984 *The Social Logic of Space*. Cambridge: Cambridge University Press.

Hingley, Richard
  1990 Domestic Organisation and Gender Relations in Iron Age and Romano-British Households. In *The Social Archaeology of Houses*. Ross Samson, ed. Pp. 125–47. Edinburgh: Edinburgh University Press.

Hodder, Ian
  1986 *Reading the Past*. Cambridge: Cambridge University Press.
  1989 This Is Not an Article about Material Culture as Text. *Journal of Anthropological Archaeology* 8:250–69.

Joyce, Rosemary A.
  2002 *The Languages of Archaeology*. Oxford: Blackwell.

Jundi, Sophia, and J. D. Hill
  1997 Brooches and Identities in First Century AD Britain: More Than Meets the Eye? In *TRAC 97, Proceedings of the Seventh Annual Theoretical Roman Archaeology Conference Nottingham 1997.* Colin Forcey, John Hawthorne, and Robert Witcher, eds. Pp. 125–37. Oxford: Oxbow.
Kinchin, Juliet
  1996 Interiors: Nineteenth-Century Essays on the "Masculine" and the "Feminine" Room. In *The Gendered Object.* Pat Kirkham, ed. Pp. 12–29. Manchester: Manchester University Press.
Kirkham, Pat, and Judy Attfield
  1996 Introduction. In *The Gendered Object.* Pat Kirkham, ed. Pp. 1–11. Manchester: Manchester University Press.
Lorentz, K. O.
  In press The Malleable Body: Headshaping in Greece and the Surrounding Regions. In *New Directions in the Skeletal Biology of Greece.* S. C. Fox, C. Bourbou, and L. Schepartz, eds. Athens: Wiener Laboratory, American School of Classical Studies in Athens.
Moore, Jenny, and Eleanor Scott, eds.
  1997 *Invisible People and Processes: Writing Gender and Childhood into European Archaeology.* London: Leicester University Press.
Morris, Meaghan
  1992 Great Moments in Social Climbing: King Kong and the Human Fly. In *Sexuality and Space.* Beatriz Colomina, ed. Pp. 1–51. New York: Princeton Architectural Press.
Nelson, Sarah Milledge
  1997 Gender in Archaeology: Analyzing Power and Prestige. Walnut Creek, CA: AltaMira Press.
Neugebauer, J.-W.
  1991 *Die Nekropole F Von Gemeinlebarn, Niederösterreich: Untersuchungen zu den Bestattungssitten und zum Grabraub in der ausgehenden Frühbronzezeit in Niederösterreich südlich der Alten Donau zwischen Enns und Wienerwald.* Römisch-Germanische Forschungen 49. Mainz: Philipp Von Zabern.
Nevett, Lisa C.
  1994 Separation or Seclusion? Towards an Archaeological Approach to Investigating Women in the Greek Household in the Fifth to Third Centuries BC. In *Architecture and Order: Approaches to Social Space.* Mike Parker Pearson and Colin Richards, eds. Pp. 98–112. London: Routledge.
  2001 *House and Society in the Ancient Greek World.* Cambridge: Cambridge University Press.
Oliver, Laurent
  1992 The Tomb of Hochdorf. *Archaeological Review from Cambridge* 11(1):51–63.

Olsen, Bjørnar
    2003   Material Culture after Text: Re-membering Things. *Norwegian Archaeological Review* 36(2):87–104.

Parker Pearson, Mike
    1996   Food, Fertility and Front Doors: Houses in the First Millennium BC. In *The Iron Age in Britain and Ireland: Recent Trends*. In Timothy Champion and John Collis, eds. Pp. 117–32. Sheffield: J. R. Collis Publications.
    1999   Food, Sex and Death: Cosmologies in the British Iron Age with Particular Reference to East Yorkshire. *Cambridge Archaeological Journal* 9(1):43–69.

Parker Pearson, Mike, and Colin Richards, eds.
    1994   *Architecture and Order: Approaches to Social Space*. London: Routledge.

Porter, Gaby
    1991   Partial Truths. In *Museum Languages: Objects and Texts*. Gaynor Kavanagh, ed. Pp. 103–17. Leicester: Leicester University Press.
    1996   Seeing through Solidity: A Feminist Perspective on Museums. In *Theorizing Museums*. Sharon Macdonald and Gordon Fyfe, eds. Pp. 105–26. Oxford: Blackwell.

Preece, Rosemary
    1996   "Equal to Half a Man": Women in the Coalmining Industry. In *Women in Industry and Technology: From Prehistory to the Present Day*. Amanda Devonshire and Barbara Wood, eds. Pp. 155–61. London: Museum of London.

Rega, Elizabeth
    1997   Age, Gender and Biological Reality in the Early Bronze Age Cemetery at Mokrin. In *Invisible People and Processes*. Jenny Moore and Eleanor Scott, eds. Pp. 229–47. London: Leicester University Press.

Riegel, Henrietta
    1996   Into the Heart of Irony: Ethnographic Exhibitions and the Politics of Difference. In *Theorizing Museums*. Sharon Macdonald and Gordon Fyfe, eds. Pp. 83–104. Oxford: Blackwell.

Roach, M. E., and J. B. Eicher
    1979   The Language of Personal Adornment. In *The Fabrics of Culture*. Justine M. Cordwell and Ronald A. Schwarz, eds. Pp. 7–21. New York: Mouton.

Sandahl, Jette
    1995   Proper Objects among Other Things. *Nordisk Museologi* 1995(2):97–106.

Schama, Simon
    1988   *The Embarrassment of Riches: An Interpretation of Dutch Culture in the Golden Age*. Berkeley: University of California Press.

Shennan, Stephen J.
    1993   Commodities, Transactions and Growth in the Central-European Early Bronze Age. *Journal of European Archaeology* 1(2):59–72.

Sofaer, Joanna
    2006   *The Body as Material Culture*. Cambridge: Cambridge University Press.

Sofaer-Derevenski, Joanna
 1997 Linking Age and Gender as Social Variables. *Ethnographisch-Archäologische Zeitschrift* 38(3–4):485–93.

Sofaer-Derevenski, Joanna, and Marie Louise Stig Sørensen
 2002 Becoming Cultural: Society and the Incorporation of Bronze. In *Metals and Society*. Barbara Ottoway and Emma C. Wager, eds. Pp. 117–21. Bar International Series 1061. Oxford: Bar International.

Sørensen, Marie Louise Stig
 1997 Reading Dress: The Construction of Social Categories and Identities in Bronze Age Europe. *Journal of European Archaeology* 5(1):93–114.
 2000 *Gender Archaeology*. Cambridge: Polity Press.
 2004 Stating Identities: The Use of Objects in Rich Bronze Age Graves. In *Explaining Social Change: Studies in Honour of Colin Renfrew*. John Cherry, Chris Scarre, and Stephen Shennan, eds. Pp. 167–76. Cambridge: McDonald Institute.
 2004 The Interconnection of Age and Gender: A Bronze Age Perspective. In *Von der Geburt bis zum Tode: Individuelle und gesellschaftliche Dimensionen von Alter und Geschlecht in der Urgeschichte*. Ruth Struwe and Linda Owen, eds. Pp. 327–338. *Ethnographisch-Archäologische Zeitschrift* 45, 2004, Heft 2.

Spector, Janet
 1991 What This Awl Means: Towards a Feminist Archaeology. In *Engendering Archaeology: Women and Prehistory*. Joan W. Gero and Margaret W. Conkey, eds. Pp. 388–406. Oxford: Blackwell.
 1993 *What This Awl Means: Feminist Archaeology at a Wahpeton Dakota Village*. St. Paul: Minnesota Historical Society Press.

Stalsberg, Anne
 1991 Women as Actors in North European Viking Trade. In *Social Approaches to Viking Studies*. Ross Samson, ed. Pp. 75–83. Glasgow: Cruithne Press.
 2001 Visible Women Made Invisible: Interpreting Varangian Women in Old Russia. In *Gender and the Archaeology of Death*. Bettina Arnold and Nancy L. Wicker, eds. Pp. 65–79. Walnut Creek, CA: AltaMira Press.

Struwe, Ruth and Linda Owen, eds.
 2004 *Von der Geburt bis zum Tode: Individuelle und gesellschaftliche Dimensionen von Alter und Geschlecht in der Urgeschichte*. *Ethnographisch-Archäologische Zeitschrift* 45, 2004, Heft 2.

Taylor, Lou
 2002 *The Study of Dress History*. Manchester: Manchester University Press.

Tilley, Christopher
 1994 *A Phenomenology of Landscape: Places, Paths and Monuments*. London: Berg.

Treherne, Paul
 1995 The Warrior's Beauty: The Masculine Body and Self-Identity in Bronze Age Europe. *Journal of European Archaeology* 3(1):105–44.

Tringham, Ruth
 1991 Households with Faces: The Challenge of Gender in Prehistoric Architectural

Remains. In *Engendering Archaeology: Women and Prehistory*. Joan W. Gero and Margaret W. Conkey, eds. Pp. 93–131. Oxford: Blackwell.

Wall, Diana diZerega
1994   *The Archaeology of Gender: Separating the Spheres in Urban America*. New York: Plenum.

Weinstein, Rosemary
1996   Women Pewterers of London 1500–1800. In *Women in Industry and Technology: From Prehistory to the Present Day*. Amanda Devonshire and Barbara Wood, eds. Pp. 125–29. London: Museum of London.

Wright, Rita P.
1991   Women's Labor and Pottery Production in Prehistory. In *Engendering Archaeology: Women and Prehistory*. Joan W. Gero and Margaret W. Conkey, eds. Pp. 194–223. Oxford: Blackwell.
1996   Technology, Gender, and Class: Worlds of Difference in Ur III Mesopotamia. In *Gender and Archaeology*. Rita P. Wright, ed. Pp. 79–110. Philadelphia: University of Pennsylvania Press.

Yeğenoğlu, Meyda
1998   *Colonial Fantasies: Towards a Feminist Reading of Orientalism*. Cambridge: Cambridge University Press.

Gender and Archaeological Mortuary Analysis

4

BETTINA ARNOLD

IDEALIZED SOCIAL RELATIONSHIPS are concretized in burial ritual in many ethnographically as well as archaeologically documented societies (Bahn 2003:4). Gender, as a virtually universal form of social categorization, is one of the most frequently encountered forms of mortuary differentiation and can be expressed in a wide range of ways, from burial location through the orientation of the body to specific sets of grave goods associated with a particular gender. Just as gender has increasingly become an integral part of archaeological analysis in general, archaeology continues to inform gender studies, particularly in terms of understanding the materiality of gender (Sørensen 2000:72). In the case of funerary archaeology, which has been described as "a crucial element of any research into past gender categorizations" (Parker Pearson 2000:96), this dialectic is especially important. The relationship between the representation of gender in the mortuary record and in the living population is not a straightforward one, however. "In particular, the mortuary context tells us that the individual seen by archaeologists represents not only a woman [or man], as constructed by the gender ideologies of her [or his] time, but specifically a *dead* woman [or man], going to her [or his] grave. Thus, the artifacts accompanying her [him] are not just associated with the idea of femininity [masculinity], but are the objects appropriate to her [his] transition from the living to the dead" (Tarlow 1999:178). Death as a transitional process not only separates the individual from her or his community but to some degree also confounds the ability of archaeologists to draw inferences between the burial record and the living society. At the same time, burial evidence remains one of the most evocative sources of information regarding past gender configurations available to us, and the inferential difficulty inherent in all mortuary analysis should not preclude its use in the interpretation of social systems in the past.

Brief History of Gender and Mortuary Archaeology

Some of the earliest explicit attempts to engender archaeological mortuary analysis were initiated in Scandinavia (Arnold and Wicker 2001:viii). The 1979 conference in Bergen titled "Were They All Men?" was certainly one of the first to articulate a growing sense of dissatisfaction with the state of archaeological interpretation from a gendered perspective. This was followed by several Anglo-American publications, notably the article by Conkey and Spector (1984) and the 1988 *Archaeological Review* issue dedicated entirely to gender (Lucy 1997:153).

Medieval archaeologists, particularly in Britain (Härke 1990, 1992; Lucy 1995, 1997; Pader 1982; Stoodley 1999), have also been engaged in engendered mortuary analysis for some time, but their publications are rarely referenced by prehistoric archaeologists, and not all the applications developed in this text-aided subfield are relevant for prehistorians. Nevertheless, several of the medieval studies are potentially of great interest to archaeologists working in earlier periods, and I will discuss some of them here and later in this chapter. Ellen Jane Pader (1982:129) was one of the first Anglo-Saxon scholars to develop an approach to mortuary analysis that included a consideration of gender configurations "from a structural perspective, concluding that sex-based relations could be seen to be articulated by constraints placed on the distribution of artifact classes, artifacts and skeletal positioning, and that these relations differed between cemeteries" (Lucy 1997:152). For some reason, archaeologists working in prehistoric and Roman Britain have been relatively unaffected by these developments in medieval archaeology and the archaeology of Roman Britain (with some exceptions, notably Parker Pearson), and there have been relatively few attempts at engendered mortuary analyses. "Feminist critique, which had developed in social anthropology and other social sciences since the 1970s, has, until now, had very little impact on the agendas of Anglo-Saxon archaeology. In contrast, studies of the Scandinavian Iron Age, the chronologically equivalent period on the other side of the North Sea, have been in the forefront of the development of feminist and gender archaeologies" (Lucy 1997:150; Dommasnes 1982, 1987, 1991; Gibbs 1987; Hjørungsdal 1991, 1994; Høgestøl 1986; Stalsberg 1984, 1987a, 1987b).

A significant problem is the fact that there is little or no overlap or information exchange between archaeological subfields, which leads to much duplication of effort and tends to block the transfer of potentially valuable data between these different areas of research. Researchers working on mortuary ritual in early medieval England or continental Europe rarely interact directly with scholars investigating mortuary ritual in prehistoric Europe or the British Isles, and the gap is even wider between North American scholars and their counterparts in the

Old World (Arnold 2002c:417–20; Sørensen 2000:16–17). Classical archaeologists tend to focus on their own citation circles and only infrequently venture into the wilds of the prehistoric mortuary literature. Naturally there are some exceptions, but these are usually scholars who have migrated temporally, geographically, or in terms of discipline (sometimes all three) in the course of their careers, and while the bibliographies of their publications do serve as bridges between subfields, in general this has not tended to have much of an impact on the state of inquiry in general.

For example, Classical and Near Eastern archaeologists concerned with gender have tended to focus primarily on the analysis of texts and imagery; there are very few studies that attempt to engender mortuary analysis on the basis of bioarchaeological data or grave good analyses (but see Bolger and Serwint 2002; Keswani 2004; Strömberg 1993). One of the few exceptions is the volume edited by Ruth D. Whitehouse (1998), which includes several chapters that engage in engendered mortuary analysis (Brown 1998). In her introduction to the volume, Whitehouse indicates the extent of this divide: "Although the title of the volume employs the inclusive term 'Italian Archaeology,' the majority of the papers deal with prehistory or protohistory and none are concerned with anything later than early Classical Archaeology. This was not my choice: I included classical and medieval archaeologists in my mailings, for both the seminar and the publication, but received offers mainly from prehistorians" (Brown 1998:1). She attributes this mainly to the fact that "in later periods work on gender has tended to focus on textual sources and on art, with few explicitly archaeological studies" (Brown 1998:1). She makes another point in this introduction that is worth pondering: she was unable at the time the volume was being organized to find any Italian archaeologists working on any aspect of gender archaeology (Brown 1998:2; Vida 1998) and expresses the hope "that this will be the last volume on the topic to depend solely on Anglo-American contributions" (Whitehouse 1998:2).

A review article by Carol Meyers (2003) outlines the history of gender studies in Syro-Palestinian archaeology and discusses some of the reasons why this area of study has lagged behind other temporal and geographic areas (but see Wright 1996:79–110). She confirms that "for the most part the practice of excavation in the eastern Mediterranean and the nature of the interpretation of excavated remains have barely been touched by the paradigm shift in the academy that has brought gender into the mainstream of scholarly discourse in most humanities and social science disciplines" (Meyers 2003:185). She argues that this neglect is due in part to the fact that the agenda for fieldwork and interpretation in Near Eastern archaeology has been set by the agenda of the textual sources, which tend to be male generated and male dominated in this part of the world (Meyers

2003:187), and concludes as follows: "Clearly the traditional research goals of Syro-Palestinian archaeology have not been congenial to the recovery of data that can contribute to the identification of gendered forms of behavior and thus to the social dynamics of human beings inhabiting the ancient sites" (Meyers 2003:187). Significantly, however, Meyers focuses mainly on settlement data in her discussion, which underscores the relative neglect of burial evidence, apart from elite interments, in this part of the world.

Sarah Nelson (2002:73) describes gender as a "relatively new topic in Asian archaeology" as well, and while much of her own research has dealt with mortuary analysis in Korea and China (Nelson 1993, 1997) and there have been other engendered analyses of Asian mortuary data (Higham 2002; Jiao 2001; Linduff 2002), the great potential of this region to contribute to the development of theoretical and methodological approaches to gender and mortuary studies has yet to be fully realized. It is no coincidence that a geographic shift toward eastern Europe and central Asia is currently under way in Anglo-American archaeology or that there is an increasing number of research projects in those regions focusing on mortuary analysis (Hanks, Smith, Alcock and Cherry, and so on). East will soon meet West, at least in archaeological terms, and mortuary analysis is one area that should flourish as a result.

North American archaeologists have been actively involved in engendering archaeological practice since at least the late 1980s, but even here there have been relatively few attempts to develop approaches specific to mortuary analysis (Arnold and Wicker 2001:ix). Gender configurations are implicitly addressed by a number of North American researchers who are known especially for their mortuary research (Buikstra et al. 1986; Carr 1995; Charles 1995; Charles and Buikstra 1983, 2002; Goldstein 1995; among others), but in general explicit analyses of gender in the mortuary context are conspicuous by their absence. Several chapters published in *Gender and the Archaeology of Death* (Crass 2001; Doucette 2001; Hamlin 2001; Hollimon 2001; O'Gorman 2001) demonstrate the potential of such studies. The situation in Central America is similar, with most of the emphasis placed on engendered analysis of iconography or systems of production (Joyce 1996, 1998; but see Joyce 1999; see also Brumfiel 1991; but see McCafferty and McCafferty 1994).

Gender Is a Verb

Gender as both category and practice is constructed as well as lived (Sørensen 2000:65). The frequent invocation of performance theory and agency in publications dedicated to gender studies in various disciplines (Feree et al. 1998; Joyce

1998; McNay 2000; Moore and Scott 1997; Nelson and Rosen-Ayalon 2002; Ortner 1996; Sørensen 2000; Sweely 1999), including engendered archaeological mortuary analysis (Arnold 2001, 2002b; Cannon 2005; Chapman 2000; Effros 2003; Härke 2000; among others), is an indication of the fluidity of the concept of gender and its social expression. As Marie Louise Stig Sørensen (2000:70–71) has suggested, "Gender is a process, a set of behavioral expectations or an effect, but it is not a thing."

A number of researchers have productively applied the work of Judith Butler (1990, 1993) to their investigations of gender as a performance as well as a process. This approach has been particularly fruitful in the interpretation of representations of the human form (see, e.g., Joyce 1996; Wicker and Arnold 1999:5–74). The body in the mortuary context can be viewed as a particular form of representation, distinguishable from wall paintings or sculpture mainly by the organic nature of many of the elements of the gender coding arranged in the burial and by the partial or complete decay of the body itself, simultaneously a literal sedimentation and disintegration of bodily practice (Joyce 1996). The *chaîne opératoire* concept, originally generated in the context of lithic analysis, has also been applied to mortuary ritual, implicitly invoking the concept of this aspect of social interaction as "a set of connected practices that produces a deliberate meaningful space that can be compared to narration" (Sørensen 2000:88; see Olivier 1992:59–60).

In addition to the "gender as process/performance" concept, there is also the problem of social identity as palimpsest. Since layers of meaning make up individual identity, with the various layers interacting differently at different stages of the life cycle and in different contexts, age, status, and individual versus group identity are all potentially enmeshed with gender in ways that make attempts to isolate it for analysis neither possible nor desirable. Ultimately, it is the way in which these variables interact with one another that should be the primary focus of any social analysis of mortuary practices.

Walking the Talk: Approaches to Engendered Mortuary Analysis

Sørensen makes the point that it is the materiality of gender in the archaeological record that makes it a potentially productive form of inquiry into the construction and evolution of past gender configurations. She suggests that mortuary ritual is perhaps ideally suited as an arena of investigation of the ontogeny of gender as a social construction precisely because in death various forms of social categorization, including gender, are idealized in concrete form, what she calls the "visualization and ideological reproduction of gender systems" (Sørensen 2000:85). A complicating factor in the application of such concepts is the problem of analytical scale. There are several scales of analysis in engendered mortuary analysis, as is also true for mortuary analysis in general:

Level 1: Cemetery landscape
Level 2: Cemetery
Level 3: Form of disposal
Level 4: Position/orientation of body/remains
Level 5: Spatial distribution of objects in graves
Level 6: Type/number/material of grave goods

At any one of these levels, gender distinctions may or may not be expressed and, if present, may be expressed to varying degrees. As Sørensen (2000:92) correctly points out, "Burials, since these are situations in which many societies most strongly and explicitly reflect upon and renegotiate identities and relationships, necessarily involve a response to gender (even if the burial appears to ignore gender this in itself constitutes a particular interpretation of gender)."

Although archaeologists tend to create an artificial distinction between settlement and mortuary remains, in fact whether or not such a division exists is culturally specific. In many past cultures, there are close connections between the house and death and between domestic structures and mortuary structures, from Bronze Age European house urns (Sørensen 2000:156ff.) and Sarmatian burial chambers (Härke 2000:184–85) to the Oneota burials associated with longhouses in the midcontinent of North America (O'Gorman 2001) and the multichambered burial compounds of Sicán in Peru (Shimada et al. 2004). Human skeletal remains are frequently found in domestic contexts, often disarticulated and incomplete but nevertheless crossing that line between the world of the dead and the living. These associations are complex and may reflect geographic as well as kin-based spatial relationships between individuals, distinctions that often include gender as a distinguishing variable. Temporal and geographic variables affect all six of the levels of analysis outlined previously. As Cannon (2005:41) has argued, "Burial treatments are known to vary among individuals and to change over time . . . but these sources of variability are more often controlled for in the process of interpretation than viewed as both the source of structural variation and a focus of interpretation in their own right."

The differential preservation of bone in archaeological contexts has tended to result in most gender assignments being made on the basis of grave goods rather than skeletal material in any case. That this is potentially problematic, leading to circular reasoning at best and a complete misinterpretation of the evidence at worst, has been pointed out by several researchers working with cultures in which gender was weakly differentiated or gender distinctions were not marked in mortuary ritual (Crass 2001; Weglian 2001). Text-aided archaeological interpretation seems particularly prone to privileging grave goods over physical remains in assigning gender to burials. As Lucy (1997:154) has pointed out for Anglo-Saxon burial archaeology, "A determination of gender based on associated grave goods is almost always preferred over biological sexing of the skeleton," particularly since so much of the sexing data tends to be based on nineteenth- or early twentieth-century determinations of material since discarded and not available for reanalysis. Under those circumstances, it seems best to avoid the term "sex" when describing mortuary contexts where preservation or identification are dubious while bearing in mind that although gender may manifest itself as a primarily dichotomous system in prehistoric contexts, the possibility of multiple permutations must be considered as well (Arnold 2002b). In a sense, the body itself is perhaps best viewed mainly as a particular form of grave good whose relationship (male bodied or female bodied) may or may not coincide with the gender code(s) represented by the other elements of the burial assemblage. As Sørensen (2000:132; emphasis added) puts it, "If with a particular society swords are a masculine and masculating item, then the contexts within which swords were deposited can be interpreted as related to or commenting upon masculinity independently of the sex (and sexuality) of the person with whom the object was associated and also *irrespective of whether the remains of a person are in fact present.*"

The ongoing debate about whether sex and gender should be treated as distinct categories differently constituted (i.e., one is phenotypic while the other is socioculturally determined) or whether this distinction can be made at all (Hubbard 1990; Kessler 1998; Walker and Cook 1998; among others) creates an additional layer of interpretive complexity. One solution is to acknowledge the contingent nature of both sex and gender since even biological sex (traditionally viewed as strictly dichotomous) should be considered a continuum rather than a binary category set (Arnold 2002b:239–40).

Ultimately, skeletal morphology must be considered in any mortuary analysis if bone preservation allows this. Sexing skeletal remains is dependent on a number of variables, not all of which can be controlled for by archaeologists (Lucy 2000:65–74). These include the following:

1. Preservation
2. Age of the individual at death
3. Degree of sexual dimorphism in a given population
4. Degree of bias inherent in the analysis

Poor preservation is far more typical than well-preserved skeletal remains, and infants and children remain difficult to sex, even though some progress has been made in refining the standards of sexing children and neonates (see, e.g., Loth and Henneberg 2001). Since sex determination is based on a series of morphological markers and the range of variation within and between the sexes can be considerable with regard to most of them, individuals who fall into the zone between the "male" and "female" ends of the spectrum have always been a problem (Henderson 1989). In a much-cited study, Kenneth Weiss (1972) was able to demonstrate that in cases where sex identification was ambiguous, there was a 12 percent bias in favor of classifying such individuals as male. This problem can to some degree be mitigated by double-blind studies in which the identification is made by at least two independent specialists without prior knowledge of the mortuary assemblage. Sex identification through the analysis of nuclear DNA may be an option in a small number of cases, but this approach is complicated by preservation as well as contamination issues. Moreover, genetic analyses are expensive and time consuming and in spite of their early promise have yet to replace more conventional methods of determining sex.

When sex can be identified on the basis of skeletal remains with some degree of certainty (in cemeteries with good adult skeletal preservation, the accuracy rate can be as high as 97 percent [Molleson and Cox 1993:91]), it should be compared to the gender categories identified on the basis of grave goods. If more than two genders existed in a prehistoric society, this should be reflected in the correlation between phenotypically identifiable sex and gender if the latter is represented in mortuary ritual. The presence of multiple genders, then, can be archaeologically recognized only under relatively ideal conditions. Unfortunately, in a large number of burials—sometimes 50 percent or more of the graves in a given cemetery population in prehistoric European contexts (the Anglo-Saxon cemetery sample analyzed by Lucy [1997: 157] is fairly typical, but see also Burmeister [2000] for an Iron Age population in Germany in which gender was strongly marked in mortuary contexts)—the grave goods may not be indicative of gender, or there may be no grave goods preserved at all. The Iron Age cemeteries of Las Cogotas and La Osera in Iberia are a good example. More than 50 percent of the graves in both cemeteries contained no grave goods at all, and of those that did contain grave goods, the majority did not contain gender-specific items (Lorrio and Zapatero 2005:fig. 29).

In such cases, other variables, including orientation or body position, may provide clues as to a range of social distinctions, including gender. However, societies in which gender is not reflected in mortuary ritual are known ethnographically, and it can be assumed that gender configurations existed in past societies that are not represented in the ethnographic record today, so the goal must be to identify the range of patterns present in each context, at the level of the cemetery, the region, and the time period, before attempting to interpret the gender configurations represented in the mortuary record. As Lucy (1997:155) has argued, "The relationship between grave goods, gender and sex must be investigated, not assumed."

A good example of the complexities of engendering mortuary analysis is the "female warrior" phenomenon. Although the best-known manifestation is probably the so-called Amazons of Ukraine and the Caucasus, who first appear in the accounts of Hippocrates and Herodotus of armed female warriors, there are New World versions as well (Fraser 1988; Hollimon 2001; Parker Pearson 2000:99–101; Taylor 1996:199–205). While the Iron Age "warrior women" of Scythia and Sauromatia are by now well documented by extensive weapons sets that include armor, spears, arrows, and shields (not, however, swords) in conjunction with skeletal evidence for trauma and stress markers from repetitive activity like riding and archery (Davis Kimball 2002; Rolle 1989; Rolle et al. 1991; Taylor 1996:201–2), this can be a tricky interpretive category for several reasons. One of the main problems is distinguishing between injuries sustained as a noncombatant and those received in battle. As the fictional character Éowyn, "shield-maiden of Rohan," says in the recent film version of J. R. R. Tolkien's epic *The Two Towers*, "The women of Rohan learned long ago that those who do not wear swords can still die upon them."

Traumatic injuries inflicted by sword, spear, ax, or arrow do not necessarily constitute evidence that the individual who suffered those injuries sustained them while engaging actively in warfare. Raiding and similar small-scale violent interactions were common in many prehistoric (and historic) societies, and a single individual could survive a number of sequential injuries simply by being in the wrong place at the wrong time. To claim that a category of "female warrior" existed in a prehistoric society, several lines of evidence should ideally be present in the female burial population (a large sample size is also useful):

1. Evidence in more than one or two cases of traumatic injury forensically consistent with battle. Examples include injuries sustained while on horseback or a preponderance of injuries (some healed premortem) to the front of the body.
2. Evidence for repetitive stress markers consistent with the use of weapons (archery, horseback riding, and swordplay would all leave distinctive signatures if engaged in for a sufficient amount of time).
3. Grave goods marking warrior status, including weapons and possibly other material culture associated with "maleness."

4. Ethnographic or contemporary written records describing such a phenomenon. If all these lines of evidence are present, a strong case can be made for a category of "female warrior" in the society in question. If not, caution is indicated.

Multiple burials are an example of another problematic mortuary category. Defined as graves containing the remains of more than one individual (not including mass, collective, or communal burials, which belong to a different category of interment, usually containing the remains of more than ten persons), multiple burials are frequently interpreted in an unconsidered and stereotypical fashion. For example, graves containing the remains of a woman and a subadult are usually interpreted as mother and child, while burials with an adult male and an adult female are typically described as husband and wife. In the latter case, the assumption is usually made that the male individual represents the primary interment, while the female is merely an accompanying "object" much like the other grave goods. There have been relatively few attempts to analyze this category of burial in a systematic fashion (but see Keswani 2004; Lucy 2000:82; Oeftiger 1984), which is unfortunate since it clearly has the potential to be an extremely informative source on prehistoric social configurations, including gender.

The ideal situation—one in which skeletal remains are well preserved and analyzed independently by several specialists, isotope and genetic analysis can be carried out, the number of systematically excavated burials is large, grave goods are part of an elaborate mortuary display, and there is iconographic and textual evidence of gender configurations—is unfortunately very rare. One of very few examples where at least some of these criteria are present is a project involving the analysis of a recently excavated complex of 1,000-year-old Middle Sicán shaft tombs on the northern coast of Peru (Shimada et al. 2003), which integrates analyses of mitochondrial DNA, odontological analysis (an approach often combined with genetic data [Alt 1997; Alt et al. 1995; Scott and Turner 1997]), developmental health, diet, placement of interred individuals, and associated grave goods to provide a window into the social organization of this particular complex society. However, even when not all of these sources of evidence are available, it is possible to engage in engendered mortuary analysis, as I hope to show in the case study presented later in this chapter.

Related to but distinct from mortuary ritual is the testimony of the body itself, or what remains after the disposal ceremony is carried out and various taphonomic processes have acted on the skeletal material (Grauer and Stuart-Macadam 1998). The bones themselves contain a record of what was consumed (in terms of both food and drink) by the individual in life, making a range of determinations possible: where the person grew up (Budd et al. 2004; Lucy 2004), what kinds of foods the person had regular access to (Parkington 1991; Richards 2000; Sobolik 1994), the reproductive role of the individual (Bentley 1996; Buikstra et al. 1986), and whether the person experienced dietary stress, disease, or injury during his or her lifetime (Roberts and Manchester 1995; Wood et al. 1992). If bone preservation is good enough, these are specific facts about the deceased that can be definitively determined without the need for reference to ethnographic analogy. On the other hand, once the scale of the inquiry shifts from the determination of an individual's life history to the subsistence patterns represented by the skeletal remains of a population, moving beyond the simple description of those patterns requires recourse to some kind of societal model. The fact that women in a given cemetery apparently ate less meat than men, for example, can be observed and described, but not interpreted, solely on the basis of the skeletal remains (Arnold, in press).

Many of the activities engaged in or suffered by individuals are inscribed on the skeletal remains themselves. Examples include the following:

1. Evidence for differential pathologies (Cohen and Bennett 1998). For example, at certain times and places in European prehistory, women exhibit greater number of parry fractures to the lower arm, which suggests high levels of domestic abuse, while men tend to exhibit weapon-induced injuries to a greater degree than women.
2. Evidence for differential repetitive stress markers with respect to type and degree of bone deformation. In many ethnographically documented preindustrial societies, women or men are engaged in more labor tasks, fewer labor tasks for longer periods, or only certain kinds of tasks. In precontact Mesoamerica and in the Neolithic Near East, for example, women exhibit characteristic deformation of the knees and shoulders consistent with hours spent grinding corn on stone mortars, while the right arm and upper body of a male blacksmith buried with his tools in Iron Age Britain was twice the size of the left arm and side. Recent publications like Jane Peterson's (2002) study of musculoskeletal stress markers, tooth wear, dental trauma, and caries in Natufian populations illustrate what such evidence can tell us about "gender and labor at the dawn of agriculture."
3. Evidence for differential nutritional stress (Cohen and Bennett 1998). In some societies, women or men had access to certain foods in greater quantities at certain periods during their lives, and the chemical signatures of the foods they consumed can be recovered from their skeletal remains. In some Mesoamerican and South American skeletal populations, for exam-

ple, men seem to have had access to more meat in their diets than women, suggesting (in conjunction with other evidence) that they may have enjoyed a higher status in society (Hastorf and Johannessen 1993). Differential wear and differential presence of caries can also provide insights into possibly gender-based dietary patterns (Lillie 1997).

4. Evidence for differential demographic representation in the burial record. In a demographically normal population, women should be represented in slightly higher numbers than men. If an archaeological burial population deviates from the expected pattern, some sort of cultural, preselection behavior must be the cause. Examples include selective infanticide (Scott 2001; Wicker 1998) or disposal of some or all members of one gender in a way that is not represented in the mortuary record. The segregated burial of suicides, unbaptized infants, and other individuals viewed as deviant in Christian communities is an obvious example, but another relatively common phenomenon ethnographically speaking is the special treatment of women who have died in childbirth (Baum 1999:105–6; Schwidetzky 1965:231). This may be represented by the absence of such individuals in the "normative" cemetery population or by their special deposition in anomalous contexts, such as caves or other locations. On the other hand, as Baum (1999:106) points out, at some point, so-called anomalous burials should be considered simply another form of normative deposition, given a sufficient number of individuals, as in the case of the numerous skeletal remains in caves and rock shelters dating to the European Iron Age.

Cemeteries may also be segregated by gender or profession, among other criteria. For example, female burials marked by brooches, needles, and curved utility knives and male burials containing swords, spears, shields, and long knives are concentrated in separate sections of first-century B.C. to first-century A.D. Iron Age cremation cemeteries in northern Germany and southern Jutland (Parker Pearson 2000:12).

5. Evidence for differential care (Cohen and Bennett 1998). This includes the differential healing of fractures, a higher incidence of disease, or a higher incidence of certain preventable diseases that indicate that little or no care is available for some groups while others have access to it, occasionally based on gender (Czarnetzki 1996).
6. Evidence that allows us to reconstruct fertility in the archaeological record, in turn allowing inferences to be drawn regarding women's reproductive roles in past societies (Buikstra et al. 1986). Gillian Bentley's (1996:24) research on the relationship between reproduction, production, and social

roles in prehistoric societies, especially foraging groups, makes it clear that female social roles, including contributions to production, are often linked to reproduction in ethnographic contexts and must therefore be considered in the interpretation of societies that are accessible to us only through archaeological evidence. She draws on the field of reproductive ecology, which investigates ecological factors that affect fertility, including disease, nutritional status, and workloads (Bentley 1996:25). Osteological markers related to fertility include the occurrence of sexually transmitted diseases that affect fertility, the mean ages for the onset of menarche and menopause, the length of birth intervals and/or lactation, diachronic changes in women's nutritional status related to pregnancy and lactation, age at weaning of infants, and so on (Bentley 1996:30–35). Bentley acknowledges that her results are drawn mainly from hunting and gathering societies and suggests that similar studies might be productively applied for complex, food producing societies as well (Bentley 1996:26).

7. Evidence for the movement of people, whether at the level of the individual or the group (Alt 1997; Alt et al. 1995; Anthony 1990; Arnold, in press; Konigsberg and Buikstra 1995:194–201; among others). Genetic studies have only recently begun to take into consideration the possibility that male and female mobility patterns might have been different enough consistently enough through time to have had an effect on the patterns seen in mtDNA and Y chromosome data (Arnold, in press; Gibbons 2000). Differences in the migration rate of males and females would be expected to influence the geographic patterns and relative level of diversity on the Y chromosome, autosomes, and mtDNA (Seielstad et al. 1998:278). Most of the discrepancy between Y chromosome and mtDNA and autosomal variation can be explained by a higher female than male migration rate due to patrilocality and the tendency for a wife to move into her husband's natal household (Seielstad et al. 1998:278). If, therefore, smaller numbers of men in prehistory moved longer distances (macromovement) while larger numbers of women moved shorter distances (micromovement) on a regular enough basis, this should produce different patterns of genetic variation for males and females (Alt et al. 1995; Konigsberg and Buikstra 1995:194). Isotope analysis also promises to provide new directions for research in this area. This form of analysis is based on the principle that what individuals ingest in the form of food or drink, including water, leaves chemical traces in the bones and teeth that can provide clues regarding everything from diet to the place in which an individual spent his or her formative years. Dietary isotope analysis can reveal the

relative proportions of protein derived from meat as compared to plant food (Hastorf 1991), seafood as compared to terrestrial protein sources, and so on. The carbon and strontium isotope ratios found in teeth, on the other hand, have been used to determine whether some individuals in cemeteries might not be local, patterns that could reveal gender distinctions that might in turn be used to generate models of residence or other social configurations (Lucy 2004). In most cases, such studies also reveal the complex interplay between status and gender (Rega 1997:238–39; Sørensen 2000:121).

The analysis of gender-specific mobility on the basis of archaeologically recoverable material culture patterns rests on a number of assumptions, among them the possibility of identifying "regional" patterns in the material marking of other social categories (including age, marital status, and occupation)—which could be interpreted as mapping ethnic distinctions (Reinhold 2003)—as well as gender differences in mortuary practices and the material culture associated with such differences (MacBeth 1993). For example, one would expect to see greater variability in female mortuary assemblages than in male assemblages in patrilocal societies in which gender was strongly marked in life as well as in death and where regional differences were reflected in costume and personal ornament, assuming that the newly married woman was permitted or required to retain the costume of her natal community.

Whether women retained the material culture markers of their natal community or reproduced them in their husband's community (e.g., in the form of pottery or textiles) would affect the archaeological visibility of such movement, and the patterns should vary depending on whether female mobility was restricted to certain social strata. The degree to which mortuary costume mirrored the costume of the living is also a factor (Brandt 1998:277). Archaeologists must develop methods of distinguishing these various forms of material culture marking from one another to avoid conflating the different archaeologically documented forms of intercommunity contact (Olausson 1988:19; Schier 1998:510).

In addition to the question of scale (including temporal and geographic variation), an engendered mortuary analysis must also take into consideration the interconnectedness of gender and a number of other variables related to social identity, notably age and status (Burmeister 1997; 2000; Hamlin and Redfern 2004; Müller 1994a, 1994b, 1994c; Rega 1997; Sofaer-Derevenski 1997; Stavish 2004). Too often, gender is analyzed and presented as independent of other social categories, resulting in a seriously skewed representation of the ways in which such identities are constituted and expressed in material form. For example, gender and power are inextricably linked in contemporary societies, yet archaeologists have only recently begun to recognize that this was also the case in the past, a realization that has led to the development of much more complex theoretical and methodological approaches to gender in archaeological interpretation (Clark 2000; Hays-Gilpin and Whitley 1998; Kästner 1997; Kehoe 1999; Moore and Scott 1997; Nelson 2002; Silverblatt 1991; Sullivan 2001; Sweely 1999). The interpretive difficulties archaeologists face are due primarily to the fact that when gender and power are combined with additional social and ideological variables, they may morph in ways that have no contemporary analogues. Archaeology poses special challenges to interpretation in the area of gender studies in part because gender and power are inextricably linked, and as a result gender can be understood only if viewed through the lens of power relationships. How power is constituted may vary considerably, however, and it should not be automatically assumed that the primary basis for such distinctions was economic, that is, based on wealth. In fact, there is good evidence to suggest that at least in western, central, and eastern Europe following the advent of metal technology, age and age-associated rites of passage such as marriage and parenthood may have played a more important role than wealth with respect to the material marking of difference in the form of costume (Arnold 2004; Burmeister 2000; Lucy 2000:87–90; Reinhold 2003:29).

Archaeologists interested in mapping gender and power relations have several sources available to them, and each of these sources can be evaluated for the degree to which gender relations are tied to the expression of power relationships. In archaeological terms, this association manifests itself in terms of visibility, both intentional (who is represented in the archaeological record and in what ways) and taphonomical (certain sources of information are more likely to be preserved than others). For example, the consistent archaeological invisibility of certain groups of people (including but not limited to nonpersons, such as slaves; children, especially infants; and, to varying degrees, women) has recently become the focus of systematic study in the archaeological literature (Moore and Scott 1997; Nelson 1999).

Ultimately, it is gender ideology (Spector and Whelan 1991) that is expressed in prehistoric European burial contexts more frequently than gender roles, in the sense that relatively few individuals are buried with implements or tools, while in the majority of complex societies in prehistoric Europe, masculinity was signaled by weapons and femininity by specific combinations of personal ornament. Weapons can, of course, be considered tools, but they are a problematic category since their symbolic significance appears to override their functional meaning in mortuary contexts in many societies—that is, they tend to communicate masculinity without necessarily representing the functional category "warrior" (Härke 1990:33; Stoodley 1999:77–78; Strömberg 1993:108).

Another confounding phenomenon is the so-called neutral burial category, that is, graves whose contents (especially when skeletal remains are not preserved and sexing is not an option) do not communicate a particular gender association (Parker Pearson 2000:97). Several researchers have noted that individuals in this category often account for more than half the burials in a given cemetery population (Arnold, in press; Brush 1988; Burmeister 2000; Lorrio and Zapatero 2005:fig. 29; Lucy 1997; Stoodley 1999:76)), which means that inferences regarding gender configurations are often being made without reference to a significant segment of the population. The assumption is that burials in which gender is not visibly marked in mortuary contexts differ with respect to some other variable or set of variables: age, status, social role, ethnicity, or a combination of these. However, considering how common this "neutral" subset of burial populations seems to be, it is significant that thus far as a category such graves have tended to be ignored—they are present in the graphs and tables of archaeological publications but are deemphasized or rationalized in the discussion and interpretation.

The differential archaeological visibility of a particular gender category compared to others is another problem since not all elements of costume, personal ornament, or mortuary assemblages are imperishable. This may result in an overrepresentation of one group compared to others that might have been present but are not archaeologically identifiable. Associating greater visibility in contemporary archaeological contexts with greater importance in past social contexts is not uncommon in the interpretation of the mortuary record, and this can lead to some egregious distortions of social configurations. For example, in the Iron Age of west-central Europe, weapon-bearing (usually adult) men (buried with bronze or iron swords, dagger, spears, or axes as well as defensive equipment) and adult women or girls with metal (bronze or iron), amber, jet, coral, glass, or other imperishable personal ornament are overrepresented in the archaeological record compared to boys, adult males not buried with weapons, or adult females or girls not buried with imperishable grave goods (Arnold 2004, in press).

Case Study: Iron Age Europe

By 600 B.C., Iron Age Europe was characterized by hierarchically organized societies in which the basis of social power was agrarian and also based to varying degrees on pastoral wealth, especially in the form of cattle. Status differences appear to have been marked mainly in the form of costume, including personal ornament and weaponry. Archaeologically less visible features such as hairstyle, body ornamentation (e.g., tattooing), and status-specific textile colors and patterns can be assumed to have been in use as well. The few systematic attempts to outline gender and power configurations have thus far all been in the realm of mortuary studies, partly because Iron Age societies evidently chose to demarcate such distinctions on their own bodies rather than expressing them in the form of settlement structures (Arnold 2004). Although there is disagreement as to the precise nature of their political structure—were they complex chiefdoms or early states?—most archaeologists would agree that age, gender roles, and status differences were both recognized and marked in these Iron Age societies. As Sofaer-Derevenski (1997:196) has pointed out, "Material culture influences gender development since it acts as a reflector of gender and is associated with culturally defined gender stereotypes from a very early age."

Some of these distinctions were marked in very consistent ways through space and time. For example, infants, especially neonates, are not represented in formal burial contexts during the Iron Age, suggesting that the definition of personhood was age dependent to some extent and that before a certain age individuals were not considered fully human. Typically their remains are found in informal contexts in settlements, including rubbish pits, abandoned structures, and ditches. While children are occasionally found buried in west-central European Iron Age mounds, the grave goods found in these burials are typically of above-average quality and quantity. Infants are found very rarely, and then always newborns in association with an adult female of childbearing age, suggesting that the deaths were simultaneous.

Gender distinctions were tied to costume in consistent ways as well, although the individual elements of the costume varied through time and space. Where large samples with good skeletal preservation are available, such as at the sites of Hallstatt (Hodson 1990; Kromer 1959), Münsingen-Rain (Müller 1998), or Wederath-Belginum (Haffner 1989), grave good assemblages can be correlated with the anthropological identification of sex, providing a basis for comparison with burial contexts in which physical anthropological analysis is not possible because of poor preservation or complete calcination of cremated bone.

The association between maleness and weapons, particularly swords, daggers, and spears, in the West Hallstatt zone (Burmeister 2000), and defensive armor, including helmets and breastplates as well as axes, in the East Hallstatt zone (Potrebica 2001) is clearly represented in the archaeological as well as the documentary record, even though there are regional and temporal variations in the vocabulary of maleness. Male personal ornament also tends to be distributed asymmetrically, so that when ring jewelry is present (bracelets, hair rings, or earrings) in biologically male graves, it tends to be found on only one side of the body (i.e., only left wrist, left upper arm, or, depending on handedness, right wrist and right upper arm and left or right ear or side of the head) (Arnold 2002a). In male burials, the wheels tend to remain on the vehicle, and the body is placed either on or under the wagon or chariot. Regularly patterned "female" costume elements include ankle rings, more than one earring, symmetrically distributed ring ornaments (especially bracelets) as well as hair, bonnet, or veil ornaments and, if a wagon is present, the separation of the wheels from the vehicle body. Also significant is the higher frequency of beads of glass, amber, jet, and other materials as well as various amulets, including unworked natural objects, in female burials. Even though male graves do contain such items, they occur in fewer male graves and in smaller numbers than in female burials. Interestingly, children's burials also frequently contain amulets and unmodified natural items (Pauli 1975), suggesting that women, probably mainly those of childbearing age, and children were seen as being more vulnerable and requiring greater protection than men. Whether this interpretation can be extrapolated to the realm of gender ideology to argue that women were viewed on a par with children and therefore inferior to men appears doubtful. Nevertheless, apart from Ludwig Pauli (1972, 1975), very few researchers have attempted a systematic study of the amulet category and its distribution in the mortuary context, and given the much larger database available now, the topic should be revisited. Obviously, regional and temporal variations exist with regard to all these gender-specific grave good categories, but it is possible to claim that gender in the European Iron Age was marked through personal ornament and weaponry as well as the regularized placement of certain categories of objects within burials (Arnold 2001, 2004, in press).

This gender "vocabulary" intersects with the vocabulary of status in the sense that elites in the uppermost tier contain the entire suite of high-status markers, such as gold neckings, Mediterranean imports (including metal drinking vessels), wheeled vehicles, and/or horse trappings (a four-wheeled wagon in the late Hallstatt period and a two-wheeled chariot in the La Tène), regardless of gender. The same elements mark paramount status whether the deceased individual was male or female. This is interesting because it suggests that even though there are smaller numbers of female paramount elites, the material culture correlates of their social personae do not differ qualitatively from their male counterparts, and it can be postulated that they had similar rights and responsibilities.

In addition, the presence of individuals whose anthropologically determined sex does not correspond to the gender assigned to their grave good assemblage suggests that more than two institutionalized gender categories existed in Iron

Age Europe (Arnold 2002b). Both biologically female individuals with "male" gendered grave goods and biologically male individuals with "female" gendered grave goods are known, but whether they constitute separate gender categories or represent a single "gender transforming" category is unknown. Stoodley's (1999:76) discussion of this phenomenon in Anglo-Saxon burials in Britain is relevant here:

> The interpretation of these individuals though is problematic. Were they fully accepted members of the gender category signaled by their assemblages? Moreover, did their communities allow the burial of individuals with assemblages that were contrary to their sex? If this were the case, then these burials were blurring the gender boundaries through their possession of a kit usually confined to the opposite sex. Or did they constitute a recognized separate, perhaps special group of people, who were permitted to transcend social boundaries? Contravening social rules by adopting the kit of the opposite gender to their sex would have made a clear statement concerning their special role/status. This would be an example of a third gender. The problem will by now be clear: as the same medium is used for both a blurred and a third gender, how can we know which is in evidence?

Significantly, although the numbers of such ambiguous burials are never very high (e.g., Stoodley estimates that masculine females represent 0.37 percent of his sample and feminine males 2.08 percent), they are represented in virtually every prehistoric and early historic European burial tradition (Breitsprecher 1987:tables 1 and 2; Knüsel and Ripley 2000). To clarify this phenomenon, significantly more would have to be known about gender configurations and about Iron Age social structure more generally. More recent studies are just beginning to systematically investigate the topic on a regional basis (Burmeister 1997, 2000), building on and responding to the pioneering efforts of researchers like Ludwig Pauli (1972, 1975) and a handful of others.

New Directions

A significant problem is the tendency of many researchers to either shoehorn all burials into one of two dichotomous sex/gender categories, ignoring or minimizing ambiguous mortuary assemblages that suggest the presence of a suprabinary gender system (Arnold 1991, 2002b; Lucy 1997:161; Stoodley 1999:76), or, conversely, the tendency to reject the presence of dichotomous binary gender systems in the past while emphasizing individual agency to a degree that comes dangerously close to temporal ethnocentrism (Sørensen 2000:55–56, 65). The richly varied forms of gender expression represented in the archaeological record tend to be obscured by various forms of contemporary preconceptions regarding gender configurations that are conceived of either as immutable and universal or as endlessly negotiated and ambiguous. As Moira Gatens (1996:35) has pointed out, "The privileged relation which each individual has to her or his own body does *not* include a privilege over its construction." Sørensen (2000:50) summarizes Gatens's perspective as follows: "This means that bodies are sexed, and that society recognizes 'its' bodies as differently sexed. She [Gatens] also shows that it is significant to accept that societies, despite transgressionary practices and contrary to personal experiences, in general see bodies as variations upon male and female." I have discussed the construction of chronocentrist limitations in the interpretation of past gender configurations:

> Prehistoric peoples constructed sex and gender on the basis of observed morphological or behavioral features. They could not have distinguished between individuals on the basis of chromosomal features if those features had no phenotypical or behavioral manifestations, for example. At least as important, our 20th-century [now 21st-century] political agendas and concerns were not theirs. (Arnold 2002:240)

To paraphrase Liam de Paor (1986:12), nobody lived, loved, or died in prehistory to prove a point about the present.

A related point is that as archaeologists we are dependent on the recognition of patterns and must be careful when arguing from exceptional examples to general social conventions. At the same time, the fact that a binary system of gender categorization is the dominant pattern in a given cemetery population should not blind us to the possibility that other categories existed as well. The same can be said for the so-called biological imperative that is rejected by many feminists as an explanation for the widespread presence of patriarchal social systems. As Sørensen (2000:67) correctly points out, "Universals do not imply that there will be no exceptions, merely that something is found worldwide in many different contexts and that in all of these the particular phenomenon is common. That women can give birth to children is thus a universal phenomenon despite some women being unable [or choosing not] to do so." In much the same way, as Sørensen (2000:91) also argues, wholesale rejection of traditional ideas about gendered objects, such as swords being male and personal ornament being female, is not the answer; "rather it is the recognition of their contextual genesis that is called for."

Just as problematic, in my opinion, are more recent attempts to identify individual sexual identity on the basis of archaeological evidence, one of the main themes of the 2004 Chacmool Conference titled "Qu(e)erying Archaeology." It is no coincidence that eleven of the fourteen case studies in Schmidt and Voss's (2000) *Archaeologies of Sexuality* are drawn from text-aided contexts, and only one makes use of prehistoric burial evidence (Schmidt 2003:224–25). Apart from the fact that the question of the extent to which agency can be archaeologically identified remains unresolved (Arnold 2001; Dobres and Robb 2000), not all social systems rely on sexual identity or the choice of sexual partner in characterizing gender (Arnold 2002b:247). Ironically, traditional, androcentric interpretations have tended to invoke sexual identity when attempting to reconcile "anomalous" sex/gender associations. The interpretation of the Early Iron Age high-status burial of Vix as a "transvestite priest" (Arnold 1991) or the characterization of an Anglo-Saxon "double weapon burial as evidence for homosexuality, rather than accepting the sexing of one of the skeletons as possibly female" (Lucy 1997:161) are just two examples. While it can be assumed that a small percentage of individuals in any prehistoric population may have exhibited biologically indeterminate or ambiguous sexual characteristics, they would not have been sufficiently numerous to constitute a normative category of sex identification (Parker Pearson 2000:96; Rega 1997:242). On the other hand, because the way in which different cultures treat such individuals can vary considerably, from selective infanticide to the creation of positions of social importance, the visibility in the mortuary context of sex/gender disjunction can be revealing in and of itself.

One of the primary ongoing goals of engendered mortuary analysis should be to ensure that past gender configurations are allowed to speak to us through the archaeological record as unencumbered as possible by the concerns and agendas of today. Physical anthropologist Linda Hurcombe (1995:96) makes this point in her discussion of the pedagogical challenges of teaching students about the evolution of the division of labor by sex and why the available evidence suggests that most men were probably hunters: "To say that such ideas are sexist is to miss the point of sexual dimorphism as an evolutionary strategy and to be biased by our own cultural experience of the *status* of activities. The female students wanted women to be seen as hunters because this was the task *they* valued more." While projecting current perspectives regarding the construction of gender onto past social systems in archaeological interpretation is clearly inevitable to some degree and while all archaeological data are potentially subject to various forms of manipulation, both conscious and unconscious, the tremendous variety of past gender configurations and the varied degree to which these are expressed in mortuary ritual dictate caution. We should try to avoid speaking for the archaeological record, even when what it has to say may not reflect contemporary attitudes toward the role of the individual in constructing identities, including gender.

Only in this way can mortuary archaeology contribute fully to the continuing exploration and discussion of gender and its material expression in past as well as present societies.

References

Alt, Kurt
- 1997 *Odontologische Verwandtschaftsanalyse: Individuelle Charakteristika der Zähne in Ihrer Bedeutung für Anthropologie, Archäologie und Rechtsmedizin.* Stuttgart: Gustav Fischer.

Alt, Kurt, Martina Munz, and Werner Vach
- 1995 Hallstattzeitliche Grabhügel im Spiegel ihrer biologischen und sozialen Strukturen am Beispiel des Hügelgräberfeldes von Dattingen, Kr. Breisgau-Hochschwarzwald. *Germania* 73(2):281–316.

Anthony, David
- 1990 Migration in Archaeology: The Baby and the Bathwater. *American Anthropologist* 92:895–914.

Arnold, Bettina
- 1991 The Deposed Princess of Vix: The Need for an Engendered European Prehistory. In *The Archaeology of Gender*. Proceedings of the 22nd Annual Chacmool Conference. D. Walde and N.D. Willows, eds. Pp. 366–74. Calgary: Department of Archaeology, University of Calgary.
- 2001 The Limits of Agency in the Analysis of Elite Celtic Iron Age Burials. *Journal of Social Archaeology* 1(2):211–23.
- 2002a A Landscape of Ancestors: The Space and Place of Death in Iron Age West-Central Europe. In *The Space and Place of Death*. H. Silverman and D. B. Small, eds. Pp. 129–44. Archaeological Papers of the American Anthropological Association 11. Washington, DC: American Anthropological Association.
- 2002b "Sein und Werden": Gender as Process in Mortuary Ritual. In *In Pursuit of Gender: Worldwide Archaeological Approaches*. Sarah Nelson and Myriam Rosen-Ayalon, eds. Pp. 239–56. Walnut Creek, CA: AltaMira Press.
- 2002c A Transatlantic Perspective on German Archaeology. In *Archaeology, Ideology and Society: the German Experience*. 2nd ed. Heinrich Härke, ed. Pp. 401–25. Frankfurt: Peter Lang.
- 2004 Machtbeziehungen und Geschlechterdifferenz in der vorgeschichtlichen Eisenzeit Europas. In *Machtbeziehungen, Geschlechterdifferenz und Religion*. Bernhard Heininger, Stephanie Böhm, and Ulrike Sals, eds. Pp. 9–34. Münster: LIT Verlag.
- 2005 Mobile Men, Sedentary Women? Material Culture as a Marker of Regional and Supra-Regional Interaction in Early Iron Age Southwest Germany. In *Celts on the Margin: Studies in European Cultural Interaction 7th c. BC–1st c. AD. Essays in Honor of Zenon Wozniak*. Halina Dobrzanska, J. V. S. Megaw, and Pau-

lina Poleska, eds. Pp. 17–26. Krakow: Institute of Archaeology and Ethnology of the Polish Academy of the Sciences.

In press Fieldwork in the Country of Death: Mortuary Variability and Archaeological Inference. In *Archaeological Concepts for the Study of the Cultural Past*. Alan Sullivan, ed. Salt Lake City: University of Utah Press.

Arnold, Bettina, and Nancy L. Wicker, eds.
  2001 *Gender and the Archaeology of Death*. Walnut Creek, CA: AltaMira Press.
Bahn, Paul, ed.
  2003 *Written in Bones: How Human Remains Unlock the Secrets of the Dead*. Toronto: Firefly.
Baum, Norbert
  1999 Die Dietersberghöhle bei Egloffstein, Kr. Forchheim—von der Opferhöhle zum Bestattungsplatz. *Prähistorische Zeitschrift* 74(1):79–121.
Bentley, Gillian R.
  1996 How Did Prehistoric Women Bear "Man the Hunter"? Reconstructing Fertility from the Archaeological Record. In *Gender and Archaeology*. Rita P. Wright, ed. Pp. 23–51. Philadelphia: University of Pennsylvania Press.
Bolger, Diana R., and Nancy J. Serwint, eds.
  2002 *Engendering Aphrodite: Women and Society in Ancient Cyprus*. Boston: American Society for Oriental Research.
Brandt, Helga
  1998 Frauen in der keltischen Eisenzeit. In: *Frauen—Zeiten—Spuren*. Bärbel Auffermann and Gerd-Christian Weniger, eds. Pp. 271–301. Mettmann: Neandertal Museum.
Breitsprecher, Ute
  1987 Zum Problem der geschlechtsspezifischen Bestattungen in der römischen Kaiserzeit: Ein Beitrag zur Forschungsgeschichte und Methode. BAR International Series 376. Oxford: British Archaeological Reports.
Brown, Keri A.
  1998 Gender and Sex: Distinguishing the Difference with Ancient DNA. In *Gender and Italian Archaeology: Challenging Stereotypes*. Ruth D. Whitehouse, ed. Pp. 35–44. London: Accordia Research Institute/University College London.
Brumfiel, Elizabeth M.
  1991 Weaving and Cooking: Women's Production in Aztec Mexico. In *Engendering Archaeology: Women and Prehistory*. Joan Gero and Margaret Conkey, eds. Pp. 224–51. Cambridge: Blackwell.
Brush, Karen
  1988 Gender and Mortuary Analysis in Pagan Anglo-Saxon Archaeology. *Archaeological Review from Cambridge* 7:76–89.
Budd, Paul, Andrew Millard, Carolyn Chenery, Sam Lucy, and Charlotte Roberts
  2004 Investigating Population Movement by Stable Isotope Analysis: A Report from Britain. *Antiquity* 78(299):127–41.

Buikstra, Jane, Lyle Konigsberg, and Jill Bullington
  1986 Fertility and the Development of Agriculture in the Prehistoric Midwest. *American Antiquity* 51:528–46.
Burmeister, Stefan
  1997 Zum sozialen Gebrauch von Tracht: Aussagemöglichkeiten hinsichtlich des Nachweises von Migrationen. *Ethnologisch-Archäologische Zeitschrift* 38:177–203.
  2000 *Geschlecht, Alter und Herrschaft in der Späthallstattzeit Württembergs.* Tübinger Schriften zur Ur- und Frühgeschichtlichen Archäologie Band 4. New York: Waxmann Münster.
Butler, Judith
  1990 *Gender Trouble: Feminism and the Subversion of Identity.* New York: Routledge.
  1993 *Bodies That Matter: On the Discursive Limits of "Sex."* New York: Routledge.
Cannon, Aubrey
  2005 Gender, Agency, and Mortuary Fashion. In *Interacting with the Dead: Perspectives on Mortuary Archaeology for the New Millennium.* Gordon F. M. Rakita, Jane E. Buikstra, Lane A. Beck, and Sloan R. Williams, eds. Pp. 41–65. Gainesville: University Press of Florida.
Carr, Christopher
  1995 Mortuary Practices: Their Social, Philosophical-Religious, Circumstantial and Physical Determinants. *Journal of Archaeological Method and Theory* 2(2):105–200.
Chapman, John
  2000 Tensions at Funerals: Social Practice and the Subversion of Community Structure in Later Hungarian Prehistory. In *Agency in Archaeology.* Marcia-Ann Dobres and John E. Robb, eds. Pp. 169–95. London: Routledge.
Charles, Douglas K.
  1995 Diachronic Regional Social Dynamics: Mortuary Sites in the Illinois Valley/American Bottom Region. In *Regional Approaches to Mortuary Analysis.* Lane A. Beck, ed. Pp. 77–100. New York: Plenum.
Charles, Douglas K., and Jane E. Buikstra
  1983 Archaic Mortuary Sites in the Central Mississippi Drainage: Distribution, Structure, and Behavioral Implications. In *Archaic Hunters and Gatherers in the American Midwest.* James L. Phillips and James A. Brown, eds. Pp. 117–45. New York: Academic Press.
  2002 Siting, Sighting and Citing the Dead. In *The Space and Place of Death.* Helaine Silverman and David B. Small, eds. Pp. 13–25. Arlington, VA: Archaeological Papers of the American Anthropological Association.
Clark, John E.
  2000 Towards a Better Explanation of Hereditary Inequality: A Critical Assessment of Natural and Historic Human Agents. In *Agency in Archaeology.* Marcia-Anne Dobres and John Robb, eds. Pp. 92–112. London: Routledge.

Cohen, M. N., and S. Bennett
  1998 Skeletal Evidence for Sex Roles and Gender Hierarchies in Prehistory. In *Reader in Gender Archaeology*. Kelley Hays-Gilpin und David S. Whitely, eds. Pp. 297–318. London: Routledge.
Conkey, Margaret W., and Janet Spector
  1984 Archaeology and the Study of Gender. *Archaeological Advances in Method and Theory* 7:1–38.
Crass, Barbara A.
  2001 Gender and Mortuary Analysis: What Can Grave Goods Really Tell Us? In *Gender and the Archaeology of Death*. Bettina Arnold and Nancy L. Wicker, eds. Pp. 105–18. Walnut Creek, CA: AltaMira Press.
Czarnetzki, Alfred
  1996 *Stumme Zeugen ihrer Leiden: Paläpathologische Befunde*. Tübingen: Attempto Verlag.
Davis Kimball, Jeanine
  2002 *Warrior Women: An Archaeologist's Search for History's Hidden Heroines*. New York: Warner Books.
de Paor, Liam
  1986 *The Peoples of Ireland: From Prehistory to Modern Times*. London: Hutchinson and Co.
Dobres, Marcia-Ann, and John E. Robb, eds.
  2000 *Agency in Archaeology*. London: Routledge.
Dommasnes, L. H.
  1982 Late Iron Age in Western Norway: Female Roles and Ranks as Deduced from an Analysis of Burial Customs. *Norwegian Archaeological Review* 15:1–2, 70–84.
  1987 Male/Female Roles and Ranks in Late Iron Age Norway. In *Were They All Men? An Examination of Sex Roles in Prehistoric Societies*. R. Bertelsen, A. Lillehammer, and J.-R. Naess, eds. Pp. 65–78. Stavanger: Arkeologisk Museum i Stavanger.
  1991 Women, Kinship and the Basis of Power in the Norwegian Viking Age. In *Social Approaches to Viking Studies*. Ross Samson, ed. Pp. 65–73. Glasgow: Cruithne Press.
Doucette, Dianna L.
  2001 Decoding the Gender Bias: Inferences of Atlatls in Female Mortuary Contexts. In *Gender and the Archaeology of Death*. Bettina Arnold and Nancy L. Wicker, eds. Pp. 159–78. Walnut Creek, CA: AltaMira Press.
Effros, Bonnie
  2003 *Merovingian Mortuary Archaeology and the Making of the Middle Ages*. Berkeley: University of California Press.
Ferree, Myra Marx, Judith Lorbeer, and Beth B. Hess, eds.
  1998 *Revisioning Gender*. Thousand Oaks, CA: Sage.

Fraser, Antonia
    1988   *The Warrior Queens.* New York: Vintage Books.

Gatens, Moira
    1996   *Imaginary Bodies: Ethics, Power, and Corporeality.* London: Routledge.

Gibbons, A.
    2000   Europeans Trace Ancestry to Paleolithic People. *Science* 290 (November 10):1080–81.

Gibbs, L.
    1987   Identifying Gender Representation in the Archaeological Record: A Contextual Study. In *The Archaeology of Contextual Meanings.* Ian Hodder, ed. Pp. 79–89. Cambridge: Cambridge University Press.

Goldstein, Lynne
    1995   Landscapes and Mortuary Practices: A Case for Regional Perspectives. In *Regional Approaches to Mortuary Analysis.* Lane A. Beck, ed. Pp. 101–24. New York: Plenum.

Grauer, Anne L., and Patricia Stuart-Macadam, eds.
    1998   *Sex and Gender in Paleopathological Perspective.* Cambridge: Cambridge University Press.

Haffner, Alfred
    1989   *Gräber—Spiegel des Lebens: Totenbrauchtum der Kelten und Römer.* Mainz: Philipp von Zabern Verlag.

Hamlin, Christine
    2001   Sharing the Load: Gender and Task Division at the Windover Site. In *Gender and the Archaeology of Death.* Bettina Arnold and Nancy L. Wicker, eds. Pp. 119–36. Walnut Creek, CA: AltaMira Press.

Hamlin, Christine, and Rebecca Redfern
    2004   The Dead of Dorset: Potentials and Problems with Engendered Mortuary Analysis. Paper presented at the 15th Anniversary Gender Conference, Chacmool 2004, University of Calgary, Calgary, November 11–14.

Härke, Heinrich
    1990   "Warrior Graves"? The Background of the Anglo-Saxon Weapon Burial Rite. *Past and Present* 126:22–43.
    1992   Changing Symbols in a Changing Society: The Anglo-Saxon Weapon Burial Rite in the Seventh Century. In *The Age of Sutton Hoo: The Seventh Century in North-Western Europe.* Martin Carver, ed. Pp. 149–62. Woodbridge: Boydell.
    2000   Die Darstellung von Geschlechtergrenzen im frühmittelalterlichen Grabritual: Normalität oder Problem? In *Grenze und Differenz im Frühen Mittelalter.* Walter Pohl and Helmut Reimitz, eds. Pp. 181–96. Wien: Verlag der Österreichischen Akademie der Wissenschaften.

Hastorf, Christine A.
    1991   Gender, Space and Food in Prehistory. In *Engendering Archaeology: Women and*

Prehistory. Joan M. Gero and Margaret W. Conkey, eds. Pp. 132–62. Oxford: Basil Blackwell.

Hastorf, Christine A., and Sissell Johannessen
   1993   Pre-Hispanic Political Change and the Role of Maize in the Central Andes of Peru. *American Anthropologist* 95:115–38.

Hayes-Gilpin, Kelley, and David S. Whitely, eds.
   1998   *Reader in Gender Archaeology.* London: Routledge.

Henderson, J.
   1989   Pagan Saxon Cemeteries: A Study of the Problems of Sexing by Grave Goods and Bones. In *Burial Archaeology: Current Research, Methods and Development.* Charlotte A. Roberts and Frances Lee and John Bintliff, eds. Pp. 77–83. BAR British Series 211. Oxford: British Archaeological Reports.

Higham, Charles F. W.
   2002   Women in the Prehistory of Mainland Southeast Asia. In *In Pursuit of Gender: Worldwide Archaeological Approaches.* Sarah M. Nelson and Myriam Rosen-Ayalon, eds. Pp. 207–24. Walnut Creek, CA: AltaMira Press.

Hjørungsdal, T.
   1991   Det skjulte kjønn: Patriarkal tradisjon og feministisk visjon i arkeologien belyst med focus på en jernalderkontekst. *Acta Archaeologica Ludensia Series in 8* 19:1–188.
   1994   Poles Apart: Have There Been Any Male or Female Graves? *Current Swedish Archaeology* 2:141–49.

Hodson, Frank
   1990   *Hallstatt—The Ramsauer Graves: Quantification and Analysis.* Bonn: Rudolf Habelt Verlag.

Høgestøl, M.
   1986   Endringer i sosial posisjon hos jernalders kvinner. *Kvinner i Arkeologi i Norge* 3:49–58.

Hollimon, Sandra
   2001   Warfare and Gender in the Northern Plains: Osteological Evidence of Trauma Reconsidered. In *Gender and the Archaeology of Death.* Bettina Arnold and Nancy L. Wicker, eds. Pp. 179–94. Walnut Creek, CA: AltaMira Press.

Hubbard, Ruth
   1990   *The Politics of Women's Biology.* New Brunswick, NJ: Rutgers University Press.

Hurcombe, Linda
   1995   Our Own Engendered Species. *Antiquity* 69:87–100.

Jiao, Tianlong
   2001   Gender Studies in Chinese Neolithic Archaeology. In *Gender and the Archaeology of Death.* Bettina Arnold and Nancy L. Wicker, eds. Pp. 51–64. Walnut Creek, CA: AltaMira Press.

Joyce, Rosemary A.
   1996   The Construction of Gender in Classic Mayan Monuments. In *Gender and*

Archaeology. Rita P. Wright, ed. Pp. 167–95. Philadelphia: University of Pennsylvania Press.
1998 Performing the Body in Pre-Hispanic Central America. *Res* 33:147–65.
1999 Social Dimensions of Preclassic Burials. In *Ritual Behavior, Social Identity and Cosmology in Pre-Classic Mesoamerica.* David C. Grove and Rosemary A. Joyce, eds. Pp. 15–47. Washington, DC: Dumbarton Oaks.

Kästner, Sibylle
1997 Rund ums Geschlecht: Ein Überblick zu feministischen Geschlechtertheorien und deren Anwendung auf die archäologische Forschung. In *Vom Knochenmann zur Menschenfrau: Feministische Theorie und archäologische Praxis.* Sigrun M. Karlisch and Sibylle Kästner, eds. Pp. 13–35. Münster: Agenda Verlag.

Kehoe, Alice
1999 A Resort to Subtler Contrivances. In *Manifesting Power: Gender and the Interpretation of Power in Archaeology.* Tracy L. Sweely, ed. Pp. 17–29. London: Routledge.

Kessler, Suzanne
1998 *Lessons from the Intersexed.* New Brunswick, NJ: Rutgers University Press.

Keswani, Priscilla
2004 *Mortuary Ritual and Society in Bronze Age Cyprus.* London: Equinox.

Knüsel, Christopher, and Kathryn Ripley
2000 The *Berdache* or Man-Woman in Anglo-Saxon England and Early Medieval Europe. In *Social Identity in Early Medieval Britain.* William O. Frazer and Andrew Tyrrell, eds. Pp. 157–91. London: Leicester University Press.

Konigsberg, Lyle W., and Jane E. Buikstra
1995 Regional Approaches to the Investigation of Past Human Biocultural Structure. In *Regional Approaches to Mortuary Analysis.* Lane A. Beck, ed. Pp. 191–219. New York: Plenum.

Kromer, Karl
1959 *Das Gräberfeld von Hallstatt.* Firenze: Sansoni.

Lillie, Malcolm C.
1997 Women and Children in Prehistory: Resource Sharing and Social Stratification at the Mesolithic-Neolithic Transition in Ukraine. In *Invisible People and Processes: Writing Gender and Childhood into European Archaeology.* Jenny Moore and Eleanor Scott, eds. Pp. 213–28. London: Leicester University Press.

Linduff, Kathy
2002 Women's Lives Memorialized in Burial in Ancient China at Anyang. In *In Pursuit of Gender: Worldwide Archaeological Approaches.* Sarah M. Nelson and Myriam Rosen-Ayalon, eds. Pp. 257–88. Walnut Creek, CA: AltaMira Press.

Lorrio, Alberto J., and Gonzalo Ruiz Zapatero
2005 The Celts in Iberia: An Overview. *E-Keltoi* 6:167–254.

Loth, Susan R., and Maciej Henneberg
2001 Sexually Dimorphic Mandibular Morphology in the First Few Years of Life. *American Journal of Physical Anthropology* 115(2):179–86.

Lucy, Sam J.
  1995 The Anglo-Saxon Cemeteries of East Yorkshire. Ph.D. diss., Cambridge University.
  1997 Housewives, Warriors and Slaves? Sex and Gender in Anglo-Saxon Burials. In *Invisible People and Processes: Writing Gender and Childhood into European Archaeology*. Jenny Moore and Eleanor Scott, eds. Pp. 150–68. London: Leicester University Press.
  2000 *The Anglo-Saxon Way of Death: Burial Rites in Early England*. Stroud: Sutton.
  2004 Gender and Identity in Medieval Britain. Paper presented at the 15th Anniversary Gender Conference, Chacmool 2004, University of Calgary, Calgary, November 11–14.
Macbeth, H.
  1993 Ethnicity and Human Biology. In *Social and Biological Aspects of Ethnicity*. M. Chapman, ed. Pp. 47–91. Oxford: Oxford University Press.
McCafferty, Sharisse, and Geoffrey McCafferty
  1994 Engendering Tomb 7 at Monte Alban. *Current Anthropology* 35(2):143–66.
McNay, Lois
  2000 *Gender and Agency*. Cambridge: Polity Press.
Meyers, Carol
  2003 Engendering Syro-Palestinian Archaeology: Reasons and Resources. *Near Eastern Archaeology* 66(4):185–97.
Molleson, T., and M. Cox
  1993 *The Spitalfields Project. Volume II: The Anthropology: The Middling Sort*. CBA Research Report 86. York: Council for British Archaeology.
Moore, Jenny, and Eleanor Scott
  1997 *Invisible People and Processes: Writing Gender and Childhood into European Archaeology*. London: Leicester University Press.
Müller, Felix, ed.
  1998 Münsingen-Rain, ein Markstein der keltischen Archäologie: Funde, Befunde und Methoden im Vergleich. Bern: Bernisches Historisches Museum.
Müller, Johannes
  1994a Altersorganisation und Westhallstatt: Ein Versuch. *Ethnographisch-Archäologische Zeitschrift* 35:220–40.
  1994b Bestattungsformen als Spiegel dualer Organisation in prähistorischen Gesellschaften? *Mitteilungen Berliner Gesellschaft Anthropologie, Ethnologie, Urgeschichte* 15:81–88.
  1994c Zur sozialen Gliederung der Nachbestattungsgemeinschaft vom Magdalenenberg bei Villingen. *Prähistorische Zeitschrift* 1994(2):122–75.
Nelson, Sarah M.
  1993 Gender Hierarchy and the Queens of Silla. In *Sex and Gender Hierarchies*. Barbara Diane Miller, ed. Pp. 297–315. Cambridge: Cambridge University Press.

1997 *Gender in Archaeology: Analyzing Power and Prestige.* Walnut Creek, CA: AltaMira Press.

2002 Ideology, Power and Gender: Emergent Complex Society in Northeastern China. In *In Pursuit of Gender: Worldwide Archaeological Approaches.* Sarah M. Nelson and Myriam Rosen-Ayalon, eds. Pp. 73–80. Walnut Creek, CA: AltaMira Press.

Nelson, Sarah M., and Myriam Rosen-Ayalon, eds.
2002 *In Pursuit of Gender: Worldwide Archaeological Approaches.* Walnut Creek, CA: AltaMira Press.

Oeftiger, Claus
1984 *Mehrfachbestattungen im Westhallstattkreis: Zum Problem der Totenfolge.* Bonn: Antiquitas.

O'Gorman, Jodie A.
2001 Life, Death and the Longhouse: A Gendered View of Oneota Social Organization. In *Gender and the Archaeology of Death.* Bettina Arnold and Nancy L. Wicker, eds. Pp. 23–50. Walnut Creek, CA: AltaMira Press.

Olausson, D.
1988 Dots on a Map: Thoughts about the Way Archaeologists Study Prehistoric Trade and Exchange. In *Trade and Exchange in Prehistory: Studies in Honor of Berta Stjernquist.* Birgitta Hårdh, L. Larsson, D. Olausson, and R. Petré, eds. Pp. 15–24. Lund: Lunds Universitets Historiska Museum.

Olivier, Laurent
1992 The Tomb of Hochdorf. *Archaeological Review from Cambridge* 11(1):51–63.

Ortner, Sherry
1996 *Making Gender: The Politics and Erotics of Culture.* Boston: Beacon Press.

Pader, Ellen Jane
1982 *Symbolism, Social Relations and the Interpretation of Mortuary Remains.* BAR British Series 130. Oxford: British Archaeological Reports.

Parker Pearson, Michael
2000 *The Archaeology of Death and Burial.* College Station: Texas A&M University Press.

Parkington, John E.
1991 Approaches to Dietary Reconstruction in the Western Cape: Are You What You Have Eaten? *Journal of Archaeological Science* 18:331–42.

Pauli, Ludwig
1972 Untersuchungen zur Späthallstattkultur in Nordwürttemberg: Analyse eins Kleinraumes im Grenzbereich zweier Kulturen. *Hamburger Beiträge zur Archäologie* 2(1):1–166.

1975 *Keltischer Volksglaube: Amulette und Sonderbestattungen am Dürrnberg bei Hallein und im eisenzeitlichen Europa.* Munich: C. H. Beck'sche Verlagsbuchhandlung.

Peterson, Jane
2002 *Sexual Revolutions: Gender and Labor at the Dawn of Agriculture.* Walnut Creek, CA: AltaMira Press.

Potrebica, Hrvoje
   2001   Some Aspects of the Warrior Concept in the Eastern Hallstatt Circle. *Prehistoria 2000* 1(1):62–81.
Rega, Elizabeth
   1997   Age, Gender and Biological Reality in the Early Bronze Age Cemetery at Mokrin. In *Invisible People and Processes: Writing Gender and Childhood into European Archaeology*. Jenny Moore and Eleanor Scott, eds. Pp. 229–47. London: Leicester University Press.
Reinhold, Sabine
   2003   Traditions in Transition: Thoughts on Late Bronze Age and Early Iron Age Burial Costumes from the Northern Caucasus. *European Journal of Archaeology* 6(1):25–54.
Richards, Michael P.
   2000   Human Consumption of Plant Foods in the British Neolithic: Direct Evidence from Bone Stable Isotopes. In *Plants in Neolithic Britain and Beyond*. Andrew S. Fairbairn, ed. Pp. 123–35. Oxford: Oxbow Monograph.
Roberts, Charlotte A., and Keith Manchester
   1995   *The Archaeology of Disease*. 2nd ed. Stroud: Sutton.
Rolle, Renate
   1989   *The World of the Scythians*. London: Batsford.
Rolle, Renate, Michael Müller-Wille, and Kurt Schietzel, eds.
   1991   *Das Gold der Steppe: Archäologie der Ukraine*. Neumünster: Karl Wachholtz Verlag.
Sangmeister, Eduard
   1994   Einige Gedanken zur Sozialstruktur im Westhallstattgebiet. *Marburger Studien zur Vor- und Frühgeschichte* 16:523–34.
Schier, Wolfram
   1998   Fürsten, Herren, Händler? Bemerkungen zu Wirtschaft und Gesellschaft der westlichen Hallstattkultur. In *Archäologische Forschungen in urgeschichtlichen Siedlungslandschaften: Festschrift für Georg Kossack zum 75. Geburtstag*. Hans-Jörg Küster, Amei Lang, and Peter Schauer, eds. Pp. 493–514. Regensburg: Universitätsverlag Regensburg.
Schmidt, Robert A.
   2003   Shamans and Northern Cosmology: The Direct Historical Approach to Mesolithic Sexuality. In *Archaeologies of Sexuality*. Robert A. Schmidt and Barbara L. Voss, eds. Pp. 220–35. London: Routledge.
Schmidt, Robert A., and Barbara L. Voss
   2003   *Archaeologies of Sexuality*. London: Routledge.
Schwidetzky, I.
   1965   Sonderbestattungen und ihre paläodemographische Bedeutung. *Homo* 16:230–47.
Scott, Eleanor
   2001   Killing the Female? Archaeological Narratives of Infanticide. In *Gender and the*

Archaeology of Death. Bettina Arnold and Nancy L. Wicker, eds. Pp. 1–22. Walnut Creek, CA: AltaMira Press.

Scott, G. Richard, and Christy G. Turner II
 1997 *The Anthropology of Modern Human Teeth.* Cambridge: Cambridge University Press.

Seielstad, M. T., E. Minch, and Luigi Cavalli-Sforza
 1998 Genetic Evidence for a Higher Female Migration Rate in Humans. *Nature Genetics* 20(November):278–80.

Shimada, Izumi, Ken-ichi Shinoda, Julie Farnum, Robert Corrucini, and Hirokatsu Watanabe
 2004 An Integrated Analysis of Pre-Hispanic Mortuary Practices: A Middle Sicán Case Study. *Current Anthropology* 45(3):369–402.

Silverblatt, Irene
 1991 Interpreting Women in States: New Feminist Ethnohistories. In *Gender at the Crossroads of Knowledge: Feminist Anthropology in the Postmodern Era.* Micaela di Leonardo, ed. Pp. 140–71. Berkeley: University of California Press.

Sobolik, Kristin D., ed.
 1994 *Paleonutrition: The Diet and Health of Prehistoric Americans.* Center for Archaeological Investigations Occasional Paper 22. Carbondale: Southern Illinois University Press.

Sofaer-Derevenski, Joanna
 1997 Linking Age and Gender as Social Variables. *Ethnologisch-Archäologische Zeitschrift* 38:485–93.

Sørensen, Marie Louise Stig
 2000 *Gender Archaeology.* Cambridge: Polity Press.

Spector, Janet, and Mary Whelan
 1991 Incorporating Gender into Archaeology Courses. In *Gender and Anthropology: Critical Reviews for Research and Teaching.* Sandra Morgan, ed. Pp. 65–94. Washington, DC: American Anthropological Association.

Stalsberg, Anne
 1984 Skandinaviske Vikingtidsfunn fra Russland med saerlig vekt påkvinnefunnere: Et bidrag til kvinne-arkeologien. *Unitekst fagskrift* 6:68–102.
 1987a The Implications of the Women's Finds for the Understanding of the Activities of the Scandinavians in Russia during the Viking Age. *Kvinner i Arkeologi i Norge* 5:33–49.
 1987b The Interpretation of Women's Objects of Scandinavian Origin from the Viking Period Found in Russia. In *Were They All Men? An Examination of Sex Roles in Prehistoric Societies.* R. Bertelsen, A. Lillehammer, and J.-R. Naess, eds. Pp. 89–101. Stavanger: Arkeologisk Museum i Stavanger.

Stavish, Patricia
 2004 "Women and Children First": The Distribution of Grave Goods in the La Tène Cemetery at Münsingen-Rain, Switzerland. Paper presented at the 15th Anniversary Gender Conference, Chacmool 2004, University of Calgary, Calgary, November 11–14.

Stoodley, Nick
  1999   *The Spindle and the Spear: A Critical Enquiry in the Construction and Meaning of Gender in the Early Anglo-Saxon Burial Rite.* BAR British Series 288. Oxford: Archaeopress.
Strömberg, Agneta
  1993   *Male or Female? A Methodological Study of Grave Gifts as Sex-Indicators in Iron Age Burials from Athens.* Jonsered: Paul Åströms Förlag.
Sullivan, Lynn P.
  2001   Those Men in the Mounds: Gender, Politics and Mortuary Practices in Late Prehistoric Eastern Tennessee. In *Archaeological Studies of Gender in the Southeastern United States.* Jane M. Eastman und Christopher B. Rodning, eds. Pp. 101–26. Gainesville: University Press of Florida.
Sweely, Tracy L., ed.
  1999   *Manifesting Power: Gender and the Interpretation of Power in Archaeology.* London: Routledge.
Tarlow, Sarah
  1999   *Bereavement and Commemoration: An Archaeology of Mortality.* Oxford: Blackwell.
Taylor, Timothy
  1996   *The Prehistory of Sex.* New York: Bantam Books.
Vida, M. Carmen
  1998   The Italian Scene: Approaches to the Study of Gender. In *Gender and Italian Archaeology: Challenging Stereotypes.* Ruth D. Whitehouse, ed. Pp. 15–22. London: Accordia Research Institute/University College London.
Walker, Phillip L., and Della Collins Cook
  1998   Gender and Sex: Vive la Difference! *American Journal of Physical Anthropology* 106:255–59.
Weglian, Emily
  2001   Grave Goods Do Not a Gender Make: A Case Study from Singen am Hohentwiel, Germany. In *Gender and the Archaeology of Death.* Bettina Arnold and Nancy L. Wicker, eds. Pp. 137–58. Walnut Creek, CA: AltaMira Press.
Weiss, Kenneth M.
  1992   On Systematic Bias in Skeletal Sexing. *American Journal of Physical Anthropology* 37:239–50.
Whitehouse, Ruth D., ed.
  1998   *Gender and Italian Archaeology: Challenging Stereotypes.* London: Accordia Research Institute/University College London.
Wicker, Nancy L.
  1998   Selective Female Infanticide as Partial Explanation for the Dearth of Women in Viking Age Scandinavia. In *Violence and Society in the Early Medieval West.* Guy Hallsall, ed. Pp. 205–21. Woodbridge: Boydell.
Wicker, Nancy L., and Bettina Arnold
  1999   *From the Ground Up: Beyond Gender Theory in Archaeology.* Proceedings of the Fifth

Gender and Archaeology Conference. BAR International Series 812. Oxford: Archaeopress.

Wood, J. W., George R. Milner, H. C. Harpending, and K. M. Weiss
  1992   The Osteological Paradox: Problems of Inferring Prehistoric Health from Skeletal Samples. *Current Anthropology* 33:343–70.

Wright, Rita P.
  1996   Technology, Gender and Class: Worlds of Difference in Ur III, Mesopotamia. In *Gender and Archaeology*. Rita P. Wright, ed. Pp. 79–110. Philadelphia: University of Pennsylvania Press.

The Engendered Household 5

JULIA A. HENDON

THE STUDY OF BOTH GENDER and households became integral to archaeological research in the 1980s. Although the household has been an important focus of gender research, not all household archaeology has adopted an engendered perspective. Thus, studies of gender in a household context and studies of the household form overlapping but not identical bodies of research. Archaeological research on the household intersects with the archaeological study of gender for four reasons. First is the household's association with the domestic group. The domestic group has responsibilities for economic production and social reproduction in many societies. The household becomes an institution through which people of different genders and ages interact on a regular basis. Second is the connection to a particular spatial locus—called for convenience the *dwelling area* (intended as a shorthand for residential space where people live on a more or less permanent basis and that may take many forms, including buildings and open spaces). Dwelling areas provide an identifiable location often used over long periods of time. Third is the scale of the social formation. This allows for finer-grained analyses of action and identity that may be contrasted with large-scale political and social structures. And finally is opportunity for comparison across classes, status groups, wealth differences, ethnicity, or other aspects of social relations and structure created by the existence of multiple households within society. In this chapter, I discuss how and why the household is a useful social formation and scale of analysis for archaeologists interested in gender. Investigation of women's and men's socially meaningful action in a domestic context has led to a richer and more nuanced understanding of issues relating to status, identity, and role.

Defining Gender in Studies of the Household

In most household-based research that also considers gender, gender is defined as a social construct that differs from biological sex, and discussion focuses on socially defined men and women. Although consideration of women's activities, role, and status figures prominently in this body of scholarship in order to rectify the lack of attention paid to women in previous scholarship (Joyce and Claassen 1997), it has also taken up the challenge of multiple social actors, such as men and women, adults and children, and the effects of differences in class, social status, wealth, or ethnicity on households (see, e.g., Allison 2003; Axelsson 1999; Bertelsen et al. 1987; Crown 2000b; Lightfoot et al. 1998; Malan 1997; Mrozowski et al. 2000; Robin 2002b; Tringham 1994; Wood 2002; Woolf 1997). The multiethnic nineteenth-century settlement of Fort Ross in California has been studied by Kent Lightfoot, Antoinette Martinez, and Ann Schiff (Lightfoot et al. 1998) to determine how daily practices informed by gender, ethnicity, and class differences become the basis for the negotiation of intimate and larger-scale social relations and identities. It should be pointed out that household archaeologists not interested in gender have not in fact focused only on men's activities; instead, they have generally not discussed people at all, preferring to treat the household as a single entity or irreducible unit of behavioral analysis. Gender archaeologists' insistence on women has thus had the welcome effect of making their studies of the household more "enpeopled" and of demonstrating the value of studying the day-to-day lives of people, with positive consequences for our understanding of social dynamics at multiple social scales (Hendon 2004).

Social relations among household members, who would be of different genders, ages, and seniority; their role in economic production; and the implications of the often unequal relationship between households or between households and the larger community or the state have proved to be productive ways of investigating the roles, status, and power of different social actors within society. A recognition of the value of studying ancient societies at different social scales or levels of analysis has also contributed to archaeological interest in day-to-day life as manifested in the activities and interactions of men and women in a household setting. These developments have grown in tandem with larger shifts in theoretical orientation in the discipline away from ecological, functionalist, or other deterministic paradigms. Among the multiplicity of perspectives that have emerged, those based on some version of practice theory "in which human intentionality matters" (Ortner 2001:272) and political economy or the study of "the organization of production and exchange that underlies and supports a system of power" (Brumfiel 2001:58) have been productive (see Brumfiel 1992; Cowgill 1993; Hendon 1996, 2004; Pauketat 2001). Crucial to these engendered household studies has been a focus on households as groups of people, not just economic or social cooperative units, or "households with faces" in Ruth Tringham's (1991) evocative phrase. The idea of collectivity inherent in social science approaches to the household must be balanced with the focus on individuals or types of social actors common to studies of gender, as must the degree to which gender is a matter of difference or inequality (Morgan 1999).

The Household from a Social Science Perspective: Definitions and Debates

Standard social science definitions of the household emphasize economic cooperation, coresidence, and responsibility for domestic tasks (Abercrombie et al. 2000; Guyer 1981, 1997; Johnson 2000; Netting et al. 1984; Yanagisako 1979). Household members are economically interdependent through their participation in activities related to production and consumption. They are involved in decision making about the allocation of their own and other members' time, skills, and resources. Household members are coresident because they share a dwelling or some sort of living space; in more general terms, households are marked by residential propinquity (Bender 1967). Residential propinquity does not mean that all members must live "under one roof" or all occupy one structure that we would identify as a house. Residential propinquity may result from functionally differentiated structures, such as kitchens or storage buildings, or from several multipurpose buildings ("houses") arranged in such a way as to form a spatially related area. Features of the built or used environment, such as barriers, orientation of structures, location of shrines, or paths, may be used to define the social framework. The most basic obligations of household members are domestic and, at a minimum, entail a significant responsibility for social reproduction, which may include child rearing, and for food preparation and consumption. In short, the term "household" is often used to refer primarily to an economic entity or, more precisely, a social entity with important economic functions. This may be only one way of approaching the household (Beaudry 1984; Svensson 1998), but it is the one that archaeologists have found most congenial. The household has even been associated with a mode of production, the domestic or household mode of production, and its ability to generate surplus evaluated in the context of evolutionary models of social and political change (Costin 1991; Saitta 1984).

Archaeology's long-standing interest in economic processes and its focus on material remains, among which dwellings often figure prominently, provided the original impetus behind household archaeology (Wilk and Rathje 1982a, 1982b). Household archaeology has become a prolific area of investigation applied to ancient, past, and historical societies in many world areas. The bulk of this household-related research has been carried out by North American–trained archaeologists writing in English, with some research by European and Latin

American scholars also evident (see Allison 1999; Ashmore and Wilk 1988; Haugen 1987; Hendon 1996, 2004; MacEachern et al. 1989; Manzanilla 1990; Robin 2003; Santley and Hirth 1993; Smith 1993; Svensson 1998).

The household's rise to prominence may be traced in part to increasing dissatisfaction with attempts to identify patterns of descent, postmarital residence, and other staples of kinship analysis archaeologically. Its rise relates to the move away from kinship studies and the questioning of commonly used definitions of the family in anthropology (Netting et al. 1984; Yanagisako 1979). These critiques did not eliminate the need to study the economic and social relations and activities of small-scale groups, but they demonstrated convincingly that anthropologists could not assume these people formed a family and would not be able to answer their research questions by focusing only on descent, genealogy, and kinship (Bender 1967; Carter 1984).

The lower level of interest by archaeologists trained outside the North American tradition in applying the term "household" or in identifying their work as household archaeology does not mean that they ignore dwellings or are uninterested in questions of domestic relations and activities, including those connected to gender. Archaeologists have discussed dwellings, *unidades domesticas* or *habitacionales*, *la maisonnée*, or the *oikos* without worrying so much about the need to distinguish between families and households that has affected British and American sociologists or cultural anthropologists (Forest 1997; Goldberg 1999; Hingley 1990; Manzanilla 1986, 1990; Nevett 1999; Svensson 1998; Uruñuela and Plunket Nagoda 1998).

Debated Elements of the Definition of the Household

Coresidence

As might be expected when social scientists attempt to turn a folk concept dominant in their own social and cultural milieu into a systematic and widely applicable analytical concept, these elements of economic interdependence, coresidence, and domesticity have been debated and disputed. Cultural anthropologists have given a great deal of attention to the question of coresidence. Anthropology's commitment to making visible the variety of social arrangements across cultures makes it less comfortable with standard sociological definitions of the household as "one or more people who share common living circumstances, especially in sharing a dwelling and/or facilities for preparing food" (Johnson 2000:145) or "a single person or group sharing living accommodation" (Abercrombie et al. 2000:166). According to Jane Guyer (1997:245),

> "Household" derives from the English version of feudalism, where each "holding" (of land) was identified with a house and its inhabitants, which was geographically fixed and had some social permanence. . . . Although most societies have domestic groups of some kind, only some have this particular institution, and the English term "household" translates poorly [into other languages].

In some societies, people sharing residential space may not constitute an economic unit or share responsibility for domestic tasks. Economic and social connections and responsibilities may be organized in ways that link together people living not only apart from one another but at some distance as well (Guyer 1981; Netting et al. 1984; Yanagisako 1979). Two possible solutions to the problems of definition and generalizability have been proposed. One is to accept that the term "household" must be defined using some other criteria than residence (Carter 1984; Netting et al. 1984; Wilk and Rathje 1982b). The other is to suggest that the definition of "household" be restricted to "economic units based on common residence" (Guyer 1997:245). These solutions clearly have different consequences. The first approach retains the household as a universal type of social formation or institution but requires that the details of residential organization be specified for each situation. The second affirms the association between the social institution and a particular spatial location but rejects the assumption that the household may be seen as a universal as well as fundamental social formation present in every society. The household becomes historically contingent rather than an ideal type.

In an early discussion of the usefulness of the household to archaeologists, Richard Wilk and William Rathje (1982b) viewed the household as universal but cautioned against assuming coresidence—although they noted the connection often does pertain. Most archaeologists engaged in household archaeology have adopted this viewpoint while ignoring the caution. At best, they acknowledge the issue but set it aside because they do not see how they would study a social group in the absence of some identifiable spatial locus. Guyer's definition provides an effective alternative perspective that moves archaeology's focus on residential space or propinquity beyond mere expediency. If the household is historical and cultural, not ontological or universal, then the archaeologist must evaluate the probability of the existence of a household society (or a society with households) by asking whether the group living in the dwelling or residential space constitutes an economic unit (Hendon 2004).

Domesticity, Public/Private, and Household Relations

The economic role of the household is generally defined in terms of production, consumption, and allocation of resources (Guyer 1981). Its status as a unit implies that household members do not act solely on the basis of their individual wants or desires. Instead, they cooperate with one another in order to benefit the group through mechanisms of sharing and by making decisions that put the group first. While economists are generally content to subsume all this under the rubric of economic behavior, it is clear to anthropologists that we are really talking about a set of social relations and structures through which economic tasks and relations are enacted and justified. Household economics are not merely a set of behaviors. "While a household can be defined by the activities it performs and by its shape and size, it can also be defined as a symbolic entity" (Netting et al. 1984:xxix). Anthony Carter (1984:47) has referred to these activities as "culturally recognized tasks," those shared economic and social activities that are culturally recognized as the province of the coresidential domestic group. Responsibility for the enactment of these tasks becomes central to why people define themselves as a group that we would label households.

An important part of the economic and social purpose of the household are domestic tasks and responsibilities, making the household the locus of domestic labor. Like household, domestic is a folk or "commonsense" category that social scientists have taken over for analytical purposes (Wilk and Netting 1984). In the process, specification of the meaning of domestic tasks has been debated in much the same way as the definition of household. As noted previously, social reproduction, including childbearing and child rearing, and food preparation on behalf of all household members are often taken as the minimal elements of domestic tasks (Yanagisako 1979). Both sociologists and anthropologists have pointed out that responsibilities for raising children may be organized in other ways involving people who do not live together and who do not form an economic unit. Some households may in fact not contain children at all and may never have done so. People who are coresident may not have share food together or expect that someone is responsible for preparing food for all to share. Once again, the expectation that it should be possible to create a clearly defined ideal type that does not overlap with other types of social institutions or groups is confounded by the realities of the historical and cultural variety documented by anthropology, sociology, and social history. On the other hand, as with economic production more generally, food production and consumption are activities that archaeologists can identify through the material record.

A more serious problem with the concept of the domestic has been raised by feminist scholars in several disciplines. Because domestic activities in capitalist economies are subsumed under the term "housekeeping," are "stereotyped as nonproductive" (Wilk and Netting 1984:6–7), and are unremunerated, they are often assumed to be irrelevant to an understanding of larger-scale social or political structures or developments. They may even be seen as an uninteresting aspect of the household's economic function. Bender (1967:498–99) notes that "as a folk concept, our term 'domestic' refers to those activities associated with the household or the home. Furthermore, it connotes female activities more than male activities." If this folk concept is not examined critically, the household risks becoming "an analytical heading that tends to submerge women and their work within undifferentiated, closed household organizational systems" (Netting et al. 1984:xxv).

This assumption has also been propped up by the adoption by anthropologists of another folk concept, one that has its roots in nineteenth-century middle-class Euro-American values. It has been used to create an analytical division of society into separate domains, the domestic and the political or politico-jural, or private and public spheres of activity:

> Underlying the politico-jural domain are jural norms guaranteed by "external" or "public" sanctions which may ultimately entail force. In contrast, the domestic . . . domain is constrained by "private" affective and moral norms, at the root of which is the fundamental axiom of prescriptive altruism. (Yanagisako 1979:187)

Early work by feminist anthropologists accepted this division and used women's restriction to the domestic sphere and their symbolic association with hearth, home, and reproduction to explain women's universal subordination (e.g., Ortner 1974; Rosaldo 1974). The work by Sherry Ortner and Michelle Rosaldo sparked a great deal of research by feminist scholars, resulting in the realization that these ideas can be situated in a particular historical and cultural context out of which much anthropological and historical research has come but that does not necessarily apply to the societies being studied (Marti 1993; Ortner 1996; Reverby and Helly 1992; Rosaldo 1980; Silverblatt 1995; Wylie 1992). Once again, a set of contingent ideas was generalized into a universal contrast: "women everywhere dominated by men [and] everywhere inhabiting a separate social domain" (di Leonardo 1991:229).

These issues have created something of a quandary for feminist scholars and those interested in gender. By using the household as the focus of research on women, is one merely reinforcing existing stereotypes on women's place in society or perpetuating the naive extension of Victorian ideals about womanhood and female nature that have found their way into analytical models of society? At the same time, it is clear that people's involvement in household relations and activities can form an important part of their daily life and play a role in how they give meaning to their lived experience. Thus, any interest in the study of what people did a lot of the time requires some consideration of household-level action and interaction. Furthermore, practice-based approaches to the study of society suggest that all action is meaningful, not just what takes place in particular social contexts or spatial settings (Bourdieu 1977).

Moreover, the ability to define households in part through a particular spatial setting has proved enormously productive for the project of engendering and enpeopling the past. Thus, like most archaeologists, those focused on the study of gender have continued to endorse a framework that views society as made up of different arenas of social action that are often associated with distinctive areas of the built environment or the landscape. These areas provide a setting in which people interact; although the associations between kind of setting and kinds of interactions are to some degree fluid and variable, it is nevertheless the case that particular configurations may be established (see Tringham 1994, 1995). Focusing on one such area or social formation, such as the dwelling area or the household, does not imply that households are best studied in isolation from the larger society of which they are a part (Beaudry 1984; Haugen 1987; Hendon 2002). Such a focus does indicate that something worthwhile may be learned by considering the particular social scale and set of relationships. The issue is not so much the labels employed but the meanings connected with those labels that impede understanding. While studying households could do no more than result in a conservative reification of women's apolitical status (e.g., Hayden 1992), gendered research has in fact for the most part worked against this point of view by asking, What is the nature of the relations among members of these culturally defined task groups?

Social Action and Interaction at the Household Level

Gender Attribution

Research focused on practice and political economy insists on a close engagement with the material record and its meaning. The cultural logic of households may be carried out through the study of the "mutually constituting" (Birdwell-Pheasant and Lawrence-Zúñiga 1999:4) relationship between houses, people, action, material culture, and meaning, or practice. In what ways does gender organize production and give meaning to social action as part of a process that produces not only material goods but also social relations and identities? This question was first approached by focusing on gender attribution, or the identification of activities associated with women carried out in a household setting.

A division of labor by gender (and age) is a common organizational mechanism for households, but what is actually done varies. Central to an identification of "women's work" is an understanding of how cultural expectations about gender make salient or emphasize certain forms of action as gendered. Like any archaeologist attempting to address interpretive questions, gender-focused archaeologists have used those mainstays of the discipline, specific and general analogy. Multiple lines of evidence for particular societies or time periods, including written sources, visual imagery, and burial practices, have been employed to determine what kinds of activities were women expected to engage in and with which they were associated (Allison 2003; Axelsson 1999; Costin 1996; Dommasnes 1987; Goldberg 1999; Hegmon et al. 2000; Hendon 1997; Malan 1997; Mills 2000; Nevett 1999; VanDerwarker and Detweiler 2002; Wall 2000; Wood 2002). Such lines of evidence are not always available, of course, but when they are, they have proved extremely helpful in identifying some range of activities that were given significance as female work. Research on preconquest Mesoamerican societies, for example, has noted the insistent association between female gender and cloth production in indigenous and European writings and in a variety of large- and small-scale forms of visual representation (Brumfiel 1991, 1996; Hendon 1997; Joyce 1993, 2000a). Such associations do not preclude variation based on social status or assume that all women did was weave. In fact, a range of activities and occupations are attested for women (Hendon 1999), and practices such as farming required the participation of all household members in patterned ways (Robin 2002a). These associations do create a cultural expectation that has implications for what socially defined women did in the course of their daily lives.

The identification of weaving as a gendered process does not even mandate that only individuals who we would recognize as biologically female engaged in these activities. Spindle whorls, taken as a marker of involvement in cloth production and female gender, have been found in some burials in Mesoamerica containing skeletons sexed as biologically male. Elizabeth Brumfiel (2001) has suggested that such burials at the site of Cholula reflect the impact of a historical process, the increasing tribute demands of the Aztec state that required households or communities to bring more people into the production system. Since gender is a social construct, it does not necessarily equate with biological sex (itself not as independent of cultural expectations as often assumed), and participation by biological males does not by itself call into question the association of female gender and textile production. While the participation by males may masculinize a formerly feminine technology, it is equally possible that the participants may become feminized through their adoption of a particular productive role or that the gender associations may be unaffected; it all depends on the cultural, social, and historical context (see Lerman et al. 2003).

Gender attribution research has also looked to the possibility of more general associations between women and domestic tasks as a way to augment or substitute for culturally or historically specific information. The search for such associations is fraught with the potential for reification of our own assumptions about women and folk notions about domesticity discussed earlier. However, cross-cultural comparison has provided strong support for an association between women and certain kinds of food preparation (for fuller discussion, see Crown 2000c; Mills 2000). In reviewing research on gender and the household, what does emerge is a high degree of self-awareness on the part of the researchers about the importance of supporting claims for gendered work or activities through a careful process of analogy and analysis.

Gender and Space

An important consequence of efforts to identify material correlates of women's and men's activities has been to seriously call into question notions of male and female space. The idea that certain parts of a dwelling area or the social landscape more generally may have strong symbolic associations with gender is not in itself problematic (Low and Lawrence-Zúñiga 2003). However, application of this possibility has generally been informed by an unreflexive structuralism that assumes the existence of binary opposition between male and female space that does not take into account how meaning is created through practice in a dynamic and often spatialized process. Static assumptions about gendered space have also led to simplistic notions of how such space would be used, notions contradicted by studies of spatial associations. Lisa Nevett's (1999) analysis of the distribution of female-associated artifacts in houses at Olynthos, Greece, combined with a study of other sources of information such as vase paintings, has led her to take issue with the standard interpretation of written sources. She argues that female members of the *oikos*, or household, were not confined to one section of the house, nor did men and women occupy separate quarters while at home:

> Women were present throughout the house as their activities required, and . . . there was no need for a specific room to be set aside for them. This does not exclude the possibility that certain areas would have been more frequented by the female members of the household than others. . . . There is, however, a conceptual difference between suggesting that an area was specifically set aside for the use of women, and that it was habitually used by them. (Nevett 1999:71)

Marilyn Goldberg's (1999) examination of the Athenian house and household agrees with Nevett's conclusions. Goldberg's analysis also raises the issue of who controls the attempt to propagate certain kinds of behaviors or attitudes as societal norms. She notes that the written sources tell us about power relations between men and women and about the attitudes of elite, educated men in Athenian society as they do about the use of space. Archaeological evidence, however, indicates that these attitudes and relations did not result in women living in seclusion. Studying space as a dynamic arena in which concepts of gender are negotiated and defined through practice, as opposed to representing some fixed deep structure, allows archaeologists to consider questions of power and multiple meanings (Moore 1996).

The use of domestic space has also been addressed for the pre-Columbian Maya through the study of dwelling areas of high-status elites and farmers. In a study of the distribution of weaving tools and food preparation activities, especially corn grinding, in an elite residential area at Copan, Honduras, I found that

> women ground maize, cooked, wove, or spun in close proximity to those people, male or female, who manufactured obsidian tools, shell ornaments, or bone items, and carried out rituals. . . . Such differences cannot be used to define a symbolically meaningful segregated "women's space."
> . . . In other words, the gendering of space achieves cultural significance only in certain contexts. . . . During the Classic period, it is public space under the control of the ruler which is most visibly gendered. (Hendon 1997:42–44)

Work on the location of women's activities at the farming hamlet of Ceren, El Salvador, by Tracy Sweely (1999a) argues for some separation of activities by function that may in turn have led to members of the same gender interacting frequently as when women gathered to grind corn. Distribution of spinning and weaving tools and materials between houses at the site also suggests that some households may have been specializing in the production of certain kinds of thread or cloth (Beaudry-Corbett and McCafferty 2002). Both studies, however, show no patterns of spatial exclusion or restriction by gender. Research on another Maya farming community, Chan Noohol in Belize, confirms the lack of restriction or exclusion by gender. Based on artifact and ecofact associations and soil chemistry analysis, Cynthia Robin (2002a, 2002b) has identified open-air work areas near houses and agricultural areas:

> People who were making tools and people who were preparing food were doing these activities in the same space, regardless of whether or not they were the same or different people or whether they were working there simultaneously or sequentially. . . . People who were involved in agriculture were able to see, talk, or call to people who were preparing food and making stone tools. (Robin 2002a:29)

Engendering Production and Consumption

While gender attribution studies have been fundamental to the development of an engendered household, they represent only one part of the process. The fact that we cannot divvy up all possible tasks by gender has led some to assume that we cannot discuss gender in the absence of unequivocal attributions. If activities do not fall neatly into a male or female sphere of operation or if a supposedly female activity is performed by men under some circumstances or if the archaeological data are ambiguous, this naive perspective assumes that all is lost. But this perspective also assumes that the only goal is to identify what specific women did at specific points in time in specific places.

If, however, we attempt to consider issues of time, labor, and scale of production in order to understand how gender, as a set of ideas, can be a fundamental organizing principle, we move beyond the identification of who did what to modeling the consequences of household-level choices or needs for its members of all genders. Economic production by household members when it occurs at home often involves other members. Rita Wright's (1991) study of pottery production in South Asia demonstrates how certain household members, in this case adult males, may be seen as "the potters"; that is to say, making pottery is their occupation. At the same time, others (here adult females and children) carry out crucial roles in the production process on a regular basis. Similar assistance by Aztec men and children in home-based cloth production made them integral to the process but did not make them weavers (Hicks 1994). Barbara Mills (2000:306) argues that "the probability that more members of the household participated in the production activity can be scaled according to increasing intensity of production." She suggests that changes in the scale or location of production may be used to argue for more or less gendered organization. Such changes may carry important implications for the allocation of people's time, skill, and energy. The development of pottery vessels and their adoption as the main food-processing and storage containers in the American Southwest meant that women's workloads increased as they took on responsibility for the preparation of different kinds of foods or different preparation techniques as well as the production of the containers themselves (Crown 2000c; Crown and Wills 1995). Brumfiel (1991) has noted how food habits changed in Mexico under Aztec rule during a time of increased tribute demands on households. The shift to meals based on corn tortillas rather than stews or porridge made more work for women even as they had to increase their weaving output. But the use of tortillas made for foods that were more transportable and allowed at least some household members to work away from home as part of their tribute obligations.

Identifying and interpreting actions relating to production and consumption by household members thus becomes crucial to an understanding of how household members interacted with one another, negotiated their identities, and formed part of larger spatial, social, and political groups. In many societies, past and present, the dwelling area is frequently also the place of work. While industrialization may have created a disjunction between home and work, some forms of production continue to be associated with the home even under global capitalism. The presence of items not manufactured by the household itself in association with the dwelling has been crucial to studies of how households interacted with the larger community or other societies. Political economy models typically focus on specialized production or production for exchange and emphasize the production of what are variously known as nonutilitarian, prestige, wealth, status, or luxury goods (Brumfiel 1987; Brumfiel and Earle 1987; Costin 1991, 1993, 1996). Practice-based approaches are more likely to find relevance in the production of items of daily use, including food, as well as in the ways that production for exchange is organized (Allison 2003; Lightfoot et al. 1998; Meadows 1999; Silliman 2001). The production, exchange, and use of "ordinary goods" (Smith 1999) can be equally significant in the creation and maintenance of multiple group identities and affiliations. Historical archaeologists have focused on how the household becomes a primary locus of consumption as capitalism develops in nineteenth-century North America. Diana Wall (2000) has demonstrated how class-based issues of taste and decorum encouraged the development of consumption practices that are early forms of consumerism among women in nineteenth-century New York City even at the height of the dominance of the separate-spheres, women-as-angels-of-the-hearth ideology.

Households and Identity

An intensive focus on what people, especially women, do in a household setting undermines the assumption that the household is best approached as a unit rather than as a set of people. Central to this approach is the assumption that someone functions as a head of household who not only serves as the representative of all household members in the public sphere but also has the greatest ability to make decisions. Differences in decision-making ability, in the ability to allocate the time and labor of others, and to otherwise enforce prescriptive altruism have long been assumed to connect to differences in age, gender, and seniority within the household. Such differences may be seen as one of the most fundamental forms of inequality in society (Blanton 1995); they certainly represent a common source of disagreement and negotiation by household members (McKie et al. 1999). Feminist economists and anthropologists have asked, What is the best way to model household relations? Are they best viewed as a form of moral economy, characterized by reciprocity and altruism, or as a kind of political economy, marked by self-interest and power struggles (Cheal 1989)? The agendas and interests of people differentiated by age, gender, role, and the ability to impose their wishes do not always coincide (Collier 1974; Hart 1992; Moore 1992). Although recognizing the interdependence of household members, this scholarship has argued that cooperation may result from differences in power or may mask ways in which household members work against or counter to others. This scholarship has also questioned whether decisions are always made at the level of the household as a whole (with the implication that there is one member whose decisions carry the greatest weight).

Archaeologists have joined other social scientists in approaching the domestic group as made up of social actors differentiated by age, gender, role, and power whose agendas and interests do not always coincide (Hart 1992; Hendon 1996; Moore 1992; Wilk 1989). Hadley Kruczek-Aaron (2002) places the material remains of a nineteenth-century New York household in the context of documented disagreements between father and daughter and between family and servants. Her analysis demonstrates the degree to which household members viewed their interactions and material practices in very different ways. Households may differ in terms of how decisions are made and how much weight is put on the contributions of various members (Svensson 1998; Wilk 1989). From this perspective, the household as a collective social formation becomes something that must be actively reproduced through practice. Dwelling areas and the domestic setting are not merely neutral locations or containers for useful activities. They become a space in which and through which certain kinds of social relations and identities are defined and given prominence through meaningful action that draws on ideas about gender, age, and other variables, such as class, into socially constructed identities that were sometimes reinforced by the cultural hegemonies of the state. The effort of producing cloth by Aztec and Maya women was legitimated through an ideology that posited a complementary relationship between social identities important to the political economy of the Aztec state and Maya polities. These identities seem to balance the male gendered role of warrior with the female one of weaver. These identities were enacted through practice (including state-mandated military training and taxation), validated through periodic ritual, and idealized through visual representation.

It must be recognized that research on dwellings (as broadly defined here) provides insight into only some aspects of household activities and interactions (Fish 2000; Hendon 1997). One way that archaeologists have made creative use of this is by using the consistent material correlate provided by the dwelling area as a useful point of reference against which to contrast the meaning of the same activities occurring in different spatial contexts. Food preparation, for example, takes on a different social significance when performed away from the dwelling and has been interpreted as evidence for women's involvement in larger-scale social, religious, or political events or relationships (Hastorf 1991; Hegmon et al. 2000; Mobley-Tanaka 1997; VanDerwarker and Detwiler 2002). Analysis of plant remains from trash pits at the Coweeta Creek site, a prehistoric and protohistoric Cherokee town in North Carolina, suggests to Amber VanDerwarker and Kandace Detwiler (2002) that women prepared food in two different locations: in association with domestic structures and near the townhouse, a structure used for ritual, social, and political interactions among members of the community. Their results suggest a greater female presence in this more "public" space than might be expected given the townhouse's frequent association with male political leaders.

Historical archaeologists have shown how class and ethnic variation in the United States affected not only household composition and activities but also the values associated with these differences, with direct implications for acceptable female behavior (Spencer-Wood 1999; Wood 2002). Moreover, middle-class stereotypes (which often approached the level of racist fantasy) about how working-class and immigrant households deviated from proper forms of organization and gender roles served as one way to maintain class and ethnic (or racial) divides that had implications for employment as well as more general social attitudes. Margaret Wood's study of the mining community of Berwind, Colorado, shows that the CF & I coal company's decision to provide housing for married workers and company-supervised boardinghouses for single male employees was part of a strategy to inculcate a set of middle-class values about individualism, loyalty to the company, capitalism, and domesticity that would discourage collective action and strikes on the work front. In the process, women who had earlier contributed to household support through taking in boarders lost a vital source of income.

Prestige and Power

Underlying much of the research discussed so far has been a concern with women's status in the household and society. This concern often takes the form of a focus on prestige and power. Both of these terms are broad and subject to a range of meanings, both folk and analytical (Crown 2000a; Hendon 1999; Lamphere 2000; Ortner 1996). Rather than construe power as something certain people have or as a particular capacity, practice or political economy perspectives start from the premise that "power is an effect of the operation of social relations" (Moore 1996:205). Studying power, therefore, needs to take a multiscalar approach (O'Donovan 2002; Sweely 1999b). The household represents one level of social relations and interaction where differences in relations of power are enacted not only through the control of such tangible factors as material resources or labor (Blanton 1995) but also through the identities that are defined and inscribed through routinized quotidian and periodic action, much of which occurs as part of household daily practice (Joyce 2000a, 2000b; Kokkinidou and Nikolaidou 1997; Robin 2002b; Tringham 1994).

Considering power dynamics within the household or at the scale of the household may yield insights into how households or certain household members acquired or reproduced social status or economic wealth in the larger context of their community or society. Feasting has become a focus of archaeological theorizing on these issues because it provides a mechanism for creating enduring social obligations between individuals or groups that involve the transfer of material resources. Such transfers and obligations raise the possibility of accumulation or control of surplus. Control may in turn lead to more permanent forms of inequality (Bray 2003; Dietler and Hayden 2001). Successful feasts require the ability to mobilize the labor of many people, both men and women. The gender dynamics of these occasions have begun to be an important area of study and offer the possibility of deepening our understanding of household relations (Fung 1995; Gero 1991; Hendon 2003).

Discussion of power frequently considers not just what people were able to do but also how social roles, action, or identities were accorded greater value or significance. As with power, consideration of prestige has moved from assuming a single form of evaluation or ranking to a perspective that sees prestige structures as multiple and based on a variety of forms of social evaluation (Hendon 1999). Gender is a frequent factor in such systems of evaluation although not the only one. It is not unusual for certain forms of prestige to be hegemonic and given more visibility with society as a whole; at the same time, counterhegemonic structures may develop in the same society that resist the hegemonic ones (Lamphere 2000). Patricia Crown and Suzanne Fish (1996) postulate that Hohokam women's status changed over time based in part on the enclosure of patios and houses, making these day-to-day activities less visible. Under these circumstances, houses and the domestic setting become not just a neutral location for activities but also a space within which certain kinds of social relations and identities are defined, created, and emphasized through meaningful action. The connection between visibility and status in southwestern Native American societies is further developed by Michelle Hegmon, Scott Ortman, and Jeannette Mobley-Tanaka (Hegmon et al. 2000) in a discussion of how gendered differences in status and prestige may be reflected in and created by the location and spatial setting of various activities or events. Their analysis attempts to assess autonomy, prestige, and power, and they find that women's autonomy seems to decrease as social hierarchies become more entrenched; thus, some women were of high status but had relatively less autonomy. Although, as the authors acknowledge, the apparent negative relationship between autonomy and prestige may be in part an artifact of how they have defined these terms, their study shows a careful attention to how the complexities of social status may be reflected in daily practice.

Participation in ritual events or exclusion from ritual spaces has emerged as one aspect of social life that archaeologists focus on when considering status. Of particular interest has been whether women were excluded from "public" ritual occasions or nondomestic ritual spaces, such as the Cherokee townhouse mentioned previously. Sweely's (1999a) Ceren data lead her to conclude that women were not excluded from ritual structures. Hegmon et al. (2000) note the association between kivas, subterranean ritual structures, and corn-grinding areas or rooms as suggestive of women's involvement in ritual life (see also Mobley-Tanaka 1997).

Concluding Thoughts

Out of this body of research and debate, it is possible to extract an archaeologically useful and empirically valid definition of the household: a coresident domestic group that functions as an economic unit in that the relations and interactions of its members provide a way to organize production, allocate resources, and structure consumption. These activities sustain household members by providing them access to resources. Production and consumption refers to something as basic as alimentation but does not stop there. Furthermore, the kinds of productive and consumptive activities may vary among households in the same society since other factors may affect household size, composition, and responsibilities. Households are, after all, only one kind of social formation, and membership in a household does not represent the only group to which its members may belong or associate themselves with. Household size and composition within a society may be affected by social status, wealth, class, occupation, seasonal cycles, or other factors.

In reviewing recent scholarship on the household and gender for this chapter, four themes emerge as central. One theme is the identification, meaning, and significance, both socially and economically, of women's activities. Another is the debate over the very existence of a division into public and private spheres of society and, if such a division reflects some social reality, what is its meaning. A third theme is the study of the economic and social implications of women's participation in production and consumption of goods and resources. The final theme considers the factors affecting or contributing to women's prestige, status, or power in society. These four themes are overlapping and interdependent. All are ultimately concerned with the social (and political) implications of economic activities. All assume a connection between social identity, action, and the location of that action. All take as a starting assumption that women's social position is likely to be different from that of men, but all are interested in complicating and disrupting facile claims of universal female subordination. And all share a conviction in the value of studying actions and interactions formerly considered too small in scale, too common in occurrence, and too intimate in psychological affect to contribute to models of social evolution or the explanation of culture change.

References

Abercrombie, Nicholas, Stephen Hill, and Bryan S. Turner
    2000   *The Penguin Dictionary of Sociology*. 4th ed. London: Penguin.
Allison, Penelope M., ed.
    1999   *The Archaeology of Household Activities*. London: Routledge.
Allison, Penelope M.
    2003   The Old Kinchega Homestead: Doing Household Archaeology in Outback New South Wales, Australia. *International Journal of Historical Archaeology* 7:161–94.
Ashmore, Wendy, and Richard R. Wilk
    1988   Household and Community in the Mesoamerican Past. In *Household and Com-*

munity in the Mesoamerican Past. Richard R. Wilk and Wendy Ashmore, eds. Pp. 1–27. Albuquerque: University of New Mexico Press.

Axelsson, Susanne
    1999 "Peopling" the Farm: Engendering Life at a Swedish Iron Age Settlement. In *From the Ground Up: Beyond Gender Theory in Archaeology*. Nancy L. Wicker and Bettina Arnold, eds. Pp. 93–102. BAR International Series 812. Oxford: Archaeopress.

Beaudry, Mary C.
    1984 Archaeology and the Historical Household. *Man in the Northeast* 28:27–38.

Beaudry-Corbett, Marilyn, and Sharisse McCafferty
    2002 Spindle Whorls: Household Specialization at Ceren. In *Ancient Maya Women*. Traci Ardren, ed. Pp. 52–67. Walnut Creek, CA: AltaMira Press.

Bender, Donald R.
    1967 A Refinement of the Concept of Household: Families, Co-Residence, and Domestic Function. *American Anthropologist* 69:493–504.

Bertelsen, Reidar, Arnvid Lillehammer, and Jenny-Rita Næss, eds.
    1987 *Were They All Men? An Examination of Sex Roles in Prehistoric Society*. Stavanger: Arkeologisk Museum.

Birdwell-Pheasant, Donna, and Denise Lawrence-Zúñiga
    1999 Introduction: Houses and Families in Europe. In *House Life: Space, Place and Family in Europe*. Donna Birdwell-Pheasant and Denise Lawrence-Zúñiga, eds. Pp. 1–35. Oxford: Berg.

Blanton, Richard E.
    1995 The Cultural Foundations of Inequality in Households. In *Foundations of Social Inequality*. T. Douglas Price and Gary M. Feinman, eds. Pp. 105–27. New York: Plenum.

Bourdieu, Pierre
    1977 *Outline of a Theory of Practice*. Richard Nice, trans. Cambridge: Cambridge University Press.

Bray, Tamara L., ed.
    2003 *The Archaeology and Politics of Food and Feasting in Early States and Empires*. New York: Kluwer Academic/Plenum.

Brumfiel, Elizabeth M.
    1987 Consumption and Politics at Aztec Huexotla. *American Anthropologist* 89:676–86.
    1991 Weaving and Cooking: Women's Production in Aztec Mexico. In *Engendering Archaeology: Women and Prehistory*. Joan M. Gero and Margaret W. Conkey, eds. Pp. 224–51. Oxford: Basil Blackwell.
    1992 Breaking and Entering the Ecosystem—Gender, Class, and Faction Steal the Show. *American Anthropologist* 94:551–67.
    1996 Figurines and the Aztec State: Testing the Effectiveness of Ideological Domi-

nation. In *Gender and Archaeology*. Rita P. Wright, ed. Pp. 143–66. Philadelphia: University of Pennsylvania Press.

2001 Asking about Aztec Gender: The Historical and Archaeological Evidence. In *Gender in Pre-Hispanic America*. Cecelia F. Klein, ed. Pp. 57–85. Washington, DC: Dumbarton Oaks.

Brumfiel, Elizabeth M., and Timothy K. Earle
1987 Specialization, Exchange, and Complex Societies: An Introduction. In *Specialization, Exchange, and Complex Societies*. Elizabeth M. Brumfiel and Timothy K. Earle, eds. Pp. 1–9. Cambridge: Cambridge University Press.

Carter, Anthony T.
1984 Household Histories. In *Households: Comparative and Historical Studies of the Domestic Group*. Robert M. Netting, Richard M. Wilk, and Eric J. Arnould, eds. Pp. 44-83. Berkeley: University of California Press.

Cheal, David
1989 Strategies of Resource Management in Household Economies: Moral Economy or Political Economy? In *The Household Economy: Reconsidering the Domestic Mode of Production*. Richard R. Wilk, ed. Pp. 11–22. Boulder, CO: Westview.

Collier, Jane F.
1974 Women in Politics. In *Woman, Culture, and Society*. Michelle Z. Rosaldo and Louise Lamphere, eds. Pp. 89–96. Palo Alto, CA: Stanford University Press.

Costin, Cathy L.
1991 Craft Specialization: Issues in Defining, Documenting, and Explaining the Organization of Production. *Archaeological Method and Theory* 3:1–56.
1993 Textiles, Women, and Political Economy in Late Prehispanic Peru. *Research in Economic Anthropology* 14:3–28.
1996 Exploring the Relationship between Gender and Craft in Complex Societies: Methodological and Theoretical Issues of Gender Attribution. In *Gender and Archaeology*. Rita P. Wright, ed. Pp. 111–40. Philadelphia: University of Pennsylvania Press.

Cowgill, George L.
1993 Beyond Criticizing New Archeology. *American Anthropologist* 95:551–73.

Crown, Patricia L.
2000a Gendered Tasks, Power, and Prestige in the Prehispanic American Southwest. In *Women and Men in the Prehispanic Southwest: Labor, Power, and Prestige*. Patricia L. Crown, ed. Pp. 3–41. Santa Fe, NM: School of American Research Press.

Crown, Patricia L., ed.
2000b *Women and Men in the Prehispanic Southwest: Labor, Power, and Prestige*. Santa Fe, NM: School of American Research Press.

Crown, Patricia L.
2000c Women's Role in Changing Cuisine. In *Women and Men in the Prehispanic Southwest: Labor, Power, and Prestige*. Patricia L. Crown, ed. Pp. 221–66. Santa Fe, NM: School of American Research Press.

Crown, Patricia L., and Suzanne K. Fish
  1996   Gender and Status in the Hohokam Pre-Classic to Classic Tradition. *American Anthropologist* 98:803–17.
Crown, Patricia L., and W. H. Wills
  1995   The Origins of Southwestern Ceramic Containers: Women's Time Allocation and Economic Intensification. *Journal of Anthropological Research* 51:173–86.
Dietler, Michael, and Brian Hayden, eds.
  2001   *Feasts*. Washington, DC: Smithsonian Institution Press.
di Leonardo, Micaela
  1991   Women's Culture and Its Discontents. In *The Politics of Culture*. Brett Williams, ed. Pp. 219–42. Washington, DC: Smithsonian Institution Press.
Dommasnes, Liv Helga
  1987   Male/Female Roles and Ranks in Late Iron Age Norway. In *Were They All Men? An Examination of Sex Roles in Prehistoric Society*. Reidar Bertelsen, Arnvid Lillehammer, and Jenny-Rita Næss, eds. Pp. 65–77. Stavanger: Arkeologisk Museum.
Fish, Suzanne K.
  2000   Farming, Foraging, and Gender. In *Women and Men in the Prehispanic Southwest: Labor, Power, and Prestige*. Patricia L. Crown, ed. Pp. 169–96. Santa Fe, NM: School of American Research Press.
Forest, Jean Daniel
  1997   Maison, maisonnée et structure sociale en Mésopotamie préhistorique (6è–4è millénaire). *al-Rafidan* 18:81–91.
Fung, Christopher D.
  1995   Domestic Labor, Gender and Power on the Mesoamerican Frontier. In *Debating Complexity*. Proceedings of the 26th Annual Chacmool Conference. D. Meyer, P. Dawson, and D. Hanna, eds. Pp. 65–75. Calgary: Chacmool Archaeological Association.
Gero, Joan M.
  1991   Who Experienced What in Prehistory? A Narrative Explanation from Queyash, Peru. In *Processual and Postprocessual Archaeologies: Multiple Ways of Knowing the Past*. Robert W. Preucel, ed. Pp. 126–39. Occasional Paper 10. Carbondale: Center for Archaeological Investigations, Southern Illinois University.
Goldberg, Marilyn Y.
  1999   Spatial and Behavioural Negotiation in Classical Athenian City Houses. In *The Archaeology of Household Activities*. Penelope M. Allison, ed. Pp. 142–61. London: Routledge.
Guyer, Jane I.
  1981   Household and Community in African Studies. *African Studies Review* 24(2/3):87–137.
  1997   Households. In *The Dictionary of Anthropology*. Thomas Barfield, ed. Pp. 245–46. Oxford: Blackwell.

Hart, Gillian
  1992   Imagined Unities: Constructions of "the Household" in Economic Theory. In *Understanding Economic Processes*. Sutti Ortiz and Susan Lees, eds. Pp. 111–29. Monograph in Economic Anthropology 10. Lanham, MD: University Press of America.

Hastorf, Christine A.
  1991   Gender, Space, and Food in Prehistory. In *Engendering Archaeology: Women and Prehistory*. Joan M. Gero and Margaret W. Conkey, eds. Pp. 132–59. Oxford: Basil Blackwell.

Haugen, Inger
  1987   Concentrating on Women: Introduction to a Debate in Social Anthropology. In *Were They All Men? An Examination of Sex Roles in Prehistoric Society*. Reidar Bertelsen, Arnvid Lillehammer, and Jenny-Rita Næss, eds. Pp. 15–21. Stavanger: Arkeologisk Museum.

Hayden, Brian
  1992   Observing Prehistoric Women. In *Exploring Gender through Archaeology: Selected Papers from the 1991 Boone Conference*. Cheryl Claassen, ed. Pp. 33–47. Monographs in World Prehistory 11. Madison, WI: Prehistory Press.

Hegmon, Michelle, Scott G. Ortman, and Jeannette L. Mobley-Tanaka
  2000   Women, Men, and the Organization of Space. In *Women and Men in the Prehispanic Southwest: Labor, Power, and Prestige*. Patricia L. Crown, ed. Pp. 43–90. Santa Fe, NM: School of American Research Press.

Hendon, Julia A.
  1996   Archaeological Approaches to the Organization of Domestic Labor: Household Practice and Domestic Relations. *Annual Review of Anthropology* 25:45–61.
  1997   Women's Work, Women's Space and Women's Status among the Classic Period Maya Elite of the Copan Valley, Honduras. In *Women in Prehistory: North America and Mesoamerica*. Cheryl Claassen and Rosemary A. Joyce, eds. Pp. 33–46. Philadelphia: University of Pennsylvania Press.
  1999   Multiple Sources of Prestige and the Social Evaluation of Women in Prehispanic Mesoamerica. In *Material Symbols: Culture and Economy in Prehistory*. John E. Robb, ed. Pp. 257–76. Occasional Paper 26. Carbondale: Center for Archaeological Investigations, Southern Illinois University.
  2002   Social Relations and Collective Identities: Household and Community in Ancient Mesoamerica. In *The Dynamics of Power*. Maria O'Donovan, ed. Pp. 273–300. Occasional Paper 30. Carbondale: Center for Archaeological Investigations, Southern Illinois University.
  2003   Feasting at Home: Community and House Solidarity among the Maya of Southeastern Mesoamerica. In *The Archaeology and Politics of Food and Feasting in Early States and Empires*. Tamara L. Bray, ed. Pp. 203–33. New York: Kluwer Academic/Plenum.
  2004   Living and Working at Home: The Social Archaeology of Household Pro-

duction and Social Relations. In *A Companion to Social Archaeology*. Lynn Meskell and Robert W. Preucel, eds. Pp. 272–86. Malden, MA: Blackwell.

Hicks, Frederic
    1994   Cloth in the Political Economy of the Aztec State. In *Economies and Polities in the Aztec Realm*. Mary G. Hodge and Michael E. Smith, eds. Pp. 89–111. Albany: Institute for Mesoamerican Studies, State University of New York.

Hingley, Richard
    1990   Domestic Organisation and Gender Relations in Iron Age and Roman-British Households. In *The Social Archaeology of Houses*. Ross Samson, ed. Pp. 125–47. Edinburgh: Edinburgh University Press.

Johnson, Allan G.
    2000   *The Blackwell Dictionary of Sociology*. 2nd ed. Malden, MA: Blackwell.

Joyce, Rosemary A.
    1993   Women's Work: Images of Production and Reproduction in Pre-Hispanic Southern Central America. *Current Anthropology* 34:255–74.
    2000a   *Gender and Power in Prehispanic Mesoamerica*. Austin: University of Texas Press.
    2000b   Girling the Girl and Boying the Boy: The Production of Adulthood in Ancient Mesoamerica. *World Archaeology* 31:4/3–83.

Joyce, Rosemary A., and Cheryl Claassen
    1997   Women in the Ancient Americas: Archaeologists, Gender, and the Making of Prehistory. In *Women in Prehistory: North American and Mesoamerica*. Cheryl Claassen and Rosemary A. Joyce, eds. Pp. 1–14. Philadelphia: University of Pennsylvania Press.

Kokkinidou, Dimitra, and Marianna Nikolaidou
    1997   Body Imagery in the Aegean Neolithic: Ideological Implications of Anthropomorphic Figurines. In *Invisible People and Processes: Writing Gender and Childhood into European Archaeology*. Jenny Moore and Eleanor Scott, eds. Pp. 88–112. London: Leicester University Press.

Kruczek-Aaron, Hadley
    2002   Choice Flowers and Well-Ordered Tables: Struggling over Gender in a Nineteenth-Century Household. *International Journal of Historical Archaeology* 6:173–85.

Lamphere, Louise
    2000   Gender Models in the Southwest: A Sociocultural Perspective. In *Women and Men in the Prehispanic Southwest: Labor, Power, and Prestige*. Patricia L. Crown, ed. Pp. 379–401. Santa Fe, NM: School of American Research Press.

Lerman, Nina E., Ruth Oldenziel, and Arwen P. Mohun
    2003   Introduction: Interrogating Boundaries. In *Gender and Technology*. Nina E. Lerman, Ruth Oldenziel, and Arwen P. Mohun, eds. Pp. 1–9. Baltimore: The Johns Hopkins University Press.

Lightfoot, Kent, Antoinette Martinez, and Ann M. Schiff
    1998   Daily Practice and Material Culture in Pluralistic Social Settings: An Archae-

ological Study of Culture Change and Persistence from Fort Ross, California. *American Antiquity* 63:199–222.

Low, Setha M., and Denise Lawrence-Zúñiga
  2003 Locating Culture. In *The Anthropology of Space and Place: Locating Culture*. Setha M. Low and Denise Lawrence-Zúñiga, eds. Pp. 1–47. Malden, MA: Blackwell.

MacEachern, Scott, D. J. W. Archer, and R. D. Garvin, eds.
  1989 *Households and Communities*. Proceedings of the 21st Annual Chacmool Conference. Calgary: Department of Archaeology, University of Calgary.

Malan, Antonia
  1997 The Material World of Family and Household. In *Our Gendered Past: Archaeological Studies of Gender in Southern Africa*. Lyn Wadley, ed. Pp. 273–301. Johannesburg: Witwatersrand University Press.

Manzanilla, Linda, ed.
  1986 *Unidades habitacionales mesoamericanas y sus áreas de actividad*. Mexico City: Instituto de Investigaciones Antropológicas, UNAM.

Manzanilla, Linda
  1990 Niveles de análisis en el estudio de unidades habitacionales. *Revista Española de Antropología Americana* 20:9–18.

Marti, Judith
  1993 Introduction. In *The Other Fifty Percent: Multicultural Perspectives on Gender Relations*. Mari Womack and Judith Marti, eds. Pp. 179–83. Prospect Heights, IL: Waveland.

McKie, Linda, Sophia Bowlby, and Susan Gregory
  1999 Connecting Gender, Power, and the Household. In *Gender, Power and the Household*. Linda McKie, Sophia Bowlby, and Susan Gregory, eds. Pp. 3–21. New York: St. Martin's Press.

Meadows, Karen
  1999 The Appetites of Households in Early Roman Britain. In *The Archaeology of Household Activities*. Penelope M. Allison, ed. Pp. 101–20. London: Routledge.

Mills, Barbara J.
  2000 Gender, Craft Production, and Inequality. In *Women and Men in the Prehispanic Southwest: Labor, Power, and Prestige*. Patricia L. Crown, ed. Pp. 301–43. Santa Fe, NM: School of American Research Press.

Mobley-Tanaka, Jeannette L.
  1997 Gender and Ritual Space during the Pithouse to Pueblo Transition: Subterranean Mealing Rooms in the North American Southwest. *American Antiquity* 62:437–48.

Moore, Henrietta
  1992 Households and Gender Relations: The Modeling of the Economy. In *Understanding Economic Processes*. Sutti Ortiz and Susan Lees, eds. Pp. 131–48. Monograph in Economic Anthropology 10. Lanham, MD: University Press of America.

1996 *Space, Text, and Gender: An Anthropological Study of the Marakwet of Kenya.* New York: Guilford Press.

Morgan, David
1999 Gendering the Household: Some Theoretical Considerations. In *Gender, Power and the Household.* Linda McKie, Sophia Bowlby, and Susan Gregory, eds. Pp. 22–40. New York: St. Martin's Press.

Mrozowski, Stephen A., James A. Delle, and Robert Paynter
2000 Introduction. In *Lines That Divide: Historical Archaeologies of Race, Class, and Gender.* James A. Delle, Stephen A. Mrozowski, and Robert Paynter, eds. Pp. xi–xxxi. Knoxville: University of Tennessee Press.

Netting, Robert M., Richard M. Wilk, and Eric J. Arnould
1984 Introduction. In *Households: Comparative and Historical Studies of the Domestic Group.* Robert M. Netting, Richard M. Wilk, and Eric J. Arnould, eds. Pp. xiii–xxxviii. Berkeley: University of California Press.

Nevett, Lisa C.
1999 *House and Society in the Ancient Greek World.* Cambridge: Cambridge University Press.

O'Donovan, Maria
2002 Grasping Power: A Question of Relations and Scales. In *The Dynamics of Power.* Maria O'Donovan, ed. Pp. 19–34. Occasional Paper 30. Carbondale: Center for Archaeological Investigations, Southern Illinois University.

Ortner, Sherry B.
1974 Is Female to Male as Nature Is to Culture? In *Women, Culture, and Society.* Michelle Z. Rosaldo and Louise Lamphere, eds. Pp. 67–88. Palo Alto, CA: Stanford University Press.
1996 *Making Gender: The Politics and Erotics of Culture.* Boston: Beacon Press.
2001 Commentary: Practice, Power and the Past. *Journal of Social Archaeology* 1:271–80.

Pauketat, Timothy R.
2001 Practice and History in Archaeology: An Emerging Paradigm. *Anthropological Theory* 1:73–98.

Reverby, Susan M., and Dorothy O. Helly
1992 Introduction: Converging on History. In *Gendered Domains: Rethinking Public and Private in Women's History.* Dorothy O. Helly and Susan M. Reverby, eds. Pp. 1–24. Ithaca, NY: Cornell University Press.

Robin, Cynthia
2002a Gender and Maya Farming: Chan Noohol, Belize. In *Ancient Maya Women.* Traci Ardren, ed. Pp. 12–30. Walnut Creek, CA: AltaMira Press.
2002b Outside of Houses: The Practices of Everyday Life at Chan Noohol, Belize. *Journal of Social Archaeology* 2:245–68.
2003 New Directions in Classic Maya Household Archaeology. *Journal of Archaeological Research* 11(4):279–356.

Rosaldo, Michelle
 1974 Women, Culture, and Society: A Theoretical Overview. In *Women, Culture, and Society*. Michelle Z. Rosaldo and Louise Lamphere, eds. Pp. 17–42. Palo Alto, CA: Stanford University Press.
 1980 The Use and Abuse of Anthropology: Reflections on Cross-Cultural Understandings. *Signs* 5:389–417.
Saitta, Dean J.
 1984 The Archaeology of Households: Alternative Approaches. *Man in the Northeast* 28:1–8.
Santley, Robert S., and Kenneth G. Hirth
 1993 Household Studies in Western Mesoamerica. In *Prehispanic Domestic Units in Western Mesoamerica: Studies of the Household, Compound, and Residence*. Robert S. Santley and Kenneth G. Hirth, eds. Pp. 3–17. Boca Raton, FL: CRC Press.
Silliman, Stephen
 2001 Agency, Practical Politics and the Archaeology of Culture Contact. *Journal of Social Archaeology* 1:190–209.
Silverblatt, Irene
 1995 Lessons of Gender and Ethnohistory in Mesoamerica. *Ethnohistory* 42:639–50.
Smith, Michael E.
 1993 New World Complex Societies: Recent Economic, Social, and Political Studies. *Journal of Archaeological Research* 1:5–41.
Smith, Monica L.
 1999 The Role of Ordinary Goods in Premodern Exchange. *Journal of Archaeological Method and Theory* 6:109–35.
Spencer-Wood, Suzanne M.
 1999 The World of the Household: Changing Meanings of the Domestic Sphere in the Nineteenth Century. In *The Archaeology of Household Activities*. Penelope M. Allison, ed. Pp. 162–89. London: Routledge.
Svensson, Eva
 1998 Expanding the Household. *Lund Archaeological Review* 4:85–100.
Sweely, Tracy L.
 1999a Gender, Space, People and Power at Ceren, El Salvador. In *Manifesting Power: Gender and the Interpretation of Power in Archaeology*. Tracy L. Sweely, ed. Pp. 153–71. London: Routledge.
 1999b Introduction. In *Manifesting Power: Gender and the Interpretation of Power in Archaeology*. Tracy L. Sweely, ed. Pp. 1–14. London: Routledge.
Tringham, Ruth
 1991 Households with Faces: The Challenge of Gender in Prehistoric Architectural Remains. In *Engendering Archaeology: Women and Prehistory*. Joan M. Gero and Margaret W. Conkey, eds. Pp. 93–131. Oxford: Basil Blackwell.
 1994 Engendered Places in Prehistory. *Gender, Place and Culture* 1:169–203.
 1995 Archaeological Houses, Households, Housework and the Home. In *The Home:*

Words, Interpretations, Meanings, and Environments. David N. Benjamin, ed. Pp. 79–107. Aldershot: Avebury.

Uruñuela Ladrón de Guevara, Gabriela, and Patricia Plunket Nagoda
    1998   Áreas de actividad en unidades domésticas del Formativo terminal en Tetimpa, Puebla. *Arqueología* 20:3–19.

VanDerwarker, Amber M., and Kandace R. Detwiler
    2002   Gendered Practice in Cherokee Foodways: A Spatial Analysis of Plant Remains from the Coweeta Creek Site. *Southeastern Archaeology* 21:21–28.

Wall, Diana diZerega
    2000   Family Meals and Evening Parties: Constructing Domesticity in Nineteenth-Century Middle-Class New York. In *Lines That Divide: Historical Archaeologies of Race, Class, and Gender.* James A. Delle, Stephen A. Mrozowski, and Robert Paynter, eds. Pp. 109–41. Knoxville: University of Tennessee Press.

Wilk, Richard M.
    1989   Decision Making and Resource Flows within the Household: Beyond the Black Box. In *The Household Economy: Reconsidering the Domestic Mode of Production.* Richard R. Wilk, ed. Pp. 23–52. Boulder, CO: Westview.

Wilk, Richard M., and Robert M. Netting
    1984   Households: Changing Forms and Functions. In *Households: Comparative and Historical Studies of the Domestic Group.* Robert M. Netting, Richard M. Wilk, and Eric J. Arnould, eds. Pp. 1–28. Berkeley: University of California Press.

Wilk, Richard M., and William L. Rathje, eds.
    1982a   *Archaeology of the Household: Building a Prehistory of Domestic Life.* Special issue of *American Behavioral Scientist* 25:617–39.

Wilk, Richard M., and William L. Rathje
    1982b   Household Archaeology. In *Archaeology of the Household: Building a Prehistory of Domestic Life.* Richard R. Wilk and William L. Rathje, eds. Special issue of *American Behavioral Scientist* 25:617–39.

Wood, Margaret C.
    2002   Women's Work and Class Conflict in a Working-Class Coal-Mining Community. In *The Dynamics of Power.* Maria O'Donovan, ed. Pp. 66–87. Occasional Paper 30. Carbondale: Center for Archaeological Investigations, Southern Illinois University.

Woolf, Alex
    1997   At Home in the Long Iron-Age: A Dialogue between Households and Individuals in Cultural Reproduction. In *Invisible People and Processes: Writing Gender and Childhood into European Archaeology.* Jenny Moore and Eleanor Scott, eds. Pp. 68–74. London: Leicester University Press.

Wright, Rita
    1991   Women's Labor and Pottery Production in Prehistory. In *Engendering Archaeology: Women and Prehistory.* Joan M. Gero and Margaret W. Conkey, eds. Pp. 31–54. Oxford: Blackwell.

Wylie, Alison
    1992   Feminist Theories of Social Power: Some Implications for a Processual Archaeology. *Norwegian Archaeological Review* 25:51–68.

Yanagisako, Sylvia J.
    1979   Family and Household: The Analysis of Domestic Groups. *Annual Review of Anthropology* 8:161–205.

Gender and Landscapes 6

WENDY ASHMORE

> *We can ponder an empowering and often gendered landscape, while recognizing that the gendering of the elements will surely vary across cultures, and meanings will shift and change depending on context, and on people's variable knowledge.*
>
> (BENDER 1998:44–45)

TAKING A CUE FROM Bender's comment, I suggest that archaeological landscapes are commonly if not universally gendered. If so, then, the question is not whether they are but rather under what circumstances, in what ways, and by whom.

Substantive responses to the refocused questions first require defining what a landscape is. In archaeology and other fields, the concept can be described simultaneously as slippery, contentious, and absolutely fundamental. Gosden and Head (1994:114–15) insightfully characterized the term as usefully ambiguous. The focus of inquiry may vary, highlighting economy and land use, social ordering, ritual and belief, or some combination of the foregoing. Paraphrasing Wilson and David (2002:5–6), the proliferation of recent work defines landscape in three principal ways: (1) as a measurable, physical world independent of human signification; (2) as a painterly representation of the world; and (3) as meaningful, socially constructed places involving bodily and cognitive experience.

What differs most among perspectives and definitions are positivist as compared with humanist stances and, by extension, the range of topics thereby deemed appropriate for consideration in landscape study (e.g., Anschuetz et al. 2001; Ashmore 2004; Bender 1993; Fisher and Thurston 1999; Knapp and Ashmore 1999; Layton and Ucko 1999). Recognition of gender in landscapes emerges most often in more humanistic treatments, of Wilson and David's third kind.

The landscapes with and among which people interact include topographic features in both earth and water forms as well as subterranean zones and the overarching sky. Wind and weather also figure in landscape experience. Although this kind of inclusiveness is necessary conceptually for the fullest understanding, not all components are equally accessible to archaeologists' investigation. And with regard to recognizing gender, inference is never direct. It does, however, draw on a range of cues and clues, some tangible in the archaeological record, others nonmaterial evidence from oral histories, ethnohistories, ethnographies, and social theory.

The sections that follow identify aspects of landscape gendering for closer consideration. These are intended as provisional responses to questions phrased at the outset—the who, how, and when of landscape gendering. The categories are no more than working analytical constructs, however, and, as will quickly become clear, expressions in each category overlap with those in others.

Landscapes from a Gendered Gaze

An initial answer to who genders landscape is that Western analysts do. That is, scholars have called attention repeatedly to the whole notion of landscape as a product of the rise of capitalism and its attendant social inequities, especially in class and gender (e.g., Bender 1999; Cosgrove 1984; Olwig 1993; Thomas 2001). Through the advent of landscape painting and the linear perspective that permitted such imagery, wealthy landowners could commission portraits of their holdings. Not only did this distinctly "Western gaze" objectify the surrounding world, distancing and removing it from direct experience, the vantage also marked possession and feminization of landscape by the men who contracted for the works. "Just as western painting defines men as the active producers and viewers of images, while women are passive objects of visual pleasure, so landscape is feminized" (Thomas 2001:169, citing S. Ford). In other words, the mere concept of landscape is loaded with connotations both of control and of hierarchical gender relations. That this may not be exclusively a Western perspective is noteworthy (e.g., Faust 2003, concerning Aztec imagery) but does not remove concern for acknowledging and seeking to neutralize the effective hold of Western intellectual traditions on landscape thinking.

As fundamentally, the Cartesian heritage in the "gaze" customarily constrains us to recognize only two sexes and two genders, female and male, and in archaeological writing about embodied sex and gender, it is women and women's bodies that are singled out for scrutiny (Faust 2003; Joyce 2004; Meskell 1996:4–5). Just as feminist archaeology and the archaeology of gender are not "just about women," so must study of gendering in landscapes continue to move beyond seeking female and male elements—and only those. Third genders and androgyny are among alternatives that may have been recognized by the societies we seek to understand, as are gender identities that change during the life cycle or with social circumstance (e.g., Fausto-Sterling 1992; Joyce 2004; Moore 1993; Talalay 2005; Yates 1993).

A further testament to the strength of Cartesian thinking, structuralist approaches figure frequently in inquiries on gender, including treatments of landscape. Although not all such works follow Lévi-Strauss in seeking timeless, universal binary oppositions, reduction of analytic categories to female and male nonetheless can appear to simplify a search for patterns—and thereby to facilitate recognizing structure. This fact should not obviate using structuralist analyses, but they might best be treated as "first forays" in search of meaning (e.g., Conkey 2001; see also Ashmore 2002).

Despite some attempts to move beyond dichotomies, then, many analysts still focus unsurprisingly on one or both of two genders. Moreover, findings seem most often to imply either competition or complementarity between female and male roles, whether the implication is intended or only apparent (compare Hays-Gilpin 2004:150). Commonplace assertions, these analytical categorizations constitute another legacy of Cartesian thinking and belie the constant negotiations more plausibly shaping socially constructed gender relations in ancient society as today (e.g., Ashmore 2002; Joyce 2004; Pyburn 2004).

Gendered Embodiment of Landscape

Inasmuch as the first entity a human experiences is her or his own body, it is hardly surprising that landscapes are embodied in human and gendered terms. Allusions to "Mother Earth" and "Mother Nature" are widespread cross-culturally and often said to tap primeval ideas about a gendered universe. Certainly, for the Greeks, Earth, or Gaia (or *Gê*) was female (e.g., Cole 2004:23). Some strands of the modern "Goddess movement" promote belief in a primordial gynocentric world, as do a number of current writers about feminist spirituality. Drawing in part on the archaeological record (especially but far from solely from the writings of Marija Gimbutas), multiple authors describe a "Great Cosmic Mother" as constituting the original "religion of the earth" (e.g., Gadon 1989; Plaskow and Christ 1989; Sjöö and Mor 1991). From this vantage, women's bodies and bodily functions model and are models for the seasonal round, lunar cycles, and the earth's fertility. Other authors, however, vigorously decry what they see as unfounded arguments, uncritical appropriation of archaeological data; they argue instead that it is far more complicated to interpret the often ambiguous and subtle evidence for ancient beliefs gendering landscape and the earth (e.g., Anthony 1995; Goodison and Morris 1998; Meskell 1995, 1998).

If not primordial, however, a concept of "Mother Earth" certainly emerges frequently in beliefs among more recent societies that are attested archaeologically, notably in the Americas. Even there, some have cautioned that gendering landscape as embodied deities is more intricate than simply a division between female, male, or other genders. For example, Hays-Gilpin (2000) points to the complexity of gendered embodiments among Acoma, Navajo, and other Native American deities and to the possibility that some of the specific ideas crystallized in their current forms as recently as the past few centuries. Nevertheless, among the Inca half a millennium ago, histories and oral accounts indicate that Pachamama was emphatically and unambiguously Earth Mother, whose reproductive potentials were realized by actions of her male counterpart, Illapa, the god of thunder or lightning (Silverblatt 1987). Her "daughters were emblems of the specifics of highland [Andean] bounty—maize, . . . potatoes, . . . coca, . . . even metals . . . and clay (Silverblatt 1987:25). Mamacocha, a descendant of the moon, was "Mother Sea" and the source of all water, whether manifest as rivers, springs, rain clouds, or irrigation (Silverblatt 1987:48). As always, the crucial point is critical evaluation of evidence for the impact of gender, not simply presuming from overgeneral analogies, Freudian (or other social) theory, or what seems "common sense."

Other societies gendered landscapes in contrasting ways. Indeed, Roth calls attention to quite different gendering of fertility, fecundity, sexuality, and their expressions in the landscape. In specific grounds for her argument, ancient Egyptian texts credit males with creativity in reproduction; after receiving the male seed, females served simply as receptacles, making no creative contributions to the child. Material representations of Egyptian fecundity were usually identified as male, depicted with male genitalia, but also with breasts and bellies suggestive of pregnancy. According to Roth (2000:195), the reason for such portrayal relates directly to landscape along the Nile

> and is rooted in the nature of its resulting agricultural cycle. In most parts of the world, the earth is made fertile by rain from the sky. By analogy with human reproduction, the sky is viewed as an active male deity, from which comes the rain that penetrates the passive and female mother earth and causes her to bring forth new life. The rain is crucial, but the creative power resides in the earth. The sky is thus gendered male and the mother earth, female.
>
> In Egypt, by contrast, the earth was fertilized by the annual flood of

the Nile. . . . The water and silt, which renewed the land and made the drops grow, came not from the sky but from the earth. Grammatically, both the earth and the floodwaters were regarded as males, and the deities that personified them . . . were also male.

The Egyptian sky was female, however, her nude body arching across the recumbent earth, stimulating his erection and thereby his acts of procreation and creation (Roth 2000:195). The two landscape forces were complementary but not equal; again, situated evidence is the key to implicating gender-related distinctions.

Elsewhere as well, celestial bodies and the sky itself were commonly gendered, as indicated in text and imagery. Sun, moon, Venus, other stars, and whole constellations were ascribed gendered identities. Sun and moon do often form a male and female pair, usually interpreted as reflecting culture-specific (if not more generalized) ideas of male potency and women's menstrual cycle resembling lunar cycles. And the same astral body can have different genders under different conditions, as when the usually female Maya moon assumes a dual-sexed identity (Taube 1992:64–68) or "becomes male at the time of the full moon" (Milbrath 1999:32). And where Western views identify lunar topography as depicting a "man in the moon," the Maya recognize a rabbit, companion to the Moon Goddess, in pre-Columbian imagery more than a millennium ago as well as today (e.g., Milbrath 1999:32, 119–20; Schele and Miller 1983). And among the Aztec, the tribal origin story pits the sun against the moon and stars, all in a context of gendered siblings. As Huitzilopochtli, the Aztec patron deity, lies in his mother's womb, his sister and "400" (i.e., countless) brothers plot to prevent his birth. Overhearing their conspiracy, he leaps, full grown, from the womb, slaying and dismembering his sister, Coyolxauhqui, and sending his brothers fleeing his wrath. The story is frequently glossed as the birth of the sun (Huitzilopochtli), whose brightness and heat cause the death of the moon (his sister) and of the stars (the brothers). It is a tale embodied materially in the Aztec Templo Mayor, where the bodies of those whose hearts were extracted, to feed and sustain the sun with their blood, were thrown down the temple steps toward the sculpture depicting the dismembered Coyolxauhqui. As Faust (2003) argues, this is one aspect of gendering in the Aztec celestial landscape, in which women are portrayed as dangerous and threatening and must be controlled or even destroyed to safeguard the continuity of the world (see also Brumfiel 1996).

Writing of "sexual cosmology," Olwig (1993:316) captures the larger situation concisely: "It is readily apparent to any farmer that there is something going on between the sky and the earth which is critical to the fertility of the land."

What remains to archaeologists interested in gender is to determine, insofar as possible, what it was that ancient people, farmers and otherwise, inferred about what was going on in earth, sky, or both. Gender may be embodied in landscape, but its expression is not necessarily universal in presence and definitely not universalized in form. It is certainly the case that recognized instances of gendered landscape embodiment have been considered most often as tropes for human reproduction, expressing aspects of anatomy and social relations. But they are also cast in other terms that equate proper maintenance of gender relations as critical to the world's survival, let alone prosperity. Whatever the story told, analysts typically identify two sexes and two genders, if sometimes recognizing situated, changeable, or ambiguous categories. Rarely, however, are identities portrayed as negotiated social states; rather, they tend to be cast as expressions of idealized roles and relations, unchanging models for human emulation.

Gendered Activity Spaces on the Landscape

A more directly materialist approach designates areas within landscapes as domains of gendered activities. The inferences are based most often in ethnographic analogy and presumptions about division of labor in antiquity and, more specifically, the gendering of particular kinds of artifacts, features, and the activities they represent. Such inference is widely recognized as difficult at best. It not only risks presumptive gender ascriptions but also risks trivializing any such ascriptions as more mechanical than a reflection of negotiated roles in socially fluid contexts (e.g., see critiques by Robin 2002). Nevertheless, provisionally identifying gendered activity arenas in the landscape can suggest some of the lines along which roles were negotiated and how gender figured in social practices.

For example, in a structural analysis of Inuit belief and myth, McGhee (1977) describes the gendering of landscape and seasons such that women are linked to the sea, winter, and marine life, while land, summer, and terrestrial game are the world of men. Among artifacts in Thule archaeological assemblages of Inuit ancestors, most objects were made from bone and antler. Ivory, however, was less easily acquired and more difficult to work: that raw material was limited to very particular items—marine hunting weapons, implements for life on the winter ice, sewing kits, and personal ornaments. Based on information in Inuit ethnographies, McGhee links the ancient Thule ivory objects to women, even though some—especially for sea hunting—were used by men in modern times. Accounts from the Alaskan northern coast may shed light on the apparent inconsistency just noted in that Bodenhorn (1993) reports that a northern coast woman's ability to call sea mammals is deemed responsible for her husband's success in the hunt. In this sense, the material hunting implements are used by men but seem, in part, an extension of women's facilitating role and a sign of complementarity in fostering family and community well-being.

From ethnographic, ethnohistoric, and archaeological research in northwestern Tanzania, Schmidt (1983, 1997) paints a striking picture of gendered and sexualized landscapes of iron smelting in the seventeenth century A.D., perhaps extending back two millennia in time. Adjacent to archaeological discovery of an ancient smelting furnace of the mid-first millennium B.C., the region's most prominent shrine is today known as Kaiija, meaning "the place of the forge." Oral history and myth describe erection of an iron tower at that forge that had fallen long ago. Modern place-names there and in the vicinity for rivers, villages, and landforms are rich in punning allusions in their joint association with iron smelting, sexual reproduction, and gender relations. In local vocabulary independent of Freudian analysis, the iron tower is considered a phallus. Its collapse metaphorically and nominally stands for a particular stage in sexual intercourse wherein the phallus beats on a woman's genitalia and thereby elicits vaginal fluid. Apparently further reducing ambiguity about the symbolism, the name for this fluid is also the name of the river adjoining the iron tower site. Moving across the landscape, from the elevated location of the tower toward lower-lying swampland and lake, the place-names continue to evince sequential stages in sexual intercourse, especially involving movements of the phallus.

During ethnoarchaeological reenactments of smelting, the men eschewed sexual relations, and women, especially menstruating women, were prohibited from contact with the smelting site and furnace. The risks for violation of these self-imposed taboos were stated in terms that linked failed smelting with reproductive breakdown, from miscarriage to sterility. Schmidt (1997:214) summarizes that "the cosmic iron tower is a symbol of human and economic fecundity." It is also inferentially a statement of normative behavior between two genders. In this highly gendered landscape, men have the kind of procreative force noted earlier in ancient Egyptian views and iconography, and relations with women are distinctly hierarchical.

A different picture emerges among the Mono Indians of California, where Jackson (1991) identified bedrock mortars as women's acorn-processing stations and argued that the seasonal movement across the landscape was structured by returns to where the mortars had been created and remained available. Here women's work structured the annual round and thereby contributed to affirming the wider importance of women's roles in Mono society. Productivity was not the domain solely of women, but the gendered landscape is consistent with more egalitarian or "balanced" gender relations than those implied in other examples.

Gendered activity realms can also be identified in landscape imagery. Writing of the Minoan Bronze Age, for example, Rehak (1999) describes gendered landscape iconography in Thera frescoes. In multiple images within the same building, women of varied life stages are shown with animals and diverse plants, especially saffron crocus. Like the women, the crocus is illustrated at various life stages, as bud and blossom, singly and by the basketful. Yellow coloring of the women's hands, feet, and mouths, as well as the presence of crocus blossoms in their hair, all suggest participation in gathering the saffron as dyestuff and food. In contrast, men portrayed in adjacent rooms occupy quite different scenes, with few or no landscape elements. Intriguingly, the youngest boy shown is painted with eye and skin colors (blue-streaked and yellow-orange, respectively) suggestive of carotene deficiency. Because saffron is high in carotenes and vitamins A and B, Rehak (1999:13) proposes that the gendered distribution of motifs and colors as well as the inclusion with women of other potentially medicinal plants all imply that females had a "detailed knowledge of the medicinal properties of saffron." Such knowledge would have benefited at least them and their families, and the frescoes' prominence suggests material acknowledgment for women's contributions to health and economy in Minoan society. As with the Mono interpretation, landscape-related activities implicate ideals of gender complementarity, with gender ranking relegated to background or unstated expression (e.g., perhaps in differential access to the frescoed chambers as well as manifestations in other venues and genres).

For Greek society in the time of Hesiod, text analyses point to strong gendering of landscape in which women's activities contributed to unifying society in political and ritual terms. As one instance, while the most important sanctuaries of Artemis, the goddess of the wilderness and of fertility, were located in the countryside, their replicas in cities "protected the city by creating a unity between the center and its borderlands" (Cole 2004:196). That is, processions of women ritually crossed the expanse from rural to urban realms; in so doing, the "females who walked unmolested . . . tested with their own bodies the security of the whole population [and] expressed the confidence and security of a community safe from incursion and confident in its own future" (Cole 2004:228). Although the ancient processions have little material trace, the sanctuaries remain, with their social and political significance clarified by textual records.

In many instances, however, recognizing gendered activities in archaeological landscapes is somewhere between challenging and impossible. The risk of presumptive gender attribution seems too great, unless there is demonstrable or strongly inferable continuity with more thoroughly documented societies and practices. Drawing on such continuities and specific accounts from California and the Great Basin, for example, Whitley (1998:18) finds that "rock-art sites were feminine-gendered places, even though they were primarily (if not exclusively) used by male shamans." The terms used to describe these shamans' portals were strongly feminine: *choishishiu*, female dog, signifying a spirit helper; *pachki*, the color red, associated in particular with menstrual blood; and *taiwan*, "basketry gambling tray, made by women and used by them in the women's walnut dice game" (Whitley 1998:18–19). Moreover, many of the rock-art images and the forms of the sites themselves are said to be vaginas. Whitley and others interpret some of the imagery as male shamans' acts to control dangerous or unruly forces, including those pertaining to women. Inversion of gender associations is acknowledged in other circumstances as a means of manipulating social relations and identities.

The gendering of the region's landscape itself offers a more encompassing explanation for associating male-gendered actors with feminine forms and words through which to act: "When the [ethnographically documented] masculine symbolism of mountain peaks is . . . matched against the [likewise, ethnographically documented] feminine symbolism of rock-art sites, the symbolic logic of rock-art site *distribution* becomes apparent. Rock-art sites as feminine places only logically fit within the feminine-gendered portions of the supernatural landscape: rock outcrops and caves, and water sources, found at relatively lower elevations" (Whitley 1998:23; emphasis added). In other words, gender is identified as a structuring principle operating in multiple social spheres in this region, most of whose recognition relies wholly on the strength of ethnographic records.

Marking Gender on Landscape

Gender marks landscapes in many ways. Landscapes are rich in meanings conveyed orally through stories, poems, songs, and other genres (e.g., Basso 1984, 1996). Of themselves, however, these do not leave material traces and are quite elusive for archaeological inquiry. The Mono bedrock mortars are one instance of material marking; the western North American rock art is another. Indeed, the best-known forms of material signs in the landscape are rock art and architecture or other monuments.

Rock-art research has exploded in quantity and sophistication in recent years. As a genre, rock art comprises human-made marks on nonportable stone surfaces, including pictographs applied onto rock and petroglyphs cut into rock (Taçon and Chippindale 1998:6). Gendered imagery has been noted virtually worldwide, from Australia and southern Africa to Europe and the Americas. Mural imagery of Paleolithic European caves is widely known if not always well understood; its study has been somewhat of a bellwether for inquiry elsewhere, and gender and sexuality were early themes in its interpretation (e.g., Bahn 1986; Conkey 2001). The most concerted consideration of gender in rock art to date is Hays-Gilpin's (2004) aptly named volume *Ambiguous Images*. As the title implies, rock art may offer what some observers see as clear and "obvious" depictions, while to others the same imagery is opaque—or simply ambiguous.

Monuments on the landscape have suggested gendered meanings in both prehistoric and historical contexts. Neolithic monuments on landscapes of southern England and the island of Malta have attracted particular attention from scholars and the wider public. Some have viewed the tombs and temples of Malta as embodiments of the Great Goddess, as her habitations, and as places for celebrating feminine principles (e.g., Biaggi 1994; but see alternatives and critiques by Malone et al. 1993; Stoddart et al. 1993). The buildings' plans are said to outline women's bodies, emphasizing the womb and other anatomical elements associated with female fecundity. Parallel interpretations have been made for monuments and landscapes at Silbury and Avebury in southern England (Dames 1976, 1977). Too often, however, these interpretations seem to place more interpretive weight on the evidence than it can be expected to bear.

In a more complicated set of arguments about landscapes of Neolithic Europe, Hodder (1984, 1990) has interpreted spatial bounding as, in part, reflective of gender relations. Arguing not for a primeval conceptualization of the world, he attends specifically to the advent of sedentary, food-producing societies and separation of tamed domestic shelter from untamed and dangerous spaces beyond. Houses and burial sites are the monuments that mark bounding of the landscape. Initially, Hodder (1984:62) argued explicitly that the internal arrangement of the longhouses and their furnishings placed women's activities deep inside, farthest away from the entry—and, by extension, from others. In the same essay, he asserted that elongated trapezoidal houses were models for the forms of long megalithic tombs, monuments frequently viewed as constituting claims to land tenure. The transformation in construction emphasis he linked to shifts in social strategies and implicated gender relations as fundamental:

> In the first phase the domestic context is the central focus of competing claims to reproductive resources. Material culture is used to form a world in which women are to be emphasised, celebrated but controlled as reproducers of the lineage, and in which women and extra-lineage ties have a central importance. In the second phase the domestic context is withdrawn from its central focus by changes in material culture, and these changes are part of the developing social control of productive resources.

Competing claims to the inheritance of those resources, whether land or livestock, are restricted by de-emphasising and devaluing the domestic context, the role of women as reproducers and the extra-lineage ties. (1984:66)

In a subsequent, more comprehensive study, the argument shifted emphasis, and gender receded as a factor directly mediating structure, especially at the scale of landscapes. Although maintaining "that early Neolithic material symbolism is involved in the celebration and control of the wild, and that the control relates to social power through the representation of male and female and through the organization of domestic space" (Hodder 1990:10–11), he recognized greater ambiguity and variability in the roles that gender identities and relations contributed to the mix (Hodder 1990:9–10, 68, 308; see also Bradley 1998; Hamilton 2000). Changes in inference in this one instance are emblematic, in many ways, of the shifts to more fluid and complex theorizing that has emerged in the interim. The same shifts are consistent with growing suspicion of inferences about gendered space that hint at replicating modern ideas, assigning men to the outdoors and women to the house (e.g., critique by Talalay 2005). Such statements apply to understanding gender and social identities more generally as well as treatments of rock art and monuments on the landscape.

Landscapes of Gendered Cosmology and History

People come to know landscapes by living within and moving across them. Landscapes become vested with history and social identity of its inhabitants, often embodying understandings of social origins and cosmology (e.g., Ingold 1973; Knapp and Ashmore 1999; Tilley 1994). Prominent features of topography come to signify episodes and actors in the deep social past as well as from more recent times. Dreaming Tracks of Australia are perhaps the most widely recognized specific manifestations linking present and past through landscape (e.g., Taçon 1999). Parallel evidence or strong inference that history and cosmology were mapped on the land is virtually worldwide in occurrence, often but not always marked materially with rock art or monuments (e.g., Bradley 1993, 1997, 1998; Graham-Campbell 1994; Hays-Gilpin 2004; Richards 1996; van de Guchte 1999). Taçon (1999:37) notes that visually dramatic kinds of places tend to attract attention in the landscape:

Often these are places where concepts of an upper world, a lower world and the earth plain come together visually in a striking manner. These are places where the center of the world may be experienced, where an *axis mundi* is located.

With or without material marking, landscapes sometimes implicate gender references in cosmology and history. For example, near the site of Vingen, in southern Norway, Mandt suggests imaginatively that

> the entire layout of the Vingen landscape may have characterized the site as something different from the profane world. When approaching the outlet of the tiny fjord, one gets the impression of passing through a "gate," of being let into a secluded, almost secret, and even a little awe-inspiring, space. The whole scenario could be construed as a hierophany, as nature's representation of the female body: the fjord is the narrow birth canal between the woman's thighs—that is the hillsides—and the water of life is streaming from above—from the very habitat of the red deer. And in clear view from the enclosed Vingen space is Hornelen, its peak—almost like a phallus—reaching right into the firmament. (quoted by Hays-Gilpin 2004:159)

Unfortunately, as Hays-Gilpin notes, little or no independent evidence can be cited to support or refute this specific interpretation. As attractive as it is in light of comments like Taçon's, the account falters by seeming to reify what must remain only one plausible scenario.

In other instances, however, oral or written histories can be invoked to understand landscape meanings and gendered beliefs. In indigenous societies of Mesoamerica, for example, the universe is "perceived, at least by some, as formed during the creation with pliant cords stretched out as on a giant loom" (Klein 1982:4). Acts of creation in daily life are microcosmic reenactments of primordial creation, and whether building a house, laying out a cornfield, or setting up a loom, proper completion or performance of the action situates the people in an orderly universe. Weaving on the back-strap loom of the Maya and their neighbors is traditionally women's work. According to the *Popol Vuh*, the seventeenth-century document recording Quiché Maya creation, a

> textile itself, like the skyearth [universe], the milpa [cornfield], and the house, has four sides and four corners. The backstrap loom, unlike the European treadle loom, permits selvages on all four sides, since the warp threads pass continuously back and forth between one loom bar and the other without being cut.... Further, it should be noted that the process of weaving (-*quem*-), as distinct from plaiting, netting, or lacing (all -*jitz'o*-),

involves the intersection of two distinct systems of threads, just as the measuring out of the skyearth involves two distinct systems of solar movements. (Tedlock and Tedlock 1985:128)

In other words, because weaving and textiles are viewed as means by which the cosmos and the order and continuity of social life are ritually and materially reproduced, women (i.e., as weavers) are on a par with men (i.e., as creators of milpa space) and with the primordial gods of creation (Ashmore 2002:240; Morris 1986). With regard to Maya landscapes, then, gender structures the creation and perpetual recreation of the properly constituted world.

Just as cosmic and historical actors are gendered, so then can landscapes incorporate gender expressions, integral to the record of society's heritage recorded in the earth, water, and sky. Once again, the challenge for archaeologists is to draw from a strong array of evidence, situated as salient for the particular landscapes under study. As Ingold (1993:172) phrases this in a different but relevant context, "Meaning is there to be *discovered* in the landscape, if only we know how to attend to it. Every feature . . . is a potential clue, a key to meaning rather than a vehicle for carrying it."

Concluding Thoughts

At the outset of this chapter, I asserted that archaeological landscapes were commonly gendered and suggested that it would be more productive to ascertain under what circumstances, in what ways, and by whom aspects of gender were ascribed. The foregoing review offers initial assessment of how archaeologists have approached these questions. Discussions of landscape and gender are relatively dispersed and their authors theoretically diverse.

With regard to who genders landscapes, archaeologists have acknowledged that while considerable attribution seems to have occurred in antiquity, intellectual and political traditions have socialized Western scholars to a pervasive "gendering" gaze at the outset of analysis. Some have sought to break free of this perspective, but it remains a matter for concern.

With regard to how landscapes have been gendered in the past, the four overlapping ways recognized in the literature are embodiment of sex and gender in landscape forms, differentiating landscape space by gender-linked activities, physically marking landscapes with gender-related images and monuments, and constituting gendered aspects of cosmology and history in the landscape.

Finally, with regard to the circumstances under which gender is expressed in archaeological landscapes, the situations are perhaps most commonly portrayed as normative statements of status quo, idealizations of proper human gender identities, roles, and relations. Some manifestations, such as Jackson's analysis of Mono bedrock mortars, seem principally to acknowledge what gendered individuals do in society, without either moral exhortation or direct indications of either equal or hierarchical relations. In others, gendered roles are relatively explicitly identified and accorded public recognition with variable degrees of what appear to be alternately appreciation or threat of dire consequences. When there is danger, women are commonly the named source, as in Aztec cosmology and East African iron-smelting landscapes. Negotiation of gender identities and roles is recognized infrequently, Whitley's discussion of far-western North American rock-art landscapes being perhaps the closest approximation in the materials reviewed here. Authors who are most explicit about the subtleties and fluidity of gender have not generally tackled issues of gender and landscape, with the notable exception of rock-art research (e.g., Hays-Gilpin 2004; Yates 1993).

Although many investigators have boldly opened new ways of thinking about landscape and about gender and the authors cited in this chapter have made strongly productive and provocative contributions to understanding landscape and gender jointly, more concerted forays will surely repay efforts. There is certainly ample room for more of the pondering of which Bender writes in the epigraph to this chapter and for going beyond pondering to develop our concrete understanding.

Acknowledgments

I am grateful to Sarah Milledge Nelson for inviting me to participate in this volume and thank her and Mitch Allen for encouragement and understanding. Conversations with Chelsea Blackmore and Kata Faust have been invaluable in my thinking about landscapes in recent years and in formulating thoughts for this chapter. Thanks to Jane Buikstra for extended communication on this and other topics and for critical reading at critical times. As always, I am immensely grateful to Tom Patterson, for encouragement and gentle but consistently insightful critique and for being my rock of morale support.

References

Anschuetz, Kurt F., Richard H. Wilshusen, and Cherie L. Scheick
    2001   An Archaeology of Landscapes: Perspectives and Directions. *Journal of Archaeological Research* 9:157–211.

Anthony, David
    1995   Nazi and Eco-Feminist Prehistories: Ideology and Empiricism in Indo-Euro-

pean Archaeology. In *Nationalism, Politics, and the Practice of Archaeology*. Philip L. Kohl and Clare Fawcett, eds. Pp. 82–96. Cambridge: Cambridge University Press.

Ashmore, Wendy
2002   Encountering Maya Women. In *Ancient Maya Women*. Traci Ardren, ed. Pp. 229–45. Walnut Creek, CA: AltaMira Press.
2004   Social Archaeologies of Landscape. In *A Companion to Social Archaeology*. Lynn Meskell and Robert W. Preucel, eds. Pp. 255–71. Oxford: Blackwell.

Bahn, Paul G.
1986   No Sex, Please, We're Aurignacians. *Rock Art Research* 3:99–105.

Basso, Keith H.
1984   "Stalking with Stories": Names, Places, and Moral Narratives among the Western Apache. In *Text, Play, and Story: The Construction and Reconstruction of Self and Society*. Stuart Plattner and Edward M. Bruner, eds. Pp. 19–55. Washington, DC: American Ethnological Society.
1996   *Wisdom Sits in Places: Landscape and Language among the Western Apache*. Albuquerque: University of New Mexico Press.

Bender, Barbara, ed.
1993   *Landscape: Politics and Perspectives*. Oxford: Berg.

Bender, Barbara
1998   *Stonehenge: Making Space*. Oxford: Berg.
1999   Subverting the Western Gaze: Mapping Alternative Worlds. In *The Archaeology and Anthropology of Landscape: Shaping Your Landscape*. Peter J. Ucko and Robert Layton, eds. Pp. 31–45. London: Routledge.

Biaggi, Christina
1994   *Habitations of the Great Goddess*. Manchester, CT: Knowledge, Ideas and Trends.

Bodenhorn, Barbara
1993   Gendered Spaces, Public Places: Public and Private Revisited on the North Slope of Alaska. In *Landscape: Politics and Perspectives*. Barbara Bender, ed. Pp. 169–203. Oxford: Berg.

Bradley, Richard
1993   *Altering the Earth: The Origins of Monuments in Britain and Continental Europe*. The Rhind Lectures 1991–92. Monograph Series, no. 8. Edinburgh: Society of Antiquaries of Scotland.
1997   *Rock Art and the Prehistory of Atlantic Europe: Signing the Land*. London: Routledge.
1998   *The Significance of Monuments: On the Shaping of Human Experience in Neolithic and Bronze Age Europe*. London: Routledge.

Brumfiel, Elizabeth M.
1996   Figurines and the Aztec State: Testing the Effectiveness of Ideological Domination. In *Gender and Archaeology*. Rita P. Wright, ed. Pp. 143–66. Philadelphia: University of Pennsylvania Press.

Cole, Susan Guettel
   2004   *Landscapes, Gender, and Ritual Space: The Ancient Greek Experience*. Berkeley: University of California Press.

Conkey, Margaret W.
   2001   Structural and Semiotic Approaches. In *Handbook of Rock Art Research*. David S. Whitley, ed. Pp. 273–310. Walnut Creek, CA: AltaMira Press.

Cosgrove, Denis E.
   1984   *Social Formation and Symbolic Landscape*. London: Croom Helm.

Dames, Michael
   1976   *The Silbury Treasure: The Great Goddess Rediscovered*. London: Thames and Hudson.
   1977   *The Avebury Cycle*. London: Thames and Hudson.

Faust, Katherine A.
   2003   Body-Landscape Metaphors: The Coyolxauhqui Relief as an Index of Human and Environmental Connectivity. Paper presented at the 102nd annual meeting of the American Anthropological Association, Chicago.

Fausto-Sterling, Anne
   1992   *Myths of Gender: Biological Theories about Women and Men*. Rev. ed. New York: Basic Books.

Fisher, Christopher T., and Tina L. Thurston, eds.
   1999   Special Section: Dynamic Landscapes and Socio-Political Process: The Topography of Anthropogenic Environments in Global Perspective. *Antiquity* 73:630–88.

Gadon, Elinor W.
   1989   *The Once and Future Goddess*. New York: HarperSanFrancisco.

Goodison, Lucy, and Christine Morris, eds.
   1998   *Ancient Goddesses: The Myths and the Evidence*. London: British Museum Press.

Gosden, Chris, and Lesley Head
   1994   Landscape—A Usefully Ambiguous Concept. *Archaeology in Oceania* 29:113–16.

Graham-Campbell, James, ed.
   1994   Archaeology of Pilgrimage. *World Archaeology* 26(1) (whole issue).

Hamilton, Naomi
   2000   The Conceptual Archive and the Challenge of Gender. In *Towards Reflexive Method in Archaeology: The Example at Çatalhöyük*. Ian Hodder, ed. Pp. 95–99. Cambridge: McDonald Institute for Archaeological Research.

Hays-Gilpin, Kelley A.
   2000   Beyond Mother Earth and Father Sky: Sex and Gender in Ancient Southwestern Visual Arts. In *Reading the Body: Representations and Remains in the Archaeological Record*. Alison E. Rautman, ed. Pp. 165–86. Philadelphia: University of Pennsylvania Press.
   2004   *Ambiguous Images: Gender and Rock Art*. Walnut Creek, CA: AltaMira Press.

Hodder, Ian
    1984   Burials, Houses, Women and Men in the European Neolithic. In *Ideology, Power and Prehistory*. Daniel Miller and Christopher Tilley, eds. Pp. 51–68. Cambridge: Cambridge University Press.
    1990   *The Domestication of Europe: Structure and Contingency in Neolithic Societies*. Oxford: Blackwell.

Ingold, Tim
    1993   The Temporality of the Landscape. *World Archaeology* 25:152–74.

Jackson, Thomas L.
    1991   Pounding Acorn: Women's Production as Social and Economic Focus. In *Engendering Archaeology: Women and Prehistory*. Joan M. Gero and Margaret W. Conkey, eds. Pp. 301–25. Oxford: Blackwell.

Joyce, Rosemary A.
    2004   Embodied Subjectivity: Gender, Femininity, Masculinity, Sexuality. In *A Companion to Social Archaeology*. Lynn Meskell and Robert W. Preucel, eds. Pp. 82–95. Oxford: Blackwell.

Klein, Cecilia
    1982   Woven Heaven, Tangled Earth: A Weaver's Paradigm of the Mesoamerican Cosmos. In *Ethnoastronomy and Archaeoastronomy in the American Tropics*. Anthony F. Aveni and Gary Urton, eds. *Annals of the New York Academy of Sciences* 385:1–35.

Knapp, A. Bernard, and Wendy Ashmore
    1999   Archaeological Landscapes: Constructed, Conceptualized, Ideational. In *Archaeologies of Landscape: Contemporary Perspectives*. Wendy Ashmore and A. Bernard Knapp, eds. Pp. 1–30. Oxford: Blackwell.

Layton, Robert, and Peter J. Ucko
    1999   Introduction: Gazing on the Landscape and Encountering the Environment. In *The Archaeology and Anthropology of Landscape: Shaping Your Landscape*. Peter J. Ucko and Robert Layton, eds. Pp. 1–20. London: Routledge.

Malone, Caroline, Anthony Bonanno, Tancred Gouder, Simon Stoddart, and David Trump
    1993   The Death Cults of Prehistoric Malta. *Scientific American* 269(6):110–17.

McGhee, Robert
    1977   Ivory for the Sea Woman: The Symbolic Attributes of a Prehistoric Technology. *Canadian Journal of Archaeology* 1:141–49.

Meskell, Lynn
    1995   Goddesses, Gimbutas and *New Age* Archaeology. *Antiquity* 69:74–86.
    1996   The Somatization of Archaeology: Discourses, Institutions, Corporeality. *Norwegian Archaeological Review* 29:1–16.
    1998   Oh My Goddess! *Archaeological Dialogues* 5:126–42.

Milbrath, Susan
    1999   *Star Gods of the Maya: Astronomy in Art, Folklore, and Calendars*. Austin: University of Texas Press.

Moore, Henrietta L.
  1993 The Differences Within and the Differences Between. In *Gendered Anthropology*. Teresa del Valle, ed. Pp. 193–204. London: Routledge.

Morris, Walter F.
  1986 Maya Time Warps. *Archaeology* 39(3):52–59.

Olwig, K. R.
  1993 Sexual Cosmology: Nation and Landscape at the Conceptual Interstices of Nature and Culture; or, What Does Landscape Really Mean? In *Landscape: Politics and Perspectives*. Barbara Bender, ed. Pp. 307–43. Oxford: Berg.

Plaskow, Judith, and Carol P. Christ, eds.
  1989 *Weaving the Visions: New Patterns in Feminist Spirituality*. New York: HarperCollins.

Pyburn, K. Anne
  2004 Rethinking Complex Society. In *Ungendering Civilization*. K. Anne Pyburn, ed. Pp. 1–46. London: Routledge.

Rehak, Paul
  1999 The Aegean Landscape and the Body: A New Interpretation of the Thera Frescoes. In *From the Ground Up: Beyond Gender Theory in Archaeology*. Nancy L. Wicker and Bettina Arnold, eds. Pp. 11–22. BAR International Series 812. Oxford: Archaeopress.

Richards, Colin
  1996 Henges and Water: Towards an Elemental Understanding of Monumentality and Landscape in Late Neolithic Britain. *Journal of Material Culture* 1:313–36.

Robin, Cynthia
  2002 Gender and Maya Farming: Chan Nòohol, Belize. In *Ancient Maya Women*. Traci Ardren, ed. Pp. 12–30. Walnut Creek, CA: AltaMira Press.

Roth, Ann Mary
  2000 Father Earth, Mother Sky: Ancient Egyptian Beliefs about Conception and Fertility. In *Reading the Body: Representations and Remains in the Archaeological Record*. Alison E. Rautman, ed. Pp. 187–201. Philadelphia: University of Pennsylvania Press.

Schele, Linda, and Jeffrey H. Miller
  1983 *The Mirror, the Rabbit, and the Bundle: "Accession" Expressions from the Classic Maya Inscriptions*. Studies in Pre-Columbian Art and Archaeology, 25. Washington, DC: Dumbarton Oaks.

Schmidt, Peter R.
  1983 An Alternative to a Strictly Materialist Perspective: A Review of Historical Archaeology, Ethnoarchaeology, and Symbolic Approaches in African Archaeology. *American Antiquity* 48:62–79.
  1997 *Iron Technology in East Africa: Symbolism, Science, and Archaeology*. Bloomington: Indiana University Press.

Silverblatt, Irene
    1987   *Moon, Sun, and Witches: Gender Ideologies and Class in Inca and Colonial Peru.* Princeton, NJ: Princeton University Press.

Sjöö, Monica, and Barbara Mor
    1991   *The Great Cosmic Mother: Rediscovering the Religion of the Earth.* 1987. Reprint, New York: HarperCollins.

Stoddart, Simon, Anthony Bonanno, Tancred Gouder, Caroline Malone, and David Trump
    1993   Cult in an Island Society: Prehistoric Malta in the Tarxien Period. *Cambridge Archaeological Journal* 3:3–19.

Taçon, Paul S. C.
    1999   Identifying Ancient Sacred Landscapes in Australia: From Physical to Social. In *Archaeologies of Landscape: Contemporary Perspectives.* Wendy Ashmore and A. Bernard Knapp, eds. Pp. 33–57. Oxford: Blackwell.

Taçon, Paul S. C., and Christopher Chippindale
    1998   An Archaeology of Rock-Art through Informed Methods and Formal Methods. In *The Archaeology of Rock-Art.* Christopher Chippindale and Paul S. C. Taçon, eds. Pp. 1–10. Cambridge: Cambridge University Press.

Talalay, Lauren E.
    2005   The Gendered Sea: Iconography, Gender, and Mediterranean Prehistory. In *The Archaeology of Mediterranean Prehistory.* Emma Blake and A. Bernard Knapp, eds. Pp. 130–55. Oxford: Blackwell.

Taube, Karl A.
    1992   *The Major Gods of Ancient Yucatan.* Studies in Pre-Columbian Art and Archaeology, 32. Washington, DC: Dumbarton Oaks.

Tedlock, Barbara, and Dennis Tedlock
    1985   Text and Textile: Language and Technology in the Arts of the Quiché Maya. *Journal of Anthropological Research* 41:121–46.

Thomas Julian
    2001   Archaeologies of Place and Landscape. In *Archaeological Theory Today.* Ian Hodder, ed. Pp. 165–86. Cambridge: Polity Press.

Tilley, Christopher
    1994   *A Phenomenology of Landscape: Places, Paths, and Monuments.* Oxford: Berg.

van de Guchte, Maarten
    1999   The Inca Cognition of Landscape: Archaeology, Ethnohistory, and the Aesthetic of Alterity. In *Archaeologies of Landscape: Contemporary Perspectives.* Wendy Ashmore and A. Bernard Knapp, eds. Pp. 149–68. Oxford: Blackwell.

Whitley, David S.
    1998   Finding Rain in the Desert: Landscape, Gender and Far Western North American Rock-Art. In *The Archaeology of Rock-Art.* Christopher Chippindale

and Paul S. C. Taçon, eds. Pp. 11–29. Cambridge: Cambridge University Press.

Wilson, Meredith, and Bruno David
    2002   Introduction. In *Inscribed Landscapes: Marking and Making Place*. Bruno David and Meredith Wilson, eds. Pp. 1–9. Honolulu: University of Hawai'i Press.

Yates, T.
    1993   Frameworks for an Archaeology of the Body. In *Interpretive Archaeology*. C. Tilley, ed. Pp. 31–72. Oxford: Berg.

Gender, Heterarchy, and Hierarchy

7

JANET E. LEVY

THE TERM "HETERARCHY" was introduced to archaeology by Carole L. Crumley in 1979 and expanded by her in later publications (Crumley 1979, 1995; Crumley and Marquardt 1987; and elsewhere). Crumley introduced the term as critique of evolutionary approaches to prehistoric social complexity. That perspective, according to Crumley, privileges the concepts of hierarchy and stratification and neglects other potential concepts of social complexity. It is striking that while the concept of heterarchy has been adopted by a variety of archaeologists, it has been little used in analyses of gender or gender relationships in the prehistoric world (but see Levy 1995, 1999a). As will become clear in this chapter, any examination of gender through the perspective of heterarchy also opens up discussion of the relationship of gender to hierarchy, ranking, and stratification. Concepts of heterarchy and gender together encourage a revision of our understanding of social complexity.

Background

Crumley (1987b:158) defines *heterarchy* as "structures are heterarchical when each element is either unranked relative to other elements or possesses the *potential* for being ranked in a number of different ways." She says further that *hierarchy* is a subset of *heterarchy* and that "the ultimate in complexity is not hierarchy but the play between hierarchy and heterarchy: across space, through time, and in the human mind" (163). Crumley cites the first use of the concept of heterarchy in the work of Warren McCulloch, a pioneer in artificial intelligence, who created the term in 1945 to describe the function of the human brain as "reasonably orderly ... [but] not organized hierarchically" (157). From this arises Crumley's critique of many social evolutionary studies that, according to her, conflate complexity with structure, structure with order, and order with hierarchy: "This conflation of hierarchy with order makes it difficult to imagine, much less recognize and study, patterns of relations that are complex but not hierarchical" (Crumley 1995:3).

Crumley also links the concept of heterarchy to her discussion of scale: "the 'grain' of a unit of analysis relative to the matrix as a whole" (Marquardt and Crumley 1987:2). She and colleagues emphasize a multiscalar approach to analysis of landscape and social boundaries, pointing out that a region may be heterogeneous at one scale and homogeneous at another, hierarchical at one scale and heterarchical at another (5). Similarly, a location can be both an edge and a center, depending on the scale (15).

Outside of archaeology, the concept of heterarchy turns up in a surprising variety of scholarly contexts. A recent search for the term turned up references in periodicals as diverse as *Forest Policy and Economics*, *Journal of International Management*, *Computers in Industry*, *Netherlands Journal of Zoology*, *Journal of Common Market Studies*, *Memory*, and *Trends in Ecology and Evolution*. Within the field of international management, heterarchy has come to be seen as a new style of organization and management, potentially more effective in a globalized world than traditional hierarchical models. For example, "As a result, organizational design needs to be less hierarchical (and more heterarchical), with shifting positions and relationships, much more lateral sharing of knowledge, the development of shared vision across the organization, and more consensual forms of decision making" (Egelhoff 1999:22). Stark (2001:75, n. 9) states, "As a more general process heterarchy refers to a process in which a given element—a statement, a deal, an identity, an organizational building-block, or sequences of genetic, computer, or legal code—is simultaneously expressed in multiple cross-cutting networks. . . . [A]uthority is no longer delegated vertically but rather emerges laterally (77). . . . [H]eterarchies make assets of ambiguities" (78). Thus, understandings of heterarchy converge on a sense of entities, patterns, or institutions characterized by fluid but orderly complexity that may or may not be ranked in a linear fashion. The concept emphasizes cross-cutting, lateral patterns of relationships. It is linked to concepts of scale. Thus, it is a potentially powerful concept in analyses of gender, a social variable that may reinforce or cross-cut a variety of social relationships and may be salient at different scales of social organization (e.g., household, community, and polity).

Heterarchy in Anthropology and Archaeology

Crumley and others have applied heterarchy to specific archaeological data in the areas of landscape archaeology and settlement pattern. For example, Crumley and colleagues (Crumley 1994; Crumley and Marquardt 1987) analyze landscape, environment, and human adaptation in pre-Roman and Roman Iron Age France through the lens of heterarchy. Scarborough and colleagues (2003) use the concept in their book-long analysis of settlement pattern, environmental diversity, and economic specialization in the east-central Yucatán Peninsula, focusing on who controls/manages/manipulates key natural resources (Scarborough et al. 2003:xiii) within a pattern of dispersed settlement and land use but complex political economy (3).

Joyce and Hendon (2000) apply heterarchy to a detailed analysis of differing settlement patterns and community structures in Late Classic (ca. A.D. 300–900) Honduras. They note that "multiple scales of variation and multiple principles of settlement organization" (157) reflect the complexity of human choices within different social systems: "conscious actors using architecture to write different forms of community onto the landscape" (154).

In addition to landscape and settlement studies, archaeologists have applied the concept of heterarchy to prehistoric economic relationships (Potter and King 1995) and craft production (Ehrenreich 1995) as well as more directly to questions of social structure, social organization, and social change (McIntosh 1999; Mills 2000; Sastre 2002; White 1995). Sociocultural anthropologists have apparently paid little attention to the concept, although Bidney (1947) quoted McCulloch's article shortly after it was published. A volume by Znoj (2005) analyzes gender, kinship, and community in a matrilineal society in Sumatra through the lens of heterarchy.

A final point in this review is that a variety of authors propose similar perspectives without using the term "heterarchy." For example, Derevenski (2000:399) says, "The relationship between horizontal and vertical differentiation may therefore be more complex than has hitherto been realized within archaeology." And Crown (2000:18) argues, "First, status is highly context specific, so that an individual may have high status in one situation with one group of people and low status in another with another group of people." These perspectives and others suggest a widespread frustration with what McIntosh (1999:1) calls archaeology's "preoccupation with the development of vertical control hierarchies." Based on the bibliography consulted for McIntosh's paper, one might argue that the frustration is especially marked among female archaeologists, hinting at the interrelationship of heterarchy and gender.

Critiques of Heterarchy

Several critiques of heterarchy have been proposed. Brumfiel (1995) suggests that the term is useful and can expand perspectives on prehistoric social systems but that it is underspecified and not clearly defined (Brumfiel 1995:125); analyses of heterarchy would benefit from more precise attention to the structural contexts in which it develops (127). Similarly, Thomas (1994) suggests that the label of heterarchy is applied too loosely to be very helpful.

Another critique is found in the debate between Rautman (1998) and McGuire and Saitta (1996; Saitta and McGuire 1998) on western Pueblo social organization. In their original article, Saitta and McGuire propose a dialectical approach that demonstrates that both prehistoric and historic pueblo societies "embodied *both* consensual and hierarchical social relations" (McGuire and Saitta 1996:198) and that "tension between equality and hierarchy conditioned an internal dynamic that governed the aggregation and fissioning of communities in late pueblo prehistory" (209). Rautman (1998) points out that this kind of complexity sounds like heterarchy and, further, has implications for scale of analysis. In response, Saitta and McGuire (1998), while not rejecting the concept out of hand, declare that it is static and not helpful on issues of causality. They also state (1998:335) that the term does not "capture our interest in the 'lived experience' of ancestral pueblo people." The latter point would presumably be rejected by Brumfiel (1995:129), who suggests, "Certainly, heterarchy creates complexity in the lives of individuals." By integrating heterarchy and gender, I hope to respond to some of these critiques by showing how heterarchy can indeed illuminate the lives of individuals and how we can specify some of the archaeological correlates of heterarchy.

Gender and Heterarchy in Archaeology

The analytical strategy of heterarchy is relevant to a number of core topics in gender studies in archaeology: division of labor, gender diversity, ranking, social evolution, and, perhaps, organization of fieldwork. Heterarchy shares with gender analysis the quality of disruption: disrupting implicit assumptions about human social systems, social complexity, and social change. I will start by discussing the integration of gender and heterarchy within the topics of gender diversity, social agency, and division of labor.

Gender Diversity and Heterarchy

A key topic in most general discussions of gender in anthropology and archaeology is illumination of the range of diversity of gender (and sexual) identities beyond the modern Western dichotomous model of male and female. A dichotomous model lends itself too easily to conclusions of either gender hierarchy or gender complementarity (Gero and Scattolin 2002) because it is difficult to conceptualize two units or categories as anything other than either equal or not equal. The concept of heterarchy, in contrast, urges the consideration of greater diversity, including multiple categories of gender and sexual identity and multiple ways that individuals within these categories may interact. Thus, the focus on lateral differentiation and complexity, which is a core component of a heterarchical approach, is equally relevant to examination of diversity of gender and sexual identities within a prehistoric society. Indeed, one can argue that the implicit quality of disruption that is characteristic of heterarchy, as noted previously, is also explicitly characteristic of many discussions of gender diversity, especially from the perspective of queer archaeology (Dowson 2000).

Crumley's discussions of heterarchy, although not focused on gender, suggest several ways that heterarchy encourages an active examination of gender diversity. She (1995:2; 1987a) refers to shifting and cross-cutting boundaries—social, linguistic, climatic, administrative, and so on—that characterize different scales of human interaction. Here she is generally referring to landscape, but the boundaries of gender and sexual identities may also be conceptualized as shifting, cross-cutting, and salient at different scales (see also Gero and Scattolin 2002:170). On the one hand, this encourages the study of the intersection of age and status with gender (see the case study later in this chapter). On the other hand, it encourages the broader examination of third genders, fourth genders, "two-spirits," and diverse sexualities. In this context, Hollimon (2000, 2001) points out that gender is considered potentially temporary and flexible in some cultures, in part because of its links to age, spiritual practice, and labor activities. Thus, it may be that the age at death of an individual will influence the burial program not only as an independent variable but also as one that works together with biological sex and/or gender.

For example, while some prehistoric cultures practiced clearly differentiated ("bounded") burial scenarios for males and females, other cultures were more heterarchical, with body position, grave type, and accompanying goods (among other possible factors) varying on the basis of multiple, cross-cutting social factors (e.g., Derevenski 2002). The archaeological visibility of third-gender individuals may well vary, depending on the degree of differentiation or heterarchy in burial programs. Any specific archaeological case may represent a society where dichotomous gender identities were emphasized or one where there was more diversity in gender identities. Examples of the latter are proposed in a number of situations, including Mesolithic Scandinavia (R. Schmidt 2000), Early Bronze Age central Europe (Weglian 2001), central North America in the late prehistoric period (Emerson 2003), and elsewhere in North America in early historic periods

(Holliman 2000, 2001). However, there is no a priori reason to expect that third genders were universally recognized or memorialized.

In fact, Arnold (2002) has persuasively argued that a proposed identification of third-gender individuals (most frequently "berdache" or biological males in female gender roles) can be a way of ignoring or denying certain roles, especially leadership roles, to women. She discusses this regarding the well-known Iron Age burial from Vix in eastern France, which contains a skeleton identified as a biological female accompanied by some typical female-associated artifacts and several extraordinary artifacts associated with leadership positions in other so-called princely burials. Certain archaeologists have identified the buried individual as a male transvestite priest (Arnold 1991, 2002), but Arnold (2002: 252) points out, "We need to distinguish between patterned sex/gender disjunction in burial and the reluctance of a largely male archaeological establishment to accept the possibility that particular women as women may have achieved considerable social power under certain circumstances."

There is quite a lot of ethnographic and ethnohistoric evidence that third-gender individuals are often seen as controlling special ritual and supernatural powers (e.g., Emerson 2003; Price 2001). Thus, identification of such individuals and their role(s) in society may be strengthened in some cases by identification within graves of ritual objects, remains of psychoactive substances (and their paraphernalia, such as pipes), anomalous grave positions, and/or anomalous appearance, all of which might denote supernatural power. Knüsel (2002) suggests that the elite individual in the Iron Age Vix burial is indeed a female and indeed a leader; further, he argues that she is distinguished by a series of striking skeletal anomalies that would have impacted her ability to move around. He feels, on the basis of historic and ethnographic data, that this strengthens her identification as one whose leadership position is based on ritual power.

Shamanistic and other ritual practice are often associated with ideas of transformation in general, including from human to animal (or to bird) as well as from male to female (Price 2001; see also Emerson 2003). An archaeological example may be found in the late prehistoric images of "eagle dancers" or "hawk men" found in the central and southeastern United States. These humans, costumed or transformed to birds, are almost always identified as males; however, in some cases a costumed figure with breasts faces one without breasts (Brown 1982; see also Levy 1999a), suggesting complex intertwining themes of human/bird and male/female. Shamanism disrupts boundaries between human world and natural world and between natural world and supernatural world, as focus on gender diversity disrupts an entrenched dichotomous model and as heterarchy disrupts traditional culture evolutionary models.

Overall, then, the concept of heterarchy as a first step encourages the case-by-case examination of gender and sexual diversity and analysis of fluctuations in such identities as well as of the interconnections of these identities with other aspects of social organization.

Gender, Heterarchy, and Agency

Dobres and Robb (2000a) point out that there have been many definitions of *agency* in the context of archaeology. In any case, concepts of agency focus on the active involvement of individuals within a social system, differentially participating in, strengthening, challenging, and resisting the structural constraints of environment, values, and institutions: "people's practical engagement with the world" (Dobres and Robb 2000b:5). Concepts of agency entail attention to scale, as the saliency of individuals varies, depending on the scale of the phenomenon being examined (Dobres and Robb 2000b: 11; Gero and Scattolin 2002; Hodder 2000). Concepts of agency also suggest attention to performance (Robb 2001), which is relevant to both gender identity and status position.

Although the development of ideas about agency in anthropology are related, in part, to expanding feminist theory, it has been noted that gender in general and women in particular are frequently missing from agency-focused analyses (Gero 2000; Ortner 2001). The methodology for examining agency in the archaeological record must focus on detailed variability in material remains of the past but is underdeveloped (Brumfiel 2000; Robb 2001).

Even this simplified description of agency approaches in archaeology suggests links both to gender perspectives and to the concept of heterarchy. First, a focus on agency is congruent with examination of diversity in gender and sexual identities. Both emphasize the importance of variability among individuals, negotiation of identity and individual action in changing social circumstances, and the importance of performance and display in establishing individual identity and action. In this latter regard, agency links as well to archaeological studies of the body (Rautman 2000).

Further, as heterarchy is linked to and relevant to study of gender and sexual diversity, so it is congruent with agency as well. Smith (2001:167) points this out as he argues that to understand past human societies, we need to think about "multiple relationships among various structurally embedded social positions (e.g., elite institutions, grassroots social groups) and plurally sited individuals (that is, individuals located as profoundly in heterarchical roles as hierarchical ones)." That is, heterarchy—as does agency—encourages an examination of social variability, flexibility, and complexity at different scales (individual, community, and cross-community institution). Heterarchy also—as does agency, at least in principle—encourages an interest in lateral relationships as well as vertical ones. Heterarchy—as does agency—encourages a focus on active performance as a means of establishing and/or contesting a variety of salient social identities and relationships. Some relationships will be hierarchical in nature (e.g., a tribute payer and a tribute receiver), some will be balanced or lateral or collaborative (e.g., an independent craft worker in textiles and one in ceramics), and some will probably have elements of both patterns at different times (e.g., a parent and a child) or will be characterized by some other pattern I cannot at the moment imagine.

Finally, any of the variable social relationships that both heterarchy and agency encourage us to look at in detail may well have important gender components. Thus, I would disagree profoundly with Saitta and McGuire (1998: 335) when they say that heterarchy does not capture the lived experience of people's lives. The qualities of flexibility, fluctuation, and negotiation that are intrinsic to the concept of heterarchy are directly relevant to an individual's lived experience. In fact, heterarchy leads us to consider just how complex an individual's—a gendered and sexual individual's—lived experience may be.

Gender, Heterarchy, and Division of Labor

So far, the discussion of gender and heterarchy has been quite abstract. One way to make the discussion more concrete is to look at division of labor in the frame of gender and heterarchy. Just as interested archaeologists have struggled to move beyond dichotomous views of gender, we have also struggled to escape a tendency toward dichotomous views of the division of labor, such as that men hunt and women gather, men make lithics, women make pottery (but only in household craft situations), men trade, women cook, and so on. A heterarchical approach to division of labor will emphasize cross-cutting boundaries, lateral relationships as well as vertical ones, and multiple scales of analysis. That is, rather than assume a specific division of labor or specific trajectory of increasing specialization over time, we should consider evidence for variable organization of labor within family, community, and region. For example, Potter and King (1995:28) argue that ceramic and lithic production and distribution among the Classic period Maya are heterarchical: "To summarize, ceramic and lithic data suggest that Maya production and exchange occurred within two-cross-cutting systems," one of which was centrally controlled and one of which was not and both of which involved both categories of artifacts.

Mills (1995) makes several illuminating and relevant points about gendered division of labor on the basis of a study of Zuni pottery production and silver working in historic times. First, she makes a key point that there are often "hidden producers," where more than one person is involved in production of craft items (e.g., gathering clay, mixing clay, forming vessels, polishing, painting, gathering fuel, building kilns, and supervising firing); however, social authorship is focused on one individual, in fact, one gendered individual (Mills 1995:150). Mills also points out that as craft production becomes more central to household economies, more members of the family, presumably gendered members, participate in craft work (167). One of the counterintuitive implications of this pattern is that, at least in the Zuni case, more specialized craft production is *less* gendered. So with increasing commercial success through the twentieth century, Zuni pottery making, which had been originally part time and gendered female, became a more full-time craft practiced by both males and females. Furthermore, as silver work grew from a part-time to a full-time craft, it developed from a craft limited to a small number of males to one practiced by multiple members of families, including children.[1]

Finally, Mills points out that third-gender individuals may participate in both ostensibly male and ostensibly female activities; We'wha, the well-known Zuni third-gender person, was an accomplished potter at a time when most pottery was produced by women, produced weaving on both male- and female-style looms, and participated in male ritual activities (Mills 1995:151, summarizing from Roscoe 1991).

Mills's work encourages a heterarchical perspective on a gendered division of labor in archaeological cases: diverse participants in fluctuating and diverse relationships. It should be an open question whether craft work and other tasks were highly gendered, and it should be an open question whether specialization implies a single producer for each object or multiple, collaborative producers. In fact, there are very few craft production sequences that one can imagine that do *not* involve multiple contributors (certain kinds of lithic production might be one). Where we have evidence to suspect third-gender individuals, the association between craft production and gender is likely to be even more complex. Mills (1995:161) notes that in earlier stages of Zuni pottery and silver manufacture, when production was part time but highly gendered, the results look *more* specialized because there is less design variability. In later phases, when production is more full time and less gendered, there is more diversity of form and design. Thus, the interrelationships among specialization, production, and gender are clearly complex and flexible.

An archaeological example, although less well developed than Mills's work, can be drawn from metallurgy in Late Bronze Age Denmark (Levy 1991, 1995).

The archaeological evidence suggests at least three locales for production of bronze artifacts as well as variable production techniques, including casting in clay molds, casting in stone molds, and lost wax casting as well as hammering and engraving designs. Some types of bronze artifacts were produced in ordinary habitation sites, apparently in a household setting, as seen in the distribution of relevant finds. Other artifact types were apparently produced in another setting because almost all the stone molds are found outside of habitation sites; finally, there are certain, very elaborate artifacts for which we have no direct archaeological evidence for the locale of their manufacture. This suggests that they were produced in a third, specialized setting.

Metallurgical production not only included casting molten metal but must have included gathering and preparing fuel, producing clay and stone molds and wax models, hammering and polishing cast items, and engraving decoration on cast objects—all tasks that could be accomplished by household members of different genders and perhaps ages. I describe this pattern of craft work as heterarchical because the evidence suggests multiple contexts of production, lateral relationships between individuals at different stages of production, and different scales of distribution of bronze artifacts. The production of the most lavish artifacts may well have been controlled by an elite, while other bronze artifacts were widely produced and distributed; both the hierarchical pattern and the heterarchical pattern are real and important.

Despite Randsborg's (1986:148) claim that Danish metallurgy must have been male dominated, the full pattern of production of bronze objects probably included males, females, and perhaps third-gender individuals. He rests his argument on ethnographic evidence, but a careful examination of that evidence, most influentially in Africa, reveals the biases of both male observers and male metal workers (P. Schmidt 1998) that often hide women's contributions. While casting was a significant part of the technology, another significant phase of production must have been crafting the detailed, apparently symbolic, engraved designs on cast items; this is a task that requires an aesthetic sense, a steady hand, and perhaps special ritual knowledge but no obvious sex-linked qualities.

As Mills (1995) notes, it may be the Western cultural emphasis on autonomous artisanship that masks the likely complexity of production sequences in prehistory. Thus, the idea of increasing craft specialization is implicitly linked to increasing hierarchy of individuals, usually male individuals. But it should remain an open question whether objects are completely made and controlled by single individuals in any particular prehistoric case. Where production evidence turns up in household settings, the likelihood is that more than one household member was significantly involved in production. That is, as noted previously, the *scale* of a particular phenomenon is relevant to understanding the nature of its complexity.

Gender, Heterarchy, and Hierarchy

Finally, this interconnection of heterarchy, gender, and division of labor again turns attention to the common but usually implicit conflation of complexity with hierarchy. As noted earlier, Crumley's original goal in introducing the concept of heterarchy was to critique simplistic understandings of social complexity and, in particular, critique the conflation of complexity and hierarchy. While others have adopted this critique (e.g., McIntosh 1999; O'Reilly 2003; Sastre 2002), gender has rarely been incorporated into the critique. A volume edited by Pyburn (2004b) provides insight into a way to expand Crumley's critique through the incorporation of gender.

Pyburn and contributors originate their critique of cultural evolutionary studies of prehistoric and early historic complex societies with an analogy to Wolf's (1982) concept of "people without history." That is, all or almost all ethnographic observations of political systems, division of labor, and gendered social roles are tainted by the bias or lack of access of Western, Christian, male observers and/or by the sociocultural, political, and economic changes caused by contact with Western, Christian, patriarchal colonizers (for similar perspectives, see also Howell 1995; Kent 1998). Thus, first in early ethnographic accounts and later in archaeological utilizations of these accounts, women are "people without history" (Pyburn 2004a:6); that is, how they really lived, what they really did with much of their time, and how they participated in political structures are simply not known. Thus, most evolutionary studies of states either explicitly or implicitly give the impression that "the status of women, though clearly not uniform across time and space, is nevertheless thought to be uniformly subordinate throughout human history" (7). Often, this subordination is linked to women's child-rearing responsibilities (this is the commonly proposed reason why women do not participate in metallurgy), but Pyburn points out, on the basis of her own experience in a nonindustrialized Maya village, that "adults do not take care of small children. Infants are cared for by 8- to 10-year olds (both boys and girls)" (17). It has also been noted by a variety of other scholars that even if women do have extra child-rearing responsibilities, they are not raising children for their entire lives.

In terms of archaeological interpretation, these assumptions oversimplify the complexity of social roles, the cross-cutting of different social variables, and the potential for autonomous, powerful women: "it seems a likely possibility that the manner in which states are defined and identified archaeologically is based on sexist assumptions about what behavior counts as political, what organizations function as economic, and what material culture indicates either" (Pyburn 2004a:29). For example, standard interpretations of Viking graves suggests that when tools are found in men's graves, they indicate occupation of the deceased; however, when tools are found in women's graves, they are said to indicate the status or occupation of the *family* (Mortensen 2004). (This, by the way, is a convention I followed in earlier research [Levy 1982:79] where it was critiqued by Sørensen [1992].) Or, in analyses of early Sumerian states, secular power is a priori given higher status than ritual power. Thus, automatically, women—who could hold the highest ritual positions—are seen as subordinate in the political system: "Rather than considering the relations between different aspects of power . . . , archaeologists constantly separate these fields and rank them in terms of superiority and inferiority, as is done with the 'public' and the 'private'" (Al-Zubaidi 2004:128). Knüsel (2002) independently makes a similar point, suggesting that the separation of secular and ritual power is a recent development probably derived from competition between church and state in early modern Europe but is not an appropriate concept in most prehistoric cases.

By adopting the concept of heterarchy, an archaeologist is encouraged to look not at classifications (e.g., chiefdom/state or corporate/network, although these can be helpful concepts at times) but rather at cross-cutting variables of status, influence, and power and the fluctuations between and among them. These variables will include ritual influence, economic control, political power, age, lineage, and—most relevant to this discussion—gender. Analyses of chiefly societies often focus on the chiefs alone (e.g., Kristiansen 1991), but surely everyone else—90 percent or more of the population—was out and about, interacting, producing, worshiping, resisting, and contributing to the archaeological record. No chief could manage or even survive without the activities of all those other people. While the activities and roles of women will obviously vary from case to case, they must have been active agents at many levels of complex societies. By focusing on heterarchy rather than hierarchy, we are encouraged to consider the intertwining roles of women, men, and third and fourth genders in the establishment of influence, power, and inequality.

The key point here is to emphasize that complexity and fluctuation in social roles is probably more often the rule than the exception in human societies. While focusing on one or more "chiefs" or "craft specialists" or "ritual specialists" is a starting point, analysis must consider the cross-cutting and fluctuating roles that individuals play within the communities of different scale that they participate in. While being a female may be most relevant within the household, being a craft producer may be more relevant at the level of the local community and being a ritual specialist more relevant at the regional level.

A heterarchical perspective on questions of social change or social evolution in prehistoric societies improves our analysis. By emphasizing lateral social differentiation, we escape a conflation of complexity and "progress" with hierarchy. Such a conflation not only denies the complexity of daily lives in a variety of social systems but also, as implied by Pyburn (2004b) and colleagues, frequently eliminates women from interpretations of political life or even public life. Prehistoric Denmark can again provide an example.

Kristiansen (1984:85) says about Neolithic Denmark, "The system's evolutionary potential was not released until the introduction of bronze." Elsewhere (Kristiansen 1991:39), he says about Bronze Age Denmark, "The core components of Iron Age social organization were developed during the late Bronze Age, but their potential was constrained by the tribal rationality of Bronze Age society." The implication here is that societies that reach their potential (like good children) are those that develop more centralized and hierarchical political structures. But, we might ask, Potential for what or for whom? Further, in his discussion of Bronze Age Denmark, Kristiansen (1991:30–31, 38) labels the Late Bronze Age (ca. 1100–600 B.C.) as a period of "consolidation and decline" as opposed to an Early Bronze Age (ca. 1600–1100 B.C.) expansion phase. Notably, the earlier period is marked by the deposition of bronze wealth in the form of swords and other weapons in mostly male burials, while the later period is marked by the deposition of bronze wealth in the form of ornaments worn by women in hoards, not burials. The two periods are certainly *different*, but the latter period is a "decline" only if male competition and hierarchy alone count as complex and interesting.

Thus, with heterarchy, we are encouraged to always incorporate analyses of lateral social differentiation—including gender differentiation—and social relations into study of social change. In order to understand social change, it is essential to understand the life courses of diverse categories of people in a prehistoric society. Further, we are encouraged to examine explicitly the interactions of vertical and horizontal social relations. Increasing economic inequality, to suggest one example, may both derive from these complex interactions and influence their further development. Even in state societies, perhaps characterized by significantly hierarchical economic and political structures, lateral social relationships must impact daily lives, and daily lives must impact the development of nonegalitarian relationships and, of course, the creation of the archaeological record. Derevenski (2000) suggests that the first metallurgy developed in central Europe not just because of technological innovation but also to respond to social needs in a time of "exceptionally complex life course trajectories" (394): "Instead, the use of metal in the Copper Age was a socio-cultural response to perceptions of the life course and developments in the categorization of the person" (402).

A Small Case Study: Late Bronze Age Denmark

Bronze Age Denmark has been mentioned a number of times as demonstrating some themes within the study of heterarchy and gender. At this point, let me expand the case study. During the Late Bronze Age (ca. 1100–600 B.C.) in Denmark, all burials are cremations and the grave goods tend to be small and infrequent; there is almost no skeletal information available. However, during the same period, a large number of bronze and gold objects are deposited in hoards, that is, collections of artifacts purposefully deposited outside of graves or domestic settlements. The hoards are frequently deposited in bogs or other damp settings and include tools, weapons, and a large number of ornaments as well as special items, such as feasting equipment, military gear, horse gear, large musical horns (*lurs*), and other rare items (illustrations can be found in Coles and Harding 1979:491–532). The *lurs*, military items, and some of the feasting equipment are found in hoards without any other objects, and the horse gear and some of the cups and feasting equipment are found in hoards containing more "personal" items as well. There are good reasons to accept that many of these hoards were ritual deposits of some kind, and most of the artifacts show evidence of having been used in life.

Bronze Ornaments, Hierarchy, and Heterarchy

One can (and, in fact, I did [Levy 1982:59–67]) analyze these hoards as markers of hierarchy within a chiefdom with the chiefly class marked especially by the feasting equipment and military objects (such as bronze shields); it was implicit that the highest rank was assumed to be male (see also Kristiansen 1984, 1991; Randsborg 1986). However, a reappraisal of the material suggests that a perspective informed by both heterarchy and gender is more revealing. The largest sample comes from the chronological phase in the middle of the Late Bronze Age, when hoards are dominated by ornaments; 101 individual sets of ornaments are found in eighty-one hoards.[2] These range from a pair of neck rings or arm rings (i.e., a single artifact type) to sets of two artifact types (e.g., a necking and two arm rings) and up to five artifact types (necking, armoring, brooch, belt plate [attached to the front of the belt], and "hanging vessel" [attached to the back of the belt]). Table 7.1 shows the patterns.

First, it is clear that the ornament sets are organized in a roughly pyramidal

Table 7.1. Danish Late Bronze Age Ornament Sets

Sets of Bronze Ornaments[1]	No. of sets	No. of combinations	No. of possible combinations[2]
HV-BP-NR-AR-F (4)	4	1	1
HV-F-NR-AR HV-BP-NR-AR HV-BP-F-NR HV-BP-F-AR (7) (3) (1) (1)	12	4	5
HV-F-NR HV-NR-AR HV-BP-AR HV-BP-NR (3) (10) (6) (4)	23	4	20
F-AR NR-AR F-NR HV-F HV-BP BP-AR HV-NR HV-AR BP-NR (2) (9) (1) (2) (5) (1) (4) (4) (1)	29	9	20
NR-NR AR-AR HV-HV (20) (6) (7)	33	3	5

[1] NR = neck ring; AR = arm ring; HV = "hanging vessel" (a belt ornament attached at the back); BP = "belt plate" (a belt ornament attached at the front); F = "fibula" (an elaborate brooch); (x) = number of examples known.
[2] $n!/r!(n-r)!$, where n = total number of artifact types (i.e., five) and r = number of artifact types in each set.

fashion, with more simple sets and fewer complex ones. Second, the table suggests that the combinations are nonrandom choices. At all levels where there are diverse options for combinations (i.e., all levels except the "top" one), not all the possible options have been utilized; further, some combinations are much more common than others. Indeed, there seem to be constraints on how the specific ornaments can be combined; for example, it is rare to find an ornament set containing a belt plate without a hanging vessel (two examples), but it is common to find the reverse, a hanging vessel without a belt plate (thirty examples, not including the seven sets that consist of hanging vessels alone). I have argued elsewhere (Levy 1982:69–74) that these sets represent sumptuary goods that indicate a variety of status positions.

There is certainly a degree of ranking demonstrated here, and the special items, such as feasting equipment, may denote one or more superordinate ranks. The ranking likely includes an economic aspect, as the objects are prestige goods of some kind made of relatively rare, imported resources. The ranking is also likely based on criteria other than economic, for the weight of some of the less complex sets is greater than that of some of the more complex ones. As metal weight can be a rough proxy of economic value here, complexity of display is not always positively correlated with economic value; both economic value and social value are being represented in complex ways. Thus, this set of archaeological data indicates at least two (and possibly several) axes of vertical differentiation.

There must also be several axes of horizontal differentiation, including sex and gender, demonstrated by the apparently nonrandom variability in artifact combinations across each level of complexity. For example, some of the variability in Bronze Age female costume has been attributed to marital status (Eskildsen and Lomborg 1976; Sørensen 1991:125). There is also limited evidence to assign different artifact types to males or females. That evidence suggests that the two kinds of belt ornaments were worn only by women. Evidence about the other three types is less clear; all three were certainly worn by women, but some were probably worn by men as well. There has not been any explicit examination of whether third- or fourth-gender individuals might also have participated in these displays.

Other material variables, such as associated artifacts, may reflect other social factors. Bronze sickles are found in some of these hoards, ornamental bronze horse gear in others, and cups or other feasting equipment in still others. Perhaps it was relevant how the objects were arranged, although these data are limited (most of the hoards were discovered by ordinary citizens, many in the nineteenth or early twentieth century, and there is no information about their arrangement); sometimes the metal objects are found within a large pottery vessel, while in other cases the objects were found in a careful pile without any container. In addition, while many of the hoards were found in wet places, there are differences in the locales of deposition. These differences may denote other social variables. Intensive analysis of the covariation of these factors may yield new patterns.

Discussion

Thus, patterns of material variability within this data set suggest that a variety of social variables were important enough to structure personal display in life and in ritual deposition. The variables of horizontal differentiation may include sex, gender, age, kinship status, ritual status, political role, work specialization, and so on. Although there is not space to analyze the variability in detail, I can suggest that the rarest ornament combinations, those that include a belt plate without a hanging vessel, might represent third-gender individuals; these individuals were wearing an object ordinarily affiliated with women only but in a rare combination—not with the other female ornament that is commonly associated with the belt plate but rather with an ornament that may be worn by both males and females. Other combinations may denote age groupings, kinship status, leadership position (e.g., personal items associated with feasting equipment or horse gear), and/or occupation.

The preliminary analysis given here was at a large scale, lumping data from all over Denmark. Another step in the analysis would be to focus the scale more narrowly. As a start, the distribution maps of these hoards and ornament sets demonstrate that they are not distributed evenly across Denmark (Levy 1982:72–74). In my original analysis, I said about this, "The ornament sets are not distributed evenly over Denmark, but at least three levels of ornament sets are found in each three relatively distinct areas (Zealand, Funen, northern Jutland). The organization of sumptuary sets differs in detail in each of these areas, but the inferred existence of several social ranks in each area is supported" (Levy 1982:74). Clearly, my interest was focused on hierarchy; further analysis might benefit from closely examining just how the organization of these ornament sets and associated artifacts does differ from region to region and the implications of those differences for understanding aspects of lateral or horizontal complexity, not just vertical differentiation.

Another perspective on these finds links heterarchy, gender, and agency. The ornament sets (as well as weapons and other objects) were worn by individuals. The objects represented not only economic resources and a variety of social statuses, but many probably also had symbolic significance. The symbolic or ritual significance could be communicated by color and sound as well as by engraved motifs (Levy 1999b). Both wearing these objects and depositing them in ritual contexts entailed performance at some level. Of course, it is social agents who create and participate in performances. But, to go further, it is heterarchical situations that encourage performance because individuals are manipulating the social resources available to them within a flexible and fluctuating social context. Perhaps this is especially true in those contexts, such as societies traditionally labeled as ranked, middle level, or chiefdoms, where ranking and stratification are evolving or changing and where status must be continually negotiated and asserted. Wolf (1990:593) reminds us that the cultural structures that establish some persons as more powerful than others must be repeatedly negotiated and actively maintained: "The cultural assertion that the world is shaped in this way and not in some other has to be repeated and enacted, lest it be questioned and denied."

Joyce (2000) and Derevenski (2000) provide other archaeological examples (Mesoamerica and central Europe, respectively) of variability in archaeologically recovered dress and ornament that identify cross-cutting and interacting age, gender, and status positions. Joyce's subtitle is "the *production* of adulthood in ancient Mesoamerica" (emphasis added). This production is clearly through dress, appearance, and performance, as it seems to be in Bronze Age Denmark as well.

The Danish hoards can be (and have been [Levy 1982:79; see also Randsborg 1986]) accepted as markers of family status and/or as markers of a general hierarchical social model. But this falls into the trap noted by Mortensen (2004) previously: men's objects are seen as marking their own status, while women's objects are seen as marking family or community status. By utilizing a heterarchical perspective, the significance of social factors beyond simply ranking—including gender—are emphasized. Women displayed and controlled significant economic and ritual resources in the objects found in the hoards, apparently including feasting equipment and horse gear. This suggests significant influence and rank; if we credit this rank simply to women's families, we implicitly impose an androcentric perspective and a passivity on women without providing well-thought-out justifications. Males also controlled a variety of economic and ritual resources, and it is certainly possible that third-gender individuals did as well. The challenge now is to seek further evidence in the archaeological record and analyze further how these variables of social role, rank, and influence interacted.

This rich set of finds from one period of the Danish Bronze Age demonstrates the advantage of a heterarchical perspective, especially when this analysis is integrated with examination of other parts of the archaeological record, such as the evidence of metalworking discussed previously. First, both the vertical and the lateral axes of social variability are considered. There is evidence of hierarchy, and this is real, but the lateral differentiation is real as well and had a daily life significance that must be considered. Second, because multiple axes of social variability are emphasized, sex and gender become important foci of research, as they must have been significant parameters of Bronze Age daily life. Where both rank and gender are considered, we are encouraged to develop a more nuanced understanding of status and rank that does not implicitly privilege males as the only active participants in high rank. Third, a multiscalar approach is encouraged; for example, one should ask how the subregions within a quite homogeneous cultural area, such as Bronze Age Denmark, differed in construction and expression of social differentiation. Given that there seems to have been communication between all the subregions (e.g., based on similar design motifs across the whole area), how might the internal social differences influence interaction and social change?

The Future

There are a number of challenges for continuing research into heterarchy and gender. First, there has been progress in specifying how heterarchy appears in the archaeological record. For example, Joyce and Hendon (2000) discuss certain landscape signatures of heterarchy. I have suggested here some ways to look at artifact data in a heterarchical perspective, examining variability that is both vertical in quality (e.g., number, size, or weight) and horizontal in quality (e.g., alternate decoration or combination). Derevenski (2002:206) provides another example, looking at the variable grave patterns of the Beaker period (ca. 2600–2000 B.C.) in southern England: "The construction of gender through the contrasting intersections between sex and other forms of difference is inherently volatile since it does not merely reflect other relations of power but is constantly contested and transformed."

Nevertheless, more work will improve our understanding of how heterarchy appears in the archaeological record in different cases. In the case of gender studies specifically, research will certainly utilize burial and habitation evidence and may benefit from ethnographic studies made richer and more critical by an understanding of the biases of current data (Pyburn 2004b). Data from biological anthropology may also contribute. For example, Peterson's (2002) work with musculoskeletal stress markers can contribute to a richer understanding of variability of occupation within a community. As she notes, these modifications of the human skeleton can provide data about labor activity that are independent of ethnographic analogy. For example, Peterson argues that activity patterns of men and women in the Levant are more similar in the early Neolithic than in the preceding Natufian (end of the period of foraging); this is due to more reorganization of male activities than female ones (Peterson 2002:73–74). In contrast, at the beginning of the Early Bronze Age, although populations overall were less robust than earlier, there appears to be more sex-based division of labor (145). There is clearly not a linear development here.

Other specialist analyses, such as compositional studies, may have a role to play. One can imagine a hierarchical situation where pots of one specific compositional pattern, perhaps from distant clays, are found in elite contexts and pots made of another, nearby clay are found in nonelite contexts. In contrast, Simon and Ravesloot (1995) suggest that the wide variability in composition of pots found in Salado (ca. A.D. 1250–1450 in Arizona) graves can be linked to a range of lateral social relationships participated in by the deceased; pots made of different clays come from dispersed individuals and groups related in a variety of ways to the deceased: "we have the potential to uncover the social framework by which Salado culture was woven together" (122), a nice metaphor for heterarchy.

Second, it may be informative to extend the notion of heterarchy to studies of gender and practice within the profession of archaeology. Conkey and Gero (1997) note the hierarchical—and often androcentric—structure of archaeological fieldwork and the impact of this structure on interpretation of the archaeological record. An explicitly heterarchical approach to fieldwork may yield very different results and provide more openings in archaeological practice for voices of women and others: "Instead, feminist practice might offer multiple interpretive judgments and evaluations at each nonreversible step of investigation, and coordinate multiple strategies and objectives of different co-investigators into the research of nonrenewable archaeological resources" (Conkey and Gero 1997:429). It remains an open question if this kind of approach, whether one calls it feminist, heterarchical, or postprocessual, can be pulled off in practice. One possible exemplar is the Çatalhöyük project in central Turkey, where multiple voices and fluid relations are explicitly encouraged: "One implication of this is that conclusions are always momentary, fluid and flexible as new relations are considered; being interactive in the sense of creating information that can be questioned and approached from different angles; being multivocal, plural, open or transparent so that a diversity of people can participate in the discourse about the archaeological process" (Hodder 1996).

Third, the concept of heterarchy can contribute to study of symbols and symbolism in the archaeological record. The focus in heterarchy on lateral differentiation and on multiscalar analysis links to Turner's (1969) concept of multivocal symbols. A single symbolic motif may have, in Turner's terms, exegetical, operational, and positional meanings, the interactions of which intensify the significance of the symbol. Hays-Gilpin (1995:134) suggests that iconography is "ambiguous by its very nature." Or, as sociologist Stark (2001:77) says in a rather different context, "Heterarchies make assets of ambiguities." This reference reminds us of the heterarchy of diverse gender identifications within different societies and the link of third- and fourth-gender individuals to ritual systems. Symbolism and ideology are significant aspects of archaeological gender studies; a heterarchical approach to symbols has the potential to enrich this topic.

Finally, there remains work to be done on applying a heterarchical perspective to analysis of culture change. Heterarchy is a rich and dense way to describe social complexity, and we can start by looking for evidence of interaction between lateral and vertical differentiation as an impetus for culture change. Certain situations may generate especially intense interaction between vertical and lateral; Crumley (1994:184) suggests that climatic conditions will have an effect here, as will times of economic stimulation (Crumley 1987b:418), perhaps including periods of new technologies and/or contact with previously unfamiliar populations.

Further, the heterarchical perspective allows a consideration of culture change that escapes the value-laden concepts of decline or collapse (Crumley 1995:4), concepts often fraught with ethnocentric and androcentric bias. Heterarchy alone does not cause culture change. Rather, a heterarchical perspective encourages investigators to focus on a broader set of social factors and gendered social players in examining culture change.

Conclusion

Because of heterarchy's emphasis on both lateral and vertical differentiation, it opens up analysis specifically to considerations of sex and gender. Thus, a heterarchical perspective discourages narratives about the past that focus on society as a whole, which usually privileges (implicitly or explicitly) the actions of only a small, usually male segment of the prehistoric population. Heterarchy requires that we keep several balls in the air at once, acknowledging fluctuations and flexibility within and interconnections among power, gender, agency, and social change.

Acknowledgments

Many thanks to Sarah Nelson for inviting me to join this project and continuing thanks to Carole Crumley, Patty Jo Watson, Joan Gero, Cheryl Claassen, Gregory Starrett, and others who have improved my research and writing on gender and other topics. My research in Denmark was supported by the American-Scandinavian Foundation, Washington University–St. Louis, and the University of North

Carolina at Charlotte. I have many debts, intellectual, practical, and personal, to a wide range of colleagues in Scandinavia.

Notes

1. Mills (1995:160) notes that while this change in labor organization did occur within a commercial context linked to capitalist markets, it happened without centralized control. Her research focused on independent, family-based producers, not the producers employed by jobbers located in the city of Gallup.

2. There were a total of 125 hoards from this period identified in 1975. The ornament sets are found both alone and combined with other objects in eighty-one hoards included in the analysis. In addition to these eighty-one hoards, four other hoards contain examples of these ornament types, but the objects cannot be easily divided into individual sets; while I believe that these four hoards do contain such sets, the objects from these four hoards are not included in the analysis. Some of the remaining hoards from this period contain bronze axes, swords, and/or spear points but no ornaments; others contain distinctive and unique items, such as shields or the *lurs* (trumpets). These clearly can and should be incorporated into a fuller analysis. The chronological period to which these objects are assigned (Montelius Period V) covers 150 to 200 years. Clearly, all the hoards cannot be contemporaneous; however, these objects cannot be dated to finer divisions within the period, so they are treated here as contemporary. For more information on the hoards in general, see Levy (1982). For general information on the Bronze Age in Denmark, see Coles and Harding (1979). Pictures are also available in Kristiansen (1984).

References

Al-Zubaidi, Layla
    2004   Tracing Women in Early Sumer. In *Ungendering Civilization*. K. Anne Pyburn, ed. Pp. 117–35. New York: Routledge.

Arnold, Bettina
    1991   The Deposed Princess of Vix: The Need for an Engendered European Prehistory. In *The Archaeology of Gender*. Proceedings of the 22nd Annual Chacmool Conference. Dale Walde and Noreen D. Willows, eds. Pp. 366–74. Calgary: Department of Archaeology, University of Calgary.
    2002   "Sein und Werden": Gender as Process in Mortuary Ritual. In *In Pursuit of Gender: Worldwide Archaeological Approaches*. Sarah Milledge Nelson and Myriam Rosen-Ayalon, eds. Pp. 239–56. Walnut Creek, CA: AltaMira Press.

Bidney, David
    1947   Human Nature and the Cultural Process. *American Anthropologist* 49:375–99.

Brown, Catherine
    1982   On the Gender of the Winged Being on Mississippian Period Copper Plates. *Tennessee Anthropologist* 7(1):1–8.

Brumfiel, Elizabeth M.
>   1995   Heterarchy and the Analysis of Complex Societies: Comments. In *Heterarchy and the Analysis of Complex Societies*. Robert M. Ehrenreich, Carole L. Crumley, and Janet E. Levy, eds. Pp. 125–31. Archaeological Papers of the American Anthropological Association 6. Washington, DC: American Anthropological Association.
>   2000   On the Archaeology of Choice: Agency Studies as a Research Stratagem. In *Agency in Archaeology*. Marcia-Anne Dobres and John E. Robb, eds. Pp. 249–55. New York: Routledge.

Coles, John, and Anthony F. Harding
>   1979   *The Bronze Age in Europe*. London: Methuen.

Conkey, Margaret W., and Joan M. Gero
>   1997   Programme to Practice: Gender and Feminism in Archaeology. *Annual Review of Anthropology* 26:411–37.

Crown, Patricia L.
>   2000   Gendered Tasks, Power, and Prestige in the Prehispanic American Southwest. In *Women and Men in the Prehispanic Southwest*. Patricia L. Crown, ed. Pp. 3–42. Santa Fe, NM: School of American Research Press.

Crumley, Carole L.
>   1979   Three Locational Models: An Epistemological Assessment of Anthropology and Archaeology. In *Advances in Archaeological Method and Theory*. Vol. 2. Michael B. Schiffer, ed. Pp. 141–73. New York: Academic Press.
>   1987a Celtic Settlement before the Conquest: The Dialectics of Landscape and Power. In *Regional Dynamics: Burgundian Landscapes in Historical Perspective*. Carole L. Crumley and William H. Marquardt, eds. Pp. 403–29. San Diego: Academic Press.
>   1987b A Dialectical Critique of Hierarchy. In *Power Relations and State Formation*. Thomas C. Patterson and Christine W. Gailey, eds. Pp. 155–69. Washington, DC: American Anthropological Association.
>   1994   The Ecology of Conquest: Contrasting Agropastoral and Agricultural Societies' Adaptations to Climatic Change. In *Historical Ecology: Cultural Knowledge and Changing Landscapes*. Carole L. Crumley, ed. Pp. 183–202. Santa Fe, NM: School of American Research Press.
>   1995   Heterarchy and the Analysis of Complex Societies. In *Heterarchy and the Analysis of Complex Societies*. Robert M. Ehrenreich, Carole L. Crumley, and Janet E. Levy, eds. Pp. 1–6. Archaeological Papers of the American Anthropological Association 6. Washington, DC: American Anthropological Association.

Crumley, Carole L., and William H. Marquardt, eds.
>   1987   *Regional Dynamics: Burgundian Landscapes in Historical Perspective*. San Diego: Academic Press.

Derevenski, Joanna Sofaer
>   2000   Rings of Life: The Role of Early Metalwork in Mediating the Gendered Life Course. *World Archaeology* 31:389–406.

2002 Engendering Context: Context as Gendered Practice in the Early Bronze Age of the Upper Thomas Valley, UK. *European Journal of Archaeology* 5:191–211.

Dobres, Marcia-Anne, and John E. Robb, eds.
2000a *Agency in Archaeology*. New York: Routledge.

Dobres, Marcia-Anne, and John E. Robb
2000b Agency in Archaeology: Paradigm or Platitude? In *Agency in Archaeology*. Marcia-Anne Dobres and John E. Robb, eds. Pp. 3–17. New York: Routledge.

Dowson, Thomas A.
2000 Why Queer Archaeology? An Introduction. *World Archaeology* 32:161–65.

Egelhoff, William G.
1999 Organizational Equilibrium and Organization Change: Two Different Perspectives on the Multinational Enterprise. *Journal of International Management* 5:15–33.

Ehrenreich, Robert M.
1995 Early Metalworking: A Heterarchical Analysis of Industrial Organization. In *Heterarchy and the Analysis of Complex Societies*. Robert M. Ehrenreich, Carole L. Crumley, and Janet E. Levy, eds. Pp. 33–40. Archaeological Papers of the American Anthropological Association 6. Washington, DC: American Anthropological Association.

Emerson, Thomas A.
2003 Materializing Cahokia Shamans. *Southeastern Archaeology* 22:135–54.

Eskildsen, L., and Ebbe Lomborg
1976 Giftetanker. *Skalk* 5:18–26.

Gero, Joan M.
2000 Troubled Travels in Agency and Feminism. In *Agency in Archaeology*. Marcia-Anne Dobres and John E. Robb, eds. Pp. 34–39. New York: Routledge.

Gero, Joan M., and M. Cristina Scattolin
2002 Beyond Complementarity and Hierarchy: New Definitions for Archaeological Gender Relations. In *In Pursuit of Gender: Worldwide Archaeological Approaches*. Sarah Milledge Nelson and Myriam Rosen-Ayalon, eds. Pp. 155–72. Walnut Creek, CA: AltaMira Press.

Hays-Gilpin, Kelley
1995 Gender Ideology and Ritual Activities. *Journal of Anthropological Research* 51:91–135.

Hodder, Ian
1996 Glocalising Catal: Towards Postprocessual Methodology. Paper presented at the Theoretical Archaeology Group, Liverpool. Electronic document, http://www.catalhoyuk.com/TAG_papers/ian.htm, accessed December 14, 2005.

2000 Agency and Individuals in Long-Term Processes. In *Agency in Archaeology*. Marcia-Anne Dobres and John E. Robb, eds. Pp. 21–33. New York: Routledge.

Hollimon, Sandra E.
2000 Archaeology of the *'Aqui*: Gender and Sexuality in Prehistoric Chumash Soci-

ety. In *Archaeologies of Sexuality.* Robert A. Schmidt and Barbara L. Voss, eds. Pp. 179–96. London: Routledge.
2001 The Gendered Peopling of North America: Addressing the Antiquity of Systems of Multiple Genders. In *The Archaeology of Shamanism.* Neil S. Price, ed. Pp. 123–34. New York: Routledge.

Howell, Todd L.
1995 Tracking Zuni Gender and Leadership Roles across the Contact Period. *Journal of Anthropological Research* 51:125–47.

Joyce, Rosemary A.
2000 Girling the Girl and Boying the Boy: The Production of Adulthood in Ancient Mesoamerica. *World Archaeology* 31:473–83.

Joyce, Rosemary A., and Julia A. Hendon
2000 Heterarchy, History, and Material Reality: "Communities" in Late Classic Honduras. In *The Archaeology of Communities: A New World Perspective.* Marcello A. Canuto and Jason Yaeger, eds. Pp. 143–60. New York: Routledge.

Kent, Susan
1998 Gender and Prehistory in Africa. In *Gender in African Prehistory.* Susan Kent, ed. Pp. 9–21. Walnut Creek, CA: AltaMira Press/Sage.

Knüsel, Christopher J.
2002 More Circe Than Cassandra: The Princess of Vix in Ritualized Social Context. *European Journal of Archaeology* 5:275–308.

Kristiansen, Kristian
1984 Ideology and Material Culture: An Archaeological Perspective. In *Marxist Perspectives in Archaeology.* Matthew Spriggs, ed. Pp. 72–100. Cambridge: Cambridge University Press.
1991 Chiefdoms, States and Systems of Social Evolution. In *Chiefdoms: Economy, Power and Ideology.* Timothy Earle, ed. Pp. 16–43. Cambridge: Cambridge University Press.

Levy, Janet E.
1982 *Social and Religious Organization in Bronze Age Denmark.* BAR International Series 124. Oxford: British Archaeological Reports.
1991 Metalworking Technology and Craft Specialization in Bronze Age Denmark. *Archaeomaterials* 5:55–74.
1995 Heterarchy in Bronze Age Denmark: Settlement Pattern, Gender, and Ritual. In *Heterarchy and the Analysis of Complex Societies.* Robert M. Ehrenreich, Carole L. Crumley, and Janet E. Levy, eds. Pp. 41–54. Archaeological Papers of the American Anthropological Association 6. Washington, DC: American Anthropological Association.
1999a Gender, Power, and Heterarchy in Middle-Level Societies. In *Manifesting Power: Gender and the Interpretation of Power in Archaeology.* Tracy Sweely, ed. Pp. 62–78. New York: Routledge.
1999b Metals, Symbols, and Society in Bronze Age Denmark. In *Material Symbols:*

  Culture and Economy in Prehistory. John Robb, ed. Pp. 205–23. Occasional Paper 26. Carbondale: Center for Archaeological Investigations, Southern Illinois University.

Marquardt, William H., and Carole L. Crumley
 1987 Theoretical Issues in the Analysis of Spatial Patterning. In *Regional Dynamics: Burgundian Landscapes in Historical Perspective.* Carole L. Crumley and William H. Marquardt, eds. Pp. 1–18. San Diego: Academic Press.

McGuire, Randall H., and Dean J. Saitta
 1996 Although They Have Petty Captains, They Obey Them Badly: The Dialectics of Prehispanic Western Pueblo Organization. *American Antiquity* 61:197–216.

McIntosh, Susan Keech
 1999 Pathways to Complexity: An African Perspective. In *Beyond Chiefdoms: Pathways to Complexity in Africa.* Susan Keech McIntosh, ed. Pp. 1–30. Cambridge: Cambridge University Press.

Mills, Barbara J.
 1995 Gender and the Reorganization of Historic Zuni Craft Production: Implications for Archaeological Interpretation. *Journal of Anthropological Research* 51:149–72.
 2000 Alternate Models, Alternate Strategies: Leadership in the Prehispanic Southwest. In *Alternative Leadership Strategies in the Prehispanic Southwest.* Barbara J. Mills, ed. Pp. 3–18. Tucson: University of Arizona Press.

Mortensen, Lena
 2004 The "Marauding Pagan Warrior" Woman. In *Ungendering Civilization.* K. Anne Pyburn, ed. Pp. 94–116. New York: Routledge.

O'Reilly, Dougald J. W.
 2003 Further Evidence of Heterarchy in Bronze Age Thailand. *Current Anthropology* 44:300–307.

Ortner, Sherry B.
 2001 Commentary: Practice, Power and the Past. *Journal of Social Archaeology* 1:271–78.

Peterson, Jane
 2002 *Sexual Revolutions: Gender and Labor at the Dawn of Agriculture.* Walnut Creek, CA: AltaMira Press.

Potter, Daniel R., and Eleanor M. King
 1995 A Heterarchical Approach to Lowland Maya Socioeconomics. In *Heterarchy and the Analysis of Complex Societies.* Robert M. Ehrenreich, Carole L. Crumley, and Janet E. Levy, eds. Pp. 17–32. Archaeological Papers of the American Anthropological Association 6. Washington, DC: American Anthropological Association.

Price, Neil S.
 2001 An Archaeology of Altered States: Shamanism and Material Culture Studies.

In *The Archaeology of Shamanism*. Neil S. Price, ed. Pp. 3–16. New York: Routledge.

Pyburn, K. Anne
  2004a Introduction: Rethinking Complex Society. In *Ungendering Civilization*. K. Anne Pyburn, ed. Pp. 1–46. New York: Routledge.

Pyburn, K. Anne, ed.
  2004b *Ungendering Civilization*. New York: Routledge.

Randsborg, Klavs
  1986 Women in Prehistory: The Danish Example. *Acta Archaeologica* 1984:143–54.

Rautman, Alison E.
  1998 Hierarchy and Heterarchy in the American Southwest: A Comment on McGuire and Saitta. *American Antiquity* 63:325–33.

Rautman, Alison E., ed.
  2000 *Reading the Body: Representations and Remains in the Archaeological Record*. Philadelphia: University of Pennsylvania Press.

Robb, John
  2001 Steps to an Archaeology of Agency. Paper presented at the Agency Workshop, November 2001, University College, London. Electronic document, http://www.arch.cam.ac.uk/~jer39/theory/agency2.html, accessed October 14, 2004.

Roscoe, Will
  1991 *The Zuni Man-Woman*. Albuquerque: University of New Mexico Press.

Saitta, Dean J., and Randall H. McGuire
  1998 Dialectics, Heterarchy, and Western Pueblo Social Organization. *American Antiquity* 63:334–36.

Sastre, Inés
  2002 Forms of Social Inequality in the Castro Culture of North-West Iberia. *European Journal of Archaeology* 5:213–48.

Scarborough, Vernon L., Fred Valdez Jr., and Nicholas Dunning, eds.
  2003 *Heterarchy, Political Economy, and the Ancient Maya: The Three Rivers Region of the East-Central Yucatán Peninsula*. Tucson: University of Arizona Press.

Schmidt, Peter
  1998 Reading Gender in the Ancient Iron Technology of Africa. In *Gender in African Prehistory*. Susan Kent, ed. Pp. 139–62. Walnut Creek, CA: AltaMira Press/Sage.

Schmidt, Robert A.
  2000 Shamans and Northern Cosmology: The Direct Historical Approach to Mesolithic Sexuality. In *Archaeologies of Sexuality*. Robert A. Schmidt and Barbara L. Voss, eds. Pp. 220–35. London: Routledge.

Simon, Arleyn W., and John C. Ravesloot
  1995 Salado Ceramic Burial Offerings: A Consideration of Gender and Social Organization. *Journal of Anthropological Research* 51:103–24.

Smith, Adam T.
    2001   The Limitations of Doxa: Agency and Subjectivity from an Archaeological Point of View. *Journal of Social Archaeology* 1:155–71.

Sørensen, Marie-Louise Stig
    1991   The Construction of Gender through Appearance. In *The Archaeology of Gender*. Proceedings of the 22nd Annual Chacmool Conference. Dale Walde and Noreen D. Willows, eds. Pp. 121–29. Calgary: Department of Archaeology, University of Calgary.
    1992   Gender Archaeology and Scandinavian Bronze Age Studies. *Norwegian Archaeological Review* 25:31–49.

Stark, David
    2001   Ambiguous Assets for Uncertain Environments: Heterarchy in Postsocialist Firms. In *The Twenty-First-Century Firm: Changing Economic Organization in International Perspective*. Paul Di Maggio, ed. Pp. 69–104. Princeton, NJ: Princeton University Press.

Thomas, Julian
    1994   AAA Annual Meeting, Washington DC. *Anthropology Today* 10(1):21.

Turner, Victor
    1969   *The Ritual Process*. Chicago: Aldine.

Weglian, Emily
    2001   Grave Goods Do Not a Gender Make: A Case Study from Singen am Hohentwiel, Germany. In *Gender and the Archaeology of Death*. Bettina Arnold and Nancy L. Wicker, eds. Pp. 137–55. Walnut Creek, CA: AltaMira Press.

White, Joyce C.
    1995   Incorporating Heterarchy into Theory on Socio-Political Development: The Case for Southeast Asia. In *Heterarchy and the Analysis of Complex Societies*. Robert M. Ehrenreich, Carole L. Crumley, and Janet E. Levy, eds. Pp. 101–24. Archaeological Papers of the American Anthropological Association 6. Washington, DC: American Anthropological Association.

Wolf, Eric R.
    1982   *Europe and the People Without History*. Berkeley: University of California Press.
    1990   Distinguished Lecture: Facing Power—Old Insights, New Questions. *American Anthropologist* 92:586–96.

Znoj, Heinzpeter
    2005   *Heterarchy and Domination in Highland Jambi: The Contest for Community in a Matrilinear Society*. London: Kegan Paul.

Gender and Ethnoarchaeology 8

KATHRYN WEEDMAN

Between 1960 and 1966, Hanna and Barbera produced a cartoon series, *The Flintstones*, which appropriately reveals Western gender ideologies and the ease with which we transport them into the past. As a cartoon, *The Flintstones* is a tool of enculturation; among other aspects of life, it demonstrates to our youth our idealized gender roles. Wilma Flintstone and Betty Rubble (the female leading roles) serve as archetypes by cooking, cleaning, gossiping, and caring for their children within their homes, but it is questionable whether they represent the Stone Age women they are supposed to portray. Their husbands, Fred and Barney, leave every day to work in the stone quarry, and when they are not "working," they are meandering out in the world taking risks and getting into trouble. These gender roles clearly reflect those of Western industrialism, marked by a period in which men were first called out of agricultural work in the household context to work in factories (Stone and McKee 1998:29–38). In the industrial age, manhood was achieved and measured against economic prosperity gained through individualistic, competitive, and aggressive behavior. By default, women were expected to care for the domestic sphere and to create a balance for men by being social, noncompetitive, nonaggressive, and passive.

The Flintstones does not represent a reality in either the past or the present. Obviously, people did not exist at the same time as dinosaurs, nor are telephones made out of ram horns or sinks filled through elephant trunks. These are anachronisms and mixings of domains: the present (realities and imaginations) and several documented pasts. The mixing of the past and the present is obvious in the material culture and the text (i.e., the music and dialogue) of *The Flintstones* cartoon. However, in many ways, *The Flintstones* represents a portrait of the past that is often mimicked or perhaps encouraged by archaeological literature, illustrations, and museum exhibits (Gifford-Gonzalez 1993b; Moser 1993; Weedman 2004). As Gifford-Gonzalez (1993b:31) stated, "To those of us conversant with thirty years' hunter-gatherer studies and with feminist critiques of 'Man the Hunter', the cumulative perspective on women and men in the landscape bears a peculiarly Western, woman's-place-is-in-the-home, cultural stamp." When archaeologists ascribe names to artifacts and features, such as hunting spear and digging stick, they imply an unspoken meaning, including the gender of the producer. We describe the past as we see it in the present, reducing them to sameness (mixing two separate domains), which is a specific form of analogy called metonymy (Schmidt 1997:28–30). Since the day when objects were recognized as products of past human activities, we have been engaged in the process of metonymy; hence, both the past and the present have revolved around heavily Eurocentric and androcentric ideologies (Orme 1981:1–16; Schmidt 1997; Trigger 1989).

Archaeology is a tool of enculturation; we enter it to learn about ourselves, where we came from, and how we behaved, and we pass this knowledge on to our children through books, museum exhibits, and television shows. We search in the past for our humanity; thus, our past is filtered through our perceptions of how we live today, including our gender roles; if it were not, it is questionable whether we would still consider the past as relevant or even interesting in the present. In essence, our reconstructions of the past are a reflection of the present, and we can broaden our interpretations of the past only through studies of present-day people and their material culture (i.e., ethnoarchaeology). Ethnoarchaeology, as the study of living peoples and their relationship to their material culture to provide models for translating the past, offers an opportunity for ascertaining alternative gender identities and their reflection in material culture and use of space. Ethnoarchaeological studies have the potential to allow us to escape Eurocentric and androcentric interpretations and reconstructions of the past by focusing on emic perspectives (David 1992b; Schmidt 1997). The goals of this chapter are to explore how ethnoarchaeological studies of gender reflect the diversity of feminist theories and define gender, how ethnoarchaeologists methodologically study gender, how they view gender as reflected in the past, and to what extent ethnoarchaeology has served as a source for identifying alternative genders.

Feminism, Defining Gender, and Ethnoarchaeological Theories

Four decades ago, Ortner (1974) argued that gender roles are rooted in the essentials of reproduction, and since this time feminist anthropologists have sought worldwide examples that offer a distinction between gender and sex to "denaturalize gender asymmetry" (Morris 1995:568). Explanations for the status, role, and identity of women outlined in cultural anthropology (di Leonardo 1991) largely mirror those in other disciplines, such as biology and political science (Jaggar 1983; Rosser 1992), including liberal feminism, existential feminism, Marxist feminism, socialist feminism, essentialist feminism, and, more recently, postmodern queer theory and performance theory. For the most part, feminist cultural studies confirm that there is a universal male/female dichotomy, that gender correlates with biological sex, that gender is intertwined with cultural and racial power relations, and that men tend to disempower the feminine (Power and Watts 1997; Visweswaran 1997). In our androcentric culture, it is not surprising to find that most studies in gendered archaeology adopted a feminist approach that emphasized finding women in the archaeological record (Conkey and Gero 1997), which has resulted in correlating gender with biological sex (Voss 2000; but for exceptions, see Hollimon 1997; Matthews 2000). Voss (2000) argues that feminist archaeologists may remain conservative because of the fear that deconstructing sex and gender may destabilize archaeological reconstructions that rely on the naturalization of the dichotomy as an absolute truth rather than as symbolic ambiguity.

The earliest studies that discuss the possible visibility of differences in gender roles as reflected in space and material culture were written by cultural anthropologists (Beck 1978; Bourdieu 1973; Draper 1975; Dupire 1963). These studies of pastoral, forager, and agricultural societies emphasized symmetry, complementarity, and equality between the sexes and dissimilarity to Western gender ideologies but reinforced the concept of a binary male/female set. Furthermore, to some extent the female authors discussed the imposition of particular gender roles as a result of contact with the West emphasizing either change (Beck 1978; Draper 1975) or cultural retention (Dupire 1963). Dupire (1963) provided an explanation for gender through a study of Fulani language and practice. Bourdieu (1973) also emphasized that while there is a male/female dichotomy represented in the use and symbolic meaning of household space, it is a reversal of the order of the outside world that indicated a balance and symmetry and overlap of the sexes. These early studies exemplify an understanding of gender through ritual practice, serving as the forebears for gendered performance theory (Bourdieu 1977; Butler 1990; Foucault 1978, 1980).

Ethnoarchaeology, as the disciplinary slip between cultural and archaeological studies and the present and the past, should provide us with alternative worldviews concerning the relationship between sex and gender and a means for viewing gendered practices through material culture in the past. David and Kramer (2001:34) note that ethnoarchaeologists generally do not explicitly reveal their theoretical perspective, and this may be even more true in studies of gender, where early gendered studies were masked under titles related to activity areas (Kent 1984) and demographics (David 1971). This is not a criticism of the authors but simply reflects the resistance to gender-focused studies among archaeologists in the 1970s and early 1980s. However, even a review of current ethnoarchaeological studies fails to reveal research that either defines gender or outlines a particular feminist perspective (for exceptions, see Kent 1998; Lyons 1992; Moore 1986:166–73). Instead, ethnoarchaeological theoretical perspectives reflect the paradigmatic changes in anthropological and archaeological thought, and their understanding of gender becomes evident through the questions researchers ask and the answers. Before the 1970s, there were few attempts in archaeology to incorporate women into prehistory because the emphasis was on structural continuity and evolutionary development, and the past was basically a mirror of a non-Western society filtered through Western ideology. Reconstructions were exceptionally androcentric, and few if any contributions to societal change or progress were attributed to women (for a notable exception, see Murray 1949). For instance, although even the earliest documented ethnoarchaeological studies focused on women potters (Bunzel 1929; Colton 1953; Cushing 1886), there is no attempt to understand gender roles in particular cultural context, as the gender/sex of men and women is viewed as a given. In these studies, not only was the male/female division taken for granted, but it was assumed that because women make pots in the present, they must also have made them in the past, which marked these studies as clearly entrenched in the direct historical approach.

Since the early 1970s, archaeologists and ethnoarchaeologists have engaged in the general comparative, discontinuous or universal-core approach, which was a reaction against direct historical, evolutionary, and diffusionistic models that failed to appreciate the uniqueness of the past (Clark 1953; Cunningham 2003; Gould 1974, 1977; Willey 1953). The general comparative approaches were similar in that they shared a belief that there are prime movers or single regularities that drive culture and transcend time; however, which real things structured behavior is disputed, especially between processual, contextual/ideological, and evolutionary models (Cunningham 2003; Kosso 1991; Wylie 2000:228). In the processual ethnoarchaeological studies of the 1970s, there is a clear assumption that a gendered division of labor equaled a sexual division of labor (Binford 1978b, 1987; Hayden 1979; Yellen 1976, 1977). The goal of these early processual studies was to generate "objective" cross-cultural generalities and norms in the performance of forager activities, primarily hunting and stone-tool production and use, and to discern from these regularities the subsequent artifact form and distribution. Ironically, although the goal of ethnoarchaeology of that time was to create cross-cultural models for testing against the past rather than directly explaining the past, these early ethnoarchaeological studies continued to view gender roles as a stagnant representation of present-day Western gender. Women are mentioned in passing as adjunct to men in butchering, hunting, or fishing activities (Binford 1978b:152) and as gatherers (Yellen 1976, 1977) and stone-tool producers (Hayden 1979:183–86). However, the emphasis was not on deciphering how gendered division of labor affected the archaeological patterning but rather on how activities transcended time and space. Hence, there were no efforts to examine historical context or to understand indigenous ideology, especially concerning gender, because the ascription of gender roles to each sex was viewed as natural universal constants.

By the 1980s, almost a decade after cultural anthropologists began to focus on denaturalizing sex from gender, processual ethnoarchaeologists began to look at gender as a cultural construction. Janes's (1983, 1989) description of the overlap between activities and space between men and women suggested that gender was not biologically determined in Dene culture. Janes (1983:78) stated that the Dene greatly value the male hunter but that actual behavior does not reflect ideology because to do so would be "maladaptive in an environment where survival . . . is still contingent upon mastery of a wide range of practical skills." He also contended that ethnohistory must be more fully studied to comprehend the influences of Europeans and history on gender relationships and ideology. Kent (1984, 1990, 1995, 1998, 1999), unlike Janes, saw little value in incorporating a historical perspective and took a much stronger processual position that ethnoarchaeology needs to focus on cross-cultural generalizations rather than on specific historical contextual cases. Her search for gender in cross-cultural regularities and generalizations would seem at odds with the idea that gender is a cultural construction, and in fact her writings reflect this struggle. In one publication, Kent (1990:149) relinquished the cultural construction of gender and the visibility of gendered use of space to only more complex societies, as such less complex societies base gendered division of labor on sex. However, Kent (1998:40) later argued that behavior and thus gender are not biologically determined but rather that the sociopolitical organization of the culture system determined gender. These views do not necessarily represent a contradiction but a westernized evolutionary perspective that there are non-Western societies that are less complex and that base gender roles on biology/nature rather than culture. Interestingly, Kent (1999) specifically argued that her perspective is not Eurocentric even with the heavy evolutionary overtones. She stated that power in egalitarian societies is meaningless because no one has more power than another; it is Western ideology that has projected a higher value on hunting as more masculine and projected it onto foraging cultures, thus perpetuating the idea that there was a division of labor and space in past foraging societies. Kent, as one of the few researchers to dedicate her career to ethnoarchaeology, should also be commended for her lifelong commitment to ethnoarchaeological studies of gender.

Contextual/interpretive ethnoarchaeology emphasized social practices and material culture as a specific system of signs that reflect the ideological structure (Hodder 1977, 1982, 1987; Schmidt 1978, 1983, 1997:23–44, 1998). The goal was to find not regularities but an understanding of meanings through material culture and its spatial distribution (i.e., context). Contextual ethnoarchaeology also stressed symbolic continuity through time by relying on structuralism, which outlines that there are universal binary oppositions, including male/female. While the male/female dichotomy may be a constant, what symbolizes this core binary opposition in ideology and practice was culture specific. As with cultural studies of gender, ethnoarchaeological contextual studies emphasized the differences that were produced by several different social processes. For example, Hodder (1977) and Herbich (1987) offered that homogeneous ceramic style may be produced by women potters in either patrilineal virilocal societies, where there are ideological pressures on women to conform in their married communities, or in matrilocal societies, where mother and daughter reside and produce pots together. Furthermore, according to Hodder (1982:83–84, 139–40), because of male dominance, women bonded and silently renegotiated their positions through the material world. Thus, Hodder viewed women as visible because women have a different ideology or worldview from men. David (1971) believed that men are invisible and that women are visible not because they silently bond through material culture but because most structures were built for women's activities. In contrast, based on her ethnoarchaeological research among the Endo of Kenya, Moore (1986:188) stated that men and women do not have a separate ideology and that materials do not reflect the true nature of gender relations. In Endo culture, males dominated and were represented obscuring male/female tensions. Donley-Reid's study of the Swahili (Donley 1982; Donley-Reid 1987, 1990a, 1990b) also emphasized male power as reflected in male control of female use of space. Lyons (1990, 1991, 1992) concurred that among her studies in northern Cameroon, space and materials in male-oriented societies are likely to reflect male dominance. However, Lyons states that ideology is not static and that through their activities and practices women make themselves known materially and spatially. Schmidt's (1996a, 1996b, 1997, 1998) work also emphasized the flexibility in gender ideology through time and space, indicating that anomalies and contradictions in male and female material and spatial representation are the key to understanding change in gendered relations as social constructions.

Proponents of evolutionary models insisted that all individuals (males and females) make their decisions on the basis of efficiency and effectiveness shaped by natural selection (Broughton and O'Connell 1999; O'Connell 1995:209). Several ethnoarchaeological studies of foragers in East Africa (Hawkes et al. 1997) and South America (Hurtado et al. 1985) by behavioral ecologists indicated that the activities that women do or do not engage in are a direct reflection of their biology and their need to enhance offspring survival, which results in their low-risk behavior. Likewise, essentialist feminists state that women are different from men because of their biology, specifically their secondary sex characteristics and reproduction system that extend to their visual-spatial ability, verbal ability, physical traits, and mental traits (Kirsch 1993; Rosser 1992). However, Gifford-Gonzalez (1993a) argued that behavioral ecological approaches have not gone far enough and fail to examine the contributions women make in hunting acquisition, transport, processing, and storage and how men, women, and children's contributions to a household together result in benefits.

Postmodern philosophers argue that Western culture has a limited perception of the world because it focuses on a center—an origin, a truth, or an ideal form (Bourdieu 1977; Derrida 1978). The presence of a center creates binary oppositions in which the privileged side (male) freezes the play marginalizing the other (female). At the forefront of this movement, feminists identified women as marginalized in past and present scientific theories, research questions, and analyses (Harding 1998; Stepan 1986). Cultural anthropologists in the past two decades have suggested that sex, like gender, is a social category and thus an entry point for understanding systems of meaning and power (Visweswaran 1997). While many ethnoarchaeological studies attempt to reveal women as the "marginalized other," none has examined gender outside the male/female dichotomy or explicitly examined their respective cultures in terms of either Western or non-Western notions of feminism.

Gender and Ethnoarchaeological Methodologies

There is little doubt that in the past decade, the focus on gender in the past has proliferated and often includes either reference to ethnohistorical documentation or cross-cultural regularities drawn from ethnographies in support of archaeological interpretations (e.g., Boismier 1991; Crass 2001; chapters in Frink et al. 2002; Galloway 1997; Spector 1983; chapters in Walde and Willows 1991). Ethnohistory, either written or oral, is an important part of ethnoarchaeological studies and is utilized to expose anomalies and change in symbolic systems related to gender (Schmidt 1997, 1998) and the impact of colonial markets and ideology on gender relations (Frink 2005; Jarvenpa and Brumbach 1995; Webley 1997, 2005). Archaeologists eager to incorporate women or gender into their interpretations rarely acknowledge the difficulties in assessing the historic and ethnographic records they use for their models. As exceptions, Kehoe (1983), Spector (1983), Larson (1991), and Gifford-Gonzalez (1998) pointed out that until the 1980s it was standard practice for men to be ethnographers with male informants. All acknowledge that it may have been difficult for male researchers to work with women participants because the latter may have anticipated disrespect. Thus, earlier text may inherently have a gendered bias that reflected the researcher's own cultural and gendered interests rather than representing the gender ideology, tasks, and roles of the community studied. Larson (1991) indicated that a careful reexamination of the literature usually indicates the presence of women but that we need to be more careful with the language we use and more cognizant of how common knowledge and practice can mute variation and meaning. In Chase's (1991) attempt to sidestep this issue, she considered only works authored by women or husband-and-wife teams, reasoning that female ethnographers have improved access to female informants and would obtain more sincere information.

Most ethnoarchaeological studies that specifically focused on gender at the outset were conducted by women (e.g., Donley-Reid, Kent, Lyons, and Moore, with the exception of the work of Brumbach and Jarvenpa) with male researchers realizing the importance of gender in their works but not taking gender as the focal point (e.g., David, Hodder, Schmidt). In cultural anthropological studies, the sex of the interviewer and participant has been a topic of methodological discussion in the form of the questions: what is the experience of female researchers, and should male researchers study only male participants and female only female participants (Flinn et al. 1998; Golde 1986b; Gregory 1984; Warren 1988; Wolf 1996). Researchers have argued that women are less threatening because of their biology or because women as oppressed citizens share a common experience and thus have greater insight into other women's lives (Golde 1986a; Hartsock 1987). Others suggested that a closer bond or friendship could lead to such an intimate rapport and bond that they had difficulty separating out what information they should ethically reveal (Stacey 1991). Female ethnographers also have indicated that women researchers may accrue an ambiguous status in fieldwork situations as asexual, honorary male, or pseudomale because of their race, class, and Western identity (Bujra 1975; Warren 1988:26). Women studying their own non-Western cultures found that they may receive access in a patriarchal society only through accompaniment by father, husband, and brothers and were expected to adhere more strictly to gender roles (Berik 1996; Gupta 1979). Interestingly, in order to cope with the presence of a female boss in a very patriarchal society, my younger male assistants chose to refer to me as mother. Kent

(1984:17–19) indicated that she received the status of daughter or close friend in her ethnoarchaeological studies of the Navajo, Spanish American, and Euro-American households, enabling her to participate closely and relate on informal rather than formal terms; however, it also limited her participation in some male activities. Kent (1984:17) also stated that she chose the matrilineal Navajo as one of her study groups because "being a woman did not interfere with my observation and participation in most activities."

The sex and gender of translators/research assistants may also affect the access that researchers have to indigenous gender ideologies. Gould (1971), Brumbach and Jarvenpa (1990), and David and Kramer (2001) have all discussed the importance of research assistants for language translation, location of sites, and interpretation of artifacts and features. However, Lyons (1992:6–7) laments difficulties finding female translators/research assistants because educating women is not highly valued, and thus few speak nonindigenous languages. I experienced similar problems while working in southern Ethiopia, as few women attended school past the age of ten, and most had household and agricultural commitments and little time for wage labor. Thus, there were virtually no women to act as translators or research assistants. I found, however, that female participants seemed uninhibited by the presence of a male translator and even openly conveyed to me incidents concerning their personal lives that they did not share with foreign male researchers. Lyons (1992:7) stated that in her ethnoarchaeological study in northern Cameroon, she had difficulty interviewing female participants concerning household and grave construction because these areas belonged to the realm of men. However, she was able to interview women concerning craft production, marketing, beer making, and features concerning their activity areas.

Ethnoarchaeological studies of gender vary considerably in the amount of time spent from eleven days (Chang 1988) to eleven months (Lyons 1992) and into multi-year longitudinal studies (Janes 1983, 1989; Kent 1984, 1999; Schmidt 1978, 1997), broadly reflecting the duration of ethnoarchaeological studies in general. Janes (1989) reports that his longitudinal studies provided him with multiple observations of activities that varied over time and in space that he otherwise would not have ascertained. Regardless of the time spent in the field, the most common means of deriving spatial and material gendered evidence was through directed and open interviews and participant observation (Hodder 1982; Janes 1983; Jarvenpa and Brumbach 1995; Kent 1984; Lyons 1992; Schmidt 1997). Brumbach and Jarvenpa (1995, 1997a, 1997b) and Frink (2005) suggest that examining activities through the task system, where, via interviews and observation, the interviewer records each specific phase/stage, produces a more nuanced understanding of gendered activities. Constructing maps of activity areas also was a popular means for collecting information concerning gendered control and location of resources and activities (Chang 1988; Janes 1983; Kent 1984; Yellen 1977). Jarvenpa and Brumbach 1995; Brumbach and Jarvenpa 1997a, 1997b) showed their maps to participants who were asked to reveal the location of structures and activities at archaeological sites. Bowser and Patton (2004) combined their GPS-constructed maps locating distances between households against kinship and networking information to determine the strength of male and female alliances and their corresponding spatial representation. Similarly, I (Weedman 2005) compared household and village location against kinship and other forms of female alliance against stone-tool variation to examine the relationship between lithic variability and space. Several researchers considered life histories important for ascertaining changes in gender relationships related to stage of life (Hodder 1982:18; Jarvenpa and Brumbach 1995). Others, especially processual and behavioral ecologists, engaged in focal person studies in which the researcher followed and timed the activities of specific individuals to determine sex-specific activities and the time allocated to these activities (Chang 1988; Hawkes et al. 1997; Hurtado et al. 1985; Janes 1983).

Ethnoarchaeological writings rarely revealed the gender relationships, contrasts and similarities in ideologies, or ethical issues raised between the researchers, their assistants, and participants. However, the type of method used was more commonly found in articles related to gender than is seen overall in ethnoarchaeological literature (for a review, see Arthur and Weedman 2005). The latter may be a reflection on the predominance of female authors, who overall in archaeological studies have reported anxiety related to their work being disputed and tend to be more concerned with methods of data collection (Beaudry and White 1994; Ford and Hundt 1994; Lutz 1990). Ethnoarchaeologists need to be more explicit about their relationships, and this may serve not only to contextualize better the work but also to provide a more fluid opening into other realms of gender identity.

Gender in the Present Projected into the Past

In the past decade, the number of articles and chapters in edited volumes attempting to identify the presence of women and gender differences in the archaeological record has grown significantly. Primarily, gender is identified through space and specific material forms, burials, rock art, and figurines (see chapters in Claassen and Joyce 1997; Donald and Hurcombe 2000; Gero and Conkey 1991; Linduff and Sun 2004; Nelson and Rosen-Ayalon 2002; Wadley 1997; Wright 1996). The following section outlines the contributions of ethnoarchaeology to interpreting gender in the past. While there have been a few studies that focus on the visibility of gender in mortuary practices (David 1992a; Hodder 1982:163–84) and personal adornment (Hodder 1977, 1982:75–85; Lyons 1989, 1998), the majority of ethnoarchaeological studies examine the intersection of gender and the use of space and craft production.

Gendered Division of Labor and Use of Household Space

In Western society, we believe that there are differences between males and females and assign each sex with specific material culture, tasks/activities, and spaces, and this belief is so enculturated that we believe it to be natural. In 1984, Kent wrote the first ethnoarchaeological cross-cultural study of household activity areas and the gendered use of space, supporting the concept that Euro-Americans have sex-specific space and material culture. Kent offered that the differences between Euro-American, Spanish American, and Navajo households are related to sociopolitical complexity. Cultural anthropologist Maxine Margolis (2000) argued that the strict male:female division of labor and space (female/domestic:male/public) that we now view as natural in Euro-American culture is a result of industrialism. Interestingly, in Kent's study of Euro-American households, the head female had no full-time employment outside the household (one wife worked as a nurse part time on the weekends), while in the nine Navajo families (except one household where the woman was blind) and two Spanish American households, the women either produced crafts or worked outside the household. While I wish not to dispute Kent's results, which support our ideal of the "American dream household" where women stay at home, it is important to understand the magnitude with which historical and ideological contexts and our own Euro-American desires to idealize the past affect our perception of gender. In this shadow, archaeologists have overlain our Western ideology of male/competitive/public:female/docile/domestic on to the past. In this section, I address how ethnoarchaeological studies of the division of labor and use of space in non-Western societies broaden our understanding of gender visibility in the archaeological record.

FORAGERS   In prehistoric foraging societies, women were invisible because the materials associated with their gendered activities are perishable (Isaac 1989). Men as hunters and toolmakers were the only visible sex in the past; even at identified home bases or living floors (i.e., household contexts), women and children were immaterial. In the 1970s, feminist ethnographic studies of hunter-gatherers and the division of labor tended to counter the strict archaeological division of male/public/hunter/provider with female/domestic/gatherer/ nurturer and the emphasis on males and male activities as propelling human evolution (Bodenhorn 1990; Draper 1975; Ember 1978; Estioko-Griffin and Griffin 1975; Slocum 1975). These studies exposed women's participation in hunts and as the main food providers through gathering. In contrast, Draper's (1975) study of the !Kung San (Khoisan speakers) indicated that while men and women engaged in different but mutual activities, the space and materials they used for these activities overlapped as a result of the small amount of household space. Subsequent ethnoarchaeological studies of the !Kung of southern Africa concurred with Draper. For instance, Yellen's (1976, 1977:91–97) ethnoarchaeological study among the Dobe !Kung suggested that while men hunted and women gathered, these activities occurred outside the household and left few if any marks on the landscape. Furthermore, within !Kung households, activities and their products were intermixed, and there were no distinct separated gendered areas. Kent's (1990, 1998) studies of the Kutse San indicated that small-scale hunter-gatherers did not consistently segregate space or architecture by gender or by activity. Hence, men and women "without stigma" regularly collected wild plants, hunted small animals, collected water and firewood, and tended to small livestock. Kent (1999) argued that in Western society, hunting is associated with manliness, prestige, and danger, which is not a concept held by non-Western societies.

While Kent (1999:34) scoffed at the idea that hunting is more dangerous than gathering, Hurtado et al. (1985) and Hawkes et al. (1997; see also O'Connell et al. 1991) argued that females are gatherers because it minimizes risks to offspring, while enhancing male productivity. O'Connell et al.'s (1991) study of the Hadza of Tanzania (Khoisan speakers) revealed that behavior associated with refuse importantly reflects gendered activities, which are based on the female need to stay close to home to minimize risks to children. Males were more closely associated with weapons maintenance and its resulting refuse in peripheral communal areas, whereas women produced refuse associated with food processing and tool maintenance in the central communal areas and in households. Women swept the communal areas and households, which would result in male visibility in peripheral areas but female activity areas virtually void of material culture. Thus, in communal and household contexts, it would not be possible to distinguish sex-related activity areas. Hurtado et al.'s (1985) study of the Ache (Tupi speakers) of eastern Paraguay indicated that unlike the !Kung model, women did not provide most of the calories consumed by the group. Their research indicated that among the Ache, child care restraints were the primary means for the division of labor. Nursing women were less efficient foragers than nonnursing women, and as the number of weaned dependents increased, so did a woman's food production. They argued that because infant mortality was high, women began to choose less risky behavior that resulted in a lower mortality rate for infants. However, in the past, infant mortality may have been lower and women's contribution to food production higher. Hawkes et al. (1997) agreed that women participate in activities to enhance reproductive success; however, among the Hadza of Tanzania, nursing mothers did not spend either more or less time foraging than nonnursing mothers. However, because of the presence of a new child, more calories were needed. The authors offered that female relatives with an interest in survival of the children, including mother's mother, sisters, husband's mother, and great-grandmothers, increased their foraging time when a newborn arrives. Thus, the division of labor that rendered females as gatherers and child care providers, even after menopause, consisted of behaviors geared toward increasing survivorship.

Ethnoarchaeological studies of Arctic peoples disagree over the visibility of men and women in space and material culture. Binford's study of the Nunamiut (Eskimo-Aleut speakers) of Alaska (Binford 1978a, 1978b:152, 158–59) indicated that there were different areas associated with different activities and that both residential and male special purpose sites are visible, while women's activities of butchering, processing, and distributing were simply adjunct to men's. Janes's (1983:71–80, 1989) study of the Dene (Na-Dene speakers) of the Mackenzie Basin, Northwest Territories, Canada, supports Binford's work that it is safest to assume the presence of sex-specific activities at temporary hunting camps, which are predominantly male. Janes argued that because of differences in life experiences and because the same household spaces were used at different times for different tasks by males and females, the gendered use of space would not be visible in households. Chang's (1988) study of an Alaskan Inupiat fish camp also indicated that although men and women have separate tasks and equipment, there is not a spatial segregation of work. Brumbach and Jarvenpa's (1997a, 1997b; Jarvenpa and Brumbach 1995) studies of the Chipewyan (Na-Dene speakers) of Saskatchewan, Canada, disputed the idea that women are invisible in the Arctic and attempt to level the field by adding women. They used the task approach and life cycle approaches to look more closely at men and women's activities and the visibility of gender. While in agreement with Binford and Janes that bush-centered kill sites more often represent male activities, they believed that these types of sites are ephemeral. In contrast, transformation sites, where together men and women process animals, are more highly visible because of the types of material culture used and the length of occupation. Furthermore, women are the primary hunters of rabbits and other animals closer to home (within three to five kilometers), and their hunting activities may be more visible in village/settlement (village-centered hunting) context than those of men, who tend to kill a few large animals far removed from the village. Within village sites, there was also a distinct use of space representing female materials and female activities. Male activities tend to occur outside the village context, making their activities invisible in villages, though their materials for these external activities are stored in specific locations within a village. Their studies also indicated, like Hurtado et al. (1985), that women participate to different degrees in the different stages of hunting (locating, stalking, dispatching, butchering, and distributing), depending on their stage in the life cycle, and that most women outside of childbearing years participate in hunting. They used census data to indicate that before European contact, women bore fewer children and probably were involved more in hunting activities.

Finally, there have been two recent ethnoarchaeological studies of the division of labor in Asia, a region of the world where there are very few studies of gender in ethnoarchaeology. Although within Binford's (1987) and O'Connell's (1987) studies of site formation among the Alyawara (Australian speakers) of Australia we find embedded information concerning the sexual division of labor and space, there is either an emphasis on male activities (Binford) or a lack of details outlining differences between male and female space (O'Connell). Gargett and Hayden's (1991) research concerning the Pintupi (Australian speakers) of Australia indicated that because of the high value of female contribution to the diet (60 to 90 percent including protein), postmartial residence in this patrilineal society is initially matrilocal. Only after the death of a man's parents and in his elder years does he return to his clan estate. Thus, household aggregation is most commonly associated with mother–daughter relationships. Cooper's (1994, 2000) studies of the Onge (Andamanese speakers) hunter-gatherers of Little Andaman, India, explored interhousehold gender. The Onge live in fishing/hunting camps and temporary encampments, and as a result there are no archaeological habitation sites but rather shell refuse middens that also contain other types of material culture. She determined that while men were responsible mostly for heavier work associated with hunting, such as setting nets and building weirs and traps, women were also hunters and fishers. Furthermore, children also contributed significantly to the diet. Cooper suggested that the allocation of tasks according to sex and age is arranged to meet efficiency in production.

FARMERS Ethnographers and archaeologists have argued that with the beginning of food production and increased sedentism (Bar-Yosef 1995; Draper 1975; Ehrenberg 1989) or with changes in forager economic and technological organization (Kent 1995), there is a more sharply defined sexual division of labor. Although women are quite clearly associated with plant gathering in forager societies, at the onset of agriculture either men or neutral agents are associated with food production. Again, much of this is a result of Western ideology, which envisions the male as farmer and the female as farmwife. The adherence and projection of our Western division of agricultural labor has already been demonstrated through the obscuring of women's roles in non-Western agriculture, leading to the misunderstanding in education programs and loan agencies associated with development and aid organizations outside the West (Lewis 1984; Rubbo 1975; Spring 2000). For example, in an article that is labeled as ethnoarchaeological but that actually is ethnographic, Casey (1991) outlined the division of labor and gender roles in the agricultural society of Mamprugu in northern Ghana as strongly contrasting Western ideals. Casey points out that in Mamprugu society, women are not confined to the household and are expected to earn income, indicating that men and women are economically autonomous and that gender is not correlated with biological sex. Recent archaeological reconstructions have begun to acknowledge women as farmers (Ehrenberg 1989; Watson and Kennedy 1991), drawing into question the spaces and materials they used in prehistoric contexts. The ethnographic and ethnoarchaeological studies of agrarian division of labor and use of space are concentrated in Africa and Central and South America.

One of the most widely cited ethnographic works that described the gendered use of space in an agrarian patrilineal society is Bourdieu's "The Berber House" (1973). Bourdieu contends that the rectangular Algerian Berber (Afro-Asiatic speakers) house in Kabyle is a metaphor for organization of the universe, which is divided into homologous oppositions including male/public:female/private/nature/darkness. But the house blurs this dichotomy because although the house is female/private as opposed to male/public, there are defined male and female objects and spaces within the house that are complementary, and the house is also a reversal of the order of the outside world, which is controlled by men. An earlier ethnoarchaeological study by David (1971) also examined an agrarian Muslim North African village for the gendered use of space but determined that men and children were mostly invisible in households, while women were visible. David studied thirty-six patrilineal Fulani (Niger-Congo speakers) households in the village of Bé in northern Cameroon to derive an archaeological model for population estimates. David suggested that the number of women in a village could be estimated on the basis of the number of structures with hearths and the number of water storage pots since only women cooked and collected water. Guest quarters and men's quarters were virtually devoid of materials, making men virtually invisible in the archaeological record, though males as heads of family may be counted by the number of granaries present.

Diane Lyons has been working on ethnoarchaeological studies of gender in agrarian West African societies for the past fifteen years. Lyons (1989, 1990, 1991, 1992, 1996, 1998) worked in the village of Dela in northern Cameron, comprised of four ethnic groups (the Mura, Urza, and the Muslim Shuw and Muslim Wandala of the Afro-Asiatic speakers). Her work outlined how women's symbolic and ideological status as daughters, wives, and cowives in different cultures and religions is practically expressed in household organization of space. In the Muslim households, men were expected to provide all resources for their wives and children (through hired labor); hence, women did not work in the fields or produce crafts as non-Muslim women in the region did. Each wife stored her resources within her own separate square dwelling, and there was little cooperation between wives. In the non-Muslim households, the roundhouses were arranged around a central area where there was cooperative family labor, storage of grains, and a family shrine. In households where there was husband–wife cooperation for economic and reproductive value, there also was sharing of space among cowives, whereas in households with cowife competition, there were restricted spaces. Lyons (1989) presented further evidence that there was a connection between the cultural construction of time, gender, and the separation of male and female household space. The patrilineal Mura's exogamous marriage patterns forced women to break continuity with their father's ancestors, denying them legitimate land rights and justifying their inferiority to men. Men spent their time cultivating ancestral fields and ensuring continuity of his patrilineage; hence, sexual relationships and the birth of children occurred in a man's house. His house was located facing east, where the sun rises, so that he would know when to rise to start working in the fields. Women spent their time cooking and with other household tasks that they performed in a separate structure. Female/kitchen houses were located facing west, where the sun sets, so that a woman knew when to prepare the family meal. Furthermore, men buried medicine bundles, bones, and entrails of rooster at the threshold of the household entrance and sleeping hut and near their granaries to protect them from the witchcraft of other men and their own wives (Lyons 1989, 1998). There was no evidence that women buried items to protect themselves from their cowives. In addition, women prepared all food and beverages in decorated pots to protect men and guests from potential danger.

Donley-Reid's (1990a, 1990b; née Donley 1982, 1987) ethnoarchaeological study was situated in Muslim patrilineal households in East African societies. She stated that Swahili (Niger-Congo speakers) coral houses of the seventeenth to nineteenth centuries were organized in a manner to protect the purity of women, in turn securing the purity of the family line. Donley-Reid believed that the Swahili settlements of the seventeenth to nineteenth centuries along the coast were founded by Arabs marrying indigenous African women. The main architectural structures of coral houses and mosques were associated with the freeborn plantation owners and the traders of indigenous raw products. The freeborn occupied the upper levels of the house, the female servants lived on the lower levels where trade goods were stored, the household slaves lived on the ground floor, and the plantation slaves lived in thatched houses made of coconut leaves. Freeborn women lived in purdah and were therefore contained in their veils and houses, and having a wife in purdah gave a man higher status. Freeborn fathers built coral houses for their daughters as wedding presents, and such houses enhanced their value and made them more desirable as wives to Arab traders, who were usually the father's brother's son. Space in architecture was a means to control women by elite Swahili men; as women moved up in the social economic hierarchy, they moved from thatched houses toward the inner room of a coral house, and it was the men who decided who lived where.

Hodder (1982:125–42, 155–63) studied the agrarian southeastern Kadugli-Moro (patrilineal) and Mesakin Tiwal and Qisar (matrilineal) of Sudan (all three are Niger-Congo language speakers). In all three cultures, the household consisted of a ring of houses connected by a low stone wall. The Moro compounds were highly variable but at minimum consisted of a granary where the wife slept and another structure for the husband and children. The Mesakin household usually was composed of an entrance house where women and children slept, a male sleeping house, one grinding house, one storage house, and two granaries. The granaries faced each other, and one belonged to the wife located on the right and the other to the husband located on the left. Furthermore, they hung domesticated animal skulls on the granaries, which served as symbols of male purity and strength and thus protected men against the impurity of women, who were the main producers of grain and sources of pollution and danger. The houses were painted with symbols related to fertility so that the male symbols enclosed the female. These designs replicated the interconnectedness of males and females and reflected the desire to provide ritual protection for men against women's pollutive powers.

Moore (1986) studied the agrarian patrilineal Endo (Nilo-Saharan Sudanic speakers) of the Marakwet territory of Kenya. The earthen and thatch houses of a household compound consisted of a male sleeping area, female cooking house, goat structure, store area, compound rubbish area, ash and chaff waste dump, and animal dung heap. In public situations, males would firmly express male dominance and compare women to children, indicating that they are social and jural minors. It was common when men first married for the compound to consist of a single house and a separate cooking house. However, in some instances there were claims of insufficient resources to build a cooking house. A second house also may be built when the eldest daughter reached the age of eight, as a father can no longer sleep in the same house as his daughter. However, he may choose to sleep with the livestock or to allow his daughter to sleep with friends rather than building a separate structure. Men spent most of their time with other men making arrows and other objects or roasting meat and with their cattle. Men are closely associated with their cattle and animal fertility, and thus they are buried near the household dung heap. Women, in contrast, are identified with crops, so they are buried near household chaff heaps. Ash represents house, hearth, and cooking and is linked to female fertility and the powers of womanhood. However, even burial placement is variable, depending on the cause of death, household compound space, and age of the deceased. Moore believed that men and women shared the same dominate ideology, and thus one should not expect that men and women would present two different ideologies in material culture. The Endo view men and women as having separate roles, but the material and spatial expression can alter vastly with the family and individual life cycles. Thus, Moore argued that organization of space is not a direct reflection of culture codes and meanings representing the relationship between male and female but rather is developed through practice, which is highly variable.

In ethnographic studies of Bantu settlements, Schapera (1953) and Kuper (1982) associated the cattle byre with male authority, and the deceased male ancestors were buried in this location, while females and children associated with the domestic context were buried under or near the household. Numerous archaeologists have used this central cattle-byre pattern to outline the presence and spread of Bantu-speaking peoples from central to eastern and southern Africa (Denbow 1984; Huffman 1982; Phillipson 1977). Segobye (1998) brought into question the emphasis on cattle and iron by archaeologists reconstructing trends over broad spans of time and spaces and the secondary relegation of agricultural production, which was probably the main source of subsistence and related to women's production and daily activities. Davison (1988) studied a Mopondo (Niger-Congo speakers) homestead in Pondoland, Transkei, South Africa, to examine how gender and the use of space change through time in a Bantu community. Davison argued that meaning is not inherent in spatial order or in particular artifacts but in their context and association, which is produced through social action. She noted variation through time in the function of structures with storage structures becoming temporary sleeping structures for new wives, and the wives of the sons had neither their own sleeping houses nor hearths. The division of the household into a female left side and male right side was most strictly adhered to by the daughter-in-law, who must avoid her husband's senior male relatives.

Davison stated that archaeologists need to better understand and consider the archaeological context of materials as reflecting the active role of material culture in the negotiation of social relations.

Outside Africa, there have been two major ethnoarchaeological research projects in Latin America that focused on the gendered use of space. Hayden and Cannon (1984) studied three Mayan (Mayan speakers) villages (Chanal, San Mateo Ixtatan, and Aguacatenago) in the highlands of Guatemala. Among the patrilineal Maya, women cannot own or work land and have to depend on crafts and aid from males to survive economically; there are few female-only households. Hayden and Cannon examined if the ratio of artifact types would be affected by household sex ratio. They found no correlation and suggested that most tools are so essential to the operation of a household that no matter what the sex ratio, a household cannot do without them. Nelson et al. (2002) examined in more detail the scale of women's work among the Maya in San Mateo Ixtatan, Guatemala, and their representation in the spatial organization and composition of household assemblages. For the most part, kitchen and hearth areas were the domains of women, and the rest of the residential area was shared or dominated by men. Their study indicated that women's labor did not substantially contribute to increasing the wealth of a household. Generally, there were two household trends: one in which women engaged in pottery production and wage labor and another in which women made blouses and produced other craft items. Households that produced pottery tended to have more women in the household, probably because of the labor intensity of pottery production. There was no relationships between the scale of women's income from craft/wage production and the percentage of household space committed to women's use. Mayan women spent less than 10 percent of their time on crafts and did not need much space to store their products and materials.

Bowser and Patton (2004) studied the horticultural Achuar (Jivaroan speakers) and Quichua (Quechuan speakers) peoples in the village of Conambo, Ecuador. Their study of the strength of male and female alliances determined that women and men have different alliances and that women are better predictors of spatial arrangement (see also see Gargett and Hayden 1991). Women's alliances show more cross-cutting between Achuar and Quichua, and the authors suggested "that women are better situated to act as political brokers between groups" (168). Furthermore, women's kinship relationships better predict spatial distances between households than men's, probably because of the matrilocal postmarital residence patterns. Their pole-thatch and sawn-wood houses are divided into two parts: a public area where men spend their time and receive male guests and a private kitchen area where women prepare food and beer and receive female guests. Consequently, materials belonging to men, such as hunting equipment, basket-making materials, and machetes, are stored in the rafters of the public/male area of the household. In contrast, materials for food and beer preparation are located in the private/female area as well as sleeping quarters. A woman's private space in the house is not open to visiting men but may be shared with her spouse and other male family members. There are clear boundary markers between the two areas indicated by architectural differences, decorated brewing pots (see the section "Ceramics and Calabashes" later in this chapter), and sometimes a hearth that is used by men and women.

PASTORALISTS   Gifford-Gonzalez (1998) stated that most anthropological descriptions of pastoral society are androcentric, focusing on male relationships with one another and with domesticated stock. As a result, many pastoral ethnographies are missing much of the daily activities of women and children in camp and "participating in the rich web of socially contextualized work and experience" (119). Gendered studies of pastoralist societies and the use of space are seemingly limited and can be drawn mostly from ethnographies. For instance, Beck's (1978) ethnographic studies of the Shiite Muslim Qashqa'i pastoralist in Iran indicated that the domestic context was not divided into male and female sections as was commonly noted among other Middle Eastern nomadic peoples. Men and women used the encampment differently; while men were responsible for caring for the herd, sheering, branding, feeding, collecting firewood, and agriculture, woman were responsible for milling and milk processing, weaving, care of small animals near the tent, lighting fires, bringing water, collecting wild plants, cooking, baking, and child care—they were mutually dependent on one another. While men and women engaged in different but mutual activities, the space and materials they used for these activities overlapped as a result of the small amount of space. In contrast, Dupire (1963) emphasized differences in space and material remains between the sexes among the Muslim Fulani of Niger. The Fulani considered females and males opposite yet complementary, and the arrangement of the landscape and household space symbolically mirrored the principles of sex differentiation with women and female space following men's. Among the Fulani, women take care of stock located in the domestic context and are responsible for milking and making butter, building houses, decorating calabashes, tending to the hearth, drawing water, and cooking by boiling in pots, while men herd animals away from the household and roast meat. In stark contrast to Western culture, the Fulani women selected men at dance festivals for their gracefulness and beauty, and both young men and young women have complete sexual freedom.

These differences between pastoral groups are not resolved through ethnoarchaeological studies.

Ethnoarchaeological studies of gender and pastoralists have concentrated in Kenya among the Ilchamus (Nilo-Saharan speakers; Hodder 1987) and the Dassanetch (Afro-Asiatic speakers; Gifford-Gonzalez 1993a); both present positive evidence for the identification of gender in spatial arrangements and material culture. Hodder's (1987) study of the Ilchamus pastoralist of Kenya used a structural approach to argue the division of household space as it parallels gendered division of labor and ideology. A screen divided the Ilchamus household so that in the right/back portion of the house, female activities, which included cooking, storing calabashes, storing firewood, grain, sleeping, giving birth, breast feeding, and menstruating, were hidden from men. The left/front of the household was for men and visitors. Although men view themselves as providing, supporting, and controlling the home, in practice women were in control of the domestic context, and men had little access to the right/back portion of the household. Hodder offered that through practical action, women were renegotiating their power or control, which a woman lost when she married and entered the "control" of another patrilineage. Gifford-Gonzalez (1993a) studied the Dassanetch pastoralists of Kenya and suggested that women's cooking and processing activities have long been viewed as secondary and ignored by archaeologists as factors influencing site formation. Her study indicated that transverse fracturing and jagged breaks on animal bones are the direct result of breakage after cooking and may indicate the presence of female activities.

The ethnoarchaeological research outlined here points positively toward the identification of gendered social relationships through examining archaeological context and the use of space, especially in pastoral and farming societies. In foraging societies, the invisibility of women is contested only by Jarvenpa and Brumbach (1995), who argued that women as well as men were hunters and that they had specific identifiable tools and space within village contexts. Interestingly, the theoretical explanations for the invisibility of women in forager societies rest primarily on processual schools of thought, where function and activity are viewed as superseding social relationships. Most farmer and pastoral studies were conducted by contextual or postprocessual researchers who argued that meaning is culture and context specific. In addition, while forager studies focused primarily on the southern African, Asian, and Arctic peoples, studies of farming and pastoralists centered primarily on Africa and covered a wide range of cultural and linguistic groups. With few exceptions, most of the farmer and pastoral studies were among patrilineal societies and among Muslim populations in North and East Africa. In studies of agrarian societies, there also was exceptional diversity with some studies indicating the visibility of both men and women (Bourdieu 1973; Davison 1988; Hodder 1982, 1987; Lyons 1989, 1991, 1992, 1998) and others emphasizing male construction of female space with primarily female visibility (David 1971; Donley 1982, 1987; Donley-Reid 1990a, 1990b). Moore (1986) argued that gendered activities and spaces do not accurately reflect gender relations. Among the studies in South (Bowser and Patton 2004) and Central America (Hayden and Cannon 1984; Nelson et al. 2002), there also is disagreement over women's visibility. Still, there is much to be studied concerning space and gender. In most of these studies, it is unclear whether there are other village structures or places where men and women spend their time outside the household context, how their restriction to marginalized environments (especially among foragers) may affect the use of space, and how the spread of westernization, Christianity, and Islam and socioeconomic status (class, race, caste, and so on) have affected the presence of a binary male/female system and the idea of the women's space only within the domestic context. Thus far, Kent (1984, 1990, 1998) is the only ethnoarchaeologist who has examined the gendered use of space cross-culturally, concluding that societies that are highly stratified are more likely to have discrete areas of gendered activities than those representing low levels of stratification and a less strict division of labor and space.

Gender Specialized Occupations: Craft Production and Technology

In Western society, because of our historical background in which men are the industrial outside workers, we tend to ascribe the most labor-intensive, dull, and unskilled occupations with women, including craft production (Gifford-Gonzalez 1993b). Furthermore, these crafts are viewed as only meagerly contributing to household economic status and/or a means of obtaining status as compared to male activities (reinforced by at least one ethnoarchaeological study; see Nelson et al. 2002). Costin (1996) stated that despite the significance of the gendered division of labor in craft production for structuring social and power relations in complex society, there are few systematic sustained works ascribing gender in the studies of craft production. People use craft items not only in the domestic sphere but also to mediate social, economic, political, and ritual contexts (Costin 1998). As such, they are imbued with symbolic meaning and often serve as active or passive identity markers (Hodder 1982; Sackett 1990). Artisans have an essential role in creating meaning that is manifested in the objects they create (Costin 1998). Many of the items we recover in the archaeological deposits (ceramics, iron, stone tools, beads, basketry, wooden and stone figurines, and other objects) were created by specific artisans. Thus far, the ethnoarchaeological studies of gender and craft production are limited to iron, hide working, ceramics, and calabashes. The following sections review what these studies reveal to us when gender is taken as a focal point for exposing gender and political-economic status (kinds of good produced, access to resources, and extent of control over production and selling of products), gender and the type of craft production (household, household industry, workshop, village industry, and factory industry), and gender and social/ritual status (religion, kin, linguistic, and relations to noncraftspersons).

IRON   The studies of gendered iron production focus on Bantu Niger-Congo– and Cushitic Afro-Asiatic–speaking regions of Africa (Childs 1991; Goucher and Herbert 1996; Herbert 1993; Schmidt 1996a, 1996b, 1997, 1998; Schmidt and Mapunda 1997). Although African smelters are almost always men, women contribute significantly to the labor required to prepare for smelting. Women may collect the ore and produce the charcoal, but they do not make the furnace or the tuyeres. Biology unsatisfactorily explains the allocation of male and female work roles in metalworking, as women already perform most of the strength activities of lifting and carrying. On another level, metalworking has a strong connection to women through symbolic representations of gestation and reproduction. The furnace itself is analogous to the womb. In several cultures images of females giving birth may adorn the furnace, whose shape and name metaphorically imbue the idea of childbirth. The bellows and tuyeres of the furnace continue the metaphor as they enter the female womb of the furnace, thus representing male sexuality and even sexual movement. The bloom is the successful outcome of the interaction, as is a child. Schmidt (1996a, 1996b, 1997, 1998) outlined the symbolic meaning of iron smelting in central and eastern Africa among the Haya, Pangwa, Fipa, Lungu, and Barongo. Iron is used mainly to produce tools for agricultural production. A "fertile" furnace produced large amounts of iron, which, through use, increased the fertility of the land, in turn enhancing human reproduction. Iron served as a symbol of fertility in both agricultural and human domains. Cross-culturally, the symbolic meaning of iron is reproduced through the practice of iron smelting, the shape and attributes of the furnace, and the presence of medicine pots inside the furnace containing plants or clay liquids known to cure human infertility. Archaeologically, Schmidt (1997, 1998) has recovered similar material symbols of fertility associated with Iron Age furnaces. Although he recognized an ideological continuity relating smelting to fertility, he went further and noted differences in time and space affiliated with male or female symbols, outlining changes in the level of tension between genders as a concurrent reflection of changing economic and political spheres (Schmidt

1998). The prohibition of male smelters from sexual intercourse during the smelt may be related to lineage control over iron production and to ideologies forbidding males who are husbands to commit adultery (avoiding women "spies" who may want to steal knowledge for their own lineages). A successful "fertile" smelt is dependent on avoiding the presence of menstruating "fertile" women. The control of iron production and the resources to produce iron, including clay (Childs 1988, 1989), served as the primary means for power and accumulation of wealth since agricultural productivity was in part enhanced by iron tools. Political leadership and power is closely linked in Bantu-speaking Africa with ironworking and symbolic connections between power, reproduction, and fertility (de Maret 1985; Schmidt 1997).

HIDE WORKING AND STONE TOOLS   The early ethnoarchaeological studies of stone tools reflect a gendered bias toward male knappers (e.g., Binford 1986; Clark and Kurashina 1981; Gallagher 1977; Gould 1980; Hayden 1977, 1979; Nelson 1916). This occurred despite the fact that there were clearly female stone-tool makers represented in ethnohistoric, ethnographic, and even ethnoarchaeological studies (Bird 1993; Goodale 1971; Gorman 1995; Gould 1977:166; Hayden 1977:183–86; Holmes 1919:316; Mason 1889; Murdoch 1892; Tindale 1965:246). In these accounts, women made and used stone tools for shaving hair, tattooing, woodworking, fighting sticks, digging sticks, cutting tools, spear points, incising/decorating tools, and scraping hides. Unfortunately, other than hide production, there are no detailed ethnoarchaeological studies concerning women and stone tools. A cross-cultural ascription of hide production to women using stone tools is evident in the ethnohistorical and ethnoarchaeological literature from North America (Albright 1984; Hiller 1948; Mason 1889; Murdoch 1889; Nissen and Dittemore 1974), Asia (Beyries et al. 2001; D'iatchenko and David 2002), and Africa (Brandt and Weedman 1997, 2002; Brandt et al. 1996; Webley 1990). Hence, although women are acknowledged as stone-tool makers, there is a lack of focus on them as such. From these hide-worker studies, we learn about the presence of women as knappers and about the general hide production process, but we often learn little about the gendered aspect of hide working.

It was not until Frink and Weedman's *Gender and Hide Production* (2005) that the gender of the hide-working agent was considered in terms of one's status, identity, symbolism, and authority and one's potential visibility in materials and space. The ascription of hide-working stone tools to women is not insignificant; stone scrapers are among the earliest stone tools found in the archaeological record, and the processing of hides is probably one of the earliest known industries beyond hunting and gathering. Four of the chapters in this volume are ethnoarchaeological and examine hide working among the Cup'ik (Eskimo-Aleut speakers) of western Alaska (Frink 2005); the Plains, Plateau, and Rocky Mountain Native Americans of North America (Baillargeon 2005); the Namaqua Khoikhoen (Khoisan speakers) of South Africa (Webley 2005); and the Konso and Gamo (Afro-Asiatic speakers) of southern Ethiopia (Weedman 2005). Frink (2005) offers that because gender relationships change through time and space, we need a contextualized understanding of the hide production process that involves a detailed study of the different phases/stages and how they are gendered. Today, women process seal and men larger sea mammals and fox. In particular, Frink demonstrates, how with the onset of European trade and impinging ideology, women's production was devalued and replaced with male control over fur production, storage, distribution, and trade. While Frink (2005) hints that a gendered past might be accessible, Webley (1990, 1997, 2005) submits that since both men and women scrape hides among the Namaqua Khoikhoen of South Africa and there is no difference in the materials or spaces they use, it is difficult to determine the gender/sex of the hide production agent. The Namaqua are a pastoralist society in which women hold a high economic and social status as a result of the presence of a cross-descent naming system that weakens the patrilineal descent system. Women inherit livestock and resources from their parents and thus are owners of cattle and control most of the domestic economy. Webley agrees with Kent (1984, 1990, 1998) that in small-scale noncomplex societies, there is no differentiation of space based on gender or activity. I (Weedman 2005) also argue that female hide production may be indistinguishable from male production in terms of tool type and distribution based on my study of the Gamo and Konso peoples of southern Ethiopia. Among the Konso, women use high-quality raw materials from long-distance resources and produce formal tools, contesting recent archaeological scenarios searching for female visibility in stone tools (e.g., Casey 1998; Gero 1991; Sassaman 1992). Both Gamo male hide workers and Konso female hide workers are members of agrarian patrilineal patrilocal societies. The Gamo male hide workers learn how to produce their stone tools from their fathers, and since postmarital residence patterns are virilocal, a discrete village/lineage-based scraper style is discernible and statistically viable. The Konso female hide workers learn mainly from their mothers, but they move to their husband's village after they marry. This results in nondiscrete hide-working areas within the village context, unless there are clusters of related females in a village, in which case there tends to be a significant difference between scrapers on the village level. Women's voices are not silenced or demeaned in informal and poorly crafted tools, but unfortunately this means that their tools are probably indistinguishable from men's. Finally, Baillargeon (2005) adds significantly to our understanding of the cross-cultural ascription of hide working to females through a study of Native Americans from the Plains, Rocky Mountains, and Plateau regions. He illustrates that tanning is viewed as a spiritual and ritual art in which the animal is infused with power and energy and brought back to life in respect for the fact that it gave its life for humans. This process is gendered on the physical and spiritual planes since women work the hides and concomitantly channel the soul of the animal back into the hide, thus restoring order.

CERAMICS AND CALABASHES   Ethnoarchaeological studies of ceramic production, distribution, use, and style represent the largest body of literature in ethnoarchaeological studies (Arnold 1985; Arthur 2003, in press; Burns 1993; Deal 1998; DeBoer and Lathrap 1979; Hodder 1979; Kramer 1997; Longacre 1983; Skibo 1992; Stark 2003). The ceramic ethnoarchaeology literature illustrates that women are the primary producers of ceramics in North America, Africa, Southeast Asia, and the Pacific; that men control the craft in the Mediterranean, Aegean, Middle East, South Asia, and Japan; and that men and women are potters in parts of Africa, Latin America, and the Middle East (Kramer 1985). Even in regions of the world where women dominate ceramic production today, such as Africa, there persists an androcentrism either in the lack of assignment or in the assumption of male artisans in ceramic sculpture and production (Burns 1993). Generally, there have been three areas of focus concerning gender and pottery: style as reflecting female production and learning systems, power and politics, and style as symbolic of gender relations.

One emphasis has been to link style with uxorilocal residence, female production, and learning (Deetz 1968; Longacre 1968). These early works pilfered ethnographic descriptions to assign women to pottery production and associate style with cultural or ethnic identity. Longacre's (1981) later ethnoarchaeological work among the Kalinga seemed to support this hypothesis. However, a cursory cross-cultural survey suggests that skill and age (Lathrap 1983), nonkin influences (Stanislawski 1978), the individual (Deal 1998:33–36), and women's birth cohort (Graves 1985) also affect potter style. Hodder's (1977, 1982:41–42, 83–84) studies of the Tugen, Njemps, and Pokot (all Nilo-Saharan speakers) of Kenya indicated that even in patrilineal virilocal societies where women are potters, pottery style may remain homogeneous because of ideological pressures on women to conform in their married communities. Herbich's (1987) ethnoarchaeological work among the Luo (Nilo-Saharan speakers) of Kenya contradicted the commonly held assumption that ceramic manufacturing styles reflect matrilineal lines and mother–daughter production. Among the Luo, potting was a specialized craft that women learn from their mother-in-laws or cowives and tend to conform to their techniques and style of potting. The Luo highly valued a woman's ability to adapt to the expectations of senior cowives and the mother-in-law. Thus, local ceramic traditions can be perpetuated by women who are entirely recruited from outside the community as a result of patrilocal marital residence and mother-in-law/daughter-in-law learning pattern. However, Herbich also pointed out that there are incentives and instances in which one might slightly alter ceramic design, such as tension between cowives, consumer demand, and influence from potter friends. Dietler and Herbich (1989, 1993) indicated that women are able to distinguish their own pots from others, including an assessment of the quality of the work, raw materials, forms, proportion, and decoration. They demonstrated through an operational sequence of production that style resides in rather than is added to material culture and that pots were decorated to target other women, particularly the women the potter knows. Visibility of the decoration was not related to their social display as indicated by the fact that beer drinking pots, the most socially visible vessel, tended to be less decorated than other pots in some Luo areas. Similarly, Hodder (1982:68–69) also argued that women's decoration on calabashes of the Njemps of Kenya lacked conformity to an ethnic symbol but rather reflected local relationships, especially those between women in opposition to older men as a form of "silent discourse."

In contrast to Dietler and Herbich's (1989, 1993) study, which suggested that women create signals in pottery but not on socially/public visible pots, are studies by La Violette (1995) and Bowser (2000; Bowser and Patton 2004) that emphasize women as active agents empowered with the ability to represent their identity and rearticulate gender roles through ceramic design. La Violette's (1995) research among the Mande of Mali (Niger-Congo speakers) revealed two linguistic and ethnically distinct endogamous groups of potters. The women of each of these groups actively represented their identity through different pottery production techniques, tempers, designs, and marketing strategies. Although artisans were endogamous, often Muslim Somono (fishers and farmers) women married into one of the artisan groups and became potters. Women more easily crossed cultural boundaries through marriage into artisan families and through other social and economic alliances than men. Bowser's (2000) ethnoarchaeological research among the Achuar- and Quichua-speaking peoples of Ecuador found that women made two types of pots: large pots for fermenting and storing manioc beer and bowls for consuming beer. These vessels were highly visible in the public sphere of the household and were used to bridge public/private and political/domestics contexts. The designs on the vessels reflected women's political affiliation and divisions, and they were detectable and recognized by other women. Bowser effectively resolved the androcentric argument that although women make pottery that marks identity (ethnic, political, and so on) boundaries, they are not viewed as active participants in politics. Bowser's work revealed that women whose pottery designs strongly reflect their political alliances intend to strengthen their relationships within particular groups, while women whose symbolic representation on pots is ambiguous often serve as mediators. Thus, women actively and intentionally demonstrate their political intentions and affiliations through ceramic design.

Ceramic and calabash studies also have pointed to the use of design as protective power against powerful spirits (David et al. 1988) and against women's pollutive powers (Donley-Reid 1990a; Hodder 1982). Sterner's (1992; David et al. 1988) studies of the Mandara region in northern Cameroon (Afro-Asiatic speakers) offers that although men conduct rituals, women make and create the rare ceramic vessels and their designs that are used for communicating to the spirit world. Women's power is located in their control over ceramic decoration, and this serves to protect either the people using the pottery or the contents of the vessel from spirits. Among the peoples of Nuba, Sudan, especially among the matrilineal Mesakin, there is a concern with female pollution and abilities to contradict male dominance and control (Hodder 1982:142–50). Material culture is frequently used in purification, especially at boundaries of interaction. Men decorated calabashes and gave them to women as marriage gifts or used them at feasts where women served men drinks. All the decorations on the calabashes are male in the sense that they are similar to the scarification marks seen on men that serve as protection against female power. Conversely, pottery made by women and generally used by women features designs based on female scarification, and these designs also may be related to the desire to provide ritual protection against male power. Donley-Reid (1990a) demonstrated that in early Swahili society when Arab men married African women, women were considered polluted because they brought the Arab line into question. Women's pollution was considered in relationship to birth, sexual activities, death, and food preparation, reducing their status and posing them as a powerful threat against men. Among the Swahili, decorative ceramics were used as protective devices against women's pollution. In Swahili culture, pots that held food or medicine that women cooked or transformed for men were also decorated to protect men. Furthermore, the Swahili placed porcelain plates and glass-bead plates in wall niches where they served as decoration and protection from the evil eye and malevolent spirits. Sherds were also taken off archaeological sites and used in the construction of house walls for protection. Ceramics and beads were placed in the rooms where the most polluting activities of birth and sexual intercourse took place.

Other ceramic studies demonstrate how pottery is symbolic of the human body and serves to mediate gender roles (Kreamer 1994; Welbourn 1984). Welbourn's (1984) studies of the Endo Marakwet (Nilo-Saharan speakers) pottery in Kenya indicated that in their mundane and ritual contexts, ceramic forms and designs represent the sexual division of labor. The cooking pots represented the world of women and cereal production and contrasted with men's beer pots, which symbolized bee husbandry and ritual blessing at ceremonies. Men controlled the public ritual world and viewed themselves as opposite to women, whose power was muted but practical as it was asserted in the everyday actions of providing sustenance and through reproducing new clan members. Material culture was used to enhance the boundary between male and female aspects of social existence. Similarly, Kreamer (1994) studied with the Moba of Togo (Niger-Congo speakers), among whom both men and women are potters, but each have specialization in techniques and types of object produced based on the sexual division of labor and spatial domains. Women were full-time specialists closely associated with domestic pottery for food and drink preparation and storage, representing women's space and domain in the domestic context and in gardens. Men were part-time potters/farmers and exclusively made beer pots. Men made beer pots because they were transportable and moved beyond the domestic context into social/public spaces, and men control the social and ritual uses of beer libations for ancestors. However, women made beer from millet grown by men and supplemented it by ingredients grown in women's gardens. Women had control over the production and distribution of beer, and the profits added considerably to the household income and to women's status. Kreamer suggested that the gendered pottery production among the Moba represented the struggle for economic and social power between men and women.

The ethnoarchaeological studies of gender and craft production reveal, as Costin (1996) noted in her ethnographic search, that the gendered division of labor in craft production is strong and that the allocation of tasks is remarkably idiosyncratic. Certainly, studies by Kreamer concerning ceramics and by myself concerning lithics emphasized that both men and women are capable of producing highly stylized and well-made items. Yet contextualized studies of symbolic infused materials suggest that gender status and power relationships are visible in craft materials. Changes in ethnic and gender relationships through time in Bantu-speaking Africa were actively symbolized through the practices (restricted male access, open male access, and male and female access) and material culture (form and types of symbolic male/female mediums) associated with iron smelting. In studies of hide working, researchers noted that Euro-American market demands and gender ideologies often served to undermine indigenous women's control of resources, production, and distribution. Ethnoarchaeological studies of potter societies emphasized how women used pottery form and design actively to communicate their social relationships with men and other women and their political alliances to the public. One seemingly universal point is the symbolism associating iron, ceramic, and hide production with human sexuality, fertility, and transformation regardless of whether there was male, female, or male and female control of production. In some societies, the association of fertility and power transcended into the use of materials culture to protect men from female powers and men and women from spiritual power. In many of these studies, the socioeconomic status of artisans is evaluated as part of their identity because, often within the cultural groups described, they were members of specific endogamous and ritual groups. However, few if any of these works, such as those focusing on use of space, consider how the influx of Western products or westernization, Christianity, and Islam have effected changes in artisan procurement, production, storage, and distribution (for an exception, see Frink 2005).

Ethnoarchaeology and the Current Level of Gender Integration

Wilma Flintstone and Betty Rubble would feel very comfortable in most ethnoarchaeological portrayals of material and spatial entanglements with gender. However, whether we can easily stipulate that this is a result of the influences and spread of westernization through colonialism and globalism is yet to be determined.

Ethnoarchaeological studies rarely define gender, explore women's lives in broader societal and historical contexts, incorporate non-Western or even Western interpretations of feminism, or explore the similarities and differences in gender between the researchers and the culture studied in their works. Because of the absence in defining gender, it can only be assumed that most studies reflect already entrenched Western ideals that gender reflects biological sex. The ethnoarchaeological studies, with few exceptions, discuss primarily the gender of labor within households or in terms of craft production where women are sifted into the previously excavated and discussed archaeological matrix. In many instances, especially in earlier work, gender appears not to be the initial focus of the research but merely a by-product of trying to understand "larger" issues of style, site activity and structure, and the male place in the world. Even in later studies and with few exceptions (Bowser, Lyons, and Schmidt), the focus is on what women do and how they do it and the material and spatial by-products rather than looking more closely at how women articulate themselves in the wider societal context.

With the exception of Kent (1984, 1990, 1995, 1998, 1999), there also is a reluctance to stipulate how and whether the ethnoarchaeological-derived interpretations can be applied to engender the past. Many have criticized ethnoarchaeological studies for their failure to conduct research that will be useful to archaeologists (Simms 1992). I believe that most of these criticisms come from researchers who wish to be handed specific cultural formulas that the archaeologists can plug into her or his material and spatial data, resulting in a final truth rather than an interpretation. Most ethnoarchaeologists who have focused on gender in the past two decades are interpretive/contextual postprocessualists. Thus, while they adhere to a universal male/female dichotomy, they also acknowledge the immense diversity with which this binary is reflected in spatial patterning and material culture. In summation, it is not possible to state, on the basis of current ethnoarchaeological research, whether throughout all times and spaces gender is visible in material culture and spatial arrangements.

Much frustration will arise from those who have attempted to find ethnoarchaeological research focused on gender. A great deal of this literature, including works by well-established and highly recognized authors such as Susan Kent, Ian Hodder, Nicholas David, and Peter Schmidt (note that most are male), is located in dissertations, in second- or third-tiered journals, and abundantly in edited volumes. Furthermore, many of the publications, outside of gendered titled edited volumes, use titles that obscure their gendered or ethnoarchaeological focus (or both) and instead focus on activity areas, households, power, crafts, and so on. Exceptions to this may be Bowser's (2000; Bowser and Patton 2004) work, which may demonstrate a growing acceptance of gendered studies into mainstream archaeological discourse. Still, ethnoarchaeologists focusing on gender need to make more concerted efforts (myself included) to publish their studies in mediums with wide readership. In many cases, this may still require a bit of persistence, as gender is still viewed as an aside to reconstructing past lifeways, as evident in our need to have special conference sessions, journal issues, and edited volumes. Gender is not fully integrated into ethnoarchaeological or archaeological reconstructions in academic writings, textbooks, and the classroom.

I believe that ethnoarchaeological research has made important strides in reaching the third to fourth stages necessary for creating gender friendly translations of the past (Rosser 1997:3–5). We have gone beyond the time when women were not noted (stage 1) and recognizing that most archaeologists and past visible agents are male (stage 2). We are currently struggling to identify the barriers that prevent incorporating women into the past (stage 3) and revealing their unique contributions to our past (stage 4). However, there are few studies that begin with taking women as the focal point for understanding the past through ethnoarchaeology (stage 5). Certainly, a gendered past and gendered ethnoarchaeological studies that fully incorporate both men and women is still missing (stage 6, the final stage). Writing this chapter has been an enlightening adventure, as it has exposed to me (and I hope to others) the well-worn paths in the ethnoarchaeological studies of gender and the missed crossroads. Ethnoarchaeology has great potential as the arbitrator between cultural and archaeological studies and as an instigator for developing new theories and methods concerning unique gender ideologies and the material world. It is now up to us to create longitudinal research projects that begin with socially oriented and gendered questions and to make concerted efforts to publish them.

References

Albright, Sylvia
    1984   *Tahltan Ethnoarchaeology*. Vancouver: Department of Archaeology, Simon Fraser University.

Arnold, Dean E.
    1985   *Ceramic Theory and Cultural Process*. Cambridge: Cambridge University Press.

Arthur, John W.
    2003   Beer, Food, and Wealth: An Ethnoarchaeological Use-Alteration Analysis of Pottery. *Journal of Archaeological Method and Theory* 9:331–55.
    In press   *Living with Pottery: Ceramic Ethnoarchaeology among the Gamo of Southwestern Ethiopia*. Salt Lake City: University of Utah Press.

Arthur, John, and Kathryn Weedman
    2005   Ethnoarchaeology. In *Handbook of Archaeological Methods*. Herbert Maschner and Christopher Chippendale, eds. Pp. 216–69. Walnut Creek, CA: AltaMira Press.

Baillargeon, Morgan
    2005   Hide Tanning: The Act of Reviving. In *Gender and Hide Production*. Lisa Frink and Kathryn Weedman, eds. Pp. 89–104. Walnut Creek, CA: AltaMira Press.

Bar-Yosef, Ofer
    1995   Earliest Food Producers: Pre-Pottery Neolithic (8000–5500). In *The Archaeology of Society in the Holy Land*. T. E. Levy, ed. Pp. 190–201. New York: Facts on File.

Beaudry, Mary, and Jacquelyn White
    1994   Cowgirls with the Blues? A Study of Women's Publication and the Citation of Women's Work in Historical Archaeology. In *Women in Archaeology*. Cheryl Claassen, ed. Pp. 138–58. Philadelphia: University of Pennsylvania Press.

Beck, Lois
    1978   Women among Qashqa'I Nomadic Pastoralists in Iran. In *Women in the Muslim World*. L. Beck and N. Keddie, eds. Pp. 352–73. Cambridge, MA: Harvard University Press.

Berik, Günseli
 1996 Understanding the Gender System in Rural Turkey: Fieldwork Dilemmas of Conformity and Intervention. In *Feminist Dilemmas in Fieldwork*. Diane L. Wolf, ed. Pp. 56–71. Boulder, CO: Westview.
Beyries, Sylvie, Sergev A. Vasil'ev, Francine David, Vladimir I. D'iachenko, Claudin Karlin, and Youri V. Chesnokov
 2001 Uil, a Paleolithic Site in Siberia: An Ethnoarchaeological Approach. In *Ethno-Archaeology and Its Transfers*. Sylvie Beyries and Pierre Pétrequin, eds. Pp. 9–21. Moyen Âge: CNRS-UNSA.
Binford, Lewis R.
 1978a Dimensional Analysis of Behavior and Site Structure: Learning from an Eskimo Hunting Stand. *American Antiquity* 43:330–61.
 1978b *Nunamiut Ethnoarchaeology*. New York: Academic Press.
 1986 An Alyawara Day: Making Men's Knives and Beyond. *American Antiquity* 51:547–62.
 1987 Researching Ambiguity: Frames of Reference and Site Structure. In *Method and Theory for Activity Area Research: An Ethnoarchaeological Approach*. Susan Kent, ed. Pp. 449–512. New York: Columbia University Press.
Bird, C. F. M.
 1993 Woman the Tool Maker: Evidence for Women's Use and Manufacture of Flaked Stone-Tools in Australia and New Guinea. In *Women in Archaeology: A Feminist Critique*. Hilary du Cros and Laurajane Smith, eds. Pp. 22–30. Canberra: Australian National University.
Bodenhorn, Barbara
 1990 I'm Not the Great Hunter, My Wife Is: Inupiat and Anthropological Models of Gender. *Etudes/Inuit Studies* 14(1–2):55–74.
Boismier, William A.
 1991 Site Formation among Subartic Peoples: An Ethnohistorical Approach. In *Ethnoarchaeological Approaches to Mobile Campsites: Hunter-Gatherer and Pastoralist Case Studies*. C. S. Gamble and W. A. Boismier, eds. Pp. 189–214. Ann Arbor, MI: International Monographs in Prehistory 1.
Bourdieu, Pierre
 1973 The Berber House. In *Rules and Meaning*. Mary Douglas, ed. Pp. 98–110. London: Penguin.
 1977 *Outline of a Practice of Theory*. Cambridge: Cambridge University Press.
Bowser, Brenda J.
 2000 From Pottery to Politics: An Ethnoarchaeological Study of Political Factionalism, Ethnicity, and Domestic Pottery Style in the Ecuadorian Amazon. *Journal of Archaeological Method and Theory* 7(3):219–48.
Bowser, Brenda J., and John Q. Patton
 2004 Domestic Spaces as Public Places: An Ethnoarchaeological Case Study of

Houses, Gender, and Politics in the Ecuadorian Amazon. *Journal of Archaeological Method and Theory* 11(2):157–81.

Brandt, Steven A., and Kathryn J. Weedman
  1997 The Ethnoarchaeology of Hideworking and Flaked Stone-Tool Use in Southern Ethiopia. In *Ethiopia in Broader Perspective: Papers of the XIIth International Conference of Ethiopian Studies*. Katsuyoshi Fukui, Elsei Kurimoto, and Masayoshi Shigeta, eds. Pp. 351–61. Kyoto: Shokado Book Sellers.
  2002 The Ethnoarchaeology of Hideworking and Stone-Tool Use in Konso, Southern Ethiopia: An Introduction. In *Le travail du cuir de la prehistoire à nos jours*. Frédérique Audoin-Rouzeau and Sylvie Beyries, eds. Pp. 113–30. Antibes: Editions APDCA.

Brandt, Steven A., Kathryn J. Weedman, and Girma Hundie
  1996 Gurage Hideworking, Stone-Tool Use and Social Identity: An Ethnoarchaeological Perspective. In *Essays on Gurage Language and Culture: Dedicated to Wolf Leslau on the Occasion of His 90th Birthday November 14, 1996*. Grover Hudson, ed. Pp. 35–51. Wiesbaden: Harrassowitz Verlag.

Broughton, Jack M., and O'Connell, James F.
  1999 On Evolutionary Ecology, Selectionist Archaeology, and Behavioral Archaeology. *American Antiquity* 64:153–65.

Brumbach, Hetty Jo, and Robert Jarvenpa
  1990 Archaeologist-Ethnographer-Informant Relations: The Dynamics of Ethnoarchaeology in the Field. In *Powers of Observation: Alternative Views in Archaeology*. S. M. Nelson and A. B. Kehoe, eds. Pp. 39–46. Archaeological Papers of the American Anthropological Association 2. Washington, DC: American Anthropological Association.
  1997a Ethnoarchaeology of Subsistence Space and Gender: A Subartic Dene Case. *American Antiquity* 62:414–36.
  1997b Woman the Hunter: Ethnoarchaeological Lessons from Chipewyan Life-Cycle Dynamics. In *Women in Prehistory*. Cheryl Claassen and Rosemary A. Joyce, eds. Pp. 17–32. Philadelphia: University of Pennsylvania Press.

Bujra, Janet
  1975 Women and Fieldwork. In *Women Cross-Culturally: Change and Challenge*. Ruby Rohrlich-Leavitt, ed. Pp. 551–57. The Hague: Mouton.

Bunzel, Ruth L.
  1929 *The Pueblo Potter: A Study of the Creative Imagination in Primitive Art*. Columbia University Contributions to Anthropology 8. New York: Columbia University Press.

Burns, Marla C.
  1993 Art, History and Gender: Women and Clay in West Africa. *African Archaeological Review* 11:129–48.

Butler, Judith P.
  1990 *Gender Trouble: Feminism and the Subversion of Identity*. New York: Routledge.

Casey, Joanna
   1991   One Man No Chop: Gender Roles in the Domestic Economy in Northern Ghana, West Africa. In *The Archaeology of Gender*. Proceedings of the 22nd Annual Chacmool Conference. Dale Walde and Noreen Willows, eds. Pp. 137–43. Calgary: Department of Archaeology, University of Calgary.
   1998   Just a Formality: The Presence of Fancy Projectile Points in a Basic Tool Assemblage. In *Gender in African Prehistory*. S. Kent, ed. Pp. 83–104. Walnut Creek, CA: AltaMira Press.

Chang, Claudia
   1988   Nauyalik Fish Camp: An Ethnoarchaeological Study in Activity-Area Formation. *American Antiquity* 53(1):145–57.

Chase, Sabrina
   1991   Polygyny, Architecture and Meaning. In *The Archaeology of Gender*. Proceedings of the 22nd Annual Chacmool Conference. Dale Walde and Noreen Willows, eds. Pp. 1150–58. Calgary: Department of Archaeology, University of Calgary.

Childs, S. Terry
   1988   Clay Resource Specialization in Ancient Tanzania: Implications for Cultural Process. In *Ceramic Ecology Revisited*. Charles Kolb, ed. Pp. 1–31. BAR International Series 436. Oxford: British Archaeological Reports.
   1989   Clay to Artifacts: Resource Selection in African Early Iron Age Iron-Making Technologies. In *Pottery Technology*. G. Bronitsky, ed. Pp. 139–64. Boulder, CO: Westview.
   1991   Style, Technology and Iron Smelting Furnaces in Bantu-Speaking Africa. *Journal of Anthropological Archaeology* 10:332–59.

Claassen, Cheryl, and Rosemary A. Joyce, eds.
   1997   *Women in Prehistory: North America and Mesoamerica*. Philadelphia: University of Pennsylvania Press.

Clark, J. Desmond, and Hiro Kurashina
   1981   A Study of the Work of a Modern Tanner in Ethiopia and Its Relevance for Archaeological Interpretation. In *Modern Material Culture: The Archaeology of Us*. R. A. Gould and M. B. Schiffer, eds. Pp. 303–43. New York: Academic Press.

Clark, John Graham D.
   1953   Archaeological Theories and Interpretation: Old World. In *Anthropology Today: Selections*. Sol Tax, ed. Pp. 104–21. Chicago: University of Chicago Press.

Colton, Harold S.
   1953   *Potsherds*. Bulletin 25. Flagstaff: Museum of Northern Arizona.

Conkey, Margaret W., and Joan M. Gero
   1997   Programme to Practice: Gender and Feminism in Archaeology. *Annual Review of Anthropology* 26:411–37.

Cooper, Zarine
    1994   Abandoned Onge Encampments and Their Relevance in Understanding the Archaeological Record in the Andaman Islands. In *Living Traditions: Studies in the Ethnoarchaeology of South Asia*. Bridget Allchin, ed. Pp. 235–63. New Delhi: Oxford University Press and IBH Publishing.
    2000   The Enigma of Gender in the Archaeological Record of the Andaman Islands. In *In Pursuit of Gender: Worldwide Archaeological Approaches*. Sarah M. Nelson and Myrian Rosen-Ayalon, eds. Pp. 173–86. Walnut Creek, CA: AltaMira Press.

Costin, Cathy Lynne
    1996   Exploring the Relationship between Gender and Craft in Complex Societies: Methodological and Theoretical Issues of Gender Attribution. In *Gender and Archaeology*. Rita P. Wright, ed. Pp. 111–40. Philadelphia: University of Pennsylvania Press.
    1998   Introduction: Craft and Social Identity. In *Craft and Social Identity*. Cathy Lynne Costin and Rita P. Wright, eds. Pp. 3–18. Archaeological Papers of the American Anthropological Association 8. Washington, DC: American Anthropological Association.

Crass, Barbara
    2001   Gender and Mortuary Analysis: What Can Grave Goods Really Tell Us. In *Gender and the Archaeology of Death*. Bettina Arnold and Nancy L. Wicker, eds. Pp. 105–18. Walnut Creek, CA: AltaMira Press.

Cunningham, Jeremy
    2003   Transcending the "Obnoxious Spectator": A Case for Processual Pluralism in Ethnoarchaeology. *Journal of Anthropological Archaeology* 22:389–410.

Cushing, Frank H.
    1886   *A Study of Pueblo Pottery as Illustrative of Zuni Culture Growth*. Washington, DC: Bureau of American Ethnology. Annual Report 4:467–521.

David, Nicholas
    1971   The Fulani Compound and the Archaeologist. *World Archaeology* 3(2):111–31.
    1992a   The Archaeology of Ideology: Mortuary Practices in the Central Mandara Highlands, Northern Cameroon. In *An African commitment; Papers in honor of Peter Lewis Shinnie*. Judy Sterner and Nicholas David, eds. Pp. 181–210. Calgary: University of Calgary Press.
    1992b   Integrating Ethnoarchaeology: A Subtle Realist Perspective. *Journal of Anthropological Archaeology* 11:330–59.

David, Nicholas, and Carole Kramer
    2001   *Ethnoarchaeology in Action*. Cambridge: Cambridge University Press.

David, Nicholas, Judy Sterner, and Kodzo Gavua
    1988   Why Pots are Decorated. *Current Anthropology* 29:365–89.

Davison, Patricia
    1988   The Social Use of Domestic Space in a Mpondo Homestead. *South African Archaeological Bulletin* 43:100–108.

de Maret, Pierre
    1985   The Smith's Myth and the Origin of Leadership in Central Africa. In *African Iron Working: Ancient and Traditional.* Randi Haaland and Peter Shinnie, eds. Pp. 73–87. Oslo: Norwegian University Press.
Deal, Michael
    1998   *Pottery Ethnoarchaeology in the Central Maya Highlands.* Salt Lake City: University of Utah Press.
DeBoer, Warren R., and Donald W. Lathrap
    1979   The Making and Breaking of Shipibo-Conibo Ceramics. In *Ethnoarchaeology: Implications of Ethnography for Archaeology.* Carol Kramer, ed. Pp. 102–38. New York: Columbia University Press.
Deetz, James
    1968   The Inference of Residence and Descent Rules from Archaeological Data. In *Pursuit of the Past.* Sally R. Binford and Lewis R. Binford, eds. Pp. 41–48. Chicago: Aldine.
Denbow, James
    1984   Cows and Kings: A Spatial and Economic Analysis of a Hierarchical Early Iron Age Settlement System in Eastern Botswana. In *Frontiers: Southern African Archaeology Today.* BAR International Series 207. M. Hall, M. G. Avery, D. M. Avery, M. L. Wilson, and A. J. B. Humpreys, eds. Pp. 24–39. Oxford: British Archaeological Reports.
Derrida, Jacques
    1978   Structure, Sign and Play in the Discourse of the Human Sciences. In *Writing and Difference.* Alan Bass, trans. Pp. 278–93. London: Routledge.
di Leonardo, Micaela
    1991   Introduction: Gender, Culture, and Political Economy. In *Gender at the Crossroads of Knowledge: Feminists Anthropology in the Postmodern Era.* Micaela di Leonardo, ed. Pp. 3–45. Berkeley: University of California Press.
D'iatchenko, Vladimir I., and Francine David
    2002   Le Préparation traditionnelle des peaux de poissons et de mammifères marins chez les populations de l'Extrême-Orient sibérien de langue toungouze par. In *Le Travail du Cuir: de la Prèhistoire à nos jours.* Frédérique Audoin-Rouzeau and Sylvie Beyries, eds. Pp. 175–91. Antibes: Editions APDCA.
Dietler, Michael, and Ingrid Herbich
    1989   Tich Matek: The Technology of Luo Pottery Production and the Definition of Ceramic Style. *World Archaeology* 21:148–64.
    1993   Ceramics and Ethnic Identity. In *Terre Cuite et Societe: Le ceramique, document technique, économique, culturel.* Juan-les-Pins, ed. Pp. 459–72. Antibes: Editions APDCA.
Donald, Moira, and Linda Hurcombe
    2000   Gender and Material Culture in Archaeological Perspective. New York: St. Martin's Press.

Donley, Linda W.
  1982   House Power: Swahili Space and Symbolic Markers. In *Symbolic and Structural Archaeology*. I. R. Hodder, ed. Pp. 63–73. Cambridge: Cambridge University Press.
  1987   Life in the Swahili Town House Reveals the Symbolic Meaning of Spaces and Artefact Assemblages. *African Archaeological Review* 5:181–92.
Donley-Reid, Linda W.
  1990a   The Power of Swahili Porcelain, Beads and Pottery. In *Powers of Observation: Alternative Views in Archaeology*. S. M. Nelson and A. B. Kehoe, eds. Pp. 47–59. Archaeological Papers of the American Anthropological Association 2. Washington, DC: American Anthropological Association.
  1990b   The Swahili House: A Structuring Space. In *Domestic Architecture and Use of Space*. Susan Kent, ed. Pp. 114–26. Cambridge: Cambridge University Press.
Draper, Patricia
  1975   !Kung Women: Contrasts in Sexual Egalitarianism in Foraging and Sedentary Context. In *Toward an Anthropology of Women*. Rayna Reiter, ed. Pp. 77–109. New York: Monthly Review Press.
Dupire, Marguerite
  1963   The Position of Women in a Pastoral Society. In *Women in Tropical Africa*. D. Paulme, ed. Pp. 47–92. Berkeley: University of California Press.
Ehrenberg, Margaret R.
  1989   *Women in Prehistory*. London: British Museum Publications.
Ember, Carol
  1978   Myths about Hunter-Gatherers. *Ethnology* 18:439–48.
Estioko-Griffin, Agnes, and P. Bion Griffin
  1975   Woman the Hunter: The Agta. In *Woman the Gatherer*. Frances Dahlberg, ed. Pp. 121–40. New Haven, CT: Yale University Press.
Flinn, Juliana, Leslie Marshall, and Jocelyn Armstrong
  1998   *Fieldwork and Families*. Honolulu: University of Hawai'i Press.
Ford, Anabel, and Anna Hundt
  1994   Equity in Academia—Why the Best Men Still Win: An Examination of Women and Men in Mesoamerican Archaeology. In *Equity Issues for Women in Archaeology*. M. C. Nelson, S. M. Nelson, and A. Wylie, eds. Pp. 147–56. Archaeological Papers of the American Anthropological Association 5. Washington, DC: American Anthropological Association.
Foucault, Michel
  1978   *The History of Sexuality*. New York: Vintage Books.
  1980   *Herculine Barbin*. New York: Pantheon.
Frink, Lisa
  2005   Gender and the Hide Production Process in Colonial Western Alaska. In *Gender and Hide Production*. Lisa Frink and Kathryn Weedman, eds. Pp. 89–104. Walnut Creek, CA: AltaMira Press.

Frink, Lisa, Rita S. Shepard, and Gregory A. Reinhardt, eds.
  2002   *Many Faces of Gender.* Boulder: University Press of Colorado.
Frink, Lisa, and Kathryn Weedman
  2005   *Gender and Hide Production.* Walnut Creek, CA: AltaMira Press.
Gallagher, James P.
  1977   Contemporary Stone-Tool Use in Ethiopia: Implications for Archaeology. *Journal of Field Archaeology* 4:407–14.
Galloway, Patricia
  1997   Where Have All the Menstrual Huts Gone? The Invisibility of Menstrual Seclusion in the Late Prehistoric Southeast. In *Women in Prehistory.* Cheryl Claassen and Rosemary A. Joyce, eds. Pp. 33–47. Philadelphia: University of Pennsylvania Press.
Gargett, Rob, and Brian Hayden
  1991   Site Structure, Kinship, and Sharing in Aboriginal Australia. In *The Interpretation of Archaeological Spatial Patterning.* Ellen M. Kroll and Timothy D. Price, eds. Pp. 11–32. New York: Plenum.
Gero, Joan
  1991   Genderlithics: Women's Roles in Stone-Tool Production. In *Engendering Archaeology: Women and Prehistory.* Joan M. Gero and Margaret W. Conkey, eds. Pp. 163–93. Oxford: Blackwell.
Gero, Joan M., and Margaret W. Conkey, eds.
  1991   *Engendering Archaeology: Women and Prehistory.* Oxford: Blackwell.
Gifford-Gonzalez, Diane P.
  1993a Gaps in the Zooarchaeological Analyses of Butchery: Is Gender an Issue? In From Bones to Behavior: Ethnoarchaeological and Experimental Contributions to the Interpretation of Faunal Remains. J. Hudson, ed. Pp. 181–99. Occasional Paper 21. Carbondale: Center for Archaeological Investigations, Southern Illinois University.
  1993b You Can Hide, but You Can't Run: Representation of Women's Work in Illustrations of Paleolithic Life. *Visual Anthropology Review* 9(1):22–41.
  1998   Gender and Early Pastoralist in East Africa. In *Gender in African Prehistory.* Susan Kent, ed. Pp. 115–38. Walnut Creek, CA: AltaMira Press.
Golde, Peggy
  1986a Introduction. In *Women in the Field.* Peggy Golde, ed. Pp. 1–18. Berkeley: University of California Press.
  1986b *Women in the Field.* Berkeley: University of California Press.
Goodale, Jane C.
  1971   *Tiwi Wives.* Seattle: University of Washington Press.
Gorman, Alice
  1995   Gender, Labour, and Resources: The Female Knappers of the Andaman Islands. In *Gendered Archaeology: The Second Australian Women in Archaeology Confer-*

ence. Jane Balme and Wendy Beck, eds. Pp. 87–91. Canberra: Australian National University.

Goucher, Candice L., and Eugenia W. Herbert
    1996   The Blooms of Banjeli: Technology and Gender in West African Iron Making. In *The Culture and Technology of African Iron Production*. Peter R. Schmidt, ed. Pp. 40–57. Gainesville: University Press of Florida.

Gould, Richard A.
    1971   The Archaeologists as Ethnographer: A Case Study from the Western Desert of Australia. *World Archaeology* 3:143–77.
    1974   Some Current Problems in Ethnoarchaeology. In *Ethnoarchaeology*. C. William Clewlow Jr., ed. Pp. 29–48. Berkeley: University of California Press.
    1977   Ethnoarchaeology: Or Where Do Models Come From. In *Stone-Tools as Cultural Markers*. R. V. S. Wright, ed. Pp. 162–68. Canberra: Australian Institute of Aboriginal Studies.
    1980   Living Archaeology. Cambridge University Press, Cambridge.

Graves, Michael
    1985   Ceramic Design Variation within a Kalinga Village: Temporal and Spatial Process. In *Decoding Prehistoric Ceramics*. B. A. Nelson, ed. Pp. 9–34. Carbondale: Southern Illinois University Press.

Gregory, James R.
    1984   The Myth of the Male Ethnographer and the Woman's World. *American Anthropologist* 86:316–27.

Gupta, Khadija Ansari
    1979   Travels of a Woman Fieldworker. In *The Fieldworker and the Field*. M. N. Srinivas, A. M. Shah, and E. A. Ramaswamy, eds. Pp. 103–14. Delhi: Oxford University Press.

Harding, Sandra
    1998   *Is Science Multicultural? Postcolonialisms, Feminisms, and Epistemologies*. Bloomington: Indiana University Press.

Hartsock, Nancy
    1987   The Feminist Standpoint: Developing the Ground of a Specifically Feminist Historical Materialism. In *Feminism and Methodology*. Sandra Harding, ed. Pp. 157–80. Bloomington: Indiana University Press.

Hawkes, Kristen, James F. O'Connell, and Nicholas G. Blurton Jones
    1997   Hadza Women's Time Allocation, Offspring Provisioning, and the Evolution of Long Postmenopausal Life Spans. *Current Anthropology* 38(4):551–77.

Hayden, Brian
    1977   Stone Tool Functions in the Western Desert. In *Stone Tools as Cultural Markers*. R. V. S. Wright, ed. Pp. 178–88. Canberra: Australian Institute of Aboriginal Studies.
    1979   Paleolithic Reflections. Atlantic Highlands, NJ: Humanities Press.

Hayden, Brian, and Aubrey Cannon
    1984   The Structure of Material Systems: Ethnoarchaeology in the Maya Highlands. Society of American Archaeology Papers, no. 3. Washington, DC: Society of American Archaeology.

Herbert, Eugenia W.
    1993   *Iron, Gender, and Power: Rituals of Transformation in African Societies*. Bloomington: Indiana University Press.

Herbich, Ingrid
    1987   Learning Patterns, Potter Interaction and Ceramic Style among the Luo of Kenya. *African Archaeological Review* 5:193–204.

Hiller, Wesley R.
    1948   Hidatsa Soft Tanning of Hides. *Minnesota Archaeologists* 14:4–11.

Hodder, Ian
    1977   The Distribution of Material Culture Items in the Baringo District, Western Kenya. *Man* 12:239–69.
    1979   Pottery Distributions: Service and Tribal Areas. *Pottery and the Archaeologists* 4:7–23.
    1982   *Symbols in Action: Ethnoarchaeological Studies of Material Culture*. Cambridge: Cambridge University Press.
    1987   The Meaning of Discard: Ash and Domestic Space in Baringo. In *Method and Theory in Activity Area Research*. Susan Kent, ed. Pp. 424–49. New York: Columbia University Press.

Hollimon, Sandra E.
    1997   The Third Gender in Native California: Two Spirit Undertakers among the Chumash and Their Neighbors. In *Women in Prehistory*. Cheryl Claassen and Rosemary A. Joyce, eds. Pp. 173–88. Philadelphia: University of Pennsylvania Press.

Holmes, William H.
    1919   *Handbook of Aboriginal American Antiquities Part I. The Lithic Industries*. Bulletin 60. Washington, DC: Bureau of American Ethnology.

Huffman, Thomas
    1982   Archaeology and Ethnohistory of the African Iron Age. *Annual Review of Anthropology* 11:133–50.

Hurtado, Ana Magdalena, Kristen Hawkes, Kim Hill, and Hillard Kaplan
    1985   Female Subsistence Strategies among the Ache Hunter-Gatherers of Eastern Paraguay. *Human Ecology* 13(1):1–27.

Isaac, Glynn
    1989   *The Archaeology of Human Origins*. Cambridge: Cambridge University Press.

Jaggar, Alison M.
    1983   *Feminist Politics and Human Nature*. Totowa, NJ: Rowman & Allanheld.

Janes, Robert R.
    1983   Archaeological Ethnography among Mackenzie Basin Dene, Canada. Technical Paper 28. Calgary: Arctic Institute of North America.

1989 The Organization of Household Activities at a Contemporary Dene Hunting Camp—Ten Years in Retrospect. In *Households and Communities*. Proceedings of the 21st Annual Chacmool Conference. A. S. MacEachern, D. J. W. Archer, and R. D. Garvin, eds. Pp. 517–24. Calgary: Department of Archaeology, University of Calgary.

Jarvenpa, Robert, and Hetty J. Brumbach
    1995 Ethnoarchaeology and Gender: Chipewyan Women as Hunters. *Research in Economic Anthropology* 16:39–82.

Kehoe, Alice
    1983 The Shackles of Tradition. In *The Hidden Half: Studies of Plains Indian Women*. Patricia Albers and Beatrice Medicine, eds. Pp. 53–76. Lanham, MD: University Press of America.

Kent, Susan
    1984 *Analyzing Activity Areas: An Ethnoarchaeological Study of the Use of Space*. Albuquerque: University of New Mexico Press.
    1990 A Cross-Cultural Study of Segmentation, Architecture, and the Use of Space. In *Domestic and Architecture and the Use of Space*. Susan Kent, ed. Pp. 127–52. Cambridge: Cambridge University Press.
    1995 Does Sedentization Promote Gender Inequality? A Case Study for the Kalahari. *Journal of the Royal Anthropological Institute* 1:513–36.
    1998 Invisible Gender—Invisible Foragers: Hunter Gatherer Spatial Patterning and the Southern African Archaeological Record. In *Gender in African Prehistory*. Susan Kent, ed. Pp. 39–69. Walnut Creek, CA: AltaMira Press.
    1999 Egalitarianism, Equality, and Equitable Power. In *Manifesting Power: Gender and the Interpretation of Power in Archaeology*. Tracy L. Sweely, ed. Pp. 30–48. London: Routledge.

Kirsch, Gesa E.
    1993 *Women Writing the Academy*. Carbondale: Southern Illinois University Press.

Kosso, Peter
    1991 Method in Archaeology: Middle Range Theory as Hermeneutics. *American Antiquity* 56:621–27.

Kramer, Carol
    1985 Ceramic Ethnoarchaeology. *Annual Reviews in Anthropology* 14:77–102.
    1997 Pottery in Rajasthan: Ethnoarchaeology in Two Indian Cities. Washington, DC: Smithsonian Institution Press.

Kreamer, Christine M.
    1994 Money, Power and Gender: Some Social and Economic Factors in Moba Male and Female Pottery Traditions (Northern Togo). In *Clay and Fire: Pottery in Africa*. Iowa Studies in African Art: The Stabley Conferences at the University of Iowa 4. Christopher D. Roy, ed. Pp. 189–212. Iowa City: School of Art and Art History, University of Iowa.

Kuper, Adam
  1982   *Wives for Cattle*. London: Routledge.
Larson, Mary Ann
  1991   Determining the Function of a "Men's House." In *The Archaeology of Gender*. Proceedings of the 22nd Annual Chacmool Conference. Dale Walde and Noreen Willows, eds. Pp. 165–75. Calgary: Department of Archaeology, University of Calgary.
Lathrap, Donald
  1983   Recent Shipibo-Conibo Ceramics and Their Implications for Archaeological Interpretation. In *Structure and Cognition in Art*. D. K. Washburn, ed. Pp. 25–39. New York: Cambridge University Press.
La Violette, Adrien J.
  1995   Women Craft Specialists in Jenne: The Manipulation of Mande Social Categories. In *Status and Identity in West Africa: Nyamakalaw of Mande*. D. C. Conrad and B. E. Frank, eds. Pp. 170–81. Bloomington: Indiana University Press.
Lewis, Barbara
  1984   The Impact of Development Policies on Women. In *African Women South of the Sahara*. Margaret Jean Hay and Sharon Stichter, eds. Pp. 170–82. Essex: Longman.
Linduff, Katheryn M., and Yan Sun
  2004   *Gender and Chinese Archaeology*. Walnut Creek, CA: AltaMira Press.
Longacre, William A.
  1968   Some Aspects of Prehistoric Society in East-Central Arizona. In *Pursuit of the Past*. Sally R. Binford and Lewis R. Binford, eds. Pp. 89–102. Chicago: Aldine.
  1981   Kalinga Potter: An Ethnoarchaeological Study. In *Pattern of the Past*. Ian Hodder, Glynn Isaac, Norman Hammond, eds. Pp. 49–66. Cambridge: Cambridge University Press.
  1983   *Ethnoarchaeology of the Kalinga*. Westong: Pictures of Record.
Lutz, Catherine
  1990   The Erasure of Women's Writing in Sociocultural Anthropology. *American Ethnologists* 17:611–27.
Lyons, Diane E.
  1989   Deliver Us from Evil: Protective Materials Used in Witchcraft and Sorcery Confrontation by the Mura of Doulo, Northern Cameroon. In *Cultures in Conflict: Current Archaeological Perspectives*. Proceedings of the 20th Annual Chacmool Conference. D. C. Tkaczuk and B. C. Vivian, eds. Pp. 297–302. Calgary: Archaeological Association of the University of Calgary.
  1990   Men's Houses: Women's Spaces: The Spatial Ordering of Households in Doulo, North Cameroon. In *Households and Communities*. Proceedings of the 21st Annual Chacmool Conference. Scott MacEachern, David J. W. Archer,

and Richard D. Garvin, eds. Pp. 28–34. Calgary: Department of Archaeology, University of Calgary.
1991 The Construction of Gender, Time and Space. In *The Archaeology of Gender*. Proceedings of the 22nd Annual Chacmool Conference. D. Walde and N. Willows, eds. Pp. 108–14. Calgary: Department of Archaeology, University of Calgary.
1992 Men's Houses: Women's Spaces: An Ethnoarchaeological Study of Gender and Household Design in Dela, North Cameroon. Ph.D. dissertation, Simon Fraser University.
1996 The Politics of House Shape: Round versus Rectilinear Domestic Structures in Déla, Northern Cameroon. *Antiquity* 70(268):351–67.
1998 Witchcraft, Gender, Power and Intimate Relations in Mura Compounds in Déla, Northern Cameroon. *World Archaeology* 29(3):344–62.

Margolis, Maxine L.
2000 *True to Her Nature: Changing Advice to American Women*. Prospect Heights, IL: Waveland.

Mason, Otis
1889 *Aboriginal Skin Dressing*. Washington, DC: Smithsonian Institution Press.

Matthews, Keith
2000 The Material Culture of the Homosexual Male: A Case for Archaeological Exploration. In *Gender and Material Culture in Archaeological Perspective*. Moira Donald and Linda Hurcombe, eds. Pp. 2–19. London: Macmillan.

Moore, Henrietta L.
1986 *Space, Text and Gender: An Anthropological Study of the Marakwet of Kenya*. Cambridge: Cambridge University Press.

Morris, Rosalind C.
1995 All Made Uo: Performance Theory and the New Anthropology of Sex and Gender. *Annual Review of Anthropology* 24:567–92.

Moser, Stephanie
1993 Gender Stereotyping in Pictorial Reconstructions of Human Origins. In *Women in Archaeology: A Feminist Critique*. Hillary du Cros and Laurajane Smith, eds. Pp. 75–91. Canberra: Australian National University.

Murdoch, John
1892 *Ethnological Results of the Point Barrow Expedition*. Washington, DC: Smithsonian Institution Press.

Murray, Margaret
1949 *The Splendor That Was Egypt*. London: Sidgwick and Jackson.

Nelson, Margaret, Donna Glowacki, and Annette Smith
2002 The Impact of Women on Household Economies: A Maya Case Study. In *In Pursuit of Gender: Worldwide Archaeological Approaches*. Sarah Milledge Nelson and Myriam Rosen-Ayalon, eds. Pp. 125–54. Walnut Creek, CA: AltaMira Press.

Nelson, Nels
    1916   Flint Working by Ishi. In *Holmes Anniversary Volume*. Frederick W. Hodge, ed. Pp. 397–402. New York: American Museum of Natural History.

Nelson, Sarah M., and Myriam Rosen-Ayalon
    2002   *In Pursuit of Gender: Worldwide Archaeological Approaches*. Walnut Creek, CA: AltaMira Press.

Nissen, Karen, and Margaret Dittemore
    1974   Ethnographic Data and Wear Pattern Analysis: A Study of Socketed Eskimo Scrapers. *Tebiwa* 17:67–87.

O'Connell, James F.
    1987   Alyawara Site Structure and Its Archaeological Implications. *American Antiquity* 52:74–108.
    1995   Ethnoarchaeology Needs a General Theory of Behavior. *Journal of Archaeological Research* 3:205–55.

O'Connell, James, Kristen Hawkes, and N. G. Blurton Jones
    1991   Distribution of Refuse Producing Activities at Hadza Residence Base Camps: Implications for Analyses of Archaeological Site Structure. In *The Interpretation of Archaeological Spatial Patterning*. Ellen M. Kroll and Timothy D. Price, eds. Pp. 61–76. New York: Plenum.

Orme, Bryony
    1981   *Anthropology for Archaeologists*. Ithaca, NY: Cornell University Press.

Ortner, Sherry B.
    1974   Is Female to Male as Nature Is to Culture? In *Women, Culture and Society*. Michelle Z. Rosaldo and Louise Lamphere, eds. Stanford, CA: Stanford University Press.

Phillipson, David
    1977   *The Later Prehistory of Eastern and Southern Africa*. New York: African Publishing.

Power, Camilla, and Ian Watts
    1997   The Woman with the Zebra's Penis: Gender, Mutability and Performance. *Journal of the Royal Anthropological Institute* 3:537–60.

Rosser, Sue V.
    1992   *Biology and Feminism*. New York: Twayne Publishers.
    1997   *Re-Engineering Female Friendly Science*. New York: Teachers College Press.

Rubbo, Anna
    1975   The Spread of Capitalism in Rural Colombia: Effects on Poor Women. In *Toward an Anthropology of Women*. Rayna Reiter, ed. Pp. 358–71. New York: Monthly Review Press.

Sackett, James
    1990   Style and Ethnicity in Archaeology: The Case for Isochrestism. In *The Uses of Style in Archaeology*. M. W. Conkey and C. A. Hastorf, eds. Pp. 32–43. Cambridge: Cambridge University Press.

Sassaman, Kenneth E.
  1992 Lithic Technology and the Hunter-Gatherer Sexual Division of Labor. *North American Archaeologist* 13:249–62.
Schapera, Isaac
  1953 *The Tswana*. London: Kegan Paul International.
Schmidt, Peter R.
  1978 *Historical Archaeology: A Structural Approach in African Culture*. Westport, CT: Greenwood Press.
  1983 An Alternative to a Strictly Materialist Perspective: A Review of Historical Archaeology, Ethnoarchaeology, and Symbolic Approaches in African Archaeology. *American Antiquity* 48:62–81.
  1996a Cultural Representation of African Iron Production. In *The Culture and Technology of African Iron Production*. Peter R. Schmidt, ed. Pp. 1–28. Gainesville: University Press of Florida.
  1996b Reconfiguring the Barongo: Reproductive Symbolism and Reproduction among a Work Association of Iron Smelters. In *The Culture and Technology of African Iron Production*. Peter R. Schmidt, ed. Pp. 74–127. Gainesville: University Press of Florida.
  1997 *Iron Technology in East Africa: Symbolism, Science, and Archaeology*. Bloomington: Indiana University Press.
  1998 Reading Gender in the Ancient Iron Technology of Africa. In *Gender in African Prehistory*. Susan Kent, ed. Pp. 139–62. Walnut Creek, CA: AltaMira Press.
Schmidt, Peter R., and Bertram B. M. Mapunda
  1997 Ideology and the Archaeological Record in Africa: Interpreting Symbolism in Iron Smelting Technology. *Journal of Anthropological Archaeology* 16:73–102.
Segobye, Alinah
  1998 Daughters of Cattle: The Significance of Herding in the Growth of Complex Societies in Southern Africa. In *Gender in African Prehistory*. Susan Kent, ed. Pp. 227–34. Walnut Creek, CA: AltaMira Press.
Simms, Steven R.
  1992 Ethnoarchaeology: Obnoxious Spectator, Trivial Pursuit, or the Keys to a Time Machine? In *Quandaries and Quests: Visions of Archaeology's Future*. LuAnn Wandsnider, ed. Pp. 186–98. Occasional Paper 20. Carbondale: Center for Archaeological Investigations, Southern Illinois University.
Skibo, James
  1992 *Pottery Function*. New York: Plenum.
Slocum, Sally
  1975 Woman the Gatherer: Male Bias in Anthropology. In *Toward and Anthropology of Women*. Rayna Reiter, ed. Pp. 36–50. New York: Monthly Review Press.
Spector, Janet D.
  1983 Male/Female Task Differentiation among the Hidatsa: Toward the Development of an Archaeological Approach to the Study of Gender. In *The Hidden*

Half. Patricia Albers and Beatrice Medicine, eds. Pp. 77–99. Washington, DC: University Press of America.

Spring, Anita, ed.
    2000   *Women Farmers and Commercial Ventures: Increasing Food Security in Developing Countries.* Boulder, CO: Lynne Rienner.

Stacey, Judith
    1991   Can There Be a Feminist Ethnography? In *Women's Words.* S. B. Gluck and D. Patai, eds. Pp. 111–19. New York: Routledge.

Stanislawski, Michael B.
    1978   If Pots Were Mortal. In *Explorations in Ethnoarchaeology.* Richard. A. Gould, ed. Pp. 201–28. Albuquerque: University of New Mexico Press.

Stark, Miriam T.
    2003   Current Issues in Ceramic Ethnoarchaeology. *Journal of Archaeological Research* 11:193–242.

Stepan, Nancy L.
    1986   Race and Gender: The Role of Analogy in Science. *Isis* 77:261–77.

Sterner, Judy A.
    1992   Sacred Pots and "Symbolic Reservoirs" in the Mandara Highlands of Northern Cameroon. In *An African Commitment: Papers in Honor of Peter Lewis Shinnie.* Judy Sterner and Nicholas David, eds. Pp. 171–79. Calgary: University of Calgary Press.

Stone, Linda, and Nancy P. McKee
    1998   *Gender and Culture in America.* Englewood Cliffs, NJ: Prentice Hall.

Tindale, Norman B.
    1965   Stone Implement Making among the Nakako, Ngadadjara, and Pitjandjara of the Great Western Desert. *Records of the South Australian Museum* 1965:131–64.

Trigger, Bruce G.
    1989   *A History of Archaeological Thought.* Cambridge: Cambridge University Press.

Visweswaran, Kamala
    1997   Histories of Feminist Ethnography. *Annual Review of Anthropology* 26:591–621.

Voss, Barbara
    2000   Feminism, Queer Theories, and the Archaeological Study of Past Sexualities. *World Archaeology* 32(2):180–92.

Wadley, Lynn
    1997   *Our Gendered Past.* Johannesburg: Witwatersrand University Press.
    1998   The Invisible Meat Providers: Women in the Stone Age of South Africa. In *Gender in African Prehistory.* Susan Kent, ed. Pp. 69–82. Walnut Creek, CA: AltaMira Press.

Walde, Dale, and Noreen Willows, eds.
    1991   *The Archaeology of Gender.* Proceedings of the 22nd Annual Chacmool Conference. Calgary: Department of Archaeology, University of Calgary.

Warren, Carol A. B.
    1988   *Gender Issues in Field Research*. Beverly Hills, CA: Sage.

Watson, Patty Jo, and Mary C. Kennedy
    1991   The Development of Horticulture in the Eastern Woodlands of North America: Women's Roles. In *Engendering Archaeology*. Joan M. Gero and Margaret W. Conkey, eds. Pp. 255–75. Oxford: Blackwell.

Webley, Lita
    1990   The Use of Stone Scrapers by Semi-Sedentary Pastoralist Groups in Namaqualand, South Africa. *South African Archaeological Bulletin* 45:28–32.
    1997   Wives and Sisters: Changing Gender Relations among Khoi Pastoralists in Namaqualand. In *Our Gendered Past: Archaeological Studies of Gender in Southern Africa*. Lyn Wadley, ed. Pp. 167–99. Johannesburg: Witwatersrand University Press.
    2005   Hideworking among Descendants of Khoekhoen Pastoralist in the Northern Cape, South Africa. In *Gender and Hide Production*. Lisa Frink and Kathryn Weedman, eds. Pp. 153–74. Walnut Creek, CA: AltaMira Press.

Weedman, Kathryn
    2004   Are Wilma Flintstone and Betty Rubble Archetypes for Stone Age Women? An Ethnoarchaeological Model of Women Stone-Tool Makers from Ethiopia. Paper presented at the meeting of the Society of American Archaeology, Montreal, April.
    2005   Gender and Stone-Tools: An Ethnographic Study of the Konso and Gamo Hideworkers of Southern Ethiopia. In *Gender and Hide Production*. Lisa Frink and Kathryn Weedman, eds. Pp. 175–96. Walnut Creek, CA: AltaMira Press.

Welbourn, Alice
    1984   Endo Ceramics and Power Strategies. In *Ideology, Power and Prehistory*. D. Miller and C. Tilley, eds. Pp. 17–24. Cambridge: Cambridge University Press.

Willey, Gordon R.
    1953   Archaeological Theories and Interpretation: New World. In *Anthropology Today: Selections*. Sol Tax, ed. Pp. 170–94. Chicago: University of Chicago Press.

Wolf, Diane L.
    1996   *Feminist Dilemmas in Fieldwork*. Boulder, CO: Westview.

Wright, Rita P.
    1996   *Gender and Archaeology*. Philadelphia: University of Pennsylvania Press.

Wylie, Alison
    2000   Questions of Evidence, Legitimacy, and the (Dis)Unity of Science. *American Antiquity* 65:227–37.

Yellen, John
    1976   Settlement Patters of the !Kung: An Archaeological Perspective. In *Kalahari Hunter-Gatherers: Studies of the !Kung San and Their Neighbors*. Richard B. Lee and Irvin DeVore, eds. Pp. 47–72. Cambridge, Mass.: Harvard University Press.
    1977   *Archaeological Approaches to the Present*. New York: Academic Press.

Feminist Gender Research in Classical Archaeology

SUZANNE M. SPENCER-WOOD

THIS CHAPTER SURVEYS THE DEVELOPMENT of different feminist approaches to gender research in classical archaeology. However, most gender research in classical archaeology does not specify its theoretical approach, and some gender research is not feminist. To be feminist, gender research must use feminist concepts or theory either implicitly or explicitly. Since most gender research in classical archaeology does not specify its theoretical approach, I have analyzed the feminist theoretical approaches implicit in the gender research.

Although this survey covers a number of major themes in the development of feminist classical archaeology, it is far from comprehensive. An initial problem I had in conducting this review is the definition of classical archaeology since some artifact analyses are considered archaeology, while others are considered art history. In contrast to historical archaeology, the field of classics is separated into textual analyses, classical archaeology, and art history. A number of studies use textual analysis to provide cultural context for interpretations of material culture. Some of these studies, although they are called art history, are included here because they are similar to artifactual studies in archaeology.

This chapter first outlines the early development of feminist classical archaeology within its multiple contexts. The rest of the chapter is organized according to the development of feminist theory in a process I call peeling the androcentric onion. Androcentrism can be metaphorically understood as an onion with multiple layers of reinforcing biases, from the surface of supposedly ungendered discourse through binary gender stereotypes to deeper biases in methods, paradigms, concepts, and language (Spencer-Wood 1995).

The development of feminist classical archaeology generally followed the development of feminist theory in peeling the androcentric onion. First, feminist critique of ungendered discourse revealed how women were made invisible. Then the first wave of feminist theory made historic women visible and researched the importance of women's public and domestic roles (Spencer-Wood 1995). Starting in the 1970s, the second wave of feminist theory analyzed patriarchy and as a result often just added women explicitly to stereotypic binary constructions of the past that emphasized gender difference (Bunch 1987:140). The third wave of feminist theory, starting in the 1990s, critiqued binary constructions of classical gender systems, differentiated gender ideology from practice, and analyzed the diversity of both in relationship to the complex intersections between gender, class, race, and ethnicity in classical cultures (Lorber 2001; Spencer-Wood 1995).

The Development of Feminist Classical Archaeology

Although classical archaeology is similar to prehistoric and historical archaeology in remaining largely ungendered, feminism has been developing within classics since the turn of the twentieth century. Feminist classical textual analysis developed much earlier than feminist classical archaeology. The influence of first-wave feminism in reconstructions of Roman and Greek culture from texts can be seen as early as 1909, when Frank Abbott highlighted women's increasing public roles in Roman society as a first step to telling the story of the "emancipation" of Roman women (Abbott 1909:41). Books on women in antiquity increased in the 1960s, some of which drew on the early second-wave feminist tome *The Second Sex* by Simone de Beauvoir (e.g., Cartledge 1993:64).

Gender research in classical archaeology/art history developed earlier than gender research in historical archaeology, possibly because classical archaeology is an older field. Perhaps the earliest gender research in classical archaeology was Helen Clees's (1920) book *A Study of Women in Attic Inscriptions*. As one of the first generation of female classical archaeologists, Clees undertook remedial research to make women visible in a field where the focus on men had made women largely invisible.

Since the 1960s, feminist classical archaeology developed as a result of the influences of women's studies, feminist theory, and feminist anthropology and prehistoric archaeology. Of the three stages of feminist research outlined by Wylie (1991b:31–32), feminist classical archaeology has included a few first-stage critiques of androcentrism (e.g., Brown 1993, 1997; Pomeroy 1975; Richlin 1992:xii). Pomeroy (1975) made a first-wave feminist analysis of women's public and private lives primarily from classical texts but also from some material culture. In the 1980s, first-wave feminist critiques and theory led to some further analyses of women's public roles from material culture and texts (e.g., Havelock

1982; Kampen 1982, 1991). Starting in the 1970s, the second wave of feminism led to an increase in analyses of classical texts to reveal information on women's domestic lives that was still being ignored. Second-wave feminist analyses of the material evidence of women's domestic roles still predominate (e.g., Clarke 1998; Keuls 1983; Walker 1983; Williams 1983). However, women are often only added to preceding androcentric reconstructions of classical cultures (Lyons, critiqued by Koloski-Ostrow 1997:2).

Most feminist classical archaeology is in Wylie's second stage of remedial research to recover women's lives that have been overlooked by men's reconstructions of the past (Brown 1993:257–58). Only since the mid-1980s has feminist theory been used to reconceptualize the treatment of classical Greco-Roman gender systems in classical archaeology (e.g., Koloski-Ostrow and Lyons 1997; Richlin 1992:xiii). In the 1990s, a number of joint volumes by classicists, archaeologists, and art historians have conducted more complex analyses of women as social actors from synthetic analyses of material culture and documents (e.g., Archer et al. 1994; Fantham et al. 1994; Reeder 1995). Postmodern feminist classical archaeology has begun to develop and critique the limits of second-wave feminist approaches (e.g., Goldberg 1999). Postmodern feminist theory underlies the increase in analyses of sexuality and masculinity (e.g., Richlin 1992). In general, analyses of material culture in cultural context have increased (Brown 1993:258). However, textual analysis dominates the field of feminist classics as it does the field as a whole (e.g., Cameron and Kurht 1993; duBois 1988; Hallett and Skinner 1997; McClure 2002; Pomeroy 1975).

Although the study of women in antiquity has become a subfield of classics since the 1970s, it is still not widely accepted as legitimate (Richlin 1992:xiii). Classical archaeology has been slow to adopt feminist frameworks for analyzing the importance of material culture in reinforcing the construction and maintenance of gender as a fundamental social institution. Classics as a field remains male dominated, resulting in refusals to accept symposia on feminist classical archaeology at the American Institute for Archaeology meetings as recently as 1996. An increasing interest in gender research in classical archaeology has recently developed in conjunction with the acceptance of postmodern multicultural and anticolonialist perspectives that are related to postmodern feminist theoretical approaches and postprocessualism (Brown 1997:13).

Feminist Critiques of Male Biases in Supposedly Ungendered Research

Feminist classicists have pointed out how women were excluded from ungendered ancient Greek history (Pomeroy 1975), art history (Lyons and Koloski-Ostrow

1997), and classical archaeology (e.g., Brown 1993:257; Richlin 1992:xiii). Major works in the classics have not included index entries for women. Classical archaeology draws on the traditional supposedly ungendered descriptions of cultures as monolithic wholes both in archaeology and in history.

Ungendered discourse in classics has been similar to historical archaeology in addressing ethnic and class differences before gender, which is at least as foundational to culture and society (e.g., Brown 1993:257). The traditional exclusion of women in classics led to absurd reconstructions of only two unenfranchised classes in ancient Greece: resident aliens and slaves. The fact that women could not vote was ignored because women as a whole were devalued and disappeared from the past as insignificant to men's history (Pomeroy 1975:xii). Men's accounts are usually presented as the ungendered normative experience, behavior, and viewpoint of the entire society. Classical texts were interpreted in the exclusively male academies since the Renaissance, editing out author "biases" in order to construct an idealized androcentric origin for European culture that valorized (male) public activities as the ungendered norm and devalued and subsumed women's domestic activities as subsidiary to the important public events of (men's) political history (Gutzwiller and Michelini 1991).

Classical archaeology initially developed largely to illustrate textual interpretations and often uncritically generalizes androcentric historic texts written by men as the universal meaning of material culture, including architecture and features as well as artifacts (Gutzwiller and Michelini 1991). The focus on public archaeological remains was given impetus by the focus of classical history on public events, politics, and wars (Pomeroy 1975). Thus, classical archaeology has often illustrated only a degendered men's history. Methodologically, women have been disappeared from the past by the classical archaeological practice of projecting the androcentric view in modern and classical cultures that men's public history is important while women's domestic activities are not (Gazda 1991).

Feminists have critiqued the focus of ungendered classical archaeology on large-scale public monuments and buildings as the only significant cultural remains. Although not stated in ungendered archaeology, textual sources identified public constructions and space exclusively with men. Thus, the supposedly ungendered focus of archaeology on public monuments and buildings was actually an androcentric focus on men's public accomplishments (e.g., Alcock 2002). The strength of the tradition of ungendered language is attested to by Ault and Nevett's (1999) ungendered feminist critique of the favoring of classical Greek public sites and the neglect of household archaeology. Houses were often ignored because of their devaluation as women's domestic domain. When houses were analyzed, it often was in terms of the status of the male head of household.

Feminist Critiques of Androcentric Methods in Classical Archaeology

The ability of feminists to engender classical archaeology has been hampered by the traditional focus of the field on formal stylistic classification and chronology, as critiqued by Brown (1993:257–58). The ungendered analysis of classical men's monuments and buildings has often focused on formal stylistic attributes used for chronological dating of structures to reconstruct the temporal development of the male-public parts of cities (e.g., Alcock 2002). Classical archaeologists and art historians traditionally classified pots in large historically meaningless Eurocentric etic categories such as "geometrical" and "nongeometrical" for classical Greece (e.g., Boardman 1998).

In art history, individual artifacts, such as statues of gendered human forms and pots with gendered paintings, were traditionally analyzed in a modern aesthetic framework that imposed Western interpretations and meanings on the artifacts (Broude and Garrard 1982:14; Richlin 1992:xii). The Eurocentric definition of some types of art and images as inherently "good" art and superior to other "bad" art has inhibited reflexive scholarly criticism (Lyons and Koloski-Ostrow 1997:12). Traditionally, no attempt was made to understand the meaning of artifacts from their archaeological context (Brown 1993:257–58). For instance, major classical art historians identified different Greek vase painters on the basis of variation in styles and quality of execution of the paintings, with no analysis of historical context or content (e.g., Boardman 1998, critique of approach by Robertson 1992:3).

Feminist Critiques of Androcentric Methods of Constructing Households

House sites in classical Greece and Rome have traditionally been analyzed mainly in terms of ungendered issues of architectural chronology and construction sequences on individual sites (critiqued by Nevett 1999:26). More recently, analyses of Roman houses have analyzed how they expressed the social status of the male head of household who legally owned the house site and all its occupants (Clarke 1991; Gazda 1991; Wallace-Hadrill 1994). The focus on men's display of public power through their houses emerges from ungendered language with the use of male pronouns, such as: "The design of individual rooms and the overall organization of a building, taken together, emphasized the power of its owner and provided a prestigious background against which he played his assigned social role" (Thébert 1987:392–93). In ungendered language, shared androcentric assumptions are revealed in male pronouns and ungendered terms that represent males, as when specialized household rooms were considered to reflect "the aristocrat's desire to present himself in an impressive setting" (Gazda 1991:14). One book chapter was titled "Power, Architecture, and Décor: How the Late Roman Aristocrat Appeared to His Guests" (Ellis 1991).

The Roman house was androcentrically viewed both as the center of the ungendered but assumed male owner's public civic and political activity and as "the private living quarters of the owner" (Gazda 1991:7; see also Dwyer 1991:26–29, 34). Methodologically, women, children, and slaves often have been subsumed in the term "familia," or "family," in ungendered analyses of households focusing on wealth differences attributed to the male head of household (e.g., Wallace-Hadrill 1994:91–118, 143–75). Families, especially wives and children, have traditionally been described in their relationships to the male head of household (e.g. Gazda 1991:4–5).

Classical texts that name houses for the male head of household have been reified through the archaeological practice of naming domestic sites for the surname of the male head of household and frequently providing information only about his public uses of household spaces (e.g., Dwyer 1991; Ellis 1991; Gazda 1991). Naming house sites for the male head of household subsumes and disappears the other members of the household, including women, children, and slaves. Naming sites for men reifies married women's ideal seclusion in the household under their husband's authority in both classical Greece and Rome. Women's subordinate status and lack of civil rights and formal education resulted in few records by or about women, contributing to the focus on men's more frequently documented behaviors (Nevett 1999:15).

Household spaces have usually been archaeologically interpreted according to the structuralist gender dichotomy as exclusively *either* public *or* private in ungendered discourse or *either* male-public *or* female-private in explicitly gendered accounts. Curiously, the analysis of households in classical archaeology is most often not explicitly gendered, even sometimes by feminists (cf. Meadows 1999; Nevett 1999). Most analyses of household spaces and artifacts use only the code words of "domestic" and "public" without mentioning men or women or their social relationships encoded in domestic spaces, features such as floor mosaics and painted designs on pots (e.g., Allison 1999; Ault and Nevett 1999; Gazda 1991).

Feminist Critiques of Androcentric Gender Research in Classical Archaeology

Since the Renaissance, the patriarchal gender systems of classical Greece and Rome have been described on the basis of the few surviving men's texts that androcentrically address topics such as marriage and family. Until recent postmodern feminist critiques, these texts were considered to describe actual gender practices rather than ideals. Many histories of classical Greece and Rome present gender roles as static universal norms conforming to the dominant patriarchal gender ideology in each culture (e.g., Cowell 1980). The elite patriarchal gender ideologies of classical Greece and Rome accorded women no legal rights. As in the later femme covert laws of Europe, women belonged to their fathers until they married, and then they belonged to their husbands. However, feminist research has revealed that the treatment of Greek and Roman women by their husbands was often controlled by the wife's family through the practice of retaining rights to her dowry in the event of mistreatment and resulting divorce, which appears to have been easier than in eighteenth- to nineteenth-century Europe, at least for the middle class (cf. Goldberg 1998:109; Millett 1970; Pomeroy 1975).

In classical archaeology and contextual art history, sculpture, Greek vase paintings, and Greek household spaces have been unproblematically interpreted to conform to the gender ideals and myths in classical men's texts (e.g., Boardman 1974:205–34). While the depiction of idealistic myths in Greek vase paintings and Roman wall paintings are recognized, feminists have critiqued the unproblematic interpretation of other images as descriptive of actual gender practices rather than ideals. Goldberg (1999) has argued that Greek vase paintings of elite women performing domestic tasks should be interpreted as idealistic rather than necessarily realistic since slaves performed many domestic tasks for the elite.

The dominant classical patriarchal gender ideologies were developed by elite men and do not represent the full diversity of gender ideologies or actual gender practices even among elite women and much less among middle- and working-class women. All women had some public roles that were accepted in classical cultures but ignored in the patriarchal gender ideology that dichotomized the world into opposed mutually exclusive male-public versus female-private domains (Katz 1998). As with most ideologies, the Greek and Roman patriarchal gender ideologies were idealistic overgeneralizations that overlooked how actual gender practices and alternative gender ideologies deviated from dominant ideals (Spencer-Wood 1999:168–69).

The gender dichotomy was assumed in classical Greek Aristotelian dominant gender ideology, which strongly influenced Roman gender ideology and thus later European gender ideology through Roman conquest, and the fourteenth-century rediscovery of classical Roman texts and monuments as the foundation of Renaissance academies (Lerner 1993). Feminists have critiqued how Victorian men legitimated their patriarchal gender ideology by tracing it back to the Greeks, ignoring the diversity in gender ideologies and actual practices in ancient Greece (Spencer-Wood 1999:167–68). Yet recent androcentric classical archaeology continues to uncritically interpret material culture through the lens of modern patriarchal ideology that is projected as isomorphic with classical cultures (Keuls 1985).

For instance, in classical archaeology, Stewart (1990:78) unreflexively analyzed classical nude sculptures of Aphrodite only in terms of a stereotypic binary male response. Thus, he described a "high" response in analyzing one sculpture of Aphrodite covering her pubis as modest, beautiful, and ladylike. Stewart showed a typical Victorian sensibility in his asexual response to the sculpture identified as a respectable woman. At the other extreme, Stewart described a "low" male response to less modest Aphrodite sculptures, called them "trivially coquettish," "overripe," and "whores" (Brown 1993:257–58). Stewart androcentrically projects modern binary heterosexual stereotypes of the lady versus the whore in his voyeuristic descriptions of the Aphrodite sculptures and does not recognize that he is ethnocentrically responding to them out of cultural context.

Feminist Critiques of Androcentrism in the Theoretical Paradigms

The theoretical paradigm of structuralism constructs cultures in supposedly deep inherent binary structures based on the gender dichotomy. Binary gender stereotypes have been used to dichotomize classical sites and household spaces as exclusively *either* male-public *or* female-private (Lyons and Koloski-Ostrow 1997:3). Actual gender practices have been constructed to conform to the dominant classical patriarchal gender ideologies. Stewart (1990) further projected onto classical Greek sculptures of the goddess Aphrodite the Victorian binary categorizations of women, and of men's responses to women.

Goldberg (1998:109) has critiqued the construction of classical cultures in ungendered dichotomies that are implicitly gendered. Further, she analyzed how the Western gender dichotomy led to the assumption that the supposedly ungendered public sphere was exclusively male in classical archaeology. Classical archaeology uses male-defined ungendered paradigms, viewpoints, categories of analysis, theories, and cultural language, all of which exclude women's experiences and views. With this framework identifying men as exclusively public, women's contributions to public life have been ignored, and men's contributions to domestic life have been ignored (Spencer-Wood 1999). The result has been an androcentric emphasis on the importance of men's houses for their public social and civic roles as well as an emphasis on the ways that men performed public interactions in their houses (Dwyer 1991:34).

Introduction to Feminist Theories Used in Gender Research in Classical Archaeology

Although a variety of feminist theoretical approaches have been simultaneously and usually implicitly used in classical archaeology, they will be discussed in the chronological order of the development of feminist theory. The historical development of feminist theory is simplified into three "waves," following normative practice despite the recognition that this tremendously oversimplifies the complex development of feminist theory (Nelson 2002).

Although feminists define the waves of feminist theory in a variety of ways, this chapter will use the broadest framework, one in which liberal egalitarian feminist theory is recognized to have developed out of the fifteenth-century feminist arguments for women's intellectual and educational equality, followed by movements for women's suffrage, equal pay, and other equal rights (Lerner 1993). Second-wave feminist theory developed out of nineteenth-century cultural feminism that valorized women's domesticity while analyzing the oppression of women in patriarchy (Donovan 2001:47–79). The second wave is usually identified with Betty Friedan's *Feminine Mystique* (1963), although it actually has precedents from the mid-nineteenth century. The third wave of feminist theory started with critiques of the second wave in the 1980s (Lorber 2001).

First-Wave Feminist Egalitarian Liberal Theory

Liberal egalitarian feminist theory critiques the patriarchal gender ideology that devalues women and conducts research demonstrating that women held diverse important roles in both 1) the public sphere and 2) the domestic sphere. Liberal feminist theory and research demonstrates that gender stereotypes were not universally practiced through these two different kinds of research paradigms concerning the ways that women are and historically have been social agents as much as men (Donovan 2001:17–79).

Research on the Importance of Women's Public Roles

Some feminist classical archaeologists have taken a first-wave liberal egalitarian theoretical approach to critique the universal identification of all public roles and spaces as inherently masculine with evidence that classical women also had public activities, roles, and spaces, some of which were as important as men's public activities, roles, and spaces. In many cases, the invisibility of women's public actions and roles is due to the classification of women's public roles as domestic, such as women's public marketing of domestic products or their dismissal as insignificant exceptions to the norm of domestic women (e.g., Cowell 1980:111, critiqued in Wallace-Hadrill 1994:138). The liberal egalitarian paradigm is important in showing that women's public activities and roles were not occasional and cannot be dismissed as exceptions even if they deviated from dominant gender norms or ideals. Although this paradigm does not challenge the higher status accorded the public sphere compared to the domestic sphere, it does importantly undermine the legitimation of men's dominance in the public sphere as universal, natural, and biological (Spencer-Wood 1995).

In contrast to the few elite classical Greek men's texts that have been interpreted to indicate the universal seclusion of women in their separate domestic quarters, feminist classicists and archaeologists have found both documentary and archaeological evidence that women of all classes held a variety of public roles. Women were responsible primarily for funeral rituals and acted as public mourners. Funerary vase paintings depict women as public mourners (e.g., Havelock 1982). Citizen's wives and daughters had primary roles in a number of major state religious festivals. For instance, maidens bearing a variety of ritual objects headed the public sacrificial procession in honor of the birthday of Athena, the city's tutelary deity. Girls also washed the statue of Athena and wove her robe, which is depicted on part of the Parthenon frieze. Many vase paintings illustrate the birth of Athena that women celebrated at the Panathenaea festival. Women had primary roles in rituals for goddesses who protected Athenian grain crops, Kore and Demeter. The largest public festival for Demeter, the Thesmophoria, was exclusively celebrated by citizen's wives over three days in late October. Women also celebrated the public Haloa festival in honor of Demeter and Dionysus in January and a threshing festival called Skira in July. Women's cycle of religious festivals celebrated their agricultural processing roles and were important in ritually ensuring the success of men's agricultural fieldwork. Some vase paintings illustrate women celebrating a ritual dance to Dionysus, performing a ritual at the altar to a god or goddess, and the third day of the Anthesteria festival (Buxton 1998:333–35; Katz 1998:101–8).

Archaeological reconstruction of roads and public buildings was used by Goldberg (1999) in conjunction with documentary records to map the path of women's ritual processions from shrines to goddesses. She was able to reconstruct the angle of vision and perspective that the women in the procession would have had in viewing public buildings and the landscape as they passed through it. Goldberg noted the cemeteries that the women's procession would pass. Women's ritual procession through the Athenian landscape sheds new light on the reasons for children's cemeteries to be located on roads leading to women's cult shrines, as noted by Houby-Nielsen (2000:161).

Feminists have also found neglected texts that discuss powerful public women, including queens, priestesses, a magistrate, and female warriors and leaders of armies in the Hellenistic period (Cantarella 1987:52–61; Pomeroy 1975:124). Texts note women's public importance as priestesses to goddesses and as oracles for two leading male gods, Zeus at Dodona, and the most important classical oracular shrine to Apollo at Delphi. Priestess was the only public office open to women, and women were priestesses for more than forty major cults in classical Athens. Further, the priestess of Athena Polias, Athens' patron deity, officiated at the most important of the state festivals and at times had the power to influence political decisions, as did the female oracles (Blundell 1995:134–35, 160–65). These texts identify women with public monuments and temples, such as the Parthenon and the large complex on Mount Olympus, where men went to get political predictions from the female oracle.

Classical Greek myths about Amazons defeating men could be empowering for Greek women, although vase paintings more often show men defeating Amazons. Herodotus's accounts of Amazons have been supported by weapons found in large numbers of female graves excavated in the Caucasus and Scythia. Among the Sauromatians in the Caucasus, 20 percent of the burials were of female warriors with weapons and battle injuries, and forty female warrior graves have been found in Scythia. A couple of female graves also include tall headdresses, portable altars, mirrors, and other items that suggest they were priestesses (Davis-Kimball 1997; Rolle 1989:88–89).

The importance of the Amazons as well as Athena for women's empowerment is suggested by their use to decorate a knee guard used in working wool. A painting on one side of the knee guard depicts Amazons preparing for battle by taking up shields and weapons, suggesting an analogy with preparing for wool working by donning the knee guard as shield. The other side depicts women working wool, interpreted as embodiments of the goddess Athena Ergane, the worker (Katz 1998:101). The analogy between Amazons at war and women working wool indicates that both may have been viewed as heroic public roles by the classical Greeks.

Although there was no public education for Athenian girls as there was for boys (Adkins and Adkins 1997:218, 153–55), documents and vase paintings show that many elite women did learn to read and write and keep household accounts (Katz 1998:130). Further, a number of Greek women were unusual in gaining an academic education and becoming renowned Greek poets and philosophers. Four vases and two coins from the island of Lesbos have been found depicting the famous poet Sappho by name, although she is not depicted reading her poetry (Snyder 1997). Female philosophers were accepted by men of the

Socratic school, which held that women could be intellectual equals of men, in support of the legendary female scholar and hetaera Aspasia (Keuls 1985:198–99). Some female philosophers practiced their egalitarian beliefs in relationships with male egalitarian philosophers or with women. In contrast to misogynist philosophers such as Aristotle, the Cynics and Pythagoreans took the revolutionary position that women and men had the same virtues so that women had the capacity to participate in public governance of society (Cantarella 1987:63–76, 91–93). In addition, Pythagorus founded and operated his famous school with his wife and accepted female as well as male students.

According to Katz's calculations, the majority of classical Greek citizen's wives engaged in small businesses, whether as wool workers, tavern keepers, or petty traders of foodstuffs such as bread or items such as garlands and perfumes. One vase painting depicts a woman selling perfume to a slave who then gives it to her mistress. Women's business transactions were restricted by law to small amounts no more than three times the daily wage of skilled workmen. As a result, women were petty traders of perfume, while men owned large perfume businesses (Katz 1998:117–18). Inscriptions on funerary monuments have identified a few Greek women doctors (Kampen 1982:70). Some court documents record that women worked the agricultural fields when necessary, such as in times of war. Some documents and vase paintings show that women were nurses and midwives (Nevett 1999:16).

Some vase paintings show women drawing water at public fountains. These women have problematically been identified as courtesans rather than citizens' wives on the basis of a few elite men's texts stating that (elite) women were secluded in houses and the typical hetaera names given the women on one vase, such as "yielding," "hither," and "little snub-nose" (Williams 1983:103–5). However, Keuls (1985:235–40) found literature recording complaints by citizens' wives about problems with unsavory characters encountered when drawing water in fountain houses. She also notes that foreign wives, called *metics*, were paid to go to the public fountains to draw water.

The only potentially lucrative area of trade largely under classical Greek women's control was the sex trade. Courtesans, called hetaerae, were learned female companions hired by men for symposia discussions. Courtesans could charge one hundred times the daily wage of a skilled workman. *Pornai*, or ordinary prostitutes, were mostly slaves who were paid about the same amount as a skilled workman and worked in brothels most often run by a man but also some women. Vase paintings illustrate both graphic sex scenes of naked prostitutes and men and other scenes of dressed women interpreted as hetaerae at men's parties called symposia, relaxing, and receiving men (Katz 1998:117–19; Sutton 1992; Williams 1983).

Roman archaeology does not provide the amount of vase painting of ordinary life that is available for classical Greece. Feminist Roman archaeologists have found carvings and documents showing that Roman women held a variety of public occupations. Documents record some women taking public political action to get sumptuary legislation passed and then to establish a women's court concerned with questions of dress and women's use of carriages. Some middle-class women operated businesses, including a large brick business producing bricks marked with the name of the woman owner and her daughter. Tomb inscriptions are dedicated to some famous late Roman female singers, composers, mimes, and flute players. Other inscriptions mention that some Roman women were in charge of large estates or were weavers, costumers, seamstresses, washwomen, fishmongers, and barmaids. The most frequent inscriptions involved a variety of trades connected with making and repairing clothing (Abbott 1909:45–51, 96–99).

Classical Roman relief carvings outside stores and on temples and funerary monuments have been found showing women in public roles, including doctors, obstetricians, midwives, nurses, hairdressers, artisans, textile producers, metalworkers, and sellers of produce in public markets. While saleswomen and salesmen appear to have the same status because of similarity in clothing and size, female doctors are not depicted as gods as are male doctors, and female textile producers and artisans are usually depicted as mythological rather than real. Roman women's work is more fully documented in texts and inscriptions than in art, which expressed the emphasis on women's domestic roles in the dominant ideology rather than women's diverse public roles in actual practice (Kampen 1982:70–74, 64–68).

Research on the Importance of Women's Domestic Roles

In this paradigm, feminists seek evidence of the importance of women's social agency in domestic roles to correct androcentric devaluations of women's domestic work. Feminists seek and find evidence that women's domestic roles in many cases either are as important as men's public roles or are significant to men's public roles or the culture in general. This paradigm derives from cultural feminist theory valorizing women's domestic roles (Donovan 2001:47–78).

Both documentary data and archaeological data indicate the importance of women's domestic production to classical cultures. Goldberg (1998:109) has pointed to the importance of the house as the primary locus of all production in the agriculturally based classical cultures. One classical Greek man's text portrayed marriage as a partnership and pointed out that a wife who was a prudent household manager could contribute more than half the income of a household of the wealthiest class (Pomeroy 1998:185).

Many of classical Greek women's household agricultural products were essential to the classical Greek economy, including production of textiles, bread and other foodstuffs, and processing vegetables, all of which some women sold in public markets. A female figurine making bread has been found (Katz 1998:133). The high value placed on women's textiles is evident in vase paintings of women spinning, weaving, and wearing clothes with woven designs, as well as the Parthenon frieze depicting preparation of a garment for the statue of Athena by women and men. Women's fine cloth was a gift to the gods (Blundell 1995:60–61; Nevett 1999:14).

In contrast to the exclusive identification of men with public roles in much classical archaeology, some texts and material culture show men performing domestic tasks in public. The importance of women's textile production is emphasized by a carving on the Parthenon frieze showing the folding of cloth by a bearded man and a child. Younger (1997) identified the child as a boy because of his exposed buttocks, which was not permitted for respectable girls, although other classicists have argued that it is a girl because textiles were women's work. However, men could commercialize women's domestic tasks into public businesses. By the end of the fifth century, a number of men were famous as bakers who sold their products in specialized Athenian bread markets (Katz 1998:133–35; Keuls 1985).

In Roman culture, women's household textile production was also important to the culture as a whole. Bread production shifted from women in the home to commercial businesses controlled by men in later Roman times (Cowell 1980:86) In Roman houses in Pompeii, Allison (1999:60–61) argued that the forecourts, which had previously been considered exclusively male public spaces, actually housed cupboards holding (women's) domestic utensils.

Research on Mothering and Child Rearing

Reconstructions of lifeways in classical cultures based on historic texts usually stress marriage and the family. In patriarchal classical Greece and Rome, women who bore sons were praised, while more than one daughter was not valued. Husbands had the power of life and death over family members, and female infanticide or sale was not uncommon (Cowell 1980:35). Babies in classical Greek vase paintings are almost invariably depicted naked and male in scenes showing slaves handing the baby to his elite mother, whose high status was depicted in having provided a male child (Keuls 1985:110–13). Recent gender research on classical artifacts has addressed previously neglected topics of mothering and childhood.

Classical Greek literary texts portray mothers' frequent deaths in childbirth as analogous to the heroic death of men in battle. Tomb carvings portray these mothers holding, but not suckling, naked male babies (Keuls 1985:138–41). Material representations of mothers and others nursing infants have been analyzed and problematized by Bonfante (1997). She found that representations of mothers nursing were rare in the formal art of both Greek and Roman civilization. Classical texts revealed that nursing was considered animalistic, primitive, and therefore uncivilized. Therefore, formal Greek and Roman art often represented animals nursing people, including the iconic statue of the twins who founded Rome nursing from a she-wolf. Neither the Greek gods nor elite or respectable bourgeois Greek or Roman women suckled their infants but instead had wet nurses. Terra-cotta figurines of wet nurses portray them as big breasted, old, and ugly, in contrast to statues and vase paintings of elite women as small breasted and pretty. Classical Greek art valorizes the young boyish-looking female body in parallel with its focus on boys. Greek documents record the practice of mothers binding their daughters' breasts to conform to the slender ideal. Elite women from the classical cultures through the Renaissance and the nineteenth century sought to preserve their youthful figures by not breast-feeding. Although formal Roman art generally copied Greek formal art, including the rarity of depictions of nursing women, Bonfante found more portrayals of nursing mothers in classical Italy because of the longevity of a goddess cult.

Conceptions of childhood are suggested by a number of classical Greek artifacts that have been interpreted as toys, including miniature four-wheeled platforms carrying horses, a wheeled mule with rider and amphorae, and a miniature beehive, granary, or pot with holes at the pointed end for use as a pendant (Williams 2000). Reilly's (1997) research has critiqued the Western ethnocentric interpretation of miniature female images carved on Athenian girls' gravestone reliefs as dolls. She differentiates terra-cotta dolls that have little breast development and jointed arms and legs from the sexually adult miniature female images that usually do not have arms or lower legs. Reilly concludes that the miniature adult female torsos presented to or held by girl children in grave bas-reliefs were votive figures representing the girl's participation in a socioreligious custom designed to form her character and body into proper and healthy femininity. The dedication of such votive figures became very popular in mid-fifth-century B.C. healing cults and made a statement that the girl buried in the grave was being brought up to become a proper feminine woman, in contrast to the popular Greek myth that girls who did not achieve menarche would become mad, refuse to marry, and attempt suicide. Houby-Nielson (2000) found that children's cemeteries in classical Athens were located close to city gates and roads that led to female cult shrines.

Second-Wave Feminist Theoretical Projections of Patriarchal Gender Ideology

The second wave of feminist theory, starting in the 1970s, involved projecting modern or historically dominant patriarchal gender ideology onto other cultures to interpret women's roles as universally domestic and subordinate to men's universally public roles (e.g., Ortner 1974; Rosaldo 1974; Rosaldo and Lamphere 1974). Rosaldo (1980) reflexively critiqued how she and others projected Victorian gender ideology to construct gender systems in other cultures as simplistic asymmetrical dichotomies.

Second-wave feminist gender research uncritically accepts classical men's accounts of a binary gender system as actual historic practice and reads the gender dichotomy into archaeological data. Second-wave feminist classical archaeologists have divided house spaces into exclusively *either* women's spaces *or* men's spaces (e.g., Fantham et al. 1994, critiqued by Goldberg 1999; Walker 1983).

On the basis of a number of documents, women were associated with rooms with hearths, storerooms with amphorae and other large jars, and workrooms with loom weights used in weaving cloth. Women's sleeping quarters are not often identified because one account specified that they were on the second story and thus are seldom preserved (Walker 1983:84, 91). Vase paintings of well-dressed women performing domestic chores such as spinning, weaving, relaxing, taking nude male babies from servants, and eating alone behind closed doors have been interpreted as depicting the women's quarters (Keuls 1983:215).

The *andron*, where men met for parties, called symposia, with hetaerae, has been ideally identified as the largest, most elaborately decorated room with a mosaic floor, close access to the public street, and an off-center door to accommodate masonry benches along two walls to support the wooden couches where men traditionally reclined for their symposia (Walker 1983:91). In some cases, the *andron* and an adjacent room or courtyard with paved or mosaic floor have been identified as the men's quarters (Keuls 1985:210–15; Walker 1983:84). Vase paintings of men holding wine cups reclining on couches with well-dressed women who sometimes play flutes or other instruments have been interpreted as depictions of symposia in the *andron* (Keuls 1985:212–13).

Third-Wave Postmodern Feminist Theoretical Approaches to Gender Research

Postmodern feminist theory critiques the second-wave structuralist approach of uncritically projecting elite Western patriarchal gender dichotomies as the universal reality of actual gender practices (e.g., Amos and Parmer 1984; Mohanty 1988; Spelman 1988). In postmodern feminist theory, gender ideologies are distinguished from the diversity of actual practices (Spencer-Wood 1992, 1991:243–44; 1994:182; 1999:168–69, 173). Postmodern multicultural feminism, queer theory, and masculinity theory destabilize the heterosexist gender dichotomy by theorizing gender and sexuality as fluid multiple identities, practices, and performances at the intersections of gender, class, race, ethnicity, religion, and other social variables (Butler 1990; Hill 1990; Lorber 2001:203; Nicholson 1990).

Diversity in Classical Gender Ideologies

In contrast to the second-wave analysis only of the elite patriarchal gender ideology, some feminist classicists and classical archaeologists have researched the diversity in the classical gender ideologies of men and indications of alternative gender ideologies materialized by some women. Feminists have critiqued the modern interpretation of Aristotle's misogynist Stoic school as the dominant gender ideology. The dominance of this ideology of gender dichotomy was constructed by Victorian men to legitimate their separate spheres of gender ideology (Spencer-Wood 1999:167–68). Feminist research has recovered a number of neglected philosophical schools with more egalitarian gender ideology, including the Socratic school, which held that women could be the intellectual equals of men, and the Cynic and Pythagorean schools, which held that women were capable of governing society because they had the same virtues as men. In contrast, Aristotelian philosophy argued that women's virtues were domestic and physical, while men's virtues included rational thought and the ability to govern, justifying the legal exclusion of women from education and formal politics (Cantarella 1987:52–61). Aristotelian gender ideology was used to legitimate misogynist gender ideology and practices from classical Greek times through much of the nineteenth century in Western cultures.

There is some documentary and archaeological evidence of Greek women's alternative gender ideologies that valorized women and their roles. Women's diverse cultic shrines and their already mentioned control of some major religious festivals indicate that women controlled ideologies that were materialized to celebrate women's powers. Archaeological excavations on the island of Lesbos have found structures with caches of female figurines that have been interpreted as women's rituals and religion at a temple.

Postmodern Gendered Household Research in Contrast to Classical Patriarchal Gender Ideology

Classical household archaeology has progressed from second-wave structuralist constructions of household spaces to embody to the dominant patriarchal gender ideology to postmodern analyses of variability in the gendered use of household spaces. Allison (1999) has critiqued the use of historic texts to interpret Roman household spaces and artifacts according to the mutually exclusive dichotomy of male-public versus female-domestic. She made a feminist ungendered critique of the assumption, based on a few men's texts, that all household courtyards were male-controlled spaces with chests for storing valuables and gold that belonged to Roman male household heads. Instead, Allison found textual references to the use of courtyard chests for storing domestic equipment. On the basis of texts by Vitruvius, recent research has recognized the oversimplification involved in previous analyses of Roman houses into public versus private family areas (Longfellow 2000:25). Both feminists and nonfeminists have concluded that rooms in Roman houses had multiple flexible uses and cannot be exclusively associated with *either* men *or* women (Allison 2004:156). Roman house rooms blended public and private functions, blurring the ideal boundary (Wallace-Hadrill 1994:9, 138).

Laurence (1994:127, 131) has agreed that there was no gendered dichotomy in the identification of elite Roman household spaces. However, instead of interpreting temporal change in gendered room use as fluidity and lack of mutually exclusive gender spaces, Laurence has analyzed a gender dichotomy in the use of spaces that was temporal rather than spatial. Laurence interprets household reception and dining spaces as used exclusively by men for public-political activities in the mornings and evenings. When the male head of house went out to transact business or politics in the forum and the public baths in the middle of the day, household spaces became exclusively female spaces used for domestic tasks.

Goldberg (1999) critiqued the inadequacy of the previous structuralist paradigm used to universally interpret classical Greek house spaces to conform to the patriarchal gender dichotomy (e.g., Vernant 1983). She critiqued Hoepfner and Schwander's (1994:22–50:fig. 33) uniform reconstruction of a block of classical Athenian houses with women's quarters on the second floor and a hearth in the main living room of every house despite the lack of archaeological evidence for the women's quarters or hearths in all the houses. Goldberg pointed out that one of the houses analyzed into separate spaces by Walker was identified as two houses by the excavator. Keuls (1985:210) states in her analyses of a house floor plan in Athens and two in Olynthus that these were among the few houses where the floor plan could be determined, raising issues concerning the breadth of applicability of her binary gendered analysis of these floor plans. One wonders whether the clarity of the floor plans analyzed by Keuls (1985) and by Walker (1983) are more the result of their reconstruction and representation rather than an accurate depiction of the actual arrangement of more ambiguous archaeological remains.

Goldberg critiqued the second-wave focus on a universalized cultural gender dichotomy and a lack of consideration of intermediary categories as well as individual social agency in manipulating cultural ideals. She critiqued the failure to consider how class, age, religion, and status of women would mediate and alter the applicability of elite patriarchal ideals (Versnel 1987). Further, she critiqued the projection of elite gender ideology to construct fixed gender boundaries rather than address how these boundaries were negotiated (e.g., Sanders 1990).

Goldberg (1999) analyzed the diversity and fluidity in the use of household spaces over time due to variables such as household size, composition, family life cycle, and variation in daily activities. She found documentary references showing the ease with which room functions were altered. Artifacts only occasionally indicated gendered room use, as in the case of loom weights used by women that were found concentrated in one room in only two Athenian houses (Jameson 1990:186, cited in Goldberg 1999:149). In contrast to the frequent identification of house courtyards as male public space (e.g., Keuls 1985; Walker 1983), loom weights associated with women have sometimes been found in courtyards. Nevett (1994) and Jameson (1990) have argued that women worked in house courtyards preparing raw grains and vegetables as well as weaving. Goldberg points out that the devaluation of domestic sites in classical archaeology led to poor records of the locations of finds within many excavated houses.

Goldberg (1999) discusses the evidence that excavated Athenian houses did not all have a room with the distinctive features identified as the *andron* for men's symposia, including a mosaic floor and stone benches for couches. One court document recorded that the *andron* in his house was moved upstairs when the bedroom was moved downstairs, demonstrating that it was not always a fixed space. Goldberg differentiates men's idealistic statements about gender-segregated spaces such as the *andron*, from its actual mixed-gender use, involving women who prepared the space and brought food and drink, as well as the hetaerae who lounged there with the men.

In contrast to the few elite men's documents claiming that women were secluded in a women's quarters or *gunaikonitis*, Goldberg (1999) notes that excavated house sites have not yielded any particular rooms with concentrations of artifacts identified with women, such as mirrors or jewelry. Further, Goldberg pointed out that some documents record changes in room functions, in one case involving the wife's bedroom being shifted from upstairs to downstairs to facilitate caring for a new baby. Clearly there were no fixed women's quarters in that house. Vase paintings of women engaged in a range of domestic activities need to be interpreted not as literally showing a fixed women's quarters but rather as economically depicting women's typical actions

Goldberg constructs classical Greek household spaces as fluid in their gendered uses and functions. Although for much of the day, men may have been out of the house farming or politicking, leaving the house to women and their work, Goldberg points out that courtyards were used by women as well as men. Therefore, strange men and women entering the house at the courtyard would have seen women, who were supposed to be secluded in the women's quarters, according to a few classical men's texts. Further, strangers often had to walk across the courtyard to reach the *andron*. Goldberg postulates that strangers may have ignored women working in the courtyard or that the women may have veiled their faces.

Nevett (1999) also critiqued the fixed structuralist identification of domestic spaces in classical Greek houses as *either* male *or* female. Instead, she compared a large number of house structures in different time periods and regions to show change through time and a high degree of variability in house size that probably related to wealth and social position. Variability in house structure and room access suggested control of social interaction between family and outsiders and possibly between genders or kin. Further, Nevett analyzed locations of artifacts in context to discuss possible gendered uses of household space. She found evidence that women and men used most areas of houses to differing degrees or frequencies. Evidence was found of segregation of sets of rooms in some houses, which could be interpreted as the women's quarters in the inner house, segregated from the men's quarters with an entrance onto the street. However, the configurations of rooms could also be explained by the desire to segregate family from strangers and visitors. Nevett pointed to the importance of the outside door to the house separating the household from nonhousehold people and the interior door in some houses separating private family space from public space. Goldberg (1999:154–55) has further pointed out that the off-center location of some house doors meant that outsiders could not see directly into the courtyard, while in other houses the door location meant that they could see people in the courtyard, which might well include women who, according to the elite gender ideology, were not to be seen by strangers.

Feminist Material Analyses of Sexual Identities and Practices in Classical Cultures

Classical archaeologists may have been the first to analyze material evidence of sexuality, including diversity in sexualities, sexual identities, and sexual practices, due to depictions of both homosexual and heterosexual sex acts and sexuality on classical Greek and Roman artifacts, from vases and sculptures to floor mosaics and wall paintings. However, discourse on sexuality was long taboo in the classics, and many of the few studies conducted before the 1970s were written in Latin (Richlin 1992:xiii). Dover's (1978) seminal *Greek Homosexuality* drew on images as well as texts but retained a male gaze. Groundbreaking feminist research on sexuality and aggression in Roman humorous texts (Richlin 1983) was followed by a radical feminist theoretical approach to research on classical Greek images and texts concerned with male sexual domination (Keuls 1985). In the 1990s, a number of studies of sexuality in classical Greece and Rome combined structuralist approaches of Detienne, Vernant, and Foucault with a more contextual anthropological approach positing that sexual experiences in antiquity were radically different from those in modern Western cultures (e.g., Halperin 1990; Halperin et al. 1990; Winkler 1990).

One of the earliest feminist analyses, by Williams (1983:97–100), proposed to unreflectively learn about Greek women's lives from Athenian painted vase designs portraying women and men in a variety of activities. She identifies vases picturing nude hetaerae learning to dance from a dressed madam and another of hetaerae washing at a fountain. A more questionable identification is made of a dressed hetaerae receiving two men, the first of whom has a bag apparently of money that she interpreted as payment for sex either for himself or for his son behind him. However, it is not clear what the woman is being paid for, and the other side of the vase shows the man paying another woman interpreted as his wife (Keuls 1985:153–87). Williams importantly questions whether dressed women need always be interpreted as respectable women. She notes that hetaerae could be depicted on two vases showing clothed women relaxing and playing the harp, one including the child-sized god Eros. Williams points out that the pottery district in Athens was also renowned for its brothels, so the male potters had a lot of opportunity to observe and paint the lives of the often wealthy hetaerae. Finally, Williams argues that the vases were made by men from and for the male gaze. As she put it, "Athenian vase painting was essentially a man's view of a man's point of view" (Williams 1983:105). Williams's research interestingly shifts from an apparently unreflectively first-wave feminist reading of vase paintings as evidence of women's lives to raising postmodern issues about the identity of the vase painters and the clothed women they painted. Finally, she discusses the male view of the vase painters in creating scenes from a male viewpoint or gaze.

Feminist classical archaeologists may have been the earliest to explicitly apply postmodern feminist theory to analyze the diversity in material depictions of sexual activities, sexuality, and sexual identities due to complex intersections of gender and class as well as temporal changes. Richlin (1992) edited *Pornography and Representation in Greece and Rome* with an introduction combining postmodern theoretical approaches of textual analysis and representation with second-wave radical feminist theorizing about the connections between pornography, sexual identities, and the oppression of women through objectification and violence. Richlin (1992:xiv–xviii) also discusses the feminist pro-pornography backlash, which includes a liberal defense of individual rights, and the lesbian sadomasochists who argue against legislating sexuality. Richlin and other authors in her volume discuss the diversity in sexual acts, sexuality, and sexual identities depicted in classical Greek and Roman paintings and texts.

Richlin's analysis of the feminist debate over pornography resonates with the debate among classical archaeologists about whether different sexual images were pornographic for the Greeks and Romans. Chapters in Richlin range from those considering all sexual themes on classical Greek vases as pornography (Sutton 1992) to those considering pornography too strong a word for some Greek images (Shapiro 1992) to questioning the classification of Roman heterosexual images as pornography (Myerowitz 1992).

Sutton (1992:7–31) analyzes sexual themes painted on fourth- to sixth-century Greek vases from a woman's viewpoint. However, he ethnocentrically describes as "hard-core" pornography the 575–450 B.C. explicit images of misogynistic heterosexual sex acts, including forcing women to have various types of sex. Keuls (1985:187–97) discusses not only these vase paintings but also others that depicted hetaerae and prostitutes in affectionate poses with customers, which she ethnocentrically labels as the myths of the happy hooker, noble prostitute, or whore with the golden heart. Sutton ethnocentrically describes the later courting and wedding scenes as "soft-core" pornography, including both homosexual pederastic courting scenes with partially clothed or nude boys, popular from 550 to 480 B.C., and heterosexual courting scenes (480–450 B.C.) and wedding scenes (450–400 B.C.), both with fully clothed women. He points out that abuse is extremely rare in the pederastic homosexual courting scenes and are absent in the romantic heterosexual courting, wedding, and abduction scenes involving respectable women. Sutton discusses how the targeted audience and gaze for the vases shifts from showing a male-centered viewpoint on sex to depictions of heterosexual courting in which women have the power to choose and even initiate gift giving and female-centered depictions of domestic scenes, including women preparing for weddings.

Shapiro (1992:61–63, 70) focuses on classical Greek vase paintings of courting scenes involving pederastic homosexual men pursuing or giving gifts to partially clothed or naked boys whom he androcentrically calls "coy" and "playful." He makes an ethnocentric analogy between the way the boys are portrayed and modern pinup girls, which he does not consider to be pornographic. By the mid-fifth century, homosexuality was viewed as the old-fashioned antidemocratic and elitist sexuality, and images of the god Eros shift from depicting him pursuing boys to pursuing girls.

Williams's earlier interpretations of vase paintings raises questions about whether the women are interpreted as respectably preparing for weddings just because they are clothed and whether they could rather be hetaerae preparing for symposia. One of the vase paintings Sutton shows could also be interpreted as a lesbian scene since it involves four women, one of whom is standing and supporting or pushing the miniature male god Eros toward a seated woman facing her and playing the harp. Sutton interpreted this woman as a bride without clear reason.

Finally, Sutton (1992:21–24) interprets the development of vase paintings of nude bathers in the second half of the fourth century as due to the innovative and iconoclastic nude sculpture of Aphrodite of Knidos. Sutton discussed how the paintings of nude bathers shifted from being painted for men on the inside of wine cups to being painted for women because they are on vases that were usually used by women. Sutton questions whether paintings of all nude women can be identified as hetaerae and states that some of these painted vases were meant for use by respectable women. However, he also mentions that the water vases with nude bathers would have been used in the public baths, which were akin to modern massage parlors, implying that these vases might have been used by less respectable women.

Other research has analyzed women's sexual powers from classical Greek documents and paintings. A number of documents record the wealth that powerful hetaerae could achieve, and vase paintings include depictions of men coming to brothels to pay for hetaerae (Keuls 1985:153–87). Some statues depict women or hermaphrodites who in myths lifted their skirts to expose their genitals as a source of power, following the model of men, who are most often depicted on vases and in sculpture with exposed genitals signaling their social dominance (Ajootian 1997). Vases further depict women exposing their genitals as a source of sexual power to arouse men or centaurs (Cohen 1997:70). Bonfante (1997) discusses the awe and terror that the bared breast evoked for the Greeks because of its magical sexual and maternal powers connected to life and death. Cohen (1997) researched how sculptures and vase paintings express the power of women outside the norm to disrupt the social order, indicated by the exposed breasts of Amazons, the goddess Athena in battle, women in Bacchic dancing, divine lovemaking, and prostitutes as well as women's exposed breasts as loss of power in the social disruption of rape scenes. In literature, mothers exposed their breasts to inspire their sons to defend them in war. Some vase paintings depict women with bared breasts attacking men or gods (Keuls 1985:380).

Myerowitz (1992:137–54) questions whether Roman wall paintings of heterosexual sex acts are pornographic. She argues that these scenes are not pornographic because no sadism or abuse of women is shown and women and men are equally objectified and have equal social agency as sexual actors. Further, women were shown only in profile rather than the full frontal display for the gaze of the male spectator and voyeur, which is found in later European art. Finally, the paintings were not hidden away for private male voyeurism but were publicly displayed on house walls, especially in bedrooms, where women as well as men viewed them. Myerowitz (1992:151) argues that Romans viewed sex as part of women's domain of pregnancy and childbirth.

Myerowitz (1992:151–52) critiques the problem of applying modern feminist theories to anachronistically interpret Roman material culture. At the same time, she understands Susanne Kappeler's feminist analysis in arguing that all representation is sexist when men hold the mirror and control the viewpoint objectifying women. Myerowitz herself at one point interprets Roman wall paintings of sex acts as the transformation of sexuality from female nature to masculine culture, which is a second-wave feminist binary structuralist construction of gender. She points out that women wrote books instructing women on how to objectify themselves for the male gaze through sexual positions preferred by men (Myerowitz 1992:136).

In contrast to Myerowitz, Koloski-Ostrow (1997) uses the popularity of the theater in Nero's time to interpret mythological scenes painted on the walls of Pompeiian houses as theatrical stage sets meant for voyeurism. Koloski-Ostrow found mythological scenes of men and gods controlling passive women, as when Paris is shown persuading Helen to go with him to Troy. In another scene, Cassandra is shown powerless in attempting to warn the Trojans about the Trojan horse. However, in another scene, a man is about to be killed by dogs for viewing a goddess naked. The mythological scenes portray gendered asymmetries of power in contrast to the sex scenes analyzed by Myerowitz. It could be further noted that many of the Roman myths were actually Greek myths that were adopted and that brought with them the gender divisions and conflicts in classical Greek culture that were expressed in myths.

Clarke (1998:13–17, 276–78) has attempted to eliminate ethnocentrism by taking an anthropological approach in analyzing the meaning of sexual images to Romans on the basis of the contexts in which the images of sex acts are displayed as well as contemporary texts concerning sex. He found a variety of sexual identities and relationships depicted according to class, status, and ethnic differences. He argues against assuming that Roman images of sex are self-evident and can be read from our cultural viewpoint. Clarke cautions against projecting modern Western values to create anachronistic distorted interpretations of the past. At the same time, he recognizes his use of the term "lovemaking," for sex acts could be understood as a nonneutral term that romanticizes sex from a Western perspective.

Clarke (1998:13, 195, 278) asks for whom Roman images of sex were erotic and points out that this depends on the cultural context. He found that Roman laws against premarital sex and adultery were only to address the elite concerns over legitimate heirs and did not apply to sex with people of lower status. There was no uniform Christian moral standard and no Christian guilt over sex for enjoyment. A wide variety of sex acts were displayed in public spaces and houses, where they were seen by women and children as well as men. Frescoes in public baths displayed sex acts undertaken not only for men but also for women, such as cunnilingus and lesbian sex. A brothel, called a lupanar, was identified from the small cubicles or cribs with built-in stone plastered beds and depictions of sex scenes that were often exaggerated and more crudely painted than the small sexually explicit paintings found in a few rooms in houses. It would seem that Romans addressed sex more openly than Christians. Further, children as well as women were permitted to view a variety of sex acts based on the sexual identities of people from different classes, ethnic groups, and sexual orientations. Clarke does the most to destabilize and "queer" Western heterosexist interpretations of Roman depictions of sex acts.

Applications of Masculinity Theories in Classical Archaeology

Feminist masculinity theories have analyzed the Western cultural construction of a normative heterosexual hypermasculinity that valorizes and institutionalizes male domination through violence. Hypermasculinity would seem to be illustrated in Greek vase paintings of myths and men's misogynistic treatment of prostitutes, showing rape, forced sex, and beatings (Keuls 1985:47–55, 180–86; Sutton 1992:11–13).

The ideology of hypermasculinity has been contrasted with postmodern research demonstrating diversity in masculine identities, experiences, behaviors, and actual performance of masculine roles. Feminist masculinity theory and research further addresses how men's institutionalized privileges and domination benefit all men—and particular groups of men more than others. Feminist masculinity research has demonstrated the institutionalization of dominance by some groups of men not only over educational and economic resources but also over other men as well as women (Lorber 2001:163–78).

Classical Greek vase paintings depict an ideology of masculinity valorizing homosexuality (575–480 B.C.). The valorization of homosexuality is interpreted from the affection shown in pederastic courting scenes of older bearded men giving gifts to and pursuing unbearded youths. Homosexuality was further legitimated in vase paintings of the main god Zeus pursuing the boy-god Gannymead (Shapiro 1992). The valorization of homosexuality provides a new perspective on Greek men's texts defining ideal masculinity as the "same-mindedness" and interdependence of autonomous citizen men (Morris 2000:155), while women were excluded from being citizens because they lacked male virtues according to Aristotle (Pomeroy 1975).

Classical Greek vase paintings depict a shift in the ideology of masculinity to valorizing male deference to clothed respectable women in courting and wedding scenes (480–400 B.C.). Vase paintings depicting women's domestic work behind closed doors in the women's quarters or entering the half-opened door to a bedroom (Keuls 1983, 1985:98–129) both represent men's control over women that was valorized in idealistic documents associating masculinity with the responsible pious male citizen head of household, who was married with children and a self-sufficient farmer who owned his own land (Hanson 1995:87–88; Morris 2000:115–49). Second-wave feminist classical archaeologists projected the ideal of masculine control of women to divide excavated foundations of houses into segregated male-public spaces and women's private quarters that had no access to the outside and that restricted access to the rest of the house (e.g., Keuls 1985; Walker 1983).

The Romans shared some similar masculine ideals as heads of households controlling their wives, children, and slaves. In fact, Roman men had the power to put members of their family to death, which was more power than Greek men had, except for female infanticide. Roman freemen also shared masculine ideals as citizens and as warriors for the state. However, classical Roman explicit sexual scenes are more often egalitarian than Greek sex scenes (Myerowitz 1992).

Roman sex scenes showed women as well as men willingly participating, in contrast to Greek scenes. Rome borrowed the Greek gods and goddesses and as a result depicted the same mythological scenes of rape.

The Future

Feminist classical archaeology has generally followed the development of feminist theory. Therefore, it can be hoped that second-wave analyses projecting the dominant historic patriarchal ideology as the universal actual gender practice will be increasingly replaced with third-wave feminist analyses of the diversity and fluidity in classical gender systems. A start has been made in constructing a richer picture of the complexity and change in classical gender systems. Most research so far has addressed class differences in gendered household spaces and consumer choices. Clarke (1988) has shown that it is also possible to address ethnic differences in houses in classical Roman culture. Perhaps it would also be possible to find ethnic areas in classical Greek cities that would reveal some ethnic differences in house design or artifacts. It is hoped that research on the negotiation and fluidity of gender identities and sexual orientations will continue to develop.

The explicit use of feminist theory in the classics has increased from Pomeroy (1975) to Keuls (1985), Richlin (1992), and Lyons and Koloski-Ostrow (1997). It is hoped that this review has demonstrated that further insight can be gained by the explicit application of feminist theory in gender research in classical archaeology.

Acknowledgments

I would like to thank the following colleagues for their generous assistance in providing me with information on gender research in feminist classical archaeology: Pim Allison, Marilyn Goldberg, Claire Lyons, and Lynn Meskell. My deepest thanks to Sarah Nelson for encouraging me to write this chapter. Of course, any errors are mine.

References

Abbott, Frank F.
    1909   *Society and Politics in Ancient Rome: Essays and Sketches*. New York: Scribner's.
Adkins, Lesley, and Roy A. Adkins
    1997   *Handbook to Life in Ancient Greece*. New York: Facts on File.
Ajootian, Aileen
    1997   The Only Happy Couple: Hermaphrodites and Gender. In *Naked Truths:*

Women, Sexuality and Gender in Classical Art and Archaeology. A. O. Koloski-Ostrow and C. L. Lyons, eds. Pp. 220–43. London: Routledge.

Alcock, Susan E.
    2002   *Archaeologies of the Greek Past: Landscape, Monuments, and Memories.* Cambridge: Cambridge University Press.

Allison, Penelope M.
    1999   Labels for Ladles: Interpreting the Material Culture of Roman Households. In *The Archaeology of Household Activities: Gender Ideologies, Domestic Spaces and Material Culture.* Penelope M. Allison, ed. Pp. 57–78. London: Routledge.
    2004   *Pompeian Households: An Analysis of Material Culture.* Monograph 42. Los Angeles: Costen Institute of Archaeology, University of California, Los Angeles.

Amos, Valerie, and Pratibha Parmer
    1984   Challenging Imperial Feminism. *Feminist Review* 17(autumn):3–19.

Archer, L. J., S. Fischler, and M. Wyke, eds.
    1994   *Women in Ancient Societies: "An Illusion of the Night."* New York: Routledge.

Ault, Bradley A., and Lisa C. Nevett
    1999   Digging Houses: Archaeologies of Classical and Hellenistic Greek Domestic Assemblages. In *The Archaeology of Household Activities: Gender Ideologies, Domestic Spaces and Material Culture.* Penelope M. Allison, ed. Pp. 43–57. London: Routledge.

Blundell, S.
    1995   *Women in Ancient Greece.* London: British Museum Press.

Boardman, John
    1974   *Athenian Black Figure Vases.* London: Thames and Hudson.
    1998   *Early Greek Vase Painting: 11th–6th Centuries B.C.* London: Thames and Hudson.

Bonfante, Larissa
    1997   Nursing Mothers in Classical Art. In *Naked Truths: Women, Sexuality and Gender in Classical Art and Archaeology.* A. O. Koloski-Ostrow and C. L. Lyons, eds. Pp. 174–97. London: Routledge.

Broude, N., and M. Garrard, eds.
    1982   *Feminism and Art History: Questioning the Litany.* New York: Harper and Row.

Brown, Shelby
    1993   Feminist Research in Archaeology: What Does It Mean? Why Is It Taking so Long? In *Feminist Theory and the Classics.* Sorkin Rabinowitz and Amy Richlin, eds. Pp. 238–71. New York: Routledge.
    1997   "Ways of Seeing" Women in Antiquity: An Introduction to Feminism in Classical Archaeology and Ancient Art History. In *Naked Truths: Women, Sexuality and Gender in Classical Art and Archaeology.* A. O. Koloski-Ostrow and C. L. Lyons, eds. Pp. 1243. London: Routledge.

Bunch, Charlotte
    1987   *Passionate Politics: Essays 1968–1986—Feminist Theory in Action.* New York: St. Martin's Press.

Butler, Judith
    1990   *Gender Trouble: Feminism and the Subversion of Identity.* London: Routledge.
Buxton, Richard
    1998   Religion and Myth. In *The Cambridge Illustrated History of Ancient Greece.* Paul Cartledge, ed. Pp. 320–45. Cambridge: Cambridge University Press.
Cameron, Averil, and Amélie Kuhrt
    1993   *Images of Women in Antiquity.* Detroit: Wayne State University Press.
Cantarella, Eva
    1987   *Pandora's Daughters: The Role and Status of Women in Greek and Roman Antiquity.* Baltimore: The Johns Hopkins University Press.
Cartledge, Paul
    1993   *The Greeks: A Portrait of Self and Others.* New York: Oxford University Press.
Clarke, John R.
    1991   *The Houses of Roman Italy 100 B.C.–A.D. 250: Ritual, Space and Decoration.* Berkeley: University of California Press.
    1998   *Looking at Lovemaking: Constructions of Sexuality in Roman Art 100 B.C.–A.D. 250.* Berkeley: University of California Press.
Clees, Helen
    1920   *A Study of Women in Attic Inscriptions.* New York: Columbia University Press.
Cohen, Beth
    1997   Divesting the Female Breast of Clothes in Classical Sculpture. In *Naked Truths: Women, Sexuality and Gender in Classical Art and Archaeology.* A. O. Koloski-Ostrow and C. L. Lyons, eds. Pp. 66–93. London: Routledge.
Collins, Patricia Hill
    1990   *Black Feminist Thought: Knowledge, Consciousness, and the Politics of Empowerment.* Boston: Unwin Hyman.
Cowell, Frank R.
    1980   *Life in Ancient Rome.* New York: Putnam.
Davis-Kimball, Jeannine
    1997   Sauro-Sarmatian Nomadic Women: New Gender Identities. *Journal of Indo-European Studies* 25:327–44.
Donovan, Josephine
    2001   *Feminist Theory: The Intellectual Traditions.* 3rd ed. New York: Continuum.
Dover, K. J.
    1978   *Greek Homosexuality.* Cambridge, MA: Harvard University Press.
duBois, Page
    1988   *Sowing the Body: Psychoanalysis and Ancient Representations of Women.* Chicago: University of Chicago Press.
Dwyer, Eugene
    1991   The Pompeian Atrium House in Theory and in Practice. In *Roman Art in the Private Sphere: New Perspectives on the Architecture and Décor of the Domus, Villa, and*

Insula. E. K. Gazda, ed., assisted by A. E. Haeckl. Pp. 25–49. Ann Arbor: University of Michigan Press.

Ellis, Simon P.
   1991   Power, Architecture, and Décor: How the Late Roman Aristocrat Appeared to His Guests. In *Roman Art in the Private Sphere: New Perspectives on the Architecture and Décor of the Domus, Villa, and Insula.* E. K. Gazda, ed., assisted by A. E. Haeckl. Pp. 117–35. Ann Arbor: University of Michigan Press.

Fantham, E., H. P. Foley, N. B. Kampen, S. B. Pomeroy, and H. A. Shapiro, eds.
   1994   *Women in the Classical World: Image and Text.* New York: Oxford University Press.

Gazda, Elaine K.
   1991   Introduction. In *Roman Art in the Private Sphere: New Perspectives on the Architecture and Décor of the Domus, Villa, and Insula.* E. K. Gazda, ed., assisted by A. E. Haeckl. Pp. 1–25. Ann Arbor: University of Michigan Press.

Goldberg, Marilyn Y.
   1998   Deceptive Dichotomy: Two Case Studies. In *Redefining Archaeology: Feminist Perspectives.* Mary Casey, Denise Donlon, Jeanette Hope, and Sharon Welfare, eds. Pp. 107–13. Canberra: ANH Publications, Research School of Pacific and Asian Studies, Australian National University.
   1999   Spatial and Behavioural Negotiation in Classical Athenian City Houses. In *The Archaeology of Household Activities: Gender Ideologies, Domestic Spaces and Material Culture.* Penelope M. Allison, ed. Pp. 142–62. London: Routledge.

Gutzwiller, Kathryn J., and Ann N. Michelini
   1991   Women and Other Strangers: Feminist Perspectives in Classical Literature. In *(En)Gendering Knowledge: Feminists in Academe.* Joan E. Hartman and Ellen Messer-Davidow, eds. Pp. 66–85. Knoxville: University of Tennessee Press.

Hallett, Judith P., and Marilyn B. Skinner, eds.
   1997   *Roman Sexualities.* Princeton, NJ: Princeton University Press.

Halperin, David M.
   1990   *One Hundred Years of Homosexuality.* New York: Routledge.

Halperin, David M., John J. Winkler, and Froma Zeitlin, eds.
   1990   *Before Sexuality: The Construction of Erotic Experience in Ancient Greece.* Princeton, NJ: Princeton University Press.

Hanson, V. D.
   1995   *The Other Greeks: The Family Farm and the Agrarian Roots of Western Civilization.* New York: Free Press.

Havelock, Christine M.
   1982   Mourners on Greek Vases: Remarks on the Social History of Women. In *Feminism and Art History: Questioning the Litany.* Norma Broude and Mary D. Garrard, eds. Pp. 45–63. New York: Harper and Row.

Hoepfner, W., and Schwander, E. L.
   1994   *Haus und statdt im klassischen Griechenland.* Munich: Deutscher Kunstverlag.

Houby-Nielsen, Sanne
 2000 Child Burials in Ancient Athens. In *Children and Material Culture*. Joanna S. Derevenski, ed. Pp. 151–67. London: Routledge.

Jameson, M.
 1990 Domestic Space in the Greek City-State. In *Domestic Architecture and the Use of Space*. Susan Kent, ed. Pp. 92–113. Cambridge: Cambridge University Press.

Kampen, Natalie B.
 1982 Social Status and Gender in Roman Art: The Case of the Saleswoman. In *Feminism and Art History: Questioning the Litany*. Norma Broude and Mary D. Garrard, eds. Pp. 63–79. New York: Harper and Row.
 1991 Between Public and Private: Women as Historical Subjects in Roman Art. In *Women's History and Ancient History*. Sarah Pomeroy, ed. Pp. 218–48. Chapel Hill: University of North Carolina Press.

Katz, Marilyn
 1998 Women, Children and Men. In *The Cambridge Illustrated History of Ancient Greece*. Paul Cartledge, ed. Pp. 100–39. Cambridge: Cambridge University Press.

Keuls, Eva
 1983 Attic Vase-Painting and the Home Textile Industry. In *Ancient Greek Art and Iconography*. Warren G. Moon, ed. Pp. 209–30. Madison: University of Wisconsin Press.
 1985 *The Reign of the Phallus: Sexual Politics in Ancient Athens*. New York: Harper and Row.

Koloski-Ostrow, Ann Olga
 1997 Violent Stages in Two Pompeian Houses: Imperial Taste, Aristocratic Response, and Messages of Male Control. In *Naked Truths: Women, Sexuality and Gender in Classical Art and Archaeology*. A. O. Koloski-Ostrow and C. L. Lyons, eds. Pp. 243–67. London: Routledge.

Koloski-Ostrow, Ann Olga, and Claire L. Lyons, eds.
 1997 *Naked Truths: Women, Sexuality and Gender in Classical Art and Archaeology*. New York: Routledge.

Laurence, Ray
 1994 *Roman Pompeii: Space and Society*. London: Routledge.

Lerner, Gerda
 1993 *The Creation of Feminist Consciousness: From the Middle Ages to Eighteen-Seventy*. New York: Oxford University Press.

Longfellow, Brenda
 2000 A Gendered Space? Location and Function of Room 5 in the Villa of the Mysteries. In *The Villa of the Mysteries in Pompeii*. Elaine K. Gazda, ed. Pp. 24–38. Ann Arbor: Kelsey Museum of Archaeology and the University of Michigan Museum of Art.

Lorber, Judith
 2001 *Gender Inequality: Feminist Theories and Politics*. 2nd ed. Los Angeles: Roxbury.

Lyons, Claire L., and Olga Koloski-Ostrow
    1997   Introduction. In *Naked Truths: Women, Sexuality and Gender in Classical Art and Archaeology*. A. O. Koloski-Ostrow and C. L. Lyons, eds. Pp. 1–12. London: Routledge.
McClure, Laura K., ed.
    2002   *Sexuality and Gender in the Classical World: Readings and Sources*. Oxford: Blackwell.
Meadows, Karen
    1999   The Appetites of Households in Early Roman Britain. In *The Archaeology of Household Activities: Gender Ideologies, Domestic Spaces and Material Culture*. Penelope M. Allison, ed. Pp. 101–21. London: Routledge.
Millett, Kate
    1970   *Sexual Politics: A Surprising Examination of Society's Most Arbitrary Folly*. Garden City, NY: Doubleday.
Mohanty, Chandra T.
    1988   Under Western Eyes: Feminist Scholarship and Colonial Discourse. *Feminist Review* 30(autumn):61–88.
Morris, Ian
    1994   *Classical Greece: Ancient Histories and Modern Archaeologies*. Cambridge: Cambridge University Press.
    2000   *Archaeology as Cultural History: Words and Things in Iron Age Greece*. London: Blackwell.
Myerowitz, Molly
    1992   The Domestication of Desire: Ovid's *Parva Tabella* and the Theater of Love. In *Pornography and Representation in Greece and Rome*. Amy Richlin, ed. Pp. 131–58. New York: Oxford University Press.
Nelson, Sarah M.
    2002   Gender in Archaeology: The Professional Is Political. Paper presented at the 2002 Centennial Meetings of the American Anthropological Association, New Orleans.
Nevett, Lisa C.
    1994   Separation or Seclusion: Towards an Archaeological Approach to Investigating Women in the Greek Household in the Fifth to Third Centuries B.C. In *Architecture and Order: Approaches to Social Space*. M. Parker Pearson and C. Richards, eds. Pp. 98–112. London: Routledge.
    1999   *House and Society in the Ancient Greek World*. Cambridge: Cambridge University Press.
Nicholson, Linda J., ed.
    1990   *Feminism/Postmodernism*. New York: Routledge.
Ortner, Sherry B.
    1974   Is Female to Male as Nature Is to Culture? In *Woman, Culture and Society*. Michelle Z. Rosaldo and Louise Lamphere, eds. Pp. 67–88. Stanford, CA: Stanford University Press.

Pomeroy, Sarah B.
   1975   *Goddesses, Whores, Wives and Slaves: Women in Classical Antiquity*. New York: Schocken Books.
   1998   The Contribution of Women to the Greek Domestic Economy: Rereading Xenophon's Oeconomicus. In *Feminisms in the Academy*. Donna C. Stanton and Abigail J. Stewart, eds. Pp. 180–99. Ann Arbor: University of Michigan Press.

Reeder, E., ed.
   1995   *Pandora: Women in Classical Greece*. Princeton, NJ: Princeton University Press.

Reilly, Joan
   1997   Naked and Limbless: Learning about the Feminine Body in Ancient Athens. In *Naked Truths: Women, Sexuality and Gender in Classical Art and Archaeology*. A. O. Koloski-Ostrow and C. L. Lyons. Pp. 154–74. London: Routledge.

Richlin, Amy
   1983   *The Garden of Priapus: Sexuality and Aggression in Roman Humor*. New Haven, CT: Yale University Press.
   1992   Introduction. In *Pornography and Representation in Greece and Rome*. Amy Richlin, ed. Pp. xi–xxiv. New York: Oxford University Press.

Robertson, Charles M.
   1992   *The Art of Vase-Painting in Classical Athens*. Cambridge: Cambridge University Press.

Rolle, Renate
   1989   *The World of the Scythians*. F. G. Walls, trans. Berkeley: University of California Press. Originally published in German in 1980.

Rosaldo, Michele Zimbalist
   1980   The Use and Abuse of Anthropology: Reflections on Feminism and Cross-Cultural Understanding. *Signs* 5(3):389–417.
   1974   Woman, Culture, and Society: A Theoretical Overview. In *Woman, Culture and Society*. Michelle Z. Rosaldo and Louise Lamphere, eds. Pp. 17–42. Stanford, CA: Stanford University Press.

Rosaldo, Michele Z., and Louise Lamphere
   1974   Introduction. In *Woman, Culture and Society*. Michelle Z. Rosaldo and Louise Lamphere, eds. Pp. 1–16. Stanford, CA: Stanford University Press.

Sanders, D.
   1990   Behavioral Conventions and Archaeology: Methods for the Analysis of Ancient Architecture. In *Domestic Architecture and the Use of Space*. Susan Kent, ed. Pp. 43–72. Cambridge: Cambridge University Press.

Shapiro, H. A.
   1992   Eros in Love: Pederasty and Pornography in Greece. In *Pornography and Representation in Greece and Rome*. Amy Richlin, ed. Pp. 53–73. New York: Oxford University Press.

Snyder, Jane M.
    1997   Sappho in Attic Vase Painting. In *Naked Truths: Women, Sexuality and Gender in Classical Art and Archaeology.* A. O. Koloski-Ostrow and C. L. Lyons, eds. Pp. 108–20. London: Routledge.

Spelman, Elizabeth
    1988   *Inessential Woman: Problems of Exclusion in Feminist Thought.* Boston: Beacon Press.

Spencer-Wood, Suzanne M.
    1991   Toward an Historical Archaeology of Domestic Reform. In *The Archaeology of Inequality.* R. McGuire and R. Paynter, eds. Pp. 231–86. Oxford: Basil Blackwell.
    1992   A Feminist Program for a Non-Sexist Archaeology. In *Quandaries and Quests: Visions of Archaeology's Future.* LuAnn Wandsnider, ed. Pp. 98–113. Occasional Paper 20. Carbondale: Center for Archaeological Investigations, Southern Illinois University.
    1994   Diversity in 19th Century Domestic Reform: Relationships among Classes and Ethnic Groups. In *"Those of Little Note": Gender, Race and Class in Historical Archaeology.* Elizabeth Scott, ed. Tucson: University of Arizona Press.
    1995   Toward the Further Development of Feminist Historical Archaeology. *World Archaeological Bulletin* 7:118–36.
    1999   The World Their Household: Changing Meanings of the Domestic Sphere in the Nineteenth Century. In *The Archaeology of Household Activities: Gender Ideologies, Domestic Spaces and Material Culture.* Penelope M. Allison, ed. Pp. 162–89. London: Routledge.

Stewart, Andrew
    1990   *Greek Sculpture: An Exploration.* New Haven, CT: Yale University Press.

Sutton, Robert F., Jr.
    1992   Pornography and Persuasion on Attic Pottery. In *Pornography and Representation in Greece and Rome.* Amy Richlin, ed. Pp. 3–36. New York: Oxford University Press.

Thébert, Y.
    1987   Private Life and Domestic Architecture in Roman Africa. In *A History of Private Life: I. From Pagan Rome to Byzantium.* P. Veyne, ed. Pp. 313–410. Cambridge, MA: Belknap Press.

Vernant, J. P.
    1983   Hestia-Hermes: The Religious Expression of Space and Movement in Ancient Greece. In *Myth and Thought.* J. P. Vernant, ed. Pp. 127–75. London: Routledge and Kegan Paul.

Versnel, H. S.
    1987   Wife and Helpmate: Women of Ancient Athens in Anthropological Perspective. In *Sexual Asymmetry.* J. Blok and P. Mason, eds. Pp. 59–86. Amsterdam: Gieben.

Walker, Susan
    1983   Women and Housing in Classical Greece: The Archaeological Evidence. In *Images of Women in Antiquity*. Averil Cameron and Amélie Kuhrt, eds. Pp. 81–91. Detroit: Wayne State University Press.

Wallace-Hadrill, Andrew
    1994   *Houses and Society in Pompeii and Herculaneum*. Princeton, NJ: Princeton University Press.

Williams, Dyfri
    1983   Women on Athenian Vases: Problems of Interpretation. In *Images of Women in Antiquity*. Averil Cameron and Amélie Kuhrt, eds. Pp. 92–107. Detroit: Wayne State University Press.
    2000   Of Geometric Toys, Symbols and Votives. In *Periplous: Papers on Classical Art and Archaeology Presented to Sir John Boardman*. G. R. Tsetskhladze, A. N. J. W. Prag, and A. M. Snodgrass, eds. Pp. 388–97. London: Thames and Hudson.

Winkler, John J.
    1990   *The Constraints of Desire: The Anthropology of Sex and Gender in Ancient Greece*. New York: Routledge.

Wylie, Alison
    1991   Gender Theory and the Archaeological Record: Why Is There No Archaeology of Gender? In *Engendering Archaeology: Women and Prehistory*. J. M. Gero and M. W. Conkey, eds. Pp. 31–54. Oxford: Basil Blackwell.

Younger, John G.
    1997   Gender and Sexuality in the Parthenon Frieze. In *Naked Truths: Women, Sexuality and Gender in Classical Art and Archaeology*. A. O. Koloski-Ostrow and C. L. Lyons, eds. Pp. 120–54. London: Routledge.

IDENTITIES II

The Prism of Self: Gender and Personhood   10

BONNIE J. CLARK AND LAURIE A. WILKIE

As FEMINIST ARCHAEOLOGISTS have continued to develop more sophisticated approaches and understandings of gender, they have recognized with increasing frequency that gender intersects with and is shaped by a range of other social identities. This intellectual position is drawn from the works of third-wave feminists (e.g., Butler 1990, 1993; Collins 2000; Giddings 1984; Spelman 1988), particularly those who examine the experiences of minority women. Spelman (1988:15) articulated this most eloquently when she observed, "One's gender identity is not related to one's racial and class identity as the parts of pop-bead necklaces are related, separable and insertable in other 'strands' with different racial and class 'parts.'" Instead, these facets of social identity are articulated and interface in complex ways that lead to the embodied experience of self. This is not to say that gender is not an important construct but, rather, that we weaken our interpretations when we fail to recognize how gender is shaped by life course, status, and other social positions.

Like many other archaeologists (e.g., Fowler 2004; Gillespie 2000; Joyce 2000a, 2004, 2006; Knapp 1988; Meskell 1999, 2002, 2004; Meskell and Joyce 2003), we have come to believe that the pursuit of archaeologies of "personhood" will allow us to better realize the potentials of engendered and feminist archaeologies. One way to construct multidimensional archaeological interpretations is to create archaeologies that recognize finer grains of social difference. Gender, age, rank, race, and other identities would be all part of a socially situated and performed persona. Such an approach would allow us to shift from considerations of gross categories, such as "woman," to a consideration of socially constructed roles that incorporate gender, such as "mother." In this chapter, we will also argue that the concept of personhood provides a new avenue of interpretive inquiry for understanding sexism and racism in the material record.

While there are a growing number of archaeologists who are explicitly constructing archaeologies of personhood, there are other archaeological projects that are also complementary to this work. For instance, a growing number of studies focus on archaeologies of childhood (e.g., Ardren and Hutson, 2006; Joyce 2000b; Moore and Scott 1997; Sofaer-Derevenski 2000; Yamin 2002). These studies examine a particular stage in the life cycle while also exploring how children learn gender and other roles. Still other scholars are studying other aspects of social difference, such as racism (e.g., Epperson 2004; Orser 2000), ethnogenesis and creolization (e.g., Ferguson 1992; Lightfoot et al. 1997; Wilkie and Farnsworth 1999), and social stratification or class identities (e.g., Wood 2004; Wurst and Fitts 1999). There exists, of course, a large body of literature on gender (e.g., Galle and Young 2004; Gero and Conkey 1991; Gilchrist 1999) and sexuality (e.g., Schmidt and Voss 2000; Voss 2000).

These works (and others like them) are looking at particular aspects of social identity that are components of personhood. Archaeologies of personhood should not be seen as replacing archaeologies of gender, sexuality, life course, or other axes of difference. Instead, archaeologies of personhood should be seen as a framework of understanding through which anthropological archaeology can integrate these dimensions of social identity in a meaningful and holistic way.

Archaeologists have been drawn to the notion of personhood for a variety of reasons. "Personhood" provides an important alternative to the Western notion of the "individual"—an autonomous and independently motivated and intentioned actor. Archaeologists have often been guilty of projecting the notion of individualism into the pasts they study. To do so ignores the complex ways of knowing and being that shape social life in other cultural and chronological settings. Personhood emphasizes humans as situated in a series of social relations and entanglements that define who they are within a community (Gillespie 2000; Meskell 1999). Personhood recognizes that the human experience is an embodied one (Joyce 2004, 2006; Meskell and Joyce 2003). Susan Gillespie (2000) sees archaeologies of personhood as conceptual means of bridging the divide between actor and society in a way that focuses on social dimensions of actors. Fowler (2004:5) sees the study of personhood as a necessary component of a humanized archaeology that recognizes culture as "socially manipulated and consumed in heterogeneous ways."

Despite differences in theoretical orientation, archaeologies of personhood share several important features. First, authors are concerned about shedding the Western notion of the individual as well as the Western notion of the mind/body dichotomy (see especially Meskell and Joyce 2003). Instead, personhood is seen as a way of interrogating materials for evidence of how embodied actors engaged in discursive social relationships. Second, scholars recognize that there are two facets to personhood—the person as a socially constructed collection of identities versus the unique lived life experiences of particular persons. This is an important distinction, for it is fully possible to be a unique individual person but not have personhood, just as personhood can be conveyed on animals or objects that are clearly not human beings. Ethnographers, particularly explicitly feminist ones, have conducted detailed investigations of the interplay of gender and elements of personhood (for overviews, see Collier and Yanagisako 1987; di Leonardo 1991; Howell and Melhuus 1993). Like other scholars, we turn to ethnographic examples to illustrate the rich and diverse ways that personhood is constructed cross-culturally, briefly discussing examples from the Ashanti, Navajo, and Tchambuli.

Ashanti and the Life Course

Working among the Ashanti people of Ghana in the early twentieth century, R. S. Rattray (1932) found that personhood did not begin at birth, for the physical world parallels that of the spirit world. When a child is born into this world, a ghost mother is losing her baby. Following birth, the infant occupies an uncertain space, between two worlds, not fully rooted in either. Hair is cut from the baby's head and is called ghost hair; the first excrement is referred to as "ghost excreta." Armlets and amulets are put on the baby. These actions serve to root the child in this world. The eight days following birth are crucial, for, in Rattray's words, "During this period no one is very certain whether the infant is going to turn out a human child or prove, by dying before this period has elapsed, that it was never anything more than some wandering ghost" (59). If the child dies before the eighth day, the body may be disfigured and buried in the village midden heap, which also served as the women's latrine. Children who had not achieved the age of puberty were buried in a similar way and referred to as "pot children," based on the nature of their burial in ceramic pots. These individuals were not afforded the full funeral rites reserved for adolescents and adults. In the case of infant death, parents gave the appearance of celebrating to discourage the ghost mother from sending another child it had no intention of leaving to live in the world.

In this example, we can see that personhood is developed as part of a maturation process. Only on achieving certain rites of passage is Ashanti personhood fully established. There are clear material correlates with each step. Life cycle is too often ignored in archaeological interpretations. There are important exceptions (see Gilchrist 1999, 2000; Joyce 2000a, 2004; Meskell 1999, 2002, 2004; Meskell and Joyce 2003; Wilkie 2003). Indeed, King (2006) suggests that residents of early post-Classic coastal Oaxaca may have held ideas about children and personhood similar to that of the Ashanti. Her excavations revealed that while adults were kept linked to households through burial under house floors, children were buried outside, either under patios or even beyond the residential areas. While some archaeologists have begun to look at childhood (e.g., Ardren and Hutson, 2006; Sofaer-Derevenski 2000), there is little consideration of other stages of life; in effect, to borrow Tringham's (1991) descriptor, the archaeological past is peopled with ageless blobs. Archaeologists must attempt, then, to identify transformative moments in the life cycle, whether marked by rites of passage or other course of life events. This is not an impossible task. In studying an African American midwife's assemblage, Wilkie (2004) has correlated the ritualized use of particular materials to specific stages of labor, delivery, and postpartum protection of the infant.

The Navajo and the Personhood of Nonhumans

Personhood is not limited to people. In Navajo life, aspects of personhood can be attributed to plants, animals, and objects that other cultures might define as inanimate. Schwarz (1997) argues that the ways that Navajo personhood is entwined with the physical space of the matrilineal home is an underlying tension in the Navajo–Hopi land dispute. The connection to one's matrilineal home is established prenatally and then in infancy, when the afterbirth and umbilical cord are buried at the matrilineal home.

The placement of the umbilical cord is particularly important for the child's future occupation. One informant told Schwarz that umbilical cords anchor babies to the earth. Navajo return to the matrilineal home frequently, including for ceremonies. Schwarz observes that the physical relocation of Navajo from their matrilineal homes literally leaves them anchorless in the world, leading to increased incidence of alcoholism, depression, and family instability. The relocatees are literally robbed of their personhood.

This case makes two important points for our consideration. First, personhood is a quality that can be conferred on inanimate objects and places. In addition, human body parts and substances can also be conferred with the status of personhood. This is not as foreign a concept to Western culture as it may first appear. After all, the abortion debate in the United States makes clear that some would confer personhood on embryos rather than on adult women. Similarly, death does not necessarily denote the end of a person's social obligations, but may only mark another transformation in their personhood. This is clearly illustrated in Gillespie's (2000) consideration of funerary ritual in Mesoamerica and Meskell and Joyce's (2003) discussion of human–animal hybrids in Egyptian and Mesoamerican art and religion.

The Tchumbali and Depersonalized Persons

Being a person does not guarantee one personhood. Among the Tchumbali of Papua New Guinea, Gewertz (1984) found that to allow for her to move in both the men's and the women's houses of this society, the elders had redefined her as a nonperson. She writes, "They agreed that I was probably not a woman at all, but a strange creature who grew male genitals upon donning trousers. My husband, they thought, was a '*man bilong sem*'—a man of shame—meaning a feminized male. And our daughter, they decided, was not born of our union but had been acquired unnaturally, perhaps purchased from a stranger who needed money. After all, two normally fertile people would have produced many more children by our advanced ages" (618). Gewertz was at first confused by this description and first tried to understand it as a redefining of her gender position. In time, she came to understand that, as an ambiguously sexed creature who was unable to contribute offspring to a patriclan, she was a social nonentity. "I was . . . a differentiated individual, an autonomous self. . . . Yet from the Tchambuli perspective, an individual has no significant reality, and hence no power, apart from his or her relationships" (618).

This example is of particular interest to this work because it illustrates an aspect of personhood not always discussed in the archaeological literature. Not only can society convey personhood, but it can also deny it. For those of us who grapple with racism, sexism, and class inequalities in the archaeology of the recent past, this allows us to recognize that these are not dehumanizing processes as much as they are depersonalizing processes. Patterson (1982) has written about slavery cross-culturally and through time being the experience of "social death." The Maya execution of prisoners of war has been presented as a ritualized stripping of their personhood (Meskell and Joyce 2003). Handler (1996) has suggested that treatment of one woman's grave at Newton Plantation was in keeping with the treatment of witch's burials in Africa. Even in death, this person had much potential for harm to her community, and her burial was designed to contain the malevolence of her person.

Archaeologies of the Contextualized Self and Archaeobiography

For our purposes, we consider an archaeology of personhood to be the archaeology of a socially contextualized self. This contextual self encompasses the experiences, expectations, and rights a person derives from ascribed and achieved statuses or identities. Gender, age, lineal associations, marriage, parental, occupation, political, caste, and other statuses converge to create a socially situated persona. We are explicit on this point because we think it is necessary for archaeologists to recognize that personhood is constructed within the constraints of a given community. Achievement, for some individuals, may be explicitly limited by their ascribed statuses. For instance, consider an enslaved person—the recognition of their achievements will always be shaped by perceptions of the potentials of persons in that ascribed role. Aspects of personhood, such as race, sex, age, ethnicity, and occupation, can be ascribed by society. Subaltern groups may hold notions of their own community's personhood that are in conflict with dominant ideologies. Archaeology, then, has the opportunity to explore the discursive relationship between structure and agent through competing personhoods. "Personhood" provides a framework through which we can look at responses to racism and sexism.

The goal of studying the contextual self is not so much to identify specific persons or the "smallest social unit" (see Flannery 1976; Hill and Gunn 1977) as to recognize at a finer grain of analysis the diversity of subject positions that existed in past societies. Within any society, there will be multiple people who occupy similar social statuses and spaces. In our consideration of personhood, we also want to discuss an additional dimension—that of the actual self. The actual self is the differentiated individual whose own experiences, attitudes, and inherent human uniqueness distinguish one from others who may occupy the same social statuses and spaces. This is not to say that the actual self is without social situatedness; rather, because of particular archaeological circumstances, dimensions of that person's unique humanity and agency are available to us. We will refer to archaeologies that include considerations of the actual self (in addition to the contextual self) as "archaeobiographies" (Clark 1996). The actual self cannot be studied, however, without consideration of the contextual self. Archaeobiography, then, represents the consideration of a completely embodied person and their lived life.

Amache Ochinee Prowers: A Case Study in Archaeobiography

Archaeobiography is perhaps most easily pursued within historical archaeology. Certainly that was implied when the concept was originally conceived as "a narrative that uses documentary records, material culture and excavated artifacts to tell the story of a specific person during a specific time" (Clark 1996:14). The first examination termed an archaeobiography (although certainly not the first to pursue this line of research) focused on the life of Amache Ochinee Prowers (Clark

1996). Her story was one particularly well suited to an approach that combined a concern for a specific lived life (biography) and the materials remains associated with that life (archaeology).

Born on the Great Plains of North America in the mid-1840s, Amache was the daughter of Ochinee or Lone Bear (*Nah'ku'uk'ihu'us*), a Southern Cheyenne sub-chief. In her teens, Amache married John Prowers, a Euroamerican Indian trader. While in her twenties, Amache and her growing family moved to the small town of Boggsville, Colorado. Located along the Mountain Branch of the Santa Fe Trail, Boggsville served as the center for several ranching operations as well as a destination on the trail. Amache's husband John built on his trading experience by opening a store in the Prowers' house to serve travelers on the trail. Amache would host such travelers as well as accommodate the visits of her own family. Her natal band often pitched their tipis adjacent to her house on their travels between the newly established Southern Cheyenne reservation in Oklahoma and traditional hunting and fishing grounds in Colorado.

Amache lived at a time of great change for the Cheyenne and for the country in which they uneasily resided. The choices she made, especially to marry outside her tribe but to continue relations with them, placed her in a delicate position, especially when her father was one of the over 200 Southern Cheyenne killed in the Sand Creek Massacre of 1864. If individual lives can contribute to our understanding of history, hers is certainly one of import. But history alone cannot tell her story. Although Amache could fluently speak three languages—Cheyenne, English, and Spanish—she was illiterate. The documents of her life include a scattering of legal papers regarding her husband's estate, several photographs, and the remembrances of her children and grandchildren. Historical syntheses and public memory (prior to archaeological research) focused on Amache's assimilation into Euroamerican society. A plaque below her picture in the Bent County courthouse claims that she was respected by that society "due to the strenuous effort of the Cheyenne woman to adapt herself to white man's ways." To truly understand her personhood, unfiltered by racism or nostalgia, we must turn to the material record.

A series of excavations both inside and surrounding the Prowers house at Boggsville have helped to recover the material record of Amache's life (Carrillo et al. 1993, 1994). Despite public memory of an assimilated Amache, her children's private memories suggest that Amache was not, in fact, "giving up her own way of life" (Hurd 1957). She continued to practice elements of Cheyenne foodways, including the gathering and processing of wild plants and game. To date, no botanical studies have been performed at the site, but the recovery of a broken pestle from the deposits implies that Amache engaged in Cheyenne methods of food preparation often enough to require replenishing her tools. Seed beads were recovered throughout the house and yard, suggesting that Amache continued to either wear or produce beaded clothing. That she had this skill is supported by accounts that state that her marriage arrangements included gifts of items she beaded herself (Hurd 1957).

The material record, however, also speaks to some of Amache's activities that were completely undocumented. Of import for wider disciplinary discussions is that fact that a number of lithics were recovered from discretely historic deposits at the Prowers house. These include fragments of two formal tools, several utilized flakes, and a number of pieces of debitage. The ethnographic record points out that a number of lithic tools were part of Cheyenne women's tool kits, including hide scrapers, implements for cutting meat, and knives with which to sharpen their digging sticks. Anthropologist Stan Hoig (1989:25) asserts, "The many chores performed by Cheyenne women required a variety of tools that they devised themselves."

We have, it is hoped, moved forward as a discipline since 1991, when Joan Gero, rhetorically speaking, had to jump up and down to call attention to the fact that women, whose tasks so often involve the use of stone tools, were likely making them as well (Gero 1991). Certainly recent research on hide workers in Ethiopia indicates that women there are involved in all stages of lithic procurement, production, and use (Brandt and Weedman 2000). Amache spent much of her time significantly spatially separated from other Cheyenne. If her stone tools needed sharpening or refurbishing, she would have had to do it herself. That Amache would have continued to use and maintain stone tools at Boggsville fits into what we know of her from written and material sources.

Individual artifacts are tangible pieces of the past. Yet when we are trying to say something about cultural continuity and change and especially the creation and manipulation of ethnic identities, their meanings can be ambiguous. As Lightfoot (1995:207) has contended, when it comes to ethnically pluralistic settlements like Boggsville, "it is clear that simply computing the percentage of European and native artifacts in archaeological deposits tells us little about the process of culture change." Indeed, many "traditional" activities can be more than adequately pursued using adopted material culture. However, an emphasis on the organization and use of space can allow us to identify key cultural values less likely to be masked by outward material signs.

Boggsville, at first blush, is not visibly different from settlements in Missouri, where John Prowers hailed from (fig. 10.1). The buildings there exhibit the symmetry of typical Anglo structures of the time, at least as seen from the front. Both the Prowers' house and that of their neighbors, the Boggses, feature the neoclassi-

Figure 10.1. Historic sketch of Boggsville from an illustrated supplement of the *Bent County Democrat*, Spring 1888.

cal touches that identify them as territorial-style architecture. However, both houses are made of adobe—not surprising given that the majority of women who lived at this site were Hispanic women from Taos, New Mexico (Clark 1997). That the Anglo veneer was very important to the settlers is clear in that both houses were "tattooed," the plaster painted with a design to make them look, from a distance, like they were built of cut stone. In addition to the use of adobe, another Hispanic element of the houses was their U-shape plans, with rooms built around a courtyard in hacienda style.

The orientation of the courtyard at the Boggs house makes sense according to the formal layout of the settlement and from an environmental standpoint. As one approaches from the river following the formal, tree-lined entry, the symmetry of the Boggs house holds. The courtyard faces south and is thus both warmed by the sun and protected from the wind. The Prowers courtyard, on the other hand, conforms to neither that layout nor environmental factors. As one approached the settlement, one would have seen right into the courtyard. Facing east as it does, it is almost always in the shade.

If one takes into account only the elements of Hispanic and Anglo architecture, the orientation of the Prowers house makes no sense. But if one factors in Cheyenne practice, it becomes much more legible. Domestic space reflects the rituals of daily life. One of the rituals that is the most critical to everyday Cheyenne functioning is *niv'stan'y'vo*, the supplications to the cardinal points of the compass. Like members of many Plains Indian groups, Amache was probably always aware of her orientation to cardinal directions. The Prowers house, with its east-facing courtyard, mirrors a Cheyenne encampment. The camp circle and the tipis themselves opened to the east or southeast. That configuration allowed the Cheyenne to greet the sun daily as it rose in the east (Grinnell 1962). The U-shaped Prowers house similarly opened up to the east, enabling Amache to continue this ritual in her daily practice. Despite the almost inconceivable nature of such a proposition, it appears that the Prowers house is a blending of Anglo and Cheyenne architecture.

This case study of an archaeobiography speaks to some of the promise of the approach. Rather than telling a story about personhood in the abstract, it examines the idea through the lived experience of a real, embodied person. It is one thing to say that the United States has always been a place of ethnic diversity. It is another to envision Amache Prowers sitting in her Victorian-era house grinding buffalo meat and greeting both travelers on the Santa Fe Trail and the rising sun in the east.

This course of research coincides with Beaudry's (1991) call to reinvent historical archaeology. We must recognize, she claims, that "the details of human

ering and childhood as examples of lived and embodied social relationships at two very different sites: La Placita in Colorado and Clifton Plantation in the Bahamas. In both case studies, the people at the center of the study have been denied some aspect of personhood by the larger society of which they are a part.

For the enslaved people of Clifton, the British legal system defined them as nonpersons—chattel—with no rights over their children or families. They had no rights over even their own bodies. As many feminist scholars have demonstrated (e.g., Collins 2000; Davis 1983; Giddings 1984; Roberts 1997), for women this denial of personhood led to the most outrageous sexual exploitation and abuse. Within the quarters, the enslaved people were a culturally heterogeneous group and, on the basis of ethnohistoric literature from West and Central Africa, were likely to have held a variety of conflicting notions of personhood. In the slave quarters, then, we have the potential to see how new understandings of personhood and value are constructed within a Creole community situated within the system of British enslavement.

The Hispanic population of La Placita faced racism as well, although of a systemically less structured nature than that experienced by enslaved peoples. Hispanics, too, were denied their full share of rights, especially those related to citizenship. In particular, the territorial expansion of the United States into what was once Mexico led to a spiral of disenfranchisement and land loss. Hispanic families in this area continue to pursue social and economic strategies in the face of disempowerment, strategies that in their material component are available to archaeologists. In these case studies, we demonstrate how we can begin the project of the study of personhood in subaltern groups.

Mothering and Childhood at Clifton Plantation

Clifton was one of three plantations owned by Loyalist William Wylly. Wylly was the attorney general of the Bahamas, and, while not an abolitionist, he was an advocate of the amelioration movement that swept through the Caribbean in the late eighteenth and early nineteenth centuries. Clifton, home to somewhere around seventy enslaved and apprenticed persons at its peak, was Wylly's grand social experiment—a place where he could put into practice what he considered to be an enlightened slaveholding philosophy (Wilkie and Farnsworth 2005).

Clifton was managed according to the "Rules of Clifton Plantation," which outlined labor and behavioral expectations to which Wylly held his enslaved people and what treatment they could expect if they followed the rules. The rules emphasized monogamy, faithfulness in marriage, engagement in Christian worship, commitment to a strong work ethic, and the demonstration of economic

life are as important as broad generalizations" (3). In fact, she goes on, the greatest potential of historical archaeology is "to help us bring to light and to understand the life history of one site and its inhabitants," eventually creating "a more and more complex mosaic" (20). Such work shifts the attention of the field from "totalizing frameworks . . . to cultural actors" (21). Archaeobiography, where it is possible, shifts the focus to an even smaller scale, telling us about not just cultural actors but also a specific, embodied, cultural actor and their lived experience.

As Meskell (1998, 2002, 2004), Meskell and Joyce (2003), and Gillespie (2000) have amply demonstrated, this level of archaeological resolution is not limited to archaeologies of the recent past. These archaeologies do require, however, a commitment to drawing on a wide range of evidentiary lines. For instance, textual archaeologies, by which we mean archaeologies that draw on written or oral sources as an evidentiary line, are in a unique situation regarding the study of personhood. Texts can provide insights into the variety of social identities and positions recognized by a group. In addition, through texts, we can come to understand the important transitions used to mark different stages in the life cycle. Through textual sources, we can find ourselves in the position of studying historically documented persons, thus allowing for the study of actual selves.

Bioarchaeology provides another line of evidence that provides a window into differentiated individuals. Hodder's (2000) consideration of the ice man is an outstanding example of such work. Bioarchaeologists have been able to do very particular kinds of archaeobiography. They construct individual life histories from skeletal materials, compiling both a catalog of single-episode life misfortunes or alternations, like a fracture or tooth shaping, and a chronicle of ongoing routines resulting in long-term changes to skeletal health or form. Arthritis, joint deterioration, malnutrition, excessive musculature, foot binding, ongoing health problems, and so on leave a documentary record inscribed on the bone. Combined with what Blakey (2001) refers to as a biocultural approach, the individual's embodied experiences can be understood within the time and place one lived.

Gender and Personhood Collide: Mothering and Childhood in the Archaeological Record

"Mother" is a cross-culturally constructed social persona that has received little attention from archaeologists. It is also a role situated in webs of generational, gender, kinship, and rank relations. One of the shortcomings of many archaeologies of childhood has been the isolation of children in the analyses from the wider social community that ultimately defined them as children. We will discuss moth-

initiative on the part of the enslaved people. In return, Wylly promised Clifton's population opportunities for outside work and trade, good accommodations, set rations, land for families to farm, and literacy training. It is interesting to note that while Wylly dictated many aspects of proper behavior, he did not dictate any policies about child rearing (Wilkie and Farnsworth 2005).

While punishments for adultery are detailed, notably missing from the rules are any exemptions from work or other considerations for pregnant or lactating women. The later dispersal of the slave community by Wylly when he left the Bahamas demonstrated that he had no qualms about separating husbands from wives or parents from children. For enslaved Africans and their descendants whose native cultures emphasized the importance of ancestors and lineal relationships, the threat of separation was particularly cruel. Although the rules are silent on the role of children within the plantation community, from other documentary evidence we can derive some insight into mothering arrangements at Clifton.

To preface this case study, we want to emphasize that we are here defining mothering as a relationship between a child and an adult that provides physical and emotional nurturing, protection, and enculturation. These are needs of children that are cross-culturally universal and necessary for successful social reproduction. While in our society we often understand mothering responsibilities for a particular child or set of children as falling to a single female, this is a culturally and chronologically specific definition. Mothering duties need not fall to biological kin or, for that matter, even to women. Collins (1994) has forcefully demonstrated that many African American women perform mothering work in a variety of ways for their communities, taking responsibility for African American children in a variety of social arenas. Likewise, among the white elite in the plantation Caribbean and American South, many mothering responsibilities for white children, including such intimate acts as breast feeding, were provided by enslaved African American women (Wilkie 2003).

Wylly clearly saw labor as being sexually divided. Women were most likely to be employed as cooks and house servants, with men more likely to be fieldworkers, carpenters, and masons. In one document, Wylly clearly states that he saw the maintenance of the provisioning grounds located adjacent to the houses to be the duty of women, with assistance of their children, while men and their able sons were to pursue outside employment such as wall building (Wilkie and Farnsworth 2005). Wylly's attitudes allowed the women of Clifton a rare opportunity to be physically close to their children during their work when farming.

Children were a large part of the Clifton population. In 1818, of the at least fifty-three persons known to have been living at Clifton, at least twenty-two were children under the age of eighteen. Six children are recorded as being employed on the plantation. They worked as shepherds, cowherds, and servants and cared for milk cows. Wylly was entitled to the labor of any child over the age of five, and at least one child of this age seems to be employed attending to milk cows and dairy, with the other person in this position at Clifton being a child of age eleven. Cowherds were children between the ages of eleven and fifteen or older men and women over the age of fifty. Servants were also young, with one on Clifton being eleven (Wilkie and Farnsworth 2005). Boys were more likely than girls to be employed at a younger age. Only one girl under the age of eighteen was employed in a set task for Wylly. Young male children and nearly all female children were an important labor resource, then, for their families, not Wylly.

Given the organization of women's labor supported by Wylly as well as his underutilization of children's labor, the women of Clifton plantation would have had the ability to keep their children near them during much of the workday. Accounts from the American South and Caribbean suggest that, when possible, enslaved women preferred to keep infants and very small children with them while working, particularly children still breast-feeding (Wilkie 2003). Most ethnographic data supports Corruccini et al.'s (1985) skeletal study, which estimated weaning age to be two to three years for enslaved children. After that age, children could be more comfortably separated from their mothers, but until they were older, they would still require supervision by an older child or adult. Older children could assist in the provisioning grounds, as envisioned by Wylly, or could engage in alternate economic activities for the good of their households.

To what degree, then, does the archaeology suggest patterns of caregiving and child oversight? We will briefly focus on three areas in which archaeological evidence is suggestive of mothering practices and children's activities: the organization of house yards, the acquisition of shellfish and marine resources, and the realm of spiritual well-being and protection.

The living space immediately surrounding the house constituted the house yard and was a distinct space in both use and organization from provisioning grounds (Pulsipher 1993). House yards tend to be swept areas where activities such as cooking, eating, cleaning, weaving, socializing, and child care took place.

At Clifton, there are eight standing structures in the slave village (fig. 10.2). Extensive excavation around four of these structures by Farnsworth and Wilkie from 1996 to 2000 allowed for the study of the size and construction of house yards (Wilkie and Farnsworth 2005). Wilkie and Farnsworth found that house yards are typically swept surfaces that are slightly wider than the width of the house structure and extend as far as fifteen meters from the rear of the house. The perimeters of the yards are typified by a ring of higher trash concentrations, with the greatest amount of accumulation corresponding to the rear of the yard.

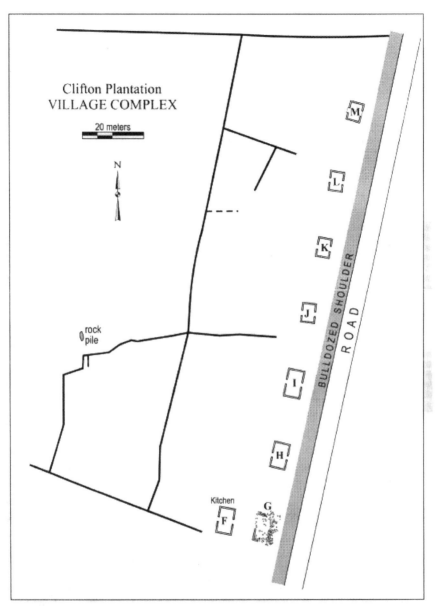

Figure 10.2. The layout of houses in the Slave Village of Clifton Plantation. Locus G was the driver's house; Locus F served as both a house and village kitchen. The remainder of the structures were single family homes.

The yard contains at least a cooking surface or structure, food preparation area, barrels for storage of drinking and washing water, and an area for eating, which in at least one case was marked by a canopy-covered structure. In the yards where kitchen buildings were identified, they tend to be located on the edge of the yard with the center areas being used for other activities. The areas immediately behind the houses featured the lowest concentrations of artifacts. Materials such as ceramics, clothing- and tobacco-related items, and food remains are typically found distributed throughout the yards despite sweeping.

At one house, a sixty-square-meter block of the yard was excavated, providing the most complete information on internal yard structure (fig. 10.3). It was this yard that provided some insight into how mothering considerations shaped the organization of space. Once the distribution of different artifact types across the extent of the yard was plotted, overlapping densities of artifacts were explored to define internal activity areas and to look at associations between architectural features in the yard and materials. A platform for a kitchen structure was found at the southern edge of the yard, and a sheltered dining area was located at the western edge. While ceramics, pipes, food remains, barrel parts, and laundry items were differentially clustered throughout the yard in patterns suggestive of different use areas, glass was recovered from only one section of the yard—a naturally occurring hole located just at the yard perimeter. From this one location, all the glass was recovered—numbering over 700 large (at least three by three centimeters) sherds.

Various reasons for this depositional pattern were contemplated. Perhaps the household was attempting to hide visible evidence of liquor consumption from the planter. Wylly had expressed disgust in a newspaper article with sailors who traded rum for provisions with the people of Clifton. There is little evidence, however, that Wylly ever spent time in the quarters but instead seems to have left all details of management up to his free-black overseer. Likewise, there were many innocent reuses for bottles that would not require them to be hidden. No bottles were recovered whole, which would have been likely if the bottles had been deposited in the hole directly after being emptied of their primary contents.

Suppose, however, that the glass was removed from the yard not because of the perceived danger of the contents but because of the perceived danger of the glass to yard occupants. Ceramics found in the yard tended to be small and did not include porcelain vessels, which may have very sharp edges when broken. Even after nearly 200 years, the edges on the glass remained sharp enough to injure excavators. If any number of small but mobile children had been tended in the yard, the glass would have been a danger to bare feet and small, curious hands.

The organization of the yard, with food preparation and consumption and

THE PRISM OF SELF 349

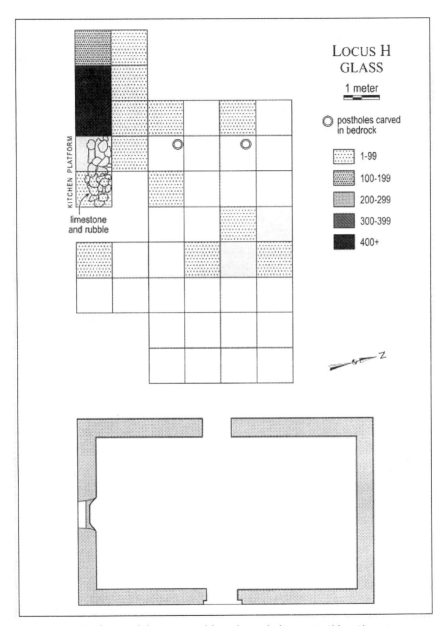

Figure 10.3. Distribution of glass recovered from the yard of Locus H, Clifton Plantation.

laundry activities consolidated along the perimeters, created an ideal surveillance zone for anyone working in those areas while facing the house. Even though employed mainly in labor benefiting her family or community rather than the planter, an enslaved person at Clifton caring for children still would have been busy with a range of other tasks. The organization of the yard space maintained a structured play zone for children that could be watched while other activities were performed. Though not at the same density, Wilkie and Farnsworth found glass to be tightly concentrated in other yards as well. This suggests that child care took place in each yard at different times, not just in one house area under a single caretaker.

Based on documentary evidence, there is reason to believe that the house at H was occupied at least through 1821 by a young African apprentice, Cudjoe, and his enslaved wife, Esther. According to an 1818 plantation slave list, the couple had two of the youngest children on the plantation, perhaps accounting for the fastidiousness of the glass collection. It may also be that Esther, as a young mother caring for two very small children, was not an efficient farmworker and instead watched other women's children in her yard. This might have led to the greater attention to potential dangers there.

Concerns for child well-being may have also shaped dietary practices at Clifton. Clifton is a coastal plantation, and the bay adjacent to the shore contains what remains one of the richest reef resources on the island of New Providence today. Shellfish and marine fish are abundant in the area. As Wilkie and Farnsworth (2005) detail elsewhere, the people of Clifton subsisted mainly on wild resources while selling domestic animals they raised in their yards and provisioning grounds at the local market. Men seemed to have taken advantage of the opportunity to earn cash from Wylly by building walls, and accounts of provisioning grounds indicate that a wide range of crops were being raised as well. Older people unable to do strenuous work and children were the most likely providers of marine resources consumed by the households. The compositions of the shellfish and fish assemblages support this contention. The vast majority of the fish recovered from Clifton were pan-sized species such as grunts, small snappers, porgies, and hinds. The fish, no matter the species, are consistent in size, suggesting the use of fishing pots. Clifton features a cliff area that abuts the sea, with the water below ranging ten to twenty feet in depth. In this area, fish swim immediately next to shore. This area would be perfect for dropping pots. Although larger fish, such as Nassau groupers and blue parrot fish, can be caught by spearfishing just a few meters from shore, these species are rare in the assemblage. Not only can pots be left unattended, thus minimizing labor involved, but, if dropped from the shore, they do not involve the same kind of risk of drowning associated with swimming.

The shellfish assemblage also supports the idea that safety concerns shaped the procurement strategy. Queen conch, a rich marine resource, is very abundant off Clifton's shore. While conch was an important part of the diet in Clifton's households, chiton, periwinkle, West Indian top shell, and tiger lucines occur to a degree not encountered at other Bahamian plantations. These are much smaller mollusks compared to conch and today are typically eaten at the beach as a snack rather than harvested for home consumption. Periwinkle and chiton are particularly difficult to harvest in any numbers because they nestle in the depths of the honeycomb rock that characterizes the shoreline. They are best removed by persons with small hands. Unlike conch, which is recovered by diving, each of the abundant species recovered from Clifton are accessible from shore. By directing that no one could enter the water while fishing or shellfish gathering, nurturers could protect children even when out of their direct oversight. Children would have been able to contribute to the family's dietary needs, but in a way that did not needlessly endanger them.

Finally, a small series of artifacts recovered from each of the houses at Clifton, beads and other potential protective devices may also be related to child care and mothering. In West Africa, beads are used to communicate multiple meanings and functions, ranging from gender or age status, ethnic identity, or religious affiliation or status (Carey 1997).

The use of "charms" or "fetishes" by African peoples was often remarked on (and misunderstood) by European visitors. Describing a group living on the Gambia River, Gray wrote in 1825, "Like all other pagans, they are very superstitious, and wear a great number of grigres, or charms round their necks, arms and legs. They are inordinately fond of red cloth, which they make use of in covering those charms." Rattray (1932) spent a great deal of effort trying to contextualize and explain the use of *suman* among the Ashanti. The *suman* is an object or series of objects that have been endowed with powers by a spiritual force, such as a deity, through a religious specialist. The components of a *suman* can widely vary but often incorporate animal parts, such as hide, bone, teeth, or claws, vegetable or animal shells, beads of different materials, fabric, and cord. The uses for *suman* can also widely vary but tend toward protective in nature and are intended for use by a single individual rather than for the protection of a corporate group (such as a lineage or a village) as shrines may be. Similar traditions of protective devices are well documented in the American South, and archaeologists have recovered materials believed to be components of such objects (Brown and Cooper 1990; Orser 1994; Wilkie 1997). Throughout the New World, the common West African practice of delaying the naming of a child until its ninth day of life was followed. Following birth, protective ornaments are placed on a newborn as a means of helping to root the child spiritually in this world.

One particular set of artifacts from House I drew our attention. From adjacent units (that otherwise contained few materials) a brass bell, a brass button, a shell button, and a comb bittersweet with a hole drilled through it—as if it were intended for stringing—were recovered. Both the bell and the shell bead are unique to the site, the only ones of their kind recovered in four excavation seasons. Comb bittersweets are very common on Clifton's beaches, and if this were a desirable ornamental object, more would have been found during excavation. The materials are not unlike protective devices described for infants and children. Were these and similar objects used to protect children from the spiritual harm that surrounded them? There are a range of objects recovered from Clifton that appear to have had uses as protective magic, including glass beads, buried coins, and other objects (Wilkie and Farnsworth 2005). The people of Clifton clearly maintained communication with persons in the spiritual realm, suggesting that indigenous understandings of personhood continued to shape discourse in the quarters.

In this case, we have briefly dealt with one aspect of mothering—that of the protection of children from harm, be that harm derived from physical or metaphysical sources. The materials from Clifton suggest much about the embodied experience of both motherhood and childhood in the context of enslavement. Arrangements of yards suggest that children were supervised in the yard spaces of homes, most likely under the surveillance of their own kin. Despite the dominant discourses that portrayed enslaved people as poor caregivers, the community employed its own value system in this arena. Likewise, food acquisition patterns also suggest a tendency toward caution and protectiveness toward young hunters and fisherfolk. Finally, the recovery of a probable protective device suggests that traditional ways of thinking about children's personhood persisted in the New World despite encounters with the religious teachings of Methodism.

Mothering and Childhood at La Placita

Although almost half a world away, the material evidence of mothering and childhood at La Placita, Colorado, bears a striking resemblance to Clifton Plantation. In particular, two elements—structured play zones and children's contributions to foodways—suggest that the strategies of subaltern families during the 1800s coalesce in instructive ways.

La Placita was a small Hispanic settlement just south of what had once been the border between Mexico and the United States. Although within U.S. territory when it was occupied in the 1880s and 1890s, the region remained part of what has been conceptualized as the "Hispano Homeland" (Nostrand 1992), and Hispanics were its majority population. Now consisting of the clustered ruins of native stone structures, La Placita was probably home to at least three different households, likely related to one another. Like the majority of Hispanic occupants of the region at that time, the people who built and occupied this settlement did not own their land. These squatters, however, are perhaps better thought of as subaltern settlers (Clark 2005), as they were pursuing traditional Hispanic land occupancy patterns legislated out of existence by the incoming U.S. government (Van Ness 1991).

Like Clifton, the work of mothering at La Placita fell almost exclusively to women but for different reasons. Indeed, not just mothering but almost all the tasks required to keep the settlement going on a day-to-day basis would have fallen on its female residents. While the enslaved men of Clifton worked the fields away from home, men in the area of the Hispano Homeland (centered in New Mexico but extending to adjacent states) were gradually less and less present in their settlements. The process whereby Hispanic men were pulled into transient labor has been elaborated by Deutsch (1987). Prior to the American takeover, many of the men of New Mexico spent time traveling either as freighters on the Santa Fe Trail or as buffalo hunters or traders with local Indians. With the American takeover came the subsequent removal of native groups, followed in the 1870s by the completion of railroads through the region. This resulted in the evaporation of many entrepreneurial opportunities for Hispanic men. Additionally, ethnocentric policies of the conquering U.S. government closed off many administrative positions formerly held by Hispanics.

This narrowing of opportunity could not have come at a worse time. The American takeover made Hispanic settlements less and less self-sufficient both through the imposition of taxes and grazing fees and through the enclosure of communal lands that had supported villages. As Deutsch (1987) documents, between 1880 and 1920, the adult and adolescent men of villages spent more and more time away as sojourning wage laborers, whether on the railroad, in mines, or as cowboys for large Anglo ranching syndicates. This is certainly suggested by the region's 1880 census, which indicates that only two of those fifteen households with male heads had as their primary occupation rancher or farmer. The other thirteen heads of household appear to be wage laborers: two are listed as farm laborers, six as general laborers, and five as herders. In six of these same households, male children were occupied as herders or laborers. Men come and go, but women and children make up the core of most households.

Material evidence at the site suggests that, like many of their neighbors, the men and possibly older boys of La Placita sojourned as wage laborers elsewhere. Although many of the site's features relate to animal husbandry, including a barn and corral, a lambing pen rock shelter, and a sheep drive line, overall the facilities at the site were modest. What was not modest were the remains of consumer goods. Over 1,100 ceramic sherds, representing a minimum of ninety-five vessels, were recovered, as well as mass-produced footwear, clothing, and tools. It is clear that the residents of the site had access to cash, more of it than could have been produced by the sheep raised there.

When women became the de facto heads of household, their workload must have increased. Not only did they need to raise children, cook, clean, and garden (all elements of established gendered divisions of labor), but they also needed to keep an eye on the stock and contend with visitors, both human and nonhuman. The material evidence of daily life at the site is a record of how women got by in a world where their work expanded because their personhood was diminished.

Child rearing, which was traditionally a dominant part of the gendered role of Hispanas, competed with new jobs they had to do, especially taking care of grazing animals. In such a situation, we might envision such women spending some of the pool of available money on items to keep children entertained. However, the artifactual evidence of toys at La Placita is quite minimal. A collapsed rubber ball and two fragments of a porcelain bisque doll were all that were recovered. Given that there are thousands of artifacts from the site, they are rare items indeed. One could use such a paucity to argue not that few toys were purchased but rather that few children were on the site. Yet in the 1880 census of the region, Hispanic households had an average of three children. Given that this was a multihousehold occupation, it is likely that there were quite a few children living at La Placita.

Children at the site seem to have figured out other ways to entertain themselves. Evidence from prehistoric sites suggests that items considered trash by adults are often used as playthings by children (Hutson and Magnoni 2002). The recycling of trash as toys would help explain some of the more puzzling items found at La Placita. It seems that a particular joy was expressed in the promise of wire. At La Placita, it gets wrapped around a range of broken items. Indeed, one of the most enigmatic of features from the site features wire wrapped around a small arch eroded out of the soft sandstone surrounding the site. Below the wire is small rock overhang enclosed with an irregular rock wall. This activity area likely represents a children's play feature, something brought up in oral histories about children's life in this area (Louden 1992). Although perhaps the work of children, the mothers of the site likely exerted influence over the feature's placement; it is on a clear line of sight from one of the domestic structures. One would, with merely a raised voice, be able to call out and be heard between the two features.

When investigating habitation areas, archaeologists should keep the spatial implications of childhood and mothering in mind. The structures of La Placita are loosely grouped around three sides of a flat terrace area. The fourth side is demarcated by a topographic break in slope that in some areas is quite steep. This settlement plan created an open arena in which the movement of children would be visible from almost all areas of the site. However, keeping the smallest children of the site from tumbling into the canyon below would have been a potential concern. Analysis of the spatial patterning of architecture and trash disposal at the site strongly suggests that the residents of the site constructed and used the open area of the site as a traditional plaza, keeping the area free from trash. A close look at the distribution of ceramic sherds (fig. 10.4) highlights that, although the majority of trash is found down the canyon, in actuality the dump begins a meter or two before the break in slope. As such, the trash could have served as a marker to smaller children that the plaza, their "safe" area of play, ended just shy of the actual terrace edge. Like those of Clifton, the mothers of La Placita were providing a structured play zone for their children, one designed for easy surveillance by busy adults.

Thinking about child rearing means thinking about children's work in addition to their play. Historians suggest that our understanding of children and childhood are radically contingent (Ariès 1962). Exactly what was expected of children in Hispanic families of this time period can at least be suggested by oral histories and ethnographies gathered during the early part of the twentieth century. These accounts imply that Hispanic children were expected to both work and play. Children assisted with many household duties, including cooking, sewing, and agricultural labors. Many chores were specifically conceptualized as children's work, particularly fetching water and tending to small animals like chickens or rabbits (Brown et al. 1978; García 1997). Alice Lopez Russell, who grew up in the early 1900s near La Placita, provides us with a firsthand account of childhood in the region (Louden 1992). Like all the children in her family regardless of gender, Alice was expected to help her mother in the kitchen. She also recalled fetching water as one of her main chores. Photographs taken in New Mexico during the early twentieth century show girls hauling water at a young age (Brown et al. 1978).

At La Placita, the water source was an enclosed seep, located off the canyon edge, below the majority of the site. The residents created a path from the edge of the plaza down to the seep, the steepest portion of which angles across a rock

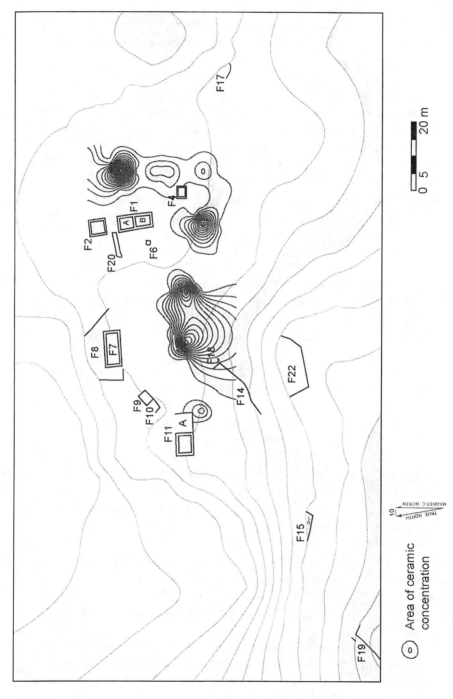

Figure 10.4. La Placita site map showing ceramic distribution.

face. Where it crosses dirt, the path is merely cleared of vegetation, but some parts exhibit serious labor investment, especially a series of steps carved into the rock. A low rock wall edges the pathway as it drops across the rock face. It would seem to serve little purpose. However, if fetching water is primarily the task of children, it takes on more import. The low rock wall made the pathway more visible and provided a psychological comfort if not actually making the path more safe. The small steps carved into the lower edge of the path are most effective for small feet and short strides.

It is clear that the mothers of La Placita invested in spatial infrastructure to increase the safety of their children. But what other compensatory measures were taken to deal with increased demands on their labor? Deutsch (1987:55) suggests that one such measure was the acquisition of new technology, in particular sewing machines and wood-burning stoves. No evidence of sewing machines was recovered from La Placita, although straight pins recovered from multiple contexts do speak to the importance of sewing. There does appear to have been a wood-burning stove used in one household, but two others went without.

The women of La Placita seem to have pursued another strategy to lessen their workload, one not envisioned by Deutsch but noted by ethnographers as common in postcolonial settings (Klein 2003). Rather than relying solely on technology, these women manipulated the social obligations of labor. Faunal evidence from the site indicates that the major sources of protein for the site's residents were wild rabbits and chickens. Both are animals associated with Hispanic children's labor. Nasario García grew up in northern New Mexico with a sojourning father. On the weekends, it was his job to kill either a chicken or a rabbit so that there would be meat with supper on the night of his father's return. As he writes, "Killing rabbits was especially painful, since I raised them; but I learned to appreciate that slaughtering or butchering animals was necessary for one's survival" (García 1997:10). There is no evidence that the cottontail rabbits at La Placita were being raised in a hutch, but it seems likely that the work of snaring or shooting them fell to children, as did the care of chickens, including gathering eggs. It is likely that children also gathered nearby wild plants, particularly piñon seeds from the tree near the seep. The overwhelming evidence of small animals at La Placita indicates that women there were delegating much of the labor of subsistence to their children. Such a strategy allowed them to focus on other aspects of their newly expanded roles.

The archaeology of both the Clifton Plantation and La Placita provides powerful insight into the lives of two very different subaltern groups. That they share so much in common speaks to the pressures of personhood under siege. When powerful outside groups claim the labor of men and older boys, it has a significant impact on women's lives. As their labor increases, women often compensate in part by relying on the work of children. Yet what children were allowed to do was conscripted, carefully managed to help ensure their safety. The safety of children was also of concern nearer the home. There, busy mothers needed to perform labor while keeping an eye on the youngest children. These mothers did their best to create structured and safe play zones for those children who had yet to be pressed into service. The results of these studies provide powerful evidence for feminist anthropologists. Modern politicians and ideologues continue to suggest the incompatibility of certain elements of personhood, especially around mothering. Although most do not overtly suggest that certain racial or ethnic positions prevent true motherhood, they blame a variety of ills on mothers who work. Of course, the wealth inequity that is one of the legacies of racism and colonization means that many mothers must work. The archaeological evidence cited here suggests that work and motherhood have never been incompatible.

Directions for the Future

The study of personhood in the past is a promising form of investigation, one that has greatly expanded in the twenty-first century. It coincides with other avenues of research both within and beyond anthropology, including studies of embodiment and postcolonial theory. Additionally, it engages with thought about agency, given that elements of a contextualized self often either conscribe or expand the potential of individual actors to engage in various social practices. Archaeologists can continue to contribute to the growing body of research in these areas, particularly given their access to data that greatly expand the temporal reach of social thought and ground it in material and spatial practices.

We hope this chapter has made it clear that for those interested in gender, archaeologies of personhood hold great potential. They promise to decenter yet at the same time reinvigorate gendered archaeology. By thinking about the prism of self, of people not with just gender but also age, kin, class, and ethnicity, we move from talking about women or men in the past to more fully realized social actors: mothers and fathers, young women, and elite elder men. The material record holds great promise for investigating the spatial elements of gendered personhood, be it the locations of rites of passage such as burials or the household spaces of parenting and childhood. When people's personhood is denied through sexism, racism, and other forms of oppression, the material world is the location of struggles and yields the evidence of strategies of resistance.

Clearly our agenda has much in common with our fellow authors in this volume. Like them—and fellow feminist researchers throughout the social sciences—we aim to expand but not abandon the goals of decades of research into gender. In 1994, feminist philosopher of science Helen Longino investigated what feminist researchers actually do. She identified a number of "theoretical virtues" (Longino 1994:476) in feminist work, including embracing complexity and eschewing single-factor causal models, trying to diffuse power, and doing work that addresses current human needs. A critical contribution of the piece is that in it Longino identifies something she calls the "bottom line requirement of feminist knowers . . . namely that they reveal or prevent the disappearing of gender" (481). Echoing Longino, we believe that an archaeology of personhood can move us forward only if pursued in such a manner that it never forgets its roots in feminist thought and never disappears gender.

References

Ardren, Traci, and Scott Hutson, eds.
    2006   *The Social Experience of Childhood in Ancient Mesoamerica.* Boulder: University Press of Colorado.

Ariès, Philippe
    1962   *Centuries of Childhood.* London: Jonathan Cape.

Beaudry, Mary C.
    1991   Reinventing Historical Archaeology. In *Historical Archaeology and the Study of American Culture.* L. A. d. Cunzo and B. L. Herman, eds. Proceedings, 1991 Winterthur Conference. Pp. 473–497. Winterthur, DE: Henry Francis du Pont Winterthur Museum.

Blakey, Michael
    2001   Bioarchaeology of the African Diaspora in the Americas: Its Origins and Scope. *Annual Review of Anthropology* 30:387–422.

Brandt, Steven A., and Kathryn J. Weedman
    2000   *Hide-Working Practices and Material Culture of Southern Ethiopia: A Cross-Cultural Comparison.* Gainesville: Department of Anthropology, University of Florida.

Brown, Kenneth, and Doreen Cooper
    1990   Structural Continuity in an African American Slave and Tenant Community. *Historical Archaeology* 24(4):7–19.

Brown, Lorin W., Charles W. Biggs, and Marta Weigle
    1978   *Hispano Folklife of New Mexico.* Albuquerque: University of New Mexico Press.

Butler, Judith
    1990   *Gender Trouble: Feminism and the Subversion of Identity.* New York: Routledge.
    1993   *Bodies That Matter: On the Discursive Limits of "Sex."* New York: Routledge.

Carey, Margaret
    1997   Gender in African Beadwork: An Overview. In *Beads and Beadmakers: Gender, Material Culture and Meaning.* L. D. Sciama and J. B. Eicher, eds. Pp. 83–93. Oxford: Berg.

Carrillo, Richard, Stephen M. Kalasz, Stephen A. Brown, Phillip L. Petersen, and Christian J. Zier
    1994   Archaeological Excavations at the Prowers House, Boggsville Historic Site (5BN363), Bent County, Colorado. Manuscript available from author.

Carrillo, Richard, Lori E. Rhodes, and Phillip L. Petersen
    1993   Historical Archaeology at Boggsville Historic Site (5BN363): Excavations Conducted to Facilitate the Restoration and Reconstruction of the Prowers House, Bent County, Colorado. Manuscript available from author.

Clark, Bonnie J.
    1996   Amache Ochinee Prowers: The Archaeobiography of a Cheyenne Woman. Master's thesis, University of Denver.
    2003   On the Edge of Purgatory: An Archaeology of Ethnicity and Gender in Hispanic Colorado. Ph.D. dissertation, University of California, Berkeley.
    2005   Lived Ethnicity: Archaeology and Identity in *Mexicano* America. *World Archaeology* 37(3):440–52.

Collier, Jane, and Sylvia J. Yanagisako, eds.
    1987   *Gender and Kinship: Essays toward a Unified Analysis.* Stanford, CA: Stanford University Press.

Collins, Patricia Hill
    1994   Shifting the Center: Race, Class, and Feminist Theorizing about Motherhood. In *Mothering: Ideology, Experience and Agency.* E. N. Glenn, G. Chang, and R. Forcey, eds. Pp. 45–66. New York: Routledge.
    2000   *Black Feminist Thought: Knowledge, Consciousness and the Politics of Empowerment.* New York: Routledge.

Corruccini, R., J. Handler, and K. Jacobi
    1985   Chronological Distribution of Enamel Hypoplasias and Weaning in a Caribbean Slave Population. *Human Biology* 57:699–711.

Davis, Angela
    1983   *Women, Race and Class.* New York: Vintage Books.

Deutsch, Sarah
    1987   *No Separate Refuge: Culture, Class, and Gender on an Anglo-Hispanic Frontier.* New York: Oxford University Press.

di Leonardo, Micaela
    1991   Introduction: Gender, Culture, and Political Economy: Feminist Anthropology in Historical Perspective. In *Gender and the Crossroads of Knowledge: Feminist Anthropology in the Postmodern Era.* M. di Leonardo, ed. Pp. 1–48. Berkeley: University of California Press.

Epperson, Terrence
    2004   Critical Race Theory and the Archaeology of the African Diaspora. *Historical Archaeology* 38(1):101–8.

Ferguson, Leland
    1992   *Uncommon Ground.* Washington, DC: Smithsonian Institution Press.

Flannery, Kent, ed.
   1976   *The Early Mesoamerican Village.* New York: Academic Press.

Fowler, Chris
   2004   *The Archaeology of Personhood: An Anthropological Approach.* London: Routledge.

Galle, J. E., and A. L. Young, eds.
   2004   *Engendering African-American Archaeology: A Southern Perspective.* Knoxville: University of Tennessee Press.

García, Nasario, ed.
   1997   *Comadres: Hispanic Women of the Rio Puerco Valley.* Albuquerque: University of New Mexico Press.

Gero, Joan
   1991   Genderlithics: Women's Roles in Stone Tool Production. In *Engendering Archaeology: Women and Prehistory.* Joan M. Gero and Margaret W. Conkey, eds. Pp. 163–93. Oxford: Blackwell.

Gero, Joan, and Margaret Conkey, eds.
   1991   *Engendering Archaeology.* Oxford: Blackwell.

Gewertz, Deborah
   1984   The Tchambuli View of Persons: A Critique of Individualism in the Works of Mead and Chodorow. *American Anthropologist* 86(3):615–29.

Giddings, Paula
   1984   *When and Where I Enter: The Impact of Black Women on Race and Sex in America.* New York: William Morrow.

Gilchrist, Roberta
   1999   *Gender and Archaeology: Contesting the Past.* London: Routledge.
   2000   Archaeological Biographies: Realizing Human Lifecycles, -Courses, and -Histories. *World Archaeology* 31(3):325–28.

Gillespie, Susan
   2000   Personhood, Agency, and Mortuary Ritual: A Case Study from the Ancient Maya. *Journal of Anthropological Archaeology* 20:71–112.

Gray, William
   1825   *Travels in Western Africa in the Years 1818, 19, 20, and 21 from the River Gambia to the River Niger.* London: John Murray.

Grinnell, George Bird
   1962   *The Cheyenne Indians: Their History and Ways of Life* I. New York: Cooper Square.

Handler, Jerome
   1996   A Prone Burial from a Plantation Slave Cemetery in Barbados, West Indies: Possible Evidence for an African-Type Witch or Other Negatively Viewed Person. *Historical Archaeology* 30(3):76–86.

Hill, James, and James Gunn, eds.
   1977   *The Individual in Prehistory: Studies of Variability in Style in Prehistoric Technologies.* New York: Academic Press.

Hodder, Ian
    2000   Agency and Individuals in Long-Term Processes. In *Agency in Archaeology*. Marcia-Anne Dobres and John Robb, eds. Pp. 21–33. London: Routledge.

Hoig, Stan
    1989   *The Cheyenne*. Indians of North America. New York: Chelsea House Publishers.

Howell, Signe, and Marit Melhuus
    1993   The Study of Kinship; the Study of Person; a Study of Gender? In *Gendered Anthropology*. T. del Valle, ed. Pp. 38–53. London: Routledge.

Hudnall, Mary Prowers
    1945   Early History of Bent County. *Colorado Magazine* 22(6):233–47.

Hurd, C. W.
    1957   *Boggsville: Cradle of the Colorado Cattle Industry*. Las Animas, CO: Boggsville Committee.

Hutson, Scott, and Aline Magnoni
    2002   Children Not at Ancient Chunchucmil, Yucatan, Mexico. Paper presented at the Annual Meeting of the American Anthropological Association, New Orleans.

Joyce, Rosemary
    2000a   *Gender and Power in Prehispanic Mesoamerica*. Texas: University of Texas.
    2000b   Girling the Girl and Boying the Boy: The Production of Adulthood in Ancient Mesoamerica. *World Archaeology* 31(3):473–83.
    2004   Embodied Subjectivity: Gender, Femininity, Masculinity, Sexuality. In *Companion to Social Archaeology*. Lynn Meskell, ed. Pp. 81–91. Oxford: Blackwell.
    2006   Feminist Theories of Embodiment and Anthropological Imagination: Making Bodies Matter. In *Feminist Anthropology: Past, Present and Future*. P. Geller and M. Stocking, eds. Philadelphia: University of Pennsylvania Press.

King, Stacie
    2006   The Marking of Age in Ancient Coastal Oaxaca. In *The Social Experience of Childhood in Ancient Mesoamerica*. T. Ardren and S. Hutson, eds. Boulder: University Press of Colorado.

Klein, Laura
    2003   *Women and Men in World Cultures*. Boston: McGraw-Hill.

Knapp, A. Bernard
    1998   Boys Will Be Boys: Masculinist Approaches to a Gendered Archaeology. In *Reader in Gender Archaeology*. K. Hays-Gilpin and D. S. Whitley, eds. Pp. 365–73. London: Routledge.

Lightfoot, Kent G.
    1995   Culture Contact Studies: Redefining the Relationship between Prehistoric and Historical Archaeology. *American Antiquity* 60(2):199–217.

Lightfoot, K., A. Martinez, and A. M. Schiff
    1997   Daily Practice and Material Culture in Pluralistic Social Settings: An Archaeological Study of Culture Change and Persistence from Fort Ross, California. *American Antiquity* 63(2):199–222.

Longino, Helen
    1994   In Search of Feminist Epistemology. *The Monist* 77(4):472–85.

Louden, Dick
    1992   Alice Lopez Russell interview. Manuscript available from the author.

Meskell, Lynn A.
    1999   *Archaeologies of Social Life*. Oxford: Blackwell.
    2002   *Private Life in New Kingdom Egypt*. Princeton, NJ: Princeton University Press.
    2004   *Object Worlds in Ancient Egypt: Material Biographies Past and Present*. London: Berg.

Meskell, Lynn A., and Rosemary A. Joyce
    2003   *Embodied Lives: Figuring Ancient Maya and Egyptian Experience*. London: Routledge.

Moore, Jenny, and Eleanor Scott, eds.
    1997   *Invisible People and Processes: Writing Gender and Childhood into European Archaeology*. London: Leicester University Press.

Nostrand, Richard
    1992   *The Hispano Homeland*. Norman: University of Oklahoma Press.

Orser, Charles E., Jr.
    1994   The Archaeology of African American Slave Religion in the Antebellum South. *Cambridge Archaeological Journal* 4(1):33–45.

Orser, Charles E., Jr., ed.
    2000   *Race and the Archaeology of Identity*. Salt Lake City: University of Utah Press.

Patterson, Orlando
    1982   *Slavery and Social Death: A Comparative Study*. Cambridge, MA: Harvard University Press.

Pulsipher, Lydia
    1993   Changing Roles in the Life Cycles of Women in Traditional West Indian Houseyards. In *Women and Change in the Caribbean: A Caribbean Perspective*. J. J. Momsen, ed. Pp. 50–64. Bloomington: Indiana University Press.

Rattray, R. S.
    1932   *The Tribes of the Ashanti Hinterland*. 2 vols. Oxford: Clarendon Press.

Roberts, Dorothy
    1997   *Killing the Black Body*. New York: Pantheon.

Schmidt, Robert, and Barbara Voss, eds.
    2000   *Archaeologies of Sexuality*. London: Routledge.

Schwarz, Maureen T.
    1996   Unraveling the Anchoring Cord: Navajo Relocation, 1974–1996. *American Anthropologist* 99(1):43–55.

Sofaer-Derevenski, Joanne, ed.
  2000   *Children and Material Culture.* London: Routledge.
Spelman, Elizabeth
  1988   *Inessential Woman: Problems of Exclusion in Feminist Thought.* Boston: Beacon Press.
Tringham, Ruth
  1990   Households with Faces: The Challenge of Gender in Prehistoric Architectural Remains. In *Engendering Archaeology.* Joan Gero and Margaret Conkey, eds. Pp. 93–131. Oxford: Blackwell.
Van Ness, John R.
  1991   *Hispanos in Northern New Mexico: The Development of Corporate Community and Multicommunity.* New York: AMS Press.
Voss, Barbara
  2000   Feminisms, Queer Theories, and the Archaeological Study of Past Sexualities. *World Archaeology* 32(2):180–92.
Wilkie, Laurie A.
  1997   Secret and Sacred: Contextualizing the Artifacts of African-American Magic and Religion. *Historical Archaeology* 31(4):81–106.
  2003   *The Archaeology of Mothering: An African-American Midwife's Tale.* New York: Routledge.
Wilkie, Laurie A., and Paul Farnsworth
  1999   Trade and the Construction of Bahamian Identity: A Multiscalar Exploration. *International Journal of Historical Archaeology* 3(4):283–320.
  2005   *Sampling Many Pots: An Archaeology of Memory and Tradition at a Bahamian Plantation.* Gainesville: University Press of Florida.
Wood, Margaret C.
  2001   Working-Class Households as Sites of Social Change. In *Household Chores and Household Choices: Theorizing the Domestic Sphere in Historical Archaeology.* K. S. Barile and J. C. Brandon, eds. Pp. 210–32. Tuscaloosa: University of Alabama Press.
Wurst, LuAnn, and Robert Fitts, eds.
  1999   Confronting Class. *Historical Archaeology* 33(1):1–195.
Yamin, Rebecca
  2002   Children's Strikes, Parent's Rights: Paterson and Five Points. *International Journal of Historical Archaeology* 6(2):113–26.

Sexuality in Archaeology

11

BARBARA L. VOSS

FOR CENTURIES, archaeologists have encountered sexually explicit materials from past cultures, but their sexual content has been either minimized or treated lasciviously. In the early 1990s, however, this situation began to change, largely through the development of feminist and gender studies in archaeology. Initially, there was little published work; individual researchers, working mainly in isolation from each other, began to circulate manuscripts and give conference papers on sex-focused research. Then, in 1996, Taylor published his ambitiously conceived and controversial monograph *The Prehistory of Sex: Four Million Years of Human Sexual Culture*. In 2000, Schmidt and Voss published their edited volume *Archaeologies of Sexuality*, and Dowson edited a *World Archaeology* issue titled "Queer Archaeologies." In the five years since then, a growing number of articles and book chapters have been published, and archaeological conferences frequently include presentations and symposia centered on sexual themes. Archaeologists are increasingly conducting investigations in which sexuality is examined as an integral aspect of the cultures they study.

The first section of this chapter, "Sexual Theories," considers the ways in which archaeologists conceptualize sexuality. It traces the relationship between sexuality studies and engendered archaeology and then turns to consider three major theories of sexuality: sexology, the sex/gender system, and queer theory. Then the chapter turns to "Sexual Topics." To date, archaeological research on sexuality can be loosely grouped around five major (and at times overlapping) themes: fertility management, homosexuality/transsexuality, prostitution, architecture and space, and sexual or erotic representations. The third section, "Sexual Cultures," discusses the work of two archaeologists—Rosemary Joyce and Lynn Meskell—who have developed rich, nuanced archaeological interpretations of sexual life in two very different times and places: Classic Maya Mesoamerica and New Kingdom Egypt.

Sexual Theories

In the mid-1980s, feminist critiques of androcentric biases in archaeology established a firm foundation for future research on sexuality. Prior to feminist interventions, most archaeological studies interpreted the past through gender stereotypes that, among other aspects, presumed a heterosexual norm, linked men to production and toolmaking and women to reproduction and child rearing, and identified men as sexually dominant and women as passive sexual objects. The feminist critique in archaeology challenged the universal applicability of these stereotypes and in doing so created possibilities for archaeological research not only on gender but also on sexuality (Conkey and Spector 1984:3–13; Gilchrist 1991; Nelson 1997:113–29; Sørensen 1988, 2000:45–52; Voss and Schmidt 2000:14–18). By separating gender roles from biological reproduction, these early feminist studies created possibilities for researching sexuality independently of reproduction. Additionally, feminist attention to the microscale demonstrated that research on interpersonal relationships—including sexual acts, sexual relations, and sexual ideologies—is neither trivial nor particularistic but instead is essential to understanding so-called macroscale topics ranging from subsistence and settlement systems to state formation and imperialism.

These early feminist archaeological studies fostered a climate within which research on sexuality became increasingly possible. As Claassen (1992:4) wrote, "There is another social function of gender to be considered and that is the social marking of sexually appropriate partners . . . if the reader accepts this social function of gender, then an archaeology of gender is an archaeology of *sexuality*." Further, it is clear through bibliographic citations that early feminist and gender-focused archaeological research was engaged with a wide range of theories of sexuality (Voss 2000b). Yet, for the most part, the topic of sexuality was rarely addressed directly. For example, many researchers examined marriage primarily as a locus of the gendered organization of labor but not as a mechanism for the social regulation of sexuality. Others used the concept of the *berdache* (Native American two-spirit) as an example of a "culturally defined gender category" (Conkey and Spector 1984:15) without discussing the ways in which two-spirit identities also reference cultural categories of sexuality. In other words, as the feminist critique matured into a program of archaeological research on gender (Conkey and Gero 1997), sexuality took a backseat. Although this may in part be attributed to what Rubin has called "sex essentialism" and "sex negativity" (Rubin 1984:275, 278; see also Voss and Schmidt 2000:3–5), it is perhaps equally attributed to the ways that certain social theories have shaped archaeological investigations of gender and sexuality.

Like all archaeological research, investigations of sexuality interpret the past through the lens of the present: deliberately, through the use of ethnographic analogies; and, less consciously, through the ways that present-day sexual norms, politics, ideologies, and identities affect researchers' conceptualization of the past. The language used to discuss sexuality today can seem so self-evident that terms such as "heterosexual," "homosexual," "masochist," or "cross-dresser" are often taken to be universal, transhistorical identity categories. Archaeological researchers without specific training in the field of sexuality studies may not be aware of the extent to which these modern, largely Euro-American sexual identity categories are relatively recent cultural phenomena. Here, I briefly discuss three of the major intellectual projects that have shaped present-day conceptions of sexuality: sexology, the sex/gender system, and gender performance theory.

Sexology

All modern academic studies of sexuality, including archaeological ones, are a legacy of sexology, a discipline that emerged in the late 1800s as part of the general expansion of taxonomic and medical sciences (Bland and Doan 1998a, 1998b). Although the research goals and practices of sexologists were diverse, a shared premise of sexology was that sexuality was an essential, enduring determinant of a person's character or identity. While religious and civil frameworks of the time focused primarily on the regulation of sexual acts and sexualized behaviors, sexologists argued that sexual acts and practices were the symptomatic expressions of durable underlying sexual dispositions. Further, these sexual dispositions were thought to cause not just sexual desires and behaviors but nonsexual preferences, habits, and behaviors as well.

Sexologists generally used the medical case-study method, in which interviews and examinations of afflicted patients were used to build profiles of the symptoms and progressions of specific diseases. Observations gathered from multiple case studies were used to develop elaborate sexual typologies. Common variables that sexologists evaluated when constructing these typologies included the patient's apparent genital sex at birth, the physical attributes of the patient's adult genitalia and other parts of the body, the patient's degree of conformance to gender norms in appearance and behavior, and the patient's sexual behavior and desires, with a specific focus on the gender(s) of the patient's real and desired sexual partners. While the case studies used were drawn primarily from urban European and American populations, they also included observations from early ethnographic studies and from reports submitted by colonial officials and missionaries working abroad (e.g., Casella 2000a). The resulting typologies were thus generally presented as universal and transhistorical categories that had been discovered through scientific research, resulting in a speciation of sexual subjects loosely parallel to the Linnaean speciation of plant and animal organisms. Most sexual identity terms used today (e.g., pedophile, transvestite, heterosexual, or homosexual) are an enduring legacy of these medical typologies.

The Sex/Gender System

If sexology generated a universalizing model of sexuality, cultural anthropology provides an alternative legacy that highlights cross-cultural variation in sexual behaviors and identities. In particular, anthropological research has focused on how sexual subjectivities are integral to cultural systems. While sexologists argued that sexuality was central to individual identity, the work of anthropologists— from Mead and Malinowski onward—expanded this premise to argue that sexuality is implicated in "almost every aspect of culture" (Malinowski 1929:xxiii).

These anthropological studies provided the empirical basis for the second dominant model operating today in sexuality studies: the sex/gender system. First articulated in Rubin's (1975) article "The Traffic in Women," the sex/gender system distinguished between sex (biological—male, female) and gender (cultural—man, woman, masculine, feminine). Subsequent anthropological research inspired by the sex/gender model focused initially on documenting the cross-cultural variability of gender roles, a project that greatly shaped the emergence of feminist and gender-focused archaeologies.

Within the sex/gender model, sexuality lurks uncomfortably in the interstices between biology and culture. Studies of sexuality within this framework have focused primarily on cultural attitudes toward men's and women's sexuality and the power dynamics of sexual relationships. Rubin (1984:267) herself articulated the limitations of the sex/gender model in this regard, intoning, "The time has come to think about sex." Rubin called for historical and political analyses to demonstrate how sexuality in general has been constructed as a stigmatized aspect of modern life and how specific sexual practices have been constructed as benign or malignant. Through reference to sexological research, Rubin advocated a "concept of benign sexual variation" in which differences in sexual practices should be viewed through an appreciation of "variation [as] a fundamental property of all life, from the simplest biological organism to the most complex human social formations" (283). As in the sex/gender system, this conceptualization of varied sexualities that are suppressed or promoted through cultural mechanisms embraces a nature/culture duality.

The theoretical prominence of the sex/gender system within archaeological studies has specific implications for the ways in which sexuality has been conceptualized in archaeological interpretations. Most positively, the sex/gender model has encouraged research on ways that sexuality varies across culture and time. However, these sexual practices and sexual identities have been treated predominantly as a function of gender rather than as a distinct aspect of social relations. Additionally, the conceptualization of sexuality as the product of a nature/cultural duality has unwittingly supported a tendency to treat reproductive, heterosexual sexual acts as natural and constant while emphasizing the cultural production of nonreproductive sexual practices and identities.

Gender Performance Theory

The nature/culture duality of the sex/gender system has been challenged by Butler's theory of gender performance. First outlined in her landmark text *Gender Trouble* (1990, reprinted in 1999) and further elaborated in various articles (e.g., Butler 1993b, 1994) and the book *Bodies That Matter* (1993a), Butler's theory of gender performativity challenges both the analytical distinction between gender and sexuality and the biological/cultural dualism of the sex/gender system model.

Butler's performance theory is complex and multifaceted and cannot be easily summarized; however, a few key points are particularly relevant here. First, Butler rejects the categorical distinction between gender and sexuality, instead arguing that both are mutually produced through a heterosexual matrix (Butler 1999:chaps. 1 and 2). The dominant discourse of heterosexuality requires a division of persons into two gender categories and simultaneously legitimizes sexual desires for the opposite gender. Through this matrix, both those with nonnormative gender identities and those whose sexual desires and practices deviate from heterosexuality are simultaneously constructed as abject persons. The heterosexual matrix is sustained by defining itself against those practices and identities that it stigmatizes and thus relies on the abject for its own existence (Butler 1993b).

Butler also questions the distinction between biological and cultural aspects of sexuality and gender. The sex/gender system rests, for example, on a claim that certain aspects of being a woman or a man are natural, yet the line between what is "cultural" or "natural" about gender and sexuality is highly contested and debated in cultural discourse. Butler thus argues that what is perceived as "natural" is delineated and fixed through cultural practices and that it is perhaps more productive to see the distinction between natural and cultural as a disciplining practice that seeks to establish certain aspects of identity as irreducible and unchangeable (Butler 1999:7–12). "There is," Butler notes, "an insistent materiality of the body, but . . . it never makes itself known or legible outside of the cultural articulation in which it appears" (Breen and Blumenfeld 2001:12).

A third element of Butler's theory is that gender and sexual identities are continually produced through social performances. Although gender and sexual identities may appear stable, the appearance of continuity is an illusion created by an endless series of mimetic repetitions, much as a film projector creates an illusion of continuity through a rapid sequence of still images being flashed on a screen. These gendered and sexual performances are not volitional in the sense that an actor might assume the identity of a character she is playing; rather, these performances are "a set of repeated acts within a highly rigid regulatory frame" (Butler 1999:43–44). It is within the gaps between these repetitions that Butler identifies potential for agency, as subjects may be able to subtly transform these mimetic performances through subversive practices like mimicry, satire, drag, exaggeration, and so on (e.g., Butler 1993a:121–40, 1999:173–77).

It would not be an understatement to note that Butler's theories of gender performance have transformed the fields of feminist/gender/sexuality studies and have shifted the terms of sexual and feminist political and social activism. One of the key effects of Butler's theories has been a profound change in sexual identification practices, especially the reclamation of the epithet "queer" (de Lauretis 1991:v). Broadly conceptualized as being oppositional to the normative heterosexual matrix, queer practices of identification generally celebrate fluidity and instability in both gender and sexual identities. Many people who previously identified (or would have been identified) as gay or lesbian or bisexual or transgendered/transsexual have adopted the moniker "queer" as a form of resistance to the taxonomic sexual identity categories that were codified and given medical and legal legitimacy through sexology (Warner 1993).

Theorizing Archaeologies of Sexuality

Archaeological research on sexual identities thus operates within this triple legacy of sexology, the sex/gender system, and gender performance theory. The greatest liability of these theories is that they were all developed to address relatively recent conditions in European and American cultures. These theories may tell us more about how we understand our sexual selves in the present day than about how people in the past may have experienced and shaped the sexual aspects of their lives. For archaeologists, this shortcoming is an opportunity. Archaeological studies of sexuality are important precisely because they illuminate the assumptions and limitations of modern theories of sexuality and, in doing so, aid in developing a practice of sexuality studies that more accurately engages with the full range and potentials of human subjectivity.

One of the biggest challenges facing archaeologists is that the categorization of "sexuality" as a distinct aspect of social relations and the premise that sexuality is a central component of social identity may both be historic products of Western modernity (Foucault 1978). On one hand, sexology, the sex/gender system, and gender performance theory provide conceptual tools that enable us to investigate sexuality in the past; on the other hand, our own predilection to view sexuality as a discrete category may blind us to other ways that sexualities were enacted in past cultures. By being aware of the historical and cultural limitation of current sexual theories, archaeologists may be able to remain open to the possibility that what we think of as "sexuality" may have been quite differently organized in the past.

A second challenge that archaeologists face in our research on sexuality consists of the tensions and contradictions among the theories of sexuality outlined here. Sexology provides a universal, medical model of sexuality; the sex/gender system provides a means for considering the ways that sexuality is biologically structured but culturally contingent; and performance theory emphasizes the social construction of sexuality. But we need not resolve the extent to which sexuality is shaped by biology or culture in order to conduct archaeological investigations of sexuality. For example, few would argue that food consumption is unrelated to biology or lacks an adaptive function, yet archaeologists also investigate how culture—including social organization, economic relationships, ethnic identities, gender ideologies, and religion, to name a few—shapes the ways that social groups and individuals produce, process, prepare, and consume food. Likewise, cultural responses to sexual desires and behaviors are so profound and varied that the relationship between biology and a specific sexual identity or practice is at most likely to be correlative rather than determinate.

Sexual Topics

These three bodies of sexuality theory—sexology, the sex/gender system, and performance theory—have provided important foundations for archaeological investigations of sexual identities. To date, archaeological research on sexuality can be loosely grouped around five major (and at times overlapping) themes: fertility management, homosexuality/transsexuality, prostitution, architecture and space, and sexual or erotic representations. This section summarizes the work that has been undertaken within each of these arenas in turn.

Reproduction in Culture: Fertility Management

Some of the earliest archaeological investigations of sexuality have centered on fertility management—a term that broadly encompasses both the production of cultural knowledge about fertility and actions that may be taken to promote or avoid conception and/or live birth of viable offspring. However, in considering fertility management as a topic within archaeological research on sexuality, it is critical not to conflate sexuality with reproduction or vice versa. There is, of course, a physiological link between reproduction and certain sexual practices—notably those that involve what Abelove (1989:126) has termed "cross-sex genital intercourse (penis in vagina, vagina around penis, with seminal emission uninterrupted)." But sexual activity is by no means limited to such practices, nor do those participating in such practices always desire conception as the outcome of sexual acts. Taylor (1996:7) posits that "for the past four million years the human line has been able to consciously separate sex from reproduction." The evidence Taylor produces to substantiate this claim is ambiguous at best, but his point that biological reproduction and sexual intercourse may have been culturally shaped long before the advent of anatomically modern humans is an important one. A growing number of studies have demonstrated that members of many animal species generally (Baghemil 2000) and of nonhuman primate species more particularly (de Waal 1989, 1995; McDonald Pavelka 1995; Vasey 1995, 1998) regularly engage in nonreproductive sexual behaviors. Vasey (1998:416–17) in particular argues that both reproductive and nonreproductive sexual behaviors are motivated largely by "mutual sexual attraction and gratification." Likewise, Taylor (1996:75) argues that for all primates (including humans), sexuality is a learned source for the exploration and expression of pleasure and power. Fertility management thus provides a means by which the reproductive aspects of sexual practices can be either enhanced or suppressed within a broader cultural context of sexuality.

Cultural practices related to fertility management include both bodily practices that are unlikely to be represented in the archaeological record and material practices that are more likely to have been preserved archaeologically. One of the most contested debates in archaeological research on sexuality centers around whether figurines and rock art from Paleolithic, Neolithic, and Mesolithic Europe and the Near East constitute evidence of rituals related to prehistoric fertility management. Selected figurines, such as the famous Venus of Willendorf, have been interpreted by some as evidence of fertility rituals or beliefs about a cosmological link between fertility and female deities—an argument that has most recently been promulgated through so-called Goddess archaeology but has its roots in earlier, nineteenth-century interpretations. As Conkey and Tringham (1995:212) have synthesized, the central argument made by many authors is that "female figurines . . . with large stomachs and so-called pendulous breasts depicted pregnancy and or lactation and therefore signified fertility and the magical desires for sexual births." Other archaeologists have extended this argument by attributing sexual meanings to other forms of prehistoric European art (e.g., Kokkinidou and Nikolaidou 1997; for discussions of varied approaches, see Bahn 1986; Bahn and Vertut 1988; Conkey 1989). The broad interpretations of prehistoric symbolic images as evidence of fertility ritual complexes have been widely challenged on both empirical and methodological grounds (Conkey and Tringham 1995; Dobres 1992; Handsman 1991; Meskell 1995, 1998b; Nelson 1990). This debate has been particularly important to the development of archaeologies of sexuality because it has introduced feminist theories of representation, the sexual gaze, and the body into archaeological interpretation.

Other archaeological investigations of fertility management have focused less on spiritual/magical practices and more on physical techniques. Taylor's survey of archaeological evidence of contraception in prehistoric Egyptian, Greek, and Bronze Age European contexts reveals a wide variety of materials used to prevent or promote reproduction. These included caustic or blocking vaginal pessaries, herbal medicines, mechanical devices used in abortions, and condoms (Taylor 1996:85–96). Archaeological investigations of more recent historical contexts in Britain and the United States have similarly recovered artifacts associated with fertility management. One of the most rigorous of these is a study of ten animal-membrane condoms recovered from a seventeenth-century garderobe (latrine) from Dudley Castle (Gaimster et al. 1996). The investigators' detailed physical analysis of the Dudley Castle specimens proved that professional production of standard-sized condoms was a well-developed craft at least a century earlier than historical records alone suggested.

Perhaps the most comprehensive archaeological study of fertility management is Wilkie's (2000, 2003) research on African American sexual magic and midwifery. Wilkie takes as her starting point a collection of artifacts that she excavated from trash deposits associated with the Perrymans, an African American family living in Mobile, Alabama, in the late nineteenth and early twentieth centuries. The maternal head of the family, Lucrecia Perryman, turned to midwifery as a means of supporting her family after her husband's death. Lay midwives in the American South served not only as medical practitioners but also as "generational and gender mediators for their communities" (Wilkie 2003:xix). Wilkie's distinctive contribution to the archaeology of fertility management and sexuality is her investigation of the ways that women during this period made decisions "to mother or not to mother" and her recognition that spiritual and medicinal practices were seamlessly integrated in the "ethnomedical tool kit" (Wilkie 2000:138) that women and men employed in preventing and promoting childbearing and in mediating tensions between the sexes. "All of these magical-medical cures indicated from the midwifery site incorporated symbols that were strongly connected with regulating sexual activity or treating the consequences of such activity. . . . The contents of a single jar of Vaseline could have been bought for use as a hair pomade, used to help cure a bout of impotence, and then used to treat a diaper rash" (Wilkie 2000:139, 133). Further, she demonstrates that fertility management can be understood only within the specific historical and cultural context within which it is practiced—in this case, within the context of the legacies of slavery, the challenges of African American life in the postbellum South, and the rise of discourses of "scientific mothering" and the increasing persecution of midwives by the American Medical Association.

Within sexuality studies as a whole, the archaeology of fertility management reminds us that even in its most "biological" moments, sexuality is produced through culture. Whether these cultural practices are spiritual, material, or both, they often involve material objects that at times literally mediate the physical surfaces of human sexual interaction. As Wilkie so powerfully demonstrates, even the most mundane, everyday artifacts can have sexual meanings and sexual functions for the people who used them.

Challenging Heteronormativity: Investigations of Homosexuality/Transsexuality

Another prominent theme in sexuality studies is research that challenges the pervasive heterosexist biases of most archaeological interpretations. The vast majority of archaeological research—including much work conducted within the framework of feminist or gender-focused archaeology—presumes heterosexual relationships (especially the nuclear family) to be the foundation of social life in past cultures. This bias persists despite the vast corpus of anthropological and historical evidence to the contrary. Heterosexism has a debilitating effect on archaeological research: in some cases, the presumption of universal heterosexuality blinds researchers to alternative and equally plausible explanations; in others, archaeological data are even distorted to support implausible interpretations (Dowson 2000; Schmidt 2002; Voss, in press; Voss and Schmidt 2000).

Efforts to correct this heterosexist bias in archaeological interpretation have been twofold. First, a body of work has emerged that seeks to expose the sexual assumptions behind archaeological interpretations. Yates's (1993) analysis of sexual representations in Scandinavian prehistoric rock art is a particularly salient example of this; he questions the conventional interpretation of certain images as a representation of heterosexual intercourse, arguing that the images could just as plausibly represent a sex act between two people of the same gender. Schmidt

(2002) traces the relationship between archaeological evidence (or lack thereof) and scholarly and popular debates about the sexuality of Ötzi, the Tyrolean "Ice Man." Reeder (2000) points out that heterosexual bias has led Egyptologists to interpret images of men in socially affectionate poses as brothers or friends, while images of men and women in similar poses are interpreted as married couples. Danielsson (2002) similarly notes that analyses of gold foil images in late Iron Age Scandinavia describe images of opposite-sex pairs as depictions of "loving couples," while same-sex pairs in similar poses are not interpreted as sexual partners. McCafferty and McCafferty (in press) examine textual and archaeological sources for evidence of nonnormative gender identities in preconquest Mexico and conclude that there existed a "range of intermediate identities" some of which were gender ambiguous (hunchbacks and dwarfs) and others sexually "deviant" (homosexuals and harlots). Cobb (in press) critiques the ways in which hunter-gatherer studies in archaeology presume the transhistorical existence of the heterosexual family group. Likewise, Dowson (in press) draws attention to the ways that museum displays and archaeological reports perpetuate a mistaken image of the heterosexual family group as the enduring constant in British history from the Mesolithic to the Anglo-Saxon period.

Second, several researchers have undertaken investigations aimed at recovering evidence of nonheterosexual identities and practices in the past. These investigations have generally focused on two modern identity categories: homosexuality (sexual desire for persons of the same gender) and transgender/transsexuality (identifying with the gender role normally performed by persons of the opposite biological sex). At times, as will be seen later in this chapter, archaeologists have conflated these two categories. This confusion is problematic but understandable. The clinical separation of gender identity from sexual object choice in modern sexual identities was one of the major intellectual products of sexology; however, many modern folk categories tend to view them as inseparable (e.g., a "fairy" is simultaneously an effeminate male and a homosexual). Here again, archaeological research struggles within the legacy of sexology while simultaneously exposing the limitations of modern sexual taxonomies.

In North America, most research challenging heteronormative biases has centered on the archaeology of so-called *berdache* and two-spirit indigenous identities. *Berdache* and two-spirit (also third- and fourth-gender) are generic anthropological terms used to conceptualize gender and sexual variance among Native North Americans. Such terms encompass a wide range of identification practices that varied significantly among different tribes. Broadly speaking, two-spirit identities are often associated with same-sex sexual practices, hermaphroditism, and transsexuality. Archaeological and ethnographic research suggest that multiple-gender/

sexuality systems may have great antiquity in North America, perhaps even originating in gendered and shamanistic practices of populations that migrated from eastern Asia and Siberia to the Americas over 10,000 years ago (Hollimon 2001).

In archaeological research, two-spirit identities were first discussed as an example of the potential diversity of sex/gender systems in the past (Claassen 1992; Duke 1991; Hollimon 1991, 1992; Whelan 1991). The earliest empirical studies of two-spirit identities centered on the analysis of mortuary evidence as a means to identify individuals in the past whose cultural gender (as identified through grave goods) differed from their physical sex (Whelan 1991). Hollimon's analysis of prehistoric Chumash burials expanded this approach by combining analysis of skeletal pathologies with distributional analysis of associated artifacts to identify a possible *'Aqí* (two-spirit) burial (Hollimon 1996, 1997). This methodology has also been used in European archaeological contexts to evaluate measures of gender dichotomy and to identify gender diversity within a cemetery population (e.g., Lucy 1997; Rega 1997; Schmidt 2000, 2001); most recently, Arnold (2002) has identified ancient DNA analysis as an additional line of evidence that can be used to investigate sex/gender configurations in mortuary contexts. These approaches to "finding" two-spirits in the archaeological record emphasize transsexuality (or, per Arnold [2002], "gender transformers") as the determinant characteristic of two-spirit identity.

More recent archaeological research has taken a more holistic view of two-spirit identities. Hollimon has reexamined the Chumash burial case to consider the relationship between gender, sexuality, religion, and occupation in *'Aqí* identity. Noting that the Chumash *'Aqí* are usually members of an undertaking guild that involves occupational, spiritual, and kin-based obligations and privileges, Hollimon suggests that designation as an *'Aqí* may relate more directly to abstinence from procreative sex acts than to a particular gendered or sexual identity. *'Aqí*, she suggests, included biological men who were transsexual, men who had sex with other men, men without children, celibates, and postmenopausal women (Hollimon 2000, in press). Prine has similarly examined two-spirit Hidatsa *miati* through close readings of ethnohistoric, ethnographic, and archaeological records. Her research indicates that *miati* individuals, who were identified as male at birth, were differentiated from their age and sex cohorts in six different ways: they changed gender at adolescence, they had specific spiritual roles, they were highly respected, they created households focused on relationships with men, they were highly productive, and they were cultural innovators. Within Hidatsa culture, *miati* played a key role in earth lodge–building ceremonies, mediating the tension between feminine earth and masculine sky. Prine thus finds archaeological indicators of the *miati* through a study of architectural remains, identifying a double-posted earth lodge that might have been a *miati* household (Prine 1997, 2000). The role of space and architecture in the production of two-spirit identities has also been considered by Perry and Joyce (2001) in their examination of Zuni *lhamana* identities. Ethnographically and historically documented *lhamana* identities evince a broad diversity of traits but generally involve biological males and females who participated in a mixture of labor and cultural practices associated with both genders and who took the role of the bigendered *Kolhamana* katsina in public ritual performances. Perry and Joyce consider the possibility that a shift in architectural practices that occurred in the Zuni region around 1200 to 1300 C.E. may also signal the crystallization of *lhamana* identities. The shift involved the construction of large plaza-oriented settlements and the movement of gender-specific everyday activities from locations inside rooms into communal plazas where rituals were also held. The public performance of gender—through both daily labor and ceremonial ritual in communal plazas—may have formalized the status of what Perry and Joyce term "gender transgressive persons."

The archaeological study of Native American two-spirit identities demonstrates the limitations of modern sexual theories. Two-spirit identities may involve sexual or gendered practices that are stigmatized today in many contexts, but within their own societies, two-spirits were as "normal" as other people. Further, it is not clear that concepts such as homosexuality or transsexuality are pertinent here. *'Aqí*, *miati*, and *lhamana* identities appear to have been shaped as much by spirituality and occupation as by gender and sexuality; further, if two-spirits occupied a *different* gender than the culturally specific categories of man or woman, they were not transsexual or transgendered, nor were their sexual relations with members of the same gender. Archaeological research on identity variation in Native North American contexts thus illuminates the methodological challenges facing archaeological research on sexuality in the past.

The same methodological challenges emerge in other studies aimed at the investigation of homosexuality in the past. How can archaeologists counter heteronormative biases without replicating the problematic ways that nonheterosexual and nonreproductive sexualities are conceptualized in the present? Unfortunately, not all archaeological research on the topic is successful in this regard. Matthews (1999:7), for example, has argued that "there is an ahistorical element in homosexual behaviour" and posits that researchers should be able to identity "common themes in the material culture of gay men," such as transvestism or exaggerated masculinity in clothing, meeting spaces where sexual encounters and exchange of partners could occur, and sex toys (which Matthews states are used "more frequently in the gay world than in the straight" [11]). While the desire to identify cross-cultural "traits" of homosexuality is understandable, such projects rely on troubling stereotypes of modern gay male life and obscure the cultural specificity of sexual practices and sexual identities. Other researchers have painstakingly worked to avoid these pitfalls. Schmidt (2002:161), in his research on Mesolithic Siberian sexuality, provides an alternative to the prevalent gender/sexual binarism, arguing instead for a "multiple sex/gender paradigm" in which the "number of sex and/or gender categories . . . cannot be assumed before analysis. Nor is there any requirement specifying the nature of categorical boundaries. In addition to discrete, non-overlapping sets, categorical variation may be continuous, such that categories grade into one another." Within this framework, Schmidt turns to the study of shamanistic identities and practices as a way of understanding prehistoric sexuality. He focuses on the "sensuous bodily experiences of shamans, and the role of the shaman as a bridge between various levels of existence" (226), including the ability to harness both male and female sexual potentials. Such work could be ephemeral or more permanent and might involve same-sex sexual relationships. But this is not an archaeology of "homosexuality"; to the contrary, Schmidt argues that for both men and women, for shamans, and for the sexual partners of all these, "sexuality in the Mesolithic was about more than mating networks. As instantiations of a sexualized cosmology, meaningful patterns of sexuality shaped how people lived and experienced their lives" (231).

Danielsson similarly turns to imagery associated with shamans in the Late Iron Age in Scandinavia. Focusing her analysis on gold foil artifacts that contain iconographic depictions of humanoid forms, she notes that such objects initially portrayed a single, mask-wearing individual of ambiguous gender. These masked figures, Danielsson suggests, most likely were representations of shamanic acts and performances in a variety of sexualized gender- and species-bending ecstatic states. In later periods, however, the gold foils increasingly depicted two individuals locked in an embrace. The unmasked figures on these later foils represented "stereotyped, aristocratic, well-to-do bodies of a man and a woman . . . (re)presenting them with conservative traits, in choice of clothes or total appearance" (Danielsson 2002:193). Danielsson argues that this transition is isometric with a literary shift that increasingly represented transgender/homosexual practices as godly rather than human practices; the changing images on the gold foil artifacts sustained "a stricter and more rigid division of gender roles in every day life, recognizable through punishment against cross-dressing, and the more easily discernible genders in grave material in the Late Iron Age compared to the Early Iron Age" (196). Archaeology, then, can not only challenge heteronormative biases of the present but also trace the historical production of disciplinary regimes that enforced gendered and sexual norms.

Historical archaeology at eighteenth- and nineteenth-century sites is contributing to a greater understanding of how the sexological terms now in common use were historically produced. Davis, for example, explores the erotic and sexual dimensions of Fonthill Abbey, a residence constructed in the early 1800s by shunned sodomite William Courtenay. At the time, Davis (2000:109) notes, "sodomy was routinely conceived rhetorically as 'pre-posterousness,' as putting ahead or before what should come below or after, inverting the natural order of social relations." Davis turns to Courtenay's unusual construction of sight lines both within and outside the building as an engagement of the desiring gaze with tropes of inversions of front and back. A second example is Casella's archaeological investigation of a nineteenth-century women's prison in Australia. Casella's excavations there revealed evidence of a black-market sexual economy—one in which both same-gender and cross-gender sexual services were part of a dense network of exchanges of food, indulgences, money, clothing, and transportation. The apex of this underground sexual economy was, paradoxically, the solitary cells, which were constructed specifically to punish repeat sexual offenders. Within the prison, Casella (2000b:214) argues, "women's sexual expression remained both opportunistic and fluidly defined. Convicts did not possess 'sexual identities' or exclusive 'persuasions,'" although most colonial officials interpreted long-term same-sex relationships among convict women as a transgressive form of heterosexuality, with a member of each couple being identified as a "pseudomale." Just as Casella's and Davis's research provides material evidence of underdocumented historic sexualities, so too has anthropologist Rubin (1991, 2000, 2002) turned to archaeological methodologies in her study of twentieth-century leathermen in San Francisco. Her diachronic and spatial analyses of gay and leather "settlement patterns" and "sites" reveals the historical production and transformation of sexual identities and practices within the shifting context of urban development.

Sexual Economies: Prostitution

As Casella's research on the sexual economy of a nineteenth-century prison suggests, commercial sex has also been central to archaeological investigations of sexuality. Archaeological studies of prostitution in North America have been spurred by the discovery of deposits from Victorian-era and turn-of-the-century brothels, parlor houses, and cribs. Significant studies include excavations of brothel sites in East Blairmore, Alberta (Lawrence Cheney 1991, 1993); Washington, D.C. (Cheek and Seifert 1994; Seifert 1991, 1994; Seifert et al. 2000); Los Angeles (Costello 2000, 2002; Costello and Praetzellis 1999; Costello et al. 1998, 1999); and Oakland (Solari 1997). Most recently, the journal *Historical Archaeology* has published a thematic issue ("Sin City") on the archaeology of prostitution (Seifert 2005).

In nearly all cases, these investigations have focused on artifacts recovered from hollow features such as privies and kitchen waste pits that are known through historic records to have been associated with brothels. In some cases, the structural remains of brothels have been recovered and recorded as well. Many of these investigations have focused on the working conditions of prostitutes and their relative economic status compared to nonbrothel households. For example, materials recovered from Los Angeles indicate that parlor house prostitutes enjoyed a substantially higher standard of living than their working-class neighbors, while the material record of crib prostitutes reflects spartan, nonresidential working conditions (Costello et al. 1998, 1999). Studies in Washington, D.C., have shown that initially, in the late 1800s, the living conditions of brothel prostitutes were roughly identical to that in adjacent nonbrothel households. However, by the early 1900s, the relative economic status of prostitutes had increased (Seifert 1994). Archaeological studies have also documented the occupational hazards of sex work through the recovery of panel medicine bottles that once contained "cures for venereal disease and pain-numbing tinctures of opium and morphine" (Costello 2002:177). The economic and occupational emphases in archaeological research on prostitution are suggestive of feminist organizing around sex work as labor from the 1970s on (Bell 1987, Nagle 1997).

Archaeological studies of prostitution have also problematized conventional scholarship about gender ideologies of the Victorian era, noting the permeability of the "separate spheres" usually associated with the female cult of domesticity (Poovey 1988, Smith-Rosenberg 1979). For example, Seifert (1991) has noted that for white working-class women in Hooker's Division, economic well-being and sexual activity were intertwined through marriage, on-the-job sexual harassment, sexual reciprocation for gifts from male friends, and sex for pay. Solari (1997) has likewise noted that for many women, prostitution was a conscious choice among a series of unattractive and equally dehumanizing alternatives. Solari has also traced the ways in which prostitution sustained the economic fabric of entire communities: people made money as brokers (procurers, pimps, and madams) and by supplying food, clothing, medicines, and liquor to brothels (Solari 1997:277–78). De Cunzo's (1995) excavation of the Magdalen Society in nineteenth-century Philadelphia expands this point by investigating the institutions that formed to oppose the spread of commercial sexuality and to provide "reform, respite, and ritual" to the "fallen" women involved in the trade.

Overwhelmingly, however, these archaeological investigations of prostitution sites have focused on the economic aspects of prostitution. What are curiously sidestepped are the sexual subjectivities of the people who lived at, worked in, and patronized these businesses. The performance piece "Red Light Voices: An Archaeological Drama of Late Nineteenth Century Prostitution" (Costello 2000) demonstrates how archaeological interpretations are radically changed when sexual subjectivities are included. Performed by Costello and her colleagues at several archaeological conferences in North America, "Red Light Voices" is a spoken-word archaeological narrative that juxtaposes historic photographs and images of artifacts from Los Angeles brothel sites with selections from oral histories and letters of prostitutes, johns, and pimps. Costello's aim in producing this drama was "to expose the human face behind our data . . . to arrive at a deeper understanding of past events by humanizing them" (Costello 2000:163).

"Red Light Voices" is notable within the genre of archaeological studies on prostitution not only in its humanistic approach but also because the drama engages with the experiences not only of women prostitutes but also of their male clients. With this one exception, archaeological studies of prostitution have focused on women—the standard of living and health practices of female prostitutes and the business acumen of madams. These studies have also presumed that the sexual transactions at brothel sites were wholly heterosexual. Here again, the legacy of sexological studies has biased archaeological research. With few exceptions, sexologists confined their discussions of prostitution to diagnosing the underlying causes of female prostitution; male patronage of female prostitutes was framed as a normal, unremarkable outgrowth of men's naturally vigorous sexual drive. Female prostitutes, on the other hand, were variously characterized in sexology as degenerate and immoral, as evidence of evolutionary atavism among the lower classes, and as the female equivalent of the male born criminal (Caplan 1998, Greenway 1998).

It is interesting that most archaeological studies of prostitution have been conducted at North American sites dating to the nineteenth and early twentieth centuries. Recently, a few papers about archaeological investigations of prostitution in other historical and geographical contexts have been presented at conferences (Chávez 2004, Levin-Richardson 2005), and it is clear from these works that there is great potential for further investigation of commercial sexuality in other archaeological settings.

Architecture and Space

Another common theme among archaeological studies in sexuality concerns architecture and space. Several examples of this have already been noted: Perry and Joyce (2001) and Prine (1997, 2000) view architecture and space as a means through which two-spirit identities were enacted and performed; Casella (1999, 2000a, 2000b, 2001), Davis (2000), Rubin (1991, 2000, 2002), and Eger (in press) likewise examine landscape, settlement patterns, viewshed, and architecture as contexts that produced and supported nonheterosexual identities and practices. Others (Chase 1991, Croucher 2004) have explored ways in which architecture and landscape participate in polygamous sexual relationships. Investigations of architecture and space provide a means for archaeologists to study the intersections between practice and representation; sexualized spaces both serve as social metaphors for sexuality and are the contexts that enable sexual performances and sexual acts.

Buchli (2000) has documented perhaps the earliest use of architectural data in an archaeology of sexuality: Soviet archaeologists in the 1920s and the 1930s turned to archaeological evidence of Paleolithic architecture as evidence of sexual relations within Friedrich Engels's vision of prehistoric communalism. The archaeological remains of Paleolithic households had immense significance for the newly formed communist society and its quest to imagine new communistic social formations, identities, and sexualities. The archaeological data recovered by Soviet archaeologists were thus used as resources by architects and planners whose designs aimed to materialize "a radical reworking of heterosexuality" (Buchli 2000:240). Buchli's archaeology of twentieth-century socialism traces the lives of individuals who lived in one such master-planned community, the Narkomfin Communal House, a structure designed and built to "ease an individual's transition towards fully socialized life" (Buchli 2000:67) through a variety of communal facilities and living quarters. Buchli's painstaking, diachronic analysis demonstrates that all space, however mundane—from laundry facilities to gymnasiums to kitchens—are constructed and experienced through shifting sexual ideologies.

Meskell (1998a, 2000) has also examined the sexualization of household space in the planned community of Dier El Medina, which housed tomb workers in New Kingdom Egypt. Her analysis of the architectural remains of workers' houses and the artifacts and imagery they contained suggest that activities in one type of room in particular—the *lit clos*, or "day bed" room—centered on married, elite, sexually potent, fertile females. The *lit clos* may have been a ritual location for sexual intercourse, conception, and childbirth; the murals usually found there incorporate erotic motifs—especially those associated with "the lives of women, and the sexual lives of mature women, at that" (Meskell 1998a:227). Meskell demonstrates that the sexual meanings of spaces are mutually produced through the physicality of the spaces themselves, the activities that occur within them, and the imagery and material culture that co-occurs within the space.

Several archaeologists have extended this argument to examine the ways in which architecture not only facilitates certain sexual meanings and practices but can also be used to control sexuality. Both Gilchrist (1994, 2000) and Voss (2000a) have particularly examined the ways that the architecture of religious institutions shaped the sexual subjectivities of the people who lived within them. Gilchrist's investigation of medieval British monasteries explores the embodied qualities of the celibacy of religious women. Architectural practices of physical enclosure—a "glorious prison" (Gilchrist 2000:93) according to one eleventh-century abbot—contributed to a process through which "the sexuality of medieval religious women was turned inside out: sexuality became an interior space, a place of elevated senses and ecstatic states of consciousness" (Gilchrist 2000:89). The enclosed environment and practices of physical asceticism enhanced the importance of visual culture, especially images of the suffering of Christ's body, which likewise showed a concern with interiority—"inner spaces, inner suffering" (Gilchrist 2000:99).

Yet, while the enclosure of medieval religious women was largely voluntary, Voss (2000a) examines the sexual confinement experienced by Native Californians in religious Spanish-colonial missions in the late 1700s and early 1800s. Colonial missionaries used architecture as a technology of sexual control. Unmarried women were prevented from having sex through confinement in a *monjerío*, or locked barracks; interethnic sexual activity was discouraged by physically segregating colonial soldiers from indigenous neighborhoods; and long adobe buildings containing single-room apartments were one means by which missionaries policed conjugal heterosexuality and enforced Catholic prohibitions against same-sex and polygamous sexual relations. Yet Native Californian oral histories highlight the contrast between official architectural intentions and the actual practices that occurred in these spaces. In particular, the locked *monjerío*, designed to protect female sexual "virtue," was in practice a space within which native girls and women were particularly vulnerable to sexual molestation by mission priests. Oral histories also recount ways that Native Californian residents of the missions were unwilling to let architectural impediments prevent sexual pleasure, arranging covert liaisons and sexual parties in the very spaces designed to effect sexual control.

Ambiguous Images: Representations of the Sexual and Erotic

Sexual and erotic representations form another body of evidence through which much archaeological research on sexuality has been produced. Several examples of this have already been discussed. Imagery from Paleolithic, Neolithic, and Mesolithic sites in Europe and the Near East are often interpreted as evidence of cultural practices related to fertility management. Critiques of heterosexism in archaeological interpretation also frequently center on reanalysis of imagery that has been previously assumed to represent heterosexual identities or practices. Gilchrist's (1994, 2000) research on medieval monasticism powerfully demonstrates how architecture and imagery together participate in the production of specific sexual subjectivities. These studies have all raised critical points in the archaeological interpretation of sexual imagery. First, they have highlighted the danger of interpreting imagery from the past through the sexual standards of the present. Today in the United States, for example, certain kinds of bodily display (exposure of the pubic region, buttocks, and female breasts) are sexually charged, but it would be a grave ethnocentric error to assume that this was always the case. Further, the sexual meanings of representations are context dependent, so that a naked human figure in a medical textbook is experienced differently by its viewers than in an art museum or a porn magazine. Second, archaeological studies of imagery need emphasize not only the context of imagery but also the production and consumption of such images. Images are not seamless reproductions of social behaviors; they are culturally constructed representations that may participate in ideological and political agendas. Viewers actively engage with visual imagery from the different subject positions they occupy. The sexual "meanings" of archaeologically recovered imagery are thus inherently ambiguous and multifaceted.

A particularly salient case in point are the so-called sex pots of ancient Peru. These sexually explicit ceramic vessels, recovered primarily from Moche funerary contexts, "are both functional clay pots, with hollow chambers for holding liquid and stirrup-shaped spouts for pouring, and works of three-dimensional sculpture [depicting] lively little figures engaged in a startling variety of acts involving the hands, nipples, genitals, anus, mouth, and tongue" (Weismantel 2004:495). The sex pots have attracted scholarly comment for decades (Gero 2004:19 provides a useful listing of previous studies). The sexual imagery on the pots centers on autoerotic and heterosexual sex acts with an emphasis on masturbation, fellatio, and anal sex; vaginal/penile intercourse is almost never depicted. This "absence" of what is generally assumed to be procreative sex has been the focus of many scholarly interpretations of the pots, which have been variously interpreted as portrayals of birth control techniques, as admonitions against forbidden sexual practices, or, because the pots are found largely in mortuary contexts, as representations of funerary sex rituals in which nonprocreative sex is symbolically associated with death.

Recently, Gero (2004) and Weismantel (2004) have each undertaken studies of the Moche sex pots that draw explicitly on feminist and queer theory. Although their approaches are quite different, both share a concern that while the pots have attracted much commentary, "the topic remains under-theorized and connotations of the 'erotic' unexamined" (Gero 2004:19). They also draw careful attention to the pots' archaeological context as funerary offerings found in burial contexts, especially the tombs of elites. The pots must be interpreted as objects commissioned by and made for elite consumers; the sexual "meanings" of the pots are thus unlikely to have been shared by all classes or ethnic groups (Weismantel 2004:500).

Weismantel's analysis of the Moche sex pots focuses on ceramics depicting heterosexual anal sex, with the man and woman lying on their sides facing the same direction (belly to back). Most Moche ceramic anal sex scenes also commonly include a tiny and shapeless third figure "who lies next to the woman's chest to breast-feed while she has sex" (Weismantel 2004:496). Weismantel challenges the commonly asserted premise that the figures on the anal sex pots are not engaged in reproductive sex. Instead, she argues, the figures might be seen as being involved in transfers of reproductive substances. Many anthropological studies have documented cultures in which sexual reproduction is seen not as a single event (of sperm meeting egg) but as a series of practices that occur over a long period of time, often involving various transfers of bodily fluids (semen, milk, or blood) into different orifices (mouth, anus, or vagina). Hence, one possible reading of the Moche anal sex pots is that "the substance that is transmitted from the man's body into the woman's as seminal fluid is the same substance that passes through her nipple into the baby's mouth; the scene depicts the movement of this nurturing fluid between three bodies, to the ultimate benefit of the infant" (499). Within this framework, other "nonreproductive" sex acts depicted on Moche pots may be similarly reinterpreted: for example, another frequent motif, that of the masturbating skeleton, may represent the intergenerational transfer of reproductive bodily fluids from the ancestors to the living (501). Weismantel concludes that Moche elite may have used these visual representations of bodily fluid transfers "to alter the definition of the reproductive act . . . [to] position the ancestors, elders, and the most powerful lineages at the center of the system that flows" (502), thus sustaining and legitimating the growing centralization of power among elite Moche lineages.

Gero's analysis of the Moche sex pots provides a different yet complementary perspective to Weismantel's. Gero compares the Moche sex pots with another assemblage of erotically charged Peruvian pottery: "copulation pots" recovered from Recuay contexts. Recuay and Moche polities were roughly contemporary, with the Moche located in coastal areas and the Recuay in the Andes. The Recuay pots, which are also found almost exclusively in mortuary contexts, represent sexuality quite differently than the Moche ones. The Recuay depict heterosexual pairs copulating belly to belly; both the male and the female figures are well dressed, but this, Gero argues, does not indicate sexual modesty but instead provides a means of marking the elite status of the copulating pair. The copulation scenes often include representations of public architecture and additional figures suggesting that the copulation was observed by an audience. "We must conclude," Gero posits, "that the Recuay copulations . . . are profoundly ritual" involving a distinctive class and status of participants. Like Weismantel, Gero views the pots as representations used by elites in their growing consolidation of power, but her comparison of the Recuay and Moche sex pots leads her to suggest that the gender politics of elite life were significantly different in the two polities: while Recuay sex pots depict complementary male–female pairs, the Moche sex pots typically depict anal and oral sex scenes in which "the focus of the interactive activity is not union and mutual pleasure but a celebration of the male orgasm . . . male orgasm emerges as both a powerful and a political act, a co-joining of maleness and powerfulness and pleasure (Gero 2004:19–20). This contrast, Gero concludes, demonstrates the significant role of "bodily ritual and embodied sensuous practice in the constitution of society" (19).

Weismantal's and Gero's reexaminations of the famed Peruvian sex pots are exemplary of other feminist archaeological research on sexually explicit representations. Marshall's (2000) reconsideration of sexually explicit prehistoric stone objects from the North American Pacific Northwest challenges earlier readings that divided these artifacts into "male" and "female" forms. Instead, she notes, the objects connote ambiguity on several registers: function is interwoven with form, aspects of woman and man are combined, and vulva and phallus intermingle. The images, Marshall suggests, refuse the binary divisions of sexuality that are often presumed in present-day cultural politics. Mayan representations of the phallus, in images of human bodies and in disembodied forms, are also regular topics of archaeological investigation; Houston (2001) has explored representations of emotions such as lust, sexual longing, and sexual disgust in phallic imagery. Many others have drawn connections between Mayan phallocentric representations of masculinity (especially penile bloodletting) and the reinforcement of male identity and state authority (Ardren, in press; Ardren and Hixson, in press; Joyce 2000a, 2000c; Meskell and Joyce 2003).

Sexual Cultures

Although the archaeology of sexuality is a relatively new undertaking, the corpus of research discussed previously fully demonstrates that archaeological remains provide a rich source of information about past sexualities. Further, archaeological investigations of past sexualities are expanding our understanding of human sexuality beyond what is imaginable from observations in the present day. The ultimate challenge for archaeologists is to integrate questions of sexuality into our studies of the whole fabric of social life in the past cultures we investigate—to fully consider Malinowski's (1929:xxiii) claim that sexuality participates in "almost every aspect of culture." This closing section discusses the research conducted by two archaeologists, Lynn Meskell and Rosemary Joyce, who perhaps have been most successful in achieving this objective. Joyce researches the Classic Maya in Mesoamerica; Meskell studies New Kingdom Egypt. Their individual scholarship on gender and sexuality in these societies is impressive in itself (Joyce 1996, 1998, 2000a, 2000b, 2000c, 2002; Meskell 1996, 1998a, 1999, 2000, 2001; Perry and Joyce 2001); most recently, they have jointly undertaken a comparative work (Meskell and Joyce 2003) that explores the embodied lives of Classic Mayan and New Kingdom Egyptian subjects.

The core project in Meskell and Joyce's comparative work is to examine "the centrality of embodied life in all its sensual and sexual specificity" (Meskell and Joyce 2003:162). In doing so, they strive to think beyond the constraints of Cartesian dualism and its foundational premise that the mind and body are ontologically separate. Classic Mayan and New Kingdom Egyptian societies existed "before and separate from the tradition that runs from Platonic to Cartesian thought, [and] give us a potential window on other ways of framing embodiment, distinct from concepts of duality, hierarchy, and rational privilege" (17). For Joyce and Meskell, sexuality and material culture are both integral to and indivisible from this investigation of embodiment: the objects that survive in the archaeological record, they argue, are not mere costumes or props or representations but "extensions of the materiality of the embodied person. This leads us to a consideration of the play of desire implied by the materialities of embodiment" (10).

Because much of the archaeological material that Meskell and Joyce engage with consists of texts and imagery, their analysis involves a substantial consideration of the sexual politics of representation. In New Kingdom Egypt, the abundant corpus of textual and iconographic materials and durable monuments and tombs have skewed archaeological interpretation to emphasize the elite perspective, which was very different from that of the majority of the populace who were illiterate and lived "in relative poverty and simplicity" (Meskell and Joyce 2003:2). Likewise, among the Classic Maya, representations are a "powerful and ambiguous source of evidence" that present "stereotypes of a universe populated primarily by young, male, subjects. They thus systematically bias our vision of ancient Maya experience" (23). In both cases, texts and representations are shaped not only by status but also by gender, specifically that of elite males. Such representations must be viewed as projects that seek to influence the ways that people understand the cultural norms they are expected to emulate and a means by which actual practices can be measured against the represented ideal (Perry and Joyce 2001:65–66). Archaeology, Meskell and Joyce (2003:4) argue, provides a valuable counterperspective that highlights household and domestic life and can "hint at more subversive trends" within each culture.

Central to this political analysis is their examination of "phallic culture" in both Mayan and Egyptian contexts. "The representation of male sexuality, although quite distinct in nature, occupies central place in both traditions, signified literally by the objectification of the penis as subject for textual and visual discourse" (Meskell and Joyce 2003:10). The Egyptian worldview centers on a "motif of bodily self-creation" (13) in which the world and many of its gods were literally brought into being through masturbatory ejaculation by the god Atum. Phallic culture was not limited to the mythical but was tied to the everyday through material objects in the form of the phallus and through representations of male bodies that emphasize or exaggerate the penis. Egyptian phallic culture was also reinforced through tropes of bodily perfection in which the female form was represented as "inherently sexualized and directed by the male gaze" (53). Unlike many cultures in which girls are asexualized, Egyptian representations show girls wearing the sexualized signifiers of female adulthood. Egyptian female sexuality, Meskell and Joyce consider, might be best understood as a continuum without sharp demarcations or rites of passage that are common in other cultures.

The centrality of the phallus in representations in the Classic Mayan world stands in contrast to that in New Kingdom Egypt, cautioning against tendencies toward universalizing or totalizing interpretations. Classic Maya representations provide images of the exposed bodies of athletic young men on homoerotic display for a politically dominant individual male. These include representations of ball-game playing, dancing, and warfare in which the erotics of the male body are highlighted through exposure of the flesh and strategic clothing that highlights the penis as it conceals it. The phallus is further emphasized through the images of penile piercing and bloodletting and "by phallic ornamentation, including three-dimensional sculptures of erect phalli up to 3 meters long" (Meskell and Joyce 2003:125). In contrast, most representations depict the female body as unsexualized and draped in clothing, with the exception of small figurines showing careful depictions of breasts and suckling infants (120–27). Further, representations of men and women figures together are unusual and when present usually depict the female gaze as directed toward the male groin. In sum, Meskell and Joyce conclude, "the bodies of young males are represented as objects for the gaze of other, centrally posed, male figures within the picture plane, and of male and female viewers of these works" (125).

In both New Kingdom Egypt and Classic Maya worlds, "phallic culture" is both complemented and contradicted by other images and texts. For example, the Egyptian worldview of phallic creation is balanced by a female sexualization of the cycle of daily life, in which the goddess Nut continuously swallows the sun and stars through her mouth and births them through her vagina. Among the Maya, there is a parallel between penile bloodletting among men and the perforation of the female tongue. The penis and semen were conceptualized as integral parts of "fluid economies," in which the emissions and emanations of the body were central to the transmission and expression of culture and power. Egyptian subjectivities emphasized the porous nature of the body, distinguishing between *mtw* (conduits for semen, air, milk, blood, urine, sweat, fragrance, disease, and spirits) and *iwf*, or flesh, including skin and genitalia. Classic Maya concepts of the body emphasized the interplay of solid and vapor, of breath, blood, and bone: raw materials that "extended personhood beyond the bounds of individual subjects" (Meskell and Joyce 2003:75). Bone, semen, spittle, blood, milk, and vaporous emanations circulated in manners that linked the living to the dead, people to animals, nobles to commoners, and kin and cohort to each other. The realm of sexual and sensual embodiment, so bounded in Western concepts of the individual subject, resists delimitation in both New Kingdom Egypt and Classic Maya contexts.

Meskell and Joyce's individual and comparative research thus demonstrates the promise of archaeological research to provide a radical perspective in sexuality studies, one that can expose and denaturalize the disciplining practices of sexology, its present-day successors, and their constraining effect on current sexualities. The very materiality of the archaeological record provides "evocative fragments of past life to think through our own cultural contexts, to understand the importance of our different legacies and refigure our own taxonomies and experiences with the recognition of cultural difference firmly in mind" (Meskell and Joyce 2003:162).

The politics of the present—as well as those of the past—have always been central to the feminist project of engendering archaeology. Archaeological research on sexuality is necessary not only because it is an integral aspect of the past cultures that archaeologists study but also because in the sexual politics of the present moment, the past is being used as a devastating rhetorical weapon by those who seek to control the sexual identities, expressions, and relationships of others. One need only consider the debates about "gay marriage" in the United States to understand this; the alleged sexual practices of ancient Greeks and

Romans, medieval Europeans, prehistoric Native Americans, and Pacific Islanders have perhaps never been received so much media attention. President Bush's call for a "marriage amendment" to the Constitution claimed that monogamous heterosexual marriage was "one of the most fundamental, enduring institutions of our civilization" (State of the Union Address, January 20, 2004). Bush's adviser, Karl Rove, later told reporters that this constitutional amendment is necessary because "we cannot allow activist local elected officials to thumb their nose at 5,000 years of human history" (Saunders 2004:B11). The research reviewed in this chapter demonstrates that archaeology is already providing an empirically rich body of knowledge that challenges the premise that any form of sexual subjectivity is inherently natural or constant. Instead, the archaeology of sexuality is demonstrating that human sexuality is more richly varied, across cultures and across time, than could have ever been imagined.

Acknowledgments

Invitations from Thomas Dowson, Eleanor Casella and Chris Fowler, Kath Sterling, and the organizers of the 2004 Chacmool Conference provided important opportunities to develop work that informed the writing of this chapter. Thanks also to Deb Cohler, Meg Conkey, Sandy Hollimon, Rosemary Joyce, Purnima Mankekar, Lynn Meskell, Robert Schmidt, Sarah Nelson, and Laurie Wilkie for many conversations and inspiration on this topic.

References

Abelove, Henry
    1989   Some Speculations on the History of Sexual Intercourse during the Long Eighteenth Century in England. *Genders* 6(fall):125–30.

Ardren, Traci
    In press   Masculinity in Classic Maya Culture. In *Que(e)rying Archaeology: The 15th Anniversary Gender Conference*. Proceedings of the 37th Annual Chacmool Archaeological Conference. Calgary: University of Calgary.

Ardren, Traci, and David R. Hixson
    In press   The Unusual Sculptures of Telantunich, Phalli and the Concept of Masculinity in Ancient Maya Thought. *Cambridge Archaeological Journal* 16(1).

Arnold, Bettina
    2002   "Sein und Werden": Gender as a Process in Mortuary Ritual. In *In Pursuit of Gender: Worldwide Archaeological Approaches*. Sarah Milledge Nelson and Myriam Rosen-Ayalon, eds. Pp. 239–56. Walnut Creek, CA: AltaMira Press.

Baghemil, Bruce
    2000   *Biological Exuberance: Animal Homosexuality and Natural Diversity*. New York: St. Martin's Press.

Bahn, P.
  1986 No Sex, Please, We're Aurignacians. *Rock Art Research* 3(2):99–120.
Bahn, P., and J. Vertut
  1988 *Images of the Ice Age*. Leicester: Winward.
Bell, Laurie, ed.
  1987 *Good Girls/Bad Girls: Feminists and Sex Trade Workers Face to Face*. Seattle: Seal Press.
Bland, Lucy, and Laura Doan, eds.
  1998a *Sexology in Culture: Labeling Bodies and Desires*. Chicago: University of Chicago Press.
  1998b *Sexology Uncensored: The Documents of Sexual Science*. Chicago: University of Chicago Press.
Breen, Margaret Soenser, and Warren J. Blumenfeld
  2001 "There Is a Person Here": An Interview with Judith Butler. *International Journal of Sexuality and Gender Studies* 6(1/2):7–23.
Buchli, Victor
  2000 Constructing Utopian Sexualities: The Archaeology and Architecture of the Early Soviet State. In *Archaeologies of Sexuality*. Robert A. Schmidt and Barbara L. Voss, eds. Pp. 236–49. London: Routledge.
Butler, Judith
  1990 *Gender Trouble: Feminism and the Subversion of Identity*. New York: Routledge.
  1993a *Bodies That Matter: On the Discursive Limits of "Sex."* New York: Routledge.
  1993b Imitation and Gender Insubordination. In *The Lesbian and Gay Studies Reader*. Henry Abelove, Michele A. Barale, and David Halpern, eds. Pp. 307–20. New York: Routledge.
  1994 Against Proper Objects. *differences* 6(2+3):1–26.
  1999 *Gender Trouble: Feminism and the Subversion of Identity*. 2nd ed. New York: Routledge.
Caplan, Jane
  1998 "Educating the Eye": The Tattooed Prostitute. In *Sexology in Culture: Labeling Bodies and Desires*. Lucy Bland and Laura Doan, eds. Pp. 100–115. Chicago: University of Chicago Press.
Casella, Eleanor Conlin
  1999 Dangerous Girls and Gentle Ladies: Archaeology and Nineteenth Century Australian Female Convicts. Ph.D. dissertation, University of California, Berkeley.
  2000a Bulldaggers and Gentle Ladies: Archaeological Approaches to Female Homosexuality in Convict Era Australia. In *Archaeologies of Sexuality*. Robert A. Schmidt and Barbara L. Voss, eds. Pp. 142–59. London: Routledge.
  2000b "Doing Trade": A Sexual Economy of 19th Century Australian Female Convict Prisons. *World Archaeology* 32(2):209–21.
  2001 Landscapes of Punishment and Resistance: A Female Convict Settlement in

Tasmania. In *Contested Landscapes: Landscapes of Movement and Exile*. Barbara Bender and Margot Winer, eds. Pp. 103–20. Oxford: Berg.

Chase, Sabrina M.
  1991 Polygyny, Architecture and Meaning. In *The Archaeology of Gender*. Proceedings of the 22nd Annual Chacmool Conference. Dale Walde and Noreen D. Willows, eds. Pp. 150–58. Calgary: Department of Archaeology, University of Calgary.

Chávez, Ulises
  2004 Cuanto Cuesta Tu Amor: La Prostitucion Entre Los Azteca. Paper presented at the Chacmool Conference: Que(e)rying Archaeology—The 15th Anniversary Gender Conference, University of Calgary, Alberta.

Cheek, Charles D., and Donna J. Seifert
  1994 Neighborhoods and Household Types in Nineteenth-Century Washington, DC: Fannie Hill and Mary McNamara in Hooker's Division. In *Historical Archaeology of the Chesapeake*. Paul A. Shackel and Barbara J. Little, eds. Pp. 267–81. Washington, DC: Smithsonian Institution Press.

Claassen, Cheryl
  1992 Questioning Gender: An Introduction. In *Exploring Gender through Archaeology: Selected Papers from the 1991 Boone Conference*. Cheryl Claassen, ed. Pp. 1–10. Madison, WI: Prehistory Press.

Cobb, Hannah
  In press A Queer Eye for the Straight Hunter Gatherer. In *Que(e)rying Archaeology: The 15th Anniversary Gender Conference*. Proceedings of the 37th Annual Chacmool Archaeological Conference. Calgary: University of Calgary.

Conkey, Margaret W.
  1989 The Structural Analysis of Paleolithic Art. In *Archaeological Thought in America*. C. C. Lamberg-Karlovsky, ed. Pp. 135–54. Cambridge: Cambridge University Press.

Conkey, Margaret W., and Ruth E. Tringham
  1995 Archaeology and the Goddess: Exploring the Contours of Feminist Archaeology. In *Feminisms in the Academy*. Donna C. Stanton and Abigail J. Stewart, eds. Pp. 199–247. Ann Arbor: University of Michigan Press.

Conkey, Margaret W., and Joan Gero
  1997 From Programme to Practice: Gender and Feminism in Archaeology. *Annual Review of Anthropology* 26:411–37.

Conkey, Margaret W., and Janet D. Spector
  1984 Archaeology and the Study of Gender. *Advances in Archaeological Method and Theory* 7:1–32.

Costello, Julia G.
  2000 Red Light Voices: An Archaeological Drama of Late Nineteenth Century Prostitution. In *Archaeologies of Sexuality*. Robert A. Schmidt and Barbara L. Voss, eds. Pp. 160–75. London: Routledge.

>   2002 Life Behind the Red Lights: Prostitution in Los Angeles, 1880–1910. In *Restoring Women's History through Historic Preservation.* Gail Dubrow and Jennifer Goodman, eds. Pp. 177–96. Baltimore: The Johns Hopkins University Press.

Costello, Julia G., and Adrian Praetzellis
>   1999 *Excavating L.A.'s Brothels.* Venice, CA: Furman Films.

Costello, Julia G., with Adrian Praetzellis, Mary Praetzellis, Judith Marvin, Michael D. Meyer, Erica S. Gibson, and Grace H. Ziesing
>   1998 *Historical Archaeology at the Headquarters Facility Project Site, the Metropolitan Water District of Southern California, Volume 1, Data Report: Recovered Data, Stratigraphy, Artifacts and Documents.* Los Angeles: Submitted to Union Station Partners on behalf of the Metropolitan Water District of Southern California, Environmental Planning Branch.

Costello, Julia G., with Adrian Praetzellis, Mary Praetzellis, Erica S. Gibson, Judith Marvin, Michael D. Meyer, Grace H. Ziesing, Sherri M. Gust, Madeleine Hirn, Bill Mason, Elain-Maryse Solari, and Suzanne B. Stewart
>   1999 *Historical Archaeology at the Headquarters Facility Project Site, the Metropolitan Water District of Southern California, Volume 2, Interpretive Report.* Los Angeles: Submitted to Union Station Partners on behalf of the Metropolitan Water District of Southern California, Environmental Planning Branch.

Croucher, Sarah
>   2004 Complex Identities on 19th Century Zanzibar. Paper presented at Theoretical Archaeology Group Conference, University of Glasgow, December 18.

Danielsson, Ing-Marie Back
>   2002 (Un)Masking Gender—Gold Foil (Dis)Embodiments in Late Iron Age Scandinavia. In *Thinking through the Body: Archaeologies of Corporeality.* Yannis Hamilakis, Mark Pluciennik, and Sarah Tarlow, eds. Pp. 85–97. New York: Kluwer Academic/Plenum.

Davis, Whitney
>   2000 The Site of Sexuality: William Beckford's Fonthill Abbey, 1780–1824. In *Archaeologies of Sexuality.* Robert A. Schmidt and Barbara L. Voss, eds. Pp. 104–13. London: Routledge.

De Cunzo, Lu Ann
>   1995 Reform, Respite, Ritual: An Archaeology of Institutions; the Magdalen Society of Philadelphia, 1800–1850. *Historical Archaeology* 29(3):1–164.

de Lauretis, Teresa
>   1991 Queer Theory: Lesbian and Gay Sexualities: An Introduction. *differences* 3(2):iii–xviii.

de Waal, Frans
>   1989 *Peacemaking among Primates.* Cambridge, MA: Harvard University Press.
>   1995 Sex as an Alternative to Aggression in the Bonobo. In *Sexual Nature/Sexual Culture.* Paul R. Abramson and Steven D. Pinkerton, eds. Pp. 37–56. Chicago: University of Chicago Press.

Dobres, Marcia-Anne
   1992   Reconsidering Venus Figurines: A Feminist Inspired Re-Analysis. In *Ancient Images, Ancient Thought: The Archaeology of Ideology*. A. Sean Goldsmith, Sandra Garvie, David Selin, and Jeannette Smith, eds. Pp. 245–62. Calgary: Archaeological Association of the University of Calgary.

Dowson, Thomas A.
   2000   Why Queer Archaeology? An Introduction. *World Archaeology* 32(2):161–65.
   In press   Que(e)rying Archaeology's Loss of Innocence. In *Que(e)rying Archaeology: The 15th Anniversary Gender Conference*. Proceedings of the 37th Annual Chacmool Archaeological Conference. Calgary: University of Calgary.

Duke, Philip
   1991   Recognizing Gender in Plains Hunting Groups: Is It Possible or Even Necessary? In *The Archaeology of Gender*. Proceedings of the 22nd Annual Chacmool Conference. Dale Walde and Noreen D. Willows, eds. Pp. 280–83. Calgary: Department of Archaeology, University of Calgary.

Eger, A. Asa
   In press   Does Function Follow Form? Architectures of Queered Space in the Roman Bathhouse. In *Que(e)rying Archaeology: The 15th Anniversary Gender Conference*. Proceedings of the 37th Annual Chacmool Archaeological Conference. Calgary: University of Calgary.

Foucault, Michel
   1978   *The History of Sexuality, Volume I: An Introduction*. Robert Hurley, trans. New York: Pantheon.

Gaimster, David, Peter Boland, Steve Linnane, and Caroline Cartwright
   1996   The Archaeology of Private Life: The Dudley Castle Condoms. *Post-Medieval Archaeology* 30:129–42.

Gero, Joan M.
   2004   Sex Pots of Ancient Peru: Post-Gender Reflections. In *Combining the Past and the Present: Archaeological Perspectives on Society*. Terje Oestigaard, Nils Anfinset, and Tore Saetersdal, eds. Pp. 3–22. BAR International Series 1210. Oxford: British Archaeological Reports.

Gilchrist, Roberta
   1991   Women's Archaeology? Political Feminism, Gender Theory and Historical Revision. *Antiquity* 65:495–501.
   1994   *Gender and Material Culture: The Archaeology of Religious Women*. New York: Routledge.
   2000   Unsexing the Body: The Interior Sexuality of Medieval Religious Women. In *Archaeologies of Sexuality*. Robert A. Schmidt and Barbara L. Voss, eds. Pp. 89–103. London: Routledge.

Greenway, Judy
   1998   It's What You Do with It That Counts: Interpretations of Otto Weininger.

In *Sexology in Culture: Labeling Bodies and Desires*. Lucy Bland and Laura Doan, eds. Pp. 26–43. Chicago: University of Chicago Press.

Handsman, Russell G.
   1991   Whose Art Was Found at Lepenski Vir? Gender Relations and Power in Archaeology. In *Engendering Archaeology: Women and Prehistory*. Joan M. Gero and Margaret W. Conkey, eds. Pp. 329–65. Cambridge, MA: Basil Blackwell.

Hollimon, Sandra E.
   1991   Health Consequences of the Division of Labor among the Chumash Indians of Southern California. In *The Archaeology of Gender*. Proceedings of the 22nd Annual Chacmool Conference. Dale Walde and Noreen D. Willows, eds. Pp. 462–69. Calgary: Department of Archaeology, University of Calgary.
   1992   Health Consequences of Sexual Division of Labor among Prehistoric Native Americans: The Chumash of California and the Arikara of the North Plains. In *Exploring Gender through Archaeology: Selected Papers from the 1991 Boone Conference*. Cheryl Claassen, ed. Pp. 81–88. Madison, WI: Prehistory Press.
   1996   Sex, Gender, and Health among the Chumash: An Archaeological Examination of Prehistoric Gender Roles. *Proceedings of the Society for California Archaeology* 9:205–8.
   1997   The Third Gender in Native California: Two-Spirit Undertakers among the Chumash and Their Neighbors. In *Women in Prehistory North American and Mesoamerica*. Cheryl Claassen and Rosemary A. Joyce, eds. Pp. 173–88. Philadelphia: University of Pennsylvania Press.
   2000   Archaeology of the 'Aqi: Gender and Sexuality in Prehistoric Chumash Society. In *Archaeologies of Sexuality*. Robert A. Schmidt and Barbara L. Voss, eds. Pp. 179–96. London: Routledge.
   2001   The Gendered Peopling of America: Addressing the Antiquity of Systems of Multiple Genders. In *The Archaeology of Shamanism*. Neil Price, ed. Pp. 123–34. London: Routledge.
   In press   Examining Third and Fourth Genders in Mortuary Contexts. In *Que(e)rying Archaeology: The 15th Anniversary Gender Conference*. Proceedings of the 37th Annual Chacmool Archaeological Conference. Calgary: University of Calgary.

Houston, Stephen D.
   2001   Decorous Bodies and Disordered Passions: Representations of Emotion among the Classic Maya. *World Archaeology* 33(2):206–19.

Joyce, Rosemary A.
   1996   The Construction of Gender in Classic Maya Monuments. In *Gender and Archaeology*. Rita P. Wright, ed. Pp. 167–98. Philadelphia: University of Pennsylvania Press.
   1998   Performing Gender in Prehispanic Central America. *RES: Anthropological Aesthetics* 33:147–65.
   2000a   *Gender and Power in Prehispanic Mesoamerica*. Austin: University of Texas Press.

2000b Girling the Girl and Boying the Boy: The Production of Adulthood in Ancient Mesoamerica. *World Archaeology* 31(3):473–83.
2000c A Precolumbian Gaze: Male Sexuality among the Ancient Maya. In *Archaeologies of Sexuality*. Robert A. Schmidt and Barbara L. Voss, eds. Pp. 263–83. London: Routledge.
2002 Desiring Women: Classic Maya Sexualities. In *Ancient Maya Gender Identity and Relations*. Lowell S. Gustafson and Amelia M. Trevelyan, eds. Pp. 329–44. Westport, CT: Greenwood Press.

Kokkinidou, Dimitra, and Maraianna Nikolaidou
1997 Body Imagery in the Aegean Mesolithic: Ideological Implications of Anthropomorphic Figurines. In *Invisible People and Processes: Writing Gender and Childhood into European Archaeology*. Jenny Moore and Eleanor Scott, eds. Pp. 88–112. London: Leicester University Press.

Lawrence Cheney, Susan
1991 Women and Alcohol: Female Influence on Recreational Patterns in the West 1880–1890. In *The Archaeology of Gender*. Proceedings of the 22nd Annual Chacmool Conference. Dale Walde and Noreen D. Willows, eds. Pp. 479–89. Calgary: Department of Archaeology, University of Calgary.
1993 Gender on Colonial Peripheries. In *Women in Archaeology: A Feminist Critique*. Hilary du Cros and Laurajane Smith, eds. Pp. 134–37. Canberra: Australian National University.

Levin-Richardson, Sarah
2005 Sex, Sight, and *Societas* in the Lupanar, Pompeii. Paper presented at Seeing the Past: Building Knowledge of the Past and Present through Acts of Seeing, Stanford Archaeology Center, Stanford University, Stanford, CA, February 5.

Lucy, S. J.
1997 Housewives, Warriors, and Slaves? Sex and Gender in Anglo-Saxon Burials. In *Invisible People and Processes: Writing Gender and Childhood into European Archaeology*. Jenny Moore and Eleanor Scott, eds. Pp. 150–68. London: Leicester University Press.

Malinowski, B.
1929 *The Sexual Life of Savages in North-Western Melanesia: An Ethnographic Account of Courtship, Marriage, and Family Life among the Natives of the Trobriand Islands, British New Guinea*. New York: Readers League of America, distributed by Eugenics Publishing Company.

Marshall, Yvonne
2000 Reading images stone b.c. *World Archaeology* 32(2):222–35.

Matthews, Keith
1999 The Material Culture of the Homosexual Male: A Case for Archaeological Exploration. In *Gender and Material Culture in Archaeological Perspective*. Moira Donald and Linda Hurcombe, eds. Pp. 3–19. London: Macmillan.

McCafferty, Sharisse D., and Geoffrey G. McCafferty
In press Alternative and Ambiguous Gender Identities in Postclassic Central Mexico. In *Que(e)rying Archaeology: The 15th Anniversary Gender Conference*. Proceedings of the 37th Annual Chacmool Archaeological Conference. Calgary: University of Calgary.

McDonald Pavelka, Mary S.
1995 Sexual Nature: What Can We Learn from a Cross-Species Perspective? In *Sexual Nature/Sexual Culture*. Paul R. Abramson and Steven D. Pinkerton, eds. Pp. 16–36. Chicago: University of Chicago Press.

Meskell, Lynn
1995 Goddesses, Gimbutas, and New Age Archaeology. *Antiquity* 69:74–86.
1996 The Somatization of Archaeology: Institutions, Discourses, Corporeality. *Norwegian Archaeological Review* 29(1):2–16.
1998a An Archaeology of Social Relations in an Egyptian Village. *Journal of Archaeological Method and Theory* 5(3):209–43.
1998b Oh, My Goddess! Archaeology, Sexuality, and Ecofeminism. *Archaeological Dialogues* 5(2):126–42.
1999 *Archaeologies of Social Life: Age, Sex, Class et cetera in Ancient Egypt*. Oxford: Blackwell.
2000 Re-em(bed)ing Sex: Domesticity, Sexuality, and Ritual in New Kingdom Egypt. In *Archaeologies of Sexuality*. Robert A. Schmidt and Barbara L. Voss, eds. Pp. 253–62. London: Routledge.
2001 *Private Life in New Kingdom Egypt*. Princeton, NJ: Princeton University Press.

Meskell, Lynn, and Rosemary A. Joyce
2003 *Embodied Lives: Figuring Ancient Maya and Egyptian Experience*. London: Routledge.

Nagle, Jill, ed.
1997 *Whores and Other Feminists*. New York: Routledge.

Nelson, Sarah Milledge
1990 Diversity of the Upper Paleolithic "Venus" Figurines and Archaeological Mythology. In *Powers of Observation: Alternative Views in Archaeology*. Sarah Milledge Nelson and Alice Kehoe, eds. Pp. 11–22. Washington, DC: American Anthropological Association.
1997 *Gender in Archaeology: Analyzing Power and Prestige*. Walnut Creek, CA: AltaMira Press.

Perry, Elizabeth M., and Rosemary A. Joyce
2001 Providing a Past for "Bodies That Matter": Judith Butler's Impact on the Archaeology of Gender. *International Journal of Sexuality and Gender Studies* 6(1/2):63–76.

Poovey, Mary
1988 *Uneven Developments: The Ideological Work of Gender in Mid-Victorian England*. Chicago: University of Chicago Press.

Prine, Elizabeth P.
   1997   The Ethnography of Place: Landscape and Culture in Middle Missouri Archaeology. Ph.D. dissertation, University of California Berkeley.
   2000   Searching for Third Genders: Towards a Prehistory of Domestic Spaces in Middle Missouri Villages. In *Archaeologies of Sexuality*. Robert A. Schmidt and Barbara L. Voss, eds. Pp. 197–219. London: Routledge.

Reeder, Greg
   2000   Same-Sex Desire, Conjugal Constructs, and the Tomb of Niankhkhnum and Khnoumhotep. *World Archaeology* 32(2):193–208.

Rega, Elizabeth
   1997   Age, Gender, and Biological Reality in the Early Bronze Age Cemetery at Mokrin. In *Invisible People and Processes: Writing Gender and Childhood into European Archaeology*. Jenny Moore and Eleanor Scott, eds. Pp. 229–47. London: Leicester University Press.

Rubin, Gayle
   1975   The Traffic in Women: Notes on the "Political Economy" of Sex. In *Toward an Anthropology of Women*. R. R. Reiter, ed. Pp. 157–210. New York: Monthly Review Press.
   1984   Thinking Sex: Notes for a Radical Theory of the Politics of Sexuality. In *Pleasure and Danger: Exploring Female Sexuality*. C. S. Vance, ed. Pp. 267–319. London: Pandora.
   1991   The Catacombs: A Temple of the Butthole. In *Leather-Folk: Radical Sex, People, Politics, and Practice*. Mark Thompson, ed. Pp. 119–41. Boston: Alyson Publications.
   2000   Sites, Settlements, and Urban Sex: Archaeology and the Study of Gay Leathermen in San Francisco, 1955–1995. In *Archaeologies of Sexuality*. Robert A. Schmidt and Barbara L. Voss, eds. Pp. 62–88. London: Routledge.
   2002   Studying Sexual Subcultures: Excavating the Ethnography of Gay Communities in Urban North America. In *Out in Theory*. Ellen Lewin and William L. Leap, eds. Pp. 17–68. Chicago: University of Illinois Press.

Saunders, Debra J.
   2004   The Homophobic Party. *San Francisco Chronicle*, November 9, B11.

Schmidt, Robert A.
   2000   Shamans and Northern Cosmology: The Direct Historical Approach to Mesolithic Sexuality. In *Archaeologies of Sexuality*. Robert A. Schmidt and Barbara L. Voss, eds. Pp. 220–35. London: Routledge.
   2001   Sex and Gender Variation in the Scandinavian Mesolithic. Ph.D. dissertation, University of California, Berkeley.
   2002   The Iceman Cometh: Queering the Archaeological Past. In *Out in Theory*. Ellen Lewin and William L. Leap, eds. Pp. 155–85. Chicago: University of Illinois Press.

Schmidt, Robert A., and Barbara L. Voss, eds.
  2000 *Archaeologies of Sexuality*. London: Routledge.
Seifert, Donna J.
  1991 Within Site of the White House: The Archaeology of Working Women. *Historical Archaeology* 25(4):82–107.
  1994 Mrs. Starr's Profession. In *Those of Little Note: Gender, Race, and Class in Historical Archaeology*. Elizabeth M. Scott, ed. Pp. 149–73. Tucson: University of Arizona Press.
Seifert, Donna J., ed.
  2005 Sin City. *Historical Archaeology* 39(1).
Seifert, Donna J., Elizabeth Barthold O'Brien, and Joseph Balicki
  2000 Mary Ann Hall's First-Class House: The Archaeology of a Capital Brothel. In *Archaeologies of Sexuality*. Robert A. Schmidt and Barbara L. Voss, eds. Pp. 117–28. London: Routledge.
Smith-Rosenberg, Carroll
  1979 The Female World of Love and Ritual: Relations between Women in Nineteenth-Century America. In *A Heritage of Her Own*. Nancy F. Cott and Elizabeth H. Pleck, eds. Pp. 311–42. New York: Simon and Schuster/Touchstone.
Solari, Elaine-Maryse
  1997 A Way of Life: Prostitution in West Oakland. In *Sights and Sounds: Essays in Celebration of West Oakland—The Results of a Focused Research Program to Augment Cultural Resources Investigations for the I-880 Cypress Replacement Project, Alameda County*. Suzanne B. Stewart and Mary Praetzellis, eds. Pp. 277–94. Sacramento: Submitted by the Anthropological Studies Center, Sonoma State University Academic Foundation, Inc., to the California Department of Transportation, District 4.
Sørensen, Marie Louise Stig
  1988 Is There a Feminist Contribution to Archaeology? *Archaeological Review from Cambridge* 7(1):9–20.
  2000 *Gender Archaeology*. Cambridge: Polity Press.
Taylor, Timothy
  1996 *The Prehistory of Sex: Four Million Years of Human Sexual Culture*. New York: Bantam Books.
Vasey, Paul L.
  1995 Homosexual Behaviour in Primates: A Review of Evidence and Theory. *International Journal of Primatology* 16:173–203.
  1998 Intimate Sexual Relations in Prehistoric: Lessons from the Japanese Macaques. *World Archaeology* 29(3):407–25.
Voss, Barbara L.
  2000a Colonial Sex: Archaeology, Structured Space, and Sexuality in Alta Califor-

nia's Spanish-Colonial Missions. In *Archaeologies of Sexuality*. Robert A. Schmidt and Barbara L. Voss, eds. Pp. 35–61. London: Routledge.

2000b Feminisms, Queer Theories, and the Archaeological Study of Past Sexualities. *World Archaeology* 32(2):180–92.

In press Looking for Gender, Finding Sexuality: A Queer Politic of Archaeology, Fifteen Years Later. In *Que(e)rying Archaeology: The 15th Anniversary Gender Conference*. Proceedings of the 37th Annual Chacmool Archaeological Conference. Calgary: University of Calgary.

Voss, Barbara L., and Robert A. Schmidt

2000 Archaeologies of Sexuality: An Introduction. In *Archaeologies of Sexuality*. Robert A. Schmidt and Barbara L. Voss, eds. Pp. 1–32. London: Routledge.

Warner, Michael, ed.

1993 *Fear of a Queer Planet: Queer Politics and Social Theory*. Minneapolis: University of Minnesota Press.

Weismantel, Mary

2004 Moche Sex Pots: Reproduction and Temporality in Ancient South America. *American Anthropologist* 106(3):495–505.

Whelan, Mary K.

1991 Gender and Historical Archaeology: Eastern Dakota Patterns in the 19th Century. *Historical Archaeology* 25:17–32.

Wilkie, Laurie A.

2000 Magical Passions: Sexuality and African-American Archaeology. In *Archaeologies of Sexuality*. Robert A. Schmidt and Barbara L. Voss, eds. Pp. 129–42. London: Routledge.

2003 *The Archaeology of Mothering: An African-American Midwife's Tale*. New York: Routledge.

Yates, T.

1993 Frameworks for an Archaeology of the Body. In *Interpretive Archaeology*. Chris Tilley, ed. Pp. 31–72. Providence, RI: Berg.

Archaeology, Men, and Masculinities   12

BENJAMIN ALBERTI

STUDYING MEN AND MASCULINITY in archaeology is a sticky proposition. While one's initial reaction may be, "Why of course! We must study masculinity alongside other aspects of gender," it quickly becomes apparent that it is not that simple. Feminist and gender archaeologies continue to reveal how "women" have been an invisible category in archaeological interpretation and history. "Men," in contrast, have always been visible, but their gender has been "unmarked." Their presence has been assumed—but assumed on the basis of a "neutral" body, unmarked by gender, race, or any other category of identity (Conkey and Spector 1984; Joyce 2004; Knapp 1998b:92; Nelson 1997:16; Wylie 1991). The genderless man comes to stand for society as a whole. The question then becomes, Can we "mark" men—give them a gender—without reinstating "man" as the universal historical subject, which would once again exclude women and subordinate men? Moreover, the inequality and violence that result from current ideas and practices associated with men and masculinity mean that to speak of "masculinity" is to invite engagement with the politics of knowledge.

The first part of the chapter considers the not entirely rhetorical question of whether we need an archaeology of masculinity at all. I argue that we need a critical study of past men and masculinities but that the framework for such studies is already in place. There is no need for a new subfield; such a move is potentially exclusionary. I further examine definitions of masculinity and point out that a certain degree of conceptual confusion exists. By disentangling such confusion, we can gain a better understanding of the ways in which masculinity and men have been understood in archaeological research. The next part of the chapter is an introduction to how men and masculinity have been understood and interpreted in archaeology. Most work on masculinity in archaeology must be inferred from general works or from work within gender archaeology. What clearly comes into focus is that issues around male bodies are at the forefront of recent work on masculinity. Ironically, this potentially presents a foundational challenge to the nascent studies of masculinity in archaeology.

A crucial issue that emerges from my discussion, addressed in the final part of the chapter, is the status of the category "masculinity." I suggest that "masculinity" or "men" may not always be the most appropriate interpretive frameworks. Indeed, the decision of whether to use the categories hinges on methodological and political concerns. I suggest two ways to proceed: either admitting the contingency of the category but using it anyway (a kind of "strategic essentialism") or being prepared to let go of the category and allow apparent ambiguity or difference in the material to drive interpretation. Borrowing a term from Fox (1998), I argue that reflexivity and the issue of "critical need"—the tension between what we want from our material and what it can tell us—should guide our decision on which path to take. The search for complete narratives of past social lives is more likely to efface differences by reproducing the historical male subject, whereas admitting the fragmentary nature of our material may prevent reification of the category "masculinity."

Do We Need an Archaeology of Masculinity?

Gutmann's (1997) observation for the status of studies of masculinity in anthropology still stands for archaeology: a quick perusal of indices in archaeological works may show women as an entry but not men. Instead, men's presence is assumed. Moreover, there are few works that focus explicitly on masculinity in archaeology. Regardless, this chapter is not intended to be a clarion call for "an" archaeology of masculinity; it is not "men's turn" (see Gutmann 1997:403). I advocate a more cautious approach by asking, Do we need an archaeology masculinity? I argue there are compelling reasons why it is important to study masculinity in archaeology. However, there are also important qualifiers, including interpretive and conceptual issues, such as whether there is anything we can recognize as "masculinity" in the archaeological record.

It has been widely recognized that accounts of past peoples have actually been accounts of normative masculinity (e.g., Conkey and Spector 1984; Scott 1997:8). Simultaneously, men have long been presented as gender neutral in archaeological accounts of the past. Archaeologists arguing for the inclusion of masculinities in archaeology echo this point, stating that to ignore masculinity is to leave the idea of an undifferentiated, universal "man" in place (Caesar 1999b:115; Foxhall 1998a; Joyce 2004; Knapp 1998b:92, 1998a). Caesar (1999b:115) states that "archaeology has neglected the complexity of masculinity and made the prehistoric man invisible through the stereotypical way of interpreting and representing the male sex." Others argue that focusing on women to the exclusion of men has had the unfortunate side effect of reinforcing the idea of a monolithic masculinity (Cornwall and Lindisfarne 1994; Knapp 1998b). Conceptually, therefore, there is a need to deconstruct the dominant concepts of "masculinity" and "man" as universal norms. Making past men's gender explicit reveals them as gendered subjects—rather than representing the whole of humanity, they can stand only for themselves.

Archaeological knowledge tends to reproduce an image of the contemporary dominant form of masculinity (see Caesar 1999a:133). The past is used as a repository of idealized archetypes that are called on by popular culture to reinforce essentialist ideas (see Joyce 2004). Caesar (1999b) points out that such "myths and stories" of man in prehistory then become active components in contemporary men's identity projects (e.g., the mythopoetic men's movement; Bly 1990; see also Middleton 1993). For example, essentialist arguments about the roots of men's aggressive sexuality that appear in the popular media use simplistic stereotyped notions of prehistoric gender arrangements to give their ideas the spurious credibility of time depth (e.g., Vedantam 2003). More sinisterly, nationalist and religious rhetoric frequently cites ideals of past male warriors and heroes (see Archetti 1998; Gutmann 1996; Mosse 1996). Thus, the "invisible man," the positive norm of masculinity in prehistory, is "a dynamic and active component in the present production of gender" (Caesar 1999a:115).

Making men's gender explicit has its own dangers. Hence, I argue that there is no need for a separate subfield ("the" archaeology of masculinity), as the necessary theoretical and conceptual frameworks are in place in feminist-inspired archaeology. Moreover, inaugurating an archaeology of masculinity has the potential to lend further solidity to an object ("masculinity") that, as discussed in this chapter, may not be a stable object of inquiry. The development of studies of masculinity in the social sciences and humanities disciplines (for overviews, see Clatterbaugh 2000; Connell 2000; Petersen 2003; in anthropology, see Gutmann 1997) has been met with skepticism by some feminists and pro-feminists (Braidotti 1994). For example, Solomon-Godeau (1995:76) signals the danger of approaching masculinity as a "newly discovered discursive object" when the fundamentals do not change but rather a newly expanded field for their deployment is offered. Moreover, as a simple "corrective" measure, it is flawed because the concepts of "men" and "masculinity" are already overvalued in Western society. Some authors have argued that the danger in creating a false equivalence between women's studies and men's studies is that men will once again be taken as representative of society as a whole (Hearn 2004; Solomon-Godeau 1995).

Carving out a disciplinary niche, or subfield, can be an aggressive process, setting up exclusions or effacements as "proper objects" (Braidotti 1994) of study are defined and boundaries are established. One of the founding fathers of the field known as New Men's Studies, Harry Brod (1987; see Cornwall and Lindisfarne 1994:29–30), reveals such a process. He argues that only men can truly understand men (Brod 1987) and ignores years of feminist scholarship, resulting in reactionary rather than critical theory and debate (Canaan and Griffin 1990; Hanmer 1990; Hearn 2004:63; Solomon-Godeau 1995:20). As Almeida (1996:143) remarks in the case of anthropology, without feminist theory and women's studies, "masculinity" would never have made an appearance on the research agenda.

Knapp (1998a, 1998b; see also Knapp and Meskell 1997) has argued for a "masculinist" archaeology informed by feminism. He states that we must include the work of "masculinist" writers partially as a corrective measure, to avoid a "gynocentric," "exclusionary, feminist world-view" (Knapp 1998a:365). In much the same way, Brod argues that "New Men's Studies can offer the necessary corrective to the 'female bias'" in feminist-inspired work (Cornwall and Lindisfarne 1994:30). The implication in both cases is that a "masculinist" perspective can challenge both androcentric and gynocentric accounts, whereas a feminist perspective merely replaces an androcentric account with a gynocentric one. Knapp's (1998a, 1998b) choice of terms is also curious; "masculinist" is not widely used in critical men's studies. In addition, it could be taken as unnecessarily antagonistic, its more common meaning being restricted to androcentric material and beliefs.

"Masculinist" perspectives have not caught on in archaeology. With Gutmann (1998:113–14), I agree that the inclusion of "masculinist" theory is not a prerequisite for either a feminist archaeology or critical studies of men and masculinity within archaeology. However, there are contributions to be made by the men's studies literature, as Knapp (1998a, 1998b) indicates. What are required, I argue, are both critical engagements with the concept of "masculinity" and the development of the means of conceptualizing sexual difference that go beyond the assumption of fixed binary categories of identity. Both these goals can be achieved through extant conceptual and theoretical frameworks within the discipline.

Defining Masculinity

There are two broad ways in which the category "masculinity" has been understood: as an "object" open to empirical analysis or as "configurations of practices" (Connell 1995, 2000). The status of the body is central to the distinction between these approaches. Practice-based approaches suggest the possibility that the category "male" is not beyond cultural intervention. Consequently, the categories on which contemporary studies of masculinity are founded may not be universally significant, in which case "masculinity" may not always be a relevant dimension of analysis in archaeological contexts.

Any interpretation of past social worlds implies an understanding of what "masculinity" means, although few authors define the term. That task is notoriously difficult—studies of men and masculinity are riddled with imprecise definitions (Connell 2000:15; Hearn 2004; MacInnes 1998; Petersen 2003). Authors frequently entirely ignore any attempt at definition, relying on implied or taken-for-granted meanings (Clatterbaugh 1998; Connell 2000:16; Gutmann 1997:385–86; Petersen 2003:58). Some of the confusion stems from whether you consider the term a descriptive or an analytical one. Problems arise when the two usages are seen as equivalent or are not clearly separated. If the term is purely descriptive, then to define masculinity is to best describe the attributes that epitomize masculine identity (i.e., a measurable list of qualities). This can lead to essentialist notions of masculinity in which certain key attributes are said to define what it means to be a man in all times and places. It quickly becomes apparent that any such description is limited to one time, one place, and one type of man. Consequently, masculinity is currently more commonly conceived of as an analytical category the content of which is culturally and historically specific. Masculinity consists of traits, behaviors, beliefs, expectations, and so on that are commonly associated with males in specific cultures and, when internalized, are a constitutive part of their identities. At the root of the term as it is conventionally used is the assumption that one's behavior reflects the type of person one is (Connell 1995:67). In effect, descriptions of masculinity often appear as a list of qualities said to characterize the category. Aggression, competitiveness, and emotional detachment are common core elements for contemporary Western countries (Petersen 2003:58), with variations of the list for other cultures. As a result, "masculinity appears as an essence or commodity, which can be measured, possessed or lost" (Cornwall and Lindisfarne 1994:12).

Even if used analytically, there remains the problem that this is a Western category of relatively recent genesis—a similar category that can be recognized as "masculinity" does not exist in many cultures (Connell 1995). Some have questioned, therefore, whether masculinity is generally applicable as a concept (Hearn 2004; MacInnes 1998). Others have argued that the inability to pin down a definition is because masculinity is not an object that can be studied empirically (Connell 1995). More recent theories of masculinity posit practice-based definitions in which the category is enacted rather than predefined by culture or society. For example, Connell (1995:44), a leading theorist in men's studies, understands masculinities to be "configurations of practice within gender relations." Ideas that have been developed to encompass this more flexible definition include "multiple masculinities," in which the term is relativized, and "hegemonic masculinity" (Carrigan et al. 1987; Connell 1987, 1995), which gets at power differentials among groups of men and between men and women as well as how the dominant form of masculinity (often elided as the way to be a man in popular discourse) maintains its position of social, economic, and political privilege. Rather than conceive of masculinity in terms of a fixed list of traits, these traits can be best understood as "tendencies and possibilities . . . that individuals have access to at different points in time" (MacInnes 1998:15). As such, there are many different notions of masculinity, often contradictory and in tension. Furthermore, in practice-based approaches, it is understood that "completely variant notions of masculinity can refer simultaneously or sequentially to the same individual" (Cornwall and Lindisfarne 1994:12).

At the heart of the tension between masculinity-as-object and masculinity-as-practice lies the sex/gender division, in which sex is a biological constant and gender is the meaning given to each sex by culture. This formulation has been challenged, opening up the category "male" to critique (see the discussion later in this chapter). Once "male" is challenged as a natural foundation for gender, it becomes hard to think of the category masculinity as universally applicable because the male–female binary is no longer a given. As Petersen (2003:58) points out, it is difficult to speak of masculinity without implying a binary notion of gender.

Archaeological Approaches to Masculinities

The following critical review of approaches to masculinity and men in archaeology reveals how the previously mentioned definitions of masculinity lie hidden in our interpretations of gender. Little of this work investigates masculinity directly. Therefore, I make explicit the understandings of masculinity implied in archaeological interpretation. I embed discussion of archaeological texts within a framework of research from other disciplines that address more directly questions of masculinity and include developments that are of interest to the archaeological study of masculinities. Also drawing from this work, recent research in archaeology brings the complexity of the category to the forefront, demonstrating the existence of a plurality of masculinities and forms of masculine identity formation. However, the underlying understanding of masculinity remains that of a quantifiable object. Other work has begun to challenge the stability and universality of the category "male," thereby exposing the interpretive limitations of the category "masculinity." What becomes clear is that it cannot be assumed that what we understand as "masculinity" is inherent in the material. Feminist-inspired theories of embodiment indicate how sexual difference may be explored without resorting to the categories "masculinity" or "male."

Work that focuses explicitly on masculinity includes general theoretical works (Alberti 1997; Caesar 1999a, 1999b; Knapp 1998a, 1998b; Knapp and Meskell 1997; Meskell 1996; Nordbladh and Yates 1990), investigations into the formation of specific masculine identities (Harrison 2002; Joyce 2000; Shanks 1996; Treherne 1995; Yates 1993), and critical research into classical masculinities (contributions to Foxhall and Salmon 1998a, 1998b; Shanks 1996). Historical periods have also produced archaeological research on masculinity (e.g., Hadley 1998a; Harrison 2002; Wilkie 1998). Furthermore, Harrison (2002) has explored experimental modes of presentation in the form of fictionalized vignettes, following the work of feminist archaeologists (e.g., Spector 1993).

"Universal Man": Essentialist Approaches to Masculinity

Essentialist approaches to masculinity have played a dual role in archaeology. First, most interpretations of masculinity in archaeology were essentialist until the advent of gender archaeology. Second, even though soundly critiqued, such approaches demonstrate the political role of interpretations of past masculinities. The search for certain key attributes of masculinity was part of the driving force behind early archaeological explorations. In terms of a framework for interpreting masculinity in the past, essentialism is limited by an inability to account for cultural or historical variation. Masculinity is seen as firmly rooted in an undifferentiated male body.

Essentialist approaches highlight key characteristics that are said to define masculinity. Irrespective of culture, history, or experience, the basis for men's behavior and identities is linked to hypothetically innate psychobiological structures, or cultural universals. Sociopolitical arrangements, such as the division of labor or organization of sexuality and reproduction, are considered epiphenomena of these innate gendered behaviors. These forms of determinism appear in many archaeological interpretations, often subtextually. They have their roots in post-Enlightenment thought and are coeval with the emergence of archaeology as a discipline. Essentialism has recently experienced a renaissance in the form of sociobiological arguments about genetically programmed behavior.

In the nineteenth and early twentieth centuries, masculinity was given a psychohistorical dimension. Protestantism and belief in scientific progress and knowledge encouraged a distinction to be made between nature and reason in which men and modernity were increasingly associated with the latter (Mosse 1996; Petersen 2003). Successful masculinity involved dominating base, animal urges through rational thought (see Connell 1994, 1995; Lloyd 1993; Seidler 1994). It was assumed that men everywhere faced the same challenge. Models of social evolution, proposed by Spencer, Morgan, and Tyler (see Trigger 1989), among others, in which human groups evolved through stages of increasing social complexity toward civilization implied a corollary psychohistorical model of the development of "mind." The psychic unity of mankind implied that all men had the potential for "cultured" (civilized) behavior and thought. Differences among men from different cultural contexts were of the nature of psychohistorical depth rather than due to individual or historicocultural difference. As such, nineteenth-century evolutionary models imply that "primitive" or prehistoric man reflected an earlier stage in the development of "modern man" both culturally and psychically.

There is an intimate relationship between masculinity and the emergence of archaeology as a discipline. The analytical structures used by archaeologists are embedded in post-Enlightenment thought, which is deeply complicit with nineteenth-century ideals of masculinity (Baker 1997:183–84; Hearn and Morgan 1990:4; Seidler 1989:2–4; Thomas 2004). This is clearly seen in the relationship among classical archaeology, contemporary ideals of masculinity, and theories of masculinity. Classical "man" was the focus of early archaeological work, the classical world being considered a gold mine of attributes of ideal masculinity, such as notions of reason, and questions of aesthetic judgment and idealized masculine beauty (Gutmann 1998; Mosse 1996). More directly, classical myths and philosophy were the inspiration for psychoanalytical theories of masculine sexual identity, including essentialist perspectives (Foxhall 1998b:2–3). Similarly, Harrison (2002) has shown how colonial ideal masculinity was consciously created through material culture. Harrison (2002) examines the manufacture of Kimberly spear points in northern Australia as a case of the mutual constitution of hybrid masculinities, those of the local Aborigine men and colonial collectors. The collector aspired to capture for himself some essence of the Aborigine man's "primitive" masculinity. An important project for future work on masculinity in archaeology, therefore, must be to critique the role played by archaeological knowledge in the contemporary identity projects of men (see Caesar 1999b).

Essentialist ideas about masculinity have reemerged in academia and in popular culture. The racism of early socioevolutionary theories has been replaced by evolutionary perspectives that root behavior in DNA and genes. This form of essentialism is particularly pervasive in popular scientific accounts of sexual difference (e.g., Baker 2000; Buss 2003). Common themes include exploring the genetic or socioevolutionary reasons for sexual behavior, violence, and hunting (e.g., Lovejoy 1981; Tiger 1969, 2000; Washburn and Lancaster 1968). There is little convincing evidence that genes or evolutionary adaptive behaviors predispose men to particular conduct or capabilities (for critiques of gender in human origins research, see Fedigan 1982; Hager 1997).

Essentialist ideas about masculinity are difficult to defend. Even if there are measurable, biological differences between men and women, trying to tie down such differences to specific conduct or capacities has proven unsuccessful (Connell 1995:46–52; Fausto-Sterling 1992). Similarly, the choice of "essence" is fairly arbitrary, depending on the theoretical leanings of the author in question (Connell 1995:69). In practice, essentialist approaches tend to focus on contemporary dominant ideals of masculinity (e.g., Gilmore 1990; see critique in Cornwall and Lindisfarne 1994:27). Archaeologically, we could only hope to find evidence of a fixed masculine "essence." Most essentialist work pre-dated the introduction of the sex/gender split into archaeology. As such, the essential attributes of masculinity were thought to emanate from within a clearly defined, universal male body.

Relativizing Masculinity: Social Construction

Social construction provided a way of thinking about masculinity that offered far greater flexibility. Most theories of social construction are based on the idea that sex and gender are two separate entities. Gendered identities and conduct are constructed by culture rather than existing within the body. Thus, variation in social arrangements and men's and women's roles cross-culturally can be explored. A limitation of this approach for exploring masculinity lies in the concept of gender used. Even though variation in "men" can be recognized, a form of essentialism remains in that the category "male" is unexplored.

A social construction theory of gender was adopted by archaeology in the 1980s (Conkey and Spector 1984) that opened the door for studies of masculinity in archaeology. However, such studies failed to materialize during this period. Given this paucity, the following is necessarily a schematic account. The meaning of "masculinity" is generally inferred rather than read directly from the texts. The focus in this section is on initial work within gender archaeology, which I inevitably falsely homogenize.

In the initial formulations of gender archaeology, "masculinity" referred to the actions and values habitually associated with males in a given culture (Conkey and Spector 1984). As such, masculinity can adhere to other people or things but must ultimately refer back to men. At times, "masculine" is used in a quantitative fashion: one can have more or less of it, as can things that are described as "masculine" (e.g., Osborne 1998). Therefore, "masculinity" can be treated as a clearly defined object that can be measured empirically and so is open to positivist approaches within archaeology (compare Joyce 2004). Material culture could be observed in association with evidence of a "male," leading to a quantifiable list of attributes that defined masculinity in that particular context. Mortuary studies, figurine analyses, and artworks were obvious realms in which such attribution could take place, as is the case with gender archaeology more broadly (Joyce 2004; Marshall 1995).

Gender was also conceived of as dichotomous, implying structural analyses: men's and women's activities could be inferred by the absence of that activity within the repertoire of the other sex. Similarly, symbolic analyses could be made by the association between "masculine" and "feminine" meanings and objects. A focus on gender "roles," combined with a general interest in materialist analysis (Voss 2000:182), and the ability to determine use wear on human skeletal remains lead to a number of studies focused on the division of labor. The relationship between material culture and gender was seen as one of reflection or ascription: particular activities, objects, and images were attributed to one or other gender. Those objects and activities then served to define "masculinity" or "femininity."

The concept of gender "identity" largely adopted in gender archaeology—that it reflects one's own feeling of being a man or a woman (Conkey and Spector 1984)—stems from work within psychoanalysis in the 1950s and 1960s, Robert Stoller (1964) being especially influential. In archaeological terms, material that is attributed to one or other sex—therefore assigning that sex a gender—is treated as the external manifestations of a stable, internal identity. Research on identity within men's studies and anthropology has also relied on Stoller's work (e.g., Gilmore 1990; Herdt 1987). Another influential source has been object-relations theories of identity formation, especially the work of Nancy Chodorow. Chodorow (1978) emphasized family dynamics as the root cause of masculine identity. She argued that boys are pushed to break their primary identification with their mothers, resulting in structures of personality that emphasize boundaries with people (see Connell 1995:20).

Chodorow's theories have been applied in archaeology to an innovative exploration of masculinity as a force for historical change. Caesar (1999b) proposes a general model of masculinity and social change based on the existence of separate male and female spheres of influence. When women attempt to occupy the male sphere, this results in the removal of the male sphere to a place where women do not yet have access, thereby maintaining male dominance and causing historical change. At the roots of her theory of gender dichotomy and hierarchy is Chodorow's notion of the boy abandoning identification with the mother (i.e., the female sphere) in search of a male object of identification. As such, masculine identity formation drives historical change.

Social construction allows for the analysis of a dynamic relationship between men and women. Gender archaeology has always focused on questions of power through the notion of gender ideology. Following Conkey and Spector (1984), gender ideologies are taken to be the meaning of male, female, sex, and reproduction in specific cultural and social contexts. In practice, ideology in gender archaeology has operated to include issues of power in a broad-based sense in which the genders interact much like classes. The relations that dominate are those between two large blocks. Often questions revolve around male domination and perhaps evidence for women's resistance and alternative ideologies (McCafferty and McCafferty 1998). Men often remain the undifferentiated dominant block or group. "Masculinity" becomes virtually synonymous with male domination (see Shanks 1996; Treherne 1995). In effect, masculinity is conflated with ideology, which is taken to be the material (often symbolic) manifestations of the undifferentiated group "men."

There are limitations to this formulation of gender. Social construction can result in a notion of gender that is static and normative. The taking on of a gendered identity through socialization or psychological development is uncomplicated and quasi-automatic. Masculine or feminine identities adhere to a man or woman through their life cycle. Questions remain concerning how to account for differences among men and for differences through the life cycle of one man. Moreover, the formulation fails to come to grips with the complexities of individual identity formation in which other categories of identity are implicated, such as race, class, age, and so on (see Meskell 2002). Men's studies authors working within this framework found that men never actually achieve "normal" masculinity, which begs the question whether these are norms at all (e.g., Metcalf and Humphries 1985). Rather, they would appear to resemble unattainable ideals. Commenting on this paradox, Connell (1995:70) asks whether the majority of men are therefore unmasculine. Even in the case of pseudo-Freudian (e.g., Stoller 1964) and object-relations theories of identity formation, in which internal conflict is at the root of the process, the assumption that there is a single structure common to the formation of masculine identity in all times and places straitjackets the theory within universalism and ethnocentrism, a criticism that has been leveled at some studies of masculinity within anthropology (e.g., Gilmore 1990; Herdt 1981, 1987; see also Cornwall and Lindisfarne 1994:32–33).

Other problems revolve around the conceptualization of "men" and "women" as dichotomous. Neither is implicated in the maintenance of the other, as they are essentially unitary and self-contained. This obscures the mutually constitutive or relational aspects of the creation of identity as well as the overlaps and commonalities between men and women (Cornwall and Lindisfarne 1994:36). Relations of power tend to be categorical: all men have power, and all women lack power. Even when questions of class are introduced into the equation, which they often are when addressing issues such as ideology, power still operates between homogeneous blocks of people.

An important limiting factor in this understanding of masculinity is the status of the body. It has been commented that fear of biologisms prevents the categories "male" and "female" from being scrutinized or considered as social constructions (Cornwall and Lindisfarne 1994:35–36; Moore 1994). In practice, sex and gender are often conflated in archaeology. Frustration has been expressed at the limitations of separately identifying sex or gender, leading some to suggest that an archaeology of gender is in fact an archaeology of sex (e.g., Marshall 1995; Sørensen 1992:35).

Multiple Masculinities: Disaggregating Men

The following work still fits within the general rubric of social construction but attempts to address some of the problems outlined in the previous section. The recognition of differences among men had previously been limited to the axes of cultural or historical difference. Research in men's studies, anthropology, and history introduced the idea that men also varied within cultures—there could be competing masculinities within a single cultural context. However, "masculinity" is still conceptualized as an identifiable, empirically measurable object residing in a "male" body. As such, the nature of the biological category "male" is not interrogated.

The weaknesses in conceiving of "man" as an undifferentiated, monolithic category in dichotomous relationship to an equally monolithic, undifferentiated "woman" quickly led to studies that began to consider variation both in terms of different kinds of men and in terms of how male subjects incorporate multiple influences in the process of identity formation. Knapp (1998a:93) has commented that the main contribution of men's studies literature to archaeology is to highlight the existence of "divergent, multiple masculinities." Historical studies have demonstrated both the contingent nature of masculinity and the plurality of forms of masculinities that exist, often side by side (e.g., Mosse 1996; Roper and Tosh 1991). Hadley, in an edited volume on masculinities in the medieval world, explores varying ideas about what men were in different historical contexts in order to "disaggregate the generality of the term 'men'" (Hadley 1998b:2) in the literature on the Middle Ages.

Historicizing the category "man" and introducing the idea of multiple masculinities breaks down the idea of men as a single oppositional category. However, it also risks producing a series of self-contained masculinities divided by race, class, sexuality, and culture. In men's studies, the concept of "hegemonic masculinity" was developed to account for relations of power and hierarchy among men as well as those between men and women (see Carrigan et al. 1987:89–100; Connell 1987, 1995; Kauffman 1994; in anthropology, see Almeida 1996). Hegemonic masculinity refers to how "particular groups of men inhabit positions of power and wealth, and how they legitimate and reproduce the social relations that generate dominance" (Carrigan et al. 1987:92). The concept has been fine-tuned to include analytic categories such as "subordinated masculinities" (e.g., homosexual men), men who are not the "frontline troops" of domination but benefit nonetheless ("complicit masculinities"), and men, often from other classes or races, who can as individuals embody the hegemonic form but lack social authority ("marginalized masculinities") (see Connell 1995:76–81).

In archaeology, the concept of "ideology," when given a gendered dimension, has sometimes been used in a broadly similar way. For instance, Robb's (1994) analysis of the development of inequality in prehistoric Italy bears a striking resemblance to Connell's formulation of the structure of hegemonic gender relationships. Robb (1994) argues for the existence of a single "male ideology" in the Eneolithic and Bronze Age in Italy. This ideology was initially used to justify male dominance over women but developed to support a male warrior elite's domination of a commoner class in the Iron Age. The same ideological model was used to justify the domination of both women and subordinate groups of men by an elite group of men. Likewise, Connell's work relies on the theoretical principle that "the relationships within genders are centered on, and can be explained by, the relationships between genders" (Demetriou 2001:343) such that the dominance of women by men provides the model or structure for the internal hierarchical ordering of masculinity and femininity.

Thinking of men's power and its ideological underpinnings in terms of the hegemony of specific groups of men or types of masculinity gets away from categorical notions of power. Connell's (1987, 1995) work on hegemonic masculinities has been developed further by Demetriou (2001; see also Archetti 1998), who, drawing on Gramsci's notion of "hegemonic bloc" and Bhaba's notion of "hybridity," formulates the concept of hegemonic masculinity as a "hybrid bloc" that unites practices from diverse masculinities rather than merely excluding or ghettoizing the subordinate and marginalized elements. The advantage of the author's approach is that it challenges the idea that masculine power is a closed, coherent and unified totality that includes no contradiction. Hybridity, Demetriou (2001) argues, leads to cunning transformations and the continuation of masculine hegemony.

The idea of a fixed, stable male identity has similarly been challenged by recognizing that the formation of the male subject is complex (Petersen 2003; Rogoff and Van Leer 1993). Object-relations theories of identity formation prioritize a unitary subject, defined by sex. Differences within a single gender category (through race, class, sexual orientation, and so on) are treated as add-ons rather than equally constitutive of the subject (see Cornwall and Lindisfarne 1994:32–33). Work by black, Chicano, and Asian men (e.g., Baca Zinn 2003; Espiritu 2003; Mac an Ghaill 1994) has led to the recognition that identity is an interpolation of differences. Similar ideas have been developed by archaeologists. Foxhall (1998a:1, 1998b) argues that a plurality of male selves existed in the classical Greek and Roman worlds. She argues that "each male self strives to be central" (Foxhall 1998a:1) by excluding others, such as effeminate men, slaves, and especially women, from the subject position. Excluded men and women have different positions in relation to the male subject. "Non-masculine" men may be derided, subjected to violence, and used as "anti-subjects" (Foxhall 1998a), but they are still men. They share a male body with their hegemonic counterparts. Subordinated men still collude with male power, whereas women's bodies disqualify them from ever becoming true subjects (Foxhall 1998b:4–5). The contributors to Foxhall and Salmon (1998a, 1998b) show clearly the nonunitary status of the category "masculinity" in antiquity.

Foxhall (1998a, 1998b) argues that the material culture and texts that constitute archaeological evidence in the classical world are complicit in the formation of ancient, male subjects. The monolithic facade—the appearance of coherence and wholeness—is an effect of reflexive male subject formation. The involvement of material culture in the active creation of dominant male subjectivity has been examined in other cultural contexts. Joyce (1996, 2000) takes figural and textual representations of male–male sexual practices in Classic Maya society as evidence of identification by a male audience with the powerful male bodies that are represented. Ritualized male bodies presented as powerful, youthful, and elaborately costumed were depicted in scenes representing all-male socialization events designed for exclusively male audiences. Joyce (2000) relates this imagery to a sexualization of masculinity and a generalized desire (by both men and women) for the male body rather than as evidence of stigmatized practices.

Bodies and the category "male" in fact occupy a slightly ambiguous status in the work on multiplicities and hegemony. On the one hand, this work shows that different bodies can be taken as evidence of different types of masculinity. For example, Foxhall (1998a:2) shows how effeminate men and slaves' bodies in the ancient world acted as antibodies. They displayed characteristics that were positively male but were negatively construed when used to typify an "Other," a non-hegemonic male. On the other hand, even though situated and marked by multiple facets of identity, the body and the sexed binary as fixed categories are still present. In men's studies, some of this confusion is revealed by Hearn's (2004) suggestion that we should be talking about "the hegemony of men" rather than hegemonic masculinities. Cornwall and Lindisfarne (1994:20) have pointed out that in their formulation of "hegemonic masculinity," Carrigan et al. (1987) elide the terms "male" and "masculinity," making that relationship seem natural and inevitable, in much the same way that sex and gender are often (unintentionally) conflated in gender archaeology. Other authors have recognized that masculinity formulated in this way becomes static, resulting in discrete blocks—groups of men and women—vying for dominance (Demetriou 2001:359; Hearn 2004:58).

Talking in terms of "masculinities" is an important step, but it does not automatically do away with masculinity as stable and unified—one simply has more stable, unitary subjects (see Dudink 1998:421). Furthermore, Petersen (2003:57) remarks that hegemonic masculinity has lost its dimension of power, simply standing for plurality or diversity. Connell has admitted that, in practice, masculinities tend to be posited as fixed "character types" battling it out for dominance (Demetriou 2001:347, n. 65). Definitions of masculinity become "additive" in the form of a fixed list of variables that are separate and relatively stable (Petersen 2003). In summary, sociological studies of men that focus on multiplicity and hegemony have added a typology of different men but have not challenged the status of the category itself (Cornwall and Lindisfarne 1994:2).

Deconstructing the Category "Male"

Essentialist and social construction approaches imply a stable object of inquiry, that there is such a thing as "masculinity" that can be measured or discovered in various cultural contexts. Social construction suggests that the specific form of masculinity may change through time but that the category itself is stable and in some sense predefined. The idea of a unitary category "man" has been challenged, but the essentialist categories "male" and "female" continue to provide the grounds for much archaeological research into gender. Recent trends in feminist-inspired archaeology and such areas as queer studies and explorations of sexuality have called into question these essentialist categories. Interestingly, the little research that deals explicitly with issues of masculinity in archaeology almost exclusively falls here, both theoretical surveys of the masculinity literature (Alberti 1997; Knapp and Meskell 1997) and specific case studies on masculinity in archaeology (Alberti 1997; Joyce 2000; Knapp and Meskell 1997; Treherne 1995; Yates 1993). I argue that the logical outcome of the critique of fixed categories is that "masculinity" becomes a highly problematic foundation for research. Consequently, I indicate research that enables us to work beyond the category yet still focus on sexed differences as an aspect of past identities.

The sex/gender division has been widely criticized for the way it essentializes sex, taken as a biological constant (Butler 1990, 1993:1–12; Grosz 1994, 1995; Moore 1994; Yanagisako and Collier 1987; in archaeology, see Alberti 2002; Joyce 2004; Meskell 1996; Nordbladh and Yates 1990; Yates 1993). Supporting social construction has led to ignoring biology as a field of inquiry. By equating sex with biology, sex and the body are seen as historically and culturally invariant. The category sex is merely a vehicle for gender. The result is that masculinity is seen as derivative of this supposed natural binary division of bodies. Furthermore, identity is thought of in terms of an internal "core" rather than as the result of active engagements with the material world (Alberti 2001; Joyce 2004).

It is widely argued that sex as much as gender is culturally constructed (see Meskell 1996). Bodies are understood and arranged according to historically and culturally specific meanings (e.g., Busby 2000; Lacqueur 1990; Strathern 1988). Anthropology has provided examples of this process, such as models of how gender can be a relational aspect of identity, in which neither masculine nor feminine essences "stick" to a body but rather pass between contextually sexed bodies (Strathern 1988). There is also evidence that, in some cultures, possession of a male body at birth is no guarantor that a child will physically develop into a male adult (e.g., Herdt 1987; Roscoe 1993). Historical studies into men's bodies also reveal that notions of male embodiment are historically contingent (Bourke 1996; Lacqueur 1990; Mosse 1996; Petersen 2003:64). As such, there are various culturally distinct ways of conceptualizing male bodies that may call into question "male" and therefore "masculinity."

The influence of culture on bodies—and the power of discourse to shape them—has been explored in archaeology through poststructuralist and practice-based theories, drawing from authors such as Foucault, Lacan, and Bourdieu, and feminist theories of embodiment, based principally on the work of Butler and Grosz (for overviews, see Joyce 2004; Meskell and Joyce 2003; Perry and Joyce 2001). There are two related ideas that run through this work that have implications for studying masculinity through archaeology: first, that bodies can escape simple sexed dichotomies, and, second, that sexual difference (and, by extension, genitality) is not always central to identity. The approach shares with other "postprocessual" work in archaeology an understanding that material culture is not just a passive medium but is actively involved in shaping human action and identity (e.g., Barrett 1988; Joyce 1998, 2001; Thomas 2000).

The limits of a binary understanding of sexual difference has been explored by Yates (1993), who has produced a densely theoretical account of the construction of male subjectivity in prehistoric Sweden. He used Lacanian and neo-Lacanian theories of the role of the body in the process of subject formation to reinterpret rock art from Göteborgs och Bohuslän. The images include representations of figure with swords, horns, and phalluses and other figures that lack these features. There are also representations of isolated calves, boats, and animals. Traditional interpretations had taken the rock art as evidence of an aggressive warrior society. Figures without weapons or phalluses were interpreted as women. According to Yates (1993:67), the formation of an aggressive masculinity resulted from certain body parts acting as "points of focus and intensity." He argues that there is no natural arrangement of the body or greater significance being accorded one part or another. Rather, society imposes an image of the body on the self, which then organizes desire and attachments. Masculinity is channeled through signs rather than being a basic property of the body. According to Yates, "Masculine identity must be guaranteed by signs applied to the surface of the body, and these signs are detachable—they do not inhere in the body, but can be separated from it" (66). He argues that identities are presented as aggressive masculinity versus ambiguity, where the second category could encompass either males or females. As such, he recognizes that a particular identity is not dependent solely on the absence or presence of genitals but rather requires other "detachable" signs to guarantee that identity. Yates's approach shares in common with Foxhall's (1998a, 1998b) work on male subjectivity a concern with how a unitary male subject is formed through the active exclusion of other possible subjects, whether male or female. This may be because both authors rely on theories of identity formation derived from Lacan, which tend toward a universal structure. The "achievement" of male subjective formation through separation and exclusion is also reminiscent of Gilmore's (1990) global model of the "achievement of masculinity" (see also Foxhall 1998b:7).

Yates has been critiqued for overrelativizing the body (Joyce 2004; Treherne 1995), a common criticism of poststructuralist theory. Connell (1995) argues that a wholly cultural account of gender is no more tenable than one based on biological determinism, as the body provides resistance to its inscription. He proposes the notion of "body reflexive practices" to bridge the gap between biological essentialism and extreme social constructionism. Connell (1995:61) argues that "bodies [are] both objects and agents of practice" and that the practices themselves form the social structures within which bodies are "appropriated and defined." In archaeology, Treherne (1995) develops a similar practice-based theory of masculine subject formation for Bronze Age European warrior societies. The warrior societies he describes show evidence that notions of beauty and the preparation and care for the body became central to male ideology during a general shift in Bronze Age Europe from a focus on communality to one in which masculine self-awareness is paramount. He argues that the body is an active part of the process of subjectification rather than being dominated by culture and language (Treherne 1995).

Treherne's work points to ways in which male identity is constituted through the interaction of bodies and material culture. However, what is missing from Connell's and Treherne's accounts is a sense of how the body can escape dualisms. Moreover, Treherne's interpretation can be criticized for being overly general and for arguing that the experience of violence is a universal constitutive element in male subject formation (Joyce 2004). The same criticism could be directed at Shanks's (1996) interpretation of proto-Korinthian imagery of hoplites.

The idea of "bodily reflexive practices" and the interplay between material culture and self-conscious subject creation are useful ways of looking at how "embodiment" is achieved. Combined with Yates's (1993:48–49) argument that the binary male–female is only one way of conceptualizing the structure of sexual identity, bodies are freed to signify in new ways. Approaches to embodiment in archaeology that draw on feminist scholarship are pushing in this direction. Central to this work is the recognition that material culture does not reflect certain categories of identity, or fixed, stable gendered divisions among people. Rather, material culture is intimately involved in the production of these categories. For example, Joyce (2004) has shown how embodiment is amenable to archaeological investigation through analyses of the connections among representations of bodies, bodily adornments that may imply physical alterations of bodies, and the development of subject positions within pre-Columbian Mesoamerican societies (Joyce 2001, 2004; Meskell and Joyce 2003). Joyce (e.g., 1998, 2001) investigates the actual process through which bodies become categorized as subjects—how they are materialized into categories—and the active role that material culture played in that process. Certain material items demonstrate a closeness and intimacy with the body that provide clues to their roles in the creation of ancient subjects. Images and representations of the body provided precedents that were called on in the reiteration of certain bodily practices. The result is a reconstruction of past subject positions that takes the materiality of their embodied existence seriously and fully integrates material culture into that process.

Questioning the universality of a binary structure to sex opens up the possibility that body parts other than genitalia may have had especial significance. For example, Alberti (2001, 2002) has noted that in Late Bronze Age Cretan art, a physical binary structure to gender is not a consistent aspect of the imagery. All bodies exhibit a similar hourglass body shape. The only clearly marked sexed characteristics are breasts, which appear in conjunction with certain clothing in the images, leading Alberti (2001) to suggest that sexed differences are only a transient aspect of categorical differences as presented in the art. In fact, thumbs appear to be of greater significance in the artwork than penises, which are entirely absent (Alberti 1997). Drawing on similar theoretical sources, Knapp and Meskell (1997) argue that androgynous figures and the lack of figures clearly represented as male among Chalcolithic (Cypriot Bronze Age) figurines is evidence that individuality was of greater contextual significance than group differences based on sex. In the case of Mesoamerican sculpture, Joyce (1998:160) recognizes hands rather than genitalia as the "bodily locus" of gender.

Deconstruction of the categories "male" and "female" has led to archaeological interpretations that stress the contingent and context-dependent formation of sexed categories and the active involvement of material culture in that process. However, bodies do not disappear when the categories are questioned. Rather, the focus moves from material culture as reflective of fixed categories of identity to one where material culture is constitutive of categories of identity. Furthermore, the terms of the debate are broadened to include the relationship between sexual difference and other forms of difference without assuming a priori that one is more central. Masculinity becomes a far less stable concept as a result. Suggesting that "male" and "masculinity" may not be relevant dimensions of analysis merely removes these objects, not the body or embodied experience of genitally differentiated bodies. Nonetheless, this work does suggest that there are logical limits to the use of "masculinity" as an analytical category.

Negotiating Masculinity

Arguing for the exclusion of "masculinity" as an a priori dimension of analysis is not merely an exercise in abstract thought. If the category is used—even when the objective is to "mark" men by giving them a gender—there is the possibility that it takes on the appearance of a universal structure. More nuanced understandings of "masculinities" do not guarantee that ideal forms will not reemerge. However, this need not mean that "masculinity" disappear entirely from interpretation. I argue there are two ways to proceed. Either the category is accepted and used as a kind of "heuristic fiction," or it is dispensed with entirely. The material evidence should drive the decision of which path to take. Adopting a reflexive approach by admitting the tension between the limitations of your material and what you desire from it may prevent the category from becoming reified.

Categorical Dilemmas

Cornwall and Lindisfarne (1994:2) argue that men's studies authors have consistently failed to dismantle categories that they take for granted. This is partly understandable. The antiessentialist critique creates quiet a dilemma for studies of masculinity, as "male" and "masculinity" can no longer be guaranteed to be universally present. An obvious reaction is the fear of erasing the categories altogether, one that I suspect is holding back men's studies from engaging fully with the implications of the poststructural critique of bodies (see Alberti 1997; Petersen 2003). This parallels Voss's (2000:186) comments on the reluctance of gender archaeology to fully critique sex, which would result in it having to relinquish its proper object, gender.

A further difficulty emerges when "masculinity" becomes the focus of inquiry, even in contexts where its presence can be assumed. At the beginning of this chapter, I stated that the concept "masculinity" must come under critical scrutiny to critique the idea of a monolithic man as well as to mark men as gendered. Ironically, this very strategy may have an undesirable side effect: by focusing attention explicitly on men, "masculinity" can become stabilized rather than destabilized. This process has been commented on in the case of historical works on masculinity, where the effort to "mark" the category has, paradoxically, led to it being reinforced (e.g., Dudink 1998, critiquing Mosse 1996). By showing masculinity as a specific historical category, it becomes stable and perhaps, once again, beyond history: "Apparently, wanting to write a history of masculinity by focusing on masculinity easily produces a perverse effect in that masculinity then quickly becomes a category of either incredible stability or a category that is somehow beyond history" (Dudink 1998:430).

The deployment of the term "masculinity" in archaeological work may be having the same effect. It is notable that the work produced to date has concentrated on violent men (e.g., Shanks 1996; Treherne 1995; Yates 1993; contributions to Foxhall and Salmon 1998a, 1998b; and work in sociobiology). A further tendency has been to conflate representations of idealized masculinity with masculinity in general. Masculinity, as it has been studied in archaeology, becomes exclusively associated with the ideal or normative form, hence losing its ability to differentiate among "masculinities."

Increased research on the connections between violence and masculinity, in both sociology and anthropology, is a crucial resource for archaeologists if we want to either disassemble the idea that masculinity and violence are synonymous or better understand that process. This focus on violent masculinity in archaeology is partly explained by the preponderance of representations of violent men as well as material culture to do with warfare. The nature of the material remains encourages a focus on images, burials, and "gendered" artifacts that suggest a connection between men and such activities, in which case we may be repeating a distortion left us by a struggle for hegemony among various forms of masculinity in the past, the hegemonic male subject leaving us evidence of his success (see Fox 1998; Foxhall 1998a). It is a mistake, therefore, to equate such evidence with a generalized masculine identity. A focus on men and violence has also privileged certain types of evidence and representations over others, leading to a lack of research on men who were not warriors, priest-kings, and the like.

If hegemonic masculinity maintains its position of privilege precisely by forcing out alternatives and declaring one type of masculinity as the normative and positively valued (in this case, violent men), then archaeology would appear to be unwittingly supporting this process by excluding alternative masculinities from research. Ironically, these alternative masculinities tend to be studied within other areas of archaeological research, including work on sexualities and queer studies.

Strategic Essentialism

Is it inevitable that when masculinity does come under scrutiny in archaeology, it restabilizes the category, lending it an air of being beyond history? Both abandoning the category altogether and continuing to use it as a heuristic device present difficulties. The former approach begs the question, With what do we replace "masculinity"? The latter runs the risk of falling foul of the tendency to associate positive values and power with the term, again subsuming marginalized or subordinated masculinities, not to mention women, however contingent the categories. Which approach is adopted should depend on the nature of the material under investigation. As such, I am in agreement with those archaeologists who contend that grand theories and overgeneralized frameworks tend to obscure rather than bring out the difference inherent in much archaeological material. A single, authoritative account of past social life is beyond our grasp (see Thomas 1996, 2000; compare Cornwall and Lindisfarne 1994:45–46). Theoretical and methodological models should be responsive enough to grow out of a hermeneutic relationship with the material evidence.

Even if masculinity is a relatively recent invention (MacInnes 1998), there is clearly cause for its use as a descriptive or analytical category in historical periods.

Dudink (1998:430) suggests that what is required is an "outflanking move" by not starting from the presumption of the historical presence of a thing identifiable as "masculinity." Dudink (1998:430) writes, "One should study around the object, questioning evidence that may or may not imply its presence; in other words, a history of masculinity that does not focus on masculinity." Such a backdoor route to studying masculinity may avoid restabilizing the category. Following this strategy suggests that we look for types of masculinities that may not be as exciting as warriors or kings. In other words, the pacifists, "stay-at-home dads," "wimps" and "layabouts" must come into interpretive focus. Contributors to Foxhall and Salmon (1998a, 1998b) have begun to address this issue for the classical world, as has Hadley (1998a) for medieval masculinities. Anthropology can provide concrete examples of practices that are not usually considered part of normative masculinity, such as alternative fathering roles, the couvade (e.g., Rival 1998), and homosexuality (e.g., Gutmann 1997:394–95; Herdt 1987, 1993). Simply recognizing the existence of practices that appear antithetical to normative masculinity (see Dowson 2000; Kimmell 1994) will broaden the terms of the debate (e.g., Joyce 2000; Voss and Schmidt 2000). In men's studies, Hearn (2004:50) argues that the category should be retained, but to avoid reifying it or refocusing our gazes exclusively on ideal forms, we should only refer to the category only in relation to women, children, other forms of masculinity, race, and so on. Locating masculinity in this way demands that attention be paid to explicitly situated subjects (see also Joyce 2004).

There will be many contexts in which the appropriateness of the category will not be clear. For example, to talk of "masculinity" in remote prehistory may make little sense. However, there is an argument to be made for its use as a heuristic device, or a "controlled fiction" (Strathern 1988). A common criticism of the antiessentialist critique is that political action becomes paralyzed if identity categories are destabilized. A response has been to use such categories strategically, employing them to achieve specific goals (Butler 1990; Petersen 2003:57). If used explicitly and critically, masculinity may serve a similar purpose in archaeological interpretation. A word of caution, though. Terms such as "queer" have been successfully strategically redeployed (see Butler 1993). But the category "masculinity" starts from a position of privilege, which puts it in a completely different relationship to power and knowledge. It is unclear whether it is possible to retain its use analytically without reinstating that same relationship of power in our interpretations.

A Methodological Corrective

The second possibility is to dispense with the category altogether. It has been remarked that archaeological evidence is inherently ambiguous (e.g., Knapp

1998a). A full critique of "masculinity" would take that ambiguity as a "tangible aspect" of the meaning of the archaeological evidence rather than a problem of methodology (see Alberti 1997; Yates 1993:47). One would not, therefore, start from the assumption that what we recognize as masculinity exists or that the analytical category "masculinity" is necessarily appropriate. Such assumptions could result in our trying to squeeze material into inappropriate interpretive frameworks. As argued previously, the sex/gender division implies a binary organization of bodies into male and female. Yates (1993) and Alberti (2001, 2002) have demonstrated how such an assumption can straitjacket the material, forcing a dualism and associated interpretations that are not inherent in the material.

To say that ridding ourselves of the category "masculinity" leaves us with few options to talk about "men" in the past would be disingenuous. Any mention of past identities is necessarily fragmentary, incomplete, and underdetermined by the evidence. Using terms that do not refer to a specific "masculine" identity but do refer to a sexed body—whether that sex is central to the identities represented or explored—is less likely to produce distortion than to redeploy a category that is heavy with meaning in the present but may not have had meaning in the past. Instead, identities and relations among persons can be built from the ground up using models that respond and are sensitive to the material in question (e.g., Joyce 2001; Meskell and Joyce 2003). Moreover, we should not expect all classes of material to be involved in every aspect of past life. For example, where monumental two-dimensional art may be involved in the enactment of power cut through with issues of hierarchy and dominance, it may not speak primarily to aspects of sexual identities. Similarly, burial goods and use-wear analyses of bones might indicate another level of interaction between things and people. Both are incomplete and will involve different usage of theory and different conceptualizations of the interrelationship between material and identity. For example, in a critique and reinterpretation of artwork from Late Bronze Age Knossos, Alberti (2001, 2002) argued that sexual difference was not central to the imagery. Consequently, the category "masculinity" seemed to be an imposition in talking about the art. This need not imply, however, that another body of material from the same period on Crete may not warrant mobilization of the category (bearing in mind the dangers of reification). Phallic imagery found at contemporary Cretan "peak sanctuaries" could indicate just such a possibility (see Peatfield 1992). Different material has different relationships to identity and sociopolitical structure, which begs for theoretical and conceptual flexibility and pluralism in approach.

Reflexivity and "Critical Need"

Studying masculinities in archaeology demands reflexivity on the part of the researcher to avoid interpretations that are reactionary rather than critical. Reflexivity refers to the process of acknowledging what it is that we want from the material and being aware of the standpoint from which knowledge is produced. Feminists and anthropologists have written on the importance of the politics of location (see Cornwall and Lindisfarne 1994:45), as have men's studies authors (e.g., Hearn 2004:62). Gender archaeology and postprocessual approaches have shown how knowledge claims are embedded in sociopolitical experience (Conkey and Gero 1991; Engelstad 1991; Shanks and Tilley 1987; Thomas 2000:3; Voss and Schmidt 2000). The gap between what our evidence says clearly and what we say of it is obviously considerable. Being open to the ambiguity of the material and to the possibility that masculinity is inappropriate for modeling past gendered lives addresses part of the issue. To further avoid exclusions inherent in the use of dominant categories, men's studies authors are following a feminist lead by calling for greater attention to be paid to the politics of knowledge and the need for reflexivity on the part of (especially male) researchers (Hearn 2004:62; Petersen 2003:55; see also Haraway 1988). Men, in general, have greater access to resources and are able to make their voices heard more easily than women, although this tendency is heavily mitigated by other aspect of social identity. This requires a degree of self-reflexivity when studying issues such as masculinity, itself so heavily involved in systems of inequality (see Hearn 2004). Men are notoriously bad at being reflexive, especially when they think they are good at being reflexive. Middleton (1993:11) has noted that "reflexivity works imperfectly for men because they don't see what they're seeing when they see themselves."

Fox (1998) has addressed the issue of reflexivity in archaeological investigations of masculinity. Even though he focuses his critique on interpretations of Athenian men, his commentary on what is at stake by attempting to study men while simultaneously not allowing the categories of "man" or "men" to eclipse historical difference has general implications. The example Fox (1998:7) examines is the thesis of the ancient Athenian as the "constrained man," proposed by Winkler (1990). Fox (1998:12) states that Winkler's enthusiasm for his object—Athenian man—led him to prematurely create a historical subject based on readings of texts without first asking what kind of subject the texts themselves were creating. In order to explain why this happened, Fox introduces the concept of "critical need"—how the desires that motivate research into past social worlds influence "the boundaries of what we study and the kinds of analysis we produce" (12). He compares the position of ancient historians who focus on gender to feminist critics who deconstruct the category "woman," the basis of the political goal that they wish to further. A parallel can also be drawn archaeologists who deconstruct the categories "man" and "woman." Echoing my argument, Fox states that "it is the insistence upon historical difference which will prevent the category of man from emerging" (12–13). Either we admit the contingency of our categories but readmit them because we consider them so important, hence dispensing with historicity, or we adhere to the goal of "reconstructing social realities" but with material that is so incomplete that clear "answers" are hard to come by (12–13). This is where "critical need" comes into play: our objectives in studying men are inseparable from the analysis. Drawing on Fox (1998:13), it may be that the category "masculinity" is present in our material only because of our desire to see it there. He argues that it is "a fantasy of narrative completion that motivates the attempts to produce a cohesive picture of the ancient self, when it is the cracks themselves which are a clear mark of a distinct historical character" (19).

Conclusions

Self-reflection on issues such as "critical need" may reduce what we say about the past, but it will also mitigate potentially destructive effects when addressing the study of masculinity. Moreover, ambiguity and uncertainty in the material may be the "cracks," or the "outflanking move," required to write a history of "men" through archaeology. Undeniably, research has successfully demonstrated the complexity wrapped up in the categories "man," "masculinity," and "male" for historical periods and in the classical world. Even so, Fox (1998) and Dudink (1998) alert us to the potential for such studies to lend greater solidity to a singular historical male subject, a process I suggest may be occurring in other areas of archaeology. Contexts that rely exclusively on nontextual evidence are even more vulnerable to imposing a category onto the material. As such, an important axiom to adopt, I suggest, is the willingness to admit that "masculinity" may not be salient in a given context. Even if we wish to afford it strategic value, I argue that there can be no archaeology of masculinity that is not simultaneously an archaeology of other historically situated and constructed subjects. The decision on whether to use the term will depend on each researcher's "critical need" and whether the local material and context warrant it.

Acknowledgments

Thank you to Sarah Nelson for providing an opportunity to develop my thinking around the issue of how to study men and masculinities through archaeology and for her patience and support. I am grateful to Rosemary Joyce for sending me unpublished work and for inspiration. My colleagues at Framingham State College provided valuable input in departmental seminars where some of these ideas were presented. Ira Silver and Lisa Eck gave continuous support and insightful commentary, for which I am hugely grateful. Many thanks to Ing-Marie Back

Danielson and Camilla Caesar, who searched for and sent materials. Thank you to Thomas Dowson and Cassie Richardson. Without Karen Alberti, this chapter would not have been completed.

References

Alberti, Benjamin
- 1997 Archaeology and Masculinity in Bronze Age Knossos. Ph.D. dissertation, University of Southampton.
- 2001 Faience Goddesses and Ivory Bull-Leapers: The Aesthetics of Sexual Difference at Late Bronze Age Knossos. *World Archaeology* 33(2):189–205.
- 2002 Gender and the Figurative Art of Late Bronze Age Knossos. In *Labyrinth Revisited: Rethinking Minoan Archaeology*. Yannis Hamilakis, ed. Pp. 98–117. Oxford: Oxbow.

Almeida, Miguel Vale de
- 1996 *The Hegemonic Male: Masculinity in a Portuguese Town*. Providence, RI: Berghahn Books.

Archetti, Eduardo
- 1998 *Masculinities: An Anthropology of Football, Polo and Tango*. Oxford: Berg.

Baca Zinn, Maxine
- 2003 Chicano Men and Masculinity. In *Men's Lives*. Michael S. Kimmel and Michael A. Messner, eds. Pp. 25–34. Boston: Allyn and Bacon.

Baker, Mary
- 1997 Invisibility as a Symptom of Gender Categories in Archaeology. In *Invisible People and Processes: Writing Gender and Childhood into European Prehistory*. Jenny Moore and Eleanor Scott, eds. Pp. 183–91. London: Leicester University Press.

Baker, Robin
- 2000 *Sperm Wars*. London: Pan Books.

Barrett, John
- 1988 Fields of Discourse: Reconstituting a Social Archaeology. *Critique of Anthropology* 7:5–16.

Bly, Robert
- 1990 *Iron John: A Book about Men*. New York: Addison-Wesley.

Bourke, Joanna
- 1996 *Dismembering the Male: Men's Bodies, Britain and the Great War*. London: Reaktion Books.

Braidotti, Rosi
- 1994 Radical Philosophies of Sexual Difference. In *The Polity Reader in Gender Studies*. Pp. 62–70. Oxford: Blackwell.

Brod, Harry
- 1987 The Case for Men's Studies. In *The Making of Masculinities: The New Men's Studies*. Harry Brod, ed. Pp. 39–62. Winchester: Allen and Unwin.

Busby, Cecilia
  2000 *The Performance of Gender: An Anthropology of Everyday Life in a South Indian Fishing Village.* London: Athlone Press.
Buss, David
  2003 *The Evolution of Desire: Strategies of Human Mating.* Philadelphia: Basic Books.
Butler, Judith
  1990 *Gender Trouble: Feminism and the Subversion of Identity.* London: Routledge.
  1993 *Bodies That Matter: On the Discursive Limits of Sex.* London: Routledge.
Caesar, Camilla
  1999a The Construction of Masculinity—The Driving Force of History: A New Way of Understanding Change in the Past. *Lund Archaeological Review* 5:117–36.
  1999b Urmannen—Den Osynliga Normen: Maskulinitetsforskning Inom Arkeologin [The Ancient Man—The Invisible Norm]. In *Han Hon Den Det: Att Integrera Genus Och Kön i Arkeologi.* Camilla Caeser, Ingrid Gustin, Elisabeth Iregren, Bodil Petersson, Elisabeth Rudebeck, Eriak Räf, and Louise Ströbeck, eds. Pp. 115–25. Institute of Archaeology Report Series 65. Lund: University of Lund.
Canaan, Joyce, and Christine Griffin
  1990 The New Men's Studies: Part of the Problem or Part of the Solution? In *Men, Masculinities and Social Theory.* Jeff Hearn and David Morgan, eds. Pp. 206–14. London: Unwin Hyman.
Carrigan, Tim, Bob Connell, and John Lee
  1987 Toward a New Sociology of Masculinity. In *The Making of Masculinities: The New Men's Studies.* Harry Brod, ed. Pp. 63–100. Winchester: Allen and Unwin.
Chodorow, Nancy
  1978 *The Reproduction of Mothering: Psychoanalysis and the Sociology of Gender.* Berkeley: University of California Press.
Clatterbaugh, Kenneth
  1998 What Is Problematic about Masculinities? *Men and Masculinities* 1(1):24–45.
  2000 Literature of the U.S. Men's Movements. *Signs: Journal of Women in Culture and Society* 25(3):883–94.
Conkey, Margaret, and Joan Gero
  1991 Tensions, Pluralities and Engendering Archaeology: Women and Prehistory. In *Engendering Archaeology.* Joan Gero and Margaret Conkey, eds. Pp. 3–30. Oxford: Basil Blackwell.
Conkey, Margaret, and Janet Spector
  1984 Archaeology and the Study of Gender. In *Advances in Archaeological Method and Theory.* Vol. 7. Michael Schiffer, ed. Pp. 1–38. New York: Academic Press.
Connell, Robert
  1987 *Gender and Power.* Cambridge: Polity Press.

    1994   Psychoanalysis on Masculinity. In *Theorizing Masculinities*. Harry Brod and Michael Kaufman, eds. Pp. 11–38. Thousand Oaks, CA: Sage.
    1995   *Masculinities*. Berkeley: University of California Press.
    2000   *The Men and the Boys*. Berkeley: University of California Press.

Cornwall, Andrea, and Nancy Lindisfarne
    1994   Dislocating Masculinity: Gender, Power, and Anthropology. In *Dislocating Masculinity: Comparative Ethnographies*. Andrea Cornwall and Nancy Lindisfarne, eds. Pp. 11–47. London: Routledge.

Demetriou, Demetrakis Z.
    2001   Connell's Concept of Hegemonic Masculinity: A Critique. *Theory and Society* 30:337–61.

Dowson, Thomas
    2000   Why Queer Archaeology? An Introduction. *World Archaeology* 32(2):161–65.

Dudink, Stefan
    1998   The Trouble with Men: Problems in the History of "Masculinity." *European Journal of Cultural Studies* 1(3):419–31.

Engelstad, Erika
    1991   Feminist Theory and Post-Processual Archaeology. In *The Archaeology of Gender*. Proceedings of the 22nd Annual Chacmool Conference. Dale Walde and Noreen D. Willows, eds. Pp. 116–20. Calgary: Department of Archaeology, University of Calgary.

Espiritu, Yen Le
    2003   All Men Are *Not* Created Equal: Asian Men in U.S. History. In *Men's Lives*. Michael S. Kimmel and Michael A. Messner, eds. Pp. 35–44. Boston: Allyn and Bacon.

Fausto-Sterling, Anne
    1992   *Myths of Gender: Biological Theories about Women and Men*. New York: Basic Books.

Fedigan, Linda
    1982   *Primate Paradigms: Sex Roles and Social Bonds*. Montreal: Eden Press.

Fox, Matthew
    1998   The Constrained Man. In *Thinking Men: Masculinity and Its Self-Representation in the Classical Tradition*. Lin Foxhall and John Salmon, eds. Pp. 6–22. London: Routledge.

Foxhall, Lin
    1998a   Introduction. In *Thinking Men: Masculinity and Its Self-Representation in the Classical Tradition*. Lin Foxhall and John Salmon, eds. Pp. 1–5. London: Routledge.
    1998b   Introduction. In *When Men Were Men: Masculinity, Power, and Identity in Classical Antiquity*. Lin Foxhall and John Salmon, eds. Pp. 1–9. London: Routledge.

Foxhall, Lin, and John Salmon, eds.
    1998a   *Thinking Men: Masculinity and Its Self-Representation in the Classical Tradition*. London: Routledge.

1998b When Men Were Men: Masculinity, Power, and Identity in Classical Antiquity. London: Routledge.

Gilmore, David
1990 Manhood in the Making: Cultural Concepts of Masculinity. New Haven, CT: Yale University Press.

Grosz, Elizabeth
1994 Volatile Bodies: Toward a Corporeal Feminism. Bloomington: Indiana University Press.
1995 Space, Time and Perversion: Essays on the Politics of Bodies. London: Routledge.

Gutmann, Matthew
1996 The Meanings of Macho: Being a Man in Mexico City. Berkeley: University of California Press.
1997 Trafficking in Men: The Anthropology of Masculinity. Annual Review of Anthropology 26:385–409.
1998 Do We Need "Masculinist" (Manly?) Defenses of Feminist Archaeology? Archaeological Dialogues 5(2):112–15.

Hadley, Dawn, ed.
1998a Masculinity in Medieval Europe. London: Longman.

Hadley, Dawn
1998b Medieval Masculinities. In Masculinity in Medieval Europe. Dawn Hadley, ed. Pp. 1–18. London: Longman.

Hager, Lori D., ed.
1997 Women in Human Evolution. London: Routledge.

Hanmer, Jalna
1990 Men, Power and the Exploitation of Women. Women's Studies International Forum 13(5):443–56.

Haraway, Donna
1988 Situated Knowledge: The Science Question in Feminism as a Site of Discourse on the Privilege of Partial Perspective. Feminist Studies 14(3):575–99.

Harrison, Rodney
2002 Archaeology and the Colonial Encounter: Kimberley Spearpoints, Cultural Identity and Masculinity in the North of Australia. Journal of Social Archaeology 2(3):352–77.

Hearn, Jeff
2004 From Hegemonic Masculinity to the Hegemony of Men. Feminist Theory 5(1):49–72.

Hearn, Jeff, and David Morgan
1990 Men Masculinities and Social Theory. In Men, Masculinities and Social Theory. Jeff Hearn and David Morgan, eds. Pp. 1–17. London: Unwin Hyman.

Herdt, Gilbert
1981 Guardians of the Flute: Idioms of Masculinity. Chicago: University of Chicago Press.

    1987   *The Sambia: Ritual and Gender in New Guinea.* New York: Holt, Rinehart and Winston.
Herdt, Gilbert, ed.
    1993   *Third Sex, Third Gender: Beyond Sexual Dimorphism in Culture and History.* New York: Zone Books.
Joyce, Rosemary
    1996   The Construction of Gender in Classic Maya Monuments. In *Gender in Archaeology: Essays in Research and Practice.* Rita Wright, ed. Pp. 167–95. Philadelphia: University of Pennsylvania Press.
    1998   Performing Gender in Pre-Hispanic Central America: Ornamentation, Representation and the Construction of the Body. *RES: Anthropological Aesthetics* 33:147–65.
    2000   A Precolumbian Gaze: Male Sexuality among the Ancient Maya. In *Archaeologies of Sexuality.* Barbara L. Voss and Robert A. Schmidt, eds. Pp. 263–83. London: Routledge.
    2001   *Gender and Power in Prehispanic Mesoamerica.* Austin: University of Texas Press.
    2004   Embodied Subjectivity: Gender, Femininity, Masculinity, Sexuality. In *Blackwell Companion to Social Archaeology.* Lynn Meskell and Robert Preucel, eds. Pp. 82–95. Oxford: Blackwell.
Kauffman, Michael
    1994   Men, Feminism, and Men's Contradictory Experiences of Power. In *Theorizing Masculinities.* Harry Brod and Michael Kaufman, eds. Pp. 142–63. Thousand Oaks, CA: Sage.
Kimmell, Michael S.
    1994   Masculinity as Homophobia: Fear, Shame, and Silence in the Construction of Gender Identity. In *Theorizing Masculinities.* Harry Brod and Michael Kaufman, eds. Pp. 119–41. Thousand Oaks, CA: Sage.
Knapp, A. Bernard
    1998a   Boys Will Be Boys: Masculinist Approaches to a Gendered Archaeology. In *Reader in Gender Archaeology.* Kelley Hays-Gilpin and David S. Whitley, eds. Pp. 365–73. London: Routledge.
    1998b   Who's Come a Long Way Baby? Masculinist Approaches to a Gendered Archaeology. *Archaeological Dialogues* 5(2):91–106.
Knapp, A. Bernard, and Lynn Meskell
    1997   Bodies of Evidence on Prehistoric Cyprus. *Cambridge Archaeological Journal* 7(2):183–204.
Laqueur, Thomas
    1990   *Making Sex: Body and Gender from the Greeks to Freud.* Cambridge, MA: Harvard University Press.
Lloyd, Genevieve
    1993   *The Man of Reason: "Male" and "Female" in Western Philosophy.* St. Paul: University of Minnesota Press.

Lovejoy, C. Owen
  1981   The Origins of Man. *Science* 211:341–50.
Mac an Ghaill, Mairtin
  1994   The Making of Black English Masculinities. In *Theorizing Masculinities*. Harry Brod and Michael Kaufman, eds. Pp. 183–99. Thousand Oaks, CA: Sage.
MacInnes, John
  1998   *End of Masculinity*. Buckingham: Open University Press.
Marshall, Yvonne
  1995   Why Do We Need Feminist Theory? Paper presented at the Institute of Field Archaeologists Annual Conference, Bradford, April 11–13.
McCafferty, Sharisse D., and Geoffrey G. McCafferty
  1998   Spinning and Weaving as Female Gender Identity in Post-Classic Mexico. In *Reader in Gender Archaeology*. Kelley Hays-Gilpin and David S. Whitley, eds. Pp. 213–30. London: Routledge.
Meskell, Lynn
  1996   The Somatization of Archaeology: Institutions, Discourses, Corporeality. *Norwegian Archaeological Review* 29(1):1–16.
  2002   The Intersections of Identity and Politics in Archaeology. *Annual Review of Anthropology* 31:279–301.
Meskell, Lynn, and Rosemary A. Joyce
  2003   *Embodied Lives: Figuring Ancient Maya and Egyptian Experience*. London: Routledge.
Metcalf, Andy, and Martin Humphries, eds.
  1985   *The Sexuality of Men*. London: Pluto Press.
Middleton, Peter
  1993   *The Inward Gaze: Masculinity and Subjectivity in Modern Culture*. London: Routledge.
Moore, Henrietta L.
  1994   *A Passion for Difference: Essays in Anthropology and Gender*. Cambridge: Polity Press.
Mosse, George L.
  1996   *The Image of Man: The Creation of Modern Masculinities*. New York: Oxford University Press.
Nelson, Sarah
  1997   *Gender in Archaeology: Analyzing Power and Prestige*. Walnut Creek, CA: AltaMira Press.
Nordbladh, Jarl, and Timothy Yates
  1990   This Perfect Body, This Virgin Text: Between Sex and Gender in Archaeology. In *Archaeology after Structuralism*. Ian Bapty and Timothy Yates, eds. Pp. 222–37. London: Routledge.
Osborne, Robin
  1998   Sculpted Men of Athens: Masculinity and Power in the Field of Vision. In *Thinking Men: Masculinity and Its Self-Representation in the Classical Tradition*. Lin Foxhall and John Salmon, eds. Pp. 23–42. London: Routledge.

Peatfield, Alan
    1992   Rural Ritual in Bronze Age Crete: The Peak Sanctuary at Atsipadhes. *Cambridge Archaeological Journal* 2(1):59–87.

Perry, Elizabeth M., and Rosemary A. Joyce
    2001   Providing a Past for *Bodies That Matter*: Judith Butler's Impact on the Archaeology of Gender. Theme Issue, "Butler Matters: Judith Butler's Impact on Feminist and Queer Studies since *Gender Trouble*," *International Journal of Sexuality and Gender Studies* 6(1–2):63–76.

Petersen, Alan
    2003   Research on Men and Masculinities: Some Implications of Recent Theory for Future Work. *Men and Masculinities* 6(1):54–69.

Rival, Laura
    1998   Androgynous Parents and Guest Children: The Huaorani Couvade. *Journal of the Royal Anthropological Institute* 4(3):619–42.

Robb, John
    1994   Gender Contradictions, Moral Coalitions, and Inequality in Prehistoric Italy. *Journal of European Archaeology* 2(1):20–49.

Rogoff, Irit, and David Van Leer
    1993   Afterthoughts . . . A Dossier on Masculinities. *Theory and Society* 22(5): 731–62.

Roper, Michael, and John Tosh, eds.
    1991   *Manful Assertions: Masculinities in Britain since 1800*. London: Routledge.

Roscoe, Will
    1993   How to Become a Berdache: Toward a Unified Analysis. In *Third Sex, Third Gender: Beyond Sexual Dimorphism in Culture and History*. Gilbert Herdt, ed. Pp. 329–72. New York: Zone Books.

Scott, Eleanor
    1997   Introduction: On the Incompleteness of Archaeological Narratives. In *Invisible People and Processes: Writing Gender and Childhood into European Archaeology*. Jenny Moore and Eleanor Scott, eds. Pp. 1–12. London: Leicester University Press.

Seidler, Victor
    1989   *Rediscovering Masculinity: Reason, Language and Sexuality*. London: Routledge.
    1994   *Unreasonable Men: Masculinity and Social Theory*. London: Routledge.

Shanks, Michael
    1996   Style and the Design of a Perfume Jar from an Archaic Greek City State. In *Contemporary Archaeology in Theory: A Reader*. Robert W. Preucel and Ian Hodder, eds. Pp. 364–93. Oxford: Blackwell.

Shanks, Michael, and Christopher Tilley
    1987   *Reconstructing Archaeology: Theory and Practice*. Cambridge: Cambridge University Press.

Solomon-Godeau, Abigail
    1995   Male Trouble. In *Constructing Masculinity*. Maurice Berger, Brian Wallis, and Simon Watson, eds. Pp. 69–76. London: Routledge.

Sørensen, Marie Louise Stig
    1992   Gender Archaeology and Scandinavian Bronze Age Studies. *Norwegian Archaeological Review* 25(1):31–49.

Spector, Janet
    1993   *What This Awl Means: Feminist Archaeology at a Wahpeton Dakota Village*. St. Paul: Minnesota Historical Society Press.

Stoller, Robert
    1964   A Contribution to the Study of Gender Identity. *International Journal of Psychoanalysis* 45:220–26.

Strathern, Marilyn
    1988   *The Gender of the Gift: Problems with Women and Problems with Society in Melanesia*. Berkeley: University of California Press.

Thomas, Julian
    1996   *Time, Culture and Identity: An Interpretive Archaeology*. London: Routledge.
    2000   Introduction: The Polarities of Post-Processual Archaeology. In *Interpretive Archaeology: A Reader*. Julian Thomas, ed. Pp. 1–18. London: Leicester University Press.
    2004   *Archaeology and Modernity*. London: Routledge.

Tiger, Lionel
    1969   *Men in Groups*. New York: Random House.
    2000   *The Decline of Males: The First Look at an Unexpected New World for Men and Women*. New York: St. Martin's Press.

Treherne, Paul
    1995   The Warrior's Beauty: The Masculine Body and Self-Identity in Bronze Age Europe. *Journal of European Archaeology* 3(1):105–44.

Trigger, Bruce
    1989   *A History of Archaeological Thought*. Cambridge: Cambridge University Press.

Vedantam, Shankar
    2003   Desire and DNA: Is Promiscuity Innate? New Study Sharpens Debate on Men, Sex and Gender Roles. *Washington Post*, August 1: A01.

Voss, Barbara L.
    2000   Feminisms, Queer Theories, and the Archaeological Study of Past Sexualities. *World Archaeology* 32(2):180–92.

Voss, Barbara L., and Robert A. Schmidt
    2000   Archaeologies of Sexuality: An Introduction. In *Archaeologies of Sexuality*. Robert A. Schmidt and Barbara L. Voss, eds. Pp. 1–32. London: Routledge.

Washburn, Sherwood, and C. S. Lancaster
    1968   The Evolution of Hunting. In *Man the Hunter*. R. B. Lee and Irvine DeVore, eds. Pp. 293–303. Chicago: Aldine.

Wilkie, Laurie
    1998   The Other Gender: The Archaeology of an Early 20th Century Fraternity. *Proceedings of the Society for California Archaeology* 11:7–11.

Winkler, John J.
    1990   *The Constraints of Desire: The Anthropology of Sex and Desire in Ancient Greece*. London: Routledge.

Wylie, Alison
    1991   Gender Theory and the Archaeological Record: Why Is There No Archaeology of Gender? In *Engendering Archaeology*. Margaret Conkey and Joan Gero, eds. Pp. 31–54. Oxford: Basil Blackwell.

Yanagisako, Sylvia, and Jane Collier
    1987   Toward a Unified Analysis of Gender and Kinship. In *Gender and Kinship*. Jane Collier and Sylvia Yanagisako, eds. Pp. 1–50. Stanford, CA: Stanford University Press.

Yates, Timothy
    1993   Frameworks for an Archaeology of the Body. In *Interpretative Archaeology*. Christopher Tilley, ed. Pp. 31–72. Oxford: Berg.

The Archaeology of Nonbinary Genders in Native North American Societies

13

SANDRA E. HOLLIMON

IN THE TWENTY YEARS since the publication of Conkey and Spector's (1984) groundbreaking work on gender and archaeology, the examination of systems of multiple genders in the archaeological record has grown. Some theoretical advances in the realms of gender, sexuality, and identity construction have provided archaeologists with new conceptual approaches to their analyses. Following the feminist critiques of science in general and archaeological theory in particular, researchers have continued to debate the meanings and manifestations of gender in the archaeological record (Voss and Schmidt 2000:14–18; Wylie 2002:185–99). Many of the recent discussions can be found in the seminal volume *Archaeologies of Sexuality* (Schmidt and Voss 2000) and in Voss (this volume). The developing approaches in archaeology that employ sexuality, performance, and queer theory are described fully in Voss (2000, 2005) and Perry and Joyce (2001). Therefore, in this chapter, I confine my discussion to the archaeological investigation of nonbinary genders in Native North American societies, north of the present Mexico–U.S. border.

Ethnographic and ethnohistoric information from Native North American societies provides evidence of nonbinary third and fourth genders, in addition to the binary genders of "woman" and "man," as defined by the specific culture. For the purposes of this discussion, third genders are expressed by individuals who are biologically male but culturally not men. Fourth genders are expressed by persons who are biologically female, but are not recognized in their societies as women. If we recognize sex as a category of bodies and gender as a category of persons, we can better understand Native North American gender systems in which individual, acquired, and ascribed traits are more important in determining gender identity than biological sex assignment (Roscoe 1998:127). These systems frequently based gender on other variables than (but not necessarily exclusive of) biologically based primary and secondary sexual characteristics. Variables such as temperament, skill or preference for work, spiritual endowment, and reproductive status appear to have been more important gender markers for nonbinary persons than for normative women and men. I use the term "normative" advisedly, for I believe that it is somewhat misleading. What some anthropologists have called supernumerary or multiple genders are equally as normative as the two categories recognized in binary gender systems.

It has been suggested that nonbinary genders have a great time depth and were most likely recognized by the original colonizing groups of North America that migrated from northeastern Asia (Hollimon 2001b:123–24; Kirkpatrick 2000:397). Therefore, archaeologists who study the material record of Native North American groups should consider nonbinary genders in their interpretations of these social systems (see also Callender and Kochems 1983:444–46; Roscoe 1998:202–3). It is an astute criticism to note that the ethnographic data do not provide detailed information on gender roles in every instance. Nevertheless, the near ubiquity of nonbinary genders in Native American societies suggests that absence of evidence for these genders in some groups (e.g., the Northeast culture area) should not be read as evidence of absence.

The studies that mention ethnographically documented nonbinary genders in their interpretations of archaeological data continue to grow (e.g., Pate 2004). However, some do not necessarily address specific analytical approaches for identifying third and fourth genders at the outset; rather, they consider the possibility somewhat after the fact. In the remainder of this chapter, I discuss examples of some of the approaches that archaeologists have employed to examine nonbinary genders in Native North American societies. I also provide some suggestions about methods that could be employed in future research.

Gender and Other Social Identities

Meskell (2001, 2002) has discussed the overlapping axes of identity and how one can study them archaeologically. She makes the very important point that it may not be possible or even appropriate to try to disentangle the various aspects of "selfhood, embodiment, and being" that derived from gender, sexuality, ethnicity, status, and age (Meskell 2002:281; see also the following discussion). In particular, the role of age in the formation, maintenance, and performance of gender identity is of increasing interests to archaeologists (e.g., Gilchrist 2000).

The covariation of gender identity and age is culturally constructed, just as are all aspects of personhood. In some societies, full human status is not granted to juveniles until a particular milestone has been passed, whether that is weaning, walking, attending school, menarche, marking a significant birthday (e.g., thirteen, sixteen, eighteen, or twenty-one years), formal initiation, marriage, or becoming a parent. These rites of passage may be the most important arenas of gender marking in a culture, especially the passage between adolescence and adulthood. Cross-culturally, the attainment of adulthood includes instruction in the proper conduct expected of adults in the given society. As such, women learn their culturally expected roles and duties, as do men. It can also be seen cross-culturally that gender roles, behaviors, and identities, especially concerning child rearing, are emphasized in this rite of passage. However, it may be only during this passage, which is frequently followed shortly by marriage for girls or young women, that gender is strongly marked.

In many prehistoric Native American societies, it may have been that women and men did not require gender marking across the entire life cycle but that nonbinary gendered persons had their gender more strongly marked during everyday lived experience. This idea, based on Bourdieu's (1977) practice theory, explains that the quotidian activities of daily life form the material patterns that archaeologists study. Perhaps archaeologists can identify distinctive dress and ornamentation, labor practices or products, or changes to the skeleton that are distinctive of nonbinary genders.

If gender signification can vary among the genders recognized by a culture, then it can also vary throughout the life cycle as mentioned previously. The final rite of passage, death, may emphasize a person's identity in a way akin to a "final statement." Mortuary analyses by definition deal with the material correlates of behaviors exhibited by living persons at the end point of another's (physical) life. However, gender is only one aspect of identity among many that can be signified.

This idea presents interesting interpretive challenges for archaeologists who examine mortuary practices. As such, they may be severely limited in detecting and interpreting gender across the entire life course because they sample only a restricted point of time in an individual's (and community's) existence. An excellent example of overcoming this obstacle is the work of Schmidt (2000, 2001, 2002), who notes that in the Southern Scandinavian Mesolithic, gender apparently was weakly marked, if marked at all, in mortuary contexts. Nevertheless, he does not contend that gender was unimportant in these societies; instead, he posits that gender may have been emphasized in social contexts other than mortuary behavior, especially ritual practices.

The possible misconstruing of gender throughout the life cycle is exemplified when we consider some ethnographic studies. The etic categories "berdache," third-gender male, or two-spirit may not be applicable to a culture's designation of gender. Goulet's (1996, 1997) northern Athapaskan studies and Stewart's (2002) work among the Netsilik demonstrate that subsuming these gender "situations" under such a simplistic taxonomy misses the subtleties of the gender contexts. When a child's gender identity changes after killing a particular game animal as an adolescent rite of passage, it is not equivalent to the lifelong nonbinary gender identity of a third-gender male. If one were to try to discern this succession of genders in a mortuary context, for instance, the interpretation may ultimately become misleading (see Crass 2001).

Additional caution must be exercised when seemingly disparate identities combine in what appears to be a single category or axis of identity. Among the Chumash of coastal California, the occupational guild of undertakers (*'aqi*) appears to have been available to persons who were third-gender males, who were postmenopausal women, who were celibate, or who were biological males who had sexual relations with men. The feature that unites these apparently distinct gender/sexuality identities is that their sexual activities (or lack thereof among the celibates) were nonprocreative (Hollimon 2000a). The *'aqi* identity incorporates spirituality, occupational specialization, and sexuality, privileging these facets of personhood over either sex or gender despite the fact that Chumash eschatology is infused with gendered concepts and actors, both human and supernatural (Hollimon 2001a, 2004).

Mortuary Studies

Some archaeologists have been considering binary genders in examining native North American mortuary data for roughly the past twenty years. This is an advance beyond the consideration of mere biological sex in mortuary analyses. However, relatively few studies have deliberately considered nonbinary genders from the outset of the research program. Instead, a fairly common occurrence is the ascription of third or fourth gender to a burial that contains accompaniments associated with the "other biological sex." In some respects, interpretations that attempt to deal with "anomalous" data play a variation on a timeworn theme in archaeological analysis: if a specific function for a class of material culture is not readily apparent, the use or meaning of the material is attributed to "ritual" or "ceremonial" contexts. While the stereotype on which this joke is based may not be as prevalent as the nonarchaeological public believes, it is still a useful analogy for my point. Some archaeologists have employed nonbinary genders or identities as something of a "trash can category," explaining ambiguous gender attributions as possible reflections of these identities. I do not argue with the employment of such interpretations; on the contrary, it is heartening to see archaeologists consider nonbinary genders at all. Instead, I argue that some archaeological interpretations merely introduce the possibility that artifact X was associated in some way with a person of such a gender identity rather than providing a more subtle, nuanced, and ultimately more contextualized explanation.

As Voss (2005) describes this method, the initial step is the determination of a normative archaeological pattern; in this case, it is the distribution of grave accompaniments. Second, artifact distributions that vary from that norm are examined as possible evidence of third-, fourth-, or *n*th-gender identities or practices. Finally, the interpretation of evidence of nonbinary genders is then supported by ethnographic and ethnohistoric textual sources. While this approach is apparently sound, Voss (2005) makes the very important point that the example of nonbinary gender identities illustrates the need for archaeologists to make a critical, firm distinction between *social* deviance and *statistical* deviation. Are nonnormative mortuary treatments merely statistical outliers in a large population study, or are they examples of particularly rich treatments that do not conform to expectations about gender identities?

Arnold (1990) discusses just such a situation concerning "the deposed princess of Vix," a spectacular Iron Age burial in Germany. Excavated in 1953, some researchers were loath to accept the biological evidence of the female sex of the burial, instead choosing to interpret the burial as that of a transvestite priest (Arnold 1990:370). Weglian (2001) describes a comparable example of burial practices in the Neolithic/Bronze Age transition in Germany. Her interpretation of atypical burials supports the identification of more than two genders in these societies.

Similarly, in her examination of the nineteenth-century Blackdog burial site in Minnesota, Whelan (1991, 1993) statistically analyzed the correlation of mortuary goods and biologically sexed skeletal remains. Whelan's interpretation of the data included the possible presence of third-gender persons who were biologically male but did not display the "standard" mortuary treatment of normative males/men exhibited in the rest of the burial population.

I suggest that this approach may be useful in the examination of nonbinary genders because it is also possible that the conflation of occupational specialization and gender might be marked in mortuary contexts. As an example, a burial from the Bering Strait site of Ekven was interpreted by the excavators as a shaman's burial because drum handles and masks were found buried with the person. Additionally, the skeleton was sexed as female, but women's and men's tools made of ivory, wood, shell, stone, and bone were included as burial accompaniments. This was the most elaborate burial at the Ekven cemetery, a site that represents the Old Bering Sea complex dating to about 2500–1500 B.P. (Arutiunov and Fitzhugh 1988:126).

It is likely that this individual was not recognized as a woman or a man or even a fourth gender in the sense that it is defined at the outset of this chapter. It is probable that the person was gendered "shaman" (or culturally designated ritual specialist). In many circumboreal indigenous societies, including North America, the ritual/medical/social role of the shaman is considered analogous to a gender. Examples come from the Inuit (Saladin D'Anglure 1992), numerous Siberian cultures (Czaplicka 1914), and perhaps Mesolithic societies in Europe (Schmidt 2000).

When identities overlap, as among ritual specialists who display gender "difference" (Bean 1976; see also Hollimon 2001b), the approaches to studying nonbinary genders may also overlap in some aspects, such as combining bioarchaeological evidence and mortuary analysis. For example, the activity-induced pathologies or musculoskeletal stress markers (MSMs) associated with an occupational specialization bring in two types of skeletal evidence. These can be combined with an examination of mortuary practices. An occupational specialist's tools may be interred as offerings, allowing interpretations of the interplay among biological sex, gender identity, and occupation. An example from the Chumash of California is described later in this chapter.

Occupational Specialization

A recurrent theme in the ethnographic descriptions of Native North American third-gender males is that their skilled craft work was finely made and highly prized. Indeed, a hallmark of both third and fourth genders is the ability or preference for work associated with "the opposite" gender. Cross-culturally, it appears that most of these persons were identified by their societies when they expressed interest or aptitude and persistently engaged in the activities considered appropriate for women (in the case of third-gender males) or men (in the case of fourth-gender females). This often occurred well before puberty, indicating that sexual behavior was a less important defining trait for nonbinary genders (Roscoe 1998:8).

There are many references in the ethnographic literature to the innovations in arts and craft work that persons of nonbinary gender achieved. However, there are relatively few instances where a material product is said to have design elements that are specific to such persons or their gender identities. There are examples of stylistic changes that are associated with a single artist, such as Hastíín Klah. Klah's innovation was to take traditional Navajo sandpainting designs and weave very large tapestries incorporating ritually important *Yeibichai* figures. Klah (1867–1937), a Navajo *nádleehí*, combined the knowledge of weaving, a woman's art, with the knowledge of religion, a domain of men. Klah also took spiritual risks by making evanescent images from the sandpainting medium into permanent designs in the tapestry (Roscoe 1998:50–51).

Senior (2000), in her examination of pottery production techniques in the Southwest, suggests that it is just such innovation that is reflected in ceramic stylistic changes. Senior's "gender-shift model of craft innovation" posits that when one gender begins to practice "another gender's" craft, either the producer will change form or the product will change form. For example, she suggests that the "social institution" of the third-gender male in some Puebloan groups actually functioned to maintain a highly gendered division of labor because the (previously) male potter has his gender reclassified by virtue of the work performed (Senior 2000:73).

Third-gender males in many Native North American societies excelled at making pottery, weaving baskets, preparing skins and hides, and other skilled crafts associated with women. However, the ability to identify the products of the labors of nonbinary gender persons in the archaeological record seems elusive. One art in which we may be able to discern the handiwork of third-gender males is the porcupine quillwork of northern Plains groups. Males who dreamed of the supernatural entity Double Woman (or her cognates) experienced a shift in gender and became third-gender males (see also the discussion later in this chapter). The difficult tasks of preparing and embroidering the quills, as well as intricate beadwork, were expected of normative women, but only Double Woman dreamers were sanctioned to use design elements that depicted the figure (Wissler 1902, 1912). Even normative women who dreamed of Double Woman were granted sexual license, which is, in one aspect, a shift in gender/sexuality identity (see DeMallie 1983).

Other aspects of clothing may provide insight in identifying third-gender material culture. In a study of the physical dimensions of a particular Lakota dress, Logan and Schmittou (1996) suggested that if the dress was worn in a traditional belted style, the wearer would be exceptionally tall. They argue that this dress was worn by a Lakota third-gender male (*winkte*) who was taller than normative women in these societies. However, in both this case and the design elements associated with Double Woman dreamers, the nondurable quality of the materials makes preservation in the archaeological record an issue. An example of Double Woman crafts that can be preserved is presented later in this chapter.

Bioarchaeological Approaches

Skeletal remains can be viewed as material culture, and the biological indicators of sex might allow inferences about gender as well (Walker and Cook 1997).

Developing technologies in skeletal analysis may provide the ability to examine relationships among biological sex, culturally constructed gender identities, and the social dimensions of mortuary practices. For example, it is increasingly possible to determine the biological sex of skeletal remains using DNA and to compare this information with the treatment of the remains in mortuary contexts. In addition, bone chemistry analysis and the examination of some nutrition-implicated pathologies could shed light on the possibility that a past population fed their girls and boys differently. This in turn has implications for the interpretation of gender dynamics in that society.

Perry (2004) considers the bioarchaeological evidence of sex-based division of labor in skeletal remains from the pre-Hispanic Southwest. Her study examined MSMs, the remodeled bone that develops in response to repetitive motion. Habitual labor may leave traces on the skeleton, and these traces can be examined with regard to female and male patterns; activities such as weaving, food production, hunting, and ceramic manufacture may be reconstructed from these MSM patterns. Perry also considers the presence of typically female MSM patterns on skeletons that are morphologically sexed as male. These may indicate that the person performed the same types of work that normative females did and may be evidence of a socially recognized third gender.

Another example comes from the Chumash of coastal southern California. While there is generally a poor fit between the "gender" of the burial accompaniments and the biological sex of a skeleton in these archaeological sites, it may be possible to use other methods to assess gender. Specifically, the combination of tools associated with an occupational specialization and the presence of activity-induced pathologies, such as osteoarthritis, may provide another avenue of interpretation. I tentatively identified two third-gender burials of relatively young biological males that showed advanced spinal degeneration that was commonly found in female skeletons. These individuals may have incurred repeated stress to the spine by use of digging sticks for harvesting tubers or digging graves. Burial accompaniments suggest that these persons may have been undertakers, an occupation staffed by third-gender males and postmenopausal women; these two graves contained basketry impressions and digging stick weights and were the only male burials in the sample ($n = 210$) to contain both of these items in the undertaker's tool kit (Hollimon 1996, 1997, 2000a).

A promising approach to the examination of skeletal remains as material culture involves the identification of traumatic injuries in sexed skeletons. A number of studies of prehistoric skeletal populations have identified statistically significant sex differences in patterns of trauma (e.g., Lambert 1997; Martin 1997; Martin and Akins 2001; Walker 1997; Wilkinson 1997). Using these patterns, it may be possible to identify third- and fourth-gender persons in skeletal populations. Biologically sexed males who display female trauma patterns may be third-gender persons, while female-sexed skeletons displaying male patterns of injury may be fourth-gender persons. My work has tentatively identified possible fourth-gender females in precontact California and the protohistoric northern Plains. In both of these areas, traumatic injuries consistent with participation in warfare as combatants have been found in female skeletons (Hollimon 1999, 2000b, 2001c). Normative women in these societies could be combatants, but ethnographic evidence also supports the possibility that at least some of these persons were fourth-gender individuals.

Household and Architectural Analysis

Household analysis has long been a focus in feminist approaches to archaeological analysis (Voss and Schmidt 2000:15). Tringham (1991:99) points out that "the analysis of social change at a microscale of the household or co-residential group or family has long been recognized as an essential scale for the study of the social relations of production." Archaeologists examining gender systems in North America have also employed this perspective.

Prine's (1997, 2000) examination of eighteenth- and nineteenth-century Hidatsa earth lodges proposes a material correlate of third-gender activities in the upper Missouri River area. Grounded in ethnographic and ethnohistoric documentation, she suggests that the Hidatsa *miati*, as cultural-ritual innovators and earth lodge builders, would express their gender identity in the homes they built for themselves. A lodge that Prine (2000:210) named "Double Post" exhibits both structural elements and size differences that make it unique among excavated Hidatsa earth lodges. She interprets the doubled post elements as a possible expression of the doubled aspects of the *miati* life path, which combined culturally defined feminine and masculine traits.

In addition, the dimensions of Double Post may indicate an unusually small household by Hidatsa standards. While an older childless couple or an elder living alone would have a lodge with four posts, they lacked the peripheral posts and the floor space exhibited by Double Post. Despite its construction, Double Post is exceptionally small, suggesting that a *miati* and spouse (and perhaps their children, adoptive or other) resided there. In contrast, a typical Hidatsa earth lodge housed three generations and their in-marrying spouses, requiring much more space than that exhibited by Double Post (Prine 2000:211).

In addition to her analysis of skeletal material, Perry examined the plaza architecture of the Southwest to argue that the Zuni third gender, *lhamana*, may have its origins around A.D. 1275 (Perry and Joyce 2001:70–71). At roughly the same time, the Katsina religion was crystallizing, at least in terms of public performances of rituals. The repetitive public performance of quotidian and ritual activities in and around large plazas would serve to create highly dualistic gender roles. In addition, these activities would help create what Perry and Joyce (2001:69) term "gender transgressive performance." Domestic and ceremonial performances that were transgressive were reinforced in the plazas, where public, integrative activities were on display (Perry and Joyce 2001:69).

Imagery and Iconography

The anthropological study of rock art provides opportunities for examining gender in archaeological contexts. Imagery as defined here refers to pictures that represent something in the physical or nonphysical world (Hays-Gilpin 2004:10). A complementary concept is that of iconography, which involves images with shared meanings and how those meanings function in particular cultural contexts (Hays-Gilpin 2004:10).

Hays-Gilpin (2004:127–46) uses such an approach to describe the iconography of certain gender/age categories in Southwest rock art. In addition to phallic flute players, she notes the wide distribution of figures with so-called butterfly hair whorls. These figures most likely depict unmarried postpubescent young women or girls and are often accompanied by female genitalia or string aprons, worn by women in ancestral Puebloan cultures. Two figures described by Hays-Gilpin may show hair whorls and penises. Although she entertains the possibility that these are depictions of female genitals or menstruation, she also considers the notion that these are representations of third-gender persons (Hays-Gilpin 2004:137).

Sundstrom (2002) has examined rock art of the northern Plains and has used oral traditions from the Lakota and Dakota to interpret the art's gender symbolism. In particular, she has focused on rock art that was most likely made by women who dreamed of Double Woman, a supernatural figure linked to dualistic aspects of womanhood (see also Hays-Gilpin 2004:93–98). These dualities include good and evil, modesty and promiscuity, and motherhood and childlessness (Sundstrom 2002:100). Women who dreamed of Double Woman could receive supernatural assistance with their skilled crafts, such as quillwork, or might receive supernatural sanction to forgo marriage and childbearing. Sundstrom (2002:102) suggests that Double Woman could display a great deal of latitude with regard to her protégés, from conforming to feminine ideals to exemplifying their exact opposites.

In addition to women, male persons might also dream of Double Woman. In this event, the person was able to adopt the clothing and lifestyle of a third gender, known in Lakota as *winkte*. The dream conferred powers similar to those attained by women who had Double Woman visions, including creativity in skilled crafts. *Winkte* also had the ability to predict the future and displayed their power by choosing auspicious names for children; parents sought the *winkte* to ensure good fortune for their children (Roscoe 1998:13–14). Although Sundstrom does not directly suggest this, it is possible to logically extend her argument. It is likely that some northern Plains rock art was made by Double Woman dreamers and that some of these persons were third gender; therefore, it is possible that third-gender persons may have been responsible for producing some of the art. The set of associated motifs that suggest Double Woman rock art include bison and deer tracks, human vulvas, handprints, footprints, and abraded grooves (Sundstrom 2002:107).

Summary

Several theoretical and methodological approaches show promise for identifying nonbinary genders in the archaeological record of Native North American societies. It is my hope that as researchers increase their examination of gender and sexuality in these cultures, they also consider the existence of nonbinary genders. In so doing, a more complete picture of these groups becomes possible.

The succession of paradigms in postprocessual archaeology has provided the opportunity for critical appraisal of many long-held and previously unexamined constructs. As an example, the use of queer theory allows us to problematize categories that were left unexamined by first-wave feminist archaeologies, such as men and masculinity (Voss 2000). As the archaeological study of gender continues its development, the subtleties and complexities of gender identities, practices, and their material manifestations will become clearer.

References

Arnold, Bettina
    1990   The Deposed Princess of Vix: The Need for an Engendered European Prehistory. In *The Archaeology of Gender*. Dale Walde and Noreen D. Willows, eds. Pp. 366–74. Calgary: University of Calgary Press.

Arutiunov, S. A., and William W. Fitzhugh
    1988   Prehistory of Siberia and the Bering Sea. In *Crossroads of Continents: Cultures of Siberia and Alaska*. William W. Fitzhugh and Aron Crowell, eds. Pp. 117–29. Washington, DC: Smithsonian Institution Press.

Bean, Lowell John
    1976   Power and Its Applications in Native California. In *Native Californians: A Theoretical Retrospective*. Lowell John Bean and Thomas C. Blackburn, eds. Pp. 407–20. Socorro, NM: Ballena Press.
Bourdieu, Pierre
    1977   *Outline of a Theory of Practice*. Cambridge: Cambridge University Press.
Callender, Charles, and Lee M. Kochems
    2000   The North American Berdache. *Current Anthropology* 24(4):443–70.
Conkey, Margaret W., and Janet D. Spector
    1984   Archaeology and the Study of Gender. *Advances in Archaeological Method and Theory* 7:1–38.
Crass, Barbara A.
    2001   Gender and Mortuary Analysis: What Can Grave Goods Really Tell Us? In *Gender and the Archaeology of Death*. Bettina Arnold and Nancy L. Wicker, eds. Pp. 105–18. Walnut Creek, CA: AltaMira Press.
Czaplicka, Marie A.
    1914   *Aboriginal Siberia*. London: Oxford University Press,.
DeMallie, Raymond J.
    1983   Male and Female in Traditional Lakota Culture. In *The Hidden Half: Studies of Plains Indian Women*. Patricia Albers and Beatrice Medicine, eds. Pp. 237–65. Lanham, MD: University Press of America.
Gilchrist, Roberta
    2000   Archaeological Biographies: Realizing Human Lifecycles, -Courses and -Histories. *World Archaeology* 31(3):325–28.
Goulet, Jean-Guy A.
    1996   The "Berdache"/"Two-Spirit": A Comparison of Anthropological and Native Constructions of Gendered Identities among the Northern Athapaskans. *Journal of the Royal Anthropological Institute* 2(4):683–701.
    1996   The Northern Athapaskan "Berdache" Reconsidered: On Reading More Than There Is in the Ethnographic Record. In *Two-Spirit People: Native American Gender Identity, Sexuality, and Spirituality*. Sue-Ellen Jacobs, Wesley Thomas, and Sabine Lang, eds. Pp. 45–68. Urbana: University of Illinois Press.
Hays-Gilpin, Kelley A.
    2004   *Ambiguous Images: Gender and Rock Art*. Walnut Creek, CA: AltaMira Press.
Hollimon, Sandra E.
    1996   Sex, Gender and Health among the Chumash of the Santa Barbara Channel Area. In *Proceedings of the Society for California Archaeology*. Vol. 9. Judith Reed, ed. Pp. 205–8. San Diego: Society for California Archaeology.
    1997   The Third Gender in Native California: Two-Spirit Undertakers among the Chumash and Their Neighbors. In *Women in Prehistory: North America and Mesoamerica*. Cheryl Claassen and Rosemary A. Joyce, eds. Pp. 173–88. Philadelphia: University of Pennsylvania Press.

1999 "They Usually Kill Some Woman": Warfare, Gender, and the Ethnographic Record in Studies of California Prehistory. Paper presented at the plenary session of the Annual Meetings of the Society for California Archaeology, Sacramento, April 3.

2000a Archaeology of the 'Aqi: Gender and Sexuality in Prehistoric Chumash Society. In *Archaeologies of Sexuality*. Robert Schmidt and Barbara Voss, eds. Pp. 179–96. London: Routledge.

2000b Sex, Health, and Gender Roles among the Arikara of the Northern Plains. In *Reading the Body: Representations and Remains in the Archaeological Record*. Alison E. Rautman, ed. Pp. 25–37. Philadelphia: University of Pennsylvania Press.

2001a Death, Gender and the Chumash Peoples: Mourning Ceremonialism as an Integrative Mechanism. In *Social Memory, Identity, and Death: Anthropological Perspectives on Mortuary Rituals*. Meredith Chesson, ed. Pp. 41–55. Archeological Papers of the American Anthropological Association 10. Washington, DC: American Anthropological Association.

2001b The Gendered Peopling of North America: Addressing the Antiquity of Systems of Multiple Genders. In *The Archaeology of Shamanism*. Neil Price, ed. Pp. 123–34. London: Routledge.

2001c Warfare and Gender in the Northern Plains: Osteological Evidence of Trauma Reconsidered. In *Gender and the Archaeology of Death*. Bettina Arnold and Nancy Wicker, eds. Pp. 179–93. Walnut Creek, CA: AltaMira Press.

2004 The Role of Ritual Specialization in the Evolution of Prehistoric Chumash Complexity. In *Foundations of Chumash Cultural Complexity*. Jeanne E. Arnold, ed. Pp. 53–63. Perspectives in California Archaeology, vol. 7. Los Angeles: Cotsen Institute of Archaeology, University of California.

Kirkpatrick, R. C.
2000 Evolution of Human Homosexual Behavior. *Current Anthropology* 41(3): 385–98.

Lambert, Patricia M.
1997 Patterns of Violence in Prehistoric Hunter-Gatherer Societies of Coastal Southern California. In *Troubled Times: Violence and Warfare in the Past*. Debra L. Martin and David Frayer, eds. Pp. 77–109. Amsterdam: Gordon and Breach.

Logan, Michael H., and Douglas A. Schmittou
1996 Identifying Berdache Material Culture: An Anthropometric Approach. *Tennessee Anthropologist* 21(1):67–79.

Martin, Debra L.
1997 Violence against Women in the La Plata River Valley (A.D. 1000–1300). In *Troubled Times: Violence and Warfare in the Past*. Debra L. Martin and David Frayer, eds. Pp. 45–75. Amsterdam: Gordon and Breach.

Martin, Debra L., and Nancy J. Akins
2001 Unequal Treatment in Life as in Death: Trauma and Mortuary Behavior at La Plata (A.D. 1000–1300). In *Ancient Burial Practices in the American Southwest*.

Douglas R. Mitchell and Judy L. Brunson-Hadley, eds. Pp. 223–48. Albuquerque: University of New Mexico Press.

Meskell, Lynn
 2001 Archaeologies of Identity. In *Archaeological Theory Today*. Ian Hodder, ed. Pp. 187–213. Cambridge: Polity Press.
 2002 The Intersections of Identity and Politics in Archaeology. *Annual Review of Anthropology* 31:279–301.

Pate, Laura
 2004 The Use and Abuse of Ethnographic Analogies in Interpretations of Gender Systems at Cahokia. In *Ungendering Civilization*. K. Anne Pyburn, ed. Pp. 71–93. New York: Routledge.

Perry, Elizabeth M.
 2004 Bioarchaeology of Labor and Gender in the Prehispanic American Southwest. Ph.D. dissertation, University of Arizona.

Perry, Elizabeth M., and Rosemary Joyce
 2001 Providing a Past for "Bodies That Matter": Judith Butler's Impact on the Archaeology of Gender. *International Journal of Gender and Sexuality Studies* 6(1/2):63–76.

Prine, Elizabeth
 1997 The Ethnography of Place: Landscape and Culture in Middle Missouri Archaeology. Ph.D. dissertation, University of California, Berkeley.
 2000 Searching for Third Genders: Towards a Prehistory of Domestic Space in Middle Missouri Villages. In *Archaeologies of Sexuality*. Robert A. Schmidt and Barbara L. Voss, eds. Pp. 197–219. London: Routledge.

Roscoe, Will
 1998 *Changing Ones: Third and Fourth Genders in Native North America*. New York: St. Martin's Press.

Saladin D'Anglure, Bernard
 1992 Rethinking Inuit Shamanism through the Concept of "Third Gender." In *Northern Religions and Shamanism*. Mihaly Hoppál and Juha Pentikäinen, eds. Pp. 146–50. Budapest: Akadémiai Kiadó.

Schmidt, Robert A.
 2000 Shamans and Northern Cosmology: The Direct Historical Approach to Mesolithic Sexuality. In *Archaeologies of Sexuality*. Robert A. Schmidt and Barbara L. Voss, eds. Pp. 1–32. London: Routledge.
 2001 "What if Gender Didn't Matter?" Gender as a Structuring Principle of Identity in the Southern Scandinavian Mesolithic. Paper presented at the 7th Gender and Archaeology Conference, Sonoma State University, Rohnert Park, October 6.
 2002 The Iceman Cometh: Queering the Archaeological Past. In *Out in Theory: The Emergence of Lesbian and Gay Anthropology*. Ellen Lewin and William L. Leap, eds. Pp. 155–85. Urbana: University of Illinois Press.

Schmidt, Robert A. and Barbara L. Voss, eds.
    2000   *Archaeologies of Sexuality*. London: Routledge.

Senior, Louise M.
    2000   Gender and Craft Innovation: Proposal of a Model. In *Gender and Material Culture in Archaeological Perspective*. Moira Donald and Linda Hurcombe, eds. Pp. 71–87. London: Macmillan.

Stewart, Henry
    2002   *Kipijuituq* in Netsilik Society: Changing Patterns of Gender and Patterns of Changing Gender. In *Many Faces of Gender: Roles and Relationships through Time in Indigenous Northern Communities*. Lisa Frink, Rita S. Shepard, and Gregory A. Reinhardt, eds. Pp. 13–25. Boulder: University Press of Colorado.

Sundstrom, Linea
    2002   Steel Awls for Stone Age Plainswomen: Rock Art, Women's Religion, and the Hide Trade on the Northern Plains. *Plains Anthropologist* 47:99–119.

Tringham, Ruth E.
    1990   Households with Faces: The Challenge of Gender in Prehistoric Architectural Remains. In *Engendering Archaeology: Women and Prehistory*. Joan Gero and Margaret W. Conkey, eds. Pp. 93–131. Oxford: Blackwell.

Voss, Barbara L.
    2000   Feminisms, Queer Theories, and the Archaeological Study of Past Sexualities. *World Archaeology* 32(2):180–92.
    2005   Sexual Subjects: Identity and Taxonomy in Archaeological Research. In *The Archaeology of Plural and Changing Identities: Beyond Identification*. Eleanor Conlin Casella and Chris Fowler, eds. Pp. 55–78. New York: Springer.

Voss, Barbara L., and Robert A. Schmidt
    2000   Archaeologies of Sexuality: An Introduction. In *Archaeologies of Sexuality*. Robert A. Schmidt and Barbara L.Voss, eds. Pp. 1–32. London: Routledge.

Walker, Phillip L.
    1997   Wife Beating, Boxing, and Broken Noses: Skeletal Evidence for the Cultural Patterning of Violence. In *Troubled Times: Violence and Warfare in the Past*. Debra L. Martin and David Frayer, eds. Pp. 145–79. Amsterdam: Gordon and Breach.

Walker, Phillip L., and Della Collins Cook
    1997   Gender and Sex: Vive la Difference. *American Journal of Physical Anthropology* 106:255–59.

Weglian, Emily
    2000   Grave Goods Do Not a Gender Make: A Case Study from Singen am Hohentwiel, Germany. In *Gender and the Archaeology of Death*. Bettina Arnold and Nancy Wicker, eds. Pp. 137–55. Walnut Creek, CA: AltaMira Press.

Whelan, Mary K.
    1991   Gender and Historical Archaeology: Eastern Dakota Patterns in the 19th Century. *Historical Archaeology* 25:17–32.

1992   Dakota Indian Economics and the Nineteenth-Century Fur Trade. *Ethnohistory* 40:246–76.

Wilkinson, Richard G.
1997   Violence against Women: Raiding and Abduction in Prehistoric Michigan. In *Troubled Times: Violence and Warfare in the Past*. Debra L. Martin and David Frayer, eds. Pp. 21–43. Amsterdam: Gordon and Breach.

Wissler, Clark
1902   Field Notes on the Dakota Indians. Department of Anthropology Archives, American Museum of Natural History, New York.
1912   Societies and Ceremonial Associations in the Oglala Division of the Teton-Dakota. *American Museum of Natural History Anthropological Papers* 11(pt. 1):1–99.

Wylie, Alison
2002   *Thinking from Things: Essays in the Philosophy of Archaeology*. Berkeley: University of California Press.

SUBSISTENCE STRATEGIES III

Gender and Human Evolution 14

DIANE BOLGER

IN THEIR GROUNDBREAKING ARTICLE "Archaeology and the Study of Gender," Conkey and Spector (1984:6) characterized reconstructions of early hominid behavior as "the most obvious case of androcentrism in archaeology both in conceptualization and mode of presentation." Unfortunately, this judgment still pertains to much of the research on human evolution today. While particular theoretical arguments and methodologies have changed in the intervening years, proponents of evolutionary theory continue to construct essentialist narratives of the human past. In terms of gender, these scenarios contain very powerful and compelling accounts of the genesis of separate spheres of male and female behavior based largely on fundamental biological differences—dichotomies, it is argued, that are so deeply rooted in the ancestral past as to be considered universally applicable to the social behavior and psychological outlook of modern humans regardless of variations between and among different social groups. Attempts to unravel or deconstruct these "origins narratives" lead directly to confrontation with many of the key issues in the archaeology of gender outlined by Conkey and Spector (1984:6–7): "presentist bias, essentialist models assuming a gendered division of labor early in prehistory, differential valuation of male and female activities, and models that generally fail to incorporate gender explicitly into constructs of the past." The principal aims of this chapter, therefore, are to examine some of the critical implications for gender of the study human origins and to assess the role of archaeological research in understanding the processes by which modern gender constructs are likely to have evolved. Although many of the critical debates about gender and evolutionary theory can be traced back to the nineteenth-century Darwinian landscape or even earlier, I have chosen as a starting point the rise of neoevolutionary theory in the early 1950s. The bulk of this chapter addresses the impact of neoevolutionary theory on the construction of two sets of biologically based narratives of human behavior that continue to exert a strong influence on archaeological interpretations of gender. The first of these traces the origin, development, and decline of "Man the Hunter," a rubric that comprises several hypothetical models of the gendered division of labor in early human societies that were extremely influential during the 1960s to 1980s. The second, more recent set of narratives consists of sociobiological models currently at the cutting edge of research in the cognitive sciences that have had an important impact on cognitive archaeology and Darwinian archaeology over the past decade. In the final section of this chapter, I explore some of the problems and prospects of constructing new explanatory models for the evolution of human behavior through which we might begin to overcome the androcentric, ethnocentric, and anachronistic bases of earlier research. I end with a detailed assessment of prospects for the participation by archaeologists in continuing debates on the conflicting roles of nature, culture, and environment in the development of hominid behavior. By engaging in these debates, archaeologists can measure the validity of current theories of gender relations in early adaptive environments by testing them against the record of our ancestral past as established by recent decades of fieldwork at a wide range of Pleistocene sites in Africa, Asia, and Europe.

In the Beginning: Modern Approaches to Human Origins

The modern study of human evolution owes its existence to a series of major developments during the 1940s and 1950s in the fields of biology, primatology, and anthropology that gave rise to new, process-oriented approaches that gradually came to replace the descriptive accounts of earlier decades. In doing so, the discipline acquired an integrated, multidisciplinary perspective that still characterizes the study of human origins today. Among these developments were the following:

- The emergence of modern evolutionary theory as a synthesis of traditional Darwinian theories of natural selection with principles of modern evolutionary biology.
- Primatological studies based on the study of animal behavior in the wild (rather than in a zoo or laboratory) that led to a greater appreciation of the social complexity of nonhuman primates and furnished new insights into similarities and differences between humans and other animals. The discovery that chimps and humans are 98 percent identical genetically has provided renewed impetus to these studies in recent years.
- The confirmation by le Gros Clark in 1949 of Dart's proposal in 1924

that *Australopithecus africanus* was a human ancestor as well as the revelation that Piltdown man was a forgery. These served as compelling challenges to racial and ethnocentric prejudices among laypersons and scientists alike that precluded the possibility that humans had evolved in Africa. Both were instrumental in establishing a more accurate account of the early stages of human development within the discipline of physical anthropology.

- The discovery by Louis and Mary Leakey at Olduvai Gorge in Tanzania of what then constituted the earliest known fossilized remains of hominids (in particular the discovery of *Zinjanthropus* in 1959 and *Homo habilis* in 1962). These discoveries quickly generated increased levels of funding for paleontological and archaeological research and created new research agendas for fossil hunters in Africa. The success of these operations is attested to by a number of outstanding discoveries such as "Lucy" and other specimens of *Australopithecus afarensis* in Ethiopia and Tanzania, the identification of several new hominid species by Meave and Richard Leakey's team at Lake Turkana in Kenya (e.g., *Australopithecus anamensis* and *Kenyanthropus platyops*), and the discovery in Chad in 2002 of a fossilized skull (provisionally classified as *Sahelanthropus tchadensis*) dating to nearly 7 million years ago.

As the result of these developments, there arose in the early 1960s a new impetus within the fields of paleoanthropology and prehistoric archaeology to explain the processes by which humans emerged as a separate species and to isolate the major factors that served as catalysts in that process, most notably an increase in brain size/intelligence as evidenced by increasing cranial capacities and the manufacture of increasingly complex stone-tool assemblages. The development of new subsistence strategies, in particular the regular inclusion of animal protein in the diet as the result of hunting, came to be regarded along with bipedality as a major factor distinguishing protohumans from nonhuman primates. In terms of sociocultural behavior, hunting was singled out as the primary reason for the greater intelligence, adaptive abilities, and social complexity of human primates. Links between hunting, intelligence, diet, and tool use, for example, were frequently diagrammed in various "feedback loops" that appeared regularly in college textbooks on physical anthropology from the 1970s to the early 1990s (e.g., Campbell 1992:249, figs. 9–11). Consequently, hunting as an adaptive strategy was allotted more evolutionary weight than simply a functional means of dietary improvement. For proponents of the hunting model, hunting technology and meat eating, together with aggression and dominance, came to be considered the very keys to the success of the genus *Homo*, and the hunting model was increasingly invoked not simply to characterize early modes of human subsistence but also to epitomize what it meant to be human. Embedded in this mode of thinking is the polarization of male and female labor and a hierarchical ranking of subsistence skills in which male activities (hunting) are positioned at the top of the evolutionary ladder and female activities (gathering) are marginalized. The development of these biased views into formal scientific hypotheses during the 1970s and 1980s is explored in detail in the following section.

Deconstructing "Man the Hunter": Technology, Subsistence, and the Sexual Division of Labor

A turning point in the study of human evolution occurred in 1950 when the eminent anthropologist and primatologist Sherwood Washburn and evolutionary biologist Theodosius Dobzhansky held a conference titled "The Origin of Man" at the renowned Symposium in Quantitative Biology at Cold Spring Harbor (Washburn 1951). One of the main objectives at this gathering of more than one hundred eminent geneticists and anthropologists was to begin to integrate modern evolutionary theory with anthropology and to shift the focus of research on human evolution from descriptive anatomy to the consideration of adaptive strategies, particularly those related to human reproduction and subsistence. Another tacit goal of the conference was political: the construction of a universal human history that was meant to combat the overt racism of American postwar society but that effectively bypassed issues of gender by lumping women and men under the generic rubric "man" (Haraway 1989:207). Several years later, Raymond Dart's imaginative reconstructions of australopithecines as aggressive hunters wielding weapons of bone, teeth, and horn (his so-called osteodontokeratic culture) captured the imagination of a number of scholars (e.g., Bartholemew and Birdsell 1953) and were adopted by the media to emphasize aggression, dominance, and territoriality—behaviors traditionally associated with males—as key factors in the success of human primates (Cartmill 1993:1–14). Later in the decade, a paper by Washburn and Avis (1958) linked the lack of estrus in females to the emergence of male–female pair bonding and monogamy, behaviors that they deemed to be hallmarks of humanity. At about the same time, primatological studies were beginning to be introduced into the emerging picture of early hominid society, first by Washburn at a Wenner-Gren conference titled "Social Life of Early Man" (1961), which included a much-cited chapter by Washburn and DeVore (1961) on the behavior of savanna baboons as a model for early hominid groups. A decade later, extensive research by Teleki (1973) drew on evidence of predation among chimpanzees to argue for the centrality of male aggression and domination as principal underlying causes of the successful emergence of humans.

The results of these and other like-minded studies were applied with increasing frequency during the 1970s and 1980s to investigations of early hominid social organization, which often focused on the differing biological and social roles of males and females. Much of this early research is now considered to be speculative, presentist, and extremely culture bound, as can readily be observed in the following fanciful reconstruction of early hominid life by French anthropologist F. M. Bergounioux, published in his contribution to *Social Life of Early Man* (1961:112):

> The first human societies were very small ethnic groups, the unit of which was the family clan. The chief at the head lived surrounded by his wife and children. His first duty was to provide for the immediate needs of his group and to defend it against anyone who attacked it. There was no need for any law except that of his will, and his authority was derived from his physical strength rather than from his intelligence or cunning.

The theoretical trajectory of these early androcentric narratives of prehistoric economic and social structures can be said to have culminated in the well-known symposium "Man the Hunter," organized by Washburn's students Lee and DeVore at Yale in 1966 (Lee and DeVore 1968), which for the first time integrated the disciplines of primatology, ethnology, archaeology, and paleoanthropology into research on early human subsistence. While explicit discussion of male and female roles in early hominid societies was curiously absent from almost all the conference papers, the importance attached to hunting, as well as the implicit assumption that a sexual division of labor existed from the time of the earliest protohumans, runs as an undercurrent throughout the book. Hunting, the collection and distribution of food and other resources at a central home base, monogamous pair bonding, a sex-based division of labor, and social organization based on a loose network of nuclear family groups were core elements in hypothetical reconstructions of the lives of our earliest ancestors, who already, it seems, bore a curious resemblance to our (modern Western) selves. With regard to subsistence and hence to the survival of the earliest known ancestral species of humans, hunting was regarded as the key factor separating humans from other primates. More than simply an innovative technological invention, hunting served as a powerful metaphor for emergent humanity in which larger brains, greater intelligence, more advanced technology, and communicative ability constituted a "great leap forward" in the struggle for the adaptive success of protohumans. "Man the Hunter" soon became a buzzword that connoted our very humanity, effectively summing up all that was important about the earliest phases of our past and helping to explain why we are who we are today.

Since men are more closely associated than women with hunting, aggression, and technological prowess in societies of the modern industrialized West, men's roles were implicitly given pride of place in these initial models of early hominid subsistence; women's roles, in contrast, appear to have been superfluous. Richard Lee's (1968) contribution to *Man the Hunter* was one of the few to place a high value on women's economic and social roles in hunting and gathering societies, a perspective he had gained from extensive ethnographic fieldwork among the Kalahari !Kung (for related research, see Lee 1979; Lee and DeVore 1976 and Lee 1979). However, his conclusions regarding the sexual division of labor among hunter-gatherers, compelling though they seem today, failed to exert a decisive impact on the overall themes of the conference or even on general statements about hunting by Lee and DeVore themselves in the introductory chapter of the book: "to date the hunting way of life has been the most successful and persistent adaptation man has ever achieved" (Lee and DeVore 1968:3), and "hunting is so universal and so consistently a male activity that it must have been a basic part of the early cultural adaptation even if it provided only a modest proportion of the food supplies" (7). Such inflated views of the role of hunting in early hominid societies, which were scarcely balanced by brief acknowledgments of the benefits of food gathering, food sharing, and women's roles in subsistence, were echoed by statements in some of the other conference papers, such as the chapter by Washburn and Lancaster (1968:293), in which they claimed that "the success of the hunting way of life has dominated the course of evolution for hundreds of thousands of years" and that "the biology, psychology and customs that separate us from the apes—all these we owe to the hunters of time past" (303).

Among the several archaeologists in attendance, Lewis Binford's (1968) contribution to *Man the Hunter* is particularly significant in terms of his central role in the construction of theoretical agendas in archaeology during the decades that followed. Processual approaches in archaeology, which were coming into vogue at the time, claimed that archaeology's proper role was as a subdiscipline of anthropology, and many archaeologists had increasingly begun to draw on ethnographic evidence in their reconstructions of early human societies. One of the crucial effects of the "Man the Hunter" symposium on the discipline of archaeology, therefore, was the transmission of received ideas concerning the sexual division of labor, the social implications of presumed biological and physical differences between the sexes, and the predominance of males in evolving patterns of economic subsistence and technological progress (such as the invention and use of tools) from ethnography and primatology to paleontology and prehistory. Ironically, however, Binford's overriding concern with rigorous methodology in the interpretation of archaeological sites served ultimately to undermine the hunting hypothesis by calling attention to its lack of substantive data (see Binford 1981, 1985, 1986, 1988, 1989).

Another eminent archaeologist participating in the conference was Glynn Isaac, then a recent Cambridge Ph.D. who was soon to become the renowned excavator of a number of important early hominid sites in Africa and a leading authority on hominid prehistory. While his conference paper said little concerning the sexual division of labor, Isaac focused on the need for archaeology to "come of age" as a discipline by moving away from typological studies of stone tools to a consideration of paleoecological factors such as diet and technology (Isaac 1968). In contrast to Binford, Isaac objected to what he regarded as the "grafting of full-fleshed . . . depictions of primate and modern human lifestyles onto early hominid bones" (Blumenschein 1991:308), and he firmly believed that questions of early hominid behavior could be answered only as the result of painstaking archaeological investigation (Isaac 1968:253). It took Isaac more than a decade to develop and implement methods of excavation and analysis that were capable of generating sufficient evidence with which to formulate and test models of early hominid behavior, and that evidence was later used to construct an alternative model to "Man the Hunter: known as the food-sharing hypothesis (discussed later in this chapter). During most of the 1970s, however, the sole voices of dissent against the hunting hypothesis came from female primatologists and anthropologists rather than archaeologists, and very little of this research was accepted for publication in mainstream anthropological journals. While only a few of these women would have considered themselves feminists, it is highly likely that the women's movement played a central role for many of them in confronting the androcentric biases inherent in much of the existing anthropological research and in helping to formulate alternative models of hominid social organization that granted women central roles in economic subsistence and political decision making. Some of these alternatives are considered in the following sections.

Challenges to the Hunting Hypothesis

While the hunting hypothesis continued to be highly influential in anthropological circles throughout the late 1960s and well into the 1970s, its obvious gender biases came under increasing attack from feminist anthropologists and other scholars who questioned the assertion that early hominid females were dependent on males for survival and were unable to accept a theory that "leaves out half of the human species" (Slocum 1975:38). In one of the first published critiques of the model, Slocum characterized it as the ethnocentric discourse of social scientists who are white, Western, and male (Slocum 1975:37; published earlier as Linton 1971). Citing ethnographic evidence such as the work by Lee among the !Kung, Slocum emphasized the importance of gathering to the survival of preindustrial groups and noted the lack of evidence, among both human and nonhuman primates, for monogamous mating behavior. The primary social bonds among such groups, she argued, would have been between mothers and infants: males, if they did in fact bring back meat to kin, would have been more likely to provision parents and siblings than mates and offspring (Slocum 1975:44).

Other studies appearing at around the same time, such as Leibowitz (1975:7), carried these arguments a step further by noting the lack of clear sex role patterns among nonhuman primates and by questioning the equation of biological differences between the sexes with polarized male/female categories of social and economic behavior. Moreover, as she and others were quick to observe, studies that draw conclusions about the roles of men and women in prehistory on the basis of the social constructs of modernity are seriously flawed since they conflate the present with the past and therefore fail to comprehend the dynamics of gender relations. This important theme has been explored in greater depth in recent years, most notably by Conkey and Williams (1991), and we shall return to it again later in this chapter. A further line of attack was launched in the late 1970s by Marxist anthropologist Eleanor Leacock, who challenged the notion of binary social categories that polarized male and female behavior at an early stage of human evolution and created hierarchical relations between men and women by ascribing differential values to male and female labor, again on the basis of modern Western values (Leacock 1978, 1983). According to Leacock, the hunting hypothesis failed to consider the dynamics of social change and equally neglected the social, historical, and cultural (rather than simply the biological) factors that may have shaped the differences in status between males and females. "Instead," she observed, "the polarization of public male authority and private female influence is taken as a given of the human condition" (Leacock 1978:248).

The androcentric bias that characterizes much of the research on human origins has, until recently, been deepened and reinforced through the integration into discussions of human evolution of primatological research, which has served to extend the present even further back in time into the "natural" world of the animal kingdom (Fedigan 1986:38–43; Haraway 1978a, 1978b; Yanagisako and Delaney 1995). Conflation of human with nonhuman primate behavior has also opened the door to sociobiological interpretations of animal behavior, which often operate within the framework of the same limited set of evolutionary constraints associated with a narrow range of reproductive strategies. This reductionist view of processes of natural selection fails to consider possible alternative factors that may have helped shape our evolutionary history. Leibowitz (1975) notes, for example, that the selective pressure for sexual dimorphism, a physical characteristic noted in varying degrees among all species of primates, may have arisen for reasons other than the conventional explanation of male dominance and aggression in competition for food and females; factors linked to life cycle events, such as energy-saving requirements by pregnant females, may also account for slower rates of female growth at the attainment of sexual maturity. Finally, if primate studies are to be brought into arguments about human patterns of social integration and dominance, greater attention needs to be paid to recent behavioral studies of nonhuman primates that focus on networking and alliance-formation strategies among female members (see the discussion later in this chapter); it has recently been demonstrated, for example, that bonobo females form coalitions that create powerful alliances, often preventing male domination in a number of social situations. As Stanford (2001:116) has observed in a review of this research, "Under conditions of female coalitional behavior, sexual equality in political power may emerge. The result of course is a very different set of social relationships than among male-dominated primates."

Alternative Models of Early Subsistence: The Narrative of "Woman the Gatherer"

Armed with ample evidence from ethnology, primatology, and social theory, critics of *Man the Hunter* began in the mid-1970s to develop alternative models of human origins that granted women more substantive roles in the successful emergence of the hominid line. Among the most influential of these was the often-cited article by Tanner and Zihlman (1976), which aimed to establish a central role for women in human evolution by establishing gathering rather than hunting as the key economic innovation that led to the survival and success of the human species. According to these authors, the basic unit of kinship in early hominid societies was not the male–female pair bond but the mother–infant relationship. Adult females gathered food to share with their offspring and transmitted valuable technical skills and complex information about the environment (Tanner and Zihlman 1976:604). The long period of dependence by young on their mothers led to increased levels of maternal investment, which in turn led to greater discrimination by adult females in choosing their mates; sexual selection in human primates, therefore, was based on female rather than male choice (590). This line of argument was developed in further articles by Zihlman (1978, 1981) as well as in some of her more recent works (1997a, 1997b, 1998) in which she stresses the necessity of developing more flexible models that consider the roles of women, men, and children in reconstructions of early hominid life as well as "a range of activities throughout the lifecycle on which natural selection acts, rather than a narrower focus on one or two of them" (Zilhman 1998:103). The importance of life cycle approaches to the study of gender and human evolution is a theme that will be taken up later in this chapter.

The importance of gathering to the early hominid diet, particularly in the early stages of human evolution, is now widely accepted, but debates continue about when hunting may have become a more regular and effective subsistence strategy. Nevertheless, few anthropologists today would support the claim by Washburn and Lancaster (1968:293) that hunting has dominated the course of human evolution. The realization that hunting arrived rather late on the economic scene, millions of years after the emergence of the earliest protohumans, and that it is very likely to have been prefaced by a long period in which crude stone tools were used as aids in scavenging activities but certainly not to hunt is now commonplace (see, e.g., recent college textbooks in physical anthropology, such as Haviland 2000; Jurmain et al. 2000). Although it is difficult to gauge the extent to which the challenges posed by Tanner, Zihlman, Leibowitz, Slocum, Leacock, and others had an impact on the decline of the hunting hypothesis, it is likely that by exposing many of its weaknesses, they helped establish and promote new research agendas that opened the door to alternative narratives about the past and furnished a more balanced view of male and female roles in models of early human subsistence.

By 1980, however, there had been little reaction among mainstream anthropologists and prehistorians to what had come to be known as the gathering hypothesis. A conference organized by Dahlberg, "Woman the Gatherer," held at Yale University in the spring of that year, sought to provide the hypothesis with the higher profile its proponents believed it deserved. In her introduction to the publication of the conference proceedings, Dahlberg (1981:10) criticized the simplistic, binary approaches adopted by most research on the sexual division of labor and observed that cross-cultural evidence demonstrates a great variety of patterns with regard to the sexual division of labor, noting that even where task differentiation between men and women exists, it is rarely rigid and inflexible. Moreover, she argued that the claim that women are not hunters can be readily refuted by a number of important ethnographic examples, such as the Mbuti and the Agta (ethnographic examples that are discussed by others in subsequent chapters of the book). The fact that women in societies such as the Agta find hunting compatible with reproductive and child-rearing activities should have prompted anthropologists to reevaluate the assumption that the sexual division of labor served as a foundation for present human society (Estiokio-Griffin and Griffin 1981:146).

Although the publication of *Woman the Gatherer* should have generated a widespread reevaluation of male and female roles in hunting and gathering activities as well as a reconsideration of the presumed centrality of hunting in early hominid societies, it in fact received no more than scant mention in textbooks and mainstream journals. For many anthropologists, the gathering hypothesis was dismissed as a biased feminist reaction to the hunting hypothesis and was therefore marginalized or entirely ignored (ironically, these same critics had never sought to challenge the hunting hypothesis on the grounds of its evident androcentric biases). Given this poor reception, it is possible that the hunting hypothesis was more extensively undermined by its own empirical weaknesses, which became increasingly clear in the face of mounting evidence from careful excavation and analysis of early hominid sites in Africa. This research ultimately demonstrated that our earliest ancestors could not have been hunters, that tools from early hominid sites could not have been effective at hunting large game, and that the crude lithic assemblages known from these sites were probably used, among other purposes, for the extraction of marrow from bones rather than for hunting. Processual archaeologists also played an important role in the demise of "Man the Hunter," for they underscored the failure of the hunting hypothesis to produce any firm evidence for hunting prior to the Upper Paleolithic period. Lewis Binford was particularly critical of theories involving hunting, food sharing at a base camp, and complex social organization and spent much time challenging what he termed "just-so" stories about the behavior of our ancestors (e.g., Binford 1981, 1985, 1986). Despite these criticisms, however, fanciful stories about the early stages of our past continued to be written throughout the 1980s. Two of the most influential of these, Lovejoy's hypothesis of male provisioning and Isaac's food-sharing hypothesis, can be viewed (in slightly different ways) as variations on the theme of "Man the Hunter."

Active Males, Passive Females: Lovejoy's Myth of Male Provisioning

In 1981, Owen Lovejoy, a paleoanthropologist specializing in hominid locomotion, published an influential article in the journal *Science* in which he argued that bipedality rather than hunting and an enlarged brain was the principal trait that made us human since it is this feature that initially distinguished hominids from nonhuman primates and because it anticipated the earliest known stone-tool assemblages by several million years (the latter were found by Johansen's team in the Awash region of Ethiopia and date to about 2.6 million years ago, while bipedality is a physical feature of hominids now thought by some paleoanthropologists to have evolved as early as 6 to 7 million years ago). Since bipedal locomotion constitutes the initial point of bifurcation between apes and humans, Lovejoy argued that we should seek to build explanatory models of early hominid behavior that are centered on this major evolutionary innovation.

In a series of articles appearing in major anthropological journals in the 1980s, Lovejoy succeeded in establishing an alternative to "Man the Hunter" that until recent years was extremely popular and influential (e.g., Lovejoy 1981, 1988; Tague and Lovejoy 1986), appearing regularly in college textbooks on physical anthropology throughout the 1980s and into the early 1990s (see, e.g., Campbell 1992 and earlier editions; Jurmain et al. 1990 and earlier editions). In these works, Lovejoy used sociobiological arguments to account for the origins of bipedality by demonstrating the emergence of fully fledged bipedal locomotion at least 4 million years ago and by linking the latter to the establishment of male–female pair bonding and male provisioning of females and offspring at a home base. The ability of protohuman females to attract long-term partners was based on their continuous sexual receptivity and on successful competition with other females (for an alternative view, see Hamilton 1984).

According to Lovejoy, everyone gained something in the process. Because females no longer needed to expend energy in the search for food, they could increase their investment in pregnancy, birth, and child rearing and could produce a greater number of offspring by decreasing birthing intervals. Males, by provisioning mates and offspring and through what Lovejoy termed "copulatory vigilance" with women who were continually sexually receptive, would gain a regular outlet for sexual activity and could rest assured that the offspring they were providing for were their own progeny. In sum, Lovejoy's hypothesis is an attempt to explain a suite of evolutionary developments by integrating the emergence of bipedal locomotion with unmediated assumptions about gender relations; in doing so, it retains the androcentric perspectives of the hunting hypothesis while shifting the content of male subsistence from hunting to gathering. While these arguments seemed convincing to some anthropologists as the result of sociobiological models in ethology (e.g., Wilson 1975), which were gaining wide acceptance during the early 1980s, for others they represented a major step backward because of their reductionist, androcentric logic. In the words of one social scientist, Lovejoy had created a model of "Man the Gatherer" in which "early hominid females were left not only four-footed, pregnant, hungry and in fear of too much exercise in their central core area, but were also left 'waiting for their man'" (Falk 1997:114).

Extensive evidence from paleoanthropology and primatology now exists with which to effectively challenge many aspects of the "male provisioning" model. In the First, several studies of fossilized remains earlier than 4.5 million years ago suggest the possibility of a long, slow transition to fully bipedal locomotion, with bipedality emerging in a forested rather than a savanna environment and anticipating the establishment of home bases and the hunter-gatherer lifestyles by millions of years (e.g., Kingdon 2003; Stern and Sussman 1983). Second, recent studies on bipedal locomotion show that less energy is expended in terrestrial movement (walking, not running), particularly for females; consequently, there is no need to invoke theories in which sedentary females are provisioned by males at a home base (Aiello and Wells 2002; Leonard and Robertson 1997). Third, female–female relationships may have been as or more important than male–female in terms of the evolution of social organization, a point that is addressed more fully later in this chapter (see Key and Aiello 1999). Finally, there is now evidence to suggest that accelerated birth intervals can harm rather than enhance reproductive success. The key to human reproductive success is "quality rather than quantity," and that is achieved through the steady production of offspring with adequate interbirth intervals. This contradicts more traditional interpretations, such as Lovejoy's, in which fertility rather than longevity is regarded as the key element in reproductive success. These arguments lay bare some of the weaknesses of narrow sociobiological models that define fitness solely in terms of reproductive output and demonstrate the importance of life history approaches to an understanding of human evolution. While Lovejoy's hypothesis figured prominently in textbooks of the 1980s and early 1990s, it has all but disappeared today in research on bipedality (the model is either given scant mention, cited as an unlikely scenario, or not mentioned at all, e.g., in Ember and Ember 1993; Haviland 2000; Jolly and White 1995; Jurmain et al. 2000; Kottak 2000; Stein and Rowe 1993).

Digging Up Difference: Isaac's Food-Sharing Hypothesis

At about the same time that Lovejoy's hypothesis was gaining wide acceptance, an alternative model of early hominid subsistence was being proposed by the prehistoric archaeologist Glynn Isaac, who was then engaged in the excavation of several hominid sites from about 1.5 million years ago near Lake Turkana in Kenya. On the basis of careful stratigraphic analyses of the remains from these and related sites (such as the so-called living floors at Olduvai Gorge) and the painstaking study of bone and stone-tool assemblages by specialist members of his team over the course of nearly a decade, Isaac constructed a model of early hominid adaptation that can be considered his most important contribution to paleoanthropology (first presented by Isaac in 1978; for a comprehensive list of his other published works as well as an assessment of Isaac's legacy, see Blumenschein 1991). The food-sharing model, as it came to be known, emphasized the exploitation of different environments by males and females who participated equally in subsistence activities and brought back food to a home base for distribution to the entire group. For Isaac, the key to the survival of early humans was not hunting or gathering but rather the sharing of food resources among the entire group, a characteristic behavior of humans that is not observed among non-human primates. Part of the appeal of the food-sharing model rested with its integration of a range of behaviors—the invention of tools, bipedalism, and greater levels of communication, intelligence, and social interaction, for example—without singling out any one factor as a "prime mover" (Isaac 1978:108). This more flexible model reflected Isaac's long-standing belief that a more broadly based model was "more readily compatible with models of human evolution that stress broadly based subsistence patterns rather than those involving intensive and voracious predation" (Isaac 1971:288).

While the food-sharing model certainly provided a more comprehensive, balanced model of early human behavior than the hunting hypothesis and the male provisioning model and managed to avoid some of their more blatant androcentric biases by acknowledging the importance of female subsistence activities in human evolution, it resembled the others in its unmediated, presentist assumptions about male and female social roles based largely on biological differences between the sexes, in its assumption of monogamous pair bonds and essentially modern "family-based" kinship structures, and in its inference of a sexual division of labor at an early stage of human evolution that associated women with the gathering of plant resources and men with the procurement of meat. As was the case with the earlier models, the polarization of male and female labor strengthened the claims of sociobiologists that disparities between men and women are inherent since they are traceable to the earliest stages of our emergence as a species; moreover, the food-sharing model failed to take into account important ethnographic evidence that demonstrates more flexible patterns of the division of labor among hunter-gatherer groups.

At around the time of his premature death in the mid-1980s, Isaac had begun to question and revise the food-sharing hypothesis, even changing its name to the "central place foraging process," which he felt made it more objective and hence more amenable to rigorous scientific testing (Blumenschein 1991:319). Even then, however, Isaac seemed to be increasingly skeptical of the ability of archaeology to provide the empirical evidence necessary to support such hypothetical reconstructions. Binford's hard-hitting criticisms of the results of Isaac's team (as well as of the Leakeys' work in East Africa) as overinterpretations of the material evidence had left unanswered the question of whether hunting existed at all among early hominid groups or whether the "sites" composed of scatters of animal bones and crude stone tools could truly be regarded as home bases (see Binford 1981, 1985, 1986, 1988, 1989). Indeed, these questions posed by Binford nearly twenty years ago remain at the forefront of archaeological inquiry into human origins today (Blumenschein 1991:320).

Current research trends in human evolution reflect to a certain degree the rigorous criticism made by nearly thirty years of research into the archaeology and anthropology of gender. One of the most influential pieces of research in this regard is an article by Gero (1991) on stone-tool production in hominid prehistory that challenges a number of long-standing, unmediated assumptions, such as the claim that males alone produced the tools that form such a large part of the archaeological record; that there was already a division of labor that excluded women from toolmaking tasks; that "tools" are equitable with "maleness" and male control of technology and the environment and, by implication, that women were somehow not strong or intelligent enough to make stone tools; that women's child care responsibilities restrict them to a limited range of repetitive, interruptible tasks that were not dangerous and did not require extensive travel; and that stone tools represent the pinnacle of prehistoric technology (with projectile points at the top of the hierarchy, bifaces in the middle, and flake tools at the bottom), thus endowing men's activities with greater social value. Elsewhere, Gero has shown that the division of labor and hierarchy of value imposed in these interpretations is highly reflective of modern gendered practices in the field of archaeology itself. To modify our interpretations of the past, we must therefore consciously change the processes and methods by which we construct those views (Gero 1985).

While remaining aware of these and other theoretical and methodological misconceptions, we must also agree with Isaac that archaeological inquiry is the discipline most capable of supplying the means by which theories about hunting, gathering, and the sexual division of labor can be fruitfully constructed. Unfortunately, just about every model proposed in previous decades to account for gender relations in the prehistoric past has been based on exaggerated distinctions between male and female anatomy, sexuality, and embodiment and on a priori inferences about the presumed behavioral correlates of those differences. The collective impact of this misengendered body of research has been enormous, and archaeologists have only just begun to deconstruct the most salient of its androcentric elements. As Conkey and Spector observed in their seminal article of

1984, "Theories of gender relations regarding production and distribution in early hominid societies should be subjects of scientific investigation rather than based on the unmediated assumptions regarding men's and women's economic roles" (7). As archaeologists continue to investigate many of these fundamental issues in the coming years, it is important that they consciously seek to avoid the many theoretical pitfalls and methodological biases that have dominated research on early hominid subsistence for more than half a century.

Gender, Cognition, and Evolution: Reconstructing the Prehistoric Mind

As the debates and controversies outlined in the previous section with regard to the gendered division of labor were in progress, new developments in evolutionary biology were beginning to filter into archaeological debate, providing fresh opportunities for incorporating sociobiological models into explanations of culture change. Although sociobiology was hardly a new idea, its reincarnation by Wilson (1975) and others in the mid-1970s, through the exploitation of concepts such as "inclusive fitness" (Hamilton 1964) and "reciprocal altruism" (Trivers 1972), began to exert a significant impact on archaeological theory since it now provided a vehicle for applying neo-Darwinian precepts to groups rather than individuals; it also threatened to sever the field of archaeology from its historical, cultural roots in the social sciences (especially anthropology) and to forge new links to the "harder" sciences of population genetics and evolutionary biology. By the early 1980s, these influences had crystallized into the formation of the subdiscipline known as neo-Darwinian archaeology, which soon split into two distinct branches known as evolutionary archaeology and behavioral ecology (for article-length reviews, see Boone and Smith 1998; Lyman and O'Brien 1998; Shennan 2004). While the intellectual focus of evolutionary archaeology has remained largely theoretical, with only a small proportion of articles devoted to specific applications (see Dunnell 1980 and the commentary by R. L. Kelly in Boone and Smith 1998:S161), research in behavioral ecology has tended to address issues of subsistence and human adaptation, such as optimal foraging models (e.g., Mithen 1990; Smith and Winterhalder 1992); in addition, since the marginal role accorded by evolutionary archaeology to cultural processes precludes the interpretation of gender categories as social constructs, behavioral ecology would appear to offer greater scope for gendered approaches since it acknowledges that the transmission of cultural variants can be attributed to factors other than natural selection (Boone and Smith 1998:S144). To date, however, it has produced very little research pertaining explicitly to gender.

In general, widespread charges by social scientists and biologists alike that sociobiological approaches (especially in their crudest forms) serve to promote sexist and racist agendas has not encouraged the integration of "naturist" principles into explanatory models of gender and human evolution. But in spite of the theoretical and methodological difficulties involved in grafting biological models onto archaeological evidence for culture change, the lack of clarity concerning the degree to which nonrandom transmission of cultural knowledge through mechanisms of social learning are deemed to have played a role in the evolution of human culture, and Dawkins's (1976:203–15) fuzzy and unsubstantiated concept of "memes" as heritable units of culture (see Shennan 2004), evolutionary approaches in archaeology have persisted as a subdiscipline of the field and have in fact been reinvigorated over the past ten to fifteen years. This is no doubt due to the assimilation of recent research in evolutionary and cognitive psychology by archaeologists who, for reasons that shall become clear later in this section, have managed to distance themselves from the more objectionable implications of sociobiological theory of the 1970s.

Cognitive aspects of human evolution have been adopted thus far by only a handful of prehistorians (e.g., Mithen 1996a; Renfrew and Scarre 1998; Shennan 2002; Steele and Shennan 1996), but they are widely regarded to be at the "cutting edge" of archaeological research and are currently receiving considerable support from academic funding bodies in the United States and the United Kingdom. Here, three major research strands have emerged: one with its roots firmly planted in traditional Darwinian principles of natural selection and reproductive success, which has been heavily influenced by recent research in evolutionary psychology (EP); another that is closely linked to cognitive psychology and concerns itself with the emergence and development of the cognitive structures ("architecture") of the human brain but is not as heavily selectionist in its outlook; and yet another, known as "dual inheritance" theory, that separates biological and cultural evolution into two distinct but interrelated strands and gives a prominent role to social learning in the diachronic transmission of culture (Boyd and Richerson 1985; Mithen 1996b). While models of cognitive evolution and dual inheritance theory are potentially important for investigating the relationships between gender and cognition in early human societies (see Hawkes 1996; Mithen 1990, 1996b), it is research in EP that is contributing most to current debates about male and female behavior within an evolutionary framework. It is therefore worthwhile to engage in a brief review of some of the central concepts of EP before turning to some of the archaeological data to which this research is currently being applied.

The Nature of Sexual Difference: Recent Developments in EP

Although many of the core elements of sociobiological theory, such as Hamilton's (1964) rule of inclusive fitness and Trivers's (1972) work on reciprocal altruism and parental investment are equally important to research in EP, current advocates of EP are at pains to show that they are not identical. For example, EP claims to have resolved the Cartesian mind–body split (often cited as a major theoretical weakness of earlier sociobiological models) by unifying the biological and nonbiological aspects of human existence. As Tooby and Cosmides (1992:21) have argued in a highly influential article, "The Psychological Foundations of Culture," which is widely acknowledged as the first comprehensive statement of the EP program, "The rich complexity of each individual is produced by a cognitive architecture, embodied in a physiological system, which interacts with the social and nonsocial world that surrounds it." Conceptual unification is attained by recognizing that "culture is the manufactured product of evolved psychological mechanisms situated in individuals living in groups" (24). Moreover, in linking social sciences with the "hard" sciences, EP claims to have overcome the inability of the social sciences to "causally locate their objects of study inside the larger network of scientific knowledge" (23). In opposition to "standard social science models," which are forever consigned by proponents of EP to the murky and rudderless realm of cultural relativism, the integrated models of EP promise the return to a principled universe replete with "grand laws and validated theories to rival those of the rest of science" (23). One does not need to consider these statements at great length, however, in order to realize that the "unification of social sciences with the rest of science" implies the assumption of the former by the latter, effectively negating "standard social science approaches" as valuable contributors to the understanding of human behavior. As a brand of sociobiology, EP reduces explanations of human behavior to static "laws" of natural selection and effectively relegates explanations of gender constructs to biological rather than cultural domains. For this reason, it has been labeled by a prominent critic in the social sciences as "neurogenetic determinism" (Rose 1998:272; see also articles in Rose and Rose 2001).

Today, more than a decade after the publication of Tooby and Cosmides's article, the literature on EP is vast and continues to grow. Limitations of space do not allow me to discuss this literature in any detail; however, mention should at least be made of some of the major works by principal proponents of EP discourse over the past ten to fifteen years: Buss (1999), Campbell (2002), Cronin (1991), Dennett (1995), Low (2000), Miller (2001), Pinker (1997), Ridley (1993, 2003), Sperber (1996), Thornhill and Palmer (2000), and Wright

(1994). While there are differences in scope and style of argumentation among these various works as well as in the degree to which they regard culture as a phenotype responsive to principles of Darwinian selection and the degree to which they vilify social science and feminist theory, they share a number of common characteristics. These include the accusation that "standard social science models" are wholly "nurturist" in orientation while ignoring the scientific "truths" of biology; the belief that the human mind is modular in its structure, a domain-specific rather than a multipurpose mechanism or a fitness-maximizing device; the consideration of a narrow range of adaptive behaviors as measures of human reproductive success, the most common being male/female differences in parental investment, sexual attraction, and strategies of mate selection; the claim that male and female adaptive behavior is essentially and fundamentally different and that the latter is linked to differences in male/female reproductive strategies that stem from basic biological differences between the sexes; a universalizing tendency that focuses exclusively on species-typical traits and ignores variation between and among different cultural groups; the speculative reconstruction of early hominid behavior without recourse to archaeological evidence; and the conflation of ancient and modern environments by using modern hunter-gatherer communities rather than early hominid species to characterize what is termed by proponents of EP as "the environment of evolutionary adaptation."

In the attempt to mollify those who would accuse EP of determinism and of failing to recognize individuals (particularly women) as active agents in their own destinies, a charge often leveled against advocates of sociobiological theory of the 1970s and 1980s, there is a growing body of research within the discipline that emphasizes the deliberate and conscious efforts (often described as "tactics" or "strategies") by individuals of both sexes to optimize their own reproductive success. For example, according to the principle of "expensive egg, cheap sperm," women are characterized in EP scenarios as "fussy" about selecting a mate since the latter will be free to exploit women's higher degree of parental investment (Campbell 2002:46). Men, on the other hand, are thought to be less fussy about mate selection since promiscuity (i.e., access to as many fertile females as possible) or even rape provides optimal conditions for male reproductive success (Campbell 2002:40; Thornhill and Palmer 2000). In another version of this scenario, Ridley (1993:236) speculates,

Deep in the mind of modern man is a simple male hunter-gatherer rule: strive to acquire power and use it to lure women who will bear heirs ... likewise, deep in the mind of a modern woman is the same basic hunter-gatherer calculator, too recently evolved to have changed much: strive to acquire a provider husband who will invest food and care in her children; strive to find a lover who can give those children first-class genes.

While this line of argumentation appears to impart a mantle of apartheid egalitarianism to the disparate and often conflicting reproductive goals of males and females as defined by EP theory, the models employed by EP in the speculative reconstructions of male and female behavior (male hunting, provisioning of female mates and offspring, constant female sexual receptivity and sexual fidelity, pair bonding, and so on) scarcely differ from those proposed by proponents of "Man the Hunter" hypotheses of the previous generation. Moreover, the apparent alibi provided by the most extreme of these scenarios for the rape of females by males (see Thornhill and Palmer 2000) reveals strong links in some quarters of EP with the more misogynist elements of earlier sociobiological theory. From an archaeological perspective, subsistence models portraying active males and passive females are no longer acceptable for reasons that have been discussed in earlier sections of this chapter. In the remainder of this section, therefore, I wish to consider and assess critically from a gendered perspective several examples of recent archaeological research that have attempted to apply some of the basic concepts of EP to archaeological data of the Paleolithic and Mesolithic periods.

Genes, Memes, and Gender: Recent Research in Evolutionary Archaeology

The most wide-ranging application of evolutionary psychology to archaeology thus far has been Stephen Shennan's *Genes, Memes and Human History* (2002). At the beginning of the book, Shennan argues for the widespread adoption by archaeologists of evolutionary theory on many of the same grounds stated by proponents of EP, namely, that archaeology is in a crisis that has resulted largely from postmodernism's rejection of "grand narrative" throughout the social sciences (Shennan 2002:10). According to Shennan, this has led archaeology into a directionless state in which "scholars show more interest in unscientific attempts to empathize with ancient peoples than in obtaining valid knowledge about the past" (Shennan 2002:book jacket). After introductory chapters in which basic principles of evolutionary psychology, behavioral ecology, and life history approaches are presented, Shennan considers the role of natural selection in long-term patterns of human subsistence (chap. 6). He then turns (chap. 7) to the subject of the evolution of male–female relations.

Like other advocates of EP, Shennan (2002:17) begins this chapter by lamenting what he sees as the "ghettoization" of feminist research, which in his view has refused to acknowledge the fundamental role of biological factors in the construction of gender relations. Male–female relations, he argues, particularly sexual relations, are central to evolutionary archaeology since they constitute the behavioral matrix in which reproductive strategies are enacted to maximize reproductive success. From the perspective of natural selection, reproductive differences and their behavioral manifestations (e.g., gender-based differences in parental investment and mate selection) are all that really matter when considering cognitive differences between males and females and thus form the thrust of all subsequent discussion in this chapter. In sum, we are presented with many of the same arguments offered by EP, some of which have been summarized here. In order to show how these ideas are currently being applied to investigations of various aspects of hominid evolution, Shennan ends the chapter (197–205) by presenting a number of examples of recent research by archaeologists and paleoanthropologists. In the pages that follow, I briefly outline a selection of recent archaeological studies that have been informed by EP. Some of these are included in Shennan's summary, and all have particular relevance to issues of gender and human evolution.

In an article that attempts to explain the sexual division of labor in early hominid societies, Hawkes (1996) attributes differences in male and female subsistence strategies to differences in parental investment, a concept proposed by Trivers (1972) and further developed by Maynard Smith (1977) and based on the principle of "expensive egg, cheap sperm" mentioned earlier (i.e., since females are capable of reproducing at maximum about once a year, they must make a greater investment of time, energy, and resources to the production of offspring than males, for whom the costs of reproduction are relatively minimal). Hawkes argues that bipolar modes of subsistence (men/hunting, women/gathering) emerged as the result of differences between male and female reproductive biology; while hunting allowed males to maximize mating opportunities by covering a wide geographical range, gathering afforded women time and energy to required to attend to the welfare of their children. Citing a number of ethnographic examples, Hawkes (1996:297) further proposes that the particular types of foraging activities engaged in by women in a given society tend to vary in accordance with child care considerations, while hunting may not always have been undertaken by males to provide for their mates and offspring but rather to maximize mating opportunities. The methodology adopted by Hawkes in this article is identical to that of EP, involving the identification of a perceived behavioral difference between males and females (in this case, hunting vs. gathering) and "explaining" its origin by recourse to sociobiological argumentation. While the hypothetical explanations she proposes may be true, there is no way to test their validity as models for human evolution since they fail to consider the physical and cultural evidence of archaeology and paleontology. For example, they neglect to account for the more than 4 million years of prehistory during which there is little evidence of hunting as a subsistence strategy. Since human reproductive biology is unlikely to have changed during that period, the adoption of hunting-gathering lifestyle must be due, at least in part, to cultural rather than biological factors.

Articles by Power and Watts (1996), and Knight (1996) propose models of collective strategizing by ancestral hominid females for the purpose of maximizing their own reproductive success. Through tactics of "sexual manipulation" and "sham menstruation," females ensured that their mates contributed a fair share to the welfare of themselves and their offspring. According to this line of reasoning, threats or actions involving the withholding of sexual favors (through sex strikes), as well as deliberate ruses to mask fertility (sham menstruation), enabled women to enhance their ability of survive by compelling mates to engage in greater levels of parental investment, including provisioning of offspring and the establishment of home bases. Although they represent a refreshing departure from standard narratives of "active male/passive female" that portray women as weak, vulnerable, and unable to fend for themselves, the speculative nature of this type of argumentation (increasingly popular in the literature on EP), as well as the degree of conscious political machination required of actors in such scenarios, renders them as implausible as the traditional androcentric models they are meant to replace. Again, the failure to develop these models in the light of archaeological evidence seriously undermines their credibility.

In an article published in *Antiquity*, Kohn and Mithen (1999) have attempted to integrate a number of aspects of EP theory with material culture of the Pleistocene by considering the form and function of Acheulian bifacial hand axes. Acheulian bifaces have a long chronological range, first appearing about 1.4 million years ago and continuing with only slight modifications for about a million years in association with fossilized remains of *Homo erectus* and several other hominid species. Archaeologists have long been puzzled about the possible function(s) of this distinctive artifact type, particularly by some of the larger examples such as those from Olduvai, which are more than twenty-eight centimeters in length (Kohn and Mithen 1999:518). While archaeologists have traditionally interpreted Acheulian hand axes as hunting and/or butchering tools or as implements for cutting wood or processing plants, Kohn and Mithen suggest a social function, namely, that they were used as sexual symbols by males and females in processes of mate selection: in addition to functioning as signals of prodigious technical ability to prospective mates, the symmetrical form of the biface may have been a desirable feature to members of the opposite sex (518–19). Recent research in cognitive psychology suggests that individuals tend to be sexually attracted to social members whose facial and other bodily features are highly symmetrical, a physical trait regarded as indicative of "good genes" (Barrett et al. 2002:111–13). On this basis, Kohn and Mithen (1999:521) speculate that the evolution of a "perceptual bias towards symmetry" may have been transferred to elements of material culture, such as the hand axes, and that the display of these technically complex, visually stimulating artifacts may have served as an effective means of attracting potential mates. On the question of whether males or females made the bifaces, the authors cite theories of sexual selection and parental investment, discussed previously, to propose that females are likely to have been the mate selectors (they are more "fussy" because of their greater levels of parental investment); consequently, it is argued, it was probably males who made the hand axes or at least the large "impractical" examples mentioned previously (522–23). In archaeological terms, there is no way to prove whether this theory is valid, and the authors fail to propose any analytical means of testing it. Logically, however, one must question the efficacy to survival of dedicating such considerable time and effort to the manufacture of elaborate tools that afforded little practical value apart from their possible use as sex charms. In addition, one questions whether the brains of protohumans such as *H. erectus* were capable of such sophisticated stratagems. If so, it seems that a million years of toolmaking might have been more profitably devoted to the development of improved strategies for survival (such as learning how to hunt) that would have been more likely to result in reliable outcomes for the "maximizing of reproductive success."

Although archaeological applications of EP have emerged only recently and have been undertaken thus far by a relatively small group of authors, it is nonetheless important to address some of the weaknesses of this research as it has been formulated to date. With the exception of the article by Kohn and Mithen, the bulk of "evidence" used to substantiate the longevity of proposed interfaces between the biological and social aspects of human behavior in the examples cited previously takes the form of speculative reconstructions that begin in the modern industrial present and purport to take a great leap backward into the (likewise modern) hunter-gatherer "past." While ethnographic studies are occasionally included in these discussions, there is a general lack of concern with integrating archaeological data. As a consequence, we are left with "just-so" stories about the past that succeed only in creating "cardboard caricatures of female activities" (Fausto-Sterling 2001:182). The study of Acheulian hand axes by Mithen and Kohn constitutes a rare attempt to integrate cognitive theory with archaeological evidence; however, more rigorous and detailed testing of their hypothesis, including contextual analysis, is needed to strengthen their case.

A number of important questions regarding the compatibility of archaeological evidence with the speculative models outlined previously were raised nearly a decade ago by Lake (1996). As archaeological inferences concerning early hominid social and economic organization must be based on careful excavation, dating, and taphonomic reconstruction of chronologically overlapping, bona-fide sites, there are enormous obstacles to overcome in order to test the hypotheses being proposed by EP models, particularly as the paleolandscape is comprised of "a series of discontinuous sediments that are extremely difficult to correlate" (Lake 1996:185–88). Whereas some psychologists have baldly pronounced the attempt to consider archaeological data (such as fossil evidence and chronology) as unnecessary and counterproductive (e.g., Miller 2001:22) and others merely pay lip service to the need to substantiate evolutionary models of human behavior with empirical evidence (e.g., Campbell 2002:12), one would expect the archaeological proponents of Darwinian models to ground their arguments in the fossil, material, and environmental record of the prehistoric past. However, this has not often proved to be the case.

In order to overcome what he sees as "the mismatch between goals and data" in interpretations of human evolution, Lake (1996:184) advocates the use of computer simulation techniques to test the validity of hypothetical reconstructions. As an example of the potential of this technique, he uses computer simulation to test hypotheses of cultural transmission and cultural learning as proposed by Boyd and Richerson (1985). In a series of computer-generated charts diagramming temporal dimensions of individual and cultural learning, such as changes in frequency of genotypes for cultural learning over 200 generations and qualitative effects over time of relationships between individual and cultural learning (Lake 1996:figs. 6.2–6.5), Lake draws several provisional conclusions about the relative impact of cultural and individual learning at various stages of human evolution (202). While computer-based methodologies such as these may eventually serve as a viable means of assessing the effects of differently scaled processes such as individual and cultural learning in the evolution, further work is clearly needed in order to achieve that goal. Moreover, despite Lake's pessimistic assessment of the ability of more traditional methods of archaeological analysis to test the validity of evolutionary models, archaeologists intent on constructing convincing interpretations of human social behavior, including gender relations, must at the very least make more rigorous attempts to do so—or run the risk of being relegated to the theoretical dustbin of evolutionary debate.

Sexing the Prehistoric Brain: Gender and Human Cognition

In addition to EP, a number of recent approaches in cognitive psychology are beginning to have an impact on archaeological research on human evolution, and some are of potential importance for issues of gender. It is surprising, however, that the first comprehensive investigation of the evolution of the human mind was written not by an archaeologist or anthropologist (or even a psychologist) but by philosopher Merlin Donald, whose *Origins of the Modern Mind*, published in 1991, has had a tremendous impact on cognitive archaeology. Reflecting on earlier theories of human cognition, Donald notes that interpretative models of higher cognitive function, regardless of whether they follow diachronic trajectories that begin with the present and work backward to nonhuman primates or vice-versa, are either "modular" or "unitary" in their approach (6). "Modular" approaches (e.g., Fodor 1983; Sperber 1996; Tooby and Cosmides 1992) take the view that the mind is comprised of a number of specific, discrete domains that operate independently of one another (the standard example used to illustrate the modular approach is the Swiss army knife). In contrast, traditional "unitary" approaches (e.g., Anderson 1983) argue for a single, integrated structure dedicated to achieving a general-purpose cognitive capacity. As an alternative to these more traditional approaches to cognition, Donald (1991:chaps. 6–8) investigates processes of human cognition within an evolutionary framework in which the minds of apes and protohumans are seen to evolve from "modular" to "unitary" structures that mirror the increase in brain size throughout the chronological range of the genus *Homo*. The most accelerated period of cognitive development, he argues, occurred with the earliest populations of *Homo sapiens* perhaps as early as 200,000 years ago and is associated with the evolution of art, language, sophisticated and varied tool technology, and the emergence of more complex levels of social organization such as the sexual division of labor (Donald 1991:208ff.). Detailed responses to some of the key ideas in *The Origin of the Modern Mind* have appeared in Noble and Davidson (1996) and in conference volumes edited by Mellars and Gibson (1996) and Renfrew and Scarre (1998).

Many of the central concepts of Donald's work have been further developed by Steve Mithen, a cognitive archaeologist whose book *The Prehistory of the Mind* (1996a) has made a valuable contribution to research on the origins and development of human cognition. According to Mithen, the "big bang" of cognitive development did not occur until about 60,000 years ago and resulted from the coalescence of multiple specialized intelligences into a single interactive unit characterized by what he terms "cognitive fluidity" (chap. 4). As Mithen has stated, "the transition to a fluid mind was neither inevitable or pre-planned," but once the transition occurred, there was no turning back (240). More significantly, it is the human capacity for cognitive fluidity that most effectively distinguishes human from nonhuman primates since it has freed cognitive processes from the rigid straitjacket of modular thought and hence from the deterministic constraints of ultra-Darwinian models such as we have just been considering.

In a more recent work, Mithen (2001:102) has posed the somewhat rhetorical question, "Why should archaeologists be concerned with the evolution of mental modularity?" He believes there are at least three good answers: first, by examining the origins and development of human cognition, we can more fully comprehend the modern human mind; second, by engaging in this research we can test the proposal that the human mind evolved in a modular fashion against the evidence of the archaeological record; and, finally, such investigation will allow us to "reconstruct" the prehistory of the mind. For the purposes of this chapter, however, it is necessary to pose a different question: why should those interested in the archaeology of gender be concerned with issues of cognitive evolution? In order to answer this question, we must first take a brief detour into recent research in cognitive psychology, which, for the past thirty years or so, has been concerned (or increasingly obsessed, it has sometimes been suggested) with cognitive differences between males and females.

Research on cognitive sex differences can be traced back to the nineteenth century to Darwin's proposal of a hierarchy of mental functions, which placed males at the higher end of the scale (reason and imagination), while women were consigned to the lower end (intuition, emotion, and instinct) (Appleman 2001:234–35). The fact that a recent book by a prominent professor at Cambridge is based on the premise that female brains are "empathizing" while male brains are "systematizing" suggests that, in some quarters at least, little has changed over the past 150 years (Baron-Cohen 2003). In addition to the proliferation of the idea of "essential differences" in male and female cognitive abilities by the media and in books on "pop psychology," a great deal of research time and funding has been expended on the attempt to demonstrate that this is the case (for detailed critiques of this research, see Fausto-Sterling 2000:chap. 5; Tavris 1992). By the same token, research emphasizing cognitive similarities between the sexes has until recently been largely ignored, and attempts in the 1970s by Ruth Bleier, former professor in neurophysiology at the University of Wisconsin, to publish critical reviews of "brain sex" research in the prestigious journal *Science* were repeatedly rejected.

Meanwhile, over the past thirty years, a virtual raft of studies employing a wide variety of methodologies, including IQ testing, PET and MRI scans, and postmortem analysis of cerebral hemispheres and the intermediary corpus callosum, as well as an even wider range of techniques applied to the brains and genitalia of rodents and other animals, have been conducted in research laboratories across Europe and the United States (for a detailed summary, see Fausto Sterling

2000:chaps. 6–8). As Tavris (1992:5) has noted, most of this research is binary in its outlook, and there has been an increasingly widespread view that cognitive differences between the sexes begin in the womb and are strongly influenced by prenatal hormones, implying that such differences are innate (see also Fausto-Sterling 2000:chap. 6). Particular attention has been focused on studies of brain lateralization that have attempted to show that males excel in right-hemisphere functions, such as visual-spatial tasks and mathematical abilities, while females are associated either with left-hemisphere functions (verbal abilities) or with a combination of both hemispheres that results in weaker right-hemisphere performance (e.g., Benbow and Stanley 1980; Geary 1996; Macoby and Jacklin 1974; Shaywitz et al. 1995; Silverman and Eals 1992; Silverman and Phillips 1998; but for opposing views, see Alper 1985; Fausto-Sterling 2000). While a detailed critique of these studies lies beyond the aims of this chapter (and in fact has been undertaken by a number of authors in recent years, including Bleier 1984; Fausto-Sterling 1992, 2000; Halpern 1992; Rosenberg 1982; Tavris 1992), it is important to emphasize a recent trend in the literature away from a focus on difference to a more balanced view that accommodates previously neglected factors, such as sampling methods, the date when the studies were carried out, and the age(s) of individuals used as test subjects, and that acknowledges the need for more cross-cultural research, as very few studies of cognitive sex differences have been conducted outside of the industrialized West (Fairweather 1976). Halpern (1992:246) argues for a "biopsychosocial perspective" that can move beyond generic, binary categories (such as right/left hemisphere, male/female, spatial/verbal, nature/nurture, and so on) by incorporating a multiplicity of biological, psychological, and social factors. Computer-assisted techniques, such as meta-analysis (e.g., Feingold 1988; Linn and Petersen 1985; Voyer et al. 1995) have also served to reverse or substantially revise many of the conclusions of earlier research on gender and cognition by factoring in a number of these variables and thereby improving the statistical base of comparison (McGuinness 1998:70–74). Today, it is far from certain that differential results in cognitive performances of males and females have any real meaningful correlation with innate mental capacities, and it is certainly the case that greater efforts are being made to devise cognitive tests that are less prone to gender bias. As research on "sexing the brain" is gradually undermined by revealing its theoretical and methodological weaknesses and as its impact on the social sciences begins to wane, scientists might now be more likely to agree with the prophetic statement made by Bleier more than twenty years ago that cognitive psychology's attempt to sex the brain was "the modern equivalent of 19th century craniology" (Bleier 1984:11–12; see also Gould 1981:103–7).

Despite the improvements in research methods cited previously, binary approaches to the study of gender and cognition continue to appear and have been given a new lease of life by the growth of EP and Darwinian archaeology. Since the models generated by this research are based on the assumption that cognitive differences between males and females arose as adaptive responses to survival mechanisms in the remote past and hence are part of "human nature," it is important for prehistorians to engage in these debates and to evaluate their strengths and weaknesses from an archaeological perspective. Mithen (2001:113) has already acknowledged the dearth of research on gender and cognitive evolution and has emphasized the need for archaeological input into these discussions in order to introduce contextual constraints of time and space, factors that are normally ignored or underplayed by psychologists. And to Isaac's often-stated belief that only archaeology is capable of directly testing theories of early hominid behavior, we now need to add that only archaeology can transform the "cardboard caricatures" of current cognitive theory into real, palpable social actors and can articulate the dynamics of gender relations in nonessentialist terms.

Gender and Human Evolution: Directions for Future Research

As we have seen in the preceding sections, the speculative narratives of early hominid behavior generated by "Man the Hunter," as well as by current approaches in evolutionary psychology and Darwinian archaeology, are implicitly based on narratives of male and female relations that reflect stereotypical gender patterns of modern industrial societies. This presentist, ethnocentric outlook, combined with a neglect of archaeological data and its requisite temporal and spatial contingencies, has resulted in generic reconstructions of the past that sever human behavior from the particular historical contexts in which identity and behavior are embedded (Bleier 1984:71; Mishler 1979; Parlee 1979). As Barrett (2000:30–31) observes, "Gender is constituted in historically and culturally specific ways . . . hence it is important to understand the specific conditions under which gender constructs are brought into being." The failure of sociobiological research to address the specific conditions under which gender relations are constructed has also fostered what Rose et al. (1984:chap. 10) have termed a "poverty of reductionism" in which complex structures such as molecules or societies are defined in terms of the discrete units of which they are composed rather than as complex totalities and in which the wide range of human adaptive behaviors is constricted to a small range of topics centering on a narrowly defined range of reproductive behaviors (see also Gould 1977).

For some proponents of neo-Darwinism, reductionism is regarded as a "necessary evil," an analytical tool that, although not ideal, furnishes the only practical, viable means of interpreting, rather than merely describing, social phenomena (Campbell 2002:17; Miller 2001:22–24). Opponents of sociobiological argumentation think differently, however, viewing humans as "creatures who are constantly re-creating our own psychic and material environments, and whose individual lives are the outcomes of an extraordinary multiplicity of intersecting causal pathways" (Rose et al. 1984:290). Reductionism reduces the richness and variety of human life and in doing so creates narratives of social behavior that dehumanize human actions (Shanks and Tilley 1987:56). As Mithen (in Boone and Smith 1998:S163) pithily noted some time ago, cognitive approaches in archaeology need to move beyond the "food and sex stuff" to consider aspects of human evolutionary history that consider issues beyond the narrow confines of reproductive success.

One way that archaeologists might begin to overcome many of the "dehumanizing" tendencies of sociobiological narratives of gender and evolution would be to introduce concepts of agency into debates about human origins (for recent examples, see Dobres 1995; Dobres and Robb 2000; Johnson 2000; McNay 2000; but for potential dangers of incorporating agency theory into gender studies, see Gero 2000). While there is clearly more work to be done to define concepts of gender and agency in archaeology, both theoretically and methodologically, and to contextualize those ideas within the framework of the archaeological record, the ability of agency theory to mediate between binary categories such as nature/culture, public/private, male/female, and individual/society provides a valuable means of modeling human behavior in evolution (both individually and in groups) from a nonreductionist perspective. For example, the concept of social agency could potentially be linked to research on cultural transmission, such as models of social learning (e.g. Boyd and Richerson 1985), or to approaches that favor concepts of egalitarianism and complementarity rather than hierarchy and dominance in the evolution of human social behavior (e.g., Erdal and Whiten 1996; Graves-Brown 1996). Agency theory can also help us appreciate more fully the temporal dimensions of social change over long periods of time as well as during the short-term changes associated with various phases of the life cycle (see the following discussion). By considering trajectories of social change at these different temporal scales, we might begin to construct narratives of gender and evolution that transcend the narrowly defined, deterministic parameters of current models by acknowledging a role for individuals and groups as agents in their own life histories.

In assessing the value of archaeological contributions to the topic of gender and human evolution, it is essential to acknowledge the important work of a number of feminist and other archaeologists who have considered these issues, either generally or in more narrowly defined contexts, in some detail. These include Conkey (1991), Gero (1991), Nelson (1997:chap. 4), articles in Hager (1997), Sørensen (2000:chap. 10), and Conkey and Spector (1984). Individually and collectively, this wide-ranging research constitutes a valuable contribution to the gendered perspective on human evolution by drawing attention to the many gender biases of traditional archaeological models of human evolution. While critical appraisals of androcentric research constitute a fundamental first step in engendering human prehistory, they need to be reinforced by the construction of new models that transcend the theoretical and methodological biases of earlier research. In the remainder of this section, therefore, I wish to consider three particular approaches to human evolution that could be integrated with current gender theory and thereby avoid the pitfalls of determinist and reductionist thinking. While these proposed areas of research are by no means new and have yielded results that could now be used in research on gender and evolution, they have yet to explicitly address issues of gender in prehistoric contexts: 1) studies of the evolution of human life history that acknowledge the importance of multiple phases of the life cycle to adaptation and survival; 2) studies of gender, technology, and material culture that focus on cooperation rather than separation of male and female subsistence activities; and 3) studies of gender and cognitive evolution that do not assume from the start the existence of significant cognitive differences between males and females.

Gender and the Evolution of Human Life Histories

Life history perspectives in human evolution embrace a wide range of interactions between physical, behavioral, and social dimensions of human life and chart their fluctuation throughout the various stages of the life cycle in accordance with environmental constraints and adaptive needs (see Bogin and Smith 2000; Fedigan 1997; Gardiner 1995; Gilchrist 2000; Key 2000; Morbeck 1997). While life history narratives are based to a considerable extent on variable aspects of male and female anatomy and could therefore be regarded as sociobiological in orientation, their focus on the dynamic and flexible nature of human behavior and decision making, as well as on the specific strategies undertaken by individuals as they negotiate their way through the life course, links them with theories of social agency and enables them to circumvent the rigid determinism and reductionism of standard sociobiological models (Morbeck 1997:6; Vitzhum 1997).

When, why, and how did modern human life cycles evolve? And in what ways did differences in the life cycles of males and females shape our evolutionary history? These are questions that form the basis of much of the current research in the field, and the results of this research are of course relevant to an understanding of gender and human evolution. Answers to these questions are complex and demand recourse to recent research on life histories of nonhuman primates, particularly those of higher primates, such as chimpanzees and bonobos, whose genetic structures closely replicate those of modern humans (Streier 2001). By the same token, the behavior of early hominids (such as *Ardipithecus* and the various species of *Australopithecus*) more closely resembles pongid behavior than that of humans, with bipedal locomotion being the only significant difference between them (Wrangham 2001). Consequently, a great deal of attention is now being paid to the role of primate behavior in the construction of life history models of human evolution (e.g., Fedigan 1997; McLeod 1997; Morbeck 1997; Streier 2001; Wrangham 2001).

As a mitigating factor to potential gender bias in this research, Fausto-Sterling (2001:49–51) has noted the increased attention given to female subjects in primatological studies during the past thirty years, a development that she feels reflects the greater numbers of female researchers who have revised or completely overturned earlier androcentric interpretations of female primate behavior. The result has been that we now know a great deal about the life histories of male and female primates, and this information can be applied to research on the reproductive and survival strategies of early hominid groups. One particularly important example is provided by longitudinal studies of Japanese macaques (Fedigan 1997; Pavelka 1997). The careful observation and study of these primates over several generations suggest that female reproductive success is most closely linked to longevity, with the key to reproductive success being not a high birthrate but the steady production of offspring with adequate interbirth intervals over a long period of time. This contradicts traditional narratives of reproductive success in which fertility rather than longevity is deemed the key adaptive element, and it consequently suggests that one of the most important elements in female reproductive fitness is the ability of females to live long and healthy lives.

Life history approaches can also contribute to an understanding of the evolution of the human mating system, a topic that has been the subject of so much recent discussion in evolutionary psychology. When did human mating behavior emerge in its present form? Wrangham (2001:40) has argued that it is likely to have occurred at a time when there was a marked decrease in sexual dimorphism of body mass since great differences (i.e., large males and smaller females) imply male competition for mates and have behavioral correlates that do not fit the human pattern. Since there is only one point in evolutionary history where a significant male reduction and female increase in body mass occur (about 1.9 million years ago with the evolution of *H. erectus*), it is highly likely that modern human mating systems also emerged at that time. More important, this example demonstrates that human evolution is a dynamic process in which physical characteristics and their behavioral correlates evolved in a mosaic rather than a unilinear fashion, and it underscores the need to analyze various types of adaptive behavior within particular temporal and spatial frameworks.

While a detailed summary of the wide array of additional research on the evolution of the human life cycle lies beyond the scope of this chapter, mention should be made of several recent life history approaches to human reproduction that have a particular bearing on gender relations. These include research on novel features of the human reproductive system, such as long periods of gestation and infancy (e.g., Ellison 2001; Key 2000), both of which are likely to have evolved as the result of encephalization (Falk 1990; Robson 2004); the considerable energy requirements of gestating females that may have played a key role in the evolution of bipedality by enhancing females' ability to nourish themselves and their offspring (Leonard and Robertson 1997); short periods of lactation in order to reduce energy demands on postpartum females that became possible as the result of the greater levels of social interaction among human primates and are likely to have had an impact on social organization (Key and Aiello 1999); and the long female postreproductive stage (menopause) that is currently being interpreted as an adaptive advantage by enabling older, experienced females to contribute to the survival of offspring and grand-offspring (for the so-called grandmothering hypothesis, see Bogin and Smith 2000:416–18; Hawkes et al. 2000). In addition, several recent studies stress the reciprocal relationships between strategies of reproduction, survival, and cognition since the ability to survive and successfully reproduce within an evolving system of complex social interactions would have placed greater demands on cognitive abilities (Erdal and Whiten 1996; Lee 1996).

The emergence of a visible archaeological record with the appearance of the earliest known stone-tool assemblages associated with the genus *Homo* provides evidence for investigating the important role of material culture in the adaptive strategies of early human populations during later phases of their evolution. Interactions between people and material culture (e.g., the manufacture and manipulation of tools in order to enhance survival) thus became an integral part of human life history from about 2.6 million years ago on. Unfortunately, life history approaches have not yet been widely adopted in archaeological research on human evolution. Mithen (2001) notes the particular lack of archaeological attention to issues of childhood and cognition in premodern societies; given the importance of childhood for the cultural transmission of gender constructs, there is also a need to develop interdisciplinary approaches between archaeology, anthropology, and developmental psychology through which we might begin to investigate how gender constructs are formed, transformed, and transmitted within particular social contexts.

Gender, Technology, and Social Organization

The potential for archaeology to contribute to our understanding of the evolution of gender relations was raised nearly a decade ago by Graves-Brown (1996). In place of the classic gendered division of labor proposed by so many earlier models, he introduced the paradigm of "complementarity" as a force in human evolution, a process by which individuals and groups fulfill different roles in the completion of a task, such as cooperative hunting and gathering by single-sex groups, cooperative child care behavior among females, and economic activities that involve both sexes. He attributes the persistence of traditional models of sexual division of labor (in particular, male provisioning models, such as Lovejoy's hypothesis) to the overstated distinction between hunting and gathering (349). In response to more recent models in evolutionary psychology, he observes, "If women could organize a sex-strike they could organize themselves to get their own food, and of course they do" and that "defense against predators is better accomplished in a group than a pair bond" (350). Female reproductive success, he believes, should be predicated on the continuous exploitation of reliable sources of nutrition rather than behaviors associated with fertility and fecundity (350; on this point as well, see Hamilton 1984).

Similar conclusions have been drawn by Key and Aiello (1999) in an article that addresses the importance of cooperative behavior in human social life. Cooperation can take many forms other than the traditional narrative of the male–female pair bond, including bonds between brothers and sisters, grandmothers and grandchildren, and parents and children as well as the bonds of friendship between individuals who are not related at all by kinship ties. While high degrees of cooperative behavior have been observed among nonhuman primates, particularly chimpanzees, nowhere has cooperation reached the level of importance achieved by humans, among whom it is highly diversified and widespread. Key and Aiello emphasize the biological bases of the evolution of cooperative behavior and demonstrate the powerful effects it is likely to have had on the evolution of human social structures. These arguments could be just as readily linked, however, to the cultural dimensions of human life, in particular to the development of tools and technology in association with the emergence of the genus *Homo*.

The socially embedded nature of technology in early human societies has been emphasized by a number of scholars in recent years (e.g., Dobres 1995; Gilchrist 1999:40–42; Ingold 1994; Lemonnier 1993; Reynolds 1993). These social approaches to material culture challenge the assumption of modern industrialists that technological achievement is largely the result of individual rather than collective endeavors since in precapitalist societies "technical relations are social" (Ingold 1994:341). Accordingly, artifacts associated with preindustrial societies should be treated as repositories of information about cultural processes involving "heterotechnic" cooperation in which technical tasks are carried out not by lone craftsmen but by a number of individuals working together (341–42). Lemonnier's (1993) concept of *chaîne opératoire* is also important in this regard for characterizing technology as a multistage process requiring the labor and skills of many individuals working interdependently. The implications of these ideas for gendered approaches to technology in human evolution are enormous since cooperative models accommodate men, women, and even children as coparticipants in technical processes.

Dobres (1995) has developed these ideas in a somewhat different direction by applying concepts of gender and social agency to the study of prehistoric technology. In a case study that considers evidence of bone and antler technologies at a number of Magdalenian sites in the eastern French Pyrénées, Dobres notes considerable intra- and intersite variation in the distribution of six artifact types as well as differences in form, function, and material. On the basis of significant local and regional variations in technical practices, she concludes that bone and antler technology was "premised on flexibility around social norms" and on this basis proposes a model of heterarchical rather than hierarchical social organization during the Upper Paleolithic (41). In addition to integrating theoretical concepts of gender and social agency with particular bodies of archaeological data, Dobres makes several important conclusions concerning gender relations in the Magdalenian without attempting to attribute specific artifacts and technical strategies to particular genders. Further application of this approach to other areas and periods of the Paleolithic would increase our understanding of the interfaces between gender and technology in other phases of human evolution and could serve as a productive methodological basis for overcoming some of the doubts expressed by Gero (2000) concerning the application of theories of social agency to archaeological studies of gender.

Gender, Evolution, and Cognition

As Mithen (2001:116) has recently asserted, archaeologists "can and must play a role in the discussions and debates about cognitive evolution" both in order to more fully understand the past mentality of humans and in order to make a significant contribution to interdisciplinary debates currently going on in the cognitive sciences. Since the latter, as we have seen earlier, have adopted a decidedly polarized model of gender relations, it is important that archaeologists become engaged in research on cognitive evolution in order to challenge the stereotypical portrayals of males and females that continue to prevail in current models of human origins.

Although the increasingly tenuous evidence for sex differences in cognitive abilities should not be entirely dismissed (Gilchrist 1999:13), the gradual erosion of earlier arguments contending that male and female brains are "hardwired differently" should now begin to encourage the development of new models of cognitive evolution based on greater degrees of sexual parity. Instead of attributing presumed cognitive differences between males and females in modern populations to differential reproductive strategies that evolved in the ancestral past, we might now begin to adopt radically different approaches that do not assume the a priori existence of cognitive sex differences and that are supported by paleobiological and archaeological data. Foley (1996:63) has traced patterns of encephalization by measuring the neocortex of extinct hominid taxa relative to modern humans. Correlation of these results with archaeological data suggests that advances in technical skills, such as improved toolmaking abilities, did not always evolve in direct proportion to enlargement of cranial capacity but that different skills and capacities evolved at different rates and times in a mosaic and nonunilinear fashion. This poses significant challenges to current theories of male and female cognition that presume that there is little or no difference in the structure of the modern human mind and that of hominids who emerged in the so-called environment of evolutionary adaptation (Tooby and Cosmides 1992). In fact, there were many adaptive environments in human prehistory, and a complex consideration of the origins and development of cognitive differences between the sexes, if those differences have indeed existed, needs to treat cognition as a dynamic process rather than a static, reified entity.

Another area of potential importance for understanding the interfaces between gender and cognition is the "creative explosion" among early modern sapient populations during the Upper Paleolithic period. While a great deal of scholarly attention has been devoted to revealing and challenging the androcentric biases of earlier interpretations of parietal and portable art (e.g., Bahn and Vertut 1997; Bailey 1994; Conkey 1991; Conkey and Williams 1991; Rice 1981; Russell 1998; Tringham and Conkey 1998), there is now a need for innovative research on the use of art and symbolism in the construction of early human social identities. Recent discoveries of a rich and complex series of cave paintings at Chauvet, skeletons painted with red ocher and sculpted images of females at Cussac (some nearly five meters in length), and large intact living floors at La Garma near Altamira replete with refuse, bone and stone tools, batons, and rudimentary stone enclosures (Bahn 2004) furnish new evidence with which to interpret the rich "iconic vocabulary" of ancestral images from a gendered perspective (Gamble 1998). In place of earlier androcentric hypotheses such as "hunting magic" to account for the apparent sudden outburst of art and creativity of early *H. sapiens*, we might begin to consider more wide-ranging explanations involved the unprecedented use of visual symbolism, by women as well as men, in the creation of social identities (for the use of red ocher as body paint in the Middle Stone Age, see, e.g., Watts 1999). These will also help reverse the marginal role traditionally granted to women in the development of art, religion, language, and other symbolic systems—cognitive achievements that have come to be regarded as hallmarks of the creativity and success of our species.

Prospects for Engendering Human Evolution: The Need for Interdisciplinary Research

While very few archaeologists are guilty of the "biophobia" attributed to "traditional social scientists" by some evolutionary psychologists (e.g., Campbell 2002:1–8; Pinker 2002; Thornhill and Palmer 2000:chap. 5; Tooby and Cosmides 1992:24), it is fair to state that archaeological contributions to human evolution have often been parochial in their overriding focus on chronology and typology as well as their lack of sufficient attention to relevant research in other fields (e.g., evolutionary biology, primatology, and cognitive psychology). Current research in the cognitive sciences is particularly important in view of some of the hypotheses that have recently been proposed in the field of evolutionary archaeology (e.g., Kohn and Mithen 1999; Shennan 2002; Steele and Shennan 1996). Here the concept of embodiment is of potential importance for integrating rather than dichotomizing the physical and cognitive aspects of human behavior (Butler 1990:chap. 1; Foucault 1978; Meskell 1998, 2000). As Gilchrist (1999:13) has recently observed, "Whether gender, social cognition or sexuality are dependent fully on biology *or* culture is no longer the issue. The interesting questions are how biological and/or cognitive difference is interpreted culturally, how this varies between societies, and how the mind and body may evolve in response to cultural definitions of gender."

In attempting to construct new models of human evolution that integrate archaeological, biological, and psychological research, there is also a need to build closer links between archaeologists, anthropologists, evolutionary biologists, and psychologists through multidisciplinary studies that can be validated through the rigorous application of empirical evidence. The potential for this type of interdisciplinary research has been demonstrated in a number of papers during the past decade (e.g., Erdal and Whiten 1996; Foley 1996; Robson-Brown 1996; Toth and Schick 1994) that integrate archaeological evidence with research in the biological and social sciences in the attempt to generate viable models for the evolution of human behavior. Unfortunately, almost all this research so far has failed to incorporate issues of gender. Since, as Thomas (1998:151) states, "the defining characteristic of humanity is not the hardware within, but the relationships between persons" and since human relationships lie at the very core of attempts to engender the prehistoric past, these are precisely the issues that research on gender and human evolution should now begin to address.

Acknowledgments

I would like to thank Sarah Nelson for inviting me to contribute to this important volume. Clive Bonsall and Eddie Peltenburg kindly read through a preliminary draft of the text and offered a number of useful and constructive comments. I naturally assume responsibility for the contents, including any errors or oversights that may occur.

References

Aiello, L. C., and J. C. K. Wells
    2002   Energetics and the Evolution of the Genus Homo. *Annual Review of Anthropology* 31:323–38.
Alper, J. S.
    1985   Sex Differences in Brain Asymmetry: A Critical Analysis. *Feminist Studies* 11(1):7–37.
Anderson, J. R.
    1983   *The Architecture of Cognition*. Cambridge, MA: Harvard University Press.
Appleman, P., ed.
    2001   *Darwin*. Norton Critical Edition. 3rd ed. New York: Norton.
Bahn, P.
    2004   New Developments in Ice-Age Art. Unpublished lecture delivered at the Department of Archaeology, University of Edinburgh, November 22.
Bahn, P., and J. Vertut
    1997   *Journey through the Ice Age*. London: Weidenfeld & Nicolson.
Bailey, D. W.
    1994   Reading Prehistoric Figurines as Individuals. *World Archaeology* 25:321–31.

Baron-Cohen, S.
  2003 *The Essential Difference*. London: Penguin.
Barrett, J. C.
  2000 Fields of Discourse: Reconstituting a Social Archaeology. In *Interpretive Archaeology: A Reader*. J. Thomas, ed. Pp. 23–32. London: Leicester University Press.
Barrett, L., R. Dunbar, and J. Lycett
  2002 *Human Evolutionary Psychology*. Basingstoke: Palgrave.
Bartholomew, G., and J. Birdsell
  1953 Ecology and the Protohominids. *American Anthropologist* 55:481–98.
Benbow, C. P., and J. C. Stanley
  1980 Sex Differences in Mathematical Ability: Fact or Artifact? *Science* 210:1262–64.
Bergounioux, F. M.
  1961 Notes on the Mentality of Primitive Man. In *Social Life of Early Man*. S. L. Washburn, ed. Pp. 106–18. London: Methuen.
Binford, L.
  1968 Methodological Considerations of the Archaeological Use of Ethnographic Data. In *Man the Hunter*. R. B. Lee and I. DeVore, eds. Pp. 268–73. Chicago: Aldine.
  1981 *Bones: Ancient Men and Modern Myths*. New York: Academic Press.
  1985 Human Ancestors: Changing Views of Their Behavior. *Journal of Anthropological Archaeology* 4:292–327.
  1986 Commentary on Bunn and Kroll's "Systematic Butchery by Plio-Pleistocene Hominids at Olduvai Gorge." *Current Anthropology* 27:444–46.
  1988 Fact and Fiction about the *Zinjanthropus* Floor: Data, Arguments and Interpretations. *Current Anthropology* 29:123–35.
  1989 *Debating Archaeology*. New York: Academic Press.
Bleier, R.
  1984 *Science and Gender: A Critique of Biology and Its Theories on Women*. New York: Pergamon Press.
Blumenschein, R. J.
  1991 Breakfast at Olorgesailie: The Natural History Approach to Early Stone Age Archaeology. *Journal of Human Evolution* 21:307–27.
Bogin, B., and B. H. Smith
  2000 Evolution of the Human Life Cycle. In *Human Biology: An Evolutionary and Biocultural Perspective*. S. Stinson, B. Bogin, R. Huss-Ashmore, and D. Rourki, eds. Pp. 377–424. New York: Wiley-Liss.
Boone, J. L., and E. A. Smith
  1998 Is It Evolution Yet? A Critique of Evolutionary Archaeology. *Current Anthropology* 39:S141–73.
Boyd, R., and P. J. Richerson
  1985 *Culture and the Evolutionary Process*. Chicago: University of Chicago Press.

Buss, D. M.
　1999　*Evolutionary Psychology: The New Science of the Mind.* Needham Heights, MA: Allyn and Bacon.
Butler, J.
　1990　*Gender Trouble: Feminism and the Subversion of Identity.* New York: Routledge.
Campbell, A.
　2002　*A Mind of Her Own: The Evolutionary Psychology of Women.* New York: Oxford University Press.
Campbell, B. G.
　1992　*Humankind Emerging.* 6th ed. New York: HarperCollins.
Cartmill, M.
　1993　*A View to a Death in the Morning: Hunting and Nature through History.* Cambridge, MA: Harvard University Press.
Conkey, M.
　1991　Contexts for Action, Contexts of Power: Material Culture and Gender in the Magdalenian. In *Engendering Archaeology: Women and Prehistory.* J. M. Gero and M. W. Conkey, eds. Pp. 57–92. Oxford: Blackwell.
Conkey, M. W., and J. D. Spector
　1984　Archaeology and the Study of Gender. In *Advances in Archaeological Theory and Methods.* Vol. 7. M. Schiffer, ed. Pp. 1–38. New York: Academic Press.
Conkey, M., with S. H. Williams
　1991　Original Narratives: The Political Economy of Gender in Archaeology. In *Gender at the Crossroads of Knowledge: Feminist Anthropology in the Postmodern Era.* M. di Leonardo, ed. Pp. 102–39. Berkeley: University of California Press.
Cronin, H.
　1991　*The Ant and the Peacock: Altruism and Sexual Selection from Darwin to Today.* New York: Cambridge University Press.
Dahlberg, F., ed.
　1981　*Woman the Gatherer.* New Haven, CT: Yale University Press.
Dawkins, R.
　1976　*The Selfish Gene.* Oxford: Oxford University Press.
Dennett, D.
　1995　*Darwin's Dangerous Idea.* London: Allen Lane/Penguin.
Dobres, M.-A.
　1995　Gender and Prehistoric Technology: On the Social Agency of Technical Strategies. *World Archaeology* 27(1):25–49.
Dobres, M.-A., and J. Robb, eds.
　2000　*Agency in Archaeology.* London: Routledge.
Donald, M.
　1991　*Origins of the Modern Mind.* Cambridge, MA: Harvard University Press.
Dunnell, R. C.
　1980　Evolutionary Theory and Archaeology. In *Advances in Archaeological Method and Theory.* Vol. 3. M. Schiffer, ed. Pp. 35–99. New York: Academic Press.

Ellison, P. T.
  2001 *On Fertile Ground: A Natural History of Human Reproduction.* Cambridge, MA: Harvard University Press.
Ember, C. R., and M. Ember
  1993 *Anthropology.* 7th ed. Englewood Cliffs, NJ: Prentice Hall.
Erdal, D., and A. Whiten
  1996 Egalitarianism and Machiavellian Intelligence in Human Evolution. In *Modelling the Early Human Mind.* P. Mellars and K. Gibson, eds. Pp. 139–50. Cambridge: McDonald Institute for Archaeological Research.
Estiokio-Griffin, A., and P. Bion Griffin
  1981 Woman the Hunter: The Agta. In *Woman the Gatherer.* F. Dahlberg, ed. Pp. 121–51. New Haven, CT: Yale University Press.
Fairweather, H.
  1976 Sex Differences in Cognition. *Cognition* 4:231–80.
Falk, D.
  1990 Brain Evolution in *Homo*: The "Radiator" Theory. *Behavioral Brain Science* 13:333–81.
  1997 Brain Evolution in Females. In *Women in Human Evolution.* L. D. Hager, ed. Pp. 114–36. London: Routledge.
Fausto-Sterling, A.
  1992 *Myths of Gender: Biological Theories about Women and Men.* New York: Basic Books.
  2000 *Sexing the Body: Gender Politics and the Construction of Sexuality.* New York: Basic Books.
  2001 Beyond Difference: Feminism and Evolutionary Psychology. In *Alas Poor Darwin: Arguments against Evolutionary Psychology.* H. Rose and S. Rose, eds. Pp. 174–89. London: Vintage Books.
Fedigan, L.
  1986 The Changing Role of Women in Models of Human Evolution. *Annual Reviews of Anthropology* 15:25–66.
  1997 Changing Views of Female Life Histories. In *The Evolving Female: A Life-History Perspective.* M. E. Morbeck, A. Galloway, and A. L. Zihlman, eds. Pp. 15–26. Princeton, NJ: Princeton University Press.
Feingold, A.
  1988 Cognitive Gender Differences Are Disappearing. *American Psychologist* 43:95–103.
Fodor, J.
  1983 *The Modularity of Mind.* Cambridge, MA: MIT Press.
Foley, R. A.
  1996 Measuring Cognition in Extinct Hominids. In *Modelling the Early Human Mind.* P. Mellars and K. Gibson, eds. Pp. 57–65. Cambridge: McDonald Institute for Archaeological Research.

Foucault, M.
    1978   *The History of Sexuality*. London: Routledge.
Gamble, C.
    1998   Foreword. In *Ancestral Images: The Iconography of Human Origins*. S. Moser. Pp. ix–xxiv. Ithaca, NY: Cornell University Press.
Gardiner, J. K.
    1995   *Provoking Agents: Gender and Agency in Theory and Practice*. Urbana: University of Illinois Press.
Geary, D. C.
    1996   Sexual Selection and Sex Differences in Mathematical Abilities. *Behavioral and Brain Sciences* 19:229–84.
Gero, J.
    1985   Socio-Politics of Archaeology and the Woman-at-Home Ideology. *American Antiquity* 50(2):342–50.
    1991   Genderlithics: Women's Roles in Stone Tool Production. In *Engendering Archaeology: Women and Prehistory*. J. M. Gero and M. W. Conkey, eds. Pp. 163–93. Oxford: Blackwell.
    2000   Troubled Travels in Agency and Feminism. In *Agency in Archaeology*. M.-A. Dobres and J. Robb, eds. Pp. 40–50. London: Routledge.
Gilchrist, R.
    1999   *Gender and Archaeology: Contesting the Past*. London: Routledge.
    2000   Archaeological Biographies: Realizing Human Lifecycles, -Courses and -Histories. *World Archaeology* 31(3):325–28.
Gould, S. J.
    1977   Biological Potentiality vs. Biological Determinism. In *Ever since Darwin*. S. J. Gould. Pp. 251–59. New York: Norton.
    1981   *The Mismeasure of Man*. New York: Norton.
Graves-Brown, P.
    1996   Their Commonwealths Are Not as We Supposed: Sex, Gender and Material Culture in Human Evolution. In *The Archaeology of Human Ancestry: Power, Sex and Tradition*. J. Steele and S. Shennan, eds. Pp. 347–60. London: Routledge.
Hager, L. D., ed.
    1997   *Women in Human Evolution*. London: Routledge.
Halpern, D. F.
    1992   *Sex Differences in Cognitive Abilities*. 2nd ed. Hillsdale, NJ: Lawrence Erlbaum Associates.
Hamilton, M. E.
    1984   Revising Evolutionary Narratives: A Consideration of Alternative Assumptions about Sexual Selection and Competition for Mates. *American Anthropologist* 86:651–62.
Hamilton, W. D.
    1964   The Genetical Evolution of Social Behaviour. *Journal of Theoretical Biology* 7:1–52.

Haraway, D.
   1978a   Animal Sociology and a Natural Economy of the Body Politic, Part I: A Political Physiology of Dominance. *Signs* 4(1):21–36.
   1978b   Animal Sociology and a Natural Economy of the Body Politic, Part II: The Past Is the Contested Zone: Human Nature and Theories of Production and Reproduction in Primate Behavior Studies. *Signs* 4(1):37–60.
   1989   *Primate Visions: Gender, Race and Nature in the World of Modern Science*. London: Routledge.

Haviland, W. A.
   2000   *Human Evolution and Prehistory*. 5th ed. Orlando: Harcourt College.

Hawkes, K.
   1996   Foraging Differences between Men and Women: Behavioural Ecology of the Sexual Division of Labour. In *The Archaeology of Human Ancestry: Power, Sex and Tradition*. J. Steele and S. Shennan, eds. Pp. 283–305. London: Routledge.

Hawkes, K., J. F. O'Connell, N. Blurton-Jones, H. Alvarez, and E. L. Charnov
   2000   The Grandmother Hypothesis and Human Evolution. In *Adaptation and Human Behavior*. L. Cronk, N. Chagnon, and W. Irons, eds. Pp. 237–58. New York: Aldine de Gruyter.

Ingold, T.
   1994   Introduction (Part V). In *Tools, Language and Cognition in Human Evolution*. K. R. Gibson and T. Ingold, eds. Pp. 337–45. Cambridge: Cambridge University Press.

Isaac, G. Ll.
   1968   Traces of Pleistocene Hunters: An East African Example. In *Man the Hunter*. R. B. Lee and I. DeVore, eds. Pp. 253–61. Chicago: Aldine.
   1971   The Diet of Early Man: Aspects of Archaeological Evidence from Lower and Middle Pleistocene Sites in Africa. *World Archaeology* 2:278–99.
   1978   The Food Sharing Behavior of Protohuman Hominids. *Scientific American* 238:90–108.

Johnson, M.
   2000   Conceptions of Agency in Archaeological Interpretation. In *Interpretive Archaeology: A Reader*. J. Thomas, ed. Pp. 211–27. London: Leicester University Press.

Jolly, C. J., and R. White
   1995   *Physical Anthropology and Archaeology*. 5th ed. New York: McGraw-Hill.

Jurmain, R., H. Nelson, L. Kilgore, and W. Trevathan
   2000   *Introduction to Physical Anthropology*. 8th ed. Stamford, CT: Wadsworth/Thomson Learning.

Jurmain, R., H. Nelson, and W. A. Turnbaugh
   1990   *Understanding Physical Anthropology and Archaeology*. 4th ed. St. Paul, MN: West.

Key, C.
   2000   The Evolution of Human Life History. *World Archaeology* 31:329–50.

Key, C. A., and L. C. Aiello
  1999 The Evolution of Social Organization. In *The Evolution of Culture*. R. Dunbar, C. Knight, and C. Power, eds. Pp. 15–33. Edinburgh: Edinburgh University Press.
Kingdon, J.
  2003 *Lowly Origin*. Princeton, NJ: Princeton University Press.
Knight, C.
  1996 Darwinism and Collective Representations. In *The Archaeology of Human Ancestry: Power, Sex and Tradition*. J. Steele and S. Shennan, eds. Pp. 331–46. London: Routledge.
Kohn, M., and S. Mithen
  1999 Handaxes: Products of Sexual Selection? *Antiquity* 73:518–26.
Kottak, C. P.
  2000 *Anthropology: The Exploration of Human Diversity*. 8th international ed. London: McGraw-Hill Higher Education.
Lake, M.
  1996 Archaeological Inference and the Explanation of Hominid Evolution. In *The Archaeology of Human Ancestry: Power, Sex and Tradition*. J. Steele and S. Shennan, eds. Pp. 184–206. London: Routledge.
Leacock, E.
  1978 Women's Status in Egalitarian Society: Implications for Social Evolution. *Current Anthropology* 19(2):247–75.
  1983 Interpreting the Origins of Gender Inequality: Conceptual and Historical Problems. *Dialectical Anthropology* 7(4):263–84.
Lee, P. C.
  1996 Inferring Cognition from Social Behaviour in Non-Humans. In *Modelling the Human Mind*. P. Mellars and K. Gibson, eds. Pp. 131–38. Cambridge: McDonald Institute for Archaeological Research.
Lee, R. B.
  1968 What Hunters Do for a Living, or, How to Make Out on Scarce Resources. In *Man the Hunter*. R. B. Lee and I. DeVore, eds. Pp. 30–48. Chicago: Aldine.
  1979 *The !Kung San: Men, Women and Work in a Foraging Society*. New York: Cambridge University Press.
Lee, R. B., and I. DeVore, eds.
  1968 *Man the Hunter*. Chicago: Aldine.
Lee, R. B., and I. DeVore
  1976 *Kalahari Hunter-Gatherers*. Cambridge, MA: Harvard University Press.
Leibowitz, L.
  1975 Perspectives on the Evolution of Sex Differences. In *Toward an Anthropology of Women*. R. R. Reiter, ed. Pp. 20–35. New York: Monthly Review Press.
Lemonnier, P.
  1993 Introduction. In *Technological Choices: Transformation in Material Cultures since the Neolithic*. P. Lemonnier, ed. Pp. 1–34. London: Routledge.

Leonard, W. R., and M. L. Robertson
    1997   Rethinking the Energetics of Bipedality. *Current Anthropology* 38(2):304–9.
Linn, M. C., and A. C. Petersen
    1985   Emergence and Characterization of Sex Differences in Spatial Ability: A Meta-Analysis. *Child Development* 56:1479–98.
Linton, S.
    1971   Woman the Gatherer: Male Bias in Anthropology. In *Women in Perspective: A Guide for Cross-Cultural Studies*. S.-E. Jacobs, ed. Pp. 9–21. Urbana: University of Illinois Press.
Lovejoy, O.
    1981   The Origin of Man. *Science* 211(23 January):341–49.
    1988   Evolution of Human Walking. *Scientific American*, November, 82–89.
Low, B.
    2000   *Why Sex Matters*. Princeton, NJ: Princeton University Press.
Lyman, R. L., and M. J. O'Brien
    1998   The Goals of Evolutionary Archaeology: History and Explanation. *Current Anthropology* 39(5):615–52.
Maccoby, E. E., and C. N. Jacklin
    1974   *The Psychology of Sex Differences*. Stanford, CA: Stanford University Press.
Maynard Smith, J.
    1977   Parental Investment—A Prospective Analysis. *Animal Behaviour* 25:1–9.
McGuinness, C.
    1998   Cognition. In *Gender and Psychology*. K. Trew and J. Kremer, eds. Pp. 66–81. New York: Arnold.
McLeod, B.
    1997   Life History, Females and Evolution: A Commentary. In *The Evolving Female: A Life-History Perspective*. M. E. Morbeck, A. Galloway, and A. L. Zihlman, eds. Pp. 270–75. Princeton, NJ: Princeton University Press.
McNay, L.
    2000   *Gender and Agency: Reconfiguring the Subject in Feminist and Social Theory*. Cambridge: Polity Press.
Mellars, P., and K. Gibson, eds.
    1996   *Modelling the Early Human Mind*. Cambridge: McDonald Institute for Archaeological Research.
Meskell, L.
    1998   The Irresistible Body and the Seduction of Archaeology. In *Changing Bodies, Changing Meanings: Studies on the Human Body in Antiquity*. D. Montserrat, ed. Pp. 139–61. London: Routledge.
    2000   Writing the Body in Archaeology. In *Reading the Body: Representations and Remains in the Archaeological Record*. A. E. Rautman, ed. Pp. 13–21. Philadelphia: University of Pennsylvania Press.

Miller, Geoffrey
    2001   *The Mating Mind: How Sexual Choice Shaped the Evolution of Human Nature*. London: Vintage Books.

Mishler, E. G.
    1979   Meaning in Context: Is There Any Other Kind? *Harvard Educational Review* 49:1–19.

Mithen, S.
    1990   *Thoughtful Foragers: A Study of Prehistoric Decision Making*. Cambridge: Cambridge University Press.
    1996a   *The Prehistory of the Mind: A Search for the Origins of Art, Religion and Science*. London: Phoenix.
    1996b   Social Learning and Cultural Tradition: Interpreting Early Palaeolithic Technology. In *The Archaeology of Human Ancestry: Power, Sex and Tradition*. J. Steele and S. Shennan, eds. Pp. 207–29. London: Routledge.
    2001   Archaeological Theory and Theories of Cognitive Evolution. In *Archaeological Theory Today*. I. Hodder, ed. Pp. 98–121. Cambridge: Polity Press.

Morbeck, M. E.
    1997   Life History, the Individual and Human Evolution. In *The Evolving Female: A Life-History Perspective*. M. E. Morbeck, A. Galloway, and A. L. Zihlman, eds. Pp. 3–14. Princeton, NJ: Princeton University Press.

Nelson, S. M.
    1997   *Gender in Archaeology: Analyzing Power and Prestige*. Walnut Creek, CA: AltaMira Press.

Noble, W., and I. Davidson
    1996   *Human Evolution, Language and Mind: A Psychological and Archaeological Inquiry*. Cambridge: Cambridge University Press.

Parlee, M. B.
    1979   Psychology and Women. *Signs* 5:121–33.

Pavelka, M. S. M.
    1997   The Social Life of Female Japanese Monkeys. In *The Evolving Female: A Life-History Perspective*. M. E. Morbeck, A. Galloway, and A. L. Zihlman, eds. Pp. 76–85. Princeton, NJ: Princeton University Press.

Pinker, S.
    1997   *How the Mind Works*. London: Penguin.
    2002   *The Blank Slate: The Modern Denial of Human Nature*. London: Allen Lane.

Power, C., and I. Watts
    1996   Female Strategies and Collective Behaviour: The Archaeology of Earliest *Homo sapiens sapiens*. In *The Archaeology of Human Ancestry: Power, Sex and Tradition*. J. Steele and S. Shennan, eds. Pp. 306–30. London: Routledge.

Renfrew, C., and C. Scarre, eds.
    1998   *Cognition and Culture: The Archaeology of Symbolic Storage*. Cambridge: McDonald Institute for Archaeological Research.

Reynolds, P. C.
    1993   The Complementation Theory of Language and Tool Use. In *Tools, Language and Cognition in Human Evolution*. K. R. Gibson and T. Ingold, eds. Pp. 407–28. Cambridge: Cambridge University Press.

Rice, P. C.
    1981   Prehistoric Venuses: Symbols of Motherhood or Womanhood? *Journal of Anthropological Research* 37:402–14.

Ridley, M.
    1993   *The Red Queen: Sex and the Evolution of Human Nature*. London: Penguin.
    2003   *Nature via Nurture: Genes, Experience and What Makes Us Human*. London: Fourth Estate.

Robson, S. L.
    2004   Breast Milk, Diet and Large Human Brains. *Current Anthropology* 45(3): 419–25.

Robson-Brown, K. A.
    1996   Systematics and Integrated Methods for the Modeling of the Pre-Modern Human Mind. In *Modelling the Early Human Mind*. P. Mellars and K. Gibson, eds. Pp. 103–17. Cambridge: McDonald Institute for Archaeological Research.

Rose, H., and S. Rose, eds.
    2001   *Alas Poor Darwin: Arguments against Evolutionary Psychology*. London: Vintage Books.

Rose, S.
    1998   *Lifelines: Biology, Freedom, Determinism*. London: Penguin.

Rose, S., R. C. Lewontin, and L. J. Kamin
    1984   *Not in Our Genes: Biology, Ideology and Human Nature*. Harmondsworth: Penguin.

Rosenberg, R.
    1982   *Beyond Separate Spheres*. New Haven, CT: Yale University Press.

Russell, P.
    1998   The Paleolithic Mother-Goddess: Fact or Fiction? In *Reader in Gender Archaeology*. K. Hayes-Gilpin and D. S. Whitley, eds. Pp. 261–68. London: Routledge.

Shanks, M., and C. Tilley
    1987   *Re-Constructing Archaeology*. Cambridge: Cambridge University Press.

Shaywitz, B. A., S. E. Shaywitz, K. R. Pugh, R. T. Constable, P. Skudlarski, R. K. Fulbright, R. A. Bronen, J. M. Fletcher, D. P. Shankweller, L. Katz, and J. C. Gore
    1995   Sex Differences in the Functional Organization of the Brain for Language. *Nature* 373:607–9.

Shennan, S.
    2002   *Genes, Memes and Human History*. London: Thames and Hudson.
    2004   Analytical Archaeology. In *A Companion to Archaeology*. J. Bintliff, ed. Pp. 3–20. Oxford: Blackwell.

Silverman, I., and M. Eals
  1992   Sex Differences in Spatial Abilities: Evolutionary Theory and Data. In *The Adapted Mind: Evolutionary Psychology and the Generation of Culture*. J. H. Barkow, L. Cosmides, and J. Tooby, eds. Pp. 533–49. Oxford: Oxford University Press.
Silverman, I., and K. Phillips
  1998   The Evolutionary Psychology of Spatial Sex Differences. In *Handbook of Evolutionary Psychology*. C. Crawford and D. L. Krebs, eds. Pp. 595–612. Mahwah, NJ: Lawrence Erlbaum Associates.
Slocum, S.
  1975   Woman the Gatherer: Male Bias in Anthropology. In *Toward an Anthropology of Women*. R. R. Reiter, ed. Pp. 36–50. New York: Monthly Review Press.
Smith, E. A., and B. Winterhalder, eds.
  1992   *Evolutionary Ecology and Human Behaviour*. New York: Aldine de Gruyter.
Sørensen, M. L. S.
  2000   *Gender Archaeology*. Cambridge: Polity Press.
Sperber, D.
  1996   *Explaining Culture: A Naturalistic Approach*. Oxford: Blackwell.
Stanford, C. B.
  2001   The Ape's Gift: Meat-Eating, Meat-Sharing and Human Evolution. In *Tree of Origin: What Primate Behavior Can Tell Us about Human Social Evolution*. F. B. M. de Waal, ed. Pp. 97–117. Cambridge, MA: Harvard University Press.
Steele, J., and S. Shennan, eds.
  1996   *The Archaeology of Human Ancestry: Power, Sex and Tradition*. London: Routledge.
Stein, P. L., and B. M. Rowe
  1993   *Physical Anthropology*. 5th ed. New York: McGraw-Hill.
Stern, J. T., and R. Sussman
  1983   The Locomotor Anatomy of *Australopithecus afarensis*. American Journal of Physical Anthropology 60:279–317.
Streier, K. B.
  2001   Beyond the Apes: Reasons to Consider the Entire Primate Order. In *Tree of Origin: What Primate Behavior Can Tell Us about Human Social Evolution*. F. B. M. de Waal, ed. Pp. 71–93. Cambridge, MA: Harvard University Press.
Tague, R., and O. Lovejoy
  1986   The Obstetric Pelvis of A. L. 288-1 (Lucy). Journal of Human Evolution 15(4):237–55.
Tanner, N., and A. L. Zihlman
  1976   Women in Evolution. Part I: Innovation and Selection in Human Origins. Signs 1(3):104–19.
Tavris, C.
  1992   *The Mismeasure of Woman*. New York: Touchstone.
Teleki, G.
  1973   *The Predatory Behavior of Wild Chimpanzees*. Lewisburg, PA: Bucknell University Press.

Thomas, J.
  1998   Some Problems with the Notion of External Symbolic Storage, and the Case of Neolithic Material Culture in Britain. In *Cognition and Culture: The Archaeology of Symbolic Storage*. C. Renfrew and C. Scarre, eds. Pp. 149–56. Cambridge: Cambridge University Press.

Thornhill, R., and C. T. Palmer
  2000   *A Natural History of Rape: Biological Bases of Sexual Coercion*. Cambridge, MA: MIT Press.

Tooby, J., and L. Cosmides
  1992   The Psychological Foundations of Culture. In *The Adapted Mind*. J. Barkow, L. Cosmides, and J. Tooby, eds. Pp. 19–136. New York: Oxford University Press.

Toth, N., and K. Schick
  1994   Early Stone Industries and Inferences regarding Language and Cognition. In *Tools, Language and Cognition in Human Evolution*. K. R. Gibson and T. Ingold, eds. Pp. 346–61. Cambridge: Cambridge University Press.

Tringham, R., and M. Conkey
  1998   Rethinking Figurines: A Critical View from Archaeology of Gimbutas, the "Goddess" and Popular Culture. In *Ancient Goddesses*. L. Goodison and C. Morris, eds. Pp. 22–45. London: British Museum Publications.

Trivers, R. L.
  1972   Parental Investment and Sexual Selection. In *Sexual Selection and the Descent of Man*. B. Campbell, ed. Pp. 136–79. Chicago: Aldine.

Vitzhum, V. J.
  1997   Flexibility and Paradox: The Evolution of a Flexibly Responsive Reproductive System. In *The Evolving Female: A Life-History Perspective*. M. E. Morbeck, A. Galloway, and A. L. Zihlman, eds. Pp. 242–58. Princeton, NJ: Princeton University Press.

Voyer, D., et al.
  1995   Magnitude of Sex Differences in Spatial Abilities: A Meta-Analysis and Consideration of Critical Variables. *Psychological Bulletin* 117(2):250–70.

Washburn, S. L.
  1951   The Analysis of Primate Evolution with Particular Reference to the Origin of Man. *Cold Spring Harbor Symposia on Quantitative Biology* 15:67–78.

Washburn, S. L., and V. Avis
  1958   Evolution of Human Behavior. In *Behavior and Evolution*. A. Roe and G. G. Simpson, eds. Pp. 421–36. New Haven, CT: Yale University Press.

Washburn, S. L., and I. DeVore
  1961   Social Behavior of Baboons and Early Man. In *Social Life of Early Man*. S. L. Washburn, ed. Pp. 91–105. London: Methuen.

Washburn, S. L., and C. S. Lancaster
  1968   The Evolution of Hunting. In *Man the Hunter*. R. B. Lee and I. DeVore, eds. Pp. 293–303. Chicago: Aldine.

Watts, I.
   1999   The Origin of Symbolic Culture. In *The Evolution of Culture*. R. Dunbar, C. Knight, and C. Power, eds. Pp. 113–36. Edinburgh: Edinburgh University Press.

Wilson, E. O.
   1975   *Sociobiology: The New Synthesis*. Cambridge, MA: Harvard University Press.

Wrangham, R. W.
   2001   Out of the Pan, into the Fire: How Our Ancestors' Evolution Depended on What They Ate. In *Tree of Origin: What Primate Behavior Can Tell Us about Human Social Evolution*. F. B. M. de Waal, ed. Pp. 121–43. Cambridge, MA: Harvard University Press.

Wright, R.
   1994   *The Moral Animal: Why We Are the Way We Are*. London: Abacus.

Yanagisako, S., and C. Delaney
   1995   *Naturalizing Power: Essays in Feminist Cultural Analysis*. London: Routledge.

Zihlman, A. L.
   1978   Women in Evolution Part 2: Subsistence and Social Organization among Early Hominids. *Signs* 4(1):4–20.
   1981   Women as Shapers of the Human Adaptation. In *Woman the Gatherer*. F. Dahlberg, ed. Pp. 75–120. New Haven, CT: Yale University Press.
   1997a   The Paleolithic Glass Ceiling: Women in Human Evolution. In *Women in Human Evolution*. L. D. Hager, ed. Pp. 91–113. London: Routledge.
   1997b   Women's Bodies, Women's Lives: An Evolutionary Perspective. In *The Evolving Female: A Life-History Perspective*. M. E. Morbeck, A. Galloway, and A. L. Zihlman, eds. Pp. 185–97. Princeton, NJ: Princeton University Press.
   1998   Woman the Gatherer: The Role of Women in Early Hominid Evolution. In *Reader in Gender Archaeology*. K. Hays-Gilpin and D. S. Whitley, eds. Pp. 91–105. London: Routledge.

Gender Dynamics in Hunter-Gatherer Society: Archaeological Methods and Perspectives

15

HETTY JO BRUMBACH AND ROBERT JARVENPA

WHAT IS THE NATURE OF gender difference and gender relations in hunter-gatherer society? More pointedly, what is our understanding of gender dynamics in hunter-gatherer societies of the past as interpreted through archaeology?

Addressing such questions is to acknowledge some formidable obstacles. Not the least of these, for most archaeologists, is the absence of living cultural systems from which to model female and male behaviors. Conventional archaeology lacks living, breathing consultants who may offer their own interpretations of female and male lives from a cultural insider's vantage point. Ethnoarchaeological studies, as well as judicious use of analogy and inference from the ethnographic and ethnohistoric record, hold promise for bridging some of these gaps. Even so, deciphering gender patterns in societies of the remote past may be akin to "working without a net."

Based in part on biological reproductive behaviors and in part on negotiated ideology and social relations, gender is deeply rooted in all societies. As Sassaman (1992:71) argues, "Gender is the primary social variable of the labor process in forager or hunter-gatherer societies." Indeed, it may be the oldest and most fundamental distinction shaping human experience. Gender dynamics among hunter-gatherers in prehistory, therefore, are central to our understanding of the human condition at large. Since 90 percent of our species' evolutionary history occurred in the context of hunting, fishing, and foraging economies, in the absence of domestication and food production, the kinds of relationships forged between women and men in those contexts are fundamental precedents in the development of human sociocultural systems generally.

To help clarify these precedents, this chapter reviews some major themes in research on gender among prehistoric hunter-gatherers.[1] What kinds of evidence or *assumptions* have archaeologists marshaled in this effort? The distinction between evidence and assumption is not trivial. As Conkey and Spector (1984:2) observe, the archaeological literature is "permeated with assumptions, assertions, and purported statements of 'fact' about gender" despite, until recently, a disinterest in formal analysis of such matters. Because hunter-gatherers occupied the earliest and longest span of prehistory, the chasm between ethnographic-ethnohistoric patterns on the one hand and the archaeological record on the other is most daunting. This gap presents formidable challenges for analysis and uses of analogy.[2] Accordingly, we seek an understanding of both overt and implicit interpretations of gender by archaeologists and the kinds and quality of information, if any, they are based on. Several broad questions emerge from and may be asked of the literature on prehistoric hunter-gatherers:

1. What is known of the sexual division of labor?
2. Are women's and men's tools and tool kits and their uses decipherable?
3. How are women's and men's activities situated in households and other spaces?
4. What do skeletal analyses reveal about the biological, demographic, and social dimensions of women's and men's lives?

While these issues are interconnected, specific studies or particular authors may focus initial attention on one question or another. Much of the literature has a frankly materialist bias, emphasizing ecological-economic infrastructure and the social relations of production that support it.[3] What are the strengths, limitations, and omissions in this literature? What more do we need to know? Are dimensions of power, prestige, and vantage point accessible to researchers?

The Great Divide? Sexual Divisions of Labor

Perhaps more than any other topic regarding prehistoric hunter-gatherers, the sexual division of labor has been a lightning rod for inappropriate analogies, muddled models, misconceptions mired in myth, and misrepresentations of data. In part, this is because what women and men did in their daily lives—or what archaeologists think they should have been doing—is an emotional projection screen inviting a plethora of hopes, fears, and biased assumptions embedded in the gender ideology of the West (Kent 1998:39).

In conventional usage, "the sexual division of labor" refers to the rules and norms that govern assignment of work to men and women in any society. Unfortunately, much discourse on this topic, particularly when related to hunting and foraging peoples, is marred by an exclusionary tone. That is, the sexual division of labor is often presented as a list of things that women cannot do, should not do, or are prohibited from doing by men (Jarvenpa and Brumbach, in press; Nelson 1997:85–111).

Gerrymandering Gender

Some landmark anthropological literature in the 1960s crystallized prevailing attitudes of the time but also influenced a subsequent generation of archaeologists. Faithful to its title, the 1968 *Man the Hunter* volume (Lee and DeVore 1968) rather dogmatically portrayed "hunting" as the exclusive role of males. In this vision of cultural evolution, men were characterized as "cooperative hunters of big game, ranging freely and widely across the landscape" (Washburn and Lancaster 1968). This exclusively male hunter model was constructed, in part, by ignoring contradictory evidence presented in the original symposium by several ethnographers and by a questionable manipulation of the content of the five original codes for subsistence economy in Murdock's (1967:154–155, cited in Lee 1968:41) *Ethnographic Atlas*.[4]

Participants in the "Man the Hunter" symposium simply reclassified the pursuit of large aquatic animals as hunting rather than fishing, and they also redefined shellfishing as gathering rather than fishing (Lee 1968:41–42). Thus, gathering now included the harvest of wild plants, small land fauna, and shellfish. Hunting was more narrowly construed to highlight the pursuit of large and mobile animals, presumably those species capable of challenging and validating a male hunter's "masculinity." In essence, by narrowing and redefining the scope of "hunting," the symposium participants eliminated women's contributions and obscured women's very real participation in a behaviorally and culturally complex enterprise.

Dahlberg's (1981) edited volume *Woman the Gatherer* served as something of a rejoinder but did this by highlighting the role of women as the gatherers of plant foods, which often contributed more than half of some foraging peoples' subsistence in tropical and temperate environments. Thus, while one of its essays demonstrated the importance of female hunters among the Agta of the Philippines (Estioko-Griffin and Griffin 1981), the volume at large has come to be best known for its discussion of women as plant gatherers "par excellence." Unfortunately, such extreme views, rendered as mutually exclusive "man the hunter" versus "woman the gatherer" models, have come to sum up the way many archaeologists interpret the economic roles of women and men.

Despite a growing literature on the topic (Endicott 1999; Estioko-Griffin and

Griffin 1981; Kelly 1995:262–70; Leacock 1981; Nelson 1980; Turnbull 1981; Watanabe 1968), the ethnographic evidence for women as hunters, and the reality of highly flexible work roles for women and men, such information has had negligible impact on archaeologists interpreting artifacts, features, and other residues at prehistoric sites. As Conkey and Spector (1984:8) have pointed out, there is a deep-seated assumption that women in prehistory were "immobilized" by pregnancy, lactation, and child care and therefore needed to be left at a home base while the males "ranged freely and widely across the landscape."

More recently, Brightman's (1996) critique of the division of labor as presented in the literature on foraging societies persuasively rejects biological or physiological determinants of gender roles. Rather, he interprets sexual divisions of labor as somewhat arbitrary ideological constructions that operate primarily to exclude women from arenas of power and prestige dominated by men (i.e., "hunting") and that women actively collude in reproducing gender asymmetries since such arrangements may be interpreted by women not as exclusion but as entitlement and complementarity.

Brightman's constructivist argument is useful in recognizing malleability in the sexual division of labor. Yet his analysis is problematic in several ways. First, women often do not accept male ideas about gender differences within their own cultures (Buckley 1982; Counts 1985), thereby calling into question the saliency of Brightman's ideas about female exclusion or marginalization, or of women's "collusion" in such matters. Second, similar to the "Man the Hunter" symposium participants, he narrowly construes "hunting" as killing, not, as we would argue, as *a comprehensive range of logistics, pursuit, dispatch, processing, and storage activities necessitating interdependent female and male labor* (Brumbach and Jarvenpa 1997b; Jarvenpa and Brumbach 1995). Even in contexts where women directly harvest or dispatch game, Brightman (1996:723) interprets these as "exceptional" or abnormal circumstances rather than flexible, adaptive behaviors. Finally, by emphasizing arenas from which women are "excluded," Brightman has perpetuated a leitmotif that has confounded research on hunter-gatherers for decades.

Why is the sexual division of labor rarely, if ever, phrased as a list of things men cannot do, should not do, or are prohibited from doing? Why are men not frequently "excluded" from vital food processing, storage, and distribution operations or from hide and clothing manufacture? In our review of the archaeological studies that follow, therefore, we invite the reader to invert familiar questions or tropes so that one may begin seeing the sexual division of labor more positively as the complex and variegated subsistence tasks *actually performed* by women and men regardless of, and sometimes in contradiction to, the normative constructions of gender fostered by their own cultures.

Behavioral Ecology Arguments

Among these tropes is the notion that specialized male hunting strategies for procuring meat have a long evolutionary history in the genus *Homo* (Smith 1999). One rendering of this idea by human behavioral ecologists is the "show-off" model of male hunting, viewing it essentially as a prestige activity linked to sexual selection (Winterhalder 2001). Such gene-centric paradigms raise many vexing questions that cannot be fully addressed here: Why is "showing off" (or the closely allied "costly signaling") not also provisioning? Is "prestige" simply the vehicle by which genes reproduce themselves? Is male hunting the only meaningful route to "prestige" in human society?

Other behavioral ecologists, however, note that women and men may seek different arrays of prey or resources in order to achieve different genetic fitness goals (Hill and Kaplan 1993).[5] Zeanah (2004) adopts the latter perspective for interpreting the division of labor and settlement patterns in the Late Holocene Carson Desert of western Nevada. Employing central place foraging models, he concludes that men logistically hunted out of residential bases that were situated to facilitate women's foraging activities in resource-rich wetland zones. Arguably, this arrangement was a way of reconciling conflicting subsistence interests between the sexes. This contrasts with previous views of Great Basin prehistory that have posited wholesale replacements of mobile hunters with semisedentary gathering peoples (Bettinger and Baumhoff 1982).[6]

Zeanah's argument also challenges Hildebrandt and McGuire's (2002) specific hypothesis that "show-off"-style, prestige-based, large game hunting by men was increasing across California and the western Great Basin between 4000 and 1000 B.P. In prior archaeological research in California, these same authors suggested that a "lack of gender polarity" in the division of labor had considerable antiquity. The pervasiveness of plant and seed-grinding "milling stones" in a range of early site contexts, they argue, indicates interchangeability or a lack of task specialization by sex (McGuire and Hildebrandt 1994).

Flexibility in Women's Work

Other archaeologists, such as Wadley (1998) in South Africa and Bird (1993) in Australia, have made insightful reappraisals of the ethnographic and ethnohistoric records for their respective areas to demonstrate indigenous women's complex and widespread involvement in a range of hunting activities, including direct harvesting of both small and large game animals, as well as toolmaking, gathering, and food processing.[7] Such fine-grained information runs counter to simple or stereotyped views of the division of labor and, thus, may be used as a source of models for more nuanced interpretations of the prehistory of South Africa and Australia. Wadley, for example, sees women's involvement as "meat providers" as highly variable and flexible. No doubt, such roles shifted along with changing gender relations linked to environmental and economic changes in Pleistocene and post-Pleistocene South Africa.

In some instances, arguments can be made for women's dominance in the direct harvest phase of activities like shellfishing, an important source of animal protein. Ethnohistoric documents attest to women's contributions in this area. Accordingly, Claassen's (1991) analysis of the Shell Mound Archaic, extending back to 8,000 B.P. in the southeastern United States, places women in a central position in the subsistence economy and society generally. Extensive shell heaps at Archaic sites, along with associated burials exhibiting preferential ritual treatment of females, suggest a prominent role for women as shellfishers. In a related study, Moss (1993) argues that while a variety of shellfish species were important food resources for prehistoric Tlingit society on the Northwest Coast, they were avoided by high-status individuals because of negative associations with laziness, poverty, and ritual impurity. There was also the danger of paralytic shellfish poisoning. Moss effectively integrates ethnographic and ethnohistoric accounts with archaeological evidence to suggest that, among Tlingit of commoner status, women depended on shellfish more than men.

While women's roles in hunting have been ignored, ironically, there is also a parallel danger in overlooking or misinterpreting the archaeological evidence for women's gathering activities. Vinsrygg (1987), for example, argues for a reinterpretation of bored or perforated stones in Stone Age sites from the Rogaland district of Norway. Rather than accepting these as "clubs" or war symbols, she interprets them as weights for digging sticks likely used by women and even children for uprooting plants in coastal areas.

Our own ethnoarchaeological work with the Chipewyan in the Canadian subarctic reveals that women's roles are far more flexible and expansive than previously believed. Women as well as men directly harvest a variety of mammals and fish. Moreover, hunting needs to be seen in context as part of a complex system of travel, preparation, and logistics preceding harvests or kills and the intricacies of butchering, processing, and distribution following kills. This full spectrum of activity is most appropriately seen as "hunting," an enterprise that produces food, clothing, tools, and other necessities of life and that requires the interdependence of female and male labor in any foraging society (Brumbach and Jarvenpa 1997b; Jarvenpa and Brumbach 1995). In a similar vein, Frink's (2002) ethnoarchaeological research among Cup'ik in western Alaska demonstrates the prominent role of women in managing multigenerational fish camps where they make complex decisions about processing and storage of fish according to species, intensity of spawning runs, and time of year. A material manifestation of this activity, albeit invisible to conventional archaeology, is women's cutting of their ownership marks on fish tails.

Ember (1975) and Hiatt (1978) assembled cross-cultural data to demonstrate an inverse correlation between men's contribution to subsistence and effective temperature. Simply put, men tend to procure more food in colder, high-latitude environments, while women's direct harvesting of food resources increases in warmer, low-latitude settings. Lee's (1968, 1979) influential work among the !Kung San, for example, demonstrates that two-thirds of the diet is plant foods gathered by women. In many other low-latitude environments, women's *and* men's plant gathering contributes significantly to the diet. Despite their prominence in gathering and also domestication of plant species from wild progenitors (Watson and Kennedy 1991), however, women receive only grudging respect for these accomplishments by archaeologists. This devaluation may derive, in part, from a Western recreational "sport hunting" model of behavior that accords prestige to those who vanquish large, dangerous animals, not to the gatherers of sessile plants.

As Halperin (1980) and Kelly (1995:262–65) argue, however, modeling subsistence as *procurement* only distorts the real labor contributions of women in processing and storing food resources, particularly in the high latitudes. Our comparative ethnoarchaeological studies in circumpolar communities reinforce this point (Jarvenpa and Brumbach 2006, in press). If archaeology is to achieve a basic understanding of women's and men's livelihoods in the past, we contend, the field must abandon Eurocentric prestige hierarchies when analyzing who did what. A preoccupation with and privileging of male hunting or even of female gathering shifts the scholarly gaze away from comprehensive social systems of provisioning toward questionable scenarios of individualistic competition and valor. We will return to these issues in the conclusion.

Tools of the Trade: Women's and Men's Gear

As discussed in the previous section, both women and men were involved in the performance of a wide range of tasks, including the harvesting of food and non-food resources, and the conversion of these items into clothing, tools, crafts items, and numerous other useful products. In order to carry out these tasks, both women and men manufactured and used a variety of tools, implements, and carriers. Part of the sexual division of labor includes the kinds and uses of such tools and facilities. Fortunately, these artifacts comprise a major part of the archaeological record left behind by hunter-gatherers.

Gender Asymmetry in Tool Visibility

Nonetheless, there appears to be significant gender asymmetry in the "visibility" of men's and women's tools and activities. Hayden (1992:42) writes, "If women have frequently been neglected in prehistory, it has largely been because of the difficulty of distinguishing their activities from males on the basis of stone tools." While this may be an accurate assessment of gender "visibility," the caution has not been applied evenly to women and men by the discipline. Most stone tools are simply assumed to have been made by men, leaving the reader to conclude that women did not make stone tools or that their tools are hard to "identify." In reviewing stone-tool manufacture, Torrence (2001:91) observes, "The gendering of hunter-gatherer stone technology has until recently been considered to be relatively unproblematic: men have been assumed to be the major, if not the only, makers and users of stone artefacts."

Some portrayals of the past have characterized the manufacture of tools and implements along stereotyped and immutable lines similar to the "man the hunter/woman the gatherer" dichotomy. For example, it has been argued that men manufactured tools of hard materials (e.g., stone, bone, antler, and ivory) while women made objects of soft items (e.g., plant fibers and animal skins) or that men made hunting and fighting weapons (e.g., knives, spear tips, and projectile points) while women produced containers and domestic items (e.g., baskets, clothing, infant carriers, and pottery). More extreme positions have emphatically argued that stone-tool manufacture was largely the occupation of men and, therefore, that most tools recovered and studied by archaeologists were made by men. Such fanciful characterizations fail to capture the behavioral realities of actual people.

While assignment of any specific tool to one gender or the other is difficult or even impossible, archaeologists rarely have problems attributing tools to men. The real crux appears to be making such attributions to women. Women are denied credit as users and producers of tools by various means. First, by (over)-emphasizing problems relating to poor preservation of organic materials, women's tools and women's production are made hard to find. Women are "hard to see" in the archaeological record, goes the argument, because women predominated in the working of soft, organic substances, which are poorly preserved. In contrast, men presumably excelled at the production of stone tools, which are more likely to be preserved. These simplistic statements about who used what materials in prehistory, however, are just as shortsighted as statements about who performed which economic activities.

Where preservation is unusually favorable, including sites characterized by extreme cold or aridity, objects of organic materials have been preserved (Ellender 1993). For example, the village site Ozette in Washington state was covered by a mud slide that preserved thousands of objects of wood and other organic material, including building materials, wooden bowls and spoons, basketry, and other craft items, thus providing a more complete picture of the material assemblage of the site's occupants. At other sites in cold and/or arid regions, preserved materials have included animal skin, wood, textiles (e.g., Ellender 1993), and even mummified remains of the people themselves. When these fuller inventories are available, it is possible to assess a broad spectrum of tools made from a variety of materials both hard and soft. Such information is a more realistic platform for interpreting the complexities of women's and men's tools and tool use.

Another way in which archaeology has colluded to exclude women from the ranks of "tool users" is by trivializing and devaluing artifacts that are attributed to women. Even when preserved, objects of organic materials are rarely accorded much respect unless they are recovered in very large numbers, such as at Ozette. For example, what is arguably the best-known bone tool from North America, the caribou leg bone hide scraper from Old Crow Flats, Yukon Territory, originally dated to 27,000 ± 3000 years B.P., was once characterized as undoubtedly "a tool created by human hands" (Jennings 1983:45). The artifact quickly faded from attention after it was more accurately dated to recent times. Yet its likely manufacture and use by a woman (the leg bone hide scraper is a quintessentially woman's tool in the ethnographic subarctic) was not considered relevant. After all, women were hard to see in the archaeological record. The object's relevance to archaeology was only its reputed antiquity.

Problems of Gender Attribution

Bird (1993:22) argues that since the economic and social roles of men and women are not biologically determined but vary both cross-culturally and through time, it "follows that in any given cultural context . . . the distribution of economic and social roles by gender should not be assumed, but rather seen as a problem worthy of exploration in its own right." Similar arguments can be made for the question of who made what tools. While gender attribution for the manufacture of specific tools may not always be possible, archaeologists should approach each situation as a fresh problem requiring a probing interpretation. This is illustrated by Wadley's (1998:80–81) residue analysis of stone tools from the South African site of Rose Cottage Cave, in which both blood and plant residues are frequently present on a single stone flake (based on Williamson's [1996] study), suggesting that a single person might be involved with both meat butchery and plant food processing. Stone flakes from another South African site, Jubilee Shelter, might have been used as arrowheads on occasion but also had plant polish on their cutting edges. Of course, the presence of plant polish does not imply that such tools were not used by men, but it does suggest that no secure gender attribution can be made (Wadley 1998:80–81).

Woman the Toolmaker

The assumption that women do not make stone tools, especially the large, formalized bifaces used for hunting and warfare, is often expressed (or implied) in the archaeological literature (see discussion in Bird 1993; Gero 1991). As Gero (1991:168) states, "The restrictive and self-fulfilling definition of stone tools as formal, standardized tools central to male activities leads to an anthropological overstatement about the importance attached to weapons, extractive tools, and hunting paraphernalia." Simply put, stone tools are *prescribed* as male by the profession. Observations of women manufacturing and using stone tools are further dismissed as "exceptions" (Bird 1993:22). In a manner parallel to gerrymandering women out of "hunting" by redefining the pursuit of small game as "collecting," the archaeological literature defines "stone tools" as elaborately produced items that are standardized, classifiable, and reproduced forms. Expedient stone tools, such as "unretouched flakes," used by women in the production of craft items are defined not as tools but as by-products from the manufacture of "real" tools (Gero 1991:165). Gero (1991), in perhaps the most influential assault on the "man the toolmaker" construct, appropriately broadens the concept of "stone tool." She insightfully notes that women can and do make stone implements but that archaeology simply does not value expedient tools as much as formalized bifaces, particularly projectile points.

Presumptions about gender hierarchy in prehistoric tool production and use parallel attitudes toward hunting and foraging work. While women may be responsible for obtaining the bulk of the food in many societies, high prestige is still accorded to the hunting of large game (particularly by archaeologists if not the hunters themselves) even when these resources provide only a small portion of a community's food supply. As a discipline, archaeology has failed to adequately address this apparent contradiction. While this issue cannot be explored in depth here, big game hunting and the apparent "prestige" that surrounds it would certainly benefit from a more probing and critical examination, one not limited by the tenets of evolutionary ecology. Gero (1991) discusses the inordinate attention paid in the literature to tools that are presumed to have been made by men for the specific purpose of killing large game animals. Such fixation on the dispatch phase of hunting is part of a Western recreational "sport hunting" model that distorts and grossly simplifies life and livelihood in hunter-forager economies (Jarvenpa and Brumbach, in press). In turn, the fascination with large, dangerous game animals has also affected, indeed compromised, archaeology's approach to the manufacture of tools.

Hunting Methods and Technologies

Archaeology's long-standing preoccupation with the dramatic confrontation of man and beast is strongly suggestive of the lurid cover art seen on some men's magazines. If hunting is to be interpreted as "male macho drama" (Gero 1993), women are excluded since a female protagonist would spoil the fun for the real men. But is this how hunting was carried out in prehistory?

More attention needs to be paid to the methods and techniques actually used by hunters of both large and small game animals. While the "man the hunter" mythos emphasizes dramatic confrontation with the large and dangerous, ethnographic and ethnohistoric accounts reveal the importance of other methods such as drives, ambushes at river crossings, poison, snares, nets, dogs, clubs, and many other techniques not characterized by direct confrontation (Casey 1998; Kehoe 1990; Kent 1998; Wadley 1998).

Kehoe (1990) notes that objects of organic materials like ropes, strings, thongs, or others she terms "lines" play pivotal roles in the harvest phase of hunting. In support of this, she cites research carried out by others, including J. E. Lips (1947), a field ethnographer among the Montagnais-Naskapi who studied critically appropriate hunting techniques. According to Kehoe (1990:27), Lips "knew that using a projectile—whether it be one pointed with stone or bone or a bullet—is the last and sometimes omitted stage of hunting, the climax after the hunters have managed to place themselves in close proximity to their prey." The devices for attaining proximity include a variety of traps, nets, and snares constructed with string, thong, and rope, that is, Kehoe's "lines." The production of ropes and lines requires the use of implements such as awls, netting shuttles, and mat and netting needles, among other tools, generally employed by women.

To illustrate the kinds of tools and implements made with the use of lines as well as tools used to manufacture the lines, Kehoe draws on Osgood's (1940) study of Ingalik material culture. More than 200 items, or almost two-thirds of the Ingalik material culture inventory, include lines in their manufacture (Osgood 1940:435; cited in Kehoe 1990:26). Kehoe believes this technology has great antiquity and demonstrates similarities between European Upper Paleolithic bone tools and the Ingalik implements described by Osgood for stripping and sewing bark and for making nets, baskets, and mats. No doubt, more awareness and study of lines would elevate women's "visibility" in the archaeological record while recognizing a larger repertoire of hunting methods and techniques employed by prehistoric peoples.

Stone-Tool Use by Women

Although fragmentary in places and often written from a male perspective, ethnohistoric and ethnographic accounts of hunter-gatherer societies document a variety of tools and materials made and used by both women and men. In societies where hunted animals make up a large part of the diet, women have been observed using large knives, hatchets, pounding stones, and other tools of hard material to butcher, pulverize, and otherwise process animal carcasses and products (Jarvenpa and Brumbach 1995, 2006). That women would attempt to butcher an animal the size of a caribou or moose, not to mention a walrus or whale, with only a utilized flake is absurd fantasy, although such tools are suitable for tailoring skin garments and other fine work. For primary butchering, large knives, hatchets, and hammerstones are far more efficient.

Bird's (1993:26) review of ethnoarchaeological studies in Australia reinforces this point. For example, Gould (1980, cited by Bird 1993:27) observes that flake knives are used by women at least as much as by men. In a related vein, Gero (1991) reviews Gould's Australian research to reveal how ethnoarchaeology can impose a male bias on stone-tool production. Thus, while Gould (1977) acknowledges use of flake knives by both genders, only males and male tasks are systematically observed.

Ethnoarchaeological research in arctic and subarctic societies demonstrates women's direct involvement in tool use and manufacture, although few stone tools are part of contemporary toolkits. Large game animals are frequently butchered by women, who use metal knives and hatchets as the tools of choice for disarticulating large sections and joints. Chipewyan women have special purpose tools for preparing animal skin hides. Today, these tools are made of wood, bone, metal, string, and leather thong (Jarvenpa and Brumbach 1995:66). Hide-making tools are wrapped in bundles of canvas, duck, or heavy cotton tightly wrapped with cord or cloth strips and stored for safekeeping.[8] The moose and caribou long bone hide scrapers in these kits are similar in form to the Old Crow Flats caribou bone flesher discussed previously. Chipewyan women also maintain log smoking and storage caches where they keep large pounding stones for pulverizing dried meat and fish and hatchets used to break up animal long bones for bone grease (Jarvenpa and Brumbach 1995:62–65).

Women in warmer, low-latitude environments also manufacture and use tools of stone and other hard materials that would be recoverable archaeologically. Gorman (1995) discusses the Andaman Islanders' interesting reversal of "traditional" sex roles in that women make stone tools, although these are used for non–food quest purposes, namely, head shaving, tattooing, and scarifying. By contrast, Andamanese men's hunting tool kits are made without lithic material but rather include implements of bamboo, wood, shell, bone, and iron.

Bird (1993:23–25) and McKell (1993) detail accounts of Australian Aboriginal women making and using tools of rough and chipped stone as well as wood. These implements were employed in a variety of tasks: cutting meat, making stone hatchets, and shaping and finishing wooden implements such as bowls, digging sticks, and fighting sticks. The hatchets were multipurpose tools used for collecting foodstuffs like honey, edible grubs, and small game. Moreover, Bird (1993:24–25) notes reports of Australian women making stone points for spears and of Tasmanian women not only making stone tools but also quarrying the stone, a toolmaking activity rarely attributed to women. Ellender (1993) describes an ossuary burial of a woman in Australia where dry conditions helped preserve organic mortuary items and other tools including a bark-fiber net bag, emu bones fashioned into split-bone knives, a quartz core, and two flakes.

A Tiwi woman on Bathurst Island used a ground edge ax while hunting that she had made herself. After describing women's use of stone tools to make digging sticks, McKell (1993:116–17) concludes, "If these stone axes were to be excavated in Australia today the archaeologist would almost always assume that they were used by men as primary tools and again by men to make secondary tools for women." As noted previously, the desire to prescribe stone tools as male is a powerful bias.

No Place Like Home: Activity Areas and Household Organization

In hunter-gatherer populations, the household is more than a reflection of society. One might argue that it *is* society. For most hunter-gatherers, the household is the center of resource production, and male–female relations form the core of economic, social, and political arrangements linking communities of households. Gender-related household or activity area analysis has been a productive research strategy for archaeologists working in arctic and subarctic contexts, for example.

Gendered Households

Reinhardt (2002) offers a statistical reanalysis and reinterpretation of a prehistoric Iñupiat subterranean dwelling destroyed by an ice override in Barrow, Alaska.

While the remarkable preservation at this well-documented site permits detailed studies of artifactual remains and architecture, Reinhardt is self-contemplative in discussing the decisions, problems, and contradictions he grappled with in converting excavated objects into quantifiable "data." He argues that the spatial distribution of artifactual material does not support earlier ideas of a clear partitioning of the dwelling into female and male "sides" or sitting areas (Newell 1984). Rather, women and children may have used most of the house floor area, with men and boys returning from a *qargi*, or men's house, to the family dwelling essentially to sleep, a pattern consistent with the ethnography of this region. Ultimately, Reinhardt urges caution in assigning gender usage or ownership to tools and residues.

In a related vein, LeMoine's (2003) analysis of Late Dorset household architecture in the eastern Canadian arctic reveals significant parallels and differences in gender roles as compared with those known from historic or ethnographic Inuit culture. In both contexts, arguably, women were the souls of the house and significant intermediaries between hunters and the animals they pursued. In the Late Dorset period, however, women may have participated more intensively in direct harvesting of small game, in sharing of labor in larger dual- or multifamily households, and in maintaining community ties during pronounced seasonal aggregations. Particularly important in this interpretation are axial features and associated hearth rows in dwellings, loci of women's activity. In LeMoine's view, women were integral to a reoccupation of the high arctic during Late Dorset times.

Whitridge (2002:172) also identifies examples of gendered space in a Classic Thule whaling village. His interpretation of the archaeological site of Qariaraqyuk, Somerset Island, identifies a detached kitchen wing he characterizes as "concealing and marginalizing a major locus of women's activities" and a *qargi* (men's communal house) that "replaced the family dwelling as the major architectural locus of men's activities." It is not entirely clear why specialized male space is interpreted as evidence for higher status while female space is interpreted as a decline in, or at least a realignment of, women's status and authority. Our own work on transformations in hunting and use of domestic space among the subarctic Chipewyan in the nineteenth and twentieth centuries indicates that increased specialization and separation of male and female economic roles does not necessarily lead to marginalization of women (Brumbach and Jarvenpa 1997a).

Asymmetries of Power?

Whitridge assumes that men derive prestige from whaling as well as from the trade goods obtained from the exchange of surplus whale products. But he makes several assumptions that need to be examined, including the notion that only men participated in the actual whale "hunt." If men indeed dominated the direct harvest phase of whale hunting, can we assume that women controlled much of the processing phases of hunting—that is, converting the carcasses into both subsistence products and valuable trade items as well as storing, managing, and distributing food? The possibility of the latter scenario gains support from ethnographic evidence from Yup'ik Eskimo communities where women not only directly harvested half the community food supply but also were regarded as the owners of the food as they dominated its storage, preparation, and distribution (Ackerman 1990). Moreover, regarding matters of domestic space, the Yup'ik men's houses actually may have contributed to men's isolation and marginalization by dispersing and separating men from their kin of both genders (Bogojavlensky and Fuller 1973).

Even so, Whitridge's work at Qariaraqyuk reminds us that the distinction between complementary gender differences and emergent asymmetries of power can be subtle. As he notes, Thule "women and men deployed their preciosities in different discursive genres, competing in effect for different kinds of cultural capital" (Whitridge 2002:190). Although this sounds like complementary gender equality, his argument about the prominent position of men in interregional systems of exchange of exotic metals points to growing differences in power and status. Whether one prefers to view this as emergent "complexity" or emergent "social asymmetry," we concur that as a fundamental structuring principle in all foraging and hunting societies, gender has been largely overlooked as a starting point for intensification and specialization in labor. We will return to the thorny issue of power and status in the concluding section of this chapter.

Somewhat different interpretations are reached in Hoffman's (2002) study of Unangan Aleut bone needles recovered from houses, among other archaeological contexts. His experiments on the production of both eyed and grooved needle forms spurred his conclusion that a change over time to grooved needles resulted from the desire of women seamstresses to produce exceptionally fine decorated clothing and gut-skin parkas. From this perspective, the garments became important status items in aboriginal trade networks and were exchanged for prestige goods like iron and amber.

Hoffman's excavations reveal concentrations of sewing needles in *large houses*, providing the connection between craft production and high-status households and, in turn, women's pivotal role in sociopolitical organization. This perspective contrasts with Whitridge in that women are seen as taking an active and conscious role in the design and production of useful tools and the crafting of high-status trade goods. In Hoffman's view, Unangan women actively participated in trade networks and gained prestige and exotic goods for themselves and their families and households.

Historical Archaeological Approaches

Other scholars have probed hunter-gatherer household organization and gender dynamics via historical archaeology and ethnoarchaeology. In such research, complementary data sets drawn from historical documents and/or native consultants' behaviors and testimony may be used to enhance interpretations of archaeological residues. Shepard's (2002) study of nineteenth-century Kuskokwim communities in Alaska analyzes changes in household social organization and division of labor triggered by European missionization. She argues that in nonstratified societies, house structures provide the clearest expression of "materialized ideology," their generalized design and layout reflecting the community's social values and ideals, a perspective shared by LeMoine (2003).

Men's and women's activities on the Kuskokwim prior to missionization were segregated into large *qasgi* (men's dormitory, communal center, and bathhouse) and small separate houses for women and children. One impact of missionization was the gradual abandonment of the *qasgi*, with the mission church becoming the focus of ceremonial life. In turn, men and women began to occupy the same domestic space, ultimately leading to a modification of dwellings and a reorientation of the spatial dimensions of activity performance.

Shepard notes that more archaeological study of mid- to late nineteenth-century houses, including the poorly documented *qasgi*, or men's house, will be needed to assess whether women's and men's living, work, and storage spaces indeed became smaller and more commingled through time. Nonetheless, Shepard's work poses a provocative question well worth pursuing in the archaeology of hunter-gatherers at large: do changes in ideas (missionization) produce changes in behavior (gender relations) that are identifiable archaeologically?

In the case of the Chipewyan of northwestern Saskatchewan, historical changes in the hunting economy, involving increased settlement centralization and logistical organization, were accompanied by a proliferation and specialization in processing and storage facilities by gender (*loretthe kwae*, or women's log smoking caches, and *t'asi thelaikoe*, or men's log storehouses)—changes that made women's special-purpose structures more visible archaeologically (Brumbach and Jarvenpa 1997a; Jarvenpa and Brumbach 1999). From this perspective, and allowing for cross-cultural differences in architecture, divergence in female and male spaces and facilities may imply increasing gender specialization but *not necessarily* marginalization of women.[9]

Household studies do not always yield clear or coherent interpretations. Shepard, for example, noted some of the unexpected patterning of faunal remains in the nineteenth-century Koyukon houses excavated by Clark (1996). In Koyukon magico-religious thought, premenopausal women are tabooed from contact with spiritually powerful bears, thus requiring an explanation for the presence of bear remains in house floors that presumably once accommodated families with women present. Aside from invoking exceptional circumstances, such as inhabiting the houses with female shamans or Iñupiat occupants, there is also the possibility—as in most societies—that some degree of behavioral flexibility operated in spite of or in contradiction to ideal norms and proscriptions.

Ambiguities and Subtleties

Indeed, the latter point is nicely reinforced by Janes's (1983) ethnoarchaeological investigations among the Willow Lake Slavey of northern Canada. While a division of labor with men as hunters and women as food processors and preparers is emphasized in Slavey ideology, *behavioral realities* are another matter. Across thirty-eight major categories of subsistence activities, nearly 35 percent of the tasks are performed by children and adults of both sexes. These include small mammal hunting, setting and checking fish nets, plucking and gutting fowl, and processing furs, among others. This flexibility and mastery of a wide range of skills by women, men, and children is highly adaptive in a demanding subarctic environment. Yet the archaeological implications may be less encouraging, at least at the intrahousehold level. As Janes (1983:79) notes, "The fact that activity areas are all nearly multifunctional at Willow Lake precludes the existence of sex-specific spaces."

In a rather novel approach to domestic space, Cooke (1998) uses hypothesized travel routes and contour lines for inferring women's and children's presence at large open prehistoric campsites in a seasonally occupied mountainous region of the Cooleman Plain of Australia. She argues that women with small children and elderly people negotiated the gentler gradients linking camps characterized by their large size and artifact diversity. While younger men may have been present at these camps, Cooke suggests they were also traversing the country via steeper routes and using camps characterized by smaller size and lesser artifact diversity.

Kent (1998) grapples insightfully with "invisibility" or lack of clear gender patterning in the spatial arrangement of residues at Late Stone Age and Early Iron Age sites in southern Africa. In the former case, she argues that early foragers simply may not have organized their culture by gender. While gendered spaces may have been of greater significance for Early Iron Age people, however, they remain elusive to the archaeologist because artifacts and features have not been provenienced with sufficient detail to allow such analysis. Kent notes that the reality of changing gender relations over time requires flexible cross-cultural ethnographic or ethnoarchaeological models for interpreting the past. Her proposition "that a consistent relationship exists between the rigidity of a division of labor that influences the use of space and objects by gender and a society's sociopolitical complexity" is an exemplar of such modeling (Kent 1998:40–41).

In a similar vein, Wadley (2000) cautions against the temptation to impose San ethnographic models on spatial patterning at Stone Age sites in South Africa. In examining the distributions of ostrich shell beads, bone points, hearths, grindstones, scrapers, flakes, and animal bone fragments, she argues that there is no compelling reason to view such spatial patterning as the product of a gendered division of labor. Rather, Wadley recommends recognition of the possibility that activities in the past may have been organized along lines of age, ability, or status, with gender distinctions playing a comparatively minor role.

Afterlife: Skeletal and Bioarchaeological Analysis

Differences in the lives of women and men often can be assessed from analyses of human skeletal remains. Cohen and Bennett (1993) summarize a range of such studies that shed light on gendered patterns of labor, physical injuries and trauma, infection and disease, nutrition, childhood stress, reproduction, and mortality, among other processes. Nonetheless, gender differences can be difficult to interpret by such means. Not enough is known about "natural" patterns to confidently differentiate between the effects of gender constructs and biological patterns. For example, there is uncertainty about how the sexes absorb nutrition, how they respond to stress, the manner in which stress is recorded, differential nutritional needs between males and females, and the confounding influence of greater stresses on women due to pregnancy and lactation (Cohen and Bennett 1993:283–84). However, despite these challenges, skeletal analysis may be a productive and insightful way of comparing the lives of women and men.

Gendered Patterns of Arthritis

Gender-specific patterns of degenerative arthritis and/or robusticity of the skeleton is one method of determining the presence and rigidity of a division of labor (Cohen and Bennett 1993). The pattern or location of degenerative joint disease may also allow inferences concerning the nature of the activities that a person engaged in while living.

Because of the difficulties of distinguishing "natural" patterns from gendered and/or cultural patterns, many studies compare skeletal health of hunter-gatherer populations with that of later agricultural peoples in the same area. According to Cohen and Bennett (1993), degenerative joint disease (DJD) and osteophytosis (arthritic changes in the spine) have been shown to increase through time as agriculture is adopted and intensified, suggesting that agriculture led to an increase in workload and physical stress when compared to the work regime of hunter-gatherers. At Dickson Mounds, Illinois, rates of both DJD and osteophytosis increased over time with the adoption of agriculture and was found to be more severe for males than for females (Goodman et al. 1984, cited in Cohen and Bennett 1993:277–78). However, a different pattern was observed at sites in Kentucky. While males from the Archaic period Indian Knoll population exhibited more pronounced vertebral arthritis than males from the later Mississippian period Hardin site, rates for females remained similar over time or increased (Cassidy 1984, cited in Cohen and Bennett 1993:278). These data suggest that not all hunter-gatherer populations were subjected to similar work stresses and that the sexual division of labor was not structured similarly across all hunter-gatherer populations.

A series of sites in Illinois dating from 6000 B.C. to A.D. 1200 indicate increased severity of arthritis for women in later populations than for the earlier Archaic populations, although the *pattern* of arthritis on the skeleton did not change. Males from these sites did not display an increase in severity, but the pattern of arthritis changed. These data suggest that women performed the same kinds of activities but in intensified form with the transition to agriculture, whereas men's work tasks changed without necessarily intensifying (Cook 1984, cited in Cohen and Bennett 1993:278). The transition to agriculture appears to have contributed to increased rates and severity of degenerative arthritis for some but not all populations as well as to changes in the patterns of arthritis (Cohen and Bennett 1993:278).

Hollimon (1992) compared skeletal populations of the fishing-collecting Chumash and the agricultural Arikara and found different patterns of DJD in both populations. Hollimon attributes these differences to divisions of labor according to gender in both populations. The percentage of Chumash men and women displaying degenerative changes was roughly equal, while Arikara males displayed almost twice the rate of DJD as Arikara females. The latter statistic may be due to a roughly seven-year difference of average age at death between Arikara males and females, with the males living longer. Among the Chumash,

Early Period women had more severe arthritis in their knees and spines than did Early Period men, while the men had more severe arthritis in their shoulders, elbows, and hands. These differences are attributed to a sexual division of labor among the Early Period Chumash where women used digging sticks and grinding implements to procure and process plant foods, while men used other tools to hunt and fish. Late Period (after A.D. 1150) women and men had similar patterns of DJD, suggesting more flexibility in gender roles. Ethnographic information from the historic period indicates that women and men were members of guilds of specialists, the membership of which cross-cut age and sex categories (Hollimon 1991).

Access to Food Resources

A common assumption regarding the consequences of a sexual division of labor among hunter-gatherers is that men and women have differential access to food resources (see note 6). It has been assumed that males, being hunters, have greater access to meat or better parts of meat because they might eat portions of the kill immediately or that women are excluded from consuming the best parts of carcasses or that women have greater access to plant foods. However, access to meat or plant foods by women and men varies considerably among different hunter-gatherer populations. Ethnographic and ethnohistoric accounts indicate that men frequently gather plant foods and that women may participate in hunts or have direct access to small game, fish, shellfish, birds, turtles, and other species that they snare or collect. Chipewyan women, who predominate in rabbit snaring, for example, often take a rest at the end of their snare line and cook one of the rabbits for a meal (Jarvenpa and Brumbach 1995:69–70). In many societies where women handle most of the processing, preservation, and management of stored foods, women may have greater access to a variety of food supplies than do men. While there does not appear to be any broad pattern of differential access to foods by gender, specific populations may demonstrate gendered differences. Some of the implications of such behaviors for nutrition in prehistory can be addressed by paleopathologists and bone chemists (Cohen and Bennett 1983).

Wadley (1998) discusses stable carbon isotope composition of human bone collagen as a marker of differences in diet, attributed to gendered work patterns and gendered access to foods. A study of skeletons from Western Cape, southern Africa, revealed few gender differences in the pre-3000 B.P. material. Stable carbon isotope compositions remained similar for both pre-3000 B.P. and post-3000 B.P. samples of female skeletons. However, the bone chemistry shifted for males of the later period. These data were interpreted to suggest that after 3000 B.P., labor became more gendered and that men ate more seal meat, fish, and other marine foods away from a home base (Sealy et al. 1992, cited in Wadley 1998:77).

Despite the previously cited changes in access to resources, studies of nutritional health among hunter-gatherer and agricultural women and men demonstrate better nutrition for the former. Cohen and Bennett (1993:281) summarize several studies of women's skeletal health that demonstrate that women in prehistoric hunter-gatherer societies suffered less from a variety of problems than did their counterparts in agricultural societies. Symptoms of anemia and other nutritional disorders, pathological bone loss, and premature osteoporosis were more pronounced in women in agricultural societies. A comparison between hunter-gatherer and agricultural skeletal samples in the Levant revealed premature osteoporosis among women in the agricultural populations (Smith et al. 1984, cited in Cohen and Bennett 1993:281). In contrast, women in the earlier Paleolithic and Mesolithic populations exhibited significantly less, if any, bone loss. Even so, such trends need to be carefully evaluated to assess the impact of increased fertility and its stresses on women in agricultural populations.

The transition to agriculture also witnessed an increase in the rates of dental caries, which were rare in earlier human populations (Cohen and Bennett 1993:281). Since diets high in carbohydrates yield higher rates of caries than diets high in fats and protein, frequencies of caries can provide dietary assessments. Walker and Erlandson's (1986) study of skeletal populations from the Northern Channel, California, uses frequencies of dental caries as an index of the ratio of proteins to carbohydrates in the diet. In earlier populations (3000–4000 B.P.), females exhibit higher rates of dental caries than do males. The authors attribute this difference to a sexual division of labor in which men had greater access to high-protein animal food through hunting while women gathered plant foods. The exploitation of plant foods is evidenced by the recovery of stone digging-stick weights used for harvesting roots and tubers. In the later part of the sequence (1820–450 B.P.), the rates of caries in men and women become more similar, a change the authors attribute to a decline in the dietary significance of plant foods and an increase among both sexes of protein, especially from small fish.

Discussion and Conclusion

Several significant generalizations about gender dynamics and the nature of work among prehistoric hunter-gatherers have emerged from the research and literature to date. The division of labor was highly variable and more flexible than commonly assumed, both within and across populations. There was no rigid or universally applicable "man the hunter/woman the gatherer" protocol, even with respect to the narrower scope of food procurement (i.e., ignoring food processing, storage, and distribution). Indeed, divisions of labor occasionally followed lines of age, ability, and experience, among other factors, rather than gender per se.

The variability and flexibility in work roles noted previously is generally supported by skeletal evidence. While arthritis and other paleopathologies afflicted women and men differently within some populations, there is no consistent gender patterning in pathologies across populations that might suggest a universal or rigid separation of female and male workloads and behaviors. Moreover, the intensification and gendered patterning of some diseases accompanying the transition to agriculture only serve to underscore the more variable and fluid situation for hunter-gatherers.

Variability and flexibility in work roles is also supported by information drawn from activity area and household analyses. While female and male sitting areas, men's houses, women's kitchen wings, and other gendered spaces are occasionally decipherable in some archaeological contexts, there is also ample evidence for widespread commingling of men's and women's activities and work areas or, alternatively, organization of work and space along lines other than gender.

Assignment of static gender categories (e.g., "female" or "male") to archaeological artifacts may bear a misleading relationship to the way such materials were employed in the real world. At best, the assignments reflect normative patterns culled from ethnohistory and ethnography. At worst, they are a kind of "best-guess" gender stereotyping based on internalized assumptions from our own cultural background. Fine-grained ethnoarchaeological accounts of actual implements and facilities in living context, including scrupulous tracking of women's and men's behaviors vis-à-vis these use histories and processing cycles, are needed to interpret how gender dynamics generate the static residues in the archaeological record. As Whitridge (2002) notes, to say that a lamp is "female" and a harpoon "male" may reflect meaningful symbolic or iconic associations. Yet these associations may obscure rather than illuminate the myriad ways such materials were actually manufactured, utilized, curated, recycled, and discarded by both women and men.

Arguably, archaeological approaches to the tools and technologies of prehistoric hunter-gatherers deserve major rethinking. The pervasive view of large stone projectile points and blades as quintessential male tools for slaying big dangerous animals is tied too closely to the Western iconic "man conquers snarling beast" cover art gracing men's magazines. At the same time, the tendency to interpret "hunting" as the fleeting moment of dispatch, or the kill, seriously distorts the complex behaviors and technologies in hunter-gatherer economies. Following Kehoe (1990), we recommend a renewed attention to "lines" and other nonlithic technologies involving preparations, travel, logistics, and management of animal movements that, ultimately, made the moment of dispatch possible. The full repertoire of procurement technologies and strategies, no doubt, required the complementary labor of women, men, and children.

If the preharvest procurement side of hunting has been seriously distorted, the postkill processing dimension of hunting has virtually been ignored by archaeologists. Ethnoarchaeological research is useful for demonstrating how postkill butchering, food processing, and storage arrangements for converting carcasses into useful food products, clothing, and implements made survival in adverse conditions possible for communities of hunter-gatherers (Jarvenpa and Brumbach 2006, in press). Much of the processing phases of hunting were managed by women. Indeed, the time investment of women's labor in such activity increases dramatically with the package size of hunted prey and is a compelling reason for decreased participation of women in the direct harvest phase of hunting in some high-latitude societies. Women were simply too busy converting carcasses into vital subsistence products. Facile arguments about women's "marginalization" and/or men's "high prestige" tend to wither in the face of such behavioral realities. Accordingly, we believe the archaeology of hunter-gatherers can come of age only with serious study of the material correlates of postkill processing, storage and distribution of food, and the implications of these dynamics for gender relations.

The last point cannot be overemphasized. Without compelling analysis of what women and men actually accomplished in their daily lives, questions about power, status, and prestige differences between the sexes cannot be addressed. Ideas about prestige hierarchies are particularly prone to contamination by gender stereotypes and biases from our own culture. Lest there be doubts on this score, one may recall how the "Man the Hunter" symposium "gerrymandered" women out of hunting by semantic manipulation of definitions. Similarly, archaeology has "downsized" or "redlined" women out of stone-tool manufacture by disassociating them from big formal lithic tools, purportedly the domain of male hunters only. Finally, the contributions of women's work in producing strings and cordage (or "lines," as noted previously) and the role these items play in hunting strategies are too often overlooked. As we have seen, the profession has a history of interpreting hunter-gatherer society in terms of women's marginalization and exclusion.

We submit that these interpretations have little resemblance to hunter-gatherer gender relations in the past or in recent history. If we inverted the logic, one might well argue that men's "show-off" or "costly-signaling" kills of large game are neither inherently prestigeful nor displays of genetic fitness but rather attempts to avoid exclusion or marginalization by women and children who represent the nurturing epicenter and future of society. Conceivably, we could build models of women's "show-off" food processing or "show-off" storage. However, there is little to be gained by replacing one set of questionable assumptions with another. Surely, *both women and men* actively negotiated their existence in hunter-gatherer societies, strategizing, coping, and making numerous decisions that facilitated their lives and livelihoods. Until the discipline removes Western gender ideology from its analysis, there can be no compelling archaeology of hunter-gatherers.

Acknowledgments

We are grateful to Sarah M. Nelson for her intellectual support and for inviting us to write this chapter. Our thinking on many of the issues discussed in this chapter has benefited from recent comparative ethnoarchaeological research generously supported by the National Science Foundation (NSF), Arctic Social Sciences Program (grant OOP-9805153). We also thank the Canadian Studies Faculty Research Grant Program, Academic Relations Office, Canadian Embassy, and the Faculty Research Awards Program, University at Albany, State University of New York, for funding an early component of our work. Special thanks are due to Fae Korsmo at NSF for her kind assistance. Our international colleagues Elena Glavatskaya, Carol Zane Jolles, and Jukka Pennanen have our gratitude for their creative collaborations. Our most profound debt is to the local people and consultants who have shared their lives and wisdom, especially to the Chipewyan of the English River First Nation, Saskatchewan, but also to the Métis of Ile à la Crosse, Saskatchewan; the Cree of Pinehouse Lake, Saskatchewan; the Khanty of the Trom'Agan area of the Surgut region of Siberia, Russia; the Sámi of Kultima, Finland; and the Iñupiaq of Little Diomede Island, Alaska. Thank you all.

Notes

1. Our survey is selective rather than exhaustive, using key monographs, journal articles, and chapters from edited symposia that best illustrate several broad themes emerging in the published literature.

2. While archaeological research is the focus of this discussion, what is known of women's and men's lives and relationships from ethnography and ethnohistory will be used to highlight, reinforce, or question arguments, themes, and analogies in the archaeological literature. By the same token, fine-grained models of gender relations derived from

ethnoarchaeological studies of living hunter-gatherers offer useful contexts for evaluating arguments about gender in the prehistoric past.

3. Arguably, a fifth question with more symbolic resonance could be added to this discussion: how are women and men identified, defined, or represented in prehistoric rock art, Upper Paleolithic cave paintings, "Venus" figurines, and other aesthetic forms? The gendered dimensions of hunter-gatherer society as expressed in art is a large and specialized area of scholarship beyond the scope of this chapter. However, see chapter 3 in this volume.

4. See Nelson (1997:86) for a discussion of the gender polarizing assumptions in Murdock's work.

5. Jochim (1988) also discusses the possibility of developing separate optimal foraging models for men and women based on their purportedly different genetic fitness goals, distinct foraging strategies, and divergent adaptive constraints. Such modeling views the individual rather than the male–female pair or some larger social form as the adaptive unit. From the vantage point of real-life hunter-gatherer families and communities, such exercises might appear oddly reductionistic. More troubling, perhaps, is that optimal foraging models fixate on energy capture, plain and simple, while ignoring the dynamics of energy flow in subsistence economies in toto, including the vast corpus of food processing, storage, and distribution activities generally handled by women.

6. See Walshe's (1998) critique of Bettinger and Baumhoff's (1982) model of Numic expansion into the Great Basin of California. She argues that their notion of a "male-rich" hunting society, marked by elaborate art and complex stone technology, being replaced by "female-rich" seed processors, with less impressive material culture, has less to do with archaeological data than with unanalyzed gender bias.

7. Similarly, Gleeson (1995) surveys ethnographers about Aboriginal Australian uses of fire with an eye toward archaeological implications. While women and men use fires somewhat differently in hunting, cooking, and toolmaking activities, the greatest gender specificity may occur in contexts involving initiation and the maintenance of large tracts of landscape defined as "female" or "male" via ritualized burning (or cleansing). In another insightful use of ethnographic evidence, Gorman's (1995) discussion of Andaman Island female stone knappers provokes a rethinking of rigid models of prehistory associating men with stone tools and meat.

8. Women in another Athapaskan-speaking group, the Tahltan of northern British Columbia, also make and use a variety of implements, including bone tools for hide preparation, which are curated as part of special-purpose "tool kits" (Albright 1999).

9. The Chipewyan historical trend toward specialized gender-segregated spaces reverses the pattern Shepard (2002) suggested for mainland western Alaskan Eskimo. The fact that the *qasgi* was not part of indigenous social structure in the central subarctic no doubt has some bearing on these divergent patterns. Even so, Whitridge's Thule kitchen and *qargi* complex could be interpreted as signs of increased specialization and separation of female and male economic roles but *not necessarily* marginalization of women.

References

Ackerman, Lillian A.
  1990   Gender Status in Yup'ik Society. *Etudes/Inuit/Studies* 14(1–2):209–21.
Albright, Sylvia
  1999   A Working Woman Needs a Good Tool Kit. In *Feminist Approaches to Pacific Northwest Archaeology*. Katherine Bernick, ed. Northwest Anthropological Research Notes, vol. 33(2):183–90. Moscow, ID.
Bettinger, R. L., and M. A. Baumhoff
  1982   The Numic Spread: Great Basin Cultures in Competition. *American Antiquity* 47(3):485–503.
Bird, C. F. M.
  1993   Woman the Toolmaker: Evidence for Women's Use and Manufacture of Flaked Stone Tools in Australia and New Guinea. In *Women in Archaeology: A Feminist Critique*. Hilary du Cros and Laurajane Smith, eds. Pp. 22–30. Canberra: Australian National University.
Bogojavlensky, Sergei, and Robert W. Fuller
  1973   Polar Bears, Walrus Hides, and Social Solidarity. *Alaska Journal* 3(2):66–76.
Brightman, Robert
  1996   The Sexual Division of Foraging Labor: Biology, Taboo, and Gender Politics. *Comparative Studies in Society and History* 38(4):687–729.
Brumbach, Hetty Jo, and Robert Jarvenpa
  1997a Ethnoarchaeology of Subsistence Space and Gender: A Subarctic Dene Case. *American Antiquity* 62(3):414–36.
  1997b Woman the Hunter: Ethnoarchaeological Lessons from Chipewyan Life-Cycle Dynamics. In *Women in Prehistory: North America and Mesoamerica*. Cheryl Claassen and Rosemary A. Joyce, eds. Pp. 17–32. Philadelphia: University of Pennsylvania Press.
Buckley, Thomas
  1982   Menstruation and the Power of Yurok Women. *American Ethnologist* 9:47–90.
Casey, Joanna
  1998   Just a Formality: The Presence of Fancy Projectile Points in a Basic Tool Assemblage. In *Gender in African Prehistory*. Susan Kent, ed. Pp. 83–103. Walnut Creek, CA: AltaMira Press.
Cassidy, Claire M.
  1984   Skeletal Evidence for Prehistoric Subsistence Change in the Central Ohio River Valley. In *Paleopathology at the Origins of Agriculture*. Mark N. Cohen and George J. Armeelagos, eds. Pp. 307–46. New York: Academic Press.
Claassen, Cheryl
  1991   Gender, Shellfishing and the Shell Mound Archaic. In *Engendering Archaeology: Women and Prehistory*. Joan M. Gero and Margaret W. Conkey, eds. Pp. 276–300. Oxford: Basil Blackwell.

Clark, A. McFadyen
    1996   Who Lived in This House? Mercury Series, Archaeological Survey of Canada Paper 153. Hull, Quebec: Canadian Museum of Civilization.
Cohen, Mark Nathan, and Sharon Bennett
    1993   Skeletal Evidence for Sex Roles and Gender Hierarchies in Prehistory. In *Sex and Gender Hierarchies*. Barbara Diane Miller, ed. Pp. 273–96. Cambridge: Cambridge University Press.
Conkey, Margaret W., and Janet D. Spector
    1984   Archaeology and the Study of Gender. In *Advances in Archaeological Method and Theory*. Vol. 7. Michael B. Schiffer, ed. Pp. 1–38. New York: Academic Press.
Cook, Delia
    1984   Subsistence and Health in the Lower Illinois Valley: Osteological Evidence. In *Paleopathology at the Origins of Agriculture*. Mark N. Cohen and George J. Armelagos, eds. Pp. 237–70. New York: Academic Press.
Cooke, Helen
    1998   Fieldwork, Mothering and the Prehistoric People of Blue Water Holes, Kosciuszko National Park. In *Redefining Archaeology: Feminist Perspectives*. Research Papers in Archaeology and Natural History, no. 29. Mary Casey, Denise Donlon, Jeannette Hope, and Sharon Wellfare, eds. Pp. 55–62. Canberra: ANH Publications, Research School of Pacific and Asian Studies, Australian National Museum.
Counts, Dorothy
    1985   Tamparonga: The Big Women of Kaliai (Papua New Guinea). In *In Her Prime: A New View of Middle-Aged Women*. J. Brown and V. Kerns, eds. Pp. 49–64. South Hadley, MA: Bergin & Garvey.
Dahlberg, Frances, ed.
    1981   *Woman the Gatherer*. New Haven, CT: Yale University Press.
Ellender, Isabel
    1993   Gender in Aboriginal Burial Practices: Evidence from Springfield Gorge Cave, Victoria. In *Women in Archaeology: A Feminist Critique*. Hilary du Cros and Laurajane Smith, eds. Pp. 104–13. Canberra: Australian National University.
Ember, Carol R.
    1975   Residential Variation among Hunter-Gatherers. *Behavior Science Research* 10:199–227.
Endicott, Karen I.
    1999   Gender Relations in Hunter-Gatherer Society. In *The Cambridge Encyclopedia of Hunters and Gatherers*. Richard B. Lee and Richard Daly, eds. Pp. 411–18. Cambridge: Cambridge University Press.
Estioko-Griffin, Agnes, and P. Bion Griffin
    1981   Woman the Hunter: The Agta. In *Woman the Gatherer*. Frances Dahlberg, ed. Pp. 121–51. New Haven, CT: Yale University Press.

Frink, Lisa
    2002   Fish Tales: Women and Decision Making in Western Alaska. In *Many Faces of Gender: Roles and Relationships through Time in Indigenous Northern Communities*. Lisa Frink, Rita S. Shepard, and Gregory A. Reinhardt, eds. Pp. 93–108. Boulder: University Press of Colorado.

Gero, Joan
    1991   Genderlithics: Women's Roles in Stone Tool Production. In *Engendering Archaeology: Women and Prehistory*. Joan M. Gero and Margaret W. Conkey, eds. Pp. 163–93. Oxford: Basil Blackwell.
    1993   The Social World of Prehistoric Facts: Gender and Power in Paleoindian Research. In *Women in Archaeology: A Feminist Critique*. Hilary du Cros and Laurajane Smith, eds. Pp. 31–40. Canberra: Australian National University.

Gleeson, C. T.
    1995   Gender and Aboriginal Fire-Use in Australia: A Preliminary Analysis of the Results of a Questionnaire. In *Gendered Archaeology: The Second Australian Women in Archaeology Conference*. Research Papers in Archaeology and Natural History, no. 26. Jane Balme and Wendy Beck, eds. Pp. 97–104. Canberra: ANH Publications, Research School of Pacific and Asian Studies, Australian National University.

Goodman, Alan, Debra Martin, George J. Armelagos, and George Clark
    1984   Health Changes at Dickson Mounds, Illinois (A.D. 950–1300). In *Paleopathology at the Origins of Agriculture*. Mark N. Cohen and George J. Armelagos, eds. Pp. 271–306. New York: Academic Press.

Gorman, Alice
    1995   Gender, Labour and Resources: The Female Knappers of the Andaman Islands. In *Gendered Archaeology: The Second Australian Women in Archaeology Conference*. Research Papers in Archaeology and Natural History, no. 26. Jane Balme and Wendy Beck, eds. Pp. 87–91. Canberra: ANH Publications, Research School of Pacific and Asian Studies, Australian National University.

Gould, Richard A.
    1977   Ethno-Archaeology: Or, Where Do Models Come From? In *Stone Tools as Cultural Markers*. R. V. S. Wright, ed. Pp. 162–77. Canberra: Australian Institute of Aboriginal Studies.
    1980   *Living Archaeology*. Cambridge: Cambridge University Press.

Halperin, Rhoda
    1980   Ecology and Mode of Production: Seasonal Variation and the Division of Labor by Sex among Hunter-Gatherers. *Journal of Anthropological Research* 36(3):379–99.

Hayden, Brian
    1992   Observing Prehistoric Women. In *Exploring Gender through Archaeology: Selected Papers from the 1991 Boone Conference*. Cheryl Claassen, ed. Pp. 33–47. Madison, WI: Prehistory Press.

Hiatt (Meehan), Betty
 1978 Woman the Gatherer. In *Woman's Role in Aboriginal Society*. F. Gale, ed. Pp. 4–15. Canberra: Australian Institute of Aboriginal Studies.

Hildebrandt, William R., and Kelly R. McGuire
 2002 The Ascendance of Hunting during the California Middle Archaic: An Evolutionary Perspective. *American Antiquity* 67(2):231–56.

Hill, Kim, and H. Kaplan
 1993 On Why Male Foragers Hunt and Share Food. *Current Anthropology* 34:701–6.

Hoffman, Brian W.
 2002 Broken Eyes and Simple Grooves: Understanding Eastern Aleut Needle Technology through Experimental Manufacture and Use of Bone Needles. In *Many Faces of Gender: Roles and Relationships through Time in Indigenous Northern Communities*. Lisa Frink, Rita S. Shepard, and Gregory A. Reinhardt, eds. Pp. 151–64. Boulder: University Press of Colorado.

Hollimon, Sandra
 1991 Health Consequences of Divisions of Labor among the Chumash Indians of Southern California. In *The Archaeology of Gender*. Proceedings of the 22nd Annual Chacmool Conference. Dale Walde and Noreen D. Willows, eds. Pp. 462–69. Calgary: Department of Archaeology, University of Calgary.
 1992 Health Consequences of Sexual Division of Labor among Prehistoric Native Americans: The Chumash of California and the Arikara of the North Plains. In *Exploring Gender through Archaeology: Selected Papers from the 1991 Boone Conference*. Cheryl Claassen, ed. Pp. 81–88. Madison, WI: Prehistory Press.

Janes, Robert R.
 1983 Archaeological Ethnography among Mackenzie Basin Dene, Canada. Technical Paper, no. 28. Calgary: Arctic Institute of North America.

Jarvenpa, Robert, and Hetty Jo Brumbach
 1995 Ethnoarchaeology and Gender: Chipewyan Women as Hunters. *Research in Economic Anthropology* 16:39–82.
 1999 The Gendered Nature of Living and Storage Space in the Canadian Subarctic. In *From the Ground Up: Beyond Gender Theory in Archaeology*. Nancy L. Wicker and Bettina Arnold, eds. Pp. 107–23. BAR International Series 812. Oxford: British Archaeological Reports.
 2006 *Circumpolar Lives and Livelihood: A Comparative Ethnoarchaeology of Gender and Subsistence*. Lincoln: University of Nebraska Press.
 In press The Sexual Division of Labor Revisited: Thoughts on Ethnoarchaeology and Gender. In *Integrating the Diversity of 21st Century Anthropology: The Life and Intellectual Legacies of Susan Kent*. Wendy Ashmore, Marcia-Anne Dobres, Sarah Nelson, and Arlene Rosen, eds. Archaeological Papers of the American Anthropological Association 17. Washington, DC: American Anthropological Association.

Jennings, Jesse D., ed.
　1983　Ancient North Americans. San Francisco: W. H. Freeman.
Jochim, Michael A.
　1988　Optimal Foraging and the Division of Labor. American Anthropologist 90:130–36.
Kehoe, Alice B.
　1990　Points and Lines. In Powers of Observation: Alternative Views in Archeology. Sarah M. Nelson and Alice B. Kehoe, eds. Pp. 23–37. Archaeological Papers of the American Anthropological Association 2. Washington, DC: American Anthropological Association.
Kelly, Robert L.
　1995　The Foraging Spectrum: Diversity in Hunter-Gatherer Lifeways. Washington, DC: Smithsonian Institution Press.
Kent, Susan
　1998　Invisible Gender—Invisible Foragers: Southern African Hunter-Gatherer Spatial Patterning and the Archaeological Record. In Gender in African Prehistory. Susan Kent, ed. Pp. 39–67. Walnut Creek, CA: AltaMira Press.
Leacock, Eleanor B.
　1981　Myths of Male Dominance. New York: Monthly Review Press.
Lee, Richard B.
　1968　What Hunters Do for a Living, or How to Make Out on Scarce Resources. In Man the Hunter. Richard B. Lee and Irven DeVore, eds. Pp. 30–48. Chicago: Aldine.
Lee, Richard B.
　1979　The !Kung San: Men, Women and Work in a Foraging Society. Cambridge: Cambridge University Press.
Lee, Richard B., and Irven DeVore, eds.
　1968　Man the Hunter. Chicago: Aldine.
LeMoine, Genevieve
　2003　Woman of the House: Gender, Architecture, and Ideology in Dorset Prehistory.
　　Arctic Anthropology 40(1):121–38.
Lips, J. E.
　1947　The Origin of Things. New York: A. A. Wyn.
McGuire, Kelly R., and W. R. Hildebrandt
　1994　The Possibilities of Women and Men: Gender and the California Milling Stone Horizon. Journal of California and Great Basin Archaeology 16(1):41–59.
McKell, Sheila
　1993　An Axe to Grind: More Ripping Yarns from Australian Prehistory. In Women in Archaeology: A Feminist Critique. Hilary du Cros and Laurajane Smith, eds. Pp. 115–20. Canberra: Australian National University.

Moss, Madonna L.
 1993 Shellfish, Gender, and Status on the Northwest Coast: Reconciling Archaeological, Ethnographic, and Ethnohistoric Records on the Tlingit. *American Anthropologist* 95(3):631–52.
Murdock, George P.
 1967 The Ethnographic Atlas: A Summary. *Ethnology* 6(2):109–236.
Nelson, Richard K.
 1980 Athapaskan Subsistence Adaptations in Alaska. In *Alaskan Native Culture and History*. Senri Ethnological Studies, no. 4. Y. Kotani and W. Workman, eds. Pp. 205–32. Osaka: National Museum of Ethnology.
Nelson, Sarah Milledge
 1997 *Gender in Archaeology: Analyzing Power and Prestige*. Walnut Creek, CA: AltaMira Press.
Newell, Raymond R.
 1984 The Archaeological, Human Biological, and Comparative Contexts of a Catastrophically Terminated Kataligaaq House at Utqiagvik, Alaska (BAR-2). *Arctic Anthropology* 21(1):5–51.
Osgood, Cornelius
 1940 Ingalik Material Culture. Yale University Publications in Anthropology, no. 22. New Haven, CT: Yale University Press.
Reinhardt, Gregory A.
 2002 Puzzling Out Gender-Specific "Sides" to a Prehistoric House in Barrow, Alaska. In *Many Faces of Gender: Roles and Relationships through Time in Indigenous Northern Communities*. Lisa Frink, Rita S. Shepard, and Gregory A. Reinhardt, eds. Pp. 121–50. Boulder: University Press of Colorado.
Sassaman, Kenneth
 1992 Gender and Technology at the Archaic-Woodland Transition. In *Exploring Gender through Archaeology: Selected Papers from the 1991 Boone Conference*. Cheryl Claassen, ed. Pp. 71–79. Madison, WI: Prehistory Press.
Sealy, J. C., M. K. Patrick, A. G. Morris, and D. Alder
 1992 Diet and Dental Caries among Later Stone Age Inhabitants of the Cape Province, South Africa. *American Journal of Physical Anthropology* 88:123–34.
Shepard, Rita S.
 2002 Changing Residence Patterns and Intradomestic Role Changes: Causes and Effects in Nineteenth Century Western Alaska. In *Many Faces of Gender: Roles and Relationships through Time in Indigenous Northern Communities*. Lisa Frink, Rita S. Shepard, and Gregory A. Reinhardt, eds. Pp. 61–79. Boulder: University Press of Colorado.
Smith, Andrew B.
 1999 Archaeology and the Evolution of Hunters and Gatherers. In *The Cambridge Encyclopedia of Hunters and Gatherers*. Richard B. Lee and Richard Daly, eds. Pp. 384–90. Cambridge: Cambridge University Press.

Smith, Patricia, Ofer Bar-Yosef, and Andrew Sillen
  1984 Archaeological and Skeletal Evidence for Dietary Change during the Late Pleistocene/Early Holocene in the Levant. In *Paleopathology at the Origins of Agriculture*. Mark N. Cohen and George J. Armelagos, eds. Pp. 101–36. New York: Academic Press.
Torrence, Robin
  2001 Hunter-Gatherer Technology: Macro- and Microscale Approaches. In *Hunter-Gatherers: An Interdisciplinary Perspective*. Catherine Panter-Brick, Robert H. Layton, and Peter Rowley-Conwy, eds. Pp. 73–98. Cambridge: Cambridge University Press.
Turnbull, Colin M.
  1981 Mbuti Womanhood. In *Woman the Gatherer*. Frances Dahlberg, ed. Pp. 205–19. New Haven, CT: Yale University Press.
Vinsrygg, Synnove
  1987 Sex-Roles and the Division of Labour in Hunting-Gathering Societies. In *Were They All Men? An Examination of Sex Roles in Prehistoric Society*. Reidar Bertelsen, Arnvid Lillehammer, and Jenny-Rita Naess, eds. Pp. 23–32. Stavanger: Arkeologisk Museum i Stavanger.
Wadley, Lynn
  1998 The Invisible Meat Providers: Women in the Stone Age of South Africa. In *Gender in African Prehistory*. Susan Kent, ed. Pp. 69–81. Walnut Creek, CA: AltaMira Press.
  2000 The Use of Space in a Gender Study of Two South African Stone Age Sites. In *Gender and Material Culture in Archaeological Perspective*. Moira Donald and Linda Hurcombe, eds. Pp. 153–68. Hampshire: Macmillan.
Walker, Philip L., and Jon M. Erlandson
  1986 Dental Evidence for Prehistoric Dietary Change on the Northern Channel Islands, California. *American Antiquity* 51(2):375–83.
Walshe, Keryn
  1998 Breeding Processors and Moribund Travellers. In *Redefining Archaeology: Feminist Perspectives*. Research Papers in Archaeology and Natural History, no. 29. Mary Casey, Denise Donlon, Jeannette Hope, and Sharon Wellfare, eds. Pp. 37–40. Canberra: ANH Publications, Research School of Pacific and Asian Studies, Australian National University.
Washburn, Sherwood, and C. S. Lancaster
  1968 The Evolution of Hunting. In *Man the Hunter*. Richard B. Lee and Irven DeVore, eds. Pp. 293–303. Chicago: Aldine.
Watanabe, Hitoshi
  1968 Subsistence and Ecology of Northern Food Gatherers with Special Reference to the Ainu. In *Man the Hunter*. Richard B. Lee and Irven DeVore, eds. Pp. 68–77. Chicago: Aldine.

Watson, Patty Jo, and Mary C. Kennedy
    1991   The Development of Horticulture in the Eastern Woodlands of North America: Women's Role. In *Engendering Archaeology: Women and Prehistory.* Joan M. Gero and Margaret W. Conkey, eds. Pp. 255–75. Oxford: Basil Blackwell.

Whitridge, Peter
    2002   Gender, Households, and the Material Construction of Social Difference: Metal Consumption at a Classic Thule Whaling Village. In *Many Faces of Gender: Roles and Relationships through Time in Indigenous Northern Communities.* Lisa Frink, Rita S. Shepard, and Gregory A. Reinhardt, eds. Pp. 165–92. Boulder: University Press of Colorado.

Williamson, B. S.
    1996   Preliminary Stone Tool Residue Analysis from Rose Cottage Cave. *Southern African Field Archaeology* 53:36–44.

Winterhalder, Bruce
    2001   The Behavioural Ecology of Hunter-Gatherers. In *Hunter-Gatherers: An Interdisciplinary Perspective.* Catherine Panter-Brick, Robert H. Layton, and Peter Rowley-Conwy, eds. Pp. 12–38. Cambridge: Cambridge University Press.

Zeanah, David W.
    2004   Sexual Division of Labor and Central Place Foraging: A Model for the Carson Desert of Western Nevada. *Journal of Anthropological Archaeology* 23:1–32.

Gender and Early Farming Societies 16

JANE D. PETERSON

GENDER STUDIES OF prehistoric farming societies are perched precariously between the detailed, often text-aided studies of complex societies and the more speculative, techno-environmental reconstructions associated with Paleolithic archaeology. Neolithic and Formative villagers often left behind an assortment of tantalizing clues—from burials, human remains, architecture, artifacts, and images—so that archaeologists feel they ought to be able to address some fairly substantial questions about the gender systems of early farmers. And these are important issues, seeing that making the transition to an agricultural economy is commonly perceived as one of the major, transformational events in the human career. How the first farmers organized their work, how they structured their relationships with family and community, and how their ideational systems shaped and reinforced gender concepts were undoubtedly critical features in the success or failure of their ventures. Yet the promise of reconstructing the gender systems from the fragmentary and static prehistoric remains has remained often illusive.

My intent is to chart the sometimes uneven progress of gender research concerning early agricultural societies. The discussion is limited to those societies that *did* depend on domesticated plants or a mix of domestic plants and animals for their livelihood but *did not* exist as part of larger state-level entities that involved institutionalized hierarchical structures. I will forefront those studies that, by virtue of theoretical insight and methodological innovation, have advanced and challenged how we think about gender in early farming societies. By doing so, I hope to provide some suggestions about conceptualizing sex roles and gender and how to overcome problems that continue to plague gender studies.

Two important trends unfold in the course of these discussions. First, while the "Neolithic Revolution" was clearly a transformative process wherever it took hold, results of gender studies suggest that the inception of settled, village farming life led to few outcomes that can be viewed as broadly generalizable across regions. Despite the strongly seductive metaphor of evolutionary change, universal (or even regional) descriptions of the effects and outcomes of the agricultural developments inevitably falter in the light of local data sets and detailed analyses. So it may seem to some that there is little we can say with certainty about gender during the rise of agriculture. I would offer, alternatively, that the variation is less a symptom of theoretical inadequacy or lack of methodological rigor but more a reflection of the stunning variety present in the data themselves—in terms of both the diversity of gender systems in place and the material ways these systems are imbued with meaning (Crown 2000a). Frequent reinterpretations and active debates indicate the incremental, sometimes awkward development of archaeological knowledge in an arena that is still experiencing substantial growing pains. Second, the past twenty years have also reminded us of the truism in anthropology that culture is holistic. It is difficult to talk about sexual roles or the sexual division of labor, for example, without considering social, economic, political, and ideological categories of gender (Dobres 2004). So it becomes increasingly clear that the most compelling studies consider multiple cultural spheres and integrate diverse data sets in their discussions of sex and gender.

I suggest that there is no one, simple solution to moving gender studies forward because there is not, one uniform limitation. Some shortcomings continue to have their roots in stereotypical projections of Western gender patterns into the past. Gender clichés are perpetuated by archaeologists who continue to claim that the search for gender is a futile pursuit and then inject assumptions about sex and gender freely into their interpretations. Yet authors who express sympathy to feminist goals and familiarity with feminist theory have sometimes presented naive, formulaic accounts as well. The archaeological record and variable preservation can also have an impact. Yet if we search out the most robust, well-preserved data sets, we do not necessarily find the most advanced gender studies. Confronting these challenges constitutes the next stage for gender studies among farming societies. And there is still an enormous potential for insightful, engendered archaeological analyses. The incentives to build a more coherent and less stereotypical gendered past are strong. As prone as we are to situate the present in the past, a more complete and unbiased view of that past clearly paves the way for thoughtful reflection and action concerning our gendered future.

Domesticating Gender

As the arbiters of culture change over the vast expanse of prehistory, we have never been hesitant about modeling gender roles, relationships, and ideologies in sweeping terms. First came the universally-applied essentialist assumptions about the roles of women and men rooted firmly in their biology and the limitations those were thought to imply. Women in farming societies were increasingly stressed by the demands imposed by larger families. Increasing sedentism fully tethered them to the "domestic" sphere. And women were less likely than ever to contribute to the technological or political developments of a group. These assumptions—and the reconstructions of Neolithic society that emerged from them—provided fodder for a first wave of critical analysis.

In 1970, Boserup published the tremendously influential study *Women's Role in Economic Development*. This pathbreaking work documented African women's massive contribution to agricultural economies and also formulated an engendered model for changing agricultural production. She claimed that women did the bulk of agricultural work in tribal societies where population levels were low, land was both abundant and collectively owned, and technology was handheld (hoe). Her typology from extensive to increasingly intensive farming was evolutionary, with demographic change and land pressure precipitating intensification and technological advance. Increased male participation coincides with the introduction of the plow.

Boserup's "female farmer" model seemed to demonstrate that women made significant productive contributions in the subsistence economy of extensive farmers. The "female farmer" model provided a basis for responding to those who supposed that modern divisions of labor were rooted in the biological limitations imposed on women by the rigors of bearing and nurturing children. And it was a powerful inferential tool for feminist researchers who were predisposed to structural-Marxist analyses (Leacock 1978, 1981; Martin and Voorhies 1975; Sacks 1974; Schlegel 1977). For many archaeologists, the model relied on technological and economic behaviors that were likely to leave material clues. Boserup's categories seemed to correspond not only with technological trajectories identifiable in the past (hoe to plow) but also with widespread social conditions in the present. This combination proved irresistible for many, and the outlines of Boserup's model are still resonant in gender accounts of prehistoric farming societies to this day.

The decline in women's agricultural contribution was viewed as a starting point for social declines. Some interpreted Boserup's model as supporting the notion that women's relegation to the domestic realm and their declining status was a historically late phenomenon associated more with the rise of private property and the state (Silverblatt 1988). Other historians and archaeologists projected the African trajectory wholesale much deeper into the prehistoric past. The onset of domestication economies served as a trigger for institutionalized sexual labor roles and further sowed the seeds of widespread social inequality between the sexes (Aaby 1977; Chevillard and LeConte 1986; Divale and Harris 1976; Ehrenberg 1989; Lerner 1986; Mears 2001; Meillassoux 1981). Accounts, often not overly burdened by data, posit a unlineal devolution of women from autonomous, valued agents to subordinate, disenfranchised objects corresponding with the rise and development of agricultural societies.

Despite its influence, Boserup's model has not survived the past thirty-five years unscathed. And the range of critiques is highly relevant to archaeological research. Foremost, the evolutionary link between an ethnographically based era of "female farming" in Africa and primitive agricultural systems writ large has crumbled under the weight of ethnographic evidence. As one example, Guyer's (1991) work among the Beti of Cameroon skillfully demonstrates how the "female farmer" model is more an artifact of the volatile social and economic conditions in the past two centuries than a result of long-term, evolutionary processes. The Beti's ancient stable crops of millet, yams, and sorghum were never produced by female labor alone. In the case of millet, men cut back tree branches, and women stacked the branches. Men placed the seeds in the ground, and women covered them with soil. Men fenced the fields, and women tended the growing crop. Only reaping was the sole domain of women. Each of these tasks took place in a ritualized context, sometimes set to music and literally choreographed. It was only with the introduction of maize and cassava and the colonial policies that encouraged their production that cultivation took on "female farming" mantle (Guyer 1991).

Results from the first wave of ethnographic research, spawned by a growing feminist interest in women's roles, reinforced Guyer's critique. Numerous geographically far-flung examples can be cited in which the productive tasks in agricultural societies do not conform to the universal, sex-segregated patterns Boserup envisioned (Bacdayan 1977; Cloud 1985; Peters 1978; Trenchard 1987). Furthermore, conceptualizing complex sets of related tasks as monolithic entities such as "farming," "hunting," or "exchange" rather that suites of smaller, related tasks often masks dual participation, complementarity, and interdigitation of men's and women's lives (i.e., Brumbach and Jarvenpa 1997 regarding hunting). These observations have not been lost on all archaeologists (see Fish 2000; Szuter 2000). But it remains all too common for archaeologists to constitute activity as monolithic chunks to be assigned to either "male" or "female" columns. Inevitably, these same accounts "snowball" into formulaic reconstructions of labor, social relationships, and power structures. From a theoretical position informed by feminism, this style of evolutionary argument is no less problematic than biological imperative models. It still maintains that gender roles are somehow rooted in fixed, essentialist capacities in men and women that map out their progress in a predetermined way over vast expanses of time and space. In sum, there are a plethora of reasons to approach evolutionary models with skepticism. My point is not that there can be no variables that are widely influential in forecasting gender but only that evolutionary models do an inadequate job of explaining known gender variability and patterning, let alone the variety likely to have been present in precolonial and preindustrial agricultural settings (sensu Leacock 1978).

In keeping with broader trends in the social sciences, archaeological gender studies increasingly embrace perspectives that stress human agency, practice, and historical contingency more than evolution (Hegmon 2003; Meade and Wiesner-Hanks 2004; Sørensen 2000). We have been reminded of Schlegel's (1977) important message that separate domains of activity and influence between the sexes do not necessarily imply a hierarchy of values associated with those domains (Claassen 1997). And the dangers of projecting etic, Western concepts of worth onto productive tasks are more often avoided (Crown 2000a). While recent studies tend to be more theoretically sophisticated and nuanced, the road is still bumpy. The process of switching paradigms has not always been graceful, nor has it ensured coherent accounts of gender. Many of the studies are aptly characterized as involving rapid intellectual reappraisal rather than deep logical consideration (Guyer 1995:26).

Lamphere (2000) has provided one particularly effective modeling effort in her synthesis of evidence from the pre-Hispanic Southwest. This model focuses on a concept of hegemony defined as both *ideas* about prestige and value and also the *practice* of exercising power (sensu Ortner 1996), combining elements of productive labor, status, and ideology. She situates the source of hegemonic influence in the realm of ritual power; which, when defined emically, should be broadly applicable to prehistoric agricultural societies outside the Southwest.

Gender relationships can be played out on a field characterized by either balanced or hierarchical hegemony. Balanced hegemony prevails when the "power associated with ritual is widely dispersed among kin groups and among men and women, and where there is little control over productive resources by kin groups whose leaders are 'important' people" (Lamphere 2000:389). Gender balance can be maintained in situations where the sexual labor is either shared or segregated (overlapping or complementary in Lamphere's words). Hierarchical hegemony, her Ritual Power Model, exists in situations where a more limited number of ritual practitioners have access to the higher prestige roles. Productive labor is likely to be more sex segregated and reinforces growing social and ideological divides. She makes a compelling case that elements of hegemony can be wrested from a range of archaeological data, albeit indirectly. I find Lamphere's model valuable as a framework to discuss a number of gender studies among prehistoric farming groups. In doing so, we are able to highlight variation in prehistoric gender systems and suggest the applicability of this model to studies outside the pre-Hispanic Southwest.

Regional Gender Case Studies

My approach in organizing a more detailed investigation into recent research trends is to highlight several broad, geographic regions. The logic of this choice rests in the publication of several influential gender volumes that review and synthesize bodies of regional data for China, Africa, North and South America, and Mesoamerica and North America (Bruhns and Stothert 1999; Claassen and Joyce 1997; Kent 1998; Linduff and Sun 2004). This format also facilitates a discussion of the influence regional research traditions has played in developing gender studies. Admittedly, the choice of the regional case studies also reflects my own familiarity with the archaeological record. My hope is that the range of Old and New World regional case studies is representative of research developments in the study of gender and farming. For readers with interests in farming societies not covered here, I direct them to the chapters in part 4 of this volume. These chapters will provide important supplemental information.

Europe (with an Emphasis on the Mediterranean Region)

The architecture of longhouses, a large corpus of figurines, mortuary data, and diverse ethnographic gleanings feature prominently in the Neolithic gender research of Europe. Economic and ideological realms have often been considered by separate authors in separate articles. There is evidence of both more sophisticated and nuanced treatments of gender and also the retention of some unproductive lines of inquiry.

One well-known vision of a pan-European gendered past was offered by Gimbutas (1974, 1989) in her examination of female figurines. Gimbutas interprets the numerous figurines as representing a religious system centered on a Great Mother Goddess, who represents concepts of fertility and life force in societies that, while egalitarian, were matrilineal and "matrifocal." There are echoes of a biological imperative model as women's position in society is centered primarily on their reproductive role. Women's downfall comes in the Bronze Age with the onslaught of male herders from the East. Archaeologists have criticized Gimbutas's data, methods, and theory related to the Goddess Culture of Old Europe (Meskell 1995). But we will limit our discussions to reworkings of the gendered implications of the figurine data.

Gimbutas's model, stretching as it does over thousands of miles and thousands of years, overlooks substantial variation in the figurines of Neolithic Europe. So it is predictable that scholars have mounted critiques of her model by analyzing the uses and meanings of specific assemblages. Concerns with fertility, particularly as it is connected with agriculture, have persisted, but alternative interpretations include considerations of figurines as territorial markers, toys, teaching aids, self-representations, good-luck charms, votives, and effigies. Talalay (1987) offers one such alternative hypothesis to explain a distinctive assemblage drawn from five sites in the northern Peloponnese. The group consists of eighteen individual female legs that appear to be as parts of broken leg pairs. A review of ethnographic and historic sources suggests that broken, paired tokens often served to identify partners in social or economic exchanges in preliterate and classical societies. Given that the legs are all sexed female, one possibility is that the legs represent the relocation of women through an exogamous marriage system (Talalay 1987:168).

Binary conceptions of sex and gender that many have imposed on figurine data have also come under fire. Talalay (2000) documents the variation in the Greek corpus. Although female figurines are the most numerous and varied—in terms of decoration, material, and position—male, dual-sexed, and sexless figurines also occur. The same is true of eastern European Neolithic figurines (Hamilton 2000). A number of possibilities in conjunction with the sexless figurines are reviewed. The figures may represent 1) individuals who subsumed or transcended sexual/gender classification (e.g., child, shaman, and so on), 2) the irrelevance of sexual classification to the image portrayed, 3) items that took on sex by the addition of perishable clothing or ornaments, or 4) individuals with sexed information that we cannot "read." Whatever the case, their interpretation is not straightforward. And these discussions encourage us to envision gender systems in which sex and gender are conceived of and represented as more multifaceted, potentially fluid categories than previously envisioned.

A second pan-European model of gender systems was put forward in Ehrenberg's *Women in Prehistory* (1989). Her reconstruction of the European Neolithic owes much to Boserup in that it identifies diminished economic production at the crux of women's disenfranchisement over time. During the Early Neolithic, women across Europe are lauded not only as the innovators of agriculture and the technologies that farming required (lithic and ceramic) but also as the main source of labor in a mixed agropastoral economy. They were socially supported by an extended matrilocal kin network and economically empowered by their control of domestic products. But by the end of the Neolithic, with the advent of the plow and increases in the importance of milk and wool, their lives had been transformed by men usurping their economic roles and relegating them to the constant drudgery of making and raising babies and the repetitive, mindless tasks of cooking and textile production. By this process, the groundwork was laid for the modern gender asymmetries seen in Western society today (Ehrenberg 1989:77). The most detailed analysis discusses the connections between family size, family structure, postmarital residence patterns, and the architectural variability of European longhouses.

There are serious problems implicit in the detailed, dichotomous sexed labor scenario on which the model is founded. Most significant, it is unsupported by any archaeological data. And since the causal mechanism for change rests in the reallocation of productive resources and labor input, these are telling. Ehrenberg is not alone in facing this dilemma. Archaeologists have been exhorted to establish an empirical basis for assigning tasks to one sex, the other, or both (Conkey and Spector 1984; Spector 1983). It is through this basic step that patterns of artifacts and features take on gendered meaning. However, this has proven a more difficult task than many first imagined. There is substantial ambiguity in our understanding of sex roles with respect to farming and herding task sets. The utility of the ethnographic record is hampered by the very diversity of sexed labor scenarios that it describes.

Whitehouse's (2002) gendered look at the data from southern Italy faces some of the same problems in discussing gendered tasks and spatial domains. Yet her model, which seeks to describe role, status, and ideology by synthesizing a wider range of archaeological materials and entertaining multiple interpretations of those data, is a good deal more satisfying. Based on grave treatments, figurines from settlement and cave deposits, and paintings on cave walls, she describes a spatially segregated but complementary gender system in which the roles, relations, and ideology of men and women were balanced (Whitehouse 2002:40–41). Men are associated with hunting by virtue of painted depictions at cave and rock-shelter locations. Only female figurines are found at settlements. Images and figurines from caves depict both males and females. And there is no evidence of status differences between the sexes from grave goods. Men and women are interpreted as having separate (off-site vs. village-based) activity spheres that also serve as the loci of ritual activity. The lack of differentiation in graves suggests that both domains are socially valued.

This preliminary engendered model is highly reminiscent of the balanced hegemony scenario previously outlined and speaks well for the value of applying Lamphere's scheme outside the pre-Hispanic Southwest. Second, the value of considering less binary classificatory systems for studying gender in Neolithic societies is reinforced. Southern Italy has its own dual-sex and sexless figurines.

Furthermore, the one significant correlation of sex in burials is that men tend to be buried on right sides and women their left. However, the rule is far from universal, as 26 percent of males and 31 percent of females are buried on the wrong side. And the lack of strict differentiation along sex lines has led authors to speculate about possible disconnects between sex and gender (Robb 1994a, 1994b). Finally, Whitehouse admits her difficulty in assigning economically important subsistence tasks by gender. Nonetheless, her discussion belies a tendency to segregate tasks by sex and lump complex task sets together. Thus, women become the cultivators, potters, and weavers and men the hunters, herders, traders, and stone-tool makers (Whitehouse 2000:39). The clear association of women's tasks with the areas close to the house and village and men's tasks to areas at greater distances affirms rather than supports her conclusion.

In looking for potential activity sphere's or specific tasks that can more safely be associated with women's work in Europe, spinning and weaving are good candidates for some regions. A Hallstatt vase from Hungary depicts groups of women spinning and weaving to musical and dance accompaniment (Barber 1994:88). Textiles themselves bear the traces of communal weaving. Crisscrossing weft threads from a man's burial cloak from Trinhoj in Jutland (ca. 1300 B.C.) demonstrates that three weavers, passing the bobbins back and forth between them, produced the garment (Barber 1994:86–87). Well-preserved textile fragments, spindle whorls, weights, and loom emplacements have begun to yield gendered insights about the social and economic contexts of weaving at the Neolithic Swiss Lake Dwelling of Robenhausen (Lillis 2004).

Africa

Archaeological gender studies are in their infancy throughout most of Africa, although the application of ethnoarchaeology, ethnohistory, and linguistics hold great promise. I know of no studies focusing on gender from early farming sites in the Sahara-savanna zone of Africa that produced the first indigenous domesticates—millet, sorghum, and African rice. A gender study of the Early Iron Age Urewe communities along Lake Victoria's lakeshore and vicinity (ca. 500 B.C.) has been conducted (Maclean 1998). Indirect evidence for farming includes the location of Urewe sites on the most fertile lands in the region and palynological sequences suggestive of human-induced deforestation. Domestic cattle and caprovine remains suggest a mixed agropastoral economy that approximates Neolithic conditions elsewhere. However, a well-developed iron-smelting technology was in place here as well and makes this case unique.

Maclean identifies four new activity sets in Urewe Early Iron Age communities: ceramic production, iron production, agricultural production, and pot cooking. Who produced the ceramics is ambiguous, although regional ethnographic accounts suggests household production is overwhelming assigned to one sex or the other. A system of joint control of agricultural production is achieved by men clearing the land and women providing all other labor. Local linguistic and ethnographic evidence support this division (Maclean 1998). The author describes pot cooking and iron smelting as a pair of emergent technologies—equally complex and equally powerful—that are linked conceptually in a developing belief system with females responsible for cooking and males for smelting. Cooking and smelting are both perceived as acts of procreation in which the application of heat changes natural objects into cultural objects (plants/animals into food and stone/ore into iron) in the same way blood and semen, when heated, produce a child (Maclean 1998:173).

The study is of note for several reasons. Maclean's emic appreciation for the social value and power associated with pot-cooking technology is important. Producing a range of cooked, nutritious foods required skills and knowledge. As the providers of cooked meals, women would have had the power to withhold food, manipulate food to cause poor health, and pollute food. Communal occasions involving cooked food would have provided arenas for displaying these skills publicly (Brumfiel 1992; Maclean 1998). The joint discussion of productive labor, technology, and symbolism produces a foundation for describing Urewe gender relations in terms of its hegemonic tendency. Lacking a discussion of ritual power per se, Maclean seems to be well on her way to describing a balanced system in which the value of men's and women's productive and symbolic realms were both intimately connected and valued.

Northern China

China presents an interesting anomaly to the historical and theoretical trends already outlined. Shelach (2004) argues that the Chinese archaeologists of the Marxist era (1960–1980) were actively discussing gender and that this concern has become less mainstream in post-Marxist times. Researchers agree that the predominant Marxist paradigm problematized the study of gender by glossing over variation in the name of universal patterns and assuming set temporal trajectories for men's and women's status. Yet Shelach describes the gender discussions of the Marxist era as producing robust, empirically based debates as well (Shelach 2004). Political agendas in the post-1980, nationalistic era have tended to marginalize gender interpretations, focusing instead on situating "Chinese-ness" in the Neolithic past (Barnes and Guo 1996; Shelach 2004). The recent publication of Linduff and Sun's *Gender and Chinese Archaeology* (2004) represents a significant event in the reintegration of gender studies into Chinese archaeology. Reexamination of robust mortuary data sets, ceramic images, figurines, and statuary feature most prominently is recent discussions.

Marxist-era models for the plethora of regional cultures identified across China typically equated Early Neolithic periods with matrilineal, egalitarian society, while Late Neolithic periods were associated with the emergence of patrilineal and patriarchal societies in which gender and social stratification emerged (Pearson and Underhill 1987). Sexual labor scenarios were constructed to accommodate the assumption that men usurped women's role in the productive economy during the Late Neolithic. As such, the expectation was that stone tools associated with cultivation (adzes and stone plowshares) would be found in males' graves and tools associated with domestic chores found in females'. Spindle whorls were typically singled out as female grave goods. Extensive samples from the Late Neolithic cemeteries of the Yangshao culture (north-central China) area and the Qijia culture (northwestern China) demonstrate that this correlation is not supported (Jiao 2001; Sun and Yang 2004). Either utilitarian grave goods are not good indicators of sexed labor patterns, or there were significant overlaps in sexed labor. In contrast, grave goods from the Late Neolithic cemetery of Dadianzi (Xiajiadian culture of eastern Inner Mongolia) lend support to traditional sexual labor divisions, as axes and arrowheads pattern consistently with males and the majority of spindle whorls occur in female graves (Wu 2004). The presence of spindle whorls in a relatively small number of male graves is never discussed, nor is the regionally variability in artifact:sex correlations.

Mortuary analyses of body position, number and type of grave goods, and labor investment in burial pits suggest that the Late Neolithic involved significant social restructuring in several parts of northern China. The distribution of grave goods and increasing numbers of exotic finds in a limited number of burials during the Late Neolithic certainly seems to suggest the emergence of distinctions between important and common people in some regions (Sun and Yang 2004; Wu 2004). How gender features in the emergent stratification is often unclear. The consideration of male/female patterning is often limited to a small subset of the burials. Double burials of adult males and females have received considerable attention in discussions of gender relations (Jiao 2001; Sun and Yang 2004; Wu 2004). During the Marxist era, this emphasis stemmed from their assumed association with the arrival of patriarchy, establishment of monogamous marriage patterns, and the resulting loss of social and economic independence for women (Sun and Yang 2004:31–32). Subsequently, they have also been used to trace changes in the status balance between the sexes. In some of the Qijia double burials, for example, female burials with skeletal elements either missing or out of anatomical position are interpreted as wives, slaves, or concubines sacrificed as part of the burial ritual (Jiao 2001; Sun and Yang 2004).

Yet mixed-sex double burials are a short-lived phenomenon limited to certain regions. In the Late Neolithic alone, single burials predominate—even at the sites with double burials. There are documented examples of double burials involving adults and children as well. And finally, mixed- and single-sex multiple burials are also part of the tradition (Jiao 2001). Thus, while site-specific cases for emerging social (and possibly gender) stratification can be built (Wu 2004), any attempt to generalize broadly about gendered mortuary patterns is quite premature.

The only discussion of human imagery on ceramics I know of briefly introduces Early Neolithic examples from the Majiayao culture. Male, female, and sexless figures occur on ceramics in burials. Images of figures that hold hands encircling bowl interiors are described as indicating men's and women's ritual dances associated with harvest, fertility, and sexual potency. One anthropomorphic jar has a female image on one side and a male on the other. This dual-sexed image and the association of both male and female painted representations on ceramics in graves suggests to some a complementary and unified conception of gender in the Majiayou Early Neolithic and is contrasted with the succeeding Late Neolithic Qijia, with its evidence for asymmetrical treatment of males and females in burials and lack of human iconography on pottery (Sun and Yang 2004:444–45).

Two ritual sites uncovered in the 1980s in northeastern China contain fascinating female-sexed figurative imagery. Both belong to the Hongshan culture of northeastern China, which flourished from 6,000 to 4,500 years ago. While most Hongshan sites consist of unpretentious Neolithic-style village sites, Dongshanzui and Niuheliang contain unique evidence of ritual elaboration and hierarchical social development in early farming contexts (Nelson 1995, 2002). Dongshanzui is a ritual site consisting of a cluster of house floors, stone platforms, and enclosures. Among these features are spread twenty clay figurine fragments, several of which are described as nude, probably pregnant females and a third that may be nursing (Jiao 2001; Nelson 2002; Pearson and Underhill 1987). Fragments of larger statues, at least one life sized, are in some cases sexed female (Jiao 2001).

Niuheliang is more accurately described as a ritual complex rather than a single site. It consists of tombs, structures, and compound enclosures stretching over eighty square kilometers. The complex does not contain a settlement component. It lies across from a low mountain shaped like the head of an animal (Barnes and Guo 1996). The tombs are considered to be elite resting places because of the effort required for their construction as well as the wealth of exotic and finely made grave goods—particularly intricate jade pieces (Barnes and Guo 1996; Nelson 1991, 2004). A large cruciform pit structure with elaborate construction and painted designs is described as the "Goddess Temple." Among the stunning finds within the temple were a painted clay mask with inlaid jade eyes and fragments of at least seven large clay statues, one estimated to be three times life size. At least one statue can be sexed female, given the presence of a breast fragment. A radiocarbon date of about 3500 B.C. situates the site in the Late Neolithic of the Hongshan culture and suggests that it may pre-date the first life-size human sculptures previously known from 3200 B.C. in Egypt (Barnes and Guo 1996).

One interpretation of Niuheliang simply assumes that the mask and statues within the complex represent the worship of female deities on which the Hongshan culture's religion centered (Jiao 2001:60). In a series of publications, Nelson has explored the political and religious significance of these images in more detail (Nelson 1991, 1995, 1996, 2002, 2004). She notes as relevant the absence of male figures at these ceremonial sites. Based on Sanday's (1981) cross-cultural research concerning gender formulations in origin myths and other religious contexts, it is difficult to deny females social power in the Hongshan cultural system where female symbolism predominates (Nelson 1991, 1996). Both ancient texts and ethnohistoric data suggest clues as to the possible sources of this power. Women may have exercised considerable leadership in spiritual life as shamans (Nelson 1996, 2002). Furthermore, women may have played important roles in the management and husbandry of pigs. While the economic importance of pig declines over the course of the Hongshan, its cultural significance is magnified as manifest through increased pig imagery and evidence for pig feasts (Nelson 1995, 2004). Working from the figurative evidence, Nelson builds compelling arguments that women were influential agents in elite Hongshan cultural circles.

Sexing the individuals in the elite tombs will certainly provide relevant data; however, results of these analyses are currently unavailable (Nelson, personal communication). If women are among the important people buried at Niuheliang, then credence is lent to a discussion of their role as central figures in elite spheres. If the burials contain only males, then the appropriation and manipulation of female imagery by males may become appropriate paths of future inquiry.

Southern Levant

As recently as 1998, well-respected figures in Levantine prehistory were cautioning that gender was all but impossible to recognize in the early prehistory of the Middle East (Bar-Yosef and Belfer-Cohen 1998:279–80). I disagree with this pessimistic forecast in light of a growing corpus of bioarchaeological work that has provided considerable insight into the activities of early farming populations. In addition to well-preserved skeletal material, the Levant boasts spectacular architectural preservation of both domestic and ritual structures. Figurative representations painted on ceramics, molded from clay, and formed with plaster on skulls are all open to gendered analyses.

In a research tradition dominated by technological and environmental analyses, statements about internal social dynamics are scarce and about sex and gender even more scarce. When pushed to consider women's activities in Neolithic societies, authors sometimes provide a litany of women's economic tasks including house construction, food preparation, water and wood gathering, planting fields, tending crops, harvesting, caring for domestic animals, cleaning, and refuse disposal (Bar-Yosef and Belfer-Cohen 1998:283). In this same account, no similar list is provided for the men. We are also told to expect that productive labor will become increasingly sex segregated with the establishment of farming communities as women are described as having new agricultural tasks and additional child care duties added to their workload. Men, meanwhile, would be increasingly involved in long-distance trade (Bar-Yosef 1995). Not only are tasks not shared, but they are spatially separate. A related point suggests that the appearance of female figurines during the Neolithic is a cultural expression for a growing dichotomy between males and females (Bar-Yosef and Belfer-Cohen 1992). The authors' recent statements regarding the inaccessibility of gender have not kept them from making some fairly specific statements on the subject in the past.

Despite these gloomy projections, a number of researchers have found productive venues to explore gender. The skeletal material from Abu Hureyra, a site in the Euphrates River valley of present-day northern Syria, was analyzed with specific attention paid to markers of occupational stress (Molleson 1994, 2000). A suite of morphological changes to the skeleton (joint faceting, degeneration of joints, and pronounced muscle attachment sites) suggested to Molleson that women spent a considerable amount of time kneeling on the floor with their toes tucked up under their feet, probably processing grain at querns. She also identified groups of females who, by virtue of distinctive dental use-wear patterns and enlarged mandibular joint surfaces, were probably involved in processing quantities of tough plant material to obtain fibers (Molleson 1994, 2000). Based on Molleson's research and the evidence showing that more women than men were buried beneath house floors, the excavators hypothesize that women's labor was closely associated with the household. They extrapolate that men would have been involved in agriculture and herding and further that men and women would have likely cooperated in labor-intensive, tightly scheduled activities like communal game drives and harvesting (Moore et al. 2000).

Two multisite analyses of Neolithic skeletal remains have suggested that Levantine sexual labor patterns might be highly localized (Eshed et al. 2003; Peterson 2002). The authors agree that Neolithic farmers had more physically demanding lifestyles than their Natufian predecessors and that new kinds of activities influenced musculature. However, they disagree on sexual divisions of labor. Osteological material from nine sites indicates to Peterson (2002) that there is little clear evidence to support a pronounced sexual division of labor during the Neolithic, as both males and females appear to have used similar muscle groups at similar levels and in similar ways. Perhaps a large number of labor-intensive tasks were shared by both sexes, or male and female tasks differed to some degree but produced similar musculature signatures. Eshed et al. (2003), in contrast, find that males in their Neolithic sample retain a high degree of muscle asymmetry in contrast to the more bilaterally symmetrical musculature of females. Since the majority of their sample comes from the coastal site of Atlit Yam (now underwater), the author proposes that paddling boats might have been a significant contributor to male musculature. The collective results suggest that sexual labor patterns varied with respect to local environments within the southern Levantine setting. Both studies provide results that occasionally suggest specific activities but more often reconstruct general activity patterns and levels. Nevertheless, even coarse-grained patterns add substantially to the discussion of sexual labor patterns.

Wright's analysis of the social contexts of food preparation and dining in Neolithic societies discusses changing men's and women's roles over time. She describes grinding and cooking as women's tasks, citing osteological and ethnographic evidence. During the earliest phase of food production (Pre-Pottery Neolithic A), grinding tools and hearths are found both indoors and outdoors representing fluid and unstructured boundaries between house and common spaces. By the Late Pre-Pottery Neolithic B, these same tools and features are found increasingly inside larger, more complicated houses in spaces that Wright describes as less accessible and out of the public eye. Following Hastorf (1991), she associates a spatial restriction of food-processing artifacts as a circumscription and control of female activities (Wright 2000:114).

This is a fascinating line of inquiry but one that needs to consider several points before its potential is fully actualized. For one, most of the structures that Wright examines have good evidence of being multistoried. The analysis of interior spaces and artifact distributions succumbs to a "tyranny of the floor plan." By this I mean that archaeologists have difficulty, in all but the most rare cases, reconstructing the arrangements of space and artifacts that occurred anywhere except on the ground floor (Peterson 2004). Furthermore, the conclusion that female activities are being controlled and circumscribed, to me, seems predicated on the notion that men are operating in different social and spatial contexts. Aside from hunting, which is becoming much less economically significant as sheep and goat domestication provide most of the needed protein, we do not have any archaeological or bioarchaeological evidence for what the men were doing. Recent osteological evidence from Çatalhöyük suggests that men were spending as much time in the smoky interior spaces as women were (Hodder 2005). Finally, our etic notions of interior spaces as "inferior," "dark," and "cramped" need to be critically examined. Considering the placement of burials under house floors, might not ground-floor rooms have been "sacred" and "powerful"?

Figurative imagery increases during the Neolithic of the southern Levant. The sculpted assemblage divides logically into larger, plaster and clay statues (thirty or more centimeters) typically found in ritual caches and smaller figurines made from clay and stone and found in domestic areas and refuse deposits. The larger statues have been interpreted as having roles in public rituals, as their size, stylized features (big eyes), and probable added garments would have made them highly visible (Garfinkel et al. 2002; Schmandt-Besserat 2004b). Examples of the large plaster statues have been described from Jericho, Nahal Hemar Cave, and 'Ain Ghazal. The most extensive collection (parts of approximately thirty-four statues) comes from two caches at 'Ain Ghazal. Morphologically, most are sexless, although three have sexual characteristics that indicate that they are female (Tubb and Grissom 1995). Examples of female images predominate among the figurines, although examples of both male and sexless figurines occur there as well (Bar-Yosef and Belfer-Cohen 1992; Miller 2002).

A recent interpretation of the proliferation of anthropomorphic images during the Neolithic revolution suggests that their meaning can be broadly interpreted. Cauvin (1997) maintains that the Neolithic revolution, rather than having its genesis in climate change or economic need, derived from a symbolic revolution grounded in a religious beliefs that placed women and bulls jointly at the apex of the prehistoric pantheon. Cauvin's position is evocative of Gimbutas at some levels, and the response to the sweeping explanatory framework in the Levant has been similar to that in Europe.

More nuanced treatments of the representations have been offered by individuals looking at the context, technology, clay composition, range of sexed types/combinations, and standardization in specific assemblages. Schmandt-Besserat describes one alternative suggested from early Babylonian texts—that the plaster statuary from 'Ain Ghazal might have functioned in ghost rituals. Ghosts featured in rituals as 1) beneficent spirits called on to remove pain by taking it with them to the underworld, 2) diviners, and 3) malevolent spirits to be exorcised

(Schmandt-Besserat 2004a). Both morphological features and contextual associations of the archaeological assemblage resonate with early historical accounts and make this hypothesis worthy of further consideration.

The largest assemblage of figurines to date comes from Sha'ar Hagolan, a village near the Sea of Gallilee (Garfinkel et al. 2002). Among the 200 figurines, a subset of seventy-four seated clay figurines has received special attention. They are designated "cowrie eyed" by virtue of their most prominent feature: long elongated oval eyes with diagonal slits. The cowrie-eyed seated figurines stand out because they appear substantially more standardized in facial and body features, apparel, and body position than the other figurines at Sha'ar Hagolan and those at other Levantine Neolithic sites as well (Miller 2002). Miller interprets the figurines as representing the Matron of Sha'ar Hagolan. As for the matron's authority, she assumes that the seated posture is linked with a position of power—as it is often assumed for male figures. Given the domestic context of finds, the matron's authority and power may hold sway primarily within the household. As to her maturity, Miller interprets the generous proportions of the lower torso and legs as being linked not with youth but with the joint effects of gravity, childbearing, and sedentism on a middle-aged body.

This interpretation is interesting and plausible but forgoes any discussion of the male cowrie-eyed figure mentioned but not illustrated (Garfinkel et al. 2002:195). In addition, there has been considerable discussion of the dual-sexed nature of these and similar figurines in the Levant and Cyprus. While the figurines have female anatomical details on the front, their overall outline and profile, when viewed from the rear, resemble phalli and glandes (Gopher and Orelle 1996; Miller 2002). Casual observations of the photographs and drawings of examples from the Sha'ar Hagolan assemblage substantiate possible dual-sex imagery in the cowrie-eyed assemblage as well. Consideration of the dual-sex interpretations does not enter into Miller's final assessment.

Less numerous than the figurines and statues from Neolithic sites are a set of figurative representations engraved on stone vessels or slabs; incised, painted, and molded in relief on ceramics; and painted on plaster floors. Garfinkel (2003) argues that these are best understood as "dancers" in religious rituals and surveys the distribution and frequency of similar imagery across the Near East and Europe from the eighth to the fourth millennium B.C. The emergence and increase in dancing motifs, beginning in the Neolithic, marks the intensification of ritual practice that would have provided the needed cohesion among members of growing agricultural villages. The decline in dancing motifs during the fourth millennium is viewed as signifying the reduction in prominence of dance in public, ritual life concomitant with the emergence of religious specialists and centralized authority. The Neolithic examples are widely distributed over space and relatively scarce. The celebrants are female, male, and sexless. While I do not always agree with the author's sex assignments (Peterson 2005), I think it is safe to say that females constitute the majority. From Neolithic objects, all-female and mixed-sex groups occur, but there are no clear examples of all-male groups. Accepting Garfinkel's premise that these are dancers, it seems reasonable to suggest that women played a significant role in Neolithic ritual sphere. But Garfinkel astutely reminds us that these images are not the equivalent of photographs of ancient rituals. The depictions on ritual and commemorative objects are realistically interpreted as reflecting the concepts *behind* the dance. The consistent uniformity in appearance, size, and posture of grouped figures is suggestive of an egalitarian ethic in which male, female, and sexless bodies had similar representational meaning at some level(s) (Garfinkel 2002).

In contrast with the communal ethic represented among the dancers, the production of plastered skulls seems to have been a Neolithic ritual that focused on the maintenance of individual identity. The postmortem removal of the skull was a common part of the Pre-Pottery Neolithic mortuary ritual. Certain of these removed skulls were slated for special treatment and subsequent reinterment. Plaster was applied to create distinctive facial features. Along with the application of pigment and inlaid items, it seems that there was an attempt to re-create individual likenesses. While this may be true, the widely held belief that these skulls represented an ancestor cult focusing on revered, male ancestors can no longer be sustained. Both CT scans and DNA analysis now indicate that skulls from women, men, and children all received this special treatment (Bonogofsky 2004). This ritual sphere is also inclusive in terms of both age and sex categories.

There is, I would argue, little evidence for a hegemonic gender hierarchy in the southern Levant. Detailed mortuary studies provide no evidence for status differentiation along sex lines during the Neolithic (Grindell 1998). Men and women are jointly participating in range of physically strenuous, habitual activities. Some sexual divisions of labor seem to be present with grinding and fiber processing being done by females and ungulate hunting probably being done by men. But there is no evidence of the bulk of agricultural work being borne by one sex or the other. Females were actively involved in domestic and community rituals that featured plaster statuary, skull plastering, and household figurines. There is some evidence for increasingly cloistered context for women's food preparation activities, but analyses need to consider both men's spaces, roof spaces, and possible emic meanings of ground-floor spaces before conclusions about the emergence of differential access to and use of public and private spaces can be sustained.

Coastal Ecuador

The Early Formative Valdivia culture of coastal Ecuador maintained sedentary village life based on multicrop agriculture. Domesticates included maize, beans, squash, and manioc. Fishing and shellfishing were important dietary components as well. During the 2,800 years that mark its development (ca. 4400–1600 B.C.), there is some evidence for emergent hereditary inequality as sites become more internally complex, evidence for ceremonialism increases, and mortuary data provides some evidence of social ranking (Zeidler 2000). Recent studies have suggested that symbolic separation between the sexes characterized household spaces and, less convincingly, daily tasks. But it is equally clear that neither separate household spheres nor the onset of incipient complexity removed females from a wide range of political and religious roles.

Efforts to differentiate the primary economic tasks of Valdivian culture are the least satisfying of recent gender efforts. Ethnographic and Spanish ethnohistoric sources have been used to establish a sexed labor pattern for the primary economic tasks. The sources are accepted grudgingly but without much critical analysis and no independent archaeological support (Bruhns and Stothert 1999). Not surprisingly, a highly segregated labor scenario emerges with men and women taking on different tasks and carrying these tasks out in different spaces. Women worked in the fields doing most of the agricultural work. They also maintained kitchen gardens and collected fish and shellfish in the mangrove swamps. Textile and, possibly, pottery production were female domains as well. Men cleared virgin agricultural land, fished in the bays and estuaries, constructed houses, hunted, and trapped (Bruhns and Stothert 1999:108). It has been suggested that a broadly diversified economy, like that of the Valdivians, would have labor and scheduling requirements likely to involve a pronounced sexual division of labor (Pearsall, in Bruhns and Stothert 1999:114).

An interest in household social organization has long been a staple of Latin American archaeology thanks to the pioneering work of Flannery, Winter, Wilk, and others. In keeping with this tradition, several attempts have been made to map gendered activities into domestic spaces and village structure. Village layout at the site of Loma Alta is described as U-shaped, with houses forming three sides around an open plaza area (Damp 1984). Using presumed associations between objects, tasks, and sexual labor divisions, Damp identifies a woman's spinning area from spindle whorls just outside the front door of one structure. Interior hearths are also assumed to be women's food production areas. Lithic debris and a broken tool on an exterior side of the house delimits a men's zone according to the author. A structural separation of male and female spheres is expanded in the interpretation of village layout using ethnographic data from the Ge Bororo of central Brazil. Damp maintains that the open plaza area, associated with the public and ceremonial aspects of village life, is associated with the "male," while the female sphere centers on the house and is considered peripheral (Damp 1984:582). While the separation of household space into male and female realms garners support from a second study, the interpretations associating male:public and female:household have been more recently challenged.

Ethnoarchaeological work among the Achuar of southeastern Ecuador has provided a basis for interpreting household spaces as well. A conceptual and functional division of house space into male and female areas is identified. Feature placement, artifact distribution, and microassemblages trampled into earthen floors from the archaeological site of Real Alto have produced parallel patterns to those observed and excavated from ethnographic settings (Stahl and Zeidler 1990; Zeidler, in Bruhns and Stothert 1999). These patterns suggest that both men and women use houses, with women's activities centering on the hearth and men's activities along the periphery. While these provide some insights into gender organization and symbolism, one might ask whether a complete picture of men's and women's lives can be constructed emphasizing households and domestic structures. In the case of Valdivia, the answer would be an emphatic no.

Real Alto (Phase 3, ca. 2800–2400 B.C.) contains several ceremonial structures on earthen platforms located in the central ceremonial district. The Charnel House stands on one of these mounds and contained a female skeleton in the central crypt, which was lined with fragmented manos and metates. The tomb complex also contained partially disarticulated and secondary interments of seven males. The group has been interpreted, most recently, as a high-status family. A hereditary component to status is suggested by the inclusion of subadults in the burials. The female burial stands out primarily because of its placement in the central ceremonial precinct of the large village (Zeidler 2000:167–68). Bruhns and Stothert (1999:100) ponder whether this woman might not have been sacrificed when the building was dedicated. While this alternative is plausible, I would note the infrequency with which male burials in similar contexts would be considered sacrificial victims.

A second inhumation from San Isidro (Phase 8, ca. 1800–1600 B.C.) is distinctive by virtue of its grave goods. A young female (age fifteen to twenty) was buried with a suite of tools highly suggestive of a shaman's ritual paraphernalia, including bat bones, a miniature incised vessel, ceremonial pieces of ground stone, and a cape or poncho made from a medium-sized feline with portions of the maxilla and mandible intact. Inside the mouth of the feline was a small figurine. It has been suggested that Valdivia figurines functioned as the repositories for spirits visited by shaman during trance (Stahl, in Zeidler 2000). Together, the burials from Real Alto's Charnel House and San Isidro suggest that women were highly visible in politico-religious aspects of Valdivian society and definitely not concerned only with preparing family meals and spinning. The archaeological evidence also mounts a substantial challenge to Damp's interpretation of women's spheres and the use of the Ge Bororo as an appropriate analogue.

The final data set to be considered are the Valdivia figurines, which have typically been interpreted as female fertility symbols. While female-sexed images predominate, once again there are examples of male and sexless images as well (Zeidler 2000:172). Figurines are found in a variety of contexts: domestic, mortuary, and ceremonial. One alternative to the fertility hypothesis describes some of the seated female figures as representations of powerful ritual practitioners (Bruhns and Stothert 1999:116). Zeidler proposes a third interpretation, suggesting that they were ritual paraphernalia used in shamanic rites, curing, and rites of passage. The predominance of female figurines suggests that a number of shamanic rituals were female focused related to life cycle changes, illness, and dangerous events like childbearing (Zeidler 2000:174). Alternatives to the fertility hypothesis reinforce the notion that women were highly visible actors in Valdivian society and support Zeidler's interpretations of the mortuary data from Real Alto's Charnel House and the San Isidro "shaman" burials.

Pre-Hispanic Southwest

Claassen (1997:77) noted that little gendered work had been conducted in southwestern archaeology. But Crown's edited volume *Women and Men in the Prehispanic Southwest* (2000b) provides readers a compilation of thoughtful studies written by researchers with long-standing interests in using gender to explore prehistoric farming societies. The Southwest is fortunate to have tremendously diverse and generally well-preserved archaeological data sets, robust regional databases, and contemporary Puebloan groups as possible analogues. Researchers have avoided some of the shortcomings discussed earlier in this chapter by a conservative approach emphasizing the "particular" over the "general."

In the context of sexual labor divisions, rather than assuming a task division for agricultural work, researchers admit that the production and distribution of corn has yet to be engendered (Spielmann 1995). Fish (2000:176–77) suggests that men and women likely shared responsibility and control for different stages of production and use of intensively managed plants. She views it likely that men's labor was pulled into agricultural pursuits as crops became a major share of diet, a view with some osteological support. Measures of cortical thickness and area indicate that Black Mesa males and females were not significantly dimorphic with respect to skeletal robusticity or muscularity. Both males and females had physically demanding lifestyles that could have resulted from participating either in the same tasks or in different tasks that required similar amounts and types of physical exertion (Martin 2000:282). Mixed-sex participation in hunting also seems likely if we view "hunting" more broadly to include small game drives, trapping, and the like (Szuter 2000:199–200).

There is wide acceptance and substantial archaeological support for assigning several tasks to one sex or the other. Bioarchaeological evidence, sex-patterned mortuary offerings, sculpted images, and regional ethnographies support sex role divisions in which women ground corn using manos and metates and men hunted using bows and arrow (Crown 2000a:224; Szuter 2000:207). The attribution of pottery production to women and loom weaving to men is more dependent on southwestern ethnography (Hegmon et al. 2000; Mills 2000; Mobley-Tanaka 1997). The argument has been made that women produced pottery vessels in response to changing sources of food and food preparation requirements (Crown and Wills 1995). These associations between sex and task provide the material bases (artifacts and features) for exploring the gendered use of space and changing gender relationships.

Issues of productive labor and status have been approached by locating the spatial domains of work within villages. Crown (2000c) argues that although women across the Southwest spent an increasing amount of time and energy preparing food, this work was valued as being critical to society's well-being and resulted in complementary status hierarchies for men and women. When status is viewed multidimensionally (as prestige, autonomy, and power), variable trajectories are uncovered for the Mogollon-Mimbres, Hohokam, and Puebloan sequences (Hegman et al. 2000). Mills (2000) makes a similar observation, finding that the increased demand for craft items in Puebloan and Hohokam settings led to different organizational strategies with different impacts on men and women. It is noteworthy that these efforts are unfettered by the devolutionary models so influential in Europe and the Near East. The lack of plow agriculture and secondary products from domestic livestock make the application of Boserupian models far less likely.

Gender ideology and its relationship with productive labor and status has been explored through a variety of media in the Southwest: rock art; pottery, textile, and basket designs; ceramic and stone figurines; and menstrual aprons/ imagery (Hays-Gilpin 2000). Mortuary remains indicate fluctuating gender hierarchies within regions and over time, with inconsistent links between the presence of gender hierarchy (male vs. female dominated) and the development of social differentiation (important people vs. commoners) (Neitzel 2000).

In a synthetic chapter concluding Crown's (2000b) volume, Lamphere (2000) suggests that four periods in the prehistory of the Southwest may have supported a more hierarchical hegemony, all of which had men at their apices. A case where hierarchical gender structures reverted to more balanced model is also included. While Lamphere's model is powerful and the database broadly integrative, there is still room for active debate about these interpretations. Discussion of a single case study illustrates this point. Relying heavily on the work by Hegmon and her coauthors, Lamphere suggests that women's prestige declined during the Pueblo IV period (post–A.D. 1300). The symbolic power of the household declined as kivas moved out of household units and into larger, aggregated community contexts. Ceremonial grinding activities, presumed to be a locus of women's power, that were once carried out in specialized mealing rooms or within kivas are increasingly secularized and carried out in open, highly visible plaza settings. This limits women's access to ritual spaces. New tools indicate that labor-intensive tortillas and piki bread making were introduced at this time, increasing women's workloads (Crown 2000c:247, 250; Hegmon et al. 2000:78–89; Mobley-Tanaka 1997:446). A hierarchical hegemony accommodates these data quite well, but the evidence from the realm of ceramic exchange networks and certain mortuary assemblages is less easy to explain.

During the Pueblo IV period, large bowls using a new glaze technology spread quickly across the Albuquerque area. Spielmann (2000:366–76) suggests that women throughout the region were integrated in a network that shared knowledge about how to make and fire these wares. At the site of Hawikku (ca. fourteenth to seventeenth centuries), dental morphology and demographic data indicate that discrete cemetery areas are associated with kin groups. Mortuary treatment and grave offerings suggest that important people (leaders) came from a small subset of the kin groups, suggesting an ascriptive element to status formation. From the 572 inhumations analyzed, eight male and three female "leaders" are identified. The male leaders consistently had grave goods that associated them with warrior roles, and two of the female leaders are described as heads of matrilines (Howell 1995). The third female "leader" had the most diverse array of grave goods, including prayer sticks, human hair (scalps), painted stones, and feathers. Zuni workmen at the site identified her as a "Medicine Priestess" based on a shrine made of shaped and painted wood, string, and feathers contained in the burial (Howell and Kintigh 1996:551). The analyses of mortuary patterns from Hawikku and glazeware ceramics from the Albuquerque area suggest that several avenues to power and prestige were still active for some women during the Pueblo IV period and may have provided considerable counterhegemonic forces.

Progress to Date

The select case studies and historical analysis of gender studies of prehistoric farming groups demonstrates remarkable (albeit uneven) progress toward more sophisticated treatments of this topic in archaeology. While a few scholars may still holdout that gender is archaeologically invisible, this position has become increasingly tenuous. As gender permeates the discussions of Neolithic and Formative societies around the globe, I sense a growing acceptance of its significance.

Task differentiation continues to pose challenges for many scholars, and it is particularly frustrating that the specifics of agricultural labor have proved so illusive. Very often we do not have a good understanding of who reaped, sowed, or milked—and arguably this may be an overly ambitious goal. The promise of fully engendering the Neolithic activity spectrum is likely to go unfulfilled. One productive trend has been to focus on more modest sets of tasks for which there are integrated data from archaeological sources, physical anthropology, and relevant ethnographies from which to infer female and male roles. Limiting the number and types of tasks discussed has left archaeologists with much to discuss. Studies that speculate on sex roles with reference to a broad range of tasks, based entirely on cross-cultural surveys or random ethnographic analogues, have failed to provide the bases for productive analyses and have tended to perpetuate unrealistic and stereotyped sexed labor scenarios.

Osteological studies of occupational stress markers have also added much to our understanding of labor patterns. The data sometimes reflect specific activities like fiber processing but often warrant more generic statements about the levels of activity, comparisons of synergistic muscle groups, or overall similarity in stress loads between males and females. Efforts to provide fine-grained interpretations from coarse-grained data leave room for injecting preconceived assumptions about labor patterns (Peterson 2002; Robb 1994c).

We can also trace a growing appreciation for the rich symbolic and ritual lives of early farmers. Researchers are actively grappling with the uses and meanings of human representations in a variety of media. Where once we had widespread acceptance that all the representations (or at least those worth depicting and discussing) were female and that all female images were fertility goddesses, we now find these same assemblages being discussed in the context of fluid gender roles, business transactions, shamanistic cures, celebrations of dance, and ghost rituals.

Evolutionary frameworks that viewed gender roles as proceeding through a series of predictable stages defined by technological, economic, and demographic variables served a generation of scholars well in their attempts to understand the processes of culture change. Unpacking the assumptions inherent in long-held theories and choosing alternatives can be an awkward process. But we have, for the most part, emerged from that process. The result is not a set of studies with a single, shared theoretical approach. They are, instead, typically informed by a variety of interests and perspectives: agency, practice theory, and the feminist critique, to name but a few. Their coherence comes not from a shared paradigm but through what Hegmon (2003:219) describes as an openness and dynamism that result from dialogue across theoretical lines. When combined with methodological rigor and an appreciation for the limitations of archaeological data, these hybrid theoretical perspectives have begun to pave the way for the next generation of gender studies.

Future Directions and Conclusions

There are several domains of inquiry that I can foresee providing fodder for future studies of gender in farming societies. The dynamic nature of gender in the human life cycle has gone largely untapped. The socialization and acculturation of children is one venue that seems promising (Morelli 1997). The role of apprenticeship in the transmission of cultural knowledge and craft is another (McClure 2004). Recently, Cannon (2004) has drawn attention to mortuary patterns suggestive of mother–daughter inheritance practices as well.

The new social roles and relationships that emerged between men and women during the Neolithic have typically been approached by trying to "gender" objects. A shift in perspective that examines how gender is made material could be a productive alternative. I am particularly drawn to studies that examine the ways in which identity is communicated through dress and adornment (Arnold 2004; Harlow 2004; Sørensen 2000). While the perishable aspects of clothing (textile, fur, and skin/hide) are often lost to time, nonperishable items can be preserved. Stone and shell items that are sewed onto clothing and headpieces or worn as jewelry can sometimes be identified. This line of inquiry might be of interest in any number of Neolithic and Formative contexts with fine-grained mortuary data sets.

Finally, in recent years, radiogenic isotopes of strontium have been used to identify immigrants among ancient populations. Strontium levels from a burial population in West Heslerton that included Neolithic/Early Bronze Age individuals suggested that some of the adult men and women were nonlocal (Montgomery et al. 2005). This method could be applicable elsewhere where the underlying geology has been mapped and is sufficiently variable to differentiate strontium signatures. The value of the application at a microregional level, the one of most significance to prehistorians interested in documenting exogamous marriage patterns for example, has yet to be documented.

The primary focus of this chapter has been to highlight the stunning variation in gender arrangements suggested by a set of geographically dispersed case studies. Historical developments provide the context for tracking the increasing theoretical eclecticism and methodological sophistication being brought to bear on archaeological gender studies. My very sincere wish is that we avoid, in the rush and pressure to generalize, the very real risk of ignoring the conspicuous variability of gender systems among early farming groups that sets our work apart as truly interesting and important.

References

Aaby, Peter
    1977   Engels and Women. *Critical Anthropology* 3(9–10):25–53.

Arnold, Bettina
    2004   Embodied Gender Performances in Early Iron Age Mortuary Ritual. Paper presented at the Chacmool Conference: Que(e)rying Archaeology—The 15th Anniversary Gender Conference, University of Calgary, Alberta, November.

Bacdayan, A. S.
    1977   Mechanistic Cooperation and Sexual Equality among the Western Bontoc. In *Social Stratification*. A. Schlegel, ed. Pp. 270–91. New York: Columbia University Press.

Barber, Elizabeth Wayland
    1994   *Women's Work: The First 20,000 Years.* New York: Norton.

Barnes, Gina, and Dashun Guo
    1996   The Ritual Landscape of "Boar Mountain" Basin: The Niuheliang Site Complex of North-Eastern China. *World Archaeology* 28:209–19.

Bar-Yosef, Ofer
    1995   Earliest Food Producers—Pre-Pottery Neolithic (8,000–5,500). In *The Archaeology of Society in the Holy Land*. T. E. Levy, ed. Pp. 190–201. New York: Facts on File.

Bar-Yosef, Ofer, and Anna Belfer-Cohen
    1992   From Foraging to Farming in the Mediterranean Levant. In *Transitions to Agriculture in Prehistory*. A. B. Gebauer and T. D. Price, eds. Pp. 21–48. Madison, WI: Prehistory Press.
    1998   Views of Gender in African Prehistory from a Middle Eastern Perspective.

In *Gender in African Prehistory.* S. Kent, ed. Pp. 279–84. Walnut Creek, CA: AltaMira Press.

Bonogofsky, Michelle
    2004   Including Women and Children: Neolithic Modeled Skulls from Jordan, Israel, Syria and Turkey. *Near Eastern Archaeology* 67:118–19.

Boserup, Ester
    1970   *Woman's Role in Economic Development.* New York: St. Martin's Press.

Bruhns, Karen Olsen, and Karen E. Stothert
    1999   *Women in Ancient America.* Norman: University of Oklahoma Press.

Brumfiel, Elizabeth M.
    1992   Distinguished Lecture in Archaeology: Breaking and Entering the Ecosystem—Gender, Class and Faction Steal the Show. *American Anthropologist* 94:551–67.

Brumbach, Hetty Jo, and Robert Jarvenpa
    1997   Ethnoarchaeology of Subsistence Space and Gender: A Subarctic Dene Case. *American Antiquity* 62:414–36.

Cannon, Aubrey
    2004   Mortuary Expressions of Mother-Daughter Inheritance and Identity. Paper presented at the Chacmool Conference: Que(e)rying Archaeology—The 15th Anniversary Gender Conference, University of Calgary, Alberta, November.

Cauvin, Jacques
    1997   *Naissance des Divinités Naissance de l'Agriculture.* Paris: CNRS.

Chevillard, N., and S. LeConte
    1986   The Dawn of Lineage Societies. In *Women's Work, Men's Property.* S. Coontz and P. Henderson, eds. Pp. 76–107. London: Verso.

Claassen, Cheryl
    1997   Changing Venue: Women's Lives in Prehistoric North America. In *Women in Prehistory.* C. Claassen and R. A. Joyce, eds. Pp. 65–87. Philadelphia: University of Pennsylvania Press.

Claassen, Cheryl, and Rosemary A. Joyce, eds.
    1997   *Women in Prehistory.* Philadelphia: University of Pennsylvania Press.

Cloud, K.
    1985   Women's Productivity in Agricultural Systems: Considerations for Project Design. In *Gender Roles in Development Projects.* C. Overholt, M. B. Anderson, K. Cloud, and J. R. Austin, eds. Pp. 17–56. West Hartford, CT: Kumarian Press.

Conkey, Margaret W., and Janet Spector
    1984   Archaeology and the Study of Gender. *Advances in Archaeological Method and Theory* 7:1–38.

Crown, Patricia L.
    2000a   Gendered Tasks, Power, and Prestige in the Prehispanic American Southwest.

In *Women and Men in the Prehispanic Southwest.* P. L. Crown, ed. Pp. 3–41. Santa Fe, NM: School of American Research Press.

Crown, Patricia L., ed.
    2000b *Women and Men in the Prehispanic Southwest.* Santa Fe, NM: School of American Research Press.

Crown, Patricia L.
    2000c Women's Role in Changing Cuisine. In *Women and Men in the Prehispanic Southwest.* P. L. Crown, ed. Pp. 221–66. Santa Fe, NM: School of American Research Press.

Crown, Patricia L., and Wirt H. Wills
    1995 The Origins of Southwestern Containers: Women's Time Allocation and Economic Intensification. *Journal of Anthropological Research* 51:173–86.

Damp, Jonathan E.
    1984 Architecture of the Early Valdivia Village. *American Antiquity* 49:573–85.

Divale, William, and Marvin Harris
    1976 Population, Warfare, and the Male Supremacist Complex. *American Anthropologist* 78:521–38.

Dobres, Marcia-Anne
    2004 Digging Up Gender in the Earliest Human Societies. In *A Companion to Gender History.* T. A. Meade and M. W. Wiesner-Hanks, eds. Pp. 211–26. Oxford: Blackwell.

Ehrenberg, Margaret R.
    1989 *Women in Prehistory.* Norman: University of Oklahoma Press.

Eshed, Vered, Avi Gopher, Ehud Galili, and Israel Hershkovitz
    2003 Musculoskeletal Stress Markers in Natufian Hunter-Gatherers and Neolithic Farmers in the Levant: The Upper Limb. *American Journal of Physical Anthropology* 122:303–15.

Fish, Suzanne K.
    2000 Farming, Foraging, and Gender. In *Women and Men in the Prehispanic Southwest.* P. L. Crown, ed. Pp. 169–96. Santa Fe, NM: School of American Research Press.

Garfinkel, Yosef
    2003 *Dancing at the Dawn of Agriculture.* Austin: University of Texas Press.

Garfinkel, Yosef, Naomi Korn, and Michele A. Miller
    2002 Art from Sha'ar Hagolan: Visions of a Neolithic Village in the Levant. In *Sha'ar Hagolan 1.* Y. Garfinkel and M. A. Miller, eds. Pp. 188–208. Oxford: Oxbow Books.

Gimbutas, Marija
    1974 *The Gods and Goddesses of Old Europe.* Berkeley: University of California Press.
    1989 Figurines and Cult Equipment: Their Role in the Reconstruction of Neolithic Religion. In *Archilleion: A Neolithic Settlement in Thessaly, Greece, 6400–5600*

BC. M. Gimbutas, S. Winn, and D. Shimabuku, eds. Monumenta Archaeologica 14. Los Angeles: Institute of Archaeology, University of California.

Gopher, A., and E. Orelle
    1996   An Alternative Interpretation for the Material Imagery of the Yarmukian, a Neolithic Culture of the Sixth Millenium BC in the Southern Levant. *Cambridge Archaeological Journal* 9:133–37.

Grindell, Beth
    1998   Unmasked Equalities: An Examination of Mortuary Practices and Social Complexity in the Levantine Natufian and Pre-Pottery Neolithic. Ph.D. dissertation, University of Arizona; Ann Arbor: University Microfilms International.

Guyer, Jane I.
    1991   Female Farming in Anthropology and African History. In *Gender at the Crossroads of Knowledge*. M. di Leonardo, ed. Pp. 257–77. Berkeley: University of California Press.
    1995   Women's Farming and Present Ethnography: Perspectives on a Nigerian Restudy. In *Women Wielding the Hoe*. D. F. Bryceson, ed. Pp. 25–46. Washington, DC: Berg.

Hamilton, Naomi
    2000   Ungendering Archaeology: Concepts of Sex and Gender in Figurine Studies in Prehistory. In *Representations of Gender from Prehistory to the Present*. M. Donald and L. Hurcombe, eds. Pp. 17–30. New York: St. Martin's Press.

Harlow, Mary
    2004   Dress and Identity at the End of the Roman Empire. Paper presented at the Chacmool Conference: Que(e)rying Archaeology—The 15th Anniversary Gender Conference, University of Calgary, Alberta, November.

Hastorf, Christine
    1991   Gender, Space and Food in Prehistory. In *Engendering Archaeology*. J. Gero and M. Conkey, eds. Pp. 131–62. Oxford: Blackwell.

Hays-Gilpin, Kelley
    2000   Gender Ideology and Ritual Activities. In *Women and Men in the Prehispanic Southwest*. P. L. Crown, ed. Pp. 91–135. Santa Fe, NM: School of American Research Press.

Hegmon, Michelle
    2003   Setting Theoretical Egos Aside: Issues and Theory in North American Archaeology. *American Antiquity* 68:213–43.

Hegmon, Michelle, Scott G. Ortman, and Jeanette L. Mobley-Tanaka
    2000   Women, Men, and the Organization of Space. In *Women and Men in the Prehispanic Southwest*. P. L. Crown, ed. Pp. 43–90. Santa Fe, NM: School of American Research Press.

Hodder, Ian
    2005   Women and Men at Çatalhöyük. *Scientific American* 15(1):34–41.

Howell, Todd L.
  1995   Tracking Zuni Gender and Leadership Roles across the Contact Period in the Zuni Region. *Journal of Anthropological Research* 51:125–47.
Howell, Todd L., and Keith W. Kintigh
  1996   Archaeological Identification of Kin Groups Using Mortuary and Biological Data: An Example from the American Southwest. *American Antiquity* 61:537–54.
Jiao, Tianlong
  2001   Gender Studies in Chinese Neolithic Archaeology. In *Gender and the Archaeology of Death*. B. Arnold and N. L. Wicker, eds. Pp. 51–62. Walnut Creek, CA: AltaMira Press.
Kent, Susan, ed.
  1998   *Gender in African Prehistory*. Walnut Creek, CA: AltaMira Press.
Lamphere, Louise
  2000   Gender Models in the Southwest: A Sociocultural Perspective. In *Women and Men in the Prehispanic Southwest*. P. L. Crown, ed. Pp. 379–401. Santa Fe, NM: School of American Research Press.
Leacock, Eleanor
  1978   Women's Status in Egalitarian Society: Implications for Social Evolution. *Current Anthropology* 19:247–75.
  1981   History, Development, and the Division of Labor by Sex. *Signs* 7:474–91.
Lerner, Gerda
  1986   *The Creation of Patriarchy*. New York: Oxford University Press.
Lillis, Jackie E.
  2004   Women and the Production of Textiles at the Neolithic Swiss Lake Dwelling Site of Robenhausen. Paper presented at the Chacmool Conference: Que(e)rying Archaeology—The 15th Anniversary Gender Conference, University of Calgary, Alberta, November.
Linduff, Katheryn M., and Yan Sun, eds.
  2004   *Gender and Chinese Archaeology*. Walnut Creek, CA: AltaMira Press.
Maclean, Rachel
  1998   Gendered Technologies and Gendered Activities in the Interlacustrine Early Iron Age. In *Gender in African Prehistory*. S. Kent, ed. Pp. 163–77. Walnut Creek, CA: AltaMira Press.
Martin, M. Kay, and Barbara Voorhies
  1975   *Female of the Species*. New York: Columbia University Press.
Martin, Debra L.
  2000   Bodies and Lives: Biological Indicators of Health Differentials and Division of Labor by Sex. In *Women and Men in the Prehispanic Southwest*. P. L. Crown, ed. Pp. 267–300. Santa Fe, NM: School of American Research Press.
McClure, Sarah B.
  2004   "Variability around the Template": Cultural Inheritance Theory and an

"Engendered" Neolithic Ceramic Technology. Paper presented at the Chacmool Conference: Que(e)rying Archaeology—The 15th Anniversary Gender Conference, University of Calgary, Alberta, November.

Meade, Teresa A., and Merry E. Wiesner-Hanks
 2004 Introduction. In *A Companion to Gender History*. T. A. Meade and M. W. Wiesner-Hanks, eds. Pp. 1–7. Oxford: Blackwell.

Mears, John A.
 2001 Agricultural Origins in Global Perspective. In *Agricultural and Pastoral Societies in Ancient and Classical History*. M. Adas, ed. Pp. 36–70. Philadelphia: Temple University Press.

Meillassoux, Claude
 1981 *Maidens, Meals, and Money*. New York: Cambridge University Press.

Meskell, Lynn
 1995 Goddesses, Gimbutas and "New Age" Archaeology. *Antiquity* 69:74–86.

Miller, Michele A.
 2002 The Function of the Anthropomorphic Figurines: A Preliminary Analysis. In *Sha'ar Hagolan I*. Y. Garfinkel and M. A. Miller, eds. Pp. 221–33. Oxford: Oxbow Books.

Mills, Barbara J.
 2000 Gender, Craft Production, and Inequality. In *Women and Men in the Prehispanic Southwest*. P. L. Crown, ed. Pp. 301–43. Santa Fe, NM: School of American Research Press.

Mobley-Tanaka, Jeanette L.
 1997 Gender and Ritual Space during the Pithouse to Pueblo Transition: Subterranean Mealing Rooms in the North American Southwest. *American Antiquity* 62:437–48.

Molleson, Theya I.
 1994 The Eloquent Bones of Abu Hureyra. *Scientific American*, August, 70–75.
 2000 People of Abu Hureyra. In *Village on the Euphrates*. A. M. T. Moore, G. C. Hillman, and A. J. Legge, eds. Pp. 301–24. Oxford: Oxford University Press.

Montgomery, Janet, Jane A. Evans, Dominic Powlesland, and Charlotte A. Roberts
 2005 Continuity or Colonization in Anglo-Saxon England? Isotope Evidence for Mobility, Subsistence Practice, and Status at West Heslerton. *American Journal of Physical Anthropology* 126:123–38.

Moore, A. M. T., G. C. Hillman, and A. J. Legge, eds.
 2000 *Village on the Euphrates*. Oxford: Oxford University Press.

Morelli, Gilda A.
 1997 Growing Up Female in a Farmer Community and a Forager Community. In *The Evolving Female*. M. E. Morbeck, A. Galloway, and A. L. Zihlman, eds. Pp. 209–19. Princeton, NJ: Princeton University Press.

Neitzel, Jill E.
 2000 Gender Hierarchies: A Comparative Analysis of Mortuary Data. In *Women and*

Men in the Prehispanic Southwest. P. L. Crown, ed. Pp. 137–68. Santa Fe, NM: School of American Research Press.

Nelson, Sarah M.
- 1991 The "Goddess Temple" and the Status of Women at Niuheliang, China. In *The Archaeology of Gender*. Proceedings of the 22nd Annual Chacmool Conference. D. Walde and N. D. Willows, eds. Pp. 302–8. Calgary: Department of Archaeology, University of Calgary.
- 1995 Ritualized Pigs and the Origins of Complex Society: Hypotheses regarding the Hongshan Culture. *Early China* 20:1–16.
- 1996 Ideology and the Formation of an Early State in Northeast China. In *Ideology and the Formation of Early States*. H. J. M. Claessen and J. G. Oosten, eds. Pp. 153–69. New York: E. J. Brill.
- 2002 Performing Power in Early China: Examples from the Shang Dynasty and the Hongshan Culture. In *The Dynamics of Power*. M. O'Donovan, ed. Pp. 151–67. Occasional Paper 30. Carbondale: Center for Archaeological Investigations, Southern Illinois University.
- 2004 *Gender in Archaeology: Analyzing Power and Prestige*. Walnut Creek, CA: AltaMira Press.

Ortner, S. B.
- 1996 *Making Gender: The Politics and Erotics of Culture*. Boston: Beacon Press.

Pearson, Richard, and Anne Underhill
- 1987 The Chinese Neolithic: Recent Trends in Research. *American Anthropologist* 89:807–22.

Peters, E. L.
- 1978 The Status of Women in Four Middle East Communities. In *Women in the Muslim World*. L. Beck and N. Keddie, ed. Pp. 311–50. Cambridge, MA: Harvard University Press.

Peterson, Jane
- 2002 *Sexual Revolutions: Gender and Labor at the Dawn of Agriculture*. Walnut Creek, CA: AltaMira Press.
- 2004 Around the House: The Use of Space in Late Pre-Pottery Neolithic B Villages in the Southern Levant. Paper presented at the 69th Annual Meeting of the Society for American Archaeology, Montreal, April.
- 2004 Review of *Dancing at the Dawn of Agriculture*. *Near Eastern Archaeology* 67:117–18.

Robb, John
- 1994a Burial and Social Reproduction in the Peninsular Italian Neolithic. *Journal of Mediterranean Archaeology* 7:27–71.
- 1994b Gender Contradictions, Moral Coalitions, and Inequality in Prehistoric Italy. *Journal of European Archaeology* 2:20–49.
- 1994c Issues in the Interpretation of Muscle Attachments. Paper presented at the Annual Meeting of the Paleoanthropology Society, Anaheim, CA, April.

Sacks, Karen
    1974   Engels Revisited: Women, the Organization of Production, and Private Property. In *Women, Culture and Society*. M. Rosaldo and L. Lamphere, eds. Pp. 207–22. Stanford, CA: Stanford University Press.
Sanday, Peggy Reeves
    1981   *Female Power and Male Dominance: On the Origins of Sexual Inequality*. Cambridge: Cambridge University Press.
Schlegel, Alice
    1977   Toward a Theory of Sexual Stratification. In *Sexual Stratification: A Cross-Cultural Review*. A. Schlegel, ed. Pp. 1–40. New York: Columbia University Press.
Schmandt-Besserat, Denise
    2004a   'Ain Ghazal Monumental Figures: A Stylistic Analysis. Electronic document, http://link.lanic.utexas.edu/menic/ghazal/ChapVI/dsp.html, accessed November 15, 2004.
    2004b   A Stone Metaphor of Creation. Electronic document, http://link.lanic.utexas.edu/menic/ghazal/ChapIV/chapter4.html, accessed November 15, 2004.
Shelach, Gideon
    2004   Marxist and Post-Marxist Paradigms for the Neolithic. In *Gender and Chinese Archaeology*. K. M. Linduff and Y. Sun, eds. Pp. 11–27. Walnut Creek, CA: AltaMira Press.
Silverblatt, Irene
    1988   Women in States. *Annual Review of Anthropology* 17:427–60.
Sørensen, Marie Louise Stig
    2000   *Gender Archaeology*. Cambridge: Polity Press.
Spector, Janet D.
    1983   Male and Female Task Differentiation among the Hidatsa: Toward the Development of an Archaeological Approach to Gender. In *The Hidden Half: Studies of Plains Indian Women*. P. Albers and B. Medicine, eds. Pp. 77–100. Washington, DC: University Press of America.
Spielmann, Katherine A.
    1995   Glimpses of Gender in the Prehistoric Southwest. *Journal of Anthropological Research* 51:91–102.
    2000   Gender and Exchange. In *Women and Men in the Prehispanic Southwest*. P. L. Crown, ed. Pp. 345–77. Santa Fe, NM: School of American Research Press.
Stahl, Peter W., and James A. Zeidler
    1990   Differential Bone-Refuse Accumulation in Food-Preparation and Traffic Areas on an Early Ecuadorian House Floor. *Latin American Antiquity* 1:150–69.
Sun, Yan, and Hongyu Yang
    2004   Gender Ideology and Mortuary Practice in Northwestern China. In *Gender and Chinese Archaeology*. K. M. Linduff and Y. Sun, eds. Pp. 29–46. Walnut Creek, CA: AltaMira Press.

Szuter, Christine R.
  2000 Gender and Animals: Hunting Technology, Ritual, and Subsistence in the Greater Southwest. In *Women and Men in the Prehispanic Southwest.* P. L. Crown, ed. Pp. 197–220. Santa Fe, NM: School for American Research Press.

Talalay, Lauren E.
  1987 Rethinking the Function of Clay Figurine Legs from Neolithic Greece: An Argument by Analogy. *American Journal of Archaeology* 91:161–69.
  2000 Archaeological Ms.conceptions: Contemplating Gender and the Greek Neolithic. In *Representations of Gender from Prehistory to the Present.* M. Donald and L. Hurcombe, eds. Pp. 3–16. New York: St. Martin's Press.

Trenchard, E.
  1987 Rural Women's Work in Sub-Saharan Africa and the Implications for Nutrition. In *The Geography of Gender in the Third World.* J. H. Momsen and J. Townsend, eds. Pp. 153–72. Albany: State University of New York Press.

Tubb, Kathryn Walker, and Carol A. Grissom
  1995 Ayn Ghazal: A Comparative Study of the 1983 and 1985 Statuary Caches. In *Studies in the History and Archaeology of Jordan V.* Pp. 435–47. Amman: Department of Antiquities.

Whitehouse, Ruth D.
  2002 Gender in the South Italian Neolithic: A Combinatory Approach. In *In Pursuit of Gender: Worldwide Archaeological Approaches.* S. M. Nelson and M. Rosen-Ayalon, eds. Pp. 15–42. Walnut Creek, CA: AltaMira Press.

Wright, Katherine I.
  2000 The Social Origins of Cooking and Dining in Early Villages of Western Asia. *Proceedings of the Prehistoric Society* 66:89–121.

Wu, Jui-man
  2004 The Late Neolithic Cemetery at Dadianzi, Inner Mongolia Autonomous Region. In *Gender and Chinese Archaeology.* K. M. Linduff and Y. Sun, eds. Pp. 47–91. Walnut Creek, CA: AltaMira Press.

Zeidler, James A.
  2000 Gender, Status, and Community in Early Formative Valdivia Society. In *The Archaeology of Communities.* M. A. Canuto and J. Yaeger, eds. Pp. 161–81. New York: Routledge.

Women, Gender, and Pastoralism 17

PAM CRABTREE

THE TRANSITION FROM FORAGING to farming represents one of the most significance changes in all of human prehistory. The nineteenth-century evolutionary anthropologists used food production, including both agriculture and animal husbandry, to distinguish savagery from barbarism in their schemes of universal social evolution. For V. Gordon Childe (1936) writing in the middle of the twentieth century, plant and animal domestication marked the beginning of the agricultural revolution. Drawing an analogy with the industrial revolution, Childe argued that the agricultural (or first) revolution represented a change in subsistence technology that affected all other aspects of human life, including settlement patterns, social relations, and ideology. Moreover, the agricultural revolution provided the economic basis for the urban (or second) revolution that produced complex, urban societies in Mesopotamia, the Indus Valley, Egypt, and the Mediterranean region (Childe 1950).

In the Eastern Hemisphere, domesticated herd animals, including sheep, goats, and cattle, played a crucial role in both Neolithic and later complex societies. Since the end of World War II, Old World archaeologists have worked diligently to identify the beginnings of animal domestication and to trace the spread of these animal domesticates throughout Eurasia. Less attention has been paid to social context in which early animal domestication took place. This chapter will attempt to examine the roles played by both women and men in early agropastoral societies. It will begin with a definition of pastoralism and a review of the archaeological evidence for the origins and spread of pastoralism in the Middle East and Europe. This chapter will then examine the roles that women and men may have played in early agropastoral societies in Eurasia and the ways that these roles may have changed through time as a result of the use of animals for secondary products, such as milk, wool, and traction (Sherratt 1981, 1983).

Pastoralism

While there is debate in the anthropological literature over the definition of pastoralism, I will follow Chang and Koster (1994:8) and define pastoralists as people "who keep herd animals and who define themselves and are defined by others as pastoralists." This is a very broad definition of pastoralism that includes nomadic pastoralism, transhumant pastoralism, and agropastoralism.

Pastoral nomads are people who practice little or no agriculture and who move their herds from place to place on a seasonal schedule. A classic ethnography of pastoral nomads is Barth's (1961) study of the Basseri in Iran. The Basseri move to high mountain pastures in the Zagros Mountains during the summer and return to the lowlands of southern Persia during the winter. Since pastoral nomads practice little or no agriculture, they are dependent on village farmers for cereals and other necessities. The rise of urbanism in the fourth millennium B.C.E. may have provided new opportunities for specialized pastoralists who could sell their excess meat and other animal products to nonfarming city dwellers (Zeder 1991).

Transhumant pastoralists combine fixed-field agriculture with mobile herding strategies. While part of the community remains in the farming village on a year-round basis, some members of the community move to seasonal pastures with their flocks and herds. Historical and ethnographic records indicate that seasonal transhumance has been practiced in the Swiss Alps since the Middle Ages (Netting 1996). In the Swiss Alps, permanent farming villages are located on the slopes. During the summer, when the high Alpine pastures are free of snow, the flocks from an entire farming village are relocated to these high pastures. The flocks are tended by a small number of men from the village who milk them and make cheeses in bulk (Netting 1996:226). Most of the population remains in the village to carry out hay making and other vital tasks. Historical and archaeological sources suggest that transhumant pastoralism may have a long history in the mountainous parts of southeastern Europe and the Alpine regions of central Europe. Transhumance, known locally as booleying, was also practiced in northwestern Ireland before the potato famine (Shanklin 1994).

Agropastoralists combine both agriculture and animal husbandry in permanent village locations. While those who favor a more restrictive definition of pastoralism may not view agropastoralists as "true" pastoralists,[1] historical evidence suggests that animal husbandry played a critical role in many ancient agropastoral societies in Eurasia. For example, in *De Bello Gallico*, Caesar remarks on the importance of cattle in both Gaul and Germany. In early Christian Ireland (from the fifth to the eighth century C.E.), historic sources indicate that "land was measured in terms of the cows it could maintain, legal compensation was reckoned in terms of cattle, a man's standing in society was determined by his wealth in cattle, and cattle raiding was a recognized form of warfare and adventure for young nobles" (Ó Curráin 1972:53). Agropastoralism has a long history in Eurasia. Archaeological evidence indicates that agropastoral villages were established about 10,000 years ago in the Middle East and that agropastoralism had spread to southeastern Europe by about 7000 B.C.E.

While pastoral societies are characterized by a wide range of mobility strategies, what all these societies have in common is that their livelihood depends on herd animals and their products. Chang and Koster (1994:9) note that "keeping herd animals requires human beings to shape their lives—socially, culturally, economically, and ideologically—in ways that are structured by an interdependence with their animals." This interdependence distinguishes pastoral societies not only from hunter-gatherer societies but also from communities that combine agriculture with hunting, such as the Mississippians of eastern North America. In order to explore the ways in which animal keeping transforms human lives, we will begin by examining the archaeological evidence for the beginnings of animal domestication in the Near East.

Identifying Animal Domestication in the Archaeological Record

Hunters and herders view animals in very different ways. Hunters are interested in acquiring dead animals and their primary products—meat, hides, sinew, and bone. Herders, on the other hand, are interested in live animals and their offspring. The shift from acquiring dead animals to maintaining flocks of live animals marks the beginning of animal domestication (Meadow 1989:81). While this represents a useful behavioral definition of animal domestication, the problem that has vexed archaeologists for over half a century is how to recognize evidence for early animal domestication in the archaeological record.

Most of our evidence for early animal domestication comes from butchered animal bones that were discarded at archaeological sites. These fragmentary remains represent refuse from meat consumption. They are therefore an indirect reflection of animal production strategies. Zooarchaeologists have used a number of criteria to identify early animal domestication in the archaeological record (for a review, see Crabtree 1993). These criteria include the appearance of an animal outside its natural range, morphological changes in the animal bones themselves, and changes in the demographic profiles or age and sex distribution of the animals that were selected for slaughter. While all these criteria have been used successfully to identify early animal domestication, each criterion has its limitations.

The appearance of animals outside their natural ranges is an obvious indication that animals are under some form of human control. Since wild goats and wild sheep are not native to Europe, the appearance of sheep and goats in southeastern Europe beginning about 9,000 years ago indicates the beginnings of pastoralism in that region. However, experiments with animal domestication are most likely to have occurred in regions where the wild ancestors of early domestic animals are found, so this criterion cannot be used to identify the earliest attempts to domesticate animals.

Morphological changes that have been used to identify animal domestication include overall body size reduction, changes in the form of the horn cores (the bones that underlie the horns), reduction in the size of the teeth and jaws, and evidence for pathological changes that may be the result of penning or tethering. The most commonly used of these criteria is overall size reduction since measurements can be taken on a wide variety of anatomical elements (Driesch 1976). Tchernov and Horowitz (1991) have suggested that size reduction may have been the result of selection for animals that would mature more quickly and reproduce more rapidly, especially in the anthropogenic environments that surrounded early farming villages. However, recent research by Zeder (2001) has indicated that, at least for goats, the supposed size reduction that accompanied early domestication may be a result changing demographic profiles of the slaughtered herds.

Demographic profiles have been used to identify early animal domestication since the 1960s. Zooarchaeologists suggested that hunting populations, interested in the dead animal and its primary products, would focus their attention on prime adult animals. Those animals would provide the highest-quality meat as well as fat and pelts (Perkins and Daly 1974:80). Herders, on the other hand, would need to maintain a small breeding population of primarily female animals. Most males would be slaughtered in late adolescence, when most of their growth had been completed. A high proportion of immature animals was therefore seen as a signature of early animal domestication.

This criterion was used rather indiscriminately in the 1960s to identify early domestic animals. Perkins (1964), for example, identified possible domestic sheep at Zawi Chemi Shanidar in northern Iraq, dating to the ninth millennium B.C.E., based on a small sample of morphologically wild sheep bones that includes a high percentage of immature specimens. Legge (1972) even suggested that gazelles might have been domesticated in Israel during the Late Pleistocene, based on a high proportion of immature animals at the Natufian site of Nahal Oren. Today, both these claims for early animal domestication are viewed with suspicion. The small sample size and the absence of morphological changes make sheep domestication at Zawi Chemi unlikely (for a critique of the evidence for sheep domestication at Zawi Chemi, see Uerpmann 1987:62–63). Although gazelles can be tamed, they cannot be herded in groups or with dogs, and they are therefore unsuitable for pastoral adaptations (Clutton-Brock 1980:171). The high proportions of young gazelles found at many Late Pleistocene sites in the Near East may be the result of hunting techniques that focused on entire herds of animals (see, e.g., Campana and Crabtree 1990; Henry 1975; Legge and Rowley-Conwy 1987).

Modern studies use demographic profiles to identify animal domestication in far more sophisticated ways. In sexually dimorphic species such as goats, measurement data can be combined with data on aging to construct demographic profiles for each species. Since a focus on live animals and their progeny leads herders to treat male and female animals differently (Meadow 1989), differences in age profiles for male and female animals may reflect the transition from hunting to herding (Hesse 1984; Zeder 2001).

The Archaeological Evidence for Early Animal Domestication in the Near East and Europe

Zooarchaeological data indicate that goats and sheep were first domesticated about 8000 B.C.E. in the Near East. Detailed analyses of the demographic data for early goats from the early eighth-millennium site of Ganj Dareh in western Iran indicates that goats were first domesticated there at about 7900 B.C. (Hesse 1984; Zeder and Hesse 2000). Early domesticated goats appear in the southern Levant at about the same time. Goats from Jericho show changes in the shape of their horn cores that may indicate incipient domestication (Clutton-Brock 1979), while a majority of the goats from the Neolithic site of 'Ain Ghazal in Jordan were killed before they reached adulthood. In addition, some of the goats from 'Ain Ghazal show evidence for arthritis, which may have resulted from poor husbandry conditions (Köhler-Rollefson et al. 1988). It is not entirely clear whether goats were independently domesticated in the southern Levant or whether they were introduced to the region from the Zagros.

Sheep appear to have been domesticated at approximately the same time as goats in the Near East. Early evidence for domestic sheep comes from a number of eighth-millennium B.C.E. sites in Syria and Anatolia. For example, the sheep from the Early Neolithic site of Bouqras in Syria show significant size decrease at a time when their numbers are increasing, leading Clason in Akkermans et al. (1983) to suggest that they were early domesticates. Recent DNA studies

(Hiendleder et al. 2002) suggest that modern domesticated sheep are derived from two different subspecies of wild mouflon (*Ovis orientalis*), indicating that the pattern of sheep domestication may be a complex one involving multiple centers of domestication.

DNA studies have shown that the pattern of cattle domestication in the Old World is quite complex. Both faunal evidence and DNA studies suggest that cattle were independently domesticated in the eastern Sahara between 8,000 and 10,000 years ago (Bradley 2003; Bradley et al. 1998; Gautier 1987). The molecular data also point to an independent domestication of zebu (humped cattle) in South Asia. The DNA evidence points to a third center for the domestication of Near Eastern and European cattle, although the location of this center has not been determined archaeologically. Domesticated cattle appear at a number of sites in the eastern Mediterranean at about 7000 B.C.E.

The cultural context in which early animal domestication took place is equally important. While early scholars such as Childe saw plant and animal domestication as a single process of transformation from foraging to farming, archaeological research conducted over the past twenty-five years has shown clearly that in the Middle East plant cultivation clearly preceded animal domestication (see, e.g., Bar-Yosef and Belfer-Cohen 1991; Moore 1982). In Syria, cereal cultivation may have begun as early as the Late Pleistocene. Hillman et al. (2001) have argued that the residents of Abu Hureyra may have begun to cultivate rye in response to a decline in the availability of wild plants during the Younger Dryas climatic event (around 11,000 B.C.E.). Evidence for early sheep and goat domestication does not appear until Period 2A (about 8000 B.C.E.), millennia after the appearance of cultivated cereal crops. In the southern Levant, plant cultivation was established during the Pre-Pottery Neolithic A (9750–8550 B.C.E.), while early animal domestication does not appear until the Middle Pre-Pottery Neolithic B (8150–7300 B.C.E.).[2] A cluster of Pre-Pottery Neolithic A sites in the lower Jordan Valley, including Gilgal (Noy 1989) and Netiv Hagdud (Bar-Yosef and Kislev 1989; Zohary 1989), has provided evidence for early barley cultivation, but these sites provide no evidence for animal domestication (Tchernov 1994). In short, in the Middle East, animal domestication was adopted by sedentary communities that had already begun to cultivate cereal crops.

The issue of why early cereal cultivators in the Middle East adopted sheep and goat pastoralism remains an important but largely unanswered question. Moore et al. (2000:497) suggest that early agricultural communities in the Middle East experienced significant population increases. As these early farming populations increased, they increased their predation of gazelle herds. As gazelles became less available to these early farming communities, Neolithic farmers turned to domestic sheep and goats as sources of meat. Using an approach based on evolutionary ecology, Alvard and Kuznar (2001:298) have suggested that animal husbandry is a form of prey conservation and that conservation is most likely to occur when long-term returns from husbandry are "higher than short term returns from hunting." In addition, a number of scholars have suggested that early domestic animals served as "walking larders" (Clutton-Brock 1989) that were used to store agricultural surpluses. Livestock manure may have also served to maintain the fertility of small agricultural plots (Halstead 1996:302).

The Near Eastern sequence of plant and animal domestication is in marked contrast to the pattern that has been established for Africa. Both archaeological evidence and DNA studies suggest that cattle pastoralism was established in eastern Africa just south of the Sahara about 8,000 to 10,000 years ago. However, agriculture was not established in the region until about 4000 B.P. Marshall and Hildebrand (2002:111) have suggested that hunter-gatherers in the eastern Sahara may have begun to domesticate cattle "to ensure their predictable availability as a food source." The highly mobile lifestyles of these early pastoralists, especially in marginal areas, worked against the adoption of cereal cultivation. Since the African pattern of animal domestication is so different from the pattern seen in the Middle East and Europe, the remainder of this chapter will focus on early pastoralists in Eurasia.

Women in Early Agropastoral Societies in the Middle East

What roles did women and men play in early agropastoral societies in the ancient Near East? While many studies of early animal domestication have focused on interpretation of the faunal data and have treated humans who domesticated these animals as "a lot of faceless blobs" (Tringham 1991:94), two early studies, one by Robert Braidwood and a second by Charles Reed, envisioned very different roles for women in early animal domestication.

Robert Braidwood was a pioneer in the study of animal and plant domestication in the Near East. In his studies of early animal and plant domestication in northern Iraq and Anatolia, he was one of the first archaeologists to make use of a multidisciplinary research team including zooarchaeologists, paleoethnobotanists, and geoarchaeologists. While Braidwood is best known for scholarly works (e.g., Braidwood and Howe 1960), he is also the author of the aptly named *Prehistoric Men* (Braidwood 1967), which served as an introductory text for archaeologists in the late 1960s and the early 1970s. The text provides the following description of life in an Early Neolithic village:

> Children and old men could shepherd the animals by day or help with the lighter work in the fields. After the crops had been harvested the younger man might go hunting and some of them would fish, but the food they brought in was only an addition to the food in the village; the villagers wouldn't starve, even if the hunters and fishermen came home empty-handed. (Braidwood 1967:113)

One wonders what Early Neolithic women and girls were doing while the men and boys planted crops, herded livestock, fished, and hunted the occasional wild animal. Presumably, the women were engaged in child care and food preparation. This vision of early agropastoral societies owes more to the world of Ozzie and Harriet in the 1950s than to the archaeological evidence for life in the Early Neolithic period.

While Braidwood's view of early agropastoral societies is an essentially androcentric one, Charles Reed, a founding father of zooarchaeology, suggests that women and girls may have played a more active role in early animal domestication. Reed (1977, 1986) notes that taming is a necessary prerequisite for animal domestication and that it is relatively easy to tame wild animals. In order for pastoralism to develop, however, a critical change in human behavior was necessary. Reed (1986:12) argues that "as long as the successful male hunter was the hero, the human social ideal, there could be no real relationships between humans and animals other than that of hunter and hunted." Reed (1977) suggests that since men were hunters, women—and especially little girls—took the first steps toward animal domestication by taming wild animals. He argues that

> little girls, increasingly as they grow, have estrogens coursing in their bloodstream; little girls play with dolls, have maternal instincts. They are not yet, as their mothers would be, inured to killing and the necessities of killing; a little girl might well adopt, protect, and tend a weaned lamb, kid, or baby pig, thus establishing that one-to-one social relationship necessary for the abolition of the flight reaction. (Reed 1977:563)

While this model allows women to play a more active role in early Near Eastern pastoralism, the model rests on untested assumptions about men's roles as hunters and the nurturing nature of women and little girls.

Reed is not alone in assuming that men were hunters and women were plant collectors in preagricultural societies in the ancient Near East. As noted previously, Henry (1975) and others have argued that preagricultural populations in the Near East hunted entire herds of gazelles. Henry (1989:215) further suggests that while these hunting strategies "would have required a substantial party of hunters, there would have been little difficulty in mustering the necessary number of adult males in a Natufian village." Henry (1989:217) further suggests that gathered cereals and nuts would have provided the bulk of the Natufian diet. Plant collecting is often assumed to have been women's work in the preagricultural Near East. For example, an illustration of plant gathering that accompanies an article on skeletal remains from the site of Abu Hureyra in Syria depicts a woman collecting plants during the Epipaleolithic, even though the skeletal remains themselves provide no evidence that women collected plants in Late Pleistocene Syria. In the Early Neolithic, men are shown as both plant cultivators and as herders of goats and sheep (Molleson 1994:75).

There is little direct archaeological evidence to suggest that men hunted animals and women gathered plants in the Near East during the Late Pleistocene. The assumption that men hunted and women gathered must be based on ethnographic parallels, especially analogies with the !Kung San as described by Lee (1968). While Lee's carefully documented study of !Kung San foraging practices has colored archaeological interpretation of ancient hunter-gatherers for over a generation, the !Kung are a particularly inappropriate analogue for ancient Near Eastern foragers. Plant remains, especially the staple mongongo nuts, are available on a year-round basis in the Kalahari, while wild wheats and barleys have a short season of availability in the Middle East. !Kung hunters generally form small hunting parties, while Near Eastern hunters stalked entire herds of gazelles. Since !Kung subsistence practices differ significantly from Epipaleolithic practices, it is unlikely that these two populations practiced similar divisions of labor.

In fact, the nature of Epipaleolithic subsistence, which is well documented archaeologically, might indicate that men and women cooperated in both hunting and gathering activities (Crabtree 1991). Hunting entire herds of animals requires substantially more labor than hunting individual animals. The animals must be driven into some kind of net, trap, or surround, and then the entire herd must be killed. Ethnographic data indicate that men and women often cooperate in communal hunting activities (see, e.g., Downs 1966). Similarly, Epipaleolithic plant-collecting activities focused on wild cereals such as wild wheats and barleys. These cereals ripen during a short three- to four-week period in the spring (Harlan 1971) and must be stored for use throughout the year. It is likely that all members of the community—men, women, and children—cooperated to maximize the harvest of these important plant resources. The nature of Late Paleolithic subsistence in the Near East does not support a strict division of labor by sex. If there is no real evidence for a sexual division of labor for preagricultural populations in the ancient Near East, then we should be highly skeptical of models for the origins of pastoralism that are based on the assumption of male hunting and female gathering.

More recent attempts to identify the sexual division of labor in early agropastoral societies have focused in human skeletal remains since repetitive activities may leave traces on bones (Molleson 1994, 2000). Molleson examined the human bones recovered from the Epipaleolithic and Early Neolithic site of Abu Hureyra in Syria. She identified changes on the articular surface of the first metatarsal that she argued were associated with prolonged use of a saddle quern to grind grain. Since a majority of these pathological changes were seen on smaller (presumably female) metatarsals, she concluded that "most of the food preparation was carried out by women" (Molleson 2000:314). She further concluded that there must have been a sexual division of labor within Early Neolithic households and that "males may have been more involved in hunting and procuring meat" (322), even though there was no specific osteological evidence to support male hunting. Molleson's conclusions have been appropriately criticized by Gilchrist (1999:44), who notes that "other explanations for the bone pathologies are not explored, and the possibility of more flexible, seasonal, or perhaps age-based divisions of labor are not considered." For our purposes, none of the osteological data shed any light on the roles that women and men (and/or boys and girls) may have played in early animal husbandry. The assumption that men played a major role in early animal husbandry (see, e.g., the image in Molleson 1994:74) is simply an assumption.

Molleson's model of the sexual division of labor in the Early Neolithic suggests that women were engaged in tasks inside the household, including not only grinding grain but also basketry and the preparation of hides. Men were engaged in a range of outside activities, including pastoralism, agriculture, and hunting. This scenario bears a striking similarity to Hodder's (1990) model for the Early European Neolithic where he contrasts the *domus*, or interior of the household, with the *agrios*, or exterior world. The model also shows similarities to the early work on the anthropology of gender that suggested that male/female dichotomies and gender hierarchies were grounded in the contrast between the world inside the household (the domestic sphere) and the outside world (the public sphere) (see Moore 1988:21–24 and references therein). Moreover, Molleson (2000:322) argues that women's "role specialization in food preparation at Abu Hureyra can be seen as a natural and inevitable development of nurturing that provided for older children and fathers." Reed used almost the same argument nearly twenty-five years earlier to explain the role of women in early animal domestication.

As an archaeological model of early agropastoral communities, Molleson's model presents several interpretive problems. First, Molleson's assumption that women were engaged primarily in food preparation rests almost entirely on a single line of evidence—that pathologies that appear to be associated with the use of a saddle quern appear more commonly on the foot bones of individuals who appear to be female. Gilchrist (1999:53) has shown that "the most convincing and nuanced readings of gender have been developed from multiple lines of evidence." Second, Molleson fails to address the roles that children might have played in early agropastoral societies. This is a striking omission since the skeletons from Abu Hureyra show that adolescents carried heavy loads, probably on their heads (Molleson 1994:71). Moreover, ethnographic and historical data suggest that children and adolescents often play important economic roles in pastoral and agricultural societies. Third, and most important from our perspective, Molleson fails to address the important question that was first raised by Reed (1977) nearly thirty years ago: how were the male gazelle hunters of the Epipaleolithic transformed into the male shepherds and goatherders of the Early Neolithic? As Reed noted many years ago, this change involves both the development of the technological knowledge involved in animal husbandry and a transformation of the ideology that surrounds animals and human–animal relationships.

The Secondary Products Revolution

The difficulty that archaeologists have had in creating models for women's and men's roles in early agropastoral societies in the Near East and Europe are highlighted when archaeologists attempt to examine the secondary products revolution (SPR) (Sherratt 1996a, 1996b) and its effects on women in early pastoral societies in Eurasia. Sherratt argued that during the mid- to late fourth millennium B.C.E., a series of fundamental changes took place in the ways that Eurasian pastoralists made use of their animals. Domestic animals, including cattle, sheep, and goats, were no longer seen primarily as sources of meat. Instead, they were used for a variety of secondary products, including milk, wool, and traction. Sherratt (1996:160–61) suggests that the SPR "separates two stages in the development of Old World agriculture: an initial stage of hoe cultivation, whose technology and transportation systems were based upon human muscle power, and in which animals were kept purely for meat; and a second stage in which plough agriculture and pastoralism can be recognized, with a technology using animal sources of energy." The use of domesticated animals for a variety of different purposes would also have increased the importance of the pastoral component in ancient economies. Since Sherratt's original model was developed more than twenty years ago, we will begin with a brief review of the archaeological evidence for the SPR (for a concise review of this evidence, see Russell 2004).

The use of animals for traction represents one of the most important technological developments of the later Neolithic (fifth and fourth millennia B.C.E.) in Eurasia. The use of animals, primarily oxen or castrated bulls, to pull light plows or ards[3] allowed farmers to expand the amount of land under cultivation. Evidence for early plowing includes plow marks preserved in buried soil surfaces and images of plowing that appear in Bronze Age rock art. In addition, zooarchaeologists have identified a series of morphological changes on cattle bones that result from traction activities (Bartosiewicz et al. 1997). In Europe, zooarchaeological evidence for traction pathologies suggests that plowing may have been established in eastern Europe as early as 4500 B.C.E. Plowing was established in northwestern Europe by 4000 B.C.E., and pictographic evidence indicates that plowing was widespread by 2500 B.C.E. (Russell 2004). Images of light plows are also well known from mid-third-millennium contexts in the eastern Mediterranean (Sherratt 1996a:165–67). The other main use for draft animals was for transportation. A wide range of archaeological data, including images and models of carts and wheel ruts, indicate that wheeled vehicles first appeared in Europe and the Near East at about 3500 B.C.E.

While the early history of animal-drawn wheeled vehicles in Eurasia is well documented and well dated, the history of early dairying is less well known. Most archaeological evidence for dairying is indirect, including ceramic vessels that may have been used for dairy products and faunal assemblages that include a high percentage of very young animals under six months of age. The faunal argument is based on the assumption that dairy herds will include a high percentage of adult female animals and that excess male calves will be slaughtered at very young ages. Sherratt (1981) initially argued that dairying was part of the SPR on the basis of changes in pottery vessel forms. He suggested that the appearance of vessels such as jugs and cups in the Late Neolithic was associated with the manipulation of liquids, including milk. Bogucki (1984, 1986), however, suggested that dairying might have a much greater antiquity, at least among temperate European pastoralists. Bogucki suggested that ceramic sieves, which are commonly recovered from Early Neolithic (ca. 5500–5000 B.C.E.) Linearbandkeramik sites in central Europe, may have been used for cheese making. While Sherratt (1996b:206) subsequently acknowledged the possibility that some dairying may have occurred in Early Neolithic societies, he argued that the quantities of milk produced must have been quite small. Following McCormick (1992), Sherratt argued that until recent times, calves must have been present in order for a cow to let down her milk. Therefore, McCormick (1992) suggested that prehistoric archaeological sites that have produced evidence for the slaughter of large numbers of very young cattle do not indicate dairying since the absence of the young calves would prevent females from lactating. This argument is problematic for several reasons. First, a cow can be induced to let down her milk by other means, such as stimulating her vagina or presenting her with a surrogate calf (Russell 2004:327). Second, ethnohistoric and archaeological sources do not confirm McCormick's assertion that faunal assemblages that include a high proportion of very young cattle indicate a meat rather than a dairy economy. For example, the archaeological and historical data for medieval Iceland and Greenland, where cattle were kept almost exclusively for dairying from the initial Viking-period settlement, consistently produce large numbers of very young cattle under six months of age (see, e.g., McGovern et al. 1996, 2001). Third, recent studies of organic residues recovered from pottery vessels from the British Isles provide direct evidence for widespread Early Neolithic dairying in northwestern Europe (Copley et al. 2003). The residue evidence indicates that dairying was established, at least in parts of Europe, well before the SPR.

The antiquity of dairying may also have important implications for our understanding of women's roles in early pastoral societies in Europe. Ethnohistoric data indicate that women played a major role in dairy production in many parts of Europe from the early Middle Ages on (see the following discussion). If women also engaged in dairying in prehistoric European societies, then women may have played an active and integral role in pastoral economies beginning in the Early Neolithic.

The final aspect of the SPR is wool production. Wild sheep and early domesticated sheep were hairy rather than woolly; their short undercoats were shed each spring. In order for sheep to be reared for wool production, genetic changes were necessary so that the wooly undercoat grew longer and was maintained throughout the year. Occasional finds of preserved textiles indicate that sheep's wool first appeared in the Middle East about 3000 B.C.E. and in Europe about 2500 B.C.E. (Russell 2004:327).

The Gender Implications of the SPR

The SPR model, as envisioned by Sherratt (1981, 1996a), has important implications for gender roles in later Neolithic agropastoral societies in Europe and the Near East. Sherratt, unlike Molleson, assumes that women would have played a primary role in Early Neolithic horticulture. He argues that "in simple hoe agriculture, the major subsistence contribution comes from female labor in sowing, weeding, and harvesting" (Sherratt 1996a:194). The SPR led to a fundamental change in the sexual division of labor. It "produced an economy dominated by men, who played a dominant role in handling large livestock either as herds or in plowing. Women became increasingly relegated to the domestic sphere" (Sherratt 1996a:196). Since women were freed from their role as food producers, they could spend more time on activities such as textile production.

The effect of this model is the same as Molleson's and even Braidwood's model for the Early Neolithic—it removes women from primary roles as pastoral producers. This model is problematic for several reasons. First, it assumes that women would have been the primary agricultural producers in Early Neolithic societies in the Middle East and Europe, and there is no clear archaeological evidence to support this assertion. Second, it assumes that men would have taken a major role in both plowing and pastoral production beginning in the Late Neolithic. While medieval historical sources from many parts of Europe indicate that plowing was a male activity, these same sources indicate that women often played a primary role in dairying. Third, it assumes that the introduction of wool sheep would have led to a new role for women as textile producers. It is important to note that while wool sheep may not have been developed until the Late Neolithic or Early Bronze Age, textiles have a much greater antiquity in Eurasia. Neolithic textiles in both the Middle East and Europe were made of flax or linen. At the site of Tybrind Vig in Denmark, Mesolithic textiles made of strings of lime and willow have recently been discovered (Anderson 2004:143), and engravings on Upper Paleolithic figurines suggest that textiles made of plant fibers may have been manufactured in the European Upper Paleolithic (Soffer et al. 2000). Textile production is not a new industry in the Late Neolithic, and the introduction of wool sheep is not likely to have radically changed women's roles. Moreover, early medieval historical sources indicate that women were often engaged in both dairying and textile production (see the following discussion).

Historical Models for Women's Roles in European Pastoral Economies

While no one wants to envision early Eurasian pastoralists as a group of faceless blobs, some alternatives are even worse. The effect of almost all the models reviewed in this chapter is to remove women from a primary role in agropastoral production. In Molleson's model for the Neolithic of the Near East, men are pastoralists and cultivators, while women are engaged in household tasks such as food preparation, basket making, and hide working. Sherratt's model for the SPR envisions men as herders and plowmen, while women are engaged in "spinning, weaving, and textile production" (Sherratt 1996a:195). Unfortunately, there is very little archaeological data to support these gender attributions. These models reify the domestic sphere/public sphere dichotomy and relegate women to a secondary role in pastoral (and agricultural) production. This need not be the case.

The historical record for medieval Europe provides evidence that women played an active role in pastoral production in many regions of the continent. As noted previously, booleying is a form of transhumance that was practiced in parts of Ireland until the early twentieth century. In the spring or early summer, cattle were moved from their winter pastures in the lowlands to summer pastures or booleys, which were often located in wooded, highland areas. Historical accounts of prefamine Ireland describe young women and men accompanying cattle and sheep to the summer pastures along with dairying vessels, spinning and carding equipment, and cooking pots (Shanklin 1994:109–10). Historical records trace the practice of booleying back to the early medieval period (ca. 400–850 C.E.).[4] The early Irish sources associate the practice of booleying with women and children and often with women of low economic and social status (Boyle 2004:95; see also Brady 1994:131; Patterson 1994:90–91). In Ireland, women and children remained in the booleys with the livestock throughout the summer, while men returned to the lowlands to protect the crops and prepare for warfare (Patterson 1994:136). The Irish sources also identify dairying, spinning, baking, and shepherding as appropriate activities for servile women (Brady 1994:131). The Irish data thus suggest that women and children played an active role in pastoral production in early medieval Ireland.

The historical records from late medieval France identify other possible roles for women in medieval agropastoral societies. In late medieval France, plowing was carried out exclusively by men. However, women were not excluded from a direct role in animal production. While men cared for the plow teams, women were responsible for the smaller livestock, such as sheep and goats as well as poultry.

Conclusion

While it would be a mistake to project models of medieval labor organization onto prehistoric Eurasian pastoral communities, the medieval data do suggest ways in which women may have played more active roles in animal husbandry and pastoral production. At present, we do not have adequate archaeological data to identify the roles played by men and women in early agropastoral communities in Eurasia. Nuanced studies of gender must be based on multiple lines of archaeological evidence, not on assumptions about the nature of women as nurturers. Zooarchaeologists have worked for forty years to develop a suite of criteria that can be used to identify early animal domestication in the archaeological record.

We need to address questions about the social organization of pastoral production with equal vigilance.

Notes

1. Dyson-Hudson and Dyson-Hudson (1980), for example, define pastoralists as individuals who rely heavily on domestic herd animals and who move their animals to pasture.

2. These dates are based on Kuijt and Goring-Morris (2002:366).

3. Light plows or ards simply scratch the surface of the soil. Heavy plows, which include a coulter, plowshare, and moldboard, do not appear in Europe and the Mediterranean until about 2,000 years ago.

4. Historical records first appear in Ireland in the early fifth century, but it is likely that the practice of booleying is even older. Only a few possible booleying sites have been identified archaeologically (Boyle 2004:95).

References

Akkermans, P. A., J. A. K. Boerma, A. T. Clason, S. G. Hill, E. Lohot, C. Meiklejohn, M. Le Mière, G. M. F. Molgot, J. J. Roodenberg, W. Waterbolk-vanRooyen, and W. Van Zeist
    1983   Bouqras Revisited: Preliminary Report on a Project in Eastern Syria. *Proceedings of the Prehistoric Society* 49:335–71.

Alvard, Michael S., and Lawrence Kuznar
    2001   Deferred Harvests: The Transition from Hunting to Animal Husbandry. *American Anthropologist* 103(2):295–311.

Anderson, S. H.
    2004   Tybrind Vig. In *Ancient Europe: 8000 B.C.–A.D. 1000: Encyclopedia of the Barbarian World*. Vol. 1. Peter Bogucki and Pam J. Crabtree, eds. Pp. 141–43. New York: Charles Scribner's Sons.

Barth, Frederik
    1961   *Nomads of South Persia: The Basseri Tribe of the Khamseh Confederacy*. Boston: Little, Brown.

Bartosiewicz, L., Wim Van Neer, and A. Lentacker
    1997   *Draught Cattle: Their Osteological Identification and History*. Annales du Musée Royale de l'Afrique Centrale, Sciences Zoologiques. Tervuren: 281.

Bar-Yosef, O., and A. Belfer-Cohen
    1991   From Sedentary Hunter-Gatherers to Territorial Farmers in the Levant. In *Between Bands and States*. S. A. Gregg, ed. Pp. 181–202. Carbondale, IL: Center for Archaeological Investigations.

Bar-Yosef, O., and M. E. Kislev
    1989   Early Farming Communities in the Jordan Valley. In *Foraging and Farming: The Evolution of Plant Exploitation.* D. R. Harris and G. C. Hillman, eds. Pp. 632–42. London: Unwin and Hyman.

Bogucki, Peter
    1984   Ceramic Sieves of the Linear Pottery Culture and Their Economic Implications. *Oxford Journal of Archaeology* 3:15–30.
    1986   The Antiquity of Dairying in Temperate Europe. *Expedition* 28(2):51–58.

Boyle, James W.
    2004   Lest the Lowliest Be Forgotten: Locating the Impoverished in Early Medieval Ireland. *International Journal of Historical Archaeology* 8(2):85–99.

Bradley, Daniel G.
    2003   Genetic Hoofprints: The DNA Trail Leading Back to the Origin of Today's Cattle. *Natural History* 112(1):36–41.

Bradley, D. G., R. T. Loftus, P. Cunningham, and D. E. MacHugh
    1998   Genetics and Domestic Cattle Origins. *Evolutionary Anthropology* 6(3):79–86.

Brady, N.
    1994   Labor and Agriculture in Early Medieval Ireland: Evidence from the Sources. In *The Work of Work: Servitude, Slavery, and Labor in Medieval England.* A. J. Frantzen and D. Moffatt, eds. Pp. 125–45. Glasgow: Cruithne Press.

Braidwood, R. J.
    1967   *Prehistoric Men.* 7th ed. Glenview, IL: Scott, Foresman.

Braidwood, R. J., et al.
    1960   *Prehistoric Investigations in Iraqi Kurdistan.* Chicago: University of Chicago Press.

Campana, D. V., and P. J. Crabtree
    1990   Communal Hunting in the Natufian of the Southern Levant: The Social and Economic Implications. *Journal of Mediterranean Archaeology* 3(2):223–43.

Chang, Claudia, and Harold A. Koster
    1994   Introduction. In *Pastoralists on the Periphery: Herders in a Capitalist World.* Claudia Chang and Harold T. Koster, eds. Pp. 1–15. Tucson: University of Arizona Press.

Childe, V. G.
    1936   *Man Makes Himself.* London: Tavistock.
    1950   The Urban Revolution. *Town Planning Review* 21(1):3–17.

Clutton-Brock, Juliet
    1979   The Mammalian Remains from Jericho Tell. *Proceedings of the Prehistoric Society* 45:135–57.
    1980   *Domesticated Animals from Early Times.* London: British Museum (Natural History) Press.

Clutton-Brock, Juliet, ed.
    1989   *The Walking Larder: Patterns of Domestication, Pastoralism, and Predation.* London: Unwin Hyman.

Copley, M. S., R. Berstan, S. Docherty, A. Mukherjee, V. Straker, S. Payne, and R. P. Evershed
    2003   The Earliest Direct Evidence for Widespread Dairying in Prehistoric Britain. *Proceedings of the National Academy of Sciences* 100(4):1524–29.

Crabtree, Pam J.
    1991   Gender Hierarchies and the Sexual Division of Labor in the Natufian Culture of the Southern Levant. In *The Archaeology of Gender.* Proceedings of the 22nd Annual Chacmool Conference. D. Walde and N. D. Willows, eds. Pp. 384–99. Calgary: Department of Archaeology, University of Calgary.
    1993   Early Animal Domestication in the Middle East and Europe. In *Archaeological Method and Theory*. Vol. 5. M. B. Schiffer, ed. Pp. 201–45. Tucson: University of Arizona Press.

Downs, J. F.
    1966   *The Two Worlds of the Washo.* New York: Holt, Rinehart and Winston.

Driesch, Angela von den
    1976   *A Guide to the Measurement of Animal Bones from Archaeological Sites.* Peabody Museum Bulletin 1. Cambridge, MA: Peabody Museum of Archaeology and Ethnology, Harvard University.

Dyson-Hudson, R., and N. Dyson-Hudson
    1980   Nomadic Pastoralism. *Annual Review of Anthropology* 9:15–61.

Gautier, A.
    1987   Prehistoric Men and Cattle in North Africa: A Dearth of Data and a Surfeit of Models. In *Prehistory of Arid North Africa.* A. E. Close, ed. Pp. 163–87. Dallas: Southern Methodist University Press.

Gilchrist, Roberta
    1999   *Gender and Archaeology: Contesting the Past.* London: Routledge.

Halstead, Paul
    1996   The Development of Agriculture and Pastoralism in Greece: When, How, Who and What? In *The Origins and Spread of Agriculture and Pastoralism in Eurasia.* D. Harris, ed. Pp. 296–309. Washington, DC: Smithsonian Institution Press.

Harlan, J.
    1971   A Wild Wheat Harvest in Turkey. *Archaeology* 20(3):197–201.

Henry, Donald O.
    1975   The Fauna in Near Eastern Archaeological Deposits. In *Problems in Prehistory: North Africa and the Levant.* F. Wendorf and A. E. Marks, eds. Pp. 379–85. Dallas: Southern Methodist University Press.
    1989   *From Foraging to Agriculture: The Levant at the End of the Ice Age.* Philadelphia: University of Pennsylvania Press.

Hesse, Brian
    1984   These Are Our Goats: The Origins of Herding in West Central Iran. In *Animals and Archaeology: 3. Early Herders and Their Flocks.* J. Clutton-Brock and C.

Grigson, eds. Pp. 243–64. BAR International Series 202. Oxford: British Archaeological Reports.

Hiendleder, S., B. Kaupe, R. Wassmuth, and A. Janke
    2002   Molecular Analysis of Wild and Domestic Sheep Questions Current Nomenclature and Provides Evidence for Domestication from Two Different Subspecies. *Proceedings of the Royal Society of London B: Biological Sciences* 269(1492): 893–904.

Hillman, G., R. Hedges, A. Moore, S. Colledge, and P. Pettit
    2001   New Evidence of Lateglacial Cereal Cultivation on the Euphrates. *The Holocene* 11(4):383–93.

Hodder, Ian
    1990   *The Domestication of Europe*. Oxford: Blackwell.

Köhler-Rollefson, I., W. Gillespie, and M. Metzger
    1988   The Fauna from Neolithic 'Ain Ghazal. In *Prehistory of Jordan: The State of Research in 1986*. A. N. Garrard and N. H. Gebel, eds. Pp. 423–30. Oxford: British Archaeological Reports, International Series 398(i).

Kuijt, Ian, and Nigel Goring-Morris
    2002   Foraging, Farming, and Social Complexity in the Pre-Pottery Neolithic of the Southern Levant: A Review and Synthesis. *Journal of World Prehistory* 16(4):363–440.

Lee, R. B.
    1968   What Hunters Do for a Living, or How to Make Out on Scarce Resources. In *Man the Hunter*. R. B. Lee and I. Devore, eds. Pp. 30–48. Chicago: Aldine.

Legge, A. J.
    1972   Prehistoric Exploitation of the Gazelle in Palestine. In *Papers in Economic Prehistory*. E. S. Higgs, ed. Pp. 119–24. Cambridge: Cambridge University Press.

Legge, A. J., and P. Rowley-Conwy
    1987   Gazelle Killing in Stone Age Syria. *Scientific American* 238(8):88–95.

Marshall, F., and E. Hildebrand
    2002   Cattle Before Crops: The Beginnings of Food Production in Africa. *Journal of World Prehistory* 16(2):99–143.

McCormick, Finbar
    1992   Early Faunal Evidence for Dairying. *Oxford Journal of Archaeology* 11(2):201–9.

McGovern, T. H., T. Amorosi, S. Perdikaris, and J. W. Woolett
    1996   Zooarchaeology of Sandnes V51: Economic Change at a Chieftain's Farm in West Greenland. *Arctic Anthropology* 33(2):94–122.

McGovern, T. H., Sophia Perdikaris, and Clayton Tinsley
    2001   Economy of Landman: The Evidence of Zooarchaeology. In *Westward to Vinland*. U. Bragason et al., eds. Pp. 154–65. Reykjavik: Nordahl Institute.

Meadow, R. H.
    1989   Osteological Evidence for the Process of Animal Domestication. In *The Walking Larder: Patterns of Domestication, Pastoralism, and Predation*. Juliet Clutton-Brock, ed. Pp. 80–89. London: Unwin Hyman.

Molleson, Theya
    1994   The Eloquent Bones of Abu Hureyra. *Scientific American* 271(2):70–75.
    2000   The People of Abu Hureyra. In *Village on the Euphrates: From Foraging to Farming at Abu Hureyra*. A. M. T. Moore, G. C. Hillman, and A. J. Legge. Pp. 301–24. Oxford: Oxford University Press.

Moore, A. M. T.
    1982   A Four-Stage Sequence for the Levantine Neolithic, ca 8500 B.C.–3750 B.C. *Bulletin of the American Schools of Oriental Research* 246:1–34.

Moore, A. M. T., G. C. Hillman, and A. J. Legge
    2000   *Village on the Euphrates: From Foraging to Farming at Abu Hureyra*. Oxford: Oxford University Press.

Moore, Henrietta L.
    1988   *Feminism and Anthropology*. Minneapolis: University of Minnesota Press.

Netting, Robert McC.
    1996   What Alpine Peasants Have in Common: Observations on Communal Tenure in a Swiss Village. In *Case Studies in Human Ecology*. Daniel G. Bates and Susan H. Lees, eds. Pp. 219–31. New York: Plenum.

Noy, T.
    1989   Gilgal I. A Pre-Pottery Neolithic Site, Israel. The 1985–1987 Seasons. *Paléorient* 15(1):15–22.

Ó Curráin, D.
    1972   *Ireland Before the Normans*. Dublin: Gill and McMillan.

Patterson, N. T.
    1994   *Cattle-Lords and Clansmen: The Social Structure of Early Ireland*. 2nd ed. Notre Dame, IN: University of Notre Dame Press.

Perkins, Dexter, Jr.
    1964   Prehistoric Fauna from Shanidar, Iraq. *Science* 144:1565–66.

Perkins, Dexter, Jr., and Patricia Daly
    1974   The Beginnings of Food Production in the Near East. In *The Old World: Early Man to the Development of Agriculture*. R. Stigler, ed. Pp. 71–97. New York: St. Martin's Press.

Reed, Charles A.
    1977   A Model for the Origin of Agriculture in the Near East. In *The Origins of Agriculture*. C. A. Reed, ed. Pp. 543–67. The Hague: Mouton.
    1986   Wild Animals Ain't So Wild, Domesticating Them Not So Difficult. *Expedition* 28(2):8–15.

Russell, Nerissa
    2004   Milk, Wool, and Traction: Secondary Animal Products. In *Ancient Europe: 8000 B.C.–A.D. 1000: Encyclopedia of the Barbarian World*. Vol. I. Peter Bogucki and Pam J. Crabtree, eds. Pp. 325–33. New York: Charles Scribner's Sons.

Shanklin, Eugenia
- 1994 "Life Underneath the Market": Herders and Gombeenmen in Nineteenth-Century Donegal. In *Pastoralists on the Periphery: Herders in a Capitalist World.* Claudia Chang and Harold T. Koster, eds. Pp. 103–21. Tucson: University of Arizona Press.

Sherratt, A. G.
- 1981 Plough and Pastoralism: Aspects of the Secondary Products Revolution. In *Pattern of the Past: Studies in Honour of David Clark.* I. Hodder, G. Isaac, and N. Hammond, eds. Pp. 261–305. Cambridge: Cambridge University Press.
- 1983 The Secondary Exploitation of Animals in the Old World. *World Archaeology* 15:90–104.
- 1996a Plough and Pastoralism: Aspects of the Secondary Products Revolution. In *Economy and Society in Prehistoric Europe: Changing Perspectives.* Andrew Sherratt, ed. Pp. 158–98. Princeton, NJ: Princeton University Press.
- 1996b The Secondary Exploitation of Animals in the Old World. In *Economy and Society in Prehistoric Europe: Changing Perspectives.* Andrew Sherratt, ed. Pp. 199–228. Princeton, NJ: Princeton University Press.

Soffer, O., J. M. Adovasio, and D. C. Hyland
- 2000 The "Venus" Figurines. *Current Anthropology* 41:511–37.

Tchernov, Eitan
- 1994 *An Early Neolithic Village in the Jordan Valley, Part II: The Fauna from Netiv Hagdud.* Cambridge, MA: Peabody Museum of Archaeology and Ethnology, Harvard University.

Tchernov, Eitan, and L. K. Horowitz
- 1991 Body Size Diminution under Domestication: Unconscious Selection in Primeval Domesticates. *Journal of Anthropological Archaeology* 10:54–75.

Tringham, Ruth E.
- 1991 Households with Faces: The Challenge of Gender in Prehistoric Architectural Remains. In *Engendering Archaeology: Women and Prehistory.* Joan M. Gero and Margaret W. Conkey, eds. Pp. 93–131. London: Basil Blackwell.

Uerpmann, Hans-Peter
- 1987 *Probleme der Neolithisierung des Mittelmeerraums.* Wiesbaden: Dr. Ludwig Reichert.

Zeder, Melinda A.
- 1991 *Feeding Cities: Specialized Animal Economy in the Ancient Near East.* Washington, DC: Smithsonian Institution Press.
- 2001 A Metrical Analysis of a Collection of Modern Goats (*Capra hircus aegargus* and *C. h. hircus*) from Iran and Iraq: Implications for the Study of Caprine Domestication. *Journal of Archaeological Science* 28(1):61–79.

Zeder, Melinda A., and Brian Hesse
- 2000 The Initial Domestication of Goats (*Capra hircus*) in the Zagros Mountains 10,000 Years Ago. *Science* 287:2254–57.

Zohary, D.
1989   Domestication of Southwest Asian Neolithic Crop Assemblage of Cereals, Pulses, and Flax: The Evidence from Living Plants. In *Foraging and Farming, the Evolution of Plant Exploitation*. D. R. Harris and G. C. Hillman, eds. Pp. 358–73. London: Unwin Hyman.

WORLD REGIONS IV

A Critical Appraisal of Gender Research in African Archaeology 18

DIANE LYONS

THIS CHAPTER CRITICALLY REVIEWS engendered archaeology of Africa's Holocene. Engendered archaeological research is distributed unevenly across the continent with regional emphasis in Egypt and southern Africa. Despite two edited volumes on the subject (Kent 1998a; Wadley 1997b), few or no gendered archaeological studies are based on materials from West, central, and North Africa or the Sahara. One should note that engendered ethnoarchaeology (not reviewed here) is represented in many regions where gendered archaeology is absent. The uneven geographic distribution of gender archaeology partly reflects problems that Connah (2001:3) identifies as inhibiting African research as a whole: poor transportation, underfunding, and political instability. As a result, basic culture history in many regions is poorly understood, and in some areas research is yet to be conducted. In addition, colonial regimes in sub-Saharan Africa often discouraged archaeological research, especially of the recent past (Robertshaw 1990). Southern Africa was a particularly pernicious example because of the extensive control of power and resources held by European settler populations (M. Hall 1996; MacEachern 1996:276; Sinclair 1990). In South Africa, apartheid policies disseminated a falsified history in the country's school curricula, a practice that contributed to the alienation of Africans from their own past (Esterhuysen 2000; Gawe and Meli 1990; Mitchell 2002:414; Pwiti and Ndoro 1999). In light of these problems, gender has not emerged as a priority in African archaeology.

Papers discussed in this chapter were selected because they explicitly attempted to engender archaeological materials. The chapter is not comprehensive, and to maximize bibliographic variety, researchers' works are sampled or overviews of their works cited. All these scholars have made important contributions to engendering Africa's past, and it is not the intention of this critique to denigrate anyone's work. This appraisal is presented to encourage discussion and interpretive rigor in future archaeological endeavors.

Gender in African Archaeology's Workplace

Only three studies specifically address the Africanist workplace, and all focus on southern Africa, a region not representative of the continent as a whole. For instance, race is a more significant issue than gender in training and hiring archaeologists in South Africa (see Wadley 1997a), where apartheid policies were enforced until 1990. But in West Africa, universities have trained indigenous archaeologists since the mid-twentieth century, and their graduates have filled academic and government posts (Kense 1990).

Wadley's (1997a) study of southern Africa's late twentieth-century workplace strives to be comparable to those conducted in Western countries, but she warns us that her database is less sophisticated. Her quantified data comes from the four (now three) South African universities offering postgraduate degrees in archaeology. Wadley states that archaeology has attracted few black South African students of either gender, and although she does not say so, these low numbers must also reflect the inferior education and restrictions that black South Africans received under apartheid policies (Esterhuysen 2000; Gawe and Meli 1990). Wadley's (1997a) data on degrees granted and employment are not quantified by race, except that only one black female and "a handful" of black male archaeologists were employed in southern Africa as of 1997. Women obtain postgraduate degrees almost on par with men (e.g., women obtained 48 percent of the Ph.D.s), but after graduation only 50 percent of these women compared to 88 percent of men gained full-time professional employment in the discipline. Nine men and two women Ph.D.s held senior teaching positions in the four university departments. Unfortunately, figures for female employment in museums and other institutions are presented with no comparable data for men or even the areas of archaeology in which men were employed. Wadley states, but without quantification, that women receive fewer fieldwork opportunities than men. Numbers for male and female authored papers in regional journals indicate that women are strongly underrepresented, figures that Wadley observes are proportional to women's full-time employment. Wadley (1997a:4) concludes that women are worse off in South Africa than in North America, citing Wylie (1993). But according to Wadley's quantified data, women hold over 20 percent of senior faculty positions in South Africa, while studies in Britain (Cane et al. 1994) and Canada (Kelley and Hill 1994) report that women fill 17 percent of faculty positions in archaeology at all ranks, and in the United States women hold 15 to 20 percent of like positions (Kramer and Stark 1994). These figures indicate that at the time of these studies, South African female academic archaeologists were doing as well as their Western colleagues. Nevertheless, Wadley's study clearly shows gender inequities in southern Africa's workplace. Undoubtedly, these disparities are rooted in South Africa's patriarchal colonial system that historical archaeologists are beginning to describe (see M. Hall 1997; Malan 1997). A better database, building on Wadley's efforts, is required to further assess the situation.

Weedman's (2001) overview of female Africanists (1860–1960) delivers an extensive bibliography for the colonial period. She describes a "chilly" academic environment where women's access to research often depended, at least initially if not entirely, on their own financial independence or close kinship with a male archaeologist. Weedman provides numerous examples of women whose scholarship was either ignored, appropriated, or belittled by male colleagues. She includes in her examples Maria Wilman and Neville Jones, who initiated the term Middle Stone Age (MSA) in 1927. The term was later popularized by Goodwin and Van Riet Lowe, but only Jones was credited for its origin. In 1950, Joan Harding attributed southern African rock art to indigenous peoples, an interpretation summarily dismissed by Abbé Breuil and James Walton, but six years later Alexander Willcox published similar ideas without citing Harding's work. Patricia Vinnicombe (1976) was the first to develop an anthropological study of rock art, but Weedman claims that in Davis's (1990) overview, Vinnicombe shares this distinction with David Lewis-Williams. However, it is important not to overstate gender bias. For example, it should be made clear that Patricia Vinnicombe (e.g., 1972, 1975) and Lewis-Williams (e.g., 1975, 1977) were publishing anthropological interpretations of rock art almost contemporaneously in the 1970s. And while Gertrude Caton-Thompson's interpretation that Africans built Great Zimbabwe was sharply condemned by the colonial government and by many local scholars (Caton-Thompson kept their published comments in a file marked "insane"), we may note that in 1906 David Randall-MacIver published conclusions similar to Caton-Thompson's that were just as unwelcome (M. Hall 1996:28–29). Both researchers' interpretations of Great Zimbabwe were rejected on racist grounds, not on the basis of their gender.

Weedman's interpretation of gender politics in the modern Africanist workplace is less specific and it is sometimes difficult to determine when she is discussing Africanists or generalizing from other studies. This distinction is important because Weedman suggests that androcentric practices in the West are extended to and are the cause of gender biases in the Africanist workplace. But her statement that "most detrimental to both women and to African prehistory is the failure to cite or seriously consider women's theories and interpretations, as is evidence by the lack of citations attributed to female archaeologists or their work" (Weedman 2001:36) is not supported by data specific to the Africanist literature.

Weedman cites 1998 membership figures for the Society of Africanist Archaeologists (SAfA), the primary international Africanist association, in which male:female representation was two to one. If SAfA's membership figures accurately reflect the number of female Africanist archaeologists, then women are significantly underrepresented as authors in the four main African archaeology journals. Male-authored articles predominate in these journals with representations ranging from 72.4 to 95.7 percent. But in the discussion of gender bias in academic posts, Weedman's distinction between female Africanist archaeologists and female archaeologists in general is again unclear. There is a "dearth" of female professors in Ph.D.-producing institutions, but although not equitable, figures cited by Weedman (2001:36) for Africanist faculty listed in the American Anthropological Association guide and South African University Internet listings show that women hold 32 percent of Africanist archaeology posts in universities. Based on these figures, women Africanists are *better* represented within their own specialization than are women in archaeology faculty positions in general (17 to 20 percent) and are proportionally represented as Africanist scholars based on membership figures for SAfA as cited previously. While the numbers support the fact that gender inequities exist, the possibility that Africanists do not fit the generalized workplace model should be explored with data specific to Africanists. What is missing from both Wadley's and Weedman's studies is a discussion of the gender imbalance among black African archaeologists. It is certainly true that there are far fewer indigenous female archaeologists than males in most African countries. Undeniably, gender relations were seriously disrupted by colonial contact (e.g., S. Hall 1998; Webley 1997), but gender asymmetries that stem from African cultural contexts also must be considered in future studies.

Shepherd (2003) investigates native labor in the colonial period through the journals and photographs of John Goodwin, one of the first professional archaeologists in sub-Saharan Africa. Laborers were almost always men who worked as field assistants, interpreters, and facilitators but are unacknowledged as individuals in site reports. Shepherd (2003:347) attributes the elision of native labor from field documentation as part of the colonial enterprise that perceived and represented Africans as idle and capable only of dirty work under careful supervision. He argues that this was part of an ideology that minimized the contribution of African labor to the success of the colonial venture. While Shepherd's observation is provocative and quotations from Goodwin's letters and field notes express the racist ideology of his day, lamentably, fieldworkers often go unacknowledged in areas of the world where race is not an issue.

A common factor in the African workplace is economic inequities between African and foreign researchers. MacEachern (1996) remarks that African researchers (regardless of gender) are in danger of becoming second-class citizens in their discipline because they do not have access to the financial resources available to foreign archaeologists and face difficulties in disseminating their research beyond the continent. The financial situation is dire not only in terms of research funding but also in providing the basic necessities to train archaeology students in African institutions (Killick 2004:110–11). Gender inequities are unlikely to take precedence in this milieu.

Engendered Archaeology in Africa's Holocene

Stone Age Hunter-Gatherers in Southern Africa

In sub-Saharan Africa, the term Late or Later Stone Age (LSA) is characterized by microlithic technology and a hunting-gathering subsistence economy. The LSA begins in the Pleistocene and ends at different times in different regions. See figure 18.1 for a map with place-names mentioned in the text.

Khoisan-speaking hunter-gatherers are referred to as San, Bushmen, or Basarwa. San is used here with the caveat that there is no consensus as to which term is the least offensive (Mitchell 2002:7–8). Strong evidence supports the San as direct descendents of LSA hunter-gatherers (Mitchell 2002), but whether San ethnography is appropriate to interpret the LSA is debated (Wilmsen 1989). San ethnography is based on a small sample of southern Africa's hunter-gatherer populations (Mitchell 2005:163), who were already affected by almost two millennia of contact with herders and farmers (Reid 2005). Khoisan-speaking pastoralists, previously called Hottentots, are now referred to as Khoe (singular) or Khoekhoe (plural). While controversial, many hold that the Khoekhoe were indigenous hunter-gatherers who adopted the use of domesticated animals from people in northern Botswana around 2000 B.P. (Mitchell 2002:227).

Considerable gender research has focused on southern Africa's LSA, but it is criticized for the use of untested (or untestable) assumptions usually pertaining to gender assignments of tasks and tools drawn uncritically from the ethnographic record (e.g., Mitchell 2001:36–37, 2005:154). For example, Wadley (1987, 1998, 2000) extensively uses San practices to interpret gender relations in LSA sites in southern Africa beginning in the Pleistocene. At Rose Cottage Cave and Jubilee Rock Shelter around 7000 B.P., Wadley (1987, 1998) interprets spatial patterning of food processing and artifact production as the result of gendered activities like those of the San, including men's and women's respective production of bone points and ostrich eggshell beads for gift-exchange practices. How-

Figure 18.1. The location of principal sites and regions in Africa of gender research discussed in the text.

ever, Mitchell (2001:166) states that there is only one such pattern at Jubilee Rock Shelter, and the spatial distribution of material remains of activities Wadley interprets as analogous to San gendered activities diverges from ethnographic spatial patterning. Somewhat comparable questions can be raised regarding Wadley's (1998) use of ethnographic materials in an interpretation of women as meat providers before 3000 B.P. Using ethnographic evidence of the Mbuti, Wadley argues that Pleistocene spear-hunting practices required that women hunted and that they received shares in the meat. Wadley suggests that women may have continued to hunt with snares even after 10,000 B.P., when bow-and-arrow hunting encouraged smaller hunting parties and the development of ethnographic concepts of game ownership and food-sharing practices. Using faunal distributions of rock hyrax at Rose Cottage Cave and ethnographic accounts of women catching small game, Wadley infers that women provided and shared hyrax with families other than their own (assuming that each hearth represents an individual family as it does in ethnographic camps), even though women do not share such game ethnographically. Wadley's assertion that women and men had equal access to meat is potentially testable, and she cites Sealy et al.'s (1992) isotopic analysis of Western Cape skeletons to do so. However, the pre–3000 B.P. sample from this collection is small and chronologically dispersed, and Sealy et al. (1992:128) state that the data are insufficient to draw substantive conclusions about diets for this period. Despite these problems, Wadley is generally recognized along with Mazel (see the following discussion) for initiating discussions of gender in LSA research in South Africa.

Kent (1998b) claims that gendered spatial segregation of activities does not occur at hunter-gatherer sites. Kent's model proposes that societies with little or no sociopolitical complexity do not segregate space by gender. She recognizes that San assign spatial areas in certain situations, including where men and women sit around the hearth at night or at weddings, but that these gendered spatial assignments break down during daily activities. Because the evidence is "confused," situational gender assignation of space is "invisible." Granting that more complex societies produce more material (especially architectural) evidence of spatial segregation for archaeologists to find, it does not follow that because gendered spaces are not visible to archaeologists that hunter-gatherers do not perceive space as gendered and use gendered space in social interaction. Kent (1998b) correctly states that archaeologists must define archaeological signatures of gender-specific spaces and activities more clearly, but she is more rigorous in her criteria for identifying gendered spaces for hunter-gatherer sites than more complex societies. For instance, when no gendered spatial distinctions are found in LSA sites, then space is not segregated by gender, but when gender-segregated space is not found in Early Iron Age (IA) sites (e.g., a more complex society), Kent explains their absence as a result of poor excavation practices. Even if this is true, there are no data to support the model.

In contrast to Wadley's interpretation that women provided meat, Mazel (1992) suggests that the shift to increased plant food exploitation between 7000 and 2000 B.P. in the Thukela Basin was a conscious strategy of women, as reliance on hunting (assumed male) was risky and caused gender inequities. Mazel argues that plant food exploitation reduced risk and increased women's status. His interpretation is framed in gender stereotypes that assert that women are socially disadvantaged where they contribute little to the food quest. As support, Mazel cites ethnographic examples of arctic and subarctic hunters with diets heavily reliant on meat, a perspective now challenged by studies (admittedly postdating Mazel's paper) that show women in these same societies to be actively involved in hunting (e.g., Brumbach and Jarvenpa 1997). Kent (1995) also states that unlike Western researchers, Botswana hunter-gatherers do not perceive hunting as "better" than collecting, and gendered tasks are flexible.

Parkington (1998) also examines gender differences in diet based on isotopic analysis and dental morphology for Western Cape skeletons from the period 3000 to 2000 B.P. (e.g., Lee Thorp et al. 1989; Sealy and van der Merwe 1988). During this period, men's diets were enriched with marine foods in contrast with women's terrestrial-based diets, a situation coincident with the production of megamiddens on the coast. Parkington (1998) views the megamiddens as products of logistical hunting strategies where men mass-processed marine resources. While occupying logistical camps, men would ingest enough marine food to cause significant differences in their diet relative to that of women. Parkington's (1998) inference of men as shellfish collectors poses an alternative to cross-cultural generalizations of women as shellfish collectors. Whatever practices caused dietary distinctions between 3000 and 2000 B.P., ethnographic food consumption practices provide potential archaeological analogies only for the period after 2000 B.P., when men's and women's diets are similar.

Other researchers link gender with specific tool types. Parkington (1998) examines Holocene stone-tool assemblages from the Western Cape that include microliths and adzes. Terminal Pleistocene woodworking was practiced with several tools, including quartz adzes, but in the Early Holocene large flake adzes made from salvaged MSA flakes became the only woodworking tool. Parkington assumes that adzes were used mainly to make and resharpen digging sticks, a tool strongly (but not exclusively) associated with women ethnographically and in rock art (Mazel 1989; Ouzman 1997). He speculates that microliths were produced and used by men and that women salvaged MSA flakes to make LSA adzes. However, since tools are not clearly assigned by sex in ethnographic accounts or in San burials (Mitchell 2005:162; Wadley 1997c), they are unreliable for doing so in past contexts. Parkington's suggestion that women scavenged rather than produced their own flakes is an androcentric notion well challenged by Casey (1998).

San and Khoekhoen ethnography is also used to infer ritual practices including finger joint amputations that occur as early as 7000 B.P. (Mitchell and Plug 1997). According to Mitchell and Plug (1997), ethnographic amputations marked both gender and ethnic identity, with joints discarded in domestic and sometimes ritual contexts. San men amputated joints from their right hand and women from their left. Cape Khoekhoe of both sexes amputated finger joints but differently from the San. Khoekhoen women practiced amputation more than men as a prerequisite for marriage, remarriage, and inheriting cattle, and their amputations were not as side specific as the San. Isolated phalanges, sometimes with cut marks, located in domestic contexts, or skeletons with all elements except distal phalanges are presented by Mitchell and Plug as potential archaeological signatures for this practice.

Southern African rock art dates from 26,000 B.P. to the early twentieth century A.D., with most dated images concentrated in the last 2,000 years (Mitchell 2002:194). The imagery is generally associated with hunter-gatherers, but some was produced and/or consumed by Khoekhoe (Dowson 1994) and Bantu agropastoralists (Prins and Hall 1994). San ethnography is extensively used to interpret the art (Davis 1990; Lewis-Williams 2000; Vinnicombe 1976), but again how far back in time is San ideology appropriate for this purpose? There are some clues. The eland is the most common image in rock art, particularly in the Drakensbergs, and its slow death by poisoned arrow is linguistically equated with the trancing shaman. In addition, the act of men hunting eland is fundamental to San metaphors of gender relations (Parkington 1998:35). Archaeological evidence for San-style bows and arrows do not occur in quantity until after 9000 B.P., so Parkington (1998) argues that shamanistic interpretations and gendered metaphors associated with men hunting eland are inappropriate before this date.

Lewis-Williams's (1981, 2000) shamanistic model is based on striking similarities between the imagery and descriptions of San shamans' trance experiences. Images are assumed to be painted by or for shaman after trances and express social norms, including stereotypes of men as hunters and shamans and women as plant food gatherers who play supportive roles in rituals (Anderson 1997). However, ethnographic evidence indicates that men, women, and children consumed and produced art (Ouzman 1997) and that one-third of all San women and half of all San men were shamans during their lifetimes (Mitchell 2002).

The importance of eland in the imagery is ascribed partly to its sexual ambivalence (Dowson 1988). Unlike other antelope, male eland have more fat than females, giving them a degree of sexual ambiguity that Dowson likens to the experience of the trancing shaman who mediates between opposing categories including human/animal and material/spiritual realms. In this liminal state, shamans are neither male nor female. Ouzman (1997) notes that bored stones and digging sticks are often considered women's tools. Bored stones occur only with female figures in rock art, but two-thirds of all human figures are "asexual" and are also associated with bored stones and digging sticks. Ouzman (1997) suggests that asexual figures are shamans and that these objects are symbols shamans use to mediate between sexually ambivalent states.

Solomon (1992) suggests women's initiation rituals, female potency, and rainmaking are just as important in rock art as shamanism. She identifies images ("mythic women") that may represent beliefs associating menstrual blood or amniotic fluid with potency for bringing rain. Stevenson (2000) also criticizes the shaman model because it assumes that men are primary agents in rituals even though many figures are not sexed. But in an analysis of therianthropes, that is, figures with human and animal characteristics, Stevenson (2000) demonstrates that many characteristics identify the animal as female.

Parkington (1998, 2002, 2003) also argues that therianthropes are not necessarily transforming shamans but represent a conflation of humans and animals, a common theme in San ideology and myth. He suggests that the imagery represents a San hunting metaphor that equates the relationship between a hunter and large meat animals (especially eland) with that of a hunter and his wife, just as the San confuse sex and hunting in their language. This metaphor is based in myth that relates a time when rules were established stating that animals and humans must marry within their own species and which foods each species could eat. Only humans could eat large game animals killed with bow and arrow. Parkington (1998, 2002) suggests that this myth is a model for the human life cycle. Beginning with initiation rites, boys are transformed into hunters and husbands; at first menstruation, girls are transformed into wives and prey. Parkington (1998) concludes that in San society, adult men are defined by hunting and women by menstruating. Gender relations are transformed when these conditions begin and when they no longer occur. Parkington (1998) suggests that the emphasis on the sexual characteristics of males and females in the images is intended to draw attention to their sexual potential and to categorize men and women by age and roles. Although Parkington argues that San view hunting and childbearing as a balance of authority, defining women by their biology and men by culture is disturbing and a view criticized by feminist scholars (see Conkey and Spector 1984).

Anderson (1997) argues that the shaman model does not account for regional variation or gender differences in rock art. His study is based on rock art sites in the southwestern Cape. Anderson (1997) assumes that Khoekhoen herders and LSA hunter-gatherers intermarried in the past but on unequal social terms (a view not shared by others, e.g., Dowson 1994; Lee and Hitchcock 1998). Anderson (1997) suggests that in the initial contact period between San and Khoekhoe, San men reacted to their declining status by smearing older fine-line hunting imagery to reassert their authority over the spiritual realm and to reemphasize the male/

hunter:female/prey metaphor within San society. During the early European colonial period, Khoekhoen women produced rock art as part of menarche rites in secluded areas, particularly caves, a practice Anderson (1997) suggests was used to affirm their ethnicity during early European colonial encounters. Women's images included red handprints, finger dots, finger smears, and crayon lines. In both cases, the images are distinctive, found in different contexts, and were produced by the gender Anderson identifies as experiencing stress in periods of culture contact.

North African Mesolithic Foragers

Archaeological terminology is not standardized in Africa, and microlithic cultures in northern Africa are called Mesolithic. Mesolithic assemblages also include pottery and grinding stones that are associated with diverse hunting-foraging-fishing peoples. Pottery was developed in Africa by non–food-producing societies, and the earliest dates for pottery come from Niger around 9500 B.P. in the south-central Sahara and from Sudan and the Libyan Sahara (ca. 9300 B.P.) (see Close 1995).

Haaland (1992, 1995, 1997) assumes that the transition to sedentism and food production begins in the Middle Nile region of Sudan in the ninth millennium B.P. with the invention of pottery, grinding stones, and other equipment used to intensively exploit fish and wild grasses. Haaland asserts that women invented pottery because women are strongly connected to pottery production and food processing cross-culturally, and she proposes a linked process between women, pottery, and sedentism in the region, reasoning that pottery increases the range of foods and nutrients available from the environment. Haaland infers that boiled foods were used to wean infants, resulting in reduced birth spacing, increased populations, and pressure to cultivate local plant foods by 6000 B.P., leading to the domestication of sorghum by 2000 B.P. She posits that women should be considered as active agents in the move to sedentism. Citing studies of recently settled hunter-gatherers in northern Canada, Haaland concludes that women carry the greatest burden in mobility and that sedentism reduces their labor. However, it is hard to imagine that women's workloads decreased with sedentism in Sudan if this process involved greater investment in cereal cultivation and processing. These activities are generally understood as labor intensive and were not part of the transition to sedentism shared by subarctic women in twentieth-century Canada.

Close (1995:31) criticizes Haaland's interpretation on archaeological grounds. Grinding stones are not "invented" in the Khartoum Mesolithic, as they are used extensively at Kubbaniya in southern Egypt by 18,000 B.P. and are contemporaneous with charred feces from infants who were fed a plant food "mush." Pottery is neither present at the site nor essential for consuming fish or grains, as fish can be roasted and Saharan pastoralists bake bread in preheated sand depressions (Close 1995:31). Evidence from Nabta Playa in southern Egypt indicates intensive wild plant use in the Early Holocene, including wild sorghum, but pottery is scarce (Barakat and el-Din Fahmy 1999; Close 1995:32; Wasylikowa and Dahlberg 1999). Close (1995:30) suggests that sedentism allowed pottery to take on a greater role in the daily lives of its makers, but functions for Mesolithic pottery, including food boiling, are not demonstrated. An assumption that women invented pots also needs greater archaeological substantiation. Although Barich (1998:113, fig. 6.4) attempts to connect designs on pots with those on women's bodies in early Saharan rock art, the "women" in the figure she presents are sexually ambiguous.

West Africa LSA: The Kintampo Complex

The Kintampo complex (ca. 4000–2000 B.P.), located in modern Ghana, provides the first evidence for decreased residential mobility in West Africa (Casey 2005). Casey (1998) examines basic (expedient) and formal stone-tool technology in the Kintampo complex and challenges interpretations that present men as producers of superior formal tools and women as the unskilled users of basic tools. In Kintampo sites, basic tools occur in all activity areas, indicating their equal use by men and women. Since basic tools can perform the tasks of formal tools, Casey asks why expend extra energy on the latter? On the basis of task allocations drawn from comparable ethnographically known societies, Casey assumes that Kintampo women were the food processors and men the hunters. She then argues that men's and women's relative mobility changed with increased sedentism during the Kintampo. Women's mobility decreased as demands on their labor increased to process plant food, and men's mobility increased in order to hunt, obtain stone, and trade. In the region today, men's hunting activities beyond the farmstead are perceived as dangerous because of exposure to supernatural forces, human strangers, and wild animals. Men protect themselves from some of these dangers with the symbolic use of charms. Most Kintampo formal stone tools are finely made projectile points that have a high probability of being lost in the forest. Casey suggests that male hunters expended energy on these points in order to communicate simple messages to spirits and people in territories beyond their control as a form of supernatural or social protection. Pottery production also increases with sedentism, and assuming that women made pottery, pots would became an important medium for women to encode and communicate information in their changing social contexts. While ethnoarchaeological studies support the active use of material culture style as a form of symbolic protection (e.g., David et al. 1988; Lyons 1998), these materials are usually effective when worn on the potential victim's body or placed in or near spaces that they occupy and on their food and beverage containers. It is unclear in Casey's study why leaving visual evidence of a man's presence outside his own territory would not provoke rather than prevent supernatural or social aggression. Nevertheless, Casey demonstrates that stylistic investment in material culture increased with sedentism. Style is invested in hunting tools and ceramics, and a gendered interpretation is compelling if ethnographic divisions of labor model those of the Kintampo.

Stone Age Pastoralists: Pastoral Neolithic (PN) in East Africa

The term Pastoral Neolithic (PN) is used in East Africa to refer to food-producing economies without agriculture (Sinclair et al. 1993). Ethnographic studies indicate that pastoralists have a constant need for labor, a problem sometimes resolved by intermarriage with foragers (Gifford-Gonzalez 1998). Gifford-Gonzalez states that androcentric models of pastoralists present intermarriage as an asymmetric relationship in which pastoralist men marry "down" to forager women but forager men cannot marry "up" to pastoralist women. The situation is hypothesized to result in increased competition among foraging men for wives and fosters the assimilation of foragers into pastoralist economies, particularly through the exchange of cattle as bride-price. But Gifford-Gonzalez (1998) argues that these models are inappropriate for the PN in Kenya around 4900 B.P., as early pastoralists would not have had the same advantages as historic groups. For instance, early PN people were unlikely to have developed many of the current strategies for risk management such as parceling out cattle to kin living in different environments, a practice that requires a large established pastoralist population. Instead, Gifford-Gonzalez suggests that bonds between early pastoralists and hunter-gatherers were more equal. She proposes that the distribution of Nderit ceramics, a technology introduced by pastoralists, may reflect symbiotic intermarriage between hunter-gatherers and pastoralists. The distribution of ceramics is currently interpreted as either the result of exchange between pastoralists and hunter-gatherers or pottery produced by mixed groups practicing herding, foraging, and farming. Without dismissing these interpretations, Gifford-Gonzalez offers an engendered third alternative. Distributions of pottery at sites with and without domestic animals may be the result of intermarriage at herding and foraging camps, respectively. She makes no claims as to which gender made the pots, but initial pottery analyses indicate that production was localized, supporting the suggestion that pastoralist potters moved between groups, not the pots.

Iron Age Research

Iron metallurgy is radiocarbon dated in West and central Africa and in the Great Lakes region to around 2600 B.P., but earlier dates from both Niger and the Great Lakes are problematic, and the origin of African iron making remains unknown (Killick 2004). Iron, pottery, plant, and animal domesticates eventually were introduced into the southern continent by agropastoralists including Bantu speakers in the early first millennium A.D.

Considerable research is vested in African iron production, and this body of work provides a well-developed model of masculinity, an important contribution to gender archaeology often criticized for its focus on women (Meskell 1999:84). Historic, ethnoarchaeological, and anthropological evidence indicates that iron production is strongly gendered in its division of labor and rituals and as symbolic practice (Barndon 1996; Herbert 1993; Schmidt 1996a, 1998). There is considerable variation despite cross-cultural commonalities in iron-smelting practices, but without exception men are the iron smelters and blacksmiths. In iron smelting, men organize the materials and labor, construct and work the furnace, and control ritual practices. Herbert (1993:54) concludes that smelting is a social act through which men appropriate agricultural production and human reproduction, and in Bantu Africa, iron production is often symbolically linked to the strength and legitimation of male rulers (Childs and Dewey 1996).

Women's participation in iron production varies by culture and other factors and can include mining, transporting, and grinding ore; preparing charcoal; preparing soil for furnace construction; bringing water and food; ritual performances; and making tuyeres and bowls for the bellows (Barndon 1996; Goucher and Herbert 1996; Schmidt 1996b, 1998). Sometimes iron production is the monopoly of men in endogamous castes and is associated with a division of tasks where men make iron and bury the dead and their wives are potters and midwives (Sterner and David 1991).

The perception that iron production is analogous to the process of human reproduction is widespread in sub-Saharan Africa and is referred to as the "reproductive paradigm" (Barndon 1996; Childs and Killick 1993; Goucher and Herbert 1996; Herbert 1993; Schmidt 1998:140; Schmidt and Mapunda 1997). Furnaces are described as being like a pregnant woman who gives birth to an iron child (Goucher and Herbert 1996; Herbert 1993; Schmidt 1996a, 1996b).

Often the furnace is built with or described linguistically as having physical characteristics that represent the female body, including breasts, vulva, and scarification patterns indicative of female rites of passage associated with birth and fertility (Barndon 1996; Collett 1993; Herbert 1993). Tuyeres and bellows, when present, are sometimes equated with penises and testes. Sexual abstinence is required of smelters who are both symbolic fathers and husbands to the furnaces (Barndon 1996), and Schmidt (1998) has observed Barongo smelters performing symbolic acts to inseminate the furnace. Individuals who break the abstinence taboo are considered to have committed adultery, an act believed to cause miscarriage in a human fetus and metaphorically of an iron bloom (Goucher and Herbert 1996). But David (2001:65) warns of inconsistencies in interpreting practices of smelters' sexual abstinence to avoid the effects of adultery in societies that are polygynous and attributing the furnace as a symbolic bride of multiple husbands where polyandry is abhorrent.

The practice of forbidding women in their fertile years or during menstruation or anyone who is sexually active from coming near the smelt is pervasive. Ritual mystification of the iron-smelting process may be a means to prevent wives who come from other groups from passing metallurgical knowledge to their male kin (Goucher and Herbert 1996; Schmidt 1998). In addition to keeping "industrial secrets," these taboos are attributed to a widespread thermodynamic metaphor (Apentiik 1997; Herbert 1993; Schmidt and Mapunda 1997:77) that perceives categories of people and activities as "hot" or "cold." Fertile women and sexually active individuals are considered "hot," and their presence near smelting furnaces, which are also "hot," results in too much heat that can compromise transformative processes in the furnace (David 2001:65).

Other practices are sometimes performed to ensure the furnace's fertility. Schmidt (1998) reports that the Pangwa, Barongo, and Haya in the Great Lakes region all place materials in the furnace floor that symbolically represent menstrual blood and semen. In the same region, these materials are considered to sustain their potency, and abandoned furnaces and slag are believed to cure human infertility (Schmidt 1998). Schmidt and Mapunda (1997) determined that all cultures in central Africa place ritual objects in the furnace floor either to protect the fertility of the furnace or to prevent malevolent forces from disrupting the smelt's success, and they identified material signatures for specific symbolic meanings (Schmidt 1998; Schmidt and Mapunda 1997). These signatures are recoverable archaeologically, and there is a growing sense that the ideology of ethnographic and historic African ironworking practices extend back to the Early IA in the Great Lakes region (Schmidt 1998; Schmidt and Mapunda 1997). This interpretation is supported by other stylistic connections between women, cooking pots, and furnace bricks in Early IA sites. For instance, clay figures portraying women giving birth are associated with a seventeenth-century furnace and early IA smelting remains in Zimbabwe (Collett 1993; MacLean 1998). However, neither iron-making practices nor gender are unchanging. Schmidt (1998) uses the ritual signatures excavated from furnaces in eastern and central Africa to demonstrate shifting ideological foci from the early IA to the twentieth century and its implications for gender and intergroup relations. Rather than imposing the ethnographic present onto the past, Schmidt tacks between ethnographic source and archaeological subject to demonstrate continuities and change through time based on material evidence.

One problem with the "reproductive paradigm" is that it overshadows other ritual practices (Herbert 1993; Schmidt 1998) and oversimplifies stages of the smelt that David (2001:64) describes as multilayered meanings and metaphors that are not necessarily interpreted or acted on uniformly by all iron-producing groups. Others suggest that the paradigm is misleading. For instance, Rowlands and Warnier (1996) claim that Cameroon's Grassfields furnaces do not represent female or male reproductive organs. They argue that the relationship between pregnancy and iron production is understood as part of broader processes of fertility for which human reproduction is not the primary model. Instead, rituals address the fertility process and the need to ensure that iron is produced in a nonviolent atmosphere to control its violent potential. Ironworkers view themselves as facilitators of the transformative process, not symbolic fathers or husbands, and their rituals and magical materials are intended to stop interference by evil forces. But David and Kramer (2001) suggest that Warnier and Rowland do not investigate the "mutually informative linkages" between technical and ritual processes of ironworking. David (2001) states that many material and proscriptive practices are metonyms intended to produce a specific technical result, including the practice of banning categories of men and women from the smelt who are "too hot."

MacLean (1998) suggests that women's domestic pot cooking is complementary to men's iron production and that both roles emerged in the Great Lakes region during the Early IA. In this period ceramics, iron production, land clearance, agricultural production, and possibly pot cooking were introduced. Her study offers some balance to Great Lake's IA research that has focused heavily on men's ironworking practices. MacLean rightly claims that technological phenomena, including iron production, must be understood as full social phenomena. Unfortunately, almost no Early IA settlements and domestic contexts have been excavated in the region (MacLean 1998), and MacLean's basic assumption that women used Early IA pots to cook food is weakened by the absence of functional analyses of these ceramics. Instead, she turns to archaeological research on ironworking to strengthen her assumption that women cooked with pots in the Early IA. Archaeological evidence links iron smelting and concepts of reproduction to the Early IA, and MacLean extends this reproductive ideology to include concepts about women and pot cooking. In the Great Lakes region, women's bodies are metaphorically linked with cooking pots and smelting furnaces. In East and southern Africa, human reproduction, iron production, and cooking are perceived as analogous heat-mediated processes that irreversibly transform natural materials into cultural products (Collett 1993). MacLean suggests that this ideology may be linked to shared decorative elements on Early IA pottery and iron-smelting furnace bricks recovered from archaeological sites in the Great Lakes region, a concept supported by Collett's (1993) work where certain motifs used in women's clothing and body scarification were found on cooking pots and smelting furnaces although the designs shared by women and pots may differ from those shared by women and furnaces. Cooking pots are also metaphorically linked to women's reproductive organs in East and southern Africa (S. Hall 1997, 1998; Lane 1998; Moore et al. 1999). However, Fowler (in press) cautions that gender symbolism is not restricted to decorative elements and some morphological characteristics of amaZulu pots are associated with men. MacLean's approach to building material links between women, cooking pots, and IA ideologies is more rigorous than assuming gender task allocation from ethnographic sources. Future work would benefit from ceramic analyses of residues and heat treatments in order to move discussions of pottery function beyond speculation. Lack of study of heat treatment of foods is partly attributed to androcentric notions that women's cooking is not of technological interest (Brumfiel 1991; Gifford-Gonzalez 1991; Lyons and D'Andrea 2003; MacLean and Insoll 1999).

But not all pots are for cooking. Berns (1993) engenders ritual pottery production in West Africa and challenges the perceived view of ceramic production that men produce art and women craft. For instance, archaeologists and art historians uncritically hold that men produced elaborate ceramic figurines in several cultures in West Africa beginning with the Nok culture in the Early IA. This interpretation excludes women from the cultural production of symbolic systems and an understanding of how gender is negotiated through the production of material culture. Berns cites considerable ethnographic evidence of Nigerian women who routinely make figurative pottery and vessels for rituals, discounting the generalization that women are rarely involved in nonhousehold pottery production.

Iron Age Pastoralists in Southern Africa (ca. A.D. 350–1850)

The Central Cattle Pattern (CCP) is a structuralist model developed by Thomas Huffman to interpret eastern Bantu IA settlements in southern Africa and is based on Kuper's (1982) ethnography of the southern Bantu. The CCP is formulated on idealized perceptions of the relative status and importance of men, women, ancestors, and cattle (Lane 1996). The men's domain is the center of the settlement and includes a cattle kraal, elite burials, communal granaries, a smithy, and a men's assembly or court. The women's domain is an outer arc of houses, kitchens, and grain bins. House interiors are spatially divided into left:right, back:front domains that are perceived, respectively, as female:male. Huffman (1996:6, 2001) argues that since the Bantu's worldview and settlement pattern are unique, the presence of the CCP in archaeological sites is direct evidence that its past occupants were Bantu speakers who shared the ethnographic Bantu's worldview. Huffman argues that the CCP was brought by Bantu-speaking pastoralists to southern Africa in the Early IA, implying that gender and other social relations represented in the CCP have not changed for 1,500 years (Huffman 2001).

Although the CCP model introduced an ideological component to the analysis of IA materials (Lane 1998), it has its critics. Later IA sites are linked historically to the ancestors of present-day groups in the region (Lane 1996), but many question the appropriateness of the model for the Early IA. First, Lane (1996) argues that the ethnographic evidence needs to be critically evaluated. Colonial anthropologists interviewed elder males whose interpretation of gender roles and rights closely matched those of colonial administrators. Anthropologists strengthened male-oriented views by presenting them as "customary law" that was then incorporated into colonial court decisions and became legal precedent (Lane 1996). Second, worldviews are not static. The ethnographic emphasis on cattle in bride-wealth payments may have increased in significance following the rinderpest epidemic in the 1890s that destroyed most herds (Lane 1996). Others (Luedke 2004; Segobye 1998) stress the importance of distinguishing between idealized behavior represented in worldviews and men's and women's actual economic contributions and domains of power. Third, Huffman's model is criticized for not explaining spatial variation observed in settlement layouts (Lane 1996; Segobye 1998). Finally, there is growing evidence that the CCP is a recent product of Later IA dynamics, including changing gender relations (S. Hall 1998; Lane 1998).

One problem is that IA settlements are rarely excavated in broad horizontal sections, a practice necessary to reveal spatial relationships useful for investigating gender (Lane 1998). Contrary to Kent (1998b), this is a problem with both Early and Later IA sites. In Later IA settlements, women's houses are poorly investigated relative to the central men's domain because the CCP model is assumed rather than tested (S. Hall 1998; Lane 1998). Lane (1998) describes how Tswana and Nguni houses are associated with women's bodies, but his gynecomorphic interpretation of Bantu settlements is not a perspective explicitly expressed by the Bantu (Huffman 2001). Simon Hall (1998) reexamined fifteenth- to nineteenth-century IA sites and emphasized women's houses. Settlements were small around 1400 to 1700 A.D., and pottery was elaborately decorated. In Tswana ethnography, women are perceived of as "hot" and potentially polluting because of their cycle of menstruation and pregnancy (S. Hall 1998:252–54). To avoid polluting certain spaces women are spatially constrained (e.g., to the compound periphery). In the early period, cooking, food processing, and consumption were not spatially segregated, and Hall (following Braithwaite's [1982] interpretation of Azande pottery) suggests that elaborately decorated pots defined boundaries between men and women and controlled potentially polluting encounters. After 1700 A.D., increased population and demands on agricultural surplus heightened tensions over landownership. Settlements became larger and aggregated, and as women's roles in food production and processing increased, their activity areas became spatially segregated. This resulted in greater predictability in men's and women's interactions, eliminating the need for elaborate pottery. Eating bowls declined in frequency, and Hall infers that men began to eat separately and from wooden containers they made for themselves. Furthermore, as men became increasingly dependent on women's agricultural production to maintain their political influence, they devalued and exerted increasing control over women's production and reproduction. Hall generalizes that when two opposing patrilineal systems interface, the material power base of the indigenous male system is undercut. Eventually, indigenous men exert greater control over women's labor and appropriate aspects of women's production as a strategy to reassert their waning influence (S. Hall 1997). Significantly, Webley (1997) describes similar dynamics for the Namaqua Khoe during the colonial period. In both studies, material objects associated with resource distribution were appropriated by men as their own economies were threatened. These studies demonstrate dynamic social relations during the IA, and S. Hall (1998) warns that Bantu ethnography is applicable only for interpreting settlements and gender for the past 300 years.

IA pastoralists are also associated with rock art. Prins and Hall (1994) provide a summary of south-central and southern Bantu rock art in which they connect specific symbols with male initiation rites and other symbols with female initiation rites, female sexual organs, divination, and rainmaking. Bantu also use color symbolism to differentiate age and gender. These symbols are all linked to concepts of fertility and are used in the "Late White" Tradition of rock art associated with these Bantu speakers. Gender-associated symbols and colors are expressed in a wide range of media, a practice noted elsewhere in Africa (e.g., Collett 1993; David et al. 1988; S. Hall 1998; Huffman 1996; Lyons 1998; MacLean 1998).

Complex Societies

Complex polities emerge at different times and places. Dynastic Egypt is the first African state (ca. 5000 B.P.), and a sequence of other states rise and fall in the northeastern quadrant of the continent from that time forward. Complex polities are widespread in sub-Saharan Africa after the late first millennium A.D., but engendered analyses are so far developed only for Great Zimbabwe, the Swahili, and the Great Lakes region.

Hassan and Smith (2002) examine sex and gender in predynastic Egypt (ca. 5300–3000 B.C.). They found that female figurines, palettes, cow and bird imagery, and the color green are associated with women in ways that anticipate the religious ideology of dynastic Egypt (Hassan and Smith 2002). At the center of this ideology is the cult of a mother goddess that symbolically links women with cows and birds (particularly ostriches) as agents of transformation and rebirth. They point out that the bull was also associated with the pharaoh in dynastic times, and the ideology of cows and bulls as sacred may extend back to the eighth millennium B.P. in the Egyptian Sahara, where sites with ritual cattle burials occur. In the predynastic, more women than men were buried with maces (symbols of power), although male hereditary rulership became the norm in dynastic Egypt. Nordström (1996), investigating mortuary remains and burial practices in A-Group culture cemeteries from Lower Nubia around 3000 B.P., also concluded that women held higher rank than men, possibly reflecting a matrilineal society. A-group had strong ties with predynastic Egypt and also had a complex and stratified society.

Poor preservation of settlements in the Nile delta and floodplain hamper direct study of nonelite domestic contexts during the dynastic period (ca. 3000–332 B.C.) (Hollis 1987; Robins 1999; Wrobel 2004), and most gendered analyses are based on textual evidence and tomb art (Bryan 1996; Robins 1999; Roehrig 1996). These interpretations focus almost exclusively on women. Texts indicate that women enjoyed rights to hold property and land, to inherit, and to generate an income (Johnson 1996; Robins 1983; Roehrig 1996). During the Middle and New Kingdoms, married women ran large estates (Robins 1999) but under their husbands' control (Bryan 1996). Textual evidence of gender equality contrasts with artistic conventions that portrayed wives as having lesser status than their husbands (Hollis 1987; Robins 1999). Women were socially recognized in tomb art nurturing young children (Wrobel 2004), but their economic roles (e.g., cloth production) were underrepresented in imagery (Roehrig 1996; Wrobel 2004).

Ancient Egyptian cosmology is enacted through sexual interactions of deities in which goddesses assisted in the transformation between life, death, and rebirth (Robins 1999; Troy 2003). Egyptian women served religious cults as entertainers, mourners, and priestesses. The Priestess of Hathor, the goddess of female sexuality, was a position of high status in the Old and Middle Kingdoms (Bryan 1996; Robins 1999). In the New Kingdom, the most powerful religious office was God's Wife of Amun-Re at Thebes. The position was usually held by the pharaoh's daughter, who acted as his representative, and entailed considerable wealth (Troy 2003). The God's Wife performed daily rituals to sexually stimulate the god Amun-Re in order to maintain the cycle of death and rebirth of the sun and the world (Robins 1983, 1999).

Male kingship was the norm in ancient Egypt, but queens acted as surrogate rulers or regents when male heirs were too young or absent (Bryan 1996; Robins 1999; Troy 2003). In the Eighteenth Dynasty, Queen Hatshepsut was made regent for Thutmose III but then transformed herself into the pharaoh by taking male titles of kingship and having herself portrayed in art as a man (Troy 2003). It is argued that Thutmose III was ill-pleased with her usurpation and defaced her images (Troy 2003). Robins (1999) argues that Hatshepsut was obliterated because she stepped outside the bounds of acceptable female behavior. But Bryan (1996) urges caution in attributing Hatshepsut's case to gender bias since Egyptians tolerated female rulers and held fluid perceptions of sexuality at least in death, when women (and men) were transformed into the male god Osiris.

Meskell (1996, 1998a, 1999) questions the narrow focus on gender in addressing identity and instead advocates for an archaeology of the individual. She criticizes poststructuralist theorists for not addressing human agency at the level of the individual and claims that it is only from the perspective of the individual skin-bound body that agents act out their cultural and social experience. The experience of gender, sexuality, and identity is dynamic and changes in an individual's lifetime through lived sensual experience as an embodied person. Gender theorists do not examine the body properly because they perceive it either as a biological organism or as separate from culturally constructed gender identities. Meskell argues that the body is a cultural object defined in law, incorporated into systems of meaning, and transformed in mourning, rites of passage, and other stages of the life cycle and death. Meskell's approach requires well-preserved bodies, a rarity in tropical Africa, although isotopic analysis of human bone is an additional method for studying individual histories (see Cox et al. 2001).

Meskell (1999) investigates burials and houses from the Eighteenth and Nineteenth Dynasties in the village of Deir el Medina. The afterlife was an important economic and ritual focus of ancient Egyptians, but funerary practices were controlled by men (Meskell 1998b, 1999). Although it is held that Egyptian women enjoyed legal parity with men, a comparison of the value and quality of goods in tombs of husbands and wives, who presumably shared equal social status, reveals that this was not so (Meskell 1998b, 1999; Robins 1999:168). As family wealth and status increased, the relative wealth of female family members declined significantly. Women and children were strongly underrepresented in Eighteenth Dynasty tombs, and although they were better represented in the Nineteenth Dynasty, they were referred to in text and art by association with a husband or father. Overall, women and children had fewer magical items and accordingly fewer expectations of the afterlife than adult male kin. Texts indicate that although Egyptian women could initiate divorce, they were not as successful as men in doing so (Meskell 1999). Divorced women often faced lives of insecurity and poverty, including little provisioning for the afterlife in the absence of male kin. In the less symbolically potent eastern necropolis, Meskell (1999) found women buried alone or together, possibly representing domestic arrangements contrary to the official heterosexual model of Egyptian couples (see also Bryan 1996; Reeder 2000). Meskell (1999) concludes that age, sex, and status were more significant in social negotiation than gender per se.

Rooms in Deir el Medina houses were oriented around elite, married, and sexually potent females (Meskell 2000). Front rooms have an "enclosed lit," often interpreted as a birthing bed, but Meskell argues that no such feature is found in images of women giving birth. Meskell suggests that these structures were cultic and associated with images that illustrate women's ritual and daily activities and stressed female roles in procreation, birth, nursing of infants, and sexuality in life, death, and the afterlife. Meskell warns that ancient Egyptian sexuality cannot be interpreted from a Western perspective.

Meskell's theoretical discussions of identity are stimulating but not entirely successful. Although she interprets individual experiences from well-preserved burials, her discussion of remains and houses is phrased in the collective experience of children, youths, women, and men that she decries in poststructuralist research. Nevertheless, Meskell's work is the most theoretically oriented and carefully considered discussion of gender and identity in the literature reviewed here.

In southern Africa, Huffman (1996) proposes that the CCP evolved into the more complex Zimbabwe Cultural Pattern (ZCP) with the rise of polities on the Zimbabwe Plateau and adjacent areas of Botswana, South Africa, and Mozambique. Zimbabwe society was stratified into nobles and commoners who had separate settlements patterns. The ZCP was the elite pattern constructed on hilltops; the CCP continued in commoner settlements below. Central cattle byres were replaced by the court and palace as the hub of political activities and the focus of sacred rulership in the ZCP, with royalty now buried on hilltops. Only a few individuals lived with the ruler in the central palace. The palace and king's wives' and nobles' compounds were protected and enclosed by guards. The male sacred ruler (*mambo*) was responsible for rainmaking and fertility rituals. He governed with his ritual sister who maintained medicines essential to his life and his ability to rule. Using ethnographic and historic records, Huffman constructs a strongly gendered cognitive map to explain the organization of space and ritual relations in Zimbabwean settlements, but his work is criticized for poor methodology in the collection and application of ethnographic evidence (Beach 1997; Denbow 1997; S. Hall 1997; Lane 1997). For instance, Huffman (1996:6) states, "To interpret Great Zimbabwe, then, we must first understand more recent settlements. This procedure minimises and in some cases eliminates the chronological gap between the ethnographic model and the archaeological data. Contrary to much misunderstanding, this is not an argument by normal analogy, but an argument about sameness." But what Huffman presents is a *false* analogy because it equates past and present (Wylie 1985) and presents Africans as unchanged (Lane 1997; Stahl 1993).

Luedke (2004) turns to the roles of commoners in gold production, an industry critical to Great Zimbabwe's international trade. In sub-Saharan Africa, women are primary agents in hoe agriculture, and Luedke cites research that suggests that prospecting for gold is related to agricultural experience, specifically the link between geological formations of gold and fertile soils. Hoes are used to mine gold, and ore is ground on grinding stones, both technologies strongly associated with women in sub-Saharan Africa. Because most of the few sexed skeletons recovered in mine shafts contemporaneous with Great Zimbabwe are female, Luedke (2004) suggests that gold mining was conducted by commoner women and was paid as tribute to the elite who controlled luxury production. While Luedke proposes that women may have obtained some wealth through gold mining, this is not the case in iron metallurgy, where women perform similar activities in ore processing (see the previous discussion). Excavation of nonelite sites is needed to clarify the social and economic roles of men and women, elite, and commoners.

The Swahili are a class-based society occupying stone towns on East Africa's coast and archipelago from southern Somalia to southern Mozambique, including parts of Madagascar and the Comoro Islands. The "Swahili culture" is known historically from the past few centuries but is based in indigenous cultural developments that extend to the eighth century A.D., with stone towns emerging in the mid-tenth century (Horton 1994). The upper class, called the Wa-ungwana, brokered the trade between the African hinterland (including Great Zimbabwe) and the Indian Ocean trade. The concept of the Swahili as a product of foreign colonies has been abandoned, although the Wa-ungwana intermarried and were strongly influenced by their Arab and other foreign trading partners (Connah 2001). Donley-Reid's (1982, 1990) interpretation of Swahili history is outdated (see Horton 1994:147), but her spatial analysis of stone houses remains useful. Coral-rag houses like those studied by Donley-Reid first appear on the coast in the fourteenth century, and Horton (1994:167) suggests that they may mark the emergence of the Wa-ungwana as a distinct group. Historically, Wa-ungwana exclusively held the right to build in stone. Donley-Reid (1982, 1990) suggests that Wa-ungwana men manipulated domestic and community space and material objects to maintain their superiority in the social hierarchy and to control trade. Stone houses conveyed a man's creditworthiness and permanence to their foreign trading partners, and foreigners could trade with Wa-ungwana partners only in the latter's home. Wa-ungwana men built coral houses as wedding presents for their daughters who were married to foreign traders. Daughters remained in their houses to ensure ongoing trade between their husband and their male kin.

Status and gender affected the built landscape in and around stone towns. Space and people became more valuable in terms of their proximity to the upper and innermost rooms of stone houses. The most valued room was the *ndani* and was occupied by Wa-ungwana women. Donley-Reid (1990) suggests that to help protect the room from polluting acts (e.g., childbirth, sexual intercourse, and death) and to maintain its ritual purity, the *ndani* was decorated with symbolic objects, including blue porcelain plates set in niches in the walls. Ritual purity and control over women's reproduction were maintained by confining women (sometimes for their entire lives) inside stone houses and particularly in the *ndani*. Wa-ungwana men were polygynous and could marry low-status and slave women. These women sometimes occupied lower status space in their husband's stone house or were provided daub-walled houses in the town. Lower-status and slave males could not live in stone houses and were further restricted from entering stone towns in the evening to prevent their contact with Wa-ungwana women (Donley-Reid 1990:119–20).

Robertshaw (1999) suggests that the evolution of the nineteenth-century Buyoro and Buganda states in the Great Lakes region was spurred on partly by the need to acquire women's labor for agricultural production, especially after the fifteenth century. Polities in the region became engaged in raiding for cattle and women. This was because these elites relied on staple surplus rather than prestige goods to bolster their power, as is inferred from archaeological remains at large centers in the region. Robertshaw suggests that the commodification of women resulted in their declining status, which was poor according to nineteenth-century historic sources. He states that women may have resisted their subordination through participation as priestesses in cults.

Future Directions

Gender archaeology has made considerable progress in Africa. The study of iron metallurgy in sub-Saharan Africa provides an excellent example of the combined use of ethnohistory, ethnoarchaeology, ethnography, and archaeology to investigate gender ideologies, relationships, and material culture production rarely equaled in gender studies. However, there is a general need for greater accountability in the use of ethnographic analogy. In my opinion, little can be said about gender in ancient societies without some degree of ethnographic analogy, but archaeologists are responsible for understanding what constitutes good analogical reasoning (see Lane 1996, 2005; Mitchell 2005:163; Stahl 1993; Wylie 1985). Stahl (1993) presents a comparative approach that tests the ethnographic source to determine how it diverges from archaeological data, including how ethnographic gender relations are shaped by colonialism and market economies (see also Stahl and Cruz 1998). Testing ethnographic sources helps avoid simple assumptions of isomorphism between gender relations in the past and present, a problem too common in the studies reviewed here. Analogical arguments can be strengthened with additional and independent lines of inquiry, including isotopic analysis of diet, spatial analysis, and gender symbolism, that cross-cut multiple forms of contextual or task-associated material culture and cultural objects (including human bodies).

Africanists must engage in theoretical debates in gender archaeology in the future. It is surprising that little attempt has been made to engender African political structures. Numerous ethnographic studies of African polities challenge widely held archaeological concepts that claim power as a male prerogative (see Nelson 2003). For instance, in sub-Saharan polities, political authority is often masculine but complemented with feminine qualities. A duality of rulership frequently involved the formal office of a queen mother or sacred sister who ruled with the male king (Bay 1995; Ifeka 1992). These women filled institutionalized offices that were integral components of power structures even where the public face of authority was masculine (Cohen 1993). In Dahomey, women were warriors and palace guards, and their military prowess was acknowledged by European colonial forces (Edgerton 2000). Several Kushite queens in Nubia, referred to by the title *Kentake* or *Kandake*, led military campaigns (including a definitive expedition against the Romans), and the tenth-century A.D. female Agaw ruler Gudit is credited with destroying the ailing Aksumite kingdom in Highland Ethiopia. Ruling queens are also part of the tradition of the Kingdom of Imerina in Madagascar. From these few examples, it is clear that women held more than nominal or occasional positions of ultimate authority in African states. In addition to public office, anthropologists describe examples of women's institutionalized and collective political action. For instance, the Igbo practice of "sitting on a man" was a strategy used by nonelite women to exert public and collective force against men who exceeded their domestic or public authority (van Allen 1997). Alternate gender categories in Africa also need to be investigated, including eunuchs, a form of slavery introduced into sub-Saharan Africa by Islam, and whose absolute loyalty to their masters allowed them to hold important political positions (Lovejoy 1983:17). Igbo "Brave Women" (McCall 1996) took wives and accumulated wealth, a direct challenge to the claim that only men can become aggrandizers because only men have wives (e.g., Clark and Blake 1995). Africanists also need to examine how gender relations were affected by the expansion of global religions. Recently, Insoll (2003) and Finneran (2002) have synthesized the impact on Africa's past of Islam and Christianity, respectively, but neither satisfactorily addresses the subject of gender in his study. In sum, with a careful and integrated approach that tests ethnographic evidence against historic and archaeological materials, African gender archaeology can provide a social approach to Africa's past and provide a basis to reevaluate archaeological theory more broadly in regard to gender and political power.

Acknowledgments

Much thanks to Drs. Nicholas David, Anne Katzenberg, and Catherine D'Andrea, who kindly provided many helpful and insightful comments for this chapter. Thanks also to Kees de Ridder, who produced figure 18.1.

References

Anderson, Gavin
    1997   Fingers and Finelines. In *Our Gendered Past*. Lyn Wadley, ed. Pp.13–69. Johannesburg: Witwatersrand University Press.

Apentiik, Rowland
　1997　Bulsa Technologies and Systems of Thought. M.A. thesis, University of Calgary.

Barakat, Hala, and Ahmed Gamal el-Din Fahmy
　1999　Wild Grasses as 'Neolithic' Food Resources in the Eastern Sahara: A Review of the Evidence from Egypt. In *The Exploitation of Plant Resources in Ancient Africa*. Marijke van der Veen, ed. Pp. 33–46. New York: Kluwer Academic/Plenum.

Barich, Barbara
　1998　Social Variability among Holocene Saharan Groups: How to Recognize Gender. In *Gender in African Prehistory*. Susan Kent, ed. Pp. 105–14. Walnut Creek, CA: AltaMira Press.

Barndon, Randi
　1996　Fipa Ironworking and Its Technological Style. In *The Culture of Technology of African Iron Production*. Peter Schmidt, ed. Pp. 58–73. Gainesville: University Press of Florida.

Bay, Edna G.
　1995　Belief, Legitimacy and the Kpojito: An Institutional History of the 'Queen Mother' in Pre-Colonial Dahomey. *Journal of African History* 36(1):1–27.

Beach, David
　1997　Review Feature: Snakes and Crocodiles: Power and Symbolism in Ancient Zimbabwe by Thomas N. Huffman. *South African Archaeological Bulletin* 52:125–27.

Berns, Marla
　1993　Art, History, and Gender: Women and Clay in West Africa. *African Archaeological Review* 11:129–48.

Braithwaite, M.
　1982　Decoration as Ritual Symbol: A Theoretical Proposal and an Ethnographic Study in Southern Sudan. In *Symbolic and Structural Archaeology*. I. Hodder, ed. Pp. 80–88. Cambridge: Cambridge University Press.

Brumbach, Hetty Jo, and Robert Jarvenpa
　1997　Ethnoarchaeology of Subsistence Space and Gender: A Subarctic Dene Case. *American Antiquity* 62(3):414–36.

Brumfiel, E. M.
　1991　Weaving and Cooking: Women's Production in Aztec Mexico. In *Engendering Archaeology*. J. Gero and M. Conkey, eds. Pp. 224–51. Oxford: Blackwell.

Bryan, Betsy
　1996　In Women Good and Bad Fortune Are on Earth: Status and Roles of Women in Egyptian Culture. In *Mistress of the House Mistress of Heaven*. Anne K. Capel and Glenn E. Markoe, eds. Pp. 25–46. New York: Hudson Hills Press.

Cane, Charlotte, Roberta Gilchrist, and Deirdre O'Sullivan
　1994　Women in Archeology in Britain: Three Papers. In *Equity Issues for Women in Archeology*. M. C. Nelson, S. M. Nelson, and Alison Wylie, eds. Pp. 91–98.

Archaeological Papers of the American Anthropological Association 5. Washington, DC: American Anthropological Association.

Casey, Joanna
   1998   Just a Formality. In *Gender in African Prehistory*. Susan Kent, ed. Pp. 83–104. Walnut Creek, CA: AltaMira Press.
   2005   Holocene Occupations of the Forest and Savanna. In *African Archaeology*. Ann Brower Stahl, ed. Pp. 225–48. Oxford: Blackwell.

Childs, S. Terry, and William J. Dewey
   1996   Forging Symbolic Meaning in Zaire and Zimbabwe. In *The Culture and Technology of African Iron Production*. Peter Schmidt, ed. Pp. 145–71. Gainesville: University Press of Florida.

Childs, S. Terry, and David Killick
   1993   Indigenous African Metallurgy: Nature and Culture. *Annual Review of Anthropology* 22:317–37.

Clark, John E., and Michael Blake
   1995   The Power of Prestige: Competitive Generosity and the Emergence of Rank Societies in Lowland Mesoamerica. In *Contemporary Archaeology in Theory*. Robert W. Preucel and Ian Hodder, eds. Pp. 258–81. Oxford: Blackwell.

Close, Angela
   1995   Few and Far Between Early Ceramics in North Africa. In *The Emergence of Pottery Technology and Innovation in Ancient Societies*. W. K. Barnett and J. W. Hoopes, eds. Pp. 23–37. Washington, DC: Smithsonian Institution Press.

Cohen, Ronald
   1993   Women, Status, and High Office in African Polities. In *Configurations of Power*. J. S. Henderson and P. J. Netherly, eds. Pp. 181–208. Ithaca, NY: Cornell University Press.

Collett, D. P.
   1993   Metaphors and Representations Associated with Precolonial Iron-Smelting in Eastern and Southern Africa. In *The Archaeology of Africa Food, Metals and Towns*. T. Shaw, P. Sinclair, B. Andah, and A. Okpoko, eds. Pp. 499–511. London: Routledge.

Conkey, M., and J. Spector
   1984   Archaeology and the Study of Gender. In *Advances in Archaeological Method and Theory 7*. M. B. Schiffer, ed. Pp. 1–38. New York: Academic Press.

Connah, G.
   2001   *African Civilizations*. 2nd ed. Cambridge: Cambridge University Press.

Cox, Glenda, Judith Sealy, Carmel Schrire, and Alan Morris
   2001   Stable Carbon and Nitrogen Isotopic Analyses of the Underclass at the Colonial Cape of Good Hope in the Eighteenth and Nineteenth Centuries. *World Archaeology* 33(1):73–97.

David, Nicholas
   2001   Lost in the Third Hermeneutic? Theory and Methodology, Objects and Rep-

resentations in the Ethnoarchaeology of African Metallurgy. *Mediterranean Archaeology* 14:49–72.

David, Nicholas, and Carol Kramer
    2001   *Ethnoarchaeology in Action*. Cambridge: Cambridge University Press.

David, Nicholas, Judy Sterner, and Kodzo Gavua
    1988   Why Pots Are Decorated. *Current Anthropology* 29(3):365–89.

Davis, Whitney
    1990   The Study of Rock Art in Africa. In *A History of African Archaeology*. Peter Robertshaw, ed. Pp. 271–95. London: James Currey.

Denbow, James
    1997   Review Feature: Snakes and Crocodiles: Power and Symbolism in Ancient Zimbabwe by Thomas N. Huffman. *South African Archaeological Bulletin* 52:128–29.

Donley-Reid, Linda W.
    1982   House Power: Swahili Space and Symbolic Markers. In *Symbolic and Structural Archaeology*. Ian Hodder, ed. Pp. 63–73. Cambridge: Cambridge University Press.
    1990   A Structuring Structure: The Swahili House. In *Domestic Architecture and the Use of Space*. S. Kent, ed. Pp. 114–26. Cambridge: Cambridge University Press.

Dowson, Thomas
    1988   Revelations of Religious Experiences: The Individual in San Rock Art. *World Archaeology* 20:116–28.
    1994   Reading Art, Writing History: Rock Art and Social Change in Southern Africa. *World Archaeology* 25(3):332–45.

Edgerton, Robert B.
    2000   *Warrior Women*. Boulder, CO: Westview.

Esterhuysen, A. B.
    2000   The Birth of Educational Archaeology in South Africa. *Antiquity* 74:159–65.

Finneran, Niall
    2002   *The Archaeology of Christianity in Africa*. Charleston, SC: Tempus.

Gawe, Stephen, and Francis Meli
    1990   The Missing Past in South African History. In *The Excluded Past: Archaeology in Education*. P. G. Stone and R. MacKenzie, eds. Pp. 98–108. London: Unwin Hyman.

Fowler, Kent
    In press   Materialising Gender: Pottery Style, Costume, and Bodily Adornment amongst the amaZulu of South Africa. In *Qu(e)erying Gender*. Proceedings of the 37th Annual Chacmool Archaeological Conference. Calgary: University of Calgary.

Gifford-Gonzalez, Diane
    1991   Gaps in Zooarchaeological Analyses of Butchery: Is Gender an Issue? In *Bones*

to Behavior: Ethnoarchaeological and Experimental Contributions of Faunal Remains. J. Hudson, ed. Pp. 181–99. Carbondale: Southern Illinois University Press.

    1998   Gender and Early Pastoralists in East Africa. In *Gender in African Prehistory*. S. Kent, ed. Pp. 115–38. Walnut Creek, CA: AltaMira Press.

Goucher, Candice L., and Eugenia W. Herbert
    1996   The Blooms of Banjeli: Technology and Gender in West African Iron Making. In *The Culture and Technology of African Iron Production*. P. Schmidt, ed. Pp. 40–57. Gainesville: University Press of Florida.

Haaland, Randi
    1992   Fish, Pots and Grain: Early and Mid-Holocene Adaptations in the Central Sudan. *African Archaeological Review* 10:43–64.
    1995   Sedentism, Cultivation, and Plant Domestication in the Holocene Middle Nile Region. *Journal of Field Archaeology* 22:157–74.
    1997   Emergence of Sedentism: New Ways of Living, New Ways of Symbolizing. *Antiquity* 71:374–85.

Hall, Martin
    1996   *Archaeology Africa*. Cape Town: David Philip.
    1997   Patriarchal Facades. In *Our Gendered Past*. Lyn Wadley, ed. Pp. 221–36. Johannesburg: Witwatersrand University Press.

Hall, Simon
    1997   Material Culture and Gender Correlations. In *Our Gendered Past*. L. Wadley, ed. Pp. 209–19. Johannesburg: Witwatersrand University Press.
    1998   A Consideration of Gender Relations in the Late Iron Age "Sotho" Sequence for the Western Highveld, South Africa. In *Gender in African Prehistory*. Susan Kent, ed. Pp. 235–58. Walnut Creek, CA: AltaMira Press.

Hassan, Fekri A., and Shelley J. Smith
    2002   Soul Birds and Heavenly Cows: Transforming Gender in Predynastic Egypt. In *In Pursuit of Gender: Worldwide Archaeological Approaches*. S. M. Nelson and M. Rosen-Ayalon, eds. Pp. 43–65. Walnut Creek, CA: AltaMira Press.

Herbert, Eugenia W.
    1993   *Iron, Gender, and Power*. Bloomington: Indiana University Press.

Hollis, Susan Tower
    1987   Women of Ancient Egypt and the Sky Goddess Nut. *Journal of American Folklore* 100(398):496–503.

Horton, Mark
    1994   Swahili Architecture, Space and Social Structure. In *Architecture and Order*. Michael Parker Pearson and Colin Richards, eds. Pp. 147–69. London: Routledge.

Huffman, Thomas N.
    1996   *Snakes and Crocodiles: Power and Symbolism in Ancient Zimbabwe*. Johannesburg: Witwatersrand University Press.

Ifeka, Caroline
    2001   The Central Cattle Pattern and Interpreting the Past. *Southern African Humanities* 13:1–17.

Ifeka, Caroline
    1992   The Mystical and Political Powers of Queen Mothers, Kings and Commoners in Nso' Cameroon. In *Persons and Powers*. S. Ardener, ed. Pp. 135–57. Oxford: Berg.

Insoll, Timothy
    2003   *The Archaeology of Islam in Sub-Saharan Africa.* Cambridge: Cambridge University Press.

Johnson, Janet H.
    1996   The Legal Status of Women in Ancient Egypt. In *Mistress of the House Mistress of Heaven*. A. K. Capel and G. E. Markoe, eds. Pp. 175–86. New York: Hudson Hills Press.

Kelley, Janem, and Warren Hill
    1994   Relationships between Graduate Training and Placement in Canadian Archeology. In *Equity Issues for Women in Archeology*. M. C. Nelson, S. M. Nelson, and A. Wylie, eds. Pp. 47–52. Archaeological Papers of the American Anthropological Association 5. Washington, DC: American Anthropological Association.

Kense, Francoise J.
    1990   Changing Paradigms, Goals and Methods in the Archaeology of Francophone West Africa. In *A History of African Archaeology*. P. Robertshaw, ed. Pp. 135–54. London: James Currey.

Kent, Susan
    1995   Does Sedentarization Promote Gender Inequality? A Case Study from the Kalahari. *Journal of the Royal Anthropological Institute*, n.s., 1:513–36.
    1998a   *Gender in African Prehistory.* Walnut Creek, CA: AltaMira Press.
    1998b   Invisible Gender—Invisible Foragers: Southern African Hunter-Gatherer Spatial Patterning and the Archaeological Record. In *Gender in African Prehistory*. S. Kent, ed. Pp. 39–68. Walnut Creek, CA: AltaMira Press.

Killick, David
    2004   What Do We Know about African Iron Working? *Journal of African Archaeology* 2(1):97–112.

Kramer, Carol, and Miriam Stark
    1994   The Status of Women in Archeology. In *Equity Issues for Women in Archeology*. M. C. Nelson, S. M. Nelson, and A. Wylie, eds. Pp. 17–22. Archaeological Papers of the American Anthropological Association 5. Washington, DC: American Anthropological Association.

Kuper, A.
    1982   *Wives for Cattle: Bridewealth and Marriage in Southern Africa.* London: Routledge and Kegan Paul.

Lane, Paul
    1996   The Use and Abuse of Ethnography in Iron Age Studies of Southern Africa. In *The Growth of Farming Communities in Africa from the Equator Southward*. J. E. G. Sutton, ed. Pp. 51–64. Nairobi: British Institute of East Africa.
    1997   Review Feature: Snakes and Crocodiles: Power and Symbolism in Ancient Zimbabwe by Thomas N. Huffman. *South African Archaeological Bulletin* 52:132–35.
    1998   Engendered Spaces and Bodily Practices in the Iron Age of Southern Africa. In *Gender in African Prehistory*. Susan Kent, ed. Pp. 179–203. Walnut Creek, CA: AltaMira Press.
    2005   Barbarous Tribes and Unrewarding Gyrations? The Changing Role of Ethnographic Imagination in African Archaeology. In *African Archaeology*. Ann Brower Stahl, ed. Pp. 24–54. Oxford: Blackwell.

Lee, Richard, and Robert K. Hitchcock
    1998   African Hunter-Gatherers: History and the Politics of Ethnicity. In *Transformations in Africa*. Graham Connah, ed. Pp. 14–45. London: Leicester University Press.

Lee Thorp, J. A., J. C. Sealy, and N. J. Van Der Merwe
    1989   Stable Carbon Isotope Ratio Differences between Bone Collagen and Bone Apatite, and Their Relationship to Diet. *Journal of Archaeological Science* 16:585–99.

Lewis-Williams, J. David
    1975   The Drakensberg Rock Paintings as an Expression of Religious Thought. In *Les religions de la prehistoire*. E. Anati, ed. Pp. 413–26. Capo di Ponte: Centro Camuno di Studi Preistorici.
    1977   Led by the Nose: Observations on the Supposed Use of Southern San Rock Art in Rain-Making Rituals. *African Studies* 36:155–59.
    1981   *Believing and Seeing: Symbolic Meanings in Southern San Rock Paintings*. London: Academic Press.
    2000   *A Cosmos in Stone*. Walnut Creek, CA: AltaMira Press.

Lovejoy, Paul
    1983   *Transformations in Slavery*. Cambridge: Cambridge University Press.

Luedke, Tracy
    2004   Gender and Agency in Economic Models of Great Zimbabwe. In *Ungendering Civilization*. K. A. Pyburn, ed. Pp. 47–70. London: Routledge.

Lyons, Diane
    1998   Witchcraft, Gender, Power and Intimate Relations in Mura Compounds in Dela, Northern Cameroon. *World Archaeology* 29(3):344–63.

Lyons, D., and A. C. D'Andrea
    2003   Griddles, Ovens and Agricultural Origins: An Ethnoarchaeological Study of Bread Baking in Highland Ethiopia. *American Anthropologist* 105(3):515–30.

MacEachern, S.
   1996   Ethnoarchaeology in Sub-Saharan Africa. *Journal of World Prehistory* 10(3):243–304.

MacLean, Rachel
   1998   Gendered Technologies and Gendered Activities in the Interlacustrine Early Iron Age. In *Gender in African Prehistory*. S. Kent, ed. Pp. 163–78. Walnut Creek, CA: AltaMira Press.

MacLean, Rachel, and Timothy Insoll
   1999   The Social Context of Food Technology in Iron Age Gao, Mali. *World Archaeology* 31(1):78–92.

Malan, Antonia
   1997   The Material World of Family and Household. In *Our Gendered Past*. L. Wadley, ed. Pp. 273–301. Johannesburg: Witwatersrand University Press.

Mazel, Aron D.
   1989   Changing Social Relations in the Thukela Basin, Natal 7000–2000 BP. *South African Archaeological Society Goodwin Series* 6:33–41.
   1992   Gender and the Hunter-Gatherer Archaeological Record: A View from the Thukela Basin. *South African Archaeological Society Goodwin Series* 47:122–26.

McCall, John C.
   1996   Portrait of a Brave Woman. *American Anthropologist* 98(1):127–36.

Meskell, Lynn
   1996   The Somatization of Archaeology: Institutions, Discourses, Corporeality. *Norwegian Archaeological Review* 29(1):1–16.
   1998a   An Archaeology of Social Relations in an Egyptian Village. *Journal of Archaeological Method and Theory* 5(3):209–43.
   1998b   Intimate Archaeologies: The Case of Kha and Merit. *World Archaeology* 29(3):363–79.
   1999   *Archaeologies of Social Life*. Oxford: Blackwell.
   2000   Re-em(bed)ding Sex: Domesticity, Sexuality, and Ritual in New Kingdom Egypt. In *Archaeologies of Sexuality*. R. Schmidt and B. Voss, eds. Pp. 253–61. London: Routledge.

Mitchell, Peter J.
   2002   *The Archaeology of Southern Africa*. Cambridge: Cambridge University Press.
   2005   Modeling Later Stone Age Societies in Southern Africa. In *African Archaeology*. Ann Brower Stahl, ed. Pp. 150–73. Oxford: Blackwell.

Mitchell, Peter J., and Ina Plug
   1997   Ritual Mutilation in Southern Africa. In *Our Gendered Past*. L. Wadley, ed. Pp. 135–66. Johannesburg: Witwatersrand University Press.

Moore, Henrietta, Todd Sanders, and Bwire Kaare
   1999   *Those Who Play with Fire*. London: Athlone Press.

Nelson, Sarah M., ed.
   2003   *Ancient Queens*. Walnut Creek, CA: AltaMira Press.

Nordström, Hans-Åke
   1996   The Nubian A-Group: Ranking Funerary Remains. *Norwegian Archaeological Review* 29(1):17–39.
Ouzman, Sven
   1997   Between Margin and Centre. In *Our Gendered Past*. L.Wadley, ed. Pp. 71–106. Johannesburg: Witwatersrand University Press.
Parkington, John
   1998   Resolving the Past Gender in the Stone Age Archaeological Record of the Western Cape. In *Gender in African Prehistory*. S. Kent, ed. Pp. 25–38. Walnut Creek, CA: AltaMira Press.
   2002   Men, Women, and Eland: Hunting and Gender among the San of Southern Africa. In *In Pursuit of Gender: Worldwide Archaeological Approaches*. S. M. Nelson and M. Rosen-Ayalon, eds. Pp. 93–117. Walnut Creek, CA: AltaMira Press.
   2003   Eland and Therianthropes in Southern African Rock Art: When Is a Person an Animal? *African Archaeological Review* 20(3):135–48.
Prins, Frans E., and Sian Hall
   1994   Expressions of Fertility in the Rock Art of Bantu-Speaking Agriculturalists. *African Archaeological Review* 12:171–203.
Pwiti, Gilbert, and Webber Ndoro
   1999   The Legacy of Colonialism: Perceptions of the Cultural Heritage in Southern Africa with Special Reference to Zimbabwe. *African Archaeological Review* 16(3):143–54.
Reeder, Greg
   2000   Same-Sex Desire, Conjugal Constructs, and the Tomb of Niankhkhnum and Khnumhotep. *World Archaeology* 32(2):193–208.
Reid, Andrew
   2005   Interaction, Marginalization, and the Archaeology of the Kalahari. In *African Archaeology*. Ann Brower Stahl, ed. Pp. 353–77. Oxford: Blackwell.
Robertshaw, P., ed.
   1990   *A History of African Archaeology*. London: James Currey.
Robertshaw, P.
   1999   Women, Labor, and State Formation in Western Uganda. In *Complex Polities in the Ancient Tropical World*. E. A. Bacus and L. J. Lucero, eds. Pp. 51–66. Archaeological Papers of the American Anthropological Association 9. Washington, DC: American Anthropological Association.
Robins, Gay
   1983   The God's Wife of Amun in the 18th Dynasty in Egypt. In *Images of Women in Antiquity*. A. Cameron and A. Khurt, eds. Pp. 65–78. London: Croom Helm.
   1999   Women in Ancient Egypt. In *Women's Roles in Ancient Civilizations*. Bella Vivante, ed. Pp. 155–87. Westport, CT: Greenwood Press.
Roehrig, Catharine H.
   1996   Some Occupations of Nonroyal Women as Depicted in Ancient Egyptian

Art. In *Mistress of the House, Mistress of Heaven*. A. K. Capel and G. E. Markoe, eds. Pp. 13–24. New York: Hudson Hills Press.

Rowlands, Michael, and Jean-Pierre Warnier
    1996   Magical Iron Technology in the Cameroon Grassfields. In *African Material Culture*. M-J Arnoldi, C. M. Geary, and K. L. Hardin, eds. Pp. 51–72. Bloomington: Indiana University Press.

Schmidt, Peter
    1996a   Cultural Representations of African Iron Production. In *The Culture and Technology of African Iron Production*. P. Schmidt, ed. Pp. 1–28. Gainesville: University Press of Florida.
    1996b   Reconfiguring the Barongo: Reproductive Symbolism and Reproduction among a Work Association of Iron Smelters. In *The Culture and Technology of African Iron Production*. P. Schmidt, ed. Pp. 74–127. Gainesville: University Press of Florida.
    1998   Reading Gender in the Ancient Iron Technology of Africa. In *Gender in African Prehistory*. S. Kent, ed. Pp. 139–62. Walnut Creek, CA: AltaMira Press.

Schmidt, Peter R., and Bertram B. Mapunda
    1997   Ideology and the Archaeological Record in Africa: Interpreting Symbolism in Iron Smelting Technology. *Journal of Anthropological Archaeology* 16(1):73–102.

Sealy, J. C., M. K. Patrick, A. G. Morris, and D. Alder
    1992   Diet and Dental Caries among Later Stone Age Inhabitants of the Cape Province, South Africa. *American Journal of Physical Anthropology* 88:123–34.

Sealy, J. C., and N. J. van der Merwe
    1988   Social, Spatial and Chronological Patterning in Marine Food Use as Determined by $\delta^{13}C$ Measurements of Holocene Human Skeletons from the South-Western Cape, South Africa. *World Archaeology* 20(1):87–102.

Segobye, Alinah
    1998   Daughters of Cattle: The Significance of Herding in the Growth of Complex Societies in Southern Africa between the 10th and 15th Centuries AD. In *Gender in African Prehistory*. S. Kent, ed. Pp. 227–33. Walnut Creek, CA: AltaMira Press.

Shepherd, Nick
    2003   "When the Hand That Holds the Trowel Is Black . . ." *Journal of Social Archaeology* 3(3):334–52.

Sinclair, Paul
    1990   The Earth Is Our History Book: Archaeology in Mozambique. In *The Excluded Past: Archaeology in Education*. P. G. Stone and R. MacKenzie, eds. Pp. 152–59. London: Unwin Hyman.

Sinclair, P. J., T. Shaw, and B. Andah
    1993   Introduction. In *The Archaeology of Africa Food, Metals and Towns*. T. Shaw, P. Sinclair, B. Andah, and A. Okpoko, eds. Pp. 1–31. London: Routledge.

Solomon, Anne
    1992   Gender, Representation, and Power in San Ethnography and Rock Art. *Journal of Anthropological Archaeology* 11:291–329.

Stahl, Ann Brower
    1993   Concepts of Time and Approaches to Analogical Reasoning in Historical Perspective. *American Antiquity* 58:235–60.

Stahl, Ann, and Maria Das Dores Cruz
    1998   Men and Women in a Market Economy. In *Gender in African Prehistory*. Susan Kent, ed. Pp. 205–26. Walnut Creek, CA: AltaMira Press.

Sterner, J., and N. David
    1991   Gender and Caste in the Mandara Highlands: Northeastern Nigeria and Northern Cameroon. *Ethnology* 30:355–69.

Stevenson, Judith
    2000   Shaman Images in San Rock Art: A Question of Gender. In *Representations of Gender from Prehistory to the Present*. M. Donald and L. Hurcombe, eds. Pp. 45–66. London: Macmillan.

Troy, Lana
    2003   She for Whom All That Is Said Is Done: The Ancient Egyptian Queen. In *Ancient Queens*. S. M. Nelson, ed. Pp. 93–116. Walnut Creek, CA: AltaMira Press.

van Allen, Judith
    1997   "Sitting on a Man": Colonialism and the Lost Political Institutions of Igbo Women. In *Perspectives on Africa*. R. R. Grinker and C. B. Steiner, eds. Pp. 536–49. Oxford: Blackwell.

Vinnicombe, Patricia
    1972   Motivation in African Rock Art. *Antiquity* 46:124–33.
    1975   The Ritual Significance of Eland (*Taurotragus oryx*) in the Rock Art of Southern Africa. In *Les religions de la prehistoire*. E. Anati, ed. Pp. 379–400. Capo di Ponte: Centro Commmuno di Studi Preistorica.
    1976   *People of the Eland*. Pietermaritzburg: University of Natal Press.

Wadley, Lyn
    1987   *Later Stone Age Hunters and Gatherers of the Southern Transvaal*. BAR International Series 380. Oxford: British Archaeological Reports.
    1997a   Introduction. In *Our Gendered Past*. Lyn Wadley, ed. Pp. 1–11. Johannesburg: Witwatersrand University Press.
    1997b   *Our Gendered Past*. Johannesburg: Witwatersrand University Press.
    1997c   Where Have All the Dead Men Gone? In *Our Gendered Past*. L. Wadley, ed. Pp. 107–33. Johannesburg: Witwatersrand University Press.
    1998   The Invisible Meat Providers. In *Gender in African Prehistory*. S. Kent, ed. Pp. 39–68. Walnut Creek, CA: AltaMira Press.
    2000   The Use of Space in a Gender Study of Two South African Stone Age Sites.

In *Gender and Material Culture in Archaeological Perspective*. M. Donald and L. Hurcombe, eds. Pp. 153–68. London: Macmillan.

Wasylikowa, Krystyna, and Jeff Dahlberg
 1999 Sorghum in the Economy of the Early Neolithic Nomadic Tribes at Nabta Playa, Southern Egypt. In *The Exploitation of Plant Resources in Ancient Africa*. M. van der Veen, ed. Pp. 11–32. New York: Kluwer Academic/Plenum.

Webley, Lita
 1997 Wives and Sisters. In *Our Gendered Past*. L.Wadley, ed. Pp. 167–208. Johannesburg: Witwatersrand University Press.

Weedman, Kathryn
 2001 Who's "That Girl": British, South African, and American Women as Africanist Archaeologists in Colonial Africa (1860s–1960s). *African Archaeological Review* 18(1):1–47.

Wilmsen, Edwin N.
 1989 *Land Filled with Flies*. Chicago: University of Chicago Press.

Wrobel, Gabriel D.
 2004 The Benefits of an Archaeology of Gender for Predynastic Egypt. In *Ungendering Civilization*. K. A. Pyburn, ed. Pp. 156–78. London: Routledge.

Wylie, Alison
 1985 The Reaction against Analogy. *In Advances in Archaeological Method and Theory 8*. M. B. Schiffer, ed. Pp. 63–111. New York: Academic Press.
 1993 Chilly Climate Issues for Women in Archaeology. In *Women in Archaeology: A Feminist Critique*. Occasional Papers in Prehistory, no. 23. H. du Cros and L. Smith, eds. Pp. 245–58. Canberra: Australian National University.

Gender in East and Southeast Asian Archaeology

19

ELISABETH A. BACUS

THE ARCHAEOLOGY OF GENDER in East and Southeast Asia is a growing area of study. Although gender studies are fairly new to these regions, there already exists research into a considerable range of issues, from gendered ideologies to the interrelations of gender and ranking in state societies. This chapter serves to highlight this work, focusing on the English-language publications (because of the author's language limitations). References to the Chinese-language literature can be found in Nelson (1997), Jiao (2001), and Linduff and Sun (2004) and to the Japanese-language literature in Ikawa-Smith (2002) (see also Habu 2004; Mizoguchi 2002). Unfortunately, it is not possible to also include here the growing body of graduate theses and papers presented at national and international conferences that further attest to the developing gender archaeology of these regions.

As the studies presented in this chapter demonstrate, a rich array of archaeological, ethnographic, and textual sources are drawn on in researching women and gender in the prehistoric and early historic periods of East and Southeast Asia, including mortuary assemblages, rock art, shell artifacts, figurines, inscriptions, legends, and ethnohistoric accounts. Many of the papers are ambitious in scope, often investigating several aspects of gender and gender relations, and represent forays into new terrain for the archaeology of China, Korea, Japan, Thailand, the Andaman Islands, and the Philippine Islands. Several themes serve to organize this overview: gendered images, gender ideology, gender roles and status, women and power in complex society, and gendered elite: intersecting identities. Alongside these archaeological investigations are studies critiquing earlier work for their essentialized and homogenized views of "women" as well as studies of archaeological practice and the presence/status of women archaeologists in East and Southeast Asia. These topics, as well as the issue of the conceptualization of gender, are considered here prior to presenting summaries of the archaeological research on gender. Concluding comments focus on future directions for the archaeology of gender in East and Southeast Asia.

Conceptualizing Gender

Archaeological studies of gender in East and Southeast Asia are primarily "womanist," that is, focused on "the actions, status, or simply presence of women in past societies" (Joyce and Claassen 1997:1). Consequently, there is little explicit discussion of how gender is or should be conceptualized and investigated. This situation may, in part, relate to research on primarily historic periods where archaeological remains are complemented by written accounts that provide information on the identities, statuses, roles, and behaviors of women (or, at least, attributed to women). In the mortuary-based studies, gender tends to be equated with sex (e.g., biologically sexed skeletons), except where an individual is identified through historical texts. Several studies are more conceptually explicit (e.g., Bacus, in press; Cuevas 2003; Shoocongdej 2002; discussed later in this chapter). They adopt the general distinction between sex as based on observable biological differences and gender as a historically specific, cultural, and social construct (albeit even perceptions of biological differences are socially constructed; e.g., Gilchrist 1999; Sørensen 2000).

The need for conceptual clarity is evident in those studies where sex and gender are used interchangeably and where gender is not understood to be a historically specific socially constructed identity that—as with the other social identities with which gender intersects—is fluid, mutable, negotiated, and possibly manipulated over the course of an individual's life and potentially at his or her death. In the first case, it results in the author's unnecessary argument for "sexing the burials" based on Dian grave goods after persuasively demonstrating gendered differences in the mortuary assemblages (Rode 2004). Only after the skeletal remains have been studied in the future can the extent to which gender and sex correlate be ascertained; such information could lead to greater understanding of gender in Dian mortuary practices. In the second case (J. Wu 2004), a clearer understanding of gender's interrelation with other social identities would have allowed the author to recognize the display of other gender–age–status distinctions in the mortuary record (see J. Wu 2004:79, 84–85).

Exposing Gender Bias in Archaeological Interpretations of the East and Southeast Asian Past

Gender-biased interpretations of the East and Southeast Asian archaeological record are identified in several studies, with some presenting new analyses and others theoretically based critiques to counter such views. A related issue receiving attention (e.g., Jiao 2001; Linduff and Sun 2004; Nelson 1998; Shelach 2004) is the dominance, until recently, of historical Marxism as the archaeological interpretive framework in China (and in North Korea, though it has received less critique in the gender archaeology literature); this tended to result in the uncritical interpretation of the Neolithic archaeological record as one of matriarchies that are subsequently replaced by patriarchal societies. While some scholars (Jiao 2001; Shelach 2004) cite the use of such a framework correlating "gender relations" to gross types of social organization as evidence of a long-standing concern with gender in Chinese archaeology, such a view lacks appreciation for how significantly different such studies are from those undertaken as part of the current archaeology of gender, a view that may stem from an undertheorized concept of gender. Comments by Sørensen (2000:37) are relevant here: it is not the acknowledgment of the existence of women, men, and children that has changed but rather the understanding of their presence, the assumptions used to assign roles and importance to genders, and the conceptualizations of women and gender. In other words, "it is the different meaning of gender that we are trying to accomplish theoretically and in its application, which has drastically transformed these concerns" (28).

Sites viewed as evidencing matriarchies, such as Majiayao in Gansu and Banpo near the Yellow River, are critically noted in the recent literature (Jiao 2001; Nelson 1997; see also Keightley 1999; Pearson 1988). Keightley (1999) considers the generally inferior status (politically and economically) of women in Neolithic and Shang China and draws attention to the need for comprehensive and reliable statistics about sex ratios, an understanding of the conditions that produced such ratios, and evidence that often supports more than a single interpretation (e.g., joint burials where the female's body has been moved may indicate the order in which people died instead of a decline in female status). Jiao (2001) also provides an empirically based critique of such interpretations. With regard to Yangshao society, in which women are argued to have played a dominant role, the evidence cited shows no clear difference among the amounts and types of grave goods found with female and male burials. Patrilineal society, subordination of females, decline of women's status, and so forth are often inferred from mixed-sex burials that are thought to represent married couples. However, Jiao's observations challenge such interpretations: mixed burials occur only in some areas of Neolithic China, it was a practice of short duration, only a small proportion of burials in any given cemetery are of this type, ownership of grave goods in these burials is difficult to ascertain and cannot be used to support interpretations that their distributions are biased against women, and flexed positions—of both males and females—are common in some sites and hence cannot be simply viewed as indicative of the subordination of women (Jiao 2001:55–57). Thus, the conventional view of early prehistoric Chinese society as matrilocal and matriarchal is not supported, nor is the view that the emergence of class society was accompanied by an overall decline in women's social status (60).

Several studies (summarized later in this chapter) reexamine sites dominated by such interpretations. Nelson (1991a) considers the meaning of female statues at Niuheliang, one of the Neolithic sites interpreted as evidencing matriarchal organization. Sun and Yang (2004) evaluate the interpretation of the Majiayao culture as one that evolved from a matrilineal society to a patrilineal/patriarchal society and that entailed the development of gender inequality. Similarly, Li (2004) seeks an alternative interpretation of gender relations to those that assume matriarchal/patriarchal organization among pastoral groups bordering early dynastic China. Worth stressing here is that critiques of androcentric bias must extend beyond a focus on matriarchies/patriarchies to include all forms of gender-biased assumptions and inferences, such as of male dominance and female subordination (Sun and Yang 2004:40, 41) and of females as passive actors (J. Wu 2004:86).

Interpretations of the Korean and Japanese archaeological record have also been the subject of gender-based critique; interpretations of the Southeast Asian archaeological record have not yet received such attention. Nelson (1991b, 1993, 2003; discussed later in this chapter) challenges the traditionally held view that the rulers of the Silla state of southeastern Korea were men (with two historically known exceptions) based on evidence of a female royal tomb. Ikawa-Smith (2002) critically reviews interpretations of the clay figurines from the Jomon period (ca. 14,500–300 B.C.) of Japan. These figurines (of more than 15,000 in number) have been the subject of research since the beginning of the late nineteenth century, and most Japanese scholars view them as mainly representations of females, though this interpretation is not without debate (see also Nagamine 1986; Ueki, cited in Habu 2004). Highlighting the need for gender-informed studies are several long-held, problematic interpretations that continue to dominate understandings of Jomon figurines, for example, "that the single most important attribute of a female is her ability to give birth, though the process is fraught with risks to the woman, the child and the demographic future of the group"; that they are "a reification of this procreative power and metaphorically symbolize productivity of the earth and nature in general; and . . . that the figurines served some important role in the Jomon society that was thought to have been ruled by magic" (Ikawa-Smith 2002:349–50). As an alternative to the mother goddess/fertility cult/sympathetic magic interpretations, Ikawa-Smith posits that the figurines "indicate tension and negotiation of power" during the Jomon. However, as she points out, this and other recently proposed ideas still need to be fully developed and tested.

Gender and Archaeological Practice in East and Southeast Asia

To date, few studies examine the social context of archaeological practice in East and Southeast Asia as it pertains to women archaeologists in these regions. A brief comment by Linduff and Sun (2004:2) indicates that there are few women archaeologists in China and even fewer who have lead positions in research. Similarly, research by Ikawa-Smith and Habu (1998, cited in Ikawa-Smith 2002) on the situation in Japan shows that "women are grossly underrepresented among those archaeologists who plan and execute archaeological investigations and who interpret and disseminate the results to students and the public" (Ikawa-Smith 2002:323). In 1995, women made up less than 3 percent of those who were admitted to the Japanese Archaeological Association, membership in which denotes an individual's professional status; a major reason for both "the stereotypical manner in which women's activities are presented in publications and museum displays directed to the general public" (323) and the virtual absence of feminist perspectives and gender archaeology in Jomon studies (Habu 2004:25). Within academia, only about 2 percent of the courses offered in Japan's archaeology programs are taught by women, even though women students are numerous in archaeology undergraduate programs and are well represented in graduate programs. The situation is improving within cultural resource management, where women archaeologists are increasing in number (from 0.3 percent in 1981 to 6.5 percent in 1992 to 10.4 percent in 1998 [the last figure is for one prefecture only]). Such a pronounced gender imbalance in Japanese archaeology is not unrelated to the "mindlessly gendered" interpretations of Jomon figurines that Ikawa-Smith also critiques in this study (see the previous discussion).

An early and thought-provoking study by Nelson (1991c) focuses on the situation for North American women archaeologists working in Asia and the Pacific. As of 1989, eight women and seventeen men worked in East and Southeast Asia. Four of the men but none of the women held positions at elite universities (with seven men in universities of the next two ranks and only one woman in a Ph.D.-granting department), from which she posits that women working in these regions are marginalized, whereas the men are viewed differently, that is, as having access to an unusual data source. The current situation of North American archaeologists working in East and Southeast Asia awaits a follow-up study.

Archaeological Investigations of Gender in East and Southeast Asia

As attested to by the publications summarized in this section, East and Southeast Asia gender archaeology involves research on diverse time periods, from the early Holocene to as recent as the mid-second millennium A.D., and across a range of themes (see figure 19.1 for location of sites and areas mentioned in this chapter). The broad themes selected here include gendered images, gender ideology, gender roles and status, women and power in complex society, and gendered elite.

Gendered Images

The studies of gendered images from China, Japan, Thailand, and the Philippines focus on clay figurines, anthropomorphic earthenware vessels, bronze decorative figures, and, in a different vein, mortuary remains. Among these is one of the earliest explicitly gender-informed interpretations of the East Asian archaeological record, Nelson's (1991a) work on the Niuheliang site in northeastern China (on ideology and symbols of elite power at Niuheliang that appear to have included yin symbolism, which, with the female statues, suggests that women were symbolically important, see also Nelson 2002). This ceremonial center of the Hongshan culture (ca. 4000–2500 calib B.C.) comprises thirteen areas of stone-mounded tombs (including high-status burials), jade ornaments, a platform-like area, and, most notably, the remains of a long, narrow, irregularly shaped building that contained fragments of statues, with most being human representations (life size and larger). Fragments of female images (hence, reference to the structure as a "goddess temple") leads Nelson to pose several questions: what is their meaning, what do they suggest about women's status, and what is the relationship between possible goddess worship and the place of women in this socially stratified society? Sanday's (1981, cited in Nelson 1991a) use of creation stories as "scripts" for interpreting gender and power relations, together with the general correlation between the presence of female origin myths and high status of women, suggests that the Niuheliang statues represent female power, status, or autonomy. Independent evidence in the form of "continuous threads in Chinese culture which could be followed back to women of power" (303), including textual accounts of female deities and evidence from the tomb of Fu Hao of the Shang dynasty (sixteenth to tenth centuries B.C.), support this interpretation. According to the oracle bones, Fu Hao was a woman of importance, possibly the king's consort or a leader of armies, suggesting that upper-class Shang women had autonomy and power. Her tomb also contained bronze mirrors of the style from the region of Niuheliang, which strengthens "the possibility of a persistent tradition of female

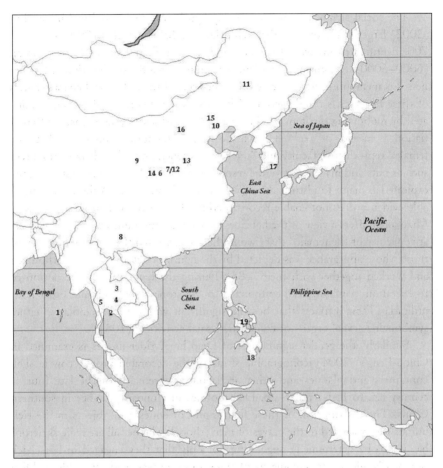

Figure 19.1. Location of archaeological sites/places mentioned in the text.
Key: **1** Chauldari and Hava Beel Cave; **2** Khok Phanom Di and Nong Nor; **3** Non Nok Tha; **4** Noen-U-Loke; **5** Tham Ta Duang, Khao Deang and Khao Plara; **6** Banpo; **7** Beizhao; **8** Dian polity; **9** Majiayao and Qijia; **10** Niuheliang; **11** Pingyang; **12** Qucun and Shangma; **13** Yinxu/Anyang; **14** Yu cemeteries; **15** Dadianzi; **16** Maoqinggou; **17** Silla state; **18** Ayub Cave; **19** the Visayas (central Philippines) (after http://alabamamaps.ua.edu/contemporarymaps/world/asia/easia2.jpg).

power" (304). While information on the sex of the skeletons is awaited, Nelson offers possible alternative conclusions: if they are all identified as female, then it would be reasonable to conclude "that women were the priestesses and perhaps the secular rulers as well as the goddesses, given the continuity to later times. . . . However, if the burials are all male, that would suggest that the high status of women as deities did not extend to social stratification" (308).

The social significance of Jomon clay figurines is considered in Mizoguchi's (2002) larger study of how the archipelago's inhabitants of 30,000 B.P. to A.D. 700 identified themselves. To understand the significance of the Earlier Jomon (6000–5000 B.P.) figurines, Mizoguchi examines what the signification of femaleness was metaphorically connected to. Since one of the only visual characteristics of these figurines is the depiction of breasts, "the networking of meanings initiated by mobilizing the item would have had at least a sex/gender-based differentiation as its *node* or *axis*" (84). He posits a metaphorical connection between females' reproductive faculty and "the yearly regeneration of predictable resources such as nuts and marine or riverine resources which . . . began to be systematically exploited as major foodstuffs during" the Earlier Jomon (84). Although the available evidence does not enable reconstruction of the way the figurines were used, Mizoguchi offers a view of the figurines as material embodiments of the "regenerative faculty of the female" that "would have constituted the identity not only of those whose appearance was depicted by the figurines but also of those who lived and worked together with them" (85). During the Later Jomon, the notion of regeneration may have been epitomized by the stone clubs/rods and other non-utilitarian lithic artifacts that became significant within the assemblage, "either symbolizing sexual organs or connoting sexual activities" (108).

Similarly, the gender significance of Dian horse-rider images is examined in Chiou-Peng's (2004) iconographic study of the decorated bronze cowrie shell containers and plaques and other archaeological remains of the late fourth-century B.C. to first-century A.D. Dian polities of Yunnan province in southern China. The distribution of these figures and of equestrian objects in the rich burials was restricted to the graves of men (though whether all are male skeletons has yet to be determined), suggesting not only that they engaged in horseback riding—"while a different means of transportation was made available to Dian women" (298)—but that it was specifically related to the elite men. The gendered creation of horsemanship appears to date back to the earliest period of Dian when the horse was introduced. Other evidence indicates the horse was neither used as a draft animal nor bred for consumption of its meat. Chiou-Peng thus concludes that horsemanship was an essential component in the culture of Dian men where, in such "stratified societies . . . military force and cavalry skills were central to the maintenance of political power by males" (312).

The visual depiction of femaleness and maleness in earthenware by inhabitants of the South Cotabato area of Mindanao Island, southern Philippines, at around 2,000 years ago is considered in Cuevas's (2003) preliminary study of anthropomorphic burial jars from the heavily disturbed site of Ayub Cave. These jars, used for secondary burial, contain the remains of multiple individuals (which itself raises intriguing methodological and interpretive issues regarding the relationship between those interred and the nature—gender, rank, and so on—of the individual portrayed as the burial jar). The bodies of the jars are formed as human torsos and are shown mainly nude, with body parts and ornaments depicted in molded and appliquéd clay, perforations, and/or paint. Many of the jar covers are shaped as human heads (ca. 149 complete and fragmentary), with some life size. Secondary sexual characteristics, specifically breasts, are prominently portrayed. Classification of approximately 150 pieces of detached breasts based on size and form—traits that would differ by age-group—enables identification of different genders and several age-groups of burial jar representations, including juvenile and adult males as well as females at the stages of puberty, adolescence, or young adult and adult. Using these results to help understand the social structure of those who produced the jars, Cueves suggests that the portrayal of different age-groups indicates that there were "changes in gender roles from childhood to adulthood" (68) and that "the representations of adult females and infants or young anthropomorphic features seem to indicate the woman's role in child tendering activities" (68). Examination of other possible gender symbols on the burial jars shows that ornamentation was not gender or age specific: jars depicting males, females, adults, and children all display pierced ears, styled hair, and bracelets and bangles on their arms.

I have explored material expressions of gender through a study of mortuary remains from Bronze Age Non Nok Tha (including burials of twenty-five male and twenty-one female adults) and several contemporary sites in northeastern Thailand (Bacus, in press). Studies arguing for the centrality of material culture to the construction, maintenance, and negotiation of gender categories and relations and of mortuary contexts as one of the principal arenas manifesting their interplay provide the framework for analyses of orientation and position of the sexed skeletons and of relationships between sex of the deceased and grave good assemblages. Results of the analysis of the early Bronze Age (ca. 2000–1500 B.C.) burials suggest that Non Nok Tha did not have a highly gendered structure as exhibited in body orientation. Similarly, statistical analysis does not indicate distinct gender categories expressed through grave good assemblages. Rather, several females and one male (possibly two) stand apart from the majority, all in different ways, suggesting that statements were being made about them as individuals; this would not preclude such statements being gender appropriate. What most of these individuals have in common relates to bronze and/or ornaments as the source of their distinctiveness: bronze bracelets, molds for making bronze axes, a bronze ax, and strands of shell beads. It may not be unreasonable to suggest that, in conjunction with their overall rarity—and, in regard to bronze, the use of imported metal and production by specialists—such items were becoming active in marking or constructing status differences that were particularly connected to females.

Changes occurred in the middle Bronze Age (ca. 1500–1000 B.C.), with some gender distinctions displayed in body positioning (but not in body orientation) and in the placement of nonornamental objects. Again, gender does not appear to have been expressed in distinct grave good assemblages, as the majority of both males and females have similar assemblages that vary somewhat in animal offerings and tools/pottery. Instead, it is a small number of individuals—accompanied by bronze, ornaments, and/or shell—who stand out from the majority. It is the presence of these items, as opposed to their abundance, that make these four to six individuals (depending on analysis) distinctive, though the quantity of items distinguishes among them, particularly in the case of bronze goods. In contrast to the earlier period, the majority of these distinctive individuals are male (whose hands were positioned differently from those of the majority of males and of all the females); the one female's greater distinctiveness is due to her seventeen bronze bracelets. The distinctiveness of their ornaments, their overall rarity across burials, the abundance of ornaments with only one individual, and, in the case of bronze bracelets and possibly shell bracelets, their occurrence across age and sex and the production of bronze by craft specialists all suggest a role in creating, displaying, and/or maintaining vertical and horizontal statuses.

Thus, while results indicate gender was not strongly expressed in mortuary contexts at Non Nok Tha, nuances of gender relations and interrelations with other social dimensions appear discernible. There is also evidence of possible gendering of craft activities (e.g., the presence of sandstone molds for the casting of bronze axes in the grave of an adult female could suggest that women were engaged in bronze crafting from the earliest period) and of heterarchical relations that other archaeologists argue characterize Bronze Age societies in Thailand (e.g., the individual distinctiveness to the burials, though less evident in the middle Bronze Age). Some of the variability identified in the analyses may indicate fluidity in gender categories, including the possibility that more than two genders were recognized. Alternatively, mortuary material culture may have had less of a role in structuring gender categories and relations at Non Nok Tha.

Gender Ideology

Gender ideology is the explicit focus of Sun and Yang's (2004) study of ideology as encoded in the mortuary ritual of the Majiayao (3300–2000 B.C.) and Qijia (2200–1700 B.C.) archaeological cultures of northwestern China. Informing their analysis of ten cemeteries with 197 male and 167 female adult burials and seven cemeteries with thirty-five double burials of male and female adults is a view of mortuary ritual as a creator and participant of the social message; an institution where political, ideological, and economic structures intermingle and compete; a ritual that can display, distort, disguise, and even deny the social reality; and as performed and controlled by the living and thus reflecting their attitudes toward gender (32). Three aspects of mortuary ritual, considered as different expressions of gender ideology, are examined. Results of the first, the relationship between tools and sex, suggest differing attitudes toward sex and gender in the various communities' mortuary rituals: the creation of a gender-neutral environment evident at five cemeteries where there is no significant association between sex and tools (and other items), an attempt "to create a concept in mortuary ritual that associated males with agricultural and craft activities and females with spinning and weaving" (35) at five cemeteries where there is a statistically significant association between spindle whorls and female burials and between other types of tools (e.g., stone chisels and axes) and male burials, and, finally, "mortuary ritual [that] was probably manipulated to favor males" (36) at one cemetery where most males were buried with tools such as stone axes and bone awls but where no artifacts are specifically associated with females.

Examination of the treatment of males and females in double burials, the second aspect, shows that among those at three Majiayao cemeteries, fourteen males and females were treated similarly in body position, placement of graves goods, and use of tomb furniture, thus expressing "an idea of sharing, rather than competing, with each other" (Sun and Yang 2004:39). However, the presence of two double burials each containing bodies in different positions (but not according to sex) indicates that "males and females . . . were no longer regarded as unified but rather as two different entities" (39). At the Qijia cemeteries, coffins were used in the fifteen double burials. At one cemetery, both the male and the female were placed inside coffins, whereas in the other two cemeteries, only the males were interred within coffins. The two spaces created by the use of a coffin lead "to an impression of segregation. . . . The female outside the coffin . . . seems to be displayed almost as a burial offering. This evidence indicates that mortuary ritual started to disfavour females" (39–40). Differences in body positions are seen in the double burials from two other sites where males were placed in an extended position and the females in a flexed position facing the male, "presenting an image of the male at the center and the female as a companion, or accessory. Clearly, the double burials suggest that mortuary ritual discriminated against women in the Qijia culture" (39–40) and "created an environment in which male's dominance and female's subordination could be easily recognized" (41).

However, Sun and Yang do not consider this practice as indicative of a patriarchal society, as argued in previous studies, since only a few of the burials have larger quantities of grave goods symbolic of wealth and social status (e.g., pig mandibles and *bi* disks); double-burial practice thus cross-cuts different social levels and was not exclusive to elite men.

Of the human/human-like images painted on Majiayao grave pottery, the last mortuary aspect examined, the male and female images are viewed—given the depiction of sexual organs—as having promoted fertility and reproduction. These figures, together with the gender-neutral ones, "indicate the Majiayao people's view of death and afterlife, connected to fertility, and presented through a metaphor for regeneration" (Sun and Yang 2004:45). The authors conclude from the various results that the region's communities projected different attitudes toward death, gender, and gender relations through their mortuary practices.

Gender Roles and Status

Several papers examine the roles and statuses of women and men, including among hunter-gatherers, pastoralists, early agricultural societies, and complex polities. To do so, they engage in analyses of material remains such as rock art, shell artifacts, grave goods, and bronze figures from sites of various periods located in the Andaman Islands, China, and Thailand. The earliest period sites investigated in regard to this issue are those in Shoocongdej's (2002) study entailing analysis of pictographs of primarily ritual and hunting scenes from late prehistoric western Thailand. More than 150 human and animal figures, rendered mainly in red ocher, are depicted on the cave and cliff walls of Tham Ta Duang, Khao Deang, and Khao Plara, the three sites examined. Dated to 4,000 to 2,000 B.P. (with Khao Plara dating slightly later than the other two contemporary sites), these rock art sites were created by food-producing communities who occasionally used them for ritual activities (with Tham Ta Duang also used as a temporary camp). It appears to have been two groups—each participating in different rock art design traditions—that created these dynamic scenes of women, men, and children.

Depictions of sexual organs and styles of hair and clothing allow classification of almost 40 percent of the human figures as male or female—both commonly found at all three sites—that then enables identification of their respective activities. The various portrayed activities include hunting, fighting with wild buffalo or bulls, possibly herding or plowing, and non–subsistence-related activities, such as walking, dancing, and ritual ceremonies. Women, unlike men, are absent from hunting scenes, the most frequently depicted activity; while the former appear associated with plowing, the latter appear associated more with wild animals and cattle herding. Men are also shown as engaged in a greater diversity of activities than women. However, in ritual activities, both are equally represented, as are children, and are shown dancing and playing music. Furthermore, women and men are depicted holding major roles in different types of ritual ceremonies: both wear elaborate dress and ornaments—interpreted as indicating positions of status or authority—in various ritual scenes. Shoocongdej (2002) suggests that these images represent the activities engaged in by men, women, and children of the late prehistoric communities that painted them (though not of domestic activities within camps or households, as they were not among the scenes depicted). Since women played important roles in rituals and the subsistence economy and participated equally with men in rituals, she concludes that women's roles and status were equal to those of men in these western Thailand communities.

Also focused primarily on Thailand, though using a different source of evidence, is Higham's (2002) investigation of women's roles and status over about 2,500 years. The central Thailand burials from Khok Phanom Di (ca. 2000–1500 B.C.) are particularly informative in this regard (see also Higham and Thosarat 1994). For the first three (of seven) mortuary phases, analysis of grave offerings does not indicate distinctions based on wealth or sex; some dietary differences between females and males existed (i.e., females had a more cariogenic and less abrasive diet than males). In the fourth phase, the situation changed: turtle carapace ornaments became exclusive to male burials, and potters' anvils accompanied some women and infants. In the following phase, there was a major break with the cessation of interment in clusters and the appearance of four extremely rich burials, one of which was of a particularly rich female interred with items such as clay cylinders, burnishing stones, pottery anvil, pottery vessels including several finely made ones of novel shape and decoration, and abundant shell jewelry (e.g., more than 120,000 shell-disk beads and shell disks). The sixth phase also included a woman interred with considerable wealth and inside a raised rectangular structure. Higham suggests that the enhanced status of women (and their preponderance in two of the putative genealogies) was due to their central economic role, specifically as pottery specialists and producers of the vessels used in exchange.

In contrast with this earlier period, the Bronze Age (ca. 1500–500 B.C.) mortuary data from several sites does not suggest differences between men and women in their burial wealth. At the site of Nong Nor, for example, analysis identifies eight of forty-nine burials, comprised of both males and females, as wealthier (e.g., greater quantity of grave goods and exotic items) than the others, a distinction not correlated with age. Only one type of grave good—grinding stones—was exclusively interred with members of one sex (male). A similar pattern is seen at the Iron Age site of Noen-U-Loke (ca. 300 B.C.–A.D. 300). It is not until the last mortuary phase that possible gender differences appeared, with iron sickles found only with female burials.

Gender roles among Andaman Islander hunter-gathers are investigated by Cooper (2002). Focusing on two sites—Chauldari shell midden located on South Andaman Island and dating to approximately 2,000 years ago and Hava Beel Cave on Baratang Island with a basal date of 1540 ± 110 years B.P. (and used by the Jarawa as recently as the 1950s)—Cooper uses direct analogy to ethnographic accounts (e.g., Man 1885; Radcliffe-Brown 1922) to define the function of artifacts and to assign gender to their users, which then allows an investigation of the sexual division of labor and the artifacts' gendered symbolic value. She argues it would be impossible to ascertain a division of labor without the use of recent accounts as "the rough distinction between men's hunting and women's gathering technologies would be confounded with the variable tool emphases of the seasonal cycle" and because midden deposits represent "the culmination of collective effort in which gender is inherently indistinguishable, having been obfuscated through variable archaeological visibility and a socio-religious system wherein such distinctions are not fostered" (185). To avoid "the epistemological pitfall of viewing gender as a static category of analysis," focus is on "objects imbued with gendered symbolism . . . with a view to understanding the characteristics of gender relationships among the Andaman Islanders" (174).

From the Chauldari site, Cooper (2002) examines bivalves with use wear on their margins and perforated shells since shell is ethnographically known to have been an important raw material for making tools and ornaments. The former are mainly of a species known to have been used in gender-specific ways, such as a knife and scraper in the hunting kit of men and in crafting of fiber nets and mats, cleaning of newborn infants, and so on by women; non–gender-specific tools included spoons. Symbolically, its value extended into, for example, the mortuary realm as a grave item held by the deceased and into men's ritual dances as an item held in the hand. Perforated shell is represented by apertures of one main gastropod species, "necklaces of which are still worn by Jarawa men and women" (177). Shellfish, however, was first and foremost a food source, and it was the women who undertook their collection and subsequent manufacture into ornaments (and who also made ornaments of other materials). The Chauldari midden also yielded a small quantity of bone and stone tools. Mostly of *Sus scrofa* (also important to the diet), the bone tools include pointed tools or gouges and barbs or arrows. Ethnographically, the former were made by either women or men, whereas the latter were made and used by men and were also used in making the scarification cuts down a male friend's back. Women also used arrows in shaving and scarification. The stone flakes and chips were used for shaving, a task undertaken generally by women. At Hava Beel Cave, the absence of pottery, tools, and faunal remains suggests that the main encampment was located outside of the cave. The small outside midden yielded faunal remains from hunting, fishing, and shellfish collecting activities. As "foraging in the shallow waters of the mangroves and along the seashore was primarily the women's responsibility," the "division of labor in such a situation . . . [is] again reflected through the distinction between the remains" (182).

Through analogy to the ethnographic sources, Cooper (2002) thus suggests that there was flexibility in the organizational characteristics of these hunter-gatherer groups. Furthermore, though a sexual division of labor existed, accounts indicate that "there was a generalized female involvement in ritual and political activities," and thus women were both "equally important to and participated fully in the symbolic activities" (183).

Division of labor and status among pastoral societies that resided along early dynastic China's frontier are examined by Li (2004). Analysis focuses on burials from the third to sixth century B.C. Pingyan site in southwestern Heilongjian province in northeastern China. Pingyan's two cemeteries, Zhuanchang and Zhandou, have yielded 118 single and multiple burials with 307 individuals (with 139 male and 107 female skeletons identified) from four phases. The presence of different ages and sexes, comprising several generations, at Zhuanchang cemetery suggests that "kinship played a significant role in the mortuary practice and that multiple burials indicated clan or family ties. Later, at the Zhandou cemetery, many double burials with the conjugal or parent-child relationships suggested the importance of the individual family in the society" (246–47).

Results suggest that male and female status at death changed over time. In Zhandou's multiple burials, males were accompanied by more grave goods than the females whose bodies faced the males suggesting "unequal status of men and women" (Li 2004:245). Such differences are not found in the earlier Zhuanchang cemetery. During the middle phase, "females were able to achieve special status that was marked by elaborate burial treatment" as indicated by the presence of a tiger-motif plaque—an elite symbol—in the graves of both a male and a female; the female was also accompanied by richer grave goods (245). Other, slightly later sites in the region exhibit a "more sharply differentiated social hierarchy" (254), indicating that gender relations varied among frontier societies. For example, the thirty-one excavated burials from Zhalainuoer (dating to no earlier than the first century A.D.) exhibit wealth distinctions in their varying number of animal sacrifices; however, there is no clear differentiation in burial goods and grave structure between male and female burials. While tasks appear to have been similarly gendered as at Pingyan, items accompanying females suggest that they engaged in hunting activities; thus, "gendering of labor was not fixed in the community" (253).

Gendered work activities appear to have existed among these frontier pastoralist-fisher-hunter communities. Weapons and hunting equipment most frequently accompanied males, whereas weaving and needlework tools are most often found in female burials. Li (2004) suggests that their presence with both sexes indicates that burials constructed "an image of men and women with shared skills" (248). The "overlapping of work activities and cooperative labor must have been more usual . . . and may suggest seasonal work patterns . . . the gendering of labor in these frontier communities must have been fluid to some degree" (255).

Women's roles and status in the Dian polity—located to the south of early dynastic China and continuing slightly later in time than the northern pastoral communities mentioned previously—are explored by Rode (2004) through a study of their mortuary remains. Among Dian grave goods are several dozen large bronze cowrie shell–containing vessels, the tops of which have detailed narrative scenes depicting human figures, animals, and structures that "encapsulate culturally specific descriptions of the people and their activities" (319). Two types of scenes are depicted on more than one vessel: combat between mounted warriors and infantry (all males) and females engaged in weaving. A similar distinction is identified in the burial assemblages—those with weapons versus those with *koushi* (belt hooks)/textile tools—and interpreted as evidence of gender polarization "consistent with the traditional division of labor ascribed to gendered tasks" (322). Using these distinct items to "sex" the burials, the associated mortuary items are then used to investigate the status of Dian women. Rode finds that "the female burials from which weaving tools and images were recovered were large interments, lavishly furnished with material wealth and symbols of power comparable to [the elite] male burials of the same period" (330). Thus, "these women enjoyed wealth, status, and authority on par with Dian men of the same period" (332). However, "gender parity" did not exist across all levels of Dian cemeteries; for example, male burials were always larger and richer in the lower-class cemeteries.

The images of gendered domains on the bronze vessels and from the grave goods depict "gender complementary, separate realms" (Rode 2004:332). "These images were made to preserve information about the deceased in life" (329), whose prestige they were meant to enhance and legitimate, and hence indicate an emphasis on both the high status of an individual and the activities that were important to the deceased, such as cloth production. Gender parity among the elite, whom these vessels accompanied, is thus attributed to women's control and supervision of cloth production that enabled them to achieve and maintain their high status, wealth, and authority; for men, positions of power and authority were gained through warfare and military prowess. Why, then, was gender parity no longer exhibited in burials subsequent to the Sinicization of central Yunnan? Rode links the decline in women's status to the decline in the prestige of the locally produced cotton cloth that resulted from the changing preference of the Dian elite for the new exotic Chinese silks. Women were thus no longer able to gain status through their independent activities and instead "would have been reduced to gaining status through their relationship to their male relatives" (336).

Women and Power in Complex Society

The relationships between women and power in complex society receive attention in studies of ancient Korea and of the protohistoric and early historic Philippines. Several papers by Nelson (1991b, 1993, 2003) focus on the former area to investigate gender and power in the state of Silla (first to seventh centuries A.D.). The discovery of the enigmatic Royal Tomb 98—a husband/wife double burial—in which the woman was buried with a gold crown suggesting that she had been the ruler presents a challenge both to our understanding of gender equality and women's status in state-level societies and to the assumption that Silla rulers were men (with two historically recorded exceptions). Combined analyses of archaeological, historical, and ethnographic evidence enable reconstruction of aspects of Silla's social, political, economic, and religious systems and provide evidence of relative gender equality. Silla was stratified into *kolpum*, or "bone ranks"—caste-like in being endogamous and composed of one or more kinship groups (1991b:104); this structure kept everyone in the same social position into which they were born. Rulers were required to come from the Holy Bone, the highest group. Significantly, it was through women "that males could establish their claim to the throne (1993:308). Sumptuary laws, listing, for example, what each gender within each rank could wear and dwell in, indicate the existence of similar rules for men and women within each bone rank and thus the absence of a gender hierarchy within each rank. They also suggest "considerable mobility for women" (1991b:104) in that they indicate that women of all ranks rode horses. Information contained in the census record supports the existence of gender equality (though with increasing domination by men over time) in that land was allocated to each male and female adult and in the greater number of women than men recorded for each village, suggesting "a preference for sons over daughters had not yet arisen" (104). Other supporting evidence includes the role of a king's sister in directing ancestor worship ceremonies, the absence of any rule of linearity to kingly succession, the possible training of women for government positions, the equal participation of women and men in village-level ceremonies, women making up the majority of those who engaged with the supernatural, the existence of many important local female deities, and the majority of recorded displays of filial piety that were concerned with mothers, not fathers.

Archaeologically, relative gender equality can be seen, for example, in the burials from regions surrounding the capital. Many of these are male–female pairs, with each person having received nearly equal treatment in their separate but overlapping mounds. Male and female nobility also appear equally represented in the burial mounds, further suggesting a lack of gender stratification. Nelson (1991b, 1993) thus reaches several conclusions about the Silla case: 1) it was a stable state with a single hierarchical system in which women always had a place in society equal to men; 2) it demonstrates that gender inequality may arise after the formation of a state and that the source of female inequality does not stem from surplus extraction, elite control of production, militarism, or generalized coercion; 3) "state-level political and economic power can coexist with relative gender equality, as long as kinship is the basic organizing principle of the elites" (1993:311); and 4) the woman interred in Tomb 98 was the ruler—the secular and possibly spiritual/ritual leader—who may have ruled jointly with her husband as the military head as suggested by the large quantity of weapons in his grave.

Nelson (2003) also considers Silla conceptualizations of power in relation to ruling queens citing Lamphere's (2002) ritual power model—where "notions of power are . . . tied to ideas about the supernatural and about ritual power" (Nelson 2003:78)—as applicable to Silla due to the evidence for the continuation of gender balance during the periods of state formation and as a conquest state. Historic accounts indicate "the elite men were not more powerful than the elite women" and that "rank at birth was more important than gender" to determining rulership (83). Myths about early kings and queens indicate that only queens were descended from a supernatural parent; these myths may refer to "a time when access to the sacred was the most important element in accessing power and that the access belonged mostly or even exclusively to women" (83). Iconographic evidence—specifically relating the crown (such as the gold one accompanying the woman in Tomb 98) to shamanism—further suggests that the base of power was supernatural and came from ritual. Furthermore, Later Han dynasty accounts describe shamans in Korea as predominantly women. Thus, Nelson argues that given that the base of power for Silla rulership was supernatural and ritual and that it was primarily women who had connections to the spirit world, it should be of no surprise that they were rulers.

I have considered the relation between women's access to prestige and power (as political authority) through a study of the political economy of early historic (1521 to early 1600s) and protohistoric (ca. tenth to early sixteenth centuries A.D.) Visayan polities of the central Philippine Islands (Bacus 2002). The study draws on two anthropological insights on contemporary gender systems in Island Southeast Asia. First, "differences between people, including men and women, are often attributed to the activities the people in question engage in or the spiritual power they exhibit or fail to exhibit" (Errington 1990:58, cited in Bacus 2002:307); thus, to understand gender requires understanding local ideas of power and prestige and how males, females, and others are mapped onto power and prestige systems. Second, women in Centrist Archipelago societies—where "male and female are viewed as basically the same sort of beings"—tend to be systematically disadvantaged in the effort to achieve prestige as a result of "practice rather than stated rules" (Errington 1990:39, 55, cited in Bacus 2002:318).

Early Spanish observations suggest that in Visayan culture of the immediate pre-Hispanic period, gender relations and images of gender were reasonably egalitarian. Elite Visayan women, described as highly praised and powerful, possibly had as many dependents and slaves as their husbands. Although Visayan women had autonomy, equality, and power in several spheres, they nonetheless do not appear to have held positions of political authority (as ruling *datu*) during the early years of Spanish contact. The Western notion of political "power," better understood as "potency" or "spiritual potency" in Island Southeast Asia—an "intangible, mysterious and divine energy which animates the universe" (Anderson 1972:7, cited in Bacus 2002:318)—may help explain this situation. Potency is something leaders seek to accumulate, and since it is invisible, it can be known only by its signs. Signs of a person's potency include large amounts of wealth and substantial numbers of followers. Prestige derives from having potency. Within hierarchical polities, power/potency can be used to support those activities (such as ceremonies) that themselves are indicators of a person's or center's potency. In the early historic Philippines, prestige was marked by items of wealth, including local and foreign goods such as gold jewelry, porcelain, silk, some iron objects, bronze gongs, and slaves; archaeological evidence suggests that some of these were also such markers during the twelfth to early sixteenth centuries. Wealth items were generally restricted to members of the *datu* nobility, and in cases where they were not, *datu* held them in greater quantity. Elite women certainly owned items of wealth. However, their direct access to these goods—and hence their ability to accumulate greater quantities of wealth—was limited (received primarily through bride-price and through inheritance). Interestingly, *baylanes* (female ritual specialists) received wealth items for their services and thus could potentially accumulate further signs of potency; by definition, they must have exhibited spiritual potency. Why, then, if this "is culturally the sine qua non for political power and authority in the archipelago," was this not the case for these women? Potency's relation to political power and authority seems to be mediated by gender.

The direct acquisition of slaves and foreign items of wealth was key to accumulating signs of potency and prestige. Although reconstruction of women in the political economy of Visayan polities indicates that women produced the goods—textiles, rice, and pottery—used in exchange with interior groups for the valuable export resources that were important to the foreign trade that ultimately provided the exotica that signified potency, women did not control, sponsor, or engage directly in this trade. Nor were women active in slave raiding. Slaves provided much of the labor, of which there appear to have been shortages, for the extractive and productive activities (e.g., pearl diving and collecting of forest products) that produced the surplus required by the elite for participating in foreign trade. Both activities, as well as warfare, were male activities; *datu* sponsored and participated in long-distance maritime trade expeditions and were the leaders in warfare and of slave raids. More important, the men who participated in these activities, regardless of whether they were lesser nobles, commoners, or slaves, received some of the acquired wealth. Amounts varied according to status. Men of all statuses thus had greater opportunities for acquiring and accumulating potent objects than women. For those men (regardless of their class) who distinguished themselves in such activities, it was possible to become *datu* since membership in this class was not strictly hereditary in the Visayas.

The limited political authority of Visayan women during the early historic period may well extend back into the early second millennium A.D., the period of increased and intensified participation in foreign trade. If slave raiding and foreign trade were activities essential to establishing political authority—and at least the latter was not regularly engaged in until the protohistoric period—then transformations in the systems of prestige and power may have occurred and should be manifested in the material record. However, understanding the relation between gender and potency/power/prestige in prehistoric and protohistoric Visayan societies awaits future research.

Gendered Elite: Intersecting Identities

The majority of current gender archaeology research focuses on intersecting identities (as displayed at death) involving the elite (though often vis-à-vis other ranked statuses) in relationship to as well as among women and men in complex societies and early states of Mongolia and China. The earliest period for which such interrelationships are examined is the Late Neolithic (ca. 1600 B.C.) at the Dadianzi site in eastern Mongolia, the focus of Jui-man Wu's (2004) investigation of the relationship of sex, age, and social status to mortuary displays. Analysis focuses on 742 mostly single interment burials (with age determined for 659 individuals and sex for 234 males and 227 females), apparently grouped according to kin. Results suggest males held higher social status given their larger graves and greater quantities of animal bones and painted ceramics in their burial niches. Males may have also "accumulated more wealth than females" (77), as their coffins contained larger quantities of natural cowrie shells, possible symbols of wealth. Some grave goods appear gender specific: axes, shovels, arrowheads, and bronze pommels, for example, were exclusive to males, suggesting that they engaged in hunting, fighting, or planting activities; spindle whorls were exclusive to female burials (though some ornaments tended to concentrate with them as well).

For the elite—who appear to have been buried in the northern area based on the distribution of very rich burial goods (e.g., a concentration of natural cowrie shells) and their proximity to one another—results indicate that larger graves and quantities of painted ceramics not only characterized male burials but also differed according to the age of the interred male, suggesting that "the older male had a high social status" (J. Wu 2004:79). Furthermore, the larger grave sizes and quantities of painted ceramics with the four females buried near the highest-status older male (and considered a family unit) suggests that "the social status of elite females . . . was related to that of elite males with whom they were attached [through marriage] and that their privileged status was because they belonged to elite family groups" (79). Gender-specific grave goods among the elite appeared only with the males, all of whom had axes.

Jui-man Wu (2004:88) concludes that in this Late Neolithic society, the social status of males was associated with that of their natal family and that "male wealth was either inherited or achieved through individual activities in their own lifetime." In comparison, female wealth and social status hierarchies "were more complicated . . . since their social status was determined through the marriage and/or ascribed from their natal family" (86), inferred, for example, from the larger grave size and presence of cowry shells with a female burial in comparison to the nearby male burial.

Women of the Shang state are the focus of several papers by Linduff (2002, 2003) and Wang (2004). The interplay of gender, status, and royal power are examined in Linduff's (2002) textual and archaeological study of Shang royal women. Analysis of literary documents—early histories and legends—provides some insights into the expectations of and appropriate roles for women, particularly those married into the ruling elite. Legends suggest that royal women in particular held positions of importance and power in social, economic, political, and religious domains; of significance was women's practice of divination, indicating their "responsibilities for maintaining contact with ancestors, whose potency in all affairs of life had to be appeased" (62). As with the textual evidence of women in early Chinese history, there is limited archaeological evidence of royal women, and it derives from only two tombs out of the thousands of dynastic period excavated tombs; both are located in Yinxu/Anyang, the last Shang capital. These tombs belong to Lady Jing and Lady Hao, both queen consorts of the late Shang king Wu Ding (ca. 1250–1200 B.C.); Lady Jing was first wife and official queen. The differences in as well as intricacies of their social positions in this polygynous marriage are evident in their tombs and grave offering, even though both were given, according to the oracle bones, the prestigious title "*mu*, or mother, and were thereby entitled them to be recorded in the ritual worship calendar and to appeal to the ancestors themselves" (69). Location of their tombs is significant in this regard: Lady Jing was buried with royalty and interred in a royal-style tomb (i.e., with a ramp) unlike Lady Hao, who nonetheless was still "afforded all the luxury of a royal Shang burial" (70). Their tombs contained an abundance of weapons, and inscriptions suggest that both managed royal agricultural lands and were military leaders. Other grave goods—musical instruments, replicas of silk worms, jade spindle whorls, and agricultural tools—suggest connections to roles "ascribed to [them] . . . as they were to their legendary forebears" (71). For example, the musical instruments were of the type associated with the inventions of Nu Wa, their legendary royal founder.

Linduff (2002) thus argues that the mortuary data demonstrate the existence of ranking among Shang women and that actual Shang women exhibited many of the strengths attributed to mythological queens in early Chinese literature. Furthermore, the mortuary ritual that they were accorded resulted from their significance to political affairs. Artifacts of frontier style and manufacture in Lady Hao's tomb suggest that she may not have been a Shang elite; "polygyny in this case must have afforded greater political status for the Shang, since this marriage . . . apparently provided a means to increased alliances and hence power over a strategic area" (70–71). Similarly, the inclusion of the largest bronze ritual vessel and other royal-style items in Lady Jing's tomb was due to her high rank as first wife and "perhaps . . . [evidence of] a cross-cousin marriage allowing a concentration of power from within the king's kin group" (71). It appears that "Shang royal women had more value and power than women in later periods" who, according to historic accounts, did not enjoy the same freedom of movement, did not have the ability to hold significant positions in the military or foreign affairs, and did not manage land. Thus, the position of Shang women may be "remnants of women's status and role in an earlier society" (72–73).

Focusing more specifically on how the Shang elite expressed sex and gender in the burial of their women, and whose perceptions were being portrayed, Linduff (2003) reconstructs the status, roles, and ethnicity of the women buried at the royal cemetery at Anyang. Inscriptional evidence suggests the statuses and roles of the buried women were varied and that the types of female burials found indicates a system of ranking (in descending order): individual tombs or ones placed near the king's burial chamber that interred the royal wives or other elite women; single, casketed tombs for lesser elite women; simple graves, probably of commoners; and those associated with royal burials or burial grounds that contained the remains of sacrificial victims (though women appear to have been sacrificed only under special circumstances). The burials richest in content belonged to royal women (see the previously mentioned summary of Linduff [2002] regarding Lady Jing and Lady Hao), though they were less rich than the king's (their husband's) tomb, which was also larger in size. Differences in rank among women also appear to have been marked by the quantity of carved bone hairpins that "signified not only social position but also a gender role and in ways not assigned to the ritual bronzes and jades that appear in both male and female tombs" (269); similarly, the quantity and type of carved bone spatulas interred with men indicated their rank. Except for this difference, the tombs of the lower-ranked elite women were comparable to those of males of the same social rank and position. Linduff thus concludes that "upper-class Shang women did have power and individual identity, and that these were recognized in burial. . . . In the context of this royal center, the memory of these women's family backgrounds and positions in society was marked in their graves" (275).

Hierarchy among Shang women is further examined in Wang's (2004) study of Anyang mortuary and inscriptional evidence. Differences in the location (e.g., which cemetery within Anyang and the spatial relationship to male royal tombs and to other women's tombs), structure, size, and presence of ramps on three royal women's tombs indicate their different ranks. Grave items also indicate "the power wielded by the deceased during her lifetime" (104); in particular, the quantity and quality of the bronze ritual vessels in their tombs "signify the power and position of these elite women in court" (95–96). The presence of the largest bronze ritual vessel in Lady Jing's tomb thus "indicates . . . circumstance when a woman belonging to the royal elite enjoyed more rank and significance than even the male elite" (101). A woman's rank, however, was due not only to her relationship to the king. Some of the bronzes in Lady Hao's tomb represented her background, "proving that she came from the 'right' lineage and from a powerful and wealthy family" (103), whereas others were tribute items from another polity "that emphasize her position in court and her political importance to the Shang" (104). Their presence indicated her connection "with national power or [that she was] responsible for business at court" (104). The burial of a female sacrificial victim whose coffin was within a king's tomb also yielded bronzes but ones without inscriptions and special design indicating "a lack of both rank and wealth" (107). Also accompanying her was a headdress more elaborate than those found with the elite women as well as other body ornaments. Wang argues that women used their sexuality in their competitions for power at court and thus that such a headdress indicates that this woman, who was later sacrificed, was able to gain the king's favor.

Status and gender differences in the slightly later Western Zhou period (eighth to eleventh centuries B.C.) Yu cemeteries (in present-day Rujiazhuang, Baoji) are examined by Jiang (2004). Focusing on two of the twenty-one undisturbed graves, the analysis is informed by a view of an individual's status as deriving from political, gender, and kinship associations; lifestyle; and economic position in regard to access and control of the means of production. Status, however, is negotiable and open to manipulation, with mortuary treatment presenting a fixed image of how a person's status and identity were viewed by the living at that point in time. Thus, mortuary practice has some "predictable features . . . reflect[ing] the status of the individual when alive" (123). Interred in the two graves was a husband and wife couple (based on the structure, layout of the corpses, and bronze inscriptions); buried in the coffin next to the husband was his concubine (as determined from the grave goods). Differences in their respective burial treatment (e.g., eight sacrificial victims—including the concubine—with the husband vs. two accompanying the wife) and the quality and diversity of their bronze grave goods (e.g., forty vs. nineteen vessels, respectively; the presence of the most important ritual vessels with the husband) indicate the higher status of the husband, not unexpected given that he was an "earl" (the third rank among Western Zhou nobles) and held the highest political status among the Yu. The dedicatory bronzes, together with the presence of more burial goods, sacrificial victims, and an independent grave, indicate that the wife held a higher status than the concubine. The husband's dedicatory bronzes to his wife, in which he linked himself to the ancestral worship of her clan, also had political significance: the Yu were not politically powerful during the Western Zhou, and a marriage alliance with the historically known powerful Jing clan would have served to strengthen the Yu. Different types of bronze vessels, as well as other grave goods, were also marked gender distinctions. Weapons and tools also identified men and positions of power; horse-and-chariot items constituted another status symbol restricted to high-ranking men. Jiang concludes from the archaeological and inscriptional evidence that the rank and status of the elite women of the Western Zhou period was relative, based on their relation to that of their husbands as well as their own family background.

Gender, status, and social hierarchy in another Western Zhou state—the Jin state (eighth to tenth centuries B.C.)—form the focus of two studies: Yong's (2004) analysis of the Jin nobility interred at the Beizhao cemetery and Huang's (2004) analysis of burials of all social classes at the Qucun and Shangma cemeteries. Yong, in addition to examining the changing status of the wives of the Jin marquises over this 200-year period, evaluates previous assumptions about women's status during the Zhou period, specifically "that a woman's social position was determined primarily by that of her husband and that throughout this period women of all social ranks were treated with less respect than men in the same rank" (161). Analysis, based on a view that status is reflected in the structure, position, and contents of an individual's tomb, focuses on nineteen tombs (eleven intact) that jointly interred the Jin marquises and their wives. Results indicate that in the earliest (early Western Zhou) of the four mortuary phases, the wives' tombs were located to the east of the husband's, suggesting that the Jin rulers did not yet consider left as related to "auspicious, *yang*, male, east and superior" and right to their opposites. This placement was reversed in subsequent phases, indicating compliance with the "Zhou ritual regulations for noble women" (166). Ramps—an indicator of rank and status—were also present on the wives' tombs during the first three phases, suggesting a relatively high status of noble women who received "the same respect as their husbands" (191), though the latter's tomb pits, burial chambers, and coffins were generally larger in size. In the final phase, the two wives' tomb pits and burial chambers were larger with their outer coffins equal to or larger than that of their husband's, suggesting that "the regulations on the sizes of burial chambers and coffins of noble women had become less rigidly followed in the Jin state by the end of the Western Zhou period, and thus, the status of the wives might have been elevated" (173–74).

Other differences and changes are seen, for example, in chariot-and-horse and other sacrifices. While in the earliest phase sacrifices were dedicated to the couple instead of to the Jin marquise alone, beginning late in the second phase the marquises' burials had fewer chariots and their wives' none. Texts indicate horses and chariots were precious gifts from the Zhou kings and may have symbolized the rank and military power of the Jin marquises, while the wives' smaller and more beautifully decorated chariots "were probably used for transportation and some special ceremonial events" (Yong 2004:175). The marquises also had larger bronze ritual vessels—another status marker of the Zhou elite that indicated the right to perform certain types of ritual ceremonies—than their wives. While the numbers diminished for both over time, inscriptions on bronze vessels from a wife's tomb of the earliest phase suggests she could commission her own bronze ritual vessels; the fewer *ding* and *gui* bronze vessels with the later-period wives in comparison "to their husbands than earlier couples . . . [suggest] that the Zhou ritual regulations became more rigid after the middle Western Zhou and that the marquises . . . and their wives both had complied with this system after that" (179). However, the wives "had more freedom in the use of new types of bronze vessels," especially during the first and last phases, suggesting that there was more flexibility in the regulations on noble women (191). Similarly, the wives' tombs also contained a great quantity and variety of jades (some exclusive to women) that were also more elaborate than those in their respective husband's tomb, and this might relate to the increasing limitations on the use of bronze ritual vessels by noble women such that "jade objects became another indicator of their status and wealth" (191). Jade shrouds, present only in the burials of the marquises and their first wives (beginning in the second phase), possibly marked status among the noblewomen. Other items exclusive to the tombs of the marquises include *zhong* bells (important in ritual ceremonies) and chime stones, both also "markers of male power in the Jin state" (184), as well as weapons and gold objects.

Although the status of the marquises' wives was generally lower than that of their husbands, Yong (2004) argues it was not static through the Zhou period as previously assumed. The changes exhibited in the status of noblewomen resulted from political circumstances; for example, beginning in the second phase, the Zhou court imposed ritual reforms that entailed greater ritual limitations on noble women, and thus the wives' status decreased. However, in the last phase, "evidence show[s] that the Zhou ritual regulations were not strictly followed. . . . Because of the increased power of vassal lords and the loss of real power of the Zhou king, or for political and diplomatic considerations [i.e., wives may have come from the Yang and Qi states], ritual regulations were violated so that the wives of the marquises of Jin enjoyed more richness and variety in their burial furnishings and burial goods" (196–97).

Huang's (2004) study of two Jin state cemeteries (Qucun and Shangma) containing more than 2,000 burials (with biological sex determined for more than 1,500 skeletons) of dukes, middle- to lower-ranked aristocrats, and commoners entails analysis of grave good categories to ascertain differences and changes in gender, status, and ranking displayed in mortuary practices. Results suggest that in the early Western Zhou, gender distinctions were made through greater quantities of bronze goods (weapons, tools, and ritual vessels) and jade items placed with male and female burials, respectively. Such a distinction marked the graves of the ducal couples as well as those of the middle to lower aristocracy, whose female burials also contained a higher proportion of the pottery vessels. The male-associated bronze weapons were "transformed into jade and stone pieces strung along with plaques into decorated necklace or pendant sets and as small life-preserving amulets" in the female burials (158). By the late Western Zhou, bronze *ge* declined, and "large jade (or stone) *ge* ... begins to reappear ... as protective staff or talisman, in tombs of high-ranking men and women, and ornamental jades begin to proliferate typologically and numerically in male burials. Aside from the addition of stringed ornamental sets, the jade (and stone) *erjue* earrings that had long been exclusive to women are now favored by men as well" (158). As usage and quantity of ornamental jades in burials of male aristocrats became similar over time to that of the female burials, a decline occurred in pottery, lacquer ware, and chariot furnishings in female burials. These changes indicate a break with the gender equality established in the early Western Zhou and the placement of "women within the same classification and ranking measure as men and used a single system of ritual regulations to redefine the relative social position of men and women" (158). The "function of ornamental jades changed from an index of the (female) owner's taste, to a symbol of the economic status of the occupant (of either gender). Accordingly, in contrast to bronze ritual vessels, even though quantity in jade artifacts does to some extent reflect social class regulation, the class system is not bound by jade usage" (158–59). By the Spring and Autumn period, burials of high and middle aristocracy had concentrations of jade and stone artifacts; jade and stone *gui* and *jue* were major items in burials across ranks and gender. Female burials, though, had fewer stone *gui* than those of males from the same period or of the same status; the earring-type *jue* reflect women's special taste in body ornamentation. Differences in their respective quantities of *jue* continued into the middle Spring and Autumn period.

As with the first paper discussed in this section, the final one, by Xiaolong Wu (2004), focuses on pastoral groups of Mongolia but of a later period. This gender-informed challenge to previous interpretations of the third- to fifth-century B.C. Maoqinggou cemetery entails reconsideration of two views: that social differentiation was based on neither age nor sex and that underlying the social structure was an acquired wealth system. Analysis focuses on seventy-nine single graves, particularly fifty-nine adult burials (with twenty-one female and thirty-eight male skeletons identified), from this cemetery "for common people of a lower rank" (206), which had two distinct groups of graves (sixty-seven graves oriented east–west and twelve oriented north–south, located mainly in the north and south areas, respectively). For the east–west graves (of thirty males and thirteen females), results suggest wealth and gender differences. The slightly larger average size and greater variation in size of the graves of females indicate a "greater inequality in energy expenditure than [for] male tombs" (208). More male graves contained pottery and animal sacrifices, the latter in larger quantities than found in the female graves, which Wu suggests were indicators of the wealth of the deceased; the particular importance of horses to a pastoral society suggests that sacrificed horse skulls, exclusive to male burials, indicate "the superior wealth, and even social status, of the deceased" (221). Female burials with animal sacrifices did not have ornaments—"the most important type of grave gift at Maoqinggou"—suggesting that these two types "were markers of certain incompatible social identities for the female; among males, they were used simultaneously to display wealth and status" (211–12). Beads from necklaces occurred more frequently and in larger quantities in female graves, whereas buckles were found primarily with males. Belt decorations, another item displaying wealth and status, also differed with small belt ornaments more common in female burials and the large and complicated ones associated mainly with male burials, though one female had the most elaborate ornaments and belt plaques of the most precious materials. Body ornaments were thus "aimed first at displaying wealth and status, instead of gender" (224). Metal weapons and tools, exclusive to some male graves, probably "marked [these] males as warriors" as well as their wealth and status among males as "tombs with weapons were also rich in other grave goods" (214). The absence of weapons in female tombs is attributed to differences in roles rather than differences in wealth between males and females; "status afforded by wealth was not hierarchical only according to gender" (214).

Xialong Wu (2004) suggests that the "acquired wealth: model thus fits the evidence from the adult male tombs—as "the well-furnished male tombs belonged to individuals older than thirty-five years, and one male of twenty-two to twenty-four years of age was buried without any grave goods" (227)—but not that of the female tombs, where several elderly females' tombs lacked grave goods, while those of some younger females were well-furnished, including that of the twenty-five-year-old female with the richest tomb. Instead, the graves of wealthy young females contained ascribed wealth; in the case of the very wealthy female, "she might have married in from another group outside of the Maoqinggou community, and her elaborate ornaments may have displayed the wealth of her natal family" (228). Thus, "while males might achieve their wealth through personal effort, females had different methods to obtain and display their wealth. This does not mean that females could not achieve wealth as males did; instead, grave goods in female tombs emphasize ascribed wealth, probably defined by women's role in marriage alliances between clans" (231).

The graves oriented north–south differed from those oriented east–west in structure (e.g., stamped fills) and were of larger size but contained fewer grave goods. Comparison of the adult burials "indicates that the females among them were better treated at death than the males" (X. Wu 2004:229); the former displayed more wealth, and two were interred in wooden coffins with one also placed inside a wooden chamber. The presence of spindle whorls in their graves "suggest a specific gender role of the female . . . and indicates females' economic and social significance" (230). The overall absence of animal sacrifices and bronze harnesses, however, suggests a different cultural tradition that coexisted with that of the east–west burials. The use of wooden chambers and coffins among the former suggest that it "was closely associated with the agricultural culture in the Central Plain area;" other graves goods (e.g., spindle whorls, agate rings) also indicate a close affinity to dynastic Chinese burials. The Maoqinggou community thus appears to have had "a mixed and complex cultural identity" (229).

Concluding Remarks: Future Directions

As this overview shows, gender archaeology in East and Southeast Asia is both challenging and enhancing our understanding of the past. Critiques of previous interpretations of the East Asian past highlight essentialized notions of women and androcentric assumptions and inferences as well as gender imbalances in archaeological practice and the link to gender-biased interpretations. Archaeological research also provides new insights on the following: gendered labor activities and status equality among early farming groups in late prehistoric Thailand, among hunter-gatherer communities in the Andaman Islands, and among early dynastic period pastoral groups in northeastern China and the Dian polity in southern China; metaphorical connections between Jomon figurines, female reproduction, and annual regeneration of food resources; few gender distinctions to Bronze Age Thailand mortuary practices; a link between high status and women's craft production and/or the control of it at Khok Phanom Di and in the Dian polity as well as between men's high status and horsemanship and warfare among the Dian and in Western Zhou states; variability in views of gender and death among communities of the Majiayao and Qijia; the high status of females, as deities and/or among the living, in Neolithic China; the mediation of potency, political power, and authority by gender in Visayan polities; gender equality in early Korean state societies; gendered wealth systems among pastoral groups of Inner Mongolia; and complex interrelations between gender and status hierarchies in early Chinese states.

These studies also illustrate areas requiring further attention. Among these are the need for greater attention to the substantial literature on the archaeology of gender, including theoretically based discussions of conceptualizations of gender, critical consideration of working assumptions (e.g., the "reflective" nature of the evidence), and elimination of androcentric and other biases. These studies provide support for the view that gender archaeology does not necessitate the development of new methodologies; however, greater methodological rigor is sometimes needed, as is attention to the significant literature on mortuary analysis.

Specialists in Chinese archaeology propose directions to further gender research in this region. For Linduff and Sun (2004), this includes the use of theoretical models that have been applied to other regions, the development of gendered social theory, and comparative studies to bring together insights from Chinese gender archaeology and from other regions of the world. Also important will be facilitating fieldwork focused on gender questions as well as disseminating results to and engaging in discussion of gender archaeology with colleagues in China. Shelach (2004), in his discussion of the "continuity" model currently dominating Chinese archaeology, criticizes it for trivializing gender and other aspects of social structure and advocates "research that focuses on the development and change of gender relations while retaining the modern notion of multilineal trajectories and taking advantage of advanced methods of data recovery and analysis" (24). Advancing gender archaeology will require better definition of those Chinese terms that have several meanings (e.g., one term that translates as both matrilocal and dualocal); more focused and a greater diversity of research questions; multiple types of evidence to include iconography and materials from domestic sites to complement the extensive reliance on mortuary remains; and "a clear paradigm on gender relations from which working hypotheses may be drawn" (26).

As archaeological research on gender in East and Southeast Asia grows, it will present further challenges to and new perspectives on these regions' prehistory and early history. In doing so, it will undoubtedly inform our larger comparative and theoretical understanding of gender, gender relations, and gender processes.

Acknowledgments

I wish to thank Sarah Nelson for inviting me to contribute to this volume and for her support of my research on gender in Southeast Asia. My thanks also to Fumiko Ikawa-Smith for references and drawing my attention to unpublished literature and to Yan Sun for assistance with locating archaeological sites on the map included in this chapter.

References

Anderson, Benedict
    1972   The Idea of Power in Javanese Culture. In *Culture and Politics in Indonesia*. C. Holt, ed. Pp. 1–69. Ithaca, NY: Cornell University Press.

Bacus, Elisabeth A.
    2002   Accessing Prestige and Power: Women in the Political Economy of Visayan Polities. In *In Pursuit of Gender: Worldwide Archaeological Approaches*. S. M. Nelson and M. Rosen-Ayalon, eds. Pp. 307–22. Walnut Creek, CA: AltaMira Press.
    In press   Expressing Gender in Bronze Age Northeast Thailand: The Case of Non Nok Tha. In *Archaeology and Women*. S. Hamilton, R. Whitehouse, and K. Wright, eds. London: University College London Press.

Chiou-Peng, Tze-huey
    2004   Horsemen in the Dian Culture of Yunnan. In *Gender and Chinese Archaeology*. K. M. Linduff and Yan Sun, eds. Pp. 289–313. Walnut Creek, CA: AltaMira Press.

Cooper, Zarine
    2002   The Enigma of Gender in the Archaeological Record of the Andaman Islands. In *In Pursuit of Gender: Worldwide Archaeological Approaches*. S. M. Nelson and M. Rosen-Ayalon, eds. Pp. 173–85. Walnut Creek, CA: AltaMira Press.

Cuevas, Nida
    2003   The Men and Women of Maitum. In *Pang-Alay: Ritual Pottery in Ancient Philippines*. C. Valdes, ed. Pp. 63–69. Makati City: Ayala Museum.

Errington, Shelly
    1990   Recasting Sex, Gender and Power: A Theoretical and Regional Overview. In *Power and Difference: Gender in Island Southeast Asia*. J. M. Atkinson and S. Errington, eds. Pp. 1–58. Palo Alto, CA: Stanford University Press.

Gilchrist, Roberta
    1999   *Gender and Archaeology: Contesting the Past*. London: Routledge.

Habu, Junko
    2004   *Ancient Jomon of Japan*. Cambridge: Cambridge University Press.

Higham, Charles
    2002   Women in the Prehistory of Mainland Southeast Asia. In *In Pursuit of Gender: Worldwide Archaeological Approaches*. S. M. Nelson and M. Rosen-Ayalon, eds. Pp. 207–24. Walnut Creek, CA: AltaMira Press.

Higham, Charles, and Rachanie Thosarat
    1994   *Khok Phanom Di: Prehistoric Adaptation to the World's Richest Habitat*. Fort Worth, TX: Harcourt Brace College Publishers.

Huang, Tsui-mei
    2004   Gender Differentiation in Jin State Jade Regulations. In *Gender and Chinese Archaeology*. K. M. Linduff and Yan Sun, eds. Pp. 137–60. Walnut Creek, CA: AltaMira Press.

Ikawa-Smith, Fumiko
    2002   Gender in Japanese Prehistory. In *In Pursuit of Gender: Worldwide Archaeological Approaches*. S. M. Nelson and M. Rosen-Ayalon, eds. Pp. 323–54. Walnut Creek, CA: AltaMira Press.

Ikawa-Smith, Fumiko, and Junko Habu
    1998   Women in Japanese Archaeology. Paper presented at the Indo-Pacific Prehistory Association 16th Congress, Melaka, Malaysia, July 1–7.

Jiang, Yu
    2004   Ritual Practice, Status, and Gender Identity: Western Zhou Tombs at Baoji. In *Gender and Chinese Archaeology*. K. M. Linduff and Yan Sun, eds. Pp. 117–36. Walnut Creek, CA: AltaMira Press.

Jiao, Tianlong
    2001   Gender Studies in Chinese Neolithic Archaeology. In *Gender and the Archaeology of Death*. B. Arnold and N. Wickers, eds. Pp. 51–62. Walnut Creek, CA: AltaMira Press.

Joyce, Rosemary, and Cheryl Claassen
    1997   Women in the Ancient Americas: Archaeologists, Gender, and the Making of Prehistory. In *Women in Prehistory: North America and Mesoamerica*. C. Claassen and R. Joyce, eds. Pp. 1–14. Philadelphia: University of Pennsylvania Press.

Keightley, David
    1999   At the Beginning: The Status of Women in Neolithic and Shang China. *Nan nü: Men, Women and Gender in Early and Imperial China* 1(1):1–62.

Lamphere, Louise
    2002   Gender Theory in Anthropology: Its Relevance for Archaeology. Paper presented at the Society for American Archaeology 67th Annual Meeting, Denver, May 20–24.

Li, Jian-jing
    2004   Gender Relations and Labor Division at the Pingyang Site. In *Gender and Chinese Archaeology*. K. M. Linduff and Yan Sun, eds. Pp. 237–55. Walnut Creek, CA: AltaMira Press.

Linduff, Katheryn
    2002   Women's Lives Memorialized in Burial in Ancient China at Anyang. In *In Pursuit of Gender: Worldwide Archaeological Approaches*. S. M. Nelson and M. Rosen-Ayalon, eds. Pp. 257–87. Walnut Creek, CA: AltaMira Press.
    2003   Many Wives, One Queen in Shang China. In *Ancient Queens: Archaeological Explorations*. S. M. Nelson, ed. Pp. 59–76. Walnut Creek, CA: AltaMira Press.

Linduff, Katheryn M., and Yan Sun
    2004   Introduction: Gender and Chinese Archaeology. In *Gender and Chinese Archaeology*. K. Linduff and Yan Sun, eds. Pp. 1–8. Walnut Creek, CA: AltaMira Press.

Man, E. H.
    1885   On the Andaman Islands, and Their Inhabitants. *Journal of the Anthropological Institute of Great Britain and Ireland* 14:253–72.

Mizoguchi, Koji
    2002   *An Archaeological History of Japan: 30,000 B.C. to A.D. 700*. Philadelphia: University of Pennsylvania Press.

Nagamine, Mitsukazu
    1986   Clay Figurines and Jomon Society. In *Windows on the Japanese Past: Studies in Archaeology and Prehistory*. R. Pearson, ed. Pp. 255–65. Ann Arbor: Center for Japanese Studies, University of Michigan.

Nelson, Sarah
    1991a   The "Goddess Temple" and the Status of Women at Niuheliang, China. In *The Archaeology of Gender*. Proceedings of the 22nd Annual Chacmool Conference. D. Walde and N. D. Willows, eds. Pp. 302–8. Calgary: Department of Archaeology, University of Calgary.
    1991b   The Status of Women in Ko-Silla: Evidence from Archaeology and Historical Documents. *Korea Journal*, summer 1991, 101–7.
    1991c   Women Archaeologists in Asia and the Pacific. In *The Archaeology of Gender*. Proceedings of the 22nd Annual Chacmool Conference. D. Walde and N. D. Willows, eds. Pp. 217–19. Calgary: Department of Archaeology, University of Calgary.
    1993   Gender Hierarchy and the Queens of Silla. In *Sex and Gender Hierarchies*. B. D. Miller, ed. Pp. 297–315. Cambridge: Cambridge University Press.
    1997   *Gender in Archaeology: Analyzing Power and Prestige*. Walnut Creek, CA: AltaMira Press.
    1998   Reflections on Gender Studies in African and Asian Archaeology. In *Gender and African Archaeology*. S. Kent, ed. Pp. 285–94. Walnut Creek, CA: AltaMira Press.
    2002   Ideology, Power, and Gender: Emergent Complex Society in Northeastern China. In *In Pursuit of Gender: Worldwide Archaeological Approaches*. S. M. Nelson and M. Rosen-Ayalon, eds. Pp. 73–80. Walnut Creek, CA: AltaMira Press.
    2003   The Queens of Silla: Power and Connections to the Spirit World. In *Ancient Queens: Archaeological Explorations*. S. Nelson, ed. Pp. 77–82. Walnut Creek, CA: AltaMira Press.

Pearson, Richard
    1988   Chinese Neolithic Burial Patterns: Problems of Method and Interpretation in Early China. *Early China* 13:1–45.

Radcliffe-Brown, A. A.
    1922   *The Andaman Islanders*. Cambridge: Cambridge University Press.

Rode, Penny
    2004   Textile Production and Female Status in Bronze Age Yunnan. In *Gender and Chinese Archaeology*. K. M. Linduff and Yan Sun, eds. Pp. 315–38. Walnut Creek, CA: AltaMira Press.

Sanday, Peggy
    1981   *Female Power and Male Dominance*. Cambridge: Cambridge University Press.

Shelach, Gideon
    2004   Marxist and Post-Marxist Paradigms for the Neolithic. In *Gender and Chinese Archaeology*. K. M. Linduff and Yan Sun, eds. Pp. 11–27. Walnut Creek, CA: AltaMira Press.

Shoocongdej, Rasmi
    2002   Gender Roles Depicted in Rock Art: A Case from Western Thailand. In *In Pursuit of Gender: Worldwide Archaeological Approaches*. S. M. Nelson and M. Rosen-Ayalon, eds. Pp. 187–206. Walnut Creek, CA: AltaMira Press.

Sørensen, Marie
    2000   *Gender Archaeology*. Cambridge: Polity Press.

Sun, Yan, and Hongyu Yang
    2004   Gender Ideology and Mortuary Practice in Northwestern China. In *Gender and Chinese Archaeology*. K. M. Linduff and Yan Sun, eds. Pp. 29–46. Walnut Creek, CA: AltaMira Press.

Wang, Ying
    2004   Ritual and Power among Court Ladies at Anyang. In *Gender and Chinese Archaeology*. K. M. Linduff and Yan Sun, eds. Pp. 95–113. Walnut Creek, CA: AltaMira Press.

Wu, Jui-man
    2004   The Late Neolithic Cemetery at Dadianzi, Inner Mongolia Autonomous Region. In *Gender and Chinese Archaeology*. K. M. Linduff and Sun Yan, eds. Pp. 47–91. Walnut Creek, CA: AltaMira Press.

Wu, Xiaolong
    2004   Female and Male Status Displayed at the Maoqinggou Cemetery. In *Gender and Chinese Archaeology*. K. M. Linduff and Yan Sun, eds. Pp. 203–35. Walnut Creek, CA: AltaMira Press.

Yong, Ying
    2004   Gender, Status, Ritual Regulations, and Mortuary Practice in the State of Jin. In *Gender and Chinese Archaeology*. K. M. Linduff and Yan Sun, eds. Pp. 161–202. Walnut Creek, CA: AltaMira Press.

Gender and Archaeology in South and Southwest Asia

20

CARLA M. SINOPOLI

THE TWO REGIONS CONSIDERED in this chapter—Southwest and South Asia—occupy very different places in the archaeological imaginations of Western readers. Southwest Asia, including the "fertile crescent" and Mesopotamia, is seen as a land of firsts and has been the focus of considerable origins-focused research—of agriculture, village life, the state, and empires. Its associations with the major religious traditions of Judaism, Christianity, and Islam (and Zoroastrianism) have made it an ancestral place for a significant portion of the world's population, creating a sense of ownership and identity that extends far beyond the region's geographic borders. In contrast, the archaeology of South Asia, including the modern countries of Afghanistan, Pakistan, Nepal, Bangladesh, India, and Sri Lanka, is largely unknown outside the region (with the exclusion of the Indus Valley or Harappan civilization, often discussed as a case of primary state formation). Despite these differences, the two areas that are the focus of this chapter share some important features beyond their geographic proximity both in their respective histories of archaeology and in the dominance of textual sources in shaping and defining research questions and interpretations of archaeological evidence.

Both Southwest and South Asia have long and rich histories of archaeological research, originating under nineteenth-century European colonialism and continuing until the present. In both also, archaeological research and archaeological remains (sites, monuments, and sculptures) figure prominently in contemporary political struggles and in the construction and contestation of diverse national, regional, ethnic, and religious identities. And, particularly for studies of states and empires of "historic periods," rich written sources—recorded on clay tablets, palm leaf documents, papyrus, and seals or inscribed on boulders, stone stele, carved images, or structures—have played important roles in shaping the directions of archaeological research and interpretations of material evidence. While these concerns are not the primary focus of this chapter, they nonetheless figure importantly throughout this review of research on gender structures, relations, ideologies, and representations in the prehistoric and early historic pasts of Southwest and South Asia.

Another similarity is that while references to what we would now refer to as gender are not uncommon in the archaeological literature from both regions, theoretically informed research focused specifically on this topic is both rare and undeveloped. This is particularly the case in South Asia, where the first overview article specifically focused on the topic was published in 2004 (Ray 2004) and includes a bibliography of only some twenty-seven citations (of which only sixteen cite specifically South Asian studies). Southwest Asia fares a little better in this regard, thanks to the contributions of scholars such as Zagarell (1986), Pollock (1991, 1999; Pollock and Bernbeck 2000), and Wright (1996, 1998), among others, but nonetheless gender is rarely a significant focus of archaeological research. In this chapter, I first discuss each region separately before moving on to some broader discussions of major themes and future potential for gender research in both.

South Asia

As noted, studies of gender have been rare in archaeological research on the prehistory and early history of South Asia. However, when the frame is broadened somewhat to consider historical, art-historical, and epigraphic work, the literature expands considerably (Boivin and Fuller 2002:205–6). Since the colonial period, art historians have been considered with sculptural representations of women and with questions of sexuality. Images of full-breasted, nearly nude goddesses (*yakshis*) on temple walls and of couples engaged in erotic activities at such sites as Khajuraho aroused the moral outrage of numerous colonial commentators, confirming European prejudices about Indian womanhood and the need for social reform. However, during nationalist struggles, before and after Indian independence, these images have been reinterpreted and valorized as powerful representations of a uniquely Indian spiritual transcendental religious aesthetic that creatively merged the "sublime and the sensual" (Guha-Thakurta 2004:255 [also broader discussions in chaps. 7 and 8 therein]). Guha-Thakurta (2004), Dehejia (1997, 1999), and Desai (1975, 2000) have written in considerable detail about changing interpretations of female temple images.

Other gender-focused discussions prominent in the colonial period concerned the ritual of sati, or self-immolation of Hindu women on the funeral pyres of their deceased husbands (Sharma 1988). Such acts were, particularly in South

India, commemorated in sculpted stone stele, or memorial stones, and here I review an important archaeological study of memorial stone distributions and meanings in the Nilgiri Hills region of inland South India. Additional gender-focused studies have examined inscriptions on Buddhist monasteries and Hindu temples to evaluate the diverse positions of women: as donors (Willis 1992), as Buddhist nuns (Skilling 2001; Willis 1985), and as "temple women" in medieval South Indian Hindu temples (Orr 2000). I will not discuss these studies in detail here since my primary focus is on archaeological analyses, but I do note that, in general, inscriptional analyses have revealed the broad range of roles held by elite women in specific historical and institutional contexts—as pilgrims, worshippers, temple functionaries, and donors to religious institutions who were able to autonomously dispose of personal wealth. Here, however, I restrict my focus to strictly archaeological studies. These largely concern the representation of human forms—in ceramic figurines and sculpture, usually interpreted in a religious framework (especially "mother goddesses"); to date, very little research has focused on social, political, or economic dimensions of gender in South Asian archaeology.

Representations of Gender

The greatest attention to gender in the South Asian archaeological literature has been in the study of female figurines, predominantly hand- and mold-made ceramic images. These are known from a wide range of sites and regions, spanning from the Neolithic village site of Mehrgarh in Baluchistan (western Pakistan) through early historic urban centers of the North Indian Ganges Basin. As in other regions of the world (see Lesure 2000, 2002), female figurines from both rural and urban contexts in South Asia have been most commonly interpreted as "mother goddesses," fertility images, or, less often, toys. Recently, however, a number of scholars have tried to push these analyses further, examining temporal changes in figurine style, associations of female figurines with other contemporary animal or human representations, and their inter- and intrasite spatial and contextual distributions.

MEHRGAH: A NEOLITHIC VILLAGE COMMUNITY   South Asia's earliest tradition of ceramic figurine production is evident at the important Neolithic settlement of Mehrgarh in Baluchistan (figure 20.1), dating from the early seventh through the early third millennium B.C. This remarkable site, excavated in the 1970s and 1980s by Jarrige et al. (1995), is the earliest Neolithic community in South Asia, with evidence for domesticated wheat and barley and domestic ani-

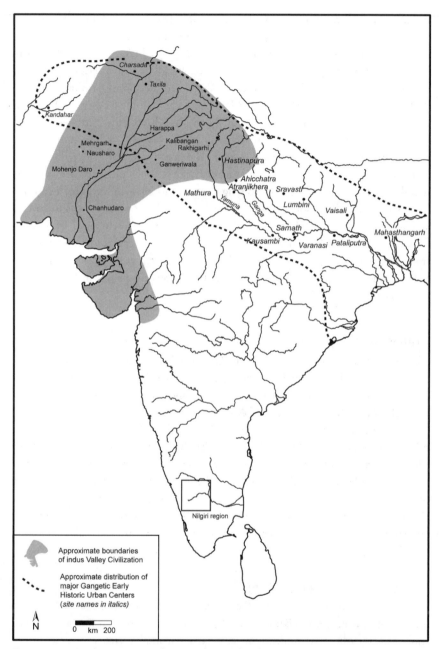

Figure 20.1. South Asia: Sites and regions discussed in the text.

mals from its lowest layers. Throughout its continuous occupation for more than four millennia, archaeologists have documented a complex sequence of architectural development and economic intensification and specialization. Developments in Baluchistan and nearby regions are generally argued to have created the conditions for the emergence of the urban Indus Valley civilization in the mid-third millennium B.C.E.

Paralleling the social and economic changes documented at Mehrgarh are changes in gendered representations of humans (Jarrige 1991). Clay figurines appear from the earliest levels at Mehrgarh (before the first ceramic vessels) and were produced throughout its entire occupation. They are relatively common, typically recovered in domestic trash and household contexts. The earliest are crude depictions of headless seated figures with outstretched legs and large hips (Jarrige 1991). Although they lack distinctive sexual features, they have been typically interpreted as female (Ardeleanu-Jansen 2002). Over time, these figures became more sophisticated and naturalistic, and by 4000 B.C., seated female figurines with elaborate hairstyles, ornaments, large hips, and pronounced breasts were being produced. No male figurines were produced during this period.

During the last phase of occupation of Mehrgarh (Period VII, ca. 2900–2600 B.C.), standing figurines appear at Mehrgarh and other nearby sites. Hairstyle and ornamentation became more elaborate, and male figurines appear for the first time, marked by genitalia, turban-like headdresses, and a pendant ornament (Ardeleanu-Jansen 2002; Jarrige 1984, 1991). Animal representations, found throughout the sequence, also became more numerous and diverse at this time. As figurines grew more complex, they also become increasingly standardized in form, suggesting large-scale production by specialists, a pattern also evident in the production of ceramic vessels. Three dominant human figurine types were produced: ornamented females, females holding babies, and standing turbaned males (Jarrige 1991:91). Similar changes are evident in figurine production in other contemporary Baluchi sites, including the large settlement of Nindowari (Jarrige 1984), a Kulli tradition site in southern Baluchistan.

Near the very end of Mehrgarh's occupation (Period VIId), a new figurine variant appeared that Jarrige (1991:92) refers to as a "composite type ... of high quality." At this time of stylistic change, female figurines decline in frequency, and standing turbaned males come to account for nearly 85 percent of all human representations (Jarrige 1991; Possehl 2002:179). In addition, females are no longer depicted holding children, though several male figurines are, perhaps reflective of changing ideologies of family, household, or property.

Both the marked changes in figurine iconography and diversity in the period immediately before state emergence and the emergence of a shared tradition of figurine production over a broad geographic area suggest that changes in gender representation were part of a larger suite of social, political, and ideological transformations. Without greater information than currently available from the suggestive publications cited previously, it is not possible to evaluate the precise nature of these changes, but the evidence does indicate that detailed analysis of the social contexts, uses, iconography, and symbolic referents (Lesure 2002) of human figurines may yield important insights into gender ideologies and gender representation in Baluchistan during a period of remarkable social, political, economic, and ideological transformation.

GENDER IN THE INDUS VALLEY CIVILIZATION: REPRESENTATIONS IN LIFE AND DEATH The Indus Valley or Harappan civilization (ca. 2600–1900 B.C.) is best known for the emergence of large urban centers and standardized material forms across a broad geographic region, including Pakistan and portions of western and northern India (fig. 20.1). Major urban sites of the period include Harappa, Mohenjo Daro, Ganweriwala (in Pakistan), and Dholavira and Rakhigarhi in India and more than 1,000 smaller sites with diagnostic Indus architecture, ceramics, or other material remains, including inscribed seals in a still unreadable script. Specialists disagree on the interpretations of Indus political organization, ideological structures, and coherence; here, I concern myself only with questions of gender, focusing on two categories of evidence that have been considered by Indus specialists: gendered representation in figurines, sculpture, and seals and mortuary data.

Figurines Ceramic figurines were produced in several sites of the Harappan or Indus Valley tradition. In general, they were far more varied than at earlier Mehrgarh and likely drew on several prior regional traditions, including those of Baluchistan discussed previously (Possehl 2002:180). While human figurines are common at Mohenjo Daro, Harappa, and several other sites in the Indus and Baluchistan regions, they are rare or absent in sites in Gujarat and India, pointing to regional variations in both the prominence of human representation and the activities in which these figurines were used. At Mohenjo Daro and Harappa, both male and female figurines were produced, probably by specialist potters (Kenoyer 1998:1, 11), with female representations generally more common than males (comprising as many as 80 percent of all human images in some areas of Mohenjo Daro; Ardeleanu-Jansen 2002:208). It is, however, not always possible to "sex" the figurines, and Possehl (2002:181) has suggested that gender ambiguity may have been a deliberate choice of figurine producers.

Indus period figurines vary considerable in form and ornamentation. Three broad categories of female figurines may be distinguished: 1) slender standing females wearing rich jewelry, short skirts or loincloths and elaborate headdresses with pannier-like protuberances that sometimes show evidence of burning; 2) large-bellied females with no ornaments; and 3) rarer "active" female figures, shown engaged in activities of daily life, including seated on cots, carrying trays or drums, or laboring. Male figurines are distinguished by beards and genitalia and typically have less elaborate ornamentation than females (Ardeleanu-Jansen 2002); they are depicted in either standing or kneeling poses.

In an ongoing effort to systematize information on figurine provenience from Mohenjo Daro (most recovered from poorly documented early twentieth-century excavations), Ardeleanu-Jansen (2002) has been attempting to reconstruct recovery contexts. Most were recovered from secondary contexts, specifically domestic trash; none came from contexts interpretable as shrines, altars, or temples. Ardeleanu-Jansen suggests that figurines were thus used predominantly in household rituals, though she recognizes that they may have served other nonreligious functions as well. Both the variability in form and ambiguity suggest that simple "mother goddess" interpretation of the female images held by earlier researchers is not valid and that these images may have served a variety of roles in Indus households.

Other Representations   Humans are also represented in a small number of larger stone figures of seated males, in a few bronze images, and on a small group of stone seals, sealing, and tablets. While some female representations are known from these materials (e.g., the two bronze "dancing" girls; Possehl 2002:113), unlike for the ceramic figurines, male images predominate. The seated stone sculptures are the largest sculptural images of the Indus tradition and are known from the urban center of Mohenjo Daro. The ten Mohenjo-Daro sculptures include five heads and five seated figures; most are damaged or broken (Ratnagar 1991:75–77). They "seem to represent a formal style of sculpture depicting a seated, bearded male with a cloak thrown over one shoulder and hands resting on the knees" (Kenoyer 1998:100). Four of the five heads, including the famous image often termed the "priest-king," are depicted with headbands, perhaps a golden fillet, similar to some found in burial contexts; some may also have had headdresses attached. It is not clear who is being represented in these images, and they are variously interpreted as rulers (Ratnagar 1991:76) or clan leaders or ancestral figures rather than deities (Kenoyer 1998:102). Most, if not all, depict males (one unbearded figure may be female but is too damaged to clearly identify; Possehl 2002).

Human or composite human–animal figures interpreted as deities appear on

Indus seals, on steatite tablets, and in some ceramic figures and masks. Most common are horned figures, including images of bearded males with large curved horns resembling those of a water buffalo, emanating from the sides of an elaborate headdress. These figures are sometimes depicted cross-legged, in a yogic-like pose, and, as in the famous "proto-Shiva" seal, are associated with fierce wild animals, such as tigers. Other male images have smaller bull-like horns and are sometimes depicted with tails and hoofed hind legs (Kenoyer 1998:102); small ceramics masks of these bullhorn figures have also been recovered. Images of horned women also occur though are less common than males.

A small number of narrative scenes are known from tablets or seals. These include, for example, a famous seal from Mohenjo Daro whose lower tier depicts a procession of seven horned figures of unidentified gender, approaching a horned male figure, standing in a space defined by a branching tree. Before him kneels another horned figure, and behind him or her stands a large bull. Other narratives depict human–animal confrontations. A terra-cotta tablet recovered in recent excavations at Harappa depicts a female, shown standing above an elephant and between two tigers, whose throats she holds in each hand (Kenoyer 1998:115). These images are not common at Indus sites and, except for the sculptures (themselves only a few feet tall), tend to occur in miniaturized forms, on small portable artifacts, suggesting use in intimate contexts of households or small groups. They certainly suggest a complex array of deities or sacred figures, predominantly but not exclusively male, probably associated with elaborate stories concerning nature, humans, and the supernatural.

Indus Mortuary Behavior Ideas about humans and gender are also visible in Indus mortuary behavior. The best evidence comes from the recent excavations of the main cemetery at Harappa, conducted by the late George Dales, Mark Kenoyer, Richard Meadow, and colleagues (see Meadow 1991). These excavations, combined with earlier work by Mortimer Wheeler, M. Rafique Mughal, and others, have yielded a sizable burial population of nearly 200 individuals from the Mature Harappan period cemetery known as R37 (Hemphill et al. 1991:139). This cemetery was used by a small segment of the population of this densely populated urban center and is not necessarily representative of the full range of Indus mortuary behavior.

Of burials from the cemetery identifiable to sex, fifty-seven are identified as male and eighty-four as female (with fifty-five unidentifiable). Deceased individuals were typically placed in rectangular graves, some in wooden coffins, and were accompanied by small numbers of grave goods, most often pottery vessels and personal ornaments. Ornament type differed by sex; women often wore shell bangles and anklets of steatite beads (Kenoyer 1998:123). Truncated conical stone amulets were also associated uniquely with adult women, perhaps markers of a unique status achieved in adulthood. Some female burials were also accompanied by bronze mirrors. Males generally had fewer grave offerings, though two adult men at Harappa had more elaborate treatment. They were buried in wooden coffins and accompanied by elaborate offerings and ornaments, including, for one, a necklace of more than 300 steatite beads and pendants and, in the other, an elaborate beaded head ornament (Kenoyer 1998:123–24).

In a preliminary analysis of the skeletal remains, Hemphill et al. (1991) examined dental and craniometric variables to examine health and biological relatedness. Overall, individuals were healthy and robust, with low incidence of traumatic injury, chronic disease, or long-term nutritional inadequacies (Possehl 2003:170). However, dental health was not quite as good, and nearly half the individuals had caries. Females had, overall, poorer dental health than males, with a significantly greater rate of caries, abscesses, and hypoplasia. The first two factors are likely a function of gendered dietary differences, while the hypoplasia indicates that girls were subject to greater nutritional stresses during growth periods than were boys (Hemphill et al. 1991:171).

Gender and the Indus Civilization   As evident from the previous discussion, considerations of gender in the first urban civilization of South Asia have been, to date, restricted largely to representation—in figurines and other images and to brief discussions of mortuary evidence. There has been little discussion of household structures, labor organization, or social or political status and roles. An important exception is a provocative study by Wright (1991), who in an article on Indus pottery production called attention to the need to consider how labor was gendered in contexts of specialized craft production occurring in household and non-household contexts. Unfortunately, to date, few have taken up her call, and while the previously discussed evidence should, I hope, indicate the considerable potential to examine gender in South Asian prehistory, as yet this potential remains largely unfulfilled.

GENDER IN HISTORICAL PERIODS IN SOUTH ASIA   As noted earlier, when we move into historical periods in South Asia, there is a somewhat richer literature concerned with issues of gender. However, much of this is text based and will not be considered here. There have been archaeological studies of figurines from early historic urban centers (e.g., Agrawal 1985; Bautze 1990), but these are generally descriptive or too readily adopt mother-goddess interpretations (for a review, see Bhardwaj 2004) and will not be discussed. However, before leaving

South Asia, one last study of gender representation should be noted—Zagarell's (2002) work on memorial stones in the Nilgiri Hills of South India.

Memorializing Heroic Sacrifice: Sati and Memorial Stones in Historic South India   The production of carved stone stelae commemorating the heroic deaths of men and women were produced throughout South India from the sixth through the eighteenth century A.D. (Settar and Sontheimer 1982). Sculptures on these typically uninscribed panels depict the deaths of warriors who died in battle or defense of their communities and of women who sacrificed their lives (and Jaina monks who committed ritual suicide) and were set up near settlements, roads, and shrines across South India. The styles and detail of memorial stones varied from region to region and over time. Most common are panels broken into multiple tiers (usually three), showing at the bottom the death of a warrior in battle; in the middle the deceased being transported to the heavens by female angels, or *apsaras*; and on the uppermost tier the deceased in heaven, usually in association with Shaivite symbols, of the lingam and bull (Nandi). Comparable to depictions of warriors are depictions of women who have committed sati, or ritual self-immolation, often depicted standing with their right arm upraised, wearing the bangles that are a mark of married status (Verghese 2000:118).

While sati has occupied a prominent place in the writings of colonial administrators and in popular imaginings of Hindu India, its practice was far more limited, determined by class, status, and particular historical circumstances (Verghese 2000). Zagarell (2002) has examined the distribution and forms of historic memorial stones in the Nilgiri Hills of southern India. Zagarell's research has focused on understanding the long-term history of human settlement in the region, and its results have challenged conventional views of the Nilgiris as a haven for isolated foraging communities that existed outside the historical trajectory of South India's expanding and contracting states and empires. Instead, inscriptions, memorial stones, and other evidence point to complex interactions between upland communities and state societies over a very long time, with significant consequences for social and economic structures, including gender.

In his examination of the sculpted hero stones from upland and lowland zones of the Nilgiri region, Zagarell presented a nuanced analysis of gender representation that acknowledged differences of class, status, and location in determining how gender ideologies and roles were conceived and portrayed. While it is likely that only people of high status were portrayed in memorial stones, the nature of these portrayals varied significantly both within and across regions. In addition, although both regions participated in shared ideologies that valued the production of memorial stones, the content of the images suggests significant differences between lowland regions that were better integrated into the political economies and ideological structures of large states and the more autonomous uplands. Thus, memorial stones in the lower reaches of the Nilgiris were typically more finely sculpted and elaborate, with priests and institutional Saivite symbols far more common than in the uplands, where images were cruder and rarely include markers of orthodox Hindu deities or priests.

In both regions, the deaths of men and women were honored, most often in the common portrayals of the heroic deaths of male warriors and the self-sacrifices of women as satis. However, in the uplands, additional images of women also occur. These depict (possibly) women armed with spears, perhaps portraying the actual roles of women in community defense in a fractious region that was both less integrated and less constrained by the dominant gender ideologies of lowland states and empires.

While Zagarell is rightly cautious in his interpretations, the importance of his analysis lies in his efforts to dissolve universal assumptions about gender roles and ideologies in South Asia and to consider historically contingent constructions in their larger social, political, and economic contexts. This small study provides a valuable model for future scholars of South Asian gender to follow.

Southwest Asia

Gender research in Southwest Asia is considerably better developed than in South Asia. While figurines and artistic representations have also loomed large in considerations of gender, particularly at sites such as Çatalhöyük and other Neolithic village communities (see the following discussion), scholars have also considered the gendered organization of labor (Peterson 2002; Wright 1996, 1998), household and kin organization (Hodder 1999; Pollock 1999), access to resources and status positions, and class (Zagarell 1986) in their assessments of changing gender structures from early agricultural villages through early urban societies. Nonetheless, the literature remains small and limited largely to two periods that I consider here: early villages of the Neolithic and Mesopotamian city-states of the fourth and third millennia B.C. (figure 20.2).

The Neolithic: Labor Organization, Gender Representation, and Community Organization

The domestication and/or adoption of domestic plants and animals and the formation of village communities have long been of interest to archaeologists working across the Middle East (e.g., Braidwood and Howe 1960; Childe 1936, 1953). Numerous early village sites have been excavated, spanning the late Pleis-

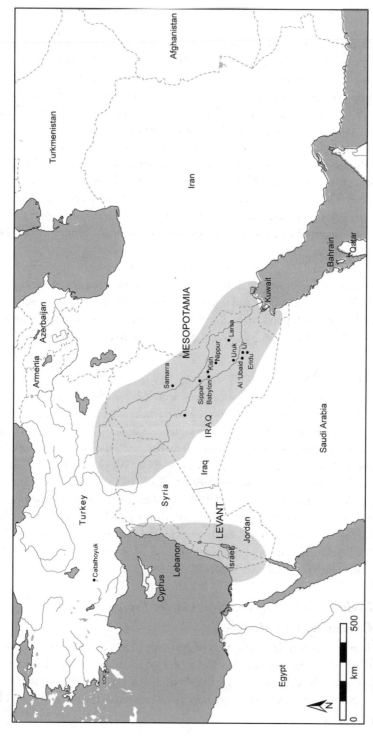

Figure 20.2. Southwest Asia: Sites and regions discussed in text.

tocene preagricultural Natufian communities of the Levant and early Holocene agricultural villages in Turkey, Iraq, Iran, Syria, Israel, and elsewhere. From the 1960s and 1970s, scholars have been interested in understanding how household and community organization was restructured during the Neolithic (e.g., Flannery 1972). Although not specifically interested in gender, these questions and their related implications concerning property, resource procurement, and labor structures touched on related issues and directed research toward larger structural and theoretical concerns, with important implications for subsequent work on changing gender roles, statuses, and ideologies. In this section, I consider several studies that have examined gender structures and ideologies in Southwest Asian Neolithic communities, focusing particularly on labor, community organization, and representation. As in South Asia, figurine studies have been prominent in discussions of gender in Southwest Asian Neolithic (e.g., Beinert 1994; Cauvin 1994; Omura 1984), often focused on fertility, "mother goddesses," and domestication. While space does not allow a detailed discussion of these studies, related issues are addressed here in the discussion of gender research centered on the important Neolithic community of Çatalhöyük.

EARLY LEVANTINE VILLAGES: CHANGING LABOR STRUCTURES The formation of agricultural communities in several regions of Southwest Asia during the early Holocene was part of a larger package of socioeconomic transformations that resulted in new relations between and among humans and their physical environment and constructed landscapes, affecting relations, values, and practices governing labor, property, the family, and sacred beliefs. Along with subsistence goods, material culture, including architecture and artifacts, was produced and consumed in new ways, creating new demands on human labor and participating actively in the production and formulation of social forms, including gender.

The changes in human practices that occurred during the Southwest Asian Neolithic are also evident in human bodies that experienced them. Peterson (2002) has evaluated gendered labor patterns in the Levantine Near East through an analysis of human skeletal remains spanning from the Natufian through Early Bronze Age periods. She focused particularly on skeletal markers of activity-related stress that resulted from regular repetitive labor activities, such as throwing, grinding, chopping, hoeing, harvesting, and so on. These data were incorporated with results from prior osteological studies of nutritional stress, trauma, dental health, and pathologies and with archaeological information on community layout, access to resources, and material culture. Peterson's sample was relatively small: 158 skeletons from fourteen sites spanning seven thousand years, from 12,500 to 5000 years B.P. Nonetheless, her work produced evidence of broad changes in gendered labor activities over a period of significant social and economic transformations and highlights the contribution of direct examination of skeletal remains for analyses of gender.

Peterson's analysis of Natufian skeletons identified several subgroups that shared common markers of activity-related stress and indicated that, with the exception of indicators of hunting, sexual difference in skeletal indicators were limited. Thus, while a significant subgroup of males had pronounced unilateral indicators of arm strength, such as would result from throwing and piercing, other males exhibited similar bilateral wear to the majority of females, indicating tasks that placed equal demands on both arms, such as grinding or raw material processing. Whether the activities that produced these markers were the same for men and women cannot be determined, but Peterson suggests they indicate occupational flexibility and a relatively weakly developed sexual division of labor. During the succeeding Neolithic period, male labor activities appear to have changed significantly, as hunting declined in importance. Both men and women were engaged in heavy physical labor. Male skeletal markers suggest such tasks as tilling, timbering, and/or grinding. Women and men also engaged in lifting and hauling of heavy burdens. By the Early Bronze Age, there was evidence for deteriorating health and nutritional status of the population overall, particularly for women, who may have lost access to resources and also experienced increased labor demands. Male musculature also was reduced compared to that of women, perhaps, Peterson suggests, indicative of greater male involvement in the less physically demanding tasks of herding rather than in agriculture. The declining physical health of women may also be linked to broader changes in gender structures and ideologies.

THE NEOLITHIC COMMUNITY OF ÇATALHÖYÜK   The late seventh-millennium B.C. Neolithic settlement of Çatalhöyük, located in the Konya Plain of south-central Turkey, has excited the interest of archaeologists and the public alike since its initial excavations in the 1960s (Mellaart 1967). Çatalhöyük is the largest known Neolithic community in Southwest Asia, with densely packed houses containing internal burials, elaborate wall art, and rich artifact assemblages, including ceramic figurines, portraying women, men, and ungendered individuals. Artistic and mortuary evidence of collective burials beneath platforms in elaborately decorated structures led Mellaart to argue that Çatalhöyük was the Middle East's first urban center and its region's supreme religious center, the inhabitants of which worshiped multiple female and male deities, among whom the "Mother Goddess" was most important. Not surprisingly, the site has excited the interest of New Age Goddess worshippers (see Barstow 1978; Hodder 1998; Meskell

1995), and the site has become an important focus of tourism and pilgrimage as well as of scholarship.

Mellaart's early interpretations of Çatalhöyük organization and ideology have been challenged on a number of grounds, and remarkable new excavations at the site, initiated in the early 1990s and directed by Hodder (1996, 2000), have provided valuable contextual evidence to refine and rethink earlier interpretations of Çatalhöyük gender structures and ideologies. Çatalhöyük's murals and wall art (including embedded bull bucrania and vulture beaks) do reveal evidence for a complex gender ideology that Hodder (1987) argues was constituted of multiple oppositions (male–female, wild–domestic, outside–inside, and life–death) that did not necessarily correlate in simple ways. Thus, while men were frequently depicted in association with wild animals and were associated with one aspect of the wild (hunting), women were visually associated with other dimensions of the wild (predators and scavengers; Hodder 1987:50) as well as with production and reproduction. Women were portrayed in figurines and murals as both life givers and life takers, associated with birth and death, respectively. Hodder situates these interpretations of Çatalhöyük symbolism and ideologies in contexts of long-term histories of domestication throughout the site's 700-year occupation, suggesting that the declining importance of figurines and murals over time correlated with increasing domestication of the natural world and "an erosion of the central importance of the wild in the symbolic constitution of social life" (55). In a later consideration of Çatalhöyük symbolism, Hodder (1999) explored finer-scale temporalities and the physical contexts of the previously described artistic behavior. In contrast with Mellaart's interpretation of specialized shrines and religious functionaries, Hodder argues that the elaborately decorated structures containing multiple internal burials were houses, the life histories of which were associated with the lives of extended families.

The community of Çatalhöyük, as the largest and most elaborate Southwest Asia Neolithic settlement excavated to date, provides rich evidence for gender ideologies and structures in a context that encourages thinking about both larger historical processes of domestication and the particularistic history of a distinctive Neolithic community.

Gender in Mesopotamia: Cities, States, Temples, and Households

Studies of gender in early Mesopotamian cities and states have addressed a variety of topics, drawing on archaeological evidence and Mesopotamian writings, including economic information of clay tablets as well as law codes and sacred texts, among others. Scholars such as Pollock (1991, 1999; Pollock and Bernbeck

2000), Wright (1996, 1998), and Zagarell (1986) have called attention to the complex relations between class, gender, and power in affecting economic and social status in early state societies, breaking down overly simplistic gender dichotomies while recognizing the significance of widely accepted dominant ideologies, including gender hierarchy, in shaping how people understood their world (Pollock and Bernbeck 2000: 151). Mesopotamian gender has also become an increasing focus of study among art historians and textual scholars, as evident in the recent two-volume publication *Sex and Gender in the Ancient Near East* (Parpola and Whiting 2002) and the work of scholars such as Asher-Greve (1985, 1997), Harris (2000), Bahrani (2001), and others. Here, I consider a subset of studies that, although they draw on both textual and material evidence, address issues that have most concerned archaeologists studying gender, including labor, households, mortuary behavior, representation, and ideology. I focus primarily on studies addressing gender in the fourth and third millennia B.C., spanning the initial development and consolidation of Mesopotamian states and empires and the rise of palace, temple, and *oikos* ("great households"; Pollock 1999) as political, economic, and ideological institutions.

GENDER AND LABOR IN SOUTHWEST ASIAN CITY-STATES Labor was highly differentiated in the urban centers and rural settlements of early Mesopotamia, structured by age, gender, and class. While gender hierarchies were everywhere operative, significant differences existed among elites and various nonelite communities (including free, semifree, and enslaved workers) in access to and control of resources and occupations. Studies of gendered production in Mesopotamia have focused particular attention on craft organization and weaving. Textiles were arguably among the most important commodities in Mesopotamian political economies and were produced exclusively by women. Other productive activities were also strongly gendered. Males worked as scribes, overseers, carpenters, basket makers, agriculturalists, fisherman, and soldiers; women also engaged in agricultural labor, such as harvesting, irrigating, winnowing, and hauling as well as in weaving (Wright 1996).

Weaving had a strong ideological loading in Mesopotamia, as it does in many other regions, and associations between weaving and womanhood are common in Sumerian myth and poetry. Nonetheless, weavers, attached to palaces, temples, and large estates, were of low social and economic status and were very poorly compensated for their labor. The development and consequences of this productive organization have been explored in some detail by Zagarell (1986) and Wright (1996, 1998; see also Maekawa 1980).

Zagarell's important article "Trade, Women, Class and Society in Ancient

Western Asia" (1986) explored the emergence of centralized institutional economies and associated state power in early dynastic period Mesopotamia, focusing particularly on female textile producers. Zagarell traced the creation of a "public/communal mode of production," fueled by attached laborers who had been disassociated from their natal households to labor in and for temples, palaces, and large estates. Of critical importance among these laborers were female weavers, whose products fueled the expansion of trade and solidification of institutional authority during the period of consolidation of state power. Although Zagarell may have overstated the dissolution of kinship in early Mesopotamia, he raised important issues on the relations between class, trade, production, and gender.

Many of these same questions were later taken up by Wright (1996, 1998) in her explorations of gendered production in institutional contexts during the highly centralized, short-lived Mesopotamian Ur III dynasty (ca. 2112–2004 B.C.). Wright, following Waetzoldt (1987), distinguished among free, semifree, and dependent workers. She focused particularly on low-status female weavers who produced goods valued both as economic commodities and, in their more elaborate forms, as luxurious garments and household textiles that could proclaim their elite owners' political and social positions. As noted previously, the importance of textiles did not, however, extend to the status of their producers, who were either semifree or enslaved workers, almost exclusively female, and of very low social and economic status. Large-scale textile production occurred in institutional settings, owned and managed by elite men (and more rarely women; Wright 1996:93), in large workshops employing dozens or hundreds of laborers. Small-scale production likely also occurred at the household level for domestic use and local exchange (Wattenmaker 1998). In institutional production, weavers and other artisans were organized into groups, for Ur III women weavers these contained twenty women under a male supervisor. Compensation for female weavers was generally low and limited to basic necessities, barley, wool, and oil (Wright 1996, citing data compiled by Waetzoldt [1987] and Maekawa [1980, 1987]). Amounts of compensation were related to the specific tasks performed (e.g., weavers earned more than spinners) and age, experience, and ethnicity. In general, rates of compensation were significantly greater for men than for women, and men were also more likely to receive additional compensation in land or supplementary foodstuffs.

GENDER AND CLASS   Both Zagarell and Wright recognized that the social and economic status of men and women in early Mesopotamia was determined by class as well as biological sex. While pronounced gender hierarchies existed across all social strata, heredity and status also were important determinants of an individual's authority and ability to control and dispose of resources and hold particular positions. Asher-Greve (2002:16) argued that primary dimensions of social stratification in Mesopotamia were by rank, status, and occupation; gender was a secondary structural principle of inequality, resulting in heterogeneous categories within larger subgroups. The result was that men were privileged over women of their class but that elite women were privileged over lower-status men and women along various juridical, economic, and social rights and privileges.

Studies of the interdynamics of class and gender have examined the ownership and use of seals inscribed with gendered personal names to evaluate the ability of women and men to engage in economic transactions (Colbow 2002; Pollock 1991), the ownership of emblems of elite status (Marcus 1993), and textual and mortuary evidence for women as officeholders, landowners, and priests (Archi 2002; Asher-Greve 2002; Pollock 1991, 1999). These studies point to complex relations between class and gender that belie simple generalizations.

Nonetheless, as Pollock and Bernbeck (2000) remind us, there was in Mesopotamia a dominant gender ideology that had important consequences for the lived experiences of men and women. They examine this ideology through both textual sources and visual imagery, particularly images on the two categories of mid-third millennium cylinder seals: naturalistic and schematic seals. Four categories of human figures are portrayed on these seals: men, women, pigtailed humans, and naked hairless individuals lacking distinctive features (Pollock and Bernbeck 2000:156). Depictions of men were more common on naturalistic seals as well as on other media, showing bearded men wearing headdresses and a net skirt. These individuals are shown in active poses (usually singly), hunting, leading processions, performing libations, or overseeing the slaughter of bound captives. Sometimes these figures are shown carrying offerings to a standing female who wears a headdress—either a goddess or a priestess. Otherwise, women are depicted as pigtailed figures who always appear in groups and often are engaged in repetitive tasks such as textile production. The genderless figures appear either singly or in groups and are depicted engaged in a variety of activities—agricultural tasks, food preparation, animal tending, hunting, in processions, and so on. Pollock and Bernbeck (2000:159–60) raise several possible interpretations for these ungendered images, which may be male or a third gender or may represent other social identities, such as age-groups. These four categories of images occur separately; men and women are not depicted together, except for males and goddesses; nonetheless, both the form and the context of the images depict hierarchical relations and suggest the existence of gender hierarchies indicated in texts and other lines of material evidence.

Summary and Conclusions

In this chapter, I have briefly reviewed the current literature on gender and archaeology in South and Southwest Asia, attempting to highlight major themes and contributions in each region. As gender has entered the mainstream of archaeological discourse in some world regions and is considered a necessary component of research interested in social, economic, ideological, and political dimensions of past human communities, in both of these regions gender research remains relatively rare. Where gender is discussed, it is often guided by unquestioned assumptions, whether about the prominence of mother goddesses in ancient societies or about divisions of labor.

However limited, the studies presented here suggest that there is considerable potential for greater theorization of gender in both regions—with their rich archaeological records, long history of research, and, for later periods, the availability of diverse written source that contain valuable insights into gender ideologies and practices. Many of the studies here concerned representation of men, women, and possible third genders in portable images, sculpture, and wall art, and systematic, contextually rich examinations of how humans are portrayed is clearly a valuable line of evidence for understanding how gender is depicted and idealized in specific historical contexts. While these dimensions may provide some insights into the lived lives of men and women, such studies require that archaeologists incorporate a much broader range of material remains into contextual studies to understand labor, access to resources, and status positions. The chapters in this volume point the way to the rich potential for a social archaeology that considers gender as an integral component of research and to the potential of that research for developing richer understandings of human history and prehistory in South and Southwest Asia.

References

Agrawal, Vasudeva S.
    1985   *Terracotta Figurines of Ahichchhatra, District Bareilly, U.P.* Varanasi: Prithivi Prakashan.

Archi, A.
    2002   The Role of Women in the Society of Ebla. In *Sex and Gender in the Ancient Near East: Proceedings of the 47th Recontre Assyriologique Internationale*. S. Parpola and R. M. Whiting, eds. Pp. 1–9. Helsinki: Neo-Assyrian Text Corpus Project.

Ardeleanu-Jansen, Alexandra
    2002   The Terracotta Figurines from Mohenjo Daro: Considerations on Tradition, Craft, and Ideology in the Harappan Civilization (c. 2400–1800 BC). In *Indian Archaeology in Retrospect. Volume 2: Protohistory: Archaeology of the Harappan Civi-*

lization. S. Settar and Ravi Korisettar, eds. Pp. 205–22. New Delhi: ICHR and Manohar Books.

Asher-Greve, Julia M.
1985 *Frauen in altsumerischer Zeit.* Malibu: Undena.
1997 The Essential Body: Mesopotamian Conceptions of the Gendered Body. *Gender and History* 9:432–61.
2002 Decisive Sex, Essential Gender. In *Sex and Gender in the Ancient Near East: Proceedings of the 47th Rencontre Assyriologique Internationale.* S. Parpola and R. M. Whiting, eds. Pp. 11–26. Helsinki: Neo-Assyrian Text Corpus Project.

Bahrani, Zainab
2001 *Women of Babylon: Gender and Representation.* London: Routledge.

Barstow, Anne
1978 The Uses of Archaeology in Women's History: James Mellaart's Work on the Neolithic Goddess at Çatal Hüyük. *Feminist Studies* 4:7–27.

Bautze, Joachim
1990 Some Observations on Female "Maurya" Terracotta Figurines. In *South Asian Archaeology 1987.* M. Taddei, ed. Pp. 611–26. Rome: Istituto Italiano per il Medio ed Estremo Oriente.

Beinert, Hans-Dieter
1994 The Human Image in the Aceramic Neolithic Period of the Middle East. In *Rituals, Rites, and Religion in Prehistory: IIIrd Daya International Conference of Prehistory.* Vol. I. W. H. Waldren, J. A. Ensenaya, and R. C. Bennard, eds. Pp. 75–103. BAR International Series 611. Oxford: British Archaeological Reports.

Bhardwaj, Deeksha
2004 Problematizing the Archaeology of Female Figurines in North-West India. In *Archaeology as History in Early South Asia.* H. P. Ray and C. M. Sinopoli, eds. Pp. 481–504. Delhi: ICHR and Aryan Books International.

Boivin, Nicole, and Dorian Fuller
2002 Looking for Post-Processual Theory in South Asian Archaeology. In *Indian Archaeology in Retrospect. Volume 4: Archaeology and Historiography. History, Theory, and Method.* S. Settar and Ravi Korisettar, eds. Pp. 181–216. New Delhi: ICHR and Manohar Books.

Braidwood, Robert J., and B. Howe
1960 *Prehistoric Investigations in Iraqi Kurdistan.* Studies in Ancient Oriental Civilization 31. Chicago: University of Chicago Press.

Cauvin, Jacques
1994 *Naissance des Divinités. Naissance de L'agriculture. La Révolution des Symboles au Néolithique.* Paris: CNRS.

Childe, V. Gordon
1936 *Man Makes Himself.* London: Watts.
1953 *New Light on the Most Ancient Near East: The Oriental Prelude to European History.* 4th ed. New York: Norton Library.

Colbow, Gudrun
    2002   Priestesses, Either Married or Unmarried and Spouses without Title: Their Seal Use and Their Seals in Sippar at the Beginning of the Second Millennium BC. In *Sex and Gender in the Ancient Near East: Proceedings of the 47th Recontre Assyriologique Internationae.* S. Parpola and R. M. Whiting, eds. Pp. 85–90. Helsinki: Neo-Assyrian Text Corpus Project.

Dehejia, Vidya, ed.
    1997   *Representing the Body: Gender Issues in Indian Art.* New Delhi: Kali for Women.
    1999   *Devi: The Great Goddess. Female Divinity in South Asian Art.* Washington, DC: Arthur M. Sackler Gallery, Smithsonian Institution.

Desai, Devangana
    1975   *Erotic Sculpture of India: A Socio-Cultural Study.* New Delhi: Tata McGraw-Hill.
    2000   *Khajuraho.* New Delhi: Oxford University Press.

Flannery, Kent V.
    1972   The Origins of the Village as a Settlement Type in Mesoamerica and the Near East. In *Man, Settlement, and Urbanism.* P. Ucko, R. Tringham, and G. Dimbleby, eds. Pp. 23–53. London: Duckworth.

Gimbutas, Marija
    1982   *The Gods and Goddesses of Old Europe, 6500–3000 BC.* London: Thames and Hudson.
    1989   *The Civilization of the Goddess: The Worlds of Old Europe.* San Francisco: Harpers.

Guha-Thakurta, Tapati
    2004   *Monuments, Objects, Histories: Institutions of Art in Colonial and Postcolonial India.* Delhi: Permanent Black.

Harris, Rivka
    2000   *Gender and Aging in Mesopotamia: The Gilgamesh Epic and Other Ancient Literature.* Norman: University of Oklahoma Press.

Hemphill, Brian E., John R. Lukacs, and Kenneth A. R. Kennedy
    1991   Biological Adaptations and Affinities of Bronze Age Harappans. In *Harappa Excavations 1986–1990: A Multidisciplinary Approach to the Third Millennium Urbanism.* Richard H. Meadow, ed. Pp. 137–82. Madison, WI: Prehistory Press.

Hodder, Ian
    1987   Contextual Archaeology: An Interpretation of Catal Hüyük and a Discussion of the Origins of Agriculture. *Bulletin of the Institute of Archaeology (London)* 24:43–56.
    1998   The Past as Passion and Play: Çatalhöyuk as a Site of Conflict in the Construction of Multiple Pasts. In *Archaeology Under Fire: Nationalism, Politics and Heritage in the Eastern Mediterranean and the Middle East.* L. Meskell, ed. Pp. 124–39. London: Routledge.
    1999   Symbolism at Çatalhöyük. In *World Prehistory: Studies in Memory of Grahame Clark.* John Coles, Robert Bewley, and Paul Mellars, eds. Pp. 177–92. Proceedings of the British Academy 99. Oxford: Oxford University Press.

Hodder, Ian, ed.
  1996 *On the Surface Çatalhöyuk 1993–1995*. Cambridge: McDonald Institute for Archaeological Research, Cambridge University.
  2000 *Towards Reflexive Method in Archaeology: The Example at Çatalhöyuk*. Cambridge: McDonald Institute of Archaeological Research, Cambridge University.
Jarrige, Catherine
  1984 Terracotta Human Figurines from Nindowari. In *South Asian Archaeology 1981*. B. Allchin, ed. Pp. 129–34. Cambridge: Cambridge University Press.
  1991 The Terracotta Figurines from Mehrgarh. In *Forgotten Cities of the Indus: Early Civilization in Pakistan from 8th to the 2nd millennium BC*. M. Jansen, M. Mulloy, and G. Urban, eds. Pp. 87–94. Mainz: Verlag Philipp von Zabern.
Jarrige, Catherine, Jean-François Jarrige, Richard H. Meadow, and Gonzague Quivron, eds.
  1995 *Mehrgarh: Field Reports 1974–1985, from Neolithic Times to the Indus Civilization*. Karachi: Department of Culture and Tourism, Government of Sind.
Kenoyer, Jonathan Mark
  1998 *Ancient Cities of the Indus Valley Civilization*. Karachi: American Institute of Pakistan Studies, Oxford University Press.
Lesure, Richard G.
  2000 A Comparative Perspective on Figurines from Early Villages. Paper presented at the Sixth Gender and Archaeology Conference, Northern Arizona University, Flagstaff, October 6–7.
  2002 The Goddess Diffracted: Thinking about the Figurines of Early Villages. *Current Anthropology* 43:587–610.
Maekawa, K.
  1980 Female Weavers and Their Children. *Sumerologica* 2:81–125.
  1987 Collective Labor Service in Gisu-Lagash: The Presargonic and Ur II Periods. In *Labor in the Ancient Near East*. M. Powell, ed. Pp. 49–71. New Haven, CT: American Oriental Society.
Marcus, Michelle
  1993 Incorporating the Body: Adornment, Gender, and Social Identity in Ancient Iran. *Cambridge Archaeological Journal* 3:157–78.
Meadow, Richard H., ed.
  1991 *Harappa Excavations 1986–1990: A Multidisciplinary Approach to the Third Millennium Urbanism*. Madison, WI: Prehistory Press.
Mellaart, James
  1967 *Çatal Hüyük: A Neolithic Town in Anatolia*. London: Thames and Hudson.
Meskell, Lynn
  1995 Goddesses, Gimbutas, and "New Age" Archaeology. *Antiquity* 69:74–86.
Omura, M.
  1984 A Reinterpretation of the Figurines of Çatal Hüyük. *Orient* 20:129–50.

Orr, Leslie C.
- 2000 *Donors, Devotees, and Daughters of God*. Oxford: Oxford University Press.

Parpola, Simo, and R. M. Whiting
- 2002 *Sex and Gender in the Ancient Near East: Proceedings of the 47th Rencontre Assyriologique Internationale*. Helsinki: Neo-Assyrian Text Corpus Project.

Peterson, Jane
- 2002 *Sexual Revolutions: Gender and Labor at the Dawn of Agriculture*. Walnut Creek, CA: AltaMira Press.

Pollock, Susan M.
- 1991 Women in a Man's World: Images of Sumerian Women. In *Engendering Archaeology*. J. Gero and M. W. Conkey, eds. Pp. 366–87. Oxford: Basil Blackwell.
- 1999 *Ancient Mesopotamia: The Eden That Never Was*. Cambridge: Cambridge University Press.

Pollock, Susan M., and Reinhard Bernbeck
- 2000 And They Said, Let Us Make Gods in Our Image: Gendered Ideology in Ancient Mesopotamia. In *Reading the Body: Representations and Remains in the Archaeological Record*. Alison E. Rautman, ed. Pp. 150–64. Philadelphia: University of Pennsylvania Press.

Possehl, Gregory L.
- 2002 *The Indus Civilization: A Contemporary Perspective*. Walnut Creek, CA: AltaMira Press.

Ratnagar, Shereen
- 1991 *Enquiries into the Political Organization of Harappan Society*. Delhi: Ravish Publishers.

Ray, Himanshu Prabha
- 2004 Gender and Archaeology: Introduction. In *Archaeology as History in Early South Asia*. Himanshu Prabha Ray and Carla M. Sinopoli, eds. Pp. 464–80. Delhi: ICHR and Aryan Books International.

Settar, S., and Gunther D. Sontheimer, eds.
- 1982 *Memorial Stones: A Study of their Origin, Significance, and Variety*. Dharwad: Institute of Indian Art History, Karnatak University.

Sharma, Arvind, ed.
- 1988 *Sati: Historical and Phenomenological Essays*. New Delhi: Manohar.

Skilling, P.
- 2001 Nuns, Laywomen, Donors, Goddesses: Female Roles in Early Indian Buddhism. *Journal of the International Association of Buddhist Studies* 24:241–73.

Verghese, Anila
- 2000 *Archaeology, Art and Religion: New Perspectives on Vijayanagara*. New Delhi: Oxford University Press.

Waetzoldt, H.
- 1987 Compensation of Craft Workers and Officials in the Ur III Period. In *Labor in the Ancient Near East*. M. A. Powell, ed. Pp. 117–42. New Haven, CT: American Oriental Society.

Wattenmaker, Patricia
    1998   Craft Production and Social Identity in Northwest Mesopotamia. In *Craft and Social Identity*. C. L. Costin and R. P. Wright, eds. Pp. 47–56. Archaeological Paper 8. Washington, DC: American Anthropological Association.

Willis, Janice D.
    1985   Nuns and Benefactresses: The Role of Women in the Development of Buddhism. In *Women, Religion and Social Change*. Y. Y. Haddad and E. B. Findly, eds. Pp. 59–85. Albany: State University of New York Press.
    1992   Female Patronage in Indian Buddhism. In *The Powers of Art: Patronage in Indian Culture*. Barbara Stoler Miller, ed. Pp. 46–53. New Delhi: Oxford University Press.

Wright, Rita P.
    1991   Women's Labor and Pottery Production in Prehistory. In *Engendering Archaeology: Women and Prehistory*. Joan M. Gero and Margaret W. Conkey, eds. Pp. 194–223. Oxford: Basil Blackwell.
    1996   Technology, Gender and Class: Worlds of Difference in Ur III Mesopotamia. In *Gender and Archaeology*. R. P. Wright, ed. Pp. 79–110. Philadelphia: University of Pennsylvania Press.
    1998   Crafting Social Identity in Ur III Southern Mesopotamia. In *Craft and Social Identity*. C. L. Costin and R. P. Wright, eds. Pp. 57–70. Archaeological Paper 8. Washington, DC: American Anthropological Association.

Zagarell, Allen
    1986   Trade, Women and Class in Ancient Western Asia. *Current Anthropology* 27(5):415–30.
    2002   Gender and Social Organization in the Reliefs of the Nilgiri Hills. In *Forager-Traders in South and Southeast Asia: Long Term Histories*. Kathleen D. Morrison and Laura L. Junker, eds. Pp. 77–104. Cambridge: Cambridge University Press.

Gender and the Disciplinary Culture of Australian Archaeology

21

CLAIRE SMITH AND EMER O'DONNELL

THE INTERSECTION OF THE feminist movement, postmodernism, and archaeology during the last quarter of the twentieth century inspired one of the most productive and challenging periods for archaeology globally. This intersection has overturned assumptions about the neutrality of archaeology, in the process offering exciting new areas of research and the promise of career paths for women. Scientific paradigms, androcentric assumptions, and a certain "homogenizing" of the past have been displaced by a concern with equity and diversity. The focus on gender as a variable, as well as the writings of women archaeologists, has been an essential driver to the postmodern movement in archaeology. Indeed, it is impossible to envisage this movement with the publications of female authors omitted or contemporary archaeology departments without at least one female lecturer. Whereas archaeology was once a dominantly male province, in 2005 women are an integral part of the social landscape. But have they achieved equity? Have gender roles changed? And in what ways has the engendering of archaeology impacted on our interpretations of the past?

This chapter focuses on these issues as they have manifested in Australian archaeology. It explores trends in the study of gender as well as changes in the employment profiles of archaeologists. While early studies in gender archaeology focused solely on women, as a first step in the redressing of androcentric biases, recently more holistic approaches have emerged that speak to gender relations, roles, and ideologies. In this chapter, these issues are discussed in terms of developments in the disciplinary culture of Australian archaeology, which offers special challenges to an archaeology of gender. Some of the major sites mentioned in the text are shown in figure 21.1.

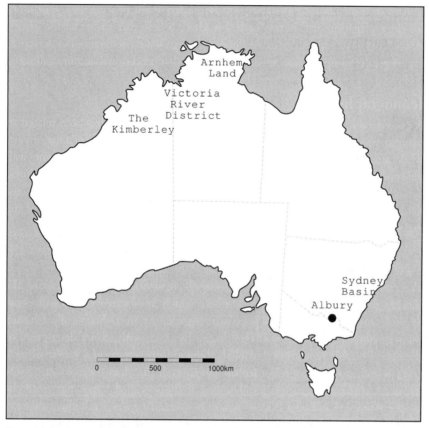

Figure 21.1. Some major sites relating to gender archaeology in Australia.

The Emergence of Gender Archaeology in Australia

To understand the emergence of gender archaeology in Australia, it is essential to understand the disciplinary culture in which it arose, was fostered, and, on occasions, foundered. Australian archaeology is a small community and has the strengths, shortcomings, and prejudices of small communities. The Australian Archaeological Association normally has around 550 members. Everyone knows or knows of everyone else. The hierarchy, while subject to generational change, is based as much on personal qualities, such as sense of humor, field skills, or an ability to generate income, as it is on publications, research programs, or institutional employment. The Australian archaeological community is better understood if considered in relation to the Australian society as a whole, which many perceive to have a strong egalitarian and antiestablishment ethos, rooted in our convict and pastoral backgrounds, and usually identified as "mateship" (Ward 2003; for critique, see also Lake 1999) but also related to a sporting prowess that could assert equality with colonial Britain (see Blainey 2001). Australians root for the underdog, bring the boaster down to earth. This antielitism (see Sawer and Hindess 2004) means that we have an ambivalent attitude to success. We both seek and reject success. We use the word "ambitious" as a derogatory term, and we are suspicious of successful people, often assuming they are unethical or corrupt even if we can't identify how. This attitude manifests in what we call the "tall poppy" syndrome, whereby successful people who stick their heads up are cut down to size (see Blainey 2001).

In Australian comedy, this antielitism manifests in titles such as "The Chaser: Striving for Mediocrity in a World of Excellence" (see http://www.chaser.com.au). In this regard, Australians are unlike Americans, who assume they are the best in the world at whatever they do, whether they are or not, or the British, who internalize a sense of superiority established in colonial times. In contrast, Australians are wary of appearing to grow too tall, and those who do succeed have to cope with both internal and external critiques of their accomplishments. In a sense, many Australians fear success.

While doing archaeology in any country is challenging, in Australia it is a particularly tough gig. Australians live in a harsh country and are a resilient people. Often, our sites are located in remote areas where survival has to be taken seriously rather than for granted. Normally, our fieldwork is done on a shoestring. We are hard on ourselves and hard on each other. We are not polite or restrained in the British or American traditions. Our conferences are small, usually only around 200 people. Our intellectual agenda is set by a relatively few individuals, often tenured staff at universities, the majority of whom are male. Usually, we say what we think, and we can be brutally frank. If we hear a conference presentation we don't like, we say so. This means that presenting a paper at our annual meetings can be a traumatic experience, especially if the topic is considered "soft," defined as such by not being the results of excavation, laboratory analysis, or survey. Part of our ethos is that you have to be tough enough to "hack it."[1] When people are criticized mercilessly—and this has happened regularly over the years—they are expected to "get over it" and continue to party (literally) afterward. We are somehow ashamed of and for those who return to their rooms or cabins to nurse hurt feelings. In an ironic turn, the critic becomes the offended party if the people they have attacked refuse to socialize afterward. Nursing your wounds is seen as a weakness, and Australian archaeologists have little tolerance for weakness.

It was into this intellectual climate that Hilary du Cros and Laurajane Smith decided to hold the first Women in Archaeology conference, in Albury, New South Wales, in 1991. Although gender was becoming a subject of inquiry in Australian archaeology during the late 1980s and early 1990s (e.g., Beck et al. 1989; Beck and Head 1990; Lawrence Cheney 1991; Smith 1991), the genesis of gender as a field of study in Australia can be tied to this conference, as can its early emphasis on women in archaeology rather than on gendered relations. Given the disciplinary culture of Australian archaeology, it is no surprise that du Cros and Smith saw the holding of this conference as a serious professional risk: "We felt immensely insecure about taking what we perceived to be a very large, politically charged and possibly a professionally fatal step" (du Cros and Smith 1993a:xviii).

There were two problems that threatened the success of this conference, both of which relate to its intellectual content. The conference had two foci, both with a public perception of being "boring" or, worse, "soft." The first focus was the professional advancement of women. In the Australian archaeology of the time, the discussion of gender inequities, especially in regard to employment, was generally interpreted as "whinging," as a process whereby women who did not have the ability or strength to make it on their own merits sought special consideration for career advancement or tried to explain away their failures. These critiques came from both women and men. The second focus was the theorizing of gender. This was a death knell, too. One of the defining characteristics of traditional Australian archaeology is a reluctance to "do" theory. While there are examples of Australian archaeologists successfully dealing with theory (e.g., Burke 1999; Colley 1998; Gorman 1993; Huchet 1991; Ireland 2002; Lydon 1999; Torrence and Clarke 2000), of course, these are atypical and mostly recent. Theory is not something that is valued highly by the Australian archaeological community as a whole. Sometimes it is considered to be the intellectual doodlings of "armchair" archaeologists, those who are too soft, either mentally or physically, to engage in fieldwork. Real archaeologists are outdoors, getting dirty and living rough. The notion of the archaeologist as hero (Moser 1995; Shanks and Tilley 1988, 1992; Zarmati 1995) or cowboy (Moser 1995; Smith 1998) is integral to how Australian archaeologists value themselves and each other. Faintly homophobic (cf. Claassen 2000), it is an image that marginalizes both women and theory:

> The cowboy archaeologist is active and must excavate, preferably deeply, into very old sites. Doing archaeology is his goal. The cowboy image not only excludes and denies the relevance of feminist issues, it questions the relevance of thinking too much about what we do as archaeologists: the doing is all that really matters. (Smith 1998:41)

Laurajane Smith contends that Australian archaeologists consider theory to be like "sand in our thongs,"[2] something that makes a simple life unnecessarily complicated or uncomfortable. She identifies a dearth of "engaged and constructive theoretical debates" within the traditional arenas of Australian archaeology and attributes this to archaeological assumptions being "too naturalised" to be viewed as problematic (Smith 1998:44).

In such a social and intellectual milieu, there was a distinct possibility that the first Women in Archaeology conference in Australia would founder. The conference, however, turned out to be a great success because of a "wind change" in the disciplinary culture of Australian archaeology. The number of female archaeologists had reached a critical mass, and they needed to talk to each other. Apart from consultants, there had been a number of female appointments to universities and senior positions in the government. Although these women were important role models to others, they still had to achieve their own individual success within systems shaped by a patriarchy that did not recognize, much less make allowances for, the additional calls, both private and professional, made on women's time.

For the female archaeologists of the time, the decision to attend the first Women in Archaeology conference was not made lightly. Many were establishing their places in universities or government institutions, and the potential penalties of attending the conference were apparent and the gains not yet established. The major possible penalty was that attending the conference could signal weakness or an inability to cope with the responsibilities of their jobs or that it would put women into an archaeological ghetto. Remember, this was at a time when there were enormous pressures on women. They were not free to do their job on an equal basis with men but were asked to be female representative(s) on a wide range of committees and were expected to take an active interest in "women's issues" as well as an inordinate share of the pastoral care of students (see Probert 2005). Thus, even when women were allowed into the game, the playing field was not leveled. While they no doubt recognized that their success or failure would impact on women in the discipline as a whole, these women could draw on little help from other women. This archaeological terrain was barely trodden much less mapped. In the early 1990s, it was clear that Australian women archaeologists needed support. In a stroke of brilliance, du Cros and Smith provided this support in the form of their keynote speakers, Meg Conkey, Joan Gero, and Alison Wylie. Each of these scholars had an established place in the international archaeological community but was still to publish major publications on gender (but see Conkey and Spector 1984).[3] Once these three were confirmed as speakers, the benefits of attending the conference outweighed the drawbacks, and the success of the conference was in hand. While this was not apparent immediately

(Meehan 1993), the impact of this conference was profound (see Casey 1998). It was during this conference that the notion arose of gender as a legitimate rather than quirky area of study in Australian archaeology.

Since that time, the study of gender has become an identifiable part of Australian archaeology, principally through the Women in Archaeology conferences but also through mainstream publications and conference presentations (see Casey 1998; Colley 2000). At the time of writing, there have been six Women in Archaeology conferences held in Australia, three of which have produced edited volumes (Balme and Beck 1995; Casey et al. 1998; du Cros and Smith 1993b). The first session on gender to be held at the annual meeting of the Australian Archaeological Association, however, did not occur until 1998. Convened by Cherrie de Leiuen and Robert Pilgrim, the title of this session, "Power and Gender in Archaeology" (de Leiuen and Pilgrim 1998), indicates a shift from the gynocentric bias of the early 1990s, which was essential to the needs of that time, to the current approach that focuses on relationships between women and men as informed by power differentials and intersection of the multiple determinants of social difference.

Engendering Australian Archaeology

The engendering of Australian archaeology has two distinct phases. The first of these focused on engendering interpretations of the past by redressing the androcentric biases that excluded women and their activities. The second, emergent phase is building on these foundations to treat gender as one of many determinants of social difference and to inquire into the multiple ways in which these dimensions intersect. The place of women in archaeology is a thread that links both phases.

As in other parts of the world (see Claassen 1992; Diaz-Andreu and Sørensen 1998; Gero and Conkey 1991; Gilchrist 1994; Moser 1993; Nelson 1997, 1998; Spector 1993; Walde and Willows 1991; Wall 1994), one of the first issues addressed by the archaeology of gender in Australia was gender bias in interpretations of the past. For many female archaeologists, the question was, Where are/were the women? The premise that women and children could not be found in the material remains of the past was based on the notion that objects commonly associated with women in the ethnographic present, such as baskets and mats made from fibers, were less likely to have endured than objects normally associated with men, such as rock art and stone tools (Haydon 1977:85; Isaac 1978:121). Consequently, one way to address or confirm gender bias in archaeological interpretations was to test this assumption. In Australia, the seminal paper in this respect was Caroline Bird's "Woman the Toolmaker: Evidence for Women's Use and Manufacture of Flaked Stone Tools in Australia and New Guinea." This paper was presented at a stone-tool conference at the University of New England in 1988. Not only did the paper challenge assumptions that stone tools were made solely by men, but it did this through drawing on a postmodern concern with the social context of production. It was not published, however, until much later (Bird 1993), at least partly because Bird felt that it would not be accepted for publication in either *Australian Archaeology* or *Archaeology in Oceania*, the principal journals for Indigenous archaeology in Australia (Bird, e-mail communication, December 20, 2004). (Note: Following the practice of Indigenous scholars [e.g., Smith 1999], I capitalize the word "Indigenous" to denote Indigenous sovereignty.) Bird's recollections give insight not only into a disciplinary culture in which the analysis of gender was considered an oddity but also into how women supported each other during this early phase of gender studies in Australian archaeology:

> I had been intrigued by an ethno-historical reference from my PhD study area to women making spear barbs and was set to thinking more generally about the issue of the social context of production and use of stone and collecting other references. Denise Gaughwin and I used to discuss gender in archaeology and among archaeologists a lot while we were working together at La Trobe and she had written a short paper for the *Artefact* on the implications of a reference from her study area to women hunting kangaroos. When the stone tool conference came up it seemed to me (perhaps naively!) that it would be a good excuse to pull it all together and challenge some assumptions. I expected the testosterone-laden nature of the conference as I have been interested in stone tool studies for long enough to notice that usually only papers on lithics by male "gung ho" rock-breakers were likely to be taken seriously in Australia. I was taken aback, however, by the hostility. On reflection, I don't think it was just the ideas that were threatening—I think it was also that a woman was standing up and expecting her ideas about lithics to be taken seriously by what I certainly felt then was very much a "boys' club." (Bird, e-mail communication, December 28, 2004)

Prior to Bird's research, instances of Aboriginal women using or making stone tools had been dismissed as "exceptions" (Bird 1993:22). This androcentric view keyed into the gender roles of researchers rather than those of the societies being recorded. In a sense, the gender roles of Aboriginal people had the potential to overturn the gendered interpretations of their pasts, providing grounds for challenging gendered assumptions in other fields of archaeology, such as historical, contact, and maritime. The importance of Bird's paper is not only that it is the first attempt to inject gender as a variable in the interpretation of the past of Aboriginal Australians but also because it inspired archaeologists to challenge gender assumptions in other spheres of study. Nevertheless, while some women publish on lithics (see Gorman 1993, 1997; Hiscock and Attenbrow 1998), men are the archaeologists with high profiles in this area (e.g., Hiscock 1988, 1996).

Another area in which the absence of women was disputed is that of rock art production. From the beginning of ethnographic research into Aboriginal culture, it had been assumed that only men in Australian Aboriginal societies produced rock art (e.g., Crawford 1968:37; Gould 1969:154). This assumption is questioned by Smith (1991) in a paper presented at the First Congress of the Australian Rock Art Research Association in 1988 and by McDonald (1992, 1995) in a study that articulated the analysis of rock art and excavated material. Smith (1991) collates a number of archival and ethnographic examples of women producing rock art in the Kimberley, Victoria River, and southern Arnhem Land regions of northern Australia (e.g., Kaberry 1939:208, 228; Mowaljarli 1992). She contends that gender is a variable that needs to be factored into rock art interpretation; that rock art may have been produced by men, women, and children; and that it may encode information on the age and gender of the artist. McDonald challenges androcentric assumptions systematically in several papers (McDonald 1992, 1995, 1998), and her (1992) analysis of both excavated material and rock art provides evidence that men, women, and children participated in the stenciling of hands and implements at a rock art site in the Sydney Basin. McDonald concludes that

> the cultural remains in the midden layer, i.e. the presence of fishhooks (ethnohistorically reported to be women's fishing apparel), shellfish, fish and small land mammals is interpreted as indicating the presence of women at this site. The more recent art phase also suggests the presence of women. This art assemblage includes stencil compositions of women's and babies' (sized) hands and digging sticks ... part of the significance of this finding is the participation of prehistoric women in the production of art, and the suggestion that art may have fulfilled a domestic role. (McDonald 1992:48)

The question that arises is, How did such erroneous gender assumptions survive for such a long period? In our view, it is due largely to a kind of "benign neglect" in the disciplinary culture of the time rather than to any kind of planned exclusion. As Balme and Beck (1993) point out, until recently constructions of gender roles in past societies were heavily influenced by Western ideologies. Androcentric assumptions survived because they were consistent with the disciplinary views of the times. The original data were based on the observations of early ethnographers, the majority of whom were European men who, appropriately enough, worked primarily with Aboriginal men. Often, these ethnographers consciously avoided inquiring into the "preserves of the other sex" (e.g., Elkin 1939:xx; see also Mountford 1976:109). This meant that many of the practices of Aboriginal women went unrecorded during that formative period when anthropological ideas about Aboriginal societies were being shaped. While there were also women ethnographers (see Marcus 1993), they were rarely employed in academic positions, and other scholars did not accept their observations when they did not concur with the disciplinary norm. For example, Kaberry (1939:208, 228) recorded women making rock paintings in the Kimberley, but this did not impinge on the idea that only men could create rock paintings imbued with spiritual power as opposed to "simple" hand stencils. Kaberry could not even convince her mentor A. P. Elkin, who wrote the introduction to her book (see Elkin 1939), much less other male scholars (e.g., Crawford 1968:37; Gould 1969:154). This is at least partly because of a robust and long-established link between men and power within the West in which interpretations that ran counter to this nexus appeared aberrant.

Another area that has been a focus of an engendered reassessment concerns the interpretation of human remains. In recent years, several studies have critically analyzed the gendered assumptions underlying the interpretation of these remains, particularly in terms of museum collections as well as the lifestyles and burial practices of Indigenous Australians. The sexing of human remains in museum collections was the focus of Donlan's (1993) study, which found a systematic bias toward males in the attribution of Aboriginal skeletal remains in collections of the Australian Museum. Other studies have addressed gendered perceptions of Indigenous health and life span. For example, Littleton (1998) found there was insufficient data to support accepted perceptions that Aboriginal women who had been buried along the Murray River had a shorter life span than men, while Hope (1998) analyzed bias in interpretations of Aboriginal burials in southern Australia. Similarly, McCardle's (2002) study of Australian Aboriginal bark burial mortuary practices in the Central Queensland Highlands challenged the notion that these burial customs had been reserved exclusively for young men and children. Contrary to previously held beliefs, her analysis showed that these remains included all age-groups and both sexes. Furthermore, McCardle's study demonstrates how a focus on the relationships between genders can lead into interesting and complex questions relating to social interactions and hierarchies.

Over the past fifteen years, the study of gender has emerged from and produced a broadening in the disciplinary foci of Australian archaeology. Archaeology in Australia has long had a processual focus on technology and the environment. In historical archaeology, for example, this is evident in works that focus on "endlessly cataloguing stamper batteries, boilers, steam engines, and water races" (Lawrence 1998:127) and a concomitant reluctance to inquire substantively into social relationships. In part, this approach derives from our colonial ties with the United Kingdom, where historical archaeology is known as industrial archaeology. It has been challenged by an engendering of Australian archaeology that necessarily involves the analysis of social relationships and dealing with the myriad facets of social identity. In historical archaeology, the study of gender has focussed on the material construction of gentility (e.g., Lydon 1995; Russell 1993, 1994; Young 1998); the status of women (e.g., Bavin 1989; Hourani 1991); the contributions of women in male-gendered spheres, such as mining (e.g., Lawrence 1998); female incarceration (e.g., Casella 2001); and constructions of national identity (e.g., Ireland 2001, 2002). Sometimes the route has been via a concern with the ethnic identities of early colonial populations (e.g., Lydon 1999; Stankowski 2002) or contact with Indigenous groups (e.g., de Leiuen 1998). All these studies are firmly grounded in the historical context of their own time and place. As Lawrence (1998:127) points out, such historical specificity is important because it "highlights the diversity of women's experiences and challenges unchanging constructions of gender and women's roles." This allows fine-grained analysis not only of women's roles but also of relationships between women and men, giving us a deeper understanding of both.

In the small community of Australian archaeology, it comes as no surprise that developments in maritime archaeology parallel those of historical archaeology. In particular, maritime archaeology has changed from a largely technological focus (e.g., McIlroy 1986; Pearson 1983; Rogers 1990) to one that also deals with the nuances of social relationships (e.g., de Leiuen 1998; Lawrence and Staniforth 1998; Staniforth et al. 2001). One of the most remarkable studies is that de Leiuen (1998, 1999), who delves into what is considered to be an archetypical male domain, the nineteenth-century whaling and sealing sites of the southern Pacific, challenging conceptions of gender roles and identifying the gendered behaviors of Indigenous women through stone tools found at contact sites. Her study highlights the fact that our understandings of gender roles, even those of the recent past, are viewed through a lens that has been shaped by the incomplete memories and historical records of Western cultures and that these understandings can be disputed and reshaped by material evidence.

Likewise, a rethinking of gender assumptions underlies Balme and Beck's (1993) analysis of the emergence of a gendered division of labor in human evolution. Balme and Beck link the assumption that there is a biological basis for the gendered division of labor to developments within the discipline of archaeology in the 1960s, which emphasized a link between sex and gender. They contend that this was the cultural basis for theories that assumed that the sex/gendered division of labor has been present from the very early stages of human evolution (e.g., Friedl 1975; Isaac and Crader 1981). These theories have endured despite social changes in Western society such as the feminist movement and, indeed, have been used to support contemporary gender role ideologies. Balme and Beck (1993) challenge such theories through disputing the fundamental assumption that there is a biological basis for the gendered division of labor. Instead, they argue that this division arose from a human need to create social distinctions. From this viewpoint, the gendered division of labor can be construed as one part of the emergence of social complexity and may have occurred much later in human evolution.

Taken together, the papers reviewed here convey the range of interests in Australian archaeology and the manner in which the archaeology of gender is transforming the discipline. Most important, the work of these researchers is a timely reminder that gender, age, and other dimensions of social identity are invisible in archaeology only if we don't make the effort to look for them.

Women as Archaeologists

As in other parts of the world, the role of women as archaeologists has been a focus of gender archaeology in Australia. There is a link between female visibility in both the past and the present: while women were being found in the remains of the past, they were marking out their own places in the present. The question we consider here is, How far have we come? Have women in Australian archaeology achieved equity in the workplace? Concern about the persistently low numbers and status of women in the archaeological workplace (Buckley 1993; Clarke 1993; Gero 1985; McGowan 1995; Truscott and Smith 1993) and in the academy generally (Collins et al. 1998; Rosser 2004; Victor and Beaudry 1992) has been evident in the literature for at least the past two decades, especially in terms of "chilly climates" that inhibit the equal advancement of minority groups (see Wylie 1993). In order to gain some insight into this issue as it presently stands in Australia, we examined the profiles of Australian universities in terms of the gender of scholars employed full time in the academy and their positions. This allowed us to identify gender bias in employment as well as the gendered aspects of promotion within the academy.

Table 21.1 shows the gender of archaeologists employed full time in Australian universities, according to position and institution, as of February 2005. In order to see the patterns more clearly, these figures are amalgamated in figure 21.2 and presented as percentages.[4] The data demonstrate that after almost two decades of concern about the low numbers of females in archaeology, women continue to be underrepresented in the full-time staff of Australian universities. Women constitute 39 percent of archaeologists in the academy, equal to the national figure for academic staff in 2003 (Australian Vice Chancellors' Committee 2004), though these are located mostly in junior positions. At the level of lecturer, the ratio of males to females is two to one, though it is getting close to equal at the level of senior lecturer. However, there appears to be a ceiling at this level, as women do not advance to senior positions at a comparable rate to men. The ratio of males to females is around four to one for associate professor and five to one for professor. In fact, only five women archaeologists in Australia hold the position of associate professor or professor. The only category in which women are more highly represented than men, at a ratio of three to two, is that of research fellow, normally supported by "soft" funding allocated to a specific project and with a limited duration. Only one institution, Flinders University, has equal female and male staff, while only one other, the University of Western Australia, has more women than men (two women and one man). It is also notable that only one institution, Charles Sturt University, employs an Aboriginal lecturer (who is male) despite the focus on Indigenous archaeology in many Australian programs. Surprisingly, several units have no women at all, and in some cases there has been a reversal in gender equity. While the archaeology program at Charles Sturt University was started by two women, Annie Clarke and Laurajane Smith (Annie Clarke, e-mail communication, January 12, 2005), it now employs only men. This pattern highlights a disciplinary bias toward males, as several units have only male faculty, while there is no unit with only female faculty. In regard to the possibility of achieving equity in the future, the most worrying figure is at the lecturer level of entry. If twice as many men as women continue to be employed at this level, the pattern of female marginalization will continue, and the academy will lose the talents of skilled people.

So how do these figures compare to those of the past? How far have women come? Comparison of the results of this study with Truscott and Smith's (1993) analysis of permanent employment in Australian archaeology shows there has been an increase in female representation at the level of lecturer, with women

Table 21.1. The Gender of Archaeologists with Full-Time Employment in Australian Universities, February 2005

Institution	Female Research Fellow	Female Lecturer	Female Senior Lecturer	Female Associate Professor	Female Professor	Male Research Fellow	Male Lecturer	Male Senior Lecturer	Male Associate Professor	Male Professor	TOTAL
Adelaide U.	0	0	1	0	0	0	0	0	0	0	1
Australian National U., Archaeology and Anthropology; RSPAS	3	0	0	0	0	3	1	1	1	3	12
Charles Darwin U.	1	0	0	0	0	0	1	0	0	0	2
Charles Sturt U.	0	0	0	0	0	0	1	1	0	0	2
Deakin U., CHC	1	0	0	0	0	0	0	0	0	1	2
Flinders U.	1	2	1	0	0	0	1	0	2	0	7
James Cook U.	0	0	1	0	0	0	1	1	1	0	4
La Trobe U.	2	0	2	1	0	1	1	3	0	2	13
Macquarie U., Ancient History	0	0	2	0	0	0	1	1	0	1	5
Monash U., Archaeology and Ancient History, CAIS, Australian Indigenous Studies, Geography and Environmental Science	2	1	0	0	0	1	0	2	0	0	6
Sydney U., Archaeology, and Heritage Studies	2	2	2	0	1	2	2	1	1	1	14
U. Melbourne, Classics and Archaeology	1	1	0	0	0	0	2	0	1	1	6
U. New England	1	0	0	1	0	1	2	0	0	3	8
U. Queensland, Social Sciences, and ATSI Unit	0	0	1	0	0	0	0	2	2	0	5
U. Western Australia	0	0	1	0	1	0	1	0	0	0	3
U. Woollongong, Earth & Environmental Sciences	0	0	0	0	1	0	0	0	0	0	1
TOTAL	14	6	11	2	3	8	14	12	9	12	91

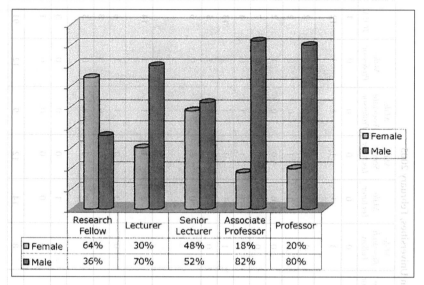

Figure 21.2. Percentage of archaeologists with full-time employment in Australian universities, according to gender and position, February 2005.

holding 25 percent (seven of twenty-eight) of these posts in 1991 and 32 percent (six of nineteen) in 2005. Truscott and Smith's amalgamation of the categories of senior lecturer and reader/associate professor shows women holding 16 percent (three of nineteen) of these posts in 1991. In 2005, women hold 45 percent (ten of twenty-two) of senior lecturer posts but only 18 percent (two of eleven) of associate lecturer posts. At the level of professor, women held 29 percent (two of seven) of posts in 1991, while in 2005 they hold 21 percent of posts (three of fourteen). These figures show that while female representation has increased at junior levels, it has reversed at the most senior level. This should not be viewed as anomalous, as comparable reversals occurred in science, mathematics, and engineering during the 1990s (see Vetter 1996). The numbers of women in senior positions in archaeology in Australian universities are still so unrepresentative as to provide evidence of continuing systemic and cultural barriers to women's progress.

These data raise several critical questions. What is the cause of this patterning? Is it general to the archaeological workplace or specific to the academy? What lessons can be learned from this?

The question of cause is a complex one since patterns in human behavior are an intersection of many factors. Certainly, a fundamental issue is the cumulative effect of behaviors such as stereotyping, exclusion and isolation, devaluation, and trivialization on women's abilities to reach their full potential. Regardless of equity legislation, such subtle discriminatory practices can create a "chilly climate" that inhibits professional advancement (see Wylie 1993). The question of female marginalization in the profession has been addressed by scholars in the context of archaeology in Australia (e.g., Beck and Head 1990; Buckley 1993; Casey 1998; Clarke 1993; Goulding et al. 1993; Phillips 1998; Truscott and Smith 1993) and globally (e.g., Conkey and Gero 1997; Ehrenberg 1989; Gero 1985, 1988; Kramer and Stark 1988; Stark 1991; Wylie 1993). The higher ratio of women to men in research positions demonstrated in the previously mentioned data may be because the flexibility of these positions makes them more attractive to women than permanent, teaching positions, but it is also likely that some women have taken this option because they have not yet obtained permanent employment. In addition, it is possible that there is a generational aspect to the pattern since many of the people who now hold positions as associate professors and professors were employed during the disciplinary cultures of the 1970s and 1980s, though the low ratio of women at entry level argues against this. It may be pertinent that in 2003 the median age for female academic staff was within the age-group of forty to forty-five compared to that of forty-five to forty-nine for men (Australian Vice Chancellors' Committee 2004).

In our view, the area of greatest concern is that of entry into the academy, where men outnumber women at a rate of two to one. The women who do not obtain a tenured post move to research fellowships, consulting, or overseas institutions. A significant number of young women, as well as young men, have taken up positions in overseas institutions in the past few years.[5] This is part of a trend in Australian society whereby around 5 percent of our population (1 million out of a population of slightly more than 20 million) live overseas (Australian Commerce and Industry 2004). While for some scholars a factor has been that research in areas such as feminist theory, identity, and postcolonial theory was not highly valued within the Australian disciplinary culture of the time (see Meskell 2003), there is no doubt that these young people are influenced by the disciplinary environment of the academy in Australia and, in particular, by their perceptions of whether they are likely to gain entry and promotion at the rate they expect. A more general study by Australian Commerce and Industry found that

> the *Push* factors for these young academics ranged across what respondents saw as the relatively low status for professionals in these areas at home and the long-term funding decline and lack of research career opportunities in

Australia. The *Pull* factors for these people revolved around better salary and career opportunities abroad. (Australian Commerce and Industry 2004:2)

Some of our best scholars, both female and male, are taking their intelligence, energy, and skills permanently to another country, a disciplinary facet of the much discussed "brain drain" of Australian academia (Hugo et al. 2001; Nicol 2000; Wood 2004). While this needs to be evaluated against the scholars with comparable skills who immigrate to Australia, we need to be concerned about the loss of skills to the Australian archaeological community from the scholars who leave permanently as against the gain in skills that would come from them acquiring experience and qualifications overseas and returning. Given the figures reported in this chapter, we expect this Australian diaspora to continue. While the academic climate may have warmed a little, it is still chilly, particularly at the upper levels.

It is difficult to determine whether the pattern described here holds across the archaeological workplace. To do this, it would be necessary to assess these issues for other forms of employment, especially those in the culture and heritage sectors. The majority of Australian archaeologists are employed by government heritage agencies or work as private consultants, dealing with cultural heritage management (Frankel 1998:27). McGowan (1995) argues that problems commonly associated with women's work, such as lower pay and unsatisfactory conditions, affect cultural heritage management workers (both women and men) because the field is female dominated and is perceived as "women's work." Goulding et al. (1993) assess the perception in Australian archaeology that women numerically dominate the cultural heritage sector. They found that "while women are more likely to be employed in cultural resource management [as opposed to the academic sector] . . . there is no gender difference on this point" (228). Writing in the early 1990s, Truscott and Smith (1993:219) record that women make up 60 percent of consultants and hold 46 percent of government cultural resource management positions. This suggests that the perception that women outnumber men in the area of cultural heritage is due to a perceived amplification of numbers as demographic parity is approached in this sector. It may also be related to the perceived status of this sector (see Clarke 1993). A similar process is likely to occur when the representation of women approaches demographic equity in the academy.

What lessons can be learned from this? First, women archaeologists who are seeking full-time employment in the academy or advancement within its ranks need to recognize that they are at a structural disadvantage. Not only are there less women in the academy, but there are systematic and cultural barriers to their advancement. There are numerous publications that offer career strategies for women (e.g., Collins et al. 1998; Chesterman 2000; Hansen 2005; Phillips 1998; Williams 2001; Zarmati 1998), and women archaeologists would do well to take full advantage of them. Second, it is essential that women in archaeology recognize that achievements are hard-won and that it is an easy matter to lose ground. In science, mathematics, and engineering, for instance, women made progress toward demographic parity and occupational equity with men in the 1970s and 1980s, but this slowed during the 1990s (Goodell 1998) and in some cases reversed (Vetter 1996). In terms of equity, the most vital issues for women are whether those who now hold fellowships will obtain permanent entry to the academy and, if they do, whether they will obtain promotion at a comparable rate to their male peers.

Related to this is the likelihood that the myths and stereotypes surrounding archaeology have marginalized women, either through excluding them from the general understanding of what is "normal" or through trivializing their achievements (Wylie 1993). The myth of the archaeologist as hero, for example, portrays an individual who is rugged, physically active, adventurous—and male (see Zarmati 1995). The popular version of this is embodied in the *Indiana Jones* novels and films and, more recently, in Nicholas Cage's performance in *National Treasure*. This is more likely to affect those people who come into the discipline more than those already there. While changing attitudes toward women in the wider society have emerged in the form of Lara Croft, the female archaeologist-hero of the film *Tomb Raider*, this is no closer to "real" archaeology. While she inscribes femininity within an active, assertive (and implicitly masculine) discourse of survival, Lara Croft does not necessarily represent liberation for female archaeologists in Australia or elsewhere. McRae (2002:135) argues that *Tomb Raider*'s success is partly a result of it being a friendlier version of feminism in an era where feminist politics is unpopular. This text "activates third wave feminism that punctuates its politics with purchases. It values fluid and flexible femininity defined through surfaces and sex appeal" (134). Moreover, the shaping of cultural norms and values by new technologies involved modular refigurations of the body that are inconsistent with a feminist agenda. The version of Lara Croft in the original video game, for instance, constructs a perfection that is biologically unattainable. A feminist biopolitics must be concerned with the narratives of gender, normalcy, and human nature that accompany new technologies. As McRae points out in terms of the Spice Girls and the re-release of *Charlie's Angels*, such formulations can highjack feminist politics in the service of dominant meanings to do with "sex appeal, fashionability and heterosexuality" (332). While the external forms change, the patriarchal core stays intact.

Finally, we consider an issue pertinent to the younger generation of female archaeologists. Given the changes that have occurred within our discipline over the past fifteen to twenty years, there is a risk that young women may consider the struggle for equity won and, moreover, that a few may wonder if there was ever a serious battle to be fought. There is risk of a neoconservatism in which successful women assume that their success is indicative of the prospect that all women can succeed if only they are willing to pay the price and women who have yet to succeed assume that they will not face unfair barriers. While female scholars succeed on their own merits, it is worthwhile remembering that there were many generations of women who had comparable merits and who tried but could not find a place in the academy (e.g., Ursula McConnel; see O'Gorman 1993). Most important, we should remember that the breaking of new ground is the hardest work of all. In Australian archaeology, this ground was broken first by scholars such as Isabel McBryde, Betty Meehan, Val Attenbrow, Sharon Sullivan, and Andrée Rosenfeld and, a little later, by Sandra Bowdler, Hilary du Cros, Lesley Head, Laurajane Smith, Jane Balme, and Wendy Beck. These are the women who created an awareness of an "empty niche" in tertiary institutions and government bodies into which younger female scholars can now be slotted (though not yet on parity with men) and who demonstrated the ability of women to succeed in Australian archaeology. Because of their hard-fought achievements, we all have it a little easier.

Gaps and Niches

While Australian archaeology has had significant advances in the field of gender, there are still gaps and niches. In this section, we identify three important aspects that Australian archaeology has yet to come to grips with. The first is the notion of sex and gender as spectrums rather than as male/female dichotomies. The second concerns the implications of gender being culturally defined. The third concerns the likelihood that there is an archaeological signature for female embodied experiences, such as menstruation and birthing.

One step that has not been taken in Australian archaeology is thinking beyond the Western hegemony of an either/or opposition for sex and gender. In gender and sexuality studies, the framing of sex and/or gender as dichotomous variables has been problematized extensively (e.g., Bassler 2004; Herdt 1996). Even the notion a male/female sexual dichotomy has been shown to be simplistic. One of the most influential papers in this respect is Anne Fausto-Sterling's (1993) article

"The Five Sexes: Why Male and Female Is Not Enough," which outlines five biological categories for sex: female, male, hermaphrodite, merm, and ferm (see also Fausto-Sterling 2000). The latter three are usually grouped under the rubric of "intersex" and are uncommon in the West, where sex of such bodies is reassigned surgically at birth or soon after. The assumption underlying such surgery, that intersexual bodies are unnatural, seems odd since intervention is the only way to make them "natural." Fausto-Sterling considers the social and political implications of these issues:

> The treatment of intersexuality in this century provides a clear example of what the French historian Michel Foucault has called biopower. The knowledge developed in biochemistry, embryology, endocrinology, psychology and surgery has enabled physicians to control the very sex of the human body. . . . On the other hand, the same medical accomplishments can be read not as progress but as a mode of discipline. Hermaphrodites have unruly bodies. They do not fall naturally into a binary classification; only a surgical shoehorn can put them there. But why should we care if a "woman," defined as one who has breasts, a vagina, a uterus and ovaries and who menstruates, also has a clitoris large enough to penetrate the vagina of another woman? Why should we care if there are people whose biological equipment enables them to have sex "naturally" with both men and women? The answers seem to lie in a cultural need to maintain clear distinctions between the sexes. Society mandates the control of intersexual bodies because they blur and bridge the great divide. Inasmuch as hermaphrodites literally embody both sexes, they challenge traditional beliefs about sexual difference: they possess the irritating ability to live sometimes as one sex and sometimes the other, and they raise the specter of homosexuality. (Fausto-Sterling 1993:24)

The point to be taken by archaeologists is that our eradication of intersexuality in the present foreshadows our failure to look for it in the past. Like the presence of women, this needs to be addressed in the present before it can be found in the past. This is not something that is being dealt with by Australian archaeology at all or one likely to be engaged in the near future.

The issues become even more complicated if we consider this in terms of gender. If there are five biologically identifiable sexes, how many genders must there be? Again, the use of spectrum as an organizing principle leaves room for female, male, transgender (those who are biologically of one sex but identify with the opposite gender)—and a plethora of "performances" in between, each of which is located within a specific historic and cultural context. Moreover, what is often considered to be "normal" is really normative in that it is what people are socialized to accept as normal. As societies and socialization change, so too do concepts of what constitutes "normal" gendered behavior. One example of that is the change since the 1950s in women's and men's gender roles in the Anglo-American countries. Furthermore, if we consider the implications of gender being culturally defined, this means that we have to engage seriously with the possibility of it having different manifestations across time and space. For archaeologists, this means taking into account the possibility of permutations that we have not considered and that do not exist in the contemporary world (e.g., Conroy 1993; Dowson 2000; Meskell 2002; Schmidt and Voss 2000).

Certainly, we are aware of some of the options that have been explored by other cultures. Greco-Roman culture, for example, viewed gender as a spectrum of qualities instead of as a dichotomy between male and female (Bassler 2004). Likewise, in seventeenth-century plays, such as those of William Shakespeare or Christopher Marlow, gender roles were blurred, and there was a greater concern with the performance of femaleness and maleness. From this viewpoint, it is more profitable to talk about male-to-male or female-to-female sexual behaviors than about men who have sex with men or women who have sex with women (cf. Naz Foundation International 2000). In India, for instance, distinctions are made between several classes of men who have sex with men: *kothis*, "feminine" men who have sex with other men; *hijra*, men, many of whom are castrated, who dress as women in both public and private spheres; *pariks*, the *kothi* label for the "husband" of a *kothi*; and *panthis*, "manly" men who have sex with other males and/or with women (Naz Foundation International 2004). The *hijra* tradition of surgical intervention to effect a "sex change" from male to female and the existence of *hijra* communities go back 4,000 years (Conway 2003). There are numerous other instances of transgendered communities worldwide in both the present and the past (see Herdt 1996; Peoples' Union for Civil Liberties, Karnata 2003:16). Perhaps it is to these communities rather than the more "fixed" classifications of the West that we should be looking for our models in interpreting the past.

The third area that has been overlooked by Australian archaeology concerns the possibility that spatial domains and artifacts, particularly those associated with ritual performance, may be related to the embodied experiences of females. While the embodied experiences of males have been a focus of much anthropological attention, those of women have been neglected. As with the production of rock paintings and stone tools, outlined previously, the embodied experiences of females have been identified by a number of early ethnographers, both women and men, but the archaeological implications of this have not been considered substantively—if at all—even when material correlates were recorded. For example, in their research among the Adnajamatana tribe of the Northern Flinders ranges in South Australia, Mountford and Harvey found that "women here are in complete possession of a wide field of ceremonial life, which covers childbirth practices, and the puberty rituals of young women" (Mountford and Harvey 1941: 155). As the rituals surrounding these life experiences translate from intimate to social domains, they become heavily inscribed with meaning and significance. This is evident even in the brief, fragmentary, and often secondhand accounts provided by early ethnographers. Mountford and Harvey (1941) provide tantalizing glimpses of birthing as a socially recognized, ritually marked female embodied performance among the Adnajamatana. They note that when a birth is impending, young people and men are sent away, while the birthing woman and her companions then go to a selected area for the birth itself. The umbilical cord is cut with a stone knife and the cord stump placed in a witchetty grub tree (Mountford and Harvey 1941:155). Spencer and Gillen (1938) record comparable rituals in their account of Aboriginal society in central Australia. They note that a birthing woman retires to *Erlukwirra*, or the women's camp. If problems arise, the husband performs rituals to expedite the birthing process, and after birth the umbilical cord is severed either with a stone knife or with the sharpened end of a digging stick. Later, the umbilical cord is made into a necklace called an *Akurlaitcha* by "swathing it with fur string," and this is then placed around the infant's neck (Spencer and Gillen 1938:466).

These are not isolated examples. Throughout the world, material, ritual, and technical correlates have been recorded for the embodied experiences of women, especially birthing. While Ford's (1964) comparative study of human reproduction identifies twelve societies that provided a special shelter for birthing, Ploss et al. (1935:571–79) identify the construction of birthing structures in nearly forty different groups located throughout the globe, each of which has its own particular cultural beliefs. The general need for a birthing structure was not, from either account, considered unusual. What was "really strange" was that "of the many travelers in recent years who have journeyed to all parts of the world, it has hardly occurred to one of them to take a photograph of such an interesting object as the birth hut" (Ploss et al. 1935:577). The use of birthing structures have been recorded in many places in the world, including the island of Nauru (Ploss et al. 1935:572), in the Gilyaks and Chukchee groups of the northern Asiatic region (Czaplicka 1969), in eastern Siberia (Kwon 1999:374), and in many Native American and Native Canadian groups (Ploss et al. 1935:575).

The enormous variety in birthing structures that has been documented can be related to cultural and environmental factors. The range of structures recorded includes wooden buildings and tents as well as brush and snow houses. There are seasonal variations in the practices of some groups. Ploss et al. (1935:575) point out that in winter, birthing women of the Chippewa and Winnebago occupy a special tent near the family hut, while in summer they retire to the woods. Similar seasonal variation in birthing practices occurs among the Iglulik groups, including the Aivilingmiut, the Iglulingmiut, the Tununermiut, and the Amitjormiut living around Danish Island (Rasmussen 1929:9). A tent is erected for birthing women in the highly mobile communities of the Hudson Bay Area (Ploss et al. 1935:575), while in Tinglit society a brush or snow house is built at the back of the main house for birthing women (Ploss et al. 1935:577).

Birthing is not the only female embodied experience that has documented social, ritual, and material correlates. In many cultures, there is material evidence of female puberty in the form of menstrual buildings that in some groups also serve as birthing areas (Galloway 1997; Hoskins 2002). The gendered values that early ethnographers placed on such buildings can be identified by Williams's (1940:142) use of the term "lesser buildings" for houses used for birthing and menstruation. A more contemporary viewpoint is apparent in Jolly's (2002) linking of female menstrual and childbirth seclusion among the Dwaio of Malaite in the Solomon Islands to ritual activity through the people's use of the term *abu*, a term also used to describe male seclusion when communicating with ancestors (Jolly 2002:21). In the same publication, Jolly (2002:167) and Fiti-Sinclair (2002:59) refer to the existence of separate structures used for the negotiation of menstruation and childbirth.

These accounts demonstrate that female embodied experiences, though intimately negotiated, have distinct social recognition and material correlates. Throughout the world, women have negotiated their embodied life experiences through spatial domains and ritualized performances. The material correlates are primarily the standing structures constructed for birthing and female puberty, though other artifacts must have been involved. The birthing and puberty structures were publicly visible and clearly identifiable within these communities, even by visiting male ethnographers. These structures were a place for rites, rituals, and the dissemination of sociocultural beliefs, providing a locus for the expression of female embodiment. The rituals that attend birthing, in particular, are among the rare cross-cultural universals (see Brown 1991) that transcend intimate and public domains simultaneously.

The question that arises is, If ethnographers have entified such structures, why haven't these been taken into account in the interpretations put forward by archaeologists? In Australia, this can be attributed to the conflation of a disciplinary culture that had few female practitioners and cultural mores of Indigenous

Australians. Early ethnographers, the majority of whom were male, expressed concerns regarding the invasive nature of their attempting to record women's experiences (e.g., Elkin 1939:xx; see also Mountford 1976:109), and, indeed, this is what prompted Elkin to encourage Kaberry to conduct her research with Aboriginal women in the Kimberly region of Western Australia (see Elkin 1939; Kaberry 1939). Moreover, gender segregation within Indigenous Australian cultures is greater than in the West (see Bell 1983, 1998; Hamilton 1980; Smith 2004), and female embodied experiences are a component of secret "women's business." For Indigenous women, the discussion of such topics with men, whether Indigenous or European, is not tenable.

Nevertheless, sufficient research exists to demonstrate that the negotiation of female experiences will leave an archaeological signature. To not factor this into our research can have serious consequences not only for the quality of archaeological analyses but also for the people who are the focus of study. For example, a failure to grapple with the gendered differences of Indigenous knowledge systems underlay controversy over the building of the Hindmarsh Island Bridge, which became the subject of a Royal Commission. Ngarrindjeri women from the region objected to this development on the grounds that the bridge's construction would disturb an important site related to secret women's business. Other Ngarrindjeri women, however, disputed this, asserting that they were unaware of this women's business. The building of the bridge was stopped while the South Australian Hindmarsh Bridge Royal Commission was held. Untrained in the way that knowledge is compartmentalized in Aboriginal cultures, the commission concluded that the claim of secret women's business was a fabrication, and the bridge was built (Stevens 1995). This debate and its outcome turned on the acknowledgment of restricted women's knowledge in Ngarrindjeri life, but little substantive research had been conducted into women's activities in this area, with most of this done by men. Outrage over the outcome prompted a substantive study by Bell (1998), but the damage had been done. In an Australian disciplinary climate that is increasingly willing to take on a social justice agenda, the recording of women's business for and under the control of Indigenous women is an obvious sphere for future research.

Our final thought here concerns relationships between power, gender, and archaeological focus. While the balance of power in archaeology has begun to shift through an engendered archaeology, archaeology still clings to an ideology that defines economic productivity as power. In itself, power is an embodied experience regardless of gender. Its expression through rites of puberty, pregnancy, birthing, death, the acquisition of food, and the construction of shelter defines its visibility. To ignore the menstruating or birthing body is to ignore a critical aspect of human life and performance. A small shift in perspective is all that is required.

Closing Thoughts

This chapter explores the emergence of and trends in the study of gender in Australian archaeology. Given the interconnected world in which archaeology now functions, much of what has occurred in Australia mirrors what has happened in other parts of the world. There are two important developments that have occurred over the past fifteen to twenty years. First, we are moving beyond the gynocentric approaches of early work (e.g., Bird 1993; Gorman 1995; Smith 1991) to develop more nuanced, complicated understandings of gender in both the past and the present. Recent approaches explicitly critique material culture in terms of both genders, and both men and women are undertaking the research (e.g., D. Bulbeck 1998; de Leiuen and Pilgrim 1998; Knapp 1998; McDonald 1998; Staniforth et al. 2001). The politics of language (Clarke 1998; Zarmati 1998) and stereotyping (Moser 1993; Zarmati 1995) also are foci. As Australian archaeologists continue to grapple with gender, they will have to attend to the fact that it is nebulous and only one facet of a social identity that includes sexual orientation, ethnicity, class, economic status, and so forth. Dealing with the many facets of social difference and their multiple intersections with each other is a complex and challenging task but one being taken up by feminist anthropologists (e.g., Conkey 2005; Feder et al. 1997; Meskell 1999; Moore 1988; Ortner 1996). Second, the disciplinary culture of Australian archaeology is changing not only in response to feminist critiques but also in response to the ongoing critique by Indigenous Australians (e.g., Birt and Copley 2005; Isaacson and Ford 2005; Langford 1983), both of which are part of a postmodern concern with the politics of domination. Although still cherishing a conservative, processual core, Australian archaeology increasingly is willing to embrace topics such as archaeological theory, postcolonialism, and the construction of identity. One outcome of this changing world is a conference environment that is less confrontational, with fewer overt arguments and less grandstanding.

The influence of third-wave feminism, which conflates an interest in the multivalent nature of human identity with a postmodern concern with the politics of domination and the deconstruction of Anglo-American values, provides the archaeology of gender with new challenges. One of the issues still to be resolved concerns the applicability of a Western model of feminism to non-Western cultures (cf. C. Bulbeck 1998; Nicholson 1990). If a first step in gender archaeology is to stop placing androcentric assumptions on our interpretations of the past, steps that must follow soon including not imposing Western notions of gender onto non-Western societies and, indeed, facing the diversity inherent in terms such as "Western." To do otherwise is to ignore the vast potential for social complexity that exists across time and space. As Meskell (1999:71) states, such an approach "regards *woman*, or *man* for that matter, as a given which is transhistorical and transcultural and constant over the trajectories of age, status and ethnicity." In the present, this is an issue of respect. When dealing with interpretations of the past, it becomes one of methodological rigor.

For archaeology, one implication is that to speak in terms of gender equality—with females and males as distinct but equal—simply imposes particular Western twenty-first-century convictions on other cultures. The Eurocentrism inherent in many Western views has been touched on by scholars in terms of the intricacies of and psychological motivations behind women's veiling in the Muslim world (Abu-Lughod 2000; Delaney 1995), in regard to the practice of clitoridectomy in some African countries (Kenyatta 1965; Toubia 1985), and in the reframing of Western feminist issues through the eyes of "other" women (C. Bulbeck 1998). Arebi addresses this issue in regard to Muslim women:

> There are three reasons why Muslim women may generally find it difficult to adopt a western model of feminism predicated on premises deemed universally applicable. Firstly, Muslim women do not perceive "family ties and kinship ties [as] a hindrance to women's liberation"; secondly, there is a resentment of "the West's identification of the problem" of Muslim women as a "religious problem"; and thirdly, wages have not necessarily functioned as a "liberating force" in the sense advocated by western feminists. (Arebi 1994:1)

If this is true for Muslim women, it is also likely to be true for Indigenous women, especially when applied to the past (cf. Colley 2000:28). Although they intersect, in many ways Indigenous and Western cultures have values and conceptualizations of the world that are deeply different. While there is enormous variation between particular cultures, Indigenous people often have different notions of time (Zimmerman 1995), of place (Smith and Burke 2004), of public and private spheres (McDonald 1998)—and of gender ideologies and roles (e.g., Bell 1983, 1998; Hamilton 1980; Kaberry 1939). In the remote communities of central and southern Arnhem Land, for instance, Indigenous women place a greater emphasis on family and kinship ties and gender segregation within the society than in the West (Smith 2004). In this region, women dress modestly, normally have one or more children by the age of twenty, and may not consider a career until they are in their early thirties, if at all. They gain gravitas and power with age: calling someone "old" is a compliment akin to saying that they are wise, so different to the conceptualization of age in the United States or Britain. In these Arnhem Land societies, unmarried women are rare. Children are a means of establishing one's place in the community and are a source of prestige and pride. Both women and men normally spend their entire lives within the network of extended family that is located in the small communities within their region (Smith 2004). To impose essentialized Anglo-American notions of gender on such societies would be spurious. While this has been recognized in some feminist research (e.g., Bowdler 1976, 1981; Colley 2000; McDonald 1992, 1995), it has not been absorbed into many mainstream analyses, as demonstrated by the Hindmarsh Island debacle. New theoretical models are needed to interpret gender relations in the pasts of such societies. As Colley (2000:28) points out, "Feminist and other critical approaches have the potential to develop a more sophisticated understanding of the use of ethnography in archaeological interpretation, and the meanings we assign to the material culture we excavate."

And new theoretical models are emerging, though perhaps not in the form that we once envisaged. Meskell highlights a recent tension in current feminism: "On the one hand, feminists align themselves with the post-structuralist deconstruction of master narratives; and, on the other, they want to create a feminine voice in opposition to the pre-existing masculine discourse" (Meskell 1999:68–69). From this viewpoint, the success of an archaeology of gender, in Australia and elsewhere, also can be viewed as its undoing. The strides we have made have entailed a reshaping of our original goals and expectations and a diffusion of focus in which women per se are less often the sole focus of study. This, in itself, is a mark of achievement. We have responded to calls to use feminist methods of inquiry to critique scientific reconstructions of the past and to use the evidence of the past to deconstruct the inevitability of contemporary conditions (e.g., Conkey 1993:11; Moser 1993). We are meeting concerns that we have a greater awareness of the dynamic nature of gender and its historical specificity (e.g., Butler 1990:4–5; Conkey and Gero 1991:9–10; Haraway 1997:28; Meskell 1999:71; Moore 1988:106; Wylie 1992:34). Increasingly, during the 1990s and the early 2000s, our studies are analyzing gender in terms of other constituents of and influences on social identity and recognizing that these are affected by individual life histories (e.g. de Leiuen 1998; Ireland 2001, 2002; Lydon 1995, 1999; McDonald 1992, 1995, 1998; Meskell 1999). It appears we are moving toward the new feminist politics called for by Haraway (1997:28) and identified by Meskell (1999:69) as "one that accepts the variable construction of identity as a methodological and political goal."

At this time, it is possible to argue that the disciplinary culture of Australian archaeology is being transformed, almost by stealth, because of the intersection of feminist, Indigenous, and postprocessual critiques. This transformation is more of an insinuation than a triumph. At a fundamental level, it is simply good sense. Moreover, our ideas of what constitutes a gendered archaeology are changing. We no longer consider this to be simply identifying women or women's behaviors in the material remains of the past (though there is still ongoing work to be done here) or being concerned with the glass ceilings that are ubiquitous (but not without significant cracks) in archaeology globally. Increasingly, gender is being seen as one part of how many people, of different genders, do archaeology, rather than the principal focus of a few, in the same way that gender is one aspect of how we all live our lives. Today, a gendered archaeology has to grapple with the multitude of other facets of human identity. This means that engendered voices must speak to class, ethnicity, sexuality, religion, economic position, and a plethora of other conditions. What is emerging is a kind of "hive archaeology," one capable of dealing with the myriad facets of social identity and their multiple intersections with each other. By engaging with the tensions located within social theories of identity, archaeologists are contributing to more nuanced, complicated understandings of gender in the past and in the present.

Acknowledgments

The genesis of this chapter was presented by Claire Smith as the Fifth Bassey Andah Memorial Lecture at the University of Ibadan, Nigeria, March 25, 2004. Claire would like to thank Bayo Folorunso, Bisi Sowunmi, Louisa Andah, and other members of the Bassey Andah Memorial Lecture Committee for inviting her to present this lecture and for their kindness during her visit. We would like to thank the members of university departments who helped us calculate up-to-date figures for their academic staff, especially Dan Potts, Iain Davidson, Jane Balme, Annie Clarke, Frank Sears, Tim Murray, Bruno David, Peter Bellwood, Matthew Spriggs, Jane Lydon, Susan Lawrence, and David Frankel. For helpful discussions or critical comments on drafts of this chapter, we thank Jane Lydon, Katrina Stankowski, Angie McGowan, Annie Ross, Heather Burke, Gary Jackson, Ian Lilley, Annie Clarke, Bruno David, John Campbell, and Alice Gorman. Annette Smith kindly checked the proofs over the Christmas period, 2005, and George Merryman was able to find humor in my depiction of the Australian archaeology disciplinary culture (but Jo Smith could only empathize with the oppressed—in Internet language, she is TSTL[6] and clearly not destined for a job in Australian archaeology).

Notes

1. To "hack it" means to endure through difficult conditions with little or no complaint.

2. In Australia, thongs are footwear, not underwear, usually worn in casual situations, such as at the beach. In some places, thongs are known as "flip-flops."

3. An advance copy of Gero and Conkey (1991) was available at the conference.

4. The data were compiled in February 2005 from information on institutional websites and cross-referenced with faculty handbooks for 2005. If we had a query, we contacted the people or departments concerned directly. In several cases where more than one department employed archaeologists, the data were combined to give a figure for the university as a whole. We excluded nonsalaried positions, such as emeritus professor or adjunct professor, and casual or sessional positions, such as tutors, and amalgamated the various categories of research fellow. In one case (University of New England), two tenured teaching staff at the level of associate professor were made professorial fellows. These were recorded as professors. The position of reader was recorded as associate professor, as it is equivalent. These data do not take into account interdisciplinary collaborations. For example, the Programme in Australian Indigenous Archaeology at Monash University regularly draws on the specialist services of both women and men from other departments (Bruno David, personal communication, January 4, 2005).

5. We could identify nine scholars in this category: Huw Barton, Judith Littleton, Peter Magee, Lynn Meskell, Stephanie Moser, Cameron Petrie, Laurajane Smith, Glen Summerhayes, and Lloyd Weeks. We excluded scholars, such as Eleanor Casella, Paul Rainbird, and Bernard Knapp, who are not Australian citizens, though they had spent extensive periods in Australian institutions before locating overseas.

6. TSTL is Internet shorthand for "too sensitive to live."

References

Abu-Lughod, Lila
    2000   *Veiled Sentiments: Honor and Poetry in a Bedouin Society*. Berkeley: University of California Press.

Arebi, Saddeka
    1994   *Women and Words in Saudi Arabia: The Politics of Literary Discourse*. New York: Columbia University Press.

Australian Commerce and Industry
    2004   Why Do One Million Australians Live Overseas? *Review* 18:1–6. Electronic document, http://www.acci.asn.au/text_files/review/r118.pdf, accessed January 5, 2005.

Australian Vice Chancellors' Committee
    2004   Other Higher Education Statistics. University Staff Profile 1996–2003. Electronic document, http://www.avcc.edu.au/content.asp?page=/publications/stats/hedstats.htm, accessed January 5, 2005.

Balme, Jane, and Wendy Beck
    1993   Archaeology and Feminism—Views on the Origins of the Division of Labour. In *Women in Archaeology: A Feminist Critique*. Hilary du Cros and Laurajane Smith, eds. Pp. 61–74. Canberra: Australian National University.

Balme, Jane, and Wendy Beck, eds.
    1995   *Gendered Archaeology: The Second Australian Women in Archaeology Conference*. Canberra: ANH Publications, Research School of Pacific and Asian Studies, Australian National University.

Bassler, Jouette
    2004   Interpreting Primal Christianity. SMU Research Faculty Profiles, Volume 11, Year 2004. Electronic document, http://www.smu.edu/newsinfo/research/2004/bassler.htm, accessed January 5, 2005.

Bavin, Louise
    1989   Behind the Facade: the Expression of Status and Class in Material Culture. *Australasian Historical Archaeology* 7:16–22.

Beck, Wendy, and Jane Balme
    1994   Gender in Aboriginal Archaeology: Recent Research. *Australian Archaeology* 39:39–46.

Beck, Wendy, and Lesley Head
    1990   Women in Australian Prehistory. *Australian Feminist Studies* 11:29–48.

Beck, Wendy, Annie Clarke, and Lesley Head, eds.
    1989   *Plants in Australian Archaeology*. Tempus 1. St. Lucia: Anthropology Museum, University of Queensland.

Bell, Diane
    1983   *Daughters of the Dreaming*. Melbourne: McPhee Gibble.
    1998   *Ngarrindjeri Wurruwarrin: A World That Is, Was, and Will Be*. Melbourne: Spinifex Press.

Bird, Caroline
    1993   Woman the Toolmaker: Evidence for Women's Use and Manufacture of Flaked Stone Tools in Australia and New Guinea. In *Women in Archaeology: A Feminist Critique*. Hilary du Cros and Laurajane Smith, eds. Pp. 22–30. Canberra: Australian National University.

Birt, Peter, and Vincent Copley
    2005   Coming Back to Country: A Conversation at Firewood Creek. In *Indigenous Archaeologies: Decolonising Theory and Practice*. Claire Smith and H. Martin Wobst, eds. Pp. 262–78. London: Routledge.

Blainey, Geoffrey
    2001   Heroes and Tall Poppies. Boyer Lecture for Australian Broadcasting Commission's Radio National. Electronic document, http://www.abc.net.au/rn/boyers/stories/s986927.htm, accessed January 5, 2005.

Bowdler, Sandra
    1976   Hook, Line and Dilly Bag: An Interpretation of an Australian Coastal Shell Midden. *Mankind* 10:248–58.

1981 Hunters in the Highlands: Aboriginal Adaptations in the Eastern Australian Uplands. *Archaeology in Oceania* 16:99–111.

Brown, Donald E.
1991 *Human Universals.* New York: McGraw-Hill.

Buckley, Kristal
1993 Cultural Resource Management and Gender Issues. In *Women in Archaeology: A Feminist Critique.* Hilary du Cros and Laurajane Smith, eds. Pp. 173–74. Canberra: Australian National University.

Bulbeck, Chilla
1998 *Re-Orienting Western Feminisms: Women's Diversity in a Post-Colonial World.* Cambridge: Cambridge University Press.

Bulbeck, David
1998 The Female Visage of Lapita. In *Redefining Archaeology: Feminist Perspectives.* Mary Casey, Denise Donlan, Jeanette Hope, and Sharon Wellfare, eds. Pp. 90–95. Canberra: ANH Publications, Research School of Pacific Studies, Australian National University.

Burke, Heather
1999 *Meaning and Ideology in Historical Archaeology: Style, Social Identity and Capitalism in an Australian Town.* New York: Plenum.

Butler, Judith
1990 *Gender Trouble: Feminism and the Subversion of Identity.* New York: Routledge.

Casella, Eleanor
2001 *Archaeology of the Ross Female Factory: Female Incarceration in Van Diemen's Land, Australia.* Hobart: Queen Victoria Museum and Art Gallery.

Casey, Mary
1998 Gender in Historical Archaeology 1991–1995: The Impact of the First Women in Archaeology Conference. In *Redefining Archaeology: Feminist Perspectives.* Mary Casey, Denise Donlan, Jeanette Hope, and Sharon Wellfare, eds. Pp. 68–73. Canberra: ANH Publications, Research School of Pacific Studies, Australian National University.

Casey, Mary, Denise Donlan, Jeanette Hope, and Sharon Wellfare, eds.
1998 *Redefining Archaeology: Feminist Perspectives.* Canberra: ANH Publications, Research School of Pacific Studies, Australian National University.

Chesterman, Colleen
2000 Women's Executive Development in Australian Higher Education: The Wexdev Model. Paper Presented at Nawe Conference, New Orleans, January. Electronic document, http://www.uts.edu.au/oth/wexdev/pdfs/womens_exec_dev.pdf, accessed January 5, 2005.

Claassen, Cheryl, ed.
1992 *Exploring Gender through Archaeology.* Philadelphia: University of Pennsylvania Press.

Clarke, Annie
    1993   CRM as Archaeological Housework: Confining Women to the Ghetto of Management. In *Women in Archaeology: A Feminist Critique*. Hilary du Cros and Laurajane Smith, eds. Pp. 91–94. Canberra: Australian National University.
    1998   Engendered Fields: The Language of the American-Australian Expedition to Arnhem Land. In *Redefining Archaeology: Feminist Perspectives*. Mary Casey, Denise Donlan, Jeanette Hope, and Sharon Wellfare, eds. Pp. 13–18. Canberra: ANH Publications, Research School of Pacific Studies, Australian National University.

Claassen, Cheryl
    2000   Homophobia and Women Archaeologists. *World Archaeology: Queer Archaeologies* 32(2):173–79.

Colley, Sarah
    1998   Engendering Pre- and Post-Contact Australian archaeology: A Theoretical Challenge. In *Redefining Archaeology: Feminist Perspectives*. Mary Casey, Denise Donlan, Jeanette Hope, and Sharon Wellfare, eds. Pp. 9–12. Canberra: ANH Publications, Research School of Pacific Studies, Australian National University.
    2000   Sisters Are Doing It for Themselves? Gender, Feminism and Australian (Aboriginal) Archaeology. In *Gender and Material Culture in Archaeological Perspective*. Linda Hurcombe and Moira Donald, eds. Pp. 20–32. London: Macmillan.

Collins, Lynn H., Joan C. Chrisler, and Kathryn Qunia, eds.
    1998   *Career Strategies for Women in Academe: Arming Athena*. Thousand Oaks, CA: Sage.

Conkey, Margaret W.
    1993   Making the Connections: Feminist Theory and the Archaeologies of Gender. In *Women in Archaeology: A Feminist Critique*. Hilary du Cros and Laurajane Smith, eds. Pp. 3–15. Canberra: Australian National University.
    2005   Dwelling at the Margins, Action at the Intersection? Feminist and Indigenous Archaeologies. *Archaeologies* 1(1):9–80.

Conkey, Margaret W., and Joan Gero
    1991   Tensions, Pluralities and Engendering Archaeology. In *Engendering Archaeology: Women and Prehistory*. Joan M. and Margaret W. Conkey, eds. Pp. 3–30. Oxford: Basil Blackwell.
    1997   Programme to Practice: Gender and Feminism in Archaeology. *Annual Review of Anthropology* 26:411–37.

Conkey, Margaret W., and Janet D. Spector
    1984   Archaeology and the Study of Gender. In *Advances in Archaeological Method and Theory* 7. Michael Schiffer, ed. Pp. 1–32. New York: Academic Press.

Conroy, Linda
    1993   Female Figurines in the Upper Palaeolithic and the Emergence of Gender. In

Women in Archaeology: A Feminist Critique. Hilary du Cros and Laurajane Smith, eds. Pp. 153–60. Canberra: Australian National University.

Conway, Linda
  2003   Reflections on the PUCL (Peoples' Union for Civil Liberties) Report. Electronic document, http://ai.eecs.umich.edu/people/conway/TS/PUCL/PUCL%20Report.html, accessed January 5, 2005.

Crawford, Ian
  1968   *The Art of the Wandjina.* Oxford: Oxford University Press.

Czaplicka, Marie A.
  1969   *Aboriginal Siberia: A Study in Social Anthropology.* Oxford: Clarendon Press.

de Leiuen, Cherrie
  1998   The Power of Gender. Honors thesis, Flinders University.

de Leiuen, Cherrie, and Robert Pilgrim
  1998   Power and Gender in Archaeology. Unpublished session rationale for annual conference of the Australian Archaeological Association, Valla Beach, New South Wales.

Delaney, Carol
  1995   Untangling the Meanings of Hair in Turkish Society. In *Off with Her Head: The Denial of Women's Identity in Myth, Religion and Culture.* Howard Eilberg-Schwartz and Wendy Doniger, eds. Pp. 53–75. Berkeley: University of California Press.

Diaz-Andreu, Margarita, and Marie Louise Stig Sørensen
  1998   *Excavating Women. A History of Women in European Archaeology.* London: Routledge.

Donlan, Denise
  1993   Imbalance in the Sex Ratio in Collections of Australian Aboriginal Remains. In *Women in Archaeology: A Feminist Critique.* Hilary du Cros and Laurajane Smith, eds. Pp. 98–103. Canberra: Australian National University.

Dowson, Thomas, ed.
  2000   *World Archaeology: Queer Archaeologies* (32)2.

du Cros, Hilary, and Laurajane Smith
  1993a   Why a Feminist Critique of Archaeology? In *Women in Archaeology: A Feminist Critique.* Hilary du Cros and Laurajane Smith, eds. Pp. xvii–xx. Canberra: Australian National University.

du Cros, Hilary, and Laurajane Smith, eds.
  1993b   *Women in Archaeology: A Feminist Critique.* Canberra: Australian National University.

Ehrenberg, Margaret
  1989   *Women in Prehistory.* Norman: University of Oklahoma Press.

Elkin, Adolphus Peter
  1939   Introduction. In *Aboriginal Woman: Sacred and Profane.* Phyllis Mary Kaberry. Pp. i–xxii. London: Routledge.

Fausto-Sterling, Anne
:   1993   The Five Sexes. *The Sciences*, March/April, 20–25.
    2000   The Five Sexes, Revisited. *The Sciences*, July/August, 18–23.
Feder, Ellen K., Mary C. Rawlinson, and Emily Zakin
:   1997   *Derrida and Feminism: Recasting the Question of Woman*. London: Routledge.
Fiti-Sinclair, Ruth
:   2002   Childbirth in Papua New Guinea Villages and in Port Moresby General Hospital. In *Birthing in the Pacific: Beyond Tradition and Modernity*. Vicki Lukere and Margaret Jolly, eds. Pp. 56–78. Honolulu: University of Hawai'i Press.
Ford, Clellan Stearns
:   1964   *A Comparative Study of Human Reproduction*. Publications in Anthropology, no. 32. New Haven, CT: Human Relations Area Files Press, Yale University.
Frankel, David
:   1998   Archaeology. In *Knowing Ourselves and Others: The Humanities in Australia into the 21st Century*. Vol. 2. Pp. 17–28. Prepared by the Australian Academy of the Humanities for the Australian Research Council Discipline Research Strategies. Canberra: National Board of Employment, Education and Training, Australian Government Publishing Services.
Friedl, Ernestine
:   1975   *Women and Men: An Anthropological View*. New York: Holt, Rinehart and Winston.
Galloway, Patricia
:   1997   Where Have All the Menstrual Huts Gone? The Invisibility of Menstrual Seclusion in the Late Prehistoric Southeast. In *Women in Prehistory: North America and Mesoamerica*. Cheryl Claassen and Rosemary A. Joyce, eds. Pp. 47–64. Philadelphia: University of Pennsylvania Press.
Gero, Joan M.
:   1985   Sociopolitics and the Woman-at-Home Ideology. *American Antiquity* 50(2):342–50.
    1988   Gender Bias in Archaeology: Here, Then and Now. In *Feminism within Science and Health Care Professions: Overcoming Resistance*. Sue V. Roser, ed. Pp. 33–43. New York: Pergamon Press.
Gero, Joan M., and Margaret W. Conkey, eds.
:   1991   *Engendering Archaeology: Women and Prehistory*. Oxford: Basil Blackwell.
Gilchrist, Roberta
:   1994   *Gender and Material Culture: The Archaeology of Religious Women*. London: Routledge.
Goodell, Joanne
:   1998   Increasing the Enrolment, Retention and Success of Female Students in Non-Traditional Areas: What Strategies Can We Use to Involve Staff in Developing a More Gender- and Culturally-Inclusive Educational Environment? In *Teaching and Learning in Changing Times, Proceedings of the 7th Annual Teaching Learning Forum, The University of Western Australia, February 1998*. Barbara Black and Nata-

lie Stanley, eds. Pp. 120–24. Perth: University of Western Australia. Electronic document, http://lsn.curtin.edu.au/tlf/tlf1998/goodell.html, accessed January 5, 2005.

Gorman, Alice C.
 1993 Theories of Prehistoric Inequality: Hobbes, Freud and Engels. In *Women in Archaeology: A Feminist Critique*. Hilary du Cros and Laurajane Smith, eds. Pp. 46–50. Canberra: Australian National University.
 1995 Gender, Labour and Resources: The Female Knappers of the Andaman Islands. In *Gendered Archaeology: The Second Australian Women in Archaeology Conference*. Jane Balme and Wendy Beck, eds. Pp. 87–91. Canberra: Division of Archaeology and Natural History, Australian National University.
 1997 Obsidian Razors from Mexico and New Guinea. *International Association for Obsidian Studies Bulletin* 19:5–6.

Gould, Richard
 1969 *Yiwara, Foragers of the Australian Desert*. London: Collins.

Goulding, Megan, Kristal Buckley, and Gabrielle Brennan
 1993 The Role of Gender in Archaeological Career Structures: A Victorian Case Study. In *Women in Archaeology: A Feminist Critique*. Hilary du Cros and Laurajane Smith, eds. Pp. 222–31. Canberra: Australian National University.

Hamilton, Annette
 1980 Dual Social Systems: Technology, Labour and Women's Secret Rites in the Eastern Western Desert of Australia. *Oceania* 51:4–19.

Hansen, Katharine
 2005 10 Powerful Career Strategies for Women. Electronic document, http://www.quintcareers.com/women_career_strategies.html, accessed January 5, 2005.

Haraway, Donna
 1997 *Modest_Witness@Second_Millenium.FemaleMale_Meets_OncoMouse™*. New York: Routledge.

Haydon, Brian
 1977 Stone Tool Functions in the Western Desert. In *Stone Tools as Cultural Markers*. Richard V. S. Wright, ed. Pp. 178–88. Canberra: Australian Institute of Aboriginal Studies.

Herdt, Gilbert, ed.
 1996 *Third Sex, Third Gender: Beyond Sexual Dimorphism in Culture and History*. New York: Zone Books.

Hiscock, Peter
 1988 A Cache of Tulas from the Boulia District of Western Queensland. *Archaeology in Oceania* 23(2):60–70.
 1996 Transformations of Upper Palaeolithic Implements in the Dabba Industry from Haua Fteah (Libya). *Antiquity* 70:657–64.

Hiscock, Peter, and Val Attenbrow
   1998   Early Holocene Backed Artefacts from Australia. *Archaeology in Oceania* 33:49–63.

Hope, Jeanette
   1998   Making up Stories: Bias in Interpretation of Aboriginal Burial Practices. In *Redefining Archaeology: Feminist Perspectives.* Mary Casey, Denise Donlan, Jeanette Hope, and Sharon Wellfare, eds. Pp. 239–45. Canberra: ANH Publications, Research School of Pacific Studies, Australian National University.

Hoskins, Janet
   2002   The Menstrual Hut and the Witch's Lair in Two Eastern Indonesian Societies. *Ethnology* 31(2):317–34.

Hourani, Pam
   1991   Spatial Organisation and the Status of Women in Nineteenth-Century Australia. *Australasian Historical Archaeology* 8:70–77.

Huchet, Bernard
   1991   Theories and Australian Prehistory: The Last Three Decades. *Australian Archaeology* 33:44–51.

Hugo, Graeme, Dianne Rudd, and Kevin Harris
   2001   Emigration from Australia: Economic Implications. Committee for Economic Development of Australia Information Paper, no. 7. Adelaide: Committee for Economic Development of Australia. Electronic document, http://www.immi.gov.au/research/publications/econimpact_1.pdf, accessed January 5, 2005.

Ireland, Tracey
   2001   An Artefact of Nation: Historical Archaeology, Heritage and Nationalism in Australia. Ph.D. dissertation, University of Sydney.
   2002   Giving Value to the Australian Historic Past. *Australasian Historical Archaeology* 20:15–25.

Isaac, Glynn
   1978   The Food Sharing Behaviour of Proto-Human Hominids. In *Human Ancestors.* Glynn L. Isaac and Richard E. Leakey, eds. Pp. 110–23. San Francisco: W. H. Freeman.

Isaac, Glynn L., and Diana C. Crader
   1981   To What Extent Were Early Hominids Carnivores? An Archaeological Perspective. In *Omnivorous Primates.* Robert Harding and Geza Teleki, eds. Pp. 27–103. New York: Columbia University Press.

Isaacson Ken, and Stephanie Ford
   2005   Looking Forward—Looking Back: Shaping a Shared Future Coming Back to Country: A Conversation at Firewood Creek. In *Indigenous Archaeologies: Decolonising Theory and Practice.* Claire Smith and H. Martin Wobst, eds. Pp. 352–65. London: Routledge.

Jolly, Margaret
  2002 Epidemiologies and Ethnographies of Motherhood in Vanuatu. In *Birthing in the Pacific: Beyond Tradition and Modernity*. Vicki Lukere and Margaret Jolly, eds. Pp. 148–77. Honolulu: University of Hawai'i Press.

Kaberry, Phyllis Mary
  1939 *Aboriginal Women: Sacred and Profane*. London: Routledge.

Knapp, A. Bernard
  1998 Boys Will Be Boys: Masculinist Approaches to a Gendered Archaeology. In *Redefining Archaeology: Feminist Perspectives*. Mary Casey, Denise Donlan, Jeanette Hope, and Sharon Wellfare, eds. Pp. 32–36. Canberra: ANH Publications, Research School of Pacific Studies, Australian National University.

Kramer, Carol, and Miriam Stark
  1988 The Status of Women in Archaeology. *Anthropology Newsletter* 29(9):1, 11–12.

Kenyatta, Jomo
  1965 *Facing Mount Kenya: The Tribal Life of Gikuyu*. New York: Vintage Books.

Kwon, Heonik
  1999 Play the Bear: Myth and Ritual in East Siberia. *History of Religions* 38(4):373–88.

Lake, Marilyn
  1999 *Getting Equal: The History of Feminism in Australia*. Sydney: Allen and Unwin.

Langford, Langford, Ros
  1983 Our Heritage—Your Playground. *Australian Archaeology* 16:1–6.

Lawrence, Susan
  1998 Approaches to Gender in the Archaeology of Mining. In *Redefining Archaeology: Feminist Perspectives*. Mary Casey, Denise Donlan, Jeanette Hope, and Sharon Wellfare, eds. Pp. 126–33. Canberra: ANH Publications, Research School of Pacific Studies, Australian National University.

Lawrence Cheney, Susan
  1991 Women and Alcohol: Female Influence on Recreational Patterns in the West 1880–1890. In *The Archaeology of Gender*. Proceedings of the Twenty-Second Annual Chacmool Conference. Dale Walde and Noreen Willows, eds. Pp. 479–89. Calgary: Department of Archaeology, University of Calgary.

Lawrence, Susan, and Mark Staniforth, eds.
  1998 *The Archaeology of Whaling in Southern Australia and New Zealand*. Archaeology Special Publication, no. 10. Gundaroo: Australasian Society for Historical Archaeology and Australian Institute for Maritime Archaeology.

Littleton, Judith
  1998 Dying for a Change. Women's Health along the Murray. In *Redefining Archaeology: Feminist Perspectives*. Mary Casey, Denise Donlan, Jeanette Hope, and Sharon Wellfare, eds. Pp. 227–33. Canberra: ANH Publications, Research School of Pacific Studies, Australian National University.

Lydon, Jane
    1995   Boarding-Houses in the Rocks: Mrs Ann Lewis' Privy, 1865. *Public History Review* 4:73–88.
    1999   *Many Inventions: The Chinese in the Rocks 1890–1930*. Melbourne: Monash Publications in History.
Marcus, Julie, ed.
    1993   *First in Their Field: Women and Australian Anthropology*. Melbourne: Melbourne University Press.
McCardle, Penny
    2002   Thesis Abstract: The Aboriginal Bark Burial Mortuary Practice of the Central Queensland Highlands. *Australian Archaeology* 54:63.
McDonald, Josephine
    1992   The Great Mackerel Rockshelter Excavation: Women in the Archaeological Record? *Australian Archaeology* 35:32–50.
    1995   Looking for a Woman's Touch: Indications of Gender in Shelter Sites in the Sydney Basin. In *Gendered Archaeology: The Second Australian Women in Archaeology Conference*. Jane Balme and Wendy Beck, eds. Pp. 92–96. Canberra: Division of Archaeology and Natural History, Australian National University.
    1998   Beyond Hook, Line and Dillybag: Gender, Economics and Information Exchange in Prehistoric Sydney. In *Redefining Archaeology: Feminist Perspectives*. Mary Casey, Denise Donlan, Jeanette Hope, and Sharon Wellfare, eds. Pp. 96–104. Canberra: ANH Publications, Research School of Pacific Studies, Australian National University.
McGowan, Angela
    1995   Working Lives: The Career Prospects and Aspirations of Men and Women Cultural Resource Managers in Tasmania. In *Gendered Archaeology: The Second Australian Women in Archaeology Conference*. Jane Balme and Wendy Beck, eds. Pp. 28–33. Canberra: Division of Archaeology and Natural History, Australian National University.
McIlroy, Jack
    1986   Bathers Bay Whaling Station, Fremantle, Western Australia. *Australasian Historical Archaeology* 4:43–50.
McRae, Leanne
    2002   Representations of Popular Cult(ture). Ph.D. dissertation, Murdoch University.
Meehan, Betty
    1993   An End and a Beginning. In *Women in Archaeology: A Feminist Critique*. Hilary du Cros and Laurajane Smith, eds. Pp. 261–62. Canberra: Australian National University.
Meskell, Lynn
    1999   *Archaeologies of Social Life: Age, Sex, Class, Etcetera in Ancient Egypt*. Social Archaeology Series. Oxford: Blackwell.

2002 The Intersections of Politics and Identity. *Annual Review of Anthropology* 31:279–301.
2003 Feminist Theory and Feminist Anthropology: What Conversations Could or Should We Be Having? Statement for the Association for Feminist Anthropology, *American Anthropological Association Newsletter*, April.

Moore, Henrietta L.
1988 *Feminism and Anthropology*. Cambridge: Polity Press.

Moser, Stephanie
1993 Gender Stereotyping in Pictorial Reconstructions of Human Origins. In *Women in Archaeology: A Feminist Critique*. Hilary du Cros and Laurajane Smith, eds. Pp. 75–92. Canberra: Australian National University.
1995 Archaeology and Its Disciplinary Culture: The Professionalisation of Australian Prehistoric Archaeology. Ph.D. dissertation, University of Sydney.

Mountford, Charles P.
1976 *Nomads of the Australian Desert*. Adelaide: Rigby.

Mountford, Charles P., and Alison Harvey
1941 Women of the Adnjamatana tribe of the Northern Flinders Ranges, South Australia. *Oceania* 12(2):155–62.

Mowaljarli, David Banggal
1992 A Ngarinyin Perspective of Repainting: Mowaljarlai's Statement to the Symposium. In *Retouch: Maintenance and Conservation of Aboriginal Rock Imagery. Proceedings of the Symposium on Retouch, First AURA Congress, Darwin 1988*. G. K. Ward, ed. Pp. 8–9. Occasional AURA Publication, no. 5. Melbourne: Australian Rock Art Research Association.

Naz Foundation International
2000 Briefing Paper 4. The Kothi Framework. Electronic document, http://www.nfi.net/NFI%20Briefing%20papers.htm, accessed January 5, 2005.
2004 Fact File I: Defining Terms Used in Working with Male-to-Male Sex. Electronic document, http://www.nfi.net/, accessed January 5, 2005.

Nelson, Sarah M.
1997 *Gender in Archaeology: Analysing Power and Prestige*. Walnut Creek, CA: AltaMira Press.
1998 Gender Hierarchy and the Queens of Silla. In *Reader in Gender Archaeology*. Kelley Hays-Gilpin and David S. Whitely, eds. Pp. 319–35. London: Routledge.

Nicholson, Linda J., ed.
1990 *Feminism/Postmodernism*. London: Routledge.

Nicol, Chris
2000 The State of Research in Australia: Brain Drain, University Research Funding and the Microelectronics Industry. Paper written specifically for the Prime Minister's Science, Engineering and Innovation Council. Electronic document, http://www.dest.gov.au/science/pmseic/documents/Microelec.pdf, accessed January 5, 2005.

Ortner, Sherry B.
   1996   *Making Gender: The Politics and Erotics of Culture.* Boston: Beacon Press.

O'Gorman, Anne
   1993   The Snake, the Serpent and the Rainbow: Ursula McConnel and Aboriginal Australians. In *First in Their Field: Women and Australian Anthropology.* Julie Marcus, ed. Pp. 84–109. Melbourne: Melbourne University Press.

Pearson, Michael
   1983   The Technology of Whaling in Australian Waters in the 19th Century. *Australasian Historical Archaeology* 1:40–54.

Peoples' Union for Civil Liberties, Karnata
   2003   Human Rights Violations against the Transgender Community: A Study of Kothi and Hijra Sex Workers in Bangalore, India—September 2003. Electronic document, http://ai.eecs.umich.edu/people/conway/TS/PUCL/PUCL%20Report.html, accessed January 5, 2005.

Phillips, Caroline
   1998   Answering the Old Boys' Club: Support Systems for Women Archaeologists. In *Redefining Archaeology: Feminist Perspectives.* Mary Casey, Denise Donlan, Jeanette Hope, and Sharon Wellfare, eds. Pp. 63–67. Canberra: ANH Publications, Research School of Pacific Studies, Australian National University.

Ploss, Hermann Heinrich, Max Bartels, and Paul Bartels
   1935   *Woman: An Historical, Gynaecological and Anthropological Compendium.* Vol. 2. Eric John Dingwall, ed. London: William Heinemann (Medical Books).

Probert, Belinda
   2005   "I Just Couldn't Fit It In": Gender and Unequal Outcomes in Academic Careers. *Gender Work and Organization* 12(1):50–72.

Rasmussen, Knud
   1929   Intellectual Culture of the Iglulik Eskimos. Translated from the Danish by William Worster. *Report of the Fifth Thule Expedition, 1921–24* 7(1):9–304.

Rogers, Brian
   1990   Derivation of Technologies Employed in Some Pre-1900 Salt Works in Eastern Australia. *Australasian Historical Archaeology* 8:36–43.

Rosser, Sue V.
   2004   *The Science Glass Ceiling: Academic Women Scientists and the Struggle to Succeed.* London: Routledge.

Russell, Penny
   1993   In Search of Woman's Place: An Historical Survey of Gender and Space in Nineteenth-Century Australia. *Australasian Historical Archaeology* 11:28–32.
   1994   *A Wish of Distinction: Colonial Gentility and Femininity.* Melbourne: Melbourne University Press.

Sawer, Marian, and Barry Hindess, eds.
   2004   *Us and Them: Anti-Elitism in Australia.* Bentley: Australian Public Intellectual Network.

Schmidt, Robert A., and Barbara L. Voss
    2000   *Archaeologies of Sexuality*. London: Routledge.
Shanks, Michael, and Christopher Tilley
    1988   *Social Theory and Archaeology*. London: Routledge.
    1992   *Reconstructing Archaeology*. London: Routledge.
Smith, Laurajane
    1998   Sand in Our Thongs: Feminism, Theory and Shoelaces. In *Redefining Archaeology: Feminist Perspectives*. Mary Casey, Denise Donlan, Jeanette Hope, and Sharon Wellfare, eds. Pp. 41–45. Canberra: ANH Publications, Research School of Pacific Studies, Australian National University.
Smith, Claire
    1991   Female Artists: The Unrecognised Factor in Sacred Rock Art Production. In *Rock Art and Prehistory: Proceedings of the 1st AURA Congress*. Paul Bahn and Andrée Rosenfeld, eds. Pp. 45–52. Oxford: Oxbow Press.
    2004   *Country, Kin and Culture: Survival of an Australian Aboriginal Community*. Adelaide: Wakefield Press.
Smith, Claire, and Heather Burke
    2004   Joining the Dots . . . Managing the Land and Seascapes of Indigenous Australia. In *Northern Ethnographic Landscapes: Perspectives from the Circumpolar Nations*. Igor Krupnik, Rachel Mason, and Tonia W. Horton, eds. Pp. 381–401. Washington, DC: Smithsonian Institution Press.
Smith, Linda Tuhawai
    1999   *Decolonizing Methodologies: Research and Indigenous Peoples*. 2nd ed. London: Zed Books.
Spector, Janet
    1993   *What This Awl Means: Feminist Archaeology at a Dakota Village*. St. Paul: Minnesota Historical Society Press.
Spencer, Baldwin, and Frank J. Gillen
    1938   *The Native Tribes of Central Australia*. London: Macmillan.
Staniforth, Mark, Susan Briggs, and Chris Lewzak
    2001   Archaeology Unearths People without History: Aboriginals, Women and Children at South Australian Shore-Based Whaling Stations. *Mains'l Haul: A Journal of Pacific Maritime History* 36(3):12–19.
Stankowski, Katrina
    2002   Polish Hill River: Cultural Identity from Material Remains. Master's thesis, Flinders University.
Stark, Miriam
    1991   The Status of Women in Archaeology. In *The Archaeology of Gender*. Proceedings of the Twenty-Second Annual Chacmool Conference. Dale Walde and Noreen Willows, eds. Pp. 87–194. Calgary: Department of Archaeology, University of Calgary.

Stevens, Iris
  1995 Report of the Hindmarsh Island Royal Commission. Adelaide: State Print.
Torrence, Robin, and Annie Clarke
  2000 Negotiating Difference: Practice Makes Theory for Contemporary Archaeology in Oceania. In The Archaeology of Difference: Negotiating Cross-Cultural Engagements in Oceania. R. Torrence and A. Clarke, eds. Pp. 1–31. One World Archaeology 38. London: Routledge.
Toubia, Nahid F.
  1985 The Social and Political Implications of Female Circumcision: The Case of the Sudan. In Women and the Family in the Middle East: New Voices of Change. Elizabeth Warnock Fernea, ed. Pp. 148–59. Austin: University of Texas Press.
Truscott, Marilyn, and Laurajane Smith
  1993 Women's Roles in the Archaeological Workforce. In Women in Archaeology: A Feminist Critique. Hilary du Cros and Laurajane Smith, eds. Pp. 217–21. Canberra: Australian National University.
Vetter, Betty M.
  1996 Myths and Realities of Women's Progress in the Sciences, Mathematics, and Engineering. In The Equity Equation: Fostering the Advancement of Women in the Sciences, Mathematics, and Engineering. Cinda-Sue Davis, Angela B. Ginorio, Carol S. Hollenshead, Barbara B. Lazarus, and Paula M. Rayman, eds. Pp. 29–56. San Francisco: Jossey-Bass.
Victor, Katherine, and Mary Beaudry
  1992 Women's Participation in American Prehistoric and Historic Archaeology: A Comparative Look at the Journals American Antiquity and Historical Archaeology. In Exploring Gender through Archaeology. Cheryl Claassen, ed. Pp. 11–21. Madison, WI: Prehistory Press.
Walde, Dale, and Noreen Willows, eds.
  1991 The Archaeology of Gender. Proceedings of the Twenty-Second Annual Chacmool Conference. Calgary: Department of Archaeology, University of Calgary.
Wall, Diana
  1994 The Archaeology of Gender: Separating the Spheres in Urban America. New York: Plenum Press.
Ward, Russell
  2003 [1958] The Australian Legend. Oxford: Oxford University Press.
Williams, Caitlan
  2001 Successful Woman's Guide to Working Smart: Ten Strengths That Matter Most. Palo Alto, CA: Davies-Black.
Williams, Frank E.
  1940 Natives of Lake Kutubu, Papua. Oceania 11(2):121–59.
Wood, Fiona
  2004 "Beyond Brain Drain": Mobility, Competitiveness and Scientific Excellence. Report prepared by Centre for Higher Education Management and Policy.

University of New England, Armidale, Australia. Distributed by Federation of Australian Scientific and Technological Societies. Electronic document, http://www.une.edu.au/sat/chemp/arms/, accessed January 5, 2005.

Wylie, Alison
- 1992 The Interplay of Evidential Constraints and Political Interests: Recent Archaeological Research on Gender. *American Antiquity* 57(1):15–35.
- 1993 Workplace Issues for Women in Archaeology: The Chilly Climate. In *Women in Archaeology: A Feminist Critique*. Hilary du Cros and Laurajane Smith, eds. Pp. 245–58. Canberra: Australian National University.

Young, Linda
- 1998 The Material Constructions of Gentility: A Context for Understanding the Role of Women in Early Nineteenth-Century Sites. In *Redefining Archaeology: Feminist Perspectives*. Mary Casey, Denise Donlan, Jeanette Hope, and Sharon Wellfare, eds. Pp. 134–37. Canberra: ANH Publications, Research School of Pacific Studies, Australian National University.

Zarmati, Louise
- 1995 Popular Archaeology and the Archaeologist as Hero. In *Gendered Archaeology: The Second Australian Women in Archaeology Conference*. Jane Balme and Wendy Beck, eds. Pp. 43–47. Canberra: Division of Archaeology and Natural History, Australian National University.
- 1998 "Archaeo-Speak": The Politics of Language in Archaeology. In *Redefining Archaeology: Feminist Perspectives*. Mary Casey, Denise Donlan, Jeanette Hope, and Sharon Wellfare, eds. Pp. 3–8. Canberra: ANH Publications, Research School of Pacific Studies, Australian National University.

Zimmerman, Larry
- 1995 We Do Not Need Your Past: Archaeological Chronology and "Indian Time" on the Plains. In *Beyond Subsistence: Plains Archaeology and the Post-Processual Critique*. Phillip Duke and Michale C. Wilson, eds. Pp. 28–45. Tuscaloosa: University of Alabama Press.

Gender Archaeology in Europe 22

RUTH WHITEHOUSE

An issue that arises in addressing the subject of gender archaeology in any area is where one should begin in the history of the discipline. Since gender is a parameter of social life that is relevant to all societies, data and interpretations that are relevant to the study of gender can be found in publications of all periods. However, I have chosen to use the current meaning of the term "gender archaeology" to refer to studies of gender that are informed by gender and feminist theory; work in this vein cannot be found before the 1970s and did not become at all common until the later 1980s and the 1990s. A second question that arises is whether to address only studies of gender in past societies or whether to include also studies of gender in the profession and practice of archaeology. As many scholars have pointed out, these two issues are intimately connected, with the androcentric interpretations of past societies both reflecting and reinforcing the androcentrism of the profession and of society at large. I have chosen to present a brief overview of published analyses of gender in the profession, plus an equally brief account of some of the most important female European archaeologists of the past whose work has generally been undervalued until recently. The main content of this chapter, however, will be devoted to studies of gender in the archaeological past of Europe. I shall begin this part with a discussion of the history and geography of gender archaeology in Europe and then move on to the theoretical frameworks employed in these studies. The accounts of the studies themselves will be organised thematically according to types of study rather than by period or region. For reasons of space and the limitations of my own expertise, I restrict myself in the main to studies of prehistory, although I do include a few case studies from the classical and Dark Age/early medieval worlds.

History and Geography of Gender Archaeology in Europe

The earliest manifestation of gender archaeology in Europe—in the sense defined previously—occurred in Scandinavia in the 1970s. A series of books and articles was published throughout the 1970s and 1980s (e.g., Dommasnes 1982; 1987; Fonnesbeck-Sandberg et al. 1972; Gejvall 1970; Gibbs 1987; Naess 1974; Thålin-Bergman 1975). A workshop on the subject of "Were They All Men? An Examination of Sex Roles in Prehistoric Society" was held in Norway in 1979, although the papers were not published until 1987 (Bertelsen et al. 1987). The main thrust of this work was to address the underrepresentation or complete absence of women both in the profession of archaeology and in archaeological accounts of past societies. The articles related to the past were concerned primarily with how to make women visible in the archaeological record and with defining female roles and male–female relations in specific cases, mostly Bronze and Iron Age societies in Scandinavia itself.

However, although several of these works by Scandinavian scholars were written in English, they had rather little impact on the Anglophone world. In 1989, Margaret Ehrenberg published her book *Women in Prehistory* and, although this work can be criticized for its remedial stance in addressing the absence of women from past studies (the "add women and stir" approach), it served to initiate interest in the subject in the United Kingdom. However, the main impact of gender ideas in the United Kingdom and to some extent elsewhere in Europe was felt in the 1990s, beginning with the publication of several edited volumes in the early part of the decade, most of them emanating from the United States or Australia (Bacus et al. 1993; Claassen 1992; du Cros and Smith 1993; Gero and Conkey 1991; Walde and Willows 1991). Of these, the most influential in Britain was probably *Engendering Archaeology* (Gero and Conkey 1991), partly perhaps because it includes case studies from European archaeology. The rapid uptake of gender studies in U.K. archaeology is indicated by a series of publications by British authors (or authors based in Britain) through the 1990s and into the present millennium. Some of these were edited volumes of papers (in chronological order, Moore and Scott 1997; Whitehouse 1998a, 1998b; Donald and Hurcombe 2000a, 2000b, 2000c), while others were single-authored monographs (again in chronological order, Gilchrist 1994, 1999; Meskell 1999; Sørensen 2000; Bolger 2003). Of these, Gilchrist (1999) and Sørensen (2000) are textbooks, which can be seen to offer rather different introductions to gender archaeology from that of the first gender archaeology textbook produced by Sarah Nelson a few years earlier (Nelson 1997b). In a recent paper (Whitehouse, in press), I argue that there is a distinctively "European" feel to these books, as well as to articles published by European authors, in contrast to their North American counterparts. This is discussed further in the section "Theoretical Approaches" later in this chapter. The development of gender archaeology has continued apace, and the number of individual articles on gender in European archaeology is now well into three figures. Moreover, although many of these articles are published in volumes of collected papers, some appear in "mainstream" archaeological journals: *American Journal of Archaeology, Antiquity, Archaeological Dialogues, Cambridge Archaeological Journal, Current Anthropology, Journal of Anthropological Research, Journal of European Archaeology, Journal of Iberian Archaeology, Journal of Mediterranean Archaeology, Journal of Social Archaeology, Norwegian Archaeological Review, Oxford Journal of Archaeology, Proceedings of the Prehistoric Society,* and *World Archaeology* have all published articles on gender archaeology in Europe. This is important because it indicates that gender archaeology is ceasing to be the "Women's studies" specialization it first was and, as Talalay puts it (2005:130), "Gender is now generally regarded as a legitimate conceptual and analytic category of archaeology."

In terms of academic political geography, much of the gender literature is based in the Anglo-American tradition and written in the English language. Indeed, several American scholars (or originally English, now based in the United States) write on European prehistory and were among the earliest to introduce gender studies into the field (e.g., Arnold 1991, 1996, 2002; Conkey 1991, 1997; Tringham 1991a, 1991b, 1994). In Europe, many scholars of different nationalities choose to write in English, especially on the subject of gender. As well as the Scandinavian scholars discussed previously who write in both English and their native languages, Trinidad Escoriza Mateu in Spain (2002) and Margarita Díaz-Andreu, for example, of Spanish nationality but now based in England, often write in English (Díaz-Andreu 1998), as does Nanno Marinatos in Greece (1987) and Dimitra Kokkinidou and Marianna Nikolaidou, based in Australia, (1997, 2000). Nonetheless, there is an incipient and growing tradition of gender archaeology literature also in other European languages: German (e.g., Karlisch et al. 1997; Wels-Weyrauch 1989, 1991), Spanish (e.g., Díaz-Andreu 1994; Escoriza Mateu 1996; Sanahuja Yll 2001). However, gender archaeology has yet to make any impression in either France or Italy (Coudart 1998:61; Vida 1998; Whitehouse 1998b:2–3).

In terms of the geographical coverage of gender studies, most areas of Europe have received some attention, though sometimes this has been on the part of scholars based outside the country in question. On the whole, the subject has developed according to the types of evidence available for an area or period rather than according to national traditions of archaeological scholarship. For instance, one focus of study in southeastern Europe and the east and central Mediterranean has been Neolithic anthropomorphic figurines, which are common in these areas. Another focus is on gender in rock art, which concentrates on the major European bodies of such art in Scandinavia, the Alpine zone, and Iberia. By contrast, gender studies of central and eastern Europe often concentrate on funerary studies of the Copper and Bronze Age periods, for which large cemeteries of single burials are known. For the same reason, mortuary analysis also dominates studies of the Iron Age in the Mediterranean and the Anglo-Saxon period in England.

Gender and Women in the Profession and Practice of Archaeology

Analysis of the (unequal) position of women within the profession of archaeology has been one aspect of growing political, specifically feminist, awareness in Europe as in the United States and Australia. The earliest articles relating to this topic formed part of the precocious Scandinavian development of the 1970s (Fonnesbeck-Sandberg et al. 1972; Holm-Olsen and Mandt-Larsen 1974). Other areas of Europe had to wait for another twenty years or more to be assessed in this way (see, including updates for Scandinavia, Champion 1998; Dommasnes 1992; Dommasnes et al. 1998; Engelstad et al. 1994; Levi 2001; Morris 1992, 1994; Nikolaidou and Kokkinidou 1998). Although the numbers vary from place to place, these articles document the fact that in every country studied in Europe, women form a minority of professional archaeologists, with Norway the only exception. Moreover, there are gender biases in the status and remuneration of jobs in archaeology, with percentages of women decreasing as the level of the job increases (the situation for Britain is documented in Aitchison 1999). Further differences emerge in the analysis of the *types* of jobs preferentially undertaken by women and men in archaeology, with women tending to concentrate on finds processing and museum work. Some studies have concentrated on specific parts of the total archaeological job scene (e.g., Hamilton's [in press] analyses of the position of women in contract field archaeology in Britain). Much of the discussion of the issues raised in these articles is concerned with the promotion of political agendas to put right the wrongs embodied in the data. However, others have raised epistemological issues about whether women and men produce different kinds of archaeological knowledge; the implications of these are general, extending beyond the scope of Europe, and are not considered here.

Another focus of recent attention has been directed toward women archaeologists of earlier generations whose contributions have previously been undervalued or entirely written out of the history of archaeology. The issue of women's absence from disciplinary history is a major theme of Díaz-Andreu and Sørensen (1998a). What has characteristically been written up until recently is a narrative with very few women players; those who are included are consistently described as exceptional individuals, emphasizing the marginal position of women in general in this story and avoiding any systematic assessment of the underlying gender politics of academe. An interesting, if profoundly unsatisfactory, response to the growing influence of feminist scholarship can be seen in the archaeological textbook used in all U.K. universities (and probably widely elsewhere) by Colin Renfrew and Paul Bahn, *Archaeology: Theories, Methods and Practice*. In the first edition (1991), *no* female archaeologist was discussed, while in the second edition (1996), Dorothy Garrod (who, perhaps not coincidentally, held the Disney Chair of Archaeology at Cambridge, which Colin Renfrew later held himself) appeared, and the photo of Louis Leakey on his own had been replaced by one showing him together with his wife, Mary. In the third edition (2000), a new spread appeared devoted to "Women Pioneers of Archaeology," providing brief biographies of six distinguished female archaeologists: Harriet Boyd Hawes, Gertrude Caton Thompson, Anna Shepard, Kathleen Kenyon, Tatiana Proskouriakoff, and Mary Leakey. This is a prime example of what is sometimes called "pseudoinclusion," with no attempt made to integrate the achievements of the chosen women into the broader account of disciplinary history. Moreover, Dorothy Garrod is not even cross-referenced in this section: presumably her inclusion in the mainstream history of archaeology negates her femininity, making her an "honorary man." The spread ends with a reference to women archaeologists who worked in Greece who are celebrated, along with their male counterparts, in a book by Hood (1998) titled *Faces of Archaeology in Greece* "with a wonderful series of portrait caricatures by Piet de Jong" (Renfrew and Bahn 2000:37). Renfrew and Bahn choose two of these caricature portraits to illustrate Virginia Grace and Hetty Goldman, both of whom worked in Greece in the early twentieth century. No male archaeologists are illustrated in this way: women really *are* different in Renfrew and Bahn's world.

In recent years, archaeologists (mostly women) have started to write about these earlier women scholars with the aim of doing belated justice to their achievements and, as Marie Louise Sørensen puts it, "reinserting this muted group into our disciplinary history" (Sørensen 2000:29). Major figures recently given biographical attention include Jane Harrison, a classical scholar who made major contributions to the study of religion (Beard 2000; Robinson 2002), and Gertrude Caton-Thompson, a British archaeologist who worked not in Europe but in Egypt and the Near East (Drower 2004). Surprisingly, no book-length biography of Dorothy Garrod, whose fieldwork was also mostly in the Near East, has yet appeared, although aspects of her career and work have been described (Davies and Charles 1999; Smith 2000). Fascinatingly, the most recent article on Garrod (Callander and Smith, in press) describes her first season of excavation at El-Wad cave in Palestine in 1929, when she not only led an all-female directorial team but also employed an almost entirely female Arab workforce; Callander and

Smith have found no trace of feminist reasoning in Garrod's writings, but at the very least the policy of employing women demonstrates a positive inclination to recognize women's abilities at all levels. Another woman archaeologist recently given full book-length treatment is Eugénie Strong, who was assistant director of the British School at Rome for sixteen years (Dyson 2004). Women who worked in European archaeology are given attention in the first book to address Europe specifically in this context: Díaz-Andreu and Sørensen (1998b), which has chapters dealing with several countries individually. For instance, Champion (1998) discusses a number of remarkable British women archaeologists of the nineteenth and earlier twentieth centuries: as well as the prehistorians, Gertrude Caton-Thompson and Dorothy Garrod, already mentioned, she discusses Amelia Edwards, who played a major role in the establishment of Egyptology as an academic discipline, through the foundation of the Egyptian Exploration Society and, posthumously, the endowment of the Edwards Chair of Egyptian Archaeology at the University College London (UCL), whose first holder was Flinders Petrie. Champion also discusses Margaret Murray, another Egyptologist who was the first woman to be employed as an archaeology lecturer in Britain (at UCL); she worked with Petrie in both Egypt and Palestine but also conducted her own excavations in Malta and Menorca. Unlike Garrod, the three London-based women—Edwards, Murray, and Caton-Thompson—were feminists and active supporters of the women's suffrage movement. Champion also discusses Kathleen Kenyon, another London-based archaeologist whose achievements have not yet been adequately acknowledged; she worked from the 1930s to the 1960s in the United Kingdom and North Africa as well as in Palestine, where her most famous excavations were at Jericho.

Another major volume to contribute to this field is Cohen and Joukowsky (2004), which includes articles on Sylvia Benton, Edith Eccles, Mercy Money-Coutts Seiradaki, Dorothy Lamb, Winifred Lamb, and Helen Waterhouse. The American women archaeologists who worked in Europe, Harriet Boyd Hawes and Edith Hall, are discussed in Bolger (1994). Harriet Boyd is also discussed by Picazo (1998), who emphasizes how she, like Dorothy Garrod, chose to work with other women. The work of one of the most influential and controversial female archaeologists of the twentieth century, Marija Gimbutas, who was of Lithuanian origin but spent most of her academic career in the United States, is discussed in Chapman (1998) and Elster (in press).

This "excavation" of women archaeologists of the past is work in progress, but already it has demonstrated that there have in fact been many women in archaeology, from the nineteenth century on. The male domination of archaeology did not prevent all women from taking part (though doubtless many were discouraged), but the contributions made by those who did enter were systematically undervalued and largely edited out of the history of the discipline.

Theoretical Approaches

Although the number and variety of publications now available challenge any kind of general summary of work in European gender archaeology, I shall nonetheless offer a brief attempt at such an overview. As I have already mentioned, European work on gender differs in some ways from that carried out in the United States. The European texts are more postprocessual than processual and reflect generically postmodern concerns: worries about "gender essentialism" in place of a largely unchallenged acceptance of women and men as analytical categories; an emphasis on "difference" rather than "power" in gender relations; predominant interests in gender representations, ideologies, and identities rather than gender roles; and an increasing emphasis on embodiment. These contrasts are of course oversimplified, but to me they do seem to have some validity and reflect more general differences between archaeology in the United States and in Europe.

The theoretical approaches used in gender archaeology in Europe, while falling mostly under a broadly postprocessual banner, are varied. Many scholars draw on feminist and gender theory, as one would expect; structuralist and poststructuralist interpretations are found; and identity and embodiment theories occur too. Some more processually oriented studies are found also, while one group of scholars in Spain is drawing on a combination of continental feminist theory and Marxism. Moreover, the goals of gender studies vary too: while there are some directed at gender roles and relations (types of study that were prominent in the first stages of gender archaeology in the United States), rather more are concerned with issues of ideology and identity from a gender perspective. The nature of gender studies in European archaeology has, in my opinion, both strengths and weaknesses, which I discuss in the concluding section of this chapter.

I would have liked to structure my discussion of the work in European gender archaeology under thematic headings such as "roles," "relations," "ideologies," and "identities." However, I have found this impractical: too many studies include more than one of these categories or make no clear distinctions between them. Rather reluctantly, I have chosen to use categories that relate mainly to the kinds of evidence discussed (although this too causes problems when authors draw on more than one type of evidence—a practice that I regard as highly desirable). The main categories will be regional studies, burial studies, gender roles in subsistence activities and craft production, gendered uses of space, and iconography (subdivided into figurine studies, rock art, and other). Sites referred to in the text are shown on the map in figure 22.1.

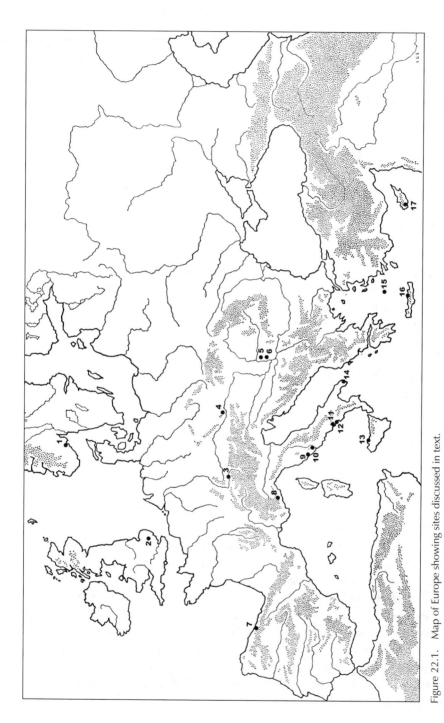

Figure 22.1. Map of Europe showing sites discussed in text.

Key: **1** Ule, **2** Barrington Edix Hill, **3** Singen, **4** Willendorf, **5** Mokrin, **6** Opovo, **7** Cueto de la Mina, **8** Mont Bégo, **9** Valcamonica and Valtellina, **10** Tarquinia, **11** Veio, **12** Sant'Abbondio, **13** Pontecagnano, **14** Grotta di Addaura, **15** Grotta di Porto Badisco, **16** Akrotiri, **17** Knossos, **18** Kissonerga

Regional Studies

No one has yet attempted to write a gender prehistory of Europe as a whole, and even regional accounts are rare. This may be due in part to the still undeveloped state of gender archaeology in Europe but is at least as much a result of the postprocessual domination of most theoretical work on European prehistory discussed previously—a framework that eschews grand narratives in favor of contextually specific studies. All the areas where broader studies of this kind have been attempted are in the Mediterranean: diachronic evolutionary accounts have been produced for Cyprus (Bolger 1992, 1993, 1996, 2002, 2003) and Italy (Robb 1994b, 1997). The same areas, Cyprus and Italy, have also been the subject of edited volumes of papers (Bolger and Serwint 2002; Whitehouse 1998a), while regional studies that aim to summarize the kinds of gender research carried out and the data available for the areas in question have been written for Italy (Whitehouse 2001) and for the Mediterranean as a whole (Talalay 2005).

The diachronic account offered by Bolger for Cyprus (summarized in Bolger 2003:191–96) depends heavily but not exclusively on the evidence of figurines (discussed further later in this chapter under "Iconography"). In the earlier Neolithic, figurines are either schematic or show ambiguous female and male features, while later in the Neolithic and into the Chalcolithic, female figurines dominate; this sequence culminates in the Middle Chalcolithic with a series of figurines emphasizing sexuality, pregnancy, and birth. Bolger argues that in this period women were highly valued for their role in biological reproduction and that many rituals were associated with birth. In the later Chalcolithic, things began to change, and the birthing rituals disappeared (with a remarkable deposit at Kissonerga, where many birthing figurines had been broken and defaced before deliberate deposition), while by the full Bronze Age, the production of female figurines had declined drastically; some figurines that do appear show females with children. Bolger suggests that this is the time that gender hierarchy begins to emerge, with women reduced to lower-status and largely domestic roles, perhaps as a result of male control over intensified agricultural production and trade. In the Late Bronze Age, when state societies (or at least high-level chiefdoms) develop and with it class-based social organization, male domination probably increased; although some elite women enjoyed high status by virtues of their class, they would still have been subordinate to elite men, and nonelite women may have been subordinated to a greater degree than previously.

Robb's accounts of the evolution of gender relations and ideologies in Italy covers a longer time span, from the Neolithic to the Iron Age, and draws for interpretation of the archaeological evidence on ethnographic analogy alone for the earlier periods and on both ethnography and backward projections from classical and later textual sources for the Iron Age. He argues that in the Neolithic, gender relations and gender symbolism were based on a balanced complementarity between male and female. Female symbols focused on the body, while male symbols focused on hunting. In the succeeding Copper and Bronze Ages, there was a marked transformation into a gender hierarchy with a dominant male ideology based on warfare. Females were still symbolized by anatomical traits and sometimes also by necklaces, while males were symbolized by weapons, initially daggers and halberds and later also axes, swords, and spears. Finally, in the Iron Age, a class-based hierarchy emerged; within this, gender asymmetry became further entrenched, but this system was cross-cut by class divisions that distinguished elite women from lower-class women as well as from men of their own class. Gender ideology of this time saw women symbolized no longer by anatomy but by ornamentation (dress and jewelry) on the one hand and spinning and weaving equipment on the other; male symbolism continued to be based on warfare, now often including defensive armor as well as weapons.

Both Bolger's and Robb's works have their critics. Frankel (1997, 2002) has argued that the evidence does not support the development of gender hierarchy (or perhaps hierarchy of any kind) in the Cypriot Bronze Age and offers alternative explanations of the changing archaeological record in terms of the presence of different ethnic groups. My own criticism of Robb's work (Whitehouse 2001:50–52) concentrates on its oversimplification of a long and complex history and also suggests—in a critique that is almost opposite that of Frankel's of Bolger's work—that Neolithic gender relations may not have been complementary but characterized to some degree by male dominance.

While it is easy to criticize these diachronic accounts, which are by definition generalizing and simplifying, they are among the very few works on gender in European prehistory to address power relations between women and men and specifically the emergence of male domination—which, one might argue, remains one of the objects of feminist research and one that only archaeology is really equipped to address.

The edited volumes (Bolger & Serwint 2002; Whitehouse 1998a) and the regional overviews (Talalay 2005; Whitehouse 2001) provide concentrations of relevant work, summaries of the current state of affairs, and takeoff points for future research.

Burial Studies

Burial studies have provided a focus for gender research in Europe from the beginning, particularly for those areas and periods where the practice of individual burial with accompanying grave goods was current. The reasons for this are clear enough: the mortuary record provides one of the few types of context where archaeologists can encounter past individuals; moreover, if skeletal remains are well preserved, the possibility arises of comparing biological sex with culturally constructed aspects of gender (expressed through grave type, orientation and position of the body, grave goods, and so on). Despite recent challenges to the validity or helpfulness of the sex/gender dichotomy, it still seems useful to be able to compare the more biological aspects of femaleness and maleness with more clearly cultural aspects. The studies vary in the way they employ the biology/culture division: some take the biology as a "bottom line," starting with the identification of sexed skeletons and then looking at what types of cultural trait can be associated with each sex; others treat the various classes of evidence, including the biological indications of sex, as independent variables, only subsequently comparing the patterns that emerge from them as studied independently. Some scholars take the view that it is possible to study gender from cultural features such as grave goods even in the absence of sexed skeletons, arguing that where clear dichotomous patterns emerge, the most likely explanation is that the differences relate to gender.

In terms of chronology and geography, we have mortuary studies that deal with gender related to the Upper Palaeolithic and Mesolithic in the Baltic (Meiklejohn et al. 2000) and the Mediterranean (Pluciennik 1998; Whitehouse 2001), the Neolithic and Copper Age of southeast Europe (Chapman 1997; Sofaer-Deverenski 1997, 2000) and the Mediterranean (Robb 1994a), the Bronze Age of central and eastern Europe (O'Shea 1995; Rega 1997, 2000; Sørensen 1991, 1997; Treherne 1995; Weglian 2001; Wels-Weyrauch 1989, 1991) and the Mediterranean (Tafuri et al. 2004), the Iron Age in central Europe (Arnold 1991, 1996, 2002) and in the Mediterranean (Strömberg 1993; Toms 1998; Vida Navarro 1992), and the Anglo-Saxon period in England (Henderson 1989; Lucy 1997, 1998; Stoodley 1999, 2000).

These studies demonstrate considerable variability. Some concentrate on the skeletal remains to extract information about life expectancy, health, diet, and movements of people from one area to another. Although using primarily biological data, the conclusions drawn have profoundly cultural implications. For instance, Rega's (1997) analysis of the skeletons from the Early Bronze Age cemetery at Mokrin, former Yugoslavia, showed that no infants under one year of age were present; this meant that babies of this age must have been given different funerary treatment from the rest of society, perhaps indicating that they were considered not yet fully human (or differently human). Rega also found that among the youngest groups represented in the cemetery, of children aged one to six, there were more females than males (these individuals could not be sexed skeletally, but, as adult burials showed strong associations between biological sex and body orientation and similar marked orientations were found in the immature skeletons, the individuals were plausibly "sexed" in this way). The dominance of females in the age-group of one to six indicates that more males than females must have died before the age of one year, and one possible explanation is that male infanticide was practiced, perhaps indicating a society in which women were highly valued either as economic providers or as a source of potential income for a kin group in a bride-wealth system.

Studies of bone chemistry have also been used to investigate gender differences, both stable isotope data and trace element data, which can be used to study both diet and patterns of mobility. In particular, the identification of specific strontium isotope signatures has been used to look at issues of migration in prehistoric Europe, especially in the context of the first farmers, where distinctions between "locals" and "immigrants" are interpreted in terms of intermarriage between colonizing male farmers and indigenous hunter-gatherer women (e.g., Bentley et al. 2003). An example of a study of trace element data is provided by Tafuri et al. (2004) in their investigation of the Middle Bronze Age cemetery of Sant'Abbondio in southwestern Italy. By comparing trace elements in the tooth enamel (which is formed over the first ten to fifteen years of life) and in the bones (representing the last years of life) of the individuals in this cemetery, a number of patterns emerged. One of these was the existence of a group of women who had grown up in an area with different ground chemistry from that of the area in which they were buried, perhaps indicating a marriage system that brought in wives from outside. Another pattern, relating to bone chemistry alone, indicated a small group of men who had an elevated level of lead in their bones, suggesting differential water intake. This is interpreted as representing repeated settlement in a different environment, which fits well with a preexisting model of this society involving transhumant pastoralism on the part of a small section of the community.

Many of the burial studies are concerned with recognizing gender ideologies by comparison of the biological sexes defined skeletally and cultural gender expressed through grave goods. A prevalent association, found in many parts of the Europe from the Bronze Age on, is that of weapons with male burials or, more accurately, with a small proportion of male burials. This is traditionally interpreted in terms of an elite warrior ideology in which male power and status are based on an association (literal or metaphorical) with prowess in warfare. Treherne (1995) offers an interesting variation on this interpretation, suggesting that traditional understandings of the term "ideology" are not adequate in this context. He describes the warrior status that emerges in the Bronze Age as a lifestyle, believed in and experienced by the men involved. He also indicates that the appearance of the warriors (their "beauty") was as much part of this lived identity (and identity in death) as the military aspect: grooming equipment such as razors and tweezers are also found in the graves.

Sørensen (1991, 1997) is also concerned with gender as constructed through appearance. In the 1991 article, the main sources of evidence she uses are the Bronze Age oak coffin burials of Denmark, with their exceptional preservation of woolen clothing, as well as the metal artifacts that survive more widely. From these burials, three different costumes seem to have been in use, one "male" and two "female" (fig. 22.2). Men seem to have worn a gown, coat, cap, and belt with leather shoes or pieces of cloth on the feet; a pin, button, or fibula held the gown together, and a bag hung from the belt; a sword or dagger may also have been attached to the belt. Both female costumes consisted of a skirt, a blouse, a belt, and a hairnet or bonnet, also with leather shoes or piece of cloth as footwear, with the whole outfit enhanced by the addition of richly decorated bronze objects.

Figure 22.2. Three different costumes in use in the Scandinavian Bronze Age: (a) male costume; (b) two different female costumes (after Sørensen 1991: 126).

The difference between the two female costumes relates to the skirts: one type is short and corded, the other long and folded. There is also evidence from surviving hair in the burials that suggest that the short skirts were associated with short hair and the long skirts with long hair. Similar distinctions are also found in other areas of northern Europe where perishable materials do not survive. In these cases, they are marked by differences in the bronze objects found in the burials. For instance, in Lüneburg, northern Germany, younger women wore only arm and ankle rings, while the older ones also had pins and fibulae. In southern Germany, Wels-Weyrauch's (1989) study showed five groups with regionally varying typologies, but in all areas the women's graves could be divided into two types, one with ornaments focussing on the chest, the other on the waist. One traditional interpretation of the differences between the two female costumes, found throughout much of the northern European Bronze Age, relates to age and/or marital status, perhaps defined in relation to men, separating potential wives from other women. However, Sørensen (2000:140) suggests that the differences were as much to do with the "differences within" (i.e., distinctions between women, marking different stages in the female life cycle) as with marking their differences from men. Sofaer-Deverenski's (2000) study of the Copper Age in the Carpathian basin also discusses metalwork in relation to gendered life cycles. In the cemeteries of this period, relatively simple copper artifacts, such as arm rings, finger rings, beads, and discs, as well as awls and daggers, were used in sophisticated ways to mark different age stages of both females and males as well as differences between them, with both gradual and sudden changes occurring.

In the Iron Age in Mediterranean Europe, as well as in Anglo-Saxon England, burial studies show clear dichotomous divisions with men defined as warriors, associated with weapons and armor, and women as cloth makers, associated with spinning and weaving equipment, such as spindle whorls, spools, and loom weights. While most scholars accept that these data do indicate ideals of manhood and womanhood in the societies in question, several scholars have been concerned to explain the anomalous graves that always occur in these cemeteries, such as female burials with male goods and vice versa or burials with both male and female goods. For instance, Vida Navarro (1992) recognized clear "weavers" and "warriors" in her analysis of an early Iron Age cemetery at Pontecagnano in southwestern Italy but argued that there was no one-to-one correlation with biological sex. One tomb of a biological male that contained a spindle whorl and a "female" fibula may have been of a man defined socially as female. In another case, a biological female was accompanied by a helmet and another "male" artifact, a plate; she was clearly not a full warrior, as she had no offensive weapons, but she might have been a woman who had acquired some aspects of male status in society. Toms (1998) also looks at Early Iron Age graves in Italy, in this case from cemeteries at Veio and Tarquinia in Etruria. She too recognizes male warriors and female spinners and weavers but points out that there were also many burials (more than 50 percent at both sites) that had no such clear gender markers. Her analysis of the warrior and weaver tombs does not suggest any correlation with age or wealth or with chronological phase or with any particular area of the cemetery; so, while some roles in society were restricted to one gender or the other, gender may not have been an overwhelmingly important social category in general. In the Anglo-Saxon context, Harrington (in press) discusses the incidence of women buried with sword-shaped weaving beaters, which clearly refer metaphorically to the actual swords buried with some men in these cemeteries. In general, the positions of weaving swords and contemporary weapon swords in burials indicate that when communities buried individuals, they actively avoided placing these two object types in the same position. However, Grave 18 at Barrington Edix Hill is an exception to this rule, and Harrington concludes that the creative potential of women in weaving was being acknowledged in this burial.

The occurrence of anomalies in the correlation of sexed skeletons and gendered grave goods is also discussed in other contexts where the possibility of third and additional genders is considered as well as sexual variations such as true hermaphroditism and pseudohermaphroditism. In a general discussion, Arnold (2002) recognizes seven possible categories of gender/sex configurations and discusses how these might be manifested in the mortuary record, while Weglian (2001) discusses some of these possibilities in her attempts to explain some anomalous graves in the Early Bronze Age cemetery of Singen in Germany.

Gender Roles in Subsistence Activities and Craft Production

While the division of labor in subsistence activities and craft practice has provided a major focus of study in American gender archaeology, they figure much less prominently in European gender studies. Nonetheless, some interesting and important studies have been carried out. There is a dilemma in studying gender roles in archaeology: on the one hand, ethnographic studies indicate that the gendered division of labor is extremely widespread in human societies at all levels of complexity and therefore that this is something we should be looking for archaeologically; on the other hand, there is no easy route to identifying who did what in the archaeologically documented past since tools and activity areas do not present themselves to us with neat gender labels. One way out of this dilemma is to extrapolate either from the burial record or from iconography. For instance, in the studies of Iron Age burials discussed in the previous section, it is assumed that women, whose graves include artifacts associated with spinning and weaving, were responsible for producing textiles.

Another example of this type of study is Johnsson et al. (2000), which looks at sickles in the Bronze and early Iron Age in Scandinavia through their associations in graves. For the earlier Bronze Age, there were few sexed skeletons, but graves were tentatively defined as male or female on the basis of other grave goods (mainly tools and weapons as opposed to ornaments); sickles, of either flint or bronze (twenty in all), were found in both female and male graves. In the later Bronze Age, the burials were mostly cremations, more than half of which could be sexed skeletally. Only five (bronze) sickles occurred in these graves, but all five were associated with male burials. At the Iron Age site of Ule in Norway, cremation burials were attributed to sex/gender categories on the basis of a mixture of sexed remains and historical analogy; all four iron sickles found at this site came from the burials of young women. Collectively, the evidence suggests that there was no timeless association of sickles (and therefore harvesting) with women, as in traditional stereotyping, but that harvesting may have been the work of men, women, or both at different times and places.

Tuohy (2000) uses burials as one source of evidence in her discussion of the so-called weaving combs of antler and bone found in Iron Age sites in southern England. These artifacts have been assumed to be weaving tools and therefore traditionally assigned to women. Tuohy's use-wear analysis suggests that they were probably used not for weaving cloth on a warp-weighted loom, as generally thought, but more probably for making braids or ornamental borders on a narrow back-strap loom. Tuohy considers the gender of both the makers and the users of these combs and concludes that either men or women or both might have made them; as to the users, associated burial evidence does link them to women, but Tuohy argues that while it is likely that women made and used braids and ornamental borders, heavier items such as belt straps or harness webbing might have been made and used by men.

An example relating to iconography, discussed later in this chapter, comes from the rock art of the Alpine area, where plowing scenes, involving plows drawn by pairs of oxen, were shown with human figures shown with marked penes; it is deduced from this that men were responsible for plowing. The problem with projecting from iconography to society is that of distinguishing between gender ideals and actual practice, which may have been rather different, with mismatches due to resistance and challenges to, or simple lack of concern with, dominant ideologies.

Another approach is to start with ethnographic analogies and, where these show strongly gendered patterns cross-culturally, to assume that these applied in the past and then to see what the implications might have been. This is the approach used both by Conkey (1991) and by Owen (2000) in their studies of technology in the European Upper Palaeolithic, especially the Magdalenian period in France and Spain. Conkey discusses what are sometimes called aggregation sites, which are sites where it is thought that groups larger than the household came together for particular purposes, and she argues that it is in contexts of this sort that sex and age differentiation are most likely to have been present. Taking the Cantabrian site of Cueto de la Mina as an example of such an aggregation site, she looks at the inventory of tools from the site and then uses ethnographic parallels to suggest how the tasks may have been divided according to gender. On this basis, men would have been responsible for making the equipment associated with big game hunting, including bone, antler, flint, and presumably wooden tools and weapons, while women (and probably children) were the prime makers of cordage, nets, and lines and the making of associated products (clothes, nets, tents and so on); they would also have been involved in shellfish collecting and preparing the shells for use attached to clothing or as independent ornaments and for making some flint tools such as scrapers for preparing hides. From this starting point, Conkey goes on to consider the tensions and negotiations that would have been necessary for the scheduling of different tasks, the organization of the labor involved, the use of space, and so on. The discussion is speculative, but through it we are given glimpses into a much more human version of Magdalenian society than traditional accounts allow. Owen's study concentrates on use-wear analysis of stone tools from Magdalenian sites in Germany and France compared with that found on experimental tools used for known purposes. The analysis showed that a high proportion (88 percent) of the tools examined had been used to process animal materials, normally male tasks in the Inuit ethnographic parallels that Owen refers to, while only 5 percent had been used for wood and only 2 percent for materials such as fish, shells, and plants, normally associated with women in the ethnographic context. Owen goes on to balance the picture of mainly male activity that emerges from the lithic analysis to consider the probable large-scale use of plant materials, considering much of the same evidence as Conkey, to conclude that women were probably involved in the production of cordage as well as objects used to produce it (including flint flakes, blades, and borers) and objects made from it (nets and possibly clothes). Both Conkey's and Owen's studies work to create a much more balanced view of Upper Palaeolithic society, with both men and women's contribution apparent, but they suffer from the fundamental problem that they depend on projecting roles recorded in the ethnographic present onto Upper Palaeolithic societies that might have been organized quite differently.

A very interesting attempt to avoid this problem appears in Sørensen's (1996) short study of Bronze Age metalworking in Europe. The title of the article, "Women as/and Metalworkers," indicates the approach adopted. Her starting point is that we do not know whether women were involved in metalworking but that we can usefully consider various alternative scenarios. She exemplifies this by taking one phase of the metalworking process, that of casting in molds. In the European Bronze Age, these molds are mostly made of clay and are often found in settlement sites. This is itself an interesting observation since, whereas metalworking is normally considered an archetypical male activity, clay working is usually thought of as female and the settlement context as domestic and therefore also female associated. Sørensen considers the following alternative scenarios:

1. If clay technologies are women's work, then women shaped the molds and designed the types; therefore, women worked with firing, women did prospecting, and women made objects used by males.
2. If men shaped the molds, then clay technologies were not exclusively women's domain; men designed the types and made objects used by women; therefore, men participated in domestic activities.
3. If clay technologies are not gender exclusive, then different stages of the production were gender exclusive or there was no gendered division of labor; therefore, the production was dependent on the cooperation of gender groups, and the planning of production involved negotiation around gender divisions and ideologies.

Sørensen does not come to any conclusion as to which of these scenarios is most likely, but her analysis shows that in any case both men and women are likely to have been involved in the total process of producing metal tools; moreover, analysis of other aspects of the archaeological record or future work with a specific research agenda might help choose between these different scenarios. I think this is an approach that has great potential and could be applied to other aspects of the archaeological record. For instance, one might consider anthropomorphic figurines (discussed later in this chapter) in these terms: were they made by women for female use, by men for male use, by both men and women for general use, and so on? We might not be able to answer these questions, but we would almost certainly come up with a variety of different interpretations of their "meaning" in these different scenarios—some of which might seem more plausible than others in the light of other aspects of the archaeological record.

Gendered Uses of Space

Ethnography shows us that space is often strongly gendered in terms of symbolism or practice or both. Therefore, this is something we should be investigating archaeologically. The problem here is similar to that affecting gender roles in production: space in the archaeological record does not come with clear gender labels. Nonetheless, gender archaeologists working in Europe, as elsewhere, have attempted to address this issue.

One response to this problem is to recognize broad dichotomous spatial patterns, interpreted in terms of structural oppositions, in the mode of structuralist anthropology. This kind of approach appears in Hodder's (1990) analysis of the Neolithic in Europe. In this book, Hodder identifies a metaphorical theme that can be traced, in changing forms, in the Neolithic as it spreads across Europe from southeast to northwest. The metaphor involves a primary opposition between the *domus* and the *agrios*, each of which has both spatial and a whole range of cultural associations. In southeastern Europe, for instance, the *domus* involves the house and is associated with furniture, plant food storage, food preparation, spinning and weaving, and figurines and is regarded by Hodder as "domestic" and symbolically female; the *agrios* is the world outside the house, associated with burial, tools and weapons, hunting, exchange, and stone- and metalworking and is regarded as "wild" and symbolically male (fig. 22.3) (Hodder 1990:44–99). Hodder modifies the simplified and static aspects of this scheme both by recognizing an overlap zone between the *domus* and the *agrios* and by incorporating ideas of change and processes of "domestication" through time of previously "wild" traits.

I also use a structuralist approach (as one of several different interpretative paradigms) in my study of caves and other underground features used for cult purposes in Italy in the Neolithic and the Copper Age (Whitehouse 1992a, 1992b:109–12). The main structural dichotomy I recognize is between the secular sphere—represented by settlement sites, which are above ground, easily accessible, light and spacious, and associated with the domestic—and the sacred sphere—characterized by the cult sites—which are underground, hidden, difficult to find and enter, and associated with the wild. There is a gender aspect to this dichotomy too since I suggest that the ritual sites constituted a largely male domain, with some of the sites at least used for initiation rites into a secret male cult. In a detailed analysis of one site, Grotta di Porto Badisco, I combine a spatial analysis of the cave, which consists of three long corridors subdivided into twelve distinct zones, and an examination of the paintings on the cave walls to suggest that the site was used for a series of initiation rites (to increasingly higher levels

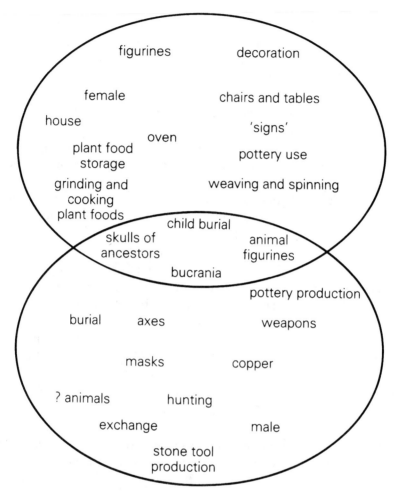

Figure 22.3. Associations of the "domus" and "agrios" in Neolithic Southeast Europe (after Hodder 1990: 69).

of secret knowledge) mapped onto the natural topography of the cave, with the most secret zones equating to the most sacred. My analysis of the figurative motifs found among the paintings indicates that both female and male figures occur in the most accessible chamber of the cave, with only male figures found further in; I argue from this that women were either excluded from the cave altogether or perhaps allowed into the one chamber only, possibly associated with first initiation.

Morter and Robb (1998) offer an analysis on a landscape scale of this same southern Italian Neolithic society that is largely compatible with the previously mentioned interpretation. They plot the human landscape in terms of concentric circles around the village, corresponding to nested social identities. Zone 1 is the house and its immediate space, zone 2 the village, zone 3 the one- to three-kilometer "catchment zone" around the village, zone 4 the intervillage zone, and zone 5 the outermost zone beyond this. They suggest that these zones corresponded, at least symbolically, to a gendered axis with the innermost zone being either gender neutral or more female and the outermost most male.

Hingley (1990) also uses a structuralist framework for his analysis of Iron Age and Romano-British houses in England. He suggests that the roundhouses characteristic of the British Iron Age were divided into a public zone that was in the center of the house near the hearth where there was space and light (under the highest part of the roof) and a private zone around the edges that was low, dark, and hidden. Unsurprisingly, he suggests a familiar association of the public space with men and the private space with women and goes on to argue that a similar division, although in different spatial arrangements, can also be recognized in the Romano-British houses of the succeeding periods.

The problem with all the interpretations just discussed is their level of generality and apparently static and unchanging nature and their consequent failure to deal with variability, individuality, change, contradiction, or resistance, all of which are major concerns of much present-day archaeology and of considerable relevance to studies of gender. The interpretations can also be criticized for what are often thought to be ethnocentric assumptions about the association of women with the domestic, private arena and men with the outside world, the public arena.

Other attempts have also been made to consider domestic space in gender terms. These include Tringham's (1991a) pioneering attempt to understand "households with faces" in the Neolithic and Copper Age of southeastern Europe. This article includes a detailed examination of the excavated archaeology of the site of Opovo but ends with an imagined account of the feelings of a Neolithic woman watching the deliberate burning of her house after the death of her husband, the household head—a contribution to developing a transgressive feminist style of writing archaeology that challenges traditional scientific norms (carried further, though not in a European context, by Spector in the same volume [1991] and later at greater length [1994]).

An example of analysis of domestic space from a later period for which written sources exist relates to the classical Greek house. Various classical Greek writers suggest a division of houses into spaces segregated by gender: the *andron*, the male dining space, and the *gynaikon*, the women's quarters, associated with cooking, weaving, and storage, appropriate for a way of life in which women lived secluded lives confined to the domestic sphere. In a pioneering study, Walker (1983) attempted to find these divisions in the archaeological record and identified possible male and female spaces in the ground plans of Greek houses on several sites. Her interpretation was challenged by Jameson (1990a, 1990b), who pointed out that while the male room, the *andron*, could be clearly identified in many cases, usually occupying a corner of the house and equipped with dining benches, there was little archaeological evidence for exclusively female spaces. Nevett (1994, 1995, 1999) offers a rather different interpretation, using, inter alia, comparison with Islamic houses in North Africa, which she argues may represent a similar kind of social organization. She suggests that only the male public area would have been exclusively gendered, with the rest of the house being available to the women; it would have been available also to male members of the household though off limits to outsiders. The *andron*, therefore, situated on the edge of the house, directly accessible from the entrance, was where men would have entertained their male guests, who would not have had to pass through or see into the rest of the house where the women would have been. On the Islamic analogy, the aim of this layout would have been to protect the honor of the women by protecting them from the gaze of unrelated men.

Another study of gender and space related to a historical society is Gilchrist's (1999:chap. 6) account of "The Contested Garden: Gender, Space and Metaphor in the Medieval English Castle." This subtle and nuanced discussion explores not only the formal division of space in the English medieval castle but also its metaphorical associations and the aspect of embodied experience, that is, what it was like to *be* a man or a woman in a medieval castle. At one level, the medieval castle is an archetypical example of a male warrior ideology associated with a society rigidly divided according to gender. We know from the documentary sources that the women of the high-ranking households that occupied the castles were secluded and occupied separate spaces from the men, situated in the innermost part of the castle, furthest from the entrance. Gilchrist's study concentrates on the garden, which was a private space provided for the female household where herbs and flowers were grown. External to the main castle building, it was nonetheless secluded and enclosed within the outer defenses. Metaphorically, enclosure was equivalent to the virginal female body; this applied particularly to the enclosure of the castle itself and even more so to the absolute enclosure of religious women in convents, but it also applied to the enclosed garden. The garden, however, was metaphorically ambivalent in medieval literature since it was also the location of lovers' trysts. It was both Paradise, associated with the Virgin Mary, and the Garden of Eden, associated with Eve, sexual temptation and the treachery of women. Literally too, the secrecy of the garden might provide the opportunity for the segregation of the sexes to be breached. It is in this sense that the garden was a "contested" space. From this analysis, we gain a more nuanced understanding of gender in upper-class medieval England than traditional accounts allow.

Iconography

A considerable component of gender archaeology in Europe has been related to iconographical analysis. Of this body of work, figurine studies form a major part, while attention has also been devoted to rock art and, to a lesser extent, wall paintings and a range of decorated artifacts. I deal here only with the prehistoric period and exclude work on classical and medieval art, which represent different fields of study, both too abundant to include here and beyond the scope of my expertise.

Figurines

We cannot consider the prehistoric European figurines without considering the mother goddess hypothesis, which has been widely and controversially influential in their interpretation—being popularly regarded as an archetypically feminist reinterpretation of prehistory. I shall begin, however, with a brief description of the data. Portable representations of the human form appear in a variety of contexts in prehistoric Europe, but for the purposes of this discussion, we can divide them into three main categories. The first is the so-called Venus figures of the Upper Palaeolithic. Some 200 or so of these small figures are known; they are mostly of stone, although bone and ivory examples also occur. They range in date from about 30,000 to 10,000 B.C., although the majority fall in the period of about 25,000 to 20,000 B.C. and are associated with Gravettian flint industries. Most of the figurines clearly depict females, and some appear pregnant and/or obese. The second category of figurines is associated with the Neolithic and Copper Age (Chalcolithic) cultures of southeastern Europe, dated about 7000 to 3500 B.C., labeled "Old Europe" by Marija Gimbutas. These figurines are predominantly of clay, although small numbers of stone examples are also known. In the core Balkan area (present-day countries of Bulgaria, Romania, Macedonia, Serbia, Ukraine, and southern Hungary), they are extremely numerous, with many thousands of known figurines; the single site of Vinca has produced some 2,000 figurines (Gimbutas 1982:22). They are also found in surrounding areas such as Greece, Italy, and Malta but in lower densities. These figurines are mainly female, but male and asexual examples also occur. They are often decorated in relief, incision, or paint. My third category is made up of the figurines of the Bronze

Age Aegean, which in fact vary considerably from the marble Cycladic figurines of the Early Bronze Age to the range of figurines found in the Minoan and Mycenaean cultures of the later Bronze Age. Figurines of all these categories have been drawn into the mother goddess debate.

THE MOTHER GODDESS HYPOTHESIS AND ITS CRITICS   The hypothesis can be summarized as follows: prehistoric societies believed in a universal mother goddess whose worship was associated with a regime of female power and authority, a lost "Golden Age" of peace, environmental harmony, and spirituality based on female values. For some women's groups, belief in a prehistoric mother goddess has become a source of empowerment for women today and has given rise to literature, art, and tourism. Although most of the literature is produced by nonarchaeologists for a general readership, it draws heavily on archaeology for validation, focusing on the work of a number of archaeologists, especially Marija Gimbutas, the Californian-based prehistorian who developed the mother goddess theory over many years until her death in 1994 (Gimbutas 1982, 1989, 1991). *Most* archaeologists, on the other hand, regard the theory as deeply flawed and believe that there are many other, more plausible interpretations of the evidence.

The origins of the mother goddess concept go back to nineteenth-century evolutionary theorizing, specifically Johann Bachofen's work *Das Mutterrecht*, published in 1861 (which translates literally as "Mother-right"). Bachofen introduced the idea of prehistoric matriarchy (i.e., female power over family and social institutions), which he regarded as a "primitive" stage of social evolution and argued that it evolved into patriarchy, which he, along with all the other (exclusively male) scholars of the time, understood as self-evidently superior to matriarchy. Subsequently, through the first half of the twentieth century, the mother goddess was an accepted part of the understanding of prehistory in the Old World, although it went out of favor in the 1960s and 1970s when it was subjected to fierce criticism by, especially, Ucko (1962, 1968) and Fleming (1969). The only major archaeologist to continue to support the mother goddess view was Marija Gimbutas, who developed the idea of "Old Europe" (southeastern Europe in the Neolithic and Copper Age), where the mother goddess and associated lifestyle flourished, until it was brought to an end by invading Indo-Europeans around 3500 B.C. who introduced male domination, warfare, and violence—in short, patriarchy (in this version, in crucial contrast to that of Bachofen, patriarchy is unequivocally a bad thing). Although Gimbutas refers to the core of "Old Europe," she frequently draws on evidence from outside its range, both geographically and chronologically: from wide areas of the Near East, for instance, and the whole of Europe and in time ranging from the Upper Palaeolithic to later prehistory and early historical times, long after the assumed arrival of the Indo-Europeans, representing, according to Gimbutas, survivals of mother goddess worship alongside later male-dominated religious systems.

Critiques of the hypothesis and specifically of Gimbutas's work have come from both outside (e.g., Fleming 1969; Hayden 1985; Ucko 1962, 1968) and within (e.g., Conkey and Tringham 1995; Meskell 1995; Talalay 1994; Tringham and Conkey 1998) the feminist movement. The more general critiques relate to inadequacies in both the data and the argumentation used by Gimbutas and by the implausibility of the hypothesis. In terms of data, the figurines are very varied not only across time and space but even within individual collections from specific areas or sites. They are certainly not universally clearly female: they sometimes include examples that are explicitly male; more frequently, there are examples that are apparently asexual, showing no clear sexual characteristics, either female or male. The style of argument adopted by Gimbutas takes the form of an assumption that the goddess hypothesis is correct, with all the evidence interpreted as supporting it. Within this framework, for instance, all the nonfemale figurines are either ignored or assumed to also represent the goddess or consort of the goddess. Such argumentation not only lacks adequate linkage to the evidence but also is impossible to refute: one either believes or does not. The goddess hypothesis also lacks plausibility on several fronts: it is unlikely that prehistoric societies over large areas and many thousands of years would have shared a single religion; it is anachronistic to think in terms of a more or less monotheistic religion for prehistory; there is no a priori reason to believe that even the definitely female figurines represent goddesses, let alone a single goddess, rather than mortal women; and, equally, there is no necessary connection between the assumed worship of a mother goddess and social organization based on female power and female values.

Feminist archaeologists have particular issues with the mother goddess hypothesis. While they are as unconvinced as nonfeminist scholars by the argument, they remain uncomfortably aware that many of the earlier, alternative interpretations of the figurines have been clearly and sometimes grossly male biased. This is particularly true of the Palaeolithic figurines, which, until recently, have been discussed by male scholars making the unquestioned assumption that they were made by male artists for male purposes. These discussions are characterized by the same tendency to objectify the female body that we find so commonly in our own society. Feminists recognize that these androcentric interpretations need challenging and that Gimbutas and her followers have served to bring this necessity to everyone's attention. Nonetheless, there are also specifically feminist criticisms to be made of the mother goddess concept. One is that it treats women as all the same, just as male-biased interpretations do; the only change is that this is now regarded as a positive thing rather than a negative one. Many feminists think we should get away from this kind of essentialism and celebrate women in all their variety and difference. In addition, the characteristics celebrated by the mother goddess movement are the very biological characteristics that men have defined women by for centuries; while it is right to reclaim these biological functions as positive experiences, we should not wish to return to a situation where women are defined exclusively in terms of sexuality and reproduction.

NEW WORK ON FIGURINES   The most basic aspect of all the new work on figurines has been an insistence on contextual specificity: the figurines show enormous variety through time and from place to place, and all cannot possibly be assumed to represent the same thing. A number of studies have looked at the issues in a general way: an issue of the *Cambridge Archaeological Journal* in 1996 had a section titled "Can We Interpret Figurines?" with articles by Bailey, Haaland and Haaland, Hamilton, Marcus, and Ucko. Other articles including general discussions are Bailey (1994, 1995), Biel (1996), Dobres (2000), Hamilton (2000), Sarenas (1998), Talalay (2000, 2005), and Tringham and Conkey (1998). One strand of this research has been to emphasize the ethnocentricity of many past interpretations, both their emphasis on rigidly dichotomous male and female genders and the suggested functions of the figurines as, inter alia, fertility symbols, pornography, substitute wives, concubines, or children's dolls, as well as mother goddesses. Under the first heading, scholars have pointed to the existence of so-called asexual figurines (showing no sexually specific anatomical features) and sexually ambiguous examples as well as clearly male and female ones and have scoured the ethnographic literature in search of multiple genders, gender transgressors, and genders defined in very different ways from our own to aid in interpretation of the prehistoric data. Under the second heading, writers have pointed out the underlying sexism (as well as ethnocentrism) of interpretations that assume not only male makers and users of female figurines but also motivations that in reality are much more likely to be historically and culturally specific than universal.

The Upper Palaeolithic figurines have been the subject of the most blatantly androcentric interpretations, perhaps both because they are most consistently rendered naked and because they are oldest and therefore thought to represent primeval ideas and behavior. However, new studies, including feminist approaches, have cast very different light on these figures (Conkey 1997; Conroy 1993; Dobres 1992, 2000; McCoid and McDermott 1996; McDermott 1996; Nelson 1997a; Rice 1981; Russell 1991, 1993). Nelson (1997a) discusses the marked biases in the general archaeological literature that focuses on the most bulbous figurines, such as the "Venus of Willendorf," often illustrated as typical of the whole category when in fact it represents the extreme end of a range from quite slender to very fat and possibly pregnant. Rice pointed out the variety in the shapes as long ago as 1981 and suggested that they corresponded to different ages and stages in the life history of women, while Nelson (1997b:160) argues that their rounded bellies may indicate simply the true shapes of most adult women who have given birth (and who do not aspire to the preternaturally thin figures of Western celebrity mothers today). In terms of whether the figurines were made by men or women, McCoid and McDermott (1996) have suggested that the artists were women and that the distorted body shapes could be the result of women looking down on their own bodies as models. This rather ingenious theory is supported by the similarity between photographs taken from this perspective and some of the figurine shapes and draws attention to the ethnocentric assumptions about naturalism and perspective present in much theorizing about prehistoric art (McCoid and McDermott 1996; McDermott 1996). However, at best, this hypothesis could account for only some of the figurines since many do not demonstrate this "distorted" perspective. Conroy (1993) uses the Upper Palaeolithic figurines in a discussion of a fundamental issue that few have addressed—the emergence of gender in the developmental history of the human species—seeing the appearance of the figurines as part of the process of symbolization that made the development of cultural ideas such as gender possible. She mentions but does not develop a point that I think deserves further attention: the absence of male figures from the Palaeolithic figurine repertoire suggests that at this time the archetypical human form was female. Perhaps in the Palaeolithic, in an inversion of the situation that feminist analysis ascribes to patriarchy, humanity was constructed as "woman" and "not woman."

Work on the figurines of the Neolithic period and later are both quite numerous and varied. We have articles on southeastern Europe (Bailey 1994, 1995, 1996; Biel 1996; Chapman 2000:68–79; Tringham and Conkey 1998), the Aegean (Kokkinidou and Nikolaidou 1997; Mina 2003, in press; Sarenas 1998; Talalay 1993, 2000, 2005; Talalay and Cullen 2002), Cyprus (Bolger 1992, 1993, 1996, 2003:chap. 4; Peltenburg 2002), and Italy (Holmes and Whitehouse 1998).

Some of the most interesting work has been geared to challenging simple dichotomous gender interpretations, particularly by considering the significance of asexual or ambiguously sexed figurines, which occur in most areas, sometimes in considerable numbers. For instance, Chapman (2000:75–79) discusses the figurines of the Copper Age Romanian Hamangia culture. These are predominantly female in their overall form and markings, with both female genitalia and breasts, but Chapman develops a point made earlier by Kokkinidou and Nikolaidou (1997:93) in relation to the Greek Neolithic that the cylindrical necks and heads of the figurines have phallic qualities (a feature found also in Cyprus; Bolger 2003:chap. 4). Since the figurines are often deliberately fragmented, the representations can "change sex," or, rather, the male aspect of what Chapman (2000) argues are hermaphrodite figures can be separated from the female part. He argues that this allows "for a spectrum of gendered identities—not merely a polarised male-female, but a range from gender-neutral to strongly hermaphrodite . . . via weakly or strongly female" (77). In a related interpretation, Holmes and Whitehouse (1998) consider the few ambiguous figurines found in Italy. Using an idea drawn from Strathern's (1988) account of belief systems in Melanesian societies in which shifting female and male essences separate, interact, and coalesce in either same-sex or cross-sex combinations, we argue that maybe a similar system existed in prehistoric Italy with appropriate domains for same sex (domestic) and cross-sex (burial and other cult) manifestations. Mina's (in press) examination of asexual figurines from Neolithic Greece considers whether they represent a separate gender. By comparison of the decorative motifs found on these figurines with those on definitely or probably female figures, she argues that they probably represented not a separate gender but rather different stages in female lives—an interpretation that parallels that deduced by Sørensen from the burial data for Bronze Age northern Europe, discussed previously. Talalay and Cullen's (2002) examination of Cypriot Bronze Age plank figurines tackles a similar issue. These figurines, which mostly lack clear anatomical sexual markings, are found in chamber tombs containing multiple burials and apparently used for generations; Talalay and Cullen argue that they represent communal solidarity rather than individual identity.

Another line of investigation has been directed at what the figurines were used for (if not mother goddesses to be worshipped) and who by, using both general arguments and contextual analysis of specific data sets. Bailey (1994) has suggested that the figurines represented individuals. Analyzing the data from Copper Age Bulgaria, he suggests that individual identity was expressed both through burials and through figurines, with male identity expressed mainly in the burial arena and female identity mainly in the domestic arena. Bolger (2003) also discusses the connection between figurines and individuals, but she emphasizes the idea of ritual practice, influenced by the ideas of Butler (1990, 1993), who understands gender in terms of performance. In the context of Cypriot Neolithic and Chalcolithic societies, Bolger (2003:111) claims that "it is highly likely that women actively engaged in rituals to maintain or elevate their own status." Many of these rituals would have been concerned with stages of the female life cycle;

this explains figurines showing stages of pregnancy and childbirth in a very different way from traditional "fertility cult" interpretations. Some very specific interpretations have also been put forward, such as Talalay's (1987) suggestion that figurines in Neolithic Greece may have been exchanged as tokens in marriage agreements.

A certain amount of work has also been carried out on the figurines of later societies, with more clearly differentiated social organization than the Neolithic and Copper Age societies discussed previously. However, these studies are usually considered in the context of a wider iconography, such as Hitchcock's (1997, 2000) work on Minoan Crete, and I shall discuss them in that context later in this chapter.

Rock Art

Apart from the Upper Palaeolithic cave art of France and Cantabrian Spain, Europe has major areas of later prehistoric art in Atlantic Europe, Scandinavia, Levantine Spain, and the Alpine area; there are also more restricted occurrences in other regions, including peninsular Italy and the islands of Sardinia and Sicily. Problems inherent in the study of rock art that apply not just to gender but to all aspects of interpretation relate to the difficulties of relating the art to other aspects of the archaeological record (i.e., to other aspects of the society that produced the art). Thus, many studies are dependent entirely on the internal evidence of the art itself (the motifs and their arrangement in relation to other motifs) and, more recently, the relationship of the art to the landscape. This limitation restricts the scope of analysis and raises the risk of circular argument.

Gender is not a new topic in analysis of rock art, and studies that discuss it appear from an early stage. However, as Russell (1991) has pointed out in the context of Upper Palaeolithic art and Díaz-Andreu (1998) in the case of Spanish Levantine art, much of this work has been in the androcentric tradition of pregender archaeology, characterized by unquestioned assumptions about how gender can be recognized in the art, that the artists were all men, and that the roles played by men and women in the societies in question corresponded to assumed universals (in fact, derived from the norms of our own society). Leroi-Gourhan's (1968) classic structuralist analysis of Upper Palaeolithic parietal art, with its recognition of male and female spheres represented by different animals species, introduced a new level of symbolic understanding to the previously rather literal interpretations but was still characterized by androcentric assumptions and stereotyping. Here I shall confine myself to discussion of some more recent studies that are informed to various degrees by gender theory and challenge some of the traditional assumptions. To some extent, this work parallels figurine studies, characterized by much more careful contextual analysis of how gender might be identified in the art, challenges to the assumption of a binary gender system, and some challenges to the view that the artists were all male. Again, as with the figurine studies, all these studies do not move in the same direction, and there are sometimes contradictory conclusions.

In the context of the Scandinavian Bronze Age rock art, early (in the sense used in this article) attempts to put gender and specifically women into the picture are articles by Mandt (1986, 1987). These are characterized by what now seem rather simplistic attempts to identify female deities and female symbols (including cup marks, trees, snakes, spirals, and rings with crosses as well as human figures shown with female genitalia) that are assumed to have a more or less universal significance connected with fertility. At the other end of the interpretative spectrum is an article by Yates (1993) on an archaeology of the body. He looks at the human figures, which have traditionally been divided into those with a penis shown, equated with men, and those without, assumed to represent women. Yates challenges the straightforward association of the penis with maleness and its absence with femaleness, which he considers a culturally specific Western notion. Instead, he argues that in Bronze Age Scandinavian society, masculine identity had to be guaranteed by signs applied to the surface of the body (the penis and also weapons on the human figures and antlers on the deer representations). Therefore, he argues that the figures lacking penes and weapons are not necessarily female: they could be male children or adolescent boys who had not yet been assigned cultural masculinity. Thus, Yates offers an interpretation diametrically opposed to that of Mandt: instead of women being found in the art, Yates's account excludes them altogether.

Another study that argues for rock art as an exclusive male domain is Barfield and Chippindale's (1997) account of the art of Mont Bégo at the western end of the Alpine chain. This art, which probably dates to the Copper and Bronze Ages, occurs at high altitudes. The art includes male figures, shown with a penis, associated with weapons (both daggers and halberds), plowing scenes (paired oxen pulling ards), and daggers and halberds by themselves and so-called cornus, which are stylized oxen shown with large horns and small bodies. Barfield and Chippindale argue that all these are male symbols and that Mont Bégo might have been used for male rites of passage, marking the achievement of adult status, when young men would have climbed to these high and remote locations to carve a symbol of their new status on the rock face (perhaps after spending a night on the mountain and/or other ordeals of initiation). The art of the Valcamonica and Valtellina in northern Italy, while showing some similarities with that of Mont Bégo, is also different in many ways: it is situated in more accessible locations; it has a much longer chronology, from Mesolithic to medieval times (with a concentration in the Copper, Bronze, and Iron Ages); and it has a much wider variety of motifs, including clearly female figures, identified by a blob in the pubic area, as well as male ones, shown with penis (fig. 22.4) (Bevan 2000). Moreover, we have in the same areas as the rock art (as well as some further afield) anthropomorphic statues known as statue-menhirs (carved in the round) or statue-stelae (incised), dated to the Copper Age with some degree of security and sharing some decorative motifs with the rock art. These monuments clearly represent humans and are variously interpreted as representing deities or ancestors; both female and male examples

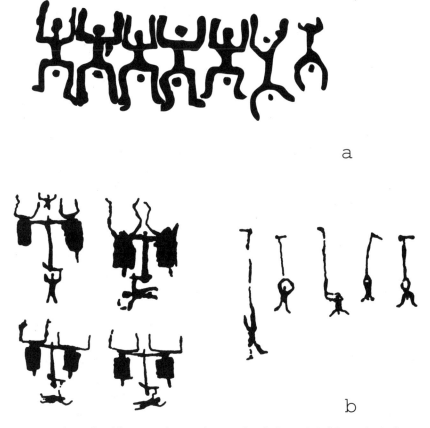

Figure 22.4. Gendered figures in Alpine rock art: (a) female figures in Val Camonica (redrawn by author from postcard; (b) male figures on Mont Bego (Barfiedl and Chippindale 1997).

occur and are depicted in clearly differentiated and mutually exclusive, ways. In some groups, the females are shown with breasts and occasionally with necklaces, while the males are shown with weapons; in others, clothing appears to be shown, with males and females shown wearing different garments and ornaments, while the men also have weapons. Various studies have considered the gender of these statues (Barfield 1995, 1998; De Marinis 1995; Harris 2003; Pedrotti 1995, 1998; Robb 1994a, 1997; Whitehouse 1992a). In 1992, I pointed to a difference between women who were shown by biological features and men shown by cultural ones (specifically weapons), in other words, a characteristic structuralist interpretation, with nature being equated with women and culture with men. Barfield criticized this account, suggesting that the statues represent clothed individuals and that breasts are shown simply because they would have protruded through clothing; he also argues that the dagger symbolizes the phallus and indeed that some of the monuments are themselves phallic in form (Barfield 1998:144). It is certainly the case that some of the monuments seem to show clothing, and Pedrotti (1998) has recognized several different regional groups in terms of clothing and ornaments, and at least some of these demonstrate gender differences. For instance, in the Valcamonica, Valtellina (central Alpine), and Atesine (eastern Alps) areas, capes with fringes occur only on male figures, while capes without fringes occur on female figures. The female figures also show differences in the number and types of ornament shown, and Pedrotti suggests that, for instance, garments with pendants attached might have indicated women of a particular status or life stage (possibly married or having had a child). None of the studies on the Alpine area give any consideration to possibilities of additional, ambiguous genders, but they do consider different stages in the life cycles of men and women, and they regard the way that gender is depicted as a matter for examination and discussion, not as a given.

An analysis that does attempt to move away from essentialist recognition of men and women in art can be found in Pluciennik's (1998:68–70) analysis of a complex Late Palaeolithic incised scene in the Sicilian cave of Grotta di Addaura. This "scene," which has provoked much discussion, appears to show a number of upright beaked figures surrounding a central pair of horizontal figures, one above the other, both shown with erect beak-like penes or possibly penis sheaths and lines, perhaps representing cords, between their backs and buttocks. This has been interpreted variously as an act of homosexual copulation or as acrobatic ritual concerned with virility or human sacrifice by ritual strangulation (in the context of fertility rituals). Pluciennik, while regarding these interpretations as ethnographically plausible, prefers to treat the engravings as fragments of narrative or myth, partly because of the evidence of erasures and repeated incisions, suggesting many reworkings of the "scene" being portrayed. These mythic elements include ideas of maleness and femaleness, with explicitly male symbols prepondering. Pluciennik warns against translating these symbolic representations in terms of men and women as biologically sexed bodies. However, the dominance of male symbols does suggest that we are concerned here with male rites, narratives, and myths in which women played no or subordinate roles.

A completely different approach is adopted by Escoriza Mateu (2002) in her study of Spanish Levantine rock art. In marked contrast to most of the work that has been conducted under the heading of gender archaeology, she disputes the utility of the concept of gender and insists on the reality of sex in the sense of differently sexed bodies as articulated by the French feminist writer Luce Irigaray. Moreover, she interprets Levantine art as the product of "the patriarchal order," characterized by representations of women that ignore or diminish the importance of women's contribution to both production and reproduction. In the art, which is now thought to date to the Neolithic period, male figures (shown with penes) are shown in scenes that depict hunting, herding, war, and ritual, while females (shown with breasts or wearing skirts, which are exclusively associated with figures with breasts) are shown clearing fields, harvesting, sowing, herding, and engaged in ritual. She argues from this that there was a sexual division of labor and that women were probably exploited (they carried out more tasks than men and more important ones from the point of view of production). They would also have borne children, vital to the reproduction of the community. She comments on the absence of images showing pregnancy or birth in the Levantine art and contrasts this with the art of the Upper Palaeolithic, where these representations occur. She interprets this as a characteristic feature of patriarchy—concealment. "The politico-ideological strategy is to hide, and to give limited social value to, females in relation to its work in the creation of the conditions for social life" (Escoriza Mateu 2002:100). This interpretation can be accused of asserting a new essentialism, insisting as it does on the absolute difference between the sexed bodies of men and women. It is also clearly based on another underlying assumption, derived from Marxist understanding, that production and reproduction are the fundamental bases of social life. These are unfashionable views in these postmodern days, but Escoriza Mateu's approach has the virtue of redirecting attention to the lives of real men and women of the past and the power relations between them—a goal that has largely disappeared from view in much of the gender archaeology literature.

Other Art

Work has been carried out on the art of some later, more complex societies. Attention has been directed to the art of fully historical periods (classical and later), where texts provide abundant information on gender to aid interpretation, but also at societies on the margin of history in which some writing occurs but which is restricted in scope or difficult to decipher. I shall discuss two examples here: the Minoans and the Etruscans.

In studies of Minoan society of the Cretan Late Bronze Age, attention has been directed at both frescoes and figurines (e.g., Alberti 2001, 2002; Hitchcock 1997, 2000; Marinatos 1987, 1993; Morris and Peatfield 2002; Rehak 1998, 1999, 2002). Talalay (2005) discusses this work, and I shall just draw out one or two points here. One is that in this area also, some scholars have challenged the binary gender structure that had been assumed in most earlier work. Hitchcock (1997) found a clear binary gender distinction in the Cretan bronze figurines but found ambiguity in some other Minoan iconography, especially wall paintings (Hitchcock 2000). In particular, she discusses the bull-leaping fresco and the "Priest-King" relief fresco, both from Knossos, where the individuals appear with white skin, a convention usually applied to females, but also have long snaky locks, kilts, and codpieces usually shown on males. Hitchcock argues that this ambiguity was deliberate and that gender ambiguity may have been part of the sanctioned social order in palatial Crete. Benjamin Alberti (2001, 2002) looks at gender in Minoan figurative art from the perspective of Butler's performance view of gendered identity. He argues that the body in Knossian iconography was not intrinsically sexed or gendered but started as a basic body template that acquired characteristics, including sexual attributes, in particular contexts, related to the performative production of gender. Another fascinating contribution is Rehak's (2002) analysis of the frescoes from Xeste 3 at Akrotiri on Thera, which he interprets as related to a female rite of passage, involving the use of saffron and perhaps involving a homoerotic element.

In relation to the Etruscans, rather a lot has been written about women in Etruscan society (e.g., Bonfante 1973a, 1973b, 1981; 1989a, 1989b, 1994; see also papers in Rallo 1989); however, these studies are in the main theory free and characterized by an unchallenged essentialism—an "add women and stir" approach. There is no doubt that such studies have cast interesting light on women in Etruscan society, such as their early role in the practice of writing (Bagnasco Gianni 1996; Hodos 1998), but they do not fall within the field of gender archaeology as defined here. A different approach is Izzet's (1998) analysis of the way in which both men and women represented themselves on sixth- to fifth-century B.C. bronze mirrors. Izzet's analysis of the scenes on the mirrors challenges the traditional view of Etruscan women as more free than their Greek counterparts, having more equal relationships with their husbands and more visible public roles. Women on the mirrors are shown being dressed, ornamented, and painted, sometimes explicitly watched by male figures. Izzet argues that they are being prepared as highly decorative luxury objects for the purposes of male erotic enjoyment and wealth display; they are also being located in the domestic arena. Men are represented very differently: male bodies, shown naked in contrast to the elaborately dressed and ornamented female bodies, are worked on from within through exercise and the associated processes of scraping, oiling, and depilating of the body; they are associated with public roles, particularly warfare and athletics. Izzet also suggests that the famous Etruscan images of couples, often cited as evidence of the "equal partnership" view, can just as easily be seen as placing women as part of men's wealth display and as erotic images for the male gaze. This objectification of women has a chronological dimension, developing more strongly from the sixth to the fourth century B.C., while in the earlier orientalizing period of the seventh century B.C., there seems to be much more gender ambiguity. Izzet's study demonstrates how a theoretically informed analysis can cast new light on gender ideologies and roles in Etruscan society even if it leads us to abandon the attractive image of empowered and equal Etruscan women (or perhaps restrict it to the early phase of Etruscan development).

Conclusions

One point that emerges from this overview is that gender archaeology in Europe is in a healthy state of rapid expansion; it is being extended to new geographical areas and new bodies of data; moreover, it is found not only in specialist volumes but also in a wide range of general archaeological journals, both national and international, indicating that the subject is now acceptable within mainstream archaeology. Nonetheless, there is no cause for complacency: large parts of European archaeological scholarship, even those that declare themselves to be concerned with social archaeology, remain untouched by the new perspectives and insights offered by gender archaeology, and there is much more work to be done. Moreover, the task ahead is not simply that of trying to persuade as yet unconvinced colleagues of the importance of gender archaeology: there are problems within gender archaeology itself, and some self-reflection is due.

In the conclusion to her survey of gender studies in the Mediterranean, Talalay (2005:145) points out that prehistorians have not yet taken up the "the range of sophisticated and theoretically informed frameworks that are now well represented in gender studies of other disciplines," which she exemplifies with agency theory and Bourdieu's concept of "doxa." It is difficult to quarrel with this critique, but I feel certain that all the more fashionable branches of theory are likely to be applied to gender studies before long. My own criticism is more conservative and refers to what we lose by not using some of the older theoretical approaches that preceded postprocessualism. As I discuss elsewhere (Whitehouse, in press), the predominantly postprocessual orientation of European gender archaeology has both positive and negative aspects. On the positive side, it focuses on contextual studies that root interpretations deep in "local knowledge" of specific past societies. The negative aspect is the rarity of studies on a large scale, showing geographical breadth or chronological duration; correspondingly, we have very few comparative analyses concerned with similarities or differences across Europe or changes and developments through time. Similarly, on the positive side, challenges to gender essentialism offer escape from ethnocentric gender stereotyping and exploration of categories and concepts well understood in anthropology and other disciplines, such as additional genders, gender transgression, gender negotiation, and gender performance. The negative aspect here is diversion from the study of the real, identifiable women and men of the past who, as both history and anthropology teach us, are likely to have lived differently gendered lives. The emphasis on "difference" rather than "power" allows us— positively—to recognize women in all their variety and individuality; negatively, it redirects attention from the traditional feminist concern with the source(s) of male dominance, which, I would argue, should still be one of our research objectives. Moreover, the concentration on "empowerment," which has replaced "power" as the dominant concept in much of the literature, denies the reality of many women's lives in many societies, subject as they have been (and still are in many places) to explicit and sometimes brutal control by men.

In addition, there is one great gap in the development of gender archaeology in Europe, and that is the virtual taboo that seems to exist on any discussion of biology, especially reproduction (Whitehouse, in press). This lacuna exists to some extent also in American gender archaeology but is at its most extreme in the European literature. Outside the context of the largely discredited mother goddess hypothesis, discussed previously, and a few of the new figurines studies, such as Bolger's work on Cyprus, there is remarkably little discussion of reproduction or motherhood as either a biological or a social phenomenon. This seems to me unfortunate since it involves ignoring something that must have been important to all societies and many individuals. It is also dangerous since it creates an apparently unbridgeable divide between gender archaeology and other disciplines that are also concerned with explaining the past. So, on the one hand, we have evolutionary biology describing a past in which it is assumed that reproductive choice is the main engine driving human history and, on the other, a gender archaeology that refuses to concern itself with reproduction at all. This problem shows no signs of being resolved at present.

Thus, there's good news and bad news. I would like to think that gender archaeologists will move forward exploiting the widest possible range of theoretical approaches from both the processual and the postprocessual repertoires as well as those that defy this kind of labeling altogether to address the widest possible range of questions about gender. There's lots of work to be done, but what an enjoyable prospect this is.

References

Aitchison, Kenneth
- 1999 *Profiling the Profession: A Survey of Archaeological Jobs in the UK*. London: Council for British Archaeology, English Heritage and Institute of Field Archaeologists.

Alberti, Benjamin
- 2001 Faience Goddesses and Ivory Bull-Leapers: The Aesthetics of Sexual Difference at Late Bronze Age Knossos. *World Archaeology* 33:189–205.
- 2002 Gender and the Figurative Art of Late Bronze Age Knossos. In *Labyrinth Revisited: Rethinking "Minoan" Archaeology*. Y. Hamilakis, ed. Pp. 98–117. Oxford: Oxbow.

Arnold, Bettina
- 1991 The Deposed Princess of Vix: The Need for an Engendered European Prehistory. In *The Archaeology of Gender*. Proceedings of the Twenty-Second Annual Chacmool Conference. D. Walde and N. D. Willows, eds. Pp. 366–74. Calgary: Department of Archaeology, University of Calgary.
- 1996 "Honorary Males" or Women of Substance? Gender, Status and Power in Iron Age Europe. *Journal of European Archaeology* 3(2):153–68.
- 2002 "Sein unde Werden": Gender as Process in Mortuary Ritual. In *In Pursuit of Gender: Worldwide Archaeological Approaches*. S. M. Nelson and M. Rosen-Ayalon, eds. Pp. 239–56. Walnut Creek, CA: AltaMira Press.

Bachofen, Johann, J.
- 1861 *Das Mutterrecht*. Basel: Benno Schwabe. (English version: *Myth, Religion and Mother Right: Selected Writings*. R. Mannheim, trans. [Princeton, NJ: Princeton University Press, 1973])

Bacus, E. A., A. W Barker, J. D. Bonevich, S. L. Dunavan, J. B. Fitzhugh, D. L. Gold, N. S. Goldman-Finn, W. Griffin, and K. M. Mudar, eds.
- 1993 *A Gendered Past: A Critical Bibliography of Gender in Archaeology*. University of Michigan Museum of Anthropology Technical Paper 25. Ann Arbor: University of Michigan Publications.

Bagnasco Gianni, Giovanna
　　1996　　*Oggetti iscritti di epoca orientalizzante in Etruria.* Florence: L. S. Olschki Editore.
Bailey, Douglass W.
　　1994　　Reading Prehistoric Figurines as Individuals. *World Archaeology* 25(3):321–31.
　　1995　　The Representation of Gender: Homology or Propaganda. *Journal of European Archaeology* 2(2):215–28.
　　1996　　The Interpretation of Figurines: The Emergence of Illusion and New Ways of Seeing. *Cambridge Archaeological Journal* 6(2):291–95.
Barfield, Lawrence
　　1995　　The Context of Statue-Menhirs. *Notizie Archeologiche Bergomensi* 3:11–20.
　　1998　　Gender Issues in North Italian Prehistory. In *Gender and Italian Archaeology: Challenging the Stereotypes.* R.D. Whitehouse, ed. Pp. 143–56. London: Accordia Research Institute and Institute of Archaeology.
Barfield, Lawrence H., and Christopher Chippindale
　　1997　　Meaning in the Later Prehistoric Rock-Engravings of Mont Bégo, Alpes-Maritimes, France. *Proceedings of the Prehistoric Society* 63:103–28.
Beard, Mary
　　2000　　*The Invention of Jane Harrison.* Revealing Antiquity, vol. 14. Cambridge, MA: Harvard University Press.
Bentley, R. Alexander, Lounès Chikhi, and T. Douglas Price
　　2003　　The Neolithic Transition in Europe: Comparing Broad Scale Genetic and Local Scale Isotopic Evidence. *Antiquity* 77:63–66.
Bertelsen, Reidar, Arnvid Lillehammer, and Jenny-Rita Naess, eds.
　　1987　　*Were They All Men? An Examination of Sex Roles in Prehistoric Society.* Stavanger: Arkeologisk Museum i Stavanger.
Bevan, Lynne
　　2000　　Women's Art, Men's Art: Gender Specific Image Selection in the Rock Art of the Valcamonica. In *Signifying Place and Space: World Perspectives of Rock Art and Landscape.* G. Nash, ed. Pp. 103–9. BAR International Series 902. Oxford: Archaeopress.
Biel, Peter F.
　　1996　　Symbolic Communication Systems: Symbols on Anthropomorphic Figurines in Neolithic and Chalcolithic Southeast Europe. *Journal of European Archaeology* 4:153–76.
Bolger, Diane L.
　　1992　　The Archaeology of Fertility and Birth: A Ritual Deposit from Chalcolithic Cyprus. *Journal of Anthropological Research* 48:145–64.
　　1993　　The Feminine Mystique: Gender and Society in Prehistoric Cypriot Studies. In *Report of the Department of Antiquities, Cyprus.* Pp. 29–42. Nicosia: Department of Antiquities.
　　1994　　Ladies of the Expedition: Harriet Boyd Hawes and Edith Hall at Work in

Mediterranean Archaeology. In *Women in Archaeology*. C. Claassen, ed. Pp. 41–50. Philadelphia: University of Pennsylvania Press.
1996 Figurines, Fertility and the Emergence of Complex Society in Prehistoric Cyprus. *Current Anthropology* 37(2):365–73.
2002 Gender and Mortuary Ritual in Chalcolithic Cyprus. In *Engendering Aphrodite: Women and Society in Ancient Cyprus*. D. Bolger and N. Serwint, eds. Pp. 67–86. Boston: American Schools of Oriental Research.
2003 *Gender in Ancient Cyprus: Narratives of Social Change on a Mediterranean Island*. Walnut Creek, CA: AltaMira Press.

Bolger, Diane, and Nancy Serwint, eds.
2002 *Engendering Aphrodite: Women and Society in Ancient Cyprus*. Cyprus American Archaeological Research Institute, Monograph 3. ASOR Archaeological Reports 7. Boston: American Schools of Oriental Research.

Bonfante, Larissa
1973a Etruscan Women: A Question of Interpretation. *Archaeology* 26(4):242–49.
1973b The Women of Etruria. *Arethus* 6(1):91–101.
1981 Etruscan Couples and Their Aristocratic Society. *Women's Studies* 8:157–87.
1989a Iconografia delle madri: Etruria e Italia antica. In *Le donne in Etruria*. A. Rallo, ed. Pp. 85–106. Rome: "L'Erma" di Bretschneider.
1989b La moda femminile etrusca. In *Ledonne in Etruria*. A. Rallo, ed. Pp. 157–71. Rome: "L'Erma" di Bretschneider.
1994 Etruscan Women. In *Women in the Classical World: Image and Text*. E. Fantham et al., eds. Pp. 243–59. Oxford: Oxford University Press.

Butler, Judith
1990 *Gender Trouble: Feminism and the Subversion of Identity*. London: Routledge.
1993 *Bodies That Matter: On the Discursive Limits of "Sex."* London: Routledge.

Callander, Jane, and Pamela J. Smith
In press Pioneers in Palestine: The Women Excavators of El-Wad Cave, 1929. In *Archaeology and Women*. S. Hamilton, R. Whitehouse, and K. Wright, eds. London: UCL Press.

Champion, Sara
1998 Women in British Archaeology. In *Excavating Women: History of Women in European Archaeology*. M. Díaz-Andreu and M. L. S. Sørensen, eds. Pp. 175–97. London: Routledge.

Chapman, John
1997 Changing Gender Relations in the Later Prehistory of Eastern Hungary. In *Invisible People and Processes: Writing Gender and Childhood into European Prehistory*. J. Moore and E. Scott, eds. Pp. 131–49. Leicester: Leicester University Press.
1998 The Impact of Modern Invasions and Migrations on Archaeological Explanation: A Biographical Sketch. In *Excavating Women: A History of Women in European Archaeology*. M. Díaz-Andreu and M. L. S. Sørensen, eds. Pp. 295–314. London: Routledge.

2000   *Fragmentation in Archaeology: Peoples, Places and Broken Objects in the Prehistory of South Eastern Europe*. London: Routledge.

Claassen, Cheryl, ed.
1992   *Exploring Gender through Archaeology: Selected Papers from the 1991 Boone Conference*. Madison, WI: Prehistory Press.

Cohen, Getzel M., and Martha S. Joukowsky, eds.
2004   *Breaking Ground: Pioneering Women Archaeologists*. Ann Arbor: University of Michigan Press.

Conkey, Margaret W.
1991   Contexts of Action, Context for Power: Material Culture and Gender in the Magdalenian. In *Engendering Archaeology: Women and Prehistory*. J. M. Gero and M. W. Conkey, eds. Pp. 57–92. Oxford: Basil Blackwell.
1997   Mobilizing Ideologies: Palaeolithic "Art," Gender Trouble, and Thinking about Alternatives. In *Women in Human Evolution*. L. D. Hager, ed. Pp. 172–207. London: Routledge.

Conkey, Margaret W., and Ruth E. Tringham
1995   Archaeology and the Goddess: Exploring the Contours of Feminist Archaeology. In *Feminisms in the Academy: Rethinking the Discipline*. D. Stanton and A. Stewart, eds. Pp. 199–247. Ann Arbor: University of Michigan Press.

Conroy, Linda P.
1993   Female Figurines of the Upper Palaeolithic and the Emergence of Gender. In *Women in Archaeology: A Feminist Critique*. H. du Cros and L. Smith, eds. Pp. 153–60. Canberra: Australia National University.

Coudart, Anick
1998   Archaeology of French Women and French Women in Archaeology. In *Excavating Women: History of Women in European Archaeology*. M. Díaz-Andreu and M. L. S. Sørensen, eds. Pp. 61–85. London: Routledge.

Davies, William, and Ruth Charles, eds.
1999   *Dorothy Garrod and the Progress of the Palaeolithic*. Oxford: Oxbow.

De Marinis, Rafaele C.
1995   Le stele antropomorfe di Aosta. *Notizie Archeologiche Bergomensi* 3:213–20.

Díaz-Andreu, Margarita
1994   Mujer y género: Nuevas tendencies dentro de la arqueología. *Arqritica* 8:17–19.
1998   Iberian Post-Palaeolithic Art and Gender: Discussing Human Representations in Levantine Art. *Journal of Iberian Archaeology* 0:33–51.

Díaz-Andreu, Margarita & Marie-Louise S. Sørensen
1998a   Excavating Women: Towards an Engendered History of Archaeology. In *Excavating Women: History of Women in European Archaeology*. M. Díaz-Andreu and M. L. S. Sørensen, eds. Pp. 1–28. London: Routledge.

Díaz-Andreu, Margarita, and Marie-Louise S. Sørensen, eds.
1998b   *Excavating Women: History of Women in European Archaeology*. London: Routledge.

Dobres, Marcia-Anne
 1992 Reconsidering Venus Figurines: A Feminist Inspired Re-Analysis. In *Ancient Images, Ancient Thought: The Archaeology of Ideology*. S. Goldsmith, S. Garvie, D. Selin, and J. Smith, eds. Pp. 245–62. Calgary: University of Calgary.
 2000 Scrutinizing the Interpreters: Feminist Perspectives on the Study and Interpretation of Ancient Female and "Goddess" Imagery. In *Deesses, Diosas, Goddesses*. Museu d'Història de Barcelona Exhibition Catalogue. Pp. 36–46. Barcelona: Ajuntament de Barcelona.

Dommasnes, Lev H.
 1982 Late Iron Age in Western Norway: Female Roles and Ranks as Deduced from an Analysis of Burial Customs. *Norwegian Archaeological Review* 15(1–2):70–84.
 1987 Male-Female Roles and Ranks in Late Iron Age Norway. In *Were They All Men? An Examination of Sex Roles in Prehistoric Society*. R. Bertelsen et al., eds. Pp. 65–77. Stavanger: Arkeologisk Museum i Stavanger.
 1992 Two Decades of Women in Prehistory and in Archaeology in Norway: A Review. *Norwegian Archaeological Review* 25(1):1–14.

Dommasnes, Lev H., E. J. Kleppe, G. Mandt, and J. Naess
 1998 Women Archaeologists in Retrospect: The Norwegian Case. In *Excavating Women: History of Women in European Archaeology*. M. Díaz-Andreu and M. L. S. Sørensen, eds. Pp. 105–24. London: Routledge.

Donald, Moira, and Linda Hurcombe, eds.
 2000a *Gender and Material Culture in Archaeological Perspective*. London: Macmillan.
 2000b *Gender and Material Culture in Historical Perspective*. London: Macmillan.
 2000c *Representations of Gender from Prehistory to the Present*. London: Macmillan.

Drower, Margaret S.
 2004 Gertrude Caton-Thompson, 1888–1985. In *Breaking Ground: Pioneering Women Archaeologists*. G. Cohen and M. S. Joukowsky, eds. Pp. 351–79. Ann Arbor: University of Michigan Press.

du Cros, Hilary, and Laurajane Smith, eds.
 1993 *Women in Archaeology: A Feminist Critique*. Canberra: Australia National University.

Dyson, Stephen L.
 2004 *Eugénie Sellers Strong: Portrait of an Archaeologist*. London: Duckworth.

Ehrenberg, Margaret
 1989 *Women in Prehistory*. London: British Museum Publications.

Elster, Ernestine S.
 In press Marija Gimbutas: Setting the Agenda. In *Archaeology and Women*. S. Hamilton, R. Whitehouse, and K. Wright, eds. London: UCL Press.

Engelstad, Erika, Gro Mandt, and Jenny-Rita Naess
 1994 Equity Issues in Norwegian Archaeology. In *Equity Issues for Women in Archaeology*. M. C. Nelson, S. M. Nelson, and A. Wylie, eds. Pp. 139–45. Archaeo-

logical Papers of the American Anthropological Association 5. Washington, DC: American Anthropological Association.

Escoriza Mateu, Trinidad
    1996   Lecturas sobre las representaciones femeninas en el arte rupestre levantino: Una revision crítica. *Arenal: Revista de Historia de las Mujeres* 3(1):5–24.
    2002   Representations of Women in Spanish Levantine Art: An Intentional Fragmentation. *Journal of Social Archaeology* 2:81–108.

Fleming, Andrew
    1969   The Myth of the Mother-Goddess. *World Archaeology* 1:247–61.

Fonnesbeck-Sandberg, E., B. Pauly Hansen, K. Jespersen, L. Bender Jørgensen, K. Løkkegård, T. Matz, U. Fraes Rasmussen, L. Slumstrup, I. Stoumann, F. Waagebech, T. Wanning, S. Wiell, L. Wienecke, and S. Ørnager
    1972   Han, hun og arkaeologien: "Arkaeologiske Studier." *Kontaktstenci* 4:5–10.

Frankel, David
    1997   On Cypriot Figurines and the Origins of Patriarchy. *Current Anthropology* 38:84.
    2002   Social Stratification, Gender and Ethnicity in Third Millennium Cyprus. In *Engendering Aphrodite: Women and Society in Ancient Cyprus*. D. Bolger and N. Serwint, eds. Pp. 171–79. Boston: American Schools of Oriental Research.

Gejvall, Nils-Gustaf
    1970   The Fisherman from Barum—Mother of Several Children: Palaeo-Anatomic Finds in the Skeleton from Bäckaskog. *Fornvännen* 95:281–89.

Gero, Joan M., and Margaret W. Conkey, eds.
    1991   *Engendering Archaeology: Women and Prehistory*. Oxford: Basil Blackwell.

Gibbs, Liv
    1987   Identifying Gender Representation in the Archaeological Record: A Contextual Study. In *The Archaeology of Contextual Meanings*. I. Hodder, ed. Pp. 79–89. Cambridge: Cambridge University Press.

Gilchrist, Roberta
    1994   *Gender and Material Culture: The Archaeology of Religious Women*. London: Routledge.
    1999   *Gender and Archaeology*. London: Routledge.

Gimbutas, Marija
    1982   *The Goddesses and Gods of Old Europe: Myths and Cult Images*. London: Thames and Hudson. (Originally published in 1974 as *The Gods and Goddesses of Old Europe*.)
    1989   *The Language of the Goddess: Unearthing the Hidden Symbols of Western Civilization*. London: Thames and Hudson.
    1991   *The Civilization of the Goddess: The World of Old Europe*. San Francisco: HarperCollins.

Haaland, G., and Randi Haaland
    1996   Levels of Meanings in Symbolic Objects. *Cambridge Archaeological Journal* 6(2):295–300.

Hamilton, Naomi
   1996   The Person Is Political. *Cambridge Archaeological Journal* 6(2):282–85.
   2000   Ungendering Archaeology: Concepts of Sex and Gender in Figurine Studies in Prehistory. In *Representations of Gender from Prehistory to the Present*. M. Donald and L. Hurcombe, eds. Pp. 17–30. London: Macmillan.

Hamilton, Sue
   In press   Women in Practice: Women in British Contract Field Archaeology. In *Archaeology and Women*. S. Hamilton, R. Whitehouse, and K. Wright, eds. London: UCL Press.

Harrington, Sue
   In press   Stirring Women, Weapons and Weaving—Aspects of Gender Identity and Symbols of Power in Early Anglo-Saxon England. In *Archaeology and Women*. S. Hamilton, R. Whitehouse, and K. Wright, eds. London: UCL Press.

Harris, Susanna
   2003   Representations of Woven Textiles in Alpine Europe during the Copper Age. In *Inhabiting Symbols: Symbol and Image in the Ancient Mediterranean*. J. B. Wilkins and E. Herring, eds. Pp. 43–84. London: Accordia Research Institute.

Hayden, Brian
   1985   Old Europe: Sacred Matriarchy or Complementary Opposition? In *Archaeology and Fertility Cult in the Ancient Mediterranean*. A. Bonanno, ed. Pp. 17–30. Amsterdam: Gruner.

Henderson, Julian
   1989   Pagan Cemeteries: A Study of the Problems of Sexing by Grave Goods and Bones. In *Burial Archaeology: Current Research, Methods and Development*. C. Roberts, F. Lee, and J. Bintliff, eds. Pp. 77–84. BAR British Series 211. Oxford: British Archaeological Reports.

Hingley, Richard
   1990   Domestic Organisation and Gender Relations in Iron Age and Romano-British Households. In *The Social Archaeology of Houses*. R. Samson, ed. Pp. 125–47. Edinburgh: Edinburgh University Press.

Hitchcock, Louise
   1997   Engendering Domination: A Structural and Contextual Analysis of Minoan Neopalatial Bronze Figurines. In *Invisible People and Processes: Writing Gender and Childhood into European Prehistory*. J. Moore and E. Scott, eds. Pp. 113–30. Leicester: Leicester University Press.
   2000   Engendering Ambiguity in Minoan Crete: It's a Drag to Be a King. In *Representations of Gender from Prehistory to the Present*. M. Donald and L. Hurcombe, eds. Pp. 69–86. London: Macmillan.

Hodder, Ian
   1990   *The Domestication of Europe*. Oxford: Blackwell.

Hodos, Tamar
   1998   The Asp's Poison: Women and Literacy in Iron Age Italy. In *Gender and Italian*

Archaeology: Challenging the Stereotypes. R. D. Whitehouse, ed. Pp. 198–208. London: Accordia Research Institute and Institute of Archaeology.

Holmes, Katie, and Ruth Whitehouse
 1998 Anthropomorphic Figurines and the Construction of Gender in Neolithic and Copper Age Italy. In *Gender and Italian Archaeology: Challenging the Stereotypes.* R. D. Whitehouse, ed. Pp. 95–126. London: Accordia Research Institute and Institute of Archaeology.

Holm-Olsen, I. M., and G. Mandt-Larsen
 1974 Kvinnens stilling I norsk arkeologi. *Kontaktstencil* 6:68–75.

Hood, R.
 1998 *Faces of Archaeology in Greece: Caricatures by Piet de Jong.* Oxford: Leopard's Head Press.

Izzet, Vedia
 1998 Holding a Mirror to Etruscan Gender. In *Gender and Italian Archaeology: Challenging the Stereotypes.* R. D. Whitehouse, ed. Pp. 209–27. London: Accordia Research Institute and Institute of Archaeology.

Jameson, Michael H.
 1990a Domestic Space in the Greek City-State. In *Domestic Architecture and the Use of Space.* S. Kent, ed. Pp. 92–113. Cambridge: Cambridge University Press.
 1990b Private Space and the Greek City. In *The Greek City from Homer to Alexander.* O. Murray and S. Price, eds. Pp. 171–95. Oxford: Clarendon Press.

Johnsson, Catherine, Karolina Ross, and Stig Welinder
 2000 Gender, Material Culture, Ritual and Gender System: A Prehistoric Example Based on Sickles. In *Gender and Material Culture in Archaeological Perspective.* M. Donald and L. Hurcombe, eds. Pp. 169–84. London: Macmillan.

Karlisch, Sigrun M., Sibyelle Kästner, and Eva-Marie Mertens, eds.
 1997 *Vom Knochenmann zur Menschenfrau: Feministiche Theorie und archäologische Praxis.* Münster: Agenda Verlag.

Kokkinidou, Dimitra, and Marianna Nikolaidou
 1997 Body Imagery in the Aegean Neolithic: Ideological Implications of Anthropomorphic Figurines. In *Invisible People and Processes: Writing Gender and Childhood into European Prehistory.* J. Moore and E. Scott, eds. Pp. 88–112. Leicester: Leicester University Press.
 2000 A Sexist Present, a Human-Less Past: Museum Archaeology in Greece. In *Gender and Material Culture in Archaeological Perspective.* M. Donald and L. Hurcombe, eds. Pp. 33–55. London: Macmillan.

Leroi-Gourhan, André
 1968 *The Art of Prehistoric Man in Western Europe.* London: Thames and Hudson.

Levi, Sara
 2001 Women's Contribution to the Field of Prehistoric Archaeology in Italy. *Origini* 23:191–222.

Lucy, Sam
  1997   Housewives, Warriors and Slaves? Sex and Gender in Anglo-Saxon Burials. In *Invisible People and Processes: Writing Gender and Childhood into European Prehistory*. J. Moore and E. Scott, eds. Pp. 150–68. Leicester: Leicester University Press.
  1998   *The Early Anglo-Saxon Cemeteries of East Yorkshire*. BAR British Series 272. Oxford: British Archaeological Reports.
Mandt, Gro
  1986   Searching for Female Deities in the Religious Manifestations of the Scandinavian Bronze Age. In *Words and Objects: Towards a Dialogue between Archaeology and History of Religion*. G. Steinsland, ed. Pp. 111–26. Oslo: Norwegian University Press.
  1987   Female Symbolism in Rock Art. In *Were They All Men? An Examination of Sex Roles in Prehistoric Society*. R. Bertelsen, A. Lillehammer, and J. R. Naess, eds. Pp. 35–52. Stavanger: Arkeologisk Museum i Stavanger.
Marcus, Joyce
  1996   The Importance of Context in Interpreting Figurines. *Cambridge Archaeological Journal* 6(2):285–91.
Marinatos, Nanno
  1987   Role and Sex Division in Rural Scenes of Aegean Art. *Journal of Prehistoric Religion* 1:23–34.
  1993   *Minoan Religion, Ritual, Image and Symbol*. Columbia: University of South Carolina Press.
McCoid, C. H., and L. McDermott
  1996   Toward Decolonizing Gender: Female Vision in the Upper Palaeolithic. *American Anthropologist*, n.s., 98(2):319–26.
McDermott, L.
  1996   Self-Representation in Upper Palaeolithic Female Figurines. *Current Anthropology* 37(2):227–75.
Meiklejohn, Christopher, Erik Brinch Petersen, and Verner Alexandersen
  2000   The Anthropology and Archaeology of Mesolithic Gender in the Western Baltic. In *Gender and Material Culture in Archaeological Perspective*. M. Donald and L. Hurcombe, eds. Pp. 222–37. London: Macmillan.
Meskell, Lynn
  1995   Goddesses, Gimbutas and "New Age" Archaeology. *Antiquity* 69:74–86.
  1999   *Archaeologies of Social Life*. Oxford: Blackwell.
Mina, Maria
  2003   Gender in Transition: Evidence and Implication from the Neolithic and Early Bronze Age Aegean. In *Inhabiting Symbols: Symbol and Image in the Ancient Mediterranean*. J. B. Wilkins and E. Herring, eds. Pp. 85–100. London: Accordia Research Institute.
  In press   Figurines without Sex; People without Gender? In *Archaeology and Women*. S. Hamilton, R. Whitehouse, and K. Wright, eds. London: UCL Press.

Moore, Jenny, and Eleanor Scott, eds.
 1997 *Invisible People and Processes: Writing Gender and Childhood into European Prehistory.* Leicester: Leicester University Press.
Morris, Christine, and Alan Peatfield
 2002 Feeling through the Body: Gesture in Cretan Bronze Age Religion. In *Thinking through the Body: Archaeologies of Corporality.* Y. Hamilakis, M. Pluciennik, and S. Tarlow, eds. Pp. 105–20. New York: Kluwer Academic/Plenum.
Morris, Elaine, ed.
 1992 *Women in British Archaeology.* Institute of Field Archaeologists Occasional Paper 4. Birmingham: Institute of Field Archaeologists.
Morris, Elaine
 1994 Extracts from *Women in British Archaeology.* In *Equity Issues for Women in Archaeology.* M. C. Nelson, S. M. Nelson, and A. Wylie, eds. Pp. 203–12. Archaeological Papers of the American Anthropological Association 5. Washington, DC: American Anthropological Association.
Morter, Jon, and John Robb
 1998 Space, Gender and Architecture in the Southern Italian Neolithic. In *Gender and Italian Archaeology: Challenging the Stereotypes.* R.D. Whitehouse, ed. Pp. 83–94. London: Accordia Research Institute and Institute of Archaeology.
Naess, Jenny-Rita
 1974 Kvinner i vikingtid. *Fra Haug ok Heidni* 2.
Nelson, Sarah M.
 1997a Diversity of the Upper Palaeolithic "Venus" Figurines and Archaeological Mythology. In *Gender in Cross-Cultural Perspective.* 2nd ed. C. B. Brettell and C. F. Sargent, eds. Pp. 67–74. Englewood Cliffs, NJ: Prentice Hall.
 1997b *Gender in Archaeology: Analyzing Power and Prestige.* Walnut Creek, CA: AltaMira Press.
Nevett, Lisa
 1994 Separation or Seclusion? Towards an Archaeological Approach to Investigating Women in the Greek Household in the Fifth to Third Centuries BC. In *Architecture and Order: Approaches to Social Space.* M. Parker Pearson and C. Richards, eds. Pp. 98–112. London: Routledge.
 1995 Gender Relations in the Classical Greek Household: The Archaeological Evidence. *Annual of the British School at Athens* 90:363–81.
 1999 *House and Society in Ancient Greece.* Cambridge: Cambridge University Press.
Nikolaidou, Marianna, and Dimitra Kokkinidou
 1998 Greek Women in Archaeology. In *Excavating Women: History of Women in European Archaeology.* M. Díaz-Andreu and M. L. S. Sørensen, eds. Pp. 235–65. London: Routledge.
O'Shea, John
 1995 Mortuary Custom in the Bronze Age of Southeastern Hungary: Diachronic

and Synchronic Perspectives. In *Regional Approaches to Mortuary Analysis*. L. Anderson Beck, ed. Pp. 125–46. New York: Plenum.

Owen, Linda R.
2000 Lithic Functional Analysis as a Means of Studying Gender and Material Culture in Prehistory. In *Gender and Material Culture in Archaeological Perspective*. M. Donald and L. Hurcombe, eds. Pp. 185–205. London: Macmillan.

Pedrotti, Anna, ed.
1995 *Le statue stele di Arco, la statuaria antropomorfa alpina nel III millennio a.C.: Abbigliamento, fibre tessili e colore*. Trento: Museo Civico di Riva del Garda and Ufficio Beni Archeologici della Provincia Autonoma di Trento.

Pedrotti, Anna
1998 Gli elementi d'abbigliamento e d'ornamento nelle statue stele dell'arco alpino. *Archéologie en Languedoc* 22:299–315.

Peltenburg, Edgar
2002 Gender and Social Structure in Prehistoric Cyprus: a Case Study from Kissonerga. In *Engendering Aphrodite: Women and Society in Ancient Cyprus*. D. Bolger and N. Serwint, eds. Pp. 53–63. Boston: American Schools of Oriental Research.

Picazo, Marina
1998 The First Women Archaeologists in Crete. In *Excavating Women: History of Women in European Archaeology*. M. Díaz-Andreu and M. L. S. Sørensen, eds. Pp. 198–213. London: Routledge.

Pluciennik, Mark
1998 Representations of Gender in Prehistoric Southern Italy. In *Gender and Italian Archaeology*. R. Whitehouse, ed. Pp. 57–82. London: Accordia Research Institute and Institute of Archaeology.

Rallo, A., ed.
1989 *Le donne in Etruria*. Rome: "L'Erma" di Bretschneider.

Rega, Elizabeth
1997 Age, Gender and Biological Reality in the Early Bronze Age Cemetery at Mokrin. In *Invisible People and Processes: Writing Gender and Childhood into European Archaeology*. J. Moore and E. Scott, eds. Pp. 229–47. Leicester: Leicester University Press.
2000 The Gendering of Children in the Early Bronze Age Cemetery at Mokrin. In *Gender and Material Culture in Archaeological Perspective*. M. Donald and L. Hurcombe, eds. Pp. 238–49. London: Macmillan.

Rehak, Paul
1998 The Construction of Gender in Late Bronze Age Aegean Art—A Prolegomenon. In *Redefining Archaeology: Feminist Perspectives*. M. Casey, D. Donlon, J. Hope, and S. Wellfare, eds. Pp. 191–98. Canberra: Australian National University Publications.
1999 The Aegean Landscape and the Body: A New Interpretation of the Thera

Frescoes. In *From the Ground Up: Beyond Gender Theory in Archaeology*. Proceedings of the Fifth Gender and Archaeology Conference. N. L. Wicker and B. Arnold, eds. Pp. 11–21. BAR International Series 812. Oxford: British Archaeological Reports.

2002   Imag(in)ing a Woman's World in Bronze Age Greece: The Frescoes from Xeste 3 at Akrotiri, Thera. In *Among Women: From the Homosocial to the Homoerotic in the Ancient World*. N. S. Rabinowitz and L. Auanager, eds. Pp. 34–59. Austin: University of Texas Press.

Renfrew, A. Colin, and Paul Bahn

1991, 1996, 2000, 2005   *Archaeology: Theories, Methods and Practice*. London: Thames and Hudson.

Rice, Patricia C.

1981   Prehistoric Venuses: Symbols of Motherhood or Womanhood? *Journal of Anthropological Research* 37(4):402–16.

Robb, John

1994a   Burial and Social Reproduction in the Peninsular Italian Neolithic. *Journal of Mediterranean Archaeology* 7:27–71.

1994b   Gender Contradictions, Moral Coalitions, and Inequality in Prehistoric Italy. *Journal of European Archaeology* 2(1):2–49.

1997   Female Beauty and Male Violence in Early Italian Society. In *Naked Truths: Women, Sexuality and Gender in Classical Art and Archaeology*. A. O. Koloski-Ostrow and C. L. Lyons, eds. Pp. 43–65. London: Routledge.

Robinson, Annabel

2002   *The Life and Work of Jane Ellen Harrison*. Oxford: Oxford University Press.

Russell, Pamela

1991   Men Only? The Myths about Paleolithic Artists. In *The Archaeology of Gender*. Proceedings of the Twenty-Second Annual Chacmool Conference. D. Walde and N. D. Willows, eds. Pp. 346–51. Calgary: Department of Archaeology, University of Calgary.

1993   The Palaeolithic Mother-Goddess: Fact or Fiction? In *Women in Archaeology: A Feminist Critique*. H. du Cros and L. Smith, eds. Pp. 93–97. Canberra: Australia National University.

Sanahuja Yll, Ma Encarna

2001   *Cuerpos Sexuados: Objetos y Prehistoria*. Barcelona: Universidad de Valencia.

Sarenas, M.

1998   Unveiling the "Female" Figurines: Critiquing Traditional Interpretations of Anthropomorphic Figurines. In *Redefining Archaeology: Feminist Perspectives*. M. Casey, D. Donlon, J. Hope, and S. Wellfare, eds. Pp. 154–64. Canberra: Australia National University.

Smith, Pamela J.

2000   Dorothy Garrod, First Woman Professor at Cambridge. *Antiquity* 74:131–86.

Sofaer-Deverenski, Joanna

1997   Age and Gender at the Site of Tiszapolgár-Basatanya, Hungary. *Antiquity* 71:875–79.

2000   Rings of Life: The Role of Early Metalwork in Mediating the Gendered Life Course. *World Archaeology* 31(3):389–406.

Sørensen, Marie Louise S.
1991   Gender Construction through Appearance. In *The Archaeology of Gender.* Proceedings of the Twenty-Second Annual Chacmool Conference. D. Walde and N. D. Willows, eds. Pp. 121–29. Calgary: Department of Archaeology, University of Calgary.
1996   Women as/and Metalworkers. In *Women in Industry and Technology: Current Research and the Museum Experience.* A. Devonshire and B. Wood, eds. Pp. 45–51. London: Museum of London.
1997   Reading Dress: The Construction of Social Categories and Identities in Bronze Age Europe. *Journal of European Archaeology* 5(1):93–114.
2000   *Gender Archaeology.* Cambridge: Polity Press.

Spector, Janet
1991   What This Awl Means: Toward a Feminist Archaeology. In *Engendering Archaeology: Women and Prehistory.* J. M. Gero and M. W. Conkey, eds. Pp. 388–406. Oxford: Basil Blackwell.
1994   *What This Awl Means: Feminist Archaeology at a Wahpeton Dakota Village.* St. Paul: Minnesota Historical Society Press.

Stoodley, Nick
1999   *The Spindle and the Spear: A Critical Enquiry into the Construction and Meaning of Gender in the Early Anglo-Saxon Burial Rite.* BAR British Series 288. Oxford: British Archaeological Reports.
2000   From the Cradle to the Grave: Age Organization and the Early Anglo-Saxon Burial Rite. *World Archaeology* 31(3):456–72.

Strathern, Marilyn
1988   *The Gender of the Gift.* Berkeley: University of California Press.

Strömberg, Agneta
1993   *Male or Female? A Methodological Study of Grave Gifts as Sex-Indicators in Iron Age Burials from Athens.* Jonsered: Paul Åströms Förlag.

Tafuri, Mary Anne, John Robb, Marisa Mastroroberto, Loretana Salvadei, and Giorgio Manzi
2004   Diet, Mobility and Residence Patterns in Bronze Age Southern Italy: Trace Element Analysis of Human Bone and Dental Analysis. *Accordia Research Papers* 9:45–56.

Talalay, Lauren E.
1987   Rethinking the Function of Clay Figurine Legs from Neolithic Greece: An Argument by Analogy. *American Journal of Archaeology* 91:161–69.
1993   *Deities, Dolls and Devices: Neolithic Figurines from Franchthi Cave, Greece.* Bloomington: Indiana University Press.
1994   A Feminist Boomerang: The Great Goddess of Greek Prehistory. *Gender and History* 6(2):165–83.

2000   Archaeological Ms.conceptions: Contemplating Gender and the Greek Neolithic. In *Representations of Gender from Prehistory to the Present*. M. Donald and L. Hurcombe, eds. Pp. 3–16. London: Macmillan.

2005   The Gendered Sea: Iconography, Gender and Mediterranean Prehistory. In *The Archaeology of Mediterranean Prehistory*. E. Blake and A. B. Knapp, eds. Pp. 130–55. Oxford: Blackwell.

Talalay, Lauren E., and Tracey Cullen

2002   Sexual Ambiguity in Plank Figures from Bronze Age Cyprus. In *Engendering Aphrodite: Women and Society in Ancient Cyprus*. D. Bolger and N. Serwint, eds. Pp. 181–95. Boston: American Schools of Oriental Research.

Thålin-Bergman, L., ed.

1975   *O forna tiders kvinnor*. Stockholm: Statens Historiska Museum.

Toms, Judith

1998   The Construction of Gender in Early Iron Age Etruria. In *Gender and Italian Archaeology*. R. Whitehouse, ed. Pp. 157–179. London: Accordia Research Institute and the Institute of Archaeology.

Treherne, Paul

1995   The Warrior's Beauty: The Masculine Body and Self-Identity in Bronze Age Europe. *Journal of European Archaeology* 3(1):105–44.

Tringham, Ruth

1991a   Households with Faces: The Challenge of Gender in Prehistoric Architectural Remains. In *Engendering Archaeology: Women and Prehistory*. J. M. Gero and M. W. Conkey, eds. Pp. 93–131. Oxford: Basil Blackwell.

1991b   Men and Women in Prehistoric Architecture. *Traditional Dwellings and Settlements Review* III:9–28.

1994   Engendered Places in Prehistory. *Gender, Place and Culture* 1:169–203.

Tringham, Ruth, and Margaret W. Conkey

1998   Rethinking Figurines: A Critical View from the Archaeology of Gimbutas, the "Goddess" and Popular Culture. In *Ancient Goddesses*. L. Goodison and C. Morris, eds. Pp. 22–45. London: British Museum Press.

Tuohy, Tina

2000   Long Handled Weaving Combs: Problems in Determining the Gender of Tool-Maker or Tool-User. In *Gender and Material Culture in Archaeological Perspective*. M. Donald and L. Hurcombe, eds. Pp. 137–52. London: Macmillan.

Ucko, Peter

1962   The Interpretation of Prehistoric Anthropomorphic Figurines. *Journal of the Royal Anthropological Institute of Great Britain and Ireland* 92(1):38–54.

1968   *Anthropomorphic Figurines of Predynastic Egypt and Neolithic Crete with Comparative Material from the Prehistoric Near East and Mainland Greece*. London: Andrew Szmidla.

1996   Mother, Are You There? *Cambridge Archaeological Journal* 6(2):300–304.

Vida Navarro, M. Carmen

1992   Warriors and Weavers: Sex and Gender in Early Iron Age Graves from Pontecagnano. *Accordia Research Papers* 3:41–53.

1998 The Italian Scene: Approaches to the Study of Gender. In *Gender and Italian Archaeology*. R. Whitehouse, ed. Pp. 15–22. London: Accordia Research Institute and Institute of Archaeology.

Walde, Dale, and Noreen D. Willows, eds.
1991 *The Archaeology of Gender*. Proceedings of the Twenty-Second Annual Chacmool Conference. Calgary: Department of Archaeology, University of Calgary.

Walker, Susan
1983 Women and Housing in Classical Greece: The Archaeological Evidence. In *Images of Women in Antiquity*. A. Cameron and A. Kuhrt, eds. Pp. 81–91. Detroit: Wayne State University Press; London: Croom Helm.

Weglian, Emily
2001 Grave Goods Do Not a Gender Make: A Case Study from Singen am Hohentwiel, Germany. In *Gender and the Archaeology of Death*. B. Arnold and N. L. Wicker, eds. Pp. 137–55. Walnut Creek, CA: AltaMira Press.

Wels-Weyrauch, Ulrike
1989 Mittelbronzezeitliche Frauentrachten in Süddeutschland. In *Dynamique du Bronze Moyen en Europe Occidentale*. Pp. 117–34. Actes du 113 Congres national des Societés savants, Strasbourg. Paris: CTHS.
1991 Die Anhänger in Südbayern. Prähistorische Bronzefunde. Abt. XI, Band 5. Munich: C. H. Beck.

Whitehouse, Ruth
1992a Tools the Manmaker: The Cultural Construction of Gender in Italian Prehistory. *Accordia Research Papers* 3:41–53.
1992b *Underground Religion: Cult and Culture in Prehistoric Italy*. London: Accordia Research Centre.

Whitehouse, Ruth, ed.
1998a *Gender and Italian Archaeology*. London: Accordia Research Institute and the Institute of Archaeology.
1998b Introduction. In *Gender and Italian Archaeology*. R. Whitehouse, ed. Pp. 1–8. London: Accordia Research Institute and the Institute of Archaeology.

Whitehouse, Ruth
2001 Exploring Gender in Prehistoric Italy. *Papers of the British School at Rome* 69:49–96.
In press Gender Archaeology and Archaeology of Women: Do We Need Both? In *Archaeology and Women*. S. Hamilton, R. Whitehouse, and K. Wright, eds. London: UCL Press.

Yates, Tim
1993 Frameworks for an Archaeology of the Body. In *Interpretative Archaeology*. C. Tilley, ed. Pp. 31–72. Oxford: Berg.

Gender and Mesoamerican Archaeology 23

ROSEMARY A. JOYCE

THE ARCHAEOLOGY OF MESOAMERICA, the culture area that spans central and southern Mexico, Guatemala, Belize and includes western Honduras and El Salvador, has been a center of development for archaeologies of gender. Thus, an examination of Mesoamerican archaeology of gender provides an overview of both the achievements and the difficulties involved in one of the major innovations in archaeology of the late twentieth century. In the pages that follow, I will identify some contributions made to Mesoamerican archaeology by thinking about gender and to the study of gender by thinking about Mesoamerica. I will sketch out a history of development that starts with relatively cautious responses to overwhelmingly androcentric models accepted until the mid-twentieth century and that proceeds to work by archaeologists who question not only androcentric views but also the assumed natural categories of analysis, like the dichotomy male and female itself. Pointing toward the future for archaeologists working in this area, I will suggest that we face continuing and even strengthening reaction from those who take androcentric views for granted and who believe that complex societies always and everywhere involve the domination of women by men. Countering this pessimistic assessment of the obstacles that remain, I will end by noting the irreversible changes that have been produced by archaeologies of gender, which will make it impossible for future generations to ignore the agency of women, indigenous understandings of sexuality and sexual difference, and the significance of cross-cutting dimensions of personhood, especially age and social status, in understanding Mesoamerican societies.

Setting the Scene: Mesoamerica in Time and Space

Mesoamerica is a somewhat arbitrary geographical region, delimited on the north by the Mexican deserts, where in the sixteenth century agricultural societies gave way to hunter-gatherers, and in the south less clearly demarcated by the "frontier" between Maya city-states and non-Maya neighbors (Joyce 2004). The definition of Mesoamerica in the twentieth century as an area of study was based on assessment of the distribution of a series of traits, not shared with societies north and south of the core region, that were understood under the models of culture-historical analysis as evidence of significant historical trajectories of development. What Mesoamerican societies presumably shared, then, were common histories of long-term engagement through which practices and values were coordinated, without political unification or ethnic or linguistic homogeneity.

While traces of human occupation in the region are much earlier, the roots of these common Mesoamerican histories are generally understood to lie in the Formative or Preclassic period (ca. 1500–200 B.C.), when, across the region, residents of villages practiced agriculture, made and used pottery vessels, and shared other technologies, such as core-blade technologies for producing obsidian tools and ground stone technologies to make tools to process seed crops, especially corn. By the middle of this early village period, public stone monuments and monumental architecture were constructed by residents of some villages, with those of the Gulf Coast Olmec archaeological culture being the earliest known examples. At this time, across Mesoamerica we see examples of material marked with graphic designs, some more naturalistic and others quite abstract, that are similar from one region to the next. These designs, engraved on pottery vessels, stone monuments, and body ornaments made of hard green stones (including jade), shell, and bone, precede the earliest examples of writing recognized by scholars and probably served in part as a form of graphic communication less tightly structured than the writing systems that developed by the end of this period.

By the Late Formative period, formal writing systems were being used by members of a number of culturally and politically independent Mesoamerican societies to inscribe texts on stone monuments in regions that included the Gulf Coast of Mexico, the highland Valley of Oaxaca, and the highlands and Pacific slope of Guatemala. In contrast, neighboring societies in the Valley of Mexico and the lowlands of Guatemala and Mexico's Yucatan Peninsula did not employ writing systems at this time, contributing to the development of a mosaic of independent city-states that dominated Mesoamerica during the succeeding Classic period (ca. 200 B.C.–A.D. 800). While clearly engaged in significant political, economic, and even social transactions, Classic centers like Teotihuacan (in central Mexico), Monte Alban (in Oaxaca), and the host of Classic lowland Maya city-states that developed in the Guatemalan and Yucatan lowlands (including Yaxchilan, Piedras Negras, Tikal, Calakmul, Caracol, and their neighbors) and in the adjacent highlands of Mexico (Palenque and Tonina), Guatemala (Kaminaljuyu) and Honduras (Copan) were independent states with differences in population size, social stratification, and economic organization.

Remarkably, while never unified, these Classic centers were apparently integrated enough that disruptions in one could contribute to instability in others. The Classic period was marked by a history of episodes when centers engaged in intensive development of monumental architecture and art followed by other episodes during which such cultural production ceased or declined. In some cases, these fluctuations can be related to specific hostile interactions with other Classic centers. Many scholars suspect that individual city-states suffered ill effects from overexploitation of local environments that were themselves dynamic and open to the influence of climactic events. While no single set of events seems to have affected the entire region, over the course of about two centuries (ca. A.D. 700–900), most of the established large Classic city-states experienced substantial disruptions in occupation and construction that in some cases led to almost total abandonment. Often these episodes of abandonment were correlated with new activity at nearby sites, most of which seem not to have approached the size of the cities they succeeded and whose population they may have drawn on in their initial episodes of development.

While conventionally described as the "collapse" of the great Classic city-states, these events did not lead to abandonment of the fundamental agricultural way of life that characterized Mesoamerica, nor did they signal a decline in political centralization across the region, even if the histories of specific city-states were brought to an end abruptly or in a lingering decline. Instead, the succeeding Postclassic period (ca. A.D. 800–1521) saw the development of a series of large city-states throughout the region, with strongly marked social, economic, and political hierarchies. In the Valley of Mexico, one of these Postclassic successor states developed into Mesoamerica's largest multi–city state, a society that grew through conquest warfare to incorporate much of the area west of the Maya region. This great polity, sometimes characterized as an "empire," was ruled from the city Tenochtitlan, occupied by people who called themselves Mexica and who today are commonly referred to as the Aztecs. With the defeat of the Mexica forces defending Tenochtitlan in A.D. 1521, the invading Spanish forces under the command of Hernan Cortes and indigenous peoples allied with them cut short the development of Aztec political power.

It would take more than a century before the last independent Maya kingdoms formally accepted Spanish imperial authority. Throughout the subsequent centuries of colonization, indigenous communities and factions within them continued to negotiate their place in the new Spanish political and social order. A large part of this negotiation concerned changes in gender roles and statuses and gendered practices that did not conform to the expectations of European administrators. While Mesoamerican archaeologists profit today from the continued presence of the descendant populations whose histories we contribute to illuminating, those present-day societies do not provide simple models for life before the disruptions of Spanish colonization.

The progress of late nineteenth- and early twentieth-century archaeological exploration was closely related to the exploration of Mesoamerica's colonial history through relocation and publication of Spanish and indigenous documents in European libraries and archives and in communities throughout the region. The first systematic ethnographies in Mesoamerica, beginning in the first decade of the twentieth century were undertaken expressly to help illuminate the archaeological heritage of what was newly appreciated to be one of the major traditions in world history. During the first half of the twentieth century, researchers seamlessly combined contemporary ethnographic descriptions, historical documents from four centuries and many different sources, and observations gleaned from archaeological excavations to create representations of timeless, idealized Mesoamerican societies. Even critiques of culture-historical approaches from the 1940s to the 1960s that led in North America to the development of processual archaeology did little to change the basic approaches current in Mesoamerica (Sabloff 1990). Archaeologists interested in gendered experience and gender identities were central in questioning such long-established approaches and in moving Mesoamerican archaeology forward.

Missing Women: Pioneers in Mesoamerican Archaeology of Gender

Robin (2003) has suggested that there were three major advances in Maya archaeology in the last half of the twentieth century: the decipherment of indigenous writing, the development of household archaeology, and the rise of an archaeology of gender. These three developments arguably all affected Mesoamerican archaeology more broadly as well, and all, as Robin notes, were involved with consideration of issues of gender. At the beginning of this trajectory stands one remarkable woman, Tatiana Proskouriakoff, and the story of Mesoamerican archaeology of gender rightly begins with her.

Proskouriakoff was employed for her skills as an artist, first by the University Museum of Pennsylvania and then by the Carnegie Institution of Washington's program on research on Maya archaeology. The projects she worked on, explorations of Classic Maya Piedras Negras and Copan and Postclassic Mayapan, were undertaken by men who drew on a model of Classic and Postclassic Maya society in which men were understood as political, religious, and social authorities dominating the public sphere, while women occupied the peripheral position of supporting male activities through their work in domestic confines. For the Maya archaeologists of Proskouriakoff's day, Classic Maya monuments were records of the religious and ritual concerns of male ritual specialists, calendar priests, and astronomers.

As Proskouriakoff worked on drawings of monumental stone sculptures, she began to question these orthodox interpretations. Instead of the deeds of male priests, she suggested that the Maya monuments recorded events in the lives of men, women, and children of the Classic Maya ruling class, arguing that the Maya were in this way no different than other known early states. Through careful analyses of the patterns of dated monuments associated in groups at the site of Piedras Negras, Proskouriakoff (1960) was led to identify each such group as recording a sequence of biographical events in the life of a specific noble, successive rulers of the site. Building on her analysis of this site (where monuments for each ruler were grouped close together), Proskouriakoff (1963, 1964) showed that the same patterns could be identified in monuments at other sites. Her advocacy of the hypothesis that these monuments recorded historical events transformed Maya archaeology. Along with that general point, she specifically identified female actors in Maya monumental art and texts and proposed that, as in kingdoms in other parts of the world, women had significant political and social status in the centuries preceding Spanish colonization.

While Proskouriakoff limited her arguments for the identification of women to Maya art, the method she used to establish such identities was highly influential across Mesoamerica. She observed that images of female deities in Postclassic Maya manuscripts, clearly identifiable as female because they were shown with bare chests with carefully depicted breasts, were labeled with a repeated sign in accompanying Maya texts (Proskouriakoff 1961). While Classic Maya images did not show women with exposed breasts, the texts on monuments showing figures wearing long robes employed the same sign as the later manuscripts referring to goddesses. English-speaking Mayanists had long identified these figures as likely to be priests, ignoring the prescient observations of Eduard and Cecelia Seler, German scholars who recognized female figures a half century before Proskouriakoff published her landmark study of women in Maya art.

Proskouriakoff's identification of noble Maya women, as part of her proposal that Classic Maya monuments commemorated human political authorities, inspired a second generation of Mesoamerican scholars who conducted detailed studies of Classic Maya art in which they recognized the presence of both men and women. While Proskouriakoff never held a formal faculty position, after the completion of the Carnegie Institution of Washington's Mayapan project she was affiliated with Harvard University's Peabody Museum. There, she was able to guide students, including the art historian Clemency Coggins and archaeologist Joyce Marcus, who soon built on the foundations Proskouriakoff provided. Almost simultaneously, these two scholars demonstrated that Classic Maya materials allowed detailed reconstruction of site-specific histories of political and social relations of men and women of the noble class.

Coggins's (1975) doctoral dissertation was a scrupulous study of the visual arts at Tikal, a site that had been the focus of investigation by the University Museum of the University of Pennsylvania since the 1950s. Framed as an exploration of the development of painting and drawing styles over time, Coggins's work went far beyond this and involved the construction of a detailed chronological framework for the site, incorporating interpretable monument data and burial assemblages. In her work, Coggins observed that inscriptions at Tikal prominently featured female actors at certain points in time. She suggested that these women were given prominence because of their roles in historical succession of political power at the site.

Marcus (1976) took a similar approach to understanding the historical events represented by inscriptions from across the Maya area. Hers was the first attempt to treat the extant Maya inscriptions as evidence of political developments among a series of interconnected cities. Following Proskouriakoff, she identified prominent women in the historical inscriptions at a number of sites, notably Piedras Negras, Yaxchilan, Tikal, and Calakmul. Marcus observed a pattern in which women from larger, arguably more important sites were named in the inscriptions of smaller, less important sites. Drawing on broader general analogy (in place of the specific analogies that dominated earlier Maya studies), she proposed that the Classic Maya world was integrated by the marriage of daughters from major centers into the ruling families at less important centers (Marcus 1987, 1992, 2001). The experiences of such noblewomen, pivotal as links in political networks and crucial as founding ancestors for later rulers, were by no means typical of the lives of all women. However, the recognition that high-level politics involved marital alliance opened the way for exploration of class-based experiences that differentiated the lives of women. Marcus noted that women rarely exercised power at the larger central sites and that they were most prominent in smaller sites, where it was still likely that they were commemorated not as political figures themselves but as the mothers of rulers.

Both Coggins and Marcus demonstrated that there was no single, static, ahistorical women's position in Maya society and, by implication, in any other Mesoamerican society. Marcus (1992, 1998, 1999, 2001) went on to explore the specifics of political, social, and gender dynamics in the history of the societies that occupied the Valley of Oaxaca from the Formative period through to the twentieth century, speakers of the Zapotec and Mixtec languages. Her long-term analyses of Oaxaca, like the shorter-term historical studies of the Classic Maya, suggested that women's relative social status was intimately related to changes in broader social relations and the emergence over time of more institutionalized social hierarchies. Women were critical points of articulation between noble families in early states, but they exercised little power themselves, and over time the degree of independent power they had was eroded by the demands of their social and political positions.

While seldom explicitly referenced, these analyses echoed studies based in Marxist frameworks that were gaining currency at the time. Like contemporary studies of women's status in the Inca Empire, these Mesoamerican analyses of the 1970s suggested that there was a directional trend in Mesoamerica toward greater disadvantage for women as social stratification increased and power was institutionalized outside familial structures (Silverblatt 1988). Explicit arguments for such an evolutionary trajectory were most forcefully made by scholars examining the relatively rich documentary record for the Aztec state, created by the first generation of colonial administrators and missionaries in the sixteenth century.

June Nash, an ethnographer of contemporary Maya societies, produced one of the first explicitly feminist analyses of pre-Hispanic gender relations by drawing on sixteenth-century documentation about the Aztecs (Nash 1978). She juxtaposed stereotyped descriptions of women's working lives recorded by the first European chroniclers with an analysis of selected Aztec sculptures, proposing an influential model of Aztec society as dominated by a misogynistic ideology through which women were disciplined as subjects of a militaristic state. The depiction of goddesses decapitated, their heads replaced by serpents, wearing necklaces of hearts and hands, was understood to materialize systematic gendered violence. This in turn was understandable as part of an overall Aztec ideology of militarism and routine submission to the power of the state (Nash 1980). Nash's understanding was echoed in an influential study of Aztec women by Rodriguez (1988) that inspired a generation of Mexican scholars to begin to examine gender relations.

Without these pioneers, there could have been no further development of gender analyses. Until they published their studies, which established that it was both fruitful and significant to ask questions about women's roles and status, there was no opening for the kinds of more nuanced questions that would quickly move to center stage in Mesoamerican archaeology of gender. Researchers working on Aztec gender relations have since proposed that these early analyses may have been influenced too much by uninterrogated biases in their source materials, produced in the first generation of colonization and based on interviews with exclusively male, noble informants. Likewise, the inevitable decline in noblewomen's ability to exercise power independently that can be derived from analyses of Maya and Oaxacan data today is understood as just one part of what must be a multiperspectival approach to gender. These advances were based on work by archaeologists seeking a wider gamut of approaches to women's roles and status in Mesoamerica who built on the work of these pioneers but also drew on new methods, new theoretical perspectives, and the material evidence of women's lives recoverable archaeologically.

The Plot Thickens: Routes to Finding Women in Mesoamerican Archaeological Sites

The next scholars interested in questions of women's status could take for granted that women had been significant political agents in Mesoamerica and that monumental art reflected that participation and changes in it over time. This contrasted with what had been the orthodox assumption, that women belonged in a domestic sector, unchanged for centuries and adequately represented by ethnographic analogues described in the twentieth century. Ethnohistorians drawing on the rich data from colonial archives, especially those describing the societies of sixteenth-century central Mexico, began to demonstrate precisely how much transformation there had been in social life and especially in gender relations, even in the first century of colonization. Women moved from central actors, property owners, and claimants to social status at the beginning of the colonial period to the kind of subordinate and dependent situation that had been taken as their timeless position (Kellogg 1986, 1988, 1993, 1995a, 1995b; Schroeder et al. 1997). If women had not been universally powerless in Mesoamerica before European colonization, then archaeologists and art historians could begin to look for these female agents and begin to define the scope of their activity in earlier centuries.

Following in the steps of the first generation of scholars of gender, the presence or absence of women in monumental images could be observed and arguments for their social importance could be based on those distributions. A flurry of publications documenting images of women have since been produced, locating women in Gulf Coast and central Mexican Olmec sites, in Classic societies of the Maya lowlands and the Guatemalan slope, and in the historical manuscripts of Oaxaca and central Mexico (e.g., Bellas 1999; Bruhns 1984, 1999; Cyphers Guillen 1984; Hamann 1997; Krochock 2002; Marcus 1987; Schele 1979; Tate

1987). Records of women in these media, understood as political documents, automatically implied that they had roles to play in political life. Most often, this was understood as implying dynastic or marriage alliance (Molloy and Rathje 1984; Schele and Mathews 1991). Only rarely did scholars following this line of analysis suggest that the women pictured exercised power independently. Even when it became clear that a few Classic Maya noblewomen were either named in texts as ruling or as exercising authority during the youth of the eventual male heir, these were explained as exceptional cases (Hewitt 1999; Josserand 2002; Thompson 1982). Clearly, while women could participate in politics in certain ways, there were bounds to their imagined freedom.

Other scholars responded to the first generation of studies by attempting to define alternative lines of evidence for the presence of women who were not subjects of monuments and their participation in social life. For the Aztecs, McCafferty and McCafferty (1988, 1999) carried out a series of influential analyses of alternative images of women that might reflect the status of a wider cross section of women. They demonstrated a close association between women's work as spinners and weavers and their self-identity as powerful subjects, contributing to the success of their social groups and ultimately society as a whole (McCafferty and McCafferty 1988, 1991). Their work transformed the study of Aztec gender relations by directing the attention of scholars to a range of artifacts that might represent gendered labor in textile production. Hendon (1991, 1992, 1997, 1999b) offered influential analyses of Classic and Preclassic Maya domestic life that similarly exploited the potential of stereotyped practice of cloth production as an index of women's actions.

These scholars were not simply interested in identifying the traces of women's action within a domestic sphere understood as subordinate to the public sphere where real politics took place. Instead, as Hendon (1996, 1999a, 2002) argued, the analysis of gendered domestic labor must be understood as documenting political action. In Mesoamerican societies, the arena of politics encompassed both the accepted public venues of plaza and street and the household, artificially circumscribed by inappropriate application of public/private dichotomies. No longer could the household be understood as private and divorced from broader economic and political activities. Brumfiel (1991, 1996a, 1996b, 1997) demonstrated in a series of careful analyses of the effects of Aztec imperial absorption of hinterland sites that the demands of the empire were felt throughout the domestic compound, where labor was reorganized in response to new economic and political realities. Brumfiel showed that the nature of food production shifted, implying that women's work in domestic spaces was reconfigured under the empire. Textile production, the activity whose gendered tool kit was so useful as a proxy for women's presence in Aztec and Maya sites, was central to political process in centralizing states, not simply a task naturally associated with women as a form of insignificant "housework." Indeed, as McCafferty and McCafferty (1994b) noted, in some situations it was arguable that textile production would be undertaken by males as well as females and that tools for textile production might be associated with males instead of females.

While monumental art could be a source for identifying noblewomen and tools for textile production could (under the right circumstances) indicate that at least some women were engaged in gender-specific production valued by the state, neither of these lines of evidence were expected to inform about the vast majority of women's lives. Most women in Mesoamerican societies did not live in the courts whose archaeological investigation has dominated scholarship for more than a century (Evans 1998, 2001; McAnany and Plank 2001). The women and men who made up the bulk of the population were presumably farmers, part-time craft producers, hunters and fishers, and practitioners of rituals to mark events in their own lives and those of their kin. It remains the fact that very few Mesoamerican archaeologists have endeavored to document the lives of the bulk of the population.

As Pyburn (1990) has noted, even the methods employed to detect sites are biased toward the more substantial stone house foundations rebuilt over generations, occupied by only a small segment of the population. Pyburn (1998) suggests that when we do explore the living sites of the bulk of the population, we will usually find it difficult to disaggregate the actions of men, women, and children who lived and worked together in these settlements. While we certainly can—and I would argue must—model these households as composed of diverse kinds of people, we cannot automatically assume that women in these past social settings carried out specific kinds of work while men maintained an exclusive focus on other tasks.

Robin (2002a, 2002b) has pursued one of the few projects intended from the start to bring the lives of the commonest of Mesoamerican people to light. Her work at the outlying agricultural hamlet of Chan Nohol, near the Classic Maya site of Xunantunich, used a variety of cutting-edge techniques to detect traces of past human action from such things as concentrations of different elements. Her research documents the work areas where agricultural products were likely processed, food prepared, and waste discarded. She shows that areas around house structures were cultivated fields and gardens and proposes that men and women collaborated in working these fields, with much less segregation of labor than assumed in conventional models.

Other archaeologists have similarly approached the remains of rural or farming communities with issues of gender in mind. Even though they cannot easily assign specific materials to male or female actors, these scholars have proposed ways to include explicit consideration of the possible experiences and contributions of women to social life in Mesoamerican villages (Pohl 1991; Pohl and Feldman 1982; Sweely 1998, 1999). Archaeologists concerned with understanding gender relations in situations where male and female activities are not clearly marked have challenges central to assumptions about gender common in Mesoamerican archaeology (Bruhns 1991; Graham 1991).

Foremost among these questionable assumptions is the identification of the goal of gender analysis as the detection of women. Gender analysis in Mesoamerican archaeology has developed from an original concern with seeing women to encompass contemporary interrogations of the concepts of stable genders and sexes themselves. These contemporary analyses contribute not just to understanding the historical developments within the region but also to understanding how gender works cross-culturally. As is the case in other world areas, archaeology of gender in Mesoamerica is providing a past that challenges the easy naturalization of contemporary gender relations. At the same time, the routinization of gender analysis risks reifying anew an equation of dichotomous, biological sex as the natural ground for dualistic genders. Examining the ways that contemporary Mesoamerican archaeology of gender is entangled in these issues should serve as an example of the pitfalls and rewards that await archaeologists working in areas with a less established tradition of this kind of analysis.

Seeing Women: Figurines, Monuments, and Human Skeletal Remains

While I began this chapter by arguing that Proskouriakoff must be credited with initiating the formal study of gender in Mesoamerican archaeology, of course gender attribution long preceded her work. Mesoamerican figurine studies, in particular, have always involved the identification of female subjects, often as the predominant or only gender represented. An examination of the changes over time in how figurines were discussed serves to demonstrate the difference that is made by adopting an explicit framework that takes gender as a research issue to be investigated rather than a natural category that can unproblematically be assumed.

Hand-modeled fired clay figurines were produced in a wide variety of styles by Mesoamericans living in Formative period or Preclassic villages, where their manufacture precedes the production of monumental stone sculpture by centuries. By the beginning of the Classic period, in many areas ceramic figurines were being produced with the assistance of molds, either to allow mass production or, as Lopiparo (2003) argues for the Ulua Valley of Honduras, to ensure reproduction of the same image regardless of level of skill. Mold-made figurines remain part of the cultural repertoire in some but not all Mesoamerican societies through to the time of the Spanish conquest. In some cases, figurines may have been produced in perishable media, either in addition to or as an alternative to fired clay; examples of wooden, bone, and shell small-scale figures are occasionally reported where preservation is good. But most discussions of figurines in Mesoamerica focus on those made of clay, which allowed delineation of physical features and details of costume.

In discussions of Formative period figurines in the first half of the twentieth century, certain localized figurine styles were singled out for their realism, for example, the Playa de los Muertos style of Honduras and the Xochipala style of Guerrero. Others were noted for their appeal to contemporary aesthetic preferences, as in the case of the "pretty lady" figurines of central Mexican sites, including Tlatilco. These figurines were modeled with narrow waists and wide busts and hips and were seen as abstractions of a girlish figure presumed to appeal to a male viewer. If they were interpreted at all, it was assumed that they served as emblems of fertility. Both the narrow waists and wider hips of central Mexican figurines and the thicker bodies of Playa de los Muertos figurines were explained through the same recourse to naturalism, as signifying stages in female reproductive cycles. The social implications of figurines as representations of stages in a female life course were never discussed, presumably because this was understood as simply recording universal female experience. Nor did such early figurine studies explore the differences in presence, absence, and frequency of figurines interpretable as images of males and those so formed that beyond an identification as human-like, no further specificity of sex was possible.

Mesoamerican Formative period figurines became a focus of gender analyses starting in the late 1970s and 1980s. What differentiated these new analyses from older studies was an explicit concern with the relationships between the sex and other attributes of these representations and the lived experiences of the people who made and used them (Follensbee 2000; Lesure 2002). In an early, influential analysis, Cyphers Guillen (1993) proposed that figurines from Chalcatzingo, Morelos, faithfully represented details of changes in the body of pregnant women. Cyphers Guillen suggested that the manufacture of these figurines was related to a concern in this agrarian society with events in the life course of women and with women's fertility. That the selection of subjects for Formative period figurines was an indication that women's lives were of specific social interest was a widely shared assumption in these analyses. Lesure (1997, 1999) proposed that the presence at Paso de la Amada of figurines depicting young standing women and older, seated, masked males and females reflected a social division of authority in which elder males and females made decisions about the lives of young women. Marcus (1998, 1999) argued that Formative figurines in Oaxaca were specific representations made and used by women in ritual veneration of their ancestors, rituals decentralized and contrasting with the ceremonies in which men participated. In my studies of Playa de los Muertos figurines, I suggested that specific stages in women's lives, especially rites of passage related to maturation, were represented in enough detail to suggest that particular women's lives were being commemorated (Joyce 2001b, 2003).

Running through all these studies of Formative period figurines was a concern about the identification of these images as intentional representations of some but not all of the people present in the societies where they were made and used. Gender identifications generally relied on a two-sex model in which the absence of explicit male genitalia was sufficient to assign a figurine a feminine sex. Occasionally, researchers noted that some proportion of the figurine assemblages they studied could not be assigned to male or female categories. This raised the possibility that Mesoamerican understandings of gender might not conform to a simple two-sex/two-gender equation (Joyce 1993, 1998, 2003).

Figurine studies have been and remain an important source of hypotheses about gendered patterns of activity not only in Formative Mesoamerican societies but also in Classic and Postclassic societies. The poses and gestures of figurines have been treated as stereotypic models that would have been emulated by living people and served as measures of gender-appropriate performance (Goldstein 1988; Joyce 1993, 1998). In highly stratified Classic (Conides 1984) and Postclassic (Brumfiel 1996a) societies, figurines have been examined as media through which ideologies of differential power were reified and contested. Figurines have been juxtaposed to representations of gendered experience in other media in Classic Maya (Joyce 1993, 2001b) and Postclassic Aztec (Brumfiel 1996a) states to expose contradictions in gender ideologies.

Contemporary Mesoamerican gender analyses question the naturalistic assumptions that underwrote previous interpretations of gender representations, whether in the form of images or texts. Writing about Aztec society, Gillespie (1989), Brown (1983), and McCafferty and McCafferty (1988, 1991) identified evidence for structural parallelism or gender complementarity in which deities, legendary figures, and even contemporary actors were understood to act as necessary halves of gendered wholes. Ideologies of gender complementarity are epitomized by pairings of male and female solar and lunar deities (Milbrath 1997; Nash 1998) and the dual-gendered maize deities (Bassie-Sweet 2002) of many

Mesoamerican societies. Human life patterned on these divine precedents ideally was represented as a form of gender balance in which stereotyped male and female actions complemented each other. In Classic Maya art, such ideologies of gender were projected through standardized pairing of adult male and female figures wearing complementary costumes and engaged in stereotyped gestures and actions (Joyce 1992, 1996, 1999, 2001c; Tate 1999). Understanding such images as ideological constructs has helped contemporary gender analysts avoid assuming that they represent an actual situation in which men's and women's actions were so circumscribed.

Ideologies of gender complementarity have provided contemporary analysts ways to begin to examine gendered relations of power. The highly elaborate costumes worn by noblewomen in some Classic Maya images are thus better considered displays of royal power than in any way typifying a gender category (Bruhns 1988). The association of iconography of warfare with women in Classic Maya art (Ayala Falcón 2002), at Cacaxtla (McCafferty and McCafferty 1994a), and among the Aztecs (Klein 1988, 1993, 1994) at least in part, arguably, represents gendered ideologies of political dominance, not misogynistic expressions of violence toward women as a category (contra Nash 1978).

Mesoamerican representations demonstrate a remarkable degree of positive valuation of female gender, whether in the form of female or dual-gendered supernatural beings (e.g., Berlo 1992; Sullivan 1982; Tate 2002) or the politically prominent noblewomen and economically and ritually active middle rank or commoner women commemorated in monumental sculpture and figurines. There are, nonetheless, legitimate questions to be asked about the degree to which, in different Mesoamerican societies, women of different classes might have been differentially disadvantaged by exploitative social, economic, and political relations (Cohodas 2002; Ruscheinsky 1995). If images are to be understood as ideologically loaded, many researchers are asking whether it is possible to more directly assess women's status through the examination of their physical remains and burial treatment.

Remarkably, while Mesoamerican mortuary analyses have long treated sex as one category of analysis, substantive studies that seek to examine gender differences or gendered experience are relatively uncommon. Writing about burials from the noble house compounds of Late Classic Copan, Storey (1998) has gradually furnished a detailed picture of declines in maternal health and rising infant mortality as that Classic city-state entered its final years. In an overview of mortuary data from Classic Maya Tikal, Haviland (1997) presents a more ambiguous picture in which social status may be more significant than sexual identity. This is also the implication of at least some of the dietary analyses of Classic Maya societies in which multiple variables, including class status, seem to be more important than sex in accounting for differences (Gerry and Chesson 2000). An extended analysis of a Formative period burial population from Tlatilco, in central Mexico, found that sex did not account statistically for any of the variation, which was much more strongly linked to age and to membership in a specific residential cluster, presumably a reasonable proxy for kin group (Joyce 2001a). While still tentative, these and other analyses suggest that we may need to reexamine our assumption that it is legitimate to seek to understand a composite female experience, especially when, as in Mesoamerica, other dimensions of social difference cross-cut sex and may have been more salient in different times and places.

Gender Trouble: Men, Women, and Others in Mesoamerican Societies

The realization that an archaeology of gender should be more than an archaeology of females has affected Mesoamerican scholarship in several ways, all of which serve to illuminate potentials for gender analysis in other archaeological traditions. A number of analyses have explored the complexity of subject positions in traditional Mesoamerican societies by examining the way that kinship relations were structured. Because the Classic Maya employed a writing system in which kin terms were recorded, these studies have emphasized examples from that society (Gillespie and Joyce 1997; Palka 1999; Robin 2001). What these analyses demonstrate is that kin roles and, by implication, gender roles were relational, fluid, and not determined by biological sex.

Fluidity and relationality are also features central to analyses that seek to understand how Mesoamerican people understood biological difference and what they made of it. Drawing on theoretical insights from feminist and queer theory, I have argued that we need to explicitly model our understanding of Mesoamerican genders as emergent in action and experience, not given and determined by biology (Joyce 2000a, 2001b; Meskell and Joyce 2003). This has led me to explore childhood in Aztec and Maya societies as a period during which, through a variety of materially evident practices of body ornamentation, dress, and labor, the bodies of young people were disciplined. In the case of the Aztecs, I suggested that the formal, public transcripts available to us suggest that gender was something that had to be shaped and formed and that was not fixed nor dichotomous. Individual children who were destined from soon after birth for a life of celibacy had more in common sexually with each other than the males and females in this group had with the other boys and girls whose lives would lead normatively to marriage and reproduction of the family. Whether we want to think of this in terms of three (or four) genders should be questioned; rather, I have suggested that Mesoamerican ideas about gender were based on understanding sexual identity as fluid, not fixed, a continuum, not a series of categories (Joyce 2001c).

Children, who were only problematically related to adult male and female genders, could develop into at least three different kinds of socially approved of sexual beings (reproductive heterosexual males, reproductive heterosexual females, and celibate males and females) in Aztec society (Joyce 2000a). There is also significant evidence from texts recorded after the Spanish conquest that Aztec youths could experience and act on same-sex desire (Kimball 1993). Labeling such gendered roles as homosexuality, a category of modern analysis that is based on a model of essential, stable, core sexual identity, is probably a mistake. Instead, what these Aztec texts—recorded as expressions of disapproval by elders for the actions of disobedient youths—direct our attention to is the entire realm of sexuality, remarkably too often left out in discussions of gender in archaeology.

Sexuality was clearly not marginal for Aztec people, who recorded detailed information about socially sanctioned women who engaged in sex with young male warriors outside of reproductive marital alliances (Arvey 1988; McCafferty and McCafferty 1999). These women (and others) were the subjects of love poetry, some of which survived and was written down in European texts (Raby 1999). Similar accounts of young men living in corporate quarters and women who engaged in sexual relations with them were mentioned for the contemporary Maya of Yucatan, although there our only sources are Spanish language accounts that condemn both parties for immorality (Joyce 2000b).

The sexuality of young men in Postclassic and Classic Maya society may itself have been more fluid than any normative heterosexual model would allow. In art, young men were routinely represented as the objects of the gaze of older men and adult women (Joyce 2000b, 2002b). These same-sex groups of youths, taking part in vigorous dances and sports, may have explicitly engaged in same-sex encounters depicted in rare sexual images in Naj Tunich cave (Stone 1995). Young men were depicted in both Maya and Aztec sources almost as objects of universal desire, their beautiful ornamented bodies the focus of older men and women and younger women (Joyce 2002a; Stone 1988). Cherished as much for their youth and activity as for their sex, these young men recall the ambiguously gendered images that have long been debated as possible evidence of a formal third or fourth gender in Mesoamerican societies.

While gender duality, androgyny, or ambiguity are noted in Aztec examples (Klein 2001), the most sustained arguments for the existence of a transgender position in Mesoamerica have been made for the Classic Maya. There, it rapidly became apparent that one of the signifiers of female costume identified by Proskouriakoff was often worn by characters who otherwise appeared to be identified as male. The same costume was worn in mythological scenes on pottery by a supernatural being identified as a maize god and by some living male and female nobles depicted in carved stone monuments (Stone 1991; Taube 1985). While an argument could be made that the human nobles were dressing as the deity and impersonating him, closer examination suggested that the maize god itself was better understood as a dual-gendered being (Bassie-Sweet 2002). The existence and valorization of such a being allowed the possibility that the human beings who dressed as this supernatural being were, through that action, aligning themselves with a sexual position that encompassed the normative, dichotomous male and female poles (Joyce 1996, 1999; Looper 2002; Reilly 2002). Mesoamerican people may have had a fundamentally different understanding of the implications of biological sex for the sexuality of human beings, and our frameworks of male/female may be doing violence to connections across those categories while ignoring distinctions within them.

Looking Backward and Forward: Reaction and the Irreversibility of Gender Analysis

Today, it is no longer possible for Mesoamerican archaeologists to ignore gender dynamics, and it clearly improves even the most traditional analyses to explicitly theorize gender difference (Brumfiel 2001; Cohodas 2002; Silverblatt 1995). But this is not to say that gender analysis has been fully accepted in the field. Particularly when gender analyses suggest that cherished assumptions derived from recent ethnography need to be reexamined or that naturalized assumptions of Euro-American researchers cannot be accepted without scrutiny, gender analysts may find themselves experiencing a backlash from those with vested interests in assuming that Mesoamerican societies in the past were divided into two categories, privileged males and subordinate females. And even if such overt reaction is not forthcoming, it is all too common to see mainstream publications ignore the work of those who are writing about the experiences of women and men in the Mesoamerican past.

The solution is not to back away from more risky work that draws the greatest opposition and simply resign oneself to repeatedly confirming the assumed invisibility of women and incapability of female agents and the homogeneity of masculinity. The kinds of questions gender analysts ask are in many ways more powerful than any specific answer we might offer to those questions. Once you ask, Why are all the subjects of Classic Maya art shown as young adults? you have irreversibly made age a question that has to be dealt with and denaturalized representation itself.

It is no longer possible for Mesoamerican archaeologists to fail to ask how women and men fared politically, economically, and socially, and these are lasting effects of asking questions about gender. The nuances of our understandings of human experience in different Mesoamerican societies will inevitably change as new objects are recovered, as new contexts are documented, and, above all, as new questions are asked. But none of this will ever make it acceptable again to simply assume that men occupied the central place in Mesoamerican societies, exercising power over housebound women who labored silently in support of a gender hierarchy determined by a two sex system. Women, men, and other genders have come out of the background and now present us with a complex social world for which we have multiple rich lines of evidence. The only thing constraining us now is our ability to ask the right questions, questions that will give these data new meaning and continue to transform our understandings.

References

Arvey, Margaret
    1988   Women of Ill-Repute in the Florentine Codex. In *The Role of Gender in Precolumbian Art and Architecture*. Virginia Miller, ed. Pp. 179–204. Lanham, MD: University Press of America.

Ayala Falcón, Maricela
    2002   Lady K'awil, Goddess O, and Maya Warfare. In *Ancient Maya Women*. Traci Ardren, ed. Pp. 105–13. Walnut Creek, CA: AltaMira Press.

Bassie-Sweet, Karen
    2002   Corn Deities and the Male/Female Principle. In *Ancient Maya Gender Identity and Relations*. Lowell Gustafson and Amy Trevelyan, eds. Pp. 169–90. Westport, CT: Greenwood Press.

Bellas, Monica L.
    1999   Women in the Mixtec Codices: Ceremonial and Ritual Roles of Lady 3 Flint. In *From the Ground Up: Beyond Gender Theory in Archaeology*. Nancy L. Wicker and Bettina Arnold, eds. Pp. 49–65. BAR International Series 812. Oxford: British Archaeological Reports.

Berlo, Janet Catherine
    1992   Icons and Ideologies at Teotihuacan: The Great Goddess Reconsidered. In *Art, Ideology and the City of Teotihuacan*. Janet C. Berlo, ed. Pp. 129–68. Washington, DC: Dumbarton Oaks.

Brown, Betty Ann
    1983   Seen but Not Heard: Women in Aztec Ritual—The Sahagun Texts. In *Text*

and Image in Pre-Columbian Art. Janet C. Berlo, ed. Pp. 119–54. BAR International Series 180. Oxford: British Archaeological Reports.

Bruhns, Karen Olson
 1984 Ladies of Cotzumalhuapa. Mexicon 6:38–39.
 1988 Yesterday the Queen Wore ... An Analysis of Women and Costume in Public Art of the Late Classic Maya. In *The Role of Gender in Precolumbian Art and Architecture*. Virginia Miller, ed. Pp. 105–34. Lanham, MD: University Press of America.
 1991 Sexual Activities: Some Thoughts on the Sexual Division of Labor and Archaeological Interpretation. In *The Archaeology of Gender*. Proceedings of the Twenty-second Annual Chacmool Conference. Dale Walde and Noreen D. Willows, eds. Pp. 420–29. Calgary: Department of Archaeology, University of Calgary.
 1999 Olmec Queens. *Yumtzilob* 11:163–89.

Brumfiel, Elizabeth M.
 1991 Weaving and Cooking: Women's Production in Aztec Mexico. In *Engendering Archaeology: Women and Prehistory*. Joan Gero and Margaret Conkey, eds. Pp. 224–51. Oxford: Basil Blackwell.
 1996a Figurines and the Aztec State: Testing the Effectiveness of Ideological Domination. In *Gender and Archaeology*. Rita Wright, ed. Pp. 143–66. Philadelphia: University of Pennsylvania Press.
 1996b Quality of Tribute Cloth: The Place of Evidence in Archaeological Argument. *American Antiquity* 61:453–62.
 1997 Tribute Cloth Production and Compliance in Aztec and Colonial Mexico. *Museum Anthropology* 21:55–71.
 2001 Asking about Aztec Gender: The Historical and Archaeological Evidence. In *Gender in Pre-Hispanic America*. Cecelia Klein, ed. Pp. 57–85. Washington, DC: Dumbarton Oaks.

Coggins, Clemency C.
 1975 Painting and Drawing Styles at Tikal: An Historical and Iconographic Reconstruction. Doctoral dissertation, Harvard University; Ann Arbor: University Microfilms International.

Cohodas, Marvin
 2002 Multiplicity and Discourse in Maya Gender Relations. In *Ancient Maya Gender Identity and Relations*. Lowell Gustafson and Amy Trevelyan, eds. Pp. 11–53. Westport, CT: Greenwood Press.

Conides, Cynthia
 1984 The Iconography of Female Figurines from Campeche: A Conceptual Approach to the Study of Maya Symbolism. Masters thesis, Columbia University.

Cyphers Guillen, Ann
 1984 Possible Role of a Woman in Formative Exchange. In *Trade and Exchange in*

        Early Mesoamerica. Kenneth G. Hirth, ed. Pp. 115–23. Albuquerque: University of New Mexico Press.
  1993   Women, Rituals, and Social Dynamics at Ancient Chalcatzingo. *Latin American Antiquity* 4:209–24.

Evans, Susan Toby
  1998   Sexual Politics in the Aztec Palace: Public, Private, and Profane. *Res* 33:166–83.
  2001   Aztec Noble Courts: Men, Women, and Children of the Palace. In *Royal Courts of the Ancient Maya. Vol. 1: Theory, Comparison, and Synthesis.* Takeshi Inomata and Stephen D. Houston, eds. Pp. 237–73. Boulder, CO: Westview.

Follensbee, Billie J.
  2000   Sex and Gender in Olmec Art and Archaeology. Doctoral dissertation, University of Maryland.

Gerry, John, and Meredith S. Chesson
  2000   Classic Maya Diet and Gender Relationships. In *Gender and Material Culture in Archaeological Perspective.* Moira Donald and Linda Hurcombe, eds. Pp. 250–64. New York: St. Martin's Press.

Gillespie, Susan D.
  1989   *The Aztec Kings: The Construction of Rulership in Mexican History.* Tucson: University of Arizona Press.

Gillespie, Susan D., and Rosemary A. Joyce
  1997   Gendered Goods: The Symbolism of Maya Hierarchical Exchange Relations. In *Women in Prehistory: North America and Mesoamerica.* Cheryl Claassen and Rosemary A. Joyce, eds. Pp. 189–207. Philadelphia: University of Pennsylvania Press.

Goldstein, Marilyn M.
  1988   Gesture, Role, and Gender in West Mexican Sculpture. In *The Role of Gender in Precolumbian Art and Architecture.* Virginia Miller, ed. Pp. 53–61. Lanham, MD: University Press of America.

Graham, Elizabeth A.
  1991   Women and Gender in Maya Prehistory. In *The Archaeology of Gender.* Proceedings of the Twenty-second Annual Chacmool Conference. Dale Walde and Noreen D. Willows, eds. Pp. 470–78. Calgary: Department of Archaeology, University of Calgary.

Hamann, Byron
  1997   Weaving and the Iconography of Prestige: The Royal Gender Symbolism of Lord 5 Flower's/Lady 4 Rabbit's Family. In *Women in Prehistory: North America and Mesoamerica.* Cheryl Claassen and Rosemary A. Joyce, eds. Pp. 153–72. Philadelphia: University of Pennsylvania Press.

Haviland, William A.
  1997   The Rise and Fall of Sexual Inequality: Death and Gender at Tikal, Guatemala. *Ancient Mesoamerica* 8:1–12

Hendon, Julia A.
- 1991 Status and Power in Classic Maya Society: An Archeological Study. *American Anthropologist* 93:894–918.
- 1992 Hilado y tejido en la epoca prehispánica: tecnologia y relaciones sociales de la producción textil. In *La indumentaria y el tejido mayas a través del tiempo*. Linda Asturias de Barrios and Dina Fernández García, eds. Pp. 7–16. Guatemala City: Museo Ixchel del Traje Indigena de Guatemala.
- 1996 Archaeological Approaches to the Organization of Domestic Labor: Household Practice and Domestic Relations. *Annual Review of Anthropology* 25:45–61.
- 1997 Women's Work, Women's Space, and Women's Status among the Classic-Period Maya Elite of the Copan Valley, Honduras. In *Women in Prehistory: North America and Mesoamerica*. Cheryl Claassen and Rosemary A. Joyce, eds. Pp. 33–46. Philadelphia: University of Pennsylvania Press.
- 1999a Multiple Sources of Prestige and the Social Evaluation of Women in Prehispanic Mesoamerica. In *Material Symbols: Culture and Economy in Prehistory*. John Robb, ed. Pp. 257–276. Occasional Paper 26. Carbondale: Center for Archaeological Investigations, Southern Illinois University.
- 1999b The Pre-Classic Maya Compound as the Focus of Social Identity. In *Social Patterns in Pre-Classic Mesoamerica*. David C. Grove and Rosemary A. Joyce, eds. Pp. 97–125. Washington, DC: Dumbarton Oaks.
- 2002 Household and State in Pre-Hispanic Maya Society: Gender, Identity, and Practice. In *Ancient Maya Gender Identity and Relations*. Lowell Gustafson and Amy Trevelyan, eds. Pp. 75–92. Westport, CT: Greenwood Press.

Hewitt, Erika A.
- 1999 What's in a Name: Gender, Power, and Classic Maya Women Rulers. *Ancient Mesoamerica* 10:251–62.

Josserand, J. Kathryn
- 2002 Women in Classic Maya Hieroglyphic Texts. In *Ancient Maya Women*. Traci Ardren, ed. Pp. 114–51. Walnut Creek, CA: AltaMira Press.

Joyce, Rosemary A.
- 1992 Images of Gender and Labor Organization in Classic Maya Society. In *Exploring Gender through Archaeology: Selected Papers from the 1991 Boone Conference*. Cheryl Claassen, ed. Pp. 63–70. Madison, WI: Prehistory Press.
- 1993 Women's Work: Images of Production and Reproduction in Pre-Hispanic Southern Central America. *Current Anthropology* 34:255–74.
- 1996 The Construction of Gender in Classic Maya Monuments. In *Gender in Archaeology: Essays in Research and Practice*. Rita Wright, ed. Pp. 167–95. Philadelphia: University of Pennsylvania Press.
- 1998 Performing the Body in Prehispanic Central America. *Res* 33:147–65.
- 1999 Symbolic Dimensions of Costume in Classic Maya Monuments: The Construction of Gender through Dress. In *Mayan Clothing and Weaving through the*

Ages. Barbara Knoke de Arathoon, Nancie L. Gonzalez, and J. M. Willemsen Devlin, eds. Pp. 29–38. Guatemala City: Museo Ixchel del Traje Indígena.

2000a   Girling the Girl and Boying the Boy: The Production of Adulthood in Ancient Mesoamerica. *World Archaeology* 31:473–83.

2000b   A Precolumbian Gaze: Male Sexuality among the Ancient Maya. In *Archaeologies of Sexuality*. Barbara Voss and Robert Schmidt, eds. Pp. 263–83. London: Routledge.

2001a   Burying the Dead at Tlatilco: Social Memory and Social Identities. In *New Perspectives on Mortuary Analysis*. Meredith Chesson, ed. Pp. 12–26. Washington, DC: Archeology Division, American Anthropological Association.

2001b   *Gender and Power in Prehispanic Mesoamerica*. Austin: University of Texas Press.

2001c   Negotiating Sex and Gender in Classic Maya Society. In *Gender in Pre-Hispanic America*. Cecelia Klein, ed. Pp. 109–41. Washington, DC: Dumbarton Oaks.

2002a   Beauty, Sexuality, Body Ornamentation and Gender in Ancient Mesoamerica. In *In Pursuit of Gender*. Sarah Nelson and Miriam Rosen-Ayalon, eds. Pp. 81–92. Walnut Creek, CA: AltaMira Press.

2002b   Desiring Women: Classic Maya Sexualities. In *Ancient Maya Gender Identity and Relations*. Lowell Gustafson and Amy Trevelyan, eds. Pp. 329–44. Westport, CT: Greenwood Press.

2003   Making Something of Herself: Embodiment in Life and Death at Playa de los Muertos, Honduras. *Cambridge Archaeological Journal* 13:248–61.

2004   Mesoamerica: A Working Model for Archaeology. In *Mesoamerican Archaeology: Theory and Practice*. Julia A. Hendon and Rosemary A. Joyce, eds. Pp. 1–42. Malden, MA: Blackwell.

Kellogg, Susan

1986   Aztec Inheritance in Sixteenth-Century Mexico City: Colonial Patterns, Prehispanic Influences. *Ethnohistory* 33:313–30.

1988   Cognatic Kinship and Religion: Women in Aztec Society. In *Smoke and Mist: Mesoamerican Studies in Memory of Thelma D. Sullivan*. J. Kathryn Josserand Karin Dakin, eds. Pp. 666–81. BAR International Series 402. Oxford: British Archaeological Reports.

1993   The Social Organization of Households among the Mexica before and after Conquest. In *Prehispanic Domestic Units in Western Mesoamerica: Studies of the Household, Compound, and Residence*. Robert Santley and Kenneth Hirth, eds. Pp. 207–24. Boca Raton, FL: CRC Press.

1995a   *Law and the Transformation of Aztec Culture, 1500–1700*. Norman: University of Oklahoma Press.

1995b   Woman's Room: Some Aspects of Gender Relations in Tenochtitlan in the Late Pre-Hispanic Period. *Ethnohistory* 42:563–76.

Kimball, G.

1993   Aztec Homosexuality—The textual Evidence. *Journal of Homosexuality* 26:7–24.

Klein, Cecelia F.
 1988 Rethinking Cihuacoatl: Aztec Political Imagery of the Conquered Woman. In *Smoke and Mist: Mesoamerican Studies in Memory of Thelma D. Sullivan*. J. Kathryn Josserand Karin Dakin, eds. Pp. 237–77. BAR International Series 402. Oxford: British Archaeological Reports.
 1993 Shield Women: Resolution of an Aztec Gender Paradox. In *Current Topics in Aztec Studies: Essays in Honor of Dr. H. B. Nicholson*. Alana Cordy-Collins and Douglas Sharon, eds. Pp. 39–64. San Diego Museum Papers, vol. 30. San Diego: San Diego Museum of Man.
 1994 Fighting with Femininity: Gender and War in Aztec Mexico. *Estudios de Cultura Nahuatl* 24:219–53.
 2001 None of the Above: Gender Ambiguity in Nahua Ideology. In *Gender in Pre-Hispanic America*. Cecelia Klein, ed. Pp. 183–253. Washington, DC: Dumbarton Oaks.
Krochock, Ruth J.
 2002 Women in the Hieroglyphic Inscriptions of Chichén Itzá. In *Ancient Maya Women*. Traci Ardren, ed. Pp. 152–70. Walnut Creek, CA: AltaMira Press.
Lesure, Richard G.
 1997 Figurines and Social Identities in Early Sedentary Societies of Coastal Chiapas, Mexico, 1550–800 B.C. In *Women in Prehistory: North America and Mesoamerica*. Cheryl Claassen and Rosemary A. Joyce, eds. Pp. 227–48. Philadelphia: University of Pennsylvania Press.
 1999 Figurines as Representations and Products at Paso de la Armada, Mexico. *Cambridge Archaeological Journal* 9:209–20.
 2002 The Goddess Diffracted. *Current Anthropology* 43:587–610.
Looper, Matthew G.
 2002 Women-Men (and Men-Women): Classic Maya Rulers and the Third Gender. In *Ancient Maya Women*. Traci Ardren, ed. Pp. 171–202. Walnut Creek, CA: AltaMira Press.
Lopiparo, Jeanne
 2003 Household Ceramic Production and the Crafting of Society in the Terminal Classic Ulúa Valley Honduras. Doctoral dissertation, University of California, Berkeley; Ann Arbor: University Microfilms International.
Marcus, Joyce
 1976 *Emblem and State in the Classic Maya Lowlands: An Epigraphic Approach to Territorial Organization*. Washington, DC: Dumbarton Oaks.
 1987 *The Inscriptions of Calakmul: Royal Marriage at a Maya City in Campeche, Mexico*. University of Michigan Museum of Anthropology Technical Report 21. Ann Arbor: University of Michigan Museum of Anthropology.
 1992 Royal Families, Royal Texts: Examples from the Zapotec and Maya. In *Mesoamerican Elites: An Archaeological Assessment*. Diane Z. Chase and Arlen F. Chase, eds. Pp. 221–41. Norman: University of Oklahoma Press.

1998   *Women's Ritual in Formative Oaxaca: Figurine-Making, Divination, Death and the Ancestors.* University of Michigan Museum of Anthropology Memoirs 33. Ann Arbor: University of Michigan Museum of Anthropology.

1999   Men's and Women's Ritual in Formative Oaxaca. In *Social Patterns in Pre-Classic Mesoamerica.* David C. Grove and Rosemary A. Joyce, eds. Pp. 67–96. Washington, DC: Dumbarton Oaks.

2001   Breaking the Glass Ceiling: The Strategies of Royal Women in Ancient States. In *Gender in Pre-Hispanic America.* Cecelia Klein, ed. Pp. 305–40. Washington, DC: Dumbarton Oaks.

McAnany, Patricia A., and Shannon Plank

2001   Perspectives on Actors, Gender Roles, and Architecture at Classic Maya Courts and Households. In *Royal Courts of the Ancient Maya. Vol. 1: Theory, Comparison, and Synthesis.* Takeshi Inomata and Stephen D. Houston, eds. Pp. 84–129. Boulder, CO: Westview.

McCafferty, Geoffrey G., and Sharisse D. McCafferty

1999   Metamorphosis of Xochiquetzal: A Window on Womanhood in Pre- and Post-Conquest Mexico. In *Manifesting Power: Gender and the Interpretation of Power in Archaeology.* Tracy Sweely, ed. Pp. 103–25. London: Routledge.

McCafferty, Sharisse D., and Geoffrey G. McCafferty

1988   Powerful Women and the Myth of Male Dominance in Aztec Society. *Archaeological Review from Cambridge* 7:45–59.

1991   Spinning and Weaving as Female Gender Identity in Post-Classic Mexico. In *Textile Traditions of Mesoamerica and the Andes: An Anthology.* Janet C. Berlo, Margot Schevill, and Edward B. Dwyer, eds. Pp. 19–44. New York: Garland.

1994a   The Conquered Women of Cacaxtla: Gender Identity or Gender Ideology? *Ancient Mesoamerica* 5:159–72.

1994b   Engendering Tomb 7 at Monte Alban: Respinning an Old Yarn. *Current Anthropology* 35:143–66.

Meskell, Lynn M., and Rosemary A. Joyce

2003   *Embodied Lives: Figuring Ancient Maya and Egyptian Experience.* London: Routledge.

Milbrath, Susan

1997   Decapitated Lunar Goddesses in Aztec Art, Myth, and Ritual. *Ancient Mesoamerica* 8:197–225.

Molloy, John P., and William L. Rathje

1974   Sexploitation among the Late Classic Maya. In *Mesoamerican Archaeology: New Approaches.* Norman Hammond, ed. Pp. 431–44. Austin: University of Texas Press.

Nash, June

1978   The Aztecs and the Ideology of Male Dominance. *Signs* 4:349–62.

1980   Aztec Women: The Transition from Status to Class in Empire and Colony. In *Women and Colonization.* Mona Etienne and Eleanor Leacock, eds. Pp. 134–48. New York: Praeger.

1998   Gendered Deities and the Survival of Culture. *History of Religions* 36:333–56.

Palka, Joel
    1999   Classic Maya Elite Parentage and Social Structure with Insights on Ancient Gender Ideology. In *From the Ground Up: Beyond Gender Theory in Archaeology*. Nancy L. Wicker and Bettina Arnold, eds. Pp. 41–48. BAR International Series 812. Oxford: British Archaeological Reports.

Pohl, Mary
    1991   Women, Animal Rearing and Social Status: The Case of the Formative Period Maya of Central America. In *The Archaeology of Gender*. Proceedings of the Twenty-second Annual Chacmool Conference. Dale Walde and Noreen D. Willows, eds. Pp. 391–99. Calgary: Department of Archaeology, University of Calgary.

Pohl, Mary, and Lawrence Feldman
    1982   The Traditional Role of Women and Animals in Lowland Maya Economy. In *Maya Subsistence*. Kent V. Flannery, ed. Pp. 295–311. New York: Academic Press.

Proskouriakoff, Tatiana
    1960   Historical Implications of a Pattern of Dates at Piedras Negras, Guatemala. *American Antiquity* 25:454–75.
    1961   Portraits of Women in Classic Maya Art. In *Essays in Pre-Columbian Art and Archaeology*. Samuel K. Lothrop et al., eds. Pp. 81–99. Cambridge, MA: Harvard University Press.
    1963   Historical Data in the Inscriptions of Yaxchilan. *Estudios de Cultura Maya* 3:149–67.
    1964   Historical Data in the Inscriptions of Yaxchilan. Part II. *Estudios de Cultura Maya* 4:177–201.

Pyburn, K. Anne
    1990   Settlement Patterns at Nohmul: Preliminary Results of Four Excavation Seasons. In *Precolumbian Population History in the Maya Lowlands*. T. Patrick Culbert and Don Rice, eds. Pp. 183–97. Albuquerque: University of New Mexico Press.
    1998   Smallholders in the Maya Lowlands: Homage to a Garden Variety Ethnographer. *Human Ecology* 26:267–86.

Raby, Dominique
    1999   Xochiquetzal en el cuicacalli: Cantos de amor y voces femeninas entre los antiguos nahuas. *Estudios de cultura nahuatl* 30:203–28.

Reilly, F. Kent
    2002   Female and Male: The Ideology of Balance and Renewal in Elite Costuming among the Classic Period Maya. In *Ancient Maya Gender Identity and Relations*. Lowell Gustafson and Amy Trevelyan, eds. Pp. 319–28. Westport, CT: Greenwood Press.

Robin, Cynthia
    2001   Kin and Gender in Classic Maya Society: A Case Study from Yaxchilan, Mex-

ico. In *New Directions in Anthropological Kinship.* Linda Stone, ed. Pp. 204–28. Lanham, MD: Rowman & Littlefield.
2002a Gender and Maya Farming: Chan Nòohol, Belize. In *Ancient Maya Women.* Traci Ardren, ed. Pp. 12–30. Walnut Creek, CA: AltaMira Press.
2002b Outside of Houses: The Practices of Everyday Life at Chan Nòohol, Belize. *Journal of Social Archaeology* 2:245–68.
2003 New Directions in Classic Maya Household Archaeology. *Journal of Archaeological Research* 11:307–56.

Rodriguez, Maria Jesus de
1988 *La mujer azteca.* Toluca: Universidad Autónoma del Estado de México.

Ruscheinsky, Lynn
1995 The Construction and Reproduction of Gender Hierarchy. In *Debating Complexity.* Proceedings of the 26th Annual Chacmool Conference. David A. Meyer, Peter C. Dawson, and Donald T. Hanna, eds. Pp. 629–34. Calgary: Chacmool Archaeological Association.

Sabloff, Jeremy
1990 *The New Archaeology and the Ancient Maya.* New York: Scientific American Library.

Schele, Linda
1979 Genealogical Documentation on the Tri-Figure Panels at Palenque. In *Tercera Mesa Redonda de Palenque.* Vol. 4. Merle Greene Robertson and Donnan Call Jeffers, eds. Pp. 41–70. San Francisco: Pre-Columbian Art Research Institute.

Schele, Linda, and Peter Mathews
1991 Royal Visits and Other Intersite Relationships among the Classic Maya. In *Classic Maya Political History: Hieroglyphic and Archaeological Evidence.* T. Patrick Culbert, ed. Pp. 226–52. Cambridge: Cambridge University Press.

Schroeder, Susan, Stephanie Wood, and R. Haskett, eds.
1997 *Indian Women of Early Mexico.* Norman: University of Oklahoma Press.

Silverblatt, Irene
1988 Women in States. *Annual Reviews in Anthropology* 17:427–60.
1995 Lessons of Gender and Ethnohistory in Mesoamerica. *Ethnohistory* 42:639–50.

Stone, Andrea J.
1988 Sacrifice and Sexuality: Some Structural Relationships in Classic Maya Art. In *The Role of Gender in Precolumbian Art and Architecture.* Virginia Miller, ed. Pp. 75–103. Lanham, MD: University Press of America.
1991 Aspects of Impersonation in Classic Maya Art. In *Sixth Palenque Round Table, 1986.* Virginia Fields, ed. Pp. 194–202. Norman: University of Oklahoma Press.
1995 *Images from the Underworld: Naj Tunich and the Tradition of Maya Cave Painting.* Austin: University of Texas Press.

Storey, Rebecca
1998 Mothers and Daughters of a Patrilineal Civilization: The Health of Females among the Late Classic Maya of Copán, Honduras. In *Sex and Gender in Paleo-*

pathological Perspective. Anne L. Grauer and Patricia Stuart-Macadam, eds. Pp. 133–48. Cambridge: Cambridge University Press.

Sullivan, Thelma
- 1982 Tlazolteotl-Ixcuina: The Great Spinner and Weaver. In *The Art and Iconography of Late Post-Classic Central Mexico.* Elizabeth Boone, ed. Pp. 7–35. Washington, DC: Dumbarton Oaks.

Sweely, Tracy L.
- 1998 Personal Interactions: The Implications of Spatial Arrangements for Power Relations at Ceren, El Salvador. *World Archaeology* 29:393–406.
- 1999 Gender, Space, People and Power at Ceren, El Salvador. In *Manifesting Power: Gender and the Interpretation of Power in Archaeology.* Tracy Sweely, ed. Pp. 155–71. London: Routledge.

Tate, Carolyn E.
- 1987 Royal Women of Yaxchilán. In *Memorias del Primer Coloquio Internacional de Mayistas: 5–10 de agosto de 1985.* Mercedes de la Garza, ed. Pp. 807–26. Mexico, D.F.: Universidad Nacional Autónoma de México, Centro de Estudios Mayas.
- 1999 Writing on the Face of the Moon: Women's Products, Archetypes and Power in Ancient Maya Civilization. In *Manifesting Power: Gender and the Interpretation of Power in Archaeology.* Tracy Sweely, ed. Pp. 81–102. London: Routledge.
- 2002 Holy Mother Earth and Her Flowery Skirt: The Role of the Female Earth Surface in Maya Political and Ritual Performance. In *Ancient Maya Gender Identity and Relations.* Lowell Gustafson and Amy Trevelyan, eds. Pp. 281–318. Westport, CT: Greenwood Press.

Taube, Karl
- 1985 The Classic Maya Maize God: A Reappraisal. In *Fifth Palenque Round Table, 1983.* Virginia Fields, ed. Pp. 171–81. San Francisco: Pre-Columbian Art Research Institute.

Thompson, Philip C.
- 1982 Dynastic Marriage and Succession at Tikal. *Estudios de cultura maya* 14:261–87.

Gender Archaeology in Native North America

24

KAREN OLSEN BRUHNS

THE NORTH AMERICAN CONTINENT is unique in archaeological studies in the amount of emphasis placed on ethnographic analogy in interpretation of the past. This has come about because indigenous societies survived until late in history and, in some cases, still survive, practicing ways of life that have been altered but that may still be still rooted in tradition. How unaffected these societies have been by the events of the past half millennium is another point and one that is, perhaps, not given enough emphasis when using ethnographic or historic documents in archaeological explanation. European societies began to influence First Nations groups in the ninth century, with the abortive attempts of the Norse to establish colonies in Newfoundland. Although relations were generally violent, some exchange of ideas and genetic material resulted and may have had influence on First Nations in the region, if only in their oral literature and mythology. However, it is a given that French and English (and Russian, for that matter) fur traders greatly modified economies and values in those nations that were involved in the fur trade and, in a sense, were responsible for the worsening position of women in the northern forests and on the Great Plains, beginning as early as the 1600s.

North America is also notable in that it provides nearly the full range of terrestrial habitats within its boundaries. From frozen tundra and extreme arctic conditions to steamy tropics to temperate rain forest to high desert, Native American cultures eventually inhabited all these environments and adapted to them culturally. Given the plant and animal crops available for domestication (or importable from adjacent regions such as Mexico and the Caribbean islands), native American agricultural systems were somewhat different from those of Eurasia, but the general processes of domestication and of the development of sedentary life were much the same as in the Old world. This suggests that gender theory derived out of studies of Old World Neolithic and Proto-Neolithic might be of use in engendering North American societies.

It is generally assumed that the development of complex societies has a major influence on gender roles, generally to the detriment of the position of women. In native North America, complex urban societies, with the possible exception of the Mississippi complex chiefdom or primitive state of Cahokia in western Illinois, were not present in aboriginal times. However, one must look at the development of chiefdoms, including complex ones, among the Hopewell-Adena, the Woodland, and the Mississippian peoples as providing expanded opportunities as well as diminished statuses for all genders and ages, as did the Chaco region during Puebloan times. This is a topic that has hardly been explored in terms of engendering the archaeological record, save in the Southwest, where increasing complexity of societies has been shown to have had mixed effects on women's roles and statuses (Crown 2000).

North America is generally divided into rough culture areas, corresponding to "types" of cultures and generalized types of environments. The *Handbook of North American Indians* (Sturtevant 1978) divides North America into the Arctic, Subarctic, Northwest Coast, California, Southwest, Great Basin, Southeast, and Northeast. These divisions only partly relate to archaeological cultural areas, based as they are on ethnography and ethnohistory, but offer a means of organizing the highly unequal and disparate studies of gender among the indigenous peoples of North America. In the following brief summary, I have lumped culture areas a bit more because of the nature of available publications in the various areas and topics (figure 24.1).

Inuit/Subarctic and Paleoindian

These geographic, cultural, and temporal periods are treated together because of their close relationship in American archaeology. Paleoindian studies are still, regrettably, one of the least engendered areas of modern prehistory, although a number of studies of known sites inhabited between approximately 15,000 and 8,000 years ago are beginning to result in a shift away from the traditional emphasis on stone projectile points and "moment of kill" in hunting in the description of Paleoindian lifeways. Given the paucity of material culture remaining in most North American terminal Pleistocene sites as well as the unfortunate focus of archaeology on the moment of the kill as the single most important aspect of hunting cultures, the varying roles of people within the earliest societies remain muddied. Moreover, tools are consistently misidentified. Kehoe (1990), in her groundbreaking article "Points and Lines," has pointed out the consistent

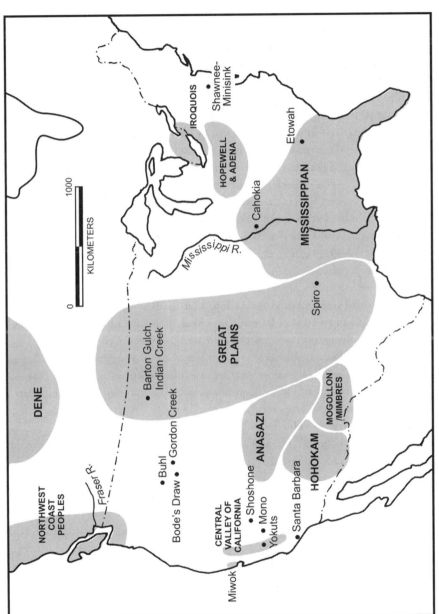

Figure 24.1. Regions in the United States, locating ethnic and cultural traditions discussed in this chapter.

misidentification of tools that probably served as implements for sewing, basketry, and even textile making as tools used by males in "the hunt." The visual presentation of pointed tools as upright phallic objects rather than oriented as they may have been used reinforces this emphasis on the moment of the kill, ignoring the organization of hunting, the preparation for the hunt, the preparation of the hunted animals, and so on. Hetty Brumbach and Robert Jarvenpa's (1997, 1997b) studies among Dene hunters in the northern forests bear strongly on the actual formation of the earliest American societies. They note that, indeed, hunting groups are formed of all women, of women and men, or of all men and that these have different time involvements and different prey animals and are spatially distinct. They also note that most hunting behavior would be invisible archaeologically. The importance of trapping, a kind of animal procurement in which women's roles is well attested, can, in fact, be traced back into the Paleoindian period. In the 1980s in northern Wyoming, a juniper wood and netting trap suitable for catching animals as large as a deer or an antelope was found (Frison et al. 1986). This trap can be dated to the seventh millennium. Although there is no evidence pertaining to who actually used this trap, a much later (and now iconic in gender archaeology illustrations) Mimbres bowl shows a pregnant woman who is bringing home an antelope that she has "gathered" (cf. the cover of Gero and Conkey 1991). It seems very likely that such procurement systems, very likely involving both women and men, were in place much earlier.

The view of Paleoindian society as being strongly male oriented, with women and children an invisible drag on settlement of the Americas, was, in part, based on evidence from kill sites with diagnostic projectile points and identifiable Pleistocene faunal remains, sites located primarily in the ancient grasslands of the North American West. This focus has militated against any study of the "nondiagnostic" flake tools also found in the kill sites and discouraged studying tool variation in the archaeological record and modeling other aspects of daily life, including women's activities. Yet Gero (1991) has cogently demonstrated that perhaps the most important tools, in terms of generality of use and economic importance, are these "unimportant" utilized flakes. Another aspect of this situation is that finding tools in association with animal bones does not necessarily indicate men hunting. These remains could equally indicate persons of either sex butchering after a communal hunt or a scavenging event and even preparation for storage or for transport by people of different genders and ages. Bruhns and Stothert (1999:31–33) point out that ethnographic studies among the Ingalik Inuit show clearly the high degree of coordination and interdependence among males and females of all ages among cold-oriented hunters and gatherers. They point out that men make more things and that women make more complicated things—such as clothing and preserved food—that men make simpler tools for women to make the complex items necessary to the survival of both (Osgood 1940). This is a subject that has hardly been touched in North American Paleoindian studies, largely, perhaps, because of the focus on hunting behaviors, commonly supposed to be limited to males despite the large (and growing) ethnographic evidence that hunting too is generally a shared activity and that who shares it is situational, not genetic (cf. Crass 2000).

As more Paleoindian living sites have been explored, variability in the earliest Americans is becoming accepted, including an acknowledgment that many peoples must have depended heavily on small game and the exploitation of plant species. This has led to an appreciation of variation in human roles within these societies. For example, studies of Indian Creek, a deeply stratified Paleoindian site in south-central Montana, show the site was occupied from late winter through early spring for some thousands of years, presumably by the same group and its descendants (Davis 1993). The largest animal hunted at Indian Creek was the bison, but far more common in numbers and in contribution to the diet were small animals: yellow-bellied marmot, prairie dogs, voles, and jack rabbits. The excavators suggest that preferentially collecting fat-bearing small animals may have been an adaptation to the hard times of late winter. Studies of the contemporary southern Chipewayan (Brumbach and Jarvenpa 1997a, 1997b) indicate that these sorts of animals are those especially hunted/trapped by women, children, and the elderly. There is evidence of numerous domestic activities at Indian Creek, including abundant refuse from stoneworking. Although the excavators identify the stone refuse as being the result of males making and maintaining stone tools, more than 85 percent of the total stone-tool inventory consists of scrapers and knives, tools used in hide and in meat or fish preparation—traditionally women's work in the northern cultures. Numbers of other Montana sites reflect similar hunting focused on small animals, while sites with good organic preservation show that plants also formed an important part of the diet. Barton Gulch, to the southwest of Indian Creek, has the remains of earth ovens. Barton Gulch has also yielded bone needles and other bone implements, grinding and pounding tools, scrapers, knives, and a great many utilized flakes. All these implements suggest that a great many different activities were being undertaken by the women and men in this site (Davis 1993).

In the northeastern United States, Paleoindian sites vary considerably in size, and some of the better-preserved indicate that people were living in small portable or quickly constructed shelters, perhaps like the wigwams or tipis of later peoples. Shawnee-Minisink in the upper Delaware Valley of Pennsylvania is one of the few sites with good plant preservation in the Northeast (McNett 1985). During the Paleoindian period, this area was a transitional zone between the boreal pine forest and the preboreal spruce and fir forest, a region not unlike that occupied by the Chipewayan peoples today. Shawnee-Minisink is apparently a late summer/early fall camp to which two families returned year after year. They worked outside around the fire place and probably used their shelters for sleeping and storage. Most tools are scrapers of various sorts, knives, spoke shaves, hammerstones, cores, and debitage. A single Clovis point knife was found. It should be pointed out that there is some debate as to whether many "projectile points" of types found in Paleoindian sites were not, in fact, knives. Still, Clovis points still serve as a temporal indicator, regardless of their actual function, and indicate the early dating of this particular site, a date that further casts doubt on the exclusive hunting adaptation of the earliest occupants of the Americas.

Plant remains at Shawnee-Minisink are varied and abundant and include amaranth, chenopods, smartweed (*Polygonum* sp.), winter cress, and a host of fruits, such as blackberries, hackberries, grapes, and hawthorn plums. Unidentified fish remains show the importance of this activity in the local subsistence system, as indeed it is—at least seasonally—among many northern foragers in both North America and Eurasia. Caribou hunting may have been practiced. The location of the camp on a known caribou migration route suggests that it was, although no caribou bone has been found. It appears that here, as in much of the northeastern woodlands, hunting was a secondary activity. Paleoindians, like later peoples in this area, were forest gatherers, supplementing their plant diet with fish, birds, rabbits, and an occasional deer or mastodon.

Situations such as these can be engendered, at least as far as admitting that women and men (and children and the elderly) all participated in a given cultural system and all contributed to it, simply because of the wide range of activities apparent in the archaeological record. As to any actual division of labor based on gender or information concerning possible gender related statuses, we must depend, as usual, on burial data. However, physical anthropological analysis, especially specialist aging and sexing of Paleoindian human remains, has been largely lacking because of both the scarcity and the generally fragmentary nature of these early finds. A rare exception to this situation is the discovery in southern Idaho of the remains of a young Paleoindian woman (age seventeen to twenty-one) dated to around 10,000 B.P. (Green et al. 1998). The burial was found in the course of gravel quarrying, and the burial ceremonies involved cannot be reconstructed, but the woman's bones were associated with a pressure flaked stemmed biface "point," a bone needle, a bone awl, and a badger baculum. Isotopic analysis suggests that this woman ate a diet heavy in both meat and fish, and enamel hypoplasia indicates periods of severe dietary stress in her life. An interesting aspect of her dental wear is that she apparently consumed foods that were highly processed in a manner that led to grit inclusion; the excavators suggest that perhaps the meat she ate was pounded into pemmican in a rough stone mortar. This find is especially interesting, as it bears on aspects of Paleoindian life, such as food processing, that are generally glossed over in the focus on the kill as the single most important event in the food procurement system. However, in general, burial data from this early time period do not provide much evidence regarding a gender-based division of labor or of status. The bifacial point found with the Buhl woman would probably have been classified as a male weapon had it been found apart from the funerary offering of a well-preserved, competently sexed skeleton. A Paleoindian burial from Gordon Creek (Colorado), dating to the eighth millennium B.C., was, in fact, originally identified as a male because of the elaboration of the reconstructable burial ritual and the worked stone and bone offerings it contained (Breternitz et al. 1971). The body of this young adult (about twenty-five years old) woman was placed tightly flexed in a red ocher–lined pit; more red ocher was scattered on her corpse, and freshly made chipped stone tools and worked elk teeth and antler objects were placed with her. The Gordon Creek woman was found before methods of ascertaining diet were developed, although her teeth too showed evidence of an abrasive diet. Another Paleoindian woman, from Sulphur Springs in southeastern Arizona, had also died in her mid-twenties to early thirties (Waters 1986). She has been dated to several thousand years later than the Gordon Creek woman. The Sulphur Springs woman was buried as a tightly flexed body and had no surviving offerings, suggesting considerable time depth to later archaic methods of disposal of the dead in this region. However, too few burials have been found in any one area to really discuss gendered differences in death-related ritual during the millennia of the first occupation of North America. What is evident is that there was considerable difference in such behavior, and one can assume that this reflects considerable differences in beliefs related both to death and to gender among the Paleoindian populations of the continent.

Another area of engendering the Paleoindian period that has received some recent attention is that of female fertility in the nomadic lifestyle (Surovell 2000). All the major theories of the populating of the Americas postulate that efficient (male) hunters attacked unwary herds of animals that had never seen humans, drastically reduced the available population, and then moved onward to repeat the slaughter, resulting in the rapid movements of human groups around the American continents and the speedy settlement of most environmental zones by *Homo sapiens*. At the same time, anthropological studies of surviving hunters and gatherers (especially in Africa) indicate low fertility and population stasis, although again most likely in response to the modern geographic and cultural containment. Surovell, however, concludes that high fertility in the Paleoindian situation could have been possible, even with high mobility, if children were helping to provide some of their own food by foraging with their mothers and if males were concentrating on high-return game.

From the known Paleoindian living sites, it seems likely that most if not all of the first Americans lived in small kin-based groups and thus that there was no need for permanent political leaders. The available evidence does not provide us with any insights into how Paleoindians negotiated roles or leadership or how these early peoples thought about femininity and masculinity. In later times, North American Indian societies showed considerable flexibility in their construction of gender categories. It seems safe to assume that some tasks at least were divided along sex lines and that others were divided by age and personal preference. It also seems likely that the tasks necessary for subsistence were assigned in a complementary fashion within family groups. Gender complementarity, including emotional, economic, and ritual interdependence, is deeply rooted in surviving Native American societies.

The North American Southwest

The cultures of the Southwest have been especially subject to the direct historic approach and ethnographic analogy of all kinds because in this region First Nations societies survive in a quasi-aboriginal manner to the present. Although the study of gender in prehistory has followed the same torturous path as in the rest of North America, the archaeological record is in many ways much richer in this northernmost outlier of Mesoamerica, largely because of the early development of representational art styles in ceramics and rock art among some cultures and the survival of sites with quantities of permanent architecture. In addition, because of the early establishment of maize agriculture and the historic and ethnographic association of women with maize food preparation, as well as the evident important role of maize in ritual, women have not been ever entirely shut out of the southwestern past.

Because of its lavish use of representational motifs, including depictions of humans, the Mimbres culture of southwestern New Mexico (ca. A.D. 200–1150) has been the focus of a number of studies that have tried to identify males and females in the art and then proceed to look at different activities, including ritual activities. Munson (2000) has used the corpus of Mimbres ceramic paintings to look at how these people chose to indicate gender differences, including supernumerary genders, as well as to differing activities among these genders. She notes that female and male clothing and headdress/hairstyles are quite different. From this initial identification, she goes on to show that there is a difference in animal procurement behaviors between males and females, with males using the bow and arrow or spear, while both sexes hunt with a throwing stick, snares, or traps. Child care is also commonly shown, although here women predominate while in ceremonial activities; even though males are more common, women and contrary genders also participate. She also notes that males are shown in a wider range of activities than are females but that the painted imagery also indicates that some women at least had access to high-status decorations and imported goods and that women associate more than men with imported macaws or parrots (although she notes that finds of psittacene birds in burials seem evenly distributed between the interments of women, men, and children).

Mimbres ceramics have also given a rare look at childbirth practices in the ancient Southwest. Hegmon and Trevathan (1996, 1997) report on a painted scene in which the child is seen coming to light face forward with its hands up, a position virtually unknown in human births. They conclude that the vessel was painted by a male unfamiliar with the human birthing process. Their conclusions have been acerbically challenged by LeBlanc (1997), Espinshade (1997), and Shaffer et al. (1997). What is interesting about the latter publication (all claim that Hegmon and Trevathan were unfamiliar with Mimbres artistic conventions) is that one Mimbres vessel shows the mother being assisted by a female midwife. These vessels, while they do not solve the question of who painted Mimbres ceramics, do enlarge our knowledge of social and medical practices in the ancient Southwest.

Just as painted ceramics have proven a fertile source of information concerning past societies' own views of women and men, so has rock art. As Hays-Gilpin (2004) notes in her ambitious cross-cultural study of rock art,, rock art has often not been taken seriously because of the problems of associating it with specific archaeological cultures and periods and even more because rock art enthusiasts are too often seen as amateurs, including women, whose interpretations are based on emotion and prior convictions (often involving extraterrestrials and "new age" beliefs). She also notes that studies of rock art have suffered from a profound Eurocentrism and the presumed obsession with fertility of the ancients. Hays-Gilpin clearly shows the variety of depictions in rock art in the American Southwest (and elsewhere) and the fact that gender and sex are often (although not invariably) shown. In the Puebloan region, she relates that although there are no ethnographic accounts of rock art being involved in puberty rituals, there are many depictions of pubescent women (identified because they wear their hair in the traditional "butterfly" whorls of the pubescent but unmarried Puebloan woman). She relates these depictions to a series of cultures in the region, beginning with Basketmaker in the early centuries A.D., and notes that similar depictions are found on pottery and on kiva murals as well as on contemporary kachina dolls. She concludes that rock art, not just the representations of young women but also those of phallic figures, flute players, and animals, may well have served an active role in merging different cultural traditions during the migration and consolidation of the pueblo peoples. Hays-Gilpin shows what uses can be made of an often intractable (in archaeological terms) art form and quite clearly concludes that rock art served different purposes within a society and continues to do so, as contemporary Hopi people use ancient rock art to reaffirm their own origin myths and beliefs.

In two slightly earlier studies, Hays-Gilpin (2000a, 2000b) used rock art, painted ceramics, and modeled figurines to look at gender ideology and ritual activities in southwestern prehistory. Despite the unevenness of the artistic record, she can demonstrate that gender hierarchies did emerge in some parts of the Southwest. She notes the association between gendered imagery and the growth of community size in various cultural traditions and suggests that in situations of tension (in this case arising from larger communities, increased task differentiation, and external contacts), artistic representations might have been used to manage tensions and renegotiate conflicts through ritual performance and artistic depictions of appropriate roles.

Ethnographic accounts of rituals in the Southwest commonly include the manipulation of portable objects in curing, hunting, and other rituals. Some objects were said to "come alive" as they were handled by shamans as part of their rituals to control power and to magically heal. This practice may extend as far back as the Archaic in the Southwest, where the peoples who lived along the lower Pecos River in western Texas created painted and engraved pebbles that were variously overpainted, repeatedly rubbed, ritually discarded, or wrapped and curated in preferred spots. The archaeological evidence suggests that these pebbles were ritual objects. The river pebbles are water worn, and Mock (1987) has argued that argues that water is linked to female processes and is the mythic home of ancestral spirits, game animals, and powerful and wise female deities. The pebbles were carefully selected for anthropomorphic or phallic pebbles and painted features such as concentric circles or spiral patterns on them. In recent times, these designs are life-producing symbols related to the cosmic order, to the point from which humans emerged from the earth, and to human reproduction, including childbirth and menstrual blood. Some pebbles seem to depict female genitals, and others show spider webs, evoking the well-known Spider Grandmother of the historic Southwest who was a powerful medicine woman with supernatural powers. Mock interprets these decorated pebbles as perhaps representing female spirits or spirit helpers. Given the paucity of information concerning social and metasocial relationships among these very early, nonagricultural, non–ceramic-making peoples, Mock's study is a welcome addition to the engenderment of the societies that succeeded the Paleoindians in this part of the world.

Studies that engender the past from purely archaeological evidence are becoming more common in the Southwest, but mainly people present their data as being from a nongendered, neutral standpoint. A major breakthrough was the 1997 School of American Research seminar, "Sex Roles and Gender Hierarchies in Middle-Range Societies: Engendering Southwestern Prehistory" (Crown 2000). This seminar looked at ways to engender southwestern society from archaeological data, including art, mortuary contexts, food preparation, and so on. Although the various presentations are not all equally successful, this volume must serve as a major resource for an engendered southwestern prehistory, especially as it concerns itself with the methodologies of studying gender and of looking at gender when using ungendered sources.

The individual papers in Crown (2000) as well as a number of other studies show that even in a situation in which gender has not been considered, engendering the archaeological record is to some extent possible. For example, if we look at the beginnings of agriculture in the Southwest, we see that it is related to the development of productive systems in Mexico and that the same processes and crops are involved. The Southwest is a land of unreliable rainfall, and Archaic populations developed a broad-spectrum foraging adaptation very early, including the manipulation of species through burning and other interventions, developing what Minnis (1985) has called "casual agriculture," that is, a mixture of agriculture with gathering/hunting, by the second millennium B.C. By the first centuries A.D., pit house villages whose occupants were fully agricultural and making ceramics were established. Crown and Wills (1995) argue that women became the ceramics makers because, with greater dependence on cultigens, the scheduling conflicts between foraging, horticulture, and food processing increased. Since one common method of dealing with workload conflicts is early weaning, by grinding cultivated seeds and cooking them into a mush, they argue that southwestern women were able to wean their infants earlier and thus achieve greater mobility as well as being relieved of the physical stress of producing milk. Because ovulation resumes when nursing lessens, early weaning has the unintended consequence of shortening the average birth interval and spurring demographic growth, which is also visible in the archaeological record. Crown and Wills also hypothesize that as women began making pottery in the Southwest, a new race of maize, more productive and more suitable for grinding, was adopted. The beginning of the use of large pots for cooking maize may reflect changes in the way food was distributed and could have favored a more equitable distribution of meat, as stews with a bit of meat assure all some access to fats and protein. Crown (2000) later elaborated on women's roles and changing cuisine as part of the School of American Research symposium. By focusing on an area in which women had traditionally worked (in this area) and by charting changing crops, vessel types and sizes, tool changes, and the contexts of these archaeologically observable aspects, she can substantially enlarge our appreciation of a dynamic subsystem and its gender correlates.

In the Mogollon region, people continued to be relatively mobile foragers and horticulturists until after A.D. 650, when a new, highly productive race of corn became available. Diehl (1996) has suggested that the Mogollon consumed increasing amounts of this maize even though it required more time to process and probably created scheduling conflicts. Because of time constraints for women, new grinding technology was adopted in the form of the Mexican trough metate with a two-handed mano. Although more efficient grinding tools, these are more costly to make and require much greater energy expenditure and fatigue by the women grinders. Diehl argues that as a result of the adoption of this technology, maize consumption increased in the Mogollon area and that this change correlated with changes in family organization, new kinds of settlements and land use, and increased trade. However, nutritional stress is also marked, although Minnis (1985) has suggested that disease load caused by crowding in nucleated settlements may be as important a factor as actual protein–calorie malnutrition.

By the Classic period (A.D. 1150–1400) in southern Arizona, Hohokam society grew more complex and showed increasing social differentiation along lines of wealth. Recent studies of Hohokam domestic production, architecture, ritual space, and burials have shown changing patterns of sexual stratification. Crown and Fish (1996:803–17) suggest that there was increasing differentiation among women in Hohokam communities in the Classic period as some women were isolated in walled compounds that limited their role in the community while promoting female integration in the family work group. The evidence summarized by McGuire (1992) indicates that the labor invested in food processing and craft production increased during the Classic period: the clay griddle (*comal*) appeared; more elaborate ceramics, including high-polished wares, were manufactured; and numerous spindle whorls demonstrated that households increased their investment in processing fiber. According to McGuire, many families abandoned the pre-Classic pit houses and elite women became separated from the rest of the community by living in large walled compounds or in residences on platform mounds. Some women in these isolated corporate groups probably enjoyed greater wealth but suffered loss of personal autonomy, although some senior women may have gained leadership roles. The grave goods indicate that female and male status was associated with different activities, represented by different sets of grave offerings. McGuire's study of the distribution of burials by sex and age at five Hohokam platform structures showed that adult females were not buried at all these sites. Furthermore, females were underrepresented in special box burials and lined-pit burials. In terms of grave goods, the researchers made a determination of grave lot value and concluded that although the remains of adult women were buried on some platforms and did occur in special burial contexts with highly valued goods, nevertheless adult males and children were buried in more valued locations with more valuable grave goods. However, there are also indications that older women were often given elaborate burials. An elderly adult female was the only woman buried in an adobe-lined pit. Another woman, between forty and fifty years of age, was interred atop the Las Colinas platform. She has been identified as a curing shaman: her pelvic area was covered with red hematite, and a leather pouch containing a large quartz crystal and asbestos was left under her head. Ethnographic analogy suggests that postmenopausal women might have participated with men in religious and political activities. Analogy also suggests that in many cases females and males may have had parallel leadership hierarchies, but these kinds of arrangements change easily and can be affected drastically by events such as warfare or conquest, as indeed they were by the invasion of Europeans and the attempted imposition of European gender norms.

The extreme emphasis on corn in the Southwest in later prehistory had other implications for prehistoric women. Corn processing in this region was women's specialty as shown by the modifications observed on female skeletons. The location of grinding bins is an important setting for understanding women's lives because these areas were used by women for many hours each day of their lives. Spielmann (1995) argues that through time there were changes in the location of bins. Data show that in the early phases of intensive agriculture, groups of bins were located in interior household settings, whereas after A.D. 1300, single bins were moved to outdoor locations in plazas and on rooftops. This shift came at the same time that mealing bins disappeared from ritual locations in kivas, suggesting a lesser or more indirect place in ritual for the female half of the population (Mobley-Tanaka 1997).

Burial analysis also shows changes in status. A study of 132 burials from two Classic period Hohokam village cemeteries (Mitchell 1991) shows that both men and women were buried together with their kin. At the Grand Canal site, subadults were found to have fewer grave goods on the whole, and adults commonly were associated with sex-specific items. Adult females were accompanied by an average of 4.8 vessels, subadults had an average of 4.1 vessels, while males had an average of 3.4 vessels. Only women were buried with more than ten vessels each. There was no significant difference in the occurrence of ornaments between adult females and males, but males had a greater number of ornaments, including marine shell and stone pendants, while subadults at Grand Canal were more likely to have ornaments than adults. At the Casa Buena site, 70 percent of the adult male tombs contained ornaments compared to only 47 percent of the female burials, and several categories of ornaments, including shell artifacts, stone pendants, and bone hairpins, were almost exclusively associated with adult males; males also got more of what the excavators decided were "ritual artifacts." Males were commonly associated with arrow points, axes, and abraders, while spindle whorls and food-processing tools such as manos and pestles were associated with adult women. The funerary rituals reconstructed at these two villages appeared egalitarian, but the contents of the tombs suggest both gender complementarity and significant social differentiation and inequality.

Burial studies also show that late prehistoric (A.D. 1350–1500) Puebloan burials at Hawikku (near Zuni) were arranged by kin group. Here the excavators identified as the burials of community leaders individuals with a greater number and diversity of burial goods or whose burial showed special body or other preparations that probably expressed the number of social roles that the individual performed in life (Howell and Kintigh 1996). Of the eleven leaders' burials found, eight were males, buried with offerings that suggest prowess in warfare (weapons and a scalp) and ritual. The three female leaders were associated with grave offerings of corn, squash, utilitarian vessels, decorated bowls, grinding equipment, baskets, shaped wood, paint-grinding stones, antler tools, gourds, decorated jars, feathers, human hair, and prayer sticks, associating women with domestic tasks and some ritual activities.

Burial analysis has also indicated that in late prehistory in the La Plata Valley (southwestern Kayenta area), some women were very badly treated. Burials of women who had died of head injuries and had been simply dumped in the grave, discarded, and not buried properly suggest systematic spousal abuse against some women (Martin 1977). These women also show physical signs of heavier work, especially grinding, much heavier than women who are found buried in proper contexts and who did not die from being beaten to death with digging sticks. This is perhaps another indication of the poor treatment of captured wives seen in other areas of North America in late prehistory.

The Midwest and Southeast

The great river valleys and temperate forests in the Midwest and the southeastern United States were the scene of early and continual cultural florescence. Here complex cultures flourished from Archaic times on (Poverty Point), collapsing only under the weight of the epidemics introduced by Hernando De Soto's genocidal explorations in 1539–1542. The Southeast and Midwest have seen considerable archaeological investigation, largely because of the complexity of the ancient cultures (and the attractiveness of their art), but, in general, engendering has been limited to "women's work" in its various aspects without much attention being paid to other aspects of the local cultures, especially engendering power and politics. This is puzzling since there are documentary sources that speak in some detail of women rulers (cf. Vega 1951), but the reigning model of chiefdoms does not apparently admit of *cacicas* as well as *caciques*.

The southeastern and midwestern Archaic cultures have been subject to a series of seminal studies (Claassen 1991; Sassaman 1992a, 1992b) that see the archaeological record as reflecting a progressive reduction of hunting to more reliable, year-round subsistence modes, such as shellfishing, fishing, and trapping small animals, coupled with a growing importance of plant resources. Tool types reflect this, as Archaic sites are characterized by large quantities of technologically simple flakes, produced easily and presumably used by women as well as men (cf. Gero 1991). Claassen has studied the involvement of both women and men and, especially, the ideological meaning of food procurement activities and their loci in Shell Mound Archaic sites along the tributaries of the Mississippi around 3500–1000 B.C. In this region, although there is no other evidence of permanent architecture, huge mounds of shell were formed by people leaving the remains of their meals on site. In these mounds, they buried their dead, suggesting that the mounds had or came to have a sacred character. The human remains from the mounds show no significant difference in health between the sexes, and while men, women, and children all had burial offerings, it is of special interest that more women than men were sprinkled with red ocher and that ceremonial items such as medicine bags, turtle shell rattles, and flutes were found with women. As people stopped constructing and using shell mounds, Claassen again has looked at agency, minimizing arguments of environmental expediency. She sees the shell mounds as more than functional refuse heaps. She claims that they are built ceremonial structures that formed the center of a ritual center visited by large groups seasonally and preferred as a burial spot. In her interpretation, shellfishing and shell mounding were both economic and religious activities important in women's lives. About 1000 B.C. with the advent of agriculture, new rituals and ideologies took their place, and shell mounds ceased to be built. Although Claassen's interpretations are highly speculative, they do model complex social change with women and men as active participants. Claassen (1997, 2002) has discussed diachronically women's changing lives, noting that strongly gendered tasks may well have not existed until intensive agriculture made its appearance (along with ceramics and textiles, all female work in later societies). She sees a strong division of labor and growing women's workloads as appearing in Middle Woodland times, with women weaning children earlier, feeding them gruels (the evidence is thinning of the walls of pots to make them more efficient cooking vessels), and using older children's labor in child care as responses to an increasing workload.

The invention of agriculture in North America is very much attached to studies of gender since in much of North America agriculture was women's work. Native North American agriculture was based at first on plants that flourish in the rich, disturbed soils around human habitations. Aside from the usual suggestions of a passively occurring "natural" domestication (which avoids having to ascribe agency to women), there have been a plethora of studies that look at possible women's role in the development and evolution of the North American agricultural system. Watson and Kennedy's (1991) classic study targets women as the specialists in harvesting wild plants. They suggest that because women possessed extensive botanical knowledge, they intentionally worked to improve seed size and increase the availability of desirable plants outside the area of their natural distribution. Late Archaic sites offer abundant evidence, including coprolites, that people were increasingly sedentary and that they consumed larger quantities of plants, both cultivated and intensively gathered from habitats near settlements. These were weedy seed plants, such as chenopods, sumpweed, maygrass, and sunflower, as well as vegetables, such as gourds and pumpkins. In burials associated with Middle Archaic earth platforms along the Illinois River, both female and male skeletons exhibit evidence of stress due to heavy work as well as the telltale signs of periodic hunger (Cassidy 1987). Despite an apparent similarity in life and work experience, females exhibited lower life expectancies than males at every age, as indeed they did throughout prehistory and into the modern period.

By the Early and Middle Woodland periods, the Adena and Hopewell peoples of the Ohio and Illinois valleys had begun to practice differential mortuary treatments, with some people being buried in wooden tombs under earthen platforms, accompanied by sumptuous grave goods that show that long-distance trade networks were in existence as well as, perhaps, specialist manufacture. Aside from ceramics manufacture, which was women's work at European contact and which has been assumed to always have been women's work, there has been no real engendering of specialist manufactures, save textiles, among the peoples of the Midwest and Southeast. In Hopewell and Adena, males tend to be buried in the focal tombs, whereas women and children are often buried in caves or in relatively simple graves, suggesting a more pronounced differentiation of social roles.

Throughout Middle Woodland times in the lower Illinois Valley, people showed gains in nutrition and health, compared to Late Archaic people, and there was no significant difference in bone strontium between females and males, suggesting that their diets were similar. By Late Woodland times, male and female activities changed. Males were eating more meat, perhaps because meat was consumed from animals killed away from home or perhaps because of ideologies about appropriate food for the two sexes. At the same time, women began to show more robust bones and muscles, a trend that continued into Mississippian times. This has been taken to indicate an ever greater participation of women in cultivation and suggests that they were fed poorly in their growing years. By the time of first European contact, virtually all agriculture was done by Native American women. Men hunted, made war, and traded, and women farmed, thus facilitating and, indeed, underwriting all the rest.

Maize was present in the eastern woodlands by 1800 B.C., but it became significant only after A.D. 800, when the Northern Flint variety of maize was developed. This crop became the basis for the development of chiefdoms along the Mississippi. In Watson and Kennedy's (1991) view, women developed this revolutionary agricultural technology. After A.D. 800 in the Late Woodland and Mississippian phases, maize became progressively more important in diets, and there was rapid cultural change and settlement growth. Skeletal evidence shows that women had more arthritis of the left arm and spine than those of earlier Woodland females. Maize farming is far harder labor than cultivation of indigenous plants. The maize-based diet brought worsening childhood health and crowding into villages because of increased competition and warfare also increased the disease load (Cook 1984), but in many regions females exhibit a progressive increase in development of the deltoid tuberosity from Middle Woodland through Mississippian times. Bridges (1991) has found that Mississippian female skeletons show increases in personal strength indicative of a major increase in workloads, whereas males showed little change in activity since the Archaic. Osteoarthritis also increased among women but not among men in the southeastern United States, reflecting the time spent by women at hard labor in late prehistoric sites. One aspect of Late Woodland gender practices that has been considered is targeted violence against women. Wilkinson (1997) has noted that with increases in warfare and increases in the workload of women, leading to perceived needs for more labor, women were commonly abducted during bellicose activities if they were of childbearing age (older women were simply clubbed to death). However, it is apparent that the life of these abducted wives was not a happy one, as the skeletons of young women show numerous signs of injuries from violence and high death rates from physical trauma. Young women, especially, show evidence of having been mistreated over long periods of time before they died. These, Wilkinson hypothesizes, were the captured women.

The Mississippian cultural tradition has been engendered basically only in the areas of agriculture and textile production (cf. Eastman and Rodning 2001). As Koehler (1997) remarks, there has been virtually no attention paid to women at all in this cultural tradition. He is interested in ritual roles and identifies in Mississippian art (ceramics, shell ornaments with elaborate iconography, and figurines), a series of figures that he identifies as early versions of later important supernaturals, especially earth and corn mothers and falcon warriors (female or third gender). Koehler can also demonstrate considerable continuity in supernatural figures from the earlier Hopewell cultural tradition, suggesting that there was continuity in supernaturals and ideologies. Another feature of the Mississippian culture is the manufacture of large stone, ceramic, and wood figures. These are usually found in female–male pairs associated with ritual architecture. The figures clearly mark differences between women and men expressed in the clothing, hairstyles, and posture (Smith 1991). Male figures have varied headgear, while females have simple long hair hanging down their backs. Females also carry a backpack, perhaps the equivalent of the Earth Mother's sacred bundle, which contained ears of corn representing the first seeds given to humankind. Very likely these figurines represent ancestral mothers and fathers, the guardians of sacred places and of specific social groups. The figurines suggest that in Mississippian ideology, gender roles were highly differentiated but that both females and males played significant parts in their cosmology. In the early historic period in southeastern society, women's and men's roles were so differentiated that, according to Smith, the two sexes were almost like different species.

Other participation in ritual by women is shown in the archaeological identification of human sacrifice. Among the historic Pawnee, one of the traditional ceremonies designed to revitalize the universe involved the commemoration of the sexual union of the Morning Star (male) and the Evening Star (female), resulting in the first girl and later all people. Historic ceremonies involved the sacrifice of a young female captive to the Evening Star. Previously it is likely that earlier young men were also sacrificed to the Morning Star. At an archaeological site on the Smoky Hill River in Kansas (ca. A.D. 1300), a burial mound was excavated and revealed the remains of a number of individuals, including a twelve-year-old female (O'Brien 1990). The mound of earth has been interpreted as the site of a sacrifice to the Evening Star. Among recent Pawnee, the ceremony involved firing arrows into the victim's body, which was then exposed, heading east, to be consumed by animals. In the prehistoric mound, archaeologists found arrow points scattered in the fill and disarticulated bones gnawed by rodents. Earlier Mississippian sites show that human sacrifice of both sexes was not unknown. The most famous, of course, is the burial of a young man in Mound

72 at Cahokia, where some sixty people accompanied the primary burial, but other sacrifices of both women and men are known (Feder 2002:173–74).

Drooker (1992) has studied Mississippian textile production through looking at textile imprints on pottery. She thinks that all women made textiles on a regular basis and can demonstrate that most textiles could easily have been woven by part-time weavers. The existence of some elaborate twined textiles, mainly at major sites such as Etowah and Spiro, suggests that there may have been more highly trained and skilled weavers who could have been, as in historic times, the wives of the chiefs producing textiles for the use of their households. Drooker speculates that skill in weaving was probably part of a woman's individual identity and an element in her prestige within the community.

Plains Indian Cultures

Although the Plains groups instantly became the icon of "The American Indian" (largely thanks to Buffalo Bill's Wild West Show and the late nineteenth-century development of the cinema), engendering these cultures has tended to confine itself to the late period and to the ethnography. Ethnohistoric studies linked with archaeological data are giving some time depth to patterns observed among the various peoples of the inland plains and adjacent forests. Spector's (1991, 1994) studies in which she has attempted to put a lost awl back into the culture and ideological universe of the Dakota are justly famous. Continuing in this technology, Sundstrom (2002) has looked at the substitution of steel awls for bone ones among Dakota and Lakota groups. Sundstrom's studies rightly insist on agency by Plains women, noting that they were not passive receivers who had no ideas or wishes. Sundstrom, as does Spector, links the awl with essential aspects of femininity and the essential role of women in the survival of her family and community. Awls were the tool used to make clothing and shelter, and although polyester and down padding have largely replaced leather clothing, even today women at powwows wear an awl case to show that they are industrious members of their community. The Siouan-speaking peoples who inhabited the forested river valleys and also the open plains have largely been characterized as bison hunters in popular mythology, but, in fact, the eastern groups were horticulturalists who also hunted, trapped, and fished. The Plains dwellers traded for maize and other agricultural products but increasingly specialized in bison hunting once the horse had been adopted. A crucial aspect of Dakota–Lakota religion is the vision quest, and there is evidence that the visions, sought by both women and men, occupied this key role in spirituality for centuries before European contact. Important among the supernaturals was Double Woman, the inventor of quillwork and a source of artistic talent among women. Dreams/visions of Double Woman were two-edged in that the dreamer was usually offered a choice, and if she chose rightly, she would become artistic, make powerful designs, and receive the benefits of being an admired woman in her community. A wrong choice would lead to a life of idleness, promiscuity, and spinsterhood. Double Woman is associated with rock art as well. Sundstrom identifies this art as a set of rock designs that include animal tracks, vulvas, footprints, and grooves, the latter made by turning bone into awls, and she identifies the artifacts found at the one properly recorded site as being women's tools (awls, pounders, and utilized flakes). The conclusion is that this rock art must have been made by women as well as used by women.

Bone tools, of course, were rapidly exchanged for steel ones as women's work providing skins for the hide trade increased in historic times. Rock art ceased to be made or at least publicized as missionaries came in. However, the association of women's work; women's valued contributions to the domestic, ritual, and international (hide trade) economy; rock art; and vision quests, especially at puberty, adds a new dimension to the study of ancestral Sioux societies.

Women's work has been looked at in Colorado, where historically Arapaho peoples moved from the plains into the mountain valleys in the summers. Work at Bode's Draw (Benedict 1993) has identified women's work camps for the bulk processing of meat, skins, processing the summer vegetables and fruits, extracting marrow, and so on. Bode's Draw has occupations dating to the Late Archaic and the Protohistoric period. This site was on a hill, not far from camp, and served as a generalized work area for women. Men at Bode's Draw are the "invisible gender."

One aspect of historic Plains society that has been disparaged by whites is the apparent heavy labor done by women while males appear to loaf. The idea of the Indian woman as an overworked drudge is popular and pervasive (cf. Weist 1983), but there are reasons to think that the foreigners' perception of a vastly unequal allocation of tasks was inaccurate. Hollimon (2000b) has explored this apparent inequity from skeletal analysis of the Arikara. She notes that women tended to die younger than males, largely because of complications of childbirth and the synergistic effects of poor nutrition and infectious diseases. However, Arikara males showed comparable patterns of degenerative joint disease, suggesting equally active laboring lives. Males also experienced greater health risks during their lifetimes, largely because of the physical dangers of warfare that led to injury and, often, premature death. Although it is evident that women had the more consistently heavy tasks of agriculture, preparation of food, fabrication of most artifacts, and child and elder care, Hollimon can show that males were not the idle peacocks that white rhetoric has painted.

Warfare is another aspect of Plains culture that can be engendered. Data from the historic period or very late prehistory show that women had varying roles to play in the bellicose aspects of their society. Most commonly, these seem to have been supportive roles or roles as victims, but women could also play more active roles as warriors, either on a permanent basis or to avenge a particular death (Medicine 1983). The institution of women warriors is mentioned in historic documents from the 1700s on, and it is evident that this was a widespread custom and found over much of North America, although most of our information comes from the Plains peoples. None of it, however, is archaeological, nor have women warriors or Manly Hearts (see the discussion later in this chapter) been identified in the archaeological record. Women victims of warfare have. Numerous sites in the Illinois and Missouri valleys show that women, as well as men, were commonly victims of warfare. At the Norris Farm site cemetery, for example, forty-three of the nearly 200 burials had signs of trauma, including embedded projectile points, massive skull injuries caused by ground stone axes, defensive trauma on arms and hands, and mutilations such as scalping and decapitation. Of five women who survived attacks (they had healed injuries), three had been scalped. Another three multiple burials contained the remains of women who had apparently been surprised while working far from the village, as carnivore damage is evident on their bones along with weapon-caused trauma (Milner et al. 1991). Likewise, a study of over 700 adult crania from middle Missouri Valley sites (dating ca. A.D. 1600–1832) shows that women had about as much chance of being scalped as men and that Arikara women in the contact period were as likely to be scalped as males, although scalping victims show a larger age differential, as women apparently were targeted in their villages by raiding parties. Scalping was, of course, the prime means of securing war trophies among the Plains tribes. Scalping may have increased with the introduction of steel knives, but evidence of scalping and the massacre of whole settlements—female, male, aged, and children alike—extends far back into the prehistoric period in North America.

During the historic period, as traditional societies broke down under foreign attack and forced missionization, some women's roles became even less enviable. Nevertheless, other women managed to turn the introduced ideologies of oppression and pollution to their own advantage, as described in a study by Galloway (1997) that suggests that the use of menstrual buildings was part of women's adaptive response to increased workloads in the historic period (both because of the fur trade and because of maize agriculture) but notes that these seclusion buildings were also the loci of ritual and crafts; women did not just stare at the wall for a week. Galloway also discusses why menstrual "huts" have not been identified in the archaeological record and how they might be and engenders a building described by the excavators as a men's house as a menstrual hut.

California/Great Basin

California and the Great Basin encompassed a variety of cultures adapted to the vast range of environments and outside contacts. Most peoples were hunters and gatherers, a way of life that continued from the first migrants into the region until the time of European invasion. Most studies of California peoples that treat gender in any manner depend heavily on ethnography and, of course, on skeletal analysis. However, gender is apparently not seen as a particularly important area of study or an essential dynamic of local First Nations societies, to the point that a recent summary of California archaeology, intended to represent the up-to-the-minute state of the field, does not mention gender at all (Arnold et al. 2004).

In central California, a pattern of subsistence change involving ever increasing dependence on gathered acorns and salmon fishing (as opposed to deer hunting) has been noted (Dickel et al. 1984) over a period from approximately 2500 B.C. to A.D. 1300. As more dependence was placed on oaks, population growth accelerated, and longevity declined. No real difference between female and male in terms of basic health is noted, but changes in women's lives are visible archaeologically. Birth spacing decreased, and adult mortality, especially that of young women, increased. During the later Archaic, unweaned babies and toddlers also began to die at an accelerating rate, apparently because of the loss of their mothers in a subsequent childbirth.

Among the California peoples, at the time of European contact (and continuing until the present), acorn processing and storage was women's work—heavy, monotonous work. It is possible, as Dickel and his colleagues suggest, that the change to a more arduous means of making a living was related to a series of draughts in which acorns formed a major reliable food source. However, focusing on acorns resulted in a more sedentary lifestyle to facilitate the processing and storage of the nuts. This innovation may be linked to population increase caused by reduced birth spacing, a situation often seen when mobile people become sedentary.

Skeletal pathologies indicate considerable biological stress among the Central Valley Archaic people. Subsistence change did *not* result in better health for the people; in fact, data from early, middle and Late Archaic skeletons show that although acute stress decreased, chronic stress increased, presumably because of inadequate nutrition and disease, resulting in increased infant and maternal death and overall higher mortality due to increased population density and disease.

Jackson's (1991) by-now classic discussion of acorn-dependent peoples in the Sierra Nevada show the importance of "women's work" in community formation and location. Jackson bases his interpretations on analogy with the ethnographically known Western Mono and other acorn-dependent peoples of central California. Jackson shows that women's food production activities were the key factor in settlement location. In late prehistory, local peoples were characterized by a settlement system involving the creation of bedrock mortars and storage silos that facilitated women's labor and production. Jackson suggests that the archaeological distribution of sites responded to women's social and resource needs. Within the big winter campsites, Jackson identifies groups of mortars around the houses and main midden area, where both men and women worked and left debris, and other mortars fifty meters away, interpreted as women's areas. This exclusive space may have been balanced by men's sweat lodges, which in the historic period were located a little distance from the main camp. In the summertime, women may have dominated the small, high-altitude sites, where men may have spent less time. In these camps, there were no isolated mortar facilities.

This interpretation of Archaic people draws attention to the importance of women's work in settlement location and form. Jackson (1991) believes that the settlement system of the late prehistoric people (and perhaps their social organization) was determined by the requirements of acorn processing. This is an important study because in most discussions of Archaic groups, men's hunting activities have been given central importance. The development of new hunting technologies (as when the bow and arrow replaced spear throwers and darts) were important events in the central California Archaic, but so was the development of acorn-processing technologies that then became the dominant factor in site location and group movement.

Dick-Bissonette (1998) has looked at gender and authority among the central Californian groups and concludes that decision making among the Yokoch (Yokuts), Mono, and Miwok was based on acorns, basketry, matrilineal use rights, and women's work groups. These aspects of society supported strongly the authority of senior women. She points out that Eurocentric ideas of how things should be have been superimposed on the prehistoric reality among these groups to present a literature that bears little resemblance to the actual structure of authority among these groups. Apparently, the acorn-based economy was best served by a matrilineal, matrilocal community group organized into households and then into larger communities. Women within these groups served not only within the household context but also as chiefs, doctors, dancers, midwives, undertakers, and so on. Moreover, because women made the baskets and baskets were essential to virtually every social aspect of California life, they literally controlled the wealth. In the archaeological context, of course, baskets do not generally survive in the archaeological context. Dick-Bissonette's research is all the more important because it clearly points out the care that must be taken with nineteenth-century European sources concerning kinship and authority within societies that had very different systems and histories than those of Eurasia.

Other gender-related studies in California archaeology have looked at the coastal-dwelling Chumash of the Santa Barbara channel. Hollimon (1992) sees evidence for both hard labor and labor-related trauma and fairly high levels of domestic violence. Lambert (1997) has also looked at Chumash osteology and sees that there is a high percentage of skull fractures represented in the archaeological population. She notes that children tend to not show signs of trauma and that adolescents have high rates of skull fracture, but they are generally healed. However, the highest percentage of skull fracture is seen in adult women. Female mortality was very high from these fractures, which she compares to studies of domestic violence deaths in modern societies and finds them analogous.

Other gender-related studies in California have concerned themselves with rock art. As summarized by Hays-Gilpin (2004:70), many southern California rock engravings and paintings are done of rocks that naturally have the appearance of female genitalia. She notes that an interpretation that has been gaining ground associates vulva forms and female figures in rock art to solar phenomena that were seen as the impregnation of the Earth Mother by a male solar deity (75). In other instances, there are well-documented (ethnographically) cases of rock art being made for encouraging pregnancy (the Pomo "baby rocks") and fertility in general, especially at puberty. Thus, there is strong association of rock art, menarche, and female fertility in the far western as well as in the southwestern United States. However, Hays-Gilpin also notes that in the interior, there is a spatial distribution of female gendered places and art, with the lower elevations being gendered female. In the Shoshonian region, it is clear that the sacred landscape is gendered and reflects the distribution of spiritual beings and powers, both beneficent and not so (153–55).

The Pacific Northwest

The Pacific Northwest, a land of temperate rain forest and rich sea resources, was historically the home of a series of indigenous groups who had highly ranked societies and who practiced sophisticated sea-oriented fishing and foraging. The arts and ritual lives of these groups have been the focus of much anthropological research, but archaeology and gender studies have lagged far behind (Bernick 1999).

Moss (1993), discussing the Tlingit, concluded that in the early historic period (the era just before and around the time of European contact), shellfishing had proportionally greater importance than it did in the nineteenth and twentieth centuries. Moss sees shellfish, however, as a not particularly prestigious food and concludes that more women than men ate shellfish and that more women and men from the lower ranks of society ate shellfish than did the highly ranked peoples of the noble lineages. Slaves consumed more shellfish than any other group. In this way, she can correlate an archaeological deposit, shell middens, with gender and class. It has been suggested that shellfish populations were somehow manipulated by their collectors to enhance desirable characteristics, but this idea has not really been pursued, even though it is known that coastal Salish women did keep white dogs (for their hair). Shellfishing lost importance in the contact period along the coast, although inland on the Columbia River Plateau (a vastly different physical environment) intensive shellfishing characterized economies and may represent women's work. Moss (1999) has reiterated her feeling that the direct historic approach, using the rich ethnographic record of the Pacific Northwest, will enable the engendering of Northwest archaeology.

Sylvia Albright's (1999) ethnoarchaeological studies among the Tahltan of northern British Columbia show that women and men have a deep knowledge of both animal and plant resources that were widely snared and trapped by both sexes. Traditionally, women and men worked together in communal hunts, and women, before white hegemony, often held high status within the society. Albright's studies are important because she details changing roles under changing circumstances (i.e., the loss of political importance by women and increased hunting by older women) and the fact that traditional tool kits were made and used by both women and men. The fact that among the Tahltan both women and men had their own tool kits is suggestive for further interpretation of stone-tool assemblages and an analysis that does not simply lump all stone tools into an anonymous, generalized assemblage thought to be characteristic of a culture.

Greaves (1999) has looked at microcore technology of the Plateau Microblade Tradition on interior British Columbia (ca. 6400–1600 B.C.). She concludes that since the vast majority of microcores are found in residential camps, they may well have been used, if not made as well, by women in preparing food for storage. She notes, however, that microcores were apparently multipurpose tools and, as such, were doubtless used by women and men.

In the same volume, Zacharias (1999) uses early documentary sources concerning the Haida to note that within the traditional class structure, nonhierarchical relations between women and men prevailed in both public and private. By establishing task differentiation, Zacharias can show that archaeological sites in this region are more likely to represent women's activity areas simply because many women's tasks were land based, unlike those of men. Pratt (1999) has critiqued several of the few reports to take gender into account among Salishan peoples, noting that, although they are a step forward, they fail to take into account the general fluidity of Salishan culture and economy in which specific tools or tool kits were highly unlikely to have been used only by a woman or a man. Bernick (1999) has critiqued the essentially androcentric reconstructions of the Marpole Phase of the Fraser River delta in which assumptions such as the passivity of women and their exclusive association with food preparation have marred understanding of this important cultural tradition.

Hays-Gilpin (2004:17–21) has compiled studies of rock are in the Plateau region (and into California) as being associated with female puberty and girls' vision quests. The time depth of such beliefs/practices is, however, not known. Marucci (1999) has considered what might be archaeological evidence of women's rituals among the British Columbia Athabaskans and some of the peoples they traded and intermarried with. She notes that menstrual seclusion is characteristic of all these peoples and that, especially, menarche was a time in which the woman was so powerful because of her physical state that she needed to be secluded to protect the others. Marucci believes, as does Galloway (1997), that one should look outside the main community boundaries for evidence of the shelters in which women stayed during menstruation. She also notes the kinds of activities (ritual and craft) that women in seclusion practiced and notes that such sites might well have culturally modified trees, pictographs, and specific types of tools, specifically women's tools, and no food waste (food taboos included a prohibition on eating fresh meat while menstruating) as well as scratchers and drinking tubes, also associated with taboos.

The Northeast

In the northeastern United States, the small amount of engendered archaeology regarding prehistoric peoples published has largely involved the matrilineal Iroquoians among whom, historically, women held strong public roles of prestige and power. Prezzano (1997) summarizes the various theories concerning Iroquois origins, including migration into an area sparsely occupied by Algonquian speakers and variations on in situ development. Origins are important in Iroquois archaeology because people see the close interaction of warfare and the existence of powerful women. Snow (1995), one of the proponents of the migration hypothesis, sees the Owasco people as the ancestors of the modern Iroquois nations, claiming that they migrated out of central Pennsylvania (Hunter Home

Phase) into New York around A.D. 900, displacing the Algonquian groups who were living there. The early Owasco people were organized into bigger family groups than their Algonquian neighbors, and they had the economic advantage of a mixed economy, based in part on the cultivation of maize, squash, and beans. The Owasco made large cooking pots, indicating that numbers of people must have eaten together. Owasco houses were large, although not as large as the later Iroquois longhouses. Snow has hypothesized that Owasco adopted a matrilocal residence pattern as part of their migration into the thinly populated northern regions. Matrilineal family organization can be adaptive in situations of migration and warfare in that it can dampen male competitiveness and violence within the group. Matrilineal segments can successfully occupy a new region without intergroup competition because hostility can be focused on an external enemy, such as, in this case, the Algonquian hunters and gatherers. In this kind of organization, men from various families marrying into and taking up residence with their wives' families become brothers-in-law to men from various lineages. This breaks up groups of potentially aggressive men who, in a patrilineal system, frequently compete among themselves.

The Iroquois, in the course of warfare, probably abducted women from the populations they were displacing. This process explains the unusual ceramic assemblages found in some sites as the captive women continued to make and use their own styles of ceramics as they lived alongside women making Owasco pottery. Late prehistoric and historic Iroquois longhouses were up to one hundred meters in length, and the people were organized in villages of as many as 500 people. When the Europeans came, they observed six to ten nuclear families per longhouse, formed around women who belonged to the same matrilineal clan segment. Women worked in family units in fields cleared by their clan brothers (who lived nearby). The heaviest cutting and clearing was done by the men, but the rest of the horticultural work was done by women: planting, hoeing, harvesting, and collecting roots, sap for maple syrup, greens, nuts, berries, and small animals. Much of this was communal work supervised by clan matrons. Men married outside their lineage, but usually within the village or a neighboring village. Men were also frequently absent from home, especially as intertribal warfare increased in later prehistory. Both the structure of the family and the absence of men gave women autonomy: the villages were the domain of women, while men were said to own the forest. Social life was characterized by separate spheres for women and men, by reciprocal obligations between the sexes, and by gender roles that were nonhierarchical. In Iroquois society, daughters may have been preferred over sons since a daughter helped increase the size and power of the household. Gender behavior can also be inferred through the analysis of Iroquois pottery, traditionally manufactured by the women. Iroquois pottery was made and discarded locally, whereas pipes, made and used by men, were spread widely over Iroquois territory. Historical data tell us that men traveled widely to exchange gifts, to trade, and to engage in diplomacy and warfare. Historic studies of the Iroquois show that women participated widely in religious activity, including the performance of sacred dances in seasonal ceremonies. In each village, women formed societies for the purpose of maintaining these traditional ceremonies. They also formed mutual aid societies to cultivate private (nonclan) plots. Iroquois mythology illustrates the division of labor by gender: women were always farmers and men hunters and warriors. When the famous Iroquois League was formed, female delegates from the dominant clan segments in each of the constituent nations named the League chiefs (sachems). The women also replaced the sachems and removed them from office when necessary. In later history, when large belts of wampum became important ritual symbols, matrons spoke through belts to the war chiefs. These female elders were not, however, matriarchs. Both female and male authority was clearly defined in this kin organized society. Women's role as food producers was in part a basis for their authority, but it was the extension of the kinship system into political life that benefited Iroquois women.

Williams and Bendremer (1997) have attempted to engender the Late Woodland/Contact period Narragansett, looking at people who both gathered plant and maritime foods and practiced agriculture. They see coastal shell middens as the result of women's activities, especially the large-scale trade in dried shellfish that is historically attested to. They aver that women also made the shell beads and the shell-tempered pottery but admit that they cannot say anything about who had control over these items in use or trade.

Supernumerary Genders

History and ethnography make it perfectly clear that the existence of so-called supernumerary genders was not uncommon among native North American peoples (cf. Roscoe 1991). However, looking for these "extra" genders in the archaeological record has been difficult. Several approaches have been tried, largely those used to try to identify any specific gender, with mixed results. Unfortunately, engendering berdaches,[1] two-spirits, or other supernumerary genders by artifacts in their funeral offerings may prove to be as fraught as similar "engendering" of women's burials has been. Assumptions concerning what is, essentially, cross-dressing in an archaeological culture may prove as wrong as they have in the British Isles, where Iron Age burials of men wearing jewelry were assumed to be the burials of followers of Cybele (who emasculated themselves and wore women's clothing) on the false assumption that local males would emulate one class of Roman males and not wear jewelry (Sherratt, in press). In addition, given that berdaches and other supernumerary genders often married and lived like others, it is difficult to see how one could engender the archaeological record in this regard without specific historic data. It is notable that the first compendium of queer archaeology (*World Archaeology* 32, no. 2, October 1, 2002) was almost in its entirety historic archaeology.

The second problem in ascertaining supernumerary genders or homosexuality in the archaeological record is simply being able to recognize any gender. Here representational art is essential, and it is notable that Munson (2000) has been able to recognize intersexed individuals in Mimbres ceramic paintings. Here hairstyle and costume are fairly strongly gendered, but there are images that show human figures wearing a mixture of women's and men's adornments or who are shown as being of one biological sex but wearing some costume indicators of the other. Munson notes that in her sample of 216 gendered individuals, she had twelve "gender-contrary" figures. Four were women with masculine traits, and eight other figures are people of unknown biological sex with both masculine and feminine traits. Munson suggests several possibilities: that these were women/ men who constituted a third gender among the Mimbres and that the others represent gender ambiguous people or people who have temporarily shifted gender. Since both males who take on women's roles and women who take on male roles are known quite widely throughout North America, all these are possible.

Depictions of sexual behavior in the artistic record are uncommon and seem to be largely relegated to rock art. Hays-Gilpin (2004:figs. 2.22, 2.23, and 2.24) illustrates a number of rock art scenes showing heterosexual intercourse and bestiality but none of homosexuality. She also illustrates (fig. 2.14) a single instance of an ambiguously sexed figure with breasts and a penis (all from the southwestern United States from varying time periods).

In the historic record of the Plains, the institutions of women warriors and Manly Hearts are well known, although, as yet, no prehistoric examples have been identified (Lewis 1941; Medicine 1983). It is not known if women who took these identities were lesbian, although they were considered somewhat different from ordinary women. Some Manly Hearts married women because a successful warrior had to have wives to help him or her in the offering of hospitality. In addition, one could become a warrior or a Manly Heart for a time and then revert to the "normal" female role. However, the institution of Manly Hearts reflects a situation in which aggression and warfare were highly valued, as was vengeance, and represents an adjustment to permit (some) women to take part in these activities in an active manner. Commonly, these women were motivated by desire for revenge against an enemy that had killed a husband or another male kinsman but could also be motivated by personal desire to achieve prestige, power, and wealth. Where we have sufficient documentation, we see that these girls began young, usually as favored children of their fathers, and were indulged and encouraged to be aggressive in games and other activities. A Manly Heart was expected to excel in aspects of life in which women usually had a nondominant role, including the acquisition of property and active performance in ceremonial. Manly Hearts were also sexually aggressive, something considered shameful in an ordinary woman. The role of manly hearted woman was not, as is sometimes claimed, analogous to the role of male berdache because no gender reversal was affected. Manly Hearts, including the famous Woman Chief of the Blackfoot, wore women's clothing and were identified sexually as women, but in terms of gender as approximating the most valued attributes of the male gender.

Hollimon (1997, 2000a) has pioneered the study of supernumerary genders among the historic and ethnographic Chumash and can extend some practices back into the prehistoric past. She notes that the third gender (*'aqi*) among the Chumash was defined as being nonprocreating and consisted of males who assumed some of the clothing and work of women and, perhaps, postmenopausal women (who continued to work and dress as women). She relates the *aqi*, who were professional undertakers, to other craft guilds among the Chumash, pointing out that the (admittedly scanty) demographic evidence for *'aqi* has them distributed in the same manner as members of other craft guilds throughout Chumash territory. Archaeological evidence does show considerable antiquity for the establishment of craft guilds, so the apparent existence of an undertakers guild, whose members were a third gender, is not surprising. Hollimon also notes that several Chumash burials may well be those of *'aqi*. Both are of relatively young men (both about eighteen years of age at the time of death). One shows the same pattern of spinal arthritis characteristic of women, perhaps reflecting his assumption of women's tasks along with the heavy work of undertaking. Another burial, belonging to the Early period (ca. 2500–600 B.C.), included both digging stick weights and basket impressions, tools associated with undertaking and funerary rituals.

Prine (2000) has studied berdaches among the protohistoric and historic Hidatsa of the northern Plains. Evaluating historic and ethnographic source material, she has turned to the large body of archaeological data generated by the Smithsonian River Basin Surveys and feels that she can with some confidence identify one earth lodge, Rock Village Feature 72, as the home of a berdache and his family. Berdaches in Hidatsa society were both heavily involved in ritual and expected to be innovators in this otherwise very traditional society. Rock Village Feature 72 is smaller than other earth lodges, thus reflecting the expected smaller family size of a berdache (they usually married older men and adopted captured children, and a berdache household seems to have generally been approximately half as large as a "normal" household). This earth lodge also has double posts, a unique feature that Prine thinks might express the double-spirited identity of the berdache (who, as part of his woman-affiliated social and economic life, would have constructed the lodge as well as lived in it). Rock Village is also geographically associated with Grandmother's Lodge, the only Hidatsa site specifically associated with the deity Village-Old-Woman, the creator who "captured" young men to become berdaches. While Prine admits that she cannot prove that this earth lodge was the home of a berdache and his family, the archaeological and geographic data strongly suggest that in this case the physical locus of a third-gender individual has been identified.

Other archaeological evidence of third genders is quite rare. Wilson (1997) reports a male in the Powers Phase Turner Cemetery buried with a ceramic vessel, an offering otherwise found only with women, and suggests that the elderly man may have been gendered female. Koehler (1997) discusses female "two-spirits," identifying a nude female warrior representation at Piney Creek (Illinois) and pointing out that "women-men" were reasonably common and tolerated the same as men who partly took the female role (berdaches). Thus, although we know from history and ethnography that supernumary genders were quite common and an accepted part of many Native America societies, locating them archaeologically has yet to be done on any regular basis. Given the importance of third genders in Native America cultures, this should be an ordinary part of archaeological interpretation, along with the recognition that there is more than one gender in human societies in general.

Gendered Archaeology in North America

As in so many fields, engendering the North American past is proceeding by fits and starts. There are genuine areas of disagreement as to what constitutes evidence and what aspects are worthy of study. Given the prevailing "cowboy" identification of (male) archaeologists in the past, convincing many in the field that looking for gender and gender-related behaviors in the archaeological record is valuable and useful is often difficult to impossible. As Bernick (1999:177) remarks in the introduction to her edited volume on gender studies in the Pacific Northwest, we all have stories to tell concerning the amazing androcentrism still present in North American archaeology. However, the growing body of studies that either focus on engendering the North American past or assume that gender is a basic dynamic of human societies and, as such, must be taken into account as part of

economy, social structure, material culture, and so on is growing rapidly and gives one hope that biological and social reality will not continue to be as scarce in American archaeology as it has been in the past.

Note

1. There has been some discussion as to whether the term berdache is an appropriate term for supernumerary genders among North American indigenous peoples. However, the lack of any other general word for this kind of third gender and the fact that individual groups had different terms and, often, somewhat different definitions of what made this third gender suggest that berdache will remain in use as a cover term at least for biological male third genders for some time to come.

References

Albright, Sylvia
    1999   A Working Woman Needs a Good Toolkit. In *Feminist Approaches to Pacific Northwest Archaeology*. Kathryn Bernick, ed. Pp. 183–90. Northwest Anthropological Research Notes, vol. 33, no. 2. Moscow, ID: NARN, Inc.

Arnold, Jeanne E., Michael R. Wals, and Sandra E. Hollimon
    2004   California Archaeology. *Journal of Archaeological Research* 12(1):1–74.

Benedict, James B.
    1993   *Excavations at Bode's Draw: A Women's Work Area in the Mountains Near Estes Park, Colorado*. Ward, CO: Center for Mountain Archaeology.

Bernick, Kathryn
    1999   A Post-Androcentric View of Fraser Delta Archaeology. In *Feminist Approaches to Pacific Northwest Archaeology*. Kathryn Bernick, ed. Pp. 235–44. Northwest Anthropological Research Notes, vol. 33, no. 2. Moscow, ID: NARN, Inc.

Bernick, Kathryn, ed.
    1999   *Feminist Approaches to Pacific Northwest Archaeology*. Northwest Anthropological Research Notes, vol. 33, no. 2. Moscow, ID: NARN, Inc.

Breternitz, David A., Alan C. Swedlund, and Duane C. Anderson
    1997   An Early Burial from Gordon Creek, Colorado. *American Antiquity* 36(2):170–81.

Bridges, Patricia S.
    1991   Skeletal Evidence of Changes in Subsistence Activities between the Archaic and Mississippian Time Periods in Northwestern Alabama. In *What Mean These Bones? Studies in Southeastern Bioarchaeology*. Mary Lucas Powell, Patricia S. Bridges, and Ana María Wagner Mires, eds. Pp. 89–101. Tuscaloosa: University of Alabama Press.

Bruhns, Karen Olsen and Karen E. Stothert
    1999   *Women in Ancient America*. Norman: University of Oklahoma Press.

Brumbach, Hetty Jo and Robert Jarvenpa
- 1997a Ethnoarchaeology of Subsistence Space and Gender: A Subarctic Dene Case. *American Antiquity* 62(3):414–36.
- 1997b Woman the Hunter: From Chipewyan Life-Cycle Dynamics. In *Women in Prehistory: North America and Mesoamerica*. Cheryl Claassen and Rosemary A. Joyce, eds. Pp. 17–32. Philadelphia: University of Pennsylvania Press.

Cassidy, Claire
- 1987 Monod Skeletal Evidence for Prehistoric Subsistence Adaptation in the Central Ohio Valley. In *Paleopathology at the Origins of Agriculture*. Mark N. Cohen and George R. Armelagos, eds. Pp. 307–45. Orlando: Academic Press.

Claassen, Cheryl P.
- 1991 Gender, Shellfishing, and the Shell Mound Archaic. In *Engendering Archaeology: Women and Prehistory*. Joan M. Gero and Margaret W. Conkey, eds. Pp. 276–300. Oxford: Basil Blackwell.
- 1997 Changing Venue: Women's Lives in Prehistoric North America. In *Women in Prehistory: North America and Mesoamerica*. Cheryl Claassen and Rosemary A. Joyce, eds. Pp. 65–87. Philadelphia: University of Pennsylvania Press.
- 2002 Mothers' Workloads and Children's Labor during the Woodland Period. In *In Pursuit of Gender: Worldwide Archaeological Approaches*. Sarah Milledge Nelson and Myriam Rosen-Ayalon, eds. Pp. 225–34. Walnut Creek, CA: AltaMira Press.

Cook, Della Collins
- 1984 Subsistence and Health in the Lower Illinois Valley: Osteological Evidence. In *Paleopathology at the Origins of Agriculture*. Mark N. Cohen and George R. Armelagos, eds. Pp. 235–69. Orlando: Academic Press.

Crass, Barbara A.
- 2000 Gender in Inuit Burial Practices. In *Reading the Body: Representations and Remains in the Archaeological Record*. Alison E. Rautman, ed. Pp. 68–76. Philadelphia: University of Pennsylvania Press.

Crown, Patricia L.
- 2000 Women's Role in Changing Cuisine. In *Women and Men in the Prehispanic Southwest*. Patricia L. Crown, ed. Pp. 221–65. Santa Fe, NM: School of American Research Press.

Crown, Patricia L., ed.
- 2000 *Women and Men in the Prehispanic Southwest*. Santa Fe, NM: School of American Research Press.

Crown, Patricia L., and Suzanne K. Fish
- 1996 Hohokam Gender and Status. *American Anthropologist* 98(4):803–17.

Crown, Patricia L., and W. H. Wills
- 1995 The Origins of Southwestern Ceramic Containers: Women's Time Allocation and Economic Intensification. *Journal of Anthropological Research* 51:173–86.

Davis, Leslie B.
   1993   Paleo-Indian Archaeology in the High Plains and Rocky Mountains of Montana. In *From Kostenki to Clovis: Upper Paleolithic-Paleindian Adaptations*. Olga Soffer and N. D. Praslov, eds. Pp. 263–77. New York: Plenum.
Dick-Bissonette, Linda E.
   1998   Gender and Authority among the Yokoch, Mono, and Miwok of Central California. *Journal of Anthropological Research* 54:49–72.
Dickel, David N., P. D. Schulz, and H. M. McHenry
   1984   Central California: Prehistoric Subsistence and Health. In *Paleopathology at the Origins of Agriculture*. Mark N. Cohen and George R. Armelagos, eds. Pp. 439–62. Orlando: Academic Press.
Diehl, Michael W.
   1996   The Intensity of Maize Processing and Production in Upland Mogollon Pithouse Villages, AD 200–1000. *American Antiquity* 61(1):102–15.
Drooker, Penelope Ballard
   1992   *Mississippian Village Textiles at Wickliffe*. Tuscaloosa: University of Alabama Press.
Eastman, Jane M. and Christopher B. Rodning, editors
   2001   *Archaeological Studies of Gender in the Southeastern United States*. Gainesville: University Press of Florida.
Espinshade, Christopher T.
   1997   Mimbres Pottery, Births, and Gender: A Reconsideration. *American Antiquity* 62(4)733–36.
Feder, Kenneth L.
   2002   *Frauds, Myths, and Mysteries*. Science and Pseudoscience in Archaeology. 4th ed. Pp. 173–74. Boston: McGraw-Hill Mayfield.
Fish, Suzanne K.
   2000   Farming, Foraging, and Gender. In *Women and Men in the Prehispanic Southwest*. Patricia L. Crown, ed. Pp. 169–96. Santa Fe, NM: School of American Research Press.
Frison, George C., R. L. Andrews, J. M. Adovasio, R. C. Carlisle, and Robert Edgar
   1986   A Late Paleoindian Animal Trapping Net from Northern Wyoming. *American Antiquity* 51(2):352–60.
Galloway, Patricia
   1997   Where Have All the Menstrual Huts Gone? The Invisibility of Menstrual Seclusion in the Late Prehistoric Southwest. In *Women in Prehistory: North America and Mesoamerica*. Cheryl Claassen and Rosemary A. Joyce, eds. Pp. 47–64. Philadelphia: University of Pennsylvania Press.
Gero, Joan M.
   1991   Genderlithics: Women's Roles in Stone Tool Production. In *Engendering Archaeology: Women and Prehistory*. Joan M. Gero and Margaret W. Conkey, eds. Pp. 163–93. Oxford: Basil Blackwell.

Gero, Joan M., and Margaret W. Conkey, eds.
   1991   *Engendering Archaeology: Women and Prehistory*. Oxford: Basil Blackwell.
Greaves, Sheila
   1999   The Cutting Edge: A New Look at Microcore Technology. In *Feminist Approaches to Pacific Northwest Archaeology*. Kathryn Bernick, ed. Pp. 235–44. Northwest Anthropological Research Notes, vol. 33, no. 2. Moscow, ID: NARN, Inc.
Green, Thomas J., Bruce Cochran, Todd W. Fenton, James C. Woods, Gene L. Thomas, Larry Tieszen, Mary Anne Davis, and Susanne J. Miller
   1998   The Buhl Burial: A Paleoindian Woman from Southern Idaho. *American Antiquity* 63(3):437–56.
Hays-Gilpin, Kelley A.
   2000a Beyond Mother Earth and Father Sky: Sex and Gender in Ancient Southwestern Visual Arts. In *Reading the Body: Representations and Remains in the Archaeological Record*. Alison E. Rautman, ed. Pp. 165–86. Philadelphia: University of Pennsylvania Press.
   2000b Gender Ideology and Ritual Activities. In *Women and Men in the Prehispanic Southwest*. Patricia L. Crown, ed. Pp. 91–136. Santa Fe, NM: School of American Research Press.
   2004   *Ambiguous Images. Gender and Rock Art*. Walnut Creek, CA: AltaMira Press.
Hegmon, Michelle, and Wenda R. Trevathan
   1996   Gender Anatomical Knowledge, and Pottery Production: Implications of an Anatomically Unusual Birth Depicted on Mimbres Pottery from Southwestern New Mexico. *American Antiquity* 61(4):747–54.
   1997   Response to Comments by LeBlanc, by Espenshade, and by Shaffer et al. *American Antiquity* 62(4):737–39.
Holliman, Sandra E.
   1992   Health Consequences of Sexual Division of Labor among Prehistoric Native Americans: The Chumash of California and the Arikara of the North Plains. In *Exploring Gender Through Archaeology: Selected Papers from the 1991 Boone Conference*. Cheryl Claassen, ed. Pp. 81–88. Madison, WI: Prehistory Press.
   1997   The Third Gender in Native California: Two-Spirit Undertakers among the Chumash and Their Neighbors. In *Women in Prehistory. North America and Mesoamerica*. Cheryl Claassen and Rosemary A. Joyce, eds. Pp. 173–88. Philadelphia: University of Pennsylvania Press.
   2000a Archaeology of the Aqi: Gender and Sexuality in Prehistoric Chumash Society. In *Archaeologies of Sexuality*. Robert A. Schmidt and Barbara L. Voss, eds. Pp. 179–96. London: Routledge.
   2000b Sex, Health, and Gender Roles among the Arikara of the Northern Plains. In *Reading the Body: Representations and Remains in the Archaeological Record*. Alison E. Rautman, ed. Pp. 25–37. Philadelphia: University of Pennsylvania Press.

Howell, Todd L., and Keith W. Kintigh
   1996   Archaeological Identification of Kin Groups Using Mortuary and Biological Data: An Example from the American Southwest. *American Antiquity* 61(3):537–34.

Jackson, Thomas L.
   1991   Pounding Acorn: Women's Production as Social and Economic Focus. In *Engendering Archaeology: Women and Prehistory*. Joan M. Gero and Margaret W. Conkey, eds. Pp. 301–28. Oxford: Basil Blackwell.

Kehoe, Alice
   1987   Points and Lines. In *Powers of Observation: Alternative Views in Archaeology*. Sarah M. Nelson and Alice B. Kehoe, eds. Pp. 23–37. Washington, DC: American Anthropological Association.

Koehler, Lyle
   1997   Earth Mothers, Warriors, Horticulturalists, Artists, and Chiefs: Women among the Mississippian and Mississippian-Oneota Peoples, A.D. 1211 to 1750. In *Women in Prehistory: North America and Mesoamerica*. Cheryl Claassen and Rosemary A. Joyce, eds. Pp. 211–26. Philadelphia: University of Pennsylvania Press.

Lambert, Patricia M.
   1997   Patterns of Violence in Prehistoric Hunter-Gatherer Societies of Coastal Southern California. In *Troubled Times: Violence and Warfare in the Past*. Debra L. Martin and David W. Frayer, eds. Pp. 77–109. Victoria: Gordon and Breach.

LeBlanc, Stephen A.
   1997   A Comment on Hegmon and Trevathan's "Gender, Anatomical Knowledge, and Pottery Production." *American Antiquity* 62(4):723–26.

Lewis, Oscar
   1941   Many-Hearted Women among the Northern Piegan. *American Anthropologist* 39(2):173–87.

Martin, Debra L.
   1977   Violence against Women in the La Plata River Valley (AD 1000–1300). In *Troubled Times: Violence and Warfare in the Past*. Debra L. Martin and David W. Frayer, eds. Pp. 45–76. Victoria: Gordon and Breach.

Marucci, Gina
   1999   Women's Ritual Sites in the Interior of British Columbia: An Archaeological Model. In *From the Ground Up: Beyond Gender Theory in Archaeology*. Nancy L. Wicker and Bettina Arnold, eds. Pp. 75–82. BAR International Series 812. Oxford: Archaeopress.

McGuire, Randall H.
   1992   *Death, Society, and Ideology in a Hohokam Community*. Boulder, CO: Westview.

McNett, Charles W., Jr.
   1985   *Shawnee Minisink: A Stratified Paleoindian-Archaic Site in the Upper Delaware Valley of Pennsylvania*. Orlando: Academic Press.

Medicine, Beatrice
    1983   "Warrior Women": Sex Alternatives for Plains Indian Women. In *The Hidden Half: Studies of Plains Indian Women*. Patricia C. Albers and Beatrice Medicine, eds. Pp. 267–80. Lanham, MD: University Press of America.

Milner, George R., Eve Anderson, and Virginia G. Smith
    1991   Warfare in Late Prehistoric West Central Illinois. *American Antiquity* 56(4):581–603.

Minnis, Paul E.
    1985   Domesticating People and Plants in the Greater Southwest. In *Prehistoric Food Production in North America*. Richard Ford, ed. Pp. 309–39. Anthropological Papers, no. 75. Ann Arbor: Museum of Anthropology, University of Michigan.

Mitchell, Douglas R.
    1991   An Investigation of Two Classic Period Hohokam Cemeteries. *North American Anthropologist* 12(2):109–27.

Mobley-Tanaka, Jeanette L.
    1997   Gender and Ritual Space during the Pithouse to Pueblo Transition: Subterranean Mealing Rooms in the North American Southwest. *American Antiquity* 62(3):437–48.

Mock, Shirley Boteler
    1987   *The Painted Pebbles of the Lower Pecos: A Study of Medium, Form, and Content*. M.A. thesis, University of Texas, San Antonio.

Moss, Madonna
    1993   Shellfish, Gender and status on the Northwest Coast: Reconciling Archaeological, Ethnographic, and Ethnohistoric Records of the Tlingit. *American Anthropologist* 95:631–52.
    1999   Engendering Archaeology in the Pacific Northwest. In *Feminist Approaches to Pacific Northwest Archaeology*. Kathryn Bernick, ed. Pp. 245–62. Northwest Anthropological Research Notes, vol. 33, no. 2. Moscow: NARN, Inc.

Munson, Marit K.
    2000   Sex, Gender, and Status: Human Images from the Classic Mimbres. *American Antiquity* 65(1):127–44.

O'Brien, Patricia J.
    1990   Evidence for the Antiquity of Gender Roles in the Central Plains Tradition. In *Powers of Observations: Alternative Views in Archaeology*. Sarah M. Nelson and Alice B. Kehoe, eds. Pp. 61–72. Archaeological Papers of the American Anthropological Association 2. Washington, DC: American Anthropological Association.

Osgood, Cornelius
    1940   *Ingalik Material Culture*. Yale University Publications in Anthropology, no. 22. New Haven, CT: Yale University Press.

Pratt, Heather
　1999　The Search for Gender in Early Northwest Coast Prehistory. In *Feminist Approaches to Pacific Northwest Archaeology*. Kathryn Bernick, ed. Pp. 229–34. Northwest Anthropological Research Notes, vol. 33, no. 2. Moscow, ID: NARN, Inc.

Prezzano, Susan C.
　1997　Warfare, Women, and Households: The Development of Iroquois Culture. In *Women in Prehistory: North America and Mesoamerica*. Cheryl Claassen and Rosemary A. Joyce, eds. Pp. 88–99. Philadelphia: University of Pennsylvania Press.

Prine, Elizabeth
　2000　Searching for Third Genders: Towards a Prehistory of Domestic Space in Middle Mississippian Moundville. In *Archaeologies of Sexuality*. Robert A. Schmidt and Barbara L. Voss, eds. Pp. 197–219. London: Routledge.

Roscoe, Will
　1991　*The Zuni Man-Woman*. Albuquerque: University of New Mexico Press.

Sassaman, Kenneth E.
　1992a　Gender and Technology at the Archaic-Woodland Transition. In *Exploring Gender Through Archaeology: Selected Papers from the 1991 Boone Conference*. Cheryl Claassen, ed. Pp. 71–80. Madison, WI: Prehistory Press.
　1992b　Lithic Technology and the Hunter-Gatherer Sexual Division of Labor. *North American Archaeologist* 13(3):249–62.

Shaffer, Brian S., Karen M. Gardner, and Harry J. Shafer
　1997　An Unusual Birth Depicted in Mimbres Pottery: Not Cracked Up to What It Is Supposed to Be. *American Antiquity* 62(4):727–32.

Sherratt, Melanie
　In press　Engendering Romano-British Cemeteries: Acknowledging Difference, Understanding the Past. Unpublished paper presented at the 15th Anniversary Gender Conference: Que(e)rying Archaeology, Chacmool 2004, University of Calgary.

Smith, Kevin E.
　1991　The Mississippian Figurine Complex and Symbolic Systems of the Southeastern United States. In *The New World Figurine Project*. Vol. 1. Terry Stocker, ed. Pp. 125–26. Provo, UT: Research Press.

Snow, Dean
　1995　Migration in Prehistory: The Northern Iroquoian Case. *American Antiquity* 60(1):59–79.

Spector, Janet D.
　1991　What This Awl Means: Towards a Feminist Archaeology. In *Engendering Archaeology: Women and Prehistory*. Joan M. Gero and Margaret W. Conkey, eds. Pp.407–11. Oxford: Basil Blackwell.

1994 *What This Awl Means: Feminist Archaeology at a Whapeton Dakota Village.* St. Paul: Minnesota Historical Society Press.

Spielmann, Katherine
   1995 Glimpses of Gender in the Prehistoric Southwest. *Journal of Anthropological Research* 51:91–102.

Sturtevant, William C., gen. ed.
   1978 *Handbook of North American Indians.* 17 vols. Washington, DC: Smithsonian Institution Press.

Sundstrom, Linea
   2002 Steel Awls for Stone Age Plainswomen: Rock Art, Religion, and the Hide Trade on the Northern Plains. *Plains Anthropologist* 47(181):99–119.

Surovell, Todd A.
   2000 Early Paleoindian Women, Children, Mobility, and Fertility. *American Antiquity* 65(3):493–508.

Vega, Garcilaso "El Inca" de la
   1951 *The Florida of the Inca.* Translated and edited by John G. and Jeannette J. Varner. Austin: University of Texas Press.

Waters, Michael R.
   1986 Sulphur Springs Woman: An Early Human Skeleton from Southeastern Arizona. *American Antiquity* 51(2):361–64.

Watson, Patty Jo, and Mary C. Kennedy
   1991 The Development of Horticulture in the Eastern Woodlands of North America: Women's Role. In *Engendering Archaeology: Women and Prehistory.* Joan M. Gero and Margaret W. Conkey, eds. Pp. 255–75. Oxford: Basil Blackwell.

Weist, Kathryn
   1983 Beast of Burden and Menial Slaves: Nineteenth Century Observations of Northern Plains Indian Women. In *The Hidden Half: Studies of Plains Indian Women.* Patricia C. Albers and Beatrice Medicine, eds. Pp. 29–52. Lanham, MD: University Press of America.

Williams, Mary Beth, and Jeffrey Bendremer
   1997 The Archaeology of Maize, Pots, and Seashells: Gender Dynamics in Late Woodland and Contact-Period New England. In *Women in Prehistory: North America and Mesoamerica.* Cheryl Claassen and Rosemary A. Joyce, eds. Pp. 136–49. Philadelphia: University of Pennsylvania Press.

Wilkinson, Richard G.
   1997 Violence against Women: Raiding and Abduction in Prehistoric Michigan. In *Troubled Times: Violence and Warfare in the Past.* Debra L. Martin and David W. Frayer, eds. Pp. 21–43. Victoria: Gordon and Breach.

Wilson, Diane
   1997 Gender, Diet, Health, and Social Status in the Mississippian Powers Phase Turner Cemetery Population. In *Women in Prehistory: North America and Mesoamer-*

ica. Cheryl Claassen and Rosemary A. Joyce, eds. Pp. 119–35. Philadelphia: University of Pennsylvania Press.

Zacharias, Sandra

1999   Feminist Methodologies in Archaeology: Implications for the Northern Northwest Coast. In *Feminist Approaches to Pacific Northwest Archaeology.* Kathryn Bernick, ed. Pp. 219–28. Northwest Anthropological Research Notes, vol. 33, no. 2. Moscow, ID: NARN, Inc.

Gender in South American Archaeology   25

VIRGINIA EBERT AND THOMAS C. PATTERSON

GENDER STUDIES IN South American archaeology are still in their infancy. While a few studies are specifically concerned with gender and its implications, many more mention biological or anatomical differences between males and females and sometimes draw inferences about health or the division of labor. Thus, the concept is relatively undeveloped in South America except for the latest periods. At the present time, most of the published data come from western South America—the area that includes northern Chile, northwestern Argentina, highland Bolivia, coastal and highland Peru, and Ecuador (e.g., Bruhns and Stothert 1999) (see figure 25.1 for a map identifying sites relevant to the text). The reconstructions of earlier societies in the area are based exclusively on archaeological data, such as mortuary analyses, skeletal remains, iconography, or the use of space; the reconstructions of the Inca state and its immediate predecessors rely on both archaeological and ethnohistorical information.

Gender refers to cultural interpretations of the significance of sexual differences; thus, it is a culturally and historically contingent system that expresses social identities, relations, and roles. It also intersects potentially with the division of labor, class structures, and other culturally constituted systems of ethnoracial identities, relations, and roles (Brumfiel 1992; Sacks 1989; Stolcke 1993). In order to understand how these articulations occurred in particular societies, it is useful to distinguish technical divisions of labor from the social division of labor. Technical divisions of labor refer to task specialization and not to social stratification. Examples of technical divisions of labor structured by gender and sharing are provided by the households of numerous lowland forest peoples of South America in which women plant and tend garden plots cleared by their husbands or cook the meat that men bring back from hunting trips (Siskind 1973). The social division of labor refers to the presence of a class structure in which the members of one social class appropriate the labor or goods produced by the members of other social classes. In the Inca state, for example, gender and class cross-

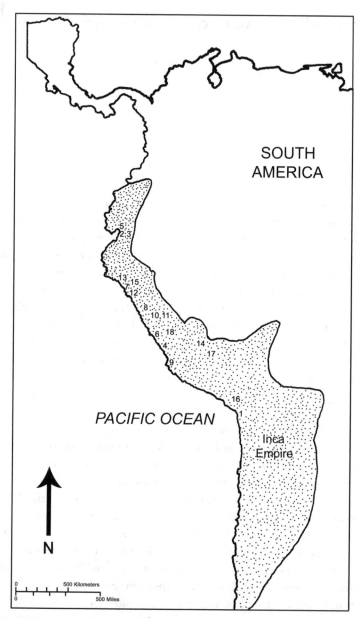

Figure 25.1. Sites and regions in western South America referred to in the text.
Key: **1** Chinchorro, **2** Las Vegas, **3** Real Alto, **4** Paloma, **5** Capa Perro, **6** Ancón-Chillón, **7** Huaca Prieta, **8** La Galgada, **9** Paracas, **10** Recuay, **11** Queyash Alto, **12** Moche polity, **13** Sipan, **14** Ayacucho, **15** Sicán polity, **16** Moquegua, **17** Cuzco (stippled area), Inca Empire.

cut one another in a complex manner. As a result, royal women or noblewomen, women who were retainers of the state, and commoner women experienced everyday life in remarkably different ways in this sixteenth-century society.

Equally significant is the concept of ethnicity. An ethnic community or group—an *ethnie* in French and *etnia* in Spanish—has a number of distinctive features that underpin and delineate the boundaries, sense of belonging, and sentiments of those individuals who claim membership. These include (1) a common or collective name known and used by members who identify and distinguish themselves from others; (2) myths of origin and descent that provide both a place of origin and a location in the world and a framework of meaning that makes sense of the community's experiences, defines its essence, inspires collective action, and allows its members to define themselves in relation to others; (3) a sense of shared history that unites successive generations, each with their own particular experiences; (4) a shared culture, such as customs, languages, arts, music, and symbols, that uniquely marks identity and boundaries; (5) an association with a symbolic, geographical center, a homeland, in which the members reside or to which they return; and (6) a sense of community and solidarity (Jones 1996; Smith 1986; Wobst 1977). Ethnicity and ethnic groups are the products of particular circumstances and have their origins in historically specific social forces (Comaroff 1987).

Archaic and Formative Cultures

Information for the early period derives from Chinchorro sites on the north coast of Chile (ca. 7000–2100 B.C.); from Las Vegas and Valdivia sites in coastal Ecuador (ca. 8200–1600 B.C.); from Yutopian, an early formative site in the chronology of northwestern Argentina (ca. 600 B.C.–A.D. 600); and from Paloma and other formative sites in coastal Peru (ca. 5000–400 B.C.).[1]

Fifteen sites on the northern coast of Chile, spanning the period from about 7000 to 2100 B.C., have yielded nearly 300 Chinchorro mummies (Arriaza 1995, 1996, 1998; Aufderheide et al. 1993; Guillén 1992; Rivera 1995). The Chinchorro sites, which reflect a maritime subsistence strategy, varied from just a few houses to about 180 and included cemeteries holding a few individuals to more than one hundred. Mummies were typically placed in shallow pits in the sand with few grave goods. The mummies are the result of a complex preparation process that involved disarticulation, the removal of organs, defleshing, and reassembly with various plants. The reassembled human body was then covered with clay or paste that was modeled to include sexual characteristics, painted, and occasionally covered with human skin and wigs. Some mummies exhibited cranial modification. The elaborate preparation of the mummies was time consuming and quite likely involved some degree of specialized knowledge, although not necessarily full-time specialists. Grave goods were diverse but utilitarian and thus do not indicate social differentiation in the communities. Further, the artificial mummification process was applied to infants, children, women, and men. At different times, the mummies of children and some adults underwent particularly elaborate treatment.

These individuals came from small, relatively sedentary, non- or preagricultural communities whose residents relied heavily on marine resources—notably sea lions, fish, and shellfish—acquired from nearby beaches, rocky headlands, and deep water. Many of the male crania had auditory exostoses, indicating prolonged periods of immersion in cold waters of the Chilean coast. This implies that there was a gendered division of labor and that men rather than women engaged in deep-sea fishing and shellfish diving. In addition, many males had stress fractures in the lumbar region, suggesting that they carried heavy objects, like large fish or small sea lions. Many female skeletons showed changes to ankle bones produced by squatting for prolonged periods, possibly to process shellfish. We infer from this that women probably collected terrestrial foods and may have harvested shellfish from shallow littoral waters.

A technical division of labor based on gender and age meant that no individual in a Chinchorro community was able to procure or produce all of the goods essential for life. It necessitated cooperation—sharing the products of one's labor with one or more members of the opposite sex and different generations in return for a portion of the products of their labor. Kinship reflects the linkage between sharing and the division of labor (Siskind 1978). Each item that was acquired or produced, such as shellfish or twined mats, potentially moved through a circuit of individuals before it was used or consumed.

The small number of people who resided in Chinchorro settlements probably meant that many camps and villages were too small to be autonomous, independent demographic entities. Thus, we infer that the various settlements of the region were linked by matrimonial mobility as men and women moved between groups to find suitable mates and that the composition of the various settlements mirrored this practice. We also infer that the relations of production and the relations of reproduction operated at different levels. While the appropriation of food and material occurred at the level of the household and perhaps the village, neither level was able to ensure demographic replacement and the continuity of the community. Their social and demographic reproduction was underwritten by relations and practices that operated between rather than within the communities. Contact with the highlands and the Amazon jungle, for example, is suggested by tool technology, camelid fur, tropical plants, and feathers from tropical birds (Arriaza 1995:47).

The residents of these communities had a number of health problems. Infant and childhood mortality was high. Many individuals were anemic because of tapeworms they acquired from eating raw or undercooked fish and sea lions. Both men and women suffered from traumatic injuries, leg bone infections, and arthritis. Some women had osteoporosis, and some men had impaired hearing because of the auditory exostoses. In spite of their numerous ailments, afflictions, and injuries, the residents of the Chinchorro communities were probably healthier than the members of later sedentary, agricultural communities in the region (Arriaza 1995:63–82).

Archaeologists investigating the Santa Elena Peninsula in coastal Ecuador have located thirty-one Las Vegas Phase sites and one hundred sites yielding Valdivia Phase cultural remains. The former date around 8200 to 5450 B.C. and the latter 4400 to 1600 B.C. (Lathrap et al. 1977; Marcos 2003; Marcos and García de Manrique 1988; Raymond 2003; Stothert 1985, 1988, 2003; Ubelaker 1980, 2003; Zeidler 2000). Virtually all discussion of the Las Vegas Phase is based on materials from Site 80, while discussion of the Valdivia Phase derives largely from Real Alto, especially the cultural remains of the Valdivia III occupation (2800–2400 B.C.).

The residents of the Las Vegas Phase communities were sedentary or semisedentary foragers who made use of a wide variety of terrestrial and marine resources (Stothert 1985, 1988). In the fifth millennium B.C., some of them may have grown gourds and possibly other plants in house gardens as one of numerous subsistence activities including foraging, fishing, and hunting. One hundred ninety-two individuals were excavated at Site 80 from primary and secondary burials as well as from three ossuaries. The numbers of males and females among the 118 sexed adults were roughly equal (Ubelaker 1980). In the ossuaries, adult males and females were equally represented; however, two-thirds of the twenty-six primary burials contained females. This suggests that deceased males and females were treated differently—that is, males may have been exhumed and moved more frequently than females, indicating different statuses or roles for female and male *ancestors* (Bruhns and Stothert 1999:62). Because of the practice of exhumation, Bruhns and Stothert have suggested that females and subadults were more likely to have durable offerings than males.

The Valdivia Phase communities engaged in diverse subsistence practices involving wild and domesticated plants, terrestrial mammals, and marine resources (fish, turtles, and shellfish). Given their geographical distribution and the ecological diversity of the Santa Elena Peninsula and its environs, there were probably subtle and potentially significant variations in subsistence activities from one settlement to another. Even slight differences of emphasis might yield significant variations in labor organization and specialization and technical divisions of labor. Within and between the contemporary settlements located in different settings, there was probably some part-time craft specialization beyond subsistence needs and the intra- or intercommunity circulation of surplus goods, such as pottery, or perhaps even labor. It is not clear whether such specialized tasks were structured by gender or age. Zeidler (2000) suggests that between 2800 and 2400 B.C. (Valdivia III), there was some degree of social differentiation or ranking within the kin-organized community at Real Alto so that at least one individual or subgroup in the town had ascribed rather than achieved status or rank. He goes on to suggest that this pattern of social differentiation was subsequently transformed and that a new pattern emerged by the beginning of the second millennium B.C. (Terminal Valdivia).

The size and spatial organization of the Real Alto settlement changed dramatically toward the middle of the third millennium B.C. The early village, which consisted of small houses around a circular or U-shaped central plaza, gave way to a ceremonial precinct with dual mounds in the middle of an elongated plaza surrounded by an outer ring of houses that were both larger and more permanent than their predecessors. The change in domestic architecture possibly reflects a shift from nuclear to extended families (Zeidler 2000). A fiesta house was built on one mound, and a charnel house was erected on the other. The principal burial in the stone-lined crypt at the charnel house was an adult female. Outside the crypt, another tomb contained an adult male and seven secondary burials of adult and subadult males. The remains of another eleven individuals were also found in the charnel house, which has been described as the locus of interment for high-status individuals (Zeidler 2000). The burial of the female with eight males has been interpreted as the sequential, sacrificial offerings of eight males to the female interred in the crypt (Lathrap et al. 1977). Klepinger (1979) has argued that the demographic characteristics of a population of seventy-two skeletons from Real Alto burials do not support the claim of male sacrifice and proposes instead that the close proximity of the skeletons at the charnel house represents a high-status family group.

The second burial discussed is that of a young adult female from the Terminal Valdivia settlement of Capa Perro. The associated grave goods—including a feline snout, a bat, a small incised pot, and a female figurine—have been linked with shamanic practices and suggest that women were engaged in these activities (Zeidler 2000). In addition, the large number of female figurines found in Valdivia houses and associated refuse deposits suggest that they may also have been integral to various domestic and shamanic rituals and, further, that these practices developed through the entire Valdivia social tradition.

In northwestern Argentina, archaeologists have excavated at the site of Yutopian (Gero and Scattolin 2002). Small, egalitarian communities with subsistence based on agriculture characterize the early formative period (ca. 600 B.C.–A.D. 600) of this area. In the central region of northwestern Argentina, exotic goods, such as specialized ceramics and articles of gold, bronze, and copper, were exchanged. The site of Yutopian contains stone constructions that probably correspond to ten groups of structures and enclosures as well as a series of agricultural terraces. Four semisubterranean house floors in one of the sectors were excavated; three of the structures share a common patio area, while the fourth sits apart from other structures and has its own partially enclosed patio area.

The focus of Gero and Scattolin's (2002) analysis is a group of grinding stones and manos from one structure and two raised, ringed hearths, one from the same structure as the grinding stones and the second from the structure that sits apart. Four grinding stones and manos were clustered together with a fifth separated from this group. The concentrated grinding stones were larger than the single one and were variable in size, area of grinding surface, and degree of use. Gero and Scattolin have inferred that they reflect communal food preparation by women, probably undertaken for multiple households or an extended household. They also note that ethnographic evidence from Andean households suggests an internal diversity of roles and relations among women in a single household. The areas around the two hearths contained plant remains signifying food and beverage preparation, again suggestive of women's work and spaces. However, one hearth was also associated with clay-soil particles turned to glass, indicative of temperatures much higher than required for cooking food. Fragmented ceramic tubes found at the second hearth were probably used to blow into the fire to intensify the heat. In addition, raw copper silicates and fragmented polished stone laminating hammers were found. In sum, then, it is likely that at least one hearth was used not only for food production for household consumption but also for some stage of producing copper artifacts for circulation outside the community.

Gero and Scattolin (2002) argue that the evidence for two disparate productive activities within the household illustrates the need for more nuanced understandings of concepts of gender and economic specialization. For the production of food, "household labor is segregated or divided by gender (i.e., a division of labor) to create separate, marked and specialized workforces that are interdependent for some vital needs," while for copper production, "household labor is integrated by gender to bind personnel into a larger operating body vis-à-vis other similar coordinated households" (Gero and Scattolin 2002:171).

Several hundred archaeological sites dating to the period before about 400 B.C. have been located on the central and north-central coasts of Peru. The focus of this section is the central coastal site of Paloma (ca. 6000–3000 B.C.), a series of slightly later settlements in the Ancón-Chillón region immediately to the north, and two sites—Huaca Prieta and La Galgada—located, respectively, on the northern coast and near farmland in the upper Santa Valley.

The subsistence economy of Paloma was dominated by fishing, littoral harvesting, hunting, and foraging (Quilter 1988). Households were the basic units of production and consumption, judging by the presence of storage pits near them and the interment of males, females, and children beneath the floors of houses that were still occupied. The skeletal remains and associated grave goods suggest a technical division of labor based on age and gender. Auditory exostoses were common among adolescent and adult males and absent in females. As noted previously, this indicates that adolescent and adult males procured deep-water resources. Tooth wear resulting from the processing of fibers indicates that females and older males made mats. The presence of weaving implements in the graves of this group further substantiates the view that the division of labor was based on both gender and age.

The health status of Paloma Phase people broadly resembled those from the northern coast of Chile. There was high infant and childhood mortality, and various age-related afflictions, like arthritis, were common. High incidences of pulmonary ailments, including tuberculosis, and the fact that lower-back problems affected both males and females and most age-groups distinguish the Paloma populations from their contemporaries in Chile. At the site of Paloma, there was a significant diminution of sexual dimorphism in musculature toward the end of the occupation (Benfer 1984, 1986, 1990; Quilter 1988).

The small size of the Paloma communities—twenty-five to seventy-five individuals—meant that they were not independent demographic units but rather that they were linked to other bands and villages in the region by the matrimonial mobility of men and women. Thus, the social and demographic reproduction of these settlements was underwritten by relations and practices that operated between communities and not within them (Patterson 1999).

In the late fourth millennium B.C., some Paloma communities added horticulture to their subsistence activities (Moseley 1975). Early cultigens—such as gourds and cotton—were not foodstuffs but rather were used to make fabrics, more efficient fishing line and nets, and net floats. These added to the productivity of fishing and allowed those communities to pursue seasonal plant cultivation that involved delayed use and consumption. This had several long-term consequences. One was the steadily increasing importance of cultivated plants in everyday diets. A second involved a spatial reorganization of work and the appearance of economically specialized fishing and farming communities in the Ancón-Chillón region of the central coast and the apparent increased circulation of goods among the settlements. Broadly contemporary sites located to the north—specifically Huaca Prieta and La Galgada—provide additional information about this new division of labor. Judging by the distribution of auditory exostoses, all the males and females at the coastal settlement of Huaca Prieta procured marine resources, and all the males and females at the inland settlement of La Galgada farmed. In this manner, the gendered division of labor that existed during the early Paloma society was transformed. This may also explain the diminished sexual dimorphism noted previously (Malina 1988; Patterson 1999; Tattersall 1985).

This spatial reorganization of labor underpinned the intensification of agricultural production on the central and north-central coasts of Peru; it also provided the foundations for the construction of nearly forty, enormous U-shaped platform mounds in the region. Each of these involved millions of person-days of labor to build and clearly drew on labor power from many neighboring settlements (Burger 1992). Some archaeologists have described these as state-based societies (e.g., Haas et al. 1987). Others have described them as kin-organized communities lacking social class structures (Burger 1992; Patterson 1999). The two perspectives involve different understandings and constructions of gender relations, gender hierarchy, and gender roles. The former viewpoint implies the existence of class structures, gender hierarchy, and differentiation between the gendered activities of elite and commoner women. The latter perspective implies that no group in the community was permanently removed from direct production, that gender hierarchy was poorly developed, and that there were minimal differences between the gendered activities of women with higher and lower status.

Early Andean States and Their Contemporaries

While there is disagreement about whether there were state-based societies in the central Andes during the second millennium B.C., there is general agreement that some existed by about 400 B.C. State formation was a patchy process that proceeded unevenly over the next thousand years. One consequence of this uneven development was that, at any given moment, the social fabric of the central Andes resembled a mosaic composed of interconnected tribes, chiefdoms, and states. A second consequence was the crystallization of ethnicity and of ethnic groups with boundaries marked by regionally distinct styles, especially pottery. This also implies that, at any given moment, there was a regional diversity in the kinds of gender relations that prevailed. Our understanding of gender identities and relations in the central Andes after about 400 B.C. is based primarily on burials and their associated grave goods and on iconographic representations.

Embroidered textiles from the Paracas Necropolis on the southern coast of Peru that date to the closing century of the first millennium B.C. provide insight into the technical divisions of labor in the organization of a craft (Bird 1961; Paul and Niles 1985). The production of the elaborately decorated Paracas fabrics began with a plain-woven cotton mantle, often many feet in length. After the cloth was woven, there were at least two subsequent stages in the creation of an embroidered mantle. First, a skilled artisan established both the overall pattern of the design and the specific design elements that would be repeated. Then a number of individuals with different skill levels embroidered the design elements on different parts of the same fabric, apparently working simultaneously. The artisans in this case are assumed to have been women because of ethnographic and historical analogy that often indicated associations of women and weaving implements, yarns, and dyes. While archaeologists often remark about the richness of Paracas-Nasca imagery and iconography on textiles and pottery, it has been noted that representations of women on pottery vessels did not occur until the middle of the fourth century A.D., limiting the degree to which the iconography of the southern Peruvian coast can be used to construct arguments about the significance of gender and gender differences (Silverman and Proulx 2002:31).

The Recuay society that developed in the Callejon de Huaylas during the middle of the first millennium A.D. was, like many neighboring groups in the central Andes, internally differentiated but probably not class stratified (Gero 2001:17, 40–43). It was not state based like the Moche polity, its nearby contemporary on the northern coast. If iconographic distinctions between males and females were blurred in earlier artistic traditions, they were now expressed in Recuay art and in the art of other societies of the first millennium A.D.; that is, gender distinctions had become salient in northern Peru. In Moche, specific individuals were probably depicted on portrait-head jars. In Recuay, however, social roles rather than individuals were represented, as men and women were differentiated by distinctive postures, gestures, activities, and associations. One common representation depicts a man with a llama. Another theme in Recuay ceramic art is a ceremony in which both men and women are participants. There is also archaeological evidence of such ceremonies near a high-status household in Queyash Alto that was closely associated with deposits containing many fine-quality ceramics, cut spondylus, women's *tupu* pins, and large quantities of butchered llama. The iconographic and archaeological evidence suggest that women prepared beer and roasted llama and served and consumed them; they also may have played panpipes and drums at the festivities. Because women were also interred beneath house floors, Gero suggests that the women of Recuay society were the protectors or nurturers of the house or kin group, while wealth in the form of llama herds and prestige were associated with a male role.

The Moche polity or polities developed on the northern coast of Peru around A.D. 300 to 400 (Bawden 1996). These were class-stratified, state-based societies. Literally hundreds of Moche tombs have been excavated. While the vast majority of these were commoners, about a dozen tombs from half a dozen sites—notably Sipan, San José de Moro, the Huaca del Sol, and the Huaca de la Luna—were lavishly furnished with hundreds of pottery vessels, silver and gold objects, and textiles. Ruling-class individuals were interred in these tombs, often with accompanying retainers or sacrificial victims.

What follows is concerned with powerful, ruling-class women, not commoner women. Vogel (2003) compares data from the tombs with Moche iconographic representations of supernatural beings on pottery, murals, and textiles. While this iconographic imagery was concerned with ritual, it also represented actual events and personages. The imagery began in the late sixth century A.D. and became increasingly more common in the seventh and eighth centuries. The tombs at Sipan contained ruling-class males who were identified with the Warrior and Owl Priest roles identified in Moche art. In addition, elite females interred at San José de Moro have been identified with priestesses in the same artistic themes. Other iconographic data indicate that women participated as musicians in these activities. This and other evidence indicates that ruling-class women played prominent roles in important ritual activities. Vogel has inferred that the power of these women extended beyond their participation in ritual; that is, they wielded political and economic power as well.

Another major episode of class and state formation occurred in the Ayacucho area of the south-central highlands of Peru toward the middle of the seventh century A.D. and was marked by the expansion of the Wari state. This involved shifts in power relations and the accumulation of wealth (Cook 2004:159–63). Burial data from Conchopata indicate that the female members of "a wealthy, intermediate elite class" were interred with a different array of goods from their male counterparts; these objects included blackware face-neck jars, copper *tupu* pins, spondylus, and turquoise. While women were not widely represented in the iconography on textiles, two depictions occur on elaborately decorated, oversized urns that are widely thought to have been used in the brewing of beer for public ceremonies. The first consists of one woman with a nude torso who appears on the interior of an urn; the other consists of two women facing one another, each clad in a long garment held in place by a belt at the waist and a *tupu* pin at the shoulder (Cook 2004:159–63). It is assumed, by analogy with later Inca society, that women made and served the beer. Both males and females were also depicted in mold-made figurines in Ayacucho. In contrast to the Moche and Recuay traditions mentioned previously, women were not portrayed breast-feeding, participating in erotic scenes, or as submissive. Cook (2004:161) suggests that "equivalent social value was assigned to male and female representations." She also suggests that "Wari artisans [intentionally] employed genres that defied easy recognition of the sexes" (160).

The Sicán polity that existed in the Lambayeque Valley on the northern coast of Peru toward the end of the first millennium A.D. was class stratified and state based. The contents of a shaft tomb near the Huaca Loro platform mound provide important insight into the class, ethnic, and gender dimensions of this society (Shimada et al. 2004). The principal individual in the tomb was a middle-aged male flanked by two groups of young adult females. There were nine individuals in each of the two groups of females, referred to as the North and South Groups. Some of the individuals in each group were primary burials, while others were secondary interments. The grave goods suggest, on the whole, that this was a high-status burial and that the different patterns of association marked culturally significant differences in the society. A textile wrapped around the principal figure extended along the floor of the tomb to the South Group women, suggesting a special relationship between them. Mitochondrial DNA (mtDNA) analyses indicate that four maternal lines are represented in the two groups of women. Those in the North Group were descended from two mothers, and those in the South Group were descended from two different women. Both mtDNA and dental trait analyses indicate the individuals in the South Group were more homogeneous than their counterparts in the North Group. There are further significant distinctions between the two groups. The South Group women were interred with locally manufactured Middle Sicán/Lambayeque pottery vessels, whereas the North Group women were interred with Moche ceramics. In addition, the health status of the South Group individuals was higher than that of members of the North Group, suggesting that there were also intraclass or interclass differences between them. The excavators have argued (1) that the women in two groups were not sacrificed and (2) that the special relation between the women of the South Group and the principal male may imply endogamy (Shimada et al. 2004:378–86).

Using burial data and associated grave goods, Clark (1993:780–94, 846, 860–64) has made two important points about gender identities in the kin-stratified communities of the Moquegua Valley in far southern Peru during the first half of the second millennium A.D. As part of the complex division of labor in the Estuquiña textile tradition, based on gender, age, ability, and other factors, she suggests that the twist direction of yarn may reflect gender differences. Her second point was that there were possibly ambiguous gender roles in the communities. One individual morphologically identified as an adult male was interred wearing items of women's apparel; his hair was also dressed in a style commonly worn by women. She suggests that this person enjoyed high status within the community. The second individual, an elderly female, was interred wearing heavily worn clothing, including several items of men's apparel. This suggests that gender blurring or ambiguity may have been linked with both age and poverty.

The Incas and Their Predecessors

The Inca empire was based on conquest and stretched nearly 3,000 miles along the Andes Mountains. From Cuzco, the imperial capital located in one of the mountain valleys of the southern highlands of Peru, the Incas exerted varying degrees of political control over peoples from the Ecuador–Colombian frontier in the north through Bolivia to central Chile and northwestern Argentina in the south. The Inca state was short lived. It took shape in the 1430s, grew explosively during the middle of the fifteenth century, and was still expanding even as it was beginning to disintegrate under the weight of its own contradictions in the 1520s on the eve of the Spanish invasion in 1532.

The expansion of the Inca state brought diverse kinds of societies—tribes, chiefdoms, and other states—under the nominal leadership of the Inca ruling class. The Incas sought to establish economic and political control over the peoples it vanquished or incorporated peacefully into the imperial state. This involved three main mechanisms: forging alliances through marriages of the Inca rulers with ruling-class women from groups that were being enmeshed in tributary relations, appropriating labor tribute from subject peoples, and creating royal estates by appropriating agricultural or pastoral lands in provincial areas.

Inca expansion and conquest had both class and gendered dimensions. Local ruling families or classes experienced incorporation differently from commoners, and women from ruling groups experienced it differently from commoner women. Relatively egalitarian groups from Jauja in the central Peruvian highlands that were incorporated into the imperial state in the 1450s were reorganized into a polity, presumably to make administration easier. The Incas also sponsored a new crop, maize, which had not been commonly grown in the Jauja region earlier. The impact of these changes can be seen in various ways. Maize production for local and state consumption involved new patterns of agricultural work. The political sphere created by the Incas involved gatherings, obligatory work, feasting, and rituals that preferentially involved men. Men's participation in the political sphere increased, at the expense of women whose public activities declined. The shift to extrahousehold activities underwrote changes in diet and in the nature of women's work within the household. Because of their participation in the public sphere, men began to consume more maize beer and meat than women. At the same time, women's work intensified as they prepared more food, especially beer, for the public feasts (Hastorf 1991).

The Inca rulers formed strategic alliances by marrying women from the ruling families of ethnic groups that were incorporated into the imperial state. This not only gave the Inca rulers access to the labor power of wives' kin but also access to lands to support their wives and the offspring from these unions. The earliest of these were the intravalley and regional alliances that were made before the rapid expansion of the state after A.D. 1440 (Bauer and Covey 2002). These marriages had three important consequences. First, they exacerbated the fact that there was no recognized and generally accepted means of succession to the Inca throne; efforts to create acceptable rules were always reactive, responses to the crises that typically occurred when rulers died or were killed. Second, marriage to an Inca ruler served to enhance the power of these women vis-á-vis their male relatives since they were largely responsible for enhancing the wealth and prestige of their kinsmen—which was the purpose of the marriages in the first place. As the wives of the rulers and the mothers of potential heirs to the throne, they and kinsmen played crucial roles in struggles over succession to the throne (Silverblatt 1976, 1987). Third, the Inca ruling class was restructured through the inclusion of children from these marriages. These children simultaneously belonged to the landholding corporations (*panaqas*) established by their Inca fathers and had allegiances through their mothers to ethnic communities in other parts of the state (Patterson 1991:69–97).

The division of labor in the Inca state was structured by age and gender as well as by social class. Like all states, the Incas were obsessed with counting and classifying subjects in order to collect labor tribute. This appears in their efforts to divide subject populations in decimal units (Julien 1982). It also appears in the censuses they conducted regularly that recorded men and women in terms of ten distinct age categories, ranging from infancy to old age. The productive activities performed by men and women shifted with age. For example, adolescents of both sexes herded; married men farmed and performed labor service for the state, including as warriors; and married women made different kinds of cloth (Rowe 1958). In addition, there were four other categories of individuals, some of which crosscut those of the census as well as each other. These were the *mitimas, camayos, yanas*, and *acllas*. The *mitimas* were men (and presumably their families) who worked in areas that were physically separated from their natal communities. The *camayos* were men who were full-time craft specialists or managers, some of whom resided and worked in their communities of origin and others who did not; both their status and specialty were apparently hereditary. The *yanas* were removed from their natal communities as young men, and most remained both physically and structurally separated from them as they toiled in later life for the Inca ruler. The *acllas* were women who had been removed from their communities of origin as young girls, and they too remained physically and structurally separated from them for the remainder of their lives (Rowe 1982).

Let us consider the *acllas* and *camayos*. The *acllas* were taken as eight- or nine-year-old girls by the Inca state from their natal communities and were placed in special houses (*acllahuasi*) in Cuzco, in one of the provincial capitals, and perhaps in other towns (Ebert 2004). Within the institution, there was an internal hierarchy that probably reflected the social origins and class position of a woman's family as well as relative age. This hierarchy underpinned the tasks that the young women eventually performed. Older *acllas*, called *mamacona*, who were most likely of Inca or noble origin, trained the girls to produce textiles and to cook food and brew beer for state-sponsored activities. In addition, some *acllas* tended agricultural fields and herds that were probably parts of the estates associated with each *acllahuasi*; others were trained as singers or musicians who presumably performed at state functions; still others worked in the state's roadside inns (*tambos*). Some *acllas* were taken or given in marriage by the Inca rulers. The *acllas* had particularly important linkages with the state cult. Every time a Temple of the Sun was established in a provincial capital, an *acllahuasi* was also built. In addition to roles as teachers and administrators in the *acllahuasi*, the *mamacona* were cloistered women dedicated to the state religious cult (Silverblatt 1987:87–108).

Acllas of the highest status wove *qompi*, the finest cloth, for the ruler and for various shrines. Fine textiles were important in the Inca state; cloth was the most highly valued product of the realm, "economically, politically, and ritually" (Costin 1998:123). It was an essential part of sacrifices, religious offerings, and rites of passage, including death (Costin 1996; Murra 1962). *Qompi* cloth was produced not only by *acllas* but also by a group of full-time male artisans called *qompicamayoq* (Costin 1996, 1998). The *qompicamayoq* were commoners from those communities, like Chupachu near Huánuco, that were renowned for their weaving skills; they worked to produce *qompi* for the Inca government in order to meet their labor obligations (Rowe 1979).

There were some striking contrasts between the two categories of full-time weavers in the Inca state. The *acllas* were recruited as young girls and may have been drawn disproportionately from elite households; they clearly had high social status in the state, at least partly because of their association with the Sun cult. The *qompicamayoq* were commoner men who wove the finest cloth to pay their labor tax. The former were permanently removed from their natal communities, while the latter retained a sense of identity and connection with their communities of origin, even in instances where they had been separated from their kin for many years. The position of *qompicamayoq* was apparently hereditary in those provinces that were renowned for their weaving skills (Costin 1998).

By claiming the right to appropriate and redistribute *acllas* (and probably *yanas*), the Inca ruler asserted control, in principle if not in practice, over the social and demographic reproduction of communities incorporated in the imperial state. The state denied the young women roles as future wives and mothers in their natal communities. By giving them in marriage to valued or desired allies, the ruler forged or cemented political ties. By giving them to the state cult, the Inca ruler enhanced their stature as they participated in various state-sponsored rituals that served to reproduce Inca culture and worldview in the provincial capitals. This new worldview provided a rationale for the changes in production relations that were taking place in the Andes.

As indicated previously, the Inca state appropriated lands in provincial areas to support the royal corporations, the state cult, the *acllahuasi*, and other state institutions. What is important here is that some ruling-class women had private, landed property. For example, Wayna Qhapaq, who ruled from A.D. 1493 to 1525, granted agricultural fields to his mother, his sons, and scores of wives. Other pieces of land on one of his estates were reputedly owned by women; however, their relationship with the Inca ruler is not clear (Niles 1999:150–52). The formation and disintegration of states created conditions for at least some individuals, including both men and women but most especially those from ruling or provincial elite backgrounds, to accumulate property, power, and wealth, as is attested in colonial period records from Peru and Ecuador (Jamieson 2000; Silverblatt 1987:114–19). During the sixteenth and seventeenth centuries, some women had considerable economic and interpersonal resources at their disposal. In the sixteenth century, some of the women were local leaders, or *kurakas* (Spalding 1998). Even though they were formally excluded from the public political sphere of the colonial government, many of them were able to call in favors from both civil and church officials if they chose to do so.

Discussion

In this chapter, we tracked gendered identities and relations over ten millennia from egalitarian kin-based communities to state-based societies. The archaeological evidence shows, however, that it is not possible to reduce the diversity of gender relations that existed in pre-Columbian South American societies to one or another of two ideal types. In social traditions as different as Chinchorro, Valdivia, and Paloma—parts of which were contemporaneous—there were demonstrable differences in gendered identities, roles, and relations. After the appearance of state-based societies in the central Andes, the uneven development of communities and their linkages with another seems to have increased both the diversity and the complexity of gender structures. This diversity and complexity was also evident in the Inca state and its colonial period successors. While archaeological data from the tropical lowlands are still scarce, the diversity and complexity of gender structures revealed in ethnohistoric and ethnographic accounts of lowland tribal and ethnic communities are enormous. Since these societies were always articulated in one way or another with those in the Andean highlands, the development of these complex, diverse structures and practices were related in some way to what happened in the highland and Pacific coastal societies discussed previously.

Thus far, the evidence concerning gender structures in pre-Columbian societies in South America is sparse and uneven. Nevertheless, asking questions about gender and its articulations with social ranking and class structures as well as with ethnicity is rewarding. The process of doing so requires that we adopt a perspective that leads to new insights about these societies.

Note

1. For consistency, we have endeavored to use dates based on calibrated radiocarbon measurements throughout this chapter.

References

Arriaza, Bernardo T.
    1995   *Beyond Death: The Chinchorro Mummies of Ancient Chile*. Washington, DC: Smithsonian Institution Press.
    1996   Preparation of the Dead in Coastal Andean Preceramic Populations. In *Human Mummies: A Global Survey of Their Status and the Techniques of Conservation*. Vol. 3. K. Spindler, K. Wilfing, E. Rastbichler-Zissernig, D. zur Nedden, and H. Nothdurfter, eds. Pp. 131–40. Vienna: Springer-Verlag.
    1998   Black and Red Chinchorro Mummies of Peru and Chile. In *Mummies: Disease and Ancient Cultures*. A. Cockburn, E. Cockburn, and T. A. Reyman, eds. Pp. 190–97. Cambridge: Cambridge University Press.

Aufderheide, A., I. Muñoz, and B. Arriaza
   1993   Seven Chinchorro Mummies and the Prehistory of Northern Chile. *American Journal of Physical Anthropology* 91(2):189–201.

Bawden, Garth
   1996   *The Moche*. Oxford: Blackwell.

Bauer, Brian, and R. Alan Covey
   2002   Processes of State Formation in the Inca Heartland (Cuzco, Peru). *American Anthropologist* 104(3):846–65.

Benfer, Robert
   1984   The Challenges and Rewards of Sedentism: The Preceramic Village of Paloma, Peru. In *Paleopathology at the Origins of Agriculture*. Mark N. Cohen and George J. Armelagos, eds. Pp. 531–58. New York: Academic Press.
   1986   Holocene Coastal Adaptations: Changing Demography and Health at the Fog Oasis of Paloma, Peru, 5,000–7,800 B.P. In *Andean Archaeology: Papers in Memory of Clifford Evans*. Ramiro M. Matos, Solveig A. Turpin, and Herbert H. Eling Jr., eds. Pp. 45–64. Monograph 27. Los Angeles: Institute of Archaeology, University of California at Los Angeles.
   1990   The Preceramic Period Site of Paloma: Bioindications of Improving Adaptation to Sedentism. *Latin American Antiquity* 1(4):284–318.

Bird, Junius B.
   1961   Textile Designing and Samplers in Peru. In *Essays in Pre-Columbian Art and Archaeology*. Samuel K. Lothrop et al., eds. Pp. 299–316. Cambridge: Harvard University Press.

Bruhns, Karen O., and Karen E. Stothert
   1999   *Women in Ancient America*. Norman: University of Oklahoma Press.

Brumfiel, Elizabeth M.
   1992   Distinguished Lecture in Archaeology: Breaking and Entering the Ecosystem—Gender, Class, and Faction Steal the Show. *American Anthropologist* 94(3):551–67.

Burger, Richard L.
   1992   *Chavin and the Origins of Andean Civilization*. London: Thames and Hudson.

Clark, Niki R.
   1993   *The Estuquina Textile Tradition: Cultural Patterning in Late Prehistoric Fabrics, Moquegua, Far Southern Peru*. Ph.D. dissertation, Washington University; Ann Arbor, MI: University Microfilms International.

Comaroff, John L.
   1987   Of Totemism and Ethnicity: Consciousness, Practice and the Signs of Inequality. *Ethnos* 52(3):301–23.

Cook, Anita G.
   2004   Wari Art and Society. In *Andean Archaeology*. Helaine Silverman, ed. Pp. 146–66. Oxford: Blackwell.

Costin, Cathy L.
 1996 Exploring the Relation between Gender and Craft in Complex Societies: Methodological and Theoretical Issues of Gender Attribution. In *Gender and Archaeology*. Rita P. Wright, ed. Pp. 111–40. Philadelphia: University of Pennsylvania Press.
 1998 Housewives, Chosen Women, Skilled Men: Cloth Production and Social Identity in the Late Prehispanic Andes. In *Craft and Social Identity*. Cathy L. Costin and Rita P. Wright, eds. Pp. 123–41. Archeological Papers of the American Anthropological Association 8, Washington, DC: American Anthropological Association.
Ebert, Virginia
 2004 Acllahuasi: Structuring Chosen Women in the Inca State. Paper presented at the Palace Women around the World Conference, University of California, Irvine, March 17–21.
Gero, Joan M.
 2001 Field Knots and Ceramic Beaus: Interpreting Gender in the Peruvian Early Intermediate Period. In *Gender in Pre-Hispanic America*. Cecelia F. Klein, ed. Pp. 15–56. Washington, DC: Dumbarton Oaks.
Gero, Joan M., and M. Cristina Scattolin
 2002 Beyond Complementarity and Hierarchy: New Definitions for Archaeological Gender Relations. In *In Pursuit of Gender: Worldwide Archaeological Approaches*. Sarah M. Nelson and Myriam Rose-Ayalon, eds. Pp. 155–71. Walnut Creek, CA: AltaMira Press.
Guillén, Sonia E.
 1992 *The Chinchorro Culture: Mummies and Crania in the Reconstruction of Preceramic Coastal Adaptation in the South Central Andes*. Ph.D. dissertation, University of Chicago; Ann Arbor, MI: University Microfilms International.
Haas, Jonathan, Shelia Pozorski, and Thomas Pozorski, eds.
 1987 *The Origins and Development of the Andean State*. Cambridge: Cambridge University Press.
Hastorf, Christine A.
 1991 Gender, Space, and Food in Prehistory. In *Engendering Archaeology: Women and Prehistory*. Joan M. Gero and Margaret W. Conkey, eds. Pp. 132–59. Oxford: Basil Blackwell.
Jamieson, Ross W.
 2000 Doña Luisa and Her Two Houses. In *Lines That Divide: Historical Archaeologies of Race, Class, and Gender*. James A. Delle, Stephen A. Mrozowski, and Robert Paynter, eds. Pp. 142–67. Knoxville: University of Tennessee Press.
Jones, Sian
 1996 *The Archaeology of Ethnicity: Constructing Identities in the Past and the Present*. London: Routledge.

Julien, Catherine J.

    1982   Inca Decimal Administration in the Lake Titicaca Region. In *The Inca and Aztec States 1400–1800: Anthropology and History*. George A. Collier, Renato I. Rosaldo, and John D. Wirth, eds. Pp. 119–51. Stanford, CA: Stanford University Press.

Klepinger, Linda

    1979   Paleodemography of the Valdivia III Phase at Real Alto, Ecuador. *American Antiquity* 44(2):305–9.

Lathrap, Donald W., Jorge G. Marcos, and James A. Zeidler

    1977   Real Alto: An Ancient Ceremonial Center. *Archaeology* 30(1):2–13.

Malina, Robert M.

    1988   Skeletal Materials from La Galgada. In *La Galgada: A Preceramic Culture in Transition*. Terence Grieder, Alberto Bueno Mendoza, C. Earle Smith Jr., and Robert M. Malina. Pp. 103–24. Austin: University of Texas Press.

Marcos, Jorge G.

    2003   A Reassessment of the Ecuadorian Formative. In *Archaeology of Formative Ecuador*. J. Scott Raymond and Richard L. Burger, eds. Pp. 7–32. Washington, DC: Dumbarton Oaks.

Marcos, Jorge G., and Mariella García de Manrique

    1988   De la dualidad fertilidad-virilidad a lo explícitamente femenino o masculino: La relación de las figurinas con los cambios en la organización social Valdivia, Real Alto, Ecuador. In *The Role of Gender in Precolumbian Art and Architecture*. Virginia E. Miller, ed. Pp. 35–52. Lanham, MD: University Press of America.

Moseley, Michael E.

    1975   *The Maritime Foundations of Andean Civilization*. Menlo Park, CA: Cummings.

Murra, John V.

    1962   Cloth and Its Functions in the Inca State. *American Anthropologist* 64(4):710–28.

Niles, Susan A.

    1999   *The Shape of Inca History: Narrative and Architecture in an Andean Empire*. Iowa City: University of Iowa Press.

Patterson, Thomas C.

    1991   *The Inca Empire: The Formation and Disintegration of a Pre-Capitalist State*. Oxford: Berg.

    1999   The Development of Agriculture and the Emergence of Formative Civilization in the Central Andes. In *Pacific Latin America in Prehistory: The Evolution of Archaic and Formative Cultures*. Michael Blake, ed. Pp. 181–88. Pullman: Washington State University Press.

Paul, Anne, and Susan A. Niles

    1985   Identifying Hands at Work on a Paracas Mantle. *Textile Museum Journal*, no. 23:5–15.

Quilter, Jeffrey
  1988   *Life and Death at Paloma: Society and Mortuary Practices in a Preceramic Peruvian Village.* Iowa City: University of Iowa Press.
Raymond, J. Scott
  2003   Social Formations in the Western Lowlands of Ecuador during the Formative. In *Archaeology of Formative Ecuador.* J. Scott Raymond and Richard L. Burger, eds. Pp. 33–67. Washington, DC: Dumbarton Oaks.
Rivera, Mario A.
  1995   The Preceramic Chinchorro Mummy Complex of Northern Chile: Context, Style, and Purpose. In *Tombs for the Living: Andean Mortuary Practices.* Tom D. Dillehay, ed. Pp. 43–78. Washington, DC: Dumbarton Oaks.
Rowe, John H.
  1958   The Age Grades of the Inca Census. In *Miscellanea Paul Rivet, octogenario dicata.* Pp. 499–522. XXXI Congreso Internacional de Americanistas, Vol. 2. México: Universidad Nacional Autónoma del México.
  1979   Standardization of Inca Tapestry Tunics. In *The Junius B. Bird Pre-Columbian Textile Conference.* Ann P. Rowe, Elizabeth P. Benson, and Anne-Louise Schaffer, eds. Pp. 239–64. Washington, DC: The Textile Museum and Dumbarton Oaks.
  1982   Inca Policies and Institutions Relating to the Cultural Unification of the Empire. In *The Inca and Aztec States 1400–1800: Anthropology and History.* George A. Collier, Renato I. Rosaldo, and John D. Wirth, eds. Pp. 93–118. Stanford, CA: Stanford University Press.
Sacks, Karen Brodkin
  1989   Toward a Unified Theory of Class, Race, and Gender. *American Ethnologist* 16(3):534–50.
Shimada, Izumi, Ken-ichi Shinoda, Julie Farnum, Robert Corruccini, and Hirokatsu Watanabe
  2004   An Integrated Analysis of Pre-Hispanic Mortuary Practices: A Middle Sicán Case Study. *Current Anthropology* 45(3):369–402.
Silverblatt, Irene
  1976   Principios de organización femenina en el Tawantinsuyu. *Revista del Museo Nacional* 42:299–340.
  1987   *Moon, Sun, and Witches: Gender Ideologies and Class in Inca and Colonial Peru.* Princeton, NJ: Princeton University Press.
Silverman, Helaine, and Donald A. Proulx
  2002   *The Nasca.* Oxford: Blackwell.
Siskind, Janet
  1973   *To Hunt in the Morning.* New York: Oxford University Press.
  1978   Kinship and Mode of Production. *American Anthropologist* 80(4):860–72.
Smith, Anthony
  1986   *The Ethnic Origins of Nations.* Oxford: Basil Blackwell.

Spalding, Karen
    1998   Constructing Identities. Yale Latin American Studies 1. New Haven, CT: Latin American Studies Center, Yale University.
Stolcke, Verena
    1993   Is Sex to Gender as Race Is to Ethnicity? In *Gendered Anthropology*. Teresa del Valle, ed. Pp. 17–37. London: Routledge.
Stothert, Karen E.
    1985   The Preceramic Vegas Culture of Coastal Ecuador. *American Antiquity* 50(4):613–37.
    1988   *La prehistoria temprana de la Peninsula de Santa Elena, Ecuador: Cultura Las Vegas*. Miscelánea Antropológica Ecuatoriana, Serie Monografía 10. Guayaquil: Banco Central del Ecuador.
    2003   Expression of Ideology in the Formative Period of Ecuador. In *Archaeology of Formative Ecuador*. J. Scott Raymond and Richard L. Burger, eds. Pp. 337–409. Washington, DC: Dumbarton Oaks.
Tattersall, Ian
    1985   The Human Skeletons from Huaca Prieta, with a Note on Exostoses of the External Auditory Meatus. In *The Preceramic Excavations at the Huaca Prieta, Chicama Valley, Peru*. Junius B. Bird, John Hyslop, and Milica D. Skinner, eds. Pp. 60–64. Anthropological Papers of the American Museum of Natural History, vol. 62, no. 1. New York: American Museum of Natural History.
Ubelaker, Douglas H.
    1980   Human Skeletal Remains from Site OGSE-80, A Pre-Ceramic Site on the Sta. Elena Peninsula, Coastal Ecuador. *Journal of the Washington Academy of Sciences* 43(6):666–77.
    2003   Health Issues in the Early Formative of Ecuador: Skeletal Biology of Real Alto. In *Archaeology of Formative Ecuador*. J. Scott Raymond and Richard L. Burger, eds. Pp. 259–87. Washington, DC: Dumbarton Oaks.
Vogel, Melissa A.
    2003   Sacred Women in Ancient Peru. In *Ancient Queens: Archaeological Explorations*. Sarah M. Nelson, ed. Pp. 117–36. Walnut Creek, CA: AltaMira Press.
Wobst, Martin
    1977   Stylistic Behavior and Information Exchange. In *For the Director: Research Essays in Honor of James B. Griffin*. Pp. 317–42. Anthropology Papers, no. 61. Ann Arbor: Museum of Anthropology, University of Michigan.
Zeidler, James A.
    2000   Gender, Status, and Community in Early Formative Valdivia Society. In *The Archaeology of Communities: A New World Perspective*. Marcello A. Canuto and Jason Yaeger, eds. Pp. 161–81. London: Routledge.

Index

Abbott, Frank, 296
Aboriginal culture: androcentric interpretations of, 697–700; and fire, 527n7; masculinity and, 408; rock art in, 698–99; skeletal remains in, 699–700; stone tools in, 697–98; Western views and, 715–16; women's secretiveness and, 713; women toolmakers in, 515
Abu Hureyra, Syria, 550
Ache culture, 258
Acheulian bifacial hand axes, 474–75
Achuar culture, 265–66, 273, 556
acllas, 867–68
acorns, 834–35
activity spaces: on landscape, 204–7; maps of, 255–56
actual self, 338
"add women and stir" approach, 4, 60, 734
Adnajamatana tribe, 711
adzes, 602
Africa: animal domestication in, 577; women and farming in, 539–40, 545–46; women and power in, 619–20. *See also specific countries and cultures*; African archaeology
African Americans: artifactual meanings and, 82; domestic realm of, 77–78; and fertility management, 373–74; mothering among, 345. *See also* slavery
African archaeology, 595–620; complex societies, 614–19; discipline of, 596–99; ethnography and, 619; future of, 619–20; Iron Age pastoralism in Southern Africa, 612–14; Iron Age research, 608–11; Kintampo complex, 606–7; North African Mesolithic foragers, 605–6; obstacles for, 595; Pastoral Neolithic in East Africa, 606–7; principal sites and regions, 600; Stone Age hunter-gatherers in Southern Africa, 599–605. *See also* Africa
age, identity and, 335, 436–37
agency: concept of, 13, 225; evolution and, 481; heterarchy and, 225–26; individual and, 615; second-wave feminist analysis of, 73–74; social, 481. *See also* performance of gender
aggregation sites, 749
aggression, evolution and, 455–56
agriculture. *See* farming
agropastoralism, 572–73, 577–81
Aiello, L. C., 485
Alberti, Benjamin, 419, 766
Albright, Sylvia, 837
Allison, Penelope M., 69, 308, 312
Almeida, Miguel Vale de, 404
Alvard, Michael S., 577
Amazons: in Greek myth, 305; Native North American, 841–42; in Plains Indian culture, 833; of Scythia and Sauromatia, 145, 305; of Ukraine and Caucasus, 145, 305
Ambiguous Images (Hays-Gilpin), 208
American Anthropological Association, 6, 598
American Institute for Archaeology, 297
American Journal of Archaeology (journal), 735

875

876 INDEX

American Medical Association, 374
Americas, gendered cosmos in, 202
amputations, 602–3
anachronism, 248, 256–76, 367, 370–71, 403, 460. *See also* assumptions about gender
analogical arguments, 619
anomalous data, 438–39
Andaman Islands, 515, 527n7, 646
Andean states, 861–65
Anderson, Gavin, 604–5
androcentrism: and anomalous sex/gender associations, 157; in art interpretation, 488; Australian archaeology and, 694, 696–701; constructions of past based on, 62; critiques of, multidisciplinary, 3; ethnoarchaeology and, 248; of evolutionary psychology, 471–72; evolutionary theory and, 453; feminist critique of, 60–65, 295–99; and figurine interpretation, 758–59; in gender research, 300–302; and households, 299–300; and hunter-gatherer societies, 525; of hunting hypothesis, 459–60; of male provisioning hypothesis, 464; methods based on, 64–65, 299; onion metaphor for, 295–96; paradigms/models based on, 17, 61–62; pastoralist research and, 266, 577–78; persistence of, 17; in primatology, 483; and rock art interpretation, 761; theoretical frameworks, epistemology, and language based on, 63, 302
Allison, Penelope, 63, 302
Almeida, Miguel, 313, 753–54
Alvard, Michael S., 577
anemia, 523
animal domestication: definition of, 573; evidence of, archaeological, 575–77; identifying in archaeological record, 573–75. *See also* pastoralism
anthropology: archaeology in relation to, 458; cultural, 249, 253, 254, 368; evolutionary theory and, 456; and gender construction, 416; heterarchy in, 220–21
Antiquity (journal), 474, 735
Aphrodite, 302

Appadurai, Arjun, 112
appearance, social construction and, 117–20
'Aqi, 376, 438, 842
archaeobiography, 337–43
Archaeological Dialogues (journal), 735
Archaeological Review (journal), 138
Archaeological Theory Today (Hodder), 17
Archaeologies of Sexuality (Schmidt and Voss), 157, 365
archaeology: as beneficiary of gender archaeology, 18; classical, 295–321; critique of, 12; historical, 59–87; textual, 343. *See also* archaeology, discipline of; gender archaeology
archaeology, discipline of: in Africa, 596–99; in Australia, 692–717; in East/Southeast Asia, 637; in Europe, 736–39; hierarchy/heterarchy in, 238; inequality in, 6–7, 17, 597, 694, 701–8, 736; information exchange in, 138–39; "Man the Hunter" symposium and, 458; masculinity and, 408; women in, 4, 6–7, 596–99, 695, 701–8, 736–39. *See also* fieldwork
Archaeology at the Millennium (Feinman and Price), 16–17
Archaeology (Fagan), 17
Archaeology in Oceania (journal), 697
Archaeology (Renfrew and Bahn), 737
architecture: other genders and, 443–44; sexuality and, 381–83; social relations and, 121–25. *See also* houses
Arctic cultures, 259–60
Ardeleanu-Jansen, Alexandra, 673
ards, 582
Arebi, Saddeka, 715
Argentina, 33, 43–44, 859
Arikara culture, 521
Aristotle, 306, 311
Arnhem Land societies, 715–16
Arnold, Bettina, 18, 224, 376, 439, 747
art. *See* craft production; figurines; grave goods; representational art; rock art; statues
Artemis, 206

art history, 295, 299
arthritis, 520–22
artifacts: children's, 69–70, 72–73, 309; classification of, ungendered, 65; gender archaeology and, 42–43; gender construction and, 113–14; interpretation of, 105; material culture and, 126; race and, 82–83; as reflection of gender, 106–8; as utterances, 128. *See also specific types;* grave goods; hoards; material culture; tools
artisans: autonomy of, as modern concept, 228; status of, 275
Arwill-Nordbladh, Elisabeth, 115, 127
Ashanti culture, 335, 351
Asher-Greve, Julia M., 684
Ashmore, Wendy, 16
Asia. *See specific countries and cultures;* East and Southeast Asian archaeology; South and Southwest Asian archaeology
Asian archaeology, 140. *See also* East and Southeast Asian archaeology; South and Southwest Asian archaeology
Asian cultures, division of labor in, 260
Aspasia, 306
assumptions about gender, 8, 41, 42, 65, 144, 156–57, 226, 504, 634–37. *See also* anachronism; androcentrism; heterosexism; stereotypes
Athens, Greece, 181
Attenbrow, Val, 708
Attfield, Judy, 115
attribution, gender. *See* gender attribution
Ault, Bradley A., 298
Australia, 408, 514, 515, 519, 527n7. *See also* Aboriginal culture; Australian archaeology
Australian Archaeological Association, 692, 696
Australian archaeology, discipline of, 692–717; androcentrism addressed in, 696–701; Australian character and, 692–93; brain drain from, 706; "chilly climate" in, 701, 705; conditions for, 693; current situation of, 714–17; entry into academy

in, 705–6; full-time employment by gender, 703, 704; gender archaeology's emergence in, 694–96; and historical archaeology, 700; and marginalization of women, 694, 702, 705, 707; sex and gender as concepts in, 708–10; women archaeologists in, 701–8
Australian Archaeology (journal), 697
Australian Rock Art Research Association, 698
Avebury, England, 208
Avis, V., 456
Awash, Ethiopia, 464
awls, 9, 63, 108, 831
Ayacucho, Peru, 863–64
Ayub Cave, Philippines, 640–41
Aztec culture: artifact decoration in, 42; gender archaeology and, 791, 793; gender construction in, 799–800; gendered cosmos in, 203; material culture and gender in, 110; sexuality in, 800; textile production in, 179, 185; tribute demands in, 179, 183

Bachofen, Johann, 756
Bacus, Elisabeth A., 641–42, 651–52
Bahn, Paul, 737
Bailey, Douglass W., 760
Baillargeon, Morgan, 271–72
Balme, Jane, 699, 701, 708
Baluchistan, 669, 671–72
Bantu culture, 264, 269–70, 612–14
Baratang Island, 646–47
Barfield, Lawrence H., 762, 764
Barich, Barbara, 606
Barrett, J. C., 480
Barth, Frederik, 572
Bar-Yosef, Ofer, 550
Basketmaker era, 40
Basseri nomads, 572
Bathurst Island, 515
Beaudry, Mary C., 85, 342–43
Beauvoir, Simone de, 296
Beck, Lois, 266

Beck, Wendy, 699, 701, 708
Beecher sisters, 69
behavioral ecology, 253, 468, 507
Belfer-Cohen, Anna, 550
Bell, Diane, 713
Bell Beaker culture: burial practices in, 116–17; dress accessories in, 119
Bender, Barbara, 199
Bender, Donald R., 177
Bendremer, Jeffrey, 840
Bennett, Sharon, 520–21, 523
Bentley, Gillian R., 148–49
Benton, Sylvia, 738
Berber culture, 261
berdaches, 224, 366, 375–76, 840–43, 844n1
Bergounioux, F. M., 457
Bernbeck, Reinhard, 684
Bernick, Kathryn, 838, 843
Berns, Marla, 611
Berwind, Colorado, 185–86
Beti culture, 540
Bhaba, Homi, 413
bias. *See* anachronism; androcentrism; assumptions about gender; stereotypes
Bidney, David, 221
bifaces, 474–75, 512
binary thinking: Australian archaeology and, 708–9; and body parts' cultural significance, 419; as Cartesian legacy, 200–201, 387; in cognitive psychology, 478–80; complementarity associated with, 222; critique of, 77; division of labor and, 226; domestic/public roles and, 70, 302; evolutionary theory and, 456–61; heterosexism of, 63; hierarchy associated with, 222; and house design, 124; second-wave feminist acceptance of, 73, 310; site designation and, 64–65; about space, 180; structuralism and, 63, 77, 180, 201, 252, 302
Binford, Lewis R., 61, 259, 260, 458–59, 463, 467
bioarchaeology: gender archaeology and, 37–38; gender differentiation and, 520; and hunter-gatherer societies, 520–23; and other genders, 441–43; and personhood, 343. *See also* human skeletal material
bipedality, 463–65
Bird, C. F. M., 8, 511, 514, 515, 697–98
birthing, 711–12, 821
Blackdog burial site, Minnesota, 439
Blakey, Michael, 343
Bleier, Ruth, 478, 479
boardinghouses, 71
Bode's Draw, Colorado, 832
body: in Australian archaeology, 710–14; dualism of mind and, 387, 470; as focus of study, 615–16; gender construction and, 113–14; Greek ideals of, 309; house as symbol of, 124–25; male-female differences, evolution of, 483–84; masculinity and, 414–19; material culture and, 127–28; in mortuary studies, 141; phenomenology and, 36; women and, 710–14
Boggsville, Colorado, 339–42
Bogucki, Peter, 582
Bolger, Diane L., 738, 741, 760
bone loss, 523
bone needles, 517
bones. *See* human skeletal material
bone tools, 511
Bonfante, Larissa, 309, 317–18
booleying, 572, 585
Boserup, Ester, 539–40
Bourdieu, Pierre, 112, 249, 261, 416, 437, 768
Bowdler, Sandra, 708
Bowser, Brenda J., 256, 265, 273–74, 277
Braidwood, Robert, 577–78
brain, 463, 477, 479, 487
Brandon, Jamie C., 82–83
breasts, meaning of, 318
Breuil, Abbé, 597
Bridges, Patricia S., 829
Bridges, Sarah T., 69
Brightman, Robert, 506

Brighton, Stephen A., 70
Britain, 734
Brod, Harry, 404
Bronze Age: Denmark, 227–28, 231–37; Early, 111–12, 116–17, 119; Late, 227–28, 231–37; Middle, 119
brooches, 120
brothels, 379–80
Bruhns, Karen Olsen, 556–57, 816, 857
Brumbach, Hetty Jo, 12, 255–56, 259, 267, 816
Brumfiel, Elizabeth, 9, 110, 179, 183, 221–22, 793
Brusasco, Paolo, 122–23
Bryan, Betsy, 615
Buchli, Victor, 382
Buganda, 618–19
built environment. *See* architecture
burial data: context and meaning of, 127; gender archaeology and, 38–40; gender construction and, 116–17; gender ideology and, 151; heterarchy and, 223; ideal situation for, 146; multiple burials as problem for, 146; neutral burial category, 152; Paleoindian, 818–19; visibility as issue for, 152. *See also* grave goods; human skeletal material; mortuary studies
Bush, George W., 390
Butler, Judith, 113, 141, 369–70
Buyoro, 618–19

Caesar, 572
Caesar, Camilla, 402–3, 410
Cage, Nicholas, 707
calabashes, 272–76
California cultures, 834–36
camayos, 867
Cambridge Archaeological Journal, 735, 758
Cambridge Cooperative Housekeeping Society, 74
Cameroon, 262, 274, 540
Cannon, Aubrey, 142, 265
caries, dental, 111, 523, 675
Carrigan, Tim, 415

Carter, Anthony, 176
Cartesian thinking, 200–201, 387, 470
Casella, Eleanor Conlin, 379
case studies: advantages/disadvantages of, 45; archaeobiography, 338–43; farming societies, 542–60; heterarchy, 232–37; mortuary study, 152–55; personhood, 344–58
Casey, Joanna, 261, 602, 606–7
Casey, Mary A., 71
Çatalhöyük, 680–81; burials in, 38–39; division of labor in, 552; gender equality in, 38–39; heterarchy in, 238; matriarchy in, 16; World Wide Web use for, 8
Caton-Thompson, Gertrude, 597, 737, 738
cattle, 576–77, 612, 616–17
Caucasus, Amazons of, 145, 305
Cauvin, Jacques, 552
cave paintings, 487–88
Central American archaeology, 140
Central Cattle Pattern (CCP), 612, 616–17
ceramics: ethnoarchaeology and, 272–76; Mimbres, 820–21, 841; Moche sex pots, 35–36, 384–86; Philippine burial jars, 640–41; Recuay copulation pots, 385–86; style of, 272–74. *See also* pottery production
cereal cultivation, 576, 605
Ceren, El Salvador, 181, 187
CF & I coal company, 185
Chacmool Conference (2004), 157
Chad, 455
chaîne opératoire, 141, 486
Champion, Sara, 738
Chang, Claudia, 259, 572, 573
change: agency and, 481; masculinity and, 410–11. *See also* evolution
Chan Noohol, Belize, 182
Chapman, John, 738, 759–60
Charles Sturt University, 702
Chase, Sabrina, 254
Chauvet, 488
Cheyenne culture, 338–42
chiefly societies, 230

childbirth, 711–12, 821
Childe, V. Gordon, 571, 576
children: artifacts of, 69–70, 72–73, 309, 354; in Ashanti culture, 335; in Aztec culture, 799–800; classical archaeology and, 308–10; at Clifton Plantation, Bahamas, 345–52; Cult of Republican Motherhood and, 77; and gender construction, 799–800; as infant caregivers, 229; at La Placita, Colorado, 352–57; in Navajo culture, 336; personhood and, 335, 336, 343–58; play landscapes of, 83–84; sexing, 144; and work, 355, 357. *See also* infants
Chile, 855–57
China: elite in, 653–59; gender ideology in, 642–44; gender roles in, 647–49; imagery in, 638–40; Late Neolithic, 547–49
Chinchorro communities, 855–57
Chiou-Peng, Tze-huey, 640
Chipewyan culture, 259, 508, 514, 518
Chippindale, Christopher, 762
Chodorow, Nancy, 410–11
Christianity, 620, 667
Chumash culture, 33, 376, 438, 521–22, 836, 842
City Beautiful movement, 79
Claassen, Cheryl, 10, 366, 508, 557, 827–28
Clark, A. McFadyen, 519
Clark, Niki R., 864–65
Clarke, Annie, 702
Clarke, John R., 319, 321
class: burial data and, 39; and depersonalization, 337; division of labor and, 853; dress and, 117–18; households and, 185; in Southwest Asia, 683–84
classical archaeology, 295–321; androcentric foundations of, 295–99; androcentric theories and, 302; and domestic realm, 307–8; first-wave feminism and, 303–10; future of, 321; and gender ideology, 300–302, 311–12; and households, 299–300, 312–14; masculinity and, 408; masculinity theories and, 319–21; methods of, 299; and mothering/child rearing, 308–10; second-wave feminism and, 310; and sexuality, 315–19; third-wave feminism and, 311–14; and women's public roles, 303–7
classics, 295–97
Clees, Helen, 296
Clifton Plantation, Bahamas, 344–52
climate, and men's subsistence contributions, 509
Close, Angela, 605–6
clothing. *See* dress
cloth production. *See* textile production
Cobb, Hannah, 375
Coggins, Clemency, 790
cognitive psychology: evolutionary archaeology and, 476–80; on males and females, 478–80, 486–88; modular versus unitary approaches in, 477; on sexual attraction, 474–75
Cohen, Beth, 318
Cohen, Getzel M., 738
Cohen, Mark Nathan, 520–21, 523
Cohodas, Marvin, 41
Collett, D. P., 611
Colley, Sarah, 716
Collins, Patricia Hill, 345
Colomina, Beatriz, 120, 125
Committee on the Status of Women in Archaeology, 6
communism, 382
comparative studies. *See* cross-cultural studies
complementarity of male-female work, 485–86
complexity, hierarchy versus heterarchy and, 219–20, 229–32
complex societies: in Africa, 614–19; art of, 766–67; in East/Southeast Asia, 649–52; in Native North America, 814; in South America, 861–65; in Southwest Asia, 681–84
compositional studies, heterarchy and, 238
computer simulation, 476
condoms, 373

Conkey, Margaret, 5, 9, 12, 47n1, 109, 138, 238, 372–73, 411, 453, 467–68, 506, 695, 749
Connah, G., 595
Connell, Robert, 405–6, 411, 413, 415, 417–18
Conroy, Linda P., 759
Constitution, U.S., 390
constructivism: basis of, 12; criticisms of, 13; masculinity and, 409–16; material culture and, 112–17; theory/data and, 12. *See also* gender construction
consumption, 182–83, 354
contact-period gender research, 75
Contemporary Archaeology in Theory (Preucel and Hodder), 17
context: ethnoarchaeology and, 252; material culture and, 108–12; personhood and, 337–38
contraception, 373
Cook, Anita G., 864
Cooke, Helen, 519
cooking, 546, 610–11. *See also* food production
Cooper, Zarine, 260, 646–47
cooperation, evolution and, 485–86
cooperative housekeeping, 74, 79
Copan, Honduras, 181
coral houses, 262–63
Cordell, Linda, 7
coresidence, 174–76
corn, 825
Cornwall, Andrea, 415, 420
Corruccini, R., 345
Cortes, Hernan, 787
Cosmides, L., 470
cosmos: gendered, 201–3; house as symbol of, 124, 261; landscape and, 209–11; weaving and, 210–11
Costin, Cathy, 16, 42, 268, 275
Courtenay, William, 379
courtesans. *See* prostitution
craft production: division of labor and, 268–69; heterarchy in, 227–28; and

meaning, 268; other genders and, 440–41; specialization in, 227–28. *See also* ceramics; pottery production; textile production
critical need, 424–25
cross-cultural studies, 34, 250–51
Crown, Patricia L., 33, 187, 221, 557, 558, 823–24, 824
Crumley, Carole L., 219–20, 223, 239
Cuerto de la Mina, Spain, 109
Cuevas, Nida, 640–41
Cullen, Tracy, 760
Cult of Female Invalidism, 77–78
Cult of Gentility, 79, 82
Cult of Home Religion, 78
Cult of Real Womanhood, 80
Cult of Republican Motherhood, 77
Cult of Single Blessedness, 80
Cult of True Womanhood/Domesticity, 78–79
cultural anthropology, 249, 253, 254, 368
cultural heritage management, in Australia, 706
culture change, heterarchy and, 239
Cup'ik culture, 508
Current Anthropology (journal), 735
cylinder seals, 684
Cynics, 306, 311
Cyprus, 741

Dahlberg, Frances, 3, 462, 505
dairying, 582–83
Dakota culture, 444, 831–32
Dales, George, 674
Damp, Jonathan E., 555–57
dancing, ritual, 553–54
Danielsson, Ing-Marie Back, 375, 378
Dart, Raymond, 456
Darwin, Charles, 478
Dassanetch culture, 267
data: construction of, 12; sources of, 11
datu, 651–52
David, Bruno, 199

David, Nicholas, 249, 252, 255, 261, 277, 609, 610
Davis, Whitney, 379, 597
Davison, Patricia, 264–65
Dawkins, R., 469
day-to-day life, as archaeological subject, 172
Death by Theory (Praetzellis), 9
De Cros, Hilary, 694
De Cunzo, Lu Ann, 67, 73, 380
Deetz, James T., 59, 62–64
degenerative joint disease (DJD), 521–22
Deir el Medina, Egypt, 616
De Jong, Piet, 737
De Leiuen, Cherrie, 696, 700
Delle, James A., 76
Demetriou, Demetrakis Z., 413–14
demographics: animal, 574–75; skeletal evidence of, 148
Dene culture, 259
Denmark, 227–28, 231–37, 745–46
dental caries, 111, 523, 675
De Paor, Liam, 156
Derevenski, Joanna Sofaer. *See* Sofaer, Joanna
The Descent of Woman (Morgan), 11
De Soto, Hernando, 827
Detwiler, Kandace, 185
Deutsch, Sarah, 353, 357
DeVore, I., 456, 457, 505
dialogic approach: to archaeology, 47n1; to material culture, 128
Dian culture, 640, 648
Díaz-Andreu, Margarita, 735, 736, 738, 761
dichotomous thinking. *See* binary thinking
Dick-Bissonette, Linda E., 835–36
Diehl, Michael W., 824
Dier El Medina, Egypt, 382
dietary analysis: of African hunter-gatherers, 602; Clifton Plantation, Bahamas, 350–51; Early Bronze Age Yugoslavia, 111–12; of hunter-gatherer societies, 522–23; isotope analysis for, 149–50; skeletal evidence of, 147–50; South Asia, 675
Dietler, Michael, 273

difference: within gender categories, 32–34; phenomenology and, 36
direct historical approach, 250
distortion, of gender in archaeology, 12
diversity: in classical gender ideologies, 311–12; heterarchy and, 222–24; postmodern theory and, 82–84
division of labor: assumptions about, 8, 226; binary thinking and, 226; complementarity versus, 485–86; critiques of, 462, 540–41, 544; cultural variation in, 257; ethnographic evidence for, 747; evolution and, 457–58, 462–63, 464, 466, 701; farmers and, 260–66; flexibility in, 507–9, 523–24; food sharing and, 466; gatherers and, 257–60; grave goods and, 39–40; heterarchy and, 226–29; households and, 179; in hunter-gatherer societies, 504–9, 579, 600–602, 646–47; hunting and, 457–58, 462–63; in iron production, 608; in Levant, 550–51, 554, 680; male provisioning and, 464; in pastoralism, 266–67, 577–81, 583–84, 647–48; in pre-Hispanic Southwest, 557–58; reproduction and, 473–74; secondary products revolution and, 583–84; skeletal evidence of, 37, 520–22; in South America, 853–61; in subsistence activities, 747–49; technical versus social, 853
DNA analysis: and animal domestication, 575–76; kinship analysis through, 864; sex identification through, 144, 376, 442. *See also* genetic analysis
Dobres, Marcia Anne, 44, 225, 486
Dobzhansky, Theodosius, 456
domestic realm: binary thinking and, 70, 302; classical archaeology and, 307–8, 310; definition of, 176; devaluation of, 177; diversity in, 77–79; household as locus of, 176–77; ideology versus practice in, 81–82, 181, 300–302, 519; importance of, 67–68, 307–8; material culture and, 109–10; mortuary remains

and, 142; public sphere and, 70–73, 177; reform ideologies and, 79–80. *See also* households; houses
Dommasnes, Liv Helga, 107, 111
Donald, Merlin, 477
Dongshanzui, China, 548
Donlan, Denise, 699
Donley-Reid, Linda W., 252, 262–63, 274, 618
Double Woman, 441, 444–45, 831–32
Dover, Kenneth, 315
Dowson, Thomas A., 365, 375, 603
Draper, Patricia, 258
Dreaming Tracks, 209
dress: composition versus wearing of, 120; other genders and, 441; social construction and, 117–20, 745–46
dress history, 118
Drooker, Penelope Ballard, 831
Du Cros, Hilary, 708
Dudink, Stefan, 422
Dupire, Marguerite, 249, 266
dwelling areas, definition of, 171. *See also* households; houses

Early Bronze Age: burial practices in, 116–17; dress accessories in, 119; material culture changes in, 111–12
East Africa, 607–8
East and Southeast Asian archaeology, 633–62; complex societies, 649–52; discipline of, 637; elite in, 652–61; future of, 661–62; gender as conceptualized in, 634; gender bias in, 634–37; gender ideology, 642–44; gender roles and status, 644–49; imagery, 638–42. *See also specific countries and cultures*
Eccles, Edith, 738
economics, households and, 173, 176
Ecuador, 265–66, 273, 555–57, 857–59
education, in Greece, 305–6
Edwards, Amelia, 738
Edwards Chair of Egyptian Archaeology, University College London, 738

Egypt: gendered cosmos in, 202–3; New Kingdom, 43, 382, 387–90; women and power in, 614–16
Egyptian Exploration Society, 738
Egyptology, 738
Ehrenberg, Margaret R., 543–44, 734
Ekven, 439–40
eland, 603, 604
elites, in Asia, 652–61
Elkin, A. P., 699, 713
Ellender, Isabel, 515
Elster, Ernestine S., 738
Ember, Carol R., 509
embodiment. *See* body
Endo culture, 263–64
Endo Marakwet culture, 275
Engels, Friedrich, 382
Engendering Archaeology (Gero and Conkey), 734
England, 754–55
Englestad, Erica, 86
epistemology: androcentric, 63; feminist, 47n1, 63, 86 (*see also* women's knowledge); postmodern, 86
equality. *See* gender equality
erasure, of gender in archaeology, 12
Erlandson, Jon M., 523
Escoriza Mateu, Trinidad, 735
Eshed, Vered, 551
essentialism: cognitive psychology and, 478–80; controversy over, 14; critiques of, 415–16; and farming societies, 539; genetics and, 407–9; masculinity and, 407–9; of second-wave feminism, 73; third-wave feminist critique of, 76
Ethiopia, 271, 464
ethnicity: classical archaeology and, 321; concept of, 855
ethnoarchaeology, 247–78; about Africa, 595; and ceramics/calabashes, 272–76; contextual/interpretive, 252; current level of gender integration in, 276–78; definition of, 248; duration of studies, 255; evolutionary theory and, 252–53; and

farmers, 260–66; and foragers, 257–60; and gender construction, 251; and hideworking, 270–72; historical development of, 249–53; and hunter-gatherer societies, 518–19; and iron production, 269–70; and male-female dichotomy, 249–53; methods of, 253–56; and pastoralism, 266–67; universalism in early, 250–51; value of, 248, 249, 503

Ethnographic Atlas (Murdock), 505

ethnography: African archaeology and, 619; applications of, 35–36; and division of labor, 747; and hunter-gatherer societies, 527n7; Native North American archaeology and, 813; on nonbinary genders, 436; and personhood, 335; problems in, 229; San, 599; time in, 45; women ethnographers, 699

ethnohistory: applications of, 35–36; ethnoarchaeology and, 253–55

Etruria, 747, 766–67

Eurocentrism, 248, 299. *See also* Western bias in archaeology

Europe: animal domestication in, 576–77; farming societies in, 542–45; Iron Age mortuary analysis in, 152–55; Neolithic, 208–9, 231, 542–45, 580. *See also specific countries and cultures*; Europe, gender archaeology in

Europe, gender archaeology in, 733–69; burial studies, 742–47; current situation of, 767–69; discipline of, 736–39; division of labor, 747–50; figurines, 755–61; history and geography of, 733–36; iconography, 755–67; regional studies, 741–42; rock art, 761–65; space as gendered, 751–55; theoretical approaches in, 739; United States practices versus, 739

everyday life, as archaeological subject, 172

evolution, 453–89; androcentrism and, 453; cognitive psychology and, 476–80; cooperation and, 485–86; critique of models of, 540–41; and division of labor, 457–58, 462–63, 464, 466, 701; ethnoarchaeology and, 252–53; evolutionary archaeology and, 472–76; evolutionary psychology and, 470–72; food sharing and, 465–66; future of research on, 480–89; gathering and, 461–63; gender construction and, 251; hierarchy/heterarchy concepts in, 219–20, 229–32; and human origins, 454–55; hunting and, 455–63; interdisciplinarity and, 488–89; life cycle and, 482–85; male development and, 408–9; male-female dichotomy and, 456–61; male provisioning and, 463–65; modern approaches to, 454–56; neo-Darwinian approaches to, 468–69; sexual dimorphism, 457

evolutionary archaeology: development of, 468; evolutionary psychology and, 470–72; recent research in, 472–76

evolutionary psychology (EP): evolutionary archaeology and, 472–76; recent developments in, 470–72

excavation practices, 612

"expensive egg, cheap sperm" principle, 471, 473

experience, phenomenology and, 36

Faces of Archaeology in Greece (Hood), 737

Fagan, Brian, 17

farming, 537–62; African case study, 545–46; Coastal Ecuador case studies, 555–57; current research situation for, 560–61; and division of labor, 260–66, 560; European case studies, 542–45; female farmer model, 539–40; future of research on, 561–62; households, 261–66; in Native North America, 828–29; Northern China case studies, 547–49; pre-Hispanic Southwest case studies, 557–60; skeletal health of farmers, 523; Southern Levant case studies, 549–54

Farnsworth, Paul, 346, 350

Faust, Katherine A., 203

Fausto-Sterling, Anne, 483, 708–9

feasting, 186
Feinman, Gary M., 16–17
female farmer model, 539–40
female warrior phenomenon, 145–46. *See also* warrior women
Feminine Mystique (Friedan), 66, 303
feminism: androcentrism critiqued by, 61–65, 295–99; and classical archaeology, 295–321; and epistemology, 47n1, 63, 86; first-wave, 66–73; gender archaeology and, 2, 5, 8–9, 13–15, 17–18, 31–32, 45–46, 47n1, 59–87, 248–49, 295; and historical archaeology, 59–87; households as subject of study for, 177–78; Marxism and, 74–76; and mother goddess hypothesis, 757–58; versus nonfeminist approaches, 59–60; and pedagogy, 9; postcolonial, 75; and postmodernism, 691; research based on, principles of, 359; risks from successes of, 708; second-wave, 73–74; third-wave, 76–85; wave metaphor for, 65; and writing, 9
ferm, 709
fertile crescent, 667
fertility: agriculture and, 542–43; figurines/rock art and, 372–73; iron production as symbolic of, 205, 269–70, 608–11; management of, 371–74; Paleoindian, 819–20; skeletal evidence of, 148–49. *See also* reproduction
fibulae, 120
fiction, 9
fieldwork: in African archaeology, 598; hierarchy/heterarchy in, 238; women's status in, 254
figurines: androcentric interpretations of, 758–59; Cypriot, 741; ethnocentric interpretations of, 758; European, 755–61; in farming societies, 542–43; as fertility symbols, 372–73; Jomon, 636–37, 639; Mesoamerican, 795–98; and mother goddess hypothesis, 755–58; in Neolithic Levant, 552–53; sexless, 543;

South Asian, 669, 671–73; from Valdivian culture, 557. *See also* statues
Finneran, Niall, 620
fire, 527n7
first-wave feminism: and classical archaeology, 303–10; and mothering/child rearing, 69–70; and public roles of women, 66–73; stereotypes exposed in, 66–73
Fish, Suzanne K., 33, 187, 557, 824
fishing: children and, 350–51; misdefinition of, 505; women engaged in, 508–9. *See also* shellfish
Fiti-Sinclair, Ruth, 712
Fitts, Robert K., 79
Five Points, New York, 84
flake knives, 514
Fleming, Andrew, 756
Flinders University, 702
The Flintstones (television show), 247
Foley, R. A., 487
Fonthill Abbey, 379
food processing, 525, 819
food production, 551. *See also* cooking
food resources, access to, 522–23
food sharing, 465–66
foraging. *See* gathering
Ford, Clellan Stearns, 711
Fort Ross, California, 172
Foucault, Michel, 127, 416, 709
fourth gender, 435. *See also* other genders
Fowler, Chris, 334
Fowler, Kent, 611
Fox, Matthew, 424–25
Foxhall, Lin, 414, 415, 417
France, 585
Frankel, David, 742
Friedan, Betty, 66, 303
Frink, Lisa, 255, 270–71, 508
Fu Hao, 638
Fulani culture, 261, 266
funerary archaeology. *See* mortuary studies

Galloway, Patricia, 833, 838
Gamo culture, 271

García, Nasario, 357
gardens: male power-garden syndrome, 64; in medieval castles, 754–55; women's role in, 70
Garfinkel, Yosef, 553–54
Gargett, Rob, 260
Garrod, Dorothy, 737–38
Gatens, Moira, 156
gathering: and division of labor, 257–60; male/female models of, 527n5; in Mesolithic North Africa, 605–6; subsistence and, 461–63; women engaged in, 461–63, 505, 508–9. *See also* hunter-gatherer societies
Gaughwin, Denise, 697
gaze, landscape gendered through, 200–201
gazelles, 574–76, 578–79
Ge Bororo culture, 556, 557
gender: artifacts and, 106–8, 113–14; changing ideologies of, 80; cognition and, 478–80, 486–88; concept of, 14–15, 59–60, 140–41, 171–73; cross-cultural study of, 34; difference and, 32–34; households and, 171–73; mortuary studies and, history of, 138–40; performance of, 33; relationships of, 14–15, 34–35; representations of, 33; sexuality and, 369; sex versus, 60, 143, 248, 368–69, 406, 412, 416, 634, 743; social categories besides, 150–51, 333, 714; as spectrum, 709–10; unmarked (*see* ungendered research, as androcentric). *See also* androcentrism; assumptions about gender; masculinity(ies); men; other genders; women
Gender and Chinese Archaeology (Linduff and Sun), 547
gender archaeology: and artifacts, 42–43; assumptions impeding, 8, 41, 42, 65, 144, 156–57, 226, 504; Australian emergence of, 694–96; beneficiaries of, 17–18; and burial data, 38–40; contributions of, 17–18, 32; controversies in, 13–15; ethnoarchaeology and, 277; European emergence of, 733–36; and farming, 537–38; future of, 45, 85–87; in global context, 9–10; history of, 2–6, 7–9; and human skeletal material, 37–38; languages for writing, 735; in Mesoamerican archaeology, 788–95; non-attributional conclusions about, 44; overview of, 1–2; pedagogy in, 9; progress in, 16–17; public questions about, 15–16; relationships as subject of, 14–15, 34–35; and representational art, 40–41; and space, 43–44; stages of, 277–78; strands of, 6–9; theory in, 10–13; and tools, 42–43; writing in, 9
gender attribution: artifacts and, 42–43; households and, 179–80; mortuary remains and, 142–44, 743–47; tools and, 511–12
gender construction: age and, 436–37; artifacts and, 113–14; body and, 113–14; burial practices and, 116–17; dress and, 117–20, 745–46; ethnoarchaeology and, 251; masculinity and, 409–16; in Mesoamerica, 799–800. *See also* constructivism; performance of gender
gender equality: in archaeological discipline, 6–7, 17, 597, 694, 701–8, 736; archaeology and, 47n1; burial data and, 38–39; in Çatalhöyük, 38–39; variability in, 33–34
gender ideology: burials as expression of, 151; changes in, 80; in classical world, 300–301, 311–12; in domestic realm, 79–82, 181, 300–302; in East/Southeast Asia, 642–44; in *The Flintstones*, 247; Jews and, 80; power and, 411–13; practice versus, 81–82, 181, 300–302, 519, 748; projected onto past, 403; religion and, 80; in Southwest Asia, 681, 684; third-wave feminism on, 81–82
gender performance theory, 369–70. *See also* performance of gender
gender research, androcentric, 300–302
general comparative approach, 250

Genes, Memes and Human History (Shennan), 472
genetic analysis: migration patterns and, 149; sex identification through, 144. *See also* DNA analysis
genetics, essentialism and, 407–9
Germany, 746
Gero, Joan M., 8, 12, 33, 42–43, 43–44, 238, 340, 384–86, 467, 512, 514, 695, 816, 859, 863
Gewertz, Deborah, 337
Ghana, 261, 606–7
Gibb, James G., 81–82
Gifford-Gonzalez, Diane, 247–48, 253, 254, 266, 267, 607
Gilchrist, Roberta, 6, 44, 115, 123–24, 383, 384, 488, 580–81, 734, 754
Gillen, Frank J., 711
Gillespie, Susan, 334
Gilmore, David, 417
Gimbutas, Marija, 16, 201, 542–43, 738, 755–58
girls, and animal domestication, 578
Glassie, Henry, 62
Gleeson, C. T., 527n7
goats, 574–77
goddesses, 16, 201, 372, 542–43, 680, 755–58
Goldberg, Marilyn, 181, 301, 302, 304, 307, 312–14
Goldman, Hetty, 737
gold production, 617
Goodwin, John, 598
Gorman, Alice, 515, 527n7
Gosden, Chris, 199
Gould, Richard A., 255, 514
Grace, Virginia, 737
Gramsci, Antonio, 413
Gräslund, Anne-Sofia, 109–10
grave goods: and division of labor in Late Neolithic China, 547; gender archaeology and, 39–40; gender attribution using, 142–44, 744–47; interpretation of, 230; Viking, 230. *See also* burial data; mortuary studies
Graves-Brown, P., 485
gray literature, 4
Great Basin, 41, 507, 834–36
Great Zimbabwe, 597, 617
Greaves, Sheila, 837
Greece: activity spaces in, 206; education in, 305; houses in, 123, 312–14, 753–54; sexuality in, 315–18; women in households in, 180–81; women's public roles in, 304–7. *See also* classical archaeology
Greek Homosexuality (Dover), 315
Griggs, Heather J., 67
Grotta di Porto Badisco, Italy, 751–52
Guatemala, 265
Gudit, 620
Guillen, Cyphers, 796
Gutmann, Matthew, 402, 404
Guyer, Jane I., 175, 540
gynaikon, 753

Haaland, Randi, 605
habitus, 112
Ḥabu, Junko, 637
Hadley, Dawn, 412–13
Hadza culture, 258–59
Hall, Edith, 738
Hall, Martin, 117
Hall, Sian, 613–14
Hall, Simon, 613
Halperin, Rhoda, 509
Halpern, D. F., 479
Hamilton, W. D., 470
Handbook of North American Indians (Sturtevant), 814
Handler, Jerome, 337
Hanen, Marcia, 9
Hansen, Julienne, 122
Hao, Lady, 654, 655
Harappan civilization, 672–75
Harding, Joan, 597
Harding, Sandra, 86–87
Harlow, Mary, 119–20

Harrington, Sue, 747
Harrison, Jane, 737
Harrison, Rodney, 408
Harvey, Alison, 711
Hassan, Fekri A., 614
Hastorf, Christine A., 44, 110
Hatshepsut, Queen, 615
Haviland, William A., 798
Hawes, Harriet Boyd, 737, 738
Hawkes, Kristen, 258, 259, 473–74
Hayden, Brian, 260, 265
Hays-Gilpin, Kelley, 40, 202, 208, 238, 444, 821–22, 836, 838, 841
Head, Lesley, 199, 708
Hearn, Jeff, 415, 422
hegemonic masculinity, 413, 421
hegemony, balanced versus hierarchical, 541
Hegmon, Michelle, 13, 17, 187, 561, 821
Hemphill, Brian E., 675
Hendon, Julia A., 16, 43, 221, 793
Henretta, J. A., 64
Henry, Donald O., 578–79
Herbert, Eugenia W., 608
Herbich, Ingrid, 252, 272–73
hermaphrodite, 709
Herodotus, 145, 305
Hesiod, 206
hetaerae, 306, 315–18
heterarchy: agency and, 225–26; applications of, 220–21; case study, 232–37; compositional studies and, 238; concept of, 219–20; in craft/metal production, 227–28; critiques of, 221–22; culture change and, 239; definition of, 219; diversity and, 222–24; division of labor and, 226–29; future of, 237–39; hierarchy in relation to, 219, 229–32; in Late Bronze Age Denmark, 232–37; skeletal evidence and, 237; symbolism and, 238–39
heterosexism: in archaeological research, 374–75; binary thinking and, 63; heterosexual matrix and, 369
Hiatt, Betty, 509

Hidatsa culture, 376–77, 443, 842–43
hideworking, 270–72, 340, 511, 514
hierarchy: evolutionary theory and, 219–20, 229–32; heterarchy in relation to, 219, 229–32; in Late Bronze Age Denmark, 232–37
Higham, Charles, 645
Hildebrand, E., 577
Hildebrandt, William R., 507
Hill, J. D., 120
Hillier, Bill, 122
Hillman, G., 576
Hindmarsh Island Bridge, Australia, 713
Hingley, Richard, 124, 753
Hippocrates, 145
Hispanics, and personhood, 344, 352–57
historical archaeology, 59–87; androcentric bias in, 61–65; and archaeobiography, 338; Australian, 700; first-wave feminism and, 66–73; future of, 85–87, 342–43; and hunter-gatherer societies, 518–19; Marxist-feminism and, 74–76; postcolonial feminism and, 75; postmodernism/third-wave feminism and, 76–85; present as influence on construction of, 403; second-wave feminism and, 73–74
Historical Archaeology (journal), 379–80
historical change. *See* change
history: landscape and, 209–11; people without, 229; present as influence on construction of, 248, 256–76, 367, 370–71, 460
Hitchcock, Louise, 766
hoards, 232–37
Hodder, Ian, 8, 17, 42, 63, 86, 208–9, 252, 263, 267, 272, 273, 277, 580, 681, 751
Hoepfner, W., 312
Hoffman, Brian W., 517
Hohokam culture, 33, 187, 824–26
Hollimon, Sandra E., 32–33, 223, 376, 521, 832, 836, 842
Holmes, Katie, 760
homosexuality, 375–79; in Greece, 316–17, 320; in India, 710

Hongshan culture, 548–49, 638–39
Hood, R., 737
Hope, Jeanette, 699
Horowitz, L. K., 574
horses, 640
Horton, Mark, 618
Hottentots, 599
households, 171–88; androcentric models of, 299–300; archaeological study of, 171, 173–74; class and, 185; in classical world, 299–300, 312–14; coresidence and, 174–76; definition of, 175–76, 187; domestic realm centered in, 176–77; economic perspective on, 173, 176; of farmers, 261–66; feminism and, 177–78; of gatherers, 257–60; gender and, 171–73; gender attribution and, 179–80; in hunter-gatherer societies, 515–16; identity and, 184–86; other genders and, 443; outwork conducted in, 71; pastoralism and, 266–67; postmodern research on, 312–14; power in, 122, 186–87; prestige in, 186–87; production and consumption in, 182–83; relations in, 184–85; social science perspective on, 173–74; space and, 68–69, 178, 180–82. *See also* domestic realm
housekeeping cooperatives, 74, 79
houses: body/cosmos symbolized by, 124–25, 261; at Clifton Plantation, Bahamas, 346–50; gender construction and, 124–25; gender relations and, 208–9; Prowers house, 340–42; seclusion and segregation in Greek, 123, 753–54. *See also* domestic realm; dwelling areas; households
Houston, Stephen D., 386
Huang, Tsui-mei, 658–59
Huffman, Thomas N., 612, 616–17
human evolution. *See* evolution
human nature: bipedality and, 463–65; brain and, 463; cognition and, 477–78; hunting and, 455–57; principle factors in, 455

human origins, 454–55, 459, 461–68, 477–78
human sacrifice, 830–31
human skeletal material: Aboriginal, 699–700; arthritis and, 520–22; and farming in Levant, 550–51; gender archaeology and, 37–38; gender differentiation and, 520; heterarchy and, 237; from hunter-gatherer societies, 520–23; and other genders, 441–43; personhood and, 343; plastered skulls, 554; repetitive stress evidence in, 147, 442, 580, 679–80; sexing, 143–44, 442, 699; in South Asia, 675; testimony of, 146–49. *See also* burial data; mortuary studies
Hungary, 545
hunter-gatherer societies, 503–27; androcentric interpretations of, 525; division of labor in, 504–9, 579, 600–602, 646–47; ethnoarchaeology and, 518–19; ethnography and, 527n7; historical archaeology and, 518–19; households and space in, 515–20; skeletal evidence of, 520–23; Southern African Stone Age, 599–605; tools in, 509–15. *See also* gathering; hunting
hunting: activities constituting, 506, 508, 524–25, 816; children engaged in, 357; critiques of emphasis on, 459–63; danger of, 258; evolution and, 455; of herds, 579; and human nature, 455–57; "kill" as focus of, 814, 816; male-female dichotomy and, 456–60, 505–7; "Man the Hunter" symposium on, 457–59, 505, 525; methods of, 513–14; prestige of, 512; processing phases of, 525, 819; scholarly emphasis on, 456–63, 505, 512–13; as "showing off," 507; subsistence and, 461–63; tools for, 512–14, 814, 816; women engaged in, 8, 260, 462, 600–601, 816–17. *See also* hunter-gatherer societies
hunting hypothesis, 455–63, 505
Hurcombe, Linda, 157

Hurtado, Ana Magdalena, 258, 260
Hutson, Scott, 63
hybridity, 413–14
hypermasculinity, 319–20

iconography, 444. *See also* representational art
identity: East/Southeast Asian elite and, 652–61; heterarchy and, 222–23; households and, 184–86; layers of, 141; masculine, 410–11, 414, 417; multiple sources of, 150–51, 333. *See also* personhood; sexual identity
ideology, representational art and, 40–41. *See also* gender ideology
Ikawa-Smith, Fumiko, 636–37
Ilchamus culture, 42, 267
imagery. *See* representational art
Inca culture, 110, 202, 865–68
India, 676–77, 710
Indiana Jones novels/films, 707
individuals, as unit of study, 615
industrial age, gender roles in, 247, 257
Indus Valley civilization, 672–75
inequality. *See* gender equality
infant mortality, 259
infants: children as caregivers for, 229; Iron Age disposal of, 153; mother-infant relationship as most significant, 461; nursing of, 309
inference, model of, 61–62
informants, gender of, 254
Ingalik culture, 513
Ingold, Tim, 211
injuries: of other genders, 442–43; of war victims, 833; of women warriors, 145, 443. *See also* repetitive stress, skeletal evidence of
Insoll, Timothy, 620
interdisciplinarity, evolutionary theory and, 488–89
intermarriage, in Pastoral Neolithic, 607–8
international management, 220
intersexuality, 709
interviews, ethnoarchaeology and, 255

Inuit culture, 204–5, 814
Inupiat culture, 259
Iñupiat culture, 515–16
Iran, 266, 572
Ireland, 572, 585
Irigaray, Luce, 765
Iron Age: in Africa, 608–14; European case study, 152–55; Late, 378
iron production, 205, 269–70, 546, 608–11
Iroquois culture, 838–40
Isaac, Glynn, 459, 465–67
Islam, 620, 667, 754
isotope analysis: of diet, 149–50; of gender, 744; migration patterns and, 149
Italy, neolithic: farming societies in, 544–45; figurines in, 760; gendered space in, 751–53; gender relations and ideologies in, 741–42; representational art in, 41; variability in gender in, 32
Izzet, Vedia, 766–67

Jackson, Andrew, 70, 72
Jackson, Louise M., 70
Jackson, Thomas L., 205, 835
Jameson, M., 313
Jameson, Michael H., 754
Janes, Robert R., 251, 259, 519
Japan, 636–37, 639
Japanese Archaeological Association, 637
Jarrige, Catherine, 669, 671
Jarvenpa, Robert, 12, 255–56, 259, 267, 816
Jauja, Peru, 865–66
Jews, gender ideologies among, 80
Jiang, Yu, 656–57
Jiao, Tianlong, 635
Jing, Lady, 654, 655
Jochim, Michael A., 527n5
Johnsson, Catherine, 748
Jolly, Margaret, 712
Jomon figurines, 636–37, 639
Jones, Neville, 597
Joukowsky, Martha S., 738
Journal of Anthropological Research, 735

Journal of European Archaeology, 735
Journal of Iberian Archaeology, 735
Journal of Mediterranean Archaeology, 735
Journal of Social Archaeology, 735
journals, women's representation in, 598
Joyce, Rosemary, 8, 40, 41, 128, 221, 236, 365, 377, 387–90, 414, 418, 444, 799–800
Jubilee Shelter, South Africa, 512, 599–600
Judaism, 667
Jundi, Sophia, 120

Kaberry, Phyllis Mary, 699, 713
Kaestner, Sibelle, 10
Kappeler, Susanne, 318
Karlisch, Sigrun, 10
Katsina religion, 377, 444
Katz, Marilyn, 306
Kehoe, Alice, 5, 7, 254, 513, 525, 814, 816
Keightley, David, 635
Kelley, Jane, 9
Kelly, Robert L., 509
Kennedy, Mary C., 828, 829
Kenoyer, Mark, 674
Kent, Susan, 251–52, 254–55, 257, 258, 268, 271, 276, 277, 519–20, 601–2
Kenya, 263–64, 267, 272–73, 275, 455, 465
Kenyon, Kathleen, 737, 738
Keuls, Eva, 306, 313, 316
Key, C. A., 485
Khao Deang, Thailand, 644
Khao Plara, Thailand, 644
Khoekhoe, 599, 602–5
Khoisan speakers, 599
Khok Phanom Di, Thailand, 645
Kinchin, Juliet, 124
King, Eleanor M., 226
King, Julia A., 81–82
King, Stacie, 335–36
Kintampo complex, West Africa, 606
Kirkham, Pat, 115
kitchens, 68–69
Klah, Hastíín, 440–41

Klepinger, Linda, 858
Knapp, A. Bernard, 404, 412, 419
knappers, 270
Knight, C., 474
knowledge, women's, 11
Knüsel, Christopher J., 224, 230
Koehler, Lyle, 830, 843
Kohn, M., 474–75
Kokkinidou, Dimitra, 735, 760
Koloski-Ostrow, Ann Olga, 318
Konso culture, 271
Korea, 649–50
Koster, Harold A., 572, 573
Koyukon culture, 519
Kramer, Carol, 249, 255, 610
Kreamer, Christine M., 275
Kristiansen, Kristian, 231
Kruczek-Aaron, Hadley, 80, 184
!Kung, 258, 458, 460, 509, 579
Kuper, Adam, 264, 612
Kuskokwim culture, 518
Kuznar, Lawrence, 577

labor. *See* division of labor; work
Lacan, Jacques, 416, 417
Lake, M., 476
Lakota culture, 441, 444–45, 831–32
Lamb, Dorothy, 738
Lamb, Winifred, 738
Lambert, Patricia M., 836
Lamphere, Louise, 541, 544, 559, 650
Lancaster, C. S., 458, 462
landscape, 199–212; activity spaces on, 204–7; definition of, 199; embodiment of, 201–4; history and, 209–11; interpretation of, 211; marking of, 207–9; who genders, 200–201
landscape painting, 199, 200
Lane, Paul, 612–13
language: androcentric, 63, 298, 299–300; gender archaeology writings and, 735; and objects as utterances, 128
La Placita, Colorado, 344, 352–57
La Plata, New Mexico, 32

Larson, Mary Ann, 254
Las Vegas Phase communities, 857
Late Dorset, 516
Late Stone Age (LSA), 599–607
Laurence, Ray, 312
La Violette, Adrien J., 273
Lawrence, Susan, 79, 700
Leacock, Eleanor, 460
Leakey, Louis, 455, 737
Leakey, Mary, 455, 737
Leakey, Meave, 455
Leakey, Richard, 455
learning, computer simulation of, 476
Le Corbusier, 125
Lee, Richard, 457, 458, 460, 505, 509, 579
legal rights, women denied, 301
Legge, A. J., 574
Leibowitz, L., 460, 461
LeMoine, Genevieve, 516
Lemonnier, P., 486
Leroi-Gourhan, André, 761
Lesure, Richard G., 796–97
Levant, 549–54, 679–80
Lévi-Strauss, Claude, 201
Lewis-Williams, David, 597, 603
lhamana, 377, 443–44
Li, Jian-jing, 636, 647
life cycle: archaeological study of, 335–36; in Ashanti culture, 335; evolution and, 482–85; gender signification and, 437; grave goods and, 40; household space and, 68; mortuary studies and, 115–16; reproduction and, 484
Lightfoot, Kent, 172, 340
Lindisfarne, Nancy, 415, 420
Linduff, Katheryn M., 547, 637, 653–55, 662
linear perspective, 200
lines, for hunting, 513–14
Lips, J. E., 513
Littleton, Judith, 699
location, phenomenology and, 36
Logan, Michael H., 441
Loma Alta, Ecuador, 555–56

Longacre, William A., 272
Longino, Helen, 359
Loos, Adolf, 125
Lopiparo, Jeanne, 796
Lovejoy, Owen, 463–65
Lucas, Michael T., 71
Lucy, Sam J., 143, 145
Luedke, Tracy, 617
Luo culture, 272–73
Lyons, Diane, 252, 255, 261–62

MacEachern, S., 599
MacLean, Rachel, 545–46, 610–11
Magdalen Asylum, Philadelphia, Pennsylvania, 73–74, 380
Magdalenian culture, 44, 486, 749
maize, 824, 829, 865
Majiayao culture, 548, 642–44
male bias. *See* androcentrism
male power-garden syndrome, 64
male provisioning, 463–65
Mali, 273
Malinowski, B., 387
Malta, 208
mamacona, 867
Mamprugu society, 261
Mande culture, 273
Mandt, Gro, 762
Manly Hearts, 841–42
"Man the Hunter" symposium (1966), 457–59, 505, 525
Mapunda, Bertram B., 609
Marcus, Joyce, 790–91, 797
Margolis, Maxine, 257
Marinatos, Nanno, 735
maritime archaeology, 700
markets, women's role in, 71
Marlow, Christopher, 710
marriage amendment, 390
Marshall, F., 577
Marshall, Yvonne, 386
Martin, Debra L., 32
Martin, Smart, 114
Martinez, Antoinette, 172

Marucci, Gina, 838
Marxism: in China, 546, 635; in Mesoamerican archaeology, 790
Marxist-feminism, 74–76
masculinity(ies), 401–25; archaeological discipline and, 408; archaeology of, 402–4, 406–7; body and, 414–19; categorical issues concerning, 420–22; classical world and, 408; construction of, 409–16; deconstruction of "male" and, 415–19; defining, 404–6, 409–10; essentialism and, 407–9; hegemonic, 413, 421; as heuristic fiction, 422; and identity, 410–11, 414, 417; ideology and, 411; iron production and, 608; material culture and, 410, 414, 418; methodological issues concerning, 419–25; power and, 411–14; reason associated with, 407–8; reflexivity in research on, 423–25; and sex/gender distinction, 406; variability in, 412–15; violence and, 420–21. *See also* masculinity theories; men
masculinity theories, 85, 319–21
material culture: body and, 127–28; context as focus of, 108–12; discourse and, 128; ethnoarchaeology and, 252; gender and, 105–29; gender construction and, 112–17; interpretation of, 105; masculinity and, 410, 414, 418; migration patterns and, 150; objects as focus of, 106–8, 126; recent developments in, 126–29; role of, in gender studies, 106–17; of space, 120–25. *See also* artifacts
mate selection, 461, 471, 474–75, 483–84
Mateu, Escoriza, 765
matrilineal organization, advantages of, 839
Matthews, Keith, 377
Mayan culture: dwelling areas in, 181–82; execution of prisoners in, 337; farming in, 35; gender archaeology and, 788–90; gendered cosmos in, 203; heterarchy in, 226; landscape and cosmology in, 210–11; representational art in, 41; sexuality in, 386, 387–90, 800; space in, 43–44, 265; textile production in, 185
Mazel, Aron D., 601–2
Mbuti culture, 600
McBryde, Isabel, 708
McCafferty, Geoffrey G., 375, 791, 794
McCafferty, Sharisse D., 375, 791, 794
McCardle, Penny, 699–700
McCoid, C. H., 759
McCormick, Finbar, 582–83
McCulloch, Warren, 219
McDermott, L., 759
McDonald, Josephine, 698
McEwan, Bonnie G., 70
McGhee, Robert, 204
McGowan, Angela, 706
McGuire, Kelly R., 507
McGuire, Randall H., 222, 226, 824–25
McIntosh, Susan Keech, 221
McKell, Sheila, 515
McRae, Leanne, 707
Meadow, Richard, 674
Meehan, Betty, 708
Mehrgarh, Baluchistan, 669, 671–72
Mellaart, James, 680–81
memes, 469
memorial stones, 676–77
men: as archaeological subject, 401–4, 406–7; reflexivity of, 424. *See also* masculinity(ies)
men's movement, 403
menstruation, 712, 833, 838
merm, 709
Meskell, Lynn, 41, 43, 365, 382, 387–90, 419, 436, 615–16, 715, 716
Mesoamerica: Classic period, 786–87; cloth production in, 46, 179; definition of, 785–86; landscape and cosmology in, 210–11; politics in, 793–94; writing systems in, 786. *See also specific countries and cultures*; Mesoamerican archaeology
Mesoamerican archaeology, 785–802; culture-historical approach in, 788; current situation of, 801–2; figurines in, 795–98;

894 INDEX

gender archaeology's emergence in, 788–95; gender construction in, 799–801; mortuary studies in, 798–99; sexuality in, 800; space/time boundaries for, 785–88
Mesolithic North Africa, 605–6
Mesolithic Siberia, 378
Mesopotamia, 681–84
metallurgy, 227–28, 231–32, 750. *See also* iron production
methodologies: androcentric, 64–65; case studies, 45; in classical archaeology, 299; comparative, 45–46; dialogic approach, 47n1; ethnoarchaeology, 253–56; ethnography/ethnohistory, 35–36, 45; explicitness about, 256; in gender archaeology, 31–46; masculinity concept and, 419–25; phenomenology, 36; postmodern, 85; reflexivity and, 423–25; researcher gender as factor in, 254–55; totalizing accounts and their critiques, 45
metonymy, 248
Meyers, Carol, 139
miati, 376–77, 443
microcores, 837
Middle Ages: architecture of, 123, 383; castles in, 754; women and pastoralism in, 585
Middle Bronze Age, 119
Middle Stone Age, 597
Middleton, Peter, 424
Midwest, American, 826–31
midwifery, 373–74
migration: material culture and, 150; skeletal evidence of, 38, 149; strontium analysis and, 561–62, 744
Miller, Michele A., 553
Mills, Barbara J., 182–83, 226–27, 228, 558
Mimbres culture, 820–21, 841
Mina, Maria, 760
mind: cognitive psychology and, 476–80; dualism of body and, 387, 470
Minnis, Paul E., 823

Minoan society, 206, 766
missionaries, Spanish, 383
Mississippian culture, 830–31
Mitchell, Peter J., 600
Mithen, Steve, 474–75, 477–78, 480, 481, 484, 486
mitimas, 867
Mizoguchi, Koji, 639
Moba culture, 275
Mobley-Tanaka, Jeannette, 187
Moche society, Peru, 35–36, 384–86, 863
Mock, Shirley Boteler, 822–23
Mogollon culture, 824
Mohenjo Daro, 672–74
Molleson, Theya, 550, 580–81
Mongolia, 653, 659–61
Mono Indians, 205
monuments, 208
Moore, A. M. T., 576
Moore, Henrietta L., 252, 263–64
Moquegua Valley, Peru, 864–65
Morgan, Elaine, 11
Mortensen, Lena, 236
Morter, Jon, 753
mortuary studies, 137–58; in American Southwest, 825–26; and artifact meanings, 127; on dress, 119; in East/Southeast Asia, 640–43, 645, 653–61; in Europe, 742–47; female warrior phenomenon and, 146; gender analysis through, 107, 111, 115–16, 141–52, 743–47; heterarchy and, 223; history of gender and, 138–40; ideal situation for, 146; Iron Age Europe case study, 152–55; issues in contemporary, 155–58; of Late Neolithic China, 547–48; levels of, 142; of Mesoamerica, 798–99; in Midwest America, 828; multiple burials and, 146; and mummies, 855–56; and neutral burial category, 152; other genders and, 144, 438–40; settlement versus mortuary remains, 142; sex and gender in, 743–44; and social constructivism, 116–17; in South America,

858, 863, 864; in South Asia, 674–75; visibility as issue for, 152. *See also* burial data; grave goods; human skeletal material
Moss, Madonna L., 508, 837
mother goddess hypothesis, 755–58
mothering: classical archaeology and, 308–10; at Clifton Plantation, Bahamas, 345–52; definition of, 345; historical archaeology and, 69–70, 72, 77–78; infant-mother relationship as most significant, 461; at La Placita, Colorado, 352–57; personhood and, 343–58; work and, 358
mouflon, 576
Mountford, Charles P., 711
Mrozowski, Stephen A., 85
MSMs, 442
Mughal, M. Rafique, 674
Mullins, Paul R., 81
multiple genders. *See* other genders
mummies, 855–56
municipal housekeeping movement, 72, 79
Munson, Marit K., 820–21, 841
Mura culture, 262
Murray, Margaret, 738
Muslims: division of labor among, 266; households of, 262–63; veiling of women, 117, 715
Myerowitz, Molly, 318

Namaqua culture, 271
Narkomfin Communal House, 382
Narragansett, 840
narrative approach, 63–64
Nash, June, 791
National Treasure (film), 707
Native Californians, 383
Native North American archaeology, 813–44; California and Great Basin, 834–36; cultural areas, 814; environmental variation and, 813; ethnography and, 813; Midwest and Southeast, 826–31; Northeast, 838–40; and other genders, 840–43; Pacific Northwest, 836–38; Paleoindian cultures, 814–20; Plains Indian cultures, 831–34; Southwest, 820–26
Native North Americans, nonbinary genders among, 375–77, 435–45. *See also specific cultures*; Native North American archaeology
Natufian culture, 579, 679–80
Navajo culture, 336, 440–41
Navarro, Vida, 746
ndani, 618
Near East: agropastoral societies in, 577–81; animal domestication in, 575–77
Near Eastern archaeology, 139–40. *See also specific countries and cultures*; Southwest Asian archaeology
needles, bone, 517
Nelson, Margaret, 265
Nelson, Sarah M., 140, 549, 636–39, 649–50, 734, 758–59
neo-Darwinian archaeology, 468, 481
Neolithic Africa, 607–8
Neolithic China, 547–49
Neolithic Europe: division of labor in, 580; farming societies in, 542–45; figurines in, 759–60; gendered space in, 751–52; hierarchy/heterarchy in, 231; monuments from, 208–9
Neolithic Revolution, 537–38, 552
Neolithic South Asia, 669, 671–72
Neolithic Southwest Asia, 549–54, 677–81
neonates, 153
neurogenetic determinism, 470
neutral, male gender as. *See* ungendered research, as androcentric
neutral burial category, 152
Nevett, Lisa, 123, 180–81, 298, 313–14, 754
New Kingdom, Egypt, 43, 382, 387–90
New Men's Studies, 404
Ngarrindjeri tribe, 713
Nikolaidou, Marianna, 735, 760
Nilgiri Hills, India, 676–77
Niuheliang, China, 548–49, 638

nomadic pastoralism, 572
nonbinary genders. *See* other genders
nonhumans, personhood of, 336
Non Nok Tha, Thailand, 641–42
nonsubsistence activities, skeletal evidence of, 38
Nördstrom, Hans-Åke, 614
North African Mesolithic gatherers, 605–6
North American archaeology, 140
Northeast, North American, 838–40
northern Plains groups, 441, 444–45
Norway, 9, 107, 734, 736
Norwegian Archaeological Review, 735
novels, 9
Nunamiut culture, 259
nursing, of infants, 309
nutrition. *See* dietary analysis

Oaxaca, 335–36
objectivism: in archaeology, 12; critique of, 63; landscape objectified by Western gaze, 200; strong objectivity, 86–87
objects. *See* artifacts
occupational specialization, 440–41
O'Connell, James F., 258, 260
Old Bering Sea complex, 439–40
Olsen, Bjørnar, 126, 128
Olwig, K. R., 203
Olynthos, Greece, 180–81
Onge culture, 260
The Origin of the Modern Mind (Donald), 477
ornaments, 232–37
Ortman, Scott, 187
Ortner, Sherry, 177, 248
Osgood, Cornelius, 513
osteophytosis, 521
osteoporosis, 523
other genders: archaeological study of, 32–33; Australian archaeology and, 709–10; binary thinking and, 63; dress of, 441; dual-sex imagery from Levant, 553; in European figurines, 759–60; heterarchy and, 223–24; household/architectural analysis and, 443–44; in Iron Age Europe, 154–55; in Mesoamerica, 799–801; mortuary analysis and, 144, 438–40; in Native North America, 375–77, 435–45, 840–43; and power, 224; and ritual, 224; skeletal evidence of, 37–38, 441–43; work and, 440–41; in Zuni culture, 227
Ötzi, the Tyrolean Ice Man, 375
Ouzman, Sven, 603–4
Owasco culture, 838–39
Owen, Linda R., 749
Oxford Journal of Archaeology, 735
Ozette, Washington, 511

Pacific Northwest, North American, 386, 836–38
Pader, Ellen Jane, 138
Paleoindian cultures, 814–20
Paleolithic architecture, 382
Paleolithic figurines, 758–59
Paloma communities, 860–61
Papua New Guinea, 337
parental investment, 473
Parkington, John, 602–4
participant observation, 255
pastoralism, 571–86; in Africa, 607–8, 612–14; agro-, 572–73, 577–81; androcentrism and, 266, 577–78; definition of, 572; division of labor in, 266–67, 577–80, 583–84, 647–48; evidence of animal domestication, 575–77; historical models for women's roles in, 585; identifying animal domestication, 573–75; nomadic, 572; and secondary products, 581–84; transhumant, 572, 585
Pastoral Neolithic in East Africa, 607–8
pathologies, skeletal evidence of, 147
patriarchy: in classical world, 300–302; concept of, 10–11; critique of, 11–12; naming practices based on, 64; second-wave feminist critique of, 73–74
Patterson, Orlando, 337
Patterson, Thomas, 5
Patton, John Q., 256, 265

Pauli, Ludwig, 154
Pawnee culture, 830
Pearson, Parker, 124
pebbles, decorated, 822–23
pedagogy, 9
Pedrotti, Anna, 764
Peirce, Melusina Fay, 74
people-object relations, 115
performance of gender: applications of, 140–41; archaeological study of, 33; cultural anthropology and, 249; material culture and, 113; skeletal evidence of, 37; space and, 120–25; theory of, 369–70. *See also* agency; gender construction
Perkins, Dexter, Jr., 574
Perry, Elizabeth M., 377, 442, 443–44
Perryman family, 70, 82, 373
personhood, 333–59; in Ashanti culture, 335; bioarchaeology and, 343; at Clifton Plantation, Bahamas, 344–52; components of, 333–34; concept of, 334–35; context and, 337–38; denial of, by society, 337, 344; future of research on, 358–59; "individual" versus, 334; in La Placita, Colorado, 344, 352–57; and mothering/child rearing, 343–58; on nonhumans, 336; research related to, 334; and textual archaeologies, 343. *See also* identity
Peru, 384–86, 860–65
Petersen, Alan, 415
Peterson, Jane, 147, 237, 551, 679–80
Petrie, Flinders, 738
phallic culture, 388–89
phenomenology: applications of, 36; drawbacks of, 36; and space/time, 121
Philippines, 640–41, 651–52
Picazo, Marina, 738
pigs, 549
Pilgrim, Robert, 696
Pingyan, China, 647
place, space versus, 121
Plains Indian cultures, 441, 444–45, 831–34

plant cultivation, 576
play landscapes, 83–84
Ploss, Hermann Heinrich, 711–12
plows, 582
Pluciennik, Mark, 764–65
political resonance, of archaeological interpretations, 12
politics: in archaeological theory, 12–13, 15, 31–32, 86–87; current, feminism and, 389; in Mesoamerica, 793–94; pottery designs and, 273–74
Pollock, Susan M., 684
Pomeroy, Sarah B., 296
porcupine quillwork, 441
pornography, 316, 318
Pornography and Representation in Greece and Rome (Richlin), 316
postcolonial feminism, 75
postmarital residence, skeletal evidence of, 38
postmodernism: on center/margins, 253; and classical archaeology, 311–14; feminism and, 691; future of, 85–87; Marxist-feminism and, 76; and masculinity theory, 85; methods of, 85; and queer theory, 85; and third-wave feminism, 76–85
postprocessualism, 13, 86, 417, 445, 739, 741; advantages/disadvantages of, 768
Potter, Daniel R., 226
pottery production: in Africa, 605–6, 611; in American Southwest, 823–24; division of labor in, 272, 275; heterarchy in, 227. *See also* ceramics
power: in Africa, 619–20; archaeological study of, 151; in East/Southeast Asia, 649–52; in Egypt, 614–16; feminist analysis of, 60; gender ideology and, 411–13; and gender relationships in Southwest, 541; in households, 186; in Iroquois culture, 840; masculinity and, 411–14; material culture and, 110; ritual and, 230, 650; secular versus ritual, 230; sexual, 317–18; spatial constructions and, 122; as spiritual potency, 651–52; third

gender and, 224; and visibility/invisibility of people, 151. *See also* prestige
Power, C., 474
practice-based approaches, 178, 183, 404–5, 418, 437
practice theory, 172
Pratt, Heather, 838
Prehistoric Men (Braidwood), 577–78
The Prehistory of Sex (Taylor), 365
The Prehistory of the Mind (Mithen), 477
present, projected onto past. *See* anachronism
prestige: in households, 186–87; of hunting, 512; stereotypes and, 525–26. *See also* power
Preucel, Robert, 17
Prezzano, Susan C., 838
Price, T. Douglas, 16–17
primatology, 454, 456, 460–61, 483
Prine, Elizabeth P., 376–77, 443, 842–43
Prins, Frans E., 613–14
private sphere. *See* domestic realm
Proceedings of the Prehistoric Society (journal), 735
processualism, 13, 250–51, 458, 463, 700
production. *See* work
Proskouriakoff, Tatiana, 737, 788–90
prostitution: archaeological study of, 379–81; in Greece, 306, 315–18; in Roman world, 319; sexology and, 381; sexuality and, 381
protective behavior: ceramic/calabash design and, 274; toward children, 335, 351–52; at Clifton Plantation, Bahamas, 345–52; powerful objects and, 351–52
Prowers, Amache Ochinee, 338–42
pseudoinclusion, 737
puberty, 712
public roles of women, 66–73, 224, 303–7
public sphere: binary thinking and, 70, 302; domestic realm and, 177
Pueblo culture, 32, 40, 222, 444, 821–22
Purser, Margaret, 75, 79
Pyburn, K. Anne, 39, 229–31, 794
Pythagoras, 306, 311

qargi, 516
Qariaraqyuk, Somerset Island, 516–17
qasgi, 518
Qashqa'i culture, 266
Qijia culture, 547–48, 642–44
qompi, 867
qompicamayoq, 867–68
quarrying, 515
queer, concept of, 370
queer theory, 85, 223
Queyash, Peru, 43
Quichua culture, 265–66, 273
quillwork, 441

race, artifacts and, 82–83
racism: as depersonalization, 337, 344; evolutionary theory and, 456; sociobiology and, 469; Zimbabwean archaeology and, 597
Randall-MacIver, David, 597
Randsborg, Klavs, 228
Rathje, William, 175
Rattray, R. S., 335, 351
Rautman, Alison E., 222
Ravesloot, John C., 238
Real Alto, Ecuador, 556–57, 858
reason, masculinity associated with, 407–8
Recuay society, Peru, 385–86, 862–63
"Red Light Voices" (Costello), 381
reductionism, neo-Darwinian, 481
Reed, Charles, 578, 580–81
Reeder, Greg, 375
reflexivity, in research, 423–25
reform women, 67–69, 72, 79–80, 84
Rega, Elizabeth, 111–12, 743–44
regional studies, in European gender archaeology, 741–42
Rehak, Paul, 206, 766
Reilly, Joan, 309
Reinhardt, Gregory A., 515–16
relativism, 86
religion: Africa and global religions, 620; gendered cosmos and, 201; gender ideology and, 80; Southwest Asia and, 667

Renfrew, Colin, 737
repetitive stress, skeletal evidence of, 147, 442, 580, 679–80
representation: artifacts as, 106–8; of gender, 33; interpretation of, 384, 387–88; of the sexual/erotic, 383–86. *See also* representational art
representational art: in American Southwest, 820–21; cognitive psychology and, 487–88; in Early Neolithic China, 548; in East/Southeast Asia, 638–42; gender archaeology and, 40–41; ideology and, 40–41; Mesopotamian cylinder seals, 684; Minoan frescoes, 766; narrative scenes, 674; in Neolithic Levant, 552–53; during Neolithic Revolution, 552; other genders and, 444–45. *See also* figurines; rock art; statues
reproduction: as archaeological subject, 768–69; cooking as symbolic of, 546, 611; division of labor and, 473–74; evolution and, 456, 460; female strategizing and, 474; iron production as symbolic of, 205, 269–70, 546, 608–11; life cycle and, 484; male versus female perspectives on, 473; mate selection and, 461, 471, 474–75, 483–84; success in, 465, 471, 473, 483, 485. *See also* fertility; sexual activity
research assistants, gender of, 255
researchers, gender of, 254–55
residential propinquity, 173
resistance, Marxist-feminism and, 75–76
Rice, Patricia C., 759
Richlin, Amy, 316
Ridley, M., 471
ritual: amputations in Africa and, 602–3; birthing and, 711–12; in classical world, 311–12; dancing in Levant, 553–54; in Egypt, 614–16; of farming societies, 560; concerning fertility, 372–73; figurines and, 760–61; and gendered space, 751–52; hideworking as, 272; in Hongshan culture, 548–49; iron production and, 609–10; menstruation and, 712, 833, 838; mortuary, 642–44; objects for, 822; power and, 230, 650; status and, 187; third gender and, 224. *See also* protective behavior
Robb, John, 741–42, 753
Robb, John E., 32, 225, 413
Robertshaw, P., 618–19
Robin, Cynthia, 35, 43, 182, 788, 794
Robins, Gay, 615
rock art: Aboriginal, 698; African, 597, 603–5, 613–14; androcentric interpretations of, 761; in California, 836; in Europe, 761–65; and fertility, 372; gendered activity spaces for, 207; gender salience in, 40, 207; interpretation of, 761, 821; and masculine identity, 417; other genders and, 444–45; sexual representations in, 374; in Southwest America, 821–22; study of, 207–8; Thai, 644–45
Rode, Penny, 648–49
Rodriguez, Maria Jesus de, 791
Roman world: dress in, 119–20; households in, 312; sexuality in, 318–19; women's public roles in, 307. *See also* classical archaeology
Rosaldo, Michelle, 177, 310
Rose, S., 470, 480
Rose Cottage Cave, South Africa, 511, 599, 601
Rosen-Ayalon, Miriam, 10
Rosenfeld, Andrée, 708
Rosser, Sue V., 277–78
Roth, Ann Mary, 202–3
Rove, Karl, 390
Rowlands, Michael, 610
Rubin, Gayle, 366, 368, 379
Rundbrief (newsletter), 10
Russell, Alice Lopez, 355
Russell, Pamela, 761

Sabloff, Jerry, 16
saffron, 206
Saitta, Dean J., 222, 226

Salado, Arizona, 238
Salishan culture, 838
San culture, 599–605
Sanday, Peggy Reeves, 549, 638
Sandler, Bernice R., 6
San Isidro, Ecuador, 556–57
Sappho, 305
Sassaman, Kenneth, 503
sati, 668–69, 676
Sauromatia, warrior women of, 145
Sausa, Peru, 44
scale, concept of, 220
scalping, 833
Scandinavia, 378, 733–34, 736
Scarborough, Vernon L., 221
Scattolin, M. Cristina, 33, 43–44, 859
Schama, Simon, 117
Schapera, Isaac, 264
Schiff, Ann, 172
Schlegel, Alice, 541
Schmandt-Besserat, Denise, 552
Schmidt, Peter R., 205, 252, 269, 277, 609–10
Schmidt, Robert A., 157, 365, 374–75, 378, 437
Schmittou, Douglas A., 441
Schwander, E. L., 312
Schwarz, Maureen T., 336
Science (journal), 463, 478
Scott, Elizabeth, 75, 76
sculptures. *See* figurines; memorial stones; statues
Scythia, warrior women of, 145, 305
Sealy, J. C., 601
seclusion, in architecture, 122–23, 180–81, 263, 313–14, 754–55
secondary products revolution (SPR), 581–84
The Second Sex (Beauvoir), 296
second-wave feminism: and classical archaeology, 310; patriarchy critiqued by, 73–74
sedentism, 605–7
Segobye, Alinah, 264

segregation, in architecture, 123, 180–81, 754
Seifert, Donna J., 65, 380
Seiradaki, Mercy Money-Coutts, 738
Seler, Cecelia, 789
Seler, Eduard, 789
self, actual, 338. *See also* identity; personhood
Senior, Louise M., 441
settlement remains, versus mortuary remains, 142
sex, biological: accuracy rate in assigning, 144; determination of, 48n2, 144, 376, 442, 699; gender versus, 60, 143, 248, 368–69, 406, 412, 416, 634, 743; intersex and, 709; mortuary determination of, 143–44
sex/gender system, 368–69
sexism: as depersonalization, 337; sociobiology and, 469
sexology, 367–68, 381
sex pots, Peruvian, 384–86
sex trade. *See* prostitution
sexual activity: iron production as symbolic of, 205, 269–70; pornography and, 316; reproduction versus, 372. *See also* reproduction
sexual attraction, 474–75
sexual identity: applicability of concept of, 156–57; heterarchy and, 222–23; sexology and, 367–68
sexuality, 365–90; and anachronism, 371; androcentric perspective on, 366; architecture and, 381–83; in classical world, 315–19; and fertility management, 371–74; gender and, 369; gender performance theory and, 369–70; homo- and trans-, 375–79; in Mayan culture, 387–90; in Mesoamerica, 800; in New Kingdom, Egypt, 387–90; politics and, 389–90; and prostitution, 379–81; representations of, 383–86; sex/gender system and, 368–69; sexology and, 367–68; study of, 365; theories of, 366–71
Shakespeare, William, 710

shamanism: among African hunter-gatherers, 603–4; Ecuadorian, 556–57; gender and, 224, 378, 439–40; and transformation, 224
Shang, China, 653–56
Shanks, Michael, 418
Shapiro, H. A., 317
Shawnee-Minisink, Pennsylvania, 817–18
sheep, 574–77, 583
Shelach, Gideon, 546, 662
shellfish, 508, 602, 837, 856
Shell Mound Archaic, 508
shell mounds, 827
Shennan, Stephen, 472–73
Shepard, Anna, 737
Shepard, Rita A., 518–19
Shepherd, Nick, 598
Sherratt, A. G., 581–84
Shoocongdej, Rasmi, 644–45
Siberia, 378
Sicán, Peru, 864
Silbury, England, 208
Silla, Korea, 649–50
Simon, Arleyn W., 238
skeletal material. *See* human skeletal material
skulls, plastered, 554
slavery, 68, 337, 344–52
Slavey culture, 519
Slocum, S., 459–60
Smith, Adam T., 225
Smith, Claire, 698
Smith, Gerrit, 80
Smith, Laurajane, 694–95, 702, 704, 706, 708
Smith, Maynard, 473
Smith, Shelley J., 614
Snow, Dean, 838–39
social agency, 481
social change. *See* change
social constructivism. *See* constructivism
socialism, 382
social science: criticisms of, 470–71; households from perspective of, 173–74
Society for American Archaeology, 6

Society for Historical Archaeology, 86
Society of Africanist Archaeologists (SAfA), 598
sociobiology, 465, 466, 468–72, 480–81
Socratic school, 306, 311
sodomy, 379
Sofaer, Joanna, 127–28, 153, 221, 231–32, 236, 237, 746
Sofaer-Derevenski, Joanna. *See* Sofaer, Joanna
Solari, Elaine-Maryse, 380
Solomon, Anne, 604
Solomon-Godeau, Abigail, 403
Sørenson, Marie Louise Stig, 141–43, 156, 635, 734, 736–38, 745, 746, 750, 760
South, Stanley, 65
South Africa, 271, 511–12, 595
South American archaeology, 853–69; Andean states, 861–65; archaic and formative cultures, 855–61; Inca culture, 865–68. *See also specific countries and cultures*
South and Southwest Asian archaeology, 667–85; regional similarities, 667; South Asia, 668–77; Southwest Asia, 677–84
South Asian archaeology, 668–77; Baluchistan, 669, 671–72; female temple imagery in, 668; figurines in, 669; historical periods, 675–77; Indus Valley, 672–75; and sati, 668–69, 676; South India, 676–77; Southwest Asian similarities to, 667. *See also specific countries and cultures*
Southeast, American, 826–31
Southeast Asian archaeology. *See* East and Southeast Asian archaeology
Southern Africa, Iron Age pastoralism in, 612–14
South India, 676–77
Southwest, American, 820–26; power in, 541; pre-Hispanic farming societies, 557–60; prestige in, 187; rock art in, 40
Southwest Asian archaeology, 677–84; figurines in, 679; Mesopotamia, 681–84; Neolithic villages, 677–81; significance of, 667; South Asian similarities to, 667.

See also specific countries and cultures; Near Eastern archaeology
space: activity spaces, 204–7, 255–56; gender archaeology and, 43–44, 180–82, 751–55; gender performance and, 120–25; household, 68–69, 178, 180–82; material culture of, 120–25; place versus, 121; segregation by gender in Africa, 601. *See also* houses; landscape
spatial syntax model, 122
specialization, in craft production, 227–28
Spector, Janet, 5, 9, 14, 18, 63, 76, 108, 138, 254, 411, 453, 467–68, 506, 831
Spelman, Elizabeth, 333
Spencer, Baldwin, 711
Spencer-Wood, Suzanne M. A., 65, 67, 68–69, 74, 77, 83–84
Spielmann, Katherine A., 559, 825
spindle whorls, 42–43, 108, 110, 115, 179
spinning. *See* spindle whorls; textile production
spirituality, gender transformations and, 375–77. *See also* ritual; shamanism
sport hunting model, 509, 513
stable carbon isotope composition, 522
Stahl, Ann Brower, 619
Stalsberg, Anne, 111
standpoint theory, 12–13
Stanford, C. B., 461
Stark, David, 238–39
statues: in Copper Age Europe, 763–64; Dian horse riders, 640; in Hongshan culture, 638; in Mississippian culture, 830; in Neolithic Levant, 552; South Asian, 673–74. *See also* figurines
status. *See* elites, in Asia; prestige
Stein, Gil, 17
stereotypes: first-wave feminist exposure of, 66–73; second-wave feminist reinforcement of, 73, 310. *See also* androcentrism; assumptions about gender
Sterner, Judy A., 274
Stevenson, Judith, 604
Stewart, Stewart, 302

Stewart-Abernathy, Leslie C., 83
Stoics, 311
Stoller, Robert, 410
Stone Age hunter-gatherers in Southern Africa, 599–605
stones, memorial, 676–77
stone tools: assumed to be men's, 510, 697; definition of, 512; first discovered, 463–64; for hideworking, 270–72; reevaluation of research on, 467; women's, 8, 340, 512, 514–15
Stoodley, Nick, 155
Storey, Rebecca, 798
storytelling. *See* narrative approach
Stothert, Karen E., 556–57, 816, 857
Strathern, Marilyn, 760
Strong, Eugénie, 738
strong objectivity, 86–87
strontium, 561–62, 744
structuralism: and binary thinking, 63, 77, 180, 201, 252, 302; ethnoarchaeology and, 252; and gendered space, 751–53
A Study of Women in Attic Inscriptions (Clees), 296
style: of ceramics, 272–74; as focus of classical archaeology, 299; other genders and, 440–41; sedentism and, 606–7
subjective aspects of research, 12, 63
subsistence: division of labor and, 747–49; food sharing and, 465–66; gathering and, 461–63; hunting and, 455–61; male provisioning and, 463–65
Sudan, 263, 274
Sullivan, Sharon, 708
suman, 351
Sumerian culture, 230
Summers, Laurence, 7
sumptuary laws, 117–18
Sun, Yan, 547, 636, 637, 642–44, 662
Sundstrom, Linea, 444–45, 831–32
supernumerary genders. *See* other genders
Sutton, Robert F., Jr., 316–17
Swahili culture, 262–63, 274, 617–18
Sweely, Tracy, 44, 181, 187

symbolism: in Çatalhöyük, 681; heterarchy and, 238–39; of iron production, 205, 269–70, 608–11; women's role in, 488
symmetry, sexual attraction and, 474–75
symposia, 306, 310, 313–14
Symposium in Quantitative Biology (1950), 456
systems theory model of culture, 61

Taçon, Paul S. C., 209–10
Tafuri, Mary Anne, 744
Tahltan culture, 837
Talalay, Lauren E., 543, 735, 760, 761, 766, 767–68
Tanner, N., 461
Tanzania, 205, 258–59, 455
task system, 255
Tavris, C., 479
Taylor, Timothy, 365, 372, 373
Tchernov, Eitan, 574
Tchumbali culture, 337
technology, in social context, 486
Teleki, G., 456
textile production: cosmology and, 210–11; earliest, 584; gender and, 115; Inca, 867–68; Mesoamerican, 46, 179; Mesoamerican archaeology, 185; Mississippian, 831; in Neolithic Europe, 545; in Peru, 862; in Southwest Asia, 682–83
textiles. *See* dress; textile production
textual archaeologies, 343
Thailand, 641–42, 644–46
Tham Ta Duang, Thailand, 644
Theoretical Archaeology Group, 5
theories: androcentric, 63, 302; Australian archaeology and, 694–95; construction of, 12; in European gender archaeology, 739; in gender archaeology, 10–13; politics and, 12–13, 15, 31–32, 86–87; of sexuality, 366–71
therianthropes, 604
things. *See* artifacts
third gender, 435. *See also* other genders
third-wave feminism: and classical archaeology, 311–14; and diversity, 82–84; essentialist critique by, 76–85; on ideology versus practice, 81–82; and inclusivity, 77; methods of, 85
Thomas, J., 489
Thomas, Julian, 222
Thukela Basin, 601–2
Thule whaling village, 516–17
Thutmose III, 615
time, space and, 121
Tingham, Ruth, 8
Tiwi culture, 515
Tlatilco, Mexico, 40, 128
Tlingit culture, 508, 837
Togo, 275
Tolkien, J. R. R., 145
Tomb 98, 649–50
Tomb Raider (film), 707
Toms, Judith, 747
Tooby, J., 470
toolmakers, women as, 8, 270–72, 340, 512–15, 697
tools: of African hunter-gatherers, 602; gender archaeology and, 42–43; gender attribution for, 511–12; hideworking, 270–72, 511, 514; in hunter-gatherer societies, 509–15; hunting, 512–14, 816; male-female dichotomy and, 510–11. *See also* stone tools; toolmakers, women as
topsy-turvy dolls, 82–83
toys, 69–70, 72–73, 309, 354
trace elements, study of, 744
traction, animals used for, 582
transhumant pastoralism, 572, 585
translators, gender of, 255
transportation, animals used for, 582
transsexuality, 375–79
trapping, 816
Treherne, Paul, 418, 744–45
Trevathan, Wenda R., 821
Tringham, Ruth, 47n1, 172, 336, 372–73, 443, 753
Trivers, R. L., 470, 473
Truscott, Marilyn, 702, 704, 706

Tuohy, Tina, 748
tupus, 42–43
Turner, Victor, 238
two-spirit identity, 375–77. *See also* berdaches
The Two Towers (film), 145

Ucko, Peter, 756
Ukraine, Amazons of, 145
Unangan Aleut culture, 517–18
ungendered research, as androcentric, 297–99, 401
United States: European gender archaeology versus that of, 739; and gender archaeology, 735. *See also specific cultures*; Native North American archaeology; Native North Americans
universalism: in early ethnoarchaeology, 250–51; masculinity and, 407–9; in theories of gender, 156
University of Western Australia, 702
Upper Paleolithic period, 487–88
Urewe culture, 545–46
utterances, objects as, 128

Valdivian culture, 555–57, 857–59
VanDerwarker, Amber, 185
Varangian women, 111
vase paintings, 301
Vasey, Paul L., 372
veils, 117, 715
Venus of Willendorf, 372, 759
victims, women as, 13
Vikings, 230
Vingen, Norway, 210
Vinnicombe, Patricia, 597
Vinsrygg, Synnøve, 508
violence: masculinity and, 420–21; against women, 829, 833
Visayan culture, 651–52
visibility/invisibility: in Arctic cultures, 259–60; burial data and, 151; for gatherers, 257; power and, 151; of tools' gender significance, 510–11; use of space and, 267–68

Vix, France, 157, 224, 439
Vogel, Melissa A., 863
Voss, Barbara L., 157, 249, 365, 383, 420, 439

Wadley, Lynn, 511–12, 520, 522–23, 596, 599–601
Walker, Madame C. J., 67
Walker, Philip L., 523
Walker, Susan, 313, 754
Wall, Diana di Zerega, 78, 79, 124, 183
Walton, James, 597
Wang, Ying, 655
war, in Plains Indian culture, 833
Warnier, Jean-Pierre, 610
Warren, Kay B., 47n1
warrior women: in Greek myth, 305; Native North American, 833, 841–42; Scythian and Sauromatian, 145, 305; Ukrainian and Caucasian, 145, 305
Washburn, Sherwood, 456, 457, 458, 462
Waterhouse, Helen, 738
Watson, Patty Jo, 828, 829
Watts, I., 474
Wa-ungwana, 618
weaning, 345, 823
weapons, gender ideology expressed through, 151–52
weaving. *See* textile production
Weber, Carmen A., 64
Webley, Lita, 271, 613
Weedman, Kathryn, 270–71, 597–98
Weglian, Emily, 439, 747
Weismantel, Mary, 35, 41, 384–85
Weiss, Kenneth, 144
Welbourn, Alice, 275
Wels-Weyrauch, Ulrike, 746
Wenner-Gren Foundation, 3, 456
"Were They All Men?" conference, 9, 734
West Africa, 262, 606–7
Western bias in archaeology, 714–16. *See also* Eurocentrism
Western Zhou period, 656–59
We'wha, 227

whale hunting, 516–17
What This Awl Means (Spector), 9, 63, 108
Wheeler, Kathleen L., 68
Wheeler, Mortimer, 674
Whelan, Mary K., 439
Whitehouse, Ruth, 14–15, 139, 544–45, 734, 742, 751, 760
Whitley, David S., 207
Whitridge, Peter, 516–17, 524
Wicker, Nancy, 18
Wilk, Richard, 175
Wilkie, Laurie A., 68, 69–70, 72, 77–78, 82, 346, 350, 373–74
Wilkinson, Richard G., 829
Willcox, Alexander, 597
Williams, Dyfri, 315–16
Williams, Frank E., 712
Williams, Mary Beth, 840
Wills, W. H., 823
Wilman, Maria, 597
Wilson, Diane, 843
Wilson, E. O., 468
Wilson, Meredith, 199
Winkler, John J., 424
winkte, 441, 445
Winters, Howard D., 40
Wolf, Eric R., 229, 236
womanism, 634
"Woman the Gatherer" conference (1980), 462–63, 505
women: in archaeological discipline, 4, 6–7, 596–99, 637, 695, 701–8, 736–39; as archaeological subject, 4, 7–8, 11, 34, 297–98; as beneficiaries of gender archaeology, 18; and dairying, 583; domestic work of, 67–68, 70–73; and embodiment, 710–14; as farmers, 539–40; as fishers, 508–9; as gatherers, 461–63, 505, 508–9; as gender archaeology subject, 14; as hunters, 8, 260, 462, 600–601, 816–17; as informants, 254; in iron production, 608; and lady-whore dichotomy, 302; legal rights not accorded, 301; as people without history, 229; public roles of, 66–73, 224, 303–7; reform, 67–69, 72, 79–80, 84; and symbolic systems, 488; as toolmakers, 8, 270–72, 340, 512–15, 697; as warriors, 145, 305, 833, 841–42. *See also* feminism; gender; gender archaeology
Women and Men in the Prehistoric Southwest (Crown), 557
Women in Archaeology conferences (Australia), 694–96
Women in Prehistory (Ehrenberg), 7, 543, 734
women's knowledge, 11. *See also* epistemology: feminist
women's movement. *See* feminism
Women's Role in Economic Development (Boserup), 539
Women's Work (Barber), 7
Wood, Margaret, 185
Woodland cultures, 828–29
wool production, 583
work: children and, 355, 357; in households, 182–83; in Inca empire, 867; mothers and, 358; other genders and, 440–41; repetitive stress evidence of, 147, 442; skeletal evidence of, 37, 520–22, 679–80; in Southwest Asia, 682–83. *See also* division of labor
World Archaeology (journal), 365, 735
World Wide Web, 8–9
Wrangham, R. W., 483
Wright, Katherine I., 551
Wright, Rita, 182
Wright, Rita P., 675, 683
writing, feminist approaches to, 9
Wu, Jui-man, 653
Wu, Xiaolong, 659–61
Wu Ding, 654
Wylie, Alison, 11–14, 61, 296–97, 695
Wylly, William, 344–46, 348

Yamin, Rebecca, 69–70
yanas, 867
Yang, Hongyu, 636, 642–44
Yates, Timothy, 374, 417, 762

Yegenoglu, Meyda, 117
Yellen, John, 258
Yentsch, Anne E., 64, 65, 68, 71
Yong, Ying, 657–58
Young, Linda, 79
Younger, John G., 308
Yucatec Maya, 35
Yugoslavia, 111, 743–44
Yup'ik Eskimo culture, 517
Yutopian, Argentina, 33, 43–44, 859

Zacharias, Sandra, 837
Zagarell, Allen, 676–77, 682–83
Zarmati, Louise, 9
Zeanah, David W., 507
zebu, 576
Zeder, Melinda A., 574
Zeidler, James A., 557, 857
Zihlman, A. L., 461–62
Zimbabwe, 38, 597, 617
Zimbabwe Cultural Pattern (ZCP), 617
Znoj, Heinzpeter, 221
zooarchaeology, 578
Zoroastrianism, 667
Zuni culture, 227, 377, 443–44

About the Contributors

Benjamin Alberti received his Ph.D. in archaeology form Southampton University in 1998. He has written on the representation of sexual difference at Late Bronze Age Knossos, Crete, and has begun to research gender, art, and materiality in late pre-Inca Northwest Argentina. He was a lecturer in archaeology at the Universidad Nacional de la Provincia de Buenos Aires, Argentina, 1999–2001, and is currently an assistant professor of anthropology at Framingham State College.

Bettina Arnold is an associate professor in the Department of Anthropology at the University of Wisconsin–Milwaukee. Her area of expertise is Early Iron Age Europe, but she has also participated in archaeological projects ranging from the Middle Bronze Age through the Roman period. Her research interests include European prehistory generally, Celtic Europe, the archaeology of gender, mortuary analysis, material culture as a system of communication, and ethical issues in archaeology, including the use and abuse of the past for political purposes. She is the coeditor, with Nancy L. Wicker, of *Gender and the Archaeology of Death* (2001) and *From the Ground Up: Beyond Gender Theory in Archaeology* (1999).

Wendy Ashmore is a professor of anthropology at the University of California, Riverside. Since receiving her Ph.D. from the University of Pennsylvania, attention to gender has joined study of settlement patterns, households, landscapes, and other aspects of space in antiquity as focus for her research and teaching, particularly with respect to the ancient Maya and their neighbors. Her publications include *Archaeologies of Landscape: Contemporary Perspectives* (coedited with A. Bernard Knapp, 1999).

Elisabeth A. Bacus is an independent scholar whose research interests include the archaeology of Southeast Asia, complex societies, political economy, gender, ceramics, and mortuary analysis. Current research projects include an archaeological investigation of early Balinese states and a mortuary-based study of social identities and relations in Bronze Age Thailand. Recent publications include "Expressing Gender in Bronze Age Northeast Thailand: The Case of Non Nok Tha" (in *Archaeology and Women*, 2006), *Archaeology of Hinduism* (edited with N. Lahirir, 2004), "Women in the Political Economy of Visayan Polities" (in *In Pursuit of Gender*, 2002), and "The Archaeology of the Philippine Islands (in *The Early Cultures of Southeast Asia*, 2004).

Diane Bolger is a research fellow in archaeology at the University of Edinburgh in Scotland and ceramic specialist for the university's projects in Cyprus and Syria. Her research interests include ceramic production and craft specialization in the prehistoric Near East and the archaeology of gender. Her main published works on gender are *Gender in Ancient Cyprus* (2003) and *Engendering Aphrodite: Women and Society in Ancient Cyprus* (2002), the latter coedited with N. Serwint. She received her Ph.D. from the University of Cincinnati in 1985.

Karen Olsen Bruhns received her Ph.D. in archaeology of Central and South America from the University of California, Berkeley. She has directed archaeological projects in Colombia, Ecuador, Nicaragua, and El Salvador and has participated in projects in Belize and Mexico. One of her books is *Women in Ancient America* (with Karen E. Stothert, 1999). She is currently the director of the Cihuatán/Las Marías Archaeological Project in El Salvador.

Hetty Jo Brumbach is an associate curator at the University of Albany, State University of New York, and Museum Associate at the New York State Museum. She is a graduate of the Buxton School, Hunter College, and the University of Albany, where she received a PhD in anthropology. Her research has focused on the Northeast United States and Canada, with interests in social archaeology, material culture and ethnicity, ceramic analysis, ethnoarchaeology, and gender. She has conducted ethnoarchaeological and ethnographic fieldwork in circumpolar communities and archaeological work in the Eastern Woodlands. Her publications include *Gaskin's Reef and River Edge South: A Multicomponent Woodland Site on the Seneca River, New York* (2003) and *Circumpolar Lives and Livelihood: A Comparative Ethnoarchaeology of Gender and Subsistence* (with Robert Jarvenpa, 2006).

Elizabeth M. Brumfiel is a professor of anthropology at Northwestern University. She holds a Ph.D. in anthropology at the University of Michigan. For the past eighteen years, she has pursued archaeological research at Xaltocan, a hinterland Aztec site in the basin of Mexico. Her edited volumes include *The Economic*

Anthropology of the State (1994) and *Factional Competition and Political Development in the New World* (with J. W. Fox, 1994).

Bonnie J. Clark is an assistant professor of anthropology at the University of Denver. She serves on the board of the National Collaborative for Women's History Sites. For over a decade, she has investigated a range of historical archaeology in western North America. She is interested in what the material record of daily life can tell us about the way people live their ethnic, gender, and class identities. She was one of the authors of *Denver: An Archaeological History* (2001).

Pam Crabtree is an associate professor at the Center for the Study of Human Origins of the Department of Anthropology, New York University. She is a zooarchaeologist who has worked on faunal materials from late prehistoric and medieval Europe, the Near East and South Asia, and historic North America. She coauthored *Exploring Prehistory: How Archaeology Reveals Our Past* (with Douglas Campana, 2005) and coedited *Ancient Europe: Encyclopedia of the Barbarian World 8000 BC–1000 AD* (with Peter Bogucki, 2004).

Virginia Ebert is a doctoral candidate in the Department of Anthropology at the University of Pennsylvania. Her current research explores the social identity of the *aqllakuna*, "chosen women" of the Inka Empire, through an examination of the *aqllawasi*, the structures in which they lived and worked. Her research in Andean archaeology integrates gender, landscape, spatial analysis, ethnohistory, and material culture. She is currently NAGPRA Research Associate with the University Museum.

Julia A. Hendon is an associate professor of anthropology in the Department of Sociology and Anthropology at Gettysburg College. A specialist in Mesoamerican archaeology with interests in household archaeology, gender, economic specialization, landscape, and the development of complex societies, her fieldwork and research has concentrated on the Classic period Maya and neighboring complex societies in northern Honduras. She is coeditor of *Mesoamerican Archaeology: Theory and Practice* (2004) and has published articles in *American Anthropologist*, *Annual Review of Anthropology*, *Latin American Antiquity*, and *Cambridge Archaeological Journal*.

Sandra E. Hollimon is a lecturer at Sonoma State University. Her Ph.D. is from the University of California, Santa Barbara. Her research interests include gender, shamanism, and emerging complexity in prehistoric California societies, especially the Chumash. Her most recent publication is "Hide Working and Changes in

Women's Status among the Arikara, 1700–1862" (in *Gender and Hide Production*, 2005).

Robert Jarvenpa is a professor and former chair of anthropology at the University of Albany, State University of New York. His research and publications focus on ecology and culture, political ecology, social and economic change, interethnic relations, sociospatial organization, decision making, and gender. He has conducted research in circumpolar communities as well as Costa Rica and the United States. He is author of *Northern Passage: Ethnography and Apprenticeship among the Subarctic Dene* (1998) and coauthor and coeditor with Hetty Jo Brumbach of the forthcoming *Circumpolar Lives and Livelihood: A Comparative Ethnoarchaeology of Gender and Subsistence*.

Rosemary A. Joyce is a professor of anthropology at the University of California, Berkeley, and has engaged in archaeological fieldwork in Honduras since 1977. She received a Ph.D. from the University of Illinois—Urbana. Her books include *Gender and Power in Prehispanic Mesoamerica* (2001), *The Languages of Archaeology* (2002), *Embodied Lives* (2003), and the hypertext *Sister Stories* (2000).

Janet E. Levy is an associate professor of anthropology at the University of North Carolina at Charlotte, where she has taught since 1980. She earned a B.A. in anthropology from Brown University and a Ph.D. in anthropology from Washington University—St. Louis. She has also taught in Illinois, Oregon, England, and Finland. In addition to gender, her interests include the prehistory of western Europe, the southeastern United States, ethics in archaeology and anthropology, and archaeometallurgy. She has served in the governance of the American Anthropological Association and Society for American Archaeology.

Diane Lyons is an assistant professor of archaeology at the University of Calgary. She holds a Ph.D. in archaeology from Simon Fraser University. She has worked on research projects in Cameroon, Ethiopia, Sudan, Canada, South America, Australia, and Hawaii. Her research interests are in the ethnoarchaeology and archaeology of gender relations, material culture style, households, and the technologies and social relations involved in food processing, preparation, and consumption.

Sarah Milledge Nelson is a John Evans Professor at the University of Denver. She works mostly in Asian archaeology. Her current project is in Liaoning Province, China, where she is surveying sites of the Hongshan period. Books include *Korean Social Archaeology* (2004) and *Gender in Archaeology, Analyzing Power and Prestige*

(2nd ed., 2004). Edited books include *Ancient Queens* (2003) and *The Archaeology of the Russian Far East* (with Y. V. Kuzmin, R. Bland, and A. Dervianko, 2006).

Emer O'Donnell is a Ph.D. student in archaeology at Flinders University of South Australia. The focus of her research is on exploration of early colonial Adelaide with particular emphasis on how women adapted their birthing systems to this new environment. She has lectured on archaeology and birthing to student midwives at Flinders Medical Center.

Thomas C. Patterson is Distinguished Professor and Chair of Anthropology at the University of California, Riverside. He is interested in contemporary social thought in archaeology and the history of anthropology. His books include *The Inca Empire: The Formation and Disintegration of a Pre-Capitalist State* (1991), *Marx's Ghost: Conversations with Archaeologists* (2003), *A Social History of Anthropology in the United States* (2001), and *Inventing Western Civilization* (1997).

Jane D. Peterson is an associate professor of anthropology at Marquette University. Her research interests focus on questions of social organization among early farming groups, particularly those in arid zones. Her analysis of household labor patterns in the Pre-Pottery Neolithic of the southern Levant led her to explore both bioarchaeological patterns in markers of occupational stress and architectural changes. Her current field site is Khirbet Hammam in southern Jordan.

Carla M. Sinopoli is a professor of anthropology and curator of Asian archaeology, University of Michigan. Her research focuses on complex societies of South Asia, political economy, material, and specialized craft production. Her most recent book is *The Political Economy of Craft Production: Crafting Empire in South India, c. 1350–1650* (2003) and *Archaeology as History: South Asia* (coedited with Himanshu P. Kay, 2004).

Claire Smith is an associate professor at Flinders University, Australia, and president of the World Archaeological Congress. Her books include *Indigenous Cultures in an Interconnected World* (coedited with Graeme K. Ward, 2000), *Country, Kin and Culture: Survival of an Australian Aboriginal Community* (2004), *The Archaeologist's Field Handbook* (with Heather Burke, 2004), and *Indigenous Archaeologies: Decolonising Archaeological Theory and Method* (coedited with H. Martin Wobst, 2005). She wrote her chapter for this volume while visiting assistant professor at Columbia University, New York.

Marie Louise Stig Sørensen earned her Ph.D. from the University of Cambridge. She is University Senior Lecturer at the Department of Archaeology, University of Cambridge, teaching and specializing in Bronze Age Europe, archaeological theory (especially gender), and archaeological heritage studies. Publications include *Gender Archaeology* (2000) and *Excavating Women: A History of Women in European Archaeology* (edited with M. Diaz-Andreu, 1998).

Suzanne M. Spencer-Wood is an associate professor of anthropology at Oakland University and an associate, Peabody Museum of Archaeology and Ethnology, Harvard University, specializing in applying feminist theory in historical archaeology and analyzing gender, class, and ethnic interactions at turn-of-the-century reform women's institutions. She organized the first two conference symposia on feminist historical archaeology in 1989 and has published in *Historical Archaeology*, *International Journal of Historical Archaeology*, and *The Landscape Journal* as well as a number of chapters in edited volumes, most recently a chapter in *Gender and Hide Production* (2005).

Barbara L. Voss is an assistant professor of cultural and social anthropology at Stanford University. She received her doctorate from the Department of Anthropology at the University of California, Berkeley, with a designated emphasis on women, gender, and sexuality. Her previous work includes *Archaeologies of Sexuality* (coedited with Robert A. Schmidt, 2000) and "Feminisms, Queer Theories, and the Archaeological Study of Past Sexualities" and "Sexual Subjects: Identity and Taxonomy in Archaeological Research" (in *The Archaeology of Plural and Changing Identities*, ed. Eleanor Conlin Casella and Chris Fowler, 2005). She currently directs the Tennessee Hollow Watershed Archaeological Project at the Presidio of San Francisco and the Market Street Chinatown project in San Jose, California.

Kathryn Weedman is a visiting assistant professor at the University of South Florida, St. Petersburg. She received her Ph.D. from the University of Florida, where she focused her ethnoarchaeological studies in Ethiopia on the relationship between social group membership and stone tool production and use. She has coedited *Gender and Hide Production* (with Lisa Frink, 2005).

Ruth Whitehouse is a professor of archaeology at the Institute of Archaeology, University College, London. For many years, she has researched on Italian and western Mediterranean prehistory, concentrating on social archaeology in general and more specifically on ritual and religion. In the past decade, she has also pursued research into gender archaeology. Major publications include *Underground*

Religion: Cult and Culture in Prehistoric Italy (1992) and an edited volume, *Gender and Italian Archaeology: Challenging the Stereotypes* (1998).

Laurie A. Wilkie is an associate professor of anthropology at the University of California, Berkeley. Her research interests include archaeological considerations of the construction of engendered, racialized, and ethnic identities in the recent past. Her published works include *Creating Freedom: Material Culture and African American Identity at Oakley Plantation, Louisiana, 1840–1950* (2000; winner of the 2001 James Mooney Book Award), *The Archaeology of Mothering: An African American Midwife's Tale* (2000; winner of the 2005 James Deetz Book Award), and, with Paul Farnsworth, *Sampling Many Pots: An Archaeology of Memory and Tradition at a Bahamian Plantation* (2005).